# Infants and Children

## *Prenatal through Middle Childhood*

Laura E. Berk     Illinois State University

**Allyn and Bacon**

Boston   London   Toronto   Sydney   Tokyo   Singapore

Editor-in-Chief, Psychology: Susan Badger
Series Editor: Laura Pearson
Series Editorial Assistant: Marnie Greenhut
Production Administrator: Marjorie Payne
Cover Designer: Suzanne Harbison
Photo Researcher: Elsa Peterson
Composition Buyer: Linda Cox
Manufacturing Buyer: Megan Cochran


ISBN 0-205-13880-2: *Infants, Children, and Adolescents* (complete text)
ISBN 0-205-15701-7: *Infants and Children: Prenatal through Early Childhood* (chapters 1–10)
ISBN 0-205-15700-9: *Infants and Children: Prenatal through Middle Childhood* (chapters 1–13)

Printed in the United States of America

10 9 8 7 6 5 4 3 2   97 96 95 94

*To my husband Ken
and my sons, David and Peter,
with love*

# Contents

**Preface**                                                    **xi**

*Part I*

## THEORY AND RESEARCH IN CHILD DEVELOPMENT

### 1. History, Theory, and Method                          1

Child Development as an Interdisciplinary,
Applied Field                                                2

Basic Themes and Issues                                      3

Organismic versus Mechanistic Child  4    Continuity
versus Discontinuity in Development  4    Nature versus
Nurture  5    A Balanced Point of View  6

Historical Foundations                                       6

Medieval Times  6    The Reformation  7
Philosophies of the Enlightenment  8    Charles
Darwin's Theory of Evolution  9    Early Scientific
Beginnings  9

Mid-Twentieth Century Influences                            12

Psychoanalytic Theory  12    Behaviorism and Social
Learning Theory  16    Piaget's Cognitive-
Developmental Theory  18

Recent Perspectives                                         22

Information Processing  22    Ethology  24
Ecological Systems Theory  25    Cross-Cultural
Research and Vygotsky's Sociocultural Perspective  28

■ *CULTURAL INFLUENCES: !Kung Infancy:*
*Acquiring Culture  30*

Comparing Child Development Theories                        29

Studying the Child                                          32

Common Methods Used to Study Children  32
General Research Designs  37    Developmental
Research Designs  40

■ *FROM RESEARCH TO PRACTICE:*
*Researchers and Practitioners as Collaborative*
*Partners  33*

Ethics in Research with Children                            42

The Chronological Approach of This Book                     44

Summary                                                     45

Important Terms and Concepts                                46

*Part II*

## FOUNDATIONS OF DEVELOPMENT

### 2. Biological and Environmental Foundations             49

Genetic Foundations                                         50

The Genetic Code  50    The Sex Cells  52
Conception  54    Boy or Girl?  55    Multiple
Births  56    Patterns of Genetic Inheritance  56

Chromosomal Abnormalities                                   62

Down Syndrome  62    Abnormalities of the Sex
Chromosomes  63

Reproductive Choices                                        65

Genetic Counseling  65    Prenatal Diagnosis and Fetal
Medicine  65    The Alternative of Abortion  68
The Alternative of Adoption  69

■ *SOCIAL ISSUES: The Pros and Cons of New*
*Reproductive Technologies  66*

Environmental Contexts for Development                      70

The Family  70    Social Class and Family
Functioning  73    The Impact of Poverty  74
Beyond the Family: Neighborhoods, Schools, Towns,
and Cities  75    The Cultural Context  77

■ *CULTURAL INFLUENCES: The Black*
*Extended Family  79*

Understanding the Relationship between Heredity
and Environment                                                 81
   The Question of "How Much?" 82    The Question
   of "How?" 84

Summary                                                         87

Important Terms and Concepts                                    88

For Further Information and Special Help                        88


3.  *Prenatal Development*                                      91

Motivations for Parenthood                                      92
   Why Have Children? 92    How Large a Family? 92
   Is There a Best Time During Adulthood to Have a
   Child? 94

Prenatal Development                                            95
   The Period of the Zygote 95    The Period of the
   Embryo 97    The Period of the Fetus 99

Prenatal Environmental Influences                              103
   Teratogens 103    Other Maternal Factors 111
   The Importance of Prenatal Health Care 116

   ■ SOCIAL ISSUES: *AIDS and Prenatal
   Development 112*

   ■ FROM RESEARCH TO PRACTICE:
   *Intervening with Prenatally Malnourished
   Infants 114*

Preparing for Parenthood                                       118
   Seeking Information 119    The Baby Becomes a
   Reality 119    Models of Effective Parenthood 119
   Practical Concerns 120    The Marital
   Relationship 120

Summary                                                        121

Important Terms and Concepts                                   122

For Further Information and Special Help                        123


4.  *Birth and the Newborn Baby*                               125

The Stages of Childbirth                                       126
   Stage 1: Dilation and Effacement of the Cervix 126
   Stage 2: Delivery of the Baby 127    Stage 3: Birth of
   the Placenta 128    The Baby's Adaptation to Labor
   and Delivery 128    The Newborn Baby's
   Appearance 128    Assessing the Newborn's Physical
   Condition: The Apgar Scale 129

Approaches to Childbirth                                       130
   Natural or Prepared Childbirth 132    Home
   Delivery 134

   ■ CULTURAL INFLUENCES: *Childbirth
   Practices Around the World 131*

Medical Interventions                                          135
   Fetal Monitoring 135    Labor and Delivery
   Medication 136    Instrument Delivery 137
   Induced Labor 137    Cesarean Delivery 138

Birth Complications                                            140
   Oxygen Deprivation 140    Preterm and Low Birth
   Weight Infants 140    Postterm Infants 143
   Understanding Birth Complications 146

   ■ SOCIAL ISSUES: *Infant Mortality in the
   United States 144*

Precious Moments After Birth                                   147

The Newborn Baby's Capacities                                  147
   Newborn Reflexes 148    Sensory Capacities 150
   Newborn States 153    Neonatal Behavioral
   Assessment 155

The Transition to Parenthood                                   157

   ■ FROM RESEARCH TO PRACTICE:
   *Postpartum Depression and the Mother–Infant
   Relationship 158*

Summary                                                        159

Important Terms and Concepts                                   160

For Further Information and Special Help                        161


*Part III*

INFANCY AND TODDLERHOOD:
THE FIRST TWO YEARS


5.  *Physical Development in Infancy
    and Toddlerhood*                                           163

Growth of the Body in the First Two Years                      164
   Changes in Body Size 164    Changes in Body
   Proportions 165    Changes in Muscle-Fat
   Makeup 166    Early Skeletal Growth 167

Brain Development                                              169
   Development of Neurons 169    Development of the
   Cerebral Cortex 170

Factors Affecting Early Physical Growth                        172
   Heredity 172    Nutrition 173    Malnutrition 175
   Affection and Stimulation 176

Changing States of Arousal                     177

Motor Development During the First Two Years    178

  The Sequence of Motor Development 178    Motor
  Skills as Complex Systems of Action 180    Maturation,
  Experience, and the Development of Motor Skills 180
  Fine Motor Development: The Special Case of Voluntary
  Reaching 181    Bowel and Bladder Control 181

■ CULTURAL INFLUENCES:
  Motor Development of African and West
  Indian Babies 182

Basic Learning Mechanisms                      185

  Classical Conditioning 185    Operant Conditioning
  187    Habituation and Dishabituation 189
  Imitation 189

■ FROM RESEARCH TO PRACTICE: The
  Mysterious Tragedy of Sudden Infant Death
  Syndrome 188

Perceptual Development in Infancy               191

  Hearing 191    Vision 192    Intermodal
  Perception 197

Understanding Perceptual Development            198

Summary                                        199

Important Terms and Concepts                   200

For Further Information and Special Help        201


6. *Cognitive Development in Infancy
   and Toddlerhood*                            203

Piaget's Cognitive-Developmental Theory         204

  Key Piagetian Concepts 204    The Sensorimotor
  Stage 206    New Research on Sensorimotor
  Development 213    Evaluation of the Sensorimotor
  Stage 215

Information Processing in the First Two Years    216

  A Model of Human Information Processing 217
  Attention and Memory 218
  Categorization Skills 219    Evaluation of
  Information Processing Findings 220

The Social Context of Early Cognitive
Development                                     221

■ FROM RESEARCH TO PRACTICE:
  Parent–Toddler Interaction and Early
  Make-Believe Play 223

Individual Differences in Early Mental
Development                                     224

  Infant Intelligence Tests 224    Early Environment and
  Mental Development 226    Early Intervention for
  At-Risk Infants and Toddlers 228

■ SOCIAL ISSUES: The Carolina
  Abecedarian Project: A Model of Infant–Toddler
  Intervention 230

Language Development During the First
Two Years                                      229

  Three Theories of Language Development 229
  Getting Ready to Talk 233    First Words 234    The
  Two-Word Utterance Phase 234    Comprehension
  Versus Production 235    Individual Differences in
  Language Development 235    Supporting Early
  Language Development 236

Summary                                        237

Important Terms and Concepts                   239

For Further Information and Special Help        239


7. *Emotional and Social Development
   in Infancy and Toddlerhood*                 241

Theories of Infant and Toddler Personality      242

  Erik Erikson: Trust and Autonomy 242    Margaret
  Mahler: Separation–Individuation 244    Similarities
  Between Erikson's and Mahler's Theories 245

Emotional Development During the First
Two Years                                      246

  The Development of Some Basic Emotions 246
  Recognizing and Responding to the Emotions of
  Others 249    The Emergence of
  Complex Emotions 249    The Beginnings of
  Emotional Self-Regulation 250

Temperament and Development                     251

  Measuring Temperament 252    The Stability of
  Temperament 253    Biological Foundations 254
  Environmental Influences 255    Temperament and
  Child Rearing: The Goodness-of-Fit Model 255

■ FROM RESEARCH TO PRACTICE:
  Difficult Children: When Parents Establish a
  "Good Fit" 257

The Development of Attachment                   256

  Theories of Attachment 257    Measuring the Security
  of Attachment 261    Cultural Variations 262
  Factors that Affect Attachment Security 263    Multiple
  Attachments 266    Attachment and Later
  Development 269

■ *CULTURAL INFLUENCES: Young Children's Attachment to Soft Objects 259*

■ *SOCIAL ISSUES: Is Infant Day Care a Threat To Attachment Security? 267*

Self-Development During the First Two Years 270

Self-Recognition 271   Categorizing the Self 273
The Emergence of Self-Control 273

Summary 275

Important Terms and Concepts 276

Milestones of Development in Infancy and Toddlerhood 277


*Part IV*

## EARLY CHILDHOOD: TWO TO SIX YEARS

### 8. *Physical Development in Early Childhood* 279

Body Growth in Early Childhood 280

Changes in Body Size and Proportions 280   Skeletal Growth 280   Asynchronies in Physical Growth 283

Brain Development in Early Childhood 284

Lateralization and Handedness 284   Other Advances in Brain Development 285

Factors Affecting Growth and Health in Early Childhood 287

Heredity and Hormonal Influences 287   Emotional Well-Being 288   Nutrition 289   Infectious Disease 290   Childhood Injuries 292

■ *SOCIAL ISSUES: Lead Poisoning in Childhood 288*

■ *CULTURAL INFLUENCES: Child Health Care in the United States and European Nations 293*

■ *FROM RESEARCH TO PRACTICE: Day Care and Infectious Disease 294*

Motor Development in Early Childhood 297

Gross Motor Development 298   Fine Motor Development 300   Factors that Affect Early Childhood Motor Skills 302

Perceptual Development in Early Childhood 304

Summary 305

Important Terms and Concepts 306

For Further Information and Special Help 306

### 9. *Cognitive Development in Early Childhood* 309

Piaget's Theory: The Preoperational Stage 310

Advances in Mental Representation 310
Make-Believe Play 311   Limitations of Preoperational Thought 312   New Research on Preoperational Thought 318   Evaluation of the Preoperational Stage 320   Piaget and Education 321

■ *FROM RESEARCH TO PRACTICE: Young Children's Understanding of Death 319*

Further Challenges to Piaget's Ideas: Vygotsky's Sociocultural Theory 322

Piaget Versus Vygotsky: Children's Private Speech 322   The Social Origins of Early Childhood Cognition 324   Vygotsky and Education 325

Information Processing in Early Childhood 325

Attention 326   Memory 327   The Young Child's Theory of Mind 329   Early Literacy and Mathematical Development 330   A Note on Academics in Early Childhood 332

Individual Differences in Mental Development During Early Childhood 334

Early Childhood Intelligence Tests 334   Home Environment and Mental Development 335   Preschool and Day Care 336   Educational Television 338

■ *SOCIAL ISSUES: Project Head Start: A Social Policy Success Story 339*

Language Development in Early Childhood 341

Vocabulary Development 341   Grammatical Development 342   Becoming an Effective Conversationalist 343   Supporting Language Learning in Early Childhood 344

Summary 346

Important Terms and Concepts 347

For Further Information and Special Help 347

### 10. *Emotional and Social Development in Early Childhood* 349

Erikson's Theory: Initiative Versus Guilt 350

Self-Development in Early Childhood 351

Foundations of Self-Concept 351   Understanding Intentions 352   The Emergence of Self-Esteem 353

Emotional Development in Early Childhood        353

Understanding Emotion 353    Improvements in
Emotional Self-Regulation 354    Changes in Complex
Emotions 355    The Development of Empathy 355

■ FROM RESEARCH TO PRACTICE: Helping
Young Children Manage Fears 356

Peer Relations in Early Childhood        358

Advances in Peer Sociability 358
First Friendships 362

Foundations of Morality in Early Childhood        363

The Psychoanalytic Perspective 363    Behaviorism
and Social Learning Theory 365    The Cognitive-
Developmental Perspective 367    The Other
Side of Morality: The Development of Aggression 368

■ SOCIAL ISSUES: Regulating Children's
Television 372

The Development of Sex Typing in Early
Childhood        371

Preschoolers' Sex-Stereotyped Beliefs and
Behavior 373    Genetic Influences on Sex Typing
374    Environmental Influences on Sex Typing 374
Sex-Role Identity 376    Raising Non-Sex-Stereotyped
Children 377

Child Rearing and Emotional and Social
Development in Early Childhood        379

Child-Rearing Styles 379    What Makes
Authoritative Child Rearing So Effective? 380
Child Maltreatment 381

Summary        384

Important Terms and Concepts        385

For Further Information and Special Help        386

Milestones of Development in Early Childhood        387


PART V

MIDDLE CHILDHOOD: SIX TO
ELEVEN YEARS

11. Physical Development in
    Middle Childhood        389

Body Growth in Middle Childhood        390

Changes in Body Size and Proportions 390    Secular
Trends in Physical Growth 392    Skeletal Growth
392    Brain Development 392

Common Health Problems in Middle Childhood        393

Vision and Hearing 394    Malnutrition 394
Obesity 394    Type A Behavior 397
Bedwetting 397    Illnesses 398
Unintentional Injuries 399

Health Education in Middle Childhood        400

■ CULTURAL INFLUENCES: Children's
Understanding of Health and Illness 401

Motor Development and Play in Middle Childhood 402

New Motor Capacities 403    Organized Games with
Rules 407    Shadows of Our Evolutionary Past 408
Physical Education 410

■ SOCIAL ISSUES: Are Adult-Organized Sports
Good for Children? 409

Summary        411

Important Terms and Concepts        412

For Further Information and Special Help        412


12. Cognitive Development in
    Middle Childhood        415

Piaget's Theory: The Concrete Operational Stage        416

Operational Thought 416    Limitations of Concrete
Operational Thought 419    New Research on
Concrete Operational Thought 419    Evaluation of
the Concrete Operational Stage 420

Information Processing in Middle Childhood        421

Attention 421    Memory Strategies 422    The
Knowledge Base and Memory Performance 424
Culture and Memory Strategies 425    The School-Age
Child's Theory of Mind 425    Self-Regulation 426
Applications of Information Processing to Academic
Learning 427

■ FROM RESEARCH TO PRACTICE:
Attention–Deficient Hyperactivity Disordered
Children 423

Individual Differences in Mental Development
During Middle Childhood        429

Defining and Measuring Intelligence 429    Explaining
Individual Differences in IQ 433    Overcoming
Cultural Bias in Intelligence Tests 436

Language Development in Middle Childhood        427

Vocabulary 437    Grammar 437    Pragmatics 438
Learning Two Languages at a Time 438

■ SOCIAL ISSUES: Bilingual Education in the
United States 440

Children's Learning in School                     441
   The Educational Philosophy 441    Teacher–Pupil
   Interaction 442    Computers in the Classroom 444
   Teaching Children with Special Needs 445

How Well Educated Are America's Children?         450

■ CULTURAL INFLUENCES: Education in
Japan, Taiwan, and the United States 451

Summary                                           453

Important Terms and Concepts                      454

For Further Information and Special Help          454


13. Emotional and Social Development in
    Middle Childhood                              457

Erikson's Theory: Industry Versus Inferiority     458

Self-Development in Middle Childhood              459
   Changes in Self-Concept 459    Development of
   Self-Esteem 460    Influences on Self-Esteem 462

Emotional Development in Middle Childhood         465

Understanding Others                              466
   Selman's Stages of Perspective-Taking 466
   Perspective-Taking and Social Behavior 466

Moral Development in Middle Childhood             468
   Learning About Justice Through Sharing 468
   Changes in Moral and Social Conventional
   Understanding 469

■ CULTURAL INFLUENCES: Children's Moral
Concepts in India and the United States 470

Peer Relations in Middle Childhood                470
   Peer Groups 471    Friendships 472
   Peer Acceptance 473

Sex Typing in Middle Childhood                    475
   School-Age Children's Sex-Stereotyped Beliefs 475
   Sex-Role Identity and Behavior 476    Cultural
   Influences on Sex Typing 476

Family Influences in Middle Childhood             477
   Parent-Child Relationships 477    Siblings 478
   Divorce 479    Remarriage 483    Maternal
   Employment 484

Some Common Problems of Development 486
   Fears and Anxieties 487    Child Sexual Abuse 488

■ FROM RESEARCH TO PRACTICE:
Children's Eyewitness Testimony 491

Stress and Coping in Middle Childhood             490

Summary                                           492

Important Terms and Concepts                      493

For Further Information and Special Help          493

Milestones of Development in Middle Childhood     495

Glossary                                          G-1

Reference                                         R-1

Index                                             I-1

# Preface

My more than twenty years of teaching child development have brought me in contact with thousands of students having diverse college majors, future goals, interests, and needs. Some are affiliated with my own department, psychology, but many come from other child-related fields—education, home economics, sociology, anthropology, and biology, to name just a few. Each semester, the professional aspirations of my students have proved to be as varied as their fields of study. Many look toward careers in applied work with children—teaching, caregiving, nursing, counseling, social work, school psychology, and program administration. Some plan to teach child development, and a few want to do research. Most hope someday to have children, while others are already parents who come with a desire to better understand their own youngsters. And almost all my students arrive with a deep curiosity about how they themselves developed from tiny infants into the complex human beings they are today.

My goal in writing this textbook is to provide a sound course of study while meeting the varied needs of students. I have provided a text that is comprehensive in its coverage of scientific knowledge and that portrays the complexities of child development in a way that captures student interest while helping them learn.

To achieve these objectives, I have grounded this book in a carefully selected body of classic and current research, which I bring to life with stories and vignettes about children and families, many of whom I have known personally. I have also used a clear, engaging writing style and included a unique pedagogical program that not only assists students in mastering information, but also stimulates them to think critically and apply what they have learned. Finally, the basic approach of this book has been shaped by my own professional and personal history as a teacher, researcher, and parent. It consists of five philosophical ingredients, which I regard as essential for students to emerge from a course with a thorough understanding of child development. I have woven each into every chapter:

1. **An understanding of major theories and the strengths and shortcomings of each.** I begin the first chapter by emphasizing that only knowledge of multiple theories can do justice to the richness of child development. As I take up each age sector and aspect of development, I present a variety of theoretical perspectives and show how research has been used to evaluate them. Discussion of contrasting theories also serves as the context for an evenhanded analysis of many controversial issues throughout the text.

2. **Knowledge of both the sequence of child development and the processes that underlie it.** I provide students with a description of the organized sequence of development along with a discussion of processes of change. An understanding of *process*—how complex combinations of biological and environmental events produce development—has been the focus of most recent research. Accordingly, the text reflects this emphasis. But new information about the timetable of change has also emerged in recent years. In many ways, the child has proved to be a far more competent being than was believed to be the case in decades past. I give thorough attention to recent evidence on the timing and sequence of development, along with its implications for process, throughout the book.

3. **An appreciation of the impact of context and culture on child development.** A wealth of new research indicates more powerfully than ever before that children live in rich physical and social contexts that affect all aspects of development. In each chapter, the student travels to distant parts of the world as I review a growing body of cross-cultural evidence. The text narrative also discusses many findings on socioeconomically and ethnically diverse children within the United States. Besides highlighting the role of immediate settings, such as family, neighborhood, and school, I make a concerted effort to underscore the impact of larger social structures—societal values, laws, and government programs—on children's well-being.

4. **A sense of the interdependency of all aspects of development—physical, cognitive, emotional, and social.** In every chapter, an integrated approach to child development is emphasized. I show how physical, cognitive, emotional, and social development are interwoven. In many instances, students are referred back to previous sections and chapters to deepen their understanding of relationships among various aspects of change.

5. **An appreciation of the interrelatedness of theory, research, and applications.** Throughout this book, I emphasize that theories of child development and the research stimulated by them provide the foundation for sound, effective practices with children. The link between theory, research, and applications is reinforced by an organizational format in which theory and research are presented first, followed by implications for practice. In addition, a new emphasis in the field—harnessing child development knowledge to shape social policies that support children's needs—is reflected in every chapter. The text addresses the current condition of children in the United States and around the world and shows how theory and research have sparked successful interventions. Many important applied topics are considered—prenatal AIDS infection, infant mortality, maternal employment nd day care, mainstreaming children with learning difficulties, bilingual education, child sexual abuse, and teenage pregnancy and childbearing, to name just a few.

## TEXT ORGANIZATION

I have chosen a chronological organization for this text. The book begins with an introductory chapter that describes the history of the field, modern theories, and research strategies. It is followed by three chapters that cover the foundations of development. Chapter 2 combines an overview of genetic and environmental influences into a single, integrated discussion of these complex determinants of development. Chapter 3 is devoted to prenatal development, Chapter 4 to birth and the newborn baby. With this foundation, students are ready to take a close look at four major age periods of development: infancy and toddlerhood, early childhood, middle childhood, and adolescence. Each of these chronological divisions contains a trio of topical chapters: physical development, cognitive development, and emotional and social development.

The chronological approach has the unique advantage of enabling students to get to know children of a given age period very well. It also eases the task of integrating the various aspects of development, since each is discussed in close proximity. At the same time, a chronologically organized book requires that theories covering several age periods by presented piecemeal. This creates a challenge for students, who must link the various parts together. To assist with this task, I remind students of important earlier achievements before discussing new developments. Also, chapters devoted to the same topic (for example, Cognitive Development in Early Childhood, Cognitive Development in Middle Childhood) are similarly organized, making it easier for students to draw connections across age periods

and construct a continuous vision of developmental change.

## SPECIAL PEDAGOGICAL FEATURES

In writing this book, I made a concerted effort to adopt a prose style that is lucid and engaging without being condescending. I frequently converse with students and encourage them to relate what they read to their own lives. In doing so, I hope to make the study of child development involving and pleasurable.

**Chapter Introductions and End-of-Chapter Summaries.** To provide students with a helpful preview of what they are about to read, I include an outline and overview of chapter content in each chapter introduction. Especially comprehensive end-of-chapter summaries, organized according to the major divisions of each chapter and highlighting key terms, remind students of key points in the text discussion.

**Brief Reviews.** Brief Reviews, which provide students with interim summaries of text content, appear at the end of major sections in each chapter. They enhance retention by encouraging students to reflect on information they have just read before moving on to a new section.

**Stories and Vignettes about Children.** To help students construct a clear image of development and to enliven the text narrative, each chronological age division is unified by case examples extending throughout the trio of chapters. For example, within the infancy and toddlerhood section, students accompany me as I sit in on periodic gatherings of three mothers and their babies, observe dramatic changes in the children's capabilities, and address their mothers' questions and concerns. Besides a set of main characters who bring unity to each age period, many additional vignettes offer vivid examples of development and diversity among children.

**Boxes.** Three types of boxes accentuate philosophical themes of this book. *Cultural Influences* boxes highlight the impact of context and culture on all aspects of development. *Social Issues* boxes discuss the condition of children in the United States and around the world and emphasize the need for sensitive social policies to ensure their well-being. *From Research in Practice* boxes integrate theory, research, and applications.

**Learning Activities.** Throughout the text narrative and within the Social Issues boxes, I encourage students to become actively involved with the material by suggesting activities that extend their understanding of child development. For example, in Chapter 1, I recommend that students keep a notebook in which they evaluate their theoretical preferences in light of research. In many places, I suggest that they observe or interview children and parents and reflect on their own experiences. Each learning activity can serve as a stimulus for class discussion or as a course assignment.

**Critical Thinking Questions.** Active engagement with the subject matter is also supported by critical thinking questions, which can be found in the margins at the end of major sections. The focus of these questions is divided between theory and applications. Many describe problematic situations faced by parents, teachers, and children and ask students to resolve them in light of what they have learned. In this way, the questions inspire high-level thinking and new insights.

**Marginal Glossary, End-of-Chapter Term List, and End-of-Book Glossary.** Mastery of terms that make up the central vocabulary of the field is promoted through a marginal glossary, and end-of-chapter term list, and an end-of-book glossary. Important terms and concepts also appear in boldface type in the text narrative.

**Concept Tables.** I have created a special series of tables that group together related concepts, summarize the important point conveyed by each, and provide vivid examples. These tables help ensure that challenging sets of concepts will be interrelated and fully understood.

**Milestone Tables.** A milestone table appears at the end of each chronological age division of the text. These tables summarize major physical, cognitive, language, and emotional and social developments of each age span.

**Additional Tables, Illustrations, and Photographs.** Additional tables are liberally included to help students grasp essential points in the text discussion, extend information on a topic, and consider applications. The many full-color illustrations throughout the book depict important theories, methods, and research findings. Photos have been carefully selected to portray the text discussion and to represent the diversity of children in the United States and around the world.

**For Further Information and Special Help.** Students in my own classes frequently ask where they can go to find out more about high-interest topics or to seek help in areas related to their own lives. To meet this need, I have included an annotated section at the end of each chapter that provides the names, addresses, and phone numbers of organizations that disseminate information about child development and offer special services.

## TEXT SUPPLEMENTS

A set of carefully prepared supplements accompanies this text. Its components support both high-quality teaching and effective student learning.

**Instructor's Resource Manual.** The Instructor's Resource Manual, prepared by Malia Huchendorf of Norman-

dale Community College, includes learning objectives, chapter outlines, chapter summaries, lecture topics and tips, classroom activities and demonstrations, connections tables that cross-reference high-interest topics discussed in several sections of the book, responses to critical thinking questions, a guide to the video and laserdisc that complement the book, additional film and media suggestions, and transparency masters.

**Test Bank.** The Test Bank, written by Christine Sartoris of Illinois State University and Carole Kremer of Hudson Valley Community College, contains over 1,600 multiple choice items. Questions are cross-referenced to Learning Objectives. For instructors who do not have enough time to choose their own test questions, premade tests of 25 items each are included. Answer justifications, which provide students with explanations of correct responses, can be found at the end of the Test Bank. It comes in both printed and computerized formats (Macintosh and IBM versions are available).

**Video and Laserdisc.** Allyn and Bacon, in cooperation with Films for the Humanities and Sciences, has provided a video and laserdisc to accompany the text. Segments average five minutes in length and are intended to launch or otherwise enhance lectures and class discussions. A Video User's Guide, which ties the film segments to the text narrative, can be found in the Instructor's Resource Manual.

**Study Guide.** I have written the Study Guide, which provides students with a comprehensive review of text content. Each chapter begins with a short summary and a list of learning objectives. These are followed by a variety of study questions, including true/false, fill-in-the-blank, matching, and short-answer essay, organized according to major headings in the text narrative. Critical thinking questions that appear in the margins of the book are reprinted in the Study Guide along with text page numbers to which students can refer as they formulate answers. Crossword puzzles assist with mastery of the vocabulary of the field. Self-tests, consisting of multiple choice, fill-in-the-blank, and true-false items, help students evaluate how well they have learned the material. Finally, each Study Guide chapter includes a list of annotated suggested readings, carefully selected to build on chapter content and to be accessible to students who are new to the field of child development.

## ACKNOWLEDGMENTS

The dedicated contributions of a great many individuals helped make this book a reality. In the months before I began writing, Allyn and Bacon sponsored focus groups in which instructors of child development discussed features of a text that would best meet their teaching goals. The insightful comments of group members were critical in shaping the organization and content of this book. I thank each of the following individuals for participating.

Carol Chamberlin
Santa Monica City College

Linda Cravensn
Moorpark College

Louise Dean
Los Angeles Valley College

Rosalind Frye
Richard J. Daley College

Robert Freudenthal
Moraine Valley Community College

Diana Hiatt
Pepperdine University

Sandy Hoffman
Oakton Community College

Barbara Kuczen-Schaller
Chicago State University

Jeri Lopton
Oxnard Community College

Maurice Page
South Suburban College

Patricia Schmolze
Los Angeles City College

Francine Smolucha
Moriane Valley Community College

Joyce West
Moriane Valley Community College

As I completed each chapter, an impressive cast of reviewers provided many helpful suggestions, constructive criticisms, and much encouragement and enthusiasm for the text. I am grateful to each one of them:

Jerry Bruce
Sam Houston State College

Kathleen Bey
Palm Beach Community College

Donald Bowers
Community College of Philadelphia

Joseph J. Campos
University of California, Berkeley

Nancy Taylor Coghill
University of Southwest Louisiana

Roswell Cox
Berea College

Janice Hartfrove-Freile
North Harris Community College

Vernon Haynes
Youngstown State University

Malia Huchendorf
Normandale Community College

Clementine Hansley Hurt
Radford University

John S. Klein
Castleton State College

Carole Kremer
Hudson Valley Community College

Gary W. Ladd
University of Illinois, Urbana-Champaign

Linda Lavine
State University of New York at Cortland

Frank Manis
University of Southern California

Cloe Merrill
Weber State University

Mary Ann McLaughlin
Clarion University of Pennsylvania

Tizarh Schutzengel
Bergen Community College

Gregory Smith
Dickinson College

Marcia Summers
Ball State University

Judith Ward
Central Connecticut State University

Shawn Ward
Le Moyne College

Alida Westman
Eastern Michigan University

Sue Williams
Southwest Texas State University

I am also indebted to colleagues at Illinois State University and Illinois Wesleyan University—Gary Creasey, Carolyn Jarvis, Patricia Jarvis, Benjamin Moore, and Mark Swerdlik—for providing consultation in areas of their expertise. Dawn Ramsburg, my graduate assistant, helped with literature reviews and securing permissions for use of copyrighted material. Joan Croce and Christine Sartoris spent many hours indexing the text. Stanford University was my academic home during the preparation of the first half of this book. I thank the School of Education for providing the necessary supports so I could engage in research and writing during my sabbatical leave.

A final word of gratitude goes to my husband, Ken, and my sons, David and Peter, both of whom have nearly completed the journey described in this book and stand on the threshold of adulthood. I have learned much from Ken, David, and Peter about parenting and child development, and they have graciously permitted me to share some of these insights in the text's vignettes. I dedicate this book, with love, to them.

Laura E. Berk

*"Adult Literacy," Samsad Begum Shilpi, 14 years, Bangladesh.*
*Reprinted by permission from The International*
*Museum of Children's Art, Oslo, Norway.*

# History, Theory, and Method

1

Child Development as an Interdisciplinary, Applied Field

Basic Themes and Issues
   *Organismic versus Mechanistic Child   Continuity versus Discontinuity in Development
   Nature versus Nurture   A Balanced Point of View*

Historical Foundations
   *Medieval Times   The Reformation   Philosophies of the Enlightenment   Charles Darwin's
   Theory of Evolution   Early Scientific Beginnings*

Mid-Twentieth Century Influences
   *Psychoanalytic Theory   Behaviorism and Social Learning Theory   Piaget's Cognitive-
   Developmental Theory*

Recent Perspectives
   *Information Processing   Ethology   Ecological Systems Theory   Cross-Cultural Research and
   Vygotsky's Sociocultural Perspective*

Comparing Child Development Theories

Studying the Child
   *Common Methods Used to Study Children   General Research Designs   Developmental
   Research Designs   Ethics in Research with Children*

The Chronological Approach of this Book

Not long ago, I left my Midwestern home to live for a year near the small city in Northern California where I spent my childhood years. One morning, I visited the neighborhood where I grew up—a place to which I had not returned since I was 12 years old. I stood at the entrance to my old schoolyard. Buildings and grounds that looked large to me as a child now seemed strangely small from my grown-up vantage point. I peered through the window of my first-grade classroom. The desks were no longer arranged in rows, but grouped in intimate clusters around the room. A computer rested against the far wall, near the spot where I once sat. I walked my old route home from school, the distance shrunken by my larger stride. I stopped in front of my best friend Kathryn's house, where we once drew sidewalk pictures, crossed the street to play kick ball, produced plays for neighborhood audiences in the garage, and traded marbles and stamps in the backyard. In place of the small shop where I had purchased penny candy stood a neighborhood day-care center, filled with the voices and vigorous activity of toddlers and preschoolers.

As I walked, I reflected on early experiences that contributed to who I am and what I am like today—weekends helping my father in his downtown clothing shop, the year during which my mother studied to become a high school teacher, moments of companionship and rivalry with my sister and brother, Sunday trips to museums and the seashore, and overnight visits to my grandmother's house where I became someone extra special.

As I passed the homes of my childhood friends, I thought of what I knew about their present lives. My close friend Kathryn, star pupil and president of our sixth-grade class—today a successful corporate lawyer and mother of two children. Shy, withdrawn Phil, cruelly teased because of his cleft lip—now owner of a thriving chain of hardware stores and member of the city council. Hulio, immigrant from Mexico who joined our class in third grade—today director of an elementary school bilingual education program and single parent of an adopted Mexican boy. And finally, my next-door neighbor Rick, who picked fights at recess, struggled with reading, repeated fourth grade, dropped out of high school, and (so I heard) moved from one job to another over the following ten years.

As you begin this course in child development, perhaps you, too, have wondered about some of the same questions that crossed my mind during that nostalgic neighborhood walk:

- What determines the features human beings share in common and those that make each of us unique—in physical characteristics, capabilities, interests, and behaviors?

- Is the infant and young child's perception of the world much the same as the adult's, or is it different in basic respects?

- Why do some of us, like Kathryn and Rick, retain the same styles of responding that characterized us as children, while others, like Phil, change in essential ways?

- How did Hulio, transplanted to a foreign culture at 8 years of age, master its language and customs and succeed in its society, yet remain strongly identified with his ethnic community?

- In what ways are children's home, school, and neighborhood experiences the same today as they were in generations past, and in what ways are they different? How does generational change—employed mothers, day care, divorce, smaller families, and new technologies—affect children's characteristics and skills?

These are central questions addressed by **child development,** a field of study devoted to understanding all aspects of human growth and change from conception through adolescence. Child development is part of a larger discipline known as **human development,** which includes all changes we experience throughout the life span. Great diversity characterizes the interests and concerns of the thousands of investigators who study child development. But all have a single goal in common: the desire to describe and identify those factors that influence the dramatic changes in young people during the first two decades of life.

---

**Child development**

A field of study devoted to understanding all aspects of human growth from conception through adolescence.

**Human development**

A field of study that includes all changes human beings experience throughout the life span.

## CHILD DEVELOPMENT AS AN INTERDISCIPLINARY, APPLIED FIELD

Look again at the questions about children listed earlier, and you will see that they are not just of scientific interest. Each is of *applied,* or practical importance, as well. In fact, scientific curiosity is just one factor that led child development to become the exciting field of study it is today. Research about development has also been stimulated by social pressures to better the lives of children. For example, the beginning of public education in the early part of this century led to a demand for knowledge about what and how to teach children of different ages. The interest of pediatricians in improving children's health required an understanding of physical growth and nutrition. The social service profession's desire to treat children's anxieties and behavior problems required information about personality and social development. And parents have continually asked for advice from child development specialists about child-rearing practices and experiences that would promote the growth of their children.

Our vast storehouse of information about child development is *interdisciplinary*; it grew through the combined efforts of people from many fields of study. Because of the need for solutions to everyday problems concerning children, academic scientists from psychology, sociology, anthropology, and biology joined forces in research with professionals from a variety of applied fields, including education, home economics, medicine, and social service, to name just a few. Today, the modern field of child development is a melting pot of contributions. Its body of knowledge is not just scientifically important, but relevant and useful.

## BASIC THEMES AND ISSUES

Before scientific study of the child, questions about children were answered by turning to common sense, opinion, and belief. Research on children did not begin until the early part of the twentieth century. Gradually it led to the construction of theories of child development, to which professionals and parents could turn for understanding and guidance. Although there are a great many definitions, for our purposes we can think of a **theory** as an orderly, integrated set of statements that describes, explains, and predicts behavior. For example, a good theory of infant-mother attachment would *describe* the behaviors that lead up to babies' strong desire to seek the affection and comfort of their mothers around 6 to 8 months of age. It would also *explain* why infants have such a strong desire. And it might also try to *predict* what might happen if babies do not develop this close emotional bond.

Theories are important for two reasons. First, they provide organizing frameworks for our observations of the child. In other words, they *interpret and give meaning* to what we see. Second, theories provide us with a sound basis for practical action. Once a theory helps us *understand* development, we are in a much better position to know *what to do* in our efforts to improve the welfare and treatment of children.

As we will see later on, theories are influenced by the cultural values and belief systems of their times. But theories differ in one important way from opinion and belief: a theory's continued existence depends on *scientific verification*. This means that the theory must be tested by using a fair set of research procedures agreed on by the scientific community.

In the field of child development, there are many theories with very different ideas about what children are like and how they develop. The study of child development provides no single truth, since investigators do not always agree on the meaning of what they see. In addition, children are complex beings; they grow physically, mentally, emotionally, and socially. As yet, no single theory has been able to explain all these aspects. Finally, the existence of many theories helps advance our knowledge, since researchers are continually trying to support, contradict, and integrate these different points of view.

In this chapter, we will introduce the major child development theories and the research strategies that have been used to test them. Then, we will return to each theory in greater detail in later parts of this book. Although there are many theories, we can easily organize them, since almost every theory takes a stand on three basic issues about childhood and child development. To help you remember these controversial issues, they are briefly summarized in Table 1.1. Let's take a close look at each one in the following sections.

**Theory**
An orderly, integrated set of statements that describes, explains, and predicts behavior.

TABLE 1.1 • Basic Issues in Child Development

| Issue | Question Raised About Development |
|---|---|
| Organismic versus mechanistic child | Are children active beings with psychological structures that underlie and control development, or are they passive recipients of environmental inputs? |
| Continuous versus discontinuous development | Is child development a matter of cumulative adding on of skills and behaviors or qualitative, stagewise change? |
| Nature versus nurture | Are genetic or environmental factors the most important determinants of child development and behavior? |

## Organismic versus Mechanistic Child

Recently, the mother of a 16-month-old boy named Angelo reported to me with amazement that her young son pushed a toy car across the livingroom floor while making a motorlike sound, "Brmmmm, brmmmm," for the first time. "We've never shown him how to do that!" exclaimed Angelo's mother. "Did he make that sound up himself," she inquired, "or did he copy it from some other child at day care?"

Angelo's mother has asked a puzzling question about the nature of children. It contrasts two basic perspectives: the organismic, or *active* position, with the mechanistic, or *passive* point of view.

**Organismic theories** assume that change is stimulated from *within the organism*—more specifically, that psychological structures exist inside the child that underlie and control development. Children are viewed as active, purposeful beings who make sense of their world and determine their own learning. For an organismic theorist, the surrounding environment supports development, as Angelo's mother did when she provided him with stimulating toys. But since children invent their own ways of understanding and responding to events around them, the environment does not bring about the child's growth.

In contrast, **mechanistic theories** focus on relationships between environmental inputs and behavioral outputs. The approach is called *mechanistic* because children's development is compared to the workings of a machine. Change is stimulated by the environment, which shapes the behavior of the child, who is a passive reactor. For example, when Angelo's playmate says "Brmmmm," Angelo responds in a likewise way. Development is treated as a straightforward, predictable consequence of events in the surrounding world.

## Continuity versus Discontinuity in Development

How can we best describe the differences in skills and behavior that exist between small infants, young children, adolescents, and adults? There are two possibilities (see Figure 1.1).

On the one hand, babies and preschoolers may respond to the world in much the same way as adults. The difference between the immature and mature being may simply be one of *amount* or *complexity* of behavior. For example, little Angelo's thinking might be just as logical and well-organized as our own. His only limitation may be that he cannot think with as many pieces of information as we can. If this is true, then changes in Angelo's thinking must be **continuous**—a process that consists of gradually adding on more of the same types of skills that were there to begin with.

---

**Organismic theory**

A theory that assumes the existence of psychological structures inside the child that underlie and control development.

**Mechanistic theory**

A theory that regards the child as a passive reactor to environmental inputs.

**Continuous development**

A view that regards development as a cumulative process of adding on more of the same types of skills that were there to begin with.

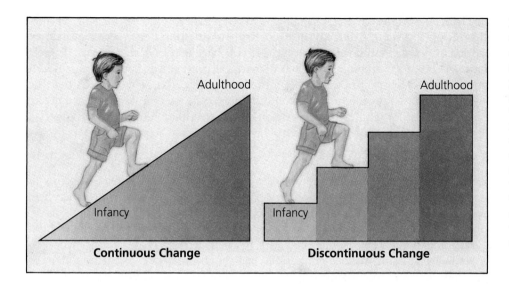

**FIGURE 1.1** • Is development continuous or discontinuous? Some theorists believe that development is a smooth, continuous process. Children gradually add more of the same types of skills. Other theorists think that development takes place in abrupt, discontinuous stages. Children change rapidly as they step up to a new level of development and then change very little for a while. With each new step, the child interprets and responds to the world in a qualitatively different way.

On the other hand, Angelo may have *unique ways of thinking, feeling, and behaving* that must be understood on their own terms—ones quite different from our own. If so, then development is a **discontinuous** process in which new ways of understanding and responding to the world emerge at particular time periods. From this perspective, Angelo may move through a series of developmental steps, each of which has unique features, until he reaches a final transformation that marks the beginning of adulthood.

Theories that accept the discontinuous perspective include a vital developmental concept: the concept of **stage.** Stages are *qualitative changes* in thinking, feeling, and behaving that characterize particular time periods of development. In stage theories, development is much like climbing a staircase, with each step corresponding to a more mature, reorganized way of functioning than the one that came before. The stage concept also assumes that children undergo periods of rapid transformation as they step up from one stage to the next, followed by plateaus during which they stand solidly within a stage. In other words, change is fairly sudden rather than gradual and always ongoing. Finally, stages are always assumed to be universal across children and cultures. That is, stage theories propose that children everywhere follow the same sequence of development. We will review some very influential stage theories later in this chapter.

*Nature versus Nurture*

Are genetic or environmental factors the most important influences on development? This is the age-old **nature-nurture controversy.** By *nature,* we mean inborn biological givens—the hereditary information we receive from our parents at the moment of conception that signals the body to grow and affects all our characteristics and skills. By *nurture,* we mean the complex forces of the physical and social world that children encounter in their homes, neighborhoods, schools, and communities.

All theories grant at least some role to both nature and nurture, but theories vary in the emphasis they place on each. For example, take a moment to consider the following questions. Is the older child's ability to think in more complex ways largely the result of an inborn timetable of growth? Or is it primarily influenced by the way parents and teachers stimulate and encourage the child? What accounts for the vast individual differences among children—in height, weight, physical coordination, intelligence, personality, and social skills? Is nature or nurture largely responsible?

**Discontinuous development**

A view in which new and different modes of interpreting and responding to the world emerge at particular time periods.

**Stage**

Qualitative changes in thinking, feeling, and behaving that characterize particular time periods of development.

**Nature–nurture controversy**

Disagreement among theorists about whether genetic or environmental factors are the most important determinants of development and behavior.

In later sections of this chapter and throughout this book, we will see that theories offer strikingly different answers to these questions. And the answers they provide are of great applied significance. If you believe that development is largely due to nature, then providing children with experiences aimed at stimulating growth would seem to be of little value. If, on the other hand, you are convinced that the environment has a profound impact on development, then you would want to offer a rich variety of learning experiences designed to help children realize their potential.

## A Balanced Point of View

So far, we have discussed the three basic issues of child development in terms of extremes—solutions on one side or the other. As we trace the unfolding of the field of child development in the rest of this chapter, you will see that the thinking of many theorists has softened. Modern ones, especially, recognize the merits of both sides. Some theories take an intermediate stand between organismic versus mechanistic and discontinuous versus continuous change. In addition, recent investigators have moved away from asking which is more important—heredity or environment. Instead, they want to know precisely *how nature and nurture work together* to influence the child's traits and capacities.

*• Why is there no single theory that can explain all aspects of child development?*

*• A school counselor advises a parent, "Don't worry about your teenager's argumentative behavior. It shows that she's beginning to see the world in a different way than she did as a young child. A rise in conflict with parents is a stage that all adolescents pass through." What stand is the counselor taking on the three basic issues about childhood and child development?*

BRIEF REVIEW   Child development is a field of study devoted to understanding human growth and change from conception through adolescence. Investigators from many disciplines have contributed to its vast knowledge base. Theories lend structure and meaning to observations of children and provide a sound basis for practical action. Almost all theories take a stand on three basic issues about what children are like and how they develop: (1) Is the child an organismic or mechanistic being? (2) Is development a continuous or discontinuous process? (3) Is nature or nurture more important in development?

Modern theories of child development are the result of centuries of change in Western cultural values, philosophical thinking about children, and scientific progress. To understand the field as it exists today, we must return to its early beginnings—to influences that long preceded scientific child study. We will see that many early ideas about children linger on as important forces in current theory and research.

## Medieval Times

In medieval times (the sixth through the fifteenth centuries), little importance was placed on childhood as a separate phase of the life cycle. The idea accepted by many theorists today, that the child's nature is unique and different from that of youths and adults, was much less common then. Instead, once children emerged from infancy, they were regarded as miniature, already-formed adults, a view called **preformationism.** This attitude is reflected in the art, language, and everyday entertainment of the times. If you look carefully at medieval paintings, you will see that children are depicted in dress and expression as immature adults. Before the sixteenth century, toys and games were not designed to occupy and amuse children but were for all people. And consider age, so important an aspect of modern personal identity that today's children can recite how old they are almost as soon as they can talk. Age

**Preformationism**
Medieval view of the child as a miniature adult.

*In this medieval painting, the young child is depicted as a miniature adult. His dress, expression, and activities resemble those of his elders. Through the fifteenth century, little emphasis was placed on childhood as a unique phase of the life cycle.* (Giraudon/Art Resource)

was unimportant in medieval custom and usage. People did not refer to it in everyday conversation, and it was not even recorded in family and civil records until the fifteenth and sixteenth centuries (Aries, 1962).

Nevertheless, faint glimmerings of the idea that children are unique emerged during medieval times. The Church defended the innocence of children and encouraged parents to provide spiritual training. Medical works had sections acknowledging the fragility of infants and children and providing special instructions for their care. And some laws recognized that children needed protection from adults who might mistreat or take advantage of them. But even though in a practical sense there was some awareness of the smallness and vulnerability of children, as yet there were no theories about the uniqueness of childhood or separate developmental periods (Borstelmann, 1983; Sommerville, 1982).

## The Reformation

In the sixteenth century, a revised image of childhood sprang from the religious movement that gave birth to Protestantism—in particular, from the Puritan belief in original sin. According to Puritan doctrine, the child was a fragile creature of God who needed to be safeguarded but who also needed to be reformed. Born evil and stubborn, children had to be civilized toward a destiny of virtue and salvation (Aries, 1962; Shahar, 1990). Harsh, restrictive child-rearing practices were recommended as the most efficient means for taming the depraved child. Infants were tightly swaddled, and children were dressed in stiff, uncomfortable clothing that held them in adultlike postures. In schools, disobedient pupils were routinely beaten by their schoolmasters (Stone, 1977).

As the Puritans emigrated from England to the United States, they brought with them the belief that child rearing was one of their most important obligations. Although they continued to regard the child's soul as tainted by original sin, they tried to promote reason in their sons and daughters so they would be able to separate right from wrong and resist temptation. The Puritans were the first to develop special reading materials for children that instructed them in religious and moral ideals. As they trained their children in self-reliance and self-control, Puritan parents gradually adopted a moderate balance between discipline and indulgence, severity and permissiveness (Pollock, 1987).

### Philosophies of the Enlightenment

The seventeenth-century Enlightenment brought new philosophies of reason and emphasized ideals of human dignity and respect. Revised ideas about childhood appeared that were more humane than those of centuries past.

*John Locke.* The writings of John Locke (1632–1704), a leading British philosopher, served as the forerunner of an important twentieth-century perspective that we will discuss shortly: *behaviorism.* Locke viewed the child as **tabula rasa.** Translated from Latin, this means blank slate or white piece of paper. According to this idea, children were not basically evil. They were, to begin with, nothing at all, and their characters could be shaped by all kinds of experiences during the course of growing up. Locke (1690/1892) described parents as rational tutors who could mold the child in any way they wished, through careful instruction, effective example, and rewards for good behavior. In addition, Locke was ahead of his time in recommending to parents child-rearing practices that were eventually supported by twentieth-century research. For example, he suggested that parents not reward children with money or sweets, but rather with praise and approval. Locke also opposed physical punishment: "The child repeatedly beaten in school cannot look upon books and teachers without experiencing fear and anger." Locke's philosophy led to a change from harshness toward children to kindness and compassion.

Look carefully at Locke's ideas, and you will see that he took a firm stand on each of the basic issues that we discussed earlier in this chapter. As blank slates, children were seen as fairly *passive* in the developmental process. The course of growth is written upon them by the environment. Locke also viewed development as *continuous.* Adultlike behaviors are gradually built up through the warm, consistent teachings of parents. Finally, Locke was a champion of *nurture*—of the power of the environment to determine whether children become good or bad, bright or dull, kind or selfish.

*Jean Jacques Rousseau.* In the eighteenth century, a new theory of childhood was introduced by the French philosopher of the Enlightenment, Jean Jacques Rousseau (1712–1778). Children, Rousseau (1762/1955) thought, were not blank slates and empty containers to be filled by adult instruction. Instead, they were **noble savages,** naturally endowed with a sense of right and wrong and with an innate plan for healthy growth. Unlike Locke, Rousseau thought children's built-in moral sense and unique ways of thinking and feeling would only be harmed by adult training. His was a permissive philosophy in which the adult should be receptive to the child's needs at each of four stages of development: infancy, childhood, late childhood, and adolescence.

Rousseau's philosophy includes two vitally important concepts that are found in modern theories. The first is the concept of *stage,* which we discussed earlier in this chapter. The second is the concept of **maturation,** which refers to a genetically determined, naturally unfolding course of growth. If you accept the notion that

**Tabula rasa**

Locke's view of the child as a blank slate whose character is shaped by experience.

**Noble savage**

Rousseau's view of the child as naturally endowed with an innate plan for orderly, healthy growth.

**Maturation**

A genetically determined, naturally unfolding course of growth.

children mature through a sequence of stages, then they cannot be preformed, miniature adults. Instead they are unique and different from adults, and their development is determined by their own inner nature. Compared to Locke, Rousseau took a very different stand on basic developmental issues. He saw children as *active* shapers of their own destiny, development as a *discontinuous* stagewise process, and *nature* as having mapped out the path and timetable of growth.

## Charles Darwin's Theory of Evolution

A century after Rousseau, another ancestor of modern child study—this time, of its scientific foundations—emerged. In the mid-nineteenth century, Charles Darwin (1809–1882), a British naturalist, joined an expedition to distant parts of the world, where he made careful observations of fossils and animal and plant life. Darwin (1859/1936) noticed the infinite variation among species. He also saw that within a species, no two individuals are exactly alike. From these observations, he constructed his famous theory of evolution.

The theory emphasized that certain species were selected by nature to survive in particular parts of the world because they had characteristics that fit with, or were adapted to, their surroundings. Other species died off because they were not as well suited to their environments. Individuals within a species who best met the survival requirements of the environment lived long enough to reproduce and pass their more favorable characteristics to future generations. Darwin's emphasis on the adaptive value of physical characteristics and behavior eventually found its way into important mid-twentieth century theories.

During his explorations, Darwin discovered that the early prenatal growth of many species was strikingly similar. This suggested that all species, including human beings, were descended from a few common ancestors. Other scientists concluded from Darwin's observation that the development of the human child, from conception to maturity, followed the same general plan as the evolution of the human species. Although this belief eventually proved to be inaccurate, efforts to chart parallels between child growth and human evolution prompted researchers to make careful observations of all aspects of children's behavior. Out of these first attempts to document an idea about development, the science of child study was born.

## Early Scientific Beginnings

***First Child Subjects—The Baby Biographies.*** Imagine yourself as a forerunner in the field of child development, confronted with observing children's growth for the first time. How might you go about this challenging task? Scientists of the late nineteenth and early twentieth centuries did what most of us would probably do in their place. They selected a convenient subject—a child of their own or of a close relative. Then, beginning in early infancy, they jotted down day-by-day descriptions and impressions of the youngster's behavior. Dozens of these baby biographies were published by the early twentieth century. In the following excerpt from one of them, the author reflects on the birth of her young niece, whose growth she followed during the first year of life:

> Its first act is a cry, not of wrath, . . . nor a shout of joy, . . . , but a snuffling, and then a long, thin, tearless á—á, with the timbre of a Scotch bagpipe, purely automatic, but of discomfort. With this monotonous and dismal cry, with its red, shriveled parboiled skin . . . , squinting, cross-eyed, pot-bellied, and bow-legged, it is not strange that, if the mother . . . has not come to love her child before birth, there is a brief interval occasionally dangerous to the child before the maternal instinct is fully aroused.
>
> It cannot be denied that this unflattering description is fair enough, and our baby was no handsomer than the rest of her kind. The little boy uncle, who had been elated

to hear that his niece resembled him, looked shocked and mortified when he saw her. Yet she did not lack admirers. I have never noticed that women (even those who are not mothers) mind a few little aesthetic defects, . . . with so many counterbalancing charms in the little warm, soft, living thing. (Shinn, 1900, pp. 20–21)

Can you tell from this passage why the baby biographies have sometimes been upheld as examples of how *not* to study children? These first investigators tended to be emotionally invested in their tiny subjects, and they seldom began their observations with a clear idea of what they wanted to find out about the child. Not surprisingly, many of the records made were eventually discarded as biased. However, we must keep in mind that the baby biographers were like explorers first setting foot on alien soil. When a field is new, we cannot expect its theories and methods to be well formulated.

The baby biographies were clearly a step in the right direction. In fact, two theorists of the nineteenth century, Darwin (1877) and the German biologist William Preyer (1882/1888), contributed to these early records of children's behavior. Preyer, especially, set high standards for making observations. He recorded what he saw immediately, as completely as possible, and at regular intervals. And he checked the accuracy of his own notes against those of a second observer (Cairns, 1983). These are the same high standards that modern researchers use when making observations of children. As a result of the biographers' pioneering efforts, in succeeding decades the child became a common subject of scientific research.

***The Normative Period of Child Study.***   G. Stanley Hall (1846–1924), one of the most influential American psychologists of the early twentieth century, is generally regarded as the founder of the child study movement (Dixon & Lerner, 1988). Inspired by Darwin's work, Hall and his well-known student Arnold Gesell (1880–1961) developed theories based on evolutionary ideas. These early leaders regarded child development as a genetically determined series of events that unfolds automatically, much like a blooming flower (Gesell, 1933; Hall, 1904).

Hall and Gesell are remembered less for their one-sided theories than for their intensive efforts to describe all aspects of child growth. Aware of the limitations of the baby biographies, Hall set out to collect a sound body of objective facts about children. This goal launched the **normative approach** to child study. In a normative investigation, measurements of behavior are taken on large numbers of children. Then age-related averages are computed to represent the typical child's development. Using this approach, Hall constructed elaborate questionnaires asking children of different ages almost everything they could tell about themselves—interests, fears, imaginary playmates, dreams, friendships, everyday knowledge, and more (White, 1992).

In the same tradition, Gesell devoted a major part of his career to collecting detailed normative information on the behavior of infants and children. His schedules of infant development were particularly complete, and revised versions continue to be used today (see Figure 1.2). Gesell was also among the first to make knowledge about child development meaningful to parents. He provided them with descriptions of motor achievements, social behaviors, and personality characteristics (Gesell & Ilg, 1943/1949, 1946/1949). Gesell hoped to relieve parents' anxieties by informing them of what to expect at each age. If, as he believed, the timetable of development is the product of millions of years of evolution, then children are naturally knowledgeable about their needs. His child-rearing advice, in the tradition of Rousseau, was a permissive approach that recommended sensitivity and responsiveness to children's cues.

***The Mental Testing Movement.***   While Hall and Gesell were developing their theories and methods in the United States, the French psychologist Alfred Binet

**Normative approach**
An approach in which age-related averages are computed to represent the typical child's development.

Points for wants
12 months

Stacks three cubes
15 months

Dumps raisin from bottle
18 months

Jumps, both feet off floor
24 months

**FIGURE 1.2** • Sample milestones from the most recent revision of Gesell's schedules of infant development. Norms on hundreds of motor, mental, language, and social skills are included. Gesell's efforts to describe the course of development continue to be useful today. (*Adapted from Knobloch, Stevens, & Malone, 1980.*)

(1857–1911) also took a normative approach to child development, but for a different reason. In the early 1900s, Binet and his colleague Theodore Simon were asked to find a way to identify retarded children in the Paris school system who needed to be placed in special classes. The first successful intelligence test, which they constructed for this purpose, grew out of practical educational concerns.

Previous attempts to create a useful intelligence test had met with little success. But Binet's effort was unique in that he began with a well-developed theory. In contrast to earlier views, which reduced intelligence to simple elements of reaction time and sensitivity to physical stimuli, Binet captured the complexity of children's thinking (Siegler, 1992). He defined intelligence as good judgment, planning, and critical reflection. Then he selected test questions that directly measured these abilities, creating a series of age-graded items that permitted him to compare the intellectual progress of different children.

In 1916, at Stanford University, Binet's test was translated into English and adapted for use with American children. It became known as the *Stanford-Binet Intelligence Scale*. Besides providing a score that could successfully predict school achievement, the Binet test sparked tremendous interest in individual differences in development. The mental testing movement was in motion. Comparisons of the intelligence test scores of children who varied in sex, ethnicity, birth order, family background, and other characteristics became a major focus of research. Intelligence tests also rose quickly to the forefront of the controversy over nature versus nurture that has continued throughout this century.

*BRIEF REVIEW*   The modern field of child development has roots dating far back into the past. In medieval times, children were regarded as miniature adults. By the sixteenth century, childhood became a distinct phase of the life cycle. The Puritan belief in original sin fostered a harsh, authoritarian approach to child rearing. During the seventeenth-century Enlightenment, Locke's "blank slate" and Rousseau's "inherently good" child promoted more humane views of children. Darwin's evolutionary ideas inspired maturational theories and the first attempts to study the child directly, in the form of baby biographies and Hall and Gesell's normative investigations. Out of the normative tradition arose Binet's first successful intelligence test and a concern with individual differences among children.

## MID-TWENTIETH CENTURY INFLUENCES

In the mid-twentieth century, the field of child development expanded into a legitimate discipline. Specialized societies were founded and research journals were launched. As child development attracted increasing interest, a variety of mid-twentieth-century theories emerged, each of which continues to have followers today. In these theories, the European concern with the inner thoughts and feelings of the child contrasts sharply with the focus of American academic psychology on scientific precision and concrete, observable behavior.

### Psychoanalytic Theory

> Early one morning in a town in northern California, the mother of a small boy of three was awakened by strange noises coming from his room. She hurried to his bed and saw him in a terrifying attack of some kind. To her it looked just like the heart attack from which his grandmother had died five days earlier. She called the doctor, who said that Sam's attack was epileptic. He administered sedatives and had the boy taken to a hospital in a near-by metropolis. . . .
>
> One month later, however, little Sam found a dead mole in the back yard and became morbidly agitated over it. His mother tried to answer his very shrewd questions as to what death was all about. He reluctantly went to sleep after having declared that his mother apparently did not know either. In the night he cried out, vomited, and began to twitch around the eyes and mouth. . . .
>
> When, two months later, a third attack occurred after the boy had accidently crushed a butterfly in his hand, the hospital added an amendment to its diagnosis: "precipitating factor: psychic stimulus." . . . Otherwise neither his birth history, nor the course of his infancy, nor his neurological condition between attacks showed specific pathology. His general health was excellent. (Erikson, 1950, pp. 25–26)

By the 1930s and 1940s, many parents came to psychiatrists and social workers with children like Sam, who suffered from serious emotional stress and difficulties in family and peer relations. The earlier normative movement had answered the question, "What are children like?" But child guidance professionals had to address the question, "How and why did children become the way they are?" to treat their difficulties. They turned for help to Freud's **psychoanalytic theory** because of its emphasis on understanding the unique developmental history of each child.

### Margin notes

• *If you could interview people of medieval times to find out whether they thought child development was a continuous or discontinuous process, how do you think they would respond?*

• *Suppose we could arrange a debate between John Locke and Jean Jacques Rousseau on the nature–nurture controversy. Summarize the argument that each of these historical figures is likely to present.*

**Psychoanalytic theory**

A perspective introduced by Freud that emphasizes the importance of sexual and aggressive drives and the unique developmental history of each child.

***Freud's Theory.***   Sigmund Freud (1856–1939), a Viennese physician, saw patients in his practice with a variety of nervous symptoms, such as hallucinations, fears, and paralyses, that appeared to have no physical basis. Seeking a cure for these troubled adults, Freud found that their symptoms could be relieved by having patients talk freely about painful events of their childhood. Using this "talking cure," he carefully examined the recollections of his patients. Startling the straightlaced Victorian society in which he lived, Freud concluded that infants and young children were sexual beings and that the way they were permitted to express their impulses lay at the heart of their adult behavior. Freud constructed his *psychosexual theory* of development on the basis of adult remembrances. It emphasizes that how parents manage their child's sexual and aggressive drives in the first few years of life is crucial for healthy personality development.

*Three Portions of the Personality.*   In Freud's theory, three parts of the personality—id, ego, and superego—become integrated during a sequence of five stages of development. The **id,** the largest portion of the mind, is inherited and present at birth. It is the source of basic biological needs and desires. The id seeks to satisfy its impulses head on, without delay. As a result, young babies cry vigorously when they are hungry, wet, or need to be held and cuddled.

The **ego**—the conscious, rational part of personality—emerges early in infancy to ensure that the id's desires are satisfied in accordance with reality. Recalling times when parents helped the baby gratify the id, the ego redirects the impulses so they are discharged on appropriate objects at acceptable times and places. Aided by the ego, the hungry baby of a few months of age stops crying when he sees his mother unfasten her clothing for breast-feeding or warm a bottle. And the more competent preschooler goes into the kitchen and gets a snack on her own.

Between 3 and 6 years of age, the **superego,** or seat of conscience, appears. It contains the values of society and is often in conflict with the id's desires. The superego develops from interactions with parents, who eventually insist that children control their biological impulses. Once the superego is formed, the ego is faced with the increasingly complex task of reconciling the demands of the id, the external world, and conscience (Freud, 1923/1974). For example, when the ego is tempted to gratify an id impulse by hitting a playmate to get an attractive toy, the superego may warn that such behavior is wrong. The ego must decide which of the two forces (id or superego) will win this inner struggle or work out a reasonable compromise, such as asking for a turn with the toy. According to Freud, the relations established between id, ego, and superego during the preschool years determine the individual's basic personality.

*Psychosexual Development.*   Freud (1938/1973) believed that, over the course of childhood, sexual impulses shift their focus from the oral to the anal to the genital regions of the body. In each stage of development, parents walk a fine line between permitting too much or too little gratification of their child's basic needs. Either extreme can cause the child's psychic energies to be *fixated,* or arrested, at a particular stage. Too much satisfaction makes the child unwilling to move on to a more mature level of behavior; too little leads the child to continue seeking gratification of the frustrated drive. If parents strike an appropriate balance, then children grow into well-adjusted adults with the capacity for mature sexual behavior, investment in family life, and rearing of the next generation. Table 1.2 briefly describes each of Freud's stages.

Freud's psychosexual theory highlighted the importance of family relationships for children's development. It was the first theory to stress the importance of early experience for later development. But Freud's perspective was eventually criticized for several reasons. First, the theory overemphasized the influence of sexual feelings in development. Second, because it was based on the problems of sexually repressed, well-to-do adults, some aspects of Freud's theory did not apply in cultures differing

**Id**
In Freud's theory, the part of the personality that is the source of basic biological needs and desires.

**Ego**
In Freud's theory, the part of the personality that directs the id's urges so they are discharged on appropriate objects and at acceptable times and places.

**Superego**
In Freud's theory, the part of the personality that is the seat of conscience and is often in conflict with the id's desires.

TABLE 1.2 • Freud's Psychosexual Stages

| Psychosexual Stage | Period of Development | Description |
|---|---|---|
| Oral | Birth–1 year | The new ego directs the baby's sucking activities toward breast or bottle. If oral needs are not met appropriately, the individual may develop such habits as thumb sucking, fingernail biting, and pencil chewing in childhood and overeating and smoking in later life. |
| Anal | 1–3 years | Young toddlers and preschoolers enjoy holding and releasing urine and feces. Toilet training becomes a major issue between parent and child. If parents insist that children be trained before they are ready or make too few demands, conflicts about anal control may appear in the form of extreme orderliness and cleanliness or messiness and disorder. |
| Phallic | 3–6 years | Id impulses transfer to the genitals, and the child finds pleasure in genital stimulation. Freud's *Oedipal conflict* for boys and *Electra conflict* for girls take place. Young children feel a sexual desire for the opposite-sex parent. To avoid punishment, they give up this desire and, instead, adopt the same-sex parent's values. As a result, the superego is formed. |
| Latency | 6–11 years | Sexual instincts die down, and the superego develops further. The child acquires new social values from adults outside the family and from play with same-sex peers. |
| Genital | Adolescence | Puberty causes the sexual impulses of the phallic stage to reappear. If development has been successful during earlier stages, it leads to marriage, mature sexuality, and the birth and rearing of children. |

*Erik Erikson*

Erik Erikson (1902–) expanded Freud's theory, emphasizing the psychosocial outcomes of development. At each psychosexual stage, a major psychological conflict is resolved. If the outcome is positive, individuals acquire personality dispositions and skills that permit them to contribute actively and constructively to society. (Olive R. Pierce/Black Star)

from nineteenth-century Victorian society. Finally, Freud's ideas were called into question because he never really studied children directly.

***Erikson's Theory.***  Several of Freud's followers took what was useful from his theory and stretched and rearranged it in ways that improved upon his vision. The most important of these neo-Freudians for the field of child development is Erik Erikson (1902–).

Although Erikson accepted Freud's basic psychosexual framework, he expanded the picture of development at each stage. First, Erikson emphasized the *psychosocial* outcomes of development—how each Freudian stage leads to the development of a unique personality and, at the same time, helps the individual become an active, contributing member of society. A series of basic psychological conflicts, each of which is resolved along a continuum from positive to negative, determines the course of development. As you can see in Table 1.3, Erikson's first five stages parallel Freud's stages. Second, Erikson did not regard important developmental tasks as limited to early childhood. He believed that they occur throughout life. Note that Erikson added three adult stages to Freud's model and was one of the first to recognize the life-span nature of development.

Finally, unlike Freud, Erikson pointed out that normal development must be understood in relation to each culture's unique life situation. For example, among the Yurok Indians (a tribe of fishermen and acorn gatherers living on the Northwest

TABLE 1.3 • Erikson's Psychosocial Stages

| Psychosocial Stage | Period of Development | Description | Corresponding Psychosexual Stage |
|---|---|---|---|
| Basic trust versus mistrust | Birth–1 year | From warm, responsive care, infants gain a sense of trust, or confidence, that the world is good. Mistrust occurs when infants have to wait too long for comfort and are handled harshly. | Oral |
| Autonomy versus shame and doubt | 1–3 years | Using new mental and motor skills, children want to choose and decide for themselves. Autonomy is fostered when parents permit reasonable free choice and do not force or shame the child. | Anal |
| Initiative versus guilt | 3–6 years | Through make-believe play, children experiment with the kind of person they can become. Initiative—a sense of ambition and responsibility—develops when parents support their child's new sense of purpose and direction. The danger is that parents will demand too much self-control, which leads to overcontrol, or too much guilt. | Phallic |
| Industry versus inferiority | 6–11 years | At school, children develop the capacity to work and cooperate with others. Inferiority develops when negative experiences at home, at school, or with peers lead to feelings of incompetence and inferiority. | Latency |
| Identity versus identity diffusion | Adolescence | The adolescent tries to answer the question, "Who am I, and what is my place in society?" Self-chosen values and vocational goals lead to a lasting personal identity. The negative outcome is confusion about future adult roles. | Genital |
| Intimacy versus isolation | Young adulthood | Young people work on establishing intimate ties to other people. Because of earlier disappointments, some individuals cannot form close relationships and remain isolated from others. | |
| Generativity versus stagnation | Middle adulthood | Generativity means giving to the next generation through child rearing, caring for other people, or productive work. The person who fails in these ways feels an absence of meaningful accomplishment. | |
| Ego integrity versus despair | Old age | In this final stage, individuals reflect on the kind of person they have been. Integrity results from feeling that life was worth living as it happened. Old people who are dissatisfied with their lives fear death. | |

coast of the United States), babies are deprived of breast-feeding for the first ten days after birth and instead are fed a thin soup from a small shell. At six months of age, infants are abruptly weaned, an event enforced, if necessary, by having the mother leave for a few days. These experiences, from our cultural vantage point, seem like cruel attempts to frustrate the child's oral needs. But Erikson pointed out that the Yurok live in a world in which salmon fill the river just once a year, a circumstance that requires the development of considerable self-restraint for survival. In this way, he showed that child-rearing experiences can only be understood by making reference to the values and requirements of the child's society as a whole.

***Contributions and Limitations of Psychoanalytic Theory.*** At this point, you are probably wondering what became of little Sam. Erikson interviewed Sam's parents and observed his behavior using the *clinical method,* which seeks to understand the unique personality of a single child. Here are some facts that Erikson discovered about Sam's case:

> Sam's grandmother had come to visit the family in its new home. There was great concern over her health, since she suffered from a weak heart. An active, vigorous boy who enjoyed teasing people, one day Sam was left in his grandmother's care. Ignoring his mother's stern warnings to behave himself, Sam climbed on a chair and fell. Sam's mother returned to find his grandmother on the floor, stricken by a heart attack. She remained ill for months and eventually died, a few days before Sam's problems began.
>
> Sam's mother had not told him the truth about his grandmother's death—only that she "had gone on a long trip north to Seattle" and that her coffin, mysteriously removed from the house one day, was packed with grandmother's books. But Sam was a bright little boy who had not seen his grandmother do much reading and who puzzled over why so many tears would be shed over a box of books.
>
> According to psychoanalytic theory, young children work through their anxieties in play, in much the same way that adults seek relief by "talking them out" with a sympathetic companion. Sam built box after box using large blocks at nursery school, experimenting with what it would be like to be locked up inside. One day, during a domino game with his therapist, Sam built a rectangular configuration, with all the dots facing inward.
>
> Erikson capitalized on the moment. "If you wanted to see the dots on your blocks, you would have to be inside that little box, like a dead person in a coffin," he explained. "When they carried your grandmother away in the coffin you probably thought that you made her die and therefore had to die yourself. That's why you built those big boxes in your school, just as you built this little one today. In fact, you must have thought you were going to die every time you had one of those attacks."
>
> "Yes," Sam answered softly, in a moment of self-reflection. Thereafter, the seizures became rare and mild occurrences. (paraphrased material and quotations from Erikson, 1950, pp. 26–32)

The clinical method, a powerful tool for studying human mental life, is one of psychoanalytic theory's great contributions. Psychoanalytic theory has also inspired research on many aspects of child development, including infant–mother attachment, aggression, sibling relationships, child-rearing practices, moral development, sex typing, and adolescent identity.

Although psychoanalytic theory did much to emphasize the importance of children's emotional health, it is no longer in the mainstream of child development research. Perhaps psychoanalytic theory became isolated from the rest of the field because it was so strongly committed to the clinical approach that it failed to consider other methods (Sears, 1975). In addition, child development researchers found it difficult to verify many psychoanalytic ideas, such as Freud's psychosexual stages (Schultz, 1975).

## Behaviorism and Social Learning Theory

At the same time that psychoanalytic theory gained in prominence, child study was also influenced by a very different perspective: **behaviorism,** a tradition consistent with Locke's tabula rasa. American behaviorism began with the work of psychologist John Watson (1878–1958) in the early part of the twentieth century. Watson wanted to create an objective science of psychology. Unlike psychoanalytic theorists, he believed in studying directly observable events—stimuli and responses—rather than the unseen workings of the mind.

**Behaviorism**

An approach that views directly observable events—stimuli and responses—as the appropriate focus of study and the development of behavior as taking place through classical and operant conditioning.

***Traditional Behaviorism.*** Watson was impressed with some studies of animal learning carried out by the famous Russian physiologist, Ivan Pavlov. Pavlov knew that dogs release saliva as an innate reflex when they are given food. But soon he noticed that his dogs were salivating before they tasted any food—when they saw the trainer who usually fed them. The dogs, Pavlov reasoned, must have learned to associate a neutral stimulus (the trainer) with another stimulus (food) that produces a reflexive response (salivation). As a result of this association, the neutral stimulus could bring about the response by itself. Anxious to test this idea, Pavlov successfully taught dogs to salivate at the sound of a bell by pairing it with the presentation of food. He had discovered *classical conditioning*.

Watson wanted to find out if classical conditioning could be applied to children's behavior. In an historic experiment, he taught Albert, a 9-month-old infant, to fear a neutral stimulus—a soft white rat—by presenting it several times with a sharp, loud sound (which naturally scared the baby). Little Albert, who at first had reached out eagerly to touch the furry rat, cried and turned his head away when he caught sight of it (Watson & Raynor, 1920). In fact, Albert's fear was so intense that researchers eventually questioned the ethics of studies like this one (an issue that we will take up later in this chapter). On the basis of findings like these, Watson concluded that environment was the supreme force in child development. Adults could mold children's behavior in any way they wished, he thought, by carefully controlling stimulus–response associations.

After Watson, American behaviorism developed along several lines. The first was Clark Hull's *drive reduction theory*. According to this view, children continually act to satisfy physiological needs and reduce states of tension. As *primary drives* of hunger, thirst, and sex are met, a wide variety of stimuli associated with them become *secondary*, or *learned drives*. For example, a Hullian theorist believes that infants prefer the closeness and attention of adults who have given them food and relieved their discomfort. To ensure adults' affection, children will acquire all sorts of responses that adults desire of them—politeness, honesty, patience, persistence, obedience, and more.

Another form of behaviorism was B.F. Skinner's (1904–1990) *operant conditioning theory*. Skinner rejected Hull's idea that primary drive reduction is the only way to get children to learn. According to Skinner, a child's behavior can be increased by following it with a wide variety of *reinforcers* besides food and drink, such as praise, a friendly smile, or a new toy. It can also be decreased through *punishment*, such as withdrawal of privileges, parental disapproval, or being sent to be alone in one's room. As a result of Skinner's work, operant conditioning became a broadly applied learning principle in child psychology. We will consider these conditioning principles more fully when we explore the infant's learning capacities in Chapter 5.

*Social Learning Theory.* Psychologists quickly became interested in whether behaviorism might offer a more direct and effective explanation of the development of children's social behavior than the less precise concepts of psychoanalytic theory. This concern sparked the emergence of **social learning theory.** Social learning theorists accepted the principles of conditioning and reinforcement that came before them. They also built on these principles, offering expanded views of how children and adults acquire new responses.

Several kinds of social learning theory emerged. The most influential was devised by Albert Bandura and his colleagues. Bandura (1977) demonstrated that *modeling*, otherwise known as imitation or observational learning, is the basis for a wide variety of children's behaviors. He recognized that children acquire many favorable and unfavorable responses simply by watching and listening to others around them. The baby who claps her hands after her mother does so, the child who angrily hits a playmate in the same way that he has been punished at home, and the teenager who wears the same clothes and hairstyle as her friends at school are all displaying observational learning.

Bandura's work continues to influence much research on children's social development. However, like changes in the field of child development as a whole, today his theory stresses the importance of *cognition,* or thinking. Bandura has shown that children's ability to listen, remember, and abstract general rules from complex sets of

*B. F. Skinner*

*B. F. Skinner (1904–1990) rejected Hull's idea that primary drive reduction is the basis of all learning. He developed an alternative learning principle, operant conditioning, that has been widely applied in the field of child development. (Chris J. Johnson/Stock Boston)*

**Social learning theory**

An approach that emphasizes the role of modeling, or observational learning, in the development of behavior.

*Through careful observations of and clinical interviews with children, Jean Piaget (1896–1980) developed his comprehensive theory of cognitive development. His work has inspired more research on children than any other single theory.*

**Behavior modification**

A set of practical procedures that combines reinforcement, modeling, and the manipulation of situational cues to change behavior.

**Cognitive-developmental theory**

An approach introduced by Piaget that views the child as actively building mental structures and cognitive development as taking place in stages.

observed behavior affects their imitation and learning. In fact, the most recent revision of Bandura's (1986, 1989) theory places such strong emphasis on how children think about themselves and other people that he calls it a *social cognitive* rather than a social learning approach. Nevertheless, he still regards modeling as the foundation for all aspects of social development.

***Contributions and Limitations of Behaviorism.*** Like psychoanalytic theory, behaviorism and social learning theory have had a major impact on applied work with children. Yet the techniques used are decidedly different. **Behavior modification** refers to procedures that combine conditioning and modeling to eliminate children's undesirable behaviors and increase their socially acceptable responses. It has largely been used with children who have serious developmental problems, such as persistent aggression and language delays (Patterson, 1982; Whitehurst et al., 1989). But behavior modification is also effective in dealing with relatively common difficulties of childhood. For example, in a recent study, preschoolers' anxious reactions during dental treatment were reduced by giving them small toys for answering questions about a story read to them while the dentist worked. Because the children could not listen to the story and kick and cry at the same time, their disruptive behaviors subsided (Stark et al., 1989).

Although the techniques of behaviorism are helpful in treating many problems, we must keep in mind that making something happen through modeling and reinforcement does not mean that these principles provide a complete account of development (Horowitz, 1987). We will see in later sections that many theorists believe that behaviorism offers too narrow a view of important environmental influences. These extend beyond immediate reinforcements and modeled behaviors to the richness of children's physical and social worlds. And, as Piaget's theory shows, behaviorism has also been criticized for underestimating children's active role in their own learning.

## Piaget's Cognitive-Developmental Theory

If there is one individual who has influenced the modern field of child development more than any other, it is the Swiss cognitive theorist Jean Piaget (1896–1980). Although American child development specialists had been aware of Piaget's work since 1930, they did not grant it much attention until the 1960s. A major reason is that Piaget's ideas and methods of studying children were very much at odds with the behaviorist tradition that dominated American psychology during the middle of the twentieth century (Beilin, 1992).

Recall that behaviorists did not study the child's mental life. In their view, thinking could be reduced to connections between stimuli and responses, and development was a continuous process, consisting of a gradual increase in the number and strength of these connections with age. In contrast, Piaget did not believe that knowledge was imposed on a passive, reinforced child. According to his **cognitive-developmental theory,** children actively construct knowledge as they manipulate and explore their world, and their cognitive development takes place in stages.

***Piaget's Stages.*** Piaget's view of development was greatly influenced by his early training in biology. Central to his theory is the biological concept of *adaptation* (Piaget, 1971). Just as the structures of the body are adapted to fit with the environment, so the structures of the mind develop over the course of childhood to better fit with, or represent, the external world. In infancy and early childhood, children's understanding is markedly different from that of adults. For example, Piaget believed that young babies do not realize that an object hidden from view—a favorite toy or even the mother—continues to exist. He also concluded that preschoolers' thinking is full of faulty logic and fantasy. For example, preschoolers commonly say that the amount of milk or lemonade changes when it is poured into a differently shaped container. And some of them insist that the images in their dreams are real objects that miraculously appear beside their beds at night! According to Piaget, children eventually revise these incorrect ideas in their ongoing efforts to achieve an *equilibrium,* or balance, between internal structures and information they encounter in their everyday worlds (Beilin, 1989; Kuhn, 1988).

In Piaget's theory, children move through four broad stages of development, each of which is characterized by qualitatively distinct ways of thinking. Table 1.4 provides a brief description of Piaget's stages. In the *sensorimotor stage,* cognitive development begins with the baby's use of the senses and movements to explore the world. These action patterns evolve into the symbolic but illogical thinking of the preschooler in the *preoperational stage.* Then cognition is transformed into the more organized reasoning of the school-age child in the *concrete operational stage.* Finally, in the *formal operational stage,* thought becomes the complex, abstract reasoning system of the adolescent and adult.

***Piaget's Methods of Study.*** Piaget devised special methods for investigating how children think. In the early part of his career, he carefully observed his three infant children and also presented them with little problems, such as an attractive object that could be grasped, mouthed, kicked, or searched for when hidden from view. From their reactions, Piaget derived his ideas about cognitive changes that take place during the first two years of life.

In studying childhood and adolescent thought, Piaget took advantage of children's ability to describe their thinking. He adapted the clinical method of psychoanalysis, conducting open-ended *clinical interviews* in which a child's initial response to a task served as the basis for the next question Piaget would ask. We will look at an example of a Piagetian clinical interview, as well as the strengths and weaknesses of this technique, when we discuss research methods later in this chapter.

In Piaget's sensorimotor stage, infants learn about the world by acting on it. As this 1-year-old takes apart, bangs, and drops these nesting cups, she discovers that her movements have predictable effects on objects and that objects influence one another in regular ways. (Erika Stone)

TABLE 1.4 • Piaget's Stages of Development

| Period of Development | Stage | Description |
|---|---|---|
| Birth–2 years | Sensorimotor | Infants "think" by acting on the world with their eyes, ears, and hands. As a result, they invent ways of solving sensorimotor problems, such as pulling a lever to hear the sound of a music box, finding hidden toys, and putting objects in and taking them out of containers. |
| 2–7 years | Preoperational | Preschool children use symbols to represent their earlier sensorimotor discoveries. Development of language and make-believe play takes place. However, thinking lacks the logical qualities of the two remaining stages. |
| 7–11 years | Concrete operational | Children's reasoning becomes logical. School-age children understand that a certain amount of lemonade or play dough remains the same even after its appearance changes. They also organize objects into hierarchies of classes and subclasses. However, thinking falls short of adult intelligence. It is not yet abstract. |
| 11 years on | Formal operational | The capacity for abstraction permits adolescents to reason with symbols that do not refer to objects in the real world, as in advanced mathematics. They can also think of all possible outcomes in a scientific problem, not just the most obvious ones. |

***Contributions and Limitations of Piaget's Theory.*** Piaget's cognitive-developmental perspective has stimulated more research on children than any other single theory. It also convinced many child development specialists that children are active learners whose minds are inhabited by rich structures of knowledge. Practically speaking, Piaget's theory encouraged the development of educational philosophies

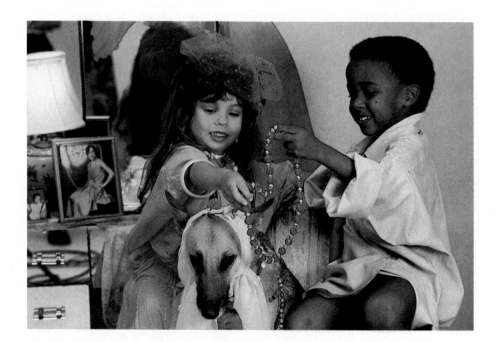

*In Piaget's preoperational stage, preschool children represent their earlier sensorimotor discoveries with symbols. Language and make-believe play develop rapidly. These 4-year-olds create an imaginative play scene with dress-up clothes and the assistance of a very cooperative family pet.* (Tom McCarthy/Stock South)

*In Piaget's concrete operational stage, school-age children think in an organized and logical fashion about concrete objects. This 8-year-old boy understands that the hamster on one side of the balance scale is just as heavy as the metal weights on the other, even though the two types of objects look and feel quite different from each other.* (Tim Davis/Photo Researchers)

and programs that emphasize children's discovery learning and direct contact with the environment. A Piagetian classroom contains richly equipped activity areas designed to stimulate children to revise their immature cognitive structures.

Despite Piaget's overwhelming contribution to child development and education, in recent years his theory has been challenged. New evidence indicates that Piaget underestimated the competencies of infants and preschoolers. We will see in later chapters that, when young children are given tasks scaled down in difficulty, their understanding appears closer to that of the older child and adult than Piaget believed. This discovery has led many investigators to conclude that the maturity of children's thinking may depend on their familiarity with the investigator's task and

*In Piaget's formal operational stage, adolescents can think logically and abstractly. As he discusses an algebraic equation with his teacher, this 14-year-old shows that he can reason with symbols that do not necessarily represent objects in the real world.* (John Lei/Stock Boston)

the kind of knowledge sampled. Finally, many studies show that children's performance on Piagetian problems can be improved with training. This finding raises questions about his assumption that discovery learning rather than adult teaching is the best way to foster development.

Today, the field of child development is divided over its loyalty to Piaget's ideas. Those who continue to find merit in Piaget's approach accept a modified view of his cognitive stages—one in which changes in children's thinking are not sudden and abrupt, but take place much more gradually than Piaget believed (Case, 1985; Fischer & Pipp, 1984). Others have given up the idea of cognitive stages in favor of a continuous approach to development—information processing—that we will take up in the next section (Gelman & Baillargeon, 1983).

*• A 6-year-old suddenly becomes frightened of the dark and refuses to go to sleep at night. How would a psychoanalyst and a behaviorist differ in their approach to treating this problem?*

*• What biological concept is emphasized in Piaget's cognitive-developmental approach? From which nineteenth-century theory did Piaget borrow this idea?*

**BRIEF REVIEW**   Three perspectives dominated child development research in the middle of the twentieth century. Child guidance professionals turned to Freud's psychoanalytic approach, and Erikson's expansion of it, for help in understanding personality development and children's emotional difficulties. Behaviorism and social learning theory use conditioning and modeling to explain the appearance of new responses and to treat behavior problems. Piaget's stage theory of cognitive development revolutionized the field with its view of children as active beings who take responsibility for their own learning.

## RECENT PERSPECTIVES

New ways of understanding the child are constantly emerging—questioning, building on, and enhancing the discoveries of earlier theories. Today, a burst of fresh approaches and research emphases, including information processing, ethology, ecological systems theory, and Vygotsky's sociocultural perspective, is broadening our understanding of children's development.

### Information Processing

During the 1970s, child development researchers became disenchanted with behaviorism as a complete account of children's learning and disappointed in their efforts to completely verify Piaget's ideas. They turned to the field of cognitive psychology for new ways to understand the development of children's thinking. Today, a leading perspective is **information processing.** It is a general approach in which the human mind is viewed as a symbol-manipulating system through which information flows (Klahr, 1989). From presentation to the senses at *input* and behavioral responses at *output,* information is actively coded, transformed, and organized.

Information processing is often thought of as a field of scripts, frames, and flowcharts. Diagrams are used to map the precise series of steps individuals use to solve problems and complete tasks, much like the plans devised by programmers to get computers to perform a series of "mental operations." Let's look at an example to clarify the usefulness of this approach. The left-hand side of Figure 1.3 shows the steps that Andrea, an academically successful 8-year-old, used to complete a two-digit subtraction problem. The right-hand side displays the faulty procedure of Jody, who arrived at the wrong answer. The flowchart approach ensures that models of child and adult thinking will be very clear. For example, by comparing the two procedures shown in Figure 1.3, we know exactly what is necessary for effective problem solving and where Jody went wrong in searching for a solution. As a result, we can pinpoint Jody's difficulties and design an intervention to improve her reasoning.

**Information processing**
An approach that views the human mind as a symbol-manipulating system through which information flows and that regards cognitive development as a continuous process.

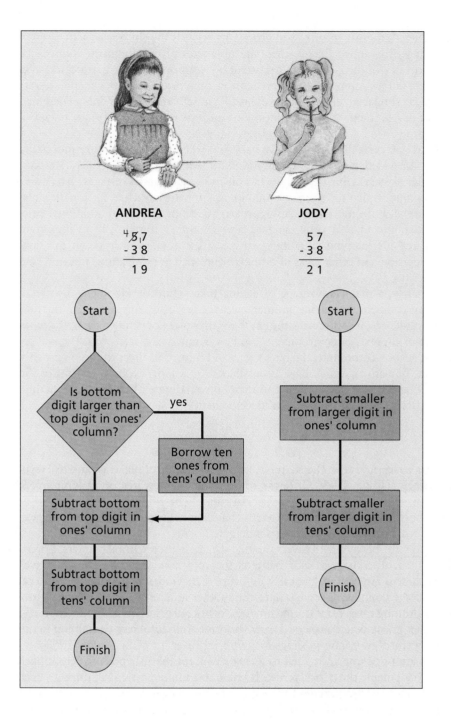

**FIGURE 1.3** • Information processing flow charts showing the steps that two 8-year-olds used to solve a math problem. In this two-digit subtraction problem with a borrowing operation, you can see that Andrea's procedure is correct, while Jody's results in a wrong answer.

A wide variety of information processing models exist. Some (like the one in Figure 1.3) are fairly narrow in that they track children's mastery of a single task. Others describe the human information processing system as a whole (Atkinson & Shiffrin, 1968; Craik & Lockhart, 1972). These general models are used as guides for asking questions about broad, age-related changes in children's thinking. For example, does a child's ability to search the environment for information needed to solve a problem become more organized and planful with age? How much new information can preschoolers hold in memory compared to older children and adults? To what extent does a child's current knowledge influence her ability to learn more?

Like Piaget's theory, information processing regards the child as an active, sense-making being. But unlike Piaget, there are no stages of development. Rather, the thought processes studied—perception, attention, memory, planning strategies, categorization of information, and comprehension of written and spoken prose—are assumed to be similar at all ages but present to a lesser extent in children. Therefore, the view of development is one of continuous increase rather than abrupt, stagewise change.

Perhaps you can tell from what we have said so far that information processing has already provided important implications for education (Hall, 1989; Resnick, 1989; Siegler, 1983a). But the theory has fallen short in some respects. Aspects of children's cognition that are not linear and logical in nature, such as imagination and creativity, are all but ignored by this approach (Greeno, 1989). In addition, critics complain that information processing isolates children's thinking from important features of real-life learning situations. So far, it has told us little about the links between cognition and other areas of development, such as motivation, emotion, and social experience.

Fortunately, a major advantage of having many child development theories is that they can compensate for one another's weaknesses. A unique feature of the final three perspectives we will discuss is the emphasis they place on *contexts for development*. The impact of context, or environment, can be examined at many levels. We will see that family, school, community, larger society, and culture all affect children's growth. In addition, human capacities have been shaped by a long evolutionary history in which our brains and bodies adapted to their surroundings. The next theory, ethology, emphasizes this biological side of development.

### Ethology

**Ethology** is concerned with the adaptive, or survival, value of behavior and its evolutionary history (Hinde, 1989). It began to be applied to research on children in the 1960s but has become even more influential today. The origins of ethology can be traced to the work of Darwin. Its modern foundations were laid by two European zoologists, Konrad Lorenz and Niko Tinbergen.

Watching the behaviors of diverse animal species in their natural habitats, Lorenz and Tinbergen observed behavior patterns that promote survival. The most well known of these is *imprinting,* the early following behavior of certain baby birds that ensures that the young will stay close to the mother and be fed and protected from danger. Imprinting takes place during an early, restricted time period of development. If the mother goose is not present during this time, but an object resembling her in important features is, young goslings may imprint on it instead (Lorenz, 1952).

Observations of imprinting led to a major concept that has been widely applied in child development: the *critical period*. It refers to a limited time span during which the child is biologically prepared to acquire certain adaptive behaviors but needs the support of an appropriately stimulating environment. Many researchers have conducted studies to find out whether complex cognitive and social behaviors must be learned during restricted time periods. For example, if children are deprived of adequate food or physical and social stimulation during the early years of life, will their intelligence be permanently impaired? If language is not mastered during the preschool years, is the child's capacity to acquire it reduced? We will answer these questions and other similar ones in later chapters.

Inspired by observations of imprinting, the British psychoanalyst John Bowlby (1969) applied ethological theory to the understanding of the human infant–caregiver relationship. He argued that attachment behaviors of babies, such as smiling, babbling, grasping, and crying, are built-in social signals that encourage the parent to approach, care for, and interact with the baby. By keeping the mother near,

**Ethology**

An approach concerned with the adaptive, or survival, value of behavior and its evolutionary history.

Konrad Lorenz (1903–1989) was one of the founders of ethology and a keen observer of animal behavior. He developed the concept of imprinting. Here, young geese who were separated from their mother and placed in the company of Lorenz during an early, critical period of development show that they have imprinted on him. They follow him about as he swims through the water, a response that promotes survival. (Nina Leen/Life Magazine. © Time, Inc.)

these behaviors help ensure that the baby will be fed, protected from danger, and provided with stimulation and affection necessary for healthy growth. The development of attachment in human infants is a lengthy process involving changes in psychological structures that lead to a deep affectional tie between caregiver and baby. As we will see in Chapter 7, it is far more complex than imprinting in baby birds. But for now, notice how the ethological view of attachment, which emphasizes the role of innate infant signals, differs sharply from the behaviorist drive reduction explanation we mentioned earlier—that the baby's desire for closeness to the mother is a learned response based on feeding.

Observations by ethologists have shown that many aspects of children's social behavior, including emotional expressions, aggression, cooperation, and social play, resemble those of our primate ancestors. Although ethology emphasizes the genetic and biological roots of behavior, learning is also considered important because it lends flexibility and greater adaptiveness to behavior. Since ethologists believe that children's behavior can best be understood in terms of its adaptive value, they seek a full understanding of the environment, including physical, social, and cultural aspects (Hinde, 1989; Miller, 1989). The next contextual perspective we will discuss, ecological systems theory, serves as an excellent complement to ethology, since it shows how various aspects of the environment, from immediate human relationships to larger societal forces, work together to affect children's development.

### Ecological Systems Theory

Urie Bronfenbrenner (1979, 1989), an American psychologist, is responsible for a new approach to child development that has risen to the forefront of the field over the past decade. **Ecological systems theory** views the child as developing within a complex *system* of relationships affected by multiple levels of the surrounding environment. To illustrate the main features of this approach, let's visit the families of two 4-year-old boys:

> Jonathan lives in a stable middle-class family with happily married parents, Susan and Jim, both of whom are employed. An active, demanding preschooler, Jonathan often strains his parents' endurance with his boundless energy and difficulty sitting still. Susan returned to work when Jonathan was 6 months old. During the day, Jonathan is

**Ecological systems theory**
Bronfenbrenner's approach, which views the child as developing within a complex system of relationships affected by multiple levels of the environment, from immediate settings of family and school to broad cultural values and programs.

*Urie Bronfenbrenner*
*Urie Bronfenbrenner is the origi-*
*nator of ecological systems theory.*
*He views the child as developing*
*within a complex system of rela-*
*tionships affected by multiple*
*levels of the surrounding environ-*
*ment, from the immediate set-*
*ting to broad cultural values,*
*laws, and customs.* (Courtesy of
Urie Bronfenbrenner, Cornell
University)

cared for in the home of a kind, patient woman who has two young children of her own. When Susan and Jim pick Jonathan up after work, they stop in to find out how his day has gone. On Saturday mornings, Jim takes Jonathan to gymnastics class, an activity that helps meet his high need for physical activity. When Jonathan's spirited behavior becomes too much for Susan, Jim quickly distracts him. And both parents set aside special times during the week to spend with their son. Susan and Jim are relieved that Jonathan's pace is beginning to slow down before he enters kindergarten next year.

Eric, an equally active child, experiences a very different kind of home life. His mother Greta was recently divorced. When Eric's dad left, Greta had trouble making ends meet. She moved to a small apartment in a low-rental neighborhood and took a job as a cashier. Greta had to find inexpensive child care for Eric quickly. She put him in a day-care center that she knew had too many children and too little supervision. But little else was available nearby, and she didn't have time to shop around. Greta misses her previous next-door neighbor, with whom she used to talk about her family problems and Eric's angry reaction to the divorce. Most days, Greta feels overwhelmed by financial worries, loneliness, the demands of her job, household chores, and Eric's increasingly defiant behavior. Evenings often end with Eric refusing to go to bed and Greta, exhausted and in tears, shouting and threatening to spank him.

Ecological systems theory highlights the many reasons that Jonathan is happy and well adjusted, while Eric is at risk for future problems. As shown in Figure 1.4, the environment is made up of four nested structures that include but extend beyond the settings in which children spend their everyday lives.

**The Microsystem.**    At the innermost level of the environment is the *microsystem,* which refers to activities and interaction patterns in the child's immediate surroundings. Bronfenbrenner emphasizes that to understand child development at this level, we must keep in mind that all relationships are *bidirectional and reciprocal.* That is, adults affect children's behavior, but children's characteristics—their personality styles and ways of thinking—also influence the behavior of adults. Both Jonathan and Eric are especially lively youngsters who would challenge the resources of just about any parent! But why are Jonathan's parents sensitive but firm, while Eric's mother is inconsistent, impatient, and punitive? To answer this question, we must look at environmental support systems that surround and influence parent–child relationships.
        Within the microsystem, interaction is affected by the presence of *third parties.* If other people in the setting are supportive, then the quality of the parent–child relationship is enhanced. Notice how Susan and Jim help one another in their parenting roles. In contrast, Greta has no one with whom to share family responsibilities and discuss Eric's needs.

**The Mesosystem.**    For children to develop at their best, child-rearing supports must also exist in the larger environment. The second level in Bronfenbrenner's theory is the *mesosystem.* It refers to connections among microsystems, such as home, school, neighborhood, and child-care center, which foster children's development. Jonathan benefits from ample mesosystem support. For example, Susan and Jim talk often with his caregiver, and Jim visits Jonathan's gymnastics class and touches base with his teacher. This is not true for Eric, whose mother has little time to check on his day-care experiences and whose caregiver has too many children to spend time with parents.

**The Exosystem.**    The *exosystem* refers to social settings that do not contain children, but that affect their experiences in immediate settings. These can be formal organizations, such as the parents' workplace or health and welfare services in the

**FIGURE 1.4** • The four layers of the environment in ecological systems theory. The microsystem refers to relations between the child and the immediate environment, the mesosystem to connections among the child's immediate settings, the exosystem to social settings that affect but do not contain the child, and the macrosystem to values, laws, and customs of the child's culture. *(Adapted from Kopp & Krakow, 1982.)*

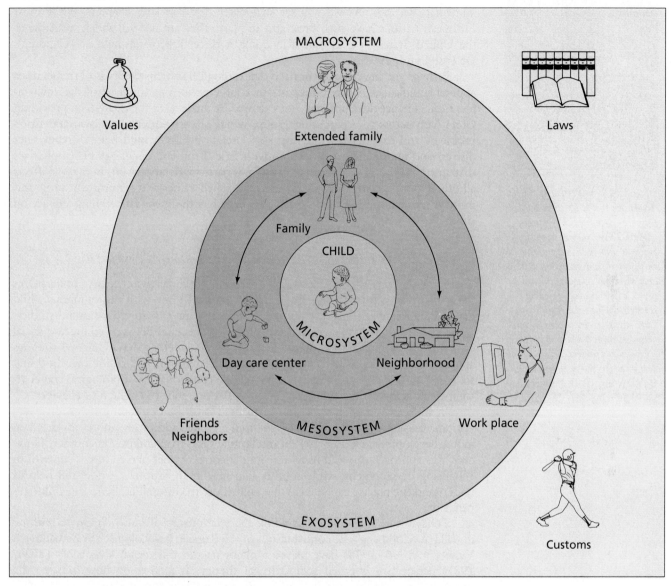

community. For example, flexible work schedules, paid maternity and paternity leave, and sick leave for parents whose children are ill are ways that work settings can help parents in their child-rearing roles and, indirectly, enhance development. Exosystem supports can also be informal, such as parents' *social networks*—friends and extended family members who provide advice, companionship, and even financial assistance. Notice how Greta lost a meaningful exosystem tie with a neighbor when she had to move. Because she has few personal and community-based relationships on which to rely, she feels isolated and unhappy. This is one reason that she has become harsh and punitive with her son (Emery, 1989).

**The Macrosystem.** The outermost level of Bronfenbrenner's model is the *macrosystem*. It is not a specific context. Instead, it refers to the values, laws, and customs

*Lev Vygotsky*
*According to the Russian psychol-*
*ogist Lev Semanovich Vygotsky*
*(1896–1934), many cognitive*
*processes and skills are socially*
*transferred from more knowledge-*
*able members of society to chil-*
*dren. Vygotsky's sociocultural*
*theory helps us understand the*
*wide variation in cognitive com-*
*petencies from culture to culture.*
*Vygotsky is pictured here with his*
*daughter.* (Courtesy of James
V. Wertsch, Clark University)

**Sociocultural theory**
Vygotsky's approach, in
which children acquire the
ways of thinking and behaving that make up a commu-
nity's culture through
cooperative dialogues with
more knowledgeable mem-
bers of that society.

of a particular culture. The priority that the macrosystem gives to children's needs affects the support they receive at lower levels of the environment. For example, in countries that require high quality standards for day care and workplace benefits for employed parents, children are more likely to have favorable experiences in their immediate settings. As we will see in greater detail in later chapters, while most European nations have such programs in place, they are not yet widely available in the United States to assist Greta in doing a better job of raising Eric (Children's Defense Fund, 1991a).

Perhaps you have already noticed that ecological systems theory is of tremendous applied significance, since it suggests that interventions at any level of the environment can enhance development. For example, at the level of the exosystem, providing Greta with access to a parenting group, where she can discuss her own and Eric's problems and experience gratifying social relationships, would help to relieve her distress and improve her relationship with Eric. Bronfenbrenner (1989) emphasizes that change at the level of the macrosystem is particularly important. Because it affects all other environmental levels, revising established values and government programs in ways more favorable to child development has the most far-reaching impact on children's well-being.

## Cross-Cultural Research and Vygotsky's Sociocultural Perspective

Ecological systems theory, as well as Erikson's psychoanalytic theory, underscores the connection between culture and development. In line with this emphasis, child development research has recently seen a dramatic increase in cross-cultural studies. Investigations that make comparisons across cultures, and between ethnic and social class groups within cultures, provide insight into whether developmental theories apply to all children or are limited to particular environmental conditions. In doing so, cross-cultural research helps us untangle the contributions of biological and environmental factors to the timing and order of appearance of children's behaviors.

In the past, cross-cultural studies focused on broad cultural differences in development—for example, whether children in one culture are more advanced in motor development or do better on intellectual tasks than children in another. However, this approach can lead us to conclude incorrectly that one culture is superior in enhancing development, while another is deficient. In addition, it does not help us understand the precise experiences that contribute to cultural differences in children's behavior.

Today, more research is examining the relationship of *culturally specific practices* to child development. The contributions of the Russian psychologist Lev Semanovich Vygotsky (1896–1934) have played a major role in this trend. Vygotsky's (1934/1987) perspective is called **sociocultural theory.** It focuses on how *culture*—the values, beliefs, customs, and skills of a social group—is transmitted to the next generation. According to Vygotsky, *social interaction*—in particular, cooperative dialogues between children and more knowledgeable members of society—is necessary for children to acquire the ways of thinking and behaving that make up a community's culture. Vygotsky believed that as adults and more expert peers help children master culturally meaningful activities, the communication between them becomes part of children's thinking. Once children internalize the essential features of these dialogues, they can use the language within them to guide their own actions and accomplish skills on their own. The young child instructing herself while working a puzzle or tying her shoes has started to produce the same kind of guiding comments that an adult previously used to help her master important tasks (Kozulin, 1990).

Perhaps you can tell from this brief description that Vygotsky's theory has been especially influential in the study of children's cognition. But Vygotsky's approach to cognitive development is quite different from Piaget's. Recall that Piaget did not regard direct teaching by adults as important for cognitive development. Instead, he emphasized children's active, independent efforts to make sense of their world. Vygotsky agreed with Piaget that children are active, constructive beings. But unlike Piaget, he viewed cognitive development as a *socially mediated process*—dependent on the support that adults and more mature peers provide as children try new tasks. In addition, Vygotsky did not regard all children as moving through the same stage sequence. Instead, he believed that social interaction leads to continuous, step-by-step changes in children's thought and behavior that can vary greatly from culture to culture.

A major finding of cross-cultural research is that cultures select different tasks for children's learning. In line with Vygotsky's theory, social interaction surrounding these tasks leads to knowledge and skills essential for success in a particular culture. For example, among the Zinacanteco Indians of southern Mexico, girls become expert weavers of complex garments at an early age through the informal guidance of adult experts (Childs & Greenfield, 1982). In Brazil, child candy sellers with little or no schooling develop sophisticated mathematical abilities as the result of buying candy from wholesalers, pricing it in collaboration with adults and experienced peers, and bargaining with customers on city streets (Saxe, 1988). And, as the research reported in Box 1.1 indicates, adults begin to encourage culturally valued skills in children at a very early age.

Findings like these reveal that children in every culture develop unique strengths that are not present in others. The field of child development has again borrowed from another discipline—anthropology—to achieve this understanding. A cross-cultural perspective reminds us that the majority of child development specialists reside in the United States, and their subjects of study are only a small minority of humankind. We cannot assume that the developmental sequences observed in our own children are "natural" or that the experiences fostering them are "ideal" without looking around the world (Laboratory of Comparative Human Cognition, 1983).

*BRIEF REVIEW*   New child development theories are constantly emerging, questioning and building on earlier discoveries. Using computerlike models of mental activity, information processing has brought exactness and precision to the study of children's thinking. Ethology highlights the adaptive, or survival, value of children's behavior and its evolutionary history. Ecological systems theory stresses that adult-child interaction is a two-way street affected by a range of environmental influences, from immediate settings of home and school to broad cultural values and programs. Vygotsky's sociocultural theory takes a closer look at social relationships that foster development. Through cooperative dialogues with mature members of society, children acquire unique, culturally adaptive competencies.

• *What shortcoming of the information processing approach is a strength of ethology, ecological systems theory, and Vygotsky's sociocultural perspective?*

• *What features of Vygotsky's sociocultural perspective make it very different from Piaget's theory?*

## COMPARING CHILD DEVELOPMENT THEORIES

In the previous sections, we reviewed seven theoretical perspectives that are major forces in modern child development research. They differ in a great many respects. First, they focus on different aspects of development. Some emphasize children's social and emotional development, while others stress important changes in children's thinking. A few, such as behaviorism, social learning theory, and ecological systems theory, discuss factors assumed to affect all aspects of children's functioning. Second, every theory takes a point of view about what the process of development is like. As we conclude our review of theoretical perspectives, take a moment to identify the stand that each theory takes on the three basic issues presented at the beginning of

## CULTURAL INFLUENCES

### Box 1.1    *!Kung Infancy: Acquiring Culture*

*I*nteraction between caregivers and infants takes different paths in different cultures. Through it, adults begin to transmit their society's values and skills to the next generation, channeling the course of future development.

Focusing on a culture very different from our own, researchers have carefully examined how caregivers respond to infants' play with objects among the !Kung, a hunting and gathering society living in the desert regions of Botswana, Africa (Bakeman et al., 1990). Daily foraging missions take small numbers of adults several miles from the campground, but most obtain enough food to contribute to group survival by working only three out of every seven days. A mobile way of life also prevents the !Kung from collecting many possessions that require extensive care and maintenance. Adults have many free hours to relax around the campfire, and they spend it in intense social contact with one another and with children (Draper & Cashdan, 1988).

In this culture of intimate social bonds and minimal property, objects are valued as things to be shared, not as personal possessions. This message is conveyed to !Kung children at a very early age. Between 6 and 12 months, grandmothers start to train babies in the importance of exchanging objects by guiding them in handing beads to relatives. The child's first words generally include *i* (here, take this) and *na* (give it to me).

In !Kung society, no toys are made for infants. Instead, natural objects, such as twigs, grass, stones, and nutshells, are always available, along with cooking implements. However, adults do not encourage babies to play with these objects. In fact, adults are unlikely to interact with infants while they are exploring objects independently. But when a baby offers an object to another person, adults become highly responsive, encouraging and vocalizing much more than at other times. Thus, the !Kung cultural emphasis on the interpersonal rather than physical aspects of

*!Kung children grow up in a hunting-and-gathering society in which possessions are a burden rather than an asset. From an early age, children experience rich, warm social contact with adults and are taught the importance of sharing. (Irven De-Vore/Anthro-Photo)*

existence is reflected in how adults interact with the very youngest members of their community.

When you next have a chance, observe the conditions under which parents react to infants' involvement with objects in your own society. How is parental responsiveness linked to cultural values? How does it compare with findings on the !Kung?

this chapter. Check your own analysis of theories against the information given in Table 1.5. If you had difficulty classifying any of them, return to the relevant section of this chapter and reread the description of that theory.

Finally, we have seen that theories have strengths and weaknesses. This may remind you of an important point we made earlier in this chapter—that no theory

TABLE 1.5 • Stance of Major Developmental Theories on Three Basic Issues in Child Development

| Theory | Organismic Versus Mechanistic Child | Continuous Versus Discontinuous Development | Nature Versus Nurture |
|---|---|---|---|
| Psychoanalytic theory | *Organismic:* Relations among structures of the mind (id, ego, and superego) determine personality. | *Discontinuous:* Stages of psychosexual and psychosocial development are emphasized. | *Both:* Innate impulses are channeled and controlled through child-rearing experiences. |
| Behaviorism and social learning theory | *Mechanistic:* Development is the result of connections established between stimulus inputs and behavioral responses. | *Continuous:* Learned behaviors increase quantitatively with age. | *Emphasis on nurture:* Learning principles of conditioning and modeling determine development. |
| Piaget's cognitive-developmental theory | *Organismic:* Psychological structures determine the child's understanding of the world. The child actively constructs knowledge. | *Discontinuous:* Stages of cognitive development are emphasized. | *Both:* Children's innate drive to discover reality is emphasized. However, it must be supported by a rich, stimulating environment. |
| Information processing | *Both:* A mechanistic, computer-like model of stimulus input and behavioral output combines with active processing structures. | *Continuous:* There is a quantitative increase in perception, attention, memory, and problem-solving skills with age. | *Both:* Maturation and learning opportunities affect information-processing capacities. |
| Ethology | *Organismic:* The infant is biologically prepared with social signals that actively promote survival. Over time, psychological structures develop that underlie infant–caregiver attachment and other adaptive behavior patterns. | *Both:* Adaptive behavior patterns increase in quantity over time. But critical periods—restricted time periods in which qualitatively distinct capacities and responses emerge fairly suddenly—are also emphasized. | *Both:* Biologically based, evolved behavior patterns are stressed, but an appropriately stimulating environment is necessary to elicit them. Also, learning can improve the adaptiveness of behavior. |
| Ecological systems theory | *Organismic:* Children's personality characteristics and ways of thinking actively contribute to their development. | *Not specified* | *Both:* Children's characteristics and the reactions of others affect each other in a bidirectional fashion. Layers of the environment influence child-rearing experiences. |
| Vygotsky's sociocultural perspective | *Organismic:* Children internalize essential features of social dialogues, forming psychological structures that they use to guide their own behavior. | *Continuous:* Interaction between the child and mature members of society leads to step-by-step changes in thought and behavior. | *Both:* Maturation and opportunities to interact with knowledgeable members of society affect the development of psychological structures and culturally adaptive skills. |

provides a complete account of development. Perhaps you found that you were attracted to some theories, but you had doubts about others. As you read more about child development research in later chapters of this book, you may find it useful to keep a notebook in which you test your own theoretical likes and dislikes against the evidence. Do not be surprised if you revise your ideas many times, just as theorists have done throughout this century. By the end of the course, you will have built your own personal perspective on child development. It might turn out to be a blend of several theories, since each viewpoint we have discussed has contributed in important ways to what we know about children. And like the field of child development as a whole, you may be left with some unanswered questions. Hopefully, they will motivate you to continue your quest to understand children in the years to come.

## STUDYING THE CHILD

In the preceding sections, we saw how theories guide the collection of information about the child, its interpretation, and its application to practices with children. In fact, research usually begins with a prediction about behavior drawn directly from a theory, or what we call an *hypothesis.* But theories and hypotheses are only the beginning of the many activities that result in sound research on child development. Conducting research according to scientifically accepted procedures involves many important steps and choices. Investigators must decide which subjects, and how many, will be asked to participate. Then they must figure out what the subjects will be asked to do and when, where, and how many times each will need to be seen. Finally, they must examine relationships and draw conclusions from their data.

In the following sections, we take a look at research strategies commonly used to study children. We begin with *research methods,* the specific activities in which subjects will be asked to participate. Then we turn to *research designs*—overall plans for research studies that permit the best possible test of the investigator's hypothesis. Finally, we discuss special ethical issues involved in doing research on children.

At this point, you may be wondering, "Why learn about research strategies? Why not leave these matters to research specialists and concentrate on what is already known about the child and how this knowledge can be applied?" There are two reasons. First, each of us must be wise and critical consumers of knowledge, not naive sponges who soak up facts about children. A basic appreciation of the strengths and weaknesses of research strategies becomes important in separating dependable information from misleading results. Second, individuals who work directly with children are sometimes in a position to carry out small-scale research studies on their own or with an experienced investigator (see Box 1.2). At other times, they may have to provide information on how well their goals for children are being realized to justify continued financial support for their programs and activities. Under these circumstances, an understanding of research becomes essential practical knowledge.

### Common Methods Used to Study Children

How does a researcher choose a basic approach to gathering information about children? Common methods in the field of child development include systematic observation, self-reports (such as questionnaires and interviews), and clinical or case studies of a single child. As you read about them, you may find it helpful to refer to Table 1.6, which summarizes the strengths and weaknesses of each method.

***Systematic Observation.*** To find out how children actually behave, a researcher may choose systematic observation. It involves observing and recording behavior as it happens. Observations of the behavior of children, and of the adults who are important in their lives, can be made in different ways. One approach is to go into the field, or natural environment, and observe the behavior of interest, a method called **naturalistic observation.**

A study of children's social development provides a good example of naturalistic observation (Barrett & Yarrow, 1977). Observing 5- to 8-year-old children at a summer camp, the researchers recorded the number of times each child provided another person with physical or emotional support in the form of comforting, sharing, helping, or expressing sympathy. The great strength of naturalistic observation in studies like this one is that investigators can see directly the everyday behaviors they hope to explain (Miller, 1987).

Naturalistic observation also has a major weakness: Not all children have the same opportunity to display a particular behavior in everyday life. In this study, some

**Naturalistic observation**
A method in which the researcher goes into the natural environment to observe the behavior of interest.

# FROM RESEARCH TO PRACTICE

## Box 1.2  *Researchers and Practitioners as Collaborative Partners*

*I*deally, researchers and practitioners should collaborate in the quest for knowledge about the child. The researcher needs to find out about behavior in the everyday environments in which teachers, caregivers, social workers, and others deal with children. And research questions and plans often benefit from the insights, suggestions, and concerns of practitioners.

In a study carried out by one of my students, this unique partnership happened. Cheryl Kinsman was interested in factors that cause children's behavior to become sex typed at an early age. At the same time, Mary Natale, a preschool teacher in our university laboratory school, wondered how to arrange activity centers in her classroom to enhance the social and play experiences of her 4- and 5-year-old pupils. Together, Cheryl and Mary selected two activity centers—the housekeeping and block areas—for special study, since these united their respective interests.

Cheryl devised a plan in which children were observed for a three-week period under Mary's original arrangement, in which the two centers, located next to each other, were separated by a high wall of shelves. Then the shelves were removed, and changes in boys' and girls' use of each area and the quality of their play were noted.

The findings revealed that boys and girls did not differ in time spent in the two settings, either before or after the shelves were removed. In fact, under each condition children of both sexes preferred the block area. But changes in aspects of their play were dramatic. Before the shelves were removed, play was highly sex typed. Children largely interacted with same-sex peers, a pattern that was particularly pronounced for boys in blocks and for girls in housekeeping. In addition, when boys entered the housekeeping area, they generally did not use its play materials. Instead, they tended to play in ways that were irrelevant to the basic purpose of the setting, such as acting out themes of King Kong or Batman.

Behavior after the divider was removed was strikingly different. Instead of sex segregation, boys and girls frequently played together. And girls, especially, engaged in more complex play, integrating materials from both settings into their fantasy themes. Finally, negative interactions between children declined after removal of the divider, perhaps because the more open play space reduced crowding and competition for materials.

As the result of this study, Cheryl learned that the design of play environments has an impact on children's sex-typed behavior. And Mary rearranged her classroom in ways that extended and enriched her pupils' social and play experiences (Kinsman & Berk, 1979).

---

children happened to be exposed to more cues for positive social responses (such as a tearful playmate), and for this reason they showed more helpful and comforting behavior. Researchers commonly deal with this difficulty by making **structured observations** in a laboratory. In this approach, the investigator sets up a cue for the behavior of interest. Since every subject is exposed to it in the same way, each has an equal opportunity to display the response. In one study, structured observations of children's helping behavior were made by having an adult "accidently" spill a box of gold stars and recording how each child reacted (Stanhope, Bell, & Parker-Cohen, 1987). This approach permits investigators to exert more control over the research situation. But the great disadvantage of structured observations is that children do not always behave in the laboratory as they do in everyday life.

The procedures used to collect systematic observations may vary considerably, depending on the nature of the research problem. Some investigators need to describe their subjects' entire stream of behavior—everything said and done for a certain time period. In one of my own studies, I wanted to find out how sensitive, responsive, and verbally stimulating caregivers were when they interacted with children in day-care centers (Berk, 1985). In this case, everything each caregiver said and did and

**Structured observation**

A method in which the researcher sets up a cue for the behavior of interest and observes that behavior in the laboratory.

TABLE 1.6 • Strengths and Weaknesses of Common Research Methods

| Method | Description | Strengths | Weaknesses |
|---|---|---|---|
| Naturalistic observation | Behavior observed in natural contexts | Observations apply to children's everyday lives | Conditions under which children are observed cannot be controlled |
| Structured observation | Behavior observed in the laboratory | Conditions of observation are the same for all children | Observations may not be typical of the way children behave in everyday life |
| Clinical interview | Flexible interviewing procedure in which the investigator obtains a complete account of the subject's thoughts | Comes as close as possible to the way subjects think in everyday life; great breadth and depth of information can be obtained in a short time period | Subjects may not report information accurately; flexible procedure makes comparison of subjects' responses difficult |
| Structured interview and questionnaire | Self-report instruments in which each subject is asked the same questions in the same way | Standardized method of asking questions permits comparisons of subjects' responses and efficient data collection and scoring | Does not yield the same depth of information as a clinical interview; responses still subject to inaccurate reporting |
| Clinical method (case study) | Combines interviews, observations, and test scores to yield a full picture of a single child's psychological functioning | Provides rich, descriptive insights into processes of development | Affected by the same problems as the clinical interview; can be biased by theoretical preferences of the researcher; conclusions cannot be applied to individuals other than the subject child |

even the amount of time she spent away from the children taking coffee breaks and talking on the phone was important. In other studies, only one or a few kinds of behavior are needed, and it is not necessary to preserve the entire behavior stream. In these instances, researchers use more efficient observation procedures in which they record only certain events or mark off behaviors on checklists.

Systematic observation provides invaluable information on how children and adults actually behave, but it tells us little about the reasoning that lies behind their responses. For this kind of information, researchers must turn to another type of method—self-reports.

***Self-Reports: Interviews and Questionnaires.*** Self-reports are techniques that ask subjects to answer questions about their abilities, feelings, beliefs, and past experiences. They range from relatively unstructured clinical interviews, the method used by Piaget to study children's thinking, to highly structured interviews, questionnaires, and tests.

Let's look at an example of a **clinical interview** in which Piaget questioned a 5-year-old child about his understanding of dreams:

Where does the dream come from?—*I think you sleep so well that you dream.*—Does it come from us or from outside?—*From outside.*—What do we dream with?—*I don't know.*—With the hands? . . . With nothing?—*Yes, with nothing.*—When you are in bed and you dream, where is the dream?—*In my bed, under the blanket. I don't really know. If it was in my stomach, the bones would be in the way and I shouldn't see it.*—Is the dream there when you sleep?—*Yes, it is in the bed beside me . . .*—You see the dream when you are in the room, but if I were in the room, too, should I see it?—*No, grownups don't ever dream.*—Can two people ever have the same dream?—*No, never.*—When the

**Clinical interview**
A method in which the researcher uses a flexible, conversational style to probe for the subject's point of view.

dream is in the room, is it near you?—*Yes, there!* (pointing to 30 cm. in front of his eyes). (Piaget, 1926/1930, pp. 97–98)

Notice how Piaget used a flexible, conversational style to encourage the child to expand his ideas. Prompts are given to obtain a fuller picture of the child's reasoning.

The clinical interview has two major strengths. First, it permits subjects to display their thoughts in terms that are as close as possible to the way they think in everyday life. Second, the clinical interview can provide a large amount of information in a fairly brief period of time. For example, in an hour-long session we can obtain a wide range of child-rearing information from a parent—much more than we could capture by observing parent–child interaction for the same amount of time.

A major weakness of the clinical interview has to do with the accuracy with which subjects report their thoughts and feelings. Some subjects, desiring to please the interviewer, may make up answers that do not represent their beliefs or experiences. And because the clinical interview depends on verbal ability and expressiveness, it may not accurately assess individuals who have difficulty putting their thoughts into words.

The clinical interview has also been criticized because of its flexibility. When questions are phrased differently for each subject, responses may be due to the manner of interviewing rather than real differences in the way subjects think about a certain topic. **Structured interviews,** in which each participant is asked the same set of questions, can eliminate this problem. In addition, these techniques are much more efficient. For example, they permit researchers to obtain written responses from an entire class of children or group of parents at the same time. Also, when structured interviews use multiple-choice, yes-no, and true-false formats, as is done on many tests and questionnaires, the answers can be tabulated by machine. However, we must keep in mind that these approaches do not yield the same depth of information

*By making structured observations in a laboratory, researchers can ensure that all subjects have the same opportunity to display the behavior of interest. But subjects may not respond in the laboratory as they do in everyday life.* (Dick Luria/FPG)

**Structured interview**

A method in which the researcher asks each subject the same questions in the same way.

as a clinical interview. And they can still be affected by the problem of inaccurate reporting.

*The Clinical Method.*    Earlier in this chapter, we discussed the **clinical method** (sometimes called the *case study approach*) as an outgrowth of psychoanalytic theory, which stresses the importance of understanding the individual child. The case of little Sam is a good example of how the clinical method brings together a wide range of information on one subject, including interview data, observations, and sometimes test scores as well. The method yields case narratives that are rich in descriptive detail and that frequently offer important insights into the processes of development.

The clinical method, like all others, has drawbacks. It is subject to the same problems as the clinical interview. Also, more than other methods, the theoretical preferences of the researcher can bias the interpretation of clinical data. Finally, investigators cannot assume that their conclusions apply to anyone other than the particular child being studied. The insights drawn from clinical investigations need to be tested further with other research methods.

*BRIEF REVIEW*    Systematic observation, self-reports, and clinical or case studies are commonly used methods in the field of child development. Naturalistic observation provides information on children's everyday behavior. But because all children do not have the same opportunity to display a particular behavior in everyday life, researchers often make structured observations in a laboratory. Self-reports clarify the reasoning behind subjects' responses. The flexible, conversational style of the clinical interview provides a wealth of information in a short period of time. Its drawbacks are that subjects may not report their thoughts accurately and comparison of subjects' responses is difficult. The structured interview is a more efficient method that questions each subject in the same way, but it does not offer the same depth of information. Clinical studies of a single child provide rich insights into the processes

• *Why is it important for students of child development and individuals who work directly with children to understand research strategies?*

• *A researcher wants to study the thoughts and feelings of children who have experienced their parents' divorce. Which method is best suited for investigating this question?*

*Using the clinical interview, this researcher asks a mother to describe her child's development. The method permits large amounts of information to be gathered in a relatively short period of time.* (Tony Freeman/Photo Edit)

**Clinical method**

A method in which the researcher attempts to understand the unique individual child by combining interview data, observations, and sometimes test scores.

of development, but these need to be tested further with methods that can be applied to more than one individual.

## General Research Designs

In deciding on a research design, investigators choose a way of setting up a study that permits them to test their hypotheses with the greatest certainty possible. Two main types of designs are used in all research on human behavior: correlational and experimental.

***Correlational Design.*** In a **correlational design,** researchers gather information on already existing groups of individuals without altering their experiences in any way. Suppose we want to answer such questions as: Does attending a day-care center promote children's friendliness with peers? Do mothers' styles of interacting with children have any bearing on children's intelligence? In these and many other instances, it is very difficult to deliberately arrange and control the conditions of interest.

The correlational design offers a way of looking at relationships between variables. But correlational studies have one major limitation: we cannot infer cause and effect. For example, if we find in a correlational study that maternal interaction does relate to children's intelligence, we would not know whether mothers' behavior actually causes intellectual differences among children. In fact, the opposite is certainly possible. The behaviors of highly intelligent children may be so attractive that they cause mothers to interact more favorably. Or a third variable that we did not even think about studying, such as amount of noise and distraction in the home, may be causing both maternal interaction and children's intelligence to change together in the same direction.

In correlational studies, and in other types of research designs, investigators often examine relationships by using a **correlation coefficient.** It is a number that describes how two measures, or variables, are associated with one another. We will encounter the correlation coefficient in discussing research findings throughout this book, so let's look at what it is and how it is interpreted. A correlation coefficient can range in value from $+1.00$ to $-1.00$. The *magnitude, or size, of the number* shows the *strength of the relationship*. A zero correlation indicates no relationship, but the closer the value is to $+1.00$ or $-1.00$, the stronger the relationship that exists. The *sign of the number* ($+$ or $-$) refers to the *direction of the relationship*. A positive sign ($+$) means that as one variable *increases,* the other also *increases*. A negative sign ($-$) indicates that as one variable *increases,* the other *decreases*.

Let's take a couple of examples to illustrate how a correlation coefficient works. In one study, a researcher found that a measure of maternal attention at 11 months of age was positively correlated with infant intelligence during the second year of life, at $+.60$. This is a moderately high correlation, which indicates that the more attentive the mothers were to their babies in infancy, the better their children did on an intelligence test several months later (Clarke-Stewart, 1973). In another study, a researcher reported that the extent to which mothers ignored their 10-month-olds' bids for attention was negatively correlated with children's willingness to comply with parental demands one year later—at $-.46$ for boys and $-.36$ for girls (Martin, 1981). These moderate correlations reveal that the more mothers ignored their babies, the less cooperative their children were during the second year of life.

Both of these investigations found a relationship between maternal behavior in the first year and children's behavior in the second year. Although the researchers suspected that maternal behavior affected the children's responses, in neither study

**Correlational design**

A research design that gathers information without altering subjects' experiences and that cannot determine cause and effect.

**Correlation coefficient**

A number, ranging from $+1.00$ to $-1.00$, that describes the strength and direction of the relationship between two variables.

could they really be sure about cause and effect. However, if we find a relationship in a correlational study, this suggests that it would be worthwhile to track down its cause with a more powerful experimental research strategy, if at all possible.

*Experimental Design.*   Unlike correlational studies, an **experimental design** permits us to determine cause and effect. In an experiment, the events and behaviors of interest are divided into two types: independent and dependent variables. The **independent variable** is the one anticipated by the investigator to cause changes in another variable. The **dependent variable** is the one that the investigator expects to be influenced by the independent variable. Inferences about cause and effect relationships are possible because the researcher directly *controls* or *manipulates* changes in the independent variable. This is done by exposing subjects to two or more treatment conditions and comparing their performance on measures of the dependent variable.

In a recent *laboratory experiment,* researchers wanted to know if quality of interaction between adults (independent variable) affects young children's emotional reactions while playing with a familiar peer (dependent variable). Pairs of 2-year-olds were brought into a laboratory set up to look much like a family home. One group was exposed to a *warm treatment* in which two adults in the kitchen spoke in a friendly way while the children played in the livingroom. A second group received an *angry treatment* in which positive communication between the adults was interrupted by an argument in which they shouted, complained, and slammed the door. Children in the angry condition displayed much more distress (such as freezing in place, anxious facial expressions, and crying). They also showed more aggression toward their playmates than did children in the warm treatment (Cummings, Iannotti, & Zahn-Waxler, 1985). The experiment revealed that exposure to even short episodes of intense adult anger can trigger negative emotion and antisocial behavior in very young children.

In experimental studies, investigators must take special precautions to control for unknown characteristics of subjects that could reduce the accuracy of their findings. For example, in the study just described, if a greater number of children who had already learned to behave in hostile and aggressive ways happened to end up in the angry treatment, we could not tell whether the independent variable or children's background characteristics produced the results. *Random assignment* of subjects to treatment conditions offers protection against this problem. By using an evenhanded procedure, such as drawing numbers out of a hat or flipping a coin, the experimenter increases the chances that children's characteristics will be equally distributed across treatment groups. Sometimes researchers combine random assignment with another technique called *matching*. In this procedure, subjects are measured ahead of time on the factor in question—in our example, aggression. Then an equal number of high- and low-aggressive subjects are randomly assigned to each treatment condition. In this way, the experimental groups are deliberately matched, or made equivalent, on characteristics that are likely to distort the results.

*Modified Experimental Designs: Field and Natural Experiments.*   Most experiments are conducted in laboratories where researchers can achieve the maximum possible control over treatment conditions. But, as we have already indicated, findings obtained in laboratories may not always apply to everyday situations. The ideal solution to this problem is to do experiments in the field as a complement to laboratory investigations. In *field experiments,* investigators capitalize on rare opportunities to randomly assign subjects to different treatments in natural settings. In the laboratory experiment that we just considered, we can conclude that the emotional climate established by adults affects children's behavior in the laboratory, but does it also do so in daily life?

**Experimental design**
A research design in which subjects are randomly assigned to treatment conditions. Permits inferences about cause and effect.

**Independent variable**
The variable manipulated by the researcher in an experiment.

**Dependent variable**
The variable that the researcher expects to be influenced by the independent variable in an experiment.

Another study helps answer this question. This time, the research was carried out in a day-care center. A caregiver deliberately acted differently while playing with two groups of preschoolers. In one condition, she helped the children in a warm and gentle style. In the other condition, she provided assistance, but her mood was cold and aloof. Observations of children's behavior revealed that preschoolers in the first group were far more likely to interact positively with each other than those in the second (Yarrow, Scott, & Waxler, 1973).

In the case of many hypotheses, researchers cannot randomly assign subjects and manipulate conditions in the real world, as these investigators were able to do. Sometimes researchers can compromise by conducting *natural experiments*. In these studies, treatments that already exist, such as different school environments, day-care centers, and preschool programs, are compared. The settings are carefully chosen to ensure that in each of them, children's characteristics are as much alike as possible. In this way, investigators rule out as best as they can alternative explanations for their treatment effects. But despite these efforts, natural experiments are unable to achieve the precision and rigor of true experimental research (Achenbach, 1978).

To help you compare the correlational and experimental designs we have discussed, Table 1.7 summarizes their strengths and weaknesses. It also includes an overview of designs for studying development, to which we now turn.

TABLE 1.7 • Strengths and Weaknesses of Common Research Designs

| Design | Description | Strengths | Weaknesses |
|---|---|---|---|
| **General Designs** | | | |
| Correlational design | Information obtained on already existing groups without altering subjects' experiences | Permits study of relationships between variables | Does not permit study of cause and effect relationships |
| Experimental design | Investigator manipulates an independent variable and looks at its effect on a dependent variable; can be conducted in the laboratory or the field | Permits study of cause and effect relationships | When conducted in the laboratory, findings may not apply to the real world; when conducted in the field, control over treatment is usually weaker than in the laboratory |
| **Developmental Designs** | | | |
| Longitudinal design | A group of subjects is studied repeatedly at different ages | Permits study of individual growth trends and relationships between early and later events and behaviors | Age-related changes may be distorted because of subject dropout, subject test-wiseness, and cohort effects |
| Cross-sectional design | Groups of subjects of different ages are studied at one point in time | More efficient than the longitudinal design | Does not permit study of individual growth trends; age differences may be distorted because of cohort effects |
| Longitudinal-sequential design | Two or more groups of children born in different years are followed over time | Permits both longitudinal and cross-sectional comparisons; reveals existence of cohort effects | May have the same problems as longitudinal and cross-sectional strategies, but the design itself helps identify difficulties |

## Developmental Research Designs

Scientists interested in child development require information about the way their subjects change over time. To answer questions about development, they must extend correlational and experimental approaches to include measurements of subjects at different ages. Longitudinal and cross-sectional designs are special *developmental* research strategies. In each, age comparisons form the basis of the research plan.

### The Longitudinal Design.

In a **longitudinal design,** a group of subjects is studied repeatedly at different ages, and changes are noted as they mature. The time spanned may be relatively short—a few months to several years—or it may be very long—a decade or even a lifetime. The longitudinal approach has two major strengths. First, since it tracks the performance of each subject over time, researchers can identify common patterns of development as well as individual differences in the paths children follow to maturity. Second, longitudinal studies permit investigators to examine relationships between early and later events and behaviors. Let's take an example to illustrate these ideas.

Recently, a group of researchers wondered whether children who display extreme personality styles—either angry and explosive or shy and withdrawn—retain the same dispositions when they become adults. In addition, they wanted to know what kinds of experiences promote stability or change in personality and what consequences these extreme dispositions have for long-term adjustment. To answer these questions, the researchers delved into the archives of the Berkeley Guidance Study, a well-known longitudinal investigation initiated in 1928 and continued over several decades (Caspi, Elder, & Bem, 1987, 1988).

Results revealed that the two personality styles were only moderately stable. Between ages 8 and 30, a good number of subjects remained the same, while others changed substantially. When stability did occur, it appeared to be due to a "snowballing effect," in which children evoked responses from adults and peers that acted to maintain their dispositions. In other words, explosive youngsters were likely to be treated with anger and hostility (to which they reacted with even greater unruliness), while shy children were apt to be ignored.

Persistence of extreme personality styles affected many areas of adult adjustment, but these outcomes were different for males and females. For men, the results of early explosiveness were most apparent in their work lives, in the form of conflicts with supervisors, frequent job changes, and unemployment. Since few women in this sample of an earlier generation worked after marriage, their family lives were most affected. Ill-tempered girls grew up to be hotheaded wives and parents who were especially prone to divorce. Sex differences in the long-term consequences of shyness were even greater. Men who had been withdrawn in childhood were delayed in marrying, becoming fathers, and establishing stable careers. Because a withdrawn, unassertive style was socially acceptable for females, women who had shy personalities showed no special adjustment problems.

### Problems in Conducting Longitudinal Research.

Despite their many strengths, longitudinal investigations pose a number of problems. For example, subjects may move away or drop out of the research for other reasons. This changes the original sample so it no longer represents the population to whom researchers would like to generalize their findings. Also, from repeated study, subjects may become "test-wise." As a result, the behavior they present to investigators may become unnatural.

But the most widely discussed threat to the accuracy of longitudinal findings is cultural-historical change, or what are commonly called **cohort effects.** Longitudinal studies examine the development of *cohorts*—children born in the same time period

**Longitudinal design**

A research design in which one group of subjects is studied repeatedly at different ages.

**Cohort effects**

The effects of cultural-historical change on the accuracy of findings: Children born in one period of time are influenced by particular cultural and historical conditions.

who are influenced by a particular set of cultural and historical conditions. Results based on one cohort may not apply to children growing up at other points in time. For example, in the study of personality styles described in the preceding section, we might ask whether the sex differences obtained are still true, in view of recent sex-role changes in our society.

*The Cross-Sectional Design.* The length of time it takes for many behaviors to change, even in limited longitudinal studies, has led researchers to turn toward a more convenient strategy for studying development. In the **cross-sectional design,** groups of subjects differing in age are studied at the same point in time.

A recent investigation provides a good illustration. Children in grades 3, 6, 9, and 12 filled out a questionnaire asking about their sibling relationships. Findings revealed that sibling interaction was characterized by greater equality and less power assertion with age. Also, feelings of sibling companionship declined during adolescence. The researchers thought that these age changes were due to several factors. As later-born children become more competent and independent, they no longer need and are probably less willing to accept direction from older siblings. In addition, as adolescents move from psychological dependence on the family to greater involvement with peers, they may have less time and emotional need to invest in siblings (Buhrmester & Furman, 1990). These are intriguing ideas about the impact of development on sibling relationships that deserve to be followed up in future research.

*Problems in Conducting Cross-Sectional Research.* The cross-sectional design is a very efficient strategy for describing age-related trends. But when researchers choose it, they are shortchanged in the kind of information they can obtain about development. Evidence about change at the level at which it actually occurs—the individual—is not available. For example, in the study of sibling relationships that we just discussed, comparisons are limited to age-group averages. We cannot tell if important individual differences exist in the development of sibling relationships, some becoming more supportive and intimate and others becoming increasingly distant with age.

Cross-sectional studies that cover a wide age span have another problem. Like longitudinal research, they can be threatened by cohort effects. For example, comparisons of 5-year-old cohorts and 15-year-old cohorts—groups of children born and raised in different time periods—may not really represent age-related changes. Instead, they may result from unique experiences associated with the time periods in which the age groups were growing up.

*Improving Developmental Designs.* To overcome some of the limitations of longitudinal and cross-sectional designs, investigators sometimes combine the two approaches. One way of doing so is the **longitudinal-sequential design.** It is composed of two or more different age groups of subjects, each of which is followed longitudinally for a number of years.

The new design has three advantages. First, it permits researchers to find out whether cohort effects are operating by comparing children of the same age who were born in different years. Using the example shown in Figure 1.5, we can compare the behaviors of the two samples when both reach ages 6 and 9. If they do not differ, then we can rule out cohort effects. Second, it is possible to do both longitudinal and cross-sectional comparisons. If outcomes are similar in both, then we can be especially confident about the accuracy of our findings. Third, the design is efficient. In the example shown in Figure 1.5, the researcher can find out about change over a 9-year period by following each cohort for just 6 years. Although the longitudinal-sequential design is used only occasionally, it provides researchers with a convenient way to profit from the strengths of both longitudinal and cross-sectional approaches.

**Cross-sectional design**

A research design in which groups of subjects of different ages are studied at the same point in time.

**Longitudinal-sequential design**

A research design with both longitudinal and cross-sectional components in which groups of subjects born in different years are followed over time.

**FIGURE 1.5** • Example of a longitudinal-sequential design. Two samples of children, one born in 1987 and the other in 1990, are observed longitudinally from 3 to 12 years of age. The design permits the researcher to check for cohort effects by comparing children of the same age who were born in different years. Also, both longitudinal and cross-sectional comparisons can be made.

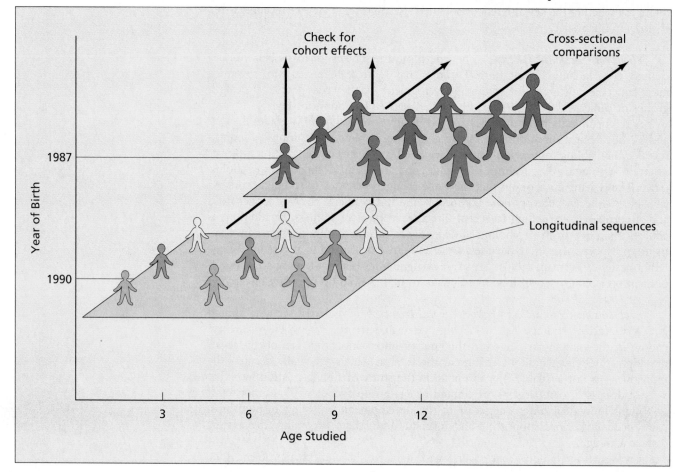

• *A researcher compares children who went to summer leadership camps with children who attended athletic camps. She finds that those who attended leadership camps are friendlier. Should the investigator tell parents that sending children to leadership camps will cause them to be more sociable? Why or why not?*

• *A researcher wants to find out if children who go to day-care centers during the first few years of life do as well in school as those who did not attend day care. Which developmental design, longitudinal or cross-sectional, is appropriate for answering this question? Explain why.*

*BRIEF REVIEW* A variety of research designs are commonly used to study children. In correlational research, information is gathered on existing groups of individuals. Investigators can examine relationships between variables, but they cannot infer cause and effect. Because experimental designs involve random assignment of subjects to treatment groups, researchers can find out if an independent variable causes change in a dependent variable. Longitudinal and cross-sectional designs are uniquely suited for studying development. In longitudinal research, subjects are studied repeatedly at different ages, an approach that provides information on individual differences in development and the relationship between early and later events and behaviors. The cross-sectional approach is more efficient because groups of subjects differing in age are studied at the same point in time. However, comparisons are limited to age-group averages. The longitudinal-sequential approach permits researchers to reap the benefits of both longitudinal and cross-sectional designs.

## Ethics in Research with Children

Research into human behavior creates ethical issues because, unfortunately, the quest for scientific knowledge can sometimes exploit people as well. When children take part in research, the ethical concerns are especially complex. Children are more vulnerable than adults to physical and psychological harm. In addition, immaturity makes it difficult or impossible for children to evaluate for themselves what participation in research will mean. For these reasons, special ethical guidelines for research on children have been developed by the federal government, by funding agencies, and by research-oriented associations such as the American Psychological Association (1968) and the Society for Research in Child Development (1990).

Table 1.8 presents a summary of children's basic research rights drawn from these guidelines. Once you have examined them, read the following research situations, each of which poses a serious ethical dilemma. What precautions do you think should be taken in each instance? Is either so threatening to children's well-being that it should not be carried out at all?

> To study the development of children's willingness to separate from their caregivers, an investigator decides to ask mothers of 1- and 2-year-olds to leave their youngsters alone for a brief time period in a strange playroom. The researcher knows that under these circumstances, some children become very upset.

> In a study of moral development, an investigator wants to assess children's ability to resist temptation by videotaping their behavior without their knowledge. Seven-year-olds are promised an attractive prize for solving some very difficult puzzles. They are also told not to look at a classmate's correct solutions, which are deliberately placed at the back of the room. If the researcher has to tell children ahead of time that cheating is being studied or that their behavior is being closely monitored, he will destroy the purpose of his study.

TABLE 1.8 • Children's Research Rights

---

**Protection from Harm**

Children have the right to be protected from physical or psychological harm in research. If in doubt about the harmful effects of research, investigators should seek the opinion of others. When harm seems possible, investigators should find other means for obtaining the desired information or abandon the research.

**Informed Consent**

Informed consent of parents as well as others who act on the child's behalf (such as school officials) should be obtained for any research involving children, preferably in writing. All research participants, including children, have the right to an explanation of all aspects of the research that may affect their willingness to participate in language appropriate to their level of understanding. Adults and children should be free to discontinue participation in research at any time.

**Privacy**

Children have the right to concealment of their identity on all information collected in the course of research. They also have this right with respect to written reports and in any informal discussions about the research.

**Knowledge of Results**

Children have the right to be informed of the results of research in terms that are appropriate to their understanding.

**Beneficial Treatments**

If experimental treatments believed to be beneficial are under investigation, children in control groups have the right to alternative beneficial treatments if they are available.

---

*Sources:* American Psychological Association, Division on Developmental Psychology, 1968; Society for Research in Child Development, Committee for Ethical Conduct in Child Development Research, 1990.

Did you find it difficult to decide on the best course of action in these examples? Virtually every committee that has worked on developing ethical principles for research has concluded that the conflicts raised by such studies cannot be resolved with simple right or wrong answers. Therefore, the ultimate responsibility for the ethical integrity of research lies with the investigator. However, researchers are advised or, in the case of federally funded research, required to seek advice from others, and special committees exist in colleges, universities, and other institutions for this purpose. These committees weigh the costs of the research to the participant in terms of time, stress, and inconvenience against its value for advancing knowledge and improving children's conditions of life (Cooke, 1982). If there are any negative implications for the safety and welfare of participants that the worth of the research does not justify, then priority is always given to the research participant.

The ethical principle of *informed consent* requires special interpretation when research subjects are children. The competence of youngsters of different ages to make choices about their own participation must be taken into account. Parental consent is meant to protect the safety of children whose ability to make these decisions is not yet fully mature. Besides parental consent, agreement of other individuals who act on children's behalf, such as institutional officials when research is conducted in schools, day-care centers, or hospitals, should be obtained. This is especially important when research includes special groups of children, such as abused youngsters, whose parents may not always represent their best interests (Thompson, 1990b).

For children 7 years and older, their own informed consent should be obtained in addition to parental consent. Around age 7, changes in children's thinking permit them to better understand simple scientific principles and the needs of others. Researchers should respect and enhance these new capacities by providing school-age children with a full explanation of research activities in language that children can understand (Ferguson, 1978; Thompson, 1990b).

Finally, young children rely on a basic faith in adults to feel secure in unfamiliar situations. For this reason, it is possible for some types of research to be particularly disturbing to them. All ethical guidelines advise that special precautions be taken in the use of deception and concealment, as occurs when researchers observe children from behind one-way mirrors, give them false feedback about their performance, or do not tell them the truth regarding what the research is all about. When these kinds of procedures are used with adults, *debriefing,* in which the experimenter provides a full account and justification of the activities, occurs after the research session is over. Debriefing should also take place with children, but it does not always work as well. Despite explanations, children may come away from the research situation with their belief in the honesty of adults undermined. Ethical standards permit deception in research with children if investigators satisfy institutional committees that such practices are necessary. Nevertheless, since deception may have serious emotional consequences for some youngsters, many child development specialists believe that its use is always unethical and that investigators should come up with other research procedures when children are involved (Cooke, 1982; Ferguson, 1978).

## THE CHRONOLOGICAL APPROACH OF THIS BOOK

With the completion of this overview of theory and research, we are ready to chart the course of child development itself. In the following chapters, the story of childhood unfolds in chronological sequence. We begin with a chapter on biological and environmental foundations—the basics of human heredity and how it combines with environmental influences to shape children's characteristics and skills. Then we turn to particular time spans of development.

There are many ways to divide the first two decades of life into separate age periods. I have chosen the following divisions because they serve as major transition points in most theories of child development. Each brings with it a diverse array of new capacities and, consequently, new social expectations of children in cultures around the world:

- Prenatal development and birth
- Infancy and toddlerhood—the first 2 years
- Early childhood—2 to 6 years
- Middle childhood—6 to 11 years
- Adolescence—11 to 20 years

Within each age period, I devote a separate chapter to each of the following aspects of development:

- Physical development—growth in body size and proportions; brain development; perceptual and motor capacities; and physical health
- Cognitive development—development of a wide variety of intellectual abilities, including attention, memory, academic and everyday knowledge, problem solving, imagination, creativity, and the uniquely human capacity to represent the world through language
- Emotional and social development—development of emotional communication, self-understanding, knowledge about other people, interpersonal skills, and moral reasoning and behavior

You are already aware from reading this first chapter that these aspects of development are not really distinct; they overlap and interact a great deal. A major advantage of discussing them as a unit within each age period is that we can easily see how they are interwoven. As our discussion proceeds, we will continuously point out relationships that exist among all aspects of development.

Finally, it is my hope that the content, organization, and instructional features of this book will help meet the needs and interests of you, its readers. Perhaps you aspire to a career in applied work with children, want to teach child development or advance its knowledge base, plan someday to raise children, are already a parent, or are simply curious about how you yourself developed from a tiny infant into the complex adult you are today. Whichever goals happen to be yours, as you embark on the study of children I wish you a stimulating and rewarding journey.

## SUMMARY

### Child Development as an Interdisciplinary, Applied Field

- **Child development** is the study of human growth and change from conception through adolescence. It is part of the larger field of **human development,** which includes all changes that take place throughout the life span.

### Basic Themes and Issues

- Child development **theories** can be organized according to the stand they take on three controversial issues: (1) Is the child an **organismic** or **mechanistic** being? (2) Is development a **continuous** process, or does it follow a series of **discontinuous stages?** (3) Is development primarily determined by **nature** or **nurture?**

### Historical Foundations

- In medieval times, children were thought of as miniature adults, a view called **preformationism.** By the sixteenth and seventeenth centuries, childhood became a distinct phase of the life cycle. However, the Puritan conception of original sin led to a harsh philosophy of child rearing.
- The Enlightenment brought new ideas favoring more humane child treatment. Locke's **tabula rasa** furnished the basis for twentieth-century behaviorism, while Rousseau's **noble savage** foreshadowed the concepts of stage and **matu-**

ration. A century later, Darwin's theory of evolution stimulated scientific child study.

• Efforts to observe the child directly began in the late nineteenth and early twentieth centuries with the baby biographies. Soon after, Hall and Gesell introduced the **normative approach,** which produced a large body of descriptive facts about children.

### Mid-Twentieth Century Influences

• In the 1930s and 1940s, child guidance professionals turned to **psychoanalytic theory** for help in understanding children with emotional problems. In Freud's theory, children develop through five psychosexual stages, during which three portions of the personality—**id, ego,** and **superego**—become integrated. Erikson built on Freud's theory by emphasizing the psychosocial outcomes of each stage and the life-span nature of development.

• Academic psychology also influenced child study. From **behaviorism** and **social learning theory** came the principles of conditioning and modeling and practical procedures of **behavior modification** with children.

• In contrast to behaviorism, Piaget's **cognitive-developmental theory** emphasizes an active child with a mind inhabited by rich structures of knowledge. Piaget's work stimulated new research on children's thinking and encouraged educational programs that emphasize discovery learning.

### New Perspectives

• The field of child development continues to seek new directions. **Information processing** views the mind as a complex, symbol-manipulating system, operating much like a computer. This approach helps investigators achieve a detailed understanding of what children of different ages do when faced with tasks and problems.

• Three modern theories place special emphasis on contexts for development. **Ethology** stresses the adaptive or survival value of behavior and its origins in evolutionary history. In **ecological systems theory,** nested layers of the environment, from immediate settings to broad cultural values and programs, are seen as major influences on children's well-being. Vygotsky's **sociocultural theory** has enhanced our understanding of cultural influences, especially in the area of cognitive development. Through cooperative dialogues with mature members of society, children acquire culturally relevant knowledge and skills.

### Studying the Child

• Common research methods in child development include systematic observation, self-reports, and the clinical or case study approach. **Naturalistic observations** are gathered in children's everyday environments, while **structured observations** take place in laboratories, where investigators deliberately set up cues to elicit the behaviors of interest.

• Self-report methods can be flexible and open-ended, like the **clinical interview.** Alternatively, **structured interviews** and questionnaires can be given, which permit efficient administration and scoring. Investigators use the **clinical method** when they desire an in-depth understanding of a single child.

• Correlational and experimental are two basic kinds of research designs. The **correlational design** examines relationships between variables as they happen to occur, without any intervention. Correlational studies do not permit statements about cause and effect. However, their use is justified when it is difficult or impossible to control the variables of interest.

• An **experimental design** can determine cause and effect. Researchers randomly assign subjects to treatment conditions and manipulate an **independent variable.** Then they determine what effect this has on a **dependent variable.** To achieve high degrees of control, most experiments are conducted in laboratories, but findings may not generalize to everyday life. Field and natural experiments are techniques used to compare treatments in natural environments.

• Longitudinal and cross-sectional designs are uniquely suited for studying development. The **longitudinal design** permits study of individual growth trends and relationships among early and later events and behaviors. The **cross-sectional design** offers an efficient approach to investigating development. However, it is limited to comparisons of age-group averages.

• Findings of longitudinal and cross-sectional research can be distorted by **cohort effects.** To overcome some of the limitations of these designs, new approaches, such as the **longitudinal-sequential design,** have been devised.

• Ethical guidelines help ensure that children's research rights are protected. Besides parental consent, researchers should seek the informed consent of children 7 years and older for research participation. The use of deception in research with children is especially risky, since it may undermine their basic faith in adults.

## IMPORTANT TERMS AND CONCEPTS

| | | |
|---|---|---|
| child development (p. 2) | discontinuous development (p. 5) | maturation (p. 8) |
| human development (p. 2) | stage (p. 5) | normative approach (p. 10) |
| theory (p. 3) | nature–nurture controversy (p. 5) | psychoanalytic theory (p. 12) |
| organismic theory (p. 4) | preformationism (p. 6) | id (p. 13) |
| mechanistic theory (p. 4) | tabula rasa (p. 8) | ego (p. 13) |
| continuous development (p. 4) | noble savage (p. 8) | superego (p. 13) |

behaviorism (p. 16)
social learning theory (p. 17)
behavior modification (p. 18)
cognitive-developmental theory (p. 18)
information processing (p. 22)
ethology (p. 24)
ecological systems theory (p. 25)
sociocultural theory (p. 28)

naturalistic observation (p. 32)
structured observation (p. 33)
clinical interview (p. 34)
structured interview (p. 35)
clinical method (p. 36)
correlational design (p. 37)
correlation coefficient (p. 37)
experimental design (p. 38)

independent variable (p. 38)
dependent variable (p. 38)
longitudinal design (p. 40)
cohort effects (p. 40)
cross-sectional design (p. 41)
longitudinal-sequential design (p. 41)

*"A Happy Childhood," Bianca Chiriloiu, 11 years, Romania. Reprinted by permission from The International Museum of Children's Art, Oslo, Norway.*

# Biological and Environmental Foundations

2

Genetic Foundations
> *The Genetic Code   The Sex Cells   Conception   Boy or Girl?   Multiple Births   Patterns of Genetic Inheritance*

Chromosomal Abnormalities
> *Down Syndrome   Abnormalities of the Sex Chromosomes*

Reproductive Choices
> *Genetic Counseling   Prenatal Diagnosis and Fetal Medicine   The Alternative of Abortion The Alternative of Adoption*

Environmental Contexts for Development
> *The Family   Social Class and Family Functioning   The Impact of Poverty   Beyond the Family: Neighborhoods, Schools, Towns, and Cities   The Cultural Context*

Understanding the Relationship between Heredity and Environment
> *The Question of "How Much?"   The Question of "How?"*

"It's a girl," announces the doctor, who holds up the squalling little creature, while her new parents gaze with amazement at their miraculous creation. "A girl! We've named her Sarah!" exclaims the proud father to eager relatives waiting by the telephone for word about their new family member. As we join these parents in thinking about how this wondrous being came into existence and imagining her future, we are struck by many questions. How could this well-formed baby, equipped with everything necessary for life outside the womb, have developed from the union of two tiny cells? What ensures that Sarah will, in due time, roll over, reach for objects, walk, talk, make friends, imagine, and create— just like every other normal child born before her? Why is she a girl and not a boy, dark-haired rather than blond, calm and cuddly instead of wiry and energetic? What difference will it make that Sarah is given a name and place in one family, community, nation, and culture rather than another?

To answer these questions, this chapter takes a close look at the foundations of development: heredity and environment. Because nature has prepared us for survival, all human beings share many features in common. Yet a brief period of time spent in the company of any child and his or her family reveals that each human being is unique. Take a moment to jot down the most obvious similarities in physical characteristics and behavior for several children and parents whom you know well. Did you find that while one child shows combined features of both parents, another resembles just one parent, while still a third is not like either parent? These directly observable characteristics are called **phenotypes.** They depend in part on the individual's **genotype**—the complex blend of genetic information transmitted from one generation to the next that determines our species and influences all our unique characteristics. Throughout life, phenotypes are also affected by the person's history of experiences in the environment.

**Phenotype**
The individual's physical and behavioral characteristics, which are determined by both genetic and environmental factors.

**Genotype**
The genetic makeup of the individual.

We begin our discussion of development at the moment of conception, an event that establishes the hereditary makeup of the new individual. In the first section of this chapter, we review basic genetic principles that help explain similarities and differences among us in appearance and behavior. Next, we turn to a variety of aspects of the environment that play a powerful role in children's lives.

As our discussion proceeds, you will quickly see that both nature and nurture are involved in all aspects of development. In fact, some findings and conclusions in this chapter may surprise you. For example, many people believe that when children inherit unfavorable characteristics, there is not much that can be done to help them. Others are convinced that when environments are harmful, the damage done to children can easily be corrected. We will see that neither of these assumptions is true. In the final section of this chapter, we take up the question of how nature and nurture *work together* to shape the course of development.

## GENETIC FOUNDATIONS

Basic principles of genetics were unknown until the mid-nineteenth century, when the Austrian monk Gregor Mendel began a series of experiments with pea plants in his monastery garden. Recording the number of times white- and pink-flowered plants had offspring with white or pink flowers, Mendel found that he could predict the characteristics of each new generation. Mendel inferred the presence of genes, factors controlling the physical traits he studied. While peas and humans may seem completely unrelated, today we know that heredity operates in similar ways among all forms of life. Since Mendel's ground-breaking observations, our understanding of how genetic messages are coded and inherited has vastly expanded.

### The Genetic Code

Each of us is made up of trillions of independent units called cells. Inside every cell is a control center, or nucleus. When cells are chemically stained and viewed through a powerful microscope, rodlike structures called **chromosomes** are visible in the nucleus. Chromosomes store and transmit genetic information. Their number varies from species to species—48 for the chimpanzee, 64 for the horse, 40 for the mouse, and 46 for the human being. Chromosomes come in matching pairs (an exception is the XY pair in males, which we will discuss shortly). Each member of a pair corresponds to the other in size, shape, and genetic functions. One is inherited from the mother and one from the father. Therefore, in humans, we speak of *23 pairs* of chromosomes residing in each human cell (see Figure 2.1).

Chromosomes are made up of a chemical substance called **deoxyribonucleic acid,** or **DNA.** In the early 1950s, James Watson and Francis Crick's (1953) discovery of the structure of the DNA molecule unlocked the genetic code. As shown in Figure 2.2, DNA is a long, double-stranded molecule that looks like a twisted ladder. Notice that each rung of the ladder consists of a specific pair of chemical substances called *bases,* joined together between the two sides. Although the bases always pair up in the same way across the ladder rungs—A with T and C with G—they can occur in any order along its sides. It is this sequence of bases that provides genetic instructions. A **gene** is actually a segment of DNA along the length of the chromosome. Genes can be of different lengths—perhaps 100 to several thousand ladder rungs long—and each differs from the next because of its special sequence of base pairs. As many as 20,000 genes may lie along a single chromosome.

A unique feature of DNA is that it can duplicate itself. This special ability makes it possible for the one-celled fertilized ovum to develop into a complex human being

---

**Chromosomes**

Rodlike structures in the cell nucleus that store and transmit genetic information.

**Deoxyribonucleic acid (DNA)**

Long, double-stranded molecules that make up chromosomes.

**Gene**

A segment of a DNA molecule that contains hereditary instructions.

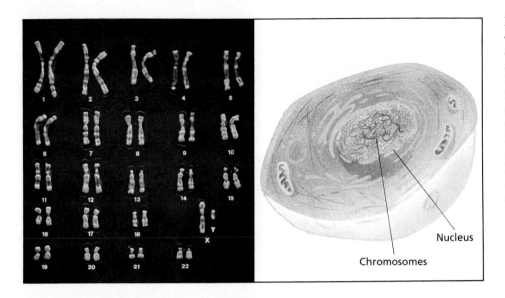

**FIGURE 2.1** • A photograph, or karyotype, of human chromosomes. The 46 chromosomes shown here were isolated from a body cell, stained, greatly magnified, and arranged in pairs according to decreasing size of the upper arm of each chromosome. Note the 23rd pair, XY: The cell donor is a male. In females, the 23rd pair would be XX. *(CNRI/ Science Photo Library/Photo Researchers)*

Nucleus

Chromosomes

**FIGURE 2.2** • DNA's ladderlike structure. The pairings of bases across the rungs of the ladder are very specific: adenine (A) always appears with thymine (T) and cytosine (C) always appears with guanine (G). Here, the DNA ladder is shown duplicating itself by splitting down the middle of its ladder rungs. Then each free base picks up a new complementary partner from the area surrounding the cell nucleus. The result is two identical strands of DNA. *(From E. Frankel, 1979,* DNA: The Ladder of Life, *New York: McGraw-Hill, p. 54. Reprinted by permission.)*

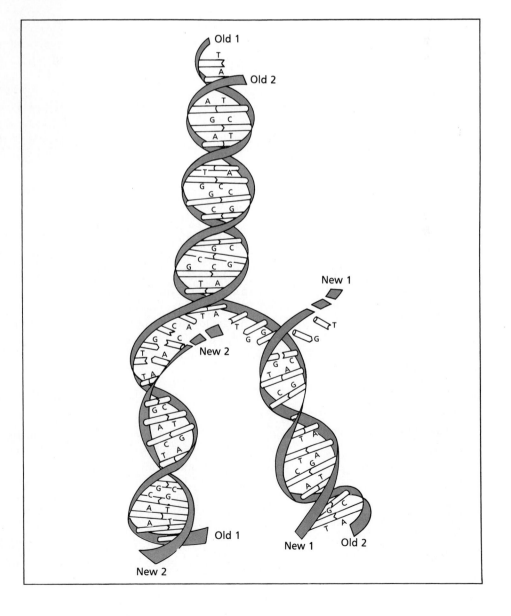

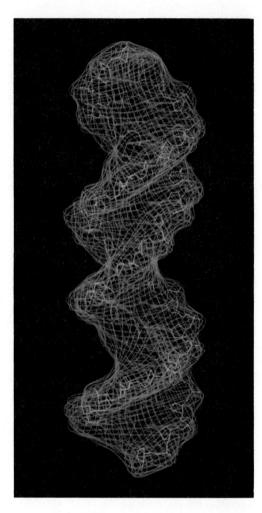

*The ladderlike appearance of DNA is evident in this computer-generated model. By simulating and color-coding the structure of DNA on a computer, scientists can rotate the image and study it from different vantage points.* (Jean-Claude Revy/Phototake)

**Mitosis**

The process of cell duplication, in which each new cell receives an exact copy of the original chromosomes.

**Gametes**

Human sperm and ova, which contain half as many chromosomes as a regular body cell.

**Meiosis**

The process of cell division through which gametes are formed and in which the number of chromosomes in each cell is halved.

**Crossing over**

Exchange of genes between chromosomes next to each other during meiosis.

composed of a great many cells. The process of cell duplication is called **mitosis.** In mitosis, the DNA ladder splits down the middle, opening somewhat like a zipper (as shown in Figure 2.2). Then each base is free to pair up with a new mate from the area surrounding the nucleus of the cell. Notice how this process creates two identical DNA ladders, each containing one new side and one old side from the previous ladder. At the level of chromosomes, during mitosis each chromosome copies itself. As a result, each new body cell contains the same number of chromosomes and the identical genetic information.

### The Sex Cells

If babies developed from the joining of two regular body cells (one from the mother and one from the father), they would have too many chromosomes to grow normally. Instead, new individuals are created when two special cells called **gametes,** or sex cells—the sperm and ovum—combine. Gametes are unique in that they contain only 23 chromosomes, half as many as a regular body cell. They are formed through a special process of cell division called **meiosis,** which halves the number of chromosomes normally present in body cells.

Meiosis takes place according to the steps in Figure 2.3. First, chromosomes pair up within the original cell, and each one copies itself. Then, a special event called **crossing over** takes place. In crossing over, chromosomes next to each other break

**FIGURE 2.3** • The cell division process of meiosis leading to gamete formation. (Here, original cells are depicted with two rather than the full complement of 23 chromosome pairs.) Meiosis creates gametes with only half the usual number of chromosomes. When sperm and ovum unite in fertilization, the first cell of the new individual (the zygote) has the correct full number of chromosomes.

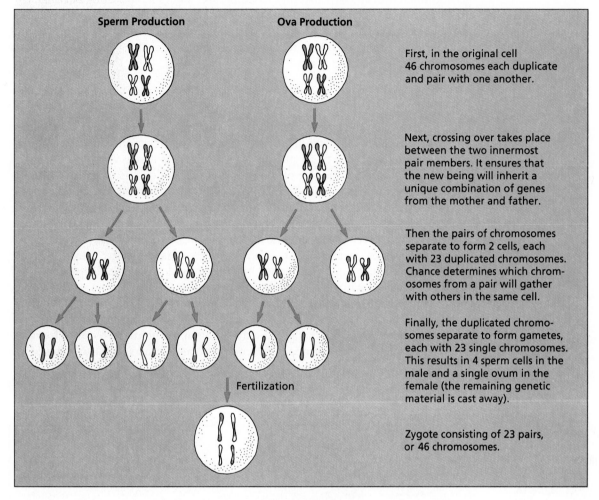

Sperm Production        Ova Production

First, in the original cell 46 chromosomes each duplicate and pair with one another.

Next, crossing over takes place between the two innermost pair members. It ensures that the new being will inherit a unique combination of genes from the mother and father.

Then the pairs of chromosomes separate to form 2 cells, each with 23 duplicated chromosomes. Chance determines which chromosomes from a pair will gather with others in the same cell.

Finally, the duplicated chromosomes separate to form gametes, each with 23 single chromosomes. This results in 4 sperm cells in the male and a single ovum in the female (the remaining genetic material is cast away).

Fertilization

Zygote consisting of 23 pairs, or 46 chromosomes.

at one or more points along their length and exchange segments, so that genes from one are replaced by genes from another. This shuffling of genes in crossing over creates new hereditary combinations. Next, the paired chromosomes separate into different cells, but chance determines which member of each pair will gather with others and eventually end up in the same gamete. Finally, in the last phase of meiosis, each chromosome leaves its duplicate and becomes part of a sex cell containing 23 chromosomes instead of the usual 46.

In the male, four sperm are produced each time meiosis occurs. Also, the cells from which the sperm arise are produced continuously throughout life. For this reason, a healthy man can father a child at any age after sexual maturity. In the female, gamete production is much more limited. Each cell division produces just one ovum. In addition, the female is born with all her ova already present in her ovaries, and she can only bear children for three to four decades. Still, there are plenty of female sex cells. About 1 to 2 million are present at birth, 40,000 remain at adolescence, and approximately 350 to 450 will mature during a woman's childbearing years (Sadler, 1990).

Look again at the steps of meiosis displayed in Figure 2.3, and notice how they ensure that a constant quantity of genetic material (46 chromosomes in each cell) is transmitted from one generation to the next. Can you also see how meiosis leads to genetic differences among offspring? Crossing over and random sorting of each member of a chromosome pair into separate sex cells mean that no two gametes will ever be the same. Meiosis explains why siblings differ from each other in appearance and behavior, while they also share features in common, since their genes come from a common pool of parental genes.

### Conception

Once formed, male and female gametes are ready to fuse with each other. The human sperm and ovum are uniquely suited for the task of reproduction. The ovum is a tiny sphere, measuring 1/175 of an inch in diameter, that is barely visible to the naked eye, appearing as a dot the size of the period at the end of this sentence. But in its microscopic world it is a giant—the largest cell in the human body. The ovum's size makes it a perfect target for the much smaller sperm, which measure only 1/500 of an inch.

About once every 28 days, in the middle of a woman's menstrual cycle, an ovum bursts from one of her *ovaries,* two walnut-sized organs located deep inside her abdomen (see Figure 2.4). Surrounded by thousands of nurse cells that will feed and protect it along its path, the ovum is drawn into one of two *fallopian tubes*—long, thin structures that lead to the hollow, soft-lined uterus. While the ovum is traveling, the spot on the ovary from which it was released—now called the *corpus luteum*—begins to secrete hormones that prepare the lining of the uterus to receive a fertilized ovum. If pregnancy does not occur, the corpus luteum shrinks, and the lining of the uterus is discarded in two weeks with menstruation (Rugh & Shettles, 1971).

**FIGURE 2.4** • Female reproductive organs. An ovum is released from the ovary and fertilized high in the fallopian tube. As the zygote begins to duplicate, it travels toward the uterus and burrows into the uterine lining.

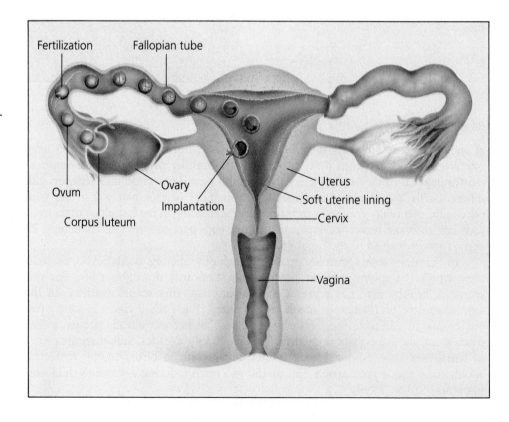

The male produces sperm in vast numbers—an average of 300 million a day—in the *testes,* two glands located in the *scrotum,* sacs that lie just behind the penis (see Figure 2.5). In the final process of maturation, each sperm develops a tail that permits it to swim long distances. During sexual intercourse, about 360 million sperm move through the *vas deferens,* a thin tube in which they are bathed in a protective fluid called *semen.* At sexual climax, semen is ejaculated from the penis into the woman's vagina. Immediately, the sperm begin to swim upstream in the female reproductive tract, through the *cervix* (opening of the uterus) and into the fallopian tube, where fertilization usually takes place. The journey is difficult, and many die. Only 300 to 500 find the ovum, if one happens to be there. The sperm have an average life of 48 hours and can lie in wait for the ovum for up to two days, while the ovum survives for up to 24 hours. Therefore, the maximum fertile period during each monthly cycle is about 72 hours long (Nilsson & Hamberger, 1990).

Only a single sperm will be successful in penetrating the surface of the enormous ovum, although others that arrive release chemicals that help break down its protective barrier. Once the winner of the race comes in contact with the ovum's inner cellular material, any remaining competitors are immediately turned away. In this way, the first cell of the new individual is formed. Called a **zygote,** it is ready to begin multiplying into a new human being.

### Boy or Girl?

Using special microscopic techniques, the 23 pairs of chromosomes in each human cell can be distinguished from one another. Twenty-two of them are matching pairs, called **autosomes.** They are numbered by geneticists from longest to shortest (refer back to Figure 2.1). The 23rd pair is made up of the **sex chromosomes,** which determine the sex of the child. In females, this pair is called XX; in males, it is called XY. The X is a relatively long chromosome, while the Y is short and carries very little

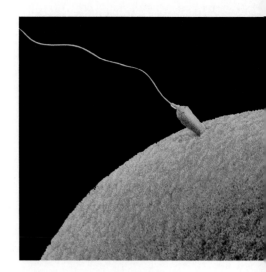

*In this photograph of fertilization taken with the aid of a powerful microscope, a tiny sperm completes its journey and starts to penetrate the surface of an enormous-looking ovum, the largest cell in the human body.* (Francis Leroy, Biocosmos/Science Photo Library/Photo Researchers)

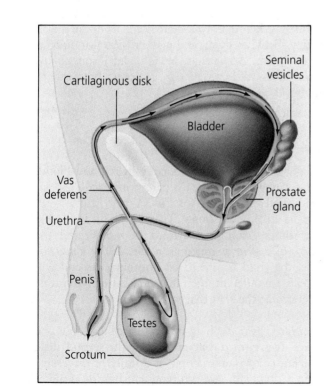

**FIGURE 2.5** • Male reproductive organs. Sperm produced in the testes move through the vas deferens, where they are mixed with semen from the prostate gland and seminal vesicles. Then they are released through the urethra in the penis.

**Zygote**

The union of sperm and ovum at conception.

**Autosomes**

The 22 matching chromosome pairs in each human cell.

**Sex chromosomes**

The 23rd pair of chromosomes, which determines the sex of the child. In females, called XX; in males, called XY.

genetic material. When gametes are formed in males, the X and Y chromosomes separate into different sperm cells. In females, all gametes carry an X chromosome. The sex of the new organism is determined by whether an X-bearing or a Y-bearing sperm fertilizes the ovum. In fact, scientists recently isolated a single gene on the Y chromosome that triggers male sexual development by switching on the production of male sex hormones. When that gene is absent, the fetus that develops is female (Page et al., 1987).

### Multiple Births

Ruth and Peter, a couple that I know well, tried for several years to have a child without success. Ruth's doctor finally prescribed a fertility drug, and twins—Jeannie and Jason—were born. Jeannie and Jason are **fraternal** or **dizygotic twins,** the most common type of multiple birth. The drug that Ruth took caused two ova to be released from her ovaries, and both were fertilized. Therefore, Jeannie and Jason are genetically no more alike than ordinary siblings. Fertility drugs are only one cause of fraternal twinning (and occasionally more offspring) in human beings. As shown in Table 2.1, other genetic and environmental factors are also involved.

There is a second way that twins can be created. Sometimes a zygote that has started to duplicate separates into two clusters of cells that develop into two individuals. These are called **identical** or **monozygotic twins** because they have the same genetic makeup. The frequency of identical twins is unrelated to the factors listed in Table 2.1. It is about the same around the world—4 out of every 1,000 births. Scientists do not know what causes this type of twinning in humans. In animals, it can be produced by temperature changes, variation in oxygen levels, and late fertilization of the ovum.

During their early years, children of single births are often healthier and develop more rapidly than do twins (Moilanen, 1989). Ruth and Peter's experience indicates why this is the case. Jeannie and Jason were born early (as most twins are)—three weeks before Ruth's due date. Like other premature infants (as we will see in Chapter 4), they required special care after birth. When the twins came home from the hospital, Ruth and Peter had to divide time between them, and neither baby got quite as much attention as the average single infant. As a result, Jeannie and Jason walked and talked several months later than other children their age, although both caught up in development by middle childhood.

### Patterns of Genetic Inheritance

Jeannie has her parents' dark, straight hair, while Jason is curly-haired and blond. Patterns of genetic inheritance—the way genes from each parent interact—explain why this is the case. Earlier we indicated that except for the XY pair in males, all chromosomes come in matching pairs called autosomes. Two forms of each gene occur at the same place on the autosomes, one inherited from the mother and one from the father. Each different form of a gene is called an **allele.** If the genes, or alleles, from both parents are alike, the child is said to be **homozygous** and will display the inherited trait. If the alleles are different, then the child is **heterozygous,** and relationships between alleles determine the trait that will appear.

**Dominant–Recessive Relationships.**　In many heterozygous pairings, only one allele affects the child's characteristics. It is termed *dominant,* while the second allele that has no effect is called *recessive.* Hair color is an example of **dominant–recessive inheritance.** The allele for dark hair is dominant (we can represent it with a capital

**Fraternal or dizygotic twins**

Twins that result from the release and fertilization of two ova. They are genetically no more alike than ordinary siblings.

**Identical or monozygotic twins**

Twins that result when a zygote, during the early stages of cell duplication, divides in two. They have the same genetic makeup.

**Allele**

Each of two forms of a gene located at the same place on the autosomes.

**Homozygous**

Having two identical alleles at the same place on a pair of chromosomes.

**Heterozygous**

Having two different alleles at the same place on a pair of chromosomes.

**Dominant–recessive inheritance**

A pattern of inheritance in which, under heterozygous conditions, the influence of only one allele is apparent.

TABLE 2.1 • Maternal Factors Linked to Fraternal Twinning

| Factor | Description |
| --- | --- |
| Ethnicity | About 8 per 1,000 births among whites, 12 to 16 per 1,000 among blacks, and 4 per 1,000 among Asians |
| Age | Rises with maternal age, peaking at 35 years, and then rapidly falls |
| Nutrition | Occurs less often among women with poor diets; occurs more often among women who are tall and overweight or of normal weight as opposed to women with slight body builds |
| Number of births | Chances increase with each additional birth |
| Exposure to fertility drugs | Treatment of infertility with the drug Clomid and various hormones increases the likelihood of multiple fraternal births, from twins to quintuplets |

*Source:* Cohen, 1984.

D), while the one for blond hair is recessive (symbolized by a small b). Children who inherit either a homozygous pair of dominant alleles (DD) or a heterozygous pair (Db) will be dark-haired, even though their genetic makeup is different. Blond hair (like Jason's) can only result from having two recessive alleles (bb). Still, heterozygous individuals (Db) with only one recessive allele can pass that trait on to their children. Therefore, they are called **carriers** of the trait.

In dominant–recessive inheritance, if we know the genetic makeup of the parents, we can predict the percentage of children in a family who are likely to display a trait or be carriers of it. Figure 2.6 shows the dominant–recessive pattern of inheritance for hair color. Note that for Jason to be blond, both Peter and Ruth must be carriers of a recessive allele (b). The figure also indicates that if Peter and Ruth decide to have more children, most are likely to be dark-haired like Jeannie.

Some human characteristics and disorders that follow the rules of dominant–recessive inheritance are given in Tables 2.2 and 2.3. As you can see from the tables, many defects and diseases are the product of recessive alleles. One of the most fre-

*These identical, or monozygotic, twins were created when a duplicating zygote separated into two clusters of cells, and two individuals with the same genetic makeup developed. Identical twins look alike, and, as we will see later in this chapter, they also tend to resemble each other in a variety of psychological characteristics.* (Porter/Image Works)

**Carrier**

A heterozygous individual who can pass a recessive gene to his or her children.

**FIGURE 2.6** • Dominant–recessive mode of inheritance as illustrated by hair color. By looking at the possible combinations of the parents' genes, we can predict that 25 percent of their children are likely to inherit two dominant genes for dark hair; 50 percent are likely to receive one dominant and one recessive gene, resulting in dark hair; and 25 percent are likely to receive two recessive genes for blond hair.

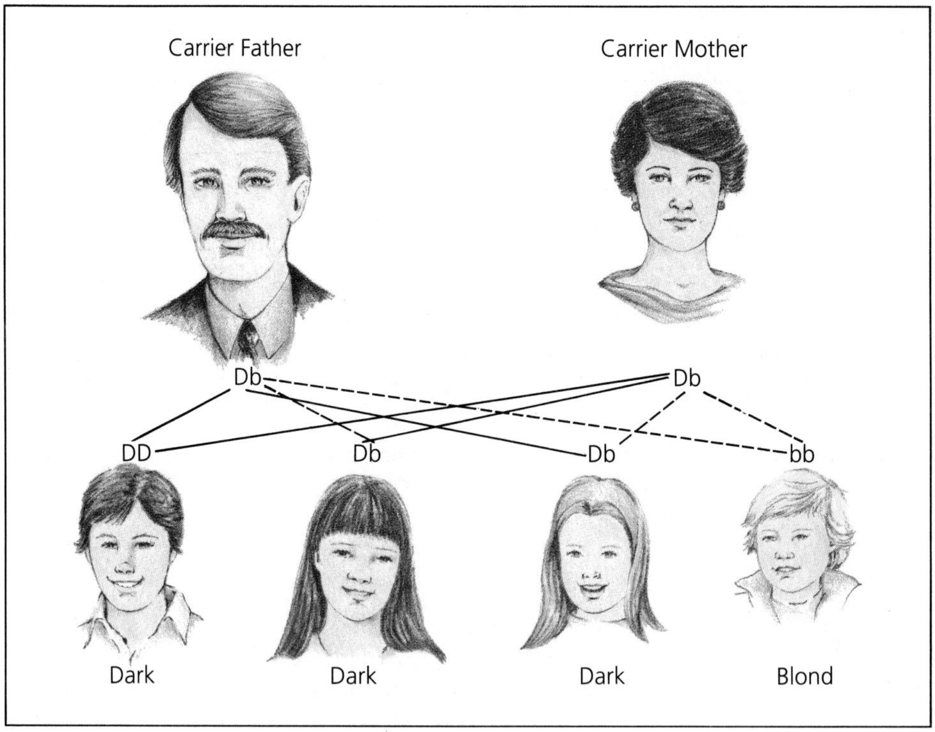

Carrier Father    Carrier Mother

Db    Db

DD    Db    Db    bb

Dark    Dark    Dark    Blond

**Codominance**

A pattern of inheritance in which both alleles, in a heterozygous combination, are expressed.

quently occurring recessive disorders is *phenylketonuria,* or *PKU.* PKU is an especially good example, since it shows that inheriting unfavorable genes does not always mean that the child's condition cannot be treated.

PKU affects the way the body breaks down proteins contained in many foods, such as cow's milk and meat. Infants born with two recessive alleles lack an enzyme that converts a harmful amino acid (phenylalanine) into a harmless by-product. Without this enzyme, an excess of phenylalanine quickly builds up and damages the central nervous system. By 3 to 5 months of age, infants with untreated PKU start to lose interest in their surroundings. By 1 year, they are permanently retarded. Most states require that every newborn be tested for PKU. If the disease is found, treatment involves placing the baby on a diet low in phenylalanine. Children who receive this treatment show near-normal levels of intelligence (Michals et al., 1988; Pietz et al., 1988).

As Table 2.3 suggests, only rarely are serious diseases due to dominant alleles. Think about why this is the case. Children who inherited the dominant allele would always develop the disorder. They would seldom live long enough to reproduce, and the harmful dominant allele would be eliminated from the family's heredity in a single generation. Note, however, that some dominant disorders do persist. One of them is *Huntington disease,* a condition in which the central nervous system degenerates. Why has this disease endured in some families? The reason is that its symptoms usually do not appear until age 35 or later, after the person has passed the dominant gene to his or her children.

*Codominance.* In some heterozygous situations, the dominant–recessive relationship does not hold completely. Instead, we see **codominance,** a pattern of inheritance in which both alleles influence the person's characteristics. The *sickle cell trait,* a heterozygous condition present in many black Africans, provides an example. *Sickle cell anemia* (see Table 2.3) occurs in full form when a child inherits two recessive

TABLE 2.2 • Examples of Dominant and Recessive Characteristics

| Dominant | Recessive |
|---|---|
| Dark hair | Blond hair |
| Curly hair | Straight hair |
| Nonred hair | Red hair |
| Facial dimples | No dimples |
| Normal hearing | Some forms of deafness |
| Normal vision | Nearsightedness |
| Farsightedness | Normal vision |
| Normal vision | Congenital eye cateracts |
| Normal color vision | Red–green color-blindness |
| Normally pigmented skin | Albinism |
| Double-jointedness | Normal joints |
| Type A blood | Type O blood |
| Type B blood | Type O blood |
| Rh positive blood | Rh negative blood |

*Source:* McKusick, 1988.

*Note:* Many normal characteristics that were previously thought to be due to dominant–recessive inheritance, such as eye color, are now regarded as due to multiple genes. For the characteristics listed here, there still seems to be fairly common agreement that the simple dominant–recessive relationship holds.

alleles. They cause the usually round red blood cells to assume a sickle shape, a response that is especially great under low oxygen conditions. The sickled cells clog the blood vessels and block the flow of blood. Individuals who have the disorder suffer severe attacks involving intense pain, swelling, and tissue damage. They generally die in the first twenty years of life, and few live past age 40. Heterozygous individuals, who have one dominant normal allele and one recessive allele, are protected from the disease under most circumstances. However, when they experience oxygen deprivation—for example, at high altitudes or after intense physical exercise—the single recessive allele asserts itself, and a temporary, mild form of the illness occurs (Sullivan, 1987).

The sickle cell allele is common among black Africans for a special reason. Carriers of it are more resistant to malaria than individuals with two alleles for normal red blood cells. In Africa, where malaria occurs often, these carriers survived and reproduced more frequently than others, leading the gene to be maintained in the black population.

*Mutation and Unfavorable Genes.* At this point, you may be asking, "How are harmful genes created in the first place?" The answer is **mutation,** a sudden but permanent change in a segment of DNA. A mutation may affect only one or two genes, or it may involve many genes, as is the case for the chromosomal disorders we will discuss shortly. Some mutations occur spontaneously, simply by chance. Others are caused by a wide variety of hazardous environmental agents that enter our food supply or are present in the air we breathe.

For many years, ionizing radiation has been known to cause mutations. Women who receive repeated doses of radiation before conception are more likely to miscarry or give birth to children with hereditary defects. Genetic abnormalities are also higher when fathers are exposed to radiation in their occupations (Schrag & Dixon, 1985). In one instance, men who worked at a reprocessing plant for nuclear fuel in England

**Mutation**
A sudden but permanent change in a segment of DNA.

TABLE 2.3 • Examples of Dominant and Recessive Diseases

| Disease | Description | Mode of Inheritance | Incidence | Treatment | Prenatal Diagnosis | Carrier Identification[a] |
|---------|-------------|---------------------|-----------|-----------|--------------------|--------------------------|
| **Autosomal Diseases** | | | | | | |
| Cooley's anemia | Pale appearance, retarded physical growth, and lethargic behavior beginning in infancy | Recessive | 1 in 500 births to parents of Mediterranean descent | Frequent blood transfusions; death from complications usually occurs by adolescence | Yes | Yes |
| Cystic fibrosis | Lungs, liver, and pancreas secrete large amounts of thick mucous, leading to breathing and digestive difficulties | Recessive | 1 in 2,000 to 2,500 Caucasian births; 1 in 16,000 African-American births | Bronchial drainage, prompt treatment of respiratory infections, and dietary management; advances in medical care allow survival with good life quality into adulthood | Yes | No |
| Phenylketonuria | Inability to neutralize a harmful amino acid contained in many food proteins causes severe central nervous system damage in the first year of life | Recessive | 1 in 8,000 births | Placement of child on a special diet controls the most harmful aspects of the disease | Yes | Yes |
| Sickle cell anemia | Abnormal sickling of red blood cells causes oxygen deprivation, pain, swelling, and tissue damage; anemia and susceptibility to infections, especially pneumonia | Recessive | 1 in 500 African-American births | Blood transfusions, painkillers, and prompt treatment of infections; no known cure: 50 percent die by age 20 | Yes | Yes |
| Tay-Sachs disease | Central nervous system degeneration with onset at about 6 months, leading to poor muscle tone, blindness, deafness, and convulsions | Recessive | 1 in 3,600 births to Jews of European descent | None; death by 3 to 4 years of age | Yes | Yes |
| Huntington disease | Central nervous system degeneration leading to muscular coordination difficulties, mental deterioration, and personality changes; symptoms usually do not appear until age 35 or later | Dominant | 1 in 18,000 to 25,000 American births | None; death occurs 10 to 20 years after symptom onset | Yes | Not applicable |
| Marfan syndrome | Tall, slender build with thin, elongated arms and legs; heart defects and eye abnormalities, especially of the lens; excessive lengthening of the body results in a variety of skeletal abnormalities | Dominant | 1 in 20,000 births | Correction of heart and eye defects sometimes possible; death from heart failure in young adulthood common | No | Not applicable |

**TABLE 2.3** • *(Continued)*

| Disease | Description | Mode of Inheritance | Incidence | Treatment | Prenatal Diagnosis | Carrier Identification[a] |
|---|---|---|---|---|---|---|
| **X-Linked Diseases** | | | | | | |
| Duchenne muscular dystrophy | Degenerative muscle disease; abnormal gait, loss of ability to walk between 7 and 13 years of age | Recessive | 1 in 3,000 to 5,000 male births | None; death from respiratory infection or weakening of the heart muscle usually occurs in adolescence | Yes | Yes |
| Hemophilia | Blood fails to clot normally; can lead to severe internal bleeding and tissue damage | Recessive | 1 in 4,000 to 7,000 male births | Blood transfusions; safety precautions to prevent injury | Yes | Yes |

*Sources:* Behrman & Vaughan, 1987; Cohen, 1984; Kainulainen et al., 1991; Martin, 1987; McKusick, 1988; Stanbury, Wyngaarden, & Frederickson, 1983.
[a]Carrier status detectable in prospective parents through blood test or genetic analyses

were found to be fathers of an unusually high number of children who developed cancer. Exposure to radiation at the plant is believed to have damaged chromosomes in the male sex cells, causing cancer in their children years later (Gardner et al., 1990). Does this mean that routine chest and dental X-rays are dangerous to future generations? Research indicates that infrequent and mild exposure to radiation does not cause genetic damage. Instead, high doses over a long period of time appear to be required.

*X-Linked Inheritance.* Males and females have an equal chance of inheriting recessive disorders carried on the autosomes, such as PKU and sickle cell anemia. But when a harmful allele is carried on the X chromosome, **X-linked inheritance** applies. Males are more likely to be affected because their sex chromosomes do not match. In females, any recessive allele on one X chromosome has some chance of being suppressed by a dominant allele on the other X. But males have only one X chromosome, and there are no corresponding alleles on the Y to override those on the X. All genes on the male's X chromosome are expressed even though they are present in only a single copy.

*Red–green color blindness* (a condition in which individuals cannot tell the difference between shades of red and green) is one example of an X-linked recessive trait. It affects males twice as often as females (Cohen, 1984). In one 3-year-old boy I know, the problem was discovered when he had difficulty learning the names of colors at nursery school. The boy's maternal grandfather was also color-blind. Although his mother was unaffected, she was a carrier who passed an X chromosome with the recessive allele to her son. Return to Table 2.3 and review those diseases that are X-linked. A well-known example is *hemophilia,* a disorder in which the blood fails to clot normally. Figure 2.7 shows its greater likelihood of inheritance by male children whose mothers carry the abnormal allele.

Besides X-linked disorders, many sex differences reveal the male to be at a disadvantage. The rates of spontaneous abortion and infant and childhood deaths are greater for males. Learning disabilities, behavior disorders, and mental retardation are also more common among boys (Richardson, Koller, & Katz, 1986). It is possible that these sex differences can be traced to the genetic code. The female, with two X chromosomes, benefits from a greater variety of genes. Nature, however, seems to have adjusted for the male's disadvantage. About 106 boys are born for every 100

**X-linked inheritance**
A pattern of inheritance in which a recessive gene is carried on the X chromosome. Males are more likely to be affected.

**FIGURE 2.7** • X-linked inheritance. In the example shown here, the allele on the father's X chromosome is normal. The mother has one normal and one abnormal allele on her X chromosomes. By looking at the possible combinations of the parents' alleles, we can predict that 50 percent of male children will have the disorder and 50 percent of female children will be carriers of it.

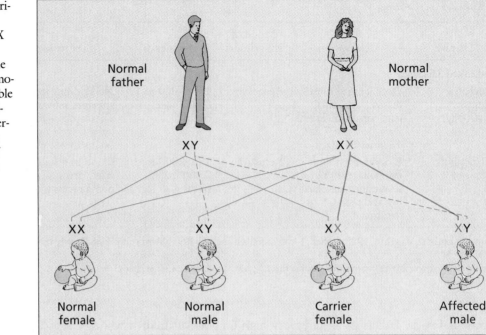

girls, and judging from miscarriage and abortion statistics, a still greater number of boys appear to be conceived (Rugh & Shettles, 1971).

*Polygenic Inheritance.* Over 1,000 human characteristics are believed to follow the rules of dominant–recessive inheritance (McKusick, 1988). In most of these cases, either people display a particular trait or they do not. Such cut-and-dried individual differences are much easier to trace to their genetic origins than characteristics that vary continuously among people. Many traits of interest to child development specialists, such as height, weight, intelligence, and personality, are of this type. People are not just tall or short, bright or dull, outgoing or shy. Instead, they show gradations between these extremes. Continuous traits like these are due to **polygenic inheritance,** in which many genes determine the characteristic in question. Polygenic inheritance is complex, and much about it is still unknown. In the final section of this chapter, we will discuss ways that have been used to infer the effect of heredity on behavior when knowledge of precise patterns of inheritance is not available.

## CHROMOSOMAL ABNORMALITIES

Besides inheriting harmful recessive alleles, abnormalities of the chromosomes are a major cause of serious developmental problems. Most chromosomal defects are the result of mistakes during meiosis when the ovum and sperm are formed. A chromosome pair does not separate properly or part of a chromosome breaks off. Since these errors involve far more DNA than problems due to single genes, they usually produce disorders with many physical and mental symptoms.

### Down Syndrome

The most common chromosomal disorder, occurring in 1 out of every 800 live births, is *Down syndrome* (Baird & Sadovnick, 1987). In most cases, it results from a failure

**Polygenic inheritance**

A pattern of inheritance in which many genes determine a characteristic.

of the 21st pair of chromosomes to separate during meiosis, so the new individual inherits three of these chromosomes rather than the normal two. In other less frequent forms, an extra broken piece of a 21st chromosome is present. In these instances, the child's characteristics can vary from practically normal to the typical characteristics of Down syndrome, depending on how much extra genetic material is present (Rosenberg & Pettigrew, 1983).

Children with Down syndrome have distinct physical features—a short, stocky build, a flattened face, a protruding tongue, almond-shaped eyes, and an unusual crease running across the palm of the hand. In addition, infants with Down syndrome are often born with eye cataracts and heart and intestinal abnormalities. Because of medical advances, fewer Down syndrome children die early than was the case in the past, but early death is still common. About 14 percent die by age 1, and 21 percent by age 10. The rest live until middle adulthood (Baird & Sadovnick, 1987).

The behavioral consequences of Down syndrome include mental retardation, speech problems, limited vocabulary, and slow motor development. These problems become more evident with age, since Down syndrome children show a gradual slowing down in development from infancy onward when compared to normal children (Kopp, 1983). Parents who give birth to a Down syndrome infant need special help in adjusting to the news that their baby is not normal and in raising their child. Effective child rearing and early intervention can make a difference in how well youngsters with Down syndrome develop (Van Dyke et al., 1990).

Why does Down syndrome occur? It rises dramatically with the mother's age, from 1 in every 1,900 births for mothers 20 to 24 years of age to 1 in every 30 births for mothers over age 45 (Baird & Sadovnick, 1987). Fathers over 40 also show an increased risk of having children with the disorder (Hook, 1980; Stene, Stene, & Stengel-Rutkowski, 1981). Geneticists believe that the sex cells gradually weaken with age so that chromosomes do not separate properly during meiosis.

## Abnormalities of the Sex Chromosomes

Other disorders of the autosomes exist besides Down syndrome, but they usually disrupt development so severely that miscarriage occurs. When such babies are born, they rarely survive beyond early childhood. In contrast, abnormalities of the sex chromosomes usually lead to fewer problems. In fact, sex chromosome disorders are often not recognized until adolescence when, in some of the deviations, puberty is delayed. The most common problems involve the presence of an extra chromosome (either X or Y) or the absence of one X chromosome in females (see Table 2.4).

A variety of myths exist about individuals with sex chromosome disorders. For example, many people believe that males with *XYY syndrome* are more aggressive and antisocial than XY males. Yet by examining Table 2.4, you will see that this is not the case. Also, it is widely believed that children with sex chromosome disorders are retarded. Yet they are not. The intelligence of XYY syndrome boys is similar to that of normal children (Stewart, 1982; Netley, 1986). And the intellectual problems of children with *triple X, Klinefelter, and Turner syndromes* are very specific. Verbal difficulties (for example, with reading and vocabulary) are common among girls with triple X and boys with Klinefelter, each of whom inherits an extra X chromosome. In contrast, Turner syndrome girls, who are missing an X, have trouble with spatial relationships. Their handwriting is poor, and they have difficulty telling right from left and finding their way around the neighborhood during the early school years. When they get to high school, they avoid courses like geometry and those that demand drawing skills (Hall et al., 1982; Netley, 1986; Pennington et al., 1982). These findings tell us that adding to or subtracting from the usual number of X chromosomes results in particular intellectual deficits. At present, geneticists do not know why this is the case.

*The flattened face and almond-shaped eyes of the younger child in this photo are typical physical features of Down syndrome. Although his intellectual development is impaired, this boy is doing well because he is growing up in a family in which his special needs are met and he is loved and accepted. (Frank Siteman/Stock Boston)*

**TABLE 2.4 • Sex Chromosomal Disorders**

| Disorder | Description | Incidence | Treatment |
|---|---|---|---|
| XYY syndrome | Inheritance of an extra Y chromosome. Typical characteristics are above-average height, large teeth, and sometimes severe acne. Intelligence, development of male sexual characteristics, and fertility are normal. | 1 in 1,000 male births | No special treatment necessary. |
| Triple X syndrome (XXX) | Inheritance of an extra X chromosome. Impaired verbal intelligence. Afflicted girls are no different in appearance or sexual development from normal age-mates, except for a greater tendency toward tallness. | 1 in 500 to 1,250 female births | Special education to treat verbal ability problems. |
| Klinefelter syndrome (XXY) | Inheritance of an extra X chromosome. Impaired verbal intelligence. Affected boys are unusually tall, have a body fat distribution resembling females, and show incomplete development of sex characteristics at puberty. They are usually sterile. | 1 in 500 to 1,000 male births | Hormone therapy at puberty to stimulate development of sex characteristics. Special education to treat verbal ability problems. |
| Turner syndrome (XO) | All or part of the second X chromosome is missing. Impaired spatial intelligence. Ovaries usually do not develop prenatally. Incomplete development of sex characteristics at puberty. Other features include short stature and webbed neck. | 1 in 2,500 to 8,000 female births | Hormone therapy in childhood to stimulate physical growth and at puberty to promote development of sex characteristics. Special education to treat spatial ability problems. |
| Fragile X syndrome | An abnormal break appears at a special place on one or both X chromosomes. Associated with mental retardation and mild facial deformities, including enlarged ears, jaw, and forehead. About 12 percent have infantile autism. | 1 in 1,500 male births and 1 in 2,000 female births | Special therapeutic programs for retarded and behavior disordered children. |

*Sources:* Bancroft, Axworthy, & Ratcliffe, 1982; Borghraef et al., 1987; Cohen, 1984; Hall et al., 1982; Ho, Glahn, & Ho, 1988; Netley, 1986; Pennington et al., 1982; Schaivi et al., 1984.

• *Two brothers, Todd and Blake, look strikingly different. Todd is tall and thin; Blake is short and stocky. What events taking place during meiosis contributed to these differences?*

• *Gilbert and Jan are planning to have children. Gilbert's genetic makeup is homozygous for dark hair; Jan's is heterozygous for blond hair. What color is Gilbert's hair? How about Jan's? What proportion of their children are likely to be dark-haired?*

One exception to the fairly mild consequences of sex chromosome abnormalities is *fragile X syndrome.* In this disorder, the X chromosome is damaged. An abnormal break appears in a special spot. Fragile X syndrome ranks second only to Down syndrome as a major genetic cause of mental retardation. It has also been linked to infantile autism, a serious emotional disorder of early childhood involving bizarre, self-stimulating behavior and delayed or absent language and communication (Ho, Glahn, & Ho, 1988).

*BRIEF REVIEW* Each individual is made up of trillions of cells. Inside each cell nucleus are chromosomes, which contain a chemical molecule called DNA. Genes are segments of DNA that determine our species and unique characteristics. Gametes, or sex cells, are formed through a special process of cell division called *meiosis* that halves the usual number of chromosomes in human cells. Then, when sperm and ovum unite at conception, each new being has the correct number of chromosomes. A different combination of sex chromosomes establishes whether a child will be boy or girl. Two types of twins—fraternal and identical—are possible. Fraternal twins are genetically no more alike than ordinary siblings, while identical twins have the same genetic makeup. Three patterns of inheritance—dominant–recessive, co-dominant, and X-linked—underlie many traits and disorders due to single genes. Characteristics that vary continuously among people, such as height and intelligence, result from the enormous complexities of polygenic inheritance, which involves a great many genes. Chromosomal abnormalities occur when meiosis is disrupted during gamete formation. Disorders of the autosomes are typically more serious than those of the sex chromosomes.

## REPRODUCTIVE CHOICES

Two years after they were married, Ted and Marianne gave birth to their first child. Kendra appeared to be a healthy and lively infant, but by 4 months her growth slowed. Diagnosed as having Tay-Sachs disease (see Table 2.3), Kendra died at 2 years of age. Ted and Marianne were devastated by Kendra's death. Although they did not want to bring another infant into the world who would endure such suffering, they badly wanted to have a child. When Ted and Marianne took walks in the neighborhood, they would see children in strollers, and tears would come to their eyes. They began to avoid family get-togethers where little nieces and nephews were constant reminders of the void in their lives.

In the past, many couples with genetic disorders in their families chose not to bear a child at all rather than risk having an abnormal baby. Today, genetic counseling and prenatal diagnosis help people make informed decisions about conceiving, carrying a pregnancy to term, or adopting a child. In addition, the legalization of abortion has meant that women, whether or not they have an increased likelihood of bearing a child with defects, can decide after conception whether they wish to give birth.

### Genetic Counseling

**Genetic counseling** helps couples who want to have a child assess their chances of giving birth to a baby with a hereditary disorder. People likely to seek it are those who know that genetic problems exist in their families or who have experienced difficulties having children, such as repeated miscarriages. The genetic counselor interviews the couple and prepares a *pedigree,* a picture of the family tree in which affected relatives are identified. The pedigree is used to estimate the likelihood that parents will have an abnormal child, using the same genetic principles we discussed earlier in this chapter. In the case of many recessive disorders (refer back to Table 2.3), medical tests can reveal whether the parent is a carrier of the harmful gene.

When all the relevant information is in, the genetic counselor helps people consider appropriate options. These include "taking a chance" and conceiving, choosing from among a variety of reproductive technologies discussed in Box 2.1, or adopting a child.

### Prenatal Diagnosis and Fetal Medicine

If couples who might bear an abnormal child decide to conceive, several **prenatal diagnostic methods**—medical procedures that permit detection of problems before birth—are available (see Table 2.5). Older women are prime candidates for *amniocentesis* or *chorionic villi biopsy* (see Figure 2.8), since the overall rate of chromosomal problems rises sharply after age 35, from 1 in every 100 to as many as 1 in every 3 pregnancies at age 48 (Hook, 1988). Except for *ultrasound* and *maternal blood analysis,* prenatal diagnosis should not be used routinely, since other methods have some chance of injuring the developing organism.

**Genetic counseling**

Counseling that helps couples assess the likelihood of giving birth to a baby with a hereditary disorder.

**Prenatal diagnostic methods**

Medical procedures that permit detection of problems before birth.

## SOCIAL ISSUES

### Box 2.1   The Pros and Cons of New Reproductive Technologies

One sixth of all married couples are infertile for a variety of reasons. Others hesitate to risk pregnancy because of a family history of genetic disease. The high incidence of reproductive problems among people who want to have children has led to alternative methods of conception and pregnancy.

For several decades, *donor insemination* (injection of sperm from an anonymous man into a woman) has been used to overcome male reproductive difficulties. In the United States alone, 20,000 children are conceived this way each year (Sokoloff, 1987). In addition, two new practices—in vitro fertilization and surrogate motherhood—have become increasingly common.

Since the first "test tube" baby was born in England in 1978, more than 5,000 infants have been created through *in vitro fertilization* (Ryan, 1989). In this method, hormones are given to a woman, stimulating ripening of several ova. These are removed surgically and placed in a dish of nutrients, to which sperm are added. Once an ovum is fertilized and begins to divide into several cells, it is injected into the mother's uterus, where, hopefully, it will implant and develop. In vitro fertilization is generally used to treat infertility in women whose fallopian tubes are permanently damaged, and it is successful for 20 percent of those who try it. These results have been encouraging enough that the technique has been expanded. By mixing and matching gametes, pregnancies can be brought about when either or both partners have a reproductive problem.

Donor insemination and in vitro fertilization appear to be physically as safe for the child as natural conception. However, serious questions have arisen about their use. Many states have no legal guidelines for these procedures. As a result, donors are not always screened for genetic or sexually transmitted diseases. In addition, only a minority of doctors keep records of donor characteristics. Yet the resulting children may someday want information about their genetic background or need it for medical reasons (Andrews, 1987; Sokoloff, 1987).

The most controversial form of medically assisted conception is *surrogate motherhood*. In this procedure, sperm from a man whose wife is infertile are used to inseminate a woman, who is paid a fee for her childbearing services. In return, the surrogate agrees to turn the baby over to the man (who is the natural father). The child is then adopted by his wife. Although most of these arrangements proceed without problems, those that end up in court highlight serious risks for all concerned. In one case, both parties rejected the handicapped infant that resulted from the pregnancy. In several others, the surrogate mother changed her mind and wanted to keep the baby. These children came into the world in midst of family conflict that threatened to last for years to come. Most surrogates already have children of their own, who may be deeply affected by the pregnancy. Knowledge that their mother would give away a baby for profit may cause these youngsters to worry about the security of their own family circumstances (McGinty & Zafran, 1988; Ryan, 1989).

Although new reproductive methods permit many barren couples to have healthy newborn babies, laws are needed to regulate them. In the case of surrogate motherhood, the ethical problems are so complex that many European governments have made the practice illegal, and some U.S. states have done so as well (McGinty & Zafran, 1988). Finally, at present nothing is known about the psychological consequences of being a product of these procedures. Research on how such children grow up, including what they know and how they feel about their origins, is important for weighing the pros and cons of these techniques.

*USE THE READER'S GUIDE to Periodical Literature* in your library to locate newspaper and magazine articles on two highly publicized surrogate motherhood cases: Baby M of New Jersey (1987) and the Calvert case of California (1990). Do you think the problems that arose in each case justify limiting or banning the practice of surrogacy?

TABLE 2.5 • Prenatal Diagnostic Methods

| Method | Description |
|---|---|
| Amniocentesis | A hollow needle is inserted through the abdominal wall to obtain a sample of fluid in the uterus. Cells are examined for genetic defects. Can be performed by 11 to 14 weeks after conception; 3 more weeks are required for test results. Small risk of miscarriage. |
| Chorionic villi biopsy | A thin tube is inserted into the uterus through the vagina or a hollow needle is inserted through the abdominal wall. A small plug of tissue is removed from the end of one or more chorionic villi, the hairlike projections on the membrane surrounding the developing organism. The cells obtained are examined for genetic defects. Can be performed at 6 to 8 weeks after conception, and results are available immediately. Entails a slightly greater risk of miscarriage than does amniocentesis. |
| Ultrasound | High-frequency sound waves are beamed at the uterus; their reflection is translated into a picture that reveals the size, shape, and placement of the fetus. By itself, permits assessment of fetal age, detection of multiple pregnancies, and identification of gross physical defects. Also used to guide amniocentesis, chorionic villi biopsy, and fetoscopy. |
| Fetoscopy | A small tube with a light source at one end is inserted into the uterus to inspect the fetus for defects of the limbs and face. Also allows a sample of fetal blood to be obtained, permitting diagnosis of such disorders as hemophilia and sickle cell anemia as well as neural defects (see below). Usually performed between 15 to 18 weeks after conception. Entails some risk of miscarriage. |
| Maternal blood analysis | By the second month of pregnancy, some of the embryo's cells enter the maternal blood stream. An elevated level of alpha-fetoprotein may indicate kidney disease, abnormal closure of the esophagus, or neural defects, such as anencephaly (absence of most of the brain) and spina bifida (bulging of the spinal cord from the spinal column). |

*Sources:* Benacerraf et al., 1988; Cohen, 1984; Rhoads et al., 1989.

Improvements in prenatal diagnosis have led to new advances in fetal medicine. Today, some medical problems are being treated before birth. For example, drugs can be delivered to the fetus by inserting a needle into the uterus. In addition, surgery has been performed to repair such problems as urinary tract obstructions and neural defects. Nevertheless, these practices remain controversial. Most are highly experimental. Although some babies are saved, the techniques frequently result in complications or miscarriage. Yet when parents are told that their unborn baby has a serious defect, they may be willing to try almost any option, even if there is only a slim chance of success. Currently, the medical profession is struggling with how to help parents make informed decisions about fetal surgery. One suggestion is that the advice of an independent counselor be provided—a doctor or nurse who understands the risks but is not involved in doing research on or performing the procedure (Kolata, 1989).

Advances in *genetic engineering* also offer new hope for correcting hereditary defects. The possibility of genetic repair of the prenatal organism is closer today than it was in the past. Researchers are mapping human chromosomes, finding the precise location of genes for specific traits and cloning (copying) these genes using chemical techniques in the laboratory. Of the 3,000 known inherited diseases, genes have been

**FIGURE 2.8** • Amniocentesis and chorionic villi biopsy. Today, more than 250 defects and diseases can be detected before birth using these procedures. (A) In amniocentesis, a needle is inserted through the abdominal wall into the uterus. Fluid is withdrawn and fetal cells are cultured, a process that takes about 3 weeks. (B) Chorionic villi biopsy can be performed much earlier in pregnancy, and results are available within 24 hours. Two approaches to obtaining a sample of chorionic villi are shown below: inserting a thin tube through the vagina into the uterus or a needle through the abdominal wall. In either of these methods, ultrasound is used for guidance. *(From K. L. Moore, 1989,* Before We Are Born, *3rd ed., Philadelphia: Saunders, p. 99. Adapted by permission.)*

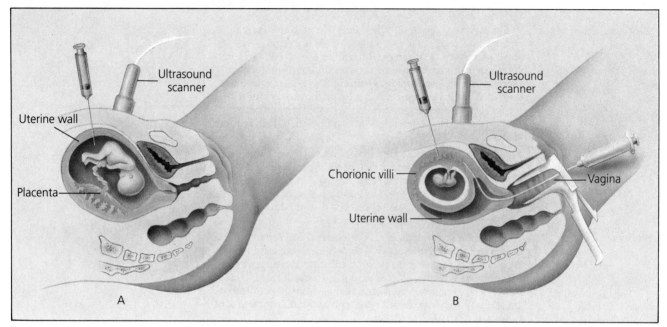

found for about 100, including Duchenne muscular dystrophy, Huntington disease, and cystic fibrosis (Caskey & McKusick, 1990). Scientists hope to use this information to identify abnormal conditions with greater accuracy before birth. Eventually, *gene splicing* (replacing a harmful gene with a good one in the early zygote or in cells in the affected part of the body) may permit defects to be permanently corrected before symptoms appear.

### The Alternative of Abortion

If prenatal diagnosis shows that the fetus has an abnormal condition that cannot be corrected, parents are faced with the difficult choice of whether or not to have an abortion. The decision to terminate a desired pregnancy is painful for all who have to make it. Parents must deal with the emotional shock of the news and decide within a very short period of time. If they choose to have an abortion, they face the grief that comes with having lost a wanted child, worries about future pregnancies, and possible guilt about the abortion itself.

Fortunately, 95 percent of developing babies examined through prenatal diagnosis are perfectly normal. It is not surprising, then, that women who accidentally become pregnant account for far more abortions than women who know their infants will be born with serious defects. Adolescents who conceive before they are mature enough to raise a child have the highest rate of abortion. In the United States, 40 percent of over one million teenage pregnancies are aborted each year (Furstenberg, Brooks-Gunn, & Chase-Lansdale, 1989).

A wealth of research suggests that being wanted by parents who have established a clear sense of direction for their own lives is important for healthy development.

As we will see in Chapter 14, adolescent girls who become pregnant usually have too many pressing concerns of their own to be effective parents. As a result, their children often have serious developmental problems. A recent study carried out in Czechoslovakia revealed that unwanted children in general—not just those born to adolescents—develop less favorably. Children of Czech mothers whose requests for an abortion had been denied were compared to controls whose mothers had not asked for an abortion. Unwanted children were less physically healthy and emotionally stable and achieved less well in school. By young adulthood, they were less satisfied with their lives, and they blamed their unhappiness on a poor relationship with their parents (David et al., 1988).

Nevertheless, science cannot inform pregnant women or society as a whole about whether abortion is a morally justifiable act. The issue of when personhood begins—at conception or sometime later during pregnancy—divides people into fiercely opposing camps. Other concerns also arise in evaluating the ethics of abortion. Is the quality of life experienced by unwanted and defective children so unfavorable that they should not be brought into the world at all? Is the burden that their care places on family members and the general public enough reason to end a pregnancy? To what extent should abortion be a woman's choice and to what extent should it be controlled by the state? These are complex questions that do not have easy answers.

## The Alternative of Adoption

Many parents who cannot have children or who are likely to pass along a genetic disorder decide to adopt. Adoption agencies try to find parents of the same race and ethnic and religious background as the child. Where possible, they also try to choose parents who are the same age as most natural parents. When matches of these kinds cannot be made, agencies place children with adoptive parents having other characteristics rather than delaying their entry into a family.

Selection of adoptive parents is important, since sometimes adoptive relationships do not work out, and the child must be removed from the home. The risk of adoption failure is greatest for handicapped children and youngsters adopted at older ages, but it is not high. Over 85 percent of these children do well in their adoptive homes. Of those who do not, 90 percent are successfully placed with a new family (Churchill, 1984; Glidden & Pursley, 1989). The outcomes are good because of careful pairing of children with parents and guidance provided to adopting families by well-trained social service professionals.

Still, adopted children have more emotional and learning difficulties than occur in the general child population (Verhulst, Althaus, & Versluis-Den Bieman, 1990). There are many reasons for this trend. The natural mother may have been unable to raise the child because of emotional problems believed to be partly genetic, such as alcoholism and schizophrenia.[1] She may have passed this tendency to her offspring. Or perhaps the mother experienced stress, poor diet, or inadequate medical care during pregnancy—factors that (as we will see in Chapter 3) can affect the child. Finally, children adopted at older ages often have a history of conflict-ridden family relationships and lack of parental affection. But raising children under any reproductive alternative entails risks, and it is still the case that most adopted children have happy childhoods and grow up to be well-adjusted, productive citizens.

As we conclude our discussion of reproductive choices, perhaps you are wondering how things turned out for Ted and Marianne. They were my next-door neighbors for many years, and I am glad to report that their story had a happy ending. Through

---

[1] Schizophrenia is a disorder involving difficulty in distinguishing fantasy from reality, hallucinations and delusions, and irrational and inappropriate behaviors.

genetic counseling, Marianne discovered a history of Tay-Sachs disease on her mother's side of the family. Ted had a distant cousin who died of the disorder. The genetic counselor explained that the chances of giving birth to another affected baby were 1 in 4. Ted and Marianne took the risk. Their son Douglas is now 10 years old. Although Douglas is a carrier of the recessive allele, he is a normal, healthy boy. In a few years, Ted and Marianne will tell Douglas about his genetic history and explain the importance of genetic counseling and testing before he has children of his own.

*• A woman over 35 has just learned that she is pregnant. Although she would like to find out as soon as possible whether her baby has a chromosomal disorder, she wants to minimize the risk of injury to the developing baby. Which prenatal diagnostic method is she likely to choose?*

*• Describe the ethical pros and cons of fetal surgery and surrogate motherhood.*

**BRIEF REVIEW**   Genetic counseling helps couples who have a history of reproductive problems or hereditary defects in their families make informed decisions about bearing a child. For those who decide to conceive, prenatal diagnostic methods permit early detection of fetal problems. Reproductive technologies, such as donor insemination, in vitro fertilization, and surrogate motherhood, are also available, but they raise serious ethical concerns. The majority of abortions are to women who accidentally become pregnant, many of them teenagers, rather than to women carrying a baby with a serious disorder. Although developmental problems are more common among adopted children than children in general, careful selection of adoptive parents and family support services make adoption successful in the large majority of cases.

## ENVIRONMENTAL CONTEXTS FOR DEVELOPMENT

Just as complex as the heredity that sets the stage for development is the child's environment—a many-layered set of influences that combine with one another to help or hinder the course of growth. Take some time at this point to think back to your own childhood and jot down a brief description of the first ten memories that come to mind. When I ask my students to do this, about half the events they describe involve their families. This emphasis on the family is not surprising, since it is the child's first and foremost context for development. But other experiences turn out to be important as well. Friends, scouting troops, clubs at church or synagogue, and successes and disappointments at school generally make the top ten.

Finally, there is one very important context that my students rarely mention. Its influence is so widespread that we seldom stop to think about it in our everyday lives. This is the broad social climate of society—its values and programs that support and protect children's development. All families need help in raising their children— safe neighborhoods, well-equipped parks and playgrounds, good schools, affordable health services, and more. And some families, because of poverty or special tragedies, need considerably more help than others.

In the following sections, we take up the role of each of these contexts in children's lives. Since they affect every age period and aspect of development, we will return to all of them in later chapters. For now, our discussion emphasizes that not just heredity, but also environments can enhance growth or create risks for children. And when a vulnerable child—a youngster with a handicap or a special disability—grows up in unfavorable child-rearing contexts, then development is seriously threatened.

### The Family

In power and breadth of influence, no context for development matches the family. The family introduces children to the physical world through the opportunities it provides for play and exploration of objects. It also creates bonds between people that are unique. The attachments children form with parents and siblings usually last a lifetime, and they serve as models for relationships in the wider world of neighborhood and school. Within the family, children also experience their first social conflicts. Discipline by parents and arguments with siblings provide children with important lessons in compliance and cooperation and opportunities to learn how to influence the behavior of others. Finally, within the family children learn the language, skills, and social and moral values of their culture.

In the section on *ecological systems theory* in Chapter 1, we saw that modern investigators view the family as a complex set of interacting relationships. The **social systems perspective** on family functioning, which has much in common with Bronfenbrenner's (1979, 1989) ecological model, grew out of researchers' efforts to describe and explain the patterns of interaction that take place in families. It regards the family as a complex system in which the behaviors of each family member affect those of others. Let's take a closer look at its basic features.

**The Family as a Social System.**   When child development specialists first studied the family in the middle part of this century, they investigated it in a very limited way. Most research focused on the mother–child relationship and emphasized one-way effects of the mother's child-rearing practices on children's behavior. Today, family systems theorists recognize that children are not mechanically shaped by the inputs of others. Instead, *bidirectional* influences exist in which the behaviors of each family member affect those of others. The very word *family system* implies that the responses of all family members are related (Kantor & Lehr, 1975; Minuchin, 1988). These system influences operate in both *direct* and *indirect* ways.

*Direct Influences.*   Keep a sharp lookout the next time you pass through the checkout counter at your local supermarket. Recently, I saw these two episodes, in which parents and children directly affected each other:

> Little Danny stood next to tempting rows of candy as his mom lifted groceries from the cart onto the counter. "Pleeeeease, can I have it, Mom?" begged Danny, holding up a large package of bubble gum. "Do you have a dollar? Just one?"

The family is a complex social system in which each person's behavior influences the behavior of others, in both direct and indirect ways. The positive mealtime atmosphere in this family is probably a product of many forces, including parents who respond to children with warmth and patience, aunts and uncles who support parents in their child-rearing roles, and children who have developed cooperative dispositions. (Michal Heron/Woodfin Camp & Assoc.)

**Social systems perspective**
A view of the family as a complex system in which the behaviors of each family member affect those of others.

"No, not today," his mother answered softly. "Remember, we picked out your special cereal. That's what I need the dollar for." Danny's mother handed him the cereal while gently taking the bubble gum from his hand and returning it to the shelf. "Here, let's pay the man," she said, as she lifted Danny into the empty grocery cart where he could see the checkout counter.

Three-year-old Meg sat in the cart while her mom transferred groceries to the counter. Meg turned around, grabbed a bunch of bananas from the cart, and started to pull them apart.

"Stop it, Meg!" shouted her mom, who snatched the bananas from Meg's hand. Meg reached for a chocolate bar while her mother wrote the check. "Meg, how many times have I told you, DON'T TOUCH!" Loosening the candy from Meg's tight little grip, Meg's mother slapped her hand. Meg's face turned red with anger as she began to wail. "Keep this up, and you'll get it when we get home," threatened Meg's mom as they left the store.

These observations fit with a wealth of research on the family system. Many studies show that when parents (like Danny's mom) are firm but patient, children tend to comply with their requests. And when children cooperate, their parents are likely to be warm and gentle in the future (Baumrind, 1983; Lewis, 1981). In contrast, when parents (like Meg's mom) discipline with harshness and impatience, children are likely to refuse and rebel. And because children's misbehavior is stressful for parents, they may increase their use of punishment, leading to more unruliness by the child (Patterson, DeBaryshe, & Ramsey, 1989). In these examples, the behavior of one family member helps sustain a form of interaction in another that either promotes or undermines children's well-being.

*Indirect Influences.* The impact of family relationships on child development becomes even more complicated when we consider that interaction between any two members is affected by others present in the setting. Recall from Chapter 1 that Bronfenbrenner called these indirect influences the effect of *third parties.* Modern researchers have become intensely interested in how a range of relationships—mother with father, parent with sibling, grandparent with parent—modifies the child's direct experiences in the family.

Third parties can serve as effective supports for child development. For example, when parents' marital relationship is warm and considerate, mothers and fathers praise and stimulate their children more and nag and scold them less. In contrast, when a marriage is tense and hostile, parents are likely to criticize and punish (Cox et al., 1989; Howes & Markman, 1989). Findings like these help us understand the stressful impact of divorce on children, a topic that we will take up in Chapter 13. Yet even when children's adjustment is strained by arguments between their parents, other family members may help restore effective interaction. Grandparents are a case in point. They can promote children's development in many ways—both directly, by responding warmly to the child, and indirectly, by providing parents with child-rearing advice, models of child-rearing skill, and even financial assistance (Cherlin & Furstenberg, 1986). Of course, like any indirect influence, grandparents can sometimes have harmful effects. If quarrelsome relations exist between parents and grandparents, then children may actually suffer.

*A Dynamic, Ever-Changing System.* The social systems approach views the interplay of forces within the family as dynamic and ever-changing. Important events, such as a move to a new neighborhood or the birth of a baby, create challenges that modify existing relationships. For example, a mother once told me that when her second child was born, her 2-year-old daughter Trina reacted (as many children do) with some "creative" attention-getting behaviors. For example, Trina would throw her cup, demand to be taken to the toilet, or squeeze into her mother's lap during the baby's feeding time. "I was exhausted from trying to take care of both children," the mother explained. "One day I stopped and listened to myself speak to Trina. I realized how impatient I'd become." The way new events affect parent–child interaction depends on the support provided by other family members as well as the age of the child. Suppose that Trina had been a school-age youngster, with many satisfying activities beyond the family, when the new baby was born. Clearly she would have responded very differently!

In addition to new events, a child's development itself is another dynamic aspect of family life. As children grow and change over time, parents must adjust their style of interaction to fit with their child's expanding abilities. When you next have a chance, notice the way that a parent relates to a tiny baby as opposed to a walking, talking toddler. During the first few months of life, much time is spent in care-giving—feeding, changing, bathing, and cuddling the infant. Within a year, things change dramatically. The 1-year-old points, shows, names objects, and makes his way through the household cupboards. In response, parents spend less time in physical care and more in talking and playing games. These new ways of interacting encourage the child's expanding motor, cognitive, and language skills (Green, Gustafson, & West, 1980).

Despite the family's flexible and changing nature, researchers have discovered some general rules about good parenting practices. As we will see in later chapters, parental *responsiveness* is repeatedly associated with better development. In infancy, responsive parents sensitively adapt their behaviors to those of the infant. They hold the baby tenderly, wait until she is ready for the next spoonful of food, and gaze into her eyes, smile, and talk softly when she indicates she is ready for social stimulation. Babies who receive such care are likely to develop into especially competent toddlers and preschoolers, both cognitively and socially (Park & Waters, 1989; Sroufe, 1983).

During childhood and adolescence, responsive parents communicate in a warm, affectionate manner and listen patiently to their youngster's point of view. And when they combine this sensitivity with another critical feature of effective parenting—*reasonable demands for mature behavior*—their children tend to be socially active and responsible and to achieve well in school (Baumrind, 1971, 1991). In fact, research examining parenting in over 180 societies indicates that a style that is warm but moderately demanding is the most common pattern around the world. Many cultures seem to have discovered for themselves the link between this style of child rearing and healthy psychological development (Rohner & Rohner, 1981).

## Social Class and Family Functioning

Although there are cross-cultural similarities in parenting practices, social class differences exist in how families rear children. When asked about qualities they would like to encourage in their youngsters, parents who work in skilled and semiskilled manual occupations (for example, machinists, truck drivers, and custodians) tend to place a higher value on external characteristics, such as obedience, neatness, and cleanliness. In contrast, white-collar and professional parents tend to emphasize inner psychological traits, such as curiosity, happiness, and self-control. These differences in values are reflected in parents' behaviors. Middle-class parents talk to and stimulate their babies more and grant them greater freedom to explore. When their children get older, they use more explanations and verbal praise. In contrast, lower-class parents are more likely to be restrictive. Because they think that infants can easily be spoiled, they limit the amount of rocking and cuddling they do (Luster, Rhoades, & Haas, 1989). Later on, commands, such as "You do that because I told you to," as well as criticism and physical punishment occur more often in low-income households (Laosa, 1981).

Social class differences in child rearing can be understood in terms of the different life conditions in low-income and middle-income families. Low-income parents often feel a sense of powerlessness and lack of influence in their relationships beyond the family. For example, at work they must obey the rules of others in positions of power and authority. When they get home, their parent–child interaction seems to duplicate these experiences, only with them in the authority roles. In contrast, middle class parents have a greater sense of control over their own lives. At work, they are used to making independent decisions and convincing others of their point of view. At home, they teach these same skills to their children (Kohn, 1979).

Education may also contribute to social class differences in child rearing. Middle-class parents' interest in developing their child's inner characteristics is probably fostered by years of higher education, during which they learned to think about abstract, subjective ideas. Finally, the greater economic security of middle-class parents frees them from the burden of having to worry about making ends meet on a daily basis. They can devote more energy and attention to their own inner characteristics and those of their children. And they can also provide many more experiences—from toys to special outings to after-school lessons—that encourage these characteristics (Hoffman, 1984).

As early as the second year of life, middle-class children are advanced in cognitive and language development over their lower-class agemates (Wachs, Užgiris, & Hunt, 1971). And throughout childhood and adolescence, middle-class children do better in school (Jencks, 1972). Child development specialists believe that social class differences in parenting practices have much to do with these outcomes.

### The Impact of Poverty

When families become so low-income that they slip into poverty, then the development of children is seriously threatened. Shirley Brice Heath (1990), an anthropologist who has spent many years studying children and families of poverty, describes the case of Zinnia Mae, who grew up in Trackton, a close-knit black community located in a small southeastern American city. As unemployment struck Trackton in the 1980s and citizens moved away, 16-year-old Zinnia Mae caught a ride to Atlanta. Two years later, Heath visited her there. By then, Zinnia Mae was the mother of three children, a 16-month-old daughter named Donna and 2-month-old twin boys. She had moved into a high-rise public housing project, one of eight concrete buildings surrounding a dirt plot scattered with broken swings, seesaws, and benches. Describing her life to Heath, Zinnia Mae said,

> "My days, you know, I just do what I can, can't get away much. . . . I can't haul (Donna) up and down those six flights of steps to get her out with them other kids, and the place here is too cramped as it is; . . . so me and Donna, we pretty much stay in here with the babies by ourselves 'cept when I get the neighbor girl to come in so I can go get some food for us to eat. . . ." (p. 504)

Each of Zinnia Mae's days was much the same. She watched TV and talked with girlfriends on the phone. The children had only one set meal (breakfast) and otherwise ate whenever they were hungry or bored. Their play space was limited to the living-room sofa and a mattress on the floor. Toys consisted of scraps of a blanket, spoons and food cartons, a small rubber ball, a few plastic cars, and a roller skate abandoned in the building. Zinnia Mae's most frequent words were, "I'm so tired." She worried about how to get papers to the welfare office, where to find a baby-sitter so she could go to the laundry or grocery, and what she would do if she located the twins' father, who had stopped sending money. She rarely had enough energy to spend time with her children.

Over the past two decades, economic changes in the United States have caused the poverty rate among families with children to climb substantially, from 15 to 20 percent. Today, more than 12 million children are affected. Families hit hardest include parents under age 25 with preschool children, the growing number of mother-only families (teenage mothers like Zinnia Mae are especially vulnerable), and racial/ethnic minorities. Poverty is as high as 51 percent among children in single-parent households, 38 percent among Hispanic children, and 44 percent among black children (Bane & Ellwood, 1989; Children's Defense Fund, 1990b).

The constant stresses that accompany poverty gradually weaken the family system. Poor families have many daily hassles—bills to pay, the car breaking down, loss of welfare and unemployment payments, something stolen from the house, to name just a few. When daily crises arise, parents become irritable, children misbehave, and hostile interactions between family members increase (Compas et al., 1989; Patterson, 1988). These outcomes are especially severe in families that must live in poor housing and dangerous neighborhoods—conditions that make day-to-day existence even more difficult (McLoyd, 1990).

Besides poverty, another problem—one that was quite uncommon a decade ago—has reduced the life chances of poor children in the United States. By the early 1990s, approximately 3 million people had no place to live. Over one-third of America's homeless population is made up of families, and 1 in every 4 homeless individuals is believed to be a child (Children's Defense Fund, 1990c). The rise in child homelessness is due to a number of factors, the most important of which is a dramatic decline in the availability of government-supported low-cost housing for the poor (Caton, 1990).

Most homeless families consist of women on their own with young children—usually under the age of 5 (Hayes, 1989). These children suffer from developmental delays and serious emotional stress (Rafferty & Shinn, 1991). Homeless youngsters also have many health problems due to inadequate diets, living outdoors or in crowded, unsanitary public shelters, and lack of immunization against childhood diseases (Wright, 1991).

An estimated 25 to 50 percent of homeless children who are old enough do not attend school (Children's Defense Fund, 1990b). Some have difficulty enrolling because they lack a permanent address or prior school records. Others do not have transportation, a change of clothes, or school supplies. And still others stay away because they are embarrassed about having no home or find it difficult to adjust to new teachers and classmates every few months. Because of poor school attendance and health and emotional problems, homeless children who do go to school achieve less well than other poor children, and they are more likely to repeat a grade (Rafferty & Shinn, 1991).

*Homelessness in the United States has risen over the past decade. Families like this one travel from place to place in search of employment and a safe and secure place to live. At night, they sleep in the family car. Homeless children are usually behind in development, have frequent health problems, and are under severe emotional stress. (Rick Browne/Stock Boston)*

## Beyond the Family: Neighborhoods, Schools, Towns, and Cities

Family systems theory emphasizes that ties between family and community are important for children's well-being. From our discussion of child poverty, perhaps you can see why this is the case. In poverty-stricken urban areas, community life is usually disrupted. Families move often, parks and playgrounds are in disarray, and community centers providing organized leisure time activities do not exist. Research indicates that child abuse and neglect are greatest in neighborhoods in which residents are dissatisfied with their community, describing it as a socially isolated place in which to live. In contrast, when family ties to the community are strong—as indicated by regular church attendance and frequent contact with friends and relatives—family stress and child adjustment problems are reduced (Garbarino & Sherman, 1980; Werner & Smith, 1982).

**Neighborhoods.** Let's take a closer look at the functions that communities serve in the lives of children by beginning with the neighborhood. What were your own childhood experiences like in the yards, streets, and parks surrounding your home?

How did you spend your time, whom did you get to know, and how important were these moments to you? To most children, the neighborhood is not just an outdoor play space; "it is a social universe" (Medrich et al., 1982, p. 33).

Neighborhoods differ in the extent to which they encourage play and exploration among children. In one study, researchers compared the impact of several neighborhoods in the same large city on children's social lives. One of them was Monterey, a well-to-do, hilly area with homes set back on large lots and streets without sidewalks. The arrangement of this neighborhood restricted children's freedom to move about and gather together. In contrast, the flat, densely populated city neighborhood of Yuba provided children with rich social experiences. Children played often in large groups, used the sidewalks and streets for spontaneous games, built secret hideaways in empty lots, and traveled together to make purchases in nearby shops (Berg & Medrich, 1980).

The resources offered by neighborhoods play an important part in children's development. One study found that the more varied children's neighborhood experiences—membership in organizations (such as scouting and 4-H), contact with adults of their grandparents' generation, visits to mother's workplace, and places to go off by themselves or with friends (a treehouse, a fort, or a neighbor's garage)—the better they scored on a battery of tests measuring social and emotional adjustment (Bryant, 1985).

*Schools.* Unlike the informal worlds of family and neighborhood, school is a formal institution designed to transmit knowledge and skills that children need to become productive members of their society. Children spend many long hours in school—6 hours a day, 5 days a week, 36 weeks a year—totaling, altogether, about 15,000 hours by graduation from high school. In fact, if we consider that many more children are entering day-care centers and preschools during the first 5 years of life that are "schoollike," then the impact of schooling begins earlier and is even more powerful than these figures suggest.

Schools themselves are complex social systems bringing together a wide variety of factors that affect many aspects of development (Goodlad, 1984; Minuchin & Shapiro, 1983). Schools differ in the quality of their physical environments—how many children are enrolled, how much space is available for work and play, and how classrooms are furnished and arranged. They also vary in their educational philosophies—whether teachers regard children as passive learners to be molded by adult instruction; as active, curious beings who determine their own learning; or somewhere in between. Finally, social life among children varies from school to school—for example, in the degree to which pupils are cooperative or competitive and in the extent to which children of different racial and ethnic groups spend time together. We will discuss the importance of all of these aspects of schooling in later chapters.

At all ages, regular contact between families and teachers supports children's development. In one study, parents who were involved in school activities and who attended parent–teacher conferences had children who showed superior academic achievement (Stevenson & Baker, 1987). Phone calls and visits to school are common among middle-class parents, whose backgrounds and values are like those of teachers. In contrast, low-income and ethnic minority parents often feel uncomfortable about coming to school (Heath, 1983, 1989). Contact between parents and teachers is also more frequent in small towns, where most citizens know each other and schools serve as centers of community life (Peshkin, 1978). Extra steps must be taken with low-income and minority families and in large urban areas to build supportive ties between family and school.

*Towns and Cities.* Besides family–school contact, other aspects of life are different for children growing up in small towns than in large cities. A well-known study examined the kinds of community settings children entered and the roles they played in a Midwestern town with a population of 700 (Barker, 1955). Many settings existed, and children were granted important responsibilities in them. For example, they helped stock shelves at Kane's Grocery Store, played in the town band, and operated the snow plow when help was short. As children joined in these activities, they did so alongside adults, who taught them the skills they needed to become responsible members of the community.

Of course, children in small towns cannot visit aquariums, take rides in subways and buses, eat pizza in Italian restaurants, go to professional baseball games, or attend orchestra concerts on a regular basis. The variety of settings is somewhat reduced in comparison to large cities. In small towns, however, children's active involvement in the community is likely to be greater. In addition, public places in small towns are safe and secure environments for children. All the streets and people are familiar, and responsible adults are present in almost all settings—a situation hard to match in today's urban environments.

Think back to the case of Zinnia Mae and her three young children, described on page 74. It reveals that community life is especially undermined in high-rise urban housing projects (Gump, 1975). In these dwellings, social contact is particularly important, since many residents have been uprooted from neighborhoods where they felt a strong sense of cultural identity and belonging. Typically, high rises are heavily populated with young single mothers, who are separated from family and friends by the cost and inconvenience of cross-town transportation. They report intense feelings of loneliness in the small, cramped apartments. At Heath's (1990) request, Zinnia Mae agreed to tape record her interactions with her children over a 2-year period. In 500 hours of tape, (other than simple directions or questions about what the children were doing) Zinnia Mae started a conversation with Donna and the boys only 18 times. Cut off from community ties, Zinnia Mae found it difficult to join in activities with her children. As a result, Donna and her brothers experienced a barren, understimulating early environment—one very different from the home and community in which Zinnia Mae herself had grown up.

## The Cultural Context

In Chapter 1, we pointed out that child development can only be fully understood when it is viewed in the larger cultural context in which it takes place. In the following sections, we expand on this important theme. First, we discuss ways in which cultural values and life conditions affect the environments in which children grow up. Second, we show how children are deeply influenced by the political and economic conditions of their nation. We will see that healthy development is critically dependent on laws and government programs that shield children from harm and foster their well-being.

**Culture and Child-Rearing Environments.**   Cultures shape family interaction, school experiences, and community settings beyond the home—in short, all aspects of the child's daily life. Many of us remain blind to aspects of our own cultural heritage until we see them in relation to the practices of others (Rogoff & Morelli, 1989).

Each year, I ask my students to think about the following question: "Who should be responsible for raising young children?" Here are some typical responses: "If parents decide to have a baby, then they should be ready to care for it." "Most people are not happy about others intruding into family life." These statements reflect a widely held opinion in the United States—that the care and rearing of children during the early years is the duty of parents, and only parents (Goffin, 1988). This view has a long history—one in which independence, self-reliance, and the privacy of family life emerged as central American values. It is one reason, among others, that the American public has been slow to accept the idea of publicly supported day care, even though the majority of mothers of young children in the United States are employed (Hayghe, 1990). This strong emphasis on individualism also helps us understand why, among middle-class families (who best represent American cultural values), only a small percentage of grandparents and other relatives participate actively and regularly in the rearing of children (Thompson et al., 1989).

Do cultures everywhere share the belief that the responsibility for early child rearing should rest in the hands of parents? Apparently not. Among the Efe hunters and gatherers of Zaire, Africa, a collective caregiving system exists in which infants are passed back and forth from one adult to another—relatives and nonrelatives alike—as often as 3 to 8 times an hour (Winn, Tronick, & Morelli, 1989). The Efe may have developed this style of infant care because their babies are unusually fussy and difficult to console. The responsibility for soothing the infant is shared among members of the group, reducing the burden placed on the baby's mother. In small agricultural societies in which mothers must spend many hours in the gardens and fields, *sibling caregiving,* in which older sisters (and sometimes brothers) take charge of younger children throughout the day, is widespread (Weisner & Gallimore, 1977).

Although American middle-class families value independence and privacy, cooperative family structures can be found in the United States. In large industrialized nations like ours, not all citizens share the same set of values. **Subcultures** exist—groups of people with beliefs and customs that differ in important ways from those of the larger culture. The values and practices of some ethnic minority groups protect children against the harmful effects of poverty. A case in point is the African-American family. As Box 2.2 indicates, the black cultural tradition of **extended family households,** in which parent and child live with one or more adult relatives, is a vital feature of black family life that has enabled its members to survive. Active and involved extended families also characterize other American minorities, such as Asian American, Native American, and Hispanic subcultures (Harrison et al., 1990).

Children growing up in different cultures also encounter unique experiences in neighborhoods and schools. Among the !Kung hunters and gatherers of Botswana, Africa, the "neighborhood" is the barren desert region surrounding the group campground. Little exists to draw children into exploration of their surroundings. Instead, they spend most of their time near home, conversing and playing with adults and peers and developing especially close bonds with others (Draper & Cashdan, 1988). Also, since !Kung children are not strong enough to keep up on lengthy hunting and gathering missions, they are "schooled" in adult work roles informally, by listening as their elders describe previous hunts and swap exciting stories and tales (Super, 1980).

Even in industrialized nations, schooling varies considerably from one culture to the next. In recent years, many investigators have looked carefully at education in Asian countries. They hope to find out why, in cross-national comparisons of mathematics and science achievement, Japanese and Chinese children are top performers, while American pupils do poorly. Indeed, as we will see in Chapter 12, many variables, including more intensive instruction, a longer school year, and more frequent communication between Asian parents and teachers, contribute to this achievement gap (Stevenson & Lee, 1990).

*Public Policies and Child Development.*   When widespread social problems arise, such as poverty, homelessness, hunger, and disease, nations attempt to solve them by developing **public policies**—laws and government programs designed to improve the condition of children and families. For example, when poverty increases and families become homeless, a country might decide to build more low-cost housing, raise the minimum wage, and increase welfare benefits. When reports indicate that many children are not achieving well in school, federal and state governments

**Subcultures**

Groups of people with beliefs and customs that differ from those of the larger culture.

**Extended family household**

A household in which parent and child live with one or more adult relatives.

**Public policies**

Laws and government programs.

# CULTURAL INFLUENCES

## Box 2.2 *The Black Extended Family*

*T*he black extended family can be traced to the African heritage of the large majority of black Americans. In many African societies, newly married couples do not start their own households. Instead, they marry into a large extended family that assists its members with all aspects of daily life. This tradition of a broad network of kinship ties travelled to the United States during the period of slavery. Since then, it has served as a protective shield against the destructive impact of poverty and racial prejudice on black family life (McLoyd, 1990; Wilson, 1989). Today, more black than white adults have relatives other than their own children living in the same household. Black parents also see more kin during the week and perceive them as more important figures in their lives, respecting the advice of relatives and caring deeply about what they think is important (Wilson, 1986).

By providing emotional support and sharing income and essential resources, the black extended family helps reduce the stress of poverty and single parenthood. In addition, extended family members often help with the rearing of children (Pearson et al., 1990). The presence of grandmothers in the households of many black teenagers and their infants protects babies from the negative influence of an overwhelmed and inexperienced mother. In one study, black grandmothers displayed more sensitive interaction with the babies of their teenage daughters than did the teenage mothers themselves. The grandmothers also provided basic information about infant development to these young mothers (Stevens, 1984). Furthermore, black adolescent mothers who live in extended families are more likely to complete high school and get a job and less likely to be on welfare than mothers living on their own—factors that return to benefit children's well-being (Furstenberg & Crawford, 1978).

Among older children, extended family living is associated with more positive adult–child interaction, better school achievement, and improved psychological adjustment (Wilson & Tolson, 1985). During adolescence, the presence of additional adults in the home reduces children's tendency to become involved in antisocial behavior (Dornbusch et al., 1985).

*Strong bonds with extended family members have helped to protect the development of many African-American children growing up under conditions of poverty and single parenthood.* (Karen Kasmauski/Woodfin Camp & Assoc.)

Finally, black extended families play an important role in transmitting black cultural values to children. Compared to black nuclear families, extended family arrangements place more emphasis on cooperation and moral and religious values (Tolson & Wilson, 1990). These factors strengthen family bonds, protect children's development, and increase the chances that the extended family life style will carry over to the next generation.

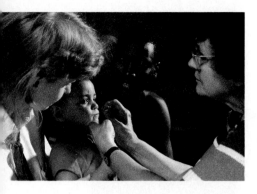

*The broad social climate of a nation has a major impact on child rearing. When governments develop sound policies and provide generous funding for child and family services, children's development is enhanced. In this public health clinic, children whose parents cannot afford private medical care receive checkups and inoculations that support healthy growth. (Bob Daemmrich/Stock Boston)*

might grant more tax money to school districts and make sure that help reaches children who need it most.

We have already seen in previous sections that, while many American children fare well, a large number grow up in environments that threaten their well-being. Despite our vast knowledge base about child development, the United States lags behind other Western nations in the creation of public policies that support children and families (Hymes, 1991). As a result, a larger proportion of American children grow up without access to adequate food, housing, medical care, day care, and educational services than is the case in most Western European nations (see Figure 2.9).

Like many people who care about children, you may be deeply disturbed by this conclusion. Why is it that the United States has not yet created conditions that protect the development of its youngest citizens? A complex set of political and economic forces is involved. Earlier we mentioned the American ideals of self-reliance and privacy. These beliefs have led government to hesitate to become involved in family matters. In addition, there is more disagreement among American than European citizens on issues of child and family policy. Americans differ sharply about government support for such programs as day care, medical benefits, and special educational services for minority youths (Wilensky, 1983). Finally, good social programs are expensive, and they must compete for a fair share of a country's economic resources. Children can easily remain unrecognized in this process, since they cannot vote or speak out to protect their own interests, as adult citizens do. They must rely on the good will of others to become an important government priority (Garwood et al., 1989).

Despite the worrisome state of America's children, progress is being made in improving their condition. In the course of this book we will discuss many successful programs that could be expanded. Another positive sign is that child development

**FIGURE 2.9** • Poverty among children in eight industrialized nations. The United States has the highest poverty rate, European countries the lowest. Those nations with low poverty rates have the most liberally funded child and family public programs. *(Adapted from Smeeding, Torrey, & Rein, 1988.)*

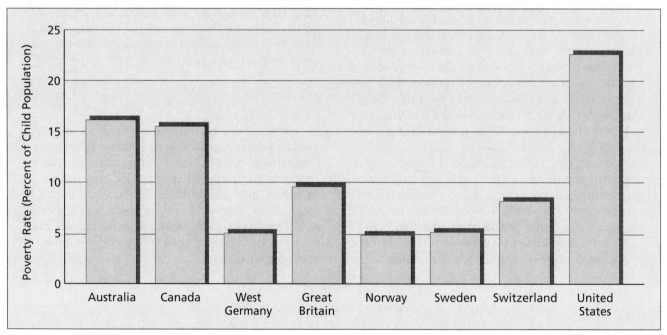

specialists are more involved than ever before in conducting research relevant to policies and communicating their findings to the country as a whole. When citizens learn about the problems of children, they may write to lawmakers, support organizations working for children's needs, or become directly involved in helping children themselves. Finally, growing awareness of the gap between what we know and what we do to improve children's everyday lives has led many investigators to become advocates for children's causes. Today, child development specialists are participating in lobbying efforts and working directly with government officials to find solutions to children's problems (Jacobs & Davies, 1991; Zigler & Finn-Stevenson, 1988). As these efforts continue, there is every reason to expect increased responsiveness to children's needs in the years to come.

*BRIEF REVIEW* Just as complex as heredity are the environments in which children grow up. First and foremost is the family—a system of mutually influencing relationships that changes over time. Child rearing in families is modified by social class, and it is seriously threatened by poverty and homelessness. A variety of additional contexts—neighborhoods that promote exploration and play, schools that establish ties with families, and communities in which children participate actively alongside adults—support development. These aspects of the environment vary considerably among cultures and subcultures. In the complex world in which we live, favorable public policies are essential for children's well-being.

• *Links between family and community are essential for children's well-being. Provide examples and research findings from our discussion that support this idea.*

• *Check your local newspaper and one or two national news magazines to see how often articles appear on the condition of children and families. Why is it important for researchers to communicate with the general public about children's needs?*

## UNDERSTANDING THE RELATIONSHIP BETWEEN HEREDITY AND ENVIRONMENT

So far in this chapter, we have discussed a wide variety of hereditary and environmental influences, each of which has the power to change the course of growth. Yet many examples exist in which children born into the same family (and who therefore share genes and environments in common) are quite different in characteristics. We also know that some children are affected more than others by their environments. Cases do exist in which a child provided with all the advantages in life does poorly, while a second child exposed to the worst of rearing conditions does well. How do scientists explain the impact of heredity and environment when they seem to work in so many different ways?

Today, all child development specialists agree that both heredity and environment are involved in every aspect of development. There is no real controversy on this point because an environment is always needed for genetic information to be expressed (Scarr, 1988). But for polygenic traits (due to many genes) like intelligence and personality, scientists are a long way from knowing the precise hereditary influences involved. They must study the impact of genes on these characteristics indirectly, and the nature-nurture controversy remains unresolved because investigators do not agree on how heredity and environment influence these complex characteristics.

Some believe that it is useful and possible to answer the question of *how much* each factor contributes to differences among children. These researchers use special methods to find out which factor plays the major role. A second group of investigators regards the question of which factor is more important as neither useful nor answerable. They believe that heredity and environment do not make separate contributions to behavior. Instead, they are always related, and the real question we need to explore is *how* they work together. Let's consider each of these two positions in turn.

## The Question of "How Much?"

Two methods—heritability estimates and concordance rates—are used to infer the importance of heredity in complex human characteristics. Each is summarized in Concept Table 2.1.

*Heritability.*    **Heritability estimates** measure the extent to which heredity is responsible for continuous traits like intelligence and personality. They are obtained from **kinship studies,** which compare the characteristics of family members. The most common type of kinship study compares identical twins, who share all their genes in common, with fraternal twins, who share only some. If people who are genetically more alike are also more similar in intelligence and personality test scores, then the researcher assumes that heredity plays an important role.

Kinship studies of intelligence provide some of the most controversial findings in the field of child development. While some experts claim a strong role for heredity, others believe that genetic factors are barely involved. Currently, most researchers support a moderate role for heredity. When many twin studies are examined, correlations between the scores of identicals are consistently higher than those of fraternals. In one summary of over 30 such investigations, the correlation for intelligence was .86 for identical twins and .60 for fraternal twins (Bouchard & McGue, 1981). Heritability estimates take these correlations and compare them, arriving at a number ranging from 0 to 1.00. The value for intelligence is about .50, which indicates that half of the individual differences in intelligence among children can be explained by differences in their genes (Loehlin, 1989). The fact that the intelligence of adopted

**CONCEPT TABLE 2.1 • Methods Used to Estimate the Importance of Heredity in Complex Characteristics**

| Concept | Important Point | Example |
|---|---|---|
| Heritability estimate | To study the role of heredity in continuous traits (such as intelligence and personality), researchers compute heritability estimates from kinship studies. A proportion that ranges from 0 to 1.00, a heritability estimate measures the extent to which individual differences in a trait are due to heredity. | By comparing the correlation of intelligence test scores for identical twins with that for fraternal twins, researchers have arrived at a heritability estimate of about .50. It indicates that heredity plays a moderate role. |
| Concordance rate | Researchers use concordance rates to study the role of heredity in traits that can be judged as either present or absent (such as emotional and behavior disorders). A concordance rate is a percentage indicating the extent to which both members of a twin pair show a trait when it is present in one pair member. By comparing concordance rates for identical and fraternal twins, researchers can estimate the importance of heredity. | Since the concordance rate for severe depression is much higher in identical than in fraternal twins, heredity probably plays an important role. |

**Heritability estimate**

A statistic that measures the extent to which continuous traits, such as intelligence or personality, can be traced to heredity.

**Kinship studies**

Studies comparing the characteristics of family members to determine the importance of heredity in complex human characteristics.

children is more strongly related to the scores of their biological parents than their adoptive parents offers further support for the role of heredity (Horn, 1983; Scarr & Weinberg, 1983).

Heritability research also reveals that genetic factors are important in personality. In fact, for aspects of personality that have been studied a great deal, such as sociability, emotional expressiveness, and activity level, heritability estimates are at about the same moderate level as that reported for intelligence (Braungart et al., 1992; Plomin, 1989).

*Concordance.* A second measure that has been used to infer the importance of heredity from twin comparisons is the **concordance rate.** It refers to the percentage of instances in which both twins show a trait when it is present in one. Researchers use it to study the contribution of heredity to characteristics that can be judged as either present or absent, such as emotional and behavior disorders. A concordance rate ranges from 0 to 100 percent. A score of 0 indicates that if one twin has the trait, the other twin never has it. A score of 100 means that if one twin has the trait, the other always has it. When a concordance rate is much higher for identical twins than for fraternal twins, then heredity is believed to play a major role. Twin studies of depression and schizophrenia show this pattern of findings. In the case of depression, the concordance rate for identical twins is 30 percent, that for fraternal twins only 6 percent. The figures are 69 percent and 13 percent for schizophrenia (Gershon et al., 1977; Kendler & Robinette, 1983). Once again, adoption studies are consistent with these results. Biological relatives of schizophrenic and depressed adoptees are more likely to share the same disorder than are adoptive relatives (Loehlin, Willerman, & Horn, 1988).

Taken together, concordance and adoption research suggests that the strong tendency for schizophrenia and depression to run in families is partly due to genetic factors (Gershon et al., 1977; Reich et al., 1987). However, we also know that environment is involved because the concordance rate for identical twins would be 100 percent if heredity were the only influence operating. In later chapters, we will see that environmental stresses, such as poverty, family conflict, and a disorganized home life, are often associated with emotional and behavior disorders in children and adolescents.

*Limitations of Heritability and Concordance.* Although heritability estimates and concordance rates provide evidence that genetic factors contribute to complex human characteristics, questions have been raised about their accuracy. Both measures are heavily influenced by the range of environments to which twin pairs have been exposed. For example, identical twins raised together under highly similar conditions have more strongly correlated intelligence test scores than those reared apart in very different environments. When the former are used to compute heritability estimates, the higher correlation causes the importance of heredity to be overestimated. To overcome this difficulty, researchers try to find twins who have been raised apart in adoptive families. But few separated twin pairs are available for study, and when they are, social service agencies often place them in advantaged homes that are similar in many ways (Bronfenbrenner & Crouter, 1983; Scarr & Kidd, 1983). Because the environments of most twin pairs do not represent the broad range of environments found in the general child population, it is often difficult to generalize heritability and concordance findings to the population as a whole.

Heritability estimates are controversial measures because they can easily be misapplied. For example, high heritabilities obtained from kinship studies have been used to suggest that racial differences in intelligence, such as the poorer performance of black children compared to whites, have a genetic basis (Jensen, 1969, 1985b). Yet this line of reasoning is widely regarded as inaccurate. Heritabilities computed

**Concordance rate**
The percentage of instances in which both members of a twin pair show a trait when it is present in one pair member. Used to study the the role of heredity in traits that can be judged as either present or absent, such as emotional and behavior disorders.

on mostly white twin samples provide no evidence about what is responsible for test score differences between the races. We have already seen that there are often large economic and cultural differences between families of different racial groups. As we will see in Chapter 12, research demonstrates that when black and white children are adopted into economically and culturally similar home environments at an early age, they do not differ in intelligence (Scarr & Weinberg, 1983).

Perhaps the most serious criticism of heritability estimates and concordance rates focuses on their usefulness. While they are interesting statistics that tell us heredity is undoubtedly involved in complex traits like intelligence and personality, they give us no precise information about how these traits develop or how children might respond when exposed to environments designed to help them develop as far as possible. Investigators who conduct heritability research argue that their studies are a first step. As more evidence accumulates to show that heredity underlies important human characteristics, then scientists can begin to ask better questions—about the specific genes involved, the way they affect development, and how their impact is modified by environmental factors.

## The Question of "How?"

According to a second perspective, heredity and environment cannot be divided into separate influences. Instead, behavior is the result of a dynamic interplay between these two forces. How do heredity and environment work together to affect development? Several important concepts shed light on this complex question. As you read about them, you may find it useful to refer to Concept Table 2.2, which provides a summary.

**Reaction Range.** The first of these ideas is **range of reaction** (Gottesman, 1963). It emphasizes that each person responds to the environment in a unique way because of his or her genetic makeup. Let's explore this idea by taking a look at

CONCEPT TABLE 2.2 • Concepts Describing How Heredity and Environment Work Together

| Concept | Important Point | Example |
|---|---|---|
| Range of reaction | Each child responds uniquely to the environment because of his or her unique genetic makeup. | Ben's intelligence increases much more than does Linda's or Ron's in an advantaged home environment (see Figure 2.10). |
| Canalization | Heredity restricts the development of some characteristics more than others. Harmful environments can also limit future development. | Motor development is more strongly canalized than is intelligence. Intelligence can become canalized when children are reared in very deprived environments. |
| Genetic–environmental correlation | Heredity affects the environments to which children are exposed. This relationship becomes stronger with age. | Parents with genes for athletic talent encourage physical exercise in their children, who may have inherited their parents' favorable genes. With age, athletically inclined children seek out physical activities. |

**Range of reaction**
Each person's unique, genetically determined response to a range of environmental conditions.

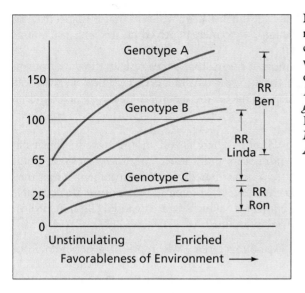

**FIGURE 2.10** • Intellectual ranges of reaction (RR) for three children in environments that vary from unstimulating to highly enriched. *(From I. I. Gottesman, 1963, "Genetic Aspects of Intelligent Behavior," in N. R. Ellis, ed.,* Handbook of Mental Deficiency, *New York: McGraw-Hill, p. 255. Adapted by permission.)*

Figure 2.10. Reaction range can apply to any characteristic; here it is illustrated for intelligence. Notice that when environments vary from extremely unstimulating to highly enriched, Ben's intelligence increases dramatically, Linda's only slightly, and Ron's hardly at all.

Reaction range highlights two important points about the relationship between heredity and environment. First, it shows that because each of us has a unique genetic makeup, we respond quite differently to the same environment. Look carefully at Figure 2.10, and notice how a poor environment results in a lower intelligence test score for Ron than Ben. Also, an advantaged environment raises Ben's score far above what is possible for Ron. Second, sometimes different genetic–environmental combinations can make two children look the same! For example, if Ben is raised in an unstimulating environment, his score will be about 100—average for children in general. Linda can also obtain this score, but to do so she must grow up in a very advantaged home. In other words, the concept of range of reaction tells us that children differ in their range of possible responses to the environment. And unique blends of heredity and environment lead to both similarities and differences in behavior.

*Canalization.* The concept of **canalization** provides another way of understanding how heredity and environment combine. Canalization is the tendency of heredity to restrict the development of some characteristics to just one or a few outcomes. A behavior that is strongly canalized follows a genetically set growth plan, and only strong environmental forces can change it (Waddington, 1957). For example, infant motor development seems to be strongly canalized, since all normal human babies eventually roll over, sit up, crawl, and walk. It takes extreme conditions to modify these behaviors or cause them not to appear. In contrast, intelligence and personality are less strongly canalized, since they respond easily to changes in the environment.

Scientists have recently expanded the notion of canalization to include environmental influences. We now know that environments can also limit development (Gottlieb, 1991). For example, when children are exposed to harmful environments early in life, there may be little that later experiences can do to change characteristics (such as intelligence) that were quite flexible to begin with. In Chapter 3, we will see that this is the case for babies born to mothers who used cocaine or drank alcohol

**Canalization**
The tendency of heredity to restrict the development of some characteristics to just one or a few outcomes.

### Sandra Scarr

*Sandra Scarr is a leading investigator of genetic and environmental contributions to complex human characteristics. Along with Kathleen McCartney, she developed broadly influential ideas about genetic–environmental correlation. Her adoption research addressing the heritability of intelligence is widely known.* (Courtesy of Sandra Scarr, University of Virginia)

**Genetic–environmental correlation**

The idea that heredity influences the environments to which individuals are exposed.

**Niche-picking**

A type of genetic–environmental correlation in which individuals actively choose environments that complement their heredity.

regularly during pregnancy. And later in this book we will find that it is also true for children who spend many years living in extremely deprived homes and institutions (Turkheimer & Gottesman, 1991).

Using the concept of canalization, we learn that genes restrict the development of some characteristics more than others. And over time, even very flexible behaviors can become fixed and canalized, depending on the environments to which children were exposed.

***Genetic–Environmental Correlation.*** There is still another way in which nature and nurture work together. Sandra Scarr and Kathleen McCartney (1983) point out that a major problem in trying to separate heredity and environment is that they are often correlated. According to the concept of **genetic–environmental correlation,** our genes influence the environments to which we are exposed (Plomin, 1986). The way this happens changes with development.

*Passive and Evocative Correlation.* At younger ages, two types of genetic–environmental correlation are common. The first is called *passive* correlation because the child has no control over it. Early on, parents provide environments that are influenced by their own heredity. For example, parents who are good athletes are likely to emphasize outdoor activities and enroll their children in swimming and gymnastics lessons at early ages. Besides getting exposed to an "athletic environment," the children may have inherited their parents' athletic ability. As a result, they are likely to become good athletes for both genetic and environmental reasons.

The second type of genetic–environmental correlation is *evocative.* Children evoke responses from others that are influenced by the child's heredity, and these responses strengthen the child's original style of responding. For example, an active, friendly baby is likely to receive more social stimulation from those around her than a passive, quiet infant. And a cooperative, attentive preschooler will probably receive more patient and sensitive interactions from parents than an inattentive, distractible child.

*Active Correlation.* At older ages, *active* genetic–environmental correlation becomes common. As children extend their experiences beyond the immediate family to school, neighborhood, and community and are given the freedom to make more of their own choices, they play an increasingly active role in seeking out environments that fit with their genetic tendencies. The well-coordinated, muscular child spends more time at after-school sports, the musically talented youngster joins the school orchestra and practices his violin, and the intellectually curious child is a well-known visitor at the local library.

This tendency to actively choose environments that complement our heredity is called **niche-picking.** Infants and young children cannot do much niche-picking, since adults select environments for them. In contrast, older children and adolescents are much more in charge of their own environments. The niche-picking idea explains why pairs of identical twins reared apart during childhood and later reunited often find, to their great surprise, that they have similar hobbies, food preferences, friendship choices, and vocations (Bouchard et al., 1990). It also helps us understand some curious longitudinal findings indicating that identical twins become somewhat more similar and fraternal twins and adopted siblings less similar from infancy to adolescence (Scarr & Weinberg, 1983; Wilson, 1983). The influence of heredity and environment is not constant but changes over time. With age, genetic factors may become more important in determining the environments we experience and choose for ourselves.

A major reason that child development specialists are interested in the nature–nurture issue is that they want to find ways to improve environments in order to help children develop as far as possible. The concepts of range of reaction, canalization, and niche-picking remind us that development is best understood as a series of complex exchanges between nature and nurture. When a characteristic is strongly determined by heredity, it can still be modified. However, children cannot be changed in any way we might desire. The success of any attempt to improve development depends on the characteristics we want to change, the genetic makeup of the child, and the type and timing of our intervention.

# SUMMARY

### Genetic Foundations

• Development begins at conception, when sperm and ovum unite to form the one-celled **zygote.** Within the cell nucleus are 23 pairs of **chromosomes.** Along their length are the **genes,** segments of **DNA** that make us distinctly human and play an important role in determining our development and characteristics.

• The **gametes** that merge to form the zygote are produced by the process of cell division known as **meiosis.** Since each zygote receives a unique set of genes from each parent, meiosis ensures that children will be genetically different from one another. Once the zygote forms, it starts to develop into a complex human being through cell duplication, or **mitosis.**

• If the fertilizing sperm carries an X chromosome, the child will be a girl; if it contains a Y chromosome, a boy will be born. **Fraternal** or **dizygotic twins** result when two ova are released from the mother's ovaries and each is fertilized. In contrast, **identical** or **monozygotic twins** develop when a zygote divides in two during the early stages of cell duplication.

• **Dominant–recessive** and **codominant** relationships are patterns of inheritance that apply to traits controlled by a single gene. When recessive disorders are **X-linked** (carried on the X chromosome), males are more likely to be affected than females. Unfavorable genes arise from **mutations,** which can occur spontaneously or be induced by hazardous environmental agents.

• Human traits that vary continuously, such as intelligence and personality, are **polygenic,** or influenced by many genes. Since the genetic principles involved are unknown, scientists must study the influence of heredity on these characteristics indirectly.

### Chromosomal Abnormalities

• The most common chromosomal abnormality is Down syndrome, which results in physical defects as well as mental retardation. Effective parenting and early intervention can improve the development of Down syndrome children.

• Disorders of the **sex chromosomes** are milder than defects of the **autosomes.** Contrary to popular belief, males with XYY syndrome are not prone to aggression. Studies of children with triple X, Klinefelter, and Turner syndromes reveal that adding to or subtracting from the usual number of X chromosomes leads to specific intellectual problems. Fragile X syndrome has been identified as a major cause of mental retardation.

### Reproductive Choices

• **Genetic counseling** helps couples at risk for giving birth to children with genetic abnormalities decide whether or not to conceive. New **prenatal diagnostic methods** make early detection of genetic problems possible. In some cases, treatment can be initiated before birth.

• When a prenatal condition cannot be corrected, some women opt for an abortion. However, the large majority of abortions are to women who accidentally become pregnant, many of them teenagers. Research indicates that unwanted children develop less favorably than other children. However, scientific studies cannot provide answers to the complex ethical questions surrounding abortion.

• Many parents who cannot conceive or who have a high likelihood of transmitting a genetic disorder decide to adopt. Although adopted children experience more developmental problems than children in general, most fare quite well.

### Environmental Contexts for Development

• Just as complex as heredity are the environments in which children grow up. The family is the child's first and foremost context for development. The **social systems perspective** emphasizes that the behaviors of each family member affect those of others. The family system is also dynamic and ever-changing, constantly adjusting to new events and developmental changes in its members.

• Two aspects of parenting promote effective development at all ages: (1) responsiveness and (2) reasonable demands for mature behavior. Although warm, moderately demanding child rearing is the most common pattern around the world, it is modified by social class. Effective parenting, along with all aspects of children's development, is seriously undermined by poverty and homelessness.

• Children profit from supportive ties between family and community. Neighborhoods that encourage play and exploration, schools that establish regular contact with parents, and communities that promote children's active participation alongside adults enhance child development.

• The values and life conditions of cultures and **subcultures** mold the environments in which children grow up. In contrast to the American middle-class family, in many cultures grandparents, siblings, and other relatives share child-rearing responsibilities. Neighborhood and school environments also vary considerably from one culture and subculture to the next.

• In the complex world in which we live, children's well-being depends on favorable **public policies.** Effective social programs are influenced by many factors, including cultural values, a nation's economic resources, and organizations and individuals that work for children's interests.

*Understanding the Relationship between Heredity and Environment*

• Scientists do not agree on how heredity and environment influence complex characteristics. Some believe that it is useful and possible to determine "how much" each factor contributes to behavior. These investigators compute **heritability estimates** and **concordance rates** from **kinship studies.**

• Other researchers believe that the important question is "how" heredity and environment work together. The concepts of **range of reaction, canalization,** and **niche-picking** remind us that development is best understood as a series of complex exchanges between nature and nurture.

## IMPORTANT TERMS AND CONCEPTS

phenotype (p. 49)
genotype (p. 49)
chromosomes (p. 50)
deoxyribonucleic acid (DNA) (p. 50)
gene (p. 50)
mitosis (p. 50)
gametes (p. 51)
meiosis (p. 51)
crossing over (p. 51)
zygote (p. 55)
autosomes (p. 55)
sex chromosomes (p. 55)
fraternal or dizygotic twins (p. 56)

identical or monozygotic twins (p. 56)
allele (p. 56)
homozygous (p. 56)
heterozygous (p. 56)
dominant–recessive inheritance (p. 56)
carrier (p. 57)
codominance (p. 58)
mutation (p. 59)
X-linked inheritance (p. 61)
polygenic inheritance (p. 62)
genetic counseling (p. 65)
prenatal diagnostic methods (p. 65)

social systems perspective (p. 71)
subcultures (p. 78)
extended family household (p. 78)
public policies (p. 78)
heritability estimate (p. 82)
kinship studies (p. 82)
concordance rate (p. 83)
range of reaction (p. 84)
canalization (p. 85)
genetic–environmental correlation (p. 86)
niche-picking (p. 86)

## FOR FURTHER INFORMATION AND SPECIAL HELP

**Causes of Mutation**

Environmental Mutagen Society
19110 Montgomery Village Avenue
Suite 310
Gaithersburg, MD 20879
(301) 869-2901

Provides information on environmental agents that cause mutation.

**Genetic Disorders**

March of Dimes Birth Defects Foundation
1275 Mamaroneck Avenue
White Plains, NY 10605
(914) 428-7100

Works to prevent genetic disorders and other birth defects through public education and community service programs.

National Genetics Foundation
P.O. Box 1374
New York, NY 10101
(212) 245-7443

Provides a referral service to university-based genetics centers for individuals and families who have or suspect they have an inherited disorder.

PKU Parents
8 Myrtle Lane
San Anselmo, CA 94960
(415) 457-4632

Provides support and education for parents of children with PKU.

National Association for Sickle Cell Disease
4221 Wilshire Blvd., Suite 360
Los Angeles, CA 90010
(213) 736-5455

Provides information and assists local groups that serve individuals with sickle cell anemia.

National Down Syndrome Congress
1800 Dempster Street
Park Ridge, IL 60068-1146
(312) 823-7550

Assists parents in finding solutions to the needs of children with Down syndrome. Local groups exist across the United States.

### Infertility

Resolve, Inc.
5 Water Street
Arlington, MA 02174-4814
(617) 643-2424

Offers counseling referral and support to persons with fertility problems.

### Adoption

National Adoption Information Clearinghouse
1400 Eye Street, Suite 600
Washington, DC 20005
(202) 842-1919

Provides information on all aspects of adoption, including children from other countries, children with special needs, and state and federal adoption laws.

### Public Policy

Children's Defense Fund
122 C Street N. W.
Washington, DC 20001
(202) 628-8787
(800) 424-9602

An active child advocacy organization. Provides information on the condition of American children and government-sponsored programs serving them.

*"A Pregnant Mother Is Dancing," Nadia, 12 years,
Austria. Reprinted by permission from The International
Museum of Children's Art, Oslo, Norway.*

# Prenatal Development

3

Motivations for Parenthood
>   *Why Have Children?   How Large a Family?   Is There a Best Time During Adulthood to*
>   *Have a Child?*

Prenatal Development
>   *The Period of the Zygote   The Period of the Embryo   The Period of the Fetus*

Prenatal Environmental Influences
>   *Teratogens   Other Maternal Factors   The Importance of Prenatal Health Care*

Preparing for Parenthood
>   *Seeking Information   The Baby Becomes a Reality   Models of Effective Parenthood*
>   *Practical Concerns   The Marital Relationship*

*A*fter months of wondering whether the time in their own lives was right, Yolanda and Jay decided to have a baby. I met them one fall in my child development class, when Yolanda was just two months pregnant. Both were full of questions: "How does the baby grow before birth? When are different organs formed? Has its heart begun to beat? Can it hear, feel, or sense our presence in other ways?" Already, Yolanda and Jay had scanned the shelves of the public library and local bookstores, picking up a dozen or more sources on pregnancy, childbirth, and caring for the newborn.

Most of all, Yolanda and Jay wanted to do everything possible to make sure that their baby would be born healthy. At one time, they believed that the developing organism was completely shielded by the uterus from any dangers in the environment. All babies born with problems, they thought, had unfavorable genes. After browsing through several pregnancy books, Yolanda and Jay realized that they were wrong. Yolanda started to wonder about her diet and whether she should keep up her daily aerobics routine. And she asked me whether an aspirin for a headache, a sleeping pill before bedtime, a glass of wine at dinnertime, or a few cups of coffee during study hours might be harmful.

In this chapter, we answer Yolanda and Jay's questions, along with a great many more that scientists have asked about the events before birth. We begin our discussion during the time period before pregnancy with these puzzling questions: Why is it that, generation after generation, most couples who fall in love and marry want to become parents? And how do they decide whether to have just one child or more than one?

Then we trace prenatal development—the 9-month period before birth. Our discussion pays special attention to environmental factors that support healthy growth as well as those that cause permanent damage. Finally, the prenatal period marks an important transitional phase in the lives of expectant parents—one that creates challenges as well as opportunities for personal growth. We take a look at ways in which couples prepare psychologically for the arrival of the baby and how a new sense of self as mother or father begins to emerge.

## MOTIVATIONS FOR PARENTHOOD

As part of her semester project for my class, Yolanda interviewed her grandmother, asking why she wanted to have children and how she settled on a particular family size. Yolanda's grandmother, whose children were born in the early 1940s, replied:

> "We didn't think much about whether or not to have children in those days. We just had them—everybody did. It would have seemed odd not to! I was 22 years old when I had the first of my four children, and I had four because—well, I wouldn't have had just one since we all thought children needed brothers and sisters, and only children could end up spoiled and selfish. Life is more interesting with children, you know. And now that we're older, we've got family we can depend on and grandchildren to enjoy. . . ."

### Why Have Children?

In some ways, the reasons given by Yolanda's grandmother for wanting children are like those of modern parents. In other ways, they are very different. In the past, the issue of whether to have children was, for many adults, "a biological given or unavoidable cultural demand" (Michaels, 1988, p. 23). Today, in Western industrialized nations, it is a matter of true individual choice. Effective birth control techniques permit adults who do not want to become parents to avoid having children in most instances. And changing social values allow people to remain childless with much less fear of social criticism and rejection than was true a generation or two ago.

When modern American couples are asked about their desire to have children, they mention a variety of advantages and disadvantages, which are listed in Table 3.1. Take a moment to consider which ones are most important to you. Although some ethnic and regional differences exist, reasons for having children that are most important to all groups include the desire for a warm, affectionate relationship and the stimulation and fun that children provide. Also frequently mentioned are growth and learning experiences that children bring into the lives of adults, the desire to have someone carry on after one's own death, and feelings of accomplishment and creativity that come from helping children grow (Hoffman, Thornton, & Manis, 1978).

American couples are also aware that having children means years of extra burdens and responsibilities. When asked about the disadvantages of parenthood, they mention "loss of freedom" most often, followed by "financial strain." Indeed, the expense of raising children is a major consideration in modern family planning. Current estimates indicate that parents spend from $86,000 to $127,000[1] to raise each child from birth through four years of college. Finally, many adults worry greatly about bringing children into a troubled world—one filled with crime, war, and pollution (Michaels, 1988).

Careful weighing of the pros and cons of having children was rare in Yolanda's grandmother's time, yet it is increasingly common today. Child development specialists view this change as positive. It means that many more couples are making informed and personally meaningful choices about becoming parents—a trend that should increase the chances that they are ready to have children and that their own lives will be enriched by their decision.

### How Large a Family?

In contrast to her grandmother, Yolanda plans to have no more than two children. And she and Jay are talking about whether to limit their family to a single child. In

[1]These figures are based on a 1980 estimate, corrected for later inflation (U.S. Department of Labor, 1992). The figure includes basic expenses related to food, housing, clothing, medical care, and education.

TABLE 3.1 • Benefits and Costs of Parenthood

| Benefits | Costs |
|---|---|
| Giving and receiving warmth and affection | Loss of freedom, being tied down |
| Experiencing the stimulation and fun that children add to life | Financial strain |
| Being accepted as a responsible and mature member of the community | Worries over children's health, safety, and well-being |
| Experiencing new growth and learning opportunities that add meaning to life | Interference with mother's employment opportunities |
| Having someone carry on after one's own death | Risks of bringing up children in a world plagued by crime, war, and pollution |
| Gaining a sense of accomplishment and creativity from helping children grow | Reduced time to spend with husband or wife |
| Learning to become less selfish and to sacrifice | Loss of privacy |
| Having offspring who help with parents' work or add their own income to the family's resources | Fear that children will turn out badly, through no fault of one's own |

Source: Michaels, 1988.

1960, the average number of children in an American family was 3.1. Today, it is 2.1, a downward trend that is expected to continue into the twenty-first century (U.S. Bureau of the Census, 1991a). In addition to more effective birth control, a major reason that family size has declined in industrialized nations is that large numbers of women are experiencing the economic and personal rewards of a career. A family size of one or two children is certainly more compatible with a woman's decision to divide her energies between work and family.

Research also indicates that modern children benefit from growing up in small families. Parents who have fewer children are more patient and use less punishment. They also have more time to devote to each child's activities, school work, and other special needs. Together, these findings may account for the fact that children who grow up in smaller families have somewhat higher intelligence test scores, do better in school, and think more positively of themselves (Wagner, Schubert, & Schubert, 1985). However, recall from Chapter 1 that a correlation between family size and children's characteristics does not tell us for sure about causation! Large families are usually less well off economically than smaller ones. Factors associated with low income—crowded housing, poor nutrition, and parental stress—may be responsible for the negative relationship between family size and children's development (Rutter & Madge, 1976). Indeed, there is evidence to support this idea. When children grow up in large, well-to-do families, they do not show the unfavorable outcomes typically associated with large family size (Page & Grandon, 1979).

Is Yolanda's grandmother right that parents who have just one child are likely to end up with a spoiled, selfish youngster? A great deal of research indicates this commonly held belief is not correct. Only children are just as socially well adjusted as children with siblings, and they also do better in school and attain higher levels of education. One reason for this trend may be that only children have somewhat more affectionate relationships with their parents than do non-only children. And they also experience more pressure at home for mastery and accomplishment. As long as these demands are not unreasonable, they seem to have positive effects on children's development (Claudy, 1984; Falbo & Polit, 1986).

Still, the one-child family has both pros and cons, as does every family life style. In a survey in which only children and their parents were asked what they liked and

TABLE 3.2 • Advantages and Disadvantages of a One-Child Family

| Advantages | | Disadvantages | |
|---|---|---|---|
| **Mentioned by Parents** | **Mentioned by Children** | **Mentioned by Parents** | **Mentioned by Children** |
| Having time to pursue one's own interests and career<br><br>Less financial pressure<br><br>Not having to worry about "playing favorites" among children | Avoiding sibling rivalry<br><br>Having more privacy<br><br>Enjoying greater affluence<br><br>Having a closer parent–child relationship | Walking a "tightrope" between healthy attention and overindulgence<br><br>Having only one chance to "make good" as a parent<br><br>Being left childless in case of the child's death | Not getting to experience the closeness of a sibling relationship<br><br>Feeling too much pressure from parents to succeed<br><br>Having no one to help care for parents when they get old |

*Source:* Hawke & Knox, 1978.

disliked about living in a single-child family, each mentioned a set of advantages and disadvantages, which are summarized in Table 3.2. The list is a useful one for parents to consider when deciding how many children would best fit their own personal and family life plans.

### Is There a Best Time During Adulthood to Have a Child?

Yolanda's grandmother had her first child in her early twenties, shortly after she was married. Yolanda became pregnant for the first time at age 28. Many people believe that giving birth during the twenties is ideal, not only because the risk of having a baby with a genetic disorder is reduced (see Chapter 2), but also because younger parents have more energy to keep up with active children.

However, as Figure 3.1 reveals, first births to women in their thirties have increased greatly over the past two decades. Many more couples are putting off

**FIGURE 3.1** • First births to American women of different ages in 1970 and 1987. The birth rate decreased over this time period for women 20 to 24 years of age, while it increased for women 25 years and older. For women in their thirties, the birth rate more than doubled. (*Adapted from U.S. Department of Health and Human Services, 1990c; Ventura, 1989.*)

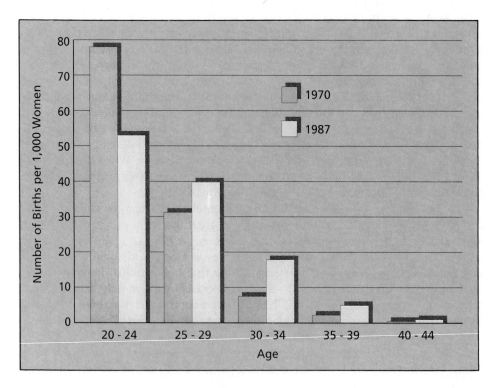

childbearing until their careers are well established and they know they can support a child (Ventura, 1989). Older parents may be somewhat less energetic than they were at an earlier age, but they are financially better off and more mature emotionally. For these reasons, they may be better able to invest in parenting (Ragozin et al., 1982). In support of this idea, when individuals who grew up with older parents are asked to reflect back on their childhoods, they often mention emotional stability as a distinct advantage (Yarrow, 1991).

Nevertheless, adult children of older parents do mention drawbacks. Some felt jealous of childhood friends because their parents seemed more active, playful, and fun loving. In addition, as they reached young adulthood, a great many began to worry about losing their parents. They had to come to terms with the fact that they would probably live much of their lives without their mothers and fathers (Yarrow, 1991).

Finally, fertility does decline with age. Older women who want to have children may find it more difficult to conceive, and a greater number of miscarriages occur with advancing age (Cohen-Overbeek et al., 1990). Although there is no best time during adulthood to begin raising children, individuals who decide to put off childbirth until well into their thirties or early forties do risk the possibility that they may not have children at all.

*BRIEF REVIEW* Today, more couples in industrialized nations weigh the pros and cons of parenthood before deciding to have children than was the case in the past. The current trend toward smaller families fits with the greater career commitment of modern women, and it also has benefits for children. Like all family life-styles, the decision to postpone childbearing to a later age has both advantages and disadvantages.

• *In what ways are couples' reasons for having children the same today as they were in Yolanda's grandmother's time? In what ways has the decision to have children changed?*

• *Rhonda and Mark are career-oriented, 35-year-old parents of an only child. They are thinking about having a second baby. What factors should they keep in mind as they decide whether to add to their family at this time in their lives?*

## PRENATAL DEVELOPMENT

During Yolanda's pregnancy, the one-celled zygote will grow into a complex human infant fully ready to be born. The vast changes that take place during these 38 weeks are usually divided into three phases: (1) the period of the zygote; (2) the period of the embryo; and (3) the period of the fetus. As we look at what happens in each, you may find it useful to refer to Table 3.3, which summarizes the milestones of prenatal development.

### The Period of the Zygote

The period of the zygote lasts about 2 weeks, from fertilization until the tiny mass of cells drifts down and out of the fallopian tube and attaches itself to the wall of the uterus. The zygote's first cell duplication is long and drawn out; it is not complete until about 30 hours after conception. Then, gradually, new cells are added at a faster rate. By the fourth day, 60 to 70 cells exist that form a hollow, fluid-filled ball called a **blastocyst** (see Figure 3.2). The cells on the inside, called the **embryonic disk,** will become the new organism; the outer ring will provide protective covering.

*Implantation.* Sometime between the seventh and ninth day, **implantation** occurs: the blastocyst burrows deep into the uterine lining. Surrounded by the woman's nourishing blood, now it starts to grow in earnest. At first, the protective outer layer multiplies fastest. A membrane, called the **amnion,** is formed that encloses

**Blastocyst**

The zygote four days after fertilization, when the tiny mass of cells forms a hollow, fluid-filled ball.

**Embryonic disk**

A small cluster of cells on the inside of the blastocyst, from which the embryo will develop.

**Implantation**

Attachment of the blastocyst to the uterine lining 7 to 9 days after fertilization.

**Amnion**

The inner membrane that forms a protective covering around the prenatal organism.

TABLE 3.3 • Major Milestones of Prenatal Development

| Trimester | Period | Weeks | Length and Weight | Major Events |
|---|---|---|---|---|
| First | Zygote | 1 | | The one-celled zygote multiplies and forms a blastocyst. |
| | | 2 | | The blastocyst burrows into the uterine lining. Structures that feed and protect the developing organism begin to form—amnion, chorion, yolk sac, placenta, and umbilical cord. |
| | Embryo | 3–4 | 1/4 inch | A primitive brain and spinal cord appear. Heart, muscles, backbone, ribs, and digestive tract begin to develop. |
| | | 5–8 | 1 inch | Many external body structures (for example, face, arms, legs, toes, fingers) and internal organs form. The sense of touch begins to develop, and the baby can move. |
| | Fetus | 9–12 | 3 inches; less than one ounce | Rapid increase in size begins. Nervous system, organs, and muscles become organized and connected, and new behavioral capacities (kicking, thumb sucking, mouth opening, and rehearsal of breathing) appear. External genitals are well formed, and the fetus's sex is evident. |
| Second | | 13–24 | 12 inches; 1.8 pounds | The fetus continues to enlarge rapidly. In the middle of this period, fetal movements can be felt by the mother. Vernix and lanugo appear to keep the fetus's skin from chapping in the amniotic fluid. All of the neurons that will ever be produced in the brain are present by 24 weeks. Eyes are sensitive to light, and the baby reacts to sound. |
| Third | | 25–38 | 20 inches; 7.5 pounds | The fetus has a chance of survival if born around this time. Continued increase in size. Lungs gradually mature. Rapid brain development causes sensory and behavioral capacities to expand. In the middle of this period, a layer of fat is added under the skin. Antibodies are transmitted from mother to fetus to protect against disease. Most fetuses rotate into an upside-down position in preparation for birth. |

*Sources:* Moore, 1989; Nilsson & Hamberger, 1990.

**Amniotic fluid**

The fluid that fills the amnion, helping to keep temperature constant and to provide a cushion against jolts caused by the mother's movement.

**Chorion**

The outer membrane that forms a protective covering around the prenatal organism. Sends out tiny fingerlike villi, from which the placenta begins to emerge.

the developing organism in **amniotic fluid.** It helps keep the temperature of the prenatal world constant and provides a cushion against any jolts caused by the woman's movement. A *yolk sac* also appears. It produces blood cells until the developing liver, spleen, and bone marrow are mature enough to take over this function (Moore, 1989).

The events of these first 2 weeks are delicate and uncertain. As many as 30 percent of zygotes do not make it through this phase. In some, the sperm and ovum do not join properly. In others, for some unknown reason cell duplication never begins. By preventing implantation in these cases, nature eliminates most prenatal abnormalities in the very earliest stages of development (Sadler, 1990).

***The Placenta and Umbilical Cord.***   By the end of the second week, another protective membrane, called the **chorion,** surrounds the amnion. From the chorion,

*During the period of the zygote, the fertilized ovum begins to duplicate at an increasingly rapid rate, forming a hollow ball of cells, or blastocyst, by the fourth day after fertilization. Here the blastocyst, magnified thousands of times, is shown burrowing into the uterine lining between the seventh and ninth day.* (© Lennart Nilsson A CHILD IS BORN/Bonniers)

tiny fingerlike *villi,* or blood vessels, begin to emerge.[2] As these villi burrow into the uterine wall, a special organ called the **placenta** starts to develop. By bringing the mother's and embryo's blood close together, the placenta will permit food and oxygen to reach the developing organism and waste products to be carried away. A membrane forms that allows these substances to be exchanged but prevents the mother's and embryo's blood from mixing directly (see Figure 3.3).

The placenta is connected to the developing organism by the **umbilical cord.** In the period of the zygote, it first appears as a primitive body stalk, but during the course of pregnancy, it grows to a length of 1 to 3 feet. The umbilical cord contains one large artery that delivers blood loaded with nutrients and two veins that remove waste products. The force of blood flowing through the cord keeps it firm, much like a garden hose, so it seldom tangles while the embryo, like a space-walking astronaut, floats freely in its fluid-filled chamber (Rugh & Shettles, 1971).

By the end of the period of the zygote, the developing organism has found food and shelter in the uterus. Already, it is a very complex being. These dramatic beginnings take place before all but the most sensitive mother knows that she is pregnant.

### The Period of the Embryo

The period of the **embryo** lasts from implantation through the eighth week of pregnancy. During these brief 6 weeks, the most rapid prenatal changes take place as the groundwork for all body structures and internal organs is laid down. Because all parts of the body are forming, the embryo is especially vulnerable to interference in healthy development. But the fact that embryonic growth takes place quickly, over a fairly short time span, helps limit opportunities for serious harm to occur.

[2]Recall from Chapter 2 that chorionic villi biopsy is the prenatal diagnostic method that can be performed earliest, by 6 to 8 weeks after conception. In this procedure, tissue from the ends of the villi are removed and examined for genetic abnormalities.

**Placenta**

The organ that separates the mother's bloodstream from the embryo or fetal bloodstream but permits exchange of nutrients and waste products.

**Umbilical cord**

The long cord connecting the prenatal organism to the placenta that delivers nutrients and removes waste products.

**Embryo**

The prenatal organism from 2 to 8 weeks after conception, during which time the foundations of all body structures and internal organs are laid down.

**FIGURE 3.2** • Development of the blastocyst. As the zygote moves down the fallopian tube, it begins to duplicate, at first slowly and then more rapidly. By the fourth day, it forms a hollow, fluid-filled ball called a blastocyst. The inner cells will become the new organism; the outer cells will provide protective covering. At the end of the first week, the blastocyst begins to implant in the uterine lining. (*From K. L. Moore, 1989,* Before we are born, *3rd ed., Philadelphia: Saunders, p. 134. Reprinted by permission.*)

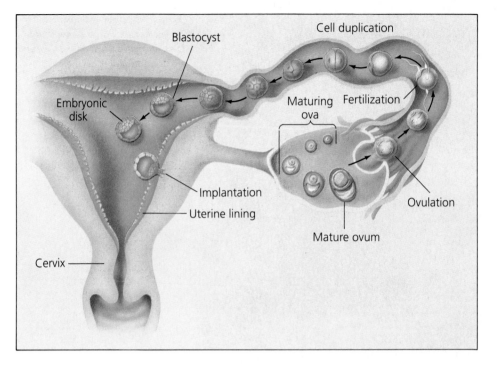

***Last Half of the First Month.*** In the first week of this period, the embryonic disk differentiates into three layers of cells: (1) the *ectoderm,* which will become the nervous system and skin; (2) the *mesoderm,* from which will develop the muscles, skeleton, circulatory system, and other internal organs; and (3) the *endoderm,* which will become the digestive system, lungs, urinary tract, and glands. These three layers give rise to all parts of the body.

**FIGURE 3.3** • Cross-section of the uterus showing the placenta. The mother's blood circulates in spaces surrounding the chorionic villi. A membrane between the two blood supplies permits food and oxygen to be delivered and waste products to be carried away. The two blood supplies do not mix directly. (*From K. L. Moore, 1989,* Before we are born, *3rd ed., Philadelphia: Saunders, p. 91. Reprinted by permission.*)

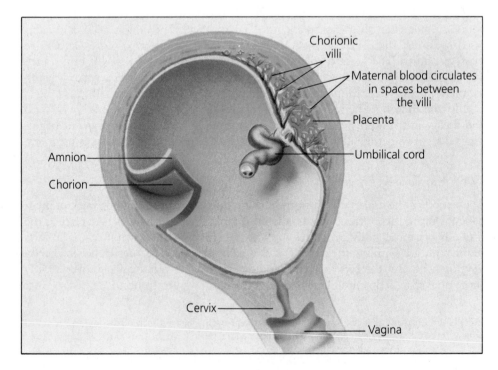

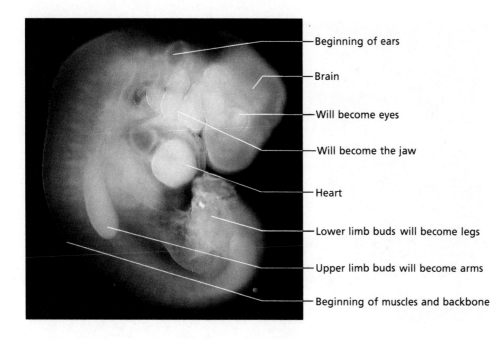

— Beginning of ears

— Brain

— Will become eyes

— Will become the jaw

— Heart

— Lower limb buds will become legs

— Upper limb buds will become arms

— Beginning of muscles and backbone

*This curled embryo is about 4 weeks old. In actual size, it is only one-fourth inch long, but many body structures have begun to form. The primitive tail will disappear by the end of the embryonic period.* (© Lennart Nilsson A CHILD IS BORN/Bonniers)

At first, the nervous system develops fastest. The ectoderm folds over to form a **neural tube,** or primitive spinal cord. At 3 1/2 weeks, the top swells to form a brain. Production of *neurons* (brain cells that store and transmit information) begins deep inside the neural tube. Once formed, neurons travel along tiny threads to their permanent locations, where they will form the major parts of the brain (Nowakowski, 1987).

While the nervous system is developing, the heart begins to pump blood around the embryo's circulatory system, and muscles, backbone, ribs, and digestive tract start to appear. At the end of the first month, the curled embryo consists of millions of organized groups of cells with specific functions, although it is only one-fourth of an inch long.

**The Second Month.**   In the second month, growth continues rapidly. The eyes, ears, nose, jaw, and neck form. Tiny buds become arms, legs, fingers, and toes. Internal organs are more distinct: the intestines grow, the heart develops separate chambers, and the liver and spleen take over production of blood cells so that the yolk sac is no longer needed. Changing body proportions cause the embryo's posture to become more upright. Now an inch long and one seventh of an ounce in weight, the embryo can already sense its world. It responds to touch, particularly in the areas of the mouth and on the soles of the feet. And it can move, although its tiny flutters are still too light to be felt by the mother (Nilsson & Hamberger, 1990).

## The Period of the Fetus

Lasting until the end of pregnancy, the period of the **fetus** is the "growth and finishing" phase. During this longest prenatal period, the developing organism begins to increase rapidly in size. As shown in Figure 3.4, the rate of body growth is extraordinary, especially from the ninth to the twentieth week (Moore, 1989).

**The Third Month.**   In the third month, the organs, muscles, and nervous system start to become organized and connected. The brain signals, and in response, the fetus kicks, bends its arms, forms a fist, curls its toes, opens its mouth, and even sucks

**Neural tube**
The primitive spinal cord that develops from the ectoderm, the top of which swells to form the brain.

**Fetus**
The prenatal organism from the beginning of the third month to the end of pregnancy, during which time completion of body structures and dramatic growth in size takes place.

*By 7 weeks, the embryo's posture is more upright. Body structures— eyes, nose, arms, legs, and internal organs—are more distinct. An embryo of this age responds to touch. It can also move, although at less than an inch long and an ounce in weight, it is still too tiny to be felt by the mother.* (© Lennart Nilsson A CHILD IS BORN/Bonniers)

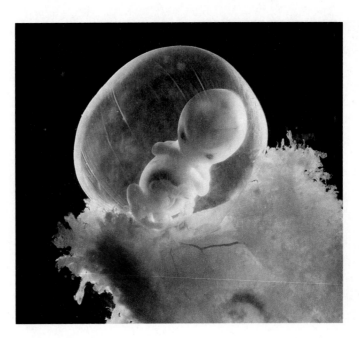

**Trimesters**

Three equal time periods in the prenatal period, each of which lasts three months.

**Vernix**

A white, cheeselike substance covering the fetus and preventing the skin from chapping due to constant exposure to the amniotic fluid.

**Lanugo**

A white, downy hair that covers the entire body of the fetus, helping the vernix stick to the skin.

its thumb. The tiny lungs begin to expand and contract in an early rehearsal of breathing movements. By the twelfth week, the external genitals are well formed, and the sex of the fetus is evident. Using ultrasound, Yolanda's doctor could see that she would have a boy (although Yolanda and Jay asked not to be told the fetus's sex). Other finishing touches appear, such as fingernails, toenails, tooth buds, and eyelids that open and close. The heartbeat is now stronger, and the doctor can hear it through a stethoscope.

Prenatal development is sometimes divided into **trimesters,** or three equal periods of time. At the end of the third month, the first trimester is complete. Two more must pass before the fetus is fully prepared to survive outside the womb.

***The Second Trimester.*** By the middle of the second trimester, between 17 and 20 weeks of age, the new being has grown large enough that its movements can be felt by the mother. If we could look inside the uterus at this time, we would find the fetus to be completely covered with a white cheeselike substance called **vernix.** It protects the skin from chapping during the long months spent bathing in the amniotic fluid. A white, downy hair covering called **lanugo** also appears over the entire body, helping the vernix stick to the skin.

At the end of the second trimester, many organs are quite well developed. And a major milestone is reached in brain development, in that all the neurons are now in place. No more will be produced in the individual's lifetime. However, *glial cells,* which support and feed the neurons, continue to increase at a rapid rate throughout the remaining months of pregnancy, as well as after birth (Nowakowski, 1987).

Brain growth means new behavioral capacities. The 20-week-old fetus can be stimulated as well as irritated by sounds. And, if a doctor has reason to look inside the uterus with fetoscopy (see Chapter 2, page 67), fetuses try to shield their eyes from the light with their hands, indicating that the sense of sight has begun to emerge (Nilsson & Hamberger, 1990). Still, a fetus born at this time cannot survive. Its lungs are quite immature, and the brain has not yet developed to the point at which it can control breathing movements and body temperature.

**FIGURE 3.4** • Rate of body growth during the fetal period. Increase in size is especially dramatic from the ninth to the twentieth week. The drawings are about one-fifth of actual size. (*From K. L. Moore, 1989,* Before we are born, *3rd ed., Philadelphia: Saunders, p. 68. Reprinted by permission.*)

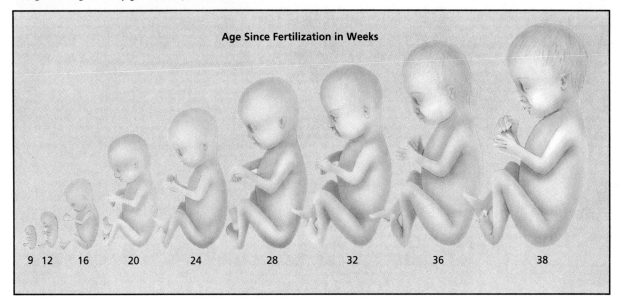

Age Since Fertilization in Weeks

9 12    16    20    24    28    32    36    38

*The Third Trimester.* The final trimester of pregnancy differs from the previous 6 months in that if born early, the fetus now has a chance for survival outside the womb. The point at which the baby can first survive is called the **age of viability.** It occurs sometime between 22 and 26 weeks (Moore, 1989). If born between the seventh and eighth month, breathing would still be a problem, and oxygen assistance would be necessary. Although the respiratory center of the brain is now mature, tiny air sacs in the lungs are not yet ready to inflate and exchange oxygen for carbon monoxide.

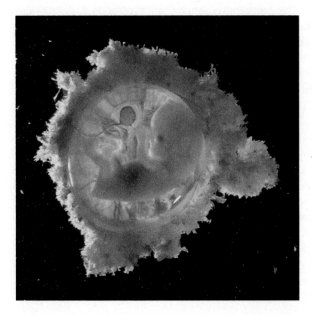

*During the period of the fetus, the organism increases rapidly in size, and body structures are completed. At 11 weeks, the brain and muscles are better connected. The fetus can kick, bend its arms, open and close its hands and mouth, and suck its thumb. Look closely, and you will see that the external genitals have begun to form. This fetus is a male.* (© Lennart Nilsson A CHILD IS BORN/Bonniers)

**Age of viability**
The age at which the fetus can first survive if born early. Occurs sometime between 22 and 26 weeks.

*At 22 weeks, this fetus is almost a foot long and slightly over a pound in weight. Its movements can be clearly felt by the mother and by other family members who place a hand on her abdomen. If born at this time, a baby has a slim chance of survival. (© Lennart Nilsson A CHILD IS BORN/Bonniers)*

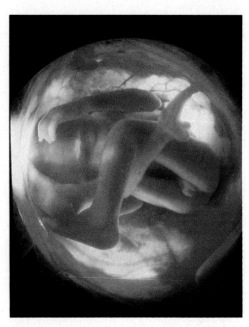

The brain continues to make great strides during the last 3 months. The *cerebral cortex,* the most highly evolved part of our brain and the seat of human intelligence, enlarges. At the same time, the fetus responds more clearly to sounds in the external world. Yolanda told me that one day, she turned on an electric mixer. The fetus reacted with a forceful startle. By 28 weeks, fetuses blink their eyes in reaction to nearby sounds (Birnholz & Benacerraf, 1983). And in the last weeks of pregnancy, they learn to prefer the tone and rhythm of their mother's voice. In one clever study, mothers were asked to read aloud Dr. Seuss's lively poem *The Cat in the Hat* to their unborn babies for the last 6 weeks of pregnancy. After birth, their infants were given a chance to suck on nipples that turned on recordings of the mother reading this poem or different rhyming stories. The infants sucked hardest to hear *The Cat in the Hat,* the sound they had come to know while still in the womb (DeCasper & Spence, 1986).

During the final 3 months, the fetus gains more than 5 pounds and grows 7 inches. As it fills the uterus, it gradually becomes less active. In the eighth month, a layer of fat is added under its skin to assist with temperature regulation. The fetus also receives antibodies from the mother's blood that protect it from illnesses that could be dangerous to the newborn, whose own immune system will not work well until several months after birth. In the last weeks, most fetuses assume an upside-down position, partly because of the shape of the uterus and because the head is heavier than the feet. Growth of the fetus starts to slow, and birth is about to take place.

*• Amy, who is 2 months pregnant, wonders how the embryo is being fed and what parts of the body have formed. Amy imagines that very little development has yet taken place. How would you answer Amy's questions? Will she be surprised at your response?*

**BRIEF REVIEW**  The vast changes that take place during pregnancy are usually divided into three periods. In the period of the zygote, the tiny one-celled fertilized ovum begins to duplicate and implants itself in the uterine lining. Structures that will feed and protect the developing organism begin to form. During the period of the embryo, the foundations for all body tissues and organs are rapidly laid down. The longest prenatal phase, the period of the fetus, is devoted to growth in size and completion of body systems. Turn back to Table 3.3 on page 96 to review the specific changes that take place during the nine months before birth.

## PRENATAL ENVIRONMENTAL INFLUENCES

Although the prenatal environment is far more constant than the world outside the womb, a great many factors can affect the developing fetus. Yolanda and Jay learned that there was much they could do to create a safe environment for their unborn child. In the following sections, we take a close look at the prenatal environment.

### Teratogens

The term **teratogen** refers to any environmental agent that causes damage during the prenatal period. It comes from the Greek word *teras,* meaning malformation or monstrosity. This label was selected because medical science first learned about harmful prenatal influences from cases in which babies had been profoundly damaged. Yet the harm done by teratogens is not always simple and straightforward. It depends on a number of factors, which are summarized in Table 3.4. First, we will see in our discussion of particular teratogens that larger doses over longer time periods usually have more negative effects. Second, the genetic makeup of the mother and baby plays an important role, since (as we indicated in Chapter 2) some individuals are better able to withstand harmful environments than are others. Third, the presence of several negative factors at once, such as poor nutrition, lack of medical care, and additional teratogens, can worsen the impact of a single harmful agent. Fourth, the effects of teratogens vary with the age of the baby at time of exposure. We can best understand this idea if we think of prenatal growth in terms of an important developmental concept to which you were introduced in Chapter 1: the **critical period.** A critical

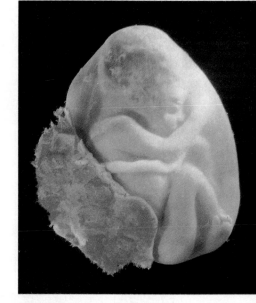

This 36-week-old fetus fills the uterus. To support its need for nourishment, the umbilical cord and placenta have grown very large. Notice the vernix (cheeselike substance) on the skin, which protects it from chapping. The fetus has accumulated a layer of fat to assist with temperature regulation after birth. In another 2 weeks, it would be full term. (© Lennart Nilsson A CHILD IS BORN/Bonniers)

TABLE 3.4 • Factors that Affect the Impact of Teratogens

| Factor | Description and Example |
|---|---|
| Amount and length of exposure | In general, the greater the amount and length of exposure, the more damage done to the embryo or fetus. Dose-related effects of this kind have been established for alcohol, smoking, and ionizing radiation. |
| Genetic makeup of mother and baby | The heredity of mother and baby affects their resistance to harmful agents. For example, cases exist in which fraternal twins have been born to drug-abusing mothers. One baby has abnormalities associated with the drug. The other does not. |
| Presence of several harmful influences | Pregnant women exposed to one harmful agent are often affected by others. For example, illegal drug users tend to have poor nutrition and more infections. The presence of these factors can worsen the impact of the drug on the embryo or fetus. |
| Time of exposure | Effects of teratogens depend on the age of the embryo or fetus. Extensive damage to body structures is most likely during the embryonic period, although some organs can still be strongly affected during the fetal period. The same teratogen can have quite different effects or no impact at all, depending on when it reaches the developing organism. |
| Delayed and indirect effects | Teratogens can have psychological consequences that are delayed or indirect. Physical defects can restrict the child's positive interactions with others and exploration of the environment. These experiences, in turn, can hinder many aspects of development. |

**Teratogen**

Any environmental agent that causes damage during the prenatal period.

**Critical period**

A limited period of time in which a part of the body or a behavior is biologically prepared to undergo rapid development and is especially sensitive to the environment.

**FIGURE 3.5** • Critical periods in prenatal development. Each organ or structure has a critical period during which its development may be disturbed. Black indicates highly sensitive periods. Pink indicates periods that are somewhat less sensitive to teratogens, although damage can occur. (*From K. L. Moore, 1989,* Before we are born, *3rd ed., Philadelphia: Saunders, p. 111. Reprinted by permission.*)

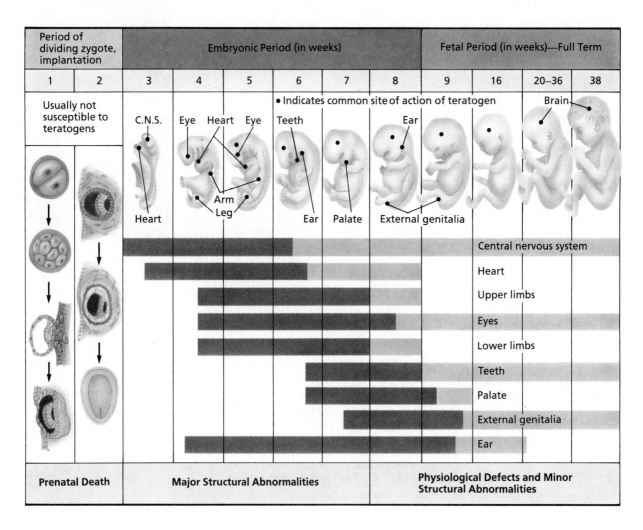

period is a limited time span in which a part of the body or a behavior is biologically prepared to undergo rapid development. During that time, it is especially sensitive to its surroundings. If the environment happens to be harmful, then damage occurs that would not have otherwise happened, and the child cannot fully recover.

Figure 3.5 provides a summary of critical periods during prenatal development. Look carefully at it, and you will see that some parts of the body, such as the brain and eye, have long critical periods that extend throughout the prenatal phase. Other critical periods, such as those for the limbs and palate, are much shorter. Figure 3.5 also indicates that we can make some general statements about the timing of harmful environmental influences. During the period of the zygote, before implantation, teratogens rarely have any impact. If they do, the tiny mass of cells is usually so completely damaged that it dies. The embryonic period is the time when serious defects are most likely to occur, since the foundations for all body parts are being laid down. During the fetal period, damage caused by teratogens is usually minor. However, some organs, such as the brain, eye, and genitals, can still be strongly affected.

Finally, the effects of teratogens are not limited to immediate physical damage. Although deformities of the body are easy to notice, important psychological consequences are harder to identify. Some may not show up until later in development. Others may take place as an indirect effect of physical damage. For example, a defect resulting from drugs the mother took during pregnancy can change reactions of others to the child as well as the child's ability to move about the environment. Over time, parent–child interaction, peer relations, and opportunities to explore may suffer. These experiences, in turn, can have far-reaching consequences for cognitive, emotional, and social development (Kopp & Kaler, 1989; Vorhees & Mollnow, 1987). Notice how an important idea about development that we discussed in earlier chapters is at work here—that of *bidirectional* influences between child and environment. Now, let's take a look at what scientists have discovered about a variety of teratogens.

*Prescription and Nonprescription Drugs.* Just about any drug taken by the mother can enter the embryonic or fetal bloodstream. In the early 1960s, the world learned a tragic lesson about drugs and prenatal development. At that time, a sedative called **thalidomide** was widely available in Europe, Canada, and South America. Although the embryos of test animals were not harmed by it, in humans it had drastic effects. When taken by mothers between the fourth to sixth week after conception, thalidomide produced gross deformities of the embryo's developing arms and legs. About 7,000 infants around the world were affected in this way (Moore, 1989). In addition, as children exposed to thalidomide grew older, a large number of them scored below average in intelligence. Perhaps the drug damaged the central nervous system directly. Or the child-rearing conditions of these severely deformed youngsters may have impaired their intellectual development (Vorhees & Mollnow, 1987).

Despite the bitter lesson of thalidomide, many pregnant women continue to take over-the-counter drugs without consulting with their doctors. Aspirin is one of the most common. Several studies suggest that repeated use of aspirin is linked to low birth weight, infant death around the time of birth, poorer motor development, and lower intelligence test scores in early childhood (Barr et al., 1990; Streissguth et al., 1987). Another frequently consumed drug is caffeine, contained in coffee. Heavy caffeine intake is associated with prematurity, miscarriage, and newborn withdrawal symptoms, such as irritability and vomiting (Aaronson & MacNee, 1989; McGowan, Altman, & Kanto, 1988).

Because children's lives are involved, we must take findings like these quite seriously. At the same time, it is important to note that we cannot yet be sure that these drugs actually cause the problems mentioned. Imagine how difficult it is to study the effects of many substances on the unborn! In the case of drugs, mothers often take more than one kind. If babies are injured, it is hard to tell which drug might be responsible or if other factors correlated with drug taking are really at fault. Until we have more information, the safest course of action is the one that Yolanda took: cut down or avoid these drugs entirely.

*Illegal Drugs.* Use of highly addictive mood-altering drugs, such as cocaine and heroin, is becoming more widespread, especially in poverty-stricken inner-city areas where they provide a temporary escape from a daily life of hopelessness. The number of "cocaine babies" born in the United States has reached crisis levels in recent years. In large cities, 10 to 17 percent of infants are affected (Frank et al., 1988; Little et al., 1989). Here is a brief account of what two of these hospitalized newborns looked like:

> Guillermo . . . has spent his whole short life crying. He is jittery and goes into spasms when he is touched. His eyes don't focus. He can't stick out his tongue, or suck. Born a week ago to a cocaine addict, Guillermo is described by his doctors as an addict him-

**Thalidomide**
A sedative widely available in Europe, Canada, and South America in the early 1960s. When taken by mothers between the fourth to sixth week after conception, it produced gross deformities of the baby's arms and legs.

self. Nearby, . . . Paul lies motionless in an incubator, feeding tubes riddling his tiny body. He needs a respirator to breathe and a daily spinal tap to relieve fluid buildup on his brain. Only one month old, he has already suffered two strokes. (Barol, 1986, p. 56)

Babies born to mothers who took cocaine, heroin, or methadone (a less addictive drug used to wean people away from heroin) are at risk for a wide variety of problems, including prematurity, low birth weight, physical defects, breathing difficulties, and death around the time of birth. These infants are, indeed, drug-addicted. Guillermo and Paul were feverish and irritable at birth. They had trouble sleeping, and their cries were abnormally shrill and piercing—a common symptom among stressed newborns that we will discuss in Chapter 4 (Chasnoff et al., 1989; Little et al., 1989). When mothers with many problems of their own must take care of these babies, who are difficult to calm down, cuddle, and feed, then behavior problems are likely to persist.

Throughout the first year of life, heroin- and methadone-exposed infants are less attentive to the environment, and their motor development is slow. After infancy, some children get better, while others remain jittery and inattentive. Researchers believe that the kind of parenting these youngsters receive may explain why there are lasting problems for some but not for others (Vorhees & Mollnow, 1987).

Unlike findings on heroin and methadone, growing evidence on cocaine suggests that large numbers of prenatally exposed babies will not recover. Recent research indicates that cocaine is linked to a specific set of physical defects. These include genital, urinary tract, kidney, and heart deformities as well as brain seizures (Chasnoff et al., 1989). Babies born to mothers who smoke crack (a cheap form of cocaine that delivers high doses quickly through the lungs) seem to be worst off in terms of low birth weight and serious damage to the central nervous system. Many show lasting emotional and behavior problems, including social withdrawal, overactivity, and aggressive outbursts (Kantrowitz, 1990; Kaye et al., 1989).

Marijuana is another illegal, mood-altering drug that is used more widely than cocaine and heroin. Although there is debate about whether it causes physical addiction in adults, babies born to women who smoked it regularly during pregnancy are addicted. They show withdrawal symptoms much like those of heroin- and cocaine-

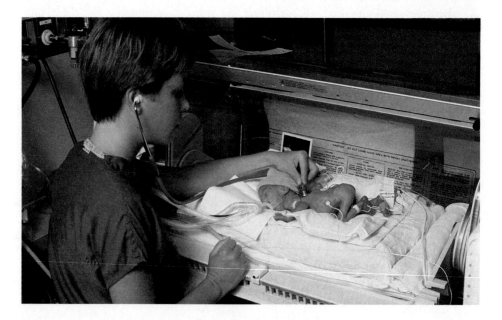

*This baby, whose mother took crack during pregnancy, was born many weeks premature. He breathes with the aid of a respirator. His central nervous system may be seriously damaged. If he survives, he is likely to show lasting emotional and behavioral problems.* (Charles Cancellare/ Picture Group)

exposed newborns. In addition, there is a slight risk of prematurity associated with marijuana (Fried et al., 1987; Lester & Dreher, 1989). These outcomes certainly put newborn babies at risk for future problems, even though long-term effects of marijuana have not been established.

*Smoking.*    In the early 1970s, when I was pregnant with my first child, I enrolled in a prenatal education class at the hospital where I would later give birth. I remember sitting in a room that was filled with smoke. Three of twelve expectant mothers lit up while waiting for class to begin. At that time, scientists already suspected that exposure to a potent addictive drug contained in cigarettes, nicotine, was dangerous to the embryo and fetus. Today, the evidence is quite clear.

The most well-known effect of smoking during pregnancy is low birth weight. But the likelihood of other serious consequences, such as prematurity, miscarriage, and infant death, is also increased. The more cigarettes a mother smokes, the greater the chances that her baby will be affected. If a pregnant woman decides to stop smoking at any time, even during the last trimester, she can help her baby. She immediately reduces the chances that the infant will be born underweight and suffer from future problems (Aaronson & MacNee, 1989; Sexton & Hebel, 1984).

Smoking during pregnancy is associated with low birth weight, prematurity, miscarriage, and infant death. During childhood, youngsters who were prenatally exposed to nicotine are at risk for attentional and learning problems. This mother can still protect her child by giving up smoking immediately. (© Will & Deni McIntyre/Photo Researchers)

Even when a baby of a smoking mother appears to be born in good physical condition, slight behavioral abnormalities may threaten the child's development. Newborns of smoking mothers are less responsive to their surroundings than other infants. For example, they turn in the direction of a sound (such as the jingle of a bell) more slowly, and they stop responding to it more quickly than babies of nonsmoking mothers (Woodson et al., 1980). An unresponsive child may not evoke the kind of interaction from others that ensures healthy psychological development. Several long-term studies report that children exposed to nicotine before birth have shorter attention spans and show poorer school achievement and increased motor activity in early and middle childhood (Naeye & Peters, 1984; Streissguth et al., 1984).

Investigators have begun to discover exactly how cigarettes harm the fetus. Nicotine causes the placenta to grow abnormally. As a result, transfer of nutrients is reduced, and the fetus gains weight poorly. Also, smoking raises the concentration of carbon monoxide in the bloodstreams of both mother and fetus. Carbon monoxide displaces oxygen from red blood cells. It damages the central nervous system and reduces birth weight in the fetuses of laboratory animals. Similar effects may occur in humans as well (Aaronson & MacNee, 1989; Nash & Persaud, 1988).

Finally, Jay made a special effort to give up cigarettes when Yolanda became pregnant. Newborn infants of fathers who smoke are also likely to be underweight! Jay realized that a smoke-filled environment at home could harm the fetus by turning Yolanda into a "passive smoker" who inhaled nicotine and carbon monoxide from the air around her (Rubin et al., 1986; Schwartz-Bickenbach et al., 1987).

*Alcohol.*    Recently, Michael Dorris (1989), a Dartmouth University anthropology professor, wrote *The Broken Cord*. In this moving story, Dorris describes what it was like to raise his adopted son Adam, whose biological mother drank heavily throughout pregnancy and died of alcohol poisoning shortly after his birth. A Sioux Indian boy, Adam was 3 years old when he came into Dorris's life. He was short and underweight and had a vocabulary of only 20 words. But Dorris was sure that with extra care and attention, Adam would overcome these problems.

Unfortunately, Adam's difficulties did not go away. Although he ate well, Adam grew slowly and remained painfully thin. He was prone to infection and had repeated brain seizures. His vocabulary did not expand like that of normal preschoolers. When he was 7, special testing revealed that Adam's intelligence was below average and that he had difficulty concentrating. At age 12, he could not add, subtract, or identify the town in which he lived.

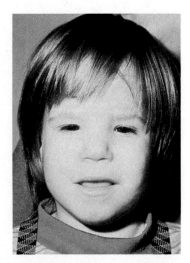

*The mother of this severely retarded boy drank heavily during pregnancy. His widely spaced eyes, thin upper lip, and short eyelid openings are typical of fetal alcohol syndrome. (Fetal Alcohol Syndrome Research Fund, University of Washington)*

**Fetal alcohol syndrome (FAS)**

A pattern of defects that results when pregnant women consume large amounts of alcohol during most or all of pregnancy. Includes mental retardation, slow physical growth, and facial abnormalities.

**Fetal alcohol effects (FAE)**

The condition of children who display some but not all of the defects of fetal alcohol syndrome. Usually their mothers drank alcohol in smaller quantities during pregnancy.

Around that time, Dorris learned the cause of Adam's problems. A counselor who worked with Native American adolescents looked at a photograph of Adam and noticed his small head, flat nose, and droopy eyelids. "FAS, too, huh?" he remarked (p. 138). Now a man in his twenties, Adam has difficulty keeping a routine job and suffers from poor judgment. He might buy something and not wait for change, open a window on a cold night and fail to close it, or wander off in the middle of a task. His case, along with many others like it, reveals that the damage done by alcohol to the embryo and fetus cannot be undone.

**Fetal alcohol syndrome (FAS)** is the scientific name for Adam's condition. Mental retardation, poor attention, and overactivity are typical of children who have the disorder. A distinct set of physical symptoms also accompanies it. These include slow physical growth and a particular pattern of facial abnormalities: widely spaced eyes, short eyelid openings, a small upturned nose, and a thin upper lip. The small heads of these children indicate that the brain has been prevented from reaching full development. Other defects—of the eyes, ears, nose, throat, heart, genitals, urinary tract, or immune system—might also be present. In all babies born with FAS, the mother drank heavily through most or all of her pregnancy (Aaronson & MacNee, 1989; Hoyseth & Jones, 1989).

Sometimes, children do not display all of the abnormalities of FAS—only some of them. In these cases, the child is said to suffer from **fetal alcohol effects (FAE).** Usually, the mothers of these children drank alcohol in smaller quantities. The particular defects of FAE children vary with the timing and length of alcohol exposure during pregnancy (Hoyseth & Jones, 1989).

How does alcohol produce its devastating effects? Researchers believe it does so in two ways. The first is by interfering with cell duplication and migration in the primitive neural tube. When the brains of FAS babies who did not survive are examined, they show a reduced number of cells and major structural abnormalities (Nowakowski, 1987). Second, large quantities of oxygen are required to metabolize alcohol in the human body. When pregnant women drink heavily, they draw oxygen away from the embryo or fetus that is vital for cell growth in the brain and other parts of the body (Vorhees & Mollnow, 1987).

Like heroin and cocaine, alcohol abuse is higher in poverty-stricken sectors of the population, especially among Native Americans. On the reservation where Adam was born, a great many children show symptoms of prenatal alcohol exposure. Unfortunately, when girls with FAS or FAE later become pregnant, the poor judgment caused by the syndrome often prevents them from understanding why they should avoid alcohol themselves. Thus, the tragic cycle is likely to repeat itself in the next generation.

At this point, you may be wondering: How much alcohol is safe during pregnancy? Is it all right to have a drink or two, either on a daily basis or occasionally? A recent study found that as little as 2 ounces of alcohol a day, taken very early in pregnancy, was associated with FAS-like facial features (Astley et al., 1992). But recall that other factors—both genetic and environmental—can make some fetuses more vulnerable to teratogenic effects. Therefore, a precise dividing line between safe and dangerous drinking levels cannot be established. Recent research shows that the more alcohol consumed during pregnancy, the poorer a child's motor coordination and intelligence at 4 years of age (Barr et al., 1990; Streissguth et al., 1989). These dose-related effects indicate that it is best for pregnant women to avoid alcohol entirely.

*Hormones.* In Chapter 2, we saw that the Y chromosome causes male sex hormones (called androgens) to be secreted prenatally, leading to formation of male reproductive organs. In the absence of male hormones, female structures develop.

Hormones are released as part of a delicately balanced system. If their quantity or timing is off, then defects of the genitals as well as other organs can occur.

Between 1945 and 1970, a synthetic hormone called **diethylstilbestrol (DES)** was widely used to prevent miscarriages in women who had a history of pregnancy problems. As the daughters of these mothers reached adolescence and young adulthood, they showed an unusually high rate of cancer of the vagina and malformations of the uterus. When they tried to have children, their pregnancies more often resulted in prematurity, low birth weight, and miscarriage than did those of non-DES-exposed women. Young men whose mothers took DES prenatally were also affected. They showed an increased risk of genital abnormalities and cancer of the testes (Linn et al., 1988; Stillman, 1982). Because of these findings, doctors no longer treat pregnant women with DES. But many children whose mothers took it are now of childbearing age, and they need to be carefully monitored by their doctors.

Sometimes mothers take other hormones that could damage the embryo or fetus. For example, occasionally a woman continues to use birth control pills during the early weeks after conception, before she knows that she is pregnant. Recent research has linked oral contraceptives to heart and limb deformities, although additional studies are needed to prove this relationship (Grimes & Mishell, 1988; Kricker et al., 1986).

*Radiation.* In Chapter 2, we saw that ionizing radiation can cause mutation, damaging the DNA in ova and sperm. When mothers are exposed to radiation during pregnancy, additional harm can come to the embryo or fetus. Defects due to radiation were tragically apparent in the children born to pregnant Japanese women who survived the bombing of Hiroshima and Nagasaki during World War II. Miscarriage, slow physical growth, an underdeveloped brain, and malformations of the skeleton and eyes were common (Michel, 1989). As we indicated in Chapter 2, research suggests that it takes large quantities of radiation over an extended period of time to damage the ovum and sperm before conception. In contrast, once prenatal development is underway, even low-level radiation from medical X-rays or leakage in the workplace may not be safe. Women need to tell their doctors if they are pregnant or trying to become pregnant before having X-ray examinations. In addition, they should avoid work environments in which they might be exposed to X-rays.

*Environmental Pollution.* Yolanda and Jay like to refinish antique furniture in their garage, and Jay is an enthusiastic grower of fruit trees in the back yard. When Yolanda became pregnant, they postponed work on several pieces of furniture, and Jay did not spray the fruit trees in the fall and spring of that year. Continuing to do so, they learned, might expose Yolanda and the embryo or fetus to chemical levels thousands of times greater than judged safe by the federal government (Samuels & Samuels, 1986).

An astounding number of potentially dangerous chemicals is released into the environment in industrialized nations. In the United States, 100,000 are in common use, and 1,000 new ones are introduced each year. Although many chemicals cause serious birth defects in laboratory animals, the impact on the human embryo and fetus is known for only a small number of them. However, a few, such as mercury, lead, and polychlorinated-biphenyls (PCBs), are established human teratogens.

*Mercury.* In the 1950s, an industrial plant released waste containing high levels of mercury into a bay providing food and water for the town of Minimata, Japan. Many children born at the time were mentally retarded and showed other serious symptoms, including abnormal speech, difficulty in chewing and swallowing, and uncoordinated movements. Autopsies of those who died revealed widespread brain damage (Vorhees & Mollnow, 1987).

**Diethylstilbestrol (DES)**
A hormone widely used between 1945 and 1970 to prevent miscarriage. Increases the chances of genital tract abnormalities and cancer of the vagina and testes in adolescence and young adulthood.

*Lead.* Pregnant women can absorb lead from car exhaust, lead-based paint flaking off the walls in old houses and apartment buildings, and other materials used in industrial occupations. High levels of lead exposure are consistently linked to prematurity, low birth weight, brain damage, and a wide variety of physical defects (Dye-White, 1986). Even a very low level of prenatal lead exposure seems to be dangerous. Affected babies show slightly poorer mental development during the first two years of life (Bellinger et al., 1987; Ernhart et al., 1985).

*Polychlorinated-Biphenyls (PCBs).* For many years, PCBs were used to insulate electrical equipment. In 1977, they were banned by the federal government after research showed that, like mercury, they found their way into waterways and entered the food supply. In one study, newborn babies of women who frequently ate PCB-contaminated fish caught in Lake Michigan were compared to newborns whose mothers ate little or no fish. The PCB-exposed babies had a variety of problems, including slightly lower than average birth weight, smaller heads (suggesting brain damage), and less interest in their surroundings (Jacobson et al., 1984). When studied again at 7 months of age, infants whose mothers ate fish during pregnancy did more poorly on memory tests (Jacobson et al., 1985). A recent follow-up at 4 years of age revealed persisting memory difficulties and lower verbal intelligence test scores (Jacobson, Jacobson, & Humphrey, 1990; Jacobson et al., 1992).

**Maternal Disease.** On her first prenatal visit, Yolanda's doctor asked if she and Jay had already had measles, mumps, chicken pox, as well as other illnesses. In addition, Yolanda was checked for the presence of several infections, and for good reason. As you can see in Table 3.5, certain diseases during pregnancy are major causes of miscarriage and birth defects.

Five percent of women catch a virus of some sort while pregnant, such as the common cold or a strain of the flu. Most of these illnesses appear to have no impact on the embryo or fetus. However, a few viruses can cause extensive damage. The best known of these is **rubella** (three-day or German measles). In the mid-1960s, a worldwide epidemic of rubella led to the birth of over 20,000 American babies with serious physical defects. Consistent with the critical period concept, the greatest damage occurs when rubella strikes during the embryonic period. Over 50 percent of

**Rubella**

Three-day German measles. Causes a wide variety of prenatal abnormalities, especially when it strikes during the embryonic period.

TABLE 3.5 • Effects of Some Infectious Diseases during Pregnancy

| Disease | Miscarriage | Physical Malformations | Mental Retardation | Low Birth Weight and Prematurity |
|---|---|---|---|---|
| **Viral** | | | | |
| Cytomegalovirus | + | + | + | + |
| Rubella | + | + | + | + |
| Chicken pox | 0 | + | + | + |
| Herpes simplex 2 (genital herpes) | + | + | + | + |
| Mumps | + | ? | 0 | 0 |
| **Bacterial** | | | | |
| Syphilis | + | + | + | ? |
| Tuberculosis | + | ? | + | + |
| **Parasitic** | | | | |
| Malaria | + | 0 | 0 | + |
| Toxoplasmosis | + | + | + | + |

*Sources:* Adapted from *Clinical genetics in nursing practice* (p. 232) by F. L. Cohen, 1984, Philadelphia: Lippincott. Reprinted by permission. Additional sources are Samson, 1988; Sever, 1983; and Vorhees, 1986.

*Key:* + = established finding, 0 = no present evidence, ? = possible effect that is not clearly established.

infants whose mothers became ill during that time show heart defects; eye cataracts; deafness; genital, urinary, and intestinal abnormalities; and mental retardation. Infection during the fetal period is less harmful, but low birth weight, hearing loss, and bone defects may still occur (Samson, 1988). Since 1966, infants and young children have been routinely vaccinated against rubella, so the number of prenatal cases today is much less than it was a generation ago. Still, 10 to 20 percent of American women of childbearing age lack the rubella antibody, so new outbreaks of the disease are still possible (Cochi et al., 1989).

The harmful effects of other common viruses are summarized in Table 3.5. The unborn baby is especially sensitive to the family of herpes viruses, for which there is no vaccine or treatment. Among these, cytomegalovirus (the most frequent prenatal infection, transmitted through repiratory or sexual contact) and herpes simplex 2 (which is sexually transmitted) are especially dangerous. In both, the virus invades the mother's genital tract, and babies can be infected either during pregnancy or at birth. Both illnesses attack the central nervous system and lead to a wide variety of physical malformations (Samson, 1988).

Several bacterial and parasitic diseases are also listed in Table 3.5. Among the most common is **toxoplasmosis,** caused by a parasite found in many animals. Pregnant women may become infected from eating raw or undercooked meat or from contact with the feces of infected cats. If the disease strikes during the first trimester, the embryo or fetus can experience eye and brain damage (Bobak, Jensen, & Zalar, 1989; Marcus, 1983). Expectant mothers can avoid toxoplasmosis by making sure that the meat they eat is well cooked. Also, pet cats should be checked for the disease and care of their litter boxes turned over to other family members during pregnancy. Outdoor garden areas that cats may have used should be avoided as well.

Finally, a relatively new but deadly viral disease that is spreading rapidly among certain sectors of the population is **acquired immune deficiency syndrome (AIDS).** Like other viruses, the AIDS virus can cross the placenta. Its impact is discussed in Box 3.1.

### Other Maternal Factors

Besides avoiding teratogens, expectant parents can support the development of the embryo or fetus by keeping track of a variety of other environmental influences. Regular exercise, good nutrition, and emotional well-being of the mother are critically important. Blood type differences between mother and fetus can create difficulties. Finally, many expectant parents wonder how a mother's age and previous births affect the course of pregnancy. We examine each of these factors in the following sections.

***Exercise.***    Yolanda continued her daily half-hour of aerobic exercise into the third trimester, although her doctor cautioned her to avoid bouncing, jolting, and jogging movements that might subject the fetus to too many shocks and startles. In fact, enjoyable physical activity, such as swimming, hiking, and aerobics, is recommended for pregnant women. Hospital-sponsored childbirth education programs frequently offer special exercise classes and suggest particular routines that help prepare for labor and delivery. Exercises that strengthen the back, abdominal, pelvic, and thigh muscles are emphasized, since the growing fetus places some strain on these parts of the body (Nilsson & Hamberger, 1990; Samuels & Samuels, 1986).

During the last trimester, when the abdomen grows very large, mothers find it difficult to move easily and freely and often need to cut back on exercise. In most cases, a mother who has remained fit during the earlier months is likely to experience fewer of the physical discomforts that arise at this time, such as back pain, upward pressure on the chest, and difficulty in breathing.

**Toxoplasmosis**
A parasitic disease caused by eating raw or undercooked meat or by contact with the feces of infected cats. During the first trimester, it leads to eye and brain damage.

**Acquired immune deficiency syndrome (AIDS)**
A relatively new viral infection that destroys the immune system. Spread through transfer of body fluids from one person to another. Can be transmitted prenatally.

## SOCIAL ISSUES

### Box 3.1   *AIDS and Prenatal Development*

First-born child of Jean and Claire, Ginette was diagnosed with AIDS when she was 6 months old. She died from respiratory infections and a failure to grow normally at 11 months of age. Immigrants from the Caribbean to Florida, Jean and Claire could not understand the social worker's explanation of why Ginette died. After all, neither parent felt sick. At that time, Claire was pregnant with a second baby. Several weeks after Ginette's death, Jeanine was born. In the meantime, friends learned that AIDS caused Ginette's death. When word spread, Jean lost his job, the family was evicted from their apartment, and friends and relatives started to avoid Jean and Claire. Over the next year, Claire gave birth to a son, Junior, and also became pregnant for a fourth time. During this pregnancy, both Claire and Jeanine began to show symptoms of AIDS infection. Claire's condition worsened. Her fourth child was born prematurely, and Claire and the baby died soon after. Jean was grief-stricken over Claire's death. Many months later, an uncle brought Jeanine and Junior to the hospital; they were eventually placed in foster care. Junior was tested for the AIDS virus. Unlike his sisters, he managed to escape it. Jean, who left the family and may have died of AIDS, was never heard from again. (paraphrased from Siebert et al., 1989, pp. 36–38)

*A*IDS is a relatively new viral disease that destroys the immune system. Affected individuals like Jean, Claire, and their children eventually die of a wide variety of illnesses that their bodies can no longer fight. Adults at greatest risk for AIDS include male homosexuals and bisexuals, users of illegal drugs who share needles, and their heterosexual partners. Transfer of body fluids from one person to another is necessary for AIDS to spread.

When women carrying the AIDS virus become pregnant, about 30 percent of the time they pass the deadly disease to the embryo or fetus. According to the U.S. Centers for Disease Control, over 3,000 childhood cases of AIDS have been diagnosed in the United States since 1981. The large majority (80 percent) are infants who received the virus before birth, often from a drug-abusing mother (Novick, 1989; Valleroy, Harris, & Way, 1990).

AIDS symptoms generally take a long time to emerge in older children and adults—up to 5 years after infection with the virus. In contrast, the disease proceeds rapidly in infants. The average age at which symptoms appear in prenatally infected babies is 6 months. Weight loss, fever, diarrhea, and repeated respiratory illnesses are common. Like Ginette, most infants survive for only 5 to 8 months after they first become ill (Minkoff et al., 1987; Task Force on Pediatric AIDS, 1989).

Research suggests that AIDS, like other viruses, can cause serious birth defects. A pattern of physical abnormalities has been linked to prenatal AIDS infection, including a prominent boxlike forehead, widely spaced and diagonally oriented eyes, thick lips, and a small head. Delayed physical and mental development are common. Infants with a greater number of these defects display AIDS symptoms sooner in the first year of life. This suggests that the deformities are caused by early prenatal transfer of the AIDS virus from mother to baby (Marion et al., 1986; Novick, 1989).

Most prenatal AIDS infants are born to urban, poverty-stricken parents. Lack of money to pay for medical treatment, rejection by relatives and friends who do not understand the disease, and anxiety about the child's future cause tremendous stress in these families. Currently, medical services for young children with AIDS and counseling for their parents are badly needed. Also, with no cure likely in the near future, widespread education of adolescents and adults about AIDS is the only way to stop continued spread of the virus to children (Task Force on Pediatric AIDS, 1989).

*EARLIER IN THIS CHAPTER,* we indicated that the same teratogen can affect babies in different ways. How are the outcomes for Jean and Claire's children consistent with this principle?

How does the case of Jean and Claire illustrate the unique problems of AIDS-affected families and their need for special medical and counseling services?

*Mild, regular exercise keeps a mother fit during pregnancy and helps her prepare for the hard physical work of labor and delivery.* (Mike Malyszko/Stock Boston)

Finally, pregnant women with health problems, such as circulatory difficulties or a history of previous miscarriages, should consult their doctors before beginning or continuing a physical fitness routine. For these mothers, exercise (especially the wrong kind) can endanger the pregnancy.

*Nutrition.* Children grow more rapidly during the prenatal period than at any other phase of development. During this time, they depend totally on the mother for nutrients to support their growth.

During World War II, a severe famine occurred in Holland, giving scientists a rare opportunity to study the impact of nutrition on prenatal development. The findings revealed that the critical period concept operates with nutrition, just as it does with the teratogens discussed earlier in this chapter. Women affected by the famine during the first trimester were more likely to have miscarriages or to give birth to babies with physical defects. When the famine struck later in pregnancy, fetuses usually survived, but many were born underweight and had small heads (suggesting an underdeveloped brain) (Stein et al., 1975).

We now know that prenatal malnutrition can cause serious damage to the central nervous system. Autopsies of malnourished babies who died at or shortly after birth reveal fewer brain cells and a brain weight that is as much as 36 percent below average. The poorer the mother's diet, the greater the loss in brain weight, especially if malnutrition occurred during the last three months of pregnancy. During that time, the brain is growing rapidly in size, and a maternal diet high in all the basic nutrients is necessary for it to reach its full potential (Naeye, Blanc, & Paul, 1973; Parekh et al., 1970; Winick, Rosso, & Waterlow, 1970).

Prenatally malnourished babies enter the world with serious behavior problems. They are apathetic and unresponsive to stimulation around them. Like drug-addicted newborns, they have a high-pitched cry that is particularly distressing to their caregivers. For this reason, the parent–infant relationship is likely to get off to a very poor start. Since malnutrition is highest in poverty-stricken areas of the world, the effects of poor nutrition quickly combine with a stressful home life. With age, low intelligence test scores and serious learning problems become increasingly apparent (Lozoff, 1989). As Box 3.2 indicates, scientists know how to intervene when poverty is the cause of inadequate diet during pregnancy, although the resources for doing so are not always available.

## FROM RESEARCH TO PRACTICE

### Box 3.2   *Intervening with Prenatally Malnourished Infants*

Margarita, 2 months pregnant with her second child, walked into a public health clinic in a rural area of Guatemala with her 6-month-old daughter Rosita in her arms. Rosita was pale and listless. Her body looked wasted, and she was several inches shorter than the average baby of her age. Because she was so poorly nourished, Rosita was less resistant to disease. She had difficulty breathing due to a respiratory infection that her body could not fight. Carlotta, the nurse on duty, noticed that Margarita was also frail, anemic, and withdrawn. In addition to poor diet, Margarita's closely spaced pregnancies had depleted her body of iron and other essential nutrients. Unless Margarita's own malnourished condition could be quickly reversed, her unborn child was in serious danger as well.

Many studies show that providing poor mothers with food supplements has a substantial impact on their health and the condition of their newborn babies. Carlotta sent Margarita to a food distribution center near the small village where she lived. Twice a day, she received a protein-rich cereal along with a high calorie drink that contained vitamins and minerals.

As a result of the food program, Margarita gained more weight during her second pregnancy than she did with her first, and her chances of miscarriage and premature birth were greatly reduced (Villar & Gonzalez-Cossio, 1986). When little Juan arrived, he was a pound and a half heavier than Rosita had been at birth. Juan also developed more quickly than his older sister—rolling over, grasping, and crawling at earlier ages (Joos et al., 1983). His active, curious behavior caused Margarita to respond to him more, and this encouraged his development even further.

When poor nutrition is allowed to continue throughout pregnancy, the malnourished baby often requires more than dietary improvement to prevent lasting problems. Rosita's tired and sometimes irritable behavior led Margarita to be less sensitive and stimulating in caring for her. As a result, Rosita became even more passive and withdrawn, and her intellectual and motor progress fell far behind that of other babies her age.

Successful intervention programs for malnourished infants must break this bidirectional cycle of apathetic mother–baby interaction. Some do so by teaching parents how to interact effectively with their infants. Margarita was fortunate to become part of a program in which a health aide visited her home regularly over a three-year period, teaching her how to play with and stimulate her children. As a result, the large difference in skills between Rosita and adequately fed children in the village was reduced (Grantham-McGregor, Schofield, & Powell, 1987).

Other interventions for prenatally malnourished babies focus on the infants. In one study, newborns were provided with a highly stimulating and responsive day care environment in addition to an enriched diet. By 15 months of age, their intellectual development was equal to that of well-nourished babies of the same socioeconomic background. And it was much more advanced than that of infants who had received only dietary supplements (Zeskind & Ramey, 1978, 1981).

Prenatal malnutrition is not just a risk factor for children born in Third World countries. It also affects many youngsters in the United States. Each year, 80,000 to 120,000 American infants come into the world seriously undernourished. The United States government does provide food packages to poverty-stricken pregnant women through its *Special Supplemental Food Program for Women, Infants, and Children.* Unfortunately, because of funding shortages, the program serves only 60 percent of those who are eligible (Children's Defense Fund, 1990d).

At this point, it is important to note that some middle-class expectant mothers are also poorly nourished. Pregnancy is not the time for a woman to worry about her figure! A weight gain of 25 to 30 pounds is normal and helps ensure the health of both mother and baby. Yet in the United States, where thinness is the feminine ideal, women often feel uneasy about gaining this much weight, and they may try to limit their food intake. When they do so, they risk their infant's development in all of the ways just described.

Finally, overweight and obesity are health hazards during pregnancy, just as they are at other times of life. A mother who tips the scales in the wrong direction at the beginning of pregnancy or who gains too much weight is at risk for high blood pressure and other complications. In addition, she is likely to find pregnancy and childbirth especially exhausting.

*Emotional State.* When women experience severe emotional stress during pregnancy, their babies are at risk for a wide variety of difficulties. Intense anxiety is associated with a higher rate of miscarriage, prematurity, low birth weight, and newborn respiratory illness. It is also related to certain physical defects, such as cleft palate and pyloric stenosis (tightening of the infant's stomach outlet, which must be treated surgically) (Norbeck & Tilden, 1983; Omer & Everly, 1988).

How can maternal stress affect the developing organism? To understand this process, think back to how your own body felt the last time you were under considerable stress. When we experience fear and anxiety, stimulant hormones are released into our bloodstream. These cause us to be "poised for action." Large amounts of blood are sent to parts of the body involved in the defensive response—the brain, heart, and muscles in the arms, legs, and trunk. Blood flow to other organs, including the uterus, is reduced. As a result, the fetus is deprived of a full supply of oxygen and nutrients. Stress hormones also cross the placenta, leading the fetus's heart rate and activity level to rise dramatically. In fact, long-term exposure to these hormones might be responsible for the irritability and digestive disturbances observed in infants of highly stressed mothers after birth (Omer & Everly, 1988). Finally, women who experience long-term anxiety are more likely to smoke, drink, eat poorly, and engage in other behaviors that harm the embryo and fetus. These factors probably contribute to the negative outcomes observed in their babies (Istvan, 1986).

It is important to note that women under severe emotional stress do not always give birth to infants with problems. The risks are greatly reduced when mothers have husbands, other family members, and friends to whom they can turn for emotional support (Norbeck & Tilden, 1983). In one study of expectant women experiencing high life stress, those who reported having people on whom they could count for help had a pregnancy complication rate of only 33 percent, compared to 91 percent for those who had few or no social supports (Nuckolls, Cassel, & Kaplan, 1972). These results suggest that finding ways to provide isolated women with supportive social ties during pregnancy can help prevent prenatal complications.

*Rh Blood Incompatibility.* When inherited blood types of mother and fetus differ, in some instances the incompatibility can cause serious problems. The most common cause of these difficulties is a blood protein called the **Rh factor.** When the mother is Rh negative (lacks the protein) and the father is Rh positive (has the protein), the baby may inherit the father's Rh positive blood type. (Recall from Table 2.2 in Chapter 2 that Rh positive blood is dominant and Rh negative blood is recessive, so the chances are good that a baby will be Rh positive.) In most pregnancies, some maternal and fetal blood cells manage to cross the placenta during the third trimester or at the time of birth, usually in small enough amounts to be quite safe. But if even a little of a fetus's Rh positive blood passes into a mother's Rh negative bloodstream, she begins to form antibodies to the foreign Rh protein. If these enter the fetus's system, they destroy red blood cells, reducing the oxygen supply to the fetus. Miscarriage, mental retardation, damage to the heart muscle, and death around the time of birth can occur.

Since it takes time for the mother to produce Rh antibodies, first-born children are rarely affected. The danger increases with each additional pregnancy. Fortunately,

**Rh factor**
A protein that, when present in the fetus's blood but not in the mother's, can cause the mother to build up antibodies. If these return to the fetus's system, they destroy red blood cells, reducing the oxygen supply to organs and tissues.

the damaging effects of Rh incompatibility can be prevented in most cases. After the birth of each Rh positive baby, Rh negative mothers are routinely given a vaccine called RhoGam, which prevents the buildup of antibodies in the mother's system. However, sometimes errors are made in maternal blood typing, and the mother's production of antibodies is not controlled. In these cases, blood transfusions can be performed immediately after birth if the baby is in danger or, if necessary, even before the baby is born (Simkin, Whalley, & Keppler, 1984).

*Maternal Age.* Earlier we indicated that women who delay having children until they are in their thirties or forties face a greater risk of infertility, miscarriage, and giving birth to babies with chromosomal defects. Are other pregnancy problems more common for older mothers?

For many years, scientists thought that aging of the mother's reproductive organs increased the likelihood of a wide variety of pregnancy complications. Recently, this idea has been questioned. New studies reveal that once serious health problems are accounted for, even women in their forties do not experience more prenatal problems than do women in their twenties (Spellacy, Miller, & Winegar, 1986; Stein, 1983). As long as an older woman is in good health, she can carry a baby successfully.

In the case of teenage mothers, does physical immaturity cause prenatal difficulties? Again, research indicates that it does not. A teenager's body is large enough and strong enough to support pregnancy. In fact, as we will see in Chapter 14, young adolescent girls grow taller and heavier and their hips broaden (in preparation for childbearing) *before* their menstrual periods begin. Nature tries to ensure that once a girl can conceive, she is physically ready to carry and give birth to a baby. Infants of pregnant teenagers are born with a higher rate of problems for quite different reasons. Many do not have access to medical care or are afraid to seek it. In addition, most pregnant teenagers come from low-income backgrounds where stress, poor nutrition, and health problems are common (Mednick, Baker, & Sutton-Smith, 1979; Roosa, 1984).

*Previous Births.* When a mother has already had several children, does her uterus start to wear out, so that more problems are experienced by later-born babies? This is another commonly held belief that has not been supported by research. One large study of over 50,000 pregnancies showed no relationship between number of previous births and the overall rate of prenatal problems (Heinonen, Slone, & Shapiro, 1977).

A few birth defects are more likely to occur in later pregnancies, but a worn-out uterus is not the cause of them. Instead, health problems have built up in these mothers over time, usually from long-term exposure to a harmful environment. Maternal alcohol abuse is a good example. Only rarely do first-born children of alcoholic mothers show all the signs of fetal alcohol syndrome. The disorder is more likely to occur in later births. As each child is born, the complications of alcoholism (poor nutrition, anemia, and liver, kidney, and pancreatic disease) make things worse and worse for the embryo and fetus. Over time, some of these mothers become so dependent on alcohol that they eat little food and actually lose weight during later pregnancies. As a result, their later-born children feed on little else besides alcohol as well (Abel, 1988; Dorris, 1989).

## The Importance of Prenatal Health Care

Yolanda had her first prenatal appointment three weeks after her first missed menstrual period. After that, she visited the doctor's office once a month until she was seven months pregnant, then twice during the eighth month. As birth grew near,

Yolanda's appointments increased to once a week. The doctor kept track of Yolanda's general health, weight gain, and the capacity of her uterus and cervix to support the fetus. The fetus's growth was also carefully monitored. During these visits, Yolanda had plenty of opportunity to ask questions, pick up literature in the waiting room, get to know the person who would deliver her baby, and plan the kind of birth experience she and Jay desired.

Yolanda's pregnancy, like most others, was uneventful. But unexpected difficulties can arise, especially if mothers have health problems to begin with. For example, women with diabetes need careful monitoring during pregnancy. The presence of extra sugar in the diabetic mother's bloodstream causes the fetus to grow larger than average, although it is physically less mature than the fetus of a non-diabetic mother. As a result, problems at birth are common for both mother and infant. Another special risk of pregnancy is **toxemia** (sometimes called *eclampsia*). In the 5 to 10 percent of women who develop this illness in the last half of their pregnancies, blood pressure increases sharply and the face, hands, and feet swell. If untreated, serious harm can result, including convulsions in the mother and death of the fetus. Usually, toxemia can be brought under control through hospitalization, bed rest, and drugs to bring the blood pressure down. If not, the baby needs to be delivered at once (Samuels & Samuels, 1986).

Unfortunately, 5 percent of pregnant women in the United States wait until the end of pregnancy to seek prenatal care or never get any at all. Financial problems are a major barrier to early prenatal care. Most women who delay going to the doctor do not receive health insurance as a fringe benefit of their jobs. Others have no insurance because they are unemployed. Although the very poorest of these mothers are eligible for government-sponsored health services, a great many women who are low-income and in need of these health benefits do not qualify (Children's Defense Fund, 1990b).

In addition to financial hardship, there are other reasons that some mothers do not seek prenatal care. In a recent study, several hundred women who first came to a public health clinic during their last trimester were asked why they waited so long. A wide variety of personal problems were mentioned, including psychological stress, the demands of taking care of other young children, and family crises. The researchers also discovered that many of their subjects were engaging in high-risk behaviors, such as smoking or gaining too little weight (Young et al., 1989). These women who had no medical attention for most of their pregnancies were among those who needed it most! Clearly, public education about the importance of early prenatal care and medical services that reach all pregnant women, especially those who are young, single, and poor, are badly needed. Table 3.6 provides a summary of "dos and don'ts" for a healthy pregnancy, based on our discussion of the prenatal environment.

*BRIEF REVIEW* Teratogens—alcohol, cigarettes, certain drugs, environmental pollutants, and diseases—can seriously harm the embryo and fetus. The effects of teratogens are complex. They depend on amount and length of exposure, the genetic makeup of mother and baby, and the presence of other harmful environmental influences. Teratogens operate according to the critical period concept. In general, greatest damage occurs during the embryonic phase, when all parts of the body are being formed. Poor maternal nutrition, severe emotional stress, and Rh blood incompatibility can also endanger the prenatal organism. As long as they are in good health, teenagers, women in their thirties and forties, and women who have given birth to several children have a high likelihood of problem-free pregnancies. Regular medical checkups are important for all expectant mothers, and they are crucial for women with a history of health difficulties.

• *Why is it especially difficult to determine the effects of some environmental agents, such as over-the-counter drugs and pollution, on the embryo and fetus?*

• *Nora, who is expecting for the first time at age 40, wonders whether she is likely to have a difficult pregnancy because of her age. How would you respond to Nora's concern?*

• *Trixie has just learned that she is pregnant. Since she has always been healthy and feels good right now, she cannot understand why the doctor wants her to come in for checkups so often. Why is early and regular prenatal care important for Trixie?*

**Toxemia**

An illness of pregnancy in which the mother's blood pressure increases sharply and her face, hands, and feet swell. If untreated, can cause convulsions in the mother and death of the baby.

TABLE 3.6 • Do's and Don'ts for a Healthy Pregnancy

| Do | Don't |
|---|---|
| Do make sure that you have been vaccinated against infectious diseases dangerous to the embryo and fetus, such as rubella, before you get pregnant. Most vaccinations are not safe during pregnancy. | Don't take any drugs without consulting your doctor. |
| Do see a doctor as soon as you suspect that you are pregnant—within a few weeks after a missed menstrual period. | Don't smoke cigarettes. If you have already smoked during part of your pregnancy, you can protect your baby by cutting down or (better yet) quitting at any time. If other members of your family are smokers, ask them to smoke outside or in areas of the household that you can easily avoid. |
| Do continue to get regular medical check-ups throughout pregnancy. | |
| Do obtain literature from your doctor, local library, and bookstore about prenatal development and care. Ask questions about anything you do not understand. | Don't drink alcohol from the time you decide to get pregnant. If you find it difficult to give up alcohol, ask for help from your doctor, local family service agency, or nearest chapter of Alcoholics Anonymous. |
| Do eat a well-balanced diet. On the average, a woman should increase her intake by 300 calories a day over her usual needs—less at the beginning and more at the end of pregnancy. Gain 25 to 30 pounds gradually. | Don't engage in activities that might expose your baby to environmental hazards, such as radiation or chemical pollutants. If you work in an occupation that involves these agents, ask for a safer assignment or a leave of absence. |
| Do keep physically fit through mild daily exercise. If possible, join a special exercise class for expectant mothers. | Don't engage in activities that might expose your baby to harmful infectious diseases, such as childhood illnesses and toxoplasmosis. |
| Do avoid emotional stress. If you are a single parent, find a relative or friend whom you can count on for emotional support. | Don't choose pregnancy as a time to go on a diet. |
| Do get plenty of rest. An overtired mother is at risk for pregnancy complications. | Don't overeat and gain too much weight during pregnancy. A very large weight gain is associated with complications. |
| Do enroll in a prenatal and childbirth education class along with the baby's father. When parents know what to expect, the 9 months before birth can be one of the most joyful times of life. | |

## PREPARING FOR PARENTHOOD

We have discussed a great many ways that normal development can be thrown off course during the prenatal period. When we consider them together, it may seem surprising that any infants are born healthy and intact, but the vast majority are. Over 90 percent of pregnancies in the United States result in normal newborn babies. For most expectant parents, the prenatal period is not a time of medical hazard. Instead, it is a period of major life change accompanied by excitement, anticipation, and looking inward. The 9 months before birth not only permit the fetus to grow, but also give men and women time to develop a new sense of themselves as mothers and fathers. This period of psychological preparation is crucial. When asked, one-third of young Americans say they do not feel ready to deal with the demands and responsibilities of parenthood (Duncan & Markman, 1988). How effectively individuals construct a new parental identity during pregnancy has important consequences for the parent–infant relationship. A great many factors contribute to the personal adjustments that take place.

## Seeking Information

We know most about how mothers adapt to the psychological challenges of pregnancy, although some evidence suggests that fathers use many of the same techniques (Colman & Colman, 1991). One common strategy is to seek information, as Yolanda and Jay did when they got books on pregnancy and childbirth and enrolled in my class. In fact, expectant mothers regard books as an extremely valuable source of information, rating them as second in importance only to their doctors. And the more a pregnant woman seeks information—by reading or in other ways, such as asking friends, consulting her own mother, or attending a prenatal class—the more confident she tends to feel about her own ability to be a good mother (Deutsch et al., 1988).

Why does information seeking promote adjustment during pregnancy? First, when people gather information about an unfamiliar event, it often becomes less threatening. Second, pregnant women who learn a great deal about what they are about to experience start to imagine themselves engaging in the activities of motherhood. For example, when they read about breast-feeding, they see themselves nursing their own baby. Expectant mothers who imagine themselves as competent caregivers make better adjustments after birth and report greater satisfaction in caring for their babies (Deutsch et al., 1986; Leifer, 1980).

## The Baby Becomes a Reality

At the beginning of pregnancy, the baby seems far off in the future. Except for a missed period and some morning sickness (nausea that most women experience during the first trimester), the woman's body has not changed much. But gradually, her abdomen enlarges, and the baby starts to become more of a reality. A major turning point occurs when expectant parents are presented with concrete proof that a fetus is, indeed, developing inside the uterus. For Yolanda and Jay, this happened 13 weeks into the pregnancy. Jay went with Yolanda to the doctor, who showed them an image of the fetus using ultrasound. As Jay described this experience, "We saw it, these little hands and feet waving and kicking. It had the cord and everything. It's really a baby in there!" Sensing the fetus's movements for the first time can be just as thrilling. Of course, the mother feels these "kicks" first, but soon after the father (and any siblings) can participate by touching her abdomen.

Mothers start to get to know the child as an individual through these first signs of life. From the vigor of its movements and its daily cycles of activity and rest, the fetus takes on the beginnings of a personality. Both parents start to dream of a relationship with the baby, to talk about names, and to make plans to welcome the newcomer into their lives.

## Models of Effective Parenthood

As pregnancy proceeds, expectant parents think about important models of parenthood in their own lives—for the woman, her mother, and for the man, his father. Research indicates that when women have had good relationships with their own mothers, they are more likely to develop positive images of themselves as mothers during pregnancy (Deutsch et al., 1988).

If their own parental relationships are mixed or negative, expectant mothers and fathers may have trouble building a healthy picture of themselves as parents. Some adults handle this problem constructively, by seeking out other examples of effective parenthood. One father named Roger shared these thoughts with his wife and several expectant couples who met regularly with a counselor to talk about their concerns during pregnancy:

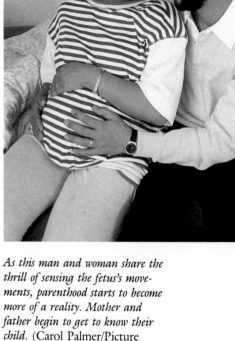

*As this man and woman share the thrill of sensing the fetus's movements, parenthood starts to become more of a reality. Mother and father begin to get to know their child. (Carol Palmer/Picture Cube)*

I rethink past experiences with my father and my family and am aware of how I was raised. I just think I don't want to do that again, I want to change that; I don't want to be like my father in that way. I wish there had been more connection and closeness and a lot more respect for who I was. For me, my father-in-law combines spontaneity, sincerity, and warmth. He is a mix of empathy and warmth plus stepping back and being objective that I want to be as a father. (Colman & Colman, 1991, p. 148)

A warm, secure relationship with their own parents is helpful to adults in developing an optimistic view of themselves as parents, but it is not a necessity. Like Roger, many people come to terms with negative experiences in their own childhoods, recognize that other options are available to them as parents, and build healthier and happier relationships with their children (Main, Kaplan, & Cassidy, 1985). Roger achieved this understanding after he participated in a special intervention program designed to help expectant mothers and fathers prepare for parenthood. Couples who take part in such programs feel better about themselves and their marital relationships, regard the demands of caring for the new baby as less stressful, and adapt more easily when family problems arise (Duncan & Markman, 1988).

### Practical Concerns

When women first learn that they are pregnant, they often wonder how long they will be able to continue many of their usual activities. Culture has a major impact on answers to this question. In the United States, women in good health often work and travel until the very end of their pregnancies, without any apparent harm to the fetus. And as long as the pregnancy has gone well, American doctors advise that sexual intercourse can be continued through most or all of the 9 months before birth (Mills, Harlap, & Harley, 1981; Samuels & Samuels, 1986).

In contrast, when a Japanese woman learns that she is pregnant, she changes her daily life considerably, out of a belief that this is necessary to protect the health of the infant. Nancy Engel (1989), an American nurse, described her experience of becoming pregnant for the first time while living in Japan:

> When I announced my pregnancy it was assumed that I would quit my teaching position and drop out of language school. My teacher told me that language study was stressful, and the increased [hormone levels] it caused were harmful to the baby. Similarly, I was advised that the noise of train travel, typing, or using a sewing machine should be avoided. My colleagues at college . . . were particularly concerned when I revealed plans to go to Thailand on vacation during the fourth month. They told me that airplane travel would cause miscarriage, and they cited numerous examples. . . . My doctor assumed that I would not engage in sexual activity, to ensure a healthy newborn. (p. 83)

As the seventh or eighth month of pregnancy approaches, the Japanese woman returns to her mother's home, where she rests until birth and recuperates for several months after the baby is born.

Although Engel could not accept these practices for herself, she realized that they were based on cultural values that hold the maternal role in high esteem and place the safety of the infant first. This investment in the child's well-being makes Japan an excellent place to have a baby. It has the lowest rate of pregnancy and birth complications in the world (Grant, 1990).

### The Marital Relationship

The most important preparation for parenthood takes place in the context of the marital relationship. Couples who are unhappy in their marriages during pregnancy continue to be dissatisfied after the baby is born (Belsky, Spanier, & Rovine, 1983; Cowan et al., 1985). Deciding to have a baby in hopes of improving a troubled marriage is a serious mistake. There is good evidence that pregnancy adds to rather than subtracts from family conflict if a marriage is in danger of falling apart (Snowden et al., 1988).

When a couple's relationship is faring well and both partners want and plan for the baby, the excitement of a first pregnancy may bring husband and wife closer together. At the same time, pregnancy does change a marriage. Expectant parents do not just add parenting to their existing responsibilities. They must adjust their established roles to make room for children. Women start to plan how they will juggle the demands of work and child rearing. Men reconsider the adequacy of their jobs and the size of the family bank account. In addition, each partner is likely to develop new expectations of the other. Women look for greater demonstrations of affection, interest in the pregnancy, and help with household chores from their husbands. They see these behaviors as important signs of the husband's continued acceptance of his wife, the pregnancy, and the baby to come (Richardson, 1983). Similarly, men are particularly sensitive to expressions of warmth from their pregnant wives. These reassure the husband that he will continue to occupy a central place in the new mother's emotional life after the baby is born (Fedele et al., 1988).

When a marriage rests on a solid foundation of love and respect, parents are well equipped to master the challenges of pregnancy. And, as we will see in the next chapter, they are also better able to adjust to the much more demanding changes that will take place in the family as soon as the baby is born.

# SUMMARY

### Motivations for Parenthood

• Today, couples in Western industrialized nations are more likely to weigh the pros and cons of becoming parents before deciding to have children than they were a generation or two ago. Parents are also having smaller families, a trend that has positive consequences for children's development.

• When couples limit their families to just one child, their youngsters are just as socially well adjusted as children who grow up with siblings. Many adults are waiting until later in their own lives to have children, when their careers are well established and they are emotionally more mature.

### Prenatal Development

• Prenatal development is usually divided into three phases. The period of the zygote lasts two weeks, from conception until the **blastocyst** is deeply **implanted** in the uterine lining. During this time, structures that will support prenatal growth begin to form. The **embryonic disk** is surrounded by the **amnion**, which is filled with **amniotic fluid.** From the **chorion,** villi emerge that burrow into the uterine wall, and the **placenta** starts to develop. The developing organism is connected to the placenta by the **umbilical cord.**

• The period of the **embryo** lasts from two to eight weeks, during which the foundations for all body structures are laid down. In the first week of this period, the **neural tube** forms, and the nervous system starts to develop. Other organs follow and also grow rapidly. At the end of this phase, the embryo responds to touch and can move.

• The period of the **fetus,** lasting until the end of pregnancy, involves a dramatic increase in body size and completion of physical structures. It is the longest prenatal phase and includes the second and third **trimesters.** By the middle of the second trimester, the mother can feel movement. The fetus becomes covered with **vernix,** which protects the skin from chapping. White downy hair called **lanugo** helps the vernix stick to the skin. At the end of the second trimester, the production of neurons in the brain is complete.

• The **age of viability** is achieved at the beginning of the final trimester, between 22 and 26 weeks. The brain continues to develop rapidly, and new sensory and behavioral capacities emerge. Gradually the lungs mature, the fetus fills the uterus, and birth is near.

### Prenatal Environmental Influences

• **Teratogens** are environmental agents that cause damage during the prenatal period. Their effects conform to the **critical period** concept. The developing organism is especially sensitive during the embryonic period, since all essential body structures are rapidly emerging. However, the impact of teratogens often differs from one case to the next, due to amount and length of exposure, the genetic makeup of mother and fetus, and the presence or absence of other harmful agents. The effects of teratogens are not limited to immediate physical damage. Serious psychological consequences may appear later in development. Some are indirectly caused by physical defects through bidirectional exchanges between child and environment.

• Drugs, alcohol, smoking, hormones, radiation, environmental pollution, and infectious diseases are teratogens that can endanger the prenatal organism. **Thalidomide,** a sedative used in the early 1960s, showed without a doubt that drugs could cross the placenta and cause serious physical damage. Babies whose mothers took heroin, methadone, or cocaine during pregnancy have withdrawal symptoms after birth and are jittery and inattentive. Cocaine is especially dangerous, since it is associated with physical defects and brain damage.

• Infants of parents who smoke are often born underweight and may display inattentiveness and learning problems in childhood. When mothers consume alcohol in large quantities, **fetal alcohol syndrome (FAS),** a disorder involving mental retardation, poor attention, overactivity, slow physical growth, and facial abnormalities, often results. Smaller amounts of alcohol may lead to some of these problems—a condition known as **fetal alcohol effects (FAE).**

• A hormone called **diethylstilbestrol (DES)** has a delayed impact on the child, increasing the chances of genital tract abnormalities and cancer of the vagina and testes in adolescence and young adulthood. Radiation, mercury, and lead can result in a wide variety of problems, including physical malformations and severe brain damage. PCBs have been linked to decreased responsiveness to the environment and memory difficulties during infancy and poorer memory and verbal intelligence in early childhood.

• Many diseases can harm the embryo and fetus. **Rubella** causes a wide variety of abnormalities, which vary with its time of occurrence during pregnancy. **Toxoplasmosis** in the first trimester may lead to eye and brain damage. **Acquired immune deficiency syndrome (AIDS)** can be transmitted prenatally and is linked to physical defects, delayed development, and early death.

• Other maternal factors can either support or complicate prenatal development. Mild, regular exercise contributes to an expectant woman's general health and readiness for childbirth. When the mother's diet is inadequate, low birth weight and brain damage are major concerns, especially if malnutrition occurs during the last three months of pregnancy.

• Emotional stress, when severe, is associated with many pregnancy complications, although its impact can be reduced by providing the mother with emotional support. If the **Rh factor** of the mother's blood is negative and the fetus's is positive, special precautions must be taken to ensure that antibodies to the Rh protein do not pass from mother to fetus.

• Maternal age and number of previous births were once thought to be major causes of pregnancy complications. Aside from the risk of chromosomal abnormalities in older women, this is not the case. Instead, poor health and environmental risks associated with poverty are the strongest predictors of pregnancy problems.

• Early and regular prenatal health care is important for all pregnant women. Unexpected difficulties can arise during pregnancy, such as **toxemia.** Prenatal care is especially critical for mothers unlikely to seek it—in particular, those who are young, single, and poor.

### Preparing for Parenthood

• Pregnancy is an important period of psychological transition. Mothers and fathers prepare for their new role by seeking information from books and other sources and becoming acquainted with the movements and daily cycles of the fetus. They also rely on effective models of parenthood as they build images of themselves as mothers and fathers.

• The most important preparation for parenthood takes place in the context of the marital relationship. During the nine months preceding birth, parents adjust their various roles and expectations of one another as they prepare to welcome the baby into the family.

## IMPORTANT TERMS AND CONCEPTS

blastocyst (p. 95)

embryonic disk (p. 95)

implantation (p. 95)

amnion (p. 95)

amniotic fluid (p. 96)

chorion (p. 96)

placenta (p. 97)

umbilical cord (p. 97)

embryo (p. 97)

neural tube (p. 99)

fetus (p. 99)

trimesters (p. 100)

vernix (p. 100)

lanugo (p. 100)

age of viability (p. 101)

teratogen (p. 103)

critical period (p. 103)

thalidomide (p. 105)

fetal alcohol syndrome (FAS) (p. 108)

fetal alcohol effects (FAE) (p. 108)

diethylstilbestrol (DES) (p. 109)

rubella (p. 110)

toxoplasmosis (p. 111)

acquired immune deficiency syndrome (AIDS) (p. 111)

Rh factor (p. 115)

toxemia (p. 117)

# FOR FURTHER INFORMATION AND SPECIAL HELP

**Prenatal Health**

National Center for Education in Maternal and Child Health
38th and R Streets, N.W.
Washington, DC 20057
(202) 625-8400

Government-sponsored agency that provides information on all aspects of maternal and child health.

**Alcohol Abuse**

National Clearinghouse for Alcohol and Drug Information
P.O. Box 2345
Rockville, MD 20852
(301) 468-2600

Government-sponsored agency that provides information on all aspects of alcohol and drug abuse.

Alcoholics Anonymous
P.O. Box 459
Grand Central Station
New York, NY 10163
(212) 686-1100

An international organization aimed at helping people recover from alcoholism. Local chapters exist in many countries.

National Council on Alcoholism
12 West 21st Street
New York, NY 10010
(212) 206-6770

Works for prevention and control of alcoholism by providing information on the problem.

**Birth Defects**

National Easter Seal Society for Crippled Children and Adults
70 E. Lake Street
Chicago, IL 60601
(312) 726-6200

Provides information on birth defects. Works with other agencies to help the disabled.

National Information Center for Children and Youth with Handicaps
P.O. Box 1492
Washington, DC 20013
(703) 893-6061

Provides information to parents and educators on services for children with handicaps.

March of Dimes Birth Defects Foundation
1275 Mamaroneck Avenue
White Plains, NY 10605
(914) 428-7100

Works to prevent birth defects through public education and community service programs.

Parents Helping Parents
535 Race Street, Suite 220
San Jose, CA 95126
(408) 288-5010

Offers a wide variety of services and educational programs to help parents raise children with special needs, including those with birth defects.

**DES**

DES Action U.S.A.
Long Island Jewish Medical Center
New Hyde Park, NY 11040
(516) 775-3450

Attempts to reach DES-exposed individuals. Offers support, counseling, and medical referral.

**AIDS**

National AIDS Information Clearinghouse
P.O. Box 6003
Rockville, MD 20850
(301) 217-0023

Government-sponsored agency that provides information about AIDS and AIDS-related services.

"Mexican Mother," Cyntia Arrieta Rodriguez, 11 years,
Mexico. Reprinted by permission from The International
Museum of Children's Art, Oslo, Norway.

# Birth and the Newborn Baby

# 4

The Stages of Childbirth
  *Stage 1: Dilation and Effacement of the Cervix   Stage 2: Delivery of the Baby   Stage 3: Birth of the Placenta   The Baby's Adaptation to Labor and Delivery   The Newborn Baby's Appearance   Assessing the Newborn's Physical Condition: The Apgar Scale*

Approaches to Childbirth
  *Natural or Prepared Childbirth   Home Delivery*

Medical Interventions
  *Fetal Monitoring   Labor and Delivery Medication   Instrument Delivery   Induced Labor   Cesarean Delivery*

Birth Complications
  *Oxygen Deprivation   Preterm and Low Birth Weight Infants   Postterm Infants   Understanding Birth Complications*

Precious Moments After Birth

The Newborn Baby's Capacities
  *Newborn Reflexes   Sensory Capacities   Newborn States   Neonatal Behavioral Assessment*

The Transition to Parenthood

A lthough Yolanda and Jay completed my course three months before their baby was born, both agreed to return the following spring to share their reactions to birth and new parenthood with my next class of students. When the long-awaited day arrived, little Joshua, who was 2 weeks old at the time, came along as well. The story that Yolanda and Jay told truly revealed that the birth of a baby is one of the most dramatic and emotional events in human experience. Jay was present throughout Yolanda's labor and delivery. Yolanda explained:

> By morning, we knew that I was in labor. It was Thursday, so we went in for my usual weekly appointment. The doctor said, yes, the baby was on the way, but it would be a while. He told us to go home and relax or take a leisurely walk and come to the hospital in three or four hours. We checked in at three in the afternoon; Joshua arrived at two o'clock the next morning. When, finally, I was ready to deliver, it went quickly; a half hour or so and some good hard pushes, and there he was! His body had stuff all over it, his face was red and puffy, and his head was misshapen, but I thought, "Oh! he's beautiful. I can't believe he's really here!"

Jay was also elated by Joshua's birth. "I wanted to support Yolanda and to experience as much as I could experience. It was awesome, indescribable," he said, holding little Joshua over his shoulder and patting and kissing him gently. "For me, it meant everything to be there."

In this chapter, we explore the experience of childbirth, from both the parents' and the baby's point of view. A generation ago when Yolanda and Jay were born, the birth process was treated more like an illness than a natural and normal part of life. Yolanda's mother remembers being left alone in a small room during most of the long hours of labor. She knew little about what was happening, was frightened by the powerful contractions of her uterus, and felt lonely and helpless. Fortunately, childbirth is rarely like this today. Women in industrialized nations have many more choices about where and how they give birth than at any time in the past, and modern hospitals often go to great lengths to make the arrival of a new baby a rewarding, family-centered event.

Joshua reaped the benefits of Yolanda and Jay's careful attention to his needs during pregnancy. He was strong, alert, and healthy at birth. Nevertheless, as we saw in Chapter 3, some mothers are at serious risk for birth complications, and even when they are not, the birth process does not always go smoothly. We will pay special attention to the problems of infants who are born underweight or arrive too early, before the prenatal period is complete. Our discussion will also examine the pros and cons of medical interventions, such as pain-relieving drugs and surgical deliveries, designed to ease a difficult birth and protect the health of mother and baby.

Finally, Yolanda and Jay spoke candidly about how, since Joshua's arrival, life at home had changed. "It's exciting and wonderful," reflected Yolanda, "but the adjustments are enormous. I wasn't quite prepared for the intensity of Joshua's 24-hour-a-day demands." In the last part of this chapter, we take a close look at the remarkable ability of newborn babies to adapt to the external world and to communicate their needs. We also consider how parents adjust to the realities of everyday life with a new baby.

## THE STAGES OF CHILDBIRTH

It is not surprising that childbirth is often referred to as labor. It is the hardest physical work that a woman may ever do. A complex series of hormonal changes initiates the process. Yolanda's whole system, which for nine months supported and protected Joshua's growth, now turned toward a new goal: getting him safely out of the uterus.

The events that lead to childbirth begin slowly in the ninth month of pregnancy and gradually pick up speed. Several signs indicate that labor is near. First, Yolanda felt the upper part of her uterus contract every once in a while. These contractions are often called *false labor* or *prelabor*, since they remain brief and unpredictable for several weeks. Second, about two weeks before birth, an event called *lightening* occurred; Joshua's head dropped down low into the uterus. The reason was that Yolanda's cervix had begun to soften, thin, and open in preparation for delivery. As a result, it no longer supported Joshua's weight so easily. Finally, a fairly sure sign that labor is only hours or days away is the *bloody show*. As the cervix widens more, the plug of mucous that sealed it during pregnancy is released, producing a reddish discharge (Samuels & Samuels, 1986). Soon after this happens, contractions of the uterus become more frequent, and mother and baby have entered the first of three stages of labor (see Figure 4.1)

### Stage 1: Dilation and Effacement of the Cervix

**Dilation and effacement of the cervix**

Widening and thinning of the cervix during the first stage of labor.

This is the longest stage of labor, lasting, on the average, 12 to 14 hours with a first baby and 4 to 6 hours with later births. **Dilation and effacement of the cervix** take place—that is, the cervix widens and thins to nothing. As a result, a clear channel from the uterus into the birth canal, or vagina, is formed. Uterine contractions that open the cervix are forceful and regular, starting out 10 to 20 minutes apart and lasting about 15 to 20 seconds. Gradually, they get closer together, occurring every

**FIGURE 4.1** • The three stages of labor. Stage 1: (A) Contractions of the uterus cause dilation and effacement of the cervix. (B) Transition is reached when the frequency and strength of the contractions are at their peak and the cervix opens completely. Stage 2: (C) The mother pushes with each contraction, forcing the baby down the birth canal, and the head appears. (D) Near the end of Stage 2, the shoulders emerge and are followed quickly by the rest of the baby's body. Stage 3: (E) With a few final pushes, the placenta is delivered.

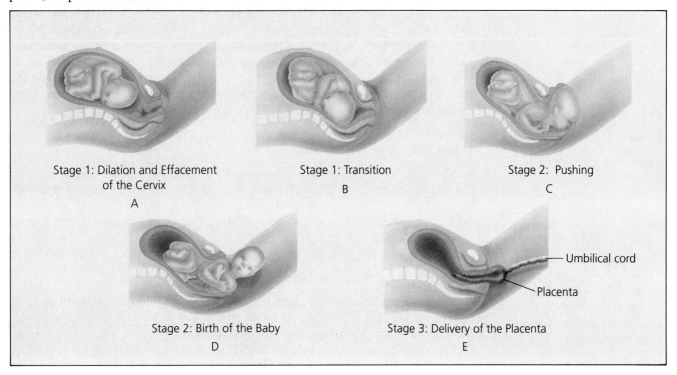

Stage 1: Dilation and Effacement of the Cervix
A

Stage 1: Transition
B

Stage 2: Pushing
C

Stage 2: Birth of the Baby
D

Stage 3: Delivery of the Placenta
E

Umbilical cord

Placenta

2 to 3 minutes. In addition, they are more powerful, continuing for as long as 60 seconds.

During this stage, there was nothing Yolanda could do to speed up the process. She was urged to relax; Jay held her hand, provided sips of juice and water, and helped her get comfortable. Throughout the first few hours, Yolanda walked, stood, or sat upright. As the contractions became more intense, she leaned against pillows or lay on her side.

The climax of the first stage of labor is a brief period called **transition,** in which the frequency and strength of contractions are at their peak and the cervix opens completely. Although transition is the most uncomfortable part of childbirth, it is especially important that the mother try to relax during this time. If she tenses or bears down with her muscles before the cervix is completely dilated and effaced, she is likely to bruise the cervix and slow down the progress of labor.

## Stage 2: Delivery of the Baby

Once the cervix is fully open, the infant is ready to be born. This second stage is much shorter than the first. It lasts about 50 minutes for a first baby and 20 minutes in later births. Strong contractions of the uterus continue, but they do not do the entire job. The most important factor is a natural urge that the mother feels to squeeze and push with her abdominal muscles. As she does so with each contraction, she forces the baby down and out.

**Transition**

Climax of the first stage of labor, in which the frequency and strength of contractions are at their peak and the cervix opens completely.

Yolanda dosed lightly between contractions. As each new wave came, "I pushed with all my might," she said. In the meantime, the doctor performed an **episiotomy,** or small incision that increases the size of the vaginal opening, permitting the baby to pass without tearing the mother's tissues. When the doctor announced that the baby's head was *crowning*—the vaginal opening had stretched around the entire head—Yolanda felt a sense of renewed energy; she knew that soon the baby would arrive. Quickly, with several more pushes, Joshua's forehead, nose, and chin emerged, then his upper body and trunk. The doctor held him up, wet with amniotic fluid and still attached to the umbilical cord. Air rushed into his lungs, and Joshua cried. When the umbilical cord stopped pulsing, it was clamped and cut. Joshua was placed on Yolanda's chest, where she and Jay could see, touch, and gently talk to him. Then he was wrapped snugly to help with temperature regulation.

### Stage 3: Birth of the Placenta

Labor comes to an end with a few final contractions and pushes. These cause the placenta to separate from the wall of the uterus and be delivered, a stage that usually lasts about 5 to 10 minutes. Yolanda and Jay were surprised at the large size of the thick 1 1/2-pound red-gray organ that had taken care of Joshua's basic needs for the previous 9 months.

### The Baby's Adaptation to Labor and Delivery

In the preceding sections, we described the events of childbirth from the outside looking in. Let's consider, for a moment, what the experience might be like for the baby. Joshua, after being squeezed and pushed for many hours, was forced to leave the warm, protective inner world of Yolanda's uterus for a cold, brightly lit external world. The strong contractions exposed his head to a great deal of pressure, and they squeezed the placenta and the umbilical cord repeatedly. Each time, Joshua's supply of oxygen was temporarily reduced.

At first glance, these events may strike you as a dangerous ordeal. Fortunately, healthy babies are well equipped to deal with the trauma of childbirth. As labor gets underway, the force of the contractions causes the infant to produce high levels of stress hormones. Recall from Chapter 3 that during pregnancy, the effects of maternal stress can endanger the baby. In contrast, during childbirth the infant's production of stress hormones is positive and adaptive. Stress hormones help the baby withstand oxygen deprivation by sending a rich supply of blood to the brain and heart. In addition, they prepare the baby to breathe effectively by causing the lungs to absorb excess liquid and expanding the bronchial tubes (passages leading to the lungs). Finally, stress hormones arouse the infant into alertness at birth. Joshua was born wide awake, ready to interact with the surrounding world (Emory & Toomey, 1988; Lagercrantz & Slotkin, 1986).

### The Newborn Baby's Appearance

What do babies look like after birth? My students asked Yolanda and Jay this question. "Come to think of it," Jay smiled, "Yolanda and I are probably the only people in the world who thought Joshua was beautiful!" The average newborn is 20 inches long and 7 1/2 pounds in weight; boys tend to be slightly longer and heavier than girls. Body proportions contribute to the baby's strange appearance. The head is very large in comparison to the trunk and legs, which are short and bowed. In fact, if your head were as large as that of a newborn infant, you would be balancing something about the size of a watermelon between your shoulders! As we will see in later chapters, the combination of a big head (with its well-developed brain) and a small

**Episiotomy**
A small incision made during childbirth to increase the size of the vaginal opening.

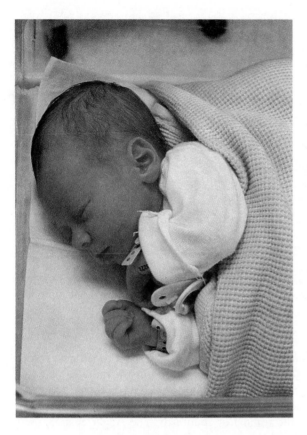

*Moments after birth, this baby, delivered in a modern American hospital, is wrapped snugly to help with temperature regulation. His head is molded from the pressure of moving down the birth canal. Although most observers would not describe newborn infants as beautiful, their pinkish glow, round face, chubby cheeks, and large forehead are characteristics that make adults feel like cuddling them. (Joseph Nettis/ Photo Researchers)*

body means that human infants learn quickly in the first few weeks and months of life. But unlike most mammals, they cannot get around on their own until much later, during the second half of the first year.

Even though newborn babies may not match the idealized image many parents created in their minds during pregnancy, some features do make them attractive. Their round faces, chubby cheeks, large foreheads, and big eyes are just those characteristics that make adults feel like picking them up and cuddling them (Berman, 1980; Lorenz, 1943). The skin is also soft and smooth, although temporary rashes may appear on the face that result from hormonal changes or plugged skin ducts. These clear up without treatment.

### Assessing the Newborn's Physical Condition: The Apgar Scale

Infants who have difficulty making the transition to life outside the uterus must be given special help at once. To quickly assess the infant's physical condition, doctors and nurses use the **Apgar Scale.** As shown in Table 4.1, a rating from 0 to 2 on each of five characteristics is made at 1 and 5 minutes after birth. An Apgar score of 7 or better indicates that the infant is in good physical condition. If the score is between 4 and 6, the baby requires special help in establishing breathing and other vital signs. If the score is 3 or below, the infant is in serious danger, and emergency medical attention is needed. Two Apgar ratings are given, since some babies have trouble adjusting at first but are doing quite well after a few minutes (Apgar, 1953).

After looking at Table 4.1, you may be wondering how infants like Joshua, who are black or are members of other dark-skinned races, can be rated on color, the last of the five Apgar signs. Color is the least dependable of the Apgar ratings. The skin tone of nonwhite babies cannot be judged easily for pinkness and blueness. However,

**Apgar Scale**
A rating used to assess the newborn baby's physical condition immediately after birth.

TABLE 4.1 · The Apgar Scale

| Sign | Score | | |
|---|---|---|---|
| | 0 | 1 | 2 |
| Heart rate | No heartbeat | Under 100 beats per minute | 100 to 140 beats per minute |
| Respiratory effort | No breathing for 60 seconds | Irregular, shallow breathing | Strong breathing and crying |
| Reflex irritability (sneezing, coughing, and grimacing) | No response | Weak reflexive response | Strong reflexive response |
| Muscle tone | Completely limp | Weak movements of arms and legs | Strong movements of arms and legs |
| Color | Blue body, arms, and legs | Body pink with blue arms and legs | Body, arms, and legs completely pink |

*Source:* Apgar, 1953.

infants of all races can be rated for a rosy glow that results from the flow of oxygen through body tissues once the baby starts to breathe, since skin tone is usually lighter at birth than the baby's inherited pigmentation.

• *What factors on both the mother's and baby's side help the newborn infant withstand the trauma of labor and delivery?*

**BRIEF REVIEW**   The hard work of labor takes place in three stages. In the first and longest stage, the cervix dilates and effaces to permit the baby to pass out of the uterus. In the second stage, the mother assists by pushing with each contraction, and the baby is born. In the third stage, the placenta is delivered. Stress hormones help the infant withstand the trauma of childbirth. The Apgar Scale is used to provide a quick rating of the baby's physical condition immediately after birth.

## APPROACHES TO CHILDBIRTH

Childbirth practices, like other aspects of family life, are molded by the society of which mother and baby are a part. The extent to which birth is affected by culture is brought into bold relief when we look at the very different approaches to childbirth around the world (see Box 4.1). Even in large Western nations, childbirth has changed dramatically over the centuries.

Before the 1800s, birth usually took place at home and was a family-centered event. Relatives, friends, and children were often present. As a result, when young people had children of their own, they knew just what to expect and were supported by other family members. The nineteenth-century industrial revolution brought greater crowding to cities along with new health problems. Childbirth moved from home to hospital, where the health of mothers and babies could be protected. Once the responsibility for childbirth was placed in the hands of doctors, women's knowledge about it was reduced, and relatives and friends were no longer welcome to participate (Lindell, 1988).

By the 1950s and 1960s, women started to question the medical procedures that came to be used routinely during labor and delivery. Many felt that frequent use of strong drugs and delivery instruments had robbed them of a precious experience and were often not necessary or safe for the baby. Gradually, a new natural childbirth movement arose in Europe and spread to the United States. Its purpose was to make hospital birth as comfortable and rewarding for mothers as possible. Today, many hospitals carry this theme further by offering birth centers that are family-centered in approach and homelike in appearance. *Free-standing birth centers,* which operate

## CULTURAL INFLUENCES

### Box 4.1  *Childbirth Practices Around the World*

*I*n cultures everywhere, birth is regarded as a special event, often magical and mysterious and cause for celebration. When we look at how tribal and village societies handle childbirth, we become aware of the wide range of ways in which babies can be ushered into the world.

Cultures vary greatly in whether they consider birth to be an illness or a natural body function. Among the Cuna Indians of Panama, childbirth is regarded as so abnormal that the pregnant mother visits the medicine man daily for drugs to help her. Throughout labor, she is constantly medicated. Cuna children are kept ignorant about the facts of life as long as possible. They are told that babies miraculously appear in the forest between deers' horns or are put on the beach by dolphins.

In contrast, the Jarara of South America and the Pukapukans of the Pacific Islands treat birth as a normal part of life. The Jarara mother gives birth in a passageway or shelter in full view of the entire community, including small children. The Pukapukan girl is so familiar with the events of labor and delivery that she can frequently be seen playing at it. Using a coconut to represent the baby, she stuffs it inside her dress, imitates the mother's pushing, and lets the nut fall at the proper moment.

In most cultures, women are assisted during childbirth, usually by two or more helpers. The type of support given varies, but in many cases, the mother is physically held from behind. Among the Mayans of the Yucatan, she is propped up by the body and arms of a woman called the "head helper," who sits in back. The helper supports the mother's weight and pushes and breathes with her during each contraction.

The majority of cultures have the mother give birth in a vertical position—sometimes on the knees, at other times, sitting, squatting, or standing. The Siriono of South America are an exception. The mother lies in a hammock slung low to the ground. A crowd of women keeps her company, standing by or sitting in nearby hammocks. Unlike the Mayan helpers, these women do not actively take part. The mother delivers the baby herself, and the infant, once born, is allowed to slide off the hammock onto the soft earth below. The mild jolt of falling a few inches is enough to stimulate the baby's first breath.

*Among the !Kung of Botswana, Africa, a mother gives birth in a sitting position, and she is surrounded by women who encourage and help her.* (Shostak/Anthro-Photo)

Sensory and physical stimulation is often provided during labor. The Laotians of Indochina and the Navaho of North America play special music for the mother. The Punjab of India rub melted butter across the mother's abdomen. Among the Comanche, warmed rocks are placed on the mother's back. The Tübatulabel Indians of California dig a trench, in which they build a fire. The trench is covered with slabs of stone, layers of earth, and mats. There, the mother lies down and gives birth.

When expectant mothers in our own culture know something about the great variety of birth practices around the world, they become more aware of their own alternatives. As a result, they may be more likely to explore childbirth options and choose ones that best fit with their own life circumstances and personal needs.

*Sources:* Jordan, 1980; Mead & Newton, 1967.

independently of hospitals and offer less in the way of back-up medical care, also exist. And a small but growing number of American women are rejecting institutional birth entirely by choosing to have their babies at home.

As indicated in Table 4.2, each of these places of childbirth—hospital delivery room, birth center, and home—has advantages and disadvantages that an expectant mother should consider before deciding where to have her baby. In the following sections, we take a closer look at two childbirth approaches that have grown in popularity in recent years: natural childbirth and home delivery.

## Natural or Prepared Childbirth

Yolanda chose **natural or prepared childbirth** as the way she wanted to have her baby. Although there are a great many natural childbirth techniques, all of them try to rid mothers of the idea that birth is a painful ordeal that requires extensive medical intervention. Most programs draw on methods developed by Grantly Dick-Read (1959) in England and Ferdinand Lamaze (1958) in France. These physicians emphasized that cultural attitudes had taught women to fear childbirth. An anxious, frightened woman in labor tenses muscles throughout her body, including those in the uterus. This turns the mild pain that sometimes accompanies strong contractions into a great deal of pain.

Yolanda and Jay enrolled in a typical natural childbirth program that was offered by a hospital birth center. The program consisted of three parts:

1. *Classes*. Yolanda and Jay attended a series of classes in which they learned about the anatomy and physiology of labor and delivery. Natural childbirth classes are based on the idea that knowledge about the birth process reduces a mother's fear.

2. *Relaxation and breathing techniques*. After each lecture, Yolanda was taught relaxation and breathing exercises aimed at counteracting any pain she might feel during uterine contractions. She also practiced creating pleasant visual images in her mind instead of thinking about the pain of childbirth.

3. *Labor coach*. While Yolanda mastered breathing and visualization techniques, Jay was taught to be a "labor coach." He learned how he could help Yolanda during childbirth—by reminding her to relax and breathe, massaging her back, supporting her body during labor and delivery, and offering words of encouragement and affection.

When natural childbirth is combined with delivery in a birth center or at home, mothers often give birth in an upright position rather than lying flat on their backs with their feet in stirrups (which is the traditional hospital delivery room practice). Doctors have become increasingly aware that gravity can speed up the second stage of labor. When mothers are upright, labor is shortened because pushing is easier and more effective. Also, the baby benefits because blood flow to the placenta is increased (Barnett, 1982). In Europe, women are typically encouraged to give birth on their sides rather than on their backs, the position most often used in United States. The side-lying position reduces the need for an episiotomy, since pressure of the baby's head against the vaginal opening is less intense (Bobak, Jensen, & Zalar, 1989).

Research comparing mothers who experience natural childbirth with those who do not suggests that there are many benefits. Mothers' attitudes toward labor and delivery are more positive, and they feel less pain (Lindell, 1988). As a result, they require less medication—usually very little or none at all (Hetherington, 1990). A study carried out in Guatemala suggests that social support may be an important part of the success of natural childbirth techniques. In a hospital in which patients were

**Natural or prepared childbirth**

An approach designed to reduce pain and medical intervention and to make childbirth a rewarding experience for parents.

TABLE 4.2 • Advantages and Disadvantages of Different Places of Birth

| Advantages | Disadvantages |
|---|---|
| **Hospital Delivery Room** | |
| Staffed by well-trained doctors and nurses | Greatest likelihood that routine medical procedures will be used, such as fetal monitoring and pain-relieving drugs |
| Emergency medical equipment and surgical procedures available | |
| Equipped to handle patients with high-risk pregnancies | Mother has least control over environment and must follow more rules |
| Intensive care for premature and ill newborns available | Hospital environment is unfamiliar and offers little privacy |
| Careful medical oversight during labor, delivery, and after birth reassures some mothers | Mother may have to remain in bed throughout labor and use a delivery table |
| Nursery care for newborn babies provides mothers with help, rest, and support | Hospital practices often minimize parents' early contact with the newborn |
| Limited visiting hours prevent mother from getting overtired | Generally more expensive than hospital birth center |
| **Hospital Birth Center**[a] | |
| Staffed by well-trained doctors and nurses | Still an environment that is unfamiliar to mothers |
| Offers an informal, homelike atmosphere in a hospital context | Still may involve some rules and medical interventions (for example, some birth centers require fetal monitoring) |
| Emergency medical equipment nearby if needed | More expensive than home delivery |
| Less likely than traditional hospital to use routine and unnecessary medical procedures | |
| Less likely than traditional hospital to have rigid rules | |
| Natural childbirth and early contact between parents and baby encouraged | |
| Mother can have family members and friends present | |
| Mother does not have to be moved from labor to delivery room | |
| Mother usually goes home sooner after birth | |
| Generally less expensive than hospital delivery room | |
| **Home Delivery** | |
| Mother is in a familiar environment that she can control | Training of medical attendants can vary widely and may not be sufficient to handle emergencies |
| Trained nurse-midwife is usually present throughout labor and delivery | Routine medical procedures and extra personnel not available if needed |
| Mother can have family members and friends present | In case of emergency, mother and baby must be transported to a hospital, delaying necessary intervention |
| Use of routine and unnecessary medical procedures unlikely | |
| Best environment for early parent–infant contact | |

*Source:* Adapted from Samuels & Samuels, 1986.
[a]For free-standing birth centers, the disadvantages listed for home delivery also apply.

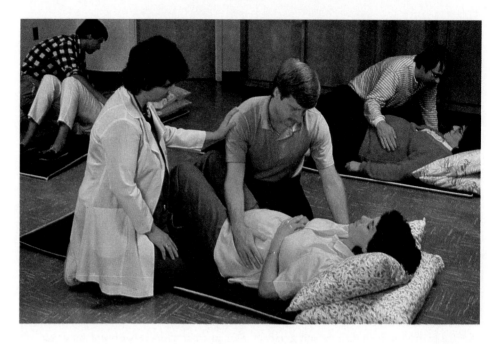

routinely prevented from having friends and relatives with them during childbirth, some mothers were randomly assigned a companion who stayed with them throughout labor, talking to them, holding their hands, and rubbing their backs to promote relaxation. These mothers had fewer birth complications, and their labors lasted half as long as those of women who did not have supportive companionship. In addition, observations in the first hour after delivery showed that mothers receiving social support were more likely to respond to their babies by talking, smiling, and gently stroking (Sosa et al., 1980).

## Home Delivery

Home birth has always been popular in certain industrialized nations, such as England, Holland, and Sweden. The number of American women choosing to have their babies at home has grown in recent years, although it is still small, amounting to about 1 percent. These mothers want to recapture the time when birth was an important part of family life (McClain, 1987). In addition, most want to avoid unnecessary medical procedures and exercise greater control over their own care and that of their babies than hospitals typically permit. Although some home births are attended by doctors, many more are handled by certified *nurse-midwives* who have degrees in nursing and additional training in childbirth management.

The joys and perils of home delivery are well illustrated by the story that Don, who painted my house as I worked on this book, told me as we took several coffee breaks together. Don is the father of four children, two of whom were born at home. "Our first child was delivered in the hospital," he said. "Even though I was present, Kathy and I found the whole atmosphere to be rigid and insensitive. We wanted a warmer, more personal environment in which to have our children." Don and Kathy's second child Cindy was born at their farmhouse, three miles out of town. A nurse-midwife was present. She coached Don, and he delivered Cindy himself. When, three years later, Kathy was in labor with Marnie, a heavy snowstorm prevented the midwife from getting to the house on time. Don delivered the baby alone, but the birth was difficult. Marnie failed to breathe for several minutes; with great effort, Don managed to revive her. The frightening memory of those moments when Marnie's

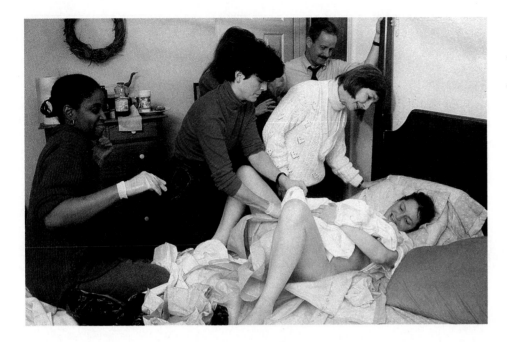

*Women who choose home birth want to share the joy of childbirth with family members, avoid unnecessary medical procedures, and exercise greater control over their own care and that of their babies. When assisted by a well-trained doctor or midwife, healthy women can give birth at home safely. (Franck Logue/Stock South)*

body was limp and blue convinced Don and Kathy to return to the hospital to have their last child. By then, the hospital's birth practices had changed greatly. Don and Kathy got to know their doctor well, and he learned that Don had delivered Cindy and Marnie. This time, Kathy's labor proceeded easily and quickly. When the baby's head crowned, the doctor stepped aside and permitted Don to bring his youngest child into the world himself.

Don and Kathy's experience raises the question of whether it is just as safe to give birth at home as in a hospital. For healthy women who are assisted by a well-trained doctor or midwife, it seems so, since complications rarely occur. However, when attendants are not carefully trained and prepared to handle emergencies, the rate of infant death is high (Schramm, Barnes, & Bakewell, 1987). When mothers are at risk for any kind of complication, the appropriate place for labor and delivery is the hospital, where life-saving treatment is available should it be needed.

## MEDICAL INTERVENTIONS

Medical interventions during childbirth are not just practiced in industrialized nations like our own. They can also be found in much smaller and simpler cultures. For example, some preliterate tribal and village societies have discovered drugs that stimulate labor and developed surgical techniques to deliver babies. Yet more so than anywhere else in the world, childbirth in the United States is a medically monitored and controlled event (Jordan, 1980; Notzon, 1990). What medical techniques are doctors likely to use during labor and delivery? When are they justified, and what dangers do they pose to mothers and babies? These are questions that we take up in the following sections.

### Fetal Monitoring

**Fetal monitors** are electronic instruments that track the baby's heart rate during labor. An abnormal heartbeat pattern may indicate that the baby is in distress due to

**Fetal monitors**
Electronic instruments that track the baby's heart rate during labor.

**FIGURE 4.2** • External fetal monitor, which is attached to the mother's abdomen and records fetal heart rate using ultrasound. This type of fetal monitoring is used routinely in American hospitals.

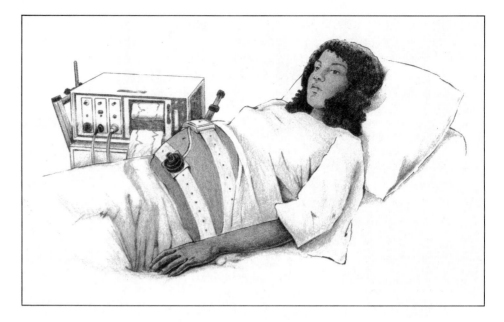

lack of oxygen and needs to be delivered immediately. Fetal monitors are required in almost all American hospitals. Two types are in common use. The most popular kind is strapped across the mother's abdomen throughout labor (see Figure 4.2). A second more accurate method involves threading a recording device through the cervix and placing it directly under the baby's scalp.

Fetal monitoring is a safe medical procedure that has been shown to save the lives of many babies when mothers have a history of pregnancy and birth complications. Nevertheless, the devices have stimulated a great deal of controversy. In mothers who have had healthy pregnancies, fetal monitoring does not reduce the rate of infant death. Some critics also point out that use of fetal monitors is linked to an increase in the number of emergency cesarean (surgical) deliveries, a practice that we will discuss shortly. They worry that fetal monitors identify many babies as in danger who, in fact, are not (Leveno et al., 1986; Prentice & Lind, 1987).

There is another reason that fetal monitors are controversial. Some women complain that the devices are uncomfortable, prevent them from moving easily, and interfere with the normal course of labor. Still, it is likely that fetal monitors will continue to be used routinely, even though they might not be necessary in most cases. Today, doctors are likely to be sued for malpractice if an infant dies or is born with problems and they cannot show that they did everything possible to protect the baby. And despite lack of evidence, some doctors firmly believe that fetal monitoring contributes to healthy outcomes in all types of mothers.

### Labor and Delivery Medication

Some form of medication is used in 80 to 95 percent of births in the United States. **Analgesias** are drugs used to relieve pain. When given during labor, the dose is usually mild and intended to help a mother relax. **Anesthesia** is a stronger type of painkiller that blocks sensation. General anesthesia, which puts the mother to sleep, is rarely used during childbirth today. More common are regional painkillers injected into the spinal column to numb the lower half of the body.

In complicated deliveries, pain-relieving drugs are essential because they permit life-saving medical interventions to be carried out. But when used routinely, they can

**Analgesia**

A mild pain-relieving drug.

**Anesthesia**

A strong painkilling drug that blocks sensation.

cause problems. Anesthesia interferes with the mother's ability to feel contractions during the second stage of labor. As a result, she may not push effectively, increasing the likelihood of an instrument delivery (see next section).

Labor and delivery medication rapidly crosses the placenta. When given in fairly large doses, it produces a depressed state in the newborn baby that may last for days. The infant is sleepy and withdrawn, sucks poorly during feedings, and is likely to be irritable when awake (Brackbill, McManus, & Woodward, 1985; Brazelton, Nugent, & Lester, 1987). One study found that mothers who received anesthesia viewed their babies as more difficult and less rewarding to care for in the weeks after birth (Murray et al., 1981).

Does the use of labor and delivery medication have a long-lasting impact on the physical and mental development of the child? Some researchers claim so (Brackbill, McManus, & Woodward, 1985), but their findings have been challenged, and contrary results exist (Broman, 1983). Nevertheless, the negative impact of these drugs on the early mother–infant relationship is good reason to limit their use.

## Instrument Delivery

**Forceps,** a metal device placed around the baby's head to pull the infant from the birth canal, have been used since the sixteenth century to speed up delivery (see Figure 4.3). A more recent instrument, the **vacuum extractor,** consists of a plastic cup placed on the baby's head attached to a suction tube. Instrument delivery is appropriate if the mother's pushing during the second stage of labor does not cause the baby to move through the birth canal in a reasonable period of time.

In the United States, forceps or vacuum extractors are used in 20 to 30 percent of births. In contrast, they are used less than 5 percent of the time in Europe. These figures suggest that instruments may be applied too freely in American hospitals (Korte & Scaer, 1990). When a doctor uses forceps to pull the baby through most or all of the birth canal, deliveries are associated with higher rates of brain damage. As a result, forceps are seldom used in this way today. However, even a low-forceps delivery (carried out when the baby is most of the way through the vagina) involves some risk of injury to the baby's head. Vacuum extractors are less likely to tear the mother's tissues than are forceps, but the risk of harming the infant is just as great (Cunningham, MacDonald, & Gant, 1989; Hanigan et al., 1990). For these reasons, neither method should be used when the mother can still be encouraged to deliver normally and there is no special reason to hurry the birth.

## Induced Labor

An **induced labor** is one that is started artificially. This is usually done by breaking the amnion or bag of waters (an event that takes place naturally in the first stage of labor) and giving the mother synthetic oxytocin, a hormone involved in stimulating contractions in laboring women.

Are there good reasons to induce labor? Yes, when continuing the pregnancy threatens the well-being of mother or baby. Too often, though, labors are induced for reasons of convenience rather than health. Perhaps the doctor is planning to go on vacation or would prefer not to be called into the hospital in the middle of the night. Parents might also desire to arrange the birth of the baby to fit with their other plans.

In healthy mothers, the onset of labor should not be scheduled like her doctor's appointment. An induced labor often proceeds differently than a naturally occurring one. The contractions are longer, harder, and closer together. The possibility of inadequate oxygen supply to the baby is increased, since there is less time between contractions for a full supply of oxygen to cross the placenta. In addition, mothers

**Forceps**
A metal device placed around the baby's head that is used to pull the infant from the birth canal.

**Vacuum extractor**
A plastic cup attached to a suction tube that is used to deliver the baby.

**Induced labor**
A labor started artificially by breaking the amnion and giving the mother a hormone that stimulates contractions.

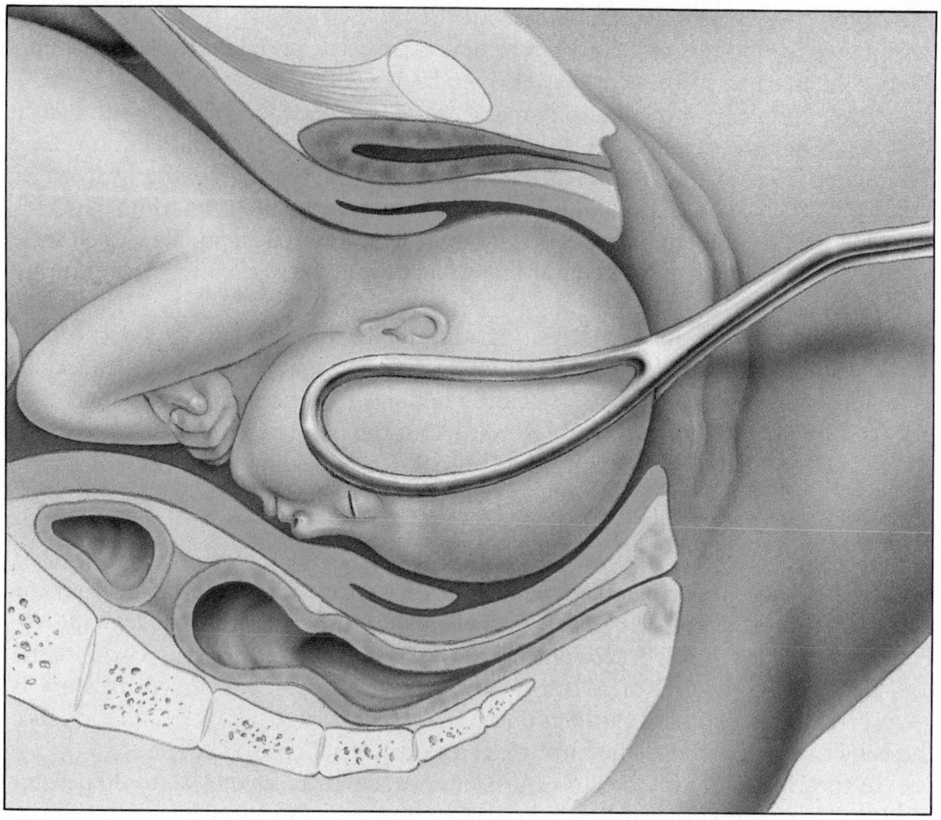

**FIGURE 4.3** • Delivery of the baby with forceps. The pressure that must be applied to pull the infant from the birth canal involves risk of injury to the baby's head. An alternative method, the vacuum extractor, is not used as often in the United States. Although vacuum extraction is less likely than forceps to injure the mother, it is just as risky for the infant. Scalp injuries caused by vacuum extraction are common.

often find it more difficult to stay in control of an induced labor, even when they have been coached in natural childbirth techniques. As a result, labor and delivery medication is likely to be used in larger amounts, and there is a greater chance of instrument delivery (Brindley & Sokol, 1988).

### Cesarean Delivery

A **cesarean delivery** is a surgical birth; the doctor makes an incision in the mother's abdomen and lifts the baby out of the uterus. Thirty years ago, cesarean delivery was rare in the United States, performed only when the life of mother or baby was in immediate danger. In 1970, 3 percent of babies were born in this way. Since that time, the cesarean rate has climbed steadily. In 1987, the practice accounted for 24.4 percent of American births, the highest rate in the world (Silver & Wolfe, 1989).

Birth complications that lead to cesarean deliveries are summarized in Table 4.3. Cesareans have always been warranted by the serious medical emergencies noted in the last entry of the table. In contrast, there is growing evidence that surgical delivery is not always needed to deal with the other four problems listed. Together, these account for over 80 percent of cesarean births.

Earlier we mentioned that fetal monitoring increases the likelihood of cesarean delivery and that some infants identified as in distress may be "false positives." Cesareans are also routinely performed when babies are in **breech position**—turned in such a way that the buttocks or feet would be delivered first. Giving birth to a breech baby through the vagina can be risky. The breech position increases the possibility that the umbilical cord may be squeezed as the large head moves through the birth canal, depriving the infant of oxygen. Head injuries are also more likely. Cesareans

**Cesarean delivery**

A surgical delivery in which the doctor makes an incision in the mother's abdomen and lifts the baby out of the uterus.

**Breech position**

A position of the baby in the uterus that would cause the buttocks or feet to be delivered first.

TABLE 4.3 • Common Reasons for Cesarean Delivery in the United States

| Reason | Percent of Cesareans |
|---|---|
| Previous cesarean | 35 |
| Abnormal labor | 28 |
| Baby in breech position | 10 |
| Infant distress due to oxygen deprivation | 10 |
| Other emergencies | 17 |
|     Serious maternal illness—diabetes, heart disease, or infection that can be transmitted to the fetus during vaginal delivery, such as herpes simplex 2 Medical emergencies, such as premature separation of the placenta from the uterus or Rh incompatibility | |

*Source:* Korte & Scaer, 1990.

are justified in many of these cases. However, the exact positioning of the infant (which can be felt by the doctor) makes a difference. Certain breech babies fare just as well with a normal delivery as they do with a cesarean (Collea, Chein, & Quilligan, 1980). Sometimes the doctor can gently turn a breech baby into a head down position during the early part of labor.

The two most common reasons for cesareans are a failure of labor to progress normally and a previous history of cesarean birth (Silver & Wolfe, 1989). Many physicians take the position that "once a cesarean, always a cesarean" because the uterine scar might rupture if the mother is permitted to deliver vaginally in a later birth. However, the surgical technique used today—a small horizontal cut in the lower part of the uterus—makes this possibility unlikely. Even when it does occur, it is not life-threatening to mother or baby (O'Sullivan et al., 1981).

Because many unnecessary cesareans are performed in the United States, pregnant women should ask questions about the procedure before choosing a doctor. When a mother does end up having a cesarean, she and her baby need extra support. The operation itself is quite safe, but it requires more time for recovery. Cesarean newborns are more likely to be sleepy and unresponsive and to have breathing difficulties. Anesthesia may have crossed the placenta, and the rush of stress hormones stimulated by labor contractions is not present to promote arousal and respiration. Any one of these factors can negatively affect the early mother–infant relationship (Cox & Schwartz, 1990).

*BRIEF REVIEW* In modern industrialized nations, a woman can choose to have her baby in a traditional hospital setting, in a birth center, or at home. Natural or prepared childbirth programs are widely available. Home births are safe for healthy women, provided attendants are well trained.

Medical interventions during childbirth are more likely to be used in the United States than anywhere else in the world. Although often justified, these procedures can cause problems. In some instances, fetal monitoring may mistakenly identify babies as distressed. Pain-relieving drugs can cross the placenta, producing a withdrawn state in the infant. Because induced labors are more difficult, they are associated with greater use of medication. Instrument deliveries involve some risk of head injury. Cesarean births require extra recovery time for the mother, and babies tend to be less alert and more likely to have breathing difficulties.

• *Use of any single medical intervention during childbirth increases the likelihood that others will also be used. Provide as many examples as you can to illustrate this idea.*

• *Sharon, a heavy smoker, has just arrived at the hospital in labor. Which one of the medical interventions discussed in the preceding sections is her doctor justified in using? (For help in answering this question, return to our discussion of effects of smoking on the fetus in Chapter 3, page 107).*

## BIRTH COMPLICATIONS

In the preceding sections and throughout Chapter 3, we indicated that some babies—in particular, those whose mothers are in poor health, who do not receive good medical care, or who have a history of pregnancy problems—are especially likely to experience birth complications. Inadequate oxygen, a pregnancy that ends too early, and a baby who is born underweight are serious problems that we have mentioned many times. Another risk factor is a pregnancy in which the baby remains in the uterus too long. Let's take a look at the impact of each of these complications on later development.

### Oxygen Deprivation

Some years ago, I got to know 2-year-old Melinda and her mother Judy, both of whom participated in a special program for handicapped infants at our laboratory school. Melinda has **cerebral palsy,** which is a general term for a variety of problems that result from brain damage before, during, or just after birth. Difficulties in muscle coordination are always involved, such as a clumsy walk, uncoordinated movements, and unclear speech. The disorder can range from very mild tremors to severe crippling accompanied by mental retardation. One out of every 500 children born in the United States has cerebral palsy. Twenty-two percent of these youngsters experienced oxygen deprivation during labor and delivery (Torfs et al., 1990).

Melinda walks with a halting, lumbering gait, and she has difficulty keeping her balance. "Some mothers don't know how the palsy happened," confided Judy, "but I do. I got pregnant accidently, and my boyfriend didn't want to have anything to do with it. I was frightened and alone most of the time. I arrived at the hospital at the last minute. Melinda was breech, and the cord was wrapped around her neck."

Squeezing of the umbilical cord, which happened in Melinda's case, is one cause of oxygen deprivation. In other instances, the birth seems to go along all right, but the baby fails to start breathing within a few minutes. Newborns can survive periods without oxygen longer than adults, but there is risk of brain damage if breathing is delayed for more than 3 minutes (Stechler & Halton, 1982). Can you think of other possible causes of oxygen deprivation that you learned about as you studied prenatal development and birth?

How do children deprived of oxygen during labor and delivery fare as they get older? Melinda's physical handicap was permanent, but otherwise she did well. The same is true for most oxygen-deprived newborns. These infants remain behind their agemates in intellectual and motor development throughout early childhood. But by the school years, most catch up in development (Corah et al., 1965; Graham et al., 1962).

When lasting problems do result, the oxygen deprivation was probably extreme. Perhaps it was caused by prenatal damage to the baby's respiratory system, or it may have happened because the infant's lungs were not yet mature enough to breathe. For example, infants born more than 6 weeks early commonly have a disorder called **respiratory distress syndrome** (otherwise known as *hyaline membrane disease*). Their tiny lungs are so poorly developed that the air sacs collapse, causing serious breathing difficulties and sometimes death. Today, mechanical ventilators keep many such infants alive. In spite of these measures, some babies suffer permanent damage from lack of oxygen, and in other cases their delicate lungs are harmed by the treatment itself (Vohr & Garcia-Coll, 1988). Respiratory distress syndrome is only one of many risks for babies born too soon, as we will see in the following section.

### Preterm and Low Birth Weight Infants

Janet, just under 6 months pregnant, and her husband Rick boarded a flight at the Hartford, Connecticut, airport, on their way to a vacation in Hawaii. Their plane was

**Cerebral palsy**

A general term for a variety of problems, all of which involve muscle coordination, that result from brain damage before, during, or just after birth.

**Respiratory distress syndrome**

A disorder of preterm infants in which the lungs are so immature that the air sacs collapse, causing serious breathing difficulties.

scheduled to make two stops before the long journey across the Pacific Ocean. In Chicago, Janet emerged from the restroom and told Rick she was bleeding. When the plane stopped again, this time in San Francisco, Janet realized she was in trouble. Rushed to a hospital, she gave birth to Keith, who weighed less than 1 1/2 pounds.

During Keith's first month, he experienced one crisis after another, all of which are common to very premature infants. Three days after birth, an ultrasound scan suggested that fragile blood vessels feeding Keith's brain had hemorrhaged, a complication that can cause brain damage. Within three weeks, Keith had surgery to close a valve in his heart, which seals automatically in full-term babies. Keith's immature immune system made infections difficult to contain. Repeated illnesses and the drugs used to treat them caused permanent hearing loss. He also had respiratory distress syndrome and was attached to a ventilator. Soon, there was evidence of lung damage, and Keith's vision was threatened because of constant exposure to oxygen. It took over three months of hospitalization for Keith's rough course of complications and treatment to ease. (paraphrased from Turiel, 1991a, pp. D13–D14)

Babies who are born 3 weeks or more before the end of a full 38-week pregnancy or who weigh less than 5 1/2 pounds (2,500 grams) have, for many years, been referred to as "premature." A wealth of research indicates that premature babies are at risk for many problems. Birth weight is the best available predictor of infant survival and healthy development. Many newborns who weigh less than 3 1/3 pounds (1,500 grams) experience difficulties that are not overcome, an effect that becomes stronger as birth weight decreases. Frequent illness, inattention, overactivity, and school learning problems are some of the problems that extend into the childhood years (McCormick, Gortmaker, & Sobol, 1990; Vohr & Garcia-Coll, 1988).

About 1 in 14 infants is born underweight in the United States. The problem can strike unexpectedly, as it did for Janet and Rick. It is highest among low-income pregnant women, especially ethnic minorities (Kopp & Kaler, 1989). These mothers, as we indicated in Chapter 3, are more likely to be undernourished and to be exposed to other harmful environmental influences—factors strongly linked to low birth weight. In addition, they often do not receive the prenatal care necessary to protect their vulnerable babies.

You may recall from Chapter 2 that prematurity is also common when mothers are carrying twins. Twins are usually born about 3 weeks early, and because of restricted space inside the uterus, they gain less weight than singleton babies after the twentieth week of pregnancy.

***Preterm versus Small for Dates.*** Although low birth weight infants face many obstacles to healthy development, individual differences exist in how well they do. Over half go on to lead normal lives—even some who weighed only a couple of pounds at birth (Vohr & Garcia-Coll, 1988). To better understand why some of these babies do better than others, researchers have divided them into two groups. The first is called **preterm.** These infants are born several weeks or more before their due date. Although small in size, their weight may still be appropriate for the amount of time they spent in the uterus. The second group is called **small for dates.** These babies are below their expected weight when length of the pregnancy is taken into account. Some small-for-dates infants are actually full term. Others are preterm infants who are especially underweight.

Of the two types of babies, small-for-dates infants usually have more serious problems. During the first year, they are more likely to die, catch infections, and show evidence of brain damage. By middle childhood, they have lower intelligence test scores, are less attentive, and achieve more poorly in school (Teberg, Walther, & Pena, 1988). Small-for-dates infants probably experienced inadequate nutrition before birth. Perhaps their mothers did not eat properly, the placenta did not function normally, or the babies themselves had defects that prevented them from growing as they should. Recall from Chapter 3 that prenatal malnutrition has serious conse-

**Preterm**
Infants born several weeks or more before their due date.

**Small for dates**
Infants whose birth weight is below normal when length of pregnancy is taken into account.

quences for children's development, and it may help to explain the lasting difficulties of many of these babies.

### Characteristics of Preterm Infants: Consequences for Caregiving.

Imagine a scrawny, thin-skinned infant whose body is only a little larger than the size of your hand. You try to play with the baby by stroking and talking softly, but he is sleepy and unresponsive. When you feed him, he sucks poorly. He is usually irritable during the short, unpredictable periods in which he is awake.

Unfortunately, the appearance and behavior of preterm babies can affect the kind of care they receive. In one study, parents were observed interacting with their preterm infants just after they arrived home from the hospital. Compared to full-term infants, preterm babies were less often held close, touched, and talked to (Goldberg, Brachfeld, & DiVitto, 1980). Those who are very ill at birth are likely to remain unresponsive and high-strung for months. When these babies are born to isolated, poverty-stricken mothers who have difficulty managing their own lives, then the chances for unfavorable outcomes are increased. In contrast, parents whose life circumstances are stable can usually overcome the stresses of caring for a preterm infant. In these cases, even sick preterm babies have a good chance of catching up in development by middle childhood (Cohen & Parmelee, 1983).

These findings suggest that how well preterm babies develop has a great deal to do with the kind of relationship established between parent and child, to which both partners contribute. If a good relationship between mother and baby can help prevent the negative effects of early birth, then intervention programs directed at supporting this relationship should help these infants recover.

### Intervening with Preterm Infants.

A preterm baby is cared for in a special bed called an *isolette*. It is a plexiglass-enclosed box in which temperature is carefully controlled, since these babies cannot yet regulate their own body temperatures effectively. Air is filtered before it enters the isolette to help protect the baby from infection. When a preterm infant is fed through a stomach tube, breathes with the aid of a respirator, and receives medication through an intravenous needle, the isolette can be very isolating indeed! Physical needs that otherwise would lead to close contact and other forms of stimulation from an adult are met mechanically. At one time

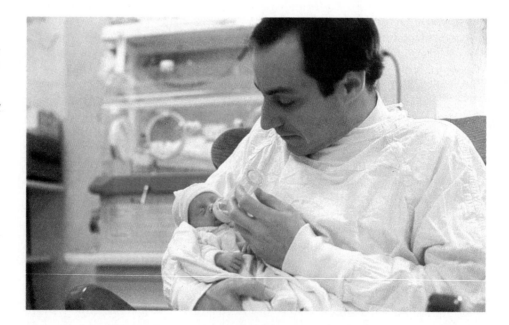

*This father feeds his preterm baby, who is only slightly larger than an adult's hand, in a hospital intensive care nursery. A good parent–infant relationship and the stimulation of touch and a soft, gentle voice are likely to help this infant recover and catch up in development. (Joseph Nettis/Photo Researchers)*

doctors believed that stimulating such a fragile baby could be harmful. Now we know that certain kinds of stimulation in proper doses can help preterm infants develop.

*Special Infant Stimulation.* In some intensive care nurseries, preterm babies can be seen rocking in suspended hammocks or lying on waterbeds—interventions designed to replace the gentle motion they would have received while being carried about in the mother's uterus. Other forms of stimulation have also been used—for example, an attractive mobile or a tape recording of a heart beat, soft music, or the mother's voice. Many studies show that these experiences promote faster weight gain, more predictable sleep patterns, and greater alertness in preterm infants during the weeks after birth (Cornell & Gottfried, 1976; Schaefer, Hatcher, & Bargelow, 1980).

Touch is an especially important form of stimulation for preterm newborns. In studies of baby animals, touching the skin releases certain brain chemicals that support physical growth. These effects are believed to occur in humans as well (Schanberg & Field, 1987). In one study, preterm infants who were gently massaged several times each day in the hospital gained weight faster and, at the end of the first year, were advanced in mental and motor development over preterm babies not given this stimulation (Field et al., 1986).

*Training Parents in Infant Caregiving Skills.* When effective stimulation helps preterm babies develop more quickly, parents are likely to feel good about their infant's growth and interact with the baby more effectively. In one program, a specially trained nurse met with mothers of low birth weight babies daily during the week before hospital discharge and in four sessions over the next 3 months. During each meeting, the nurse helped the mother appreciate her baby's unique ways of signaling readiness for interaction and discomfort and taught her to respond sensitively to the infant's cues. Then the children's mental development was carefully tracked over the next seven years. Infants of mothers who received the intervention, in comparison to infants of mothers who did not, gained steadily in mental test performance over infancy and childhood until their scores equalled those of full-term youngsters. These findings indicate that even a relatively brief effort to help mothers adjust to the care of a low birth weight baby can have long-term benefits for development (Achenbach et al., 1990).

As we conclude our discussion of preterm and low birth weight infants, I would like to tell you more about Keith, the very sick baby whom you met at the beginning of this section. Because of advanced medical technology and new ways of helping parents, many preterm infants survive and eventually catch up in development, but Keith was not one of the lucky ones. Even with the best of care, from 30 to 70 percent of babies born as early as Keith either die or end up with serious handicaps. Eventually, Keith was transferred to a hospital near Janet and Rick's home. For a while, he could be held for several hours a day outside the isolette, but soon he suffered new setbacks. He stopped gaining weight and caught more infections, and the respirator that had helped him live left his lungs so badly damaged that there was not much chance of survival. Six months after he was born, Keith died (Turiel, 1991b).

Keith's premature birth was unavoidable, but the high rate of underweight babies in the United States—one of the worst in the industrialized world—could be greatly reduced by improving the health and social conditions described in Box 4.2. Fortunately, today we can save many preterm babies, but an even better course of action would be to prevent low birth weight and infant death before they happen.

## Postterm Infants

The normal length of pregnancy is 38 weeks. Infants born after 42 weeks are **post-term.** About 10 percent of babies fall into this category. Most of these late-arriving

**Postterm**
Infants who spend a longer than average time period in the uterus—more than 42 weeks.

# SOCIAL ISSUES

## Box 4.2  *Infant Mortality in the United States*

*I*nfant mortality is an index used around the world to assess the overall health of a nation's children. It refers to the number of deaths in the first year of life per 1,000 live births. How do you think the United States compares to other industrialized nations in infant mortality? The information in Figure 4.4 may surprise you. Although the United States has the most up-to-date health care technology in the world, it has made less progress than many other countries in reducing infant deaths. Over the past three decades, it slipped down in the international rankings, from seventh in the 1950s to twenty-first at the beginning of the 1990s (U.S. Bureau of the Census, 1991). Members of America's poor racial minorities, black babies especially, are at greatest risk. Black infants are more than twice as likely as white infants to die in the first year of life (Children's Defense Fund, 1989).

**Neonatal mortality,** the rate of death within the first month of life, accounts for 67 percent of the high infant death rate in the United States. Two factors are largely responsible for neonatal mortality. The first is serious physical defects, most of which cannot be prevented. The percentage of babies born with physical defects is about the same in all racial and socioeconomic groups. The second leading cause of neonatal mortality is low birth weight, which is largely preventable. Black babies are nearly four times more likely to die because they are born early and underweight than are white infants. On an international scale, the number of underweight babies born in the United States is alarmingly high. It is greater than that of 28 other countries (Children's Defense Fund, 1990).

Why are American babies more likely to be born underweight and to die than infants in so many other nations? Experts agree that widespread poverty and weak health care programs for mothers and young children are responsible (National Commission to Prevent Infant Mortality, 1988). Except for the United States, each country listed in Figure 4.4 provides all its citizens with government-sponsored health-care benefits. And each takes extra steps to make sure that pregnant mothers and babies have access to good nutrition, high-quality medical care, and social and economic supports that promote effective parenting (Wegman, 1991).

For example, all Western European nations guarantee women a certain number of prenatal visits at very low or no cost, and their quality is regulated by national standards. In addition, a health professional routinely visits the home after a baby is born to provide counseling about infant care and to arrange additional health services. Home assistance is especially extensive in Holland. For a token fee, each mother is granted the services of a trained maternity helper, who assists with infant care, shopping, housekeeping, meal preparation, and the care of other children during the ten days after delivery (Miller, 1987).

Paid employment leave for expectant and new parents is also widely available in Western Europe. It ranges from about 2 to 10 months, depending on the country. Several nations, such as Norway, Sweden, and West Germany, permit the father to take childbirth leave if he is the principal caregiver. The period of leave can usually be extended on an unpaid basis. Additional paid leave is granted in the event of maternal or child illness (Miller, 1987).

In countries with low infant mortality rates, expectant mothers need not wonder how or where they will get health and child care assistance, or who will pay for it. The clear link between high-quality maternal and infant health services and reduced infant mortality provides strong justification for implementing similar programs in the United States.

WHY HAS THE UNITED STATES been reluctant to develop a national system of health care, while European nations have had these programs in place for many years? For help in answering this question, return to our discussion of public policies and child development in Chapter 2, pages 78–81.

List all the factors discussed in Chapter 3 and in this chapter that increase the chances that a baby will be born underweight. How many of these factors could be prevented by better health care for mothers and babies?

**FIGURE 4.4** • Infant mortality in 28 nations. Despite its advanced health care technology, the United States ranks poorly. It is twenty-first in the world, with a death rate of 10 infants per 1,000 births. (*Adapted from Wegman, 1991.*)

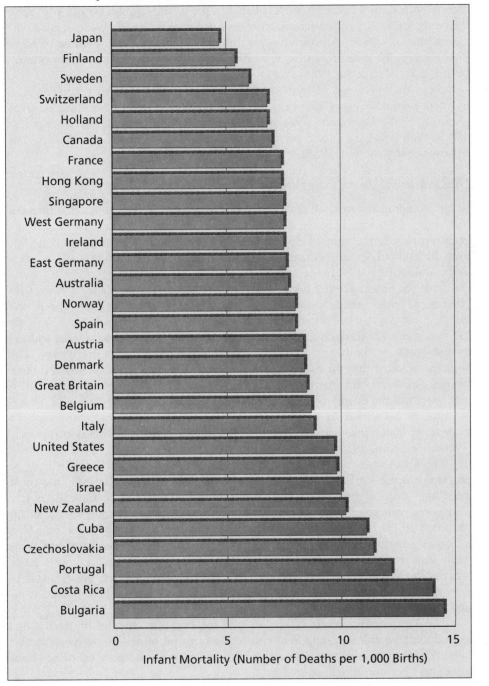

Infant Mortality (Number of Deaths per 1,000 Births)

**Infant mortality**

The number of deaths in the first year of life per 1,000 live births.

**Neonatal mortality**

The number of deaths in the first month of life per 1,000 live births.

newborns are quite normal. However, a small number start to lose weight at the end of pregnancy because the placenta no longer functions properly. As the baby becomes more overdue, the amount of amniotic fluid drops sharply. This increases the chances that the infant's movements in the uterus will squeeze the umbilical cord. Also, since the heads and bodies of postterm infants grow larger during extra weeks spent in the uterus, they may have difficulty moving through the birth canal. Because of all of these factors, the possibility of oxygen deprivation and head injuries in a postterm birth is great (Mannino, 1988).

Since the likelihood of birth complications and infant death rises steeply as a pregnancy continues past 42 weeks, doctors usually induce labor in these mothers (Resnick, 1988). Once born, most of these babies do well. Their mental development may be slightly behind during infancy and early childhood, but it generally evens out by school entry (Shime, 1988).

### Understanding Birth Complications

In the preceding sections, we discussed a variety of birth complications that threaten children's well-being. Now let's try to put the evidence together. Are there any general principles that might help us understand how infants who survive a traumatic birth are likely to develop? A landmark study carried out in Hawaii provides answers to this question.

In 1955, Emmy Werner began to follow 670 infants on the island of Kauai who experienced either mild, moderate, or severe complications at birth. Each was matched, on the basis of social class and race, with a healthy newborn. The study had two goals: (1) to discover the long-term effects of birth complications; and (2) to find out how family environments affect the child's chances for recovery. The findings indicated that the likelihood of long-term difficulties was increased if birth trauma was severe. But the most powerful clue to how well these children did in later years was the quality of their home environments. Children growing up in stable families did almost as well as those with no birth difficulties. Those exposed to poverty, family disorganization, and mentally ill parents often developed poorly (Werner & Smith, 1982).

The Kauai study tells us that as long as birth injuries are not overwhelming, a supportive home environment can restore children's growth. However, the most intriguing cases in this study were the handful of exceptions to this rule. A few youngsters with severe birth complications and very troubled families managed to surmount all the odds. Werner (1989) found that these resilient children relied on factors outside the family and within themselves to overcome stress. Some had especially attractive personalities that caused them to receive positive responses from relatives, neighbors, and peers. In other cases, a grandparent, aunt, uncle, or babysitter established a warm relationship with the child and provided the needed emotional support.

The Kauai study reveals that as long as the overall balance of life events tips toward the favorable side, children with severe birth problems can develop successfully. When negative factors outweigh positive ones, even the sturdiest of newborn babies may become a lifelong casualty.

• *Explain how the long-term outcomes reported for oxygen-deprived and preterm babies fit with the findings of the Kauai study.*

• *Sensitive care can help preterm infants recover, but unfortunately they are less likely to receive this kind of care than full-term newborns. Why is this the case?*

**BRIEF REVIEW** Birth complications can threaten children's development. Oxygen deprivation, when extreme, causes lasting brain damage. Preterm and small-for-dates babies are at risk for many problems. Providing these infants with special stimulation and teaching parents how to care for and interact with them helps restore favorable growth. The longer a postterm infant remains in the uterus, the greater the likelihood of birth difficulties. When newborns with serious complications grow up in positive social environments, they have a good chance of catching up in development.

## PRECIOUS MOMENTS AFTER BIRTH

Yolanda and Jay's account of Joshua's birth revealed that the time spent holding and touching him right after delivery was a memorable period filled with intense emotion. A mother given her infant at this time will usually stroke the baby gently, look into the infant's eyes, and talk softly (Klaus & Kennell, 1982). Observations of and interviews with fathers indicate that they respond similarly. Most are overjoyed at the birth of the baby and experience a feeling state that has been called **engrossment,** a term that captures the involvement and interest that fathers display toward their newborn child (Greenberg & Morris, 1974). Regardless of their social class or whether they participated in childbirth classes, fathers touch, look at, talk to, and kiss their newborn infants just as much as mothers. When they hold the baby, sometimes they exceed mothers in stimulation and affection (Parke & Tinsley, 1981).

Many nonhuman animals engage in specific caregiving behaviors immediately after birth that are critical for survival of the young. For example, a mother cat licks her newborn kittens and then encircles them with her body (Schneirla, Rosenblatt, & Tobach, 1963). Rats, sheep, and goats engage in similar licking behaviors. But if the mother is separated from the young during the time period following delivery, her responsiveness declines until finally she rejects the infant (Poindron & Le Neindre, 1980; Rosenblatt & Lehrman, 1963).

Do human parents also require close physical contact with their babies in the hours after birth for **bonding,** or feelings of affection and concern for the infant, to develop? A few investigators used to think so, but now we know that bonding does not depend on a precise period of togetherness in human beings (Goldberg, 1983). Some parents report sudden, deep feelings of affection for their babies on first holding them. For others, these emotions emerge gradually, over the first few weeks of life (MacFarlane, Smith, & Garrow, 1978). In adoptive parents, a warm, affectionate relationship can develop quite successfully even if the child enters the family months or years after birth (Dontas et al., 1985; Hodges & Tizard, 1989). Taken together, these findings indicate that human bonding is a complex process that depends on many factors, not just what happens during a short time interval.

Still, contact with the infant after birth might be one of several factors that helps build a good relationship between parent and baby. When nurses take the infant away after delivery, they convey a message to parents that professionals are capable of caring for the baby but mothers and fathers are not. Recent research shows that mothers learn to discriminate their own newborn baby from other infants on the basis of touch, smell, and sight (a photograph) after as little as one hour of contact (Kaitz et al., 1987, 1988, 1992). This early recognition probably facilitates responsiveness to the infant, although it is not critical for the development of a warm relationship.

Today, hospitals recognize that early contact between parents and babies can be helpful. An arrangement called **rooming in,** in which the baby stays in the mother's hospital room all or most of the time, is widely available. If parents choose not to take advantage of this option or cannot do so because the infant requires special medical attention, there is no evidence that the baby will suffer emotionally.

## THE NEWBORN BABY'S CAPACITIES

As recently as 50 years ago, scientists considered the newborn baby to be a passive, disorganized being whose world was, in the words of turn-of-the-century psychologist William James, a "blooming, buzzing confusion." The newly arrived infant, it was commonly believed, could see, hear, feel, and do very little. Today, we know that this image of an incompetent newborn is wrong. Newborn babies have a remark-

*Elated by the birth of his baby, this father displays the absorbed interest in his newborn known as engrossment.* (Erika Stone)

**Engrossment**
The father's experience of involvement and interest in the newborn baby.

**Bonding**
Parents' feelings of affection and concern for the newborn baby.

**Rooming in**
An arrangement in which the newborn baby stays in the mother's hospital room all or most of the time.

TABLE 4.4 • Some Newborn Reflexes

| Reflex | Stimulation | Response | Age of Disappearance | Function |
|---|---|---|---|---|
| Eye blink | Bright light shined at eyes or hand clap near head | Quick closing of eyelids | Permanent | Protection from strong stimulation |
| Tonic neck | Turn baby's head to one side while lying awake on back | Infant lies in a "fencing position": one arm is extended in front of eyes on side to which head is turned, other arm is flexed | 4 months | May prepare infant for voluntary reaching |
| Palmar grasp | Place finger in infant's hand and press against palm | Spontaneous grasp of adult's finger | 3 to 4 months | Prepares infant for voluntary grasping |
| Babinski | Stroke sole of foot from toe toward heel | Toes fan out and curl as foot twists in | 8 to 12 months | Unknown |
| Rooting | Stroke cheek near corner of mouth | Head turns toward source of stimulation | 3 weeks (becomes voluntary head turning at this time) | Helps infant find the nipple |
| Sucking | Place finger in infant's mouth | Rhythmic sucking of finger | Permanent | Permits feeding |
| Moro | Hold infant horizontally on back and let head drop slightly, or produce a sudden loud sound against surface supporting the infant | Infant makes an "embracing" motion by arching back, extending legs, throwing arms outward, and then bringing them in toward the body | 6 months | In human evolutionary past, may have helped infant cling to mother |
| Stepping | Hold infant under arms and permit bare feet to touch a flat surface | Infant lifts one foot after another in a stepping response | 2 months | Prepares infant for voluntary walking |

Sources: Knobloch & Pasamanick, 1974; Prechtl & Beintema, 1965.

able set of capacities that are crucial for survival and that are profoundly important in evoking the attention and care they receive from parents. In relating to the physical world and building their first social relationships, babies are active from the very start.

### Newborn Reflexes

A **reflex** is an inborn, automatic response to a particular form of stimulation. Reflexes are the newborn baby's most obvious organized patterns of behavior. Human infants come into the world with dozens of them. As Jay put Joshua down on a table in my classroom, we saw several. When Jay bumped the side of the table, Joshua reacted by flinging his arms wide and bringing them back toward his body. As Yolanda stroked Joshua's cheek, he turned his head in her direction. When she put her finger in the palm of Joshua's hand, he grabbed on tightly. Table 4.4 provides a description of the major newborn reflexes. See if you can name the ones that Joshua displayed. Then let's take a look at the meaning and purpose of these curious behaviors.

**Reflex**

An inborn, automatic response to a particular form of stimulation.

***Survival Value of Reflexes.*** Some reflexes have survival value. The rooting reflex helps a baby find the mother's nipple. Once the baby locates the nipple, imagine what it would be like if we had to teach the infant the complex lip and tongue movements involved in sucking. If sucking were not automatic, it is unlikely that our species would have survived for a single generation!

Other reflexes probably had survival value during our evolutionary past but no longer serve any special purpose. For example, the Moro or "embracing" reflex is believed to have helped infants cling to their mothers during a time period when babies were carried about all day. If the baby happened to lose support, the reflex caused the infant to embrace and, along with the grasp reflex, regain its hold on the mother's body (Kessen, 1967; Prechtl, 1958).

*Reflexes and the Development of Motor Skills.*  A few reflexes form the basis for complex motor skills that will develop later on. For example, the tonic neck reflex may prepare the baby for voluntary reaching. When infants lie on their backs in this "fencing position," they naturally gaze at the hand in front of their eyes. The reflex may encourage them to combine vision with arm movements and, eventually, reach for objects (Knobloch & Pasamanick, 1974).

The stepping reflex looks like a primitive walking response. In infants who gain weight quickly in the weeks after birth, the stepping reflex drops out because thigh and calf muscles are not strong enough to lift the baby's increasingly chubby legs. However, the capacity for stepping movements is still there. If the lower part of the infant's body is dipped in water, the reflex reappears, since the buoyancy of the water lightens the load on the baby's muscles (Thelen, Fisher, & Ridley-Johnson, 1984). When the stepping reflex is exercised regularly, babies are likely to walk several weeks earlier than if it is not practiced (Zelazo, 1983). However, there is no special need for parents to get their infants to use the stepping reflex, since all normal babies walk in due time.

*Reflexes and Early Social Relationships.*  A baby who searches for and successfully finds the nipple, sucks easily during feedings, and grasps when the hand is touched encourages parents to respond lovingly and strengthens their sense of competence as caregivers. Reflexes can also assist parents in comforting the baby, since they permit infants to control distress and amount of stimulation to some degree themselves. For example, on short trips with Joshua to the grocery store, Yolanda brought along a pacifier. If he became fussy, sucking helped quiet him until she could feed, change, or hold and rock him.

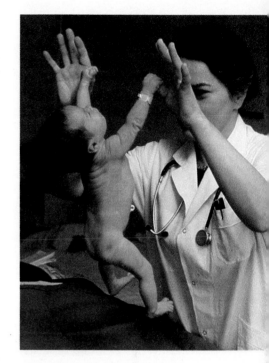

*The palmar grasp reflex is so strong during the first week after birth that many infants can use it to support their entire weight. (J. da Cunha/Petit Format/Photo Researchers)*

*This baby shows the Babinski reflex. When an adult strokes the sole of the foot, the toes fan out. Then they curl as the foot twists in. (Innervisions)*

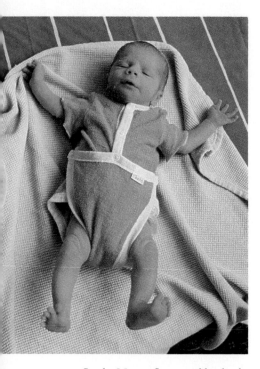

In the Moro reflex, a sudden loud sound or loss of support causes this baby to arch his back, extend his legs, throw his arms outward, and then bring them in toward the body. (Elizabeth Crews)

When held upright under the arms, newborn babies show reflexive stepping movements. (Innervisions)

The next time you have a chance to watch a young baby nursing, look carefully. You will see that the infant's sucking behavior is highly organized. Bursts of sucks separated by pauses occur, a style of feeding that is unique to the human species. Some researchers believe that this burst–pause rhythm is an evolved behavior pattern that helps parents and infants establish satisfying interaction as soon as possible. Notice what most mothers do during the baby's pause: they jiggle the infant. If you ask them why, they say that jiggling "wakes the baby up" and encourages more sucking. In response, newborn babies learn during the first few weeks of life to expect and wait for their mother's jiggle. As a result, mothers and infants build an early sequence of interaction during feeding that resembles the turn taking of human conversation. Using the primitive sucking reflex, the young baby participates in this dialogue as an active, cooperative partner (Kaye & Wells, 1980).

**The Importance of Assessing Newborn Reflexes.**    Look at Table 4.4 again, and you will see that most newborn reflexes disappear during the first 6 months of life. Scientists believe that this is due to a gradual increase in voluntary control over behavior as the cortex of the brain matures.

Pediatricians test the reflexes of infants carefully, especially if they have experienced birth trauma, because reflexes provide one way of assessing the health of the baby's nervous system. In infants who are brain damaged, reflexes may be weak or absent, or in some cases they may be exaggerated and overly rigid. Brain damage may also be indicated when reflexes persist past the point in development when they should normally disappear (Touwen, 1984).

## Sensory Capacities

What can babies perceive with the senses at birth? On his visit to my class, Joshua looked wide-eyed at my bright pink blouse and turned to the sound of his mother's voice. During feedings, he lets Yolanda know by the way he sucks that he prefers the taste of breast milk to a bottle of plain water. Clearly, Joshua has some well-developed sensory capacities. In the following sections, we explore the newborn baby's responsiveness to touch, taste, smell, sound, and visual stimulation. See Table 4.5 for a summary of these remarkable abilities.

**Touch.**    In our discussion of preterm infants, we indicated that touch helps stimulate early physical growth, and, as we will see in Chapter 7, it is important for emotional development as well. Therefore, it is not surprising that sensitivity to touch is well developed at birth. Return once more to the reflexes listed in Table 4.5. They reveal that the newborn baby responds to touch, especially around the mouth and on the palms of the hands and soles of the feet. During the prenatal period, these areas, along with the genitals, are the first to become sensitive to touch, followed by other regions of the body (Humphrey, 1978).

Reactions to temperature change are also present at birth. When Yolanda and Jay undress Joshua, he often expresses his discomfort by crying and becoming more active. Newborn babies are more sensitive to stimuli that are colder than body temperature than to those that are warmer (Humphrey, 1978).

At birth, infants are quite sensitive to pain. When male newborns are circumcised, the procedure is usually done without anesthesia because of the risk of giving pain relieving drugs to a very young infant. Babies often respond with an intense, high-pitched, stressful cry (Porter, Porges, & Marshall, 1988). In addition, heart rate and blood pressure rise, irritability increases, and the baby's sleep is disturbed for hours afterward (Anand, Phil, & Hickey, 1987). Recent research aimed at developing safe pain-relieving drugs for newborns promises to ease the severe stress of these procedures (Masciello, 1990). Doctors are becoming more aware than ever before

TABLE 4.5 • The Newborn Baby's Sensory Capacities

| Sense | Functioning in the Newborn |
|---|---|
| Touch | Responsive to touch, temperature change, and pain |
| Taste | Prefers sweetness; can distinguish sweet, salty, sour, and bitter tastes |
| Smell | Prefers the smell of a lactating woman (if breast-fed, can distinguish own mother's breast odor); reacts to the smell of certain foods in the same way as adults; can identify the location of an odor and turn away from unpleasant odors |
| Hearing | Prefers complex sounds to pure tones; can distinguish some sound patterns; recognizes differences among almost all human speech sounds; turns in the general direction of a sound; prefers high-pitched, expressive voices with rising intonation and sound of own mother's voice |
| Vision | Least well-developed sense at birth; focusing ability and visual acuity limited; scans visual field and attempts to track moving objects; color vision not yet well developed |

that small infants, just like older children and adults, cannot be treated as if they are insensitive to pain.

***Taste.*** All babies come into the world with an ability to communicate their taste preferences to caregivers. When given a sweet liquid instead of water, Joshua uses longer sucks with fewer pauses, indicating that he prefers sweetness and tries to savor the taste of his favorite food (Crook & Lipsitt, 1976). If water is made salty, Joshua shortens his sucking bursts, as if to avoid an unpleasant taste (Crook, 1978). Facial expressions also reveal that infants can distinguish among several tastes. Much like adults, newborn babies relax their facial muscles in response to sweetness, purse their lips when the taste is sour, and show a distinct archlike mouth opening when it is bitter (Steiner, 1979). These reactions are important for survival, since (as we will see in Chapter 5) the food that is ideally suited to support the infant's early growth is the sweet-tasting milk of the mother's breast.

***Smell.*** In many mammals, the sense of smell plays an important role in eating and protecting the young from predators by helping mothers and babies recognize each other. Although smell is less well developed in human beings than in other mammals, traces of its survival value are still present. In one study, newborns were exposed to the odor of their own mother's breast pad and that of a strange mother. By 6 days of age, they turned more often in the direction of the odor of their own mother (MacFarlane, 1975). The ability to recognize the mother's smell occurs only in breast-fed newborns (Cernoch & Porter, 1985). However, bottle-fed babies prefer the smell of any lactating (milk-producing) woman to the smell of a woman who is not (Makin & Porter, 1989). Newborn infants' attraction to the odor of the lactating breast probably helps them locate an appropriate food source and, in the process, learn to identify their own mother.

The reaction of the newborn baby to the smell of certain foods is surprisingly similar to that of adults, suggesting that several odor preferences are innate. For example, the smell of bananas or chocolate causes a relaxed, pleasant facial expression, while the odor of rotten eggs makes the infant frown (Steiner, 1979). Newborns can also identify the location of an odor and, if it is unpleasant, defend themselves. When a whiff of ammonia is presented to one side of the baby's nostrils, infants less than 6 days old quickly turn their heads in the other direction (Reiser, Yonas, & Wikner, 1976).

*Hearing.* Newborn infants can hear a wide variety of sounds, but they are more responsive to some than others. For example, they prefer complex sounds, such as noises and voices, to pure tones (Bench et al., 1976). In the first few days, infants can already tell the difference between a few sound patterns, such as a series of tones arranged in ascending and descending order and words they have already heard as opposed to new ones (Brody, Zelazo, & Chaika, 1984; Morrongiello, 1986).

These capacities, as well as others, indicate that the newborn baby is marvelously prepared for the awesome task of acquiring language. Tiny infants are especially sensitive to the sounds of human speech. They can make fine-grained distinctions among a wide variety of speech sounds—"ba" and "ga," "ma" and "na," and the short vowel sounds "a" and "i," to name just a few. For example, when given a nipple that turns on the "ba" sound, babies suck vigorously for a period of time, and then sucking slows down. When the sound switches to "ga," sucking picks up again, indicating that infants can detect this subtle sound difference. Using this method, researchers have found that there are only a few speech sounds that newborns cannot discriminate (Aslin, Pisoni, & Jusczyk, 1983). Infants seems to come into the world biologically prepared to respond to the sounds of any human language.

Responsiveness to sound provides support for the newborn baby's visual exploration of the environment. When an adult speaks to Joshua, he turns in the general direction of the voice. His ability to identify the precise location of a sound will improve greatly over the first 6 months and show further gains into the second year (Ashmead et al., 1991; Morrongiello, 1988).

Listen carefully to yourself the next time you talk to a young baby. You will probably speak in a high-pitched, expressive voice and use a rising tone at the ends of phrases and sentences. Adults probably communicate this way with infants because they notice that babies are more attentive when they do so. Indeed, newborns prefer human speech with these characteristics (Sullivan & Horowitz, 1983). In addition, they will suck more on a nipple to hear a recording of their own mother's voice than that of a strange woman, a preference that probably developed from hearing the muffled sounds of the mother's voice before birth (Spence & DeCasper, 1987). Infants' special responsiveness to their mother's speech encourages the mother to talk to the baby. As she does so, both readiness for language and the emotional bond between mother and child are strengthened.

*Vision.* Humans depend on vision more than any other sense for active exploration of the environment. Yet vision is the least mature of the newborn baby's senses. Visual centers in the brain as well as the eye itself continue to develop after birth. For example, cells in the *retina*, the membrane lining the inside of the eye that captures light and transforms it into messages that are sent to the brain, are not as mature or as densely packed as they will be in several months. Also, the muscles of the *lens*, that part of the eye that permits us to adjust our focus to varying distances of objects, are weak at birth (Appleton, Clifton, & Goldberg, 1975).

Because of these factors, newborn babies cannot focus their eyes as well as an adult can, and **visual acuity,** or fineness of discrimination, is limited. When you have your vision tested, the doctor provides an estimate of your visual acuity, which indicates how finely you perceive stimuli in comparison to a normal adult. Applying this same index to newborn babies, researchers have found that they perceive objects at a distance of 20 feet about as clearly as adults do at 440 to 800 feet (Appleton, Clifton, & Goldberg, 1975; Cornell & McDonnell, 1986). In addition, unlike adults (who see nearby objects most clearly), newborn babies see equally unclearly across a wide range of distances (Banks, 1980). As a result, images such as the parent's face, even from close up, look much like the blur shown in Figure 4.5.

Although newborn infants cannot yet see well, they actively explore their environment with the limited visual abilities that they have. They scan the visual field for

**Visual acuity**

Fineness of visual discrimination.

**FIGURE 4.5** • The newborn baby's limited focusing ability and poor visual acuity lead the mother's face, even when viewed from close up, to look much like the fuzzy image on the left rather than the clear image on the right. *(Varden Studios)*

interesting sights and try to track moving objects. However, their eye movements are slow and not very accurate (Aslin, 1987; Kremenitzer et al., 1979). Joshua's captivation with my pink blouse reveals that he is attracted to bright objects. Nevertheless, once newborns focus on an object, they do not examine it as thoroughly as an older infant. Instead, they tend to look only at a single feature—for example, the corner of a triangle instead of the entire shape. Although newborn babies prefer to look at colored rather than gray stimuli, they are not yet good at discriminating colors. It will take several months for color vision to improve (Teller & Bornstein, 1987).

### Newborn States

Throughout the day and night, newborn infants move in and out of five different **states of arousal,** or degrees of sleep and wakefulness, which are described in Table 4.6. During the first month, these states alternate frequently. Quiet alertness is the most fleeting. It usually moves toward fussing and crying relatively quickly. Much to the relief of their fatigued parents, newborns spend the greatest amount of time asleep—on the average, about 16 to 17 hours a day.

Although sleep is the dominant state in all newborns, striking individual differences in daily rhythms exist that affect parents' attitudes toward and interactions with the baby. A few infants sleep for long periods at an early age, increasing the rest their parents get and the energy they have for sensitive, responsive care. Babies who cry a great deal require that parents try harder to soothe them. If these efforts are not successful, parents' positive feelings for the infant and sense of competence may suffer. Babies who spend more time in the alert state are likely to receive more social stimulation. And since this state provides opportunities to explore the environment, infants who favor it may have a slight advantage in cognitive development.

Of the five states listed in Table 4.6, the two extremes—sleep and crying—have been of greatest interest to investigators. Each tells us something about normal and abnormal early development.

*Sleep.* Yolanda and Jay watched Joshua while he slept one day and wondered why his eyelids and body twitched and his rate of breathing varied, speeding up at some points and slowing down at others. "Is this how babies are supposed to sleep?" they asked, somewhat worried. "Indeed, it is," I responded.

**States of arousal**
Different degrees of sleep and wakefulness.

TABLE 4.6 • Infant States of Arousal

| State | Description | Daily Duration in Newborn |
|---|---|---|
| Regular sleep | Infant is at full rest and shows little or no body activity. The eyelids are closed, no eye movements occur, the fact is relaxed, and breathing is slow and regular. | 8–9 hours |
| Irregular sleep | Gentle limb movements, occasional stirring, and facial grimacing occur. Although the eyelids are closed, occasional rapid eye movements can be seen beneath them. Breathing is irregular. | 8–9 hours |
| Drowsiness | Infant is either falling asleep or waking up. Body is less active than in irregular sleep but more active than in regular sleep. Eyes open and close; when open, they have a glazed look. Breathing is even but somewhat faster than in regular sleep. | Varies |
| Quiet alertness | Infant's body is relatively inactive, with eyes open and attentive. Breathing is even. | 2–3 hours |
| Waking activity and crying | Infant shows frequent bursts of uncoordinated body activity. Breathing is very irregular. Face may be relaxed or tense and wrinkled. Crying may occur. | 1–4 hours |

*Source:* Wolff, 1966.

**Rapid-eye-movement (REM) sleep**

An "irregular" sleep state in which brain wave activity is similar to that of the waking state; eyes dart beneath the lids, heart rate, blood pressure, and breathing are uneven; and slight body movements occur.

**Non-rapid-eye-movement (NREM) sleep**

A "regular" sleep state in which the body is quiet and heart rate, breathing, and brain wave activity are slow and regular.

Sleep is made up of at least two states. Irregular, or **rapid-eye-movement (REM) sleep,** is the one that Yolanda and Jay happened to observe. The expression, "sleeping like a baby" was probably not meant to describe this state! During REM sleep, the brain and parts of the body are highly active. Electrical brain wave activity is remarkably similar to that of the waking state. The eyes dart beneath the lids; heart rate, blood pressure, and breathing are uneven; and slight body movements occur. In contrast, during regular or **non-rapid-eye-movement (NREM) sleep,** the body is quiet, and heart rate, breathing, and brain wave activity are slow and regular (Dittrichova et al., 1982).

Like children and adults, newborns alternate back and forth between REM and NREM sleep. However, they spend far more time in the REM state than they ever will again throughout their lives. REM sleep accounts for 50 percent of the newborn baby's sleep time. It declines steadily to 20 percent between 3 and 5 years of age, which is about the same percentage it consumes in adulthood (Roffwarg, Muzio, & Dement, 1966).

Why do young infants spend so much time in REM sleep? In older children and adults, the REM state is associated with dreaming. Babies probably do not dream, at least not in the same way we do. Young infants are believed to have a special need for the stimulation of REM sleep because they spend little time in an alert state, when they can get input from the environment. REM sleep seems to be a way in which the brain stimulates itself. Sleep researchers believe that this stimulation is vital for growth of the central nervous system. In support of this idea, the percentage of REM sleep is especially great in preterm babies, who are even less able to take advantage of external stimulation than are full-term newborns (Parmelee et al., 1967).

Because the normal sleep behavior of the newborn baby is organized and patterned, observations of sleep states can help identify central nervous system abnormalities. In infants who are brain damaged or who have experienced serious birth trauma, disturbed REM-NREM sleep cycles are often present (Theorell, Prechtl, & Vos, 1974).

*Crying.* Crying is the first way that babies communicate, letting parents know that they need food, comfort, and stimulation. During the weeks after birth, all babies seem to have some fussy periods when they are difficult to console. But most of the time, the nature of the cry helps guide parents toward its cause. The baby's cry is actually a complex stimulus that varies in intensity, from a whimper to a message of all-out distress (Gustafson & Harris, 1990). The more intense the cry, the more likely parents are to rush to the infant, anxious and worried.

Most of the time, events that cause newborn infants to cry have to do with physical needs. Hunger is the most common cause, but young infants may also cry in response to temperature change when undressed, a sudden loud sound, or a painful stimulus. Interestingly, newborn crying can also be caused by the sound of another crying baby. Some researchers believe that this response reflects an inborn ability to react to the suffering of others (Martin & Clark, 1982; Hoffman, 1988).

The next time you hear a baby cry, take a moment to observe your own mental and physical reaction. A crying baby stimulates strong feelings of arousal and discomfort in just about anyone—men and women and parents and nonparents alike (Boukydis & Burgess, 1982; Murray, 1985). The powerful effect of the infant's cry is probably innately programmed in all human beings to make sure that babies receive the care and protection they need to survive.

*To soothe her crying infant, this mother talks softly while holding the baby closely. (Lew Merrim/Monkmeyer Press)*

Although parents are not always correct in interpreting the meaning of the baby's cry, experience quickly improves their accuracy (Green, Jones, & Gustafson, 1987). Yet even when parents are fairly certain about the cause of the cry, the baby may not always calm down. Fortunately, as Table 4.7 indicates, there are many ways to soothe a crying newborn when feeding and diaper changing do not work. The technique that parents usually try first is lifting the baby to the shoulder; it is also the one that works the best. Being held upright against the parent's gently moving body not only encourages infants to stop crying, but also causes them to become quietly alert and attentive to the environment (Reisman, 1987). Other common soothing methods are offering the baby a pacifier, talking gently or singing, and swaddling (wrapping the baby's body snugly in a blanket). During some fussy periods, Yolanda and Jay took Joshua on short car rides around the neighborhood. Nestled in his car seat and soothed by the motion and hum of the car motor, Joshua fell blissfully asleep.

Like reflexes and sleep patterns, the infant's cry offers a clue to central nervous system distress. The cries of brain-damaged babies and those who have experienced prenatal and birth complications are often shrill and piercing (Lester, 1987; Zeskind & Lester, 1978, 1981). Most parents try to respond to a sick baby's urgent call for help with extra care and attention. In some cases, however, the cry is so unpleasant and the infant so difficult to soothe that parents become frustrated, resentful, and angry. Research reveals that preterm and sick babies are more likely to be abused by their parents than are healthy infants. Often these parents mention a high-pitched, grating cry as one factor that caused them to lose control and harm the baby (Boukydis, 1985; Frodi, 1985).

## Neonatal Behavioral Assessment

The many capacities described in the preceding sections have been put together into tests that permit doctors, nurses, and child development specialists to assess the behavior of the infant during the newborn period. The most widely used of

TABLE 4.7 • Ways of Soothing a Crying Newborn

| Method | Explanation |
|---|---|
| Lift the baby to the shoulder and rock or walk | Provides a combination of physical contact, upright posture, and motion. The most effective soothing technique. |
| Swaddle the baby | Restricting movement while increasing warmth often soothes a young infant. |
| Offer a pacifier | Sucking helps babies control their own level of arousal. |
| Talk softly or play rhythmic sounds | Continuous, monotonous, rhythmic sounds, such as a clock ticking, a fan whirring, or peaceful music, are more effective than intermittent sounds. |
| Take the baby for a short car ride or walk in a baby carriage; swing the baby in a cradle | Gentle, rhythmic motion of any kind helps lull the baby to sleep. |
| Massage the baby's body | Stroke the baby's torso and limbs with continuous, gentle motions (used in some non-Western cultures to relax the baby's muscles). |
| Combine several of the methods listed above | Stimulating several of the baby's senses at once is often more effective than stimulating only one. |
| If these methods do not work, permit the baby to cry for a short period of time | Occasionally, a baby responds well to just being put down and will, after a few minutes, fall asleep. |

*Sources:* Campos, 1989; Heinl, 1983; Lester, 1985; Reisman, 1987.

these tests is T. Berry Brazelton's (1984) **Neonatal Behavioral Assessment Scale (NBAS).** With it, the examiner can look at the baby's reflexes, state changes, responsiveness to physical and social stimuli, motor abilities, and other reactions.

The NBAS has been given to many infants around the world. As a result, researchers have learned a great deal about individual and cultural differences in newborn behavior and how a baby's reactions can be maintained or changed by child-rearing practices. For example, NBAS scores of Asian and Native American babies reveal that they are less irritable than Caucasian infants. Mothers in these cultures often encourage their babies' calm dispositions through swaddling, close physical contact, and nursing at the first signs of discomfort (Chisholm, 1989; Freedman & Freedman, 1969; Murett-Wagstaff & Moore, 1989). In contrast, the poor NBAS scores of undernourished infants born in Zambia, Africa, are quickly changed by the way their mothers care for them. The Zambian mother carries her baby about on her hip all day, providing a rich variety of sensory stimulation. As a result, by one week of age a once unresponsive newborn has been transformed into an alert, contented baby (Brazelton, Koslowski, & Tronick, 1976).

Can you tell from these examples why a single NBAS score is not a good predictor of later development? Since newborn behavior and parenting styles combine to shape development, *changes in NBAS scores* over the first week or two of life (rather than a single score) provide the best estimate of the baby's ability to recover from the stress of birth. NBAS "recovery curves" predict intelligence with moderate success well into the preschool years (Brazelton, Nugent, & Lester, 1987).

The NBAS has also been used to help parents get to know their infants. In some hospitals, the examination is given in the presence of parents to teach them about their newborn baby's capacities. Parents of both preterm and full-term newborns

**Neonatal Behavioral Assessment Scale (NBAS)**

A test developed to assess the behavior of the infant during the newborn period.

*Similar to women in the Zambian culture, this Efe mother of Zaire, Africa, carries her baby about all day, providing close physical contact and a rich variety of stimulation.* (Tronick/Anthro-Photo)

who participate in these programs have been found to interact more confidently and effectively with their babies (Brazelton, Nugent, & Lester, 1987). Although lasting effects on development have not been demonstrated, NBAS-based interventions are clearly useful in helping the parent–infant relationship get off to a good start.

*BRIEF REVIEW* The newborn baby is equipped with a wide variety of capacities for relating to the surrounding world. Reflexes are the infant's most obvious organized behavior patterns. Some, like sucking, have survival value, while others, like stepping, form the basis for motor skills that will develop later. The senses of touch, taste, smell, and hearing are well developed in the newborn baby. Vision is least mature, but newborns actively explore the environment with the visual abilities that they have. Infants move in and out of five states of arousal throughout the day and night. Sleep is the dominant state; young infants spend far more time in REM sleep than they will at later ages. A crying baby stimulates strong feelings of discomfort in nearby adults. Fortunately, there are many ways to soothe a crying newborn. Neonatal behavioral assessment permits doctors, nurses, and researchers to assess the remarkable capacities of the newborn baby.

• *How do the capacities of newborn babies contribute to their first social relationships? In answering this question, provide as many examples as you can.*

• *Jackie, who had a difficult birth, observes her 2-day-old daughter Kelly being given the NBAS. Kelly scores poorly on many items. Jackie wonders if this means that Kelly will not develop normally. How would you respond to Jackie's concern?*

## THE TRANSITION TO PARENTHOOD

The early weeks after a new baby enters the family are full of profound changes. The mother needs to recover from childbirth and adjust to massive hormone changes that have taken place in her body. If she is breast-feeding, energies must be devoted to working out this intimate relationship. The father also needs to become a part of this new threesome while supporting the mother in her recovery. At times, he may feel somewhat jealous of the baby, who constantly demands and gets his wife's attention (Berman & Pedersen, 1987; Jordan, 1990). While all this is going on, the tiny infant is very assertive about his urgent physical needs, demanding to be fed, changed, and

## FROM RESEARCH TO PRACTICE

Box 4.3 *Postpartum Depression and the Mother–Infant Relationship*

For as many as 50 to 80 percent of first-time mothers, the excitement of the baby's arrival gives way to an emotional letdown during the first week after delivery, a reaction known as the *postpartum* (or after-birth) *blues*. The blues are temporary. They die down as new mothers adjust to hormonal changes following childbirth, gain confidence in caring for the baby, and are reassured by their husbands, family members, and friends.

However, as many as 10 percent of women do not bounce back from childbirth so easily. They experience **postpartum depression,** mild to severe feelings of sadness and withdrawal that continue for weeks or months (Gotlib et al., 1989; Ziporyn, 1992). Stella was one of these women. Her genetic makeup may have predisposed her to develop postpartum depression, but social and cultural factors were also involved. Stella's pregnancy went well until the last month, when her husband Kyle's lack of interest in the baby caused her to worry that having a child might be a mistake. Five days after Lucy was born, Stella's mood plunged. She was anxious and weepy, overwhelmed by Lucy's needs, and angry that she no longer had control over her own schedule. When Stella approached Kyle about her own fatigue and his unwillingness to help with the baby, he snapped that she overreacted to every move he made. Stella's friends, who did not have children, stopped by once to see Lucy and did not call again.

Stella's depressed mood quickly affected her relationship with the baby. As Lucy started to spend more time awake and alert, Stella rarely smiled and talked to her. Lucy responded to Stella's sad, vacant gaze by turning away, frowning, and crying herself (Cohn et al., 1990; Tronick, 1989). Each time this happened, Stella felt guilty and inadequate as a mother, and her depression deepened. Soon Lucy showed signs of serious cognitive and emotional problems, known to affect children of depressed mothers as early as 2 months of age (Cytryn et al., 1986; Whiffen & Gotlib, 1989).

Six weeks after childbirth, Stella made a routine visit to her doctor. He sensed that she was edgy and asked what was wrong. Stella described her tearfulness, fatigue, and inability to comfort Lucy. The doctor also took note of Stella's marital problems and lack of social support—factors commonly associated with postpartum depression (Whiffen, 1988).

Stella was referred to a special treatment program for depressed mothers and their babies. A counselor worked with the family, helping Stella and Kyle with their own problems and encouraging them to be more sensitive and patient with Lucy. In most cases of postpartum depression, treatment is successful. After several months, mother, father, and baby were doing well (Steiner, 1990).

Postpartum depression strikes women of different social classes and ages equally often. About half the time, signs of the depressive mood are already present during pregnancy (Gotlib et al., 1989). Early treatment is vital, to prevent the disorder from undermining the mother–infant relationship and harming the baby's development.

---

**Postpartum depression**
Feelings of sadness and withdrawal that appear shortly after childbirth and that continue for weeks or months.

comforted at odd times of the day and night. A family schedule that was once routine and predictable is now irregular and uncertain.

Yolanda spoke candidly about the changes that she and Jay experienced:

Our emotions were running high the first few days after Joshua's birth. When we brought Joshua home, we had to come down to earth and deal with the realities of our new responsibility. Both of us were struck by how small and helpless Joshua was, and we worried about whether we would be able to take proper care of him. It took us twenty minutes to change the first diaper. I rarely feel well rested because I'm up two to four times every night, and I spend a good part of my waking hours trying to anticipate Joshua's rhythms and needs. If Jay weren't so willing to help by holding and walking Joshua, I think I'd find it much harder.

The demands of new parenthood—disrupted sleep schedules, less time for husband and wife to devote to one another, and new financial responsibilities—often lead to a mild decline in a couple's marital happiness. In addition, entry of the baby into the family usually causes the roles of husband and wife to become more traditional (Cowan & Cowan, 1988; Palkovitz & Copes, 1988). This is even true for couples like Yolanda and Jay, who are strongly committed to sex-role equality and were used to sharing household tasks. Yolanda took a leave of absence from work, while Jay's career life continued just as it had before. As a result, Yolanda spent much more time at home with the baby, while Jay focused more on his provider role. This movement toward traditional roles is hardest on new mothers who have been used to active involvement in a career (LaRossa & LaRossa, 1981). It may be one reason, among others, that women typically experience a more difficult period of adaptation to new parenthood than do men (see Box 4.3).

How long does this time of adjustment to parenthood last? One pair of counselors, who have worked with many new parents, once joked that it lasts about 15 years! Actually, when husband and wife set aside time to listen to one another and try to support each other's needs, the stress caused by new parenthood stays at manageable levels. Family relationships and routine care of the baby are worked out after a few months. Nevertheless, the counselors pointed out, "As long as children are dependent on their parents, those parents find themselves preoccupied with thoughts of their children. This does not keep them from enjoying other aspects of their lives, but it does mean that they never return to being quite the same people they were before they became parents" (Colman & Colman, 1991, p. 198).

 SUMMARY

### The Stages of Childbirth

• Childbirth takes place in three stages. In the first stage, **dilation and effacement of the cervix** occur as uterine contractions increase in strength and frequency. This stage culminates in **transition,** a brief period in which contractions are strongest and closest together and the cervix opens completely. In the second stage, the mother feels an urge to bear down with her abdominal muscles, and the baby is born. In the final stage, the placenta is delivered.

• During labor, infants produce high levels of stress hormones, which help them withstand oxygen deprivation and arouse them into alertness at birth. Newborn infants have large heads, small bodies, and facial features that make adults feel like picking them up and cuddling them. The **Apgar Scale** is used to assess the newborn baby's physical condition at birth.

### Approaches to Childbirth

• **Natural or prepared childbirth** helps reduce stress and pain for the mother during labor and delivery. As a result, most mothers require little or no medication, and they feel more positively about the birth experience.

• As long as mothers are healthy and assisted by a well-trained doctor or midwife, it is just as safe to give birth at home as in a hospital.

### Medical Interventions

• Medical interventions during childbirth are more common in the United States than anywhere else in the world. When women have a history of pregnancy and birth complications, **fetal monitors** help save the lives of many babies. However, when used routinely, they may identify infants as in danger who, in fact, are not.

• **Analgesia** and **anesthesia** are necessary in complicated deliveries. When given in large doses, these drugs produce a depressed state in the newborn that affects the early mother–infant relationship. They also increase the likelihood of an instrument delivery. **Forceps** or **vacuum extractors** can cause head injuries.

• Since **induced labors** are more difficult than naturally occurring ones, they should not be scheduled for reasons of convenience. **Cesarean deliveries** are justified in cases of medical emergency and when babies are in **breech position.** Many unnecessary cesareans are performed in the United States.

### Birth Complications

• Although most births proceed normally, serious complications can occur. A major cause of **cerebral palsy** is lack of oxygen. As long as oxygen deprivation is not extreme, most oxygen-deprived newborns catch up in development by the school years. **Respiratory distress syndrome,** which can cause permanent damage due to lack of oxygen, is common in infants who are more than six weeks premature.

• Premature births are high among low-income pregnant women and mothers of twins. **Small-for-dates** infants usually have longer-lasting problems than do **preterm** babies whose weight is appropriate for time spent in the uterus. Some interventions for preterm infants provide special stimulation in the intensive care nursery. Others teach parents how to care for and interact with these fragile babies. A major cause of **neonatal** and **infant mortality** in the United States is low birth weight.

• **Postterm** infants are at risk for serious birth complications. Therefore, doctors usually induce labor in mothers whose pregnancies have continued for more than 42 weeks.

• When babies experience birth trauma, a supportive home environment can help restore their growth. Even infants with severe birth complications can recover with the help of favorable life events.

### Precious Moments After Birth

• Human parents do not require close physical contact with the baby immediately after birth for **bonding** to occur. Nevertheless, most parents find early contact with the infant especially meaningful, and it may help them build a good relationship with the baby.

### The Newborn Baby's Capacities

• Infants begin life with remarkable skills for relating to their physical and social worlds. **Reflexes** are the newborn baby's most obvious organized patterns of behavior. Some have survival value, while others provide the foundation for voluntary motor skills that will develop later.

• The senses of touch, taste, smell, and sound are well developed at birth. Newborns are especially responsive to high-pitched expressive voices, and they prefer the sound of their mother's voice. They can distinguish almost all speech sounds in human languages.

• Vision is the least mature of the newborn's senses. At birth, focusing ability and **visual acuity** are limited. In exploring the visual field, newborn babies are attracted to bright objects, but they limit their looking to single features. The newborn infant has difficulty discriminating colors.

• Although newborns alternate frequently among five different **states of arousal,** they spend most of their time asleep. **Rapid-eye-movement (REM) sleep** provides young infants with stimulation essential for central nervous system development.

• A crying baby stimulates strong feelings of discomfort in nearby adults. Once feeding and diaper changing have been tried, lifting the baby to the shoulder is the most effective soothing technique. Many other soothing methods are helpful.

• The most widely used instrument for assessing the behavior of the newborn infant is Brazelton's **Neonatal Behavioral Assessment Scale (NBAS).** The NBAS has helped researchers understand individual and cultural differences in newborn behavior. Sometimes it is used to teach parents about their baby's capacities.

### The Transition to Parenthood

• The new baby's arrival is exciting but stressful. The demands of new parenthood often lead to a slight drop in marital happiness, and family roles become more traditional. When husband and wife are sensitive to each other's needs, adjustment problems are usually temporary, and the transition to parenthood goes well.

## IMPORTANT TERMS AND CONCEPTS

dilation and effacement of the cervix (p. 126)

transition (p. 127)

episiotomy (p. 128)

Apgar Scale (p. 129)

natural or prepared childbirth (p. 132)

fetal monitors (p. 135)

analgesia (p. 136)

anesthesia (p. 136)

forceps (p. 137)

vacuum extractor (p. 137)

induced labor (p. 137)

cesarean delivery (p. 138)

breech position (p. 138)

cerebral palsy (p. 140)

respiratory distress syndrome (p. 140)

preterm (p. 141)

small for dates (p. 141)

postterm (p. 143)

infant mortality (p. 145)

neonatal mortality (p. 145)

engrossment (p. 147)

bonding (p. 147)

rooming in (p. 147)

reflex (p. 148)

visual acuity (p. 152)

states of arousal (p. 153)

rapid-eye-movement (REM) sleep (p. 154)

non-rapid-eye movement (NREM) sleep (p. 154)

Neonatal Behavioral Assessment Scale (NBAS) (p. 156)

postpartum depression (p. 158)

## FOR FURTHER INFORMATION AND SPECIAL HELP

### General Childbirth Information

National Association of Parents and Professionals for Safe Alternatives in Childbirth
Route 1, Box 646
Marble Hill, MO 63764-9726
(314) 238-2010

Provides information on all aspects of childbirth. Places special emphasis on choosing safe childbirth alternatives.

American Foundation for Maternal and Child Health
439 East 51st Street, 4th Floor
New York, NY 10022
(212) 759-5510

Provides information on maternal and child health during the birth period.

### Independent Birth Centers

National Association of Childbearing Centers
3123 Gottschall Road
Perkiomenville, PA 18074
(215) 234-8068

Offers referrals to free-standing birth centers, which operate independently of hospitals.

### Natural Childbirth

American Society for Psychoprophylaxis in Obstetrics (ASPO)
1840 Wilson Blvd., Suite 204
Arlington, VA 22201
(703) 524-7802
(800) 368-4404

Trains and certifies instructors in Lamaze method of natural childbirth. Provides information to expectant parents.

American Academy of Husband-Coached Childbirth
P.O. Box 5224
Sherman Oaks, CA 91413
(818) 788-6662
(800) 423-2397

Certifies instructors in the Bradley method of natural childbirth, which emphasizes coaching by the husband.

### Home Birth

Association for Childbirth at Home, International
P.O. Box 430
Glendale, CA 91209
(213) 663-4996

Provides information on and support for home birth.

Informed Homebirth/Informed Birth and Parenting
P.O. Box 3675
Ann Arbor, MI 48106
(313) 662-6857

Trains and certifies home-birth attendants. Offers information to couples interested in home birth.

### Midwives

American College of Nurse-Midwives
1522 K Street, N.W.
Suite 1000
Washington, DC 20005
(202) 289-0171

Certifies nurse-midwives and provides referrals to expectant parents.

### Cesarean Delivery

Cesareans/Support, Education, and Concern, Inc.
(C/Sec, Inc.)
22 Forest Road
Framingham, MA 01701
(508) 877-8266

Provides information on and support for cesarean mothers, including vaginal birth after cesarean.

### Cerebral Palsy

United Cerebral Palsy Association
7 Penn Plaza
Suite 804
New York, NY 10001
(212) 268-6655

Provides assistance to persons with cerebral palsy and their families. Local and state chapters offer medical, therapeutic, and social services.

*"Mother and Child," Sumedha Patale Pieris, 9 years,*
*Sri Lanka. Reprinted by permission from The*
*International Museum of Children's Art, Oslo, Norway.*

# Physical Development in Infancy and Toddlerhood

5

Growth of the Body in the First Two Years
*Changes in Body Size   Changes in Body Proportions   Changes in Muscle–Fat Makeup
Early Skeletal Growth*

Brain Development
*Development of Neurons   Development of the Cerebral Cortex*

Factors Affecting Early Physical Growth
*Heredity   Nutrition   Malnutrition   Affection and Stimulation*

Changing States of Arousal

Motor Development During the First Two Years
*The Sequence of Motor Development   Motor Skills as Complex Systems of Action
Maturation, Experience, and the Development of Motor Skills   Fine Motor Development:
The Special Case of Voluntary Reaching   Bladder and Bowel Control*

Basic Learning Mechanisms
*Classical Conditioning   Operant Conditioning   Habituation and Dishabituation
Imitation*

Perceptual Development in Infancy
*Hearing   Vision   Intermodal Perception*

Understanding Perceptual Development

Within a two-day period, Lisa, Beth, and Felicia each gave birth to their first child at the same hospital. During their stay, the three mothers got to know one another. Over the next two years, they met once a month to talk over questions and concerns about the development of their babies—Byron, Rachel, and April. The mothers permitted me to sit in on several of these meetings, and I watched and listened as the infants changed from immobile lap babies into cruising 1-year-olds, and finally, into walking, talking toddlers.

As the infants grew, the mothers' conversations changed accordingly. In the beginning, they worried most about physical care—how well breast-feeding was going, how soon to introduce solid foods, and when the baby's sleep–waking schedule would become more predictable. Between 2 and 3 months, each mother noticed that her baby's daily rhythms had become more organized and patterned, and all three youngsters were much more alert. "Two months seems like a real turning point," commented Felicia. "Life is easier now that I can anticipate April's feedings and naptimes. She seems like more of a little person, and she's much more interested in the world around her."

As the infants' motor skills changed, the home setting in which the mothers gathered changed as well. By the second half of the first year, mothers and babies no longer sat quietly in pairs on the sofa. Instead, the floor was covered with toys, and all three infants crawled about, while their mothers kept a watchful eye out for coffee table corners, lamp cords, and electric sockets. Soon crawling became walking. This

*New motor skills have a dramatic impact on the baby's approach to the world. As infants sit up and begin to crawl, their whole view of the environment and capacity to explore it changes. (Margaret Miller/Photo Researchers)*

*when crawling becomes walking toddlerhood*

marked the beginning of *toddlerhood*—a period that spans the second year of life—and the children's approach to the world changed again. At first, the youngsters did, indeed, "toddle" with an awkward gait, rocking from side to side and tipping over frequently. But their faces reflected the thrill of being upright, and they explored enthusiastically. As their 2-year-old birthdays approached, the mothers reflected on the astounding changes that had taken place since the newborn period. "Byron is nearly twice as tall and four times as heavy," said Lisa. "He's starting to look more like a little boy than a baby."

This chapter traces physical growth during the first 2 years—one of the most remarkable and busiest times of development. We will see how rapid changes in the infant's body and brain support new motor skills, learning mechanisms, and perceptual capacities. Byron, Rachel, and April will join us along the way, to illustrate individual differences and environmental influences on physical development.

## GROWTH OF THE BODY IN THE FIRST TWO YEARS

The next time you have a chance, briefly observe several infants and toddlers while walking in your neighborhood or at a nearby shopping center. You will see that their capabilities are vastly different. One reason for the change in what children can do over the first 2 years is that their bodies change enormously—so much so that relatives who visit just after a baby is born and return again a year or two later often remark that the child does not seem like the same individual!

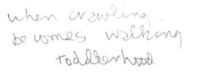

### Changes in Body Size

To parents, the most obvious signs of physical growth are changes in the size of the child's body as a whole. During the first 2 years, these changes are rapid—faster than they will be at any time after birth. As shown in Figure 5.1, by the end of the first year the infant's length is 50 percent greater than it was at birth, and by 2 years of age it is 75 percent greater. Weight shows similar dramatic gains. By 5 months of age, birth weight has doubled, at 1 year it has tripled, and at 2 years it has quadrupled.

**FIGURE 5.1** • Gains in height and weight from birth to 2 years among American children. The steep rise in these growth curves shows that children grow rapidly during this period. At the same time, wide individual differences in body size exist. Infants and toddlers who fall at the 50th percentile are average in height and weight. Those who fall at the 90th percentile are taller and heavier than 90 percent of their agemates. Those who fall at the 10th percentile are taller and heavier than only 10 percent of their peers. Note that girls are slightly shorter and lighter than boys.

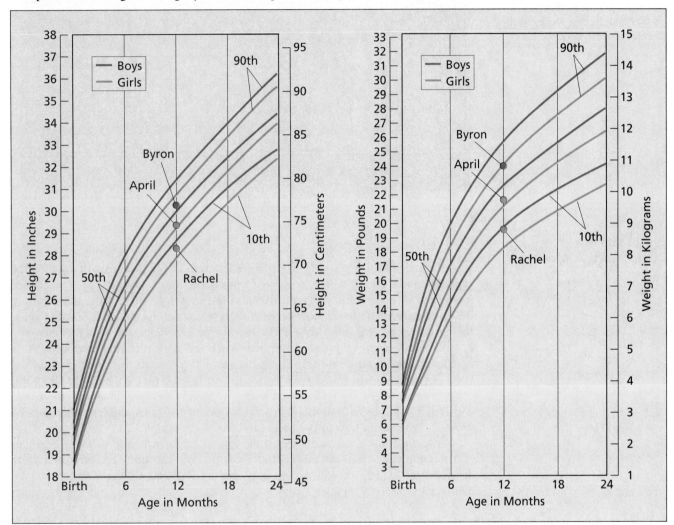

In body size, as in all aspects of development, differences among children exist. In infancy, girls are slightly shorter and lighter than boys. This small but typical sex difference continues throughout early and middle childhood, and it will be greatly magnified at adolescence. Racial differences in body size are apparent as well. Look again at Figure 5.1, and you will see that Rachel, a Japanese child, is below the growth norms (height and weight averages) for youngsters her age. In contrast, April is above average, as African-American children tend to be (Tanner, 1978b).

### Changes in Body Proportions

As the child's overall size increases, different parts of the body grow at different rates. Recall from Chapter 3 that during the prenatal period, the head develops first from the primitive embryonic disk, followed by the lower part of the body. After birth, the head and chest continue to have a growth advantage, but the baby's trunk and

**FIGURE 5.2** • Changes in body proportions from the early prenatal period to adulthood. The figure illustrates the cephalo-caudal trend of physical growth. The head gradually becomes smaller and the legs longer in proportion to the rest of the body.

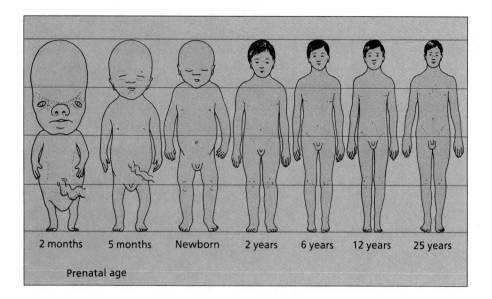

2 months    5 months    Newborn    2 years    6 years    12 years    25 years

Prenatal age

*[handwritten note: head's biggest get smaller as arms & legs get bigger]*

*[handwritten note: growth from center outward]*

legs gradually pick up speed. This organized pattern of physical growth is called the **cephalo-caudal trend,** which, translated from Latin, means head to tail. You can see it depicted in Figure 5.2. At birth, the head takes up 1/4 of the body, the legs only 1/3. Notice how the lower portion of the body catches up by age 2. At that time, the head accounts for only 1/5 and the legs for nearly 1/2 of total body length.

There is a second growth pattern that describes changes in body proportions. It is called the **proximo-distal trend,** meaning growth proceeds from the center of the body outward. Again, this is what happened during the prenatal period. The head, chest, and trunk grew first, followed by the arms and legs, and finally by the hands and feet. During infancy and childhood, growth of the arms and legs continues to proceed somewhat ahead of the hands and feet.

Concept Table 5.1 summarizes these important growth trends. Look carefully at the examples given in the table. They show that not just body growth, but motor development (which we will discuss in a later section) follows these same developmental patterns.

### Changes in Muscle–Fat Makeup

One of the most obvious changes in Byron, Rachel, and April's appearances was their transformation into round, plump babies by the middle of the first year. Body fat (most of which lies just beneath the skin) begins to increase in the last few weeks of prenatal life and continues to do so after birth, reaching a peak at about 9 months of age. Then, during the second year, toddlers start to become more slender, a trend that continues into middle childhood. This very early rise in "baby fat" helps the small infant keep a constant body temperature (Tanner, 1978b).

Muscle tissue grows according to a very different plan than fat. It increases very slowly during infancy and childhood and will not reach a peak until adolescence. Babies are not very muscular creatures, and their strength and physical coordination are limited.

As with body size, slight differences exist between boys and girls in muscle–fat makeup. From the beginning, girls have a higher ratio of fat to muscle than boys, a difference that will increase in middle childhood and become very large during adolescence (Tanner & Whitehouse, 1975).

**Cephalo-caudal trend**

An organized pattern of physical growth that proceeds from head to tail.

**Proximo-distal trend**

An organized pattern of physical growth that proceeds from the center of the body outward.

**CONCEPT TABLE 5.1 • Trends in Body Growth and Motor Control**

| Concept | Important Point | Example |
|---------|-----------------|---------|
| Cephalo-caudal trend | Parts of the body grow at different rates. Physical growth and motor control of the upper regions proceeds ahead of growth and control of the lower regions. | At birth, the baby's head is large in comparison to the trunk and legs. During the first year, infants lift their heads and chests before they sit, crawl, and walk. |
| Proximo-distal trend | Physical growth and motor control proceed from the center of the body outward. | The head, chest, and trunk grow earliest, followed by the arms and legs, and then the hands and feet. During infancy, head and chest control are achieved before control of the arms and, finally, the hands. |

## Early Skeletal Growth

Children of the same age differ in *rate* of physical growth. In other words, some make faster progress toward a mature body size than others. We cannot tell how quickly a child's physical growth is moving along just by looking at current body size, since children grow to different heights and weights in adulthood. For example, Byron is slightly larger and heavier than Rachel and April, but he is not physically more mature. In a moment, you will see why.

**General Skeletal Growth.** The best way of estimating a child's physical maturity is to use **skeletal age,** a measure of development of the bones of the body. The embryonic skeleton is first formed out of soft, pliable tissue called *cartilage*. Then, beginning in the sixth week of pregnancy, cartilage cells gradually harden into bone, a very gradual process that continues throughout childhood and adolescence. Once bones have taken on their basic shape, special growth centers called **epiphyses** appear just before birth (see Figure 5.3). In the long bones of the body, the epiphyses

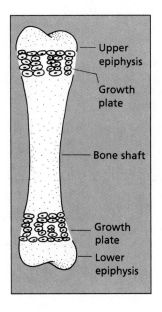

**FIGURE 5.3** • Diagram of a long bone showing upper and lower epiphyses. Cartilage cells are produced at a growth plate and gradually harden into bone. As growth continues, the epiphyses disappear. *(Reprinted by permission of the publisher from* Fetus into man, *by J. M. Tanner, Cambridge, Mass.: Harvard University Press, p. 33. Copyright © 1978 by J. M. Tanner. All rights reserved.)*

**Skeletal age**

An estimate of physical maturity based on development of the bones of the body.

**Epiphyses**

Growth centers in the bones where new cartilage cells are produced and gradually harden.

emerge at the two extreme ends of each bone. There, new cartilage cells are produced and gradually harden. As growth continues, the epiphyses get thinner and disappear. When this occurs, no more growth of the bone is possible. Skeletal age can be estimated by X-raying the bones and seeing how many epiphyses there are and the extent to which they are fused. These X-rays are compared to norms established for bone maturity based on large numbers of children (Delecki, 1985).

When the skeletal ages of infants and children are examined, they reveal that black children tend to be slightly ahead of white children at all ages. In addition, girls are considerably ahead of boys. At birth, the difference between the sexes amounts to about 4 to 6 weeks, a gap that widens over infancy and childhood and is responsible for the fact that girls reach their full body size several years before boys. Girls are advanced in development of other organs of the body as well. Their greater physical maturity may contribute to the fact that they are more resistant to harmful environmental influences throughout development. As we pointed out in Chapter 2, girls experience fewer developmental problems, and infant and childhood mortality for girls is also lower (Tanner, 1978b).

*Growth of the Skull.*   Doctors are concerned with another aspect of skeletal development when they routinely measure the head sizes of children between birth and 2 years of age. Skull growth is especially rapid during the first 2 years because of large increases in brain size. At birth, the bones of the skull are separated by six gaps, or "soft spots," called **fontanels** (see Figure 5.4). The gaps permit the bones to overlap as the large head of the baby passes through the mother's narrow birth canal. You can easily feel the largest gap, the anterior fontanel, at the top of a baby's skull. It is slightly more than an inch across. It gradually shrinks and is filled in during the second year. The other fontanels are smaller and close more quickly. As the skull bones come in contact with one another, they form *sutures,* or seams. These permit the skull to expand easily as the brain grows during the first few years of life.

FIGURE 5.4 • The skull at birth, showing the fontanels and sutures. *(Reproduced by permission from* Human growth and development throughout life: A nursing perspective, *by P. M. Hill & P. Humphrey, Delmar Publishers, Inc., p. 42. Copyright 1982.)*

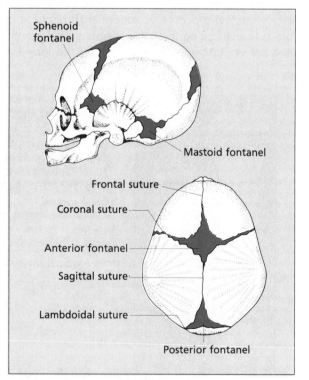

**Fontanels**

Six soft spots that separate the bones of the skull at birth.

***Appearance of Teeth.***   On the average, the baby's first tooth appears at about 6 months, although there are wide individual differences. April already had a tooth when she was born; a few infants do not get their first tooth until 1 year of age. After the first tooth erupts, new ones appear every month or two. By age 2, the child has 20 teeth. Dental development provides a rough clue to overall rate of skeletal development. A child who gets teeth early is likely to be ahead in physical maturity (Mott, James, & Sperhac, 1990).

## BRAIN DEVELOPMENT

At birth, the brain is nearer to its adult size than any other physical structure, and it continues to develop at an astounding pace throughout infancy and toddlerhood. To best understand brain growth, we need to look at it from two vantage points. The first is at the microscopic level of individual brain cells. The second is at the larger level of the cerebral cortex, the most complex brain structure and the one responsible for the highly developed intelligence of our species.

### Development of Neurons

The human brain has 100 to 200 billion **neurons,** or nerve cells, that store and transmit information, many of which have thousands of direct connections with other neurons. Neurons differ from other body cells in that they are not tightly packed together. There are tiny gaps, or **synapses,** between them where fibers from different neurons come close together but do not touch. Neurons release chemicals that cross the synapse, thereby sending messages to one another.

The basic story of brain growth concerns how neurons develop and form this elaborate communication system. In Chapter 3, we indicated that neurons are produced in the primitive neural tube of the embryo, from which they travel to form the major parts of the brain. Recall that by the end of the second trimester of pregnancy, this process is complete; no more neurons will ever again be produced. After birth, the neurons form complex networks of synaptic connections. During infancy and toddlerhood, growth of neural fibers and synapses increases at an astounding pace (Moore, 1989; Nowakowski, 1987).

Once neurons form connections, a new factor becomes important in their survival: *stimulation.* Neurons that are stimulated by input from the surrounding environment continue to establish new synapses. Those that are seldom stimulated soon die off. This suggests that appropriate stimulation of the child's brain is critically important during periods in which the formation of synapses is at its peak (Greenough, Black, & Wallace, 1987). Indeed, a great deal of animal research supports this idea. For example, there seems to be a critical period during which rich and varied visual experiences must occur for the visual centers of the brain to develop normally. If a month-old kitten is deprived of light for as brief a time as 3 or 4 days, these areas of the brain start to degenerate (Hubel & Wiesel, 1970).

At this point, you may be wondering: If no more neurons are produced after the prenatal period, what causes the dramatic increase in skull size that we mentioned earlier in this chapter? About half the brain's volume is made up of **glial cells,** which do not carry messages. Instead, their most important function is **myelinization,** a process in which neural fibers are coated with an insulating fatty sheath (called *myelin*) that improves the efficiency of message transfer. Glial cells multiply at a dramatic pace from the fourth month of pregnancy through the second year of life, after which their rate of production slows down (Spreen et al., 1984). Myelinization is responsible for the rapid gain in overall size of the brain (see Figure 5.5). By the

**Neurons**

Nerve cells that store and transmit information in the brain.

**Synapse**

The gap between neurons, across which chemical messages are sent.

**Glial cells**

Brain cells serving the function of myelinization.

**Myelinization**

A process in which neural fibers are coated with an insulating fatty sheath that improves the efficiency of message transfer.

**FIGURE 5.5** • Increase in weight of the human brain from the prenatal period to adulthood. The rise in brain weight is especially rapid between the fetal period and the child's second birthday (see red line), when glial cells are multiplying at a dramatic pace. As brain weight increases, the cortex becomes increasingly convoluted, or folded. *(From R. J. Lemire, J. D. Loeser, R. W. Leech, & E. C. Alvord, 1975, Normal and abnormal development of the human nervous system, New York: Harper & Row, p. 236. Adapted by permission.)*

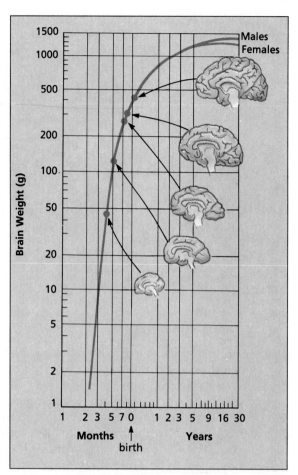

time toddlerhood is complete, the brain is already about three-fifths of its adult weight.

## Development of the Cerebral Cortex

The **cerebral cortex** is the largest structure of the human brain, accounting for 85 percent of its weight and containing the greatest number of neurons and synapses. The cortex surrounds the rest of the brain, much like a half-shelled walnut. Of all brain structures, the cerebral cortex is the last to stop growing. For this reason, it is believed to be much more sensitive to environmental influences than any other part of the brain (Suomi, 1982).

As shown in Figure 5.6, different regions of the cerebral cortex have specific functions, such as receiving information from the senses, instructing the body to move, and thinking. Scientists study the development of these regions by analyzing the chemical makeup and myelinization of the brains of young children who have died. Their findings reveal that the order in which areas of the cortex develop corresponds to the order in which various capacities emerge in the infant and growing child. For example, among areas that control body movement, the most advanced at birth is the precentral gyrus (refer again to Figure 5.6). Within it, neurons that control the head, arms, and chest mature ahead of those that control the trunk and legs. Do you recognize a familiar developmental trend? The last portion of the cortex to develop and myelinate is the frontal lobe, which is responsible for thought and consciousness. From age 2 months onward, this area functions more effectively, and

**Cerebral cortex**

The largest structure of the human brain that accounts for the highly developed intelligence of the human species.

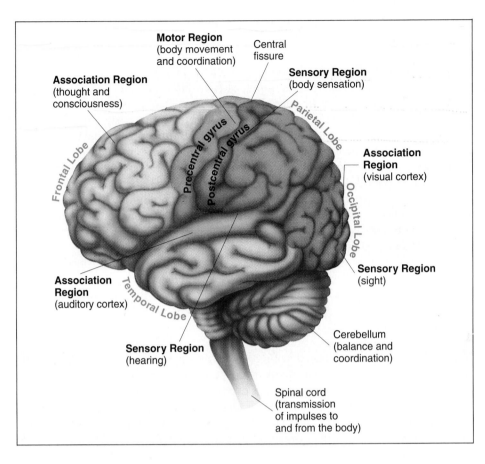

**FIGURE 5.6** • The left side of the human brain, showing the major structures of the cerebral cortex. The cortex is divided into different lobes, each of which contains a variety of regions with specific functions. *Motor regions* give direct orders to the muscles of the body, *sensory regions* receive direct input from the sense organs, and *association or "thought" regions* combine impulses from many other parts of the brain.

*[handwritten note: what is thought & consciousness and frontal & temporal function? lobes + -]*

it continues its growth for years, well into the second and third decades of life (Spreen et al., 1984).

*Lateralization of the Cortex.* Figure 5.6 shows only one *hemisphere,* or side, of the cortex. If you could turn the brain around, you would see that it has two hemispheres—left and right. Although the hemispheres look alike, they do not have precisely the same functions. Some tasks are done mostly by one hemisphere and some by the other. For example, each hemisphere receives sensory information from and controls only one side of the body—the one opposite to it. For most of us, the left hemisphere is responsible for verbal abilities (such as spoken and written language), and the right hemisphere handles emotional reactions and spatial abilities (such as judging distances, reading maps, and recognizing geometric shapes). This pattern may be reversed in left-handed people, but more often, the cortex of left-handers is less clearly specialized than that of right-handers.

Specialization of the two hemispheres is called **lateralization.** Few topics in child development have stimulated more interest than the question of when brain lateralization occurs. The reason that scientists are interested in this issue is that they want to know more about brain **plasticity.** A highly *plastic* cortex is still adaptable because many areas are not yet committed to specific functions. If a part of the brain is damaged, other parts can take over tasks that would have been handled by the damaged region. But once the hemispheres lateralize, damage to a particular region means that the abilities controlled by it will be lost forever.

Researchers used to think that lateralization of the cortex did not begin until after 2 years of age (Lenneberg, 1967). Today we know that this is not the case. Electrical brain wave recordings taken as infants react to different kinds of stimulation suggest that the hemispheres have already started to specialize at birth. Most preterm

**Lateralization**
Specialization of functions of the two hemispheres of the cortex.

**Plasticity**
The ability of other parts of the brain to take over functions of damaged regions.

and full-term newborns show greater activity in the left hemisphere while listening to speech sounds. In contrast, the right hemisphere reacts more strongly to nonspeech sounds as well as stimuli (such as a sour-tasting fluid) that cause infants to display negative emotions (Fox & Davidson, 1986; Hahn, 1987).

Although brain lateralization begins early in life, it is not yet complete. The brain gradually becomes more specialized with age (McManus et al., 1988). As a result, if the cortex of a baby less than 1 year old is damaged, it shows a remarkable ability to bounce back from injury. For example, cases exist in which infants had part or all of one hemisphere removed to control violent brain seizures. The remaining hemisphere, whether right or left, took over language and spatial functions as the child matured (Goodman & Whitaker, 1985). But because lateralization had already begun, recovery from injury was not complete. As these brain-injured infants reached middle childhood and adolescence, they showed many normal abilities, but they had difficulty with very complex verbal and spatial tasks (Dennis & Whitaker, 1976; Kohn & Dennis, 1974).

The cortex seems to be programmed from the start for the hemispheric specialization that is typical of our species. A lateralized brain is certainly adaptive. It permits a much greater variety of talents to be represented in the two hemispheres than if both sides of the cortex served exactly the same functions.

*BRIEF REVIEW*   The infant's body increases rapidly in overall size during the first 2 years of life. Different parts of the body grow at different rates, following cephalo-caudal and proximo-distal trends of development. During the first year, body fat increases much faster than muscle. The skull expands rapidly as the brain grows. Around 6 months of age, the first teeth emerge. The human brain grows faster early in development than any other organ of the body. During the first 2 years, synapses, or connections between neurons, are rapidly laid down. Myelinization is responsible for efficient communication among neurons and a dramatic increase in brain weight. The cerebral cortex is the last part of the brain to stop growing. It is also the structure most affected by stimulation. The cortex has already begun to lateralize at birth, but it retains considerable plasticity during the first year of life.

*• When Joey was born, the doctor found that his anterior fontanel had started to close prematurely. Joey had surgery to open the fontanel when he was 3 months old. From what you know about the function of the fontanels, why was early surgery necessary?*

*• Felicia commented that at 2 months of age April's daily schedule seemed more predictable, and she was much more alert. What aspects of brain development might be responsible for this change?*

## FACTORS AFFECTING EARLY PHYSICAL GROWTH

Physical growth, like other aspects of development, results from the continuous and complex interplay between heredity and environment. April, who has tall parents, is likely to be tall herself. Lisa, who constantly has to watch her weight, wonders whether Byron will have the same problem. Although all three children are growing up in homes where there is plenty to eat and they receive much love and stimulation, many infants are not so fortunate. Each of these factors affects early physical growth, as we will see in the following sections.

### Heredity

Since identical twins are much more alike in height and weight than are fraternals, we know that heredity plays a role in body size. However, this resemblance depends on when infant twins are measured. At birth, the differences in weights and lengths of identical twins are actually greater than those of fraternals. The reason is that identical twins share the same placenta, and one baby usually manages to get more nourishment. As long as negative environmental factors are not severe, the smaller baby recovers and swings back to her genetically determined path of growth within a few months (Wilson, 1976). This tendency is called **catch-up growth,** and it persists throughout childhood and adolescence.

When nutrition is adequate, height and rate of physical growth (as measured by skeletal age) are largely determined by heredity (Susanne, 1975). Body weight is also affected by genetic makeup, since the weights of adopted children correlate more strongly with those of their biological than adoptive parents. However, as far as weight is concerned, environment—in particular, nutrition—plays an especially important role (Stunkard et al., 1986).

### Nutrition

Good nutrition is important at any time of development, but it is especially critical in infancy because the baby's brain and body are growing so rapidly. Pound for pound, a young baby's energy needs are twice as great as those of an adult. This is because 25 percent of the infant's total caloric intake is devoted to growth, and extra calories are needed to keep rapidly developing organs of the body functioning properly (Pipes, 1989).

Babies do not just need enough food. They need the right kind of food. In early infancy, breast milk is especially suited to their needs, and bottled formulas try to imitate it. Later on, infants require well-balanced solid foods. If a baby's diet is deficient in either quantity or quality, growth can be permanently stunted.

***Breast- versus Bottle-Feeding.*** For thousands of years, all human babies were fed the ultimate human health food: breast milk. Only within the last hundred years has bottle-feeding been available. As formulas became easier to prepare, breast-feeding declined from the 1940s into the 1970s when over 75 percent of American infants were bottle fed. Partly as a result of the natural childbirth movement (see Chapter 4), efforts were made in the 1970s and 1980s to encourage mothers to breast-feed. Soon breast-feeding became more common, especially among well-educated, middle-class women. Today, over 60 percent of American mothers breast-feed their babies (National Center for Health Statistics, 1991).

Here are the major nutritional and health advantages of breast milk:

1. *Correct balance of fat and protein.* Compared to the milk of other mammals, human milk is higher in fat and lower in protein. This balance, as well as the unique proteins and fats contained in human milk, is ideal for a rapidly my-elinating nervous system. In contrast, the makeup of cow's milk is suited to early muscle growth (Stini et al., 1980). As we saw earlier, the natural growth pattern for human infants is to add fat quickly and muscle slowly during the first 2 years of life.

2. *Nutritional completeness.* Human milk is a complete food for young babies. A mother who breast-feeds need not add solid foods to her infant's diet until the baby is 6 months old. At that time, her baby is better able to swallow solids, and the digestive tract is mature enough to handle them. The milks of all mammals are low in iron, but the iron contained in breast milk is much more easily absorbed by the baby's system. Consequently, bottle-fed infants need iron-fortified formula, and doctors sometimes recommend giving them iron-rich solid foods by 2 to 3 months of age.

3. *Protection against disease.* Breast-feeding helps protect the young infant against disease. For 1 to 4 days before the mother's milk comes in, her breasts produce a sticky yellowish fluid called **colostrum.** Colostrum is especially high in antibodies, and the breast milk that follows also provides them. As a result, breast-fed babies have far fewer respiratory and intestinal illnesses and allergic reactions than do bottle-fed infants (American Academy of Pediatrics, 1984).

**Catch-up growth**
Physical growth that returns to its genetically determined path after being delayed by environmental factors.

**Colostrum**
The sticky yellowish fluid produced by the mother's breast before the milk comes in that is especially high in antibodies.

*Breast-feeding is especially important in developing countries, where infants are at risk for malnutrition and early death due to widespread poverty. This Huastec baby of southern Mexico is likely to grow normally during the first year because his mother decided to breast-feed.* (Jean-Gerard Sidaner/Photo Researchers)

4. *Digestibility*. Since breast-fed babies have a different kind of bacteria growing in their intestines than do bottle-fed infants, they rarely become constipated or have diarrhea.

Because of these benefits, breast-fed babies in poverty-stricken regions of the world are much less likely to be malnourished and 6 to 14 times more likely to survive the first year of life. Too often, bottle-fed infants in developing countries are given low-grade nutrients, such as rice water or highly diluted cow's and goat's milk. When formula is available, it is generally contaminated due to poor sanitation (Grant, 1990).

In industrialized nations, most women who choose breast-feeding find it to be an emotionally satisfying experience, but breast-feeding is not for everyone. Some mothers simply do not like it, or they are embarrassed by it. A few others, for physiological reasons, are unable to produce enough milk. Occasionally, there are medical reasons that prevent a mother from nursing. If she is taking certain drugs, they can be transmitted to the baby through the milk. If she has a serious viral or bacterial disease, such as AIDS or tuberculosis, she runs the risk of infecting her baby (Seltzer & Benjamin, 1990).

Breast milk is so easily digestible that a breast-fed infant becomes hungry quite often—every 1½ to 2 hours in comparison to the 3- to 4-hour schedule of the bottle-fed baby. This makes breast-feeding inconvenient for many women who are employed. However, a mother who cannot be with her baby all the time can still breast-feed or combine it with bottle-feeding. For example, Lisa returned to her job part-time when Byron was 2 months old. Before she left for work, she pumped her milk into a bottle for later feeding by his caregiver. The same technique can be used for infants who are hospitalized. Preterm infants, especially, benefit from the antibodies and easy digestibility of breast milk. Moreover, the breast milk produced for a preterm baby is different from that produced for a full-term infant. It is higher in protein and certain minerals and believed to be specially adapted to the preterm infant's growth needs (Gross, Geller, & Tomarelli, 1981).

Table 5.1 summarizes factors associated with a mother's choice of breast-feeding over bottle-feeding. Some women who cannot or do not want to breast-feed worry that they might be depriving the baby of an experience that is critical for emotional development. As we will see in Chapter 7, emotional well-being is affected by the warmth and sensitivity that accompanies infant feeding, not by the type of milk offered. Research reveals that breast- and bottle-fed youngsters show no differences in psychological development (Fergusson, Horwood, & Shanon, 1987).

***Are Chubby Babies at Risk for Later Overweight and Obesity?*** Overweight and *obesity* are common problems in industrialized nations where food is plentiful. In the United States alone, about 45 percent of adults are affected. The health risks are serious. They include high blood pressure, heart disease, diabetes, and a shorter life span (Stephenson et al., 1987). Fatness also has social and emotional consequences. As we will see in Chapter 11 when we take up obesity in detail, fat children tend to be very unhappy youngsters who are often disliked by their peers.

Byron was an enthusiastic eater from early infancy. He nursed vigorously and gained weight quickly. By 5 months, he indicated his need for solid foods by whimpering after a feeding and reaching for food from his parents' plates. Lisa had heard about research in which rats were overfed early in development. Their bodies responded by producing too many fat cells, which acted to maintain the overweight condition (Knittle & Hirsch, 1968; Winick & Noble, 1966). Like many other American women who live in a culture preoccupied with thinness, Lisa wondered: Was she overfeeding Byron and, thereby, increasing his chances of being permanently overweight?

TABLE 5.1 • Factors Associated with a Mother's Choice of Breast- Over Bottle-Feeding

---

**Maternal Attitudes**

Mother believes that breast-feeding:

    Is better for growth and health of the baby

    Is more convenient than preparing bottles

    Offers special feelings of closeness to the baby and personal satisfaction

**Family Characteristics**

Higher family income and education

Mother unemployed or employed part-time rather than full-time

Mother married rather than single (a sympathetic husband increases the likelihood of breast-feeding)

Mother's husband, friends, relatives, and doctor support the decision to breast-feed

**Pregnancy and Birth Experience**

Planned pregnancy

Early start of prenatal care

Enrollment in natural childbirth or other prenatal classes

Uncomplicated delivery

Previous success at breast-feeding

---

*Sources:* Baranowski et al., 1986; Grossman et al., 1990.

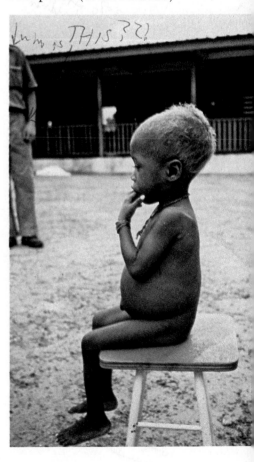

*The swollen abdomen and listless behavior of this child are classic symptoms of kwashiorkor, a nutritional illness that results from a diet very low in protein. (CNRI/Phototake)*

As yet, there is no evidence that a well-nourished human infant—even a very chubby one—can accumulate too many fat cells. Only a slight correlation exists between fatness in infancy and obesity at older ages (Roche, 1981). Most chubby infants thin out during toddlerhood and the preschool years, as weight gain slows and they become more active.

Infants and toddlers can eat nutritious foods freely, without risk of becoming too fat. In fact, parents who try to put their babies on diets may cause malnutrition (a topic we discuss next). When infants are first given solid foods, iron-fortified cereal mixed with whole milk satisfies their needs. Between 6 and 12 months, mashed and minced cooked fruits, vegetables, starches, and meats should gradually be added. Around 1 year, most infants have enough teeth to make the transition to chopped table foods, which should include all the basic food groups (Mott, James, & Sperhac, 1990).

Although a baby's food intake should not be limited, concerned parents can prevent their infants from becoming overweight children and adults in other ways. One way is to encourage good eating habits. Candy, soft drinks, french fries, and other high-calorie foods loaded with sugar, salt, and saturated fats are not appropriate treats for toddlers. When given such foods regularly, young children start to prefer them (Birch, 1990; Harris & Booth, 1987). Regular physical exercise also guards against excessive weight gain. Once toddlers learn to walk, climb, and run, parents should encourage their natural delight at being able to control their bodies by providing opportunities for physically active play.

## Malnutrition

Osita is an Ethiopian 2-year-old whose mother has never had to worry about his gaining too much weight. When she weaned him at 1 year, there was little for him to eat besides starchy rice flour cakes. Soon his belly enlarged, his feet swelled, his hair began to fall out, and a rash appeared on his skin. His bright-eyed, curious behavior vanished, and he became irritable and listless.

In developing countries where food resources are limited, malnutrition is widespread. Recent evidence indicates that 40 to 60 percent of the world's children do not get enough to eat (Lozoff, 1989). Among the 4 to 7 percent who are severely affected, malnutrition leads to two dietary diseases: marasmus and kwashiorkor.

**Marasmus** is a wasted condition of the body that usually appears in the first year of life. It is caused by a diet that is low in all essential nutrients. The disease often occurs when a baby's mother is severely malnourished. As a result, she cannot produce enough breast milk, and bottle-feeding is also inadequate. Her starving baby becomes painfully thin and is in danger of dying.

*general starvation*

Osita has **kwashiorkor.** Unlike marasmus, it is not the result of general starvation. Instead, it is due to an unbalanced diet, one that is very low in protein. Kwashiorkor usually strikes after weaning, between 1 and 3 years of age. It is common in areas of the world where children get just enough calories from starchy foods, but protein resources are scarce. The child's body responds by breaking down its own protein reserves. This causes the swelling and other symptoms that Osita experienced.

Children who manage to survive these extreme forms of malnutrition grow to be smaller in all body dimensions (Galler, Ramsey, & Solimano, 1985a). In addition, their brains are seriously affected. One long-term study of marasmic children revealed that an improved diet led to some catch-up growth in height, but the children failed to catch up in head size (Stoch et al., 1982). The malnutrition probably interfered with myelinization, causing a permanent loss in brain weight. By the time these youngsters reach middle childhood, they score low on intelligence tests, show poor fine motor coordination, and have difficulty paying attention in school (Galler et al., 1984; Galler, Ramsey, & Solimano, 1985b).

Recall from our discussion of prenatal malnutrition in Chapter 3 that poverty and stressful living conditions make the impact of poor diet even worse. We also noted that prenatal malnutrition is not confined to Third World countries. The same is true for malnutrition after birth. A recent survey revealed that over 12 percent of American children go to bed hungry at night (Food Research & Action Center, 1991). While few of these children have marasmus or kwashiorkor, their physical growth and ability to learn in school are still affected. Malnutrition is clearly a national and international crisis—one of the most serious problems confronting the human species today.

*12% American children*

*Malnutrition leads to:*

**Marasmus**

A disease usually appearing in the first year of life that is caused by a diet low in essential nutrients. Leads to a wasted condition of the body.

**Kwashiorkor**

A disease usually appearing between 1 and 3 years of age that is caused by a diet low in protein. Symptoms include an enlarged belly, swollen feet, hair loss, skin rash, and irritable, listless behavior.

*unbalanced diet*

**Inorganic failure to thrive**

A growth disorder usually present by 18 months of age that is caused by lack of affection and stimulation.

### Affection and Stimulation

We are not used to thinking of affection and stimulation as necessary for healthy physical growth, but they are just as vital to an infant as food. **Inorganic failure to thrive** is a growth disorder resulting from lack of parental love that is usually present by 18 months of age. Infants who have it show all the signs of marasmus, described in the previous section. Their bodies look wasted, and they are withdrawn and apathetic. However, no organic (or biological) cause for the baby's failure to grow can be found. Enough food is offered, and the infant does not have a serious illness.

Lana, an observant nurse, noticed signs of failure to thrive in Melanie, whose mother brought her to a public health clinic at 8 months of age. Melanie was 3 pounds lighter than she had been 2 months earlier. Lana took a close look at Melanie's behavior. Unlike most infants her age, she did not mind separating from her mother. Lana tried offering Melanie a toy, but she showed little interest. Instead, she kept her eyes on adults in the room, anxiously watching their every move. When Lana tried to interact with Melanie by looking into her eyes and smiling, Melanie turned her head away (Leonard, Rhymes, & Solnit, 1986; Oates, 1984).

The family circumstances surrounding failure to thrive help explain these typical reactions. During feeding and diaper changing, Melanie's mother sometimes acted cold and distant, at other times impatient and hostile. Melanie tried to protect herself by keeping track of her mother's whereabouts and, when her mother approached, avoiding her gaze (Haynes et al., 1983). Often an unhappy marriage or other family pressures contribute to these serious caregiving problems (Gagan, 1984). In Melanie's case, her father was an alcoholic who was out of work, and her parents argued constantly. Her mother had little energy to meet the psychological needs of Melanie and her other three children.

When treated by intervening with parents or placing the baby in a caring foster home, failure-to-thrive infants show quick catch-up growth. But if the disorder is not corrected early, the child is likely to remain small and show lasting intellectual, emotional, and social problems (Altemeier et al., 1984; Drotar & Sturm, 1988).

 **BRIEF REVIEW**   Heredity, nutrition, and affection and stimulation all contribute to early physical growth. Studies of twins show that height and weight are affected by genetic makeup. Breast milk provides babies with the ideal nutrition between birth and 6 months of age. Although bottle- and breast-fed babies do not differ in psychological development, breast-feeding protects many poverty-stricken infants against malnutrition, disease, and early death. A mother who feeds her baby nutritious foods need not worry about a chubby infant becoming an overweight child. Malnutrition is a serious global problem. When marasmus and kwashiorkor are allowed to persist, physical size, brain growth, and ability to learn are permanently affected. Inorganic failure to thrive reminds us of the close connection between sensitive, loving care and how children grow.

- *Nicki is a low-income mother who did not finish high school. Is Nicki likely to choose breast- or bottle-feeding? Why is breast milk especially important for Nicki's baby?*

- *Ten-month-old Shaun is below average in height and painfully thin. He has one of two serious growth disorders. Name them, and indicate what clues you would look for to tell which one Shaun has.*

## CHANGING STATES OF AROUSAL

Between birth and 2 years, the organization of sleep and wakefulness changes substantially, and fussiness and crying also decline. Recall from Chapter 4 that the newborn baby takes round-the-clock naps that add up to about 16 hours of sleep. The decline in total sleep time from birth to 2 years is not great; the average 2-year-old still needs 12 to 13 hours. Instead, the greatest change in sleep and wakefulness is that short periods of each are gradually put together, and they start to coincide with a night and day schedule (Berg & Berg, 1987). While the newborn baby might take 5 or 6 naps during the day, the older infant remains awake for longer daytime periods and needs fewer naps—by the second year, only one or two. Still, there are great individual differences in sleep needs that remain fairly stable over infancy and early childhood (Jacklin et al., 1980).

The changes in infants' patterns of arousal are largely due to brain maturation, but they are affected by the social environment as well. Lisa and Felicia were delighted when, around 4 months of age, their babies slept through the night. In the United States and other Western nations, night waking is regarded as inconvenient. Parents try to get their babies to sleep through by offering an evening feeding before putting them down in a separate, quiet room. In this way, they push young infants to the limits of their neurological capacities. In many Asian and African cultures, infants remain in constant physical contact with their mothers. Influenced by Japanese child-rearing customs, Beth held Rachel close for much of the day. At night, she lay in her mother's bed, sleeping and waking to nurse at will (Miyake, Chen, & Campos, 1985). For infants experiencing this type of care, the average sleep period remains constant at 3 hours, from 1 to 8 months of age. Only at the end of the first year do these babies move in the direction of an adultlike sleep-waking schedule (Super & Harkness, 1982).

More mature arousal patterns are a welcome relief to many parents, but they also bring new challenges. We will see in the following sections that the baby's growing alertness supports the development of many new motor skills and perceptual capacities. Parents must constantly adjust their caregiving to fit with the infant's rapidly changing approach to the world.

## MOTOR DEVELOPMENT DURING THE FIRST TWO YEARS

Lisa, Beth, and Felicia each kept baby books, filling them with proud notations about when the three children held up their heads, reached for objects, sat by themselves, and walked alone. Parents' enthusiasm for these achievements makes perfect sense. They are, indeed, milestones of development. With each new motor skill, babies master their bodies and the environment in a new way. For example, sitting alone grants infants an entirely different perspective on the world compared to when they spent much of the day lying on their backs and stomachs. Voluntary reaching permits babies to find out about objects by acting on them. And when infants can move on their own, their opportunities for exploration are multiplied.

Babies' motor achievements have a powerful effect on their social relationships. April was the first of the three babies to master crawling. Suddenly, Felicia had to "child-proof" the household and restrict April's movements in ways that were unnecessary when, placed on a blanket, she would stay there! A gate was installed at the top of the staircase, breakable objects removed from the coffee table, and April picked up when she crawled into places that might endanger her safety. At the same time, playful activities expanded. At the end of the first year, April and her parents played a gleeful game of hide-and-seek around the livingroom sofa. Soon after, April could turn the pages of a cardboard picture book and point while Felicia named the objects. Motor skills, social competencies, cognition, and language were developing together and supporting one another.

### The Sequence of Motor Development

*Gross motor development* refers to control over actions that help infants get around in the environment, such as crawling, standing, and walking. In contrast, *fine motor development* has to do with smaller movements, such as reaching and grasping. Figure 5.7 shows the average age at which a variety of gross and fine motor skills are achieved during infancy and toddlerhood. Most children follow this sequence fairly closely.

Notice that Figure 5.7 also presents the age ranges during which the majority of babies accomplish each skill. These indicate that although the sequence of motor development is fairly uniform across children, there are large individual differences in the rate at which motor development proceeds. Also, a baby who is a late reacher is not necessarily going to be a late crawler or walker. We would only be concerned about a child's development if a large number of motor skills were seriously delayed.

Look at Figure 5.7 once more, and you will see that there is organization and direction to the infant's motor achievements. The *cephalo-caudal trend* discussed earlier in this chapter is clearly evident. Motor control of the head comes before control of the arms and trunk, and control of the arms and trunk is achieved before control of the legs. The *proximo-distal trend* can also be seen in that head, trunk, and arm control is advanced over coordination of the hands and fingers. Because physical and motor development follow the same general sequence, the cephalo-caudal and proximo-distal trends are believed to be genetically determined, maturational patterns.

**FIGURE 5.7** • Gross and fine motor skills achieved during the first 2 years. The average age at which each skill is attained is presented, followed by the age range during which 90 percent of infants master the skill. *(From Bayley, 1969.)*

| Head erect and steady | Elevates self by arms | Rolls from side to back | Grasps cube |
| --- | --- | --- | --- |
| 6 weeks<br>3 weeks–4 months | 2 months<br>3 weeks–4 months | 2 months<br>3 weeks–5 months | 3 months, 3 weeks<br>2–7 months |
| Rolls from back to side | Sits alone | Crawls | Pulls to stand |
| 4 1/2 months<br>2–7 months | 7 months<br>5–9 months | 7 months<br>5–11 months | 8 months<br>5–12 months |
| Plays pat-a-cake | Stands alone | Walks alone | Builds tower of 2 cubes |
| 9 months, 3 weeks<br>7–15 months | 11 months<br>9–16 months | 11 months, 3 weeks<br>9–17 months | 13 months, 3 weeks<br>10–19 months |
| Scribbles vigorously | Walks up stairs with help | Jumps in place | Walks on tiptoe |
| 14 months<br>10–21 months | 16 months<br>12–23 months | 23 months, 2 weeks<br>17–30 months | 25 months<br>16–30 months |

*Like the Hopi Indians studied by Wayne and Marsena Dennis, this Shoshone baby spends the day tightly bound to a cradle board. The Dennises found that confinement to the cradle board did not hinder the development of walking. They concluded that the emergence of motor skills is largely due to biological maturation. Later studies revealed that both maturation and experience influence the course of motor development. (Victor Engelbert/Photo Researchers)*

**System of action**

In motor development, the combination of previously acquired skills to produce a more advanced skill.

## Motor Skills as Complex Systems of Action

We must be careful not to think of infant motor skills as a series of isolated, unrelated accomplishments. Earlier in this century, researchers made this mistake, but today we know that motor development is a matter of acquiring increasingly complex **systems of action.** When motor skills work as a *system,* separate abilities blend together, each cooperating with others to produce a more advanced skill. During infancy, new systems of action emerge constantly. For example, control of the head and upper chest are combined into sitting with support. Kicking, rocking on all fours, and reaching are gradually put together into crawling. Then crawling, standing, and stepping are united into walking alone (Hofsten, 1989; Pick, 1989; Thelen, 1989).

The way simple motor acts are coordinated into more effective motor systems is most obvious in the area of fine motor skills. As we will see when we discuss the development of voluntary reaching, the various components—grasping, looking, and moving the arms—at first emerge independently. Then they are combined into successful reaching for objects (Manchester, 1988). Once reaching is accomplished, it can be coordinated with other actions to produce even more complex skills, such as stacking blocks, putting objects in containers, and eating with a spoon (Connolly & Dagleish, 1989).

## Maturation, Experience, and the Development of Motor Skills

What explains the appearance of new motor skills? Over the past half-century, cross-cultural research has suggested some thought-provoking answers. The earliest of these studies, carried out in the 1930s and 1940s, led investigators to the one-sided conclusion that motor development was almost entirely due to biological maturation. For example, Wayne and Marsena Dennis (1940) studied age of walking among the Hopi Indians. Some Hopi mothers bound their infants to cradle boards, while others had given up this practice. Even though cradle board babies had no opportunity to move their trunk and legs throughout the day, they walked at the same age as unbound infants—an outcome suggesting that experience was unimportant. But note how comparisons like this one pay little attention to subtle experiences that could have affected the motor skill in question. For example, the upright position of the cradle board and the baby's opportunity to move freely when taken off it at night might have made up for lack of activity during the day.

In fact, much later in his career, when Dennis (1960) observed infants raised in very deprived Iranian institutions, he realized that early movement opportunities and a stimulating environment do contribute to motor development. The Iranian babies spent their days lying on their backs in cribs, without toys to play with. Most did not move about on their own until after 2 years of age. When, finally, they did move, the constant experience of lying on their backs led them to scoot in a sitting position rather than crawl on their hands and knees the way infants raised in families do. This preference for scooting probably slowed the infants' motor development even further. Babies who scoot come up against furniture with their feet, not their hands. Consequently, they are far less likely to pull themselves to a standing position in preparation for walking.

Turn to Box 5.1 for additional evidence on how experience affects motor development—this time, in Africa and the West Indies. Putting all these findings together, we must conclude that early motor skills, like other aspects of development, are due to complex transactions between nature and nurture. While heredity ensures that all babies will follow a similar sequence of motor development, early experience can alter this sequence to some degree. And experience can greatly change the rate at which motor milestones are reached.

## Fine Motor Development: The Special Case of Voluntary Reaching

Of all motor skills, voluntary reaching is believed to play the greatest role in infant cognitive development, since it opens up a whole new way of exploring the environment (Piaget, 1936/1952). By grasping things, turning them over, and seeing what happens when they are released, infants learn a great deal about the sights, sounds, and feel of objects.

The development of reaching and grasping, shown in Figure 5.9, provides an excellent example of how motor skills start out as gross, diffuse activity and move toward mastery of fine movements. When newborns are held in an upright posture, they direct their arms toward an object dangled in front of them. These movements are called **prereaching** because they resemble poorly coordinated swipes or swings. Like the reflexes we discussed in Chapter 4, prereaching eventually drops out, around 7 weeks of age. Then, at about 3 months, visually guided reaching appears and gradually improves in accuracy (Bushnell, 1985; Hofsten, 1984).

Once infants can reach, they start to modify the nature of their grasp. When the grasp reflex of the newborn period weakens, it is replaced by the **ulnar grasp,** a clumsy motion in which the fingers close against the palm. Around 4 to 5 months, both hands become coordinated in exploring objects. Babies of this age can hold an object in one hand while the other scans it with the tips of the fingers, and they frequently transfer objects from hand to hand (Rochat, 1989). By the end of the first year, infants use the thumb and index finger opposably in a well-coordinated **pincer grasp** (Halverson, 1931). Once the pincer grasp appears, the ability to manipulate objects greatly expands. The 1-year-old can pick up raisins and blades of grass, turn knobs, and open and close small boxes.

Like other motor milestones, voluntary reaching is affected by early experience. In a well-known study, Burton White and Richard Held (1966) found that institutionalized babies provided with a moderate amount of visual stimulation—at first, simple designs and later, a mobile hung over their cribs—reached for objects 6 weeks earlier than did infants given nothing to look at. A third group of babies provided with massive stimulation—patterned crib bumpers and mobiles at an early age—also reached sooner than did unstimulated babies. But this heavy dose of enrichment took its toll. These infants looked away and cried a great deal, and they were not as advanced in reaching as the moderately stimulated group. White and Held's findings remind us that more stimulation is not necessarily better. Trying to push infants beyond their current readiness to handle stimulation can undermine the development of important motor skills.

Toddlers are not ready for toilet training until around age 2, when they can control bladder and rectal muscles consistently. The parents of this 2-year-old boy bought a small toilet on which he can sit comfortably, and they make toileting a pleasant experience. He is likely to be fully trained within a few months. (Margaret Miller/Photo Researchers)

## Bowel and Bladder Control

More than any other aspect of early muscular development, parents wonder about bowel and bladder control. Lisa admitted that she once tried sitting Byron on a child-size potty at 15 months. "That lasted for about two seconds," she said. "Byron is so absorbed in walking and exploring right now that he doesn't have the patience to sit there, waiting for something to happen."

Two or three generations ago, many mothers tried to toilet train small infants. However, they did not really succeed in teaching anything. They only caught the baby's urine or bowel movement at a convenient moment. Toilet training is best delayed until the end of the second or beginning of the third year. Not until then can toddlers consistently identify the signals from a full rectum or bladder and wait until they are in the right place to permit these muscles to open. Research indicates that mothers who postpone training until age 2 succeed in having infants who are fully trained within 4 months. Starting earlier does not produce a more reliably

**Prereaching**

The poorly coordinated primitive reaching movements of newborn babies.

**Ulnar grasp**

The clumsy grasp of the young infant, in which the fingers close against the palm.

**Pincer grasp**

The well-coordinated grasp emerging at the end of the first year, involving thumb and forefinger opposition.

## CULTURAL INFLUENCES

### Box 5.1 *Motor Development of African and West Indian Babies*

*T*ake a quick survey of several parents with whom you are acquainted by asking: Can young babies profit from training? Should sitting, crawling, and walking be deliberately encouraged? Answers to these questions vary widely from culture to culture. Rachel's mother, who comes from Japan, believes that such efforts are unnecessary and unimportant (Caudill, 1973). But in other parts of the world, direct stimulation of motor skills is common.

Among the Baganda of Uganda and the Kipsigis of Kenya, babies hold their heads up, sit alone, and walk considerably earlier than American infants. Infant caregiving customs are believed to be responsible, since babies are advanced only in those motor skills that are trained.

As early as 1 month, the Baganda mother begins teaching her infant to sit, since children do not become true members of the Baganda community until they can sit alone properly. Between 1 and 3 months, babies are seated on the adult's lap and held with one arm around the waist. When they are 3 to 4 months old, they are placed on a mat or in a basin, and cloths are wrapped around them for support. The capacity to sit in a group promotes friendly social interaction, which Baganda adults regard as vitally important to encourage in young children. Also, early sitting is helpful to Baganda mothers. Once a baby can sit, the mother no longer needs to carry him on her back while she works in the garden. Instead, she can seat the infant nearby or assign an older sibling to watch him (Kilbride & Kilbride, 1975).

The Kipsigis teach motor skills in a similar way. As early as the first few weeks of life, Kipsigis babies spend up to 60 percent of the day in a sitting position on the mother's lap. Around 5 to 6 months, they are placed in special holes in the ground, and rolled blankets are used to keep them upright. Walking is deliberately encouraged by 1 month, when mothers start to play with their babies in a fashion called *kitwalse,* which means "to make jump." They frequently hold small infants upright on their laps and bounce them up and down. At 7 to 8 months, walking is stimulated further. Caregivers hold babies under the arms or by the hands with the feet touching the ground and slowly move them forward. Time spent practicing walking is gradually increased as the infant responds with stronger stepping movements (Super, 1981).

The West Indians of Jamaica, whose infants are also advanced in head control, sitting, and walking, do not try to train their infants in specific skills. Instead, shortly after birth, babies experience a highly stimulating, formal handling routine. As shown in Figure 5.8, the West Indian mother stretches the baby's legs, arms, and neck, vigorously massages the body after the daily bath, props the infant with cushions to encourage an upright posture, and exercises stepping responses. Asked why they use the formal handling routine, West Indian mothers refer to the traditions of their culture and the need to help babies grow up strong, healthy, and physically attractive. They also say that they want to develop flexibility of the infant's body as a way of preventing physical injury (Hopkins & Westra, 1988).

Do these observations mean that mothers everywhere should teach their babies motor skills? The practices described here are meaningful only in particular cultures. Recall from Chapter 4 that exercising infant reflexes (some of which provide the foundation for later motor skills) has no lasting impact on development. The same is true for a wide variety of motor capacities during the first 2 years of life. Nevertheless, cross-cultural research clearly demonstrates that besides heredity, cultural values and child-rearing customs contribute to the emergence and refinement of early motor skills.

**FIGURE 5.8** • West Indian mothers use a formal handling routine with their babies. Exercises practiced in the first few months include stretching each arm while suspending the baby (A); holding the infant upside-down by the ankles (B); grasping the baby's head on both sides, lifting upwards, and stretching the neck (C); and propping the infant with cushions that are gradually removed as the baby begins to sit independently (D). Later in the first year, the baby is "walked" up the mother's body (E) and encouraged to take steps on the floor while supported (F). *(Adapted from B. Hopkins & T. Westra, 1988, "Maternal handling and motor development: An intracultural study," Genetic, Social and General Psychology Monographs, 14, pp. 385, 388, 389. Reprinted with permission of the Helen Dwight Reid Educational Foundation. Published by Heldref Publications, 1319 Eighteenth St. NW, Washington, DC 20036-1802. Copyright © 1988.)*

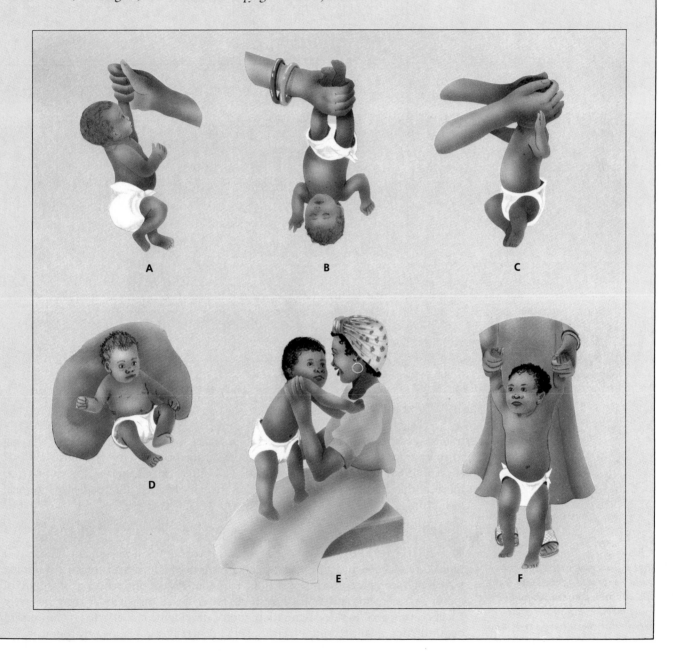

**FIGURE 5.9** • Some milestones of visually guided reaching. The average age at which each skill is attained is given. *(Ages from Bayley, 1969; Rochat, 1989.)*

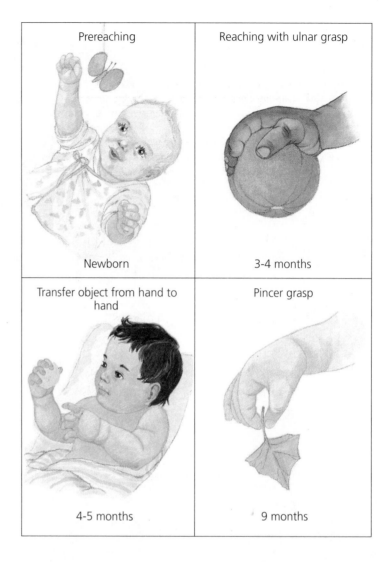

Prereaching

Newborn

Reaching with ulnar grasp

3-4 months

Transfer object from hand to hand

4-5 months

Pincer grasp

9 months

trained preschooler. The whole process just takes longer (Brazelton, 1962). Trying to toilet train too early simply amounts to "a lot of effort for not much reward" (Leach, 1989, p. 246) In addition, as we will see in Chapter 7, pressuring too much in this area, as well as in others, can negatively affect the toddler's emotional well-being.

*• Rosanne read in a magazine that infant motor development could be speeded up through exercise and visual stimulation. She hung mobiles and pictures all over her newborn baby's crib, and she massages and manipulates his body daily. Is Rosanne doing the right thing? Why or why not?*

*BRIEF REVIEW*   The overall sequence of motor development follows the cephalo-caudal and proximo-distal trends. Each new skill is a matter of developing increasingly complex systems of action. Large individual differences exist in rate of motor development, and motor milestones are achieved earlier today than they were a half century ago. Besides maturation, motor development is affected by movement opportunities, infant rearing practices, and a generally stimulating environment. Visually guided reaching begins with the uncoordinated prereaching movements of the newborn baby and gradually evolves into a refined pincer grasp around 1 year of age. Toddlers are not ready for toilet training until the end of the second or beginning of the third year.

**CONCEPT TABLE 5.2** • Basic Learning Mechanisms

| Concept | Important Point | Example |
|---|---|---|
| Classical conditioning | When a neutral stimulus is paired with a stimulus that leads to a reflexive response, eventually the neutral stimulus produces that response. This learning mechanism permits infants to build associations between stimuli that regularly occur together. | A mother often places her baby in an infant seat to feed him solid foods. Each time the baby is placed in the infant seat when it is not time to eat, he mouths and moves his head forward in preparation for feeding. |
| Operant conditioning | A behavior is followed by a stimulus that either increases (reinforces) or decreases (punishes) its occurrence. This learning mechanism enables infants to control stimuli to which they are exposed. | A mother smiles and talks gently each time her baby smiles. Soon the baby's smiling increases in frequency. A second mother frowns and speaks sharply when her baby smiles. The baby eventually stops smiling. |
| Habituation and dishabituation | When a repetitive stimulus is presented, responsiveness to it declines over time (habituation). Introduction of a new stimulus causes responsiveness to return to a high level (dishabituation). This preference for novelty increases the efficiency of learning | A baby looks with interest at a bright red ring. Soon looking decreases. Later, when shown the red ring alongside a new green one, the baby spends much more time looking at the green ring. |
| Imitation | The newborn's ability to copy the facial expressions of adults may promote positive interaction between caregiver and infant. | When a mother widens or purses her lips, a newborn infant observing her is likely to display a similar expression. |

## BASIC LEARNING MECHANISMS

*Learning* refers to changes in behavior as the result of experience. Babies come into the world with a built-in set of learning mechanisms that permit them to profit from experience immediately. Infants are capable of two basic forms of learning, which we introduced in Chapter 1: classical and operant conditioning. Now we will discuss them in greater detail. Besides conditioning, infants learn through a natural preference they have for novel stimulation. Finally, one early learning mechanism is bound to surprise you: newborn babies have a remarkable ability to imitate the facial expressions of adults. The basic ways in which infants learn are summarized in Concept Table 5.2.

### Classical Conditioning

In Chapter 4, we discussed a variety of newborn reflexes. These make **classical conditioning** possible in the young infant. In this form of learning, a new stimulus is paired with a stimulus that leads to a reflexive response. Once the baby's nervous system makes the connection between the two stimuli, then the new stimulus by itself produces the behavior.

Recall from Chapter 1 that the Russian physiologist Ivan Pavlov first demonstrated classical conditioning in some famous research he conducted with dogs (see page 17). Classical conditioning is of great value to human infants, as well as other animals, because it helps them recognize which events usually occur together in the everyday world. As a result, they can anticipate what is about to happen next, and the environment becomes more orderly and predicable (Rovee-Collier, 1987). Let's take a closer look at the steps of classical conditioning.

As Beth settled down in the rocking chair to nurse Rachel, she was in the habit of gently stroking Rachel's forehead. Soon Beth noticed that each time Rachel's forehead was stroked, she made active sucking movements. Rachel had been classically conditioned. Here is how it happened (see Figure 5.10):

**Classical conditioning**

A form of learning that involves associating a neutral stimulus with a stimulus that leads to a reflexive response.

**FIGURE 5.10** • The steps of classical conditioning. The example here shows how Rachel was classically conditioned to make sucking movements when her forehead was stroked.

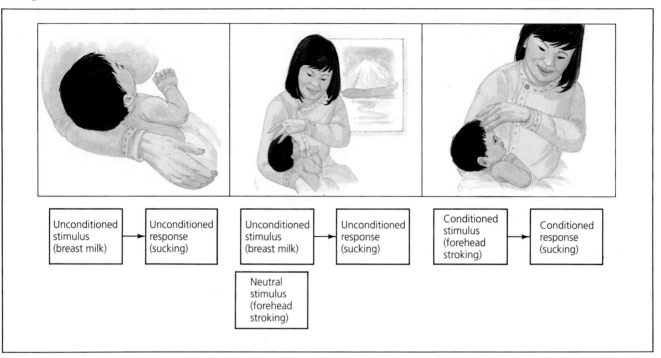

| Unconditioned stimulus (breast milk) | → | Unconditioned response (sucking) |
| Unconditioned stimulus (breast milk) | → | Unconditioned response (sucking) |
| Neutral stimulus (forehead stroking) | | |
| Conditioned stimulus (forehead stroking) | → | Conditioned response (sucking) |

**Unconditioned stimulus (UCS)**

In classical conditioning, a stimulus that leads to a reflexive response.

**Unconditioned response (UCR)**

In classical conditioning, a reflexive response that is produced by an unconditioned stimulus (UCS).

**Conditioned stimulus (CS)**

In classical conditioning, a neutral stimulus that, through pairing with an unconditioned stimulus (UCS), leads to a new response (CR).

**Conditioned response (CR)**

In classical conditioning, an originally reflexive response that is produced by a conditioned stimulus (CS).

**Extinction**

In classical conditioning, decline of the CR, as a result of presenting the CS enough times without the UCS.

*1.* Before learning takes place, an **unconditioned stimulus (UCS)** must consistently produce a reflexive, or **unconditioned response (UCR).** In Rachel's case, the stimulus of sweet breast milk (UCS) results in sucking (UCR).

*2.* To produce learning, a *neutral stimulus* that does not lead to the reflex is presented at about the same time as the UCS. Ideally, the neutral stimulus should occur just before the UCS. Beth stroked Rachel's forehead as each nursing period began. Therefore, the stroking (neutral stimulus) was paired with the taste of milk (UCS).

*3.* If learning has occurred, the neutral stimulus by itself produces the reflexive response. The neutral stimulus is then called a **conditioned stimulus (CS),** and the response it elicits is called a **conditioned response (CR).** We know that Rachel has been classically conditioned because stroking her forehead outside of the feeding situation (CS) results in sucking (CR).

If the CS is presented alone enough times, without being paired with the UCS, the CR will no longer occur. In other words, if Beth strokes Rachel's forehead again and again without feeding her, Rachel will gradually stop sucking in response to stroking. This is referred to as **extinction.** In a classical conditioning experiment, the occurrence of responses to the CS during the extinction phase shows that learning has taken place.

Although young babies can be classically conditioned, they will not respond to just any pairing of stimuli. To be easily learned, the association between a UCS and a CS must have survival value. Rachel learned quickly in the feeding situation, since learning which stimuli regularly accompany feeding improves the infant's ability to get food and survive (Blass, Ganchrow, & Steiner, 1984).

Some responses are very difficult to condition in young babies. Fear is one of them. Until the last half of the first year, infants do not have the motor skills to escape unpleasant events. Because they depend on their parents for this kind of protection, they do not have a biological need to form these associations. But between 8 and 12 months, the conditioning of fear is easily accomplished, as the famous example of little Albert, conditioned by John Watson to withdraw and cry at the sight of a furry white rat, clearly indicates. Return to Chapter 1, page 17, to review this well-known experiment. Then test your knowledge of classical conditioning by identifying the UCS, UCR, CS, and CR in Watson's study. In Chapter 7, we will discuss the development of fear, as well as other emotional reactions, in greater detail.

## Operant Conditioning

In classical conditioning, babies build up expectations about stimulus events in the environment, but they do not influence the stimuli that occur. **Operant conditioning** is quite different. In this type of learning, the infant's responses determine the kind of stimulus received. Recall from Chapter 4 that newborn babies suck differently when a nipple delivers sweet liquid as opposed to plain water. If they are given a sour-tasting fluid, they purse their lips and stop sucking entirely. When you read about this research, you were actually studying operant conditioning. A stimulus that increases the occurrence of a response is called a **reinforcer.** Removing a desirable stimulus or presenting an unpleasant one to decrease the occurrence of a response is called **punishment.** In the example just described, sweet liquid *reinforces* the sucking response, while a sour-tasting fluid *punishes* it.

Operant conditioning of newborn babies has been demonstrated in many studies. Because the young infant can only control a few behaviors, successful operant conditioning is limited to sucking and head-turning responses. However, many stimuli besides food can serve as reinforcers. For example, researchers have created special laboratory conditions in which the baby's rate of sucking on a nipple produces a variety of interesting sights and sounds. Newborns will suck faster to see visual designs or to hear music and human voices (Rovee-Collier, 1987). As these findings suggest, operant conditioning has become a powerful tool for finding out what babies can perceive.

As infants get older, operant conditioning expands to include a wider range of responses and stimuli. For example, special mobiles have been hung over the cribs of 2-month-olds. When the baby's foot is attached to the mobile with a long cord, the infant can, by kicking, make the mobile turn. Under these conditions, it takes only a few minutes for infants to start kicking vigorously (Rovee-Collier, 1984). Operant conditioning soon modifies parents' and babies' reactions to each other. As the infant gazes into the adult's eyes, the adult looks and smiles back, and then the infant looks and smiles again. The behavior of each partner reinforces the other, and as a result, both parent and baby continue their pleasurable interaction. In Chapter 7, we will see that this kind of contingent responsiveness plays an important role in the development of infant–caregiver attachment.

Recall from Chapter 1 that classical and operant conditioning originated with behaviorism, an approach that views the child as a relatively passive responder to environmental stimuli. If you look carefully at the findings described here, you will see that young babies are not passive. Instead, they use any means they can to explore and control the surrounding world. In fact, when infants' environments are so disorganized that their behavior has little or no impact on the surrounding world, serious developmental problems, ranging from intellectual retardation to apathy and depression, can result (Cicchetti & Aber, 1986; Seligman, 1975). In addition, as Box 5.2 reveals, problems in brain functioning may prevent some babies from actively learning certain lifesaving responses, leading to sudden infant death syndrome, a major cause of infant mortality.

**Operant conditioning**

A form of learning in which the infant's responses determine the kind of stimuli (reinforcer or punisher) received.

**Reinforcer**

In operant conditioning, a stimulus that increases the occurrence of a response.

**Punishment**

In operant conditioning, removing a desirable stimulus or presenting an unpleasant one to decrease the occurrence of a response.

## FROM RESEARCH TO PRACTICE

Box 5.2   *The Mysterious Tragedy of Sudden Infant Death Syndrome*

Before they went to bed, Millie and Stuart looked in on 3-month-old Sasha. She was sleeping soundly, her breathing no longer as labored as it had been 2 days before when she caught her first cold. There had been reasons to worry about Sasha at birth. She was born 3 weeks early, and it took over a minute before she started breathing. As Millie and Stuart stood over Sasha's crib, they reflected on how much she had grown and changed since those early days.

Millie awoke with a start the next morning and looked at the clock. It was 7:30, and Sasha had missed her night waking and early morning feeding. Wondering if she was all right, Millie tiptoed into the room. Sasha lay still, curled up under her blanket. She had died silently during her sleep.

Sasha was a victim of **sudden infant death syndrome (SIDS).** In industrialized nations, SIDS is the leading cause of infant mortality between 1 and 12 months of age. It accounts for over one third of these deaths in the United States (Cotton, 1990; Wilson & Neidich, 1991). Millie and Stuart's grief was especially hard to bear because no one could give them a definite answer about why Sasha died. They felt guilty and under attack by relatives, and their 5-year-old daughter Jill reacted with sorrow that lasted for months. Eventually, Millie and Stuart sought help from a support group for parents who have lost a baby. And Millie started to read about the disorder, in hopes of finding out about ways to prevent it. Here is some of what she learned:

Although the precise cause of SIDS is not known, infants who die of it show physical abnormalities from the very beginning. Early medical records of SIDS babies reveal higher rates of prematurity and low birth weight, poor Apgar scores, and limp muscle tone (Buck et al., 1989; Lipsitt, Sturner, & Burke, 1979; Shannon et al., 1987). Abnormal heart rate and respiration as well as disturbances in sleep–waking activity are also involved (Froggatt et al., 1988). At the time of death, over half of SIDS babies have a mild respiratory infection. This seems to in-crease the chances of respiratory failure in an already vulnerable baby (Cotton, 1990).

One hypothesis about the cause of SIDS is that problems in brain functioning prevent these infants from learning how to respond when their survival is threatened—for example, when respiration is suddenly interrupted (Lipsitt, 1982). Between 2 and 4 months of age, when SIDS is most likely to occur, reflexes decline and are replaced by voluntary, learned responses. Respiratory and muscular weaknesses of SIDS babies may stop them from acquiring behaviors that replace defensive reflexes. As a result, when breathing difficulties occur during sleep, they do not wake up, shift the position of their bodies, or cry out for help. Instead, they simply give in to oxygen deprivation and death.

In an effort to reduce the occurrence of SIDS, researchers are studying environmental factors associated with it. A baby of a smoking mother is 2 to 3 times more likely to die of SIDS than is an infant of a nonsmoker (Haglund & Cnattingius, 1990). Other consistent findings are that SIDS babies are more likely to sleep on their stomachs than on their backs, and often they are wrapped very warmly in clothing and blankets (Flemming et al., 1990). Why are these factors associated with SIDS? Scientists think that smoke and excessive body warmth (which can be encouraged by putting babies down on their stomachs) place a strain on the respiratory control system in the brain. In an at-risk baby, the respiratory center may stop functioning.

Can simple procedures like quitting smoking, changing an infant's sleeping position, and removing a few bed clothes prevent SIDS? More research is needed to find out for sure. In the meantime, surviving family members require a great deal of emotional support (DeFrain, Taylor, & Ernst, 1982). As Millie commented 6 months after Sasha's death, "It's the worst crisis we've ever been through. What's helped us most are the comforting words of parents in our support group who've experienced the same tragedy."

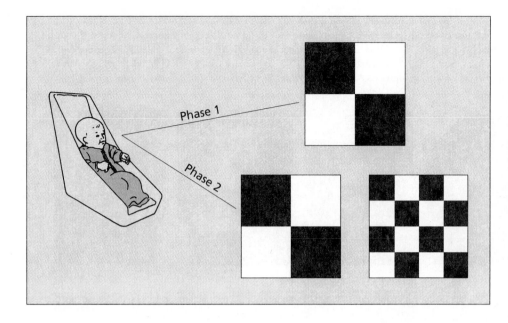

**FIGURE 5.11** • Example of how the habituation–dishabituation response can be used to study infant perception and cognition. In Phase 1, an infant is permitted to look at (habituate to) a 2 × 2 checkerboard. In Phase 2, the baby is again shown the 2 × 2 checkerboard, but this time it appears alongside a new, 4 × 4 checkerboard. If the infant dishabituates to (spends more time looking at) the 4 × 4 checkerboard, then we know the baby remembers the first stimulus and can tell that the second one is different.

### Habituation and Dishabituation

Take a moment to walk through the rooms of the library, your home, or wherever you happen to be reading this book. What did you notice? Probably those things that are new and different, such as a picture on the wall that is out of place or a piece of furniture that has been moved. At birth, the human brain is set up to be attracted to novelty. **Habituation** refers to a gradual reduction in the strength of a response due to repetitive stimulation. Looking, heart rate, and respiration may all decline, indicating a loss of interest. Once this has occurred, a new stimulus—some kind of change in the environment—causes responsiveness to return to a high level. This recovery is called **dishabituation.**

Habituation and dishabituation enable us to conserve energy by focusing our attention on those aspects of the environment we know least about. As a result, learning is more efficient (Lipsitt, 1986). By studying the stimuli to which infants of different ages habituate and dishabituate, scientists can tell much about the infant's understanding of the world. For example, a baby who first habituates to a visual pattern (such as a 2 × 2 checkerboard) and then dishabituates to a new one (a 4 × 4 checkerboard) clearly remembers the first stimulus and perceives the second one as different from it. This method of studying infant perception and cognition, which is illustrated in Figure 5.11, can be used with newborn babies—even those who are 5 weeks preterm (Rose, 1980; Werner & Siqueland, 1978). We will return to habituation research later in this chapter, when we discuss perceptual development, and in Chapter 6, when we consider infant attention and memory.

### Imitation

For many years, scientists believed that **imitation**—learning by copying the behavior of another person—was beyond the capacity of very young infants. They were not expected to imitate until several months after birth (Bayley, 1969; Piaget, 1945/1951). Then, a growing number of studies began to report that newborn babies come into the world with a primitive ability to imitate the behavior of their caregivers.

Figure 5.12 shows examples of responses obtained in two of the first studies of newborn imitation (Field et al., 1982; Meltzoff & Moore, 1977). As you can see, the babies appeared to imitate a wide variety of adult facial expressions. These results

**Sudden infant death syndrome (SIDS)**

Death of a seemingly healthy baby, who stops breathing during the night, without apparent cause.

**Habituation**

A gradual reduction in the strength of a response as the result of repetitive stimulation.

**Dishabituation**

Increase in responsiveness after stimulation changes.

**Imitation**

Learning by copying the behavior of another person. Also called modeling or observational learning.

**FIGURE 5.12** • Photographs from two of the first studies of neonatal imitation. Those on the left show 2- to 3-week-old infants imitating tongue protrusion (A), mouth opening (B), and lip protrusion (C) of an adult experimenter. Those on the right show 2-day-old infants imitating happy (D) and sad (E) adult facial expressions. *(From T. M. Field et al., 1982, "Discrimination and imitation of facial expressions by neonates," Science, 218, p. 180. Copyright 1977 by the AAAS; A. N. Meltzoff & M. K. Moore, 1977, "Imitation of facial and manual gestures by human neonates," Science, 198, p. 75. Copyright 1977 and 1982 by the AAAS.)*

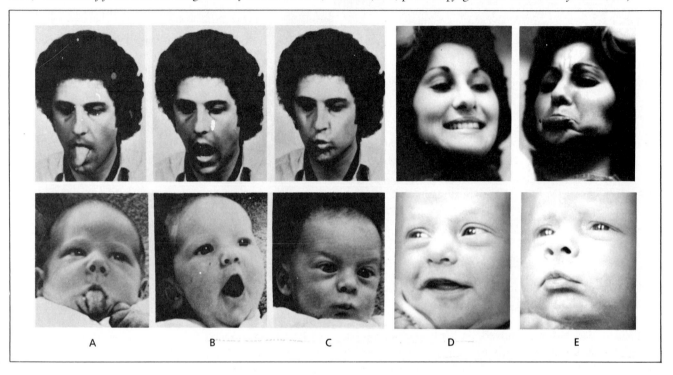

A          B          C          D          E

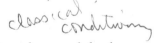

• *Byron has a music box hung on the side of his crib. Each time he pulls a lever, the music box plays a nursery tune. Which learning mechanism is the manufacturer of this toy taking advantage of?*

• *Earlier in this chapter, we indicated that infants with inorganic failure to thrive are unlikely to smile at a friendly adult. Also, they keep track of nearby adults in an anxious and fearful way. Explain these reactions using the learning mechanisms discussed in the preceding sections.*

are so extraordinary that it is not surprising they have been challenged. Other researchers who tried to get young babies to imitate were much less successful (Abravanel & Sigafoos, 1984; Kaitz et al., 1988; McKenzie & Over, 1983). Yet some of these studies included babies who were exposed to labor and delivery medication, which may interfere with this remarkable capacity. In one well-controlled investigation, babies tested minutes after a drug-free delivery, when they were bright-eyed and alert, showed clear imitation of two facial expressions: lips widened and lips pursed (Reissland, 1988). Another study of alert newborns found that besides facial expressions, they can imitate head movements as well (Meltzoff & Moore, 1989).

As we will see in Chapter 6, a baby's capacity to imitate changes greatly over the first 2 years. But however limited it is at birth, imitation provides the baby with a powerful means of learning. Through imitation, adults can get young infants to express desirable behaviors, and once they do, adults can encourage these further. In addition, adults take great pleasure in a baby who imitates their facial gestures and actions. Perhaps newborn imitation is one of those capacities that helps get the baby's relationship with parents off to a good start.

**BRIEF REVIEW**    Infants are marvelously equipped to learn immediately after birth. Through classical conditioning, infants acquire stimulus associations that have survival value. Operant conditioning permits them to control events in the surrounding world. Habituation and dishabituation reveal that infants, much like adults, are naturally attracted to novel stimulation. Finally, newborn babies' amazing ability to imitate the facial expressions of adults may promote early social interaction with caregivers.

## PERCEPTUAL DEVELOPMENT IN INFANCY

In Chapter 4, you learned that touch, taste, smell, and hearing were remarkably well developed at birth. Now let's turn to a related question: How does perception change over the first year of life?

Our discussion will focus on infant hearing and vision because almost all research addresses these two aspects of perceptual development. Unfortunately, we know little about how touch, taste, and smell develop after birth. Also, in Chapter 4 we used the word *sensation* to talk about these capacities. Now we are using the word *perception*. The reason for the change is that sensation suggests a fairly passive process— what the baby's receptors detect when they are exposed to stimulation. In contrast, perception is much more active. When we perceive, we organize and interpret what we see. As we look at the perceptual achievements of infancy, you will probably find it hard to tell where perception leaves off and thinking begins. Thus, the research we are about to discuss provides an excellent bridge to the topic of Chapter 6—infant cognitive development.

### Hearing

On Byron's first birthday, Lisa bought several tapes of nursery songs, and she turned one on each afternoon at naptime. Soon Byron let her know his favorite tune. If she put on the tape with "Twinkle, Twinkle," he stood up in his crib and whimpered until she replaced it with "Jack and Jill." Byron's behavior illustrates the greatest change that takes place in hearing over the first year of life: babies start to organize sounds into complex patterns. If two melodies differing only slightly are played, 1-year-olds can tell that they are not the same (Morrongiello, 1986).

As we will see in the next chapter, by the end of the first year infants are getting ready to talk. Around this time, they begin to organize the speech they hear into more complex units. Recall from our discussion in Chapter 4 that newborns recognize the difference between almost all sounds in human languages. By 7 months, they become sensitive to larger speech units that are critical to figuring out the meaning of what they hear. In one study, researchers recorded two versions of a mother telling a story. In the first, she spoke naturally, with pauses occurring between clauses, like this: "Cinderella lived in a great big house (pause), but it was sort of dark (pause) because she had this mean stepmother." In the second version, the mother inserted pauses in unnatural places—in the middle of clauses. She sounded like this: "Cinderella lived in a great big house, but it was (pause) sort of dark because she had (pause) this mean stepmother." Did you find it difficult to pay attention to the second of these examples? So do 7- to 10-month-olds. They clearly prefer speech with natural breaks (Hirsh-Pasek et al., 1987).

As infants become sensitive to the structure of speech, they also become familiar with its unique sounds. As a result, by 8 to 10 months they no longer discriminate sounds that are not used in their own language community (Werker, 1989). For example, Japanese newborns can easily tell the difference between "ra" and "la." But by the end of the first year, they treat these two sounds as if they were just the same. The reason is that the Japanese language does not distinguish them. As older infants pay attention to speech sounds that lead to changes of meaning in their own language, they start to ignore those that play no useful role.

## Vision

Suppose you lived in a world in which you were allowed to choose between hearing and vision, but you could not have both. Which would you select? Most people decide on vision, for good reason. More than any other sense, humans depend on vision for active exploration of the environment. Although at first the baby's visual world is fragmented, it undergoes extraordinary changes during the first 7 to 8 months of life.

Visual development is supported by rapid maturation of the eye and visual centers in the brain. Recall from Chapter 4 that the newborn baby's focusing ability and color perception are poor. By 3 months, infants can focus on objects just as well as adults can, and they can discriminate many more colors than they could at birth (Banks, 1980; Teller & Bornstein, 1987). Visual acuity (fineness of discrimination) improves steadily throughout the first year. In Chapter 4, we noted that newborns see about as clearly at 20 feet as adults do at 440 to 800 feet. By 6 months, their acuity has improved greatly, to about 20/100. At 11 months, it reaches a near-adult level (Appleton, Clifton, & Goldberg, 1975; Atkinson & Braddock, 1989). The ability to hold fixation on a moving object and track it with the eyes improves steadily over the first 6 months of life (Hainline, 1985).

As babies see more clearly and explore their visual field more adeptly, they work on figuring out the characteristics of objects and how they are arranged in space. We can best understand how they do so by examining the development of two aspects of vision: depth and pattern perception.

**Depth Perception.**   *Depth perception* is the ability to judge the distance of objects from one another and from ourselves. It is important for understanding the layout of the environment and for guiding motor activity. To reach for objects, babies must have some idea about depth. Later, when infants learn to crawl, depth perception helps prevent them from bumping into furniture and falling down staircases. However, as we will see shortly, parents are unwise to trust the baby's judgment in these situations entirely!

The earliest studies of depth perception used a well-known apparatus called the *visual cliff* (see Figure 5.13). Devised by Eleanor Gibson and Richard Walk (1960), it consists of a table covered by glass, at the center of which is a platform. On one side of the platform (the shallow side) is a checkerboard pattern just under the surface of the glass. On the other (the deep side), the checkerboard is several feet beneath the glass. The researchers placed crawling infants on the platform and asked their mothers to entice them across both the deep and shallow sides by calling to them and holding out a toy. Although the babies readily crossed the shallow side, all but a few reacted with fear to the deep side. The Gibsons concluded that around the time that infants crawl, most distinguish deep and shallow surfaces and avoid drop-offs that look dangerous (Walk & Gibson, 1961).

Gibson and Walk's research shows that crawling and avoidance of drop-offs are linked, but it does not tell us how they are related. Also, we cannot tell when depth perception first appears from studies of crawling infants. To better understand the development of depth perception, recent research has looked at babies' ability to detect particular depth cues, using methods that do not require that they crawl.

*The Emergence of Depth Perception.*   How do we know that an object is near rather than far away? Let's try some exercises to find out. Look toward the far wall while moving your head from side to side. Notice how objects close to your eye move past your field of vision more quickly than those far away. Next, pick up a small object (such as your cup) and move it toward and away from your face. Did its image grow larger as it approached and smaller as it receded? *Motion* provides us with a great deal of information about depth, and it is the first type of depth cue to which infants

**FIGURE 5.13** • The visual cliff. By refusing to cross the deep side and showing a preference for the shallow surface, this infant demonstrates the ability to perceive depth. *(William Vandivert/Scientific American)*

are sensitive. Around 3 weeks of age, babies blink their eyes defensively to an object moved toward their face that looks as if it is going to hit (Nanez, 1987). As they are carried about and as people and things turn and move before their eyes, infants learn more about depth. For example, by 3 months, motion has helped them figure out that objects are not flat shapes. Instead, they are three-dimensional (Arterberry & Yonas, 1988).

Motion is not the only important depth cue. Our eyes are separated, and each receives a slightly different view of the visual field. In children and adults, the brain blends these two images but also registers the difference between them, providing us with *binocular* (meaning two eyes) depth cues. Researchers have used ingenious methods to find out if infants are sensitive to binocular cues. One way is to project two overlapping images before the baby, who wears special goggles to ensure that each eye receives one of them. If babies make use of binocular cues, they see an organized form that they track with their eyes instead of random dots. Results reveal that binocular sensitivity emerges between 2 and 3 months and gradually improves over the first half-year (Banks & Salapatek, 1983).

We also use a final set of depth cues—the same ones that artists use to make a painting look three-dimensional. These are called *pictorial* depth cues. Examples are lines that create the illusion of perspective, changes in texture (nearby textures are more detailed than ones far away), and overlapping objects (an object partially hidden by another object is perceived to be more distant). Investigators have explored infants' sensitivity to pictorial cues by covering one eye (so the baby cannot rely on binocular vision), presenting stimuli with certain cues, and seeing which ones babies reach for. These experiments show that 7-month-old babies are sensitive to a variety of pictorial cues, but 5-month-olds are not (Yonas et al., 1986). Pictorial depth perception is last to develop, emerging around the middle of the first year.

Table 5.2 summarizes the infant's developing sensitivity to depth. Now let's turn to an important influence on depth perception: the baby's ability to move about independently.

*Independent Movement and Depth Perception.* Just before she reached the 6-month mark, April started crawling. "She's like a fearless daredevil," exclaimed Felicia to the

TABLE 5.2 • Development of Depth Perception

| Age | Perceptual Capacity |
| --- | --- |
| 3 weeks–3 months | Sensitivity to motion cues appears and improves |
| 3–6 months | Sensitivity to binocular cues appears and improves |
| 6–7 months | Sensitivity to pictorial cues appears |
| 6–11 months | Wariness of heights develops and is encouraged by the ability to move about independently |

other mothers. "If I put her down in the middle of our bed, she crawls right over the edge. The same thing's also happened by the stairs."

Will April become more wary of the side of the bed and the staircase as she becomes a more experienced crawler? Research suggests that she will. In one study, infants with more crawling experience (regardless of when they started to crawl) were far more likely to refuse to cross the deep side of the visual cliff (Bertenthal, Campos, & Barrett, 1984). Avoidance of heights, the investigators concluded, is "made possible by independent locomotion" (Bertenthal & Campos, 1987, p. 563).

Independent movement does not just influence wariness of drop-offs. It is related to other aspects of three-dimensional understanding as well. For example, crawling infants are better at remembering object locations and finding hidden objects than are their noncrawling agemates, and the more crawling experience they have, the better their performance on these tasks (Campos & Bertenthal, 1989; Kermoian & Campos, 1988). Why does crawling make such a difference? Compare your own experience of the environment when you are driven from one place to another as opposed to when you walk or drive yourself. When you move on your own, you are much more aware of landmarks and routes of travel, and you take more careful note of what things look like from different points of view. The same is true for infants. In fact, some researchers believe that crawling is so important in structuring babies' experience of the world that it may promote a new level of brain organization by strengthening important synaptic connections in the cortex (Bertenthal & Campos, 1987).

An estimated 80 to 90 percent of American parents place babies who are not yet crawling in infant "walkers" (Marcella & McDonald, 1990). These mechanical devices consist of a seat with a frame on castors in which babies can move around independently by pushing with their feet. Do walkers help stimulate development in the ways described above? Research suggests that they do (Bertenthal, Campos, & Barrett, 1984; Kermoian & Campos, 1988). However, there is no evidence that walkers have lasting effects on development, and they can be dangerous. Infants frequently tip over in them, hitting their heads. Even worse, they careen down staircases, perhaps because the frame and seat provide them with a false sense of security. Walkers account for over 23,000 injuries in the United States each year (Rieder, Schwartz, & Newman, 1986). For safety's sake, it is best not to put babies in these devices. The reorganization of experience linked to independent movement eventually takes place for all normal infants. The risks involved in trying to accelerate it far outweigh the benefits.

***Pattern Perception.*** Are young babies sensitive to the pattern, or form, of things they see, and do they prefer some patterns to others? Early research revealed that even newborns prefer to look at patterned as opposed to plain stimuli—for example, a drawing of the human face or one with scrambled facial features to a black-and-white oval (Fantz, 1961, 1963). Since then, many studies have shown that as infants get older, they prefer more complex patterns. For example, when shown black-and-white checkerboards, 3-week-old infants look longest at ones with a few large squares, whereas 8- and 14-week-olds prefer those with many squares (Brennan, Ames, & Moore, 1966). Infant preferences for many other patterned stimuli have been tested—curved versus straight lines and connected versus disconnected elements, to name just a few.

*Contrast Sensitivity.* For many years, investigators did not understand why babies of different ages find certain patterns more attractive than others. Then, a general principle was found to account for early pattern preferences. It is called **contrast sensitivity** (Banks & Ginsburg, 1985; Banks & Salapatek, 1981). *Contrast* refers to the overall quantity of light–dark transitions in a pattern. If babies are *sensitive to* (or can detect) a difference in contrast between two patterns, they will prefer the one with more contrast. To understand this idea, look at the two checkerboards in the top row of Figure 5.14. The one with many small squares has more contrast. Now look at the bottom row, which shows how these checkerboards appear to infants in the first few weeks of life. Because of their poor vision, young babies cannot see the contrast in more complex patterns. This explains why they prefer to look at large, bold checkerboards. By 2 months of age, their contrast sensitivity has improved considerably. As a result, infants start to spend much more time looking at patterns with fine details (Dodwell, Humphrey, & Muir, 1987).

Two checkerboards differing in contrast

Appearance of checkerboards to very young infants

**FIGURE 5.14** • The way two checkerboards differing in contrast look to infants in the first few weeks of life. The poor vision of very young infants prevents them from seeing the contrast in the more complex checkerboard. As a result, it appears as a dark mass, and the baby prefers to look at the pattern with large, bold squares. (*Adapted from M. S. Banks & P. Salapatek, "Infant visual perception," in M. M. Haith & J. J. Campos, eds.,* Handbook of child psychology: *Vol. 2, Infancy and developmental psychobiology, 4th ed., p. 504. Copyright 1983 by John Wiley & Sons. Reprinted by permission.*)

**Contrast sensitivity**

A general principle accounting for early pattern preferences, which states that if babies can detect a difference in contrast between two patterns, they will prefer the one with more contrast.

*Combining Pattern Elements.*   In the early weeks of life, infants respond to the separate parts of a pattern. For example, when shown drawings of human faces, 1-month-olds limit their visual exploration to the border of the stimulus, and they stare at single high-contrast features, such as the hairline or chin (see Figure 5.15). At about 2 months of age, infants start to thoroughly explore a pattern's internal features by moving their eyes quickly around the figure and pausing briefly to look at each of its parts (Bronson, 1991; Salapatek, 1975).

Once babies can detect all parts of a stimulus, they begin to combine pattern elements. In fact, infants of 6 or 7 months are so good at detecting pattern organization that they even perceive subjective boundaries that are not really present. For example, look at Figure 5.16. Seven-month-old babies perceive a square in the center of this pattern, just as you do (Bertenthal, Campos, & Haith, 1980). Older infants carry this responsiveness to subjective form even further. Nine-month-olds can detect the organized meaningful pattern in a series of moving lights that resemble a human being walking, in that they look much longer at this display than they do at upside down or disorganized versions (Bertenthal et al., 1985). Although 3- to 5-month-olds can tell the difference between these patterns, they do not show a special preference for one with both an upright orientation and a humanlike movement pattern (Bertenthal et al., 1987).

*Perception of the Human Face.*   Do newborn babies have an innate capacity to recognize and respond to the human face? Some early work suggested that they do (Fantz, 1961), but recent research indicates that they do not. Infants under 2 months do not look longer at a facial pattern than a pattern of equal complexity, such as one with scrambled facial features, largely because (as we noted earlier) 1-month-olds do not explore the internal features of a stimulus. At 2 to 3 months, when infants look at an entire pattern, they do prefer a face over scrambled arrangements (Dannemiller & Stephens, 1988; Maurer, 1985).

**FIGURE 5.15** • Visual scanning of the pattern of the human face by 1- and 2-month-old infants. One-month-olds limit their scanning to single features on the border of the stimulus, whereas 2-month-olds explore internal features. *(From P. Salapatek, 1975, "Pattern perception in early infancy." In L. B. Cohen & P. Salapatek, eds.,* Infant perception: From sensation to cognition, *New York: Academic Press, p. 201. Reprinted by permission.)*

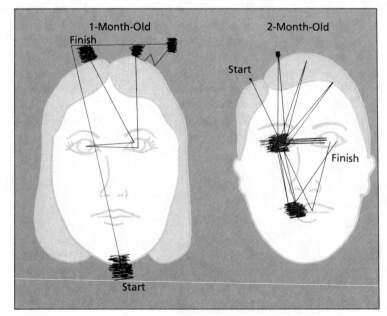

*intermodal*

The baby's tendency to search for structure in a patterned stimulus is quickly applied to face perception. By 3 months of age, infants make fine-grained distinctions among the features of different faces. For example, they can tell the difference between the photos of two strangers, even when the faces are moderately similar (Barrera & Maurer, 1981a). Around this time, babies also recognize their mother's face in a photo, since they look longer at it than the face of a stranger (Barrera & Maurer, 1981b). And by 5 months, they clearly associate a real face with a color photograph of the same person (Dirks & Gibson, 1977). In Chapter 7 we will see that as face perception improves, infants recognize and respond to the expressive behavior of others. Like many other early capacities, perception of the human face plays an important role in infants' earliest social relationships.

The development of pattern perception in general, and face perception in particular, is summarized in Table 5.3. Take a moment to note the close parallels between them. The table shows that several important developments in pattern perception take place around 2 months of age. Recall that 2 months is also a time when the cortex develops rapidly and when babies become more alert and interested in the world around them. Brain growth supports the baby's improved ability to make sense of patterned stimuli.

*Intermodal Perception*

So far, we have discussed the infant's perceptual abilities one by one. However, when we take in information from the environment, we often use **intermodal perception.** That is, we combine stimulation from more than one *modality,* or sensory system, at a time. For example, we know that the shape of an object is the same whether we see it or touch it, that lip movements are closely coordinated with the sound of a voice, and that dropping a rigid object on a hard surface will cause a sharp, banging sound.

Are young infants, like adults, capable of intermodal perception, or do they have to learn how to put different types of sensory input together? Recent evidence reveals that from the start, babies perceive the world in an intermodal fashion (Spelke, 1987). Recall that newborns turn in the general direction of a sound, and they reach for objects in a primitive way. These behaviors suggest that infants expect sight, sound, and touch to go together.

By a few weeks after birth, infants show some impressive intermodal associations. In one study, 1-month-old babies were given a pacifier to suck with either a smooth surface or a surface with nubs on it. After exploring it in their mouths, the infants were shown two pacifiers—one smooth and one nubbed. They preferred to look at the shape they had sucked, indicating that they could match touch and visual stimulation without spending months seeing and feeling objects (Meltzoff & Borton, 1979). The findings of another study revealed that by 4 months, vision and hearing are well coordinated. Infants of this age were shown two films side by side, one with two blocks banging and the other with two sponges being squashed together. At the same time, the sound track for only one of the films—either a sharp banging noise or a soft squashing sound—could be heard. Infants looked at the film that went with the sound track, indicating that they detected a common rhythm in what they saw and heard (Bahrick, 1983).

Of course, a great many intermodal matches—the way a train sounds or a teddy bear feels—must be based on experience. But what is so remarkable about intermodal development is how quickly infants acquire these associations. Most of the time, they need just one exposure to a new situation (Spelke, 1987). In addition, when researchers try to teach intermodal relationships by pairing sights and sounds that do not naturally go together, babies will not learn them (Bahrick, 1988). Intermodal perception is yet another capacity that helps infants build up an orderly, predictable perceptual world.

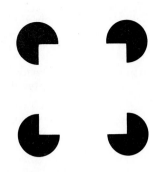

**FIGURE 5.16** • Subjective boundaries in a visual pattern. Do you perceive a square in the middle of this figure? By 7 months of age, infants do, too. *(Adapted from Bertenthal, Campos, & Haith, 1980.)*

**Intermodal perception**
Perception that combines information from more than one sensory system.

TABLE 5.3 • Development of Pattern and Face Perception

|  | 0–1 Month | 2–3 Months | 4–9 Months |
|---|---|---|---|
| Pattern perception | Preference for patterns with large elements | Preference for patterns with fine details | Detection of increasingly complex pattern arrangements |
|  | Visual exploration limited to the border of a stimulus and single features | Visual exploration of entire stimulus, including internal features |  |
|  |  | Combination of pattern elements into an organized whole |  |
| Face perception | Absence of face perception | Preference for a facial pattern over patterns with scrambled facial features | More fine-grained discrimination of faces, including ability to associate a real face with its photograph |
|  |  | Recognition of mother's face in a photo |  |

• *Five-month-old Tyrone sat in his infant seat, passing a teething biscuit from hand to hand, moving it up close to his face and far away, and finally dropping it overboard on the floor below. What aspect of visual development is Tyrone probably learning about? Explain your answer.*

• *Diane put up bright wallpaper with detailed pictures of animals in Jana's room before she was born. During the first 2 months of life, Jana hardly noticed the wallpaper. Then, around 2 months, she showed keen interest. What new visual abilities probably account for this change?*

**Differentiation theory**
The view that perceptual development involves the detection of increasingly fine-grained invariant features in the environment.

**Invariant features**
Features that remain stable in a constantly changing perceptual world.

**BRIEF REVIEW** During the first year, infants gradually organize sounds into more complex patterns, and they become sensitive to the sound patterns of their own language. Changes in visual abilities are striking. Depth perception improves as infants detect motion, binocular, and pictorial depth cues. Experience in independent movement plays an important role in avoidance of heights as well as other aspects of three-dimensional understanding. The principle of contrast sensitivity accounts for young babies' pattern preferences. As vision improves, infants perceive the parts of a pattern as an organized whole. Face perception follows the same sequence of development as pattern perception in general. Young infants have a remarkable ability to combine information across different sensory modalities.

## UNDERSTANDING PERCEPTUAL DEVELOPMENT

Now that we have reviewed the development of infant perceptual capacities, the question arises: How can we put this diverse array of amazing achievements together? Does any general principle account for perceptual development? Eleanor and James Gibson's **differentiation theory** provides a widely accepted answer. According to the Gibsons, infants actively search for **invariant features** of the environment—those that remain stable—in a constantly changing perceptual world. For example, in pattern perception, at first babies are confronted with a confusing mass of stimulation. But very quickly, they search for features that stand out along the border of a stimulus. Then they explore its internal features, and as they do so, they notice *stable relationships* among those features. As a result, they detect overall patterns. The development of intermodal perception also reflects this principle. Again, what babies seem to do is seek out invariant relationships, such as a similar tempo in an object's motion and sound, that unite information across different modalities.

The Gibsons use the word *differentiation* (which means analyze or break down) to describe their theory because over time, the baby makes finer and finer distinctions among stimuli. For example, the human face is initially perceived in terms of single, high-contrast features, such as the hairline or chin. Then eyes, nose, and mouth are detected and combined into a pattern. Soon subtle distinctions between one face and another are made, and babies can tell mother, father, and stranger apart. So one way of understanding perceptual development is to think of it as a built-in tendency to

*Summary*

search for order and stability in the surrounding world, a capacity that becomes increasingly fine-tuned with age (Gibson 1970; Gibson 1979).

As we conclude this chapter, it is only fair to note that some researchers believe that babies do not just make sense of their world by searching for invariant features. Instead, they impose *meaning* on what they perceive, constructing categories of objects and events in the surrounding environment. We have already seen the glimmerings of this cognitive point of view in some of the evidence reviewed in this chapter. For example, older babies *interpret* a familiar face as a source of pleasure and affection and a pattern of blinking lights as a moving human being. We will save our discussion of infant cognition for the next chapter, acknowledging for now that the cognitive perspective also has merit in understanding the achievements of infancy. In fact, many researchers combine these two positions, regarding infant development as proceeding from a perceptual to a cognitive emphasis over the first year of life (Salapatek & Cohen, 1987).

# SUMMARY

### Growth of the Body in the First Two Years

• Changes in height and weight are rapid during the first 2 years. Physical growth of parts of the body follows **cephalo-caudal** and **proximo-distal trends.** Body fat is laid down quickly during the first 9 months, while muscle development is slow and gradual.

• **Skeletal age,** a measure based on the number of **epiphyses** and the extent to which they are fused, is the best way to estimate the child's overall physical maturity. At birth, infants have six **fontanels,** which permit skull bones to expand as the brain grows. The first tooth emerges around 6 months of age.

### Brain Development

• Early in development the brain grows faster than any other organ of the body. During infancy, **neurons** form **synapses,** or complex communication networks, at a rapid rate. Stimulation determines which neurons will survive and which will die off. **Glial cells,** which are responsible for **myelinization,** multiply rapidly into the second year and result in large gains in brain size.

• The development of different regions of the **cerebral cortex** corresponds to the order in which various capacities emerge in the infant and child. **Lateralization** refers to specialization of the hemispheres of the cortex. In early infancy, before many regions of the cortex have taken on specialized roles, there is high brain **plasticity.** However, some brain specialization already exists at birth.

### Factors Affecting Early Physical Growth

• Physical growth results from the continuous and complex interplay between heredity and environment. Heredity contributes to body size and rate of maturation.

• Breast milk is ideally suited to the growth needs of young babies and offers protection against disease. Breast-feeding prevents malnutrition and infant death in poverty-stricken areas of the world. Breast-fed and bottle-fed babies do not differ in psychological development.

• Although overweight and obesity are widespread problems in industrialized nations, chubby babies are not at risk for accumulating too many fat cells. Trying to put a baby on a diet can endanger development.

• **Marasmus** and **kwashiorkor** are dietary diseases caused by malnutrition that affect many children in developing countries. If allowed to continue, body growth and brain development can be permanently stunted. **Inorganic failure to thrive** illustrates the importance of stimulation and affection for normal physical growth.

### Changing States of Arousal

• During infancy, short periods of sleep and wakefulness are put together, and they start to coincide with a night and day schedule. Changing arousal patterns are affected by brain development, but the social environment also plays a role. Infants in Western nations sleep through the night much earlier than those in many Asian and African cultures.

### Motor Development During the First Two Years

• Like physical development, motor development follows the cephalo-caudal and proximo-distal trends. New motor skills are a matter of combining existing skills into increasingly complex **systems of action.**

• Experience has a profound effect on motor development, as shown by research on infants raised in deprived institutions. Stimulation of infant motor abilities accounts for cross-cultural differences in motor development. During the first year, infants gradually perfect their visually guided reaching.

• Young children are not physically and psychologically ready for toilet training until the end of the second or beginning of the third year of life.

### Basic Learning Mechanisms

• Infants can be **classically conditioned** when the pairing of an **unconditioned stimulus (UCS)** and **conditioned stimulus (CS)** has survival value. Young babies are easily conditioned in the feeding situation. Classical conditioning of fear is difficult before 8 to 12 months.

• **Operant conditioning** of infants has been demonstrated in many studies. In addition to food, interesting sights and sounds serve as effective **reinforcers.**

• **Habituation** and **dishabituation** reveal that at birth babies are attracted to novelty. Newborn infants also have a primitive ability to **imitate** the facial expressions of adults.

### Perceptual Development in Infancy

• Over the first year, infants organize sounds into more complex patterns. They also become more sensitive to the sounds of their own language.

• Rapid development of the eye and visual centers in the brain supports the development of focusing, color discrimination, and visual acuity during the first half year. The ability to track a moving object also improves.

• Research on depth perception reveals that responsiveness to motion develops first, followed by sensitivity to binocular and then pictorial cues. Experience in moving about independently affects babies' three-dimensional understanding.

• **Contrast sensitivity** accounts for babies' early pattern preferences. At first, infants look at the border of a stimulus and at single features. Around 2 months, they explore the internal features of a pattern and start to combine elements together. Over time, they discriminate increasingly complex patterns. Perception of the human face follows the same sequence of development as sensitivity to other patterned stimuli.

• Research suggests that from the start, infants are capable of **intermodal perception.** They quickly combine information across sensory modalities, often after just one exposure to a new situation.

### Understanding Perceptual Development

• According to Eleanor and James Gibson's **differentiation theory,** perceptual development is a matter of searching for **invariant features** in a constantly changing perceptual world. Others take a more cognitive viewpoint in suggesting that at an early age infants impose meaning on what they perceive. Many researchers combine these two ideas.

## IMPORTANT TERMS AND CONCEPTS

| | | |
|---|---|---|
| cephalo-caudal trend (p. 166) | colostrum (p. 173) | extinction (p. 186) |
| proximo-distal trend (p. 166) | marasmus (p. 176) | operant conditioning (p. 187) |
| skeletal age (p. 167) | kwashiorkor (p. 176) | reinforcer (p. 187) |
| epiphyses (p. 167) | inorganic failure to thrive (p. 176) | punishment (p. 187) |
| fontanels (p. 168) | system of action (p. 180) | sudden infant death syndrome (SIDS) (p. 189) |
| neurons (p. 169) | prereaching (p. 181) | habituation (p. 189) |
| synapse (p. 169) | ulnar grasp (p. 181) | dishabituation (p. 189) |
| glial cells (p. 169) | pincer grasp (p. 181) | imitation (p. 189) |
| myelinization (p. 169) | classical conditioning (p. 185) | contrast sensitivity (p. 195) |
| cerebral cortex (p. 170) | unconditioned stimulus (UCS) (p. 186) | intermodal perception (p. 197) |
| lateralization (p. 171) | unconditioned response (UCR) (p. 186) | differentiation theory (p. 198) |
| plasticity (p. 171) | conditioned stimulus (CS) (p. 186) | invariant features (p. 198) |
| catch-up growth (p. 173) | conditioned response (CR) (p. 186) | |

# FOR FURTHER INFORMATION AND SPECIAL HELP

## Physical Growth and Health

Healthy Mothers, Healthy Babies
409 Twentieth Street, S. W.
Washington, D.C. 20024-2188
(202) 863-2458

A coalition of national and state organizations concerned with maternal and child health. Serves as a network through which information on nutrition, injury prevention, and infant mortality is shared.

United Nations Children's Fund (UNICEF)
3 United Nations Plaza
New York, NY 10017
(212) 326-7000

International organization dedicated to addressing the problems of children around the world. Develops and implements health and nutrition programs, campaigns to have children vaccinated against disease, and coordinates delivery of food and other aid to disaster-stricken areas.

Word Health Organization (WHO)
Avenue Appia
CH–1211 Geneva 27
Switzerland
(22) 791-2111

International health agency of the United Nations that seeks to obtain the highest level of health care for all people. Promotes prevention and treatment of disease and strives to eliminate poverty. Places special emphasis on the health needs of developing countries.

## Breast-Feeding

La Leche League International
9616 Minneapolis Avenue
Franklin Park, IL 60131
(800) LA LECHE

Provides information and support to breast-feeding mothers. Local chapters exist in many cities.

## Malnutrition

Food Research and Action Center
1319 F Street N.W., Suite 500
Washington, DC 20004
(202) 393-5060

Provides assistance to community organizations trying to make federal food programs more responsive to the needs of millions of hungry Americans. Seeks to enhance public awareness of the problems of hunger and poverty in the United States.

## Sudden Infant Death Syndrome (SIDS)

National Sudden Infant Death Syndrome Clearinghouse
8201 Greensboro Drive, Suite 600
McLean, VA 22102
(703) 821-8955

Provides information to health professionals and the public on SIDS.

National Sudden Infant Death Syndrome Foundation (NSIDSF)
10500 Little Patuxent Pkwy, #420
Columbia, MD 21044
(301) 964-8000

Provides assistance to parents who have lost a child to SIDS. Works with families and health professionals in caring for infants at risk due to heart and respiratory problems.

*"Mother and Child,"* Camilla Bergli, 6 years, Norway.
*Reprinted by permission from The International Museum
of Children's Art, Oslo, Norway.*

# Cognitive Development in Infancy and Toddlerhood

# 6

Piaget's Cognitive-Developmental Theory
*Key Piagetian Concepts   The Sensorimotor Stage   New Research on Sensorimotor Development   Evaluation of the Sensorimotor Stage*

Information Processing in the First Two Years
*A Model of Human Information Processing   Attention and Memory   Categorization Skills   Evaluation of Information Processing Findings*

The Social Context of Early Cognitive Development

Individual Differences in Early Mental Development
*Infant Intelligence Tests   Early Environment and Mental Development   Early Intervention for At-Risk Infants and Toddlers*

Language Development During the First Two Years
*Three Theories of Language Development   Getting Ready to Talk   First Words   The Two-Word Utterance Phase   Comprehension Versus Production   Individual Differences in Language Development   Supporting Early Language Development*

W hen Byron, Rachel, and April were brought together by their mothers at age 18 months, the room was alive with activity. I sat back in a corner and watched as the events of the next hour unfolded. The three spirited explorers were bent on discovery. Rachel dropped shapes through holes in a plastic box that Beth held and adjusted so the harder ones would fall smoothly into the container. Once a few shapes were inside, Rachel grabbed and shook the box, squealing with delight as the lid fell open and the shapes scattered around her. The clatter of the falling shapes attracted Byron, who picked one up, carried it to the railing at the top of the basement steps, and dropped it overboard. Byron watched with interest as the shape tumbled down the stairs, then followed it with a teddy bear, a large rubber ball, his shoe, and a spoon. In the meantime, April pulled open a drawer, unloaded a set of wooden bowls, stacked them in a pile, knocked it over, then banged two bowls together like cymbals. With each action, the youngsters seemed to be asking, "What's out here in this world? Which behavior leads to which consequence? What events can I control?"

As the toddlers experimented with things around them, I could see the beginnings of language—a whole new way of influencing the world. April was the most vocal of the three youngsters. "All gone baw!" she exclaimed as Byron tossed the bright red ball down the basement steps. Although Byron was not yet talking, he was preparing to become a speaker in many ways. A stream of babbled syllables could be heard as he moved around the room, and he skillfully used gestures to communicate his desires. A close look at Rachel revealed that the capacity to represent experience through words and gestures had opened up a whole new realm of play possibilities. Rachel could pretend. "Night-night," she said as she put her head down on her hands and closed her eyes, ever-so-pleased that in the world of make-believe, she could decide for herself when and where to go to bed.

Over the first 2 years, the small, reflexive newborn baby becomes a self-assertive, purposeful being who solves simple problems and has started to master the most amazing of human abilities—language. "How does all this happen so quickly?" asked Felicia, turning to me. In this chapter, we consider three perspectives on early cognitive development—Piaget's *cognitive-developmental theory*, *information processing*, and Vygotsky's *sociocultural theory*. We will see that each casts a different light on Felicia's question.

Lisa raised another concern. "Byron isn't talking yet, and he rarely stacks things and puts shapes in containers like Rachel and April. If he isn't developing as quickly as other children now, will that still be true when he goes to school?" Mental tests permit direct comparisons of the cognitive progress of children of the same age. We will carefully consider the usefulness of these tests during this earliest phase of development.

Our discussion concludes with the beginnings of language. We will see how toddlers' first words and word combinations build on early cognitive achievements. But very soon, new words and expressions greatly increase the speed and flexibility of human thinking. Throughout development, cognition and language are related, and they mutually support one another.

## PIAGET'S COGNITIVE-DEVELOPMENTAL THEORY

The Swiss theorist Jean Piaget is the great twentieth-century giant of cognitive development. His work led researchers all over the world to view children as busy, motivated explorers whose thinking develops as they act directly on the environment. Perhaps you remember from Chapter 1 that Piaget's theory was greatly influenced by his background in biology. He believed that over time, the child's mind forms and modifies psychological structures to achieve a better adaptive fit with reality.

### Key Piagetian Concepts

According to Piaget, between infancy and adolescence, children move through four stages of development. The most elaborate is the **sensorimotor stage,** which spans the first 2 years of life. As the name of this stage implies, Piaget believed that infants and toddlers "think" with their eyes, ears, hands, and other sensorimotor equipment. They cannot yet carry out many activities inside their heads. But by the end of toddlerhood, children are very different. At 18 months, Byron, Rachel, and April could solve practical, everyday problems and represent their experiences in speech, gesture, and play. To understand Piaget's view of how these vast changes take place, we need to look at some important Piagetian concepts, which are summarized in Concept Table 6.1. These convey Piaget's ideas about *what changes with development,* and *how cognitive change takes place.*

**What Changes with Development.** Piaget believed that *psychological structures*—the child's organized ways of making sense of experience—change with age. He referred to specific structures as **schemes.** At first, schemes are motor action patterns. For example, at age 6 months, Byron dropped objects in a fairly rigid way, simply by letting go of a rattle or teething ring in his hand. Each time, he looked with interest as the object fell on the floor in front of him. By age 18 months, Byron's

**Sensorimotor stage**

Piaget's first stage, during which infants and toddlers "think" with their eyes, ears, hands, and other sensorimotor equipment. Spans the first 2 years of life.

**Scheme**

In Piaget's theory, a specific structure, or organized way of making sense of experience, that changes with age.

**CONCEPT TABLE 6.1 • Basic Piagetian Concepts**

| Concept | Important Point | Example |
|---------|----------------|---------|
| Schemes | Specific mental structures, or organized ways of making sense of experience, that change with age. The first schemes are motor action patterns that infants and toddlers use to find out about their world. | At 1 month, Byron's "grasping scheme" was fairly rigid; he grasped anything placed in his hand in much the same way. By 4 months, he adjusted his hand opening to the size of the object offered. |
| Adaptation | The process of changing schemes by acting directly on the environment and being influenced by it as a result. Combines assimilation and accommodation. | At 20 months, April saw a kangaroo for the first time in her picture book. She tried to adapt her schemes to make sense of the object. |
| Assimilation | Interpreting the world in terms of current schemes. Children strive to assimilate, or use schemes to understand the environment. Successful use of schemes produces a state of *equilibrium*, a pleasurable cognitive condition. | At first, April applied a current scheme to the kangaroo, calling it a "bunny." |
| Accommodation | Creating new schemes or changing old ones to take into account new aspects of the environment. When children do more accommodating than assimilating, they are in a state of *disequilibrium*, or cognitive discomfort. | Later April noticed that kangaroos are not just like bunnies. She modified her scheme for interpreting the object, calling it a "funny bunny." |
| Equilibration | The back-and-forth movement between equilibrium and disequilibrium that occurs throughout development. Gradually produces more effective schemes. | As Byron modified his "grasping scheme" and April her "bunny scheme," their new cognitive structures achieved a better fit with the environment and were less likely to be challenged in the future. |
| Organization | The process of linking schemes together into a strongly interconnected system, so they can be applied jointly to the environment. | Over time, April linked her schemes for "bunnies," "kitties," and "kangaroos" together. She could easily pick out similarities and differences among them. |

*Behaviors that create work for caregivers can be important learning experiences for babies. This infant experiments with her "dropping scheme." As the food falls from her hand, she looks with interest to see how and where it lands. As a result, her sensorimotor understanding of the world expands. (By permission of Current, Inc.)*

"dropping scheme" had become much more deliberate and creative. He tossed all sorts of objects down the basement stairs, throwing some up in the air, bouncing others off walls, releasing some gently and others with all the force his little body could muster. Soon Byron's schemes will move from an *action-based level* to a *mental level*. When this happens, Byron will not just act on objects around him. He will show evidence of thinking before he acts (Ginsburg & Opper, 1988). This change, as we will see later, marks the transition from sensorimotor to preoperational thought.

***How Cognitive Change Takes Place.*** Piaget believed that two processes are responsible for changes in schemes: adaptation and organization.

*Adaptation.*    The next time you have a chance to observe infants and toddlers, notice how they tirelessly repeat actions that lead to interesting effects. For example, Byron dropped objects over and over, gradually noticing that varying the way he held his hand and the type of object released produced fascinating new results. Byron was changing his "dropping scheme" through **adaptation,** a process that involves acting directly on the environment and being influenced by it as a result.

Adaptation is made up of two complementary activities—**assimilation** and **accommodation.** During *assimilation,* we interpret the external world in terms of our current schemes. For example, when Byron dropped objects, he was assimilating them all into his sensorimotor "dropping scheme." Beth described another instance of assimilation, which occurred when Rachel visited the zoo on her second birthday. On seeing her first camel, Rachel sifted through her collection of schemes until she found one that resembled this strange new creature. "Horse!" she called out, after looking puzzled for a moment. In *accommodation,* we create new schemes or adjust old ones after noticing that our current ways of thinking do not capture the environment completely. When Byron dropped objects in different ways, he was modifying his dropping scheme to account for the varied properties of objects. And when Rachel started to refer to camels as "lumpy horses," she realized that certain characteristics of camels are not like horses and revised her "horse scheme" accordingly.

So far, we have referred to assimilation and accommodation as separate activities, but Piaget regarded them as always working together. That is, in every interchange with the environment, we interpret information using our existing structures, and we also refine them to achieve a better fit with experience. But the balance between assimilation and accommodation does vary from one time period to another. During periods in which children are not changing very much, they assimilate more than they accommodate. Piaget called this a state of cognitive *equilibrium,* implying a steady, comfortable condition. During times of rapid cognitive change, however, children are in a state of *disequilibrium,* or cognitive discomfort. They realize that new information does not fit with their current schemes, and they must do something about it. So they shift away from assimilation toward accommodation. Once they have modified their schemes, they move back toward assimilation, exercising their newly changed structures until they are ready to be modified again.

Piaget used the term **equilibration** to sum up this back-and-forth movement between equilibrium and disequilibrium throughout development. Each time it occurs, more effective schemes are produced. They take in a wider range of aspects of the environment, and there is less and less to throw them out of balance (Piaget, 1985). Because the times of greatest accommodation are the earliest ones, the sensorimotor stage is Piaget's most complex period of development.

*Organization.*    Besides adaptation, schemes change through a second process called **organization.** It takes place internally, apart from direct contact with the environment. Once children form new structures, they start to rearrange them, linking them with other schemes so they are part of a strongly interconnected cognitive system. For example, eventually Byron will relate "dropping" to "throwing" and to his developing understanding of "nearness" and "farness." And Rachel will construct a separate "camel scheme" that will be connected by similarities and differences to her understanding of horses and other animals. According to Piaget, schemes reach a true state of equilibrium when they become part of a broad network of structures that can be jointly applied to the surrounding world (Flavell, 1963; Piaget, 1936/1952).

## The Sensorimotor Stage

The difference between the newborn baby and the 2-year-old child is so vast that the sensorimotor stage is divided into six substages. Piaget's observations of his own three children served as the basis for this sequence of development. Three subjects is

---

**Adaptation**

In Piaget's theory, the process of acting directly on the environment and being influenced by it as a result.

**Assimilation**

That part of adaptation in which the external world is interpreted in terms of current schemes.

**Accommodation**

That part of adaptation in which new schemes are created and old ones adjusted to create a better fit with the environment.

**Equilibration**

In Piaget's theory, back-and-forth movement between cognitive equilibrium and disequilibrium throughout development, which leads to more effective schemes.

**Organization**

In Piaget's theory, the internal rearrangement and linking together of schemes so that they form a strongly interconnected cognitive system.

a very small sample, but Piaget watched carefully and also presented his son and two daughters with little tasks (such as hidden objects) that helped reveal their understanding of the world. In the following sections, we will first describe infant development as Piaget saw it. Then we will consider evidence indicating that in some ways, the structures of young infants are more advanced than Piaget imagined them to be.

*The Circular Reaction.*    At the beginning of the sensorimotor stage, infants know so little about the world that they cannot purposefully explore it. This presents a problem for young babies, since they need some way of adapting their first schemes. The **circular reaction** provides them with a special means of doing so. It involves stumbling onto a new experience caused by the baby's own motor activity. The reaction is "circular" because the infant tries to repeat the event again and again. As a result, a sensorimotor response that first occurred by chance becomes strengthened into a new scheme. For example, at age 2 months Rachel accidently made a smacking sound after finishing a feeding. The sound was new and intriguing, so Rachel tried to repeat it until, after a few days, she became quite expert at smacking her lips.

During the first 2 years, the circular reaction changes in several ways. At first, it is centered around the infant's own body. Later it turns outward, toward manipulation of objects. Finally, it becomes experimental and creative, aimed at producing novel effects in the environment. Piaget considered these revisions in the circular reaction so important for early cognitive development that he named the sensorimotor substages after them. You may find it helpful to refer to the summary of sensorimotor development in Table 6.1 as you read about each substage below.

TABLE 6.1 • Summary of Cognitive Development During the Sensorimotor Stage

| Sensorimotor Substage | Typical Adaptive Behaviors | Object Permanence |
|---|---|---|
| 1. Reflexive schemes (birth–1 month) | Newborn reflexes (see Chapter 4, page 148) | None |
| 2. Primary circular reactions (1–4 months) | Simple motor habits centered around the infant's own body; limited anticipation of events | None |
| 3. Secondary circular reactions (4–8 months) | Actions aimed at repeating interesting effects in the surrounding world; imitation of familiar behaviors | None |
| 4. Coordination of secondary circular reactions (8–12 months) | Intentional or goal-directed action sequences; improved anticipation of events; imitation of behaviors slightly different from those the infant usually performs | Ability to find an object in the first location in which it is hidden |
| 5. Tertiary circular reactions (12–18 months) | Exploration of the properties of objects by acting on them in novel ways; imitation of unfamiliar behaviors | Ability to search in several locations for a hidden object |
| 6. Mental representation (18 months–2 years) | Internal representation of objects and events; deferred imitation and make-believe play | Ability to find an object that has been moved while out of sight |

**Circular reaction**
In Piaget's theory, a means of building schemes in which infants try to repeat a chance event caused by their own motor activity.

**FIGURE 6.1** • The newborn baby's schemes consist of reflexes, which will gradually be modified as they are applied to the surrounding environment.

*Substage 1: Reflexive Schemes (Birth–1 Month).* Piaget regarded newborn reflexes as the building blocks of sensorimotor intelligence. As we will see in the next substage, sucking, grasping, and looking gradually change as they are applied to the surrounding environment. But at first, babies suck, grasp, and look in much the same way, no matter what experiences they encounter (see Figure 6.1). Beth reported an amusing example of Rachel's indiscriminate sucking at 2 weeks of age. She lay on the bed next to her father while he took a nap. Suddenly, he awoke with a start. Rachel had latched on and begun to suck on his back!

*Substage 2: Primary Circular Reactions—The First Learned Adaptations (1–4 Months).* Infants start to gain voluntary control over their actions by repeating chance behaviors that lead to satisfying results. This leads them to develop some simple motor habits, such as sucking their fists or thumbs and opening and closing their hands (see Figure 6.2). Babies of this substage also start to vary their behavior

**FIGURE 6.2** • At 2 months, Byron sees his hand open and close and tries to repeat this action, in a primary circular reaction.

in response to environmental demands. For example, they open their mouths differently when presented with a nipple as opposed to a spoon. Young infants also show a limited ability to anticipate events. For example, at age 3 months, when Byron awoke from his nap, he cried out with hunger. But as soon as Lisa entered the room and moved toward his crib, Byron's crying stopped. He knew that feeding time was near.

Piaget called the first circular reactions *primary,* and he regarded them as quite limited. Notice how, in the examples just given, infants' adaptations are oriented toward their own bodies and motivated by basic needs. According to Piaget, babies of this age are not yet very concerned with the effects of their actions on the external world.

### Substage 3: Secondary Circular Reactions—Making Interesting Sights Last (4–8 Months).

Think back to our discussion of motor development in Chapter 5. Between 4 and 8 months, infants sit up and become skilled at reaching for, grasping, and manipulating objects. These motor achievements play a major role in turning their attention outward toward the environment. Using the *secondary* circular reaction, infants try to repeat interesting effects in the surrounding world that are caused by their own actions. In the following illustration, notice how Piaget's 4-month-old son Laurent gradually builds the sensorimotor scheme of "hitting" over a 10-day period (see Figure 6.3):

> At 4 months 7 days [Laurent] looks at a letter opener tangled in the strings of a doll hung in front of him. He tries to grasp (a scheme he already knows) the doll or the letter opener but each time, his attempts only result in his knocking the objects (so they swing out of his reach) . . . . At 4 months 15 days, with another doll hung in front of him, Laurent tries to grasp it, then shakes himself to make it swing, knocks it accidentally, and then tries simply to hit it . . . . At 4 months 18 days, Laurent hits my hands without trying to grasp them, but he started by simply waving his arms around, and only afterwards went on to hit my hands. The next day, finally, Laurent immediately hits a doll hung in front of him. The [hitting] scheme is now completely differentiated [from grasping]. (Piaget, 1936/1952, pp. 167–168)

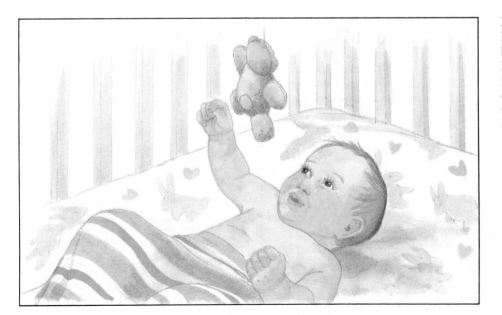

**FIGURE 6.3** • At 4 months, Piaget's son Laurent accidently hits a doll hung in front of him. He tries to recapture the interesting effect of the swinging doll. In doing so, he builds a new "hitting scheme" through the secondary circular reaction.

Improved control over their own behavior permits infants of this substage to imitate the behavior of others. However, babies under 8 months only imitate actions that they themselves have practiced many times. They cannot adapt flexibly and quickly, imitating behaviors that are new and unfamiliar (Kaye & Marcus, 1981).

***Substage 4: Coordination of Secondary Circular Reactions (8–12 Months).*** Now infants start to organize schemes. They combine secondary circular reactions into new, more complex action sequences. As a result, two landmark cognitive changes take place.

First, babies can engage in **intentional** or **goal-directed behavior.** Before this substage, actions that led to new schemes had a random, hit-or-miss quality to them. But by 8 months of age, infants have had enough practice with a variety of schemes that they combine them deliberately in the solution of sensorimotor problems. The clearest example is provided by Piaget's famous *object-hiding tasks,* in which he shows the baby an attractive object and then hides it behind his hand or under a cover. Infants of this substage can find the object. In doing so, they coordinate two schemes—"pushing" aside the obstacle and "grasping" the object.

The fact that infants can retrieve hidden objects reveals that they have begun to attain a second cognitive milestone: **object permanence,** the understanding that objects continue to exist when they are out of sight (see Figure 6.4). But awareness of object permanence is not yet complete. If an object is moved from one hiding place (A) to another (B), babies will search for it only in the first hiding place (A). Because 8- to 12-month-olds make this **AB search error,** Piaget concluded that they do not have a clear image of the object as persisting when out of sight.

Finally, Substage 4 brings two additional advances. First, infants can anticipate events much more effectively than before, and using their new capacity for intentional behavior, they sometimes try to change those experiences. For example, at 10 months Byron crawled after Lisa when she put on her coat, whimpering to keep her from leaving. Second, babies can imitate behaviors that are slightly different from those they usually perform. After watching someone else, they try to stir with a spoon, push a toy car, or drop raisins in a cup. Once again, they do so by drawing on their capacity for intentional behavior—purposefully modifying schemes to fit an observed action. This permits infants to add quickly to their schemes by copying the behavior of others (Piaget, 1945/1951).

**Intentional or goal-directed behavior**

A sequence of actions in which infants combine schemes deliberately to solve a sensorimotor problem.

**Object permanence**

The understanding that objects continue to exist when they are out of sight.

**AB search error**

The error made by 8- to 12-month-olds after an object is moved from hiding place A to hiding place B. Infants in Piaget's Substage 4 search for it only in the first hiding place (A).

**FIGURE 6.4** • Around 8 months, infants combine schemes deliberately in the solution of sensorimotor problems. They show the beginnings of object permanence, since they can find an object in the first place in which it is hidden.

***Substage 5: Tertiary Circular Reactions—Discovering New Means Through Active Experimentation (12–18 Months).*** At this substage, the circular reaction—now called *tertiary*—becomes experimental and creative. Toddlers do not just repeat behaviors that lead to familiar results. They *repeat with variation,* provoking new effects. Recall how Byron dropped objects over the basement steps, trying this, then that, and then another action in a deliberately exploratory approach (see Figure 6.5). Because they approach the world in this exploratory way, 12- to 18-month-olds are far better sensorimotor problem solvers than they were before. For example, Rachel could figure out how to fit a shape through a hole in a container by turning and twisting it until it fell through, and she discovered how to use a stick to get toys that were out of reach.

According to Piaget, this new capacity to experiment leads to a more advanced understanding of object permanence. Toddlers look in not just one, but several locations to find a hidden toy. Thus, they no longer make the AB search error. Their more flexible action patterns also permit them to imitate many more behaviors, such as stacking blocks, scribbling on paper, and making funny faces.

***Substage 6: Mental Representation—Inventing New Means Through Mental Combinations (18 Months–2 Years).*** Substage 5 is the last truly *sensorimotor* stage, since Substage 6 brings with it the ability to create **mental representations** of reali-

**FIGURE 6.5** • At 18 months, Byron dropped a variety of objects down the basement stairs, throwing some up in the air, bouncing others off the wall, releasing some gently and others forcefully, in a deliberately experimental approach. Byron displayed a tertiary circular reaction.

**Mental representation**
An internal image of an object or event not present.

ty—internal images of objects and events not present. As a result, the older toddler can solve problems through symbolic means instead of trial-and-error behavior. One sign of this new capacity is that children arrive at solutions to sensorimotor problems suddenly, suggesting that they experiment with actions inside their heads. For example, at 19 months April received a new push toy. As she played with it for the first time, she rolled it over the carpet and ran into the sofa. Faced with this problem, she paused for a moment, as if to "think," and then immediately turned the toy in a new direction. Had she been in Substage 5, she would have pushed, pulled, and bumped it in a random fashion until it was free to move again.

With the capacity to represent, toddlers arrive at a more advanced understanding of object permanence—that objects can move or be moved when out of sight. Try the following object-hiding task with an 18- to 24-month-old as well as a younger child: Put a small toy inside a box and the box under a cover. Then, while the box is out of sight, dump the toy out and show the toddler the empty box. The Substage 6 child will easily find the hidden toy. Younger toddlers are baffled by this situation.

Representation also brings with it the capacity for **deferred imitation**—the ability to remember and copy the behavior of models who are not immediately present. A famous and amusing example is Piaget's daughter Jacqueline's imitation of another child's temper tantrum:

> Jacqueline had a visit from a little boy . . . who, in the course of the afternoon, got into a terrible temper. He screamed as he tried to get out of a playpen and pushed it backwards, stamping his feet. Jacqueline stood watching him in amazement . . . . The next day, she herself screamed in her playpen and tried to move it, stamping her foot lightly several times in succession. (Piaget, 1936/1952, p. 63)

Finally, the sixth substage leads to a major change in the nature of play. Throughout the first year and a half, infants and toddlers engage in **functional play**—pleasurable motor activity with or without objects through which they practice sensorimotor schemes. At the end of the second year, children's growing capacity to represent experience permits them to engage in **make-believe play,** or pretend, in which they act out everyday and imaginary activities. The make-believe of the toddler is very simple, as Rachel's pretending to go to sleep at the beginning of this chapter indicates (see Figure 6.6). However, make-believe expands greatly in early childhood, and it is so important for psychological development that we will devote a great deal

**Deferred imitation**

The ability to remember and copy the behavior of models who are not immediately present.

**Functional play**

A type of play involving pleasurable motor activity with or without objects. Enables infants and toddlers to practice sensorimotor schemes.

**Make-believe play**

A type of play in which children pretend, acting out everyday and imaginary activities.

**FIGURE 6.6** • When Rachel engaged in make-believe by pretending to go to sleep, she created a mental representation of reality. With the capacity for mental representation, the sensorimotor stage draws to a close.

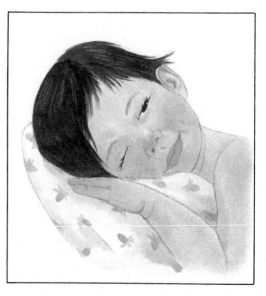

of attention to it in Chapters 9 and 10. In addition, we will return to the question of how make-believe play first emerges when we take up Vygotsky's sociocultural theory later in this chapter.

### New Research on Sensorimotor Development

Over the past 20 years, many researchers have tried to confirm Piaget's observations of sensorimotor development. New studies show that infants display certain cognitive capacities earlier than Piaget believed. Already, you have read about some of these findings. Think back to the operant conditioning research reviewed in Chapter 5. Recall that newborns will suck vigorously on a nipple that controls a variety of interesting sights and sounds, a behavior that closely resembles Piaget's secondary circular reaction. It appears that babies try to explore and control the external world much earlier than 4 to 8 months. In fact, they start to do so as soon as they are born.

Piaget may have underestimated infant capacities because he did not have the sophisticated experimental techniques for studying early cognition that we have today (Flavell, 1985). As we consider recent research on sensorimotor development as well as information processing (covered in a later section), we will see that operant conditioning and the habituation–dishabituation response have been used ingeniously to find out what the young baby knows.

***Object Permanence.*** Before 8 months of age, do babies really believe that an object spirited out of sight no longer exists? It appears not. One remarkable study found evidence for object permanence at 3 1/2 months of age, much earlier than Piaget concluded it developed! The research made use of the habituation–dishabituation response, which we discussed in Chapter 5. First, infants were habituated to a screen that rotated through a 180-degree arc, like a drawbridge (see Figure 6.7A). Then a yellow box was placed behind the screen, and two test events were presented. The first was a *possible event*, in which the screen slowly moved up from a flat position until it rested against the box, where it stopped and then returned to its original position (see Figure 6.7B). The second was an *impossible event* in which the screen began as before but miraculously continued its movement as if the box were no longer there (the experimenter secretly removed it). The screen completed a full 180-degree arc before reversing direction, returning to its original position, and revealing the box standing intact (see Figure 6.7C). Young infants dishabituated to, or looked with much greater interest and surprise at, the impossible event than the possible one. This finding suggests that young babies must have some notion of object permanence—that an object continues to exist when it is hidden from view (Baillargeon, 1987).

If 3 1/2-month-olds grasp the idea of object permanence, then what explains Piaget's finding that much older infants (who are quite capable of voluntary reaching) do not try to search for objects hidden under covers or behind an adult's hand? One explanation is that, just as Piaget's theory suggests, they cannot yet put together the separate schemes—pushing aside the obstacle and grasping the object—necessary to retrieve a hidden toy. In other words, what they *know* about object permanence is not yet *evident* in their searching behavior (Užgiris, 1973).

Once 8- to 12-month-olds actively search for a hidden object, they make the AB search error when it is hidden in more than one place. If infants are capable of finding hidden objects, then why does this error occur? For some years, researchers thought that babies had trouble remembering an object's new location after it was hidden in more than one place. But now they know that this is not the reason for the AB search error (Wellman, Cross, & Bartsch, 1987). As we will see in a later section, young infants have good memories—ones that last much longer than the few moments it takes to hide an object in a second location (Baillargeon & Graber, 1988). Why don't

**FIGURE 6.7** • Study in which infants were tested for object permanence using the habituation–dishabituation response. (A) First, infants were habituated to a screen moving through a 180-degree arc. Then two test events were presented. (B) In the possible event, the screen rotated in front of a yellow box and then rested against it, where it stopped and then returned to its original position. (C) In the impossible event, the screen slowly moved up from a flat position until it covered the yellow box and then continued its movement as if the box were no longer there, reversing direction and returning to its original position, revealing the box standing intact. Infants as young as 3 1/2 months dishabituated to the impossible event, suggesting that they understood object permanence. (*Adapted from R. Baillargeon, 1987, "Object permanence in 3-1/2- and 4-1/2-month-old infants,"* Developmental Psychology, *23, p. 656. Copyright © 1987 by the American Psychological Association. Reprinted by permission of the publisher and author.*)

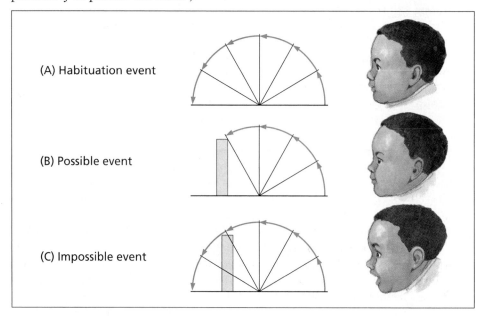

they search in the right place when given an opportunity? Once again, before 12 months infants seem to have difficulty translating what they know about an object moving from one place to another into a successful search strategy. This ability to integrate knowledge with action may depend on rapid maturation of the cortex at the end of the first year (Diamond, 1988; Goldman-Rakic, 1987).

***Deferred Imitation.*** Piaget studied deferred imitation by noting when his own three children demonstrated it in their everyday behavior. Under these conditions, a great deal has to be known about the infant's daily life to be sure that imitation has occurred. Also, some babies might be capable of deferred imitation but simply not have many opportunities to display it.

Recently, Andrew Meltzoff (1988b) brought 9-month-olds into the laboratory and deliberately tried to induce deferred imitation. The babies were shown three novel toys—an L-shaped piece of wood that could be bent, a box with a button that could be pushed, and a plastic egg filled with metal nuts that could be shaken. One group watched an adult demonstrate these actions. Several control groups were exposed to the objects or to an adult touching them, but they were not shown how to use them. When tested after a one-day delay, babies who saw the modeled actions were far more likely to engage in them than were control subjects.

Meltzoff's research reveals that deferred imitation, a form of representation, is present almost a year before Piaget expected it to be. Also, his findings show that

9-month-olds can keep not just one, but several actions in mind at the same time. By 14 months, toddlers use deferred imitation skillfully to enrich their range of sensorimotor schemes. They can retain as many as 6 modeled behaviors over a 1-week period (Meltzoff, 1988a).

### Evaluation of the Sensorimotor Stage

In view of the findings just discussed, how should we evaluate the accuracy of Piaget's sensorimotor stage? Clearly, important cognitive capacities emerge in preliminary form long before Piaget expected them to do so. At the same time, when these capacities first appear, they may not be secure enough to make a large difference in the baby's understanding of the world or to serve as the foundation for new knowledge. Piaget's substages do mark the full-blown achievement of many infant cognitive milestones, if not their first appearance. Follow-up research consistently shows that infants anticipate events, actively search for hidden objects, flexibly vary the circular reaction, and engage in make-believe within the general time frame that Piaget said they do (Corman & Escalona, 1969; Užgiris & Hunt, 1975).

The disagreements between Piaget's observations and those of recent research raise more questions about *how* early development takes place than what infants and toddlers achieve during the first 2 years. Consistent with Piaget's ideas, new research shows that motor activity does facilitate the early construction of knowledge. For example, in Chapter 5, we discussed findings indicating that babies who are experienced crawlers are better at finding hidden objects, and they also have a keener appreciation of depth on the visual cliff (see page 193). But it is possible that infants do not need to construct all aspects of their cognitive world through motor action. The beginnings of some schemes, such as object permanence and imitation, may be prewired into the human brain from the start. (Recall the research on newborn imitation discussed in Chapter 5. It supports the idea that infants are "set up" to imitate the behavior of others at birth.) Other important schemes may be constructed through purely perceptual learning—by looking and listening—rather than through acting directly on the world (Gibson & Spelke, 1983).

Finally, infants do not develop in the neat stepwise fashion implied by Piaget's theory, in which a variety of skills change together and abruptly as each new substage is attained. For example, a baby at one level of progress on imitation is likely to be at quite another on object permanence. Many sensorimotor capacities appear to develop separately and gradually, depending on the infant's rate of biological maturation and the specific experiences encountered (Harris, 1983). These ideas—that adultlike capacities are present during infancy in primitive form, that cognitive development is gradual and continuous, and that it must be described separately for each skill— serve as the basis for a major competing approach to Piaget's theory: information processing, which we take up next.

But before we turn to this alternative point of view, let's conclude our discussion of the sensorimotor stage by recognizing Piaget's enormous contributions. Although not all of his conclusions were correct, Piaget's work inspired a wealth of new research on infant cognition, including studies that eventually challenged his ideas. In addition, Piaget's observations of infants have been of great practical value. Teachers and caregivers continue to look to the sensorimotor stage for guidelines on how to create developmentally appropriate environments for infants and toddlers. Now that you are familiar with Piaget's sequence of infant development, take some time to apply it. For example, what kinds of playthings would support the building of sensorimotor and early representational schemes? Prepare your own list of infant and toddler toys and justify it by making reference to Piaget's substages. Then compare your suggestions to the ones given in Table 6.2.

*The development of deferred imitation plays a major role in enriching the young child's range of sensorimotor schemes. This toddler may have watched an older brother or sister hit a ball with a plastic bat. After storing the behavior in memory, she practices it at a later time, when her sibling is conveniently not around to prevent her from playing with the toys. (Elizabeth Crews/ The Image Works)*

TABLE 6.2 • Playthings that Support the Development of Sensorimotor and Early Representational Schemes

| From 2 Months | From 6 Months | From 1 Year |
|---|---|---|
| Crib mobile | Squeezing toys | Large dolls |
| Rattles | Nesting cups | Toy dishes |
|  | Foam rubber ball | Toy telephone |
|  | Stuffed animals (without glass or button eyes that can be swallowed) | Hammer and peg toy |
|  | Filling and emptying toys | Pull and push toys |
|  | Large and small blocks | Cars and trucks |
|  | Pots, pans, and spoons from the kitchen | Simple puzzles |
|  | Bath toys | Sand box, shovel, and pail |
|  | Picture books | Shallow wading pool and water toys |

• *Tony pushed his toy bunny through the slats of his crib onto a nearby table. Using his "pulling scheme," he tried to retrieve it, but it would not fit back through the slats. Next Tony tried jerking, turning, and throwing the bunny. Is Tony in a state of equilibrium or disequilibrium? How do you know?*

• *Mimi banged her rattle again and again on the tray of her high chair. Then she dropped the rattle, which fell out of sight on her lap, but Mimi did not try to retrieve it. Which sensorimotor substage is Mimi in? Why do you think so?*

BRIEF REVIEW According to Piaget, children actively build psychological structures, or schemes, as they manipulate and explore their world. Two processes, adaptation (which combines assimilation and accommodation) and organization, account for the development of schemes. The vast changes that take place during the sensorimotor stage are divided into six substages. The circular reaction, a special means that infants use to adapt schemes, changes from being oriented toward the infant's own body, to being directed outward toward objects, to producing novel effects in the surrounding world. During the last three substages, infants make strides in intentional behavior and understanding object permanence. By the final substage, they start to represent reality and show the beginnings of make-believe play. Recent research reveals that secondary circular reactions, object permanence, and deferred imitation are present much earlier than Piaget believed. These findings raise questions about Piaget's claim that babies must construct all aspects of their cognitive world through motor activity and that sensorimotor development takes place in stages.

## INFORMATION PROCESSING IN THE FIRST TWO YEARS

Information processing theorists agree with Piaget that children are active, inquiring beings, but otherwise their view of human thinking is decidedly different. Unlike Piaget, information processing does not provide a single, unified theory of cognitive development. Instead, it is an approach that focuses on many different aspects of thinking, from attention, memory, and categorization skills to complex problem solving.

In Chapter 1, we saw that information processing relies on scripts, frames, and flowcharts to describe the human cognitive system. Often the steps in thinking are likened to the operations a computer performs when it stores, interprets, and responds to incoming information. The computer model of human thinking is very attractive because it is explicit and precise. Information processing researchers find it useful because they are not satisfied with global concepts, like assimilation and accommodation, to describe how children think. Instead, they want to know exactly what individuals of different ages do when faced with a task or problem (Klahr, 1989; Kuhn, 1988; Siegler, 1983a).

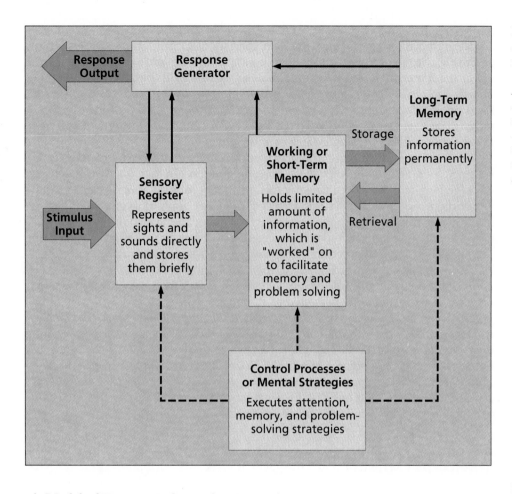

**FIGURE 6.8** • Atkinson and Shiffrin's model of the human information processing system. *(Adapted from R. M. Shiffrin & R. C. Atkinson, 1969, "Storage and retrieval processes in long-term memory."* Psychological Review, *76, p. 180. Copyright © 1969 by the American Psychological Association. Adapted by permission of the authors.)*

## A Model of Human Information Processing

Although many flowcharts of human information processing exist, Richard Atkinson and Richard Shiffrin's (1968) computerlike model has inspired more research than any other. As shown in Figure 6.8, Atkinson and Shiffrin divide the mind into three basic parts: the *sensory register, working* or *short-term memory,* and *long-term memory.* As information flows through each, it can be operated on and transformed using **control processes,** or **mental strategies.** When we use strategies to manipulate input in various ways, we increase the efficiency of thinking as well as the chances that information will be retained for later use. To understand this idea more clearly, let's take a brief look at each aspect of Atkinson and Shiffrin's model.

First, information enters the **sensory register.** Here, sights and sounds are represented directly, but they cannot be held for long. For example, take a moment to look around you and then close your eyes. An image of what you saw probably persists for a few seconds, but then it decays or disappears, unless you use mental strategies to preserve it. For example, you can *attend* to some information more carefully than others, thereby increasing the chances that the selected input will transfer to the next step of the information processing system.

The second waystation of the mind is **working** or **short-term memory.** This is the conscious part of our mental system, where we actively "work" on a limited amount of information. For example, if you are studying this book effectively, you are constantly applying control processes, or mental strategies, manipulating input in your working memory to ensure that it will be retained and available to solve problems. Perhaps you are attending to certain information that seems most important. Or you may be using a variety of memory strategies, such as taking notes,

**Control processes, or mental strategies**

In information processing, procedures that operate on and transform information, increasing the efficiency of thinking as well as the chances that information will be retained for later use.

**Sensory register**

In information processing, that part of the mental system in which sights and sounds are held briefly before they decay or get transferred to working or short-term memory.

**Working or short-term memory**

In information processing, the conscious part of the mental system, where we actively "work" on a limited amount of information to ensure that it will be retained.

repeating information to yourself, or grouping pieces of information together—a strategy much like Piaget's notion of organization. Organization is an especially effective way to remember the many new concepts flowing into your working memory at the moment. If you permit stimulus input to remain piecemeal and disconnected, you can hold very little in your working memory at once, since you must focus on each item separately. But organize it and you will not just increase your memory capacity. You will improve the chances that information will be transferred to the third, and largest, storage area of your system.

Unlike the sensory register and working memory, the capacity of **long-term memory,** our permanent knowledge base, is limitless. In fact, so much input is stored in long-term memory that we sometimes have problems in *retrieval,* or getting information back from the system. To aid retrieval, we apply strategies in long-term memory just as we do in working memory. For example, think about how information in your long-term memory is arranged. According to Atkinson and Shiffrin (1968), it is *categorized* according to a master plan based on contents, much like a "library shelving system which is based upon the contents of books" (p. 181). When information is filed in this way, it can be retrieved quite easily by following the same network of associations that was used to store it in the first place.

Information processing researchers believe that the basic structure of the human mental system is similar throughout life (Siegler, 1983a). Therefore, changes in children's thinking must be due to improvements in strategies, such as attending to information and categorizing it effectively. Do infants use these processing strategies? How does memory—so critical a part of all cognitive activity—improve over the first 2 years? These are questions that information processing researchers ask, and you will find answers to them in the following sections.

### Attention and Memory

If you think back to our discussion of perceptual development in Chapter 5, you will discover that you already know something about how attention develops in early infancy. Recall that between 1 and 2 months, infants shift from attending to a single high-contrast feature of their visual world to exploring objects and patterns more thoroughly.

Besides attending to more aspects of the environment, infants gradually become more efficient at managing their attention, taking information into their mental systems more quickly with age. The habituation–dishabituation response has been used to study this aspect of cognitive change. Recall from Chapter 5 that habituation refers to a decline in attention as babies become familiar with a stimulus. In dishabituation, attention recovers when babies are exposed to a second stimulus—one new and different from the first. Research reveals that preterm infants require a long time to habituate and dishabituate to novel stimuli—for example, 5 minutes or more for visual patterns (Werner & Siqueland, 1978). But by 5 months, babies process new information rapidly, requiring as little as 5 to 10 seconds to take in a complex visual stimulus and recognize that it is different from a second one (Fagan, 1971, 1977).

Habituation does not just tell us about changes in the efficiency of infant attention. It also provides a window into infant memory capacities. For example, infants can be exposed to a stimulus until they habituate. Then they can be shown the same stimulus at a later time. If habituation takes place more rapidly on the second occasion, this indicates that babies must recognize that they have seen the pattern before. Using this method, studies show that by 3 months of age, infants remember a visual stimulus for 24 hours (Martin, 1975). By the end of the first year, their retention increases to several days and, in the case of some stimuli (such as human faces), a few weeks (Fagan, 1973).

**Long-term memory**
In information processing, the permanent knowledge base of the mental system.

At this point, let's note that infant memory varies considerably across situations. The habituation response tells us how long babies retain a new stimulus that they view once in the strange context of the laboratory, but it underestimates their ability to remember real-world events that they can actively control. Using operant conditioning, Carolyn Rovee-Collier (1987) studied infant memory in a familiar setting— at home while babies lay in their cribs. First, 2- and 3-month-olds were taught how to make a mobile move by kicking a foot tied to it with a long cord. Then the mobile was removed, and after a week's delay, the infants were reattached to it. Right away they kicked vigorously, showing that indeed they remembered. And as long as they were reminded of the mobile's dancing motion (the experimenter briefly rotated it for the baby), infants started kicking again up to 2 weeks after they were first trained (Linde, Morrongiello, & Rovee-Collier, 1985; Rovee-Collier, Patterson, & Hayne, 1985). Much like older children and adults, babies seem to remember best when experiences take place in familiar contexts and when they participate actively (Lipsitt, 1990; Shields & Rovee-Collier, 1992).

So far, we have discussed only one type of memory—**recognition.** It is the simplest form of retrieval because all babies have to do is indicate (by looking or kicking) whether a new stimulus is identical or similar to one previously experienced. **Recall** is a second, more challenging form of memory, since it involves remembering something that is not present. To recall, you must generate an image of the absent stimulus. Can infants engage in recall? By the middle of the first year, they can. Felicia reported that one day when her husband telephoned, 7-month-old April heard his voice through the receiver and immediately crawled to the front door. April seemed to be *recalling* times when she had heard the sounds of her father's muffled voice through the door as he was about to arrive home from work (Ashmead & Perlmutter, 1980).

*Using an operant conditioning method in which babies make a mobile move by kicking a foot tied to it with a long cord, Carolyn Rovee-Collier has made many discoveries about infant learning, memory, and categorization. (Courtesy of Carolyn Rovee-Collier, Rutgers University)*

### Categorization Skills

As infants gradually remember more information, they seem to store it in a remarkably orderly fashion. Even young babies categorize stimulus events. In fact, they do so at such an early age that categorization is among the strongest pieces of evidence that babies' brains are set up from the start to structure experience in adultlike ways (Bornstein & Sigman, 1986; Mervis, 1985).

To find out about infant categorization, Rovee-Collier conducted some creative variations of her operant conditioning research, described in the previous section. This time, 3-month-olds were taught to kick to move a mobile that was made of a uniform set of stimuli—for example, small blocks, all with the letter *A* on them. After a delay, kicking returned to a high level only if the babies were shown a mobile whose elements were labeled with the same form (the letter *A*). If the form was changed (from *A*s to 2s), infants no longer kicked vigorously. While learning to make the mobile move, the babies had grouped together its features, associating the kicking response with the category "*A*" and, at later testing, distinguishing it from the category "2" (Hayne, Rovee-Collier, & Perris, 1987).

Habituation–dishabituation research has also been used to study infant categorization. The findings reveal that 9- to 12-month-olds structure objects into an impressive array of categories—food items, furniture, birds, and stuffed animals, to name just a few (Roberts, 1988; Ross, 1980; Sherman, 1985; Younger, 1985). Besides organizing the physical world, infants begin to categorize their emotional and social worlds as well. For example, 7-month-olds sort people into males and females, and they recognize the same facial expression (happiness) when it is demonstrated by different people (Caron, Caron, & Myers, 1982; Francis & McCroy, 1983).

During the second year, children become active categorizers during their play. Try giving a toddler a set of objects that differ in shape and color (such as small

**Recognition**

A type of memory that involves noticing whether a stimulus is identical or similar to one previously experienced.

**Recall**

A type of memory that involves remembering a stimulus that is not present.

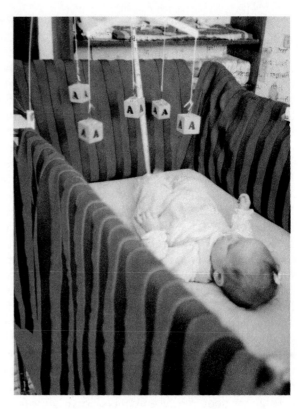

*This 3-month-old infant discovered that by kicking, he could shake a mobile made of small blocks with a letter "A" on them. After a delay, the baby continued to kick vigorously only if the mobile he saw was labeled with the same form (the letter "A"). He did not kick when given a mobile with a different form (the number "2"). The infant's behavior shows that he groups similar stimuli into categories and can distinguish the category "A" from the category "2". (Courtesy of Carolyn Rovee-Collier, Rutgers University)*

blocks) and see if any instances of spontaneous categorization occur. Research shows that around 12 months, toddlers merely touch objects that belong together, without grouping them. A little later, they form single categories. For example, when given four balls and four boxes, a 16-month-old will put all the balls together but not the boxes. And finally, around 18 months of age, toddlers can sort objects correctly into two classes. Interestingly, this advanced object-sorting behavior appears at about the same time that toddlers show a "naming explosion," or a sharp spurt in vocabulary in which they label many more objects. Perhaps toddlers are transferring their more advanced understanding of categories to the verbal plane, thereby picking up new words (Gopnik & Meltzoff, 1987a, 1987b).

### Evaluation of Information Processing Findings

The information processing research discussed in the preceding sections underscores the *continuity* of human thinking from infancy into adult life. In attending to the environment, remembering everyday events, and categorizing objects, Byron, Rachel, and April think in ways that are remarkably similar to our own, even though they are far from being the proficient mental processors we are. Findings on infant memory and categorization join with other research in challenging Piaget's view of early cognitive development as taking place in discrete stages. If 3-month-olds can hold events in memory for as long as 2 weeks and categorize stimuli around them, then they must have some ability to mentally represent their experiences. Representation seems to be another cognitive skill that does not have to wait until babies have had many months of sensorimotor experience (even though there is no dispute that it flourishes during the second year of life).

Information processing has contributed greatly to our view of the young baby as a sophisticated cognitive being. Still, it has drawbacks. Perhaps the greatest one stems from its central strength: by breaking cognition down into separate elements (such as perception, attention, and memory), information processing has had difficulty putting all these pieces back together into a broad, comprehensive theory of children's thinking. For this reason, many child development specialists still resist abandoning Piaget's ideas in favor of it. During the past decade, several attempts have been made to improve on Piaget's theory by combining it with the information processing approach. We will discuss these efforts in Chapter 12. Although none is yet widely accepted, by drawing on the strengths of both of perspectives, the field of child development may be moving closer to a new, more powerful view of how the mind of the infant and child develops (Case, 1991b).

## THE SOCIAL CONTEXT OF EARLY COGNITIVE DEVELOPMENT

If a new, broader theory eventually emerges out of Piagetian and information processing views, it is likely to be deficient in one important respect: Both approaches pay little attention to the idea that children live in rich social contexts that affect the way their cognitive world is structured. Vygotsky's sociocultural theory has brought the field of child development to this realization (Bruner, 1990; Rogoff, 1990).

Take a moment to review the short episode at the beginning of this chapter in which Rachel dropped shapes into a container. Notice that Rachel is not an independent explorer who discovers how to use the toy on her own. Instead, she learns about it with her mother's help. With Beth's support, Rachel will gradually become better at matching shapes to openings and dropping them into the container. Then she will be able to perform the activity (and others like it) on her own.

Vygotsky (1930–1935/1978) believed that complex mental activities, such as voluntary attention, memory, and problem solving, have their origins in social interaction. Through joint activities with more mature members of their society, children come to master activities and think in ways that have meaning in their culture. A special Vygotskian concept, the **zone of proximal** (or potential) **development,** explains how this happens. It refers to a range of tasks that the child cannot yet handle alone but can accomplish with the help of more skilled partners. To understand this idea, think of a sensitive teacher or parent (such as Beth) who introduces a child to a new activity. The adult picks a task that the child can master but one challenging enough that the child cannot do it by herself. Thus, the activity is especially suited for spurring development forward. Then the adult guides and supports, breaking the task down into manageable units. By joining in the interaction, the child picks up mental strategies, and her competence increases. When this happens, the adult steps back, permitting the child to take over more responsibility for the task.

As we will see in Chapters 9 and 12, Vygotsky's ideas have mostly been applied at older ages, when children become skilled at language and their ability to engage in social communication expands. But recently, Vygotsky's theory has been extended downward to infancy. In earlier parts of this book, we showed that babies are equipped with ways of ensuring that caregivers will interact with them. Then adults adjust the environment and their communication in ways that promote learning.

A study by Barbara Rogoff and her collaborators (1984) illustrates this process. The researchers watched how several adults played with Rogoff's son and daughter over the first 2 years, while a jack-in-the-box toy was nearby. In the early months, adults tried to focus the baby's attention by showing the toy and, as the bunny popped out, saying something like, "My, what happened?" By the end of the first

**Zone of proximal development**

In Vygotsky's theory, a range of tasks that the child cannot yet handle alone but can do with the help of more skilled partners.

*This mother assists her baby in making a music box work. By presenting a task within the child's zone of proximal development and fine-tuning her support to the infant's momentary needs, the mother spurs her youngster's cognitive development forward.* (Erika Stone)

year (when the baby's cognitive and motor skills had improved), interaction centered on how to use the jack-in-the-box. When the infant reached for the toy, adults guided the baby's hand in turning the crank and putting the bunny back in the box. As the youngsters became toddlers, adults helped from a distance. They used verbal instructions and gestures, such as rotating a hand in a turning motion near the crank, while the child tried to make the toy work. Research suggests that this fine-tuned support is related to cognitive competence. Infants whose mothers gently direct their attention and (as they get older) encourage them to manipulate the environment are advanced in play and language skills during the second year (Belsky, Goode, & Most, 1980; Tamis-LeMonda & Bornstein, 1989).

In previous sections of this chapter, we saw how infants create new schemes by acting on the physical world (Piaget) and how certain prewired skills become better developed as the result of infants' wide-ranging experience with objects (information processing). Vygotsky adds a third dimension to our understanding by emphasizing that important aspects of cognitive development are socially mediated. In Box 6.1, you will find additional evidence for this idea. And we will see even more in the next section, as we look at individual differences in mental development during the first 2 years.

• *When Rachel was 3 months old, she stared at a little toy dog that Beth dangled in front of her and then looked away. The next day, Beth held up the toy dog again and Rachel looked at it, but more briefly. What can we conclude about Rachel's processing of the toy?*

• *At age 18 months, Byron's father stood behind him, helping him throw a large rubber ball into a box. When Byron showed he could throw the ball, his father stepped back and let him try on his own. Using Vygotsky's ideas, explain how Byron's father is supporting his cognitive development.*

*BRIEF REVIEW*   Using flowcharts of the human mental system, information processing researchers analyze thinking into separate elements and study how each changes with age. Atkinson and Shiffrin's computerlike model divides the mind into three parts: the sensory register, working or short-term memory, and long-term memory. As information flows through the system, control processes, or mental strategies, operate on it, increasing the likelihood that information will be retained. Mental strategies gradually improve with age. Infants attend to more aspects of the environment, manage their attention more efficiently, and remember information over longer periods of time. Findings on infant categorization support the view that babies are prewired to structure experience in adultlike ways. According to Vygotsky's sociocultural theory, early cognitive development is socially mediated as adults help infants and toddlers master tasks in the zone of proximal development.

# FROM RESEARCH TO PRACTICE

## Box 6.1  *Parent–Toddler Interaction and Early Make-Believe Play*

One of my husband Ken's shared activities with our two sons when they were young was to bake pineapple upside-down cake, a favorite treat. At age 4 1/2, David was already well-versed in the process—how to arrange the pineapple slices, mix the batter, pour it into the pan, and transfer it to the oven. I remember well one Sunday afternoon when a cake was in the making. Little Peter, then 21 months old, stood on a chair at the kitchen sink, busy pouring water from one cup to another.

"He's in the way, Dad!" complained David, trying to pull Peter away from the sink. Peter let out a sharp yell and refused to budge, turning back to his pouring.

"Maybe if we let him help, then he'll give us some room at the sink," Ken suggested. As David stirred the batter, Ken poured some into a small bowl for Peter, moved his chair to the side of the sink, and handed him a spoon.

"Here's how you do it, Petey," instructed David, with an air of superiority. Peter watched as David stirred, then tried to copy his motion. When it was time to pour the batter, Ken helped Peter hold and tip the small bowl so its contents flowed into the pan.

"Time to bake it," said Ken.

"Bake it, bake it," repeated Peter, as he watched Ken slip the pan into the oven.

Several hours later, when the cake was cool and the dishes washed, we observed one of Peter's earliest instances of make-believe play. He got his pail from the sandbox and, after filling it with a handful of sand, carried it into the kitchen and put it down on the floor in front of the oven. "Bake it, bake it," Peter called to Ken. Together, father and son lifted the pretend cake inside the oven.

Historically, the emergence of make-believe play was studied in isolation from the social environment in which it usually occurs. Until recently, most researchers observed young children while playing alone. Probably for this reason, Piaget and his followers concluded that toddlers discover make-believe independently, as soon as they are capable of representational schemes. Vygotsky's theory has challenged this view. He believed that society provides children with opportunities to represent culturally meaningful activities in play. Make-believe, like other mental functions, grows out of interactions with others (Smolucha, 1992). In the example just described, Peter's capacity to represent daily events was extended when Ken drew him into the baking task and helped him act it out in play.

New research supports the idea that early make-believe is the combined result of children's readiness to engage in it and social experiences that promote it. In several recent studies, researchers compared toddlers' solitary play with their play while interacting with their mothers. In each case, toddlers engaged in more than twice as much make-believe when mothers were involved. In addition, caregiver support led early make-believe to move toward a more advanced level (Fiese, 1990; Slade, 1987; Zukow, 1986). For example, when adults actively took part, toddlers were more likely to combine representational schemes into more complex sequences, as Peter did when he put sand in the bucket ("making the batter"), carried it into the kitchen, and (with Ken's help) put it in the oven ("baking the cake").

In many cultures, adults do not spend much time playing with young children. Instead, older siblings fill in by letting toddlers join in their play and by modeling appropriate actions (Zukow, 1989). Notice how, in the episode described here, David showed Peter how to stir the batter, and Peter was quickly drawn into the baking activity.

According to Vygotsky, make-believe is a major means through which children extend their cognitive skills and learn about important activities in their culture. His theory, and the findings that support it, tell us that providing a stimulating physical environment is only part of what is necessary to promote early cognitive growth. In addition, toddlers must be invited and encouraged by their elders to become active participants in the social world around them.

*Alfred Binet*

*The French psychologist Alfred Binet (1857–1911) developed the first successful intelligence test. His work inspired the design of many new tests, including ones that measure infant mental development.* (The Bettmann Archive)

**Intelligence quotient or IQ**

A score that permits an individual's performance on an intelligence test to be compared to the performances of other individuals of the same age.

## INDIVIDUAL DIFFERENCES IN EARLY MENTAL DEVELOPMENT

When he neared age 2, Byron had only a handful of words in his vocabulary, continued to play in a less mature way than Rachel and April, and seemed restless and overactive. Lisa, increasingly concerned about Byron's progress, decided to take him to a psychological clinic where he was given one of many tests available for assessing the mental development of infants and toddlers.

The testing approach is very different from the cognitive theories we have discussed so far, which try to explain the *process* of development—how children's thinking changes over time. In contrast, designers of mental tests are much more concerned with cognitive *products*. Their aim is to measure behaviors that reflect mental development and arrive at scores that predict future performance, such as later intelligence, school achievement, and adult vocational success. Recall from Chapter 1 that this concern with prediction arose nearly a century ago, when the French psychologist Alfred Binet was asked to identify children unlikely to succeed in regular school classes. Binet's first successful intelligence test, which predicted school achievement, inspired the design of many new tests, including ones that measure intelligence at younger and younger ages. If ways could be found to identify infants and toddlers at risk for doing poorly when they reach school age, then special help could be provided early in life, when there is greatest hope of preventing later problems.

### Infant Intelligence Tests

As you can probably imagine, accurately measuring the intelligence of infants is an especially challenging task. Unlike children, babies cannot answer questions or follow directions. All we can do is present them with stimuli, coax them to respond, and observe their behavior. As a result, most infant tests consist of perceptual and motor responses along with a few tasks that tap early language and problem solving. One commonly used infant test is the *Bayley Scales of Infant Development*, designed to assess children between 2 months and 2 1/2 years. It is made up of two scales: (1) the Mental Scale, which includes such items as turning to a sound, looking for a fallen object, building a tower of cubes, and naming pictures; and (2) the Motor Scale, which assesses gross and fine motor skills, such as grasping, sitting, drinking from a cup, and jumping (Bayley, 1969).

When taking such tests, babies are not necessarily willing and cooperative. They often get hungry, distracted, or tired during the testing period. As we will see shortly, both the makeup of infant tests and the immaturity of these young test-takers affect the ability of infant tests to predict later performance. But before we examine the issue of prediction, we need to look at how intelligence test scores are computed.

***Computing Intelligence Test Scores.*** Scores on intelligence tests, whether designed for infants, children, or adults, are arrived at in much the same way. When a test is constructed, it is given to a large, representative sample of individuals. Performances of people at each age level form a *normal* or *bell-shaped curve* in which most scores fall near the center (the mean or average) and progressively fewer fall out toward the extremes. On the basis of this distribution, the test designer computes *norms,* or standards against which future test-takers can be compared. For example, the number of items that Byron passes at age 2 will be compared to that of 2-year-olds in general. If Byron does better than 50 percent of his agemates, his score will be 100, an average test score. If he exceeds most youngsters his age, his score will be much higher. If he does better than only a small percentage of 2-year-olds, his score will be much lower. Scores computed in this way are called **intelligence quotients,** or **IQs,** a term you have undoubtedly heard before. Table 6.3 describes the meaning

TABLE 6.3 • Meaning of Different IQ Scores

| Score | Percentile Rank (Child does better than . . . percent of same-age children) | |
|---|---|---|
| 70 | 2 | |
| 85 | 16 | |
| 100 (average IQ) | 50 | |
| 115 | 84 | |
| 130 | 98 | |

of a range of IQ scores. Notice how the IQ offers a way of finding out whether a child is ahead, behind, or on time (average) in mental development in relation to other children of the same age. The great majority of individuals (96 percent) have IQs that fall between 70 and 130; only a very few achieve higher or lower scores.

*Predicting Later Performance from Infant Tests.* Many people assume that IQ is a measure of inborn ability that does not change with age. Research on the stability of IQ shows that this is not the case. Despite the careful construction of many infant tests, they predict later intelligence poorly (Lewis & McGurk, 1972). In one longitudinal study, the same group of children was tested repeatedly from infancy through adolescence (McCall, Appelbaum, & Hogarty, 1973). The scores of most youngsters changed considerably. In fact, the average IQ shift between 21/2 and 17 years of age was as great as 28.5 points! In addition, high scorers during the early years were not necessarily high scorers later on.

We have already seen that infants and toddlers are especially likely to become distracted, fatigued, or bored during testing. As a result, scores often do not reflect their true abilities. But there is a second reason that early intellectual measures are not good predictors of later IQ. The perceptual and motor tasks that appear on infant tests are quite different from the test questions given to older children, which emphasize verbal, conceptual, and problem-solving skills. Because of concerns that infant test scores do not tap the same dimensions of intelligence measured at older ages, they are conservatively labeled **developmental quotients,** or **DQs,** rather than IQs.

It is important to note that infant tests do show somewhat better long-term prediction for extremely low scoring babies (Honzik, 1983). Today, infant tests are largely used for *screening*—helping to identify for further observation and intervention babies whose very low scores mean that they have a high likelihood of experiencing developmental problems in the future (Lewis & Sullivan, 1985).

Because infant tests do not predict later IQ for most children, researchers have turned to information processing for new ways to assess early mental functioning. The findings have been encouraging. Measures of infant recognition memory, based on the habituation–dishabituation response, have been found to be good predictors of IQ during the preschool years, with correlations ranging from .35 to .65 (Rose, Feldman, & Wallace, 1988). Researchers believe that recognition memory is a more effective predictor of later IQ than are traditional infant tests because it taps a basic cognitive process—response to novelty—that underlies intelligent behavior at all ages (Fagan & Montie, 1988; Fagan, Shepherd, & Knevel, 1991).

**Developmental quotient or DQ**

A score on an infant intelligence test, based primarily on perceptual and motor responses. Computed in the same manner as an IQ.

For many years, infant tests based on Piaget's theory have been available (Corman & Escalona, 1969; Užgiris & Hunt, 1975). Like recognition memory, object permanence has turned out to be a somewhat better predictor of preschool IQ than traditional measures, perhaps because it, too, reflects a basic intellectual process—problem solving (Wachs, 1975).

## Early Environment and Mental Development

In Chapter 2, we indicated that intelligence is a complex blend of hereditary and environmental influences. Because infant scores are so unstable, researchers have not been able to study genetic contributions to intelligence at such an early age. On the other hand, many studies have examined the relationship of environmental factors to infant and toddler mental test scores.

### The Home Environment.

From what you have learned so far in this chapter, what aspects of young children's home experiences would you expect to influence early mental development? To answer this question, Robert Bradley, Bettye Caldwell, and their collaborators developed the **Home Observation for Measurement of the Environment (HOME),** a checklist for gathering information about the quality of children's home lives through observation and parental interview. Factors measured by HOME during the first 3 years are listed in Table 6.4. Each is positively related to toddlers' mental test performance. In addition, high HOME scores are associated with IQ gains between 1 and 3 years of age, while low HOME scores predict declines as large as 15 to 20 points (Bradley et al., 1989).

When researchers look at different social class and ethnic groups, the findings on early home environment are much the same. Stimulation provided by the physical setting and parental encouragement, involvement, and affection repeatedly predict infant and early childhood IQ, no matter what the child's background (Bradley & Caldwell, 1982; Bradley et al., 1989).

Can the research summarized so far help us understand Lisa's concern about Byron's development? Indeed, it can. Andrew, the psychologist who tested Byron,

**Home Observation for Measurement of the Environment (HOME)**

A checklist for gathering information about the quality of children's home lives through observation and parental interview.

TABLE 6.4 • Home Observation for the Measurement of the Environment (HOME): Infant and Toddler Subscales

| Subscale | Sample Item |
|---|---|
| Emotional and verbal responsiveness of the parent | Parent caresses or kisses the child at least once during observer's visit |
| Acceptance of the child | Parent does not interfere with the child's actions or restrict the child's movements more than three times during observer's visit |
| Organization of the physical environment | Child's play environment appears safe and free of hazards |
| Provision of appropriate play materials | Parent provides toys or interesting activities for the child during observer's visit |
| Maternal involvement with the child | Parent tends to keep child within visual range and to look at the child often during observer's visit |
| Variety in daily stimulation | Child eats at least one meal per day with mother and father, according to parental report |

*Source:* Elardo & Bradley, 1981.

found that he scored slightly below average but well within normal range. Besides giving the test, Andrew interviewed Lisa about her child-rearing practices and watched her play with Byron. He noticed that Lisa, anxious about how well Byron was doing, tended to pressure him a great deal. She constantly bombarded him with questions and instructions that were not related to his ongoing actions. Andrew explained that when parents are intrusive in these ways, infants and toddlers are likely to be distractible, show less mature forms of play, and do poorly on mental tests (Bradley et al., 1989; Fiese, 1990). He coached Lisa in how to establish a sensitive give-and-take in the way that she played with Byron. At the same time, he assured her that Byron's current performance need not forecast his future development, since warm, responsive parenting that builds on toddlers' current capacities is a much better indicator of how they will do later than an early mental test score.

*Infant Day Care.* Home environments are not the only influential settings in which young children spend their days. During the past two decades, women in industrialized nations have entered the labor force in large numbers. Today, over half of American mothers with children under age 2 are employed (Children's Defense Fund, 1991d). Day care for infants and toddlers has become common, and research indicates that its quality has a major impact on mental development. In one series of studies, researchers examined the development of young children in Bermuda, where 85 percent enter day care before age 2. Verbal stimulation by caregivers and an overall rating of day-care center quality (based on many characteristics, from physical facilities to daily activities) predicted enhanced cognitive, language, and social skills during the preschool years (McCartney et al., 1985; Phillips, McCartney, & Scarr, 1987). In Sweden, children who enter high-quality day care before age 1 also show long-term benefits. They perform better in school and are viewed as especially well adjusted by their teachers in middle childhood and adolescence (Andersson, 1989, 1992).

Arrange to visit some day-care settings in your own community, and take notes on what you see. In contrast to most European countries, where day care is nationally regulated and liberally funded to ensure its high quality, reports on American day care are cause for deep concern (Kammerman, 1991). Standards are set by the states, and they vary greatly across the nation. In some places, caregivers need not have any special training in child development, and one adult is permitted to care for as many as 8 to 12 babies at once. Large numbers of infants and toddlers everywhere attend unlicensed day-care homes, where no one checks to see that minimum health and safety standards are met (Children's Defense Fund, 1991d). Children who enter poor quality day care during the first year of life and remain there during the preschool years are rated by teachers as distractible, low in task involvement, and inconsiderate of others when they reach kindergarten age (Howes, 1990).

Unfortunately, children most likely to have inadequate day care come from low-income and poverty-stricken families, where parents cannot afford to pay for the kind of services their youngsters need (Children's Defense Fund, 1991d). As a result, these children receive a double dose of vulnerability, both at home and in the day-care environment. Table 6.5 lists signs of good quality care that can be used in choosing a day-care setting for an infant or toddler. Of course, for parents to make this choice, there must be enough high quality day care available. Recognizing that American day care is in a state of crisis, Congress recently allocated additional funds to upgrade its quality and assist parents—especially those with low incomes—in paying for it (Jacobs & Davies, 1991). This is a hopeful sign, since good day care protects the well-being of all children, and it can serve as effective early intervention for youngsters whose development is at risk, much like the programs we are about to consider in the next section.

TABLE 6.5 • Signs of Good Quality Infant and Toddler Day Care

| Program Characteristics | Signs of Quality |
| --- | --- |
| Physical setting | Indoor environment is clean, in good repair, well lighted, and well ventilated. Fenced outdoor play space is available. Setting does not appear overcrowded when children are present. |
| Toys and equipment | Play materials are appropriate for infants and toddlers (see Table 6.3) and stored on low shelves within easy reach. Cribs, high chairs, infant seats, and child-sized tables and chairs are available. Outdoor equipment includes small riding toys, swings, slide, and sandbox. |
| Caregiver/child ratio | In day-care centers, caregiver/child ratio is no greater than 1 to 4. Group size (number of children in one room) is no greater than 8 infants with 2 caregivers and 12 toddlers with 3 caregivers. In day-care homes, caregiver is responsible for no more than 6 children; within this group, no more than 2 are infants and toddlers. Staffing is consistent, so infants and toddlers can form relationships with particular caregivers. |
| Daily activities | Daily schedule includes times for active play, quiet play, naps, snacks, and meals. It is flexible rather than rigid, to meet the needs of individual children. Atmosphere is warm and supportive, and children are never left unsupervised. |
| Caregiver training | Caregiver has at least some training in child development, first aid, and safety. |
| Relationships with parents | Parents are welcome anytime. Caregivers talk frequently with parents about children's behavior and development. |
| Licensing and accreditation | Day-care setting, whether a center or home, is licensed by the state. If a center, accreditation by the National Academy of Early Childhood Programs is evidence of an especially high-quality program. |

*Sources:* Berezin, 1990; National Association for the Education of Young Children, 1984.

### Early Intervention for At-Risk Infants and Toddlers

Many studies show that children of poverty are likely to show gradual declines in intelligence test scores and to achieve poorly when they reach school age (Cox, 1983; Ramey & Finkelstein, 1981). These problems are largely due to home environments that, from the earliest ages, undermine children's ability to learn and increase the chances that they will remain poor throughout their own lives. A variety of intervention programs have been developed to break this tragic cycle of poverty. Although most begin during the preschool years (we will discuss these in Chapter 9), a few start during infancy and continue to provide supports for development through early childhood.

Interventions for infants and toddlers go about the task of helping them in different ways. Some are center-based. Children come to classrooms for educational experiences, well-balanced meals, and health services designed to compensate for their underprivileged home lives. In addition, parents may receive training in child-rearing skills. The Carolina Abecedarian Project is a well-known center-based intervention; you can find out about it by reading Box 6.2. Other interventions are home-based. A skilled adult visits the home and works with parents, teaching them how to stimulate a very young child's development. In most intervention programs, participating youngsters score higher on mental tests than untreated controls by age 2—gains that persist as long as the program lasts and occasionally longer. The more intense the intervention (for example, full-day, year-round high-quality day care plus support services for parents), the greater the intellectual gains of participating children (Bryant & Ramey, 1987).

Without some form of early intervention, large numbers of children born into disadvantaged families will not reach their full potential. Recognition of this reality has recently led the United States Congress to provide limited funding for intervention services directed at infants and toddlers who already have serious developmental problems or who are at risk for them because of poverty. At present, available programs are not nearly enough to meet the need. Nevertheless, the ones that exist are a promising beginning in a new effort aimed at preventing the serious learning difficulties of millions of poor children by starting to help them at a very early age (Gallagher, 1989).

*BRIEF REVIEW* The mental testing approach arrives at IQ scores that compare a child's performance to that of same-age children. Infant intelligence tests consist largely of perceptual and motor responses, and they predict later intelligence poorly. Measures of recognition memory and object permanence show better prediction into the preschool years. Factors in the home environment—stimulation provided by the physical setting and parental encouragement, involvement, and affection—are consistently related to early test scores. High-quality day care supports mental development, while poor-quality care undermines it. Intensive early intervention for poverty-stricken infants and toddlers has been successful in producing improvements in IQ.

## LANGUAGE DEVELOPMENT DURING THE FIRST TWO YEARS

As perception and cognition improve during infancy, they pave the way for an extraordinary human achievement—language. On the average, children say their first word at 12 months of age, with a range of about 8 to 18 months (Whitehurst, 1982). Once words appear, language develops rapidly. By age 6, children are speaking in elaborate sentences and are skilled conversationalists.

To appreciate what an awesome task this is, think about the many abilities involved in your own flexible use of language. When you speak, you must select words that match the underlying concepts you want to convey. Then you must combine them into phrases and sentences based on a complex set of grammatical rules. Next, you must pronounce these utterances correctly, or you will not be understood. Finally, you must follow the rules of everyday conversation. For example, if you do not take turns, make comments that are relevant to what your partner just said, and use an appropriate tone of voice, then no matter how clear and correct your language, others may refuse to listen to you.

Infants and toddlers are still newcomers to their physical and social worlds, but they make remarkable progress in getting these skills underway. How do they manage to do so? There are several theories of how early language development takes place. Let's look at each one and evaluate them, based on what we know about the beginnings of language in the first 2 years.

### Three Theories of Language Development

In the 1950s, researchers had little notion that infants and toddlers were as competent as we know they are today. They did not take seriously the idea that very young children might be able to figure out important properties of the language they hear, just as they organize the world of objects into meaningful units. As a result, the first

• *Fifteen-month-old Joey's IQ is 115. His mother wants to know exactly what this means and what she should do at home to support his mental development. How would you respond to her questions?*

• *Using what you learned about brain growth in Chapter 5, explain why intensive intervention for poor children starting in the first 2 years has a greater impact on IQ scores than intervention beginning at a later age.*

## SOCIAL ISSUES

### Box 6.2    The Carolina Abecedarian Project: A Model of Infant–Toddler Intervention

*I*n the 1970s, an experiment was begun to find out if educational enrichment at a very early age could prevent the declines in mental development known to affect children born into extreme poverty. The Carolina Abecedarian Project identified over a hundred infants at serious risk for school failure, based on parental education and income, a history of poor school achievement among older siblings, and other family problems. Shortly after birth, the babies were randomly assigned to either a treatment or control group.

Between 3 weeks and 3 months of age, infants in the treatment group were enrolled in a full-time, year-round day-care program, where they remained until they entered school. During the first 3 years, the children received stimulation aimed at promoting motor, cognitive, language, and social skills. After age 3, the goals of the program expanded to include prereading and math concepts. At all ages, special emphasis was placed on adult–child communication. Teachers were trained to engage in informative, helpful, and nondirective interaction with the children, who were talked and read to daily. Both treatment and control children received nutrition and health services. The primary difference between them was the day-care

experience, designed to support the treatment group's mental development.

Intelligence test scores were gathered on the children regularly, and (as Figure 6.9 indicates) by 12 months the performance of the two groups began to diverge. Treatment children scored substantially higher than controls throughout the preschool years (Ramey & Campbell, 1984). Although the high-risk backgrounds of both groups led their IQs to drop during the school years, follow-up testing at ages 8 and 12 revealed that treatment children maintained their advantage in IQ over controls. In addition, at age 12 treatment youngsters were achieving considerably better in school, especially in reading, writing, and general knowledge (Campbell & Ramey, 1991; Martin, Ramey, & Ramey, 1990).

As we will see in Chapter 9, interventions that start later and last for shorter periods of time do not have this enduring impact on intelligence test scores (although they do show other long-term benefits). The findings of the Carolina Abecedarian Project, and others like it, indicate that intensive intervention beginning in infancy is the most effective way to combat the devastating effects of poverty on children's mental development.

---

two theories of how children acquire language were extreme views. One, *behaviorism,* regarded language development as entirely due to environmental influences—in particular, intensive training by parents. The second, *nativism* (meaning inborn), assumed that children were prewired to master the intricate rules of their language.

***The Behaviorist Perspective.***    The leader of this view was the well-known behaviorist B.F. Skinner (1957). He proposed that language, just like any other behavior, is acquired through *operant conditioning* (see Chapter 5, page 187). As the baby makes sounds, parents reinforce those that are most like words with smiles, hugs, and speech in return. For example, at 12 months, my older son David could often be heard babbling something like this: "book-a-book-a-dook-a-dook-a-book-a-nook-a-book-aaa." One day, I held up his picture book while he babbled away and said, "Book!" Very soon David was saying "book-aaa" in the presence of books. Some behaviorists rely on *imitation* to explain how children rapidly acquire complex utterances, such as whole phrases and sentences (Whitehurst & Vasta, 1975). And imitation can combine with reinforcement to promote language learning, as when the parent coaxes, "Say I want a cookie" and delivers praise and a treat after the toddler responds with "wanna cookie!"

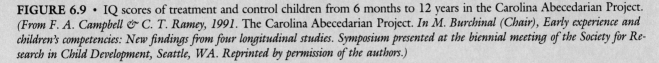

**FIGURE 6.9** • IQ scores of treatment and control children from 6 months to 12 years in the Carolina Abecedarian Project. *(From F. A. Campbell & C. T. Ramey, 1991.* The Carolina Abecedarian Project. *In M. Burchinal (Chair), Early experience and children's competencies: New findings from four longitudinal studies. Symposium presented at the biennial meeting of the Society for Research in Child Development, Seattle, WA. Reprinted by permission of the authors.)*

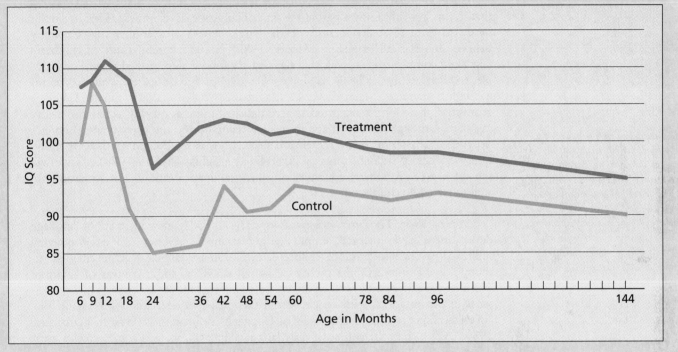

As these examples indicate, there is little doubt that reinforcement and imitation contribute to early language development. At the same time, there is wide agreement that they are not the whole story. As Felicia remarked one day, "It's amazing how creative April is with language. She combines words in ways she's never heard before, such as 'needle it' when she wants me to sew up her teddy bear and 'all gone outside' when she has to come in from the backyard." Felicia's observations reveal that young children do not just copy the speech of others. A great many things they say are not directly taught. So conditioning and imitation are best viewed as supporting early language learning rather than fully explaining it.

***The Nativist Perspective.*** Linguist Noam Chomsky (1957) was the first to recognize that even small children assume much responsibility for their own language learning. But his alternative to Skinner's view was just the opposite: a nativist theory that regards the young child's amazing language skill as etched into the structure of the human brain. Chomsky's main interest was in one aspect of language—grammar. He believed that grammatical rules are much too complex to be directly taught to or independently discovered by a young child. Instead, he argued, all children are born with a **language acquisition device (LAD)** that permits them, as soon as they have

**Language Acquisition Device (LAD)**

An innate ability that permits children, as soon as they have picked up enough words, to combine them into grammatically correct expressions.

*Noam Chomsky*
*Linguist Noam Chomsky proposed a nativist theory of language acquisition. According to Chomsky, children are born with an innate language acquisition device (LAD) that permits them to combine words into grammatically consistent utterances at an early age. (Constantine Manos/Magnum)*

learned enough words, to combine them into grammatically consistent expressions. According to Chomsky, the LAD contains a set of rules common to all languages. No matter which language children hear, they speak it in a rule-oriented fashion from the very beginning.

Are children biologically primed to acquire language? There is evidence that they are. Recall from Chapter 4 that newborn babies are remarkably sensitive to speech sounds and show a preference for listening to the human voice. In addition, children the world over reach the major milestones of language development in a similar sequence. This regularity of development certainly fits with Chomsky's idea of a biologically determined language program.

At the same time, there are serious challenges to Chomsky's theory, suggesting that it, too, provides only a partial account of language development. First, scientists have had great difficulty identifying the single system of grammar that Chomsky believes underlies all languages (Moerk, 1989). Second, careful study of children's first word combinations reveals that they do not follow grammatical rules. For example, toddlers are just as likely to say "cookie give" as "give cookie," which conforms to English grammar (Maratsos, 1983; Maratsos & Chalkley, 1980). Finally, language acquisition is no longer regarded as accomplished quite as quickly as nativist theory assumes. Although extraordinary strides are made during the early years, children's progress in mastering many sentence constructions is steady and gradual. It shows little evidence of sudden, innately determined insights (Brown, 1973). As we will see in Chapter 12, complete mastery of some grammatical rules is not achieved until well into middle childhood.

*A New View: The Interactionist Perspective.*   Today, new ideas about language development have emerged, emphasizing that innate abilities and environmental influences *interact* to produce children's extraordinary language achievements. Although several interactionist theories exist, all stress the social context of language learning. An active child, well endowed for acquiring language, observes and participates in conversations with others. From these experiences, children gradually discover the functions and regularities of language (Bohannon & Warren-Leubecker, 1989). As we chart the course of early language growth, we will come across a great deal of evidence that supports this new view. Table 6.6 provides an overview of early language milestones that we will take up in the next few sections.

TABLE 6.6 • Milestones of Language Development During the First Two Years

| Approximate Age | Milestone |
|---|---|
| 2–6 months | Infants coo, making pleasurable vowel sounds. |
| 4 months on | Infants and parents establish joint attention, and parents often verbally label what the baby is looking at. |
| 6–14 months | Infants babble, adding consonants to the sounds of the cooing period and repeating syllables. By 7 months, babbling of hearing infants starts to include many sounds of mature spoken languages. In hearing-impaired babies, speechlike babbles are delayed. |
| 6–14 months | Infants become capable of playing simple games, such as pat-a-cake and peekaboo. These provide practice in conversational turn taking and also highlight the meaning and function of spoken words. |
| 8–12 months | Infants use preverbal gestures, such as showing and pointing, to influence the behavior of others. |
| 12 months | Infants say their first recognizable word. |
| 18–24 months | Vocabulary expands from about 50 to 200 words. |
| 20–26 months | Toddlers combine two words. |

### Getting Ready to Talk

Before babies say their first word, they are preparing for language in many ways. They listen attentively to human speech, and they make speechlike sounds. As adults, we can hardly help but respond.

*This infant uses a preverbal gesture, pointing, to communicate something about these flowers. When parents label his gestures, they encourage him to add words to them. (Stan Ries/Picture Cube)*

***Cooing and Babbling.*** Around 2 months, babies begin to make vowellike noises, called **cooing** because of their pleasant "oo" quality. Gradually, consonants are added, and around 6 months **babbling** appears, in which infants repeat consonant–vowel combinations in long strings, such as "bababababa" or "nanananana."

The timing of early babbling seems to be due to maturation, since babies everywhere (even those who are deaf) start babbling at about the same age and produce a similar range of early sounds (Stoel-Gammon & Otomo, 1986). But for babbling to develop further, infants must be able to hear human speech. Around 7 months, babbling starts to include the sounds of mature spoken languages. However, if a baby's hearing is impaired, these speechlike sounds are greatly delayed. Observations of one totally deaf infant revealed a complete absence of speechlike babbles (Oller & Eilers, 1988).

When a baby coos or babbles and gazes at you, what are you likely to do? One day while I was standing in line at the post office, a mother and her 7-month-old daughter entered. As we waited, the baby babbled, and three adults—myself and two people standing beside me—started to talk to the infant. We cooed and babbled ourselves, imitating the baby, and also said such things as, "My, you're a big girl, aren't you? Out to help mommy mail letters today?" Then the baby smiled and babbled all the more. As adults interact with infants and they listen to spoken language, babbling increases, and its range of sounds expands. Through babbling, babies seem to experiment with a great many sounds that later can be blended into their first words (Elbers & Ton, 1985).

***Becoming a Communicator.*** Adults do not just interact with infants when they coo and babble. They also do so in many other situations. By age 4 months, infants start to gaze in the same direction adults are looking, and adults follow the baby's line of vision as well. When this happens, parents often comment on what the infant sees. In this way, the environment is labeled for the baby. Researchers believe that this kind of joint attention may be quite important for early language development. Infants who experience it often are likely to talk earlier and show faster vocabulary development (Dunham & Dunham, 1992; Tomasello, 1990).

Around 6 months, interaction between parent and baby begins to include give-and-take. Turn-taking games, such as pat-a-cake and peekaboo, appear. At first, the parent starts the game and the baby is an amused observer. But by 12 months, babies actively participate, exchanging roles with the parent. As they do so, they practice the turn-taking pattern of human conversation, and they also hear words paired with the actions they perform. Simple infant games like these are ideal contexts for infants to grasp the meaning and function of spoken words (Ratner & Bruner, 1978).

At the end of the first year, as infants become capable of intentional behavior, they use preverbal gestures to deliberately influence the behavior of others (Bates, 1979). If you return to the beginning of this chapter, you will see that Byron did so when he held up a toy to show it and pointed to the cupboard to get a cookie. When adults respond to babies' gestures and also label them ("Oh, you want a cookie!"), infants learn that using language quickly leads to desired results. Soon toddlers utter words along with these reaching and pointing gestures, the gestures recede, and spoken language is underway (Goldin-Meadow & Morford, 1985).

**Cooing**
Pleasant vowellike noises made by infants beginning at about 2 months of age.

**Babbling**
Repetition of consonant–vowel combinations in long strings, beginning around 6 months of age.

*First Words*

Ask several parents of toddlers to tell you which words appeared first in their children's vocabularies. Note how the words build on the sensorimotor foundations that Piaget described. Children's first words usually refer to objects that move (such as "car," "ball," "cat"), familiar actions ("bye-bye," "up," "more"), or outcomes of familiar actions ("dirty," "wet," "hot"). In their first 50 words, toddlers rarely name things that just *sit there*, like table or vase (Nelson, 1973). Sometimes early words are linked to specific cognitive achievements. For example, use of disappearance words, like "all gone," occurs at about the same time toddlers master advanced object permanence problems. And success and failure expressions, such as "there!" and "uh-oh!", appear when toddlers can solve sensorimotor problems suddenly, in Piaget's Substage 6. According to one pair of researchers, "Children seem to be motivated to acquire words that are relevant to the particular cognitive problems they are working on at the moment" (Gopnik & Meltzoff, 1986, p. 1057).

When young children first learn a new word, they often do not use it in just the way we do. Sometimes they apply the word too narrowly, an error called **underextension.** For example, at 16 months, April used the word "doll" only to refer to the worn and tattered doll that she carried around with her much of the day. A more common error is **overextension**—applying a word to a wider collection of objects and events than is appropriate. For example, when Rachel learned the word "car," she used it in the presence of a great many objects, including buses, trains, trucks, and fire engines. Toddlers' overextensions reflect a remarkable sensitivity to categorical relations. They do not overextend randomly. Instead, they apply a new word to a group of similar experiences, such as "car" to represent wheeled objects, "dog" to refer to four-legged animals, and "open" to mean opening a door, peeling fruit, and undoing shoe laces (Behrend, 1988; Clark, 1983). As children enlarge their vocabularies, they start to make finer distinctions, and overextensions gradually disappear.

*The Two-Word Utterance Phase*

At first, toddlers add to their vocabularies slowly, at a rate of 1 to 3 words a month. Over time, the number of words learned accelerates. Between 18 and 24 months, a spurt in vocabulary usually takes place. Many children add 10 to 20 new words a week (Goldfield & Reznick, 1990; Reznick & Goldfield, 1992). As vocabulary size moves toward 200 words, toddlers start to combine two words, such as "Mommy shoe," "go car," and "more cookie." These two-word utterances have been called **telegraphic speech** because like a telegram, they leave out smaller and less important words, such as "can," "the," and "to." Also, as yet there are no word endings, like "-s" and "-ed" (Brown, 1973). Even though the two-word utterance is very limited, children the world over use it to express an impressive variety of meanings (see Table 6.7).

At one time, researchers thought that there was a consistent grammar built into these expressions, but now they know that there is not. Two-word speech contains some simple formulas for use of particular words, such as "want + X" and "more + X" (which toddlers apply creatively by inserting many different words in the X position). But this does not mean that they know the rules of language, since they make many grammatical errors. For example, at 20 months, Rachel said "more hot" and "more read," but these combinations are not acceptable in English grammar (Braine, 1976; Maratsos & Chalkley, 1980).

These findings tell us that in learning to talk, toddlers are absorbed in figuring out the meanings of words and using their limited vocabularies in whatever way possible to get their thoughts across to others. This is an ambitious enough task for such a young child. But it does not take long for children to figure out basic grammat-

**Underextension**

An early vocabulary error in which a word is applied too narrowly, to a smaller number of objects and events than is appropriate.

**Overextension**

An early vocabulary error in which a word is applied too broadly, to a wider collection of objects and events than is appropriate.

**Telegraphic speech**

Toddlers' two-word utterances that, like a telegram, leave out smaller and less important words.

TABLE 6.7 • Common Meanings Expressed in Toddler's Two-Word Utterances

| Meaning | Example |
| --- | --- |
| Agent + action | "Tommy hit" |
| Action + object | "Give cookie" |
| Agent + object | "Mommy truck" (meaning mommy push the truck) |
| Action + location | "Put table" (meaning put X on the table) |
| Entity + location | "Daddy outside" |
| Entity + attribute | "Big ball" |
| Possessor + possession | "My truck" |
| Demonstrative + entity | "That doggie" |
| Notice + noticed object | "Hi mommy," "Hi truck" |
| Recurrence | "More milk" |
| Nonexistent object | "No shirt," "No more milk" |

*Source:* Brown, 1973.

ical rules. As we will see in Chapter 9, the beginnings of grammar are in place by age 2 1/2.

## Comprehension Versus Production

So far, we have focused on language **production**—the words and word combinations that children can say. What about **comprehension**—the language that children understand? At all ages, comprehension develops ahead of production. For example, the 8-month-old whose mother says, "Where's the doggie?" is likely to look around the room for the family's pet dog. And toddlers follow many simple directions, such as, "Bring me your book" or "Don't touch the lamp," even though they cannot yet express all these words in their own speech.

Why is language comprehension ahead of production? Think back to the distinction made earlier in this chapter between two types of memory—recognition and recall. Comprehension only requires that children recognize the meaning of a word, while production demands that they recall, or actively retrieve from their memories, the word as well as the concept for which it stands (Kuczaj, 1986). Language production is clearly a more difficult task. Failure to say a word does not mean that toddlers do not understand it. When we evaluate a child's language development, we need to keep both of these processes in mind. If we rely only on what children say, we will underestimate their knowledge of language.

## Individual Differences in Language Development

So far, we have discussed steps in language development that characterize children everywhere. But on the basis of what we have said about Byron, Rachel, and April, it should come as no surprise that there are great individual differences in how quickly language learning proceeds. Each child's progress results from a complex blend of biological and environmental influences. For example, earlier we saw that Byron's spoken language was delayed, in part because Lisa pressured him a great deal. But Byron is also a boy, and many studies show that girls are ahead of boys in early vocabulary growth (Jacklin & Maccoby, 1983). Besides the child's sex, personality makes a difference. Toddlers who are very reserved and cautious often wait until they understand a great deal before trying to speak. When, finally, they do speak, their vocabularies grow rapidly and they combine words almost immediately (Nelson, 1973).

**Production**

In language development, the words and word combinations that children say.

**Comprehension**

In language development, the words and word combinations that children understand.

Listen closely to what toddlers say, and you are likely to observe some striking differences in the words and phrases they produce. Young children have unique *styles* of early language learning. April (like most toddlers) used a **referential style;** her vocabulary consisted mainly of words that referred to objects. In contrast, Rachel used an **expressive style.** She produced many more pronouns and social formulas, such as "stop it," "thank you," and "I want it," which she uttered as compressed phrases, much like single words (as in "Iwannit"). Toddlers who use these styles have different early ideas about the functions of language. April thought words were for naming objects, while Rachel believed they were for talking about the feelings and needs of herself and other people. April's vocabulary grew faster, since all languages contain many more object labels than social phrases (Bates, Bretherton, & Snyder, 1988; Nelson, 1973).

What accounts for a toddler's choice of a particular language style? Once again, both biological and environmental factors seem to be involved. April had an especially active interest in exploring objects and parents who eagerly responded with names of things to her first attempts to talk. Rachel spent more time watching other people, and she listened carefully as her parents used verbal routines ("How are you?" "It's no trouble") designed to support social relationships (Furrow & Nelson, 1984; Goldfield, 1987; Nelson, 1981). The two toddlers' vocabularies gradually became more similar as they revised their first notions of what language is all about.

At what point should parents be concerned if their child does not talk or says very little? If a toddler's language is greatly delayed when compared to the norms given in Table 6.6 (page 232), then parents should consult the child's doctor or arrange for an evaluation by a speech and language therapist. Some toddlers who do not follow simple directions could have a hearing problem. A child over age 2 who has great difficulty putting thoughts into words may have a serious language disorder that requires immediate and intensive treatment (Warren & Kaiser, 1988).

## Supporting Early Language Development

There is little doubt that children are specially prepared for acquiring language, since no other species can develop as flexible and creative a capacity for communication as we can (Berko Gleason, 1989). At the same time, a great deal of evidence fits with the interactionist approach—that a rich social environment builds on young children's natural readiness to speak their native tongue. During infancy and toddlerhood, parents establish the contexts in which language development takes place. We have already seen several examples of how they capitalize on infants' native abilities—labeling objects babies look at, responding to coos and babbles, and playing social games.

Watch several parents talk to infants and toddlers, and you will find further evidence for the interactionist perspective. Adults the world over speak to young children in **motherese,** a form of language made up of short sentences with exaggerated expression and very clear pronunciation (Fernald et al., 1989; Newport, Gleitman, & Gleitman, 1977). Motherese also contains many simplified words, such as "night-night," "bye-bye," "daddy," and "tummy," that are easy for toddlers to pronounce. In addition, speakers of motherese often repeat phrases, ask questions, and give directions, perhaps as a way of checking to see if their message has been properly received. Here is an example of Felicia speaking motherese to 18-month-old April as together they get ready to leave for home:

Felicia: "Time to go, April."
April: "Go car."
Felicia: "Yes, time to go in the car. Where's your jacket?"
April: (looks around, walks to the closet) "Dacket!" (pointing to her jacket)
Felicia: "There's that jacket! Let's put it on. (helps April into the jacket) On it goes!
    Let's zip up. (zips up the jacket) Now, say bye-bye to Byron and Rachel."

**Referential style**

A style of early language learning in which toddlers use language mainly to label objects.

**Expressive style**

A style of early language learning in which toddlers use language mainly to talk about the feelings and needs of themselves and other people.

**Motherese**

A form of language used by adults to speak to young children that consists of short sentences with exaggerated expression and very clear pronunciation.

April: "Bye-bye, By-on."

Felicia: "What about Rachel? Bye to Rachel?"

April: "Bye-bye, Ta-tel (Rachel)."

Felicia: "Where's your doll? Don't forget your doll."

April: (looks around)

Felicia: "Look by the sofa. See? Go get the doll. By the sofa." (April gets the doll.)

Parents do not seem to be deliberately trying to teach children to talk when they use motherese, since many of the same speech qualities appear when adults communicate with foreigners. Motherese probably arises from adults' unconscious desire to keep young children's attention and ease their task of understanding, and it works effectively in these ways. From birth on, children prefer to listen to motherese over other kinds of adult talk (Cooper & Aslin, 1990). And parents constantly fine-tune it to fit with children's needs. Notice how Felicia used an utterance length that was just ahead of April's, creating a sensitive match between the stimulation she provided and what April was capable of understanding and producing (Bohannon & Warren-Leubecker, 1989).

Motherese contains many features shown by research to support early language development. For example, parents who frequently repeat part of their own or the child's previous utterance and use simple questions have 2-year-olds who make faster language progress (Barnes et al., 1983; Hoff-Ginsburg, 1986). But this does not mean that we should deliberately load our speech to toddlers with repetitions, questions, and other characteristics of motherese! These qualities occur naturally as adults draw young children into dialogues in which their attempts to talk are accepted as meaningful and worthwhile. Amount of conversational give-and-take between parent and child is one of the best predictors of early language development because it provides many examples of speech just ahead of the child's current level as well as a sympathetic environment in which children can try out new skills (Huttenlocher et al., 1991). In fact, a major reason that twins and later-born children often acquire early language more slowly than singletons is that they have fewer opportunities to converse with parents, who must divide their time between several youngsters (Jones & Adamson, 1987; Tomasello, Mannle, & Kruger, 1986).

Do social experiences that promote language development remind you of ones discussed earlier in this chapter that strengthen cognitive development in general? Notice how parent–child conversation and the motherese that is a part of it create a *zone of proximal development* in which children's language expands. In contrast, impatience and rejection of children's efforts to talk lead them to stop trying and result in immature language skills (Nelson, 1973). In the next chapter, we will see that the very same sensitivity to children's needs and capacities that supports cognition and language is at the heart of their emotional and social development as well.

# SUMMARY

### Piaget's Cognitive-Developmental Theory

• Influenced by his background in biology, Piaget viewed cognitive development as an adaptive process. By acting directly on the environment, children move through four stages in which internal structures achieve a better fit with external reality.

• In Piaget's theory, psychological structures, or **schemes,** change in two ways. The first is through **adaptation,** which is made up of two complementary activities—**assimilation** and **accommodation.** The second is through

**organization,** the internal rearrangement of schemes so that they form a strongly interconnected cognitive system.

• Piaget's **sensorimotor stage** is divided into six substages. Through the **circular reaction,** the newborn baby's reflexes are gradually transformed into the more flexible action patterns of the older infant and finally into the representational schemes of the 2-year-old child. During Substage 4, infants develop **intentional** or **goal-directed behavior** and begin to understand **object permanence.** By Substage 6, they become capable of **mental representation,** as shown by sudden solutions to sensorimotor problems, **deferred imitation,** and **make-believe play.**

• Although Piaget's overall sequence of sensorimotor development has been confirmed, he underestimated the capacities of young infants. Secondary circular reactions, object permanence, and deferred imitation are present earlier than Piaget believed. It is possible that infants do not have to construct all aspects of their cognitive world through motor activity. The beginnings of some schemes may be there from the start.

### Information Processing in the First Two Years

• Unlike Piaget's stage theory, information processing views development as a continuous process; the cognitive approach of children and adults is assumed to be much the same. According to Atkinson and Shiffrin, the human mental system is divided into three parts: the **sensory register, working** or **short-term memory,** and **long-term memory.** As information flows through each, **control processes,** or **mental strategies,** operate on it to increase the efficiency of thinking as well as the chances that information will be retained.

• With age, infants attend to more aspects of the environment, take information into their mental systems more quickly, and remember experiences over longer periods of time. Young infants are capable of **recognition** memory; by 7 months, they can **recall** events that are not present.

• Infants remember information in a remarkably orderly fashion. During the first year, they group stimuli into increasingly complex categories. By the second year, they become active categorizers, spontaneously sorting objects during their play.

• Information processing has contributed greatly to our view of the young baby as a sophisticated cognitive being. However, it has not yet provided us with a broad, comprehensive theory of children's thinking.

### The Social Context of Early Cognitive Development

• According to Vygotsky's sociocultural theory, complex mental functions have their origins in social interaction. By engaging in joint activities with more skilled partners, infants master tasks within the **zone of proximal development**—ones just ahead of their current capacities. As a result, cognitive competence increases.

### Individual Differences in Early Mental Development

• The mental testing approach measures intellectual development in an effort to predict future performance. **Intelligence quotients,** or **IQs,** are scores on mental tests that compare a child's performance to that of same-age children.

Infant tests consist largely of perceptual and motor responses; they predict later intelligence poorly. As a result, scores on infant tests are called **developmental quotients,** or **DQs,** rather than IQs. Tests of recognition memory and object permanence, which tap basic cognitive processes, show better predictability.

• Research using the **Home Observation for Measurement of the Environment (HOME)** shows that stimulation provided by the home environment and parental encouragement, involvement, and affection repeatedly predict early mental test scores, no matter what the child's social class and cultural background. The quality of infant and toddler day care also has a major impact on mental development. Intensive early intervention is required to prevent the gradual declines in intelligence so often experienced by poverty-stricken children.

### Language Development During the First Two Years

• Three theories provide different accounts of how young children develop language. According to the behaviorist perspective, parents train children in language skills by relying on operant conditioning and imitation. In contrast, Chomsky's nativist view regards children as naturally endowed with a **language acquisition device (LAD).** New interactionist theories offer a compromise between these extreme views, stressing that innate abilities and social contexts combine to promote language development.

• During the first year, a great deal of preparation for language takes place. Infants begin **cooing** at 2 months and **babbling** around 6 months. When adults respond to infants' coos and babbles, play turn-taking games with them, and acknowledge their preverbal gestures, they encourage language progress.

• Around 12 months, toddlers say their first word. When picking up new words, young children make errors involving **underextension** and **overextension.** Between 18 months and 2 years, two-word utterances called **telegraphic speech** appear. At all ages language **comprehension** develops ahead of **production.**

• Individual differences in early language development exist. Girls show faster progress than boys, and reserved, cautious toddlers may wait for a period of time before trying to speak. Most toddlers use a **referential style** of language learning, in which early words consist largely of names for objects. A few use an **expressive style,** in which social formulas are common and vocabulary grows more slowly.

• Adults the world over speak to young children in **motherese,** a simplified form of language that is well suited to their learning needs. Motherese occurs naturally when parents engage toddlers in conversations that accept and encourage their early efforts to talk.

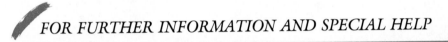

## IMPORTANT TERMS AND CONCEPTS

sensorimotor stage (p. 204)

scheme (p. 204)

adaptation (p. 206)

assimilation (p. 206)

accommodation (p. 206)

equilibration (p. 206)

organization (p. 206)

circular reaction (p. 207)

intentional or goal-directed behavior (p. 210)

object permanence (p. 210)

AB search error (p. 210)

mental representation (p. 211)

deferred imitation (p. 212)

functional play (p. 212)

make-believe play (p. 212)

control processes or mental strategies (p. 217)

sensory register (p. 217)

working or short-term memory (p. 217)

long-term memory (p. 218)

recognition (p. 219)

recall (p. 219)

zone of proximal development (p. 221)

intelligence quotient or IQ (p. 224)

developmental quotient or DQ (p. 225)

Home Observation for Measurement of the Environment (HOME) (p. 226)

language acquisition device (LAD) (p. 231)

cooing (p. 233)

babbling (p. 233)

underextension (p. 234)

overextension (p. 234)

telegraphic speech (p. 234)

production (p. 235)

comprehension (p. 235)

referential style (p. 236)

expressive style (p. 236)

motherese (p. 236)

## FOR FURTHER INFORMATION AND SPECIAL HELP

### Infant Development and Education

Association for Childhood Education International (ACEI)
11141 Georgia Avenue, Suite 200
Wheaton, MD 20902
(301) 942-2443

Organization interested in promoting good educational practice from infancy through early adolescence. Student membership is available and includes a subscription to *Childhood Education,* a bimonthly journal covering research, practice, and public policy issues.

National Association for the Education of Young Children (NAEYC)
1834 Connecticut Avenue, N.W.
Washington, DC 20005
(202) 347-0308

Organization open to all individuals interested in acting on behalf of young children's needs, with primary focus on educational services. Student membership is available and includes a subscription to *Young Children,* a bimonthly journal covering theory, research, and practice in infant and early childhood development and education.

### Early Intervention

National Center for Clinical Infant Programs
733 15th Street, N.W., Suite 912
Washington, DC 20004
(202) 347-0308

Seeks to promote optimum development of infants and toddlers through encouraging high-quality intervention services. Pub-

lishes public policy reports and a bulletin that reviews research and lists training opportunities.

High-Scope Foundation
600 N. River Street
Ypsilanti, MI 48198
(313) 485-2000

Devoted to improving development and education from infancy through the high school years. Has designed a parent–infant education program. Conducts longitudinal research to determine the effects of early intervention on development.

### Day Care

Child Care Resource and Referral, Inc.
2116 Campus Drive, S.E.
Rochester, MN 55904
(507) 287-2020

Represents more than 260 local agencies that work for high-quality day care and provide information on available services.

National Association for Family Day Care
815 15th Street, N.W., Suite 928
Washington, DC 20005
(202) 347-3356

Organization open to caregivers, parents, and other individuals involved or interested in family day care. Serves as a national voice that promotes high quality day care.

*"My Big Brother," Dai Akiyama, 4 years, Japan. Reprinted by permission from The International Museum of Children's Art, Oslo, Norway.*

# Emotional and Social Development in Infancy and Toddlerhood

# 7

Theories of Infant and Toddler Personality
    *Erik Erikson: Trust and Autonomy    Margaret Mahler: Separation–Individuation
    Similarities between Erikson's and Mahler's Theories*
Emotional Development During the First Two Years
    *The Development of Some Basic Emotions    Recognizing and Responding to the Emotions of
    Others    The Emergence of Complex Emotions    The Beginnings of Emotional Self-Regulation*
Temperament and Development
    *Measuring Temperament    The Stability of Temperament    Biological Foundations
    Environmental Influences    Temperament and Child Rearing: The Goodness-of-Fit Model*
The Development of Attachment
    *Theories of Attachment    Measuring the Security of Attachment    Cultural Variations
    Factors that Affect Attachment Security    Multiple Attachments    Attachment and
    Later Development*
Self-Development During the First Two Years
    *Self-Recognition    Categorizing the Self    The Emergence of Self-Control*

L isa, Beth, and Felicia's monthly conversations often focused on the emotional and social sides of their infants' development. As the babies turned 8 months old, Beth noticed some important changes: "For some reason, Rachel's become more fearful in the last few weeks. Recently, I took her to the airport to meet my parents, who were arriving from Japan. When they stepped off the plane and tried to hug her, she didn't return their enthusiasm, as she would have a month or two ago. Instead, she turned her head away and buried it against my shoulder. Several days later, I left Rachel with my parents for several hours—the first time I'd been away from her since she was born. She wailed as soon as she saw me head for the door. And when I returned, Rachel seemed angry. She insisted on being held but also pushed me away and continued to cry. It took 5 or 10 minutes before I was able to calm her down."

Lisa and Felicia also reported an increasing wariness of strangers and a strong desire to remain close to familiar adults in Byron and April. At the same time, each baby seemed more willful. An object removed from the hand at 5 months produced little response, but at 8 months Byron actively resisted when Lisa took away a table knife he had managed to get hold of. And he could not be consoled by a variety of toys that she offered in its place. Taken together, these reactions reflect two related aspects of personality that begin to develop during the first 2 years: *close ties to others* and *a sense of self*—an awareness of one's own separateness and uniqueness.

Our discussion begins with major theories that provide an overall picture of personality development during infancy and toddlerhood. Then we look at factors that contribute to these changes. First, we chart the general course of emotional development. As we do so, we will discover why fear and anger became more apparent in Byron, Rachel, and April's range of emotions by the end of the first year. Second, our attention turns to individual differences in temperament and personality. We will examine biological and environmental contributions to these differences and their consequences for future development.

Next, we take up attachment to the caregiver, the child's first affectional tie that develops over the course of infancy. We will see how the feelings of security that grow out of this important bond provide a vital source of support for the child's exploration, sense of independence, and expanding social relationships.

Finally, we focus on early self-development. By the end of toddlerhood, April recognized herself in mirrors and photographs, labeled herself as a girl, and showed the beginnings of self-control. "Don't touch!" she instructed herself one day as she resisted the desire to pull a lamp cord out of its socket. Cognitive advances combine with social experiences to produce these changes during the second year.

## THEORIES OF INFANT AND TODDLER PERSONALITY

In Chapter 1, we pointed out that psychoanalytic theory is no longer in the mainstream of child development research. But one of its lasting contributions has been its ability to capture the essence of personality development during each phase of life. Recall from Chapter 1 that Sigmund Freud, founder of the psychoanalytic movement, believed that psychological health and maladjustment could be traced to the early years—in particular, to the quality of the child's relationships with parents.

Return to page 14 of Chapter 1 and reread the brief description of Freud's *psychosexual stages*. During the first 3 years, he focused on how parents help their children discharge instinctual drives originating from the oral and then from the anal zone of the body. Freud's limited concern with the channeling of instincts and his neglect of important experiences after the early years came to be heavily criticized. But the basic outlines of his theory were accepted and elaborated by several noted psychoanalysts who came after him. The leader of these neo-Freudians is Erik Erikson, whose *psychosocial theory* we introduced in Chapter 1.

In the following sections, we take a closer look at the emotional and social tasks of infancy and toddlerhood, as Erikson and a second well-known psychoanalyst—Margaret Mahler—saw them. Although each emphasized somewhat different features of early experience as central to development, we will see that the two theories have much in common.

### Erik Erikson: Trust and Autonomy

Erikson (1950) characterized each Freudian stage as an inner conflict that is resolved toward the positive or negative side, depending on the child's experiences with caregivers. When parenting supports the child's needs, the first year leads to feelings of trust in others and the next 2 years lead to a sense of personal autonomy. These early attitudes provide the foundation for healthy emotional and social development throughout life.

**Basic Trust Versus Mistrust.** Freud called the first year the **oral stage**, during which infants obtain pleasure through the mouth—at first by sucking, and later, after teeth erupt, by biting and chewing. Gratification of the baby's need for food and pleasurable oral stimulation rests in the hands of the mother, whose task is to provide the right amount of oral satisfaction. If she feeds the baby when hungry, provides suitable objects for the infant to suck and bite, and weans neither too early nor too late, then energies transfer smoothly to the anal region, and the infant is prepared for the next stage of development.

**Oral stage**
Freud's first psychosexual stage, during which infants obtain pleasure through the mouth.

According to Erikson, basic trust grows out of the quality of the mother's relationship with the baby. A mother who relieves her baby's discomfort promptly and holds him tenderly, especially during feedings, promotes basic trust. (Craig Hammell/The Stock Market)

Erikson accepted Freud's emphasis on the importance of feeding, but he expanded and enriched Freud's view. A healthy outcome during infancy, Erikson believed, does not depend on the *amount* of food or oral stimulation offered, but rather on the *quality* of the mother's behavior. A mother who supports her baby's development relieves discomfort promptly and sensitively. For example, she holds the infant gently during feedings, patiently waits until the baby has had enough milk, and weans when the infant shows less interest in the breast and sucking.

Erikson recognized that no mother can be constantly and perfectly in tune with her baby's needs. Many factors affect her responsiveness—her own feelings of personal happiness, her momentary life condition (for example, whether she has one or several small children to care for), and child-rearing practices encouraged by her culture. But when the *balance of care* is sympathetic and loving, then the psychological conflict of the first year—**basic trust versus mistrust**—is resolved on the positive side. The trusting infant expects the world to be good and gratifying, so he feels confident about venturing out and exploring it. The mistrustful baby cannot count on the kindness and compassion of others, so he protects himself by withdrawing from people and things around him.

*Autonomy Versus Shame and Doubt.* During Freud's **anal stage,** instinctual energies shift to the anal region of the body. Toddlers take pleasure in retaining and releasing urine and feces at will. At the same time, society requires that elimination occur at appropriate times and places. As a result, Freud viewed toilet training, in which children must bring their anal impulses in line with social requirements, as having a crucial impact on personality development. If parents insist that children be trained before they are physically ready or wait too long before expecting self-control, an unresolved battle of wills is initiated between parent and child. Then anal conflicts persist, and instinctual energies are not free to move on to the next stage.

**Basic trust versus mistrust**

In Erikson's theory, the psychological conflict of infancy, which is resolved positively if caregiving, especially during feeding, is sympathetic and loving.

**Anal stage**

Freud's second psychosexual stage, in which toddlers take pleasure in retaining and releasing urine and feces at will.

*This 2-year-old is intent on combing his hair. Toddlers who are allowed to decide and do things for themselves in appropriate situations develop a sense of autonomy—the feeling that they can control their bodies and act competently on their own. (Brent Jones/Stock Boston)*

Erikson agreed that the parent's manner of toilet training is critical for psychological health. But he viewed bladder and bowel control as only one of a broad range of important experiences encountered by newly walking, talking toddlers. Their familiar refrains—"No!" and "Do it myself!"—reveal that they want to decide for themselves with all their powers, not just in toileting, but in other situations as well. The great conflict of this stage, **autonomy versus shame and doubt,** is resolved favorably when parents provide young children with suitable guidance and reasonable choices. A self-confident, secure 2-year-old has been encouraged not just to use the toilet, but also to eat with a spoon and to help pick up his toys. His parents do not criticize or attack him when he fails in these new skills. And they meet his assertions of independence with tolerance and understanding. For example, his mother grants him an extra five minutes to finish his play before leaving for the grocery store and waits patiently while he tries to zip his jacket. According to Erikson, the parent who is over- or undercontrolling in toileting is likely to be so in other aspects of the toddler's life as well. The outcome is a child who feels forced and shamed and who doubts his ability to control his impulses and act competently on his own.

### Margaret Mahler: Separation–Individuation

Erikson's theory describes how sensitive channeling of the baby's drives leads to positive attitudes toward others (trust) and to good feelings about the self (autonomy). Mahler carries this theme further, focusing on how the infant's early relationship with the mother provides the foundation for a sense of self that emerges in the second year (Mahler, Pine, & Bergman, 1975). According to Mahler, awareness of the self as separate and unique is the outcome of events that take place in two phases of development: symbiosis and separation–individuation.

**Symbiosis.** During the first 2 months, babies are only minimally aware of the surrounding world, spending most of the day asleep, waking when hunger and other tensions cause them to cry, and sinking back into sleep when basic needs are satisfied and discomforts are relieved. But from the second month on, the phase of **symbiosis** (meaning the blending of two people into an intimate, harmonious relationship)

**Autonomy versus shame and doubt**

In Erikson's theory, the psychological conflict of toddlerhood, which is resolved positively if parents provide young children with suitable guidance and appropriate choices.

**Symbiosis**

In Mahler's theory, the baby's intimate sense of oneness with the mother, encouraged by warm, physical closeness and gentle handling.

begins. At this time, infants become increasingly alert and interested in sights and sounds around them (see Chapter 5). But unlike the older child and adult, they do not realize that these events exist outside themselves. Instead, the self and surrounding world (including the person on whom they depend most for survival—the mother) are completely fused. According to Mahler, this oneness with the mother is a necessary first step on the way to developing a sense of self. It is promoted by the mother's responsiveness to the infant's emotional signals. As the baby cries, coos, and smiles, the mother reacts promptly and with positive emotional tone. The more she does so, the more confidently and easily the infant will separate from her during the next phase. In contrast, infants handled harshly and impatiently are likely to have great difficulty distancing themselves from their mothers.

*Separation–Individuation.* In Mahler's second phase, **separation–individuation,** the baby's capacity to physically move away from the mother triggers self-awareness (individuation). The process of separating from the mother begins around 4 to 5 months, when the infant, held in the mother's arms, leans away from her body to scan the environment. But the decisive events of this phase are crawling and then walking—that is, the baby's growing capacity to leave the mother at his/her own initiative.

*According to Mahler, walking brings a dramatic advance in separation–individuation. As she ventures further from her mother to explore the environment, this toddler becomes increasingly aware that she and her mother are distinct beings. (John Coletti/The Picture Cube)*

Newly crawling 8- to 10-month-olds venture away from the mother to explore their world, but they remain very dependent on her for emotional support. Infants of this age wander only a short distance away. They frequently look back for reassurance and return to the mother's side to reexperience the safety and security of close body contact. Yet as the crawling baby comes and goes, he experiences the mother from a new, distant vantage point and becomes dimly aware of his own separateness.

The onset of walking brings a dramatic advance in individuation. The upright posture is accompanied by greater freedom of movement and a new delight in exploration. As toddlers venture further from the mother and test their own capacities, they become even more conscious that the mother and the self are distinct beings. Around 18 months, this realization is full-blown, and at first it is frightening. Older toddlers may engage in all kinds of behaviors aimed at resisting and undoing this separateness—following and clinging to the mother, filling her lap with objects retrieved from the surrounding environment, and darting away in hopes of being chased, caught, and reminded of her continuing commitment. According to Mahler, the temper tantrums that often occur around this time—referred to as the "terrible twos" by many parents—are signs of the new self's desire to assert itself mixed with feelings of helpless dependence at not being able to manage all the challenges of the environment.

The mother's patience and reassurance eventually help toddlers surmount this temporary crisis. Between 2 and 3 years, children whose mothering experiences have been gratifying and supportive emerge from this second phase with a sturdy sense of themselves as separate persons. They are affectionate, caring, and cooperative, play energetically, and can cope with mild frustrations. And gains in representation and language (see Chapter 6) enable children to create a positive inner image of the mother that they can rely on in her absence so separations from her are easier.

### Similarities Between Erikson's and Mahler's Theories

As you read about Erikson's and Mahler's theories, undoubtedly you noticed several common themes. Each regards warm, sensitive parenting as vital for personality development. In addition, each theorist views toddlerhood as a time of budding selfhood. For Erikson, it is a stage when children achieve autonomous control over basic impulses; for Mahler, it is a period during which they learn to separate confidently from the parent. Both theorists also agree that when children emerge from

**Separation–individuation**
In Mahler's theory, the process of separating from the mother and becoming aware of the self, which is triggered by crawling and walking.

Review

the first few years without sufficient trust in caregivers and a healthy sense of individuality, the seeds are sown for adjustment problems. Adults who have difficulty establishing intimate ties to others, who are overly dependent on a loved one, or who continually doubt their own ability to meet new challenges may not have fully mastered the tasks of trust, autonomy, and individuation during infancy and toddlerhood.

Erikson and Mahler arrived at their conclusions by using the clinical method (see Chapter 1) to study normal mother–infant pairs as well as children and adults with serious emotional problems. As we examine research based on other methods in the remainder of this chapter, we will return many times to the perceptive observations of these two theorists.

*• Derek's mother fed him in a warm and loving manner during the first year. But when he became a toddler, she kept him in a playpen for many hours because he got into too much mischief while exploring freely. Use Erikson's theory to evaluate Derek's early experiences.*

*• At 18 months, Betina became clingy and dependent. She followed her mother around the house and asked to be held often. How would Mahler account for Betina's behavior? How should Betina's parents respond?*

**BRIEF REVIEW**    Erikson's and Mahler's psychoanalytic theories provide an overview of the emotional and social tasks of infancy and toddlerhood. According to Erikson, basic trust and autonomy grow out of warm, supportive parenting and reasonable expectations for impulse control during the second year. Mahler's theory suggests that sensitive exchange of emotional signals between mother and baby leads to a symbiotic bond, which provides the foundation for a confident sense of self as infants crawl and then walk on their own. Both theorists agree that the development of trust and individuality during infancy and toddlerhood have lasting consequences for personality development.

## EMOTIONAL DEVELOPMENT DURING THE FIRST TWO YEARS

In the previous chapter, I suggested that you find some time to observe several infants and parents, noting babies' increasingly effective schemes for controlling the environment and ways that adults support cognitive and language development. Now focus on another aspect of infant and caregiver behavior: the expression and exchange of emotions. While you observe, note the various emotions the infant displays, the cues you rely on to interpret the baby's feelings, and how the caregiver responds.

Over the past twenty years, researchers have conducted many observations like these to find out how effectively babies communicate their feelings and interpret those of others. They have discovered that emotions play a powerful role in organizing the events that Erikson and Mahler regarded as so important during the early years—relationships with caregivers, exploration of the environment, and discovery of the self (Barrett & Campos, 1987; Campos et al., 1983).

### The Development of Some Basic Emotions

Since infants cannot describe their feelings, researchers face a challenging task in determining exactly which emotions they are experiencing. Facial expressions seem to offer the most reliable cues. Cross-cultural evidence indicates that when looking at photographs of different facial gestures, people around the world associate them with emotions in the same way (Ekman & Friesen, 1972). These findings inspired researchers to carefully analyze infants' facial expressions in order to study the range of emotions they display at different ages. A commonly used method for doing so is illustrated in Figure 7.1.

Do infants come into the world with the ability to express a wide variety of emotions? Some investigators regard the emotional life of the newborn baby as quite limited. For example, according to one theory, separate emotions gradually emerge over the first year out of two global arousal states: the newborn baby's tendency to

**FIGURE 7.1** • Which emotions are these babies displaying? The MAX (Maximally Discriminative Facial Movement) System is a widely used method for classifying infants' emotional expressions. Facial muscle movements are carefully rated to determine their correspondence with basic feeling states. For example, cheeks raised and corners of the mouth pulled back and up signal happiness (A). Eyebrows raised, eyes widened, and mouth opened with corners pulled straight back denote fear (B). *(From Izard, 1979.)*

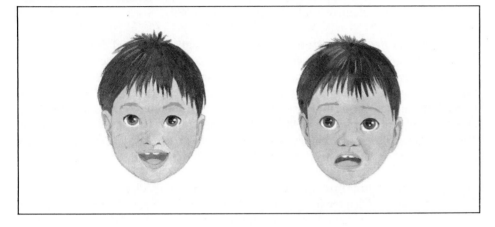

approach pleasant and withdraw from unpleasant stimulation (Fox, 1991). Other theorists believe that all the **basic emotions**—those that can be directly inferred from facial expressions, such as happiness, interest, surprise, fear, anger, sadness, and disgust—are present in the first few weeks of life (Campos et al., 1983). Observations of babies' facial gestures suggest that signs of almost all the basic emotions are present in early infancy, although each becomes more recognizable with age (Malatesta et al., 1989). Three emotions—happiness, anger, and fear—have received the most research attention. Let's see how they change over the first year.

*Happiness.* Happiness—first in terms of blissful smiles and later through exuberant laughter—contributes to many aspects of development. Infants smile and laugh when they conquer new skills, expressing their delight in cognitive and physical mastery. The smile also encourages caregivers to be affectionate as well as stimulating, so the baby will smile all the more. Happiness binds parent and baby into a warm, supportive relationship and, at the same time, fosters the infant's developing competence.

During the early weeks, newborn babies smile when full, during sleep, and in response to gentle touches and sounds, such as stroking of the skin, rocking, and the mother's soft, high-pitched voice (Emde & Koenig, 1969). By the end of the first month, infants start to smile at interesting sights, but these must be dynamic, eye-catching events, such as a bright object jumping suddenly across the baby's field of vision. Between 6 and 10 weeks, the human face evokes a broad grin called the **social smile,** which is soon accompanied by pleasurable cooing (Sroufe & Waters, 1976; Wolff, 1963). Perhaps you can already tell that early changes in smiling parallel the development of infant perceptual capacities—in particular, babies' increasing sensitivity to visual patterns, including the human face—that we discussed in Chapter 5.

Laughter, which appears around 3 to 4 months, reflects faster processing of information than smiling. But like smiling, the first laughs occur in response to very active stimuli, such as the mother saying playfully, "I'm gonna get you!" and kissing the baby's tummy. Over time, as infants understand more about their world, they laugh at events that contain more subtle elements of surprise. At 10 months, Byron

**Basic emotions**

Emotions that can be directly inferred from facial expressions, such as happiness, interest, surprise, fear, anger, sadness, and disgust.

**Social smile**

The smile evoked by the stimulus of the human face. First appears between 6 and 10 weeks.

chuckled as Lisa played a silent game of peek-a-boo, and at 1 year, he laughed heartily as she crawled on all fours and then walked like a penguin (Sroufe & Wunsch, 1972).

By the middle of the first year, infants smile and laugh more often when interacting with familiar people, a preference that supports and strengthens the parent–child bond. During the second year, toddlers deliberately use the smile as a social signal. They break their play with an interesting toy to turn around and communicate their delight to an attentive adult (Jones & Raag, 1989).

***Anger and Fear.*** Newborn babies respond with generalized distress to a variety of unpleasant experiences, including hunger, painful medical procedures, changes in body temperature, and too much or too little stimulation (see Chapter 4). During the first 2 months, fleeting expressions of anger appear as babies cry. These gradually increase in frequency and intensity, showing a sharp rise between 7 and 19 months (Izard, Hembree, & Huebner, 1987). At the same time, babies show anger in wider range of situations—for example, when an object is taken away, the mother leaves for a brief time, or the baby is put down for a nap (Shiller, Izard, & Hembree, 1986).

Like anger, fear rises dramatically after 7 months. Older infants hesitate before playing with a new toy that they would have grasped immediately at an earlier age. And, as we saw in Chapter 5, research with the visual cliff reveals that they start to show fear of heights by avoiding edges and drop-offs around this time. But the most frequent expression of fear is to unfamiliar adults, a reaction called **stranger anxiety.** Many infants and toddlers are quite wary of strangers, but not all of them are. Whether or not stranger anxiety occurs depends on a number of factors: the infant's temperament (some babies are generally more fearful), past experiences with strangers, and the situation in which baby and stranger meet (Thompson & Limber, 1991).

To understand these influences, let's return for a moment to Rachel's fearful withdrawal from her grandparents, described at the beginning of this chapter. From birth on, Rachel's mother cared for her continuously. She had little opportunity to get to know strange adults. Also, she met her grandparents for the first time in an unfamiliar environment (a crowded airport), and they rushed over and tried to hold her. Under these conditions, babies are most likely to display fearful reactions (Emde, Gaensbauer, & Harmon, 1976). Later, at home, Rachel watched with interest and approached as her grandmother sat quietly on the sofa, smiling and holding out a teddy bear. A familiar setting, the opportunity to become acquainted from a distance, and warmth and friendliness on the part of the stranger reduced Rachel's fear (Horner, 1980).

At this point, you may be wondering: Just what is the significance of this rise in fear and anger at the end of the first year? Researchers believe that these emotions have special survival value as infants' motor capacities improve. Older babies can use the energy mobilized by anger to defend themselves or overcome obstacles to blocked goals. Fear becomes especially adaptive as infants begin to crawl and walk. It keeps babies' enthusiasm for exploration in check, making it more likely that they will remain close to the caregiver's side and be careful about approaching unfamiliar people and objects. Anger and fear are also strong social signals that motivate caregivers to approach and comfort a suffering infant and, in the case of separation, may discourage them from leaving again soon.

Finally, cognitive development plays an important role in infants' angry and fearful reactions, just as it does in their expressions of happiness. Between 8 and 12 months, when (as Piaget pointed out) babies grasp the notion of intentional behavior, they have a better understanding of the cause of their frustrations. Therefore, they know at whom or what to get angry. In the case of fear, improved memories permit older infants to distinguish familiar events from strange ones better than they could before.

**Stranger anxiety**
The infant's expression of fear in response to unfamiliar adults. Appears in many babies after 7 months of age.

## Recognizing and Responding to the Emotions of Others

Infants' emotional expressions are closely tied to their ability to recognize and respond to the feelings of others. In Chapter 5, we noted that between 2 and 3 months, babies begin to inspect the internal features of faces. Around this time, they respond in kind to an adult's facial expression, spontaneously matching it in feeling tone. When the mother smiles and gently talks, babies react with interest and joy. When she displays a depressed, frozen gaze, they show sadness and look away. And when she expresses anger, infants are likely to respond with angry sounds, facial gestures, and body movements (Haviland & Lelwica, 1987; Tronick, 1989).

These observations reveal that from an early age, babies recognize and interpret emotional signals in meaningful ways, a capacity that improves over the first year (Termine & Izard, 1988). Once infants become competent at reading the emotional expressions of others, they engage in **social referencing,** in which they actively seek information about a trusted person's feelings when faced with an uncertain situation. Beginning at 8 to 10 months, when infants start to evaluate events with regard to their safety and security, social referencing occurs often. Many studies show that the mother's feeling state (happiness, fear, or anger) influences whether a 1-year-old will show wariness of strangers, play with an unfamiliar toy, or cross the deep side of the visual cliff (Hornik, Risenhoover, & Gunnar, 1987; Sorce et al., 1985; Walden & Ogan, 1988).

Social referencing provides infants with a powerful means of learning about the world through indirect experience. By recognizing and responding to caregivers' emotional cues, babies can avoid harmful situations (such as a shock from an electric outlet or a fall down a steep staircase) without first experiencing their unpleasant consequences. And through social referencing, parents teach their newly crawling and walking youngsters, whose capacity to explore the environment is rapidly expanding, how to react to a great many novel events.

## The Emergence of Complex Emotions

Besides basic emotions, human beings are capable of a second, higher-order set of feelings, including shame, embarrassment, guilt, envy, and pride. These are called **complex emotions** because each blends two or more basic emotional states. In addition, complex emotions always involve injury to or enhancement of our sense of self. For example, when we are ashamed or embarrassed, we feel negatively about ourselves, and we seem to experience sadness, anger, and fear at the same time (Campos et al., 1983).

Complex emotions first appear in the second year of life, as the sense of self emerges and toddlers become capable of combining separate emotions, in much the same way that they put together Piagetian sensorimotor schemes. By 18 months, children can be seen feeling ashamed and embarrassed as they lower their eyes, hang their heads, and hide their faces with their hands. Guilt and pride are present by age 3 (Lewis et al., 1989; Sroufe, 1979). But besides self-awareness and the capacity to experience several basic emotions at once, complex emotions require an additional ingredient: adult instruction in *when* to feel proud, ashamed, or guilty. Parents begin to provide this tutoring early, when they say to the toddler and preschooler, "My, look at how far you can throw that ball!" or "Shame on you for grabbing that toy from Billy!"

As these comments indicate, complex emotions play an important role in helping children acquire socially valued behaviors and goals. It is not surprising that the situations in which adults encourage children to experience these feelings vary considerably from culture to culture. In the United States, children are taught to feel pride over personal achievement—throwing a ball the farthest, winning a game, and (later

**Social referencing**

Relying on a trusted person's emotional reaction to decide how to respond to an uncertain situation.

**Complex emotions**

Emotions that blend two or more basic emotional states and involve injury to or enhancement of the sense of self. Examples are shame, embarrassment, guilt, envy, and pride.

*Among the !Kung of Botswana, Africa, very young children are encouraged to help and share. Perhaps this toddler already feels a sense of pride as she tries to assist her grandmother with food preparation. (Konner/Anthro-Photo)*

on) getting good grades. Among the Zuni Indians, shame and embarrassment occur in response to purely personal success, while pride is evoked by generosity, helpfulness, and sharing (Benedict, 1934a).

## The Beginnings of Emotional Self-Regulation

Besides expanding their range of emotional reactions, infants and toddlers begin to find ways to manage their emotional experiences. **Emotional self-regulation** refers to the strategies we use to adjust our emotional state to a comfortable level of intensity (Dodge, 1989; Thompson, 1990a). If you drank a cup of coffee to wake yourself up this morning, reminded yourself that an anxiety-provoking event would be over soon, or decided not to see a horror film because it might frighten you, you were engaging in emotional self-regulation.

In the early months of life, infants have only a limited capacity to regulate their emotional states. Although they can turn away from unpleasant stimulation and mouth and suck when their feelings get too intense, they are easily overwhelmed by internal and external stimuli. As a result, they depend on the soothing interventions of caregivers—lifting the distressed infant to the shoulder, rocking, and talking softly—for help in adjusting their emotional reactions.

Rapid development of the cortex (see Chapter 5) gradually increases the baby's tolerance for stimulation. Between 2 and 4 months, caregivers start to build on this capacity by initiating face-to-face play and attention to objects. In these rich interactional sequences in which emotional signals are exchanged, parents arouse pleasure in the baby while adjusting the pace of their own behavior so the infant does not become overwhelmed and distressed. As a result, the baby's tolerance for stimulation increases further (Kopp, 1989). By the end of the first year, infants' ability to move about permits them to regulate feelings more effectively by approaching or retreating from various stimuli.

As caregivers help infants regulate their emotional states, they also provide lessons in socially approved ways of expressing feelings. Beginning in the first few months, mothers match their baby's positive feelings far more often than the negative

**Emotional self-regulation**
Strategies for adjusting our emotional state to a comfortable level of intensity.

ones. In this way, they encourage happiness and discourage anger and sadness. Interestingly, boys get much more of this training than do girls. Mothers respond less often to a baby boy's cries of distress than to a girl's. The well-known sex difference— females as emotionally expressive and males as emotionally controlled—is promoted at a very tender age (Malatesta & Haviland, 1982; Malatesta et al., 1986).

By the second year, growth in representation and language leads to new ways of regulating emotions. The 18- to 24-month-old has already acquired many words for talking about feelings, such as "happy," "love," "surprised," "scary," "yucky," and "mad" (Bretherton et al., 1986; Dunn, Bretherton, & Munn, 1987). By describing their emotions, toddlers can guide the caregiver in ways that help them feel better. For example, when 2-year-old Rachel listened in on a story about monsters that Lisa was reading to Byron, she was able to tell her mother that she felt afraid:

Rachel (whining): Mommy!
Beth: What's wrong, Rachel?
Rachel: Scary.
Beth: What? The book?
Rachel: Yes. Scary book. Put away.
Beth: We can't put it away yet. Byron's looking at it.
Rachel (walking toward her mother, about to cry): Hug Rachel.

Toddlers' use of words to label feelings shows that they already have a remarkable understanding of themselves and others as emotional beings. As we will see in later chapters, development of this ability to think about feelings leads emotional self-regulation to improve greatly during early and middle childhood.

*BRIEF REVIEW*    Changes in infants' ability to express emotion and respond to the emotions of others reflect their developing cognitive capacities and serve social as well as survival functions. The social smile appears between 6 and 10 weeks, laughter around 3 to 4 months. Anger and fear gradually increase over the first year, showing a sharp rise after 7 months. Young infants match the feeling tone of their caregivers' emotional expressions. By 8 to 10 months, they engage in social referencing, actively seeking information about the caregiver's feelings when faced with an uncertain situation. Complex emotions, such as shame, embarrassment, and pride, begin to emerge in the second year as toddlers combine basic emotions and develop self-awareness. Emotional self-regulation is supported by brain maturation, improvements in cognition and language, and sensitive child-rearing practices.

## TEMPERAMENT AND DEVELOPMENT

Throughout the first year, Byron, Rachel, and April each showed joy, anger, sadness, fear, interest, and higher or lower activity levels in certain situations. But as I got to know them well, their unique patterns of emotional responding became apparent. Byron was constantly in motion. As early as the first few weeks of life, he wriggled about in his crib and squirmed vigorously on the diaper table. When he crawled and walked, his parents found themselves repeatedly chasing after him as he dropped one toy, moved on to the next, and climbed on chairs and tables. Lisa envied Beth's calm, relaxed experience with Rachel. At 7 months, she managed to sit through a lengthy family celebration at a restaurant, remaining contentedly in her high chair for almost two hours. And April's sociability was unmistakable to everyone who met her. She smiled and laughed at adults and was especially at ease in the company of other children, whom she readily approached during the second year.

When we describe one person as cheerful and upbeat, another as active and energetic, and still others as calm, cautious, or prone to angry outbursts, we are

• *Dana is planning to meet her 10-month-old niece Laureen for the first time. How should Dana expect Laureen to react? How would you advise Dana to go about establishing a positive relationship with Laureen?*

• *One of Byron's favorite games was dancing with his mother while she sang "Old MacDonald," clapping his hands and stepping from side-to-side. At 14 months, Byron danced joyfully as Beth and Felicia watched. At 20 months, he began to show signs of embarrassment—smiling, looking away, and covering his eyes with his hands. What explains this change in Byron's emotional behavior?*

referring to **temperament**—stable individual differences in quality and intensity of emotional reaction (Goldsmith, 1987). Researchers have become increasingly interested in temperamental differences among infants and children, since the child's style of emotional responding is believed to form the cornerstone of the adult personality.

The New York Longitudinal Study, initiated in 1956 by Alexander Thomas and Stella Chess, is the most comprehensive and longest-lasting study of temperament to date. A total of 141 children were followed from the first few months of life over a period that now extends well into adulthood. Results showed that temperament is a major factor in increasing the chances that a child will experience psychological problems or, alternatively, be protected from the effects of a highly stressful home life. However, Thomas and Chess (1977) also found that temperament is not fixed and unchangeable. Parenting practices can modify children's emotional styles considerably.

These findings inspired a growing body of research on temperament, including its stability, its biological roots, and its interaction with child-rearing experiences. But before we review what is known about these issues, let's look at how temperament is measured.

## Measuring Temperament

Temperament is usually assessed in one of three ways: through interviews and questionnaires given to parents; through behavior ratings by doctors, nurses, or caregivers who know the child well; or through direct observation by researchers (Bates, 1987). Sometimes, physiological measures are used to supplement these techniques. For example, we will see later that heart rate, pupil dilation, and muscle tension in response to unfamiliar events distinguish highly inhibited, shy youngsters from their very sociable counterparts (Kagan & Snidman, 1991).

Most often, parental reports are used to assess temperament because parents have a depth of knowledge about the child that cannot be matched by any other source. Information from parents has been criticized for being biased and subjective, but it is useful for understanding the way parents view and respond to their child (Sirignano & Lachman, 1985). And when parents describe a baby as extreme in some aspect of temperament, independent observations usually confirm their judgments. For example, babies regarded as irritable and difficult by their mothers do show high levels of fussing and crying (Worobey & Blajda, 1989).

In the New York Longitudinal Study, detailed descriptions of each child's behavior were collected regularly from parents. When carefully analyzed, these yielded 9 dimensions of temperament, which are summarized in Table 7.1. The researchers noticed that certain traits clustered together, producing three types of children that described a large part of their sample:

- The **easy child** (40 percent of the sample): This child quickly establishes regular routines in infancy, is generally cheerful, and adapts easily to new experiences.
- The **difficult child** (10 percent of the sample): This child is irregular in daily routines, is slow to accept new experiences, and tends to react negatively and intensely.
- The **slow-to-warm-up child** (15 percent of the sample): This child is inactive, shows mild, low-key reactions to environmental stimuli, is negative in mood, and adjusts slowly when faced with new experiences.

Notice that 35 percent of the children did not fit any of these patterns. Instead, they showed unique blends of temperamental characteristics. Although other systems for classifying temperament do exist (Buss & Plomin, 1984; Rothbart, 1981), these nine dimensions and three styles provide a fairly complete picture of the traits most often studied.

**Temperament**

Stable individual differences in quality and intensity of emotional reaction.

**Easy child**

A child whose temperament is such that he or she quickly establishes regular routines in infancy, is generally cheerful, and adapts easily to new experiences.

**Difficult child**

A child whose temperament is such that he or she is irregular in daily routines, is slow to accept new experiences, and tends to react negatively and intensely.

**Slow-to-warm-up child**

A child whose temperament is such that he or she is inactive, shows mild, low-key reactions to environmental stimuli, is negative in mood, and adjusts slowly when faced with new experiences.

TABLE 7.1 • Nine Dimensions of Temperament

| Dimension | Description and Example |
|---|---|
| Activity level | Proportion of active periods to inactive ones. Some babies are always in motion. Others move about very little. |
| Rhythmicity | Regularity of body functions. Some infants fall asleep, wake up, get hungry, and have bowel movements on a regular schedule, while others are much less predictable. |
| Distractibility | Degree to which stimulation from the environment alters behavior. Some hungry babies stop crying temporarily if offered a pacifier or a toy to play with. Others continue to cry until fed. |
| Approach/withdrawal | Response to a new object or person. Some babies accept new foods and smile and babble at strangers, while others pull back and cry on first exposure. |
| Adaptability | Ease with which the child adapts to changes in the environment. Although some infants withdraw when faced with a new experience, they quickly adapt, accepting the new food or person on the next occasion. Others continue to fuss and cry over an extended period of time. |
| Attention span and persistence | Amount of time devoted to an activity. Some babies watch a mobile or play with a toy for a long time, while others lose interest after a few minutes. |
| Intensity of reaction | Intensity or energy level of response. Some infants laugh and cry loudly, while others react only mildly. |
| Threshold of responsiveness | Intensity of stimulation required to evoke a response. Some babies startle at the slightest change in sound or lighting. Others take little notice of these changes in stimulation. |
| Quality of mood | Amount of friendly, joyful behavior as opposed to unpleasant, unfriendly behavior. Some babies smile and laugh frequently when playing and interacting with people. Others fuss and cry often. |

*Source:* Thomas, Chess, & Birch, 1970.

*Alexander Thomas*

*Stella Chess*

*Alexander Thomas and Stella Chess initiated the New York Longitudinal Study, a comprehensive investigation of temperament in which 141 children were followed from infancy into adulthood. Thomas and Chess's groundbreaking methods and findings inspired a burst of research on the role of temperament in development. (Courtesy of Stella Chess and Alexander Thomas)*

## The Stability of Temperament

It would be difficult to claim that something like temperament really exists if children's emotional styles were not stable over time. Indeed, the findings of many studies provide support for the long-term stability of temperament. An infant who scores low or high on attention span, activity level, irritability, sociability, or shyness is likely to respond in a similar way when assessed again in childhood and, occasionally, even into the adult years (Caspi, Elder, & Bem, 1987, 1988; Goldsmith & Gottesman, 1981; Kagan & Moss, 1962; Kagan, 1989; Korner et al., 1981; Riese, 1987; Ruff et al., 1990).

When the evidence as a whole is examined carefully, however, temperamental stability from one age period to the next is only modest. While quite a few children remain the same, a good number have changed when assessed again a few years later. In fact, some characteristics, such as shyness and sociability, are stable over the long term only in children at the extremes—those who are very inhibited or very outgoing to begin with (Kagan, Reznick, & Gibbons, 1989).

A story that a mother recently told me about her two daughters illustrates the finding that early temperament persists for some but not all youngsters. The older girl, Allie, was active and sociable as a baby and remained so. On moving to a new neighborhood at age 6, she boldly went from house to house knocking on doors, asking if there were any children to play with. Throughout her school years, Allie was a joiner. By the time she graduated from high school, she had been cheerleader, prom queen, president of the senior class, captain of the tennis team, and an active participant in several clubs. In contrast, Allie's younger sister Keri was shy and withdrawn. At age 3, Keri reacted to the move to a new neighborhood by hiding behind her mother when children approached. Throughout middle childhood, she needed time to "warm up"—to new foods, new people, and new challenges in school. But by eighth grade, Keri began to look different. "We were astonished when she tried out for the basketball team and made it, especially since basketball requires so much physical assertiveness," her mother commented. The following year, Keri joined the tennis team and, like her sister, became president of her high school class. Her schoolmates valued her patient, considerate style of relating to others.

The fact that early in life, children show marked individual differences in temperament suggests that biological factors play an important role. At the same time, the changes shown by children like Keri indicate that temperament can be modified by experience. Let's take a close look at genetic and environmental contributions to temperament in the following sections.

### Biological Foundations

The very word *temperament* implies a biological foundation for individual differences in personality. In recent years, many studies have compared identical with fraternal twins to find out if heredity is involved. The findings reveal that identicals are more similar than fraternals across a wide range of temperamental traits (activity level, sociability, intensity of emotional reaction, attention span, and persistence) and personality measures (introversion, extroversion, anxiety, and impulsivity) (Campos et al., 1983; Plomin, 1989; Scarr & Kidd, 1983). In Chapter 2, we indicated that heritability estimates derived from twin studies suggest a moderate role for genetic factors in temperament and personality: About half of the individual differences among us can be traced to differences in our genetic makeup.

New research on the biological basis of shyness provides further support for the importance of heredity. Early in life, children who are cautious and reserved differ in physiological reactions from those who are outgoing and emotionally expressive. Babies who eventually develop into inhibited, withdrawn toddlers show high rates of motor activity, fretting and crying when faced with new sights and sounds (Kagan & Snidman, 1991). By the end of the first year, highly stimulating, unfamiliar experiences (such as a battery-powered robot or a bingo cage filled with noisy, colorful balls) cause their hearts to race, their pupils to dilate, and their muscles to tense up. Under the same conditions, sociable babies remain relaxed and composed. Shy people are also more likely to have certain physical traits—blue eyes, thin faces, and hay fever—known to be influenced by heredity. Researchers believe that the genes controlling these characteristics may also contribute to a fearful, reactive temperamental style (Kagan, Reznick, & Snidman, 1988).

Finally, racial and sex differences in early temperament exist, again implying a role for heredity. Compared to Caucasian infants, Chinese and Japanese babies tend to be calmer, more easily soothed when upset, and better at quieting themselves (Caudill & Frost, 1975; Freedman, 1976). Rachel's capacity to remain contentedly seated in her high chair through a long family dinner certainly fits with this evidence. And Byron's high rate of activity is consistent with sex differences in emotional styles. From an early age, boys tend to be more active and daring than girls—a difference reflected in boys' higher accident rates throughout childhood and adolescence (Jacklin & Maccoby, 1983; Richardson, Koller, & Katz, 1986).

## Environmental Influences

Although hereditary influences on temperament are clear, no study has shown that infants maintain their early emotional styles in the absence of environmental supports. Instead, heredity and environment combine to strengthen the stability of temperament, since (as we saw in Chapter 2), the child's approach to the world affects the experiences to which she is exposed. To see how this works, let's take a second look at racial and sex differences in temperament.

As I watched Beth care for Rachel as a 3-month-old baby, her calm, soothing manner and use of gentle rocking and touching contrasted with Lisa and Felicia's stimulation of their infants through lively facial expressions and talking. These differences in caregiving appear repeatedly in studies comparing American with Asian infant–mother pairs (Caudill & Frost, 1975; Fogel, Toda, & Kawai, 1988; Otaki et al., 1986). The findings suggest that some differences in early temperament are encouraged by cultural beliefs and practices. When Japanese mothers are asked about their approach to child rearing, they respond that babies come into the world as independent beings who must learn to rely on their mothers through close physical contact. American mothers are likely to believe just the opposite—that they must wean the baby away from dependence into autonomy (Doi, 1973; Kojima, 1986). As a result, Japanese mothers do more comforting and American mothers more stimulating—behaviors that enhance early temperamental differences between their infants.

A similar process seems to be at work as far as sex differences in temperament are concerned. Within the first 24 hours after birth (before they could have had much experience with the baby), parents already perceive male and female newborns differently. Sons are rated as larger, better coordinated, more alert, and stronger. Daughters are viewed as softer, more awkward, weaker, and more delicate (Rubin, Provenzano, & Luria, 1974). These sex-typed beliefs carry over into the way parents treat their infants and toddlers. For example, parents more often encourage infant sons to be physically active and daughters to seek help and physical closeness. These practices promote and sustain temperamental differences between boys and girls (Fagot, 1978; Smith & Lloyd, 1978).

In families with several children, an additional influence on temperament is at work. Parents often look for and emphasize each child's unique characteristics (Plomin, 1989). You can see this in the comments parents make after the birth of a second baby: "He's so much calmer," "She's a lot more active," or "He's more sociable." Research shows that when one child in a family is viewed as easy, another is likely to be perceived as difficult, even though the second child might not be very difficult when compared to children in general (Schachter & Stone, 1985). Each child, in turn, evokes responses from caregivers that are consistent with parental views and with the youngster's actual temperamental style. These findings demonstrate that temperament and personality can only be understood in terms of complex interdependencies between genetic and environmental factors.

## Temperament and Child Rearing: The Goodness-of-Fit Model

We have already indicated that the temperaments of many children do change over time. For example, only half of shy, slow-to-warm-up babies like Keri will remain so at age 6. Even fewer will qualify as timid and withdrawn by the time they reach young adulthood, although these children rarely become highly sociable. This suggests that environments do not always act in the same direction as a child's temperament. In fact, if a child's disposition interferes with learning or getting along with others, it is important for adults to gently but consistently counteract the child's maladaptive behavior.

The concept of **goodness-of-fit** describes how temperament and environmental pressures can work together to produce favorable outcomes (Thomas & Chess, 1977). Goodness-of-fit involves creating child-rearing environments that recognize each child's temperament while helping the youngster achieve more adaptive functioning. In short, children with different temperaments have unique child-rearing needs. In the case of sociable Allie, a neighborhood rich in playmates was sufficient for her to reach out and develop rewarding friendships. But Keri's inhibited behavior required quite different handling. In infancy, her parents needed to sit quietly by, slowly drawing her into interaction with other people. And during the preschool years, surrounding her with several children at once was overwhelming. She needed one playmate at a time, help from adults in getting an activity started, and several meetings arranged by her mother until she felt comfortable with the new child. Had Keri been forced into social situations or criticized for her shyness, she might not have developed into the self-confident, popular youngster that she eventually became by early adolescence.

As Box 7.1 indicates, parenting that is in tune with the child's temperament is particularly important for difficult youngsters, who are at special risk for adjustment problems. The concept of goodness-of-fit reminds us that babies come into the world with unique dispositions that adults need to accept. Children cannot be molded in ways that do not blend with their basic styles. This means that parents can neither take full credit for their children's virtues nor be blamed for all their faults—attitudes that were common a generation ago. But parents can turn an environment that exaggerates a child's difficulties into one that builds on the youngster's strengths, helping each child master the challenges of development.

In the following sections, we will see that goodness-of-fit is also at the heart of infant–caregiver attachment. This first intimate social relationship grows out of interaction between parent and baby, to which the emotional styles of both partners contribute.

*BRIEF REVIEW*  Children's unique temperamental styles are apparent in early infancy. The long-term stability of temperament is only moderate. Some children retain their original dispositions, while others change over time. Heredity influences early temperament, but child-rearing experiences determine whether a child's emotional style is sustained or modified over time. A good fit between parenting practices and child temperament helps children whose temperaments predispose them to adjustment problems achieve more adaptive functioning.

## THE DEVELOPMENT OF ATTACHMENT

**Attachment** is the strong, affectional tie we feel for special people in our lives that leads us to feel pleasure and joy when we interact with them and to be comforted by their nearness during times of stress. By the end of the first year, infants have become attached to familiar people who have responded to their needs for physical care and stimulation. Watch babies of this age, and notice how the mother is singled out for special attention. A whole range of responses is reserved just for her. As she enters the room, the baby breaks into a broad, friendly smile. When she picks him up, he pats her face, explores her hair, and snuggles against her body. When he feels anxious or afraid, he crawls into her lap and clings closely.

Freud first suggested that the infant's emotional tie to the mother provides the foundation for all later relationships. We will see shortly that research on children deprived of an early, warm caregiving relationship supports Freud's belief in the

---

• *At age 18 months, highly active Byron climbed out of his high chair long before his meal was finished. Exasperated with Byron's behavior, his father made him sit at the table until he had eaten all his food. Soon Byron's behavior escalated into a full-blown tantrum. Using the concept of goodness-of-fit, suggest another way of handling Byron.*

**Goodness-of-fit**

An effective match between child-rearing practices and a child's temperament, leading to favorable adjustment.

**Attachment**

The strong, affectional tie that humans feel toward special people in their lives.

## FROM RESEARCH TO PRACTICE

### Box 7.1   Difficult Children: When Parents Establish a "Good Fit"

*I*n the New York Longitudinal Study, 70 percent of children who were temperamentally difficult in the early years developed serious behavior problems by middle childhood. But in no case was this outcome the result of temperament alone. Instead, it occurred because the negative behaviors of difficult children often provoked parental reactions that fit poorly with their basic dispositions. The case of Carl, one of the most difficult youngsters in the New York Longitudinal sample, shows how long-term outcomes for these children are a function of rearing experiences (Thomas & Chess, 1977).

As a baby, Carl rejected almost all new situations, such as his first bath and spoonfuls of solid food. He shrieked, cried, and struggled to get away. Yet his mother and father recognized that his behavior did not mean that they were "bad parents." To the contrary, Carl's father viewed his emotional intensity as a sign of strength and vigor. And both parents believed that if they were patient, reduced the number of new situations that Carl had to deal with at one time, and provided him with opportunities for repeated exposure, he would, in the end, adapt positively.

By the time Carl reached school age, he was doing remarkably well. The energies that he put into rebellious tantrums were now channeled constructively. He was a good student and became enthusiastically involved in several activities. One of these was playing the piano—lessons that he had asked for but (as with other new experiences) at first disliked intensely. Carl's mother had granted his request for piano instruction on one condition: that he stick to the lessons for 6 months. Held to this bargain, Carl came to love his introduction to music. His parents' patience and consistency had helped him reorganize his behavior, accept and benefit from new learning opportunities, and avoid adjustment difficulties.

Unfortunately, many difficult children are not as lucky as Carl. As infants, they are far less likely than easy babies to get sensitive care (Crockenberg, 1986). By the second year, parents of difficult children often resort to angry, punitive discipline. In response, the child reacts with defiance and disobedience (Lee & Bates, 1985). The difficult child's temperament combined with harsh, inconsistent child rearing form a poor fit that maintains and even increases the child's irritable, conflict-ridden style.

Harmony between rearing environments and child temperament is best accomplished early, before unfavorable temperament–environment relationships have had a chance to produce adjustment problems that are hard to undo. Parents of difficult infants and toddlers, especially, can benefit from interventions that encourage them to be warm and accepting while making firm, reasonable, and consistent demands for mastering new experiences and situations.

importance of the attachment bond. But attachment has also been the subject of intense theoretical debate for decades. Behaviorist and psychoanalytic theories were early views that competed with one another to explain how attachment developed. The problems with these theories eventually led to a new perspective, ethological theory, which is most popular today. As we take up each of these viewpoints, you may find it helpful to refer to the summary provided in Table 7.2.

### Theories of Attachment

**Behaviorism.**   Behaviorists believe that infants' attachment behaviors—seeking closeness to the mother, following her about, and crying and calling in her absence—are learned responses. The best-known behaviorist account is a **drive reduction** explanation that grants feeding a central role in the infant–mother relationship. As the baby's hunger (*primary drive*) is satisfied repeatedly by the mother, her presence becomes a *secondary or learned drive* because it is paired with tension relief. As a result,

**Drive reduction account of attachment**

A behaviorist view that regards the mother's satisfaction of the baby's hunger (primary drive) as the basis for the infant's preference for her (secondary drive).

TABLE 7.2 • Three Theories of Attachment

| Theory | Description |
|---|---|
| Drive reduction (behaviorism) | As the mother satisfies the baby's hunger (primary drive), her presence is paired with tension relief and becomes a secondary or learned drive. This theory has been discredited by evidence indicating that babies become attached to people who do not feed them. |
| Psychoanalytic | From warm, sensitive care, babies develop a sense of trust and a positive, inner image of the mother that enables them to separate from her and explore their world. This explanation has been criticized for placing too much emphasis on feeding and too little on the baby's contribution to the attachment bond. |
| Ethological | Attachment has evolved over the history of our species to promote survival, and both infant characteristics and quality of caregiving contribute to it. Babies move through four phases of development in which they develop a strong affectional tie to a familiar caregiver. |

*Baby monkeys reared with "surrogate mothers" from birth preferred to cling to a soft terry cloth "mother" instead of a wire mesh "mother" that held a bottle. These findings reveal that the drive reduction explanation of attachment, which assumes that the mother–infant relationship is based on feeding, is not correct.* (Martin Rogers/Stock Boston)

the baby learns to prefer all kinds of stimuli that accompany feeding, including the mother's soft caresses, warm smiles, and tender words of comfort (Sears, Maccoby, & Levin, 1957).

Although feeding is an important context in which mothers and babies build a close relationship, today we know that the attachment bond does not depend on satisfying an infant's hunger. In the 1950s, a famous study of rhesus monkeys proved the drive reduction explanation to be wrong. Baby monkeys separated from their mothers at birth and reared with terry cloth and wire mesh "surrogate mothers" spent their days clinging to the terry cloth substitute, even though the wire mesh "mother" held the bottle and infants had to climb on it to be fed. The baby monkeys preferred the terry cloth (which resembled the soft body of a monkey mother), even though it had never been paired with feeding (Harlow & Zimmerman, 1959). Observations of human infants reveal that they become attached to family members who seldom if ever feed them, including fathers, siblings, and grandparents (Schaffer & Emerson, 1964). And perhaps you have noticed that toddlers, at least in Western cultures, develop strong emotional ties to cuddly objects, such as blankets and teddy bears (see Box 7.2). Yet such objects have never played a role in infant feeding!

A second problem with the drive reduction account is that it cannot explain why the attachment relationship, once formed, tends to persist over long periods in which attachment figures are absent. Think about your own feelings of attachment for people whom you have not seen (and been reinforced by) in many months. Behaviorism would predict that your desire for closeness should *extinguish,* or disappear. Yet clearly it does not. Drive reduction has great difficulty in explaining the remarkable endurance of human attachments over time and space.

***The Psychoanalytic Perspective.*** Psychoanalytic theories, such as Erikson's and Mahler's, emphasize that the central ingredient in attachment is *the quality of the mother's interaction* with her baby. Once the infant develops a sense of trust that the mother will satisfy his needs, he can separate from her for short periods to explore the environment. Eventually the child forms a permanent, positive inner image of the mother that can be relied on for emotional support during brief absences.

Compared to behaviorism, the psychoanalytic approach provides a much richer view of the attachment bond, viewing it as critical for exploration of the environment,

# CULTURAL INFLUENCES

### Box 7.2   *Young Children's Attachment to Soft Objects*

W hen Bruce was born, he received a soft, cuddly Pooh Bear—bright yellow with a red vest and a warm, smiling face. During his first few months, Bruce's mother made the bear nod and dance before his eyes. Soon Bruce laughed merrily at the bear's antics. The bear remained a favorite source of amusement for mother and baby throughout the first year.

When Bruce walked at 12 months, his interest in nursing at his mother's breast declined while his enthusiasm for exploration increased. At the same time, Pooh Bear became a special toy, accompanying Bruce everywhere he went during the day as well as to bed at night. During moments of fatigue and frustration, Bruce pressed the bear against his face and stroked it with his fingers, as if to substitute for the warm closeness he felt when cradled in his mother's arms.

The importance to small children of special objects, such as blankets, teddy bears, and other cuddly toys, has long been recognized by parents. Such attachments are highly frequent in Western cultures, where babies sleep in a separate room at night and experience frequent daytime separations from their

mothers. In contrast, objects of attachment are entirely absent in village and tribal societies in which caregivers are continuously available to infants (Gaddini & Gaddini, 1970; Hong & Townes, 1976). This suggests that soft objects help children manage the stress of maternal separation and serve as substitutes for special people when they are not available. In support of this idea, research shows that toddlers use attachment objects as a secure base of exploration in a strange playroom, in much the same way that they depend on their mothers for support when exposed to unfamiliar environments (Passman, 1976).

Soft, cuddly toys are normal and effective sources of security during a developmental period in which children increase their physical and psychological separateness from parents. Object-attached children are just as well-adjusted as other youngsters (Mahalski, Silva, & Spears, 1985; Passman, 1987). And almost half of those who form such attachments as infants and toddlers still display them during middle childhood (Sherman et al., 1981). No harm results from allowing a child who so chooses to become dependent on a cuddly comforter.

cognitive mastery, and a sense of emotional security. Psychoanalytic theories also recognize that deep affectional bonds, once formed, can endure over separations from loved individuals.

Despite its strengths, the psychoanalytic perspective has been criticized on two grounds. First, because it builds on Freud's oral stage, (like behaviorism) it overemphasizes the importance of feeding in the attachment bond. Second, if you return to Erikson's and Mahler's theories at the beginning of this chapter, you will see that a great deal is said about the mother's contribution to the attachment relationship. But much less attention is given to the importance of the infant's characteristics and behavior. Ethological theory is unique in recognizing that babies contribute actively to ties established with their parents.

*Bowlby's Ethological Theory.*   Today, **ethological theory of attachment** is the most widely accepted view of the infant's emotional tie to the caregiver. Recall from Chapter 1 that according to ethology, many human behaviors have evolved over the history of our species because they promote survival. John Bowlby (1969), who first applied this idea to the infant–caregiver bond, was originally a psychoanalyst. As you will see shortly, his theory retains a number of psychoanalytic features. At the same time, Bowlby was inspired by Konrad Lorenz's studies of imprinting in baby geese (see Chapter 1). He believed that the human baby, like the young of other animal species, is endowed with a set of built-in behaviors that help keep the parent nearby, increasing the chances that the infant will be protected from danger. Contact with

**Ethological theory of attachment**

A theory formulated by Bowlby, which views the infant's emotional tie to the familiar caregiver as an evolved response that promotes survival.

*During the phase of "clear-cut" attachment, babies display a clear preference for the familiar caregiver, who serves as a secure base for exploration and a haven of safety to which they can return. (Erika Stone)*

**Separation anxiety**
An infant's distressed reaction to the departure of the familiar caregiver.

**Secure base**
The use of the familiar caregiver as a base from which the infant confidently explores the environment.

the parent also ensures that the baby will be fed, but Bowlby was careful to point out that feeding is not the basis for attachment. Instead, the attachment bond has strong biological roots. It can best be understood within an evolutionary framework in which survival of the species is of utmost importance.

According to Bowlby, the infant's relationship to the parent begins as a set of innate signals that call the adult to the baby's side. Over time, a true affectional bond develops, which is supported by new emotional and cognitive capacities as well as a history of warm, responsive care. The development of attachment takes place in four phases:

1. *The preattachment phase* (birth–6 weeks). A variety of built-in signals— grasping, smiling, crying, and gazing into the adult's eyes—help bring newborn babies into close contact with other human beings. Once an adult responds, infants encourage her to remain nearby, since they are comforted when picked up, stroked, and talked to softly. Babies of this age can recognize their own mother's smell and voice (see Chapter 4). However, they are not yet attached to her, since they do not mind being left in the care of a strange adult.

2. *The "attachment-in-the-making" phase* (6 weeks–6 to 8 months). During this phase, infants start to respond differently to a familiar caregiver than to a stranger. For example, at 4 months, Byron smiled, laughed, and babbled more freely when interacting with his mother and quieted more quickly when she picked him up. As infants engage in face-to-face interaction with the parent and experience relief from distress, they learn that their own actions affect the behavior of those around them. They begin to develop a sense of trust—the expectation that the caregiver will respond when signaled. But babies still do not protest when separated from the parent, despite the fact that they can recognize and distinguish her from unfamiliar people.

3. *The phase of "clear-cut" attachment* (6 to 8 months–18 months to 2 years). Now, attachment to the familiar caregiver is evident. Babies of this phase display **separation anxiety,** in that they become upset when the adult on whom they have come to rely leaves. Separation anxiety appears universally around the world after 6 months of age, increasing until about 15 months (see Figure 7.2). Its appearance suggests that infants have a clear understanding that the caregiver continues to exist when not in view. Consistent with this idea, babies who have not yet mastered Piagetian object permanence usually do not become anxious when separated from their mothers (Lester et al., 1974).

    Besides protesting the parent's departure, older infants and toddlers act more deliberately to maintain her presence. They approach, follow, and climb on her in preference to others. And they use her as a **secure base** from which to explore, venturing into the environment and then returning for emotional support, as we indicated earlier in this chapter.

4. *Formation of a reciprocal relationship* (18 months to 2 years and on). By the end of the second year, rapid growth in representation and language permits toddlers to understand some of the factors that influence the parent's coming and going and to predict her return. As a result, separation protest declines. Now children start to negotiate with the caregiver, using requests and persuasion to alter her goals rather than crawling after and clinging to her. For example, at age 2, April asked Felicia to read a story before leaving her with a babysitter. The extra time with her mother, along with a better understanding of where Felicia was going ("to a movie with Daddy") and when she would be back ("right after you go to sleep"), helped April withstand her mother's absence.

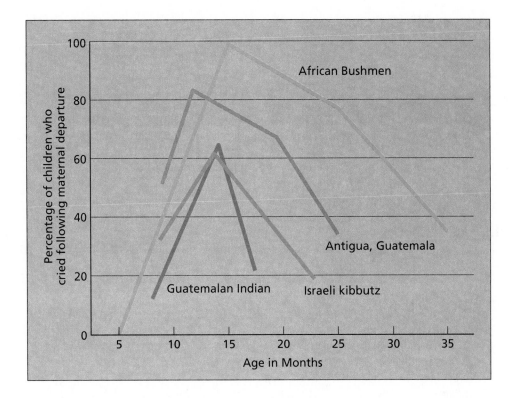

According to Bowlby (1980), out of their experiences during these four phases, children construct an inner representation of the parent–child bond that becomes a vital part of their personalities. This image serves as a model, or guide, for all future interactions—through childhood and adolescence and into adult life (Bretherton, 1990).

*Measuring the Security of Attachment*

Although virtually all family-reared babies become attached to a familiar caregiver by the second year, the quality of this relationship differs greatly from child to child. Some infants appear especially relaxed and secure in the presence of the caregiver; they know they can count on her for protection and support. Others seem more anxious and uncertain. Researchers have developed special methods for assessing attachment security so they can find out what influences it and study its impact on later development.

The **Strange Situation** is the most widely used technique for measuring the quality of attachment between 1 and 2 years of age. In designing it, Mary Ainsworth and her colleagues (1978) reasoned that if the development of attachment has gone along well, infants and toddlers should use the parent as a secure base from which to explore an unfamiliar playroom. In addition, when the parent leaves for a brief period of time, the child should show separation anxiety, and a strange adult should be less comforting than the parent. As summarized in Table 7.3, the Strange Situation takes the baby through eight short episodes in which brief separations from and reunions with the parent take place.

Observing the responses of infants to these episodes, researchers have identified a secure attachment pattern and three patterns of insecurity (Ainsworth et al., 1978; Main & Solomon, 1986). As you read about these four attachment classifications,

**Strange Situation**

A procedure involving short separations from and reunions with the mother that assesses the quality of the attachment bond.

TABLE 7.3 • Episodes in the Strange Situation

| Episode | Events | Attachment Behaviors Observed |
|---------|--------|-------------------------------|
| 1 | Experimenter introduces parent and baby to playroom and then leaves. | |
| 2 | Parent is seated while baby plays with toys. | Parent as a secure base |
| 3 | Stranger enters, is seated, and talks to parent. | Reaction to unfamiliar adult |
| 4 | Parent leaves room. Stranger responds to baby and offers comfort if upset. | Separation anxiety |
| 5 | Parent returns, greets baby, and if necessary offers comfort. Stranger leaves room. | Reaction to reunion |
| 6 | Parent leaves room. | Separation anxiety |
| 7 | Stranger enters room and offers comfort. | Ability to be soothed by stranger |
| 8 | Parent returns, greets baby, if necessary offers comfort, and tries to reinterest baby in toys. | Reaction to reunion |

*Source:* Ainsworth et al., 1978.
*Note:* Each episode lasts about 3 minutes. Separation episodes are cut short if baby becomes very upset. Reunion episodes are extended if baby needs more time to calm down and return to play.

see if you can identify the one that Rachel displayed, described at the beginning of this chapter.

- **Secure attachment.** These infants use the parent as a secure base from which to explore. When separated, they may or may not cry, but if they do, it is due to the parent's absence, since they show a strong preference for her over the stranger. When the parent returns, they actively seek contact, and their crying is reduced immediately.

- **Avoidant attachment.** These babies seem unresponsive to the parent when she is present. When she leaves, they are usually not distressed, and they react to the stranger in much the same way as the parent. During reunion, they avoid or are slow to greet the parent, and when picked up, they often fail to cling.

- **Resistant attachment.** Before separation, these infants seek closeness to the parent and often fail to explore. When she returns, they display angry, resistive behavior, sometimes hitting and pushing. In addition, many continue to cry after being picked up and cannot be easily comforted.

- **Disorganized/disoriented attachment.** This pattern seems to reflect the greatest insecurity. At reunion these infants show a variety of confused, contradictory behaviors. For example, they might look away while being held by the parent, approach her with a flat, depressed gaze, or cry out unexpectedly after having calmed down.

## Cultural Variations

Infants' reactions in the Strange Situation closely resemble their behavior when faced with parental separations in everyday life (Blanchard & Main, 1979). For this reason, the procedure has proved to be a powerful tool for assessing attachment security. However, cross-cultural evidence indicates that infants' responses may have to be interpreted differently in other cultures. For example, as Figure 7.3 indicates, German

**Secure attachment**
The quality of attachment characterizing infants who are distressed by maternal separation and easily comforted by the mother when she returns.

**Avoidant attachment**
The quality of insecure attachment characterizing infants who are usually not distressed by maternal separation and who avoid the mother when she returns.

**Resistant attachment**
The quality of insecure attachment characterizing infants who remain close to the mother before departure and display angry, resistive behavior when she returns.

**Disorganized/disoriented attachment**
The quality of insecure attachment characterizing infants who respond in a confused, contradictory fashion when reunited with their mothers.

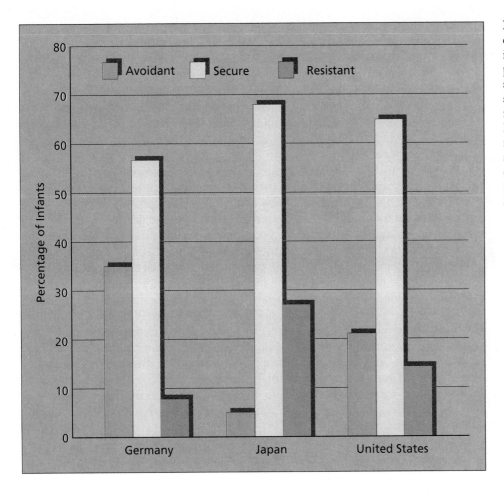

**FIGURE 7.3** • A cross-cultural comparison of infants' reactions in the Strange Situation. A high percentage of German babies seem avoidantly attached, while a substantial number of Japanese infants appear resistantly attached. Note that these responses may not reflect true insecurity. Instead, they are probably due to cultural differences in rearing practices. *(Adapted from van IJzendoorn & Kroonenberg, 1988.)*

infants show considerably more avoidant attachment than American babies do. But German parents encourage their infants to be nonclingy and independent, so the baby's behavior may be an intended outcome of cultural beliefs and practices (Grossmann et al., 1985). Did you classify Rachel's attachment behavior as resistant? An unusually high number of Japanese infants display a resistant response, but the reaction may not represent true insecurity. Japanese mothers rarely leave their babies in the care of unfamiliar people, so the Strange Situation probably creates far greater stress for them than it does for infants who frequently experience maternal separations (Miyake, Chen, & Campos, 1985; Takahashi, 1990). Despite these cultural variations, the secure pattern is still the most common attachment classification in all societies studied to date (van IJzendoorn & Kroonenberg, 1988).

### Factors that Affect Attachment Security

What factors might influence attachment security? First, simply having an opportunity to establish a close relationship with one or a few caregivers should be critically important. Second, warm, sensitive parenting should lead to greater attachment security. Third, since babies actively contribute to the attachment relationship, an infant's characteristics should make a difference in how well it proceeds. And finally, because children and parents are embedded in larger contexts, family circumstances should influence attachment quality. In the following sections, we examine each of these factors.

*Maternal Deprivation.*    The powerful effect of the baby's affectional tie to the mother is most evident when it is absent. In a series of landmark studies, René Spitz (1945, 1946) observed institutionalized babies who had been given up by their mothers between the third month and the end of the first year. The infants were placed on a large ward where they shared a nurse with at least seven other babies. In contrast to the happy, outgoing behavior they had shown before separation, they wept and withdrew from their surroundings, lost weight, and had difficulty sleeping. If a caregiver whom the baby could get to know did not replace the mother, the depression deepened rapidly.

According to Spitz, institutionalized infants experienced emotional difficulties not because they were separated from their mothers, but because they were prevented from forming a bond with one or a few adults. Other findings support this conclusion. In a recent longitudinal study, researchers followed the development of infants reared in an institution that offered a good caregiver/child ratio and a rich selection of books and toys. However, staff turnover was so rapid that the average child had a total of 50 different caregivers by the age of 4 1/2! Many of these children became "late adoptees" who were placed in homes after age 4. Since most developed deep ties with their adoptive parents, this study indicates that a first attachment bond can develop as late as 4 to 6 years of age, and perhaps even later. But throughout childhood and adolescence, these youngsters were more likely to display emotional and social problems, including an excessive desire for adult attention, "overfriendliness" to strange adults and peers, and difficulties in establishing friendships (Hodges & Tizard, 1989; Tizard & Hodges, 1978; Tizard & Rees, 1975). Although follow-ups into adulthood are necessary to be sure, these results leave open the possibility that fully normal development depends on establishing close bonds with caregivers during the first few years of life.

*Quality of Caregiving.*    Even when infants experience the closeness of one or a few caregivers, parental behavior that is insensitive to their signals and needs should lead to insecure attachment. To test this idea, researchers have related various aspects of maternal caregiving to the quality of the attachment bond. The findings of many studies reveal that securely attached infants have mothers who respond promptly to infant signals and handle their babies tenderly and carefully. In contrast, insecurely attached infants have mothers who dislike physical contact, handle them awkwardly, and behave in a "routine" manner when meeting the infant's needs (Ainsworth et al., 1978; Belsky, Rovine, & Taylor, 1984; Kiser et al., 1986).

Exactly what is it that mothers of securely attached babies do to support their infant's feelings of trust? To find out, investigators have videotaped thousands of hours of mother–infant interaction, carefully coding it for each partner's behavior toward the other. They have discovered that a special form of communication called **interactional synchrony** separates the experiences of secure from insecure babies (Isabella & Belsky, 1991). Interactional synchrony is best described as a sensitively tuned emotional dance, in which the mother responds to infant signals in a well-timed, appropriate fashion. In addition, both partners match emotional states, especially the positive ones. Watching Felicia interact with April in this way, I saw her respond to April's excited shaking of a rattle with an enthusiastic "That-a-girl!" When April babbled and looked at her mother, Felicia smiled and spoke expressively in return. When she fussed and cried, Felicia soothed with gentle touches and soft words (Stern, 1985).

It is important to note that exchanges between securely attached babies and their mothers are not always harmonious. In fact, only 30 percent of the time are they perfectly "in sync" with one another. The remaining 70 percent of the time, interactive errors occur, but both mother and baby become skilled at repairing these and returning to a synchronous state. For example, if the mother is momentarily dis-

**Interactional synchrony**

A sensitively tuned "emotional dance," in which the mother responds to infant signals in a well-timed, appropriate fashion and both partners match emotional states, especially the positive ones. Promotes secure attachment.

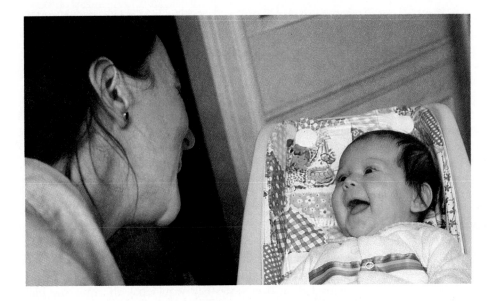

*Interactional synchrony is a sensitively tuned emotional dance in which a mother responds to her baby in a well-timed fashion, and both partners match emotional states, especially the positive ones. This harmonious exchange of emotional signals predicts secure attachment. (Julie O'Neil/The Picture Cube)*

tracted, her infant is likely to whimper and look away. This prompts the mother to turn back to the baby with a direct gaze, a smile, and a comforting sound. Through such exchanges, infants learn that they can control their interactive experiences. And the positive emotional tone that characterizes them extends to other aspects of the baby's life—to enthusiasm for exploring the environment and responsiveness to other people (Tronick, 1989; Tronick, Cohn, & Shea, 1986).

Compared to the experiences of securely attached infants, interactions of insecure babies with their mothers contain much lower rates of synchrony. Avoidant infants tend to have mothers who are overstimulating and intrusive. They might, for example, talk energetically to a baby who is looking away or falling asleep. Resistant infants experience interaction that is at the other extreme. Their mothers are minimally involved in caregiving and unresponsive to infant signals (Isabella & Belsky, 1991; Malatesta et al., 1989). It is as if avoidant babies try to escape from overwhelming, poorly paced interaction that they cannot control, while resistant infants react with anger and frustration to a lack of maternal involvement.

When caregiving is extremely inadequate, it is a powerful predictor of disruptions in attachment. Child abuse and neglect (topics that we will consider in Chapter 10) are associated with all three forms of attachment insecurity. Among maltreated infants, the most worrisome classification—disorganized/disoriented attachment—is especially high (Carlson et al., 1989). Infants of depressed mothers also show the uncertain behaviors of this pattern, mixing closeness, resistance, and avoidance while looking very sad and depressed themselves (Radke-Yarrow et al., 1985).

***Infant Characteristics.***   Since interactional synchrony is the result of a *relationship* that builds between two partners, infant characteristics should affect how easily it is established. Indeed, there is good evidence that this is the case. In Chapters 3 and 4, we saw that prematurity, birth complications, and newborn illness make caregiving more taxing for parents. However, as long as parents have the time and patience to care for a baby with special needs and the infant is not very sick, at-risk newborns fare quite well in the development of attachment security (Easterbrooks, 1989).

Infants also vary considerably in temperament, but the precise role that temperament plays in attachment security has been a matter of considerable debate. Some researchers think that temperament is largely responsible for the way that babies respond in the Strange Situation. They believe, for example, that babies who are irritable and fearful may simply react to brief separations from their mothers with intense anxiety, regardless of the parent's sensitivity to the baby (Kagan, 1989). Recent research, however, indicates that such babies are no more likley to be rated as insecurely attached in the Strange Situation than their calmer, more even-tempered counterparts (Mangelsdorf et al., 1990; Vaughn et al., 1989).

A major reason that temperament does not show a clear-cut relationship with attachment security may be that its influence depends on goodness-of-fit. From this perspective, *many* temperamental characteristics can lead to secure attachment as long as the caregiver sensitively adjusts her behavior to fit the needs of her infant (Sroufe, 1985). But when mothers' capacity to do so is strained—for example, by lack of help and encouragement from husbands, relatives, and friends—then difficult babies are at greater risk for attachment insecurity (Crockenberg, 1981). These findings reveal that conditions of family life have much to do with the kind of relationship that develops between mother and baby.

***Family Circumstances.*** Around April's first birthday, Felicia and her husband Lonnie experienced a period of great emotional strain. Lonnie was laid off his job, and constant arguments with Felicia over how they would pay the monthly bills caused him to leave the family for a time. Although Felicia tried not to let these worries affect her caregiving, April sensed the tension in the air. Several times, Felicia left April at Beth's house while she looked for employment herself. April, who had previously taken separations like these quite well, cried desperately on her mother's departure and clung for a long time after she returned. April's behavior reflects a repeated finding in the attachment literature: When families experience major life changes, such as a shift in employment or marital status, the quality of attachment often changes—sometimes in a positive and at other times in a negative direction (Thompson, Lamb, & Estes, 1982; Vaughn et al., 1989). This is an expected outcome, since family transitions affect parent–child interaction, which, in turn, influences the attachment bond. As Felicia and Lonnie resolved their difficulties, April's clinginess declined and she felt more secure.

Felicia eventually took a job; Lisa had returned to work many months before. When mothers divide their time been work and parenting and place their infants in day care, does this affect the quality of attachment? This question is an important one, since over 50 percent of American mothers with children under age 2 are employed. Box 7.3 reviews the current controversy over whether infant day care threatens attachment security.

## Multiple Attachments

We have already indicated that babies develop attachments to a variety of familiar people—not just mothers, but fathers, siblings, grandparents, and substitute caregivers as well. Although Bowlby (1969) made room for multiple attachments in his theory, he believed that infants are predisposed to direct their attachment behaviors to a single attachment figure, especially when they are distressed. Observations of infants support this idea. When an anxious, unhappy 1-year-old is permitted to choose between the mother and father as a source of comfort and security, the infant usually chooses the mother (Lamb, 1976). This preference declines over the second year of life until, around 18 months, it is no longer present. An expanding world of attachments enriches the emotional and social lives of many babies.

***Fathers.*** In Chapter 4, we saw that fathers begin to build affectionate relationships with infants shortly after birth. But over the first year of life, mothers and fathers from a variety of cultures achieve synchrony in different ways. Mothers devote more time to physical care, such as changing, bathing, and feeding. In contrast,

# SOCIAL ISSUES

## Box 7.3  *Is Infant Day Care a Threat to Attachment Security?*

Recent studies indicate that American infants placed in full-time day care (more than 20 hours per week) before 12 months of age are more likely than home-reared babies to display insecure attachment in the Strange Situation. Does this mean that infants who experience daily separations from their employed mothers and early placement in day care are at risk for developmental problems? Some researchers think so (Belsky, 1988; Belsky & Braungart, 1991; Sroufe, 1988), while others disagree (Clarke-Stewart, 1989; Scarr, Phillips, & McCartney, 1990). Yet a close look at the evidence reveals that we should be extremely cautious about concluding that day care is harmful to babies.

First, the rate of attachment insecurity among day-care infants is only slightly higher than that of control babies (34 versus 29 percent), and it is identical to the overall figure reported for children in industrialized countries around the world. In fact, most infants of employed mothers are securely attached! This suggests that the early emotional development of day-care youngsters is probably within normal range (Thompson, 1988).

Second, we have seen that family conditions affect attachment security. Many employed women find the pressures of handling two full-time jobs (work and motherhood) stressful. Some respond less sensitively to their babies because they are fatigued and harried, thereby risking the infant's security (Owen & Cox, 1988). Other employed mothers probably value and encourage their infant's independence. In these cases, avoidance in the Strange Situation may represent healthy autonomy rather than insecurity.

Finally, poor quality day care may contribute to the slightly higher rate of insecure attachment among infants of employed mothers. In one investigation, babies classified as insecurely attached to both mother and caregiver tended to be placed in day-care environments with large numbers of children and few adults,

*When caregivers are warm, responsive, and stable and infants' needs for physical care and stimulation are met, day care is unlikely to interfere with attachment security. (Carol Palmer/The Picture Cube)*

where their bids for attention were frequently ignored (Howes et al., 1988).

In summary, the research to date suggests that a small number of infants may be at risk for attachment insecurity due to inadequate day care and joint pressures of full-time employment and raising a baby experienced by their mothers. However, using this evidence to justify a reduction in infant day-care services is inappropriate. When family incomes are limited and mothers who want to work are forced to stay at home, children's emotional security is not promoted (Hock & DeMeis, 1987). Instead, it makes sense to increase the availability of high-quality day care and to educate parents about the vital role of sensitive, responsive caregiving in early emotional development.

RETURN TO CHAPTER 6 and review the signs of good quality day care on page 228. Which ones are especially important in ensuring the emotional well-being of infants and toddlers?

*When playing with their babies, fa-thers tend to engage in highly physi-cal bouncing and lifting games, especially with sons.* (Steve Starr/ Stock Boston)

fathers spend more time in playful interactions (Lamb, 1987; Roopnarine et al., 1990). Also, when mothers and fathers play with babies, their interactions tend to be different. Mothers more often provide toys, talk to infants, and initiate conventional games like pat-a-cake and peekaboo. In contrast, fathers tend to engage in more exciting, highly physical bouncing and lifting games, especially with infant sons (Yogman, 1981). In view of these differences, it is not surprising that babies tend to look to their mothers when distressed and to their fathers for playful stimulation.

Even in the eyes of parents, the view of "mother as caregiver" and "father as playmate" is widely held (Parke & Tinsley, 1981). However, this picture is changing in some families as a result of the revised work status of women. Employed mothers tend to engage in more playful stimulation of their babies than do unemployed mothers, while their husbands are somewhat more involved in caregiving (Baruch & Barnett, 1986; Pedersen et al., 1980). When fathers are the primary caregivers, they retain their arousing play style in addition to looking after the baby's physical well-being (Hwang, 1986). Such highly involved fathers are less sex-typed in their beliefs, have sympathetic, friendly personalities, and regard parenthood as an especially enriching experience. Also, a warm, gratifying marital relationship supports both parents' involvement with babies, but it is particularly important as far as fathers are concerned (Lamb, 1987; Levy-Shiff & Israelashvili, 1988).

**Siblings.**    Despite a declining family size (see Chapter 3), 80 percent of American children still grow up with at least one sibling. In a survey in which married couples were asked why they desired more than one child, the most frequently mentioned reason was sibling companionship (Bulatao & Arnold, 1977). Yet the arrival of a baby brother or sister is a difficult experience for most preschoolers, who quickly realize that now they must share the attention and affection of their parents. They often become demanding and clingy for a time and engage in instances of "deliberate naughtiness," especially when the mother is caring for the baby (Dunn & Kendrick, 1982).

TABLE 7.4 • Ways to Encourage Affectional Ties Between Infants and Their Preschool Siblings

To minimize feelings of being deprived of affection and attention, set aside time to spend with the older child. Fathers can be especially helpful in this regard, planning special outings with the preschooler and taking over care of the baby so the mother can be with the older child.

Respond patiently to the older sibling's misbehavior and demands for attention, recognizing that these reactions are temporary. Give the preschooler opportunities to feel proud of being more grown-up than the baby. For example, encourage the older child to assist with feeding, bathing, dressing, and offering toys, and show appreciation for these efforts.

Discuss the baby's feelings and intentions with the preschooler, such as: "He's so little that he just can't wait to be fed," or "He's trying to reach his rattle and can't." By helping the older sibling understand the baby's point of view, parents can promote friendly, considerate behavior.

*Sources:* Dunn & Kendrick, 1982; Howe & Ross, 1990; Spock & Rothenberg, 1985.

However, resentment about being displaced is only one feature of a rich emotional relationship that starts to build between siblings after a baby's birth. The older child can also be seen kissing, patting, and calling out "Mom, he needs you" when the baby cries—signs of growing caring and affection. By the time the baby is about 8 months old, siblings typically spend much time together. Infants of this age are comforted by the presence of their preschool-age brother or sister during short absences of the mother (Stewart, 1983). And during the second year of life, they actively join in play with the older child (Dunn, 1989).

Nevertheless, individual differences in the quality of sibling relationships appear shortly after a baby's birth and persist through early childhood (Dunn, 1989). Temperament plays an important role. For example, conflict increases when one member of a sibling pair is emotionally intense or highly active (Brody, Stoneman, & Burke, 1987; Stocker, Dunn, & Plomin, 1989). But parenting practices also have much to do with how well siblings get along. When a mother is very positive and playful with a new baby, her preschool-age child is likely to feel slighted and act in a less friendly way toward the infant. This does not mean that parents should limit the attention they give to infants, but it does indicate the importance of setting aside special times to devote to the older child. In addition, mothers who often discuss the baby's feelings and intentions have preschoolers who are more likely to comment on the infant as a person with special wants and needs. And such children behave in an especially considerate and friendly manner when interacting with the baby (Dunn & Kendrick, 1982; Howe & Ross, 1990).

A list of suggestions for promoting positive relationships between babies and their preschool siblings is given in Table 7.4. Research on brothers and sisters as attachment figures reminds us of the complex, multidimensional nature of the infant's social world. Siblings offer a rich social context in which children learn and practice a wide range of skills, including affectionate caring, conflict resolution, and control of hostile and envious feelings. Warm, enduring bonds among brothers and sisters occur especially often in large families. Having more children means that parents have less time to devote to each one, and this seems to intensify children's attachment to one another (Bossard & Boll, 1956).

### Attachment and Later Development

According to psychoanalytic and ethological theories, the inner feelings of affection and security that result from a healthy attachment relationship support all aspects of psychological development. Consistent with this view, research indicates that quality of attachment to the mother in infancy is related to cognitive and social development in early childhood. Preschoolers who were securely attached as babies show greater enthusiasm and persistence on problem-solving tasks. And such children also have relationships with peers that are especially positive (Frankel & Bates, 1990; Matas, Arend, & Sroufe, 1978; Park & Waters, 1989).

These findings have been taken by some researchers to mean that secure attachment in infancy *causes* increased autonomy and competence during later years. Yet much more evidence is needed before we can be sure of this conclusion. Earlier in this chapter, we saw that infants deprived of a familiar caregiver show long-term adjustment difficulties. But similar outcomes do not always occur for babies who do become attached but for whom the relationship is less than ideal. In some studies, insecurely attached infants became preschoolers with serious adjustment difficulties; in others they did not (Bates & Bayles, 1988; Fagot & Kavanaugh, 1990; Sroufe, 1983).

Michael Lamb and his colleagues (1985) suggest that *continuity of caregiving* determines whether attachment insecurity is linked to later problems. When parents react insensitively for a very long time, children have a good chance of becoming maladjusted. But infants and young children are resilient beings. A child who has compensating, affectional ties outside the family or whose parents' caregiving improves is likely to fare well. This suggests that efforts to create warm, responsive environments are not just important in infancy; they are also worthwhile at later ages. Indeed, we will discover that this is the case in subsequent chapters.

**BRIEF REVIEW**   Drive reduction (behaviorist) and psychoanalytic theories have been criticized for overemphasizing feeding and paying little attention to the baby's active role in establishing an attachment bond. According to ethological theory, infant–caregiver attachment has evolved to promote survival. In early infancy, babies' innate signals help keep the parent nearby. By 6 to 8 months, separation anxiety and use of the mother as a secure base from which to explore indicate that a true attachment has formed. Representation and language help toddlers tolerate separations from the parent. Research on infants deprived of a consistent caregiver suggests that fully normal development may depend on establishing a close affectional bond in the first few years of life. Interactional synchrony supports secure attachment, while insensitive caregiving is linked to attachment insecurity. Family conditions, such as a change in marital or employment status, can affect the quality of attachment. In addition to mothers, fathers and siblings are influential attachment figures. Continuity of caregiving may be more important than early attachment security in affecting long-term psychological adjustment.

• *Return to Chapter 6 and list the child-rearing practices that promote early cognitive development. How do they compare to those that foster secure attachment?*

• *Recall from Chapter 6 that Lisa tended to overwhelm Byron with questions and instructions that were not related to his ongoing actions. How would you expect Byron to respond in the Strange Situation? Explain your answer.*

• *Maggy works full-time and leaves her 14-month-old son Vincent at a day-care center. When she arrives to pick him up at the end of the day, Vincent keeps on playing and ignores her. Maggy wonders whether Vincent is securely attached. Is Maggy's concern warranted?*

## SELF-DEVELOPMENT DURING THE FIRST TWO YEARS

Infancy is a rich, formative period for the development of physical and social understanding. In Chapter 6, you learned that infants develop an appreciation of the permanence of objects—that they continue to exist when no longer in view. And in this chapter, we saw that over the first year, infants recognize and respond appropriately to others' emotions and distinguish familiar people from strangers. The fact that both objects and people achieve an independent, stable existence in infancy implies that knowledge of the self as a separate, permanent entity also emerges around this time. Once self-awareness develops, it supports a diverse array of social and emotional achievements, as we will see in the following sections.

### Self-Recognition

Felicia hung a large, plastic mirror on the side of April's crib. As early as the first few months, April smiled and returned friendly behaviors to her image. At what age did she realize that the charming baby gazing and grinning back was really herself?

To answer this question, researchers have conducted clever laboratory observations in which they expose infants and toddlers to images of themselves in mirrors, on videotapes, and in still photos. In one study, 9- to 24-month-olds were placed in front of a mirror. Then, under the pretext of wiping the baby's nose, each mother was asked to rub red dye on her infant's face. Younger infants touched the mirror as if the red mark had nothing to do with any aspect of themselves. But by 15 months, toddlers began to rub their strange-looking little red noses—a response that indicates the beginnings of self-recognition (Bullock & Lutkenhaus, 1990; Lewis & Brooks-Gunn, 1979).

By the end of toddlerhood, recognition of the self is well established. Two-year-olds look and smile more at a photo of themselves than one of another child. And almost all of them use their name or a personal pronoun ("I" or "me") to label their own image or to refer directly to themselves (Lewis & Brooks-Gunn, 1979).

How do toddlers develop an awareness of the self's existence? As yet, there is little evidence to answer this question. Many theorists believe that the beginnings of self lie in infants' developing *sense of agency*—recognition that their own actions cause objects and people to react in predictable ways. Parents who encourage babies to explore the environment and who respond to their signals in a consistent, sensitive manner help them construct a sense of agency. Then, as infants act on the environment, they notice different effects that may help them sort out self from other people and objects. For example, batting a mobile and seeing it swing in a pattern different

*This infant notices the correspondence between his own movements and the movements of the image in the mirror, a cue that helps him figure out that the grinning baby is really himself. (Paul Damien/Tony Stone/Worldwide)*

*Empathy first appears in toddlerhood. It depends on the cognitive capacity to distinguish self from other.* (Michael Kornafel/FPG)

from the infant's own actions informs the baby about the relation between self and physical world. Smiling and vocalizing at a caregiver who smiles and vocalizes back helps specify the relation between self and social world. And watching the movement of one's own hand provides still another kind of feedback—one under much more direct control than other people or objects. The contrast among these experiences may help infants build an image of self as separate from external reality (Case, 1991a; Lewis, 1991; Lewis & Brooks-Gunn, 1979).

Once self-awareness emerges, it quickly becomes a central part of children's emotional and social lives. Earlier you learned that complex emotions depend on toddlers' emerging sense of self. Self-recognition also leads to the first signs of **empathy**—the ability to understand and respond sympathetically to the feelings of others. For example, toddlers start to give to others what they themselves find comforting—a hug, a reassuring comment, or a favorite doll or blanket (Hoffman, 1984; Zahn-Waxler et al., 1992). And along with an increase in empathic behavior comes a much clearer awareness of how to upset and frustrate other people (Dunn, 1989). One 18-month-old heard her mother comment to another adult, "Anny (sibling) is really frightened of spiders. In fact, there's a particular toy spider that we've got that she just hates" (p. 107). The innocent-looking toddler ran to get the spider out of the toy box, returned, and pushed it in front of Anny's face!

**Empathy**
The ability to understand and respond sympathetically to the feelings of others.

## Categorizing the Self

Self-awareness permits toddlers to compare themselves to other people, in much the same way that they group together physical objects (see Chapter 6). Between 18 and 30 months, children categorize themselves and others on the basis of age ("baby," "boy," or "man"), sex ("boy" versus "girl" and "lady" versus "man"), and even goodness and badness ("I good girl." "Tommy mean!") (Stipek, Gralinski, & Kopp, 1990). Toddlers' understanding of these social categories is quite limited. But as soon as this knowledge appears, children use it to organize their own behavior. For example, toddlers' ability to label their own gender is associated with a sharp rise in sex-typed responses (Fagot & Leinbach, 1989). As early as 18 months, children select and play in a more involved way with toys that are stereotyped for their own sex— dolls and tea sets for girls, trucks and cars for boys. Then parents encourage these preferences further by responding more positively when toddlers display them (Caldera, Huston, & O'Brien, 1989). As we will see in Chapter 10, sex-typed behavior increases dramatically over early childhood.

## The Emergence of Self-Control

Self-awareness also provides the foundation for **self-control,** the capacity to resist an impulse to engage in socially disapproved behavior. Self-control is essential for morality, another dimension of the self that will flourish during childhood and adolescence. To behave in a self-controlled fashion, children must have some ability to think of themselves as separate, autonomous beings who can direct their own actions. And they must also have the representational and memory capacities to recall a caregiver's directive (such as, "April, don't touch that light socket!") and apply it to their own behavior (Kopp, 1987).

As these abilities mature, the first glimmerings of self-control appear in the form of **compliance.** Between 12 and 18 months, children start to show clear awareness of caregivers' wishes and expectations and can voluntarily obey simple requests and commands (Kaler & Kopp, 1990). And, as every parent knows, they can also decide to do just the opposite! One way toddlers assert their emerging sense of autonomy is by resisting adult directives. But think back to Erikson's theory, which suggests that parenting practices have much to do with a healthy sense of self. Consistent with this idea, among toddlers who experience warm, sensitive caregiving and reasonable expectations for mature behavior, opposition is far less common than compliance and cooperation (Crockenberg & Litman, 1990; Kuczynski et al., 1987).

Around 18 months, the capacity for self-control appears, and it improves steadily into early childhood. In one study, toddlers were given three tasks that required them to resist temptation. In the first, they were asked not to touch an interesting toy telephone that was within arm's reach. In the second, raisins were hidden under cups, and they were instructed to wait until the experimenter said it was all right to pick up a cup and eat a raisin. In the third, they were told not to open a gift until the experimenter had finished her work. As shown in Figure 7.4, on all three problems the ability to wait increased substantially between 18 and 30 months of age. Toddlers who were especially self-controlled were also advanced in language development. In fact, some could be seen using verbal techniques, such as singing and talking to themselves, to keep from touching the desired objects (Vaughn, Kopp, & Krakow, 1984).

Still, toddlers' control over their own actions is very fragile; it depends on constant oversight and reminders by parents. Young children also have more difficulty controlling their behavior in some situations than others. For example, waiting before engaging in a desired action (as in the tasks just described) is easier than stopping

**Self-control**

The capacity to resist a momentary impulse to engage in socially disapproved behavior.

**Compliance**

Voluntary obedience to adult requests and commands.

**FIGURE 7.4** • Age changes in resistance to temptation. Toddlers' ability to resist improves steadily between 18 and 30 months of age. *(Adapted from Vaughn, Kopp, & Krakow, 1984.)*

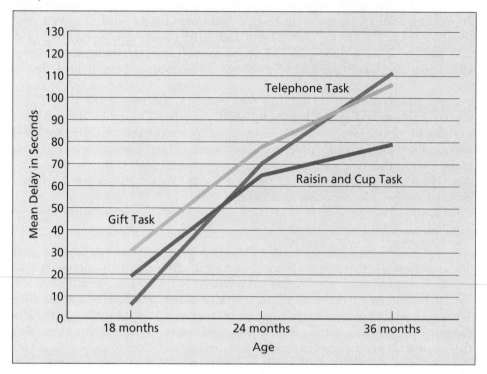

an enjoyable activity (Pressley, 1979). To get a toddler to calmly give up playing with an attractive toy to accompany the parent on an errand, several prompts ("Remember, we're going to go in just a minute") and gentle insistence are usually necessary.

As the second year of life drew to a close, Lisa, Beth, and Felicia were delighted at their youngsters' new-found capacity for compliance and self-control. It signaled that the three toddlers were ready to learn the rules of social life. As we will see in Chapter 10, advances in cognition and language, along with parental warmth and reasonable maturity demands, lead children to make tremendous strides in this area during the early childhood years.

# SUMMARY

### Theories of Infant and Toddler Personality

• The psychoanalytic theories of Erikson and Mahler capture salient features of personality development during infancy and toddlerhood. According to Erikson, warm, responsive caregiving leads infants to resolve the psychological conflict of Freud's **oral stage—basic trust versus mistrust**—on the positive side. During the **anal stage, autonomy versus shame and doubt** is resolved favorably when parents provide appropriate guidance and reasonable choices.

• According to Mahler, sensitive, loving care fosters **symbiosis**, which provides the foundation for **separation–individuation** during toddlerhood. The capacity to move away from the mother, by crawling and then walking, leads to self-awareness. Gains in representation and language permit a positive, inner image of the mother to be created that can be relied on for emotional support in her absence.

### Emotional Development During the First Two Years

• Newborn babies experience several, and perhaps all, the **basic emotions.** However, the frequency and extent to which they are expressed change with age. The **social smile** appears between 6 and 10 weeks, laughter around 3 to 4 months. Happiness strengthens the parent–child bond and reflects as well as supports cognitive and physical mastery. Anger and fear, especially in the form of **stranger anxiety,** increase after 7 months. These reactions have special survival value as infants' motor capacities improve.

• The ability to recognize and interpret the emotional expressions of others expands over the first year. Around 8 to 10 months, **social referencing** appears; infants actively seek emotional information from caregivers in uncertain situations. During toddlerhood, self-awareness and the ability to combine basic emotions provide the foundation for **complex emotions,** such as shame, embarrassment, and pride. Caregivers help infants with **emotional self-regulation** by relieving distress, engaging in stimulating play, and discouraging negative emotion.

### Temperament and Development

• Infants differ greatly in **temperament,** or style of emotional responding. Three temperamental patterns—the **easy child,** the **difficult child,** and the **slow-to-warm-up child**—were identified in the New York Longitudinal Study. Many temperamental characteristics show moderate stability over time.

• Temperament has biological roots, but child rearing has much to do with whether a child's emotional style remains the same or changes over time. The **goodness-of-fit model** describes how temperament and environmental pressures work together to affect later development. Parenting practices that create a good fit with the child's basic emotional style help difficult and withdrawn children achieve more adaptive functioning.

### The Development of Attachment

• The development of **attachment,** infants' strong affectional tie to familiar caregivers, has been the subject of intense theoretical debate. Although **drive reduction** (behaviorist) and psychoanalytic explanations exist, the most widely accepted perspective is **ethological theory of attachment.** It views attachment as a relationship that has evolved to protect infants from danger and promote survival.

• The baby contributes actively to the formation of the attachment bond. In early infancy, a set of built-in behaviors encourages the parent to remain close to the baby. Around 6 to 8 months, **separation anxiety** and use of the parent as a **secure base** from which to explore indicate that a true attachment relationship has formed. As toddlers develop representation and language, they try to alter the caregiver's coming and going through requests and persuasion rather than following and clinging. From experiences with the caregiver during the first two years, children build a positive inner image of the attachment relationship that serves as a guide for all future interactions.

• The **Strange Situation** is the most widely used technique for measuring the quality of attachment between 1 and 2 years of age. Four attachment classifications have been identified: **secure attachment, avoidant attachment, resistant attachment,** and **disorganized/disoriented attachment.**

• A variety of factors affect attachment quality. Infants deprived of affectional ties with one or a few adults show lasting emotional and social problems. Sensitive, responsive caregiving, in the form of **interactional synchrony,** promotes attachment security. Even difficult-to-care-for infants are likely to become securely attached if parents adapt their caregiving to suit the baby's needs. Family conditions, such as a change in employment or marital status, affect parent–infant interaction and, in turn, attachment security.

• Besides attachments to mothers, infants develop strong ties to fathers, usually through stimulating, playful interaction. Early in the first year, infants begin to build rich emotional relationships with siblings that mix affection and caring with rivalry and resentment. Individual differences in the quality of sibling relationships are influenced by temperament and parenting practices.

• Infants who are securely attached to their mothers show more effective cognitive and social functioning during the preschool years. However, continuity of parental care may be the critical factor that determines whether an infant who is insecurely attached shows later adjustment problems.

### Self-Development During the First Two Years

• Reactions of infants to images of themselves in mirrors, on videotapes, and in photos show that self-recognition is well-established by the end of the second year. Self-awareness permits toddlers to form primitive social categories based on age and sex. It also provides the foundation for complex emotions, empathy, and **compliance** and **self-control.**

# IMPORTANT TERMS AND CONCEPTS

oral stage (p. 242)

basic trust versus mistrust (p. 243)

anal stage (p. 243)

autonomy versus shame and doubt (p. 244)

symbiosis (p. 244)

separation–individuation (p. 245)

basic emotions (p. 247)

social smile (p. 247)

stranger anxiety (p. 248)

social referencing (p. 249)

complex emotions (p. 249)

emotional self-regulation (p. 250)

temperament (p. 252)

easy child (p. 252)

difficult child (p. 252)

slow-to-warm-up child (p. 252)

goodness-of-fit (p. 256)

attachment (p. 256)

drive reduction account of attachment (p. 257)

ethological theory of attachment (p. 259)

separation anxiety (p. 260)

secure base (p. 260)

Strange Situation (p. 261)

secure attachment (p. 262)

avoidant attachment (p. 262)

resistant attachment (p. 262)

disorganized/disoriented attachment (p. 262)

interactional synchrony (p. 264)

empathy (p. 272)

self-control (p. 273)

compliance (p. 273)

| MILESTONES OF DEVELOPMENT IN INFANCY AND TODDLERHOOD | | | |
|---|---|---|---|
| **Age** | **Physical** | **Cognitive** | **Language** | **Emotional/Social** |
| Birth–6 months | Rapid height and weight gain. Reflexes decline. Sleep organized into a day/night schedule. Holds head up, rolls over, and reaches for objects. Can be classically and operantly conditioned. Habituates to unchanging stimuli. Hearing well developed. Depth and pattern perception emerge and improve. | Repeats chance behaviors leading to pleasurable and interesting results. Displays object permanence in habituation–dishabituation task. Recognition memory for people, places, and objects improves. Able to categorize simple stimuli. | Cooing and babbling emerge. Establishes joint attention with caregiver, who labels objects and events. | Expresses basic emotions (happiness, interest, surprise, fear, anger, sadness, disgust). Social smile and laughter emerge. Matches adults' emotional expressions. Displays unique temperamental traits. |
| 7–12 months | Sits alone, crawls, and walks. Shows refined pincer grasp. Displays greater sensitivity to speech sounds of own language. Depth and pattern perception improve further. | Combines sensorimotor schemes. Engages in intentional or goal-directed behavior. Finds object hidden in one place. Capable of deferred imitation. Recall memory for people, places, and objects improves. Groups stimuli into wider range of categories. | Babbling expands to include sounds of spoken languages. Uses preverbal gestures (showing, pointing) to communicate. | Anger and fear increase in frequency and intensity. Stranger anxiety and separation anxiety appear. Uses caregiver as a secure base for exploration. Engages in social referencing. "Clearcut" attachment to caregiver appears. |
| 13–18 months | Height and weight gain rapid, but not as great as in first year. Walking better coordinated. Scribbles with pencil. Builds tower of 2–3 cubes. | Experiments with objects in a trial-and-error fashion. Finds object hidden in more than one place. Actively categorizes objects during play. | Actively joins in turn-taking games, such as pat-a-cake and peekaboo. Says first words. Makes errors of underextension and overextension. | Actively joins in play with siblings. Recognizes images of self in mirrors and on video-tape. Shows signs of empathy. Capable of compliance. |
| 19–24 months | Jumps, runs, and climbs. Manipulates objects with good coordination. Builds tower of 4–5 cubes. | Solves sensorimotor problems suddenly. Finds object moved while out of sight. Active categorization of objects during play improves. | Vocabulary increases to 200 words. Combines two words; consistent grammar not yet present. | Complex emotions (shame and embarrassment) emerge. Acquires a vocabulary of emotional terms. Starts to use language to assist with emotional self-regulation. Begins to tolerate caregiver absenses more easily. Self-recognition well-established: Uses own name or personal pronoun to label image of self. Categorizes the self and others on the basis of age and sex. Shows sex-typed toy choices. Self-control appears. |

*"Giriam Children Pounding Millet," by Suril P. Patel,
11 years, Kenya, Reprinted by permission from the International Museum of Children's Art, Oslo, Norway.*

# Physical Development in Early Childhood

**8**

Body Growth in Early Childhood
*Changes in Body Size and Proportions   Skeletal Growth   Asynchronies in Physical Growth*

Brain Development in Early Childhood
*Lateralization and Handedness   Other Advances in Brain Development*

Factors Affecting Growth and Health in Early Childhood
*Hereditary and Hormonal Influences   Emotional Well-Being   Nutrition   Infectious Disease   Childhood Injuries*

Motor Development in Early Childhood
*Gross Motor Development   Fine Motor Development   Factors that Affect Early Childhood Motor Skills*

Perceptual Development in Early Childhood

F or more than a decade, my fourth-floor office window overlooked the preschool and kindergarten play yard of our university laboratory school. Sitting at my desk, I spent many fascinating moments watching young children at play. On mild fall and spring mornings, the doors of the preschool and kindergarten swung open, and sand table, woodworking bench, easels, and large blocks spilled out into a small, fenced courtyard. Around the side of the building was a grassy area with jungle gyms, swings, a small playhouse, and a flower garden planted by the children. Beyond it, I could see a circular path lined with tricycles and wagons. Each day the setting was alive with activity.

As I looked on from my distant vantage point, the physical changes of early childhood were clearly evident. Children's bodies were longer and leaner than they had been a year or two earlier. The awkward gait of toddlerhood had disappeared in favor of more refined movements that included climbing, jumping, galloping, and skipping. Throughout the morning, children scaled the jungle gym, searched for imaginary pirates behind trees and bushes, chased one another across the play yard, and peddled tricycles vigorously over the pavement.

Just as impressive as these gross motor achievements were gains in fine motor skills. At the sand table, children built hills, valleys, caves, and roads and prepared trays of pretend cookies and cupcakes. Nearby, blocks of wood were hammered into small sculptures. And with increasing age, the paintings that hung out to dry took on greater form and detail as family members, houses, trees, birds, sky, monsters, and letterlike forms appeared in the children's colorful creations.

The years from 2 to 6 are often called "the play years," and aptly so, since play blossoms during this time and supports every aspect of development. We begin our consideration of early childhood by tracing the physical achievements of this period—growth in body size, improvements in motor coordination, and refinements in perception. Our discussion pays special attention to biological and environmental factors that support these changes, as well as to their intimate connection with other aspects of development. The preschool children whom I came to know well, first by watching from my office window and later by observing at close range in their classrooms, will provide us with many examples of developmental trends and individual differences. In this chapter, we will meet Lynette, a child so small that at age 4, she was no taller and heavier than the average 2-1/2-year-old. We will also get to know Hallie, whose impoverished home life left him vulnerable to serious health problems due to poor diet and infectious disease. Several of Lynette and Hallie's classmates will also join us along the way.

## BODY GROWTH IN EARLY CHILDHOOD

### Changes in Body Size and Proportions

Look at Figure 8.1, and you will see that the rapid increase in body size that took place in infancy tapers off into a slower pattern of growth during early childhood. On the average, 2 to 3 inches in height and about 5 pounds in weight are added each year, with boys continuing to be slightly larger than girls (Mott, James, & Sperhac, 1990). At the same time, the "baby fat" that began to decline in toddlerhood drops off further. The child gradually becomes thinner, although girls retain somewhat more body fat, and boys are slightly more muscular. As the torso lengthens and widens, internal organs tuck neatly inside, and the spine straightens. By age 5, the top-heavy, bowlegged, potbellied toddler has become a more streamlined, flat-tummied, longer-legged child with body proportions similar to that of adults (Tanner, 1978b). Consequently, posture and balance improve—changes that support the gains in motor coordination that we will take up later in this chapter.

Individual differences in body size that existed in infancy are even more apparent during early childhood. Looking down at the play yard one day, I watched 5-year-old Darryl speed around the bike path. At 48 inches in height and 55 pounds in weight, he towered over his kindergarten classmates and was, as his mother put it, "off the growth charts" at the doctor's office (the average American 5-year-old boy is 43 inches tall and weighs 42 pounds). Priti, a girl from India, and Lynette, a Caucasian child, were at the other extreme. Priti was small because of her racial heritage, Lynette and Hallie for reasons that we will discuss shortly.

The existence of racial differences in body size reminds us that growth norms for one population (those in Figure 8.1 apply to American children) are not good standards for many youngsters around the world. Consider the Efe of Zaire, an African people who normally grow to an adult height of less than 5 feet. A recent study of the early physical growth of Efe children revealed that between 1 and 6 years, their growth tapers off to a greater extent than that of American preschoolers. By age 5, the average Efe child is shorter than over 97 percent of 5-year-olds in the United States. For genetic reasons, the hormones controlling body size have less effect on Efe youngsters than they do on other children (Bailey, 1990). In view of these findings, we would be mistaken to take the Efe youngster's small stature as a sign of serious growth or health problems, although this concern is warranted for an extremely slow-growing Caucasian child, such as Lynette.

### Skeletal Growth

The skeletal changes that we discussed in Chapter 5 continue throughout early childhood. Between ages 2 and 6, approximately 45 new *epiphyses,* or growth centers in

**FIGURE 8.1** • Gains in height and weight during early childhood among American youngsters. Compared to the first 2 years of life, growth is slower. Girls continue to be slightly shorter and lighter than boys. Wide individual differences in body size exist, as the percentiles on these charts reveal. Darryl, Priti, Lynette, and Hallie's heights and weights differ greatly.

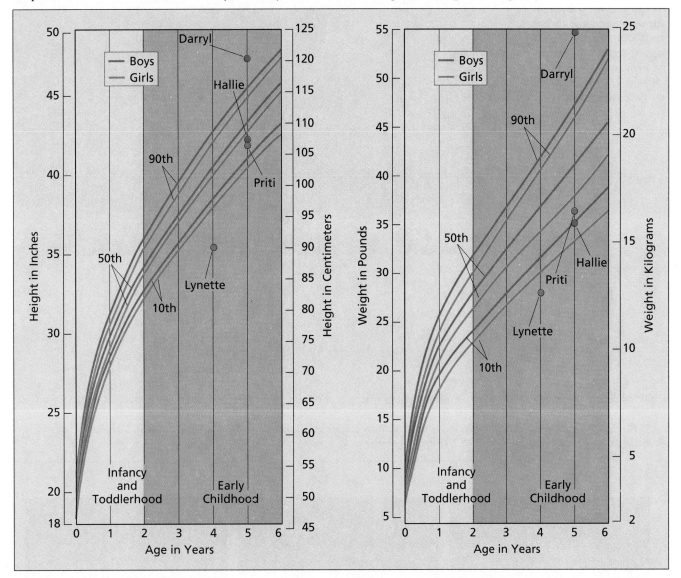

which cartilage hardens into bone, emerge in various parts of the skeleton. Others will appear in middle childhood. Figure 8.2, which shows X-rays of a girl's hand at three ages, illustrates changes in the epiphyses over time. Notice how, at age 2 1/2, wide gaps exist between the wrist bones and at the ends of the finger and arm bones. By age 5 1/2, these have filled in considerably. At age 14 1/2 (when this girl reached her adult size), the wrist and long bones are completely fused. X-rays like these permit doctors to estimate children's *skeletal age,* the best available measure of progress toward physical maturity (see Chapter 5, page 167). During early and middle childhood, information about skeletal age is helpful in diagnosing growth disorders. It also provides a rough estimate of children's chronological age in areas of the world where birth dates are not customarily recorded.

*Toddlers and 5-year-olds have very different body shapes. During early childhood, body fat declines, the torso enlarges to better accommodate the internal organs, and the spine straightens. Compared to her younger brother, this girl looks more streamlined. Her body proportions resemble those of an adult.* (Bob Daemmrich/Stock Boston)

**FIGURE 8.2** • X-rays of a girl's hand, showing skeletal maturity at three ages. Notice how the wrist bones and epiphyses on the long bones of the fingers and forearms gradually close. *(From J. M. Tanner, R. H. Whitehouse, N. Cameron, W. A. Marshall, M. J. R. Healey, & H. Goldstein, 1983, Assessment of skeletal maturity and prediction of adult height, [TW2 Method], 2nd ed., Academic Press [London, Ltd.], pp. 86–87. Reprinted by permission.)*

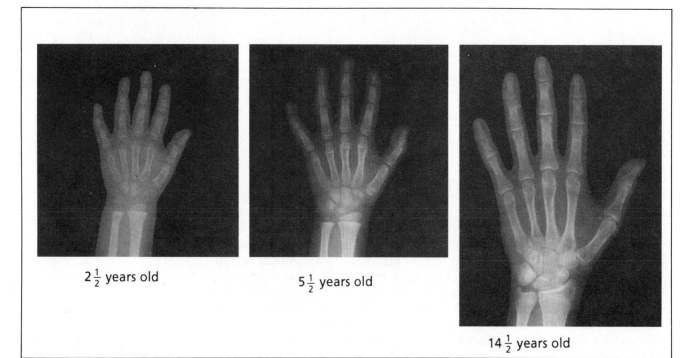

Parents and children are especially aware of another aspect of skeletal growth: maturation of the teeth. By the end of the preschool years, children start to lose their primary or "baby" teeth. The age at which they do so varies from child to child and is heavily influenced by genetic factors. Girls, who are ahead of boys in physical development, lose their primary teeth sooner. Cultural heritage also makes a difference. For example, American children get their first secondary tooth at 6 1/2 years, children in Ghana at just over 5 years, and children in Hong Kong around the sixth birthday. Environmental influences, especially prolonged malnutrition, can delay the age at which children cut their permanent teeth (Mott, James, & Sperhac, 1990).

Even though preschoolers will eventually lose their primary teeth, care of them is important, since diseased baby teeth can affect the health of permanent teeth. Consistent brushing, avoidance of sugary foods, and regular dental visits prevent tooth cavities. Since the early 1970s, childhood cavities in the United States have dropped by more than half. Today, 50 percent of children reach young adulthood with no tooth decay at all. Unfortunately, these improvements do not apply to all sectors of the American or world's population. Tooth decay remains high among low-income youngsters in the United States and among children in developing countries because of poor diet, lack of fluoridation, and inadequate health care (Louie et al., 1990).

## Asynchronies in Physical Growth

From what you have learned so far in this chapter and in Chapter 5, can you come up with a single overall description of early physical growth? If you found yourself answering "no" to this question, you are correct. Figure 8.3 shows that physical

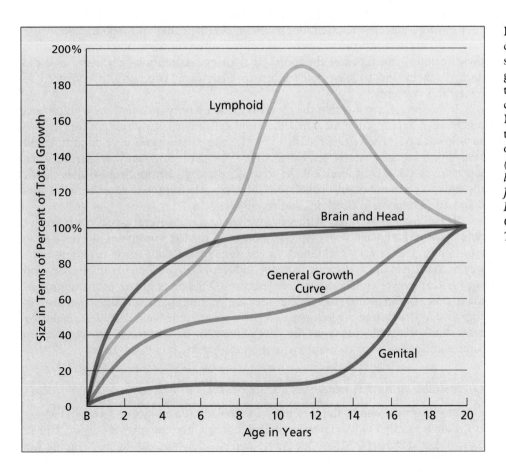

**FIGURE 8.3** • Growth of three different organ systems and tissues contrasted with the body's general growth. Growth is plotted in terms of percentage of change from birth to 20 years. Notice how the lymph tissue rises to twice its adult level by the end of childhood. Then it declines. *(Reprinted by permission of the publisher from* Fetus into man *by J. M. Tanner, Cambridge, Mass: Harvard University Press, p. 16. Copyright © 1978 by J. M. Tanner. All rights reserved.)*

growth is an *asynchronous* process. Different body systems have their own unique, carefully timed patterns of maturation. The **general growth curve** refers to change in overall body size (as measured by height and weight). It takes its name from the fact that outer dimensions of the body as well as a variety of internal organs follow the same pattern—rapid growth during infancy, slower gains in early and middle childhood, and rapid growth again during adolescence. Yet there are important exceptions to this trend. The development of the genitals shows a slight rise from birth to age 4, followed by a period of little change throughout middle childhood, after which growth is especially rapid during adolescence. In contrast, the lymph tissue (small clusters of glands found throughout the body) grows at an astounding pace in infancy and childhood, reaching a peak just before adolescence, at which point it declines. The lymph system plays a central role in the body's ability to fight infection and also assists in the absorption of nutrients from foods (Shields, 1972). Rapid early growth of lymph tissue helps ensure children's health and survival.

There is another growth trend in Figure 8.3 with which you are familiar: During the first few years, the brain grows faster than any other part of the body. Recall from Chapter 5 that the brain develops especially rapidly during infancy and toddlerhood. It continues to enlarge in size throughout early childhood, increasing from 60 percent of its adult weight at age 2 to 90 percent by age 6 (Tanner, 1978b). Let's take a look at some highlights of brain development during early childhood.

## BRAIN DEVELOPMENT IN EARLY CHILDHOOD

Between the years of 2 and 6, children gain in a wide variety of skills—physical coordination, perception, attention, memory, language, logical thinking, and imagination. Virtually all theorists agree that brain maturation contributes importantly to these changes. During early childhood, the cortex continues to *myelinate,* as it did during infancy and toddlerhood (return to Chapter 5, page 169, if you need to review this concept).

In Chapter 5, we saw that the cortex is made up of two *hemispheres* with distinct functions. A recent study measured the electrical activity of various cortical regions at different ages. The results revealed that the two hemispheres develop at different rates. For most children, the left hemisphere shows a dramatic growth spurt between 3 and 6 years and then levels off. In contrast, the right hemisphere matures slowly throughout early and middle childhood, showing a slight growth spurt between ages 8 and 10 (Thatcher, Walker, & Giudice, 1987).

These findings fit nicely with what we know about several aspects of cognitive development. Language skills (typically housed in the left hemisphere) increase at an astonishing pace in early childhood. In contrast, spatial skills (such as finding one's way from place to place, drawing pictures, and recognizing geometric shapes) develop very gradually over childhood and adolescence. Differences in rate of maturation of the two hemispheres also suggest that they are continuing to *lateralize* (specialize in cognitive functions). In the following sections, we examine brain lateralization during early childhood by focusing on the development of handedness. Then we take up some additional aspects of brain maturation during the preschool years.

### Lateralization and Handedness

One morning on a visit to the preschool, I followed the activities of 3-year-old Moira as she drew pictures, worked puzzles, joined in snack time, and played outside. Unlike most of her classmates, Moira does most things—drawing, eating, and zipping her

**General growth curve**
Curve that represents overall changes in body size—rapid growth during infancy, slower gains in early and middle childhood, and rapid growth once more during adolescence.

jacket—with her left hand. But she also performs a few activities with her right hand, such as throwing a ball.

A strong hand preference reflects the greater capacity of one side of the brain—often referred to as the individual's **dominant cerebral hemisphere**—to carry out skilled motor action. Other abilities located on the dominant side may be superior as well. In support of this idea, for right-handed people, who make up 90 percent of the population, language is housed with hand control in the left hemisphere. For the remaining 10 percent who are left-handed, language is often shared between the hemispheres, rather than located in only one. This indicates that the brains of left-handers tend to be less strongly lateralized than those of right-handers (Hiscock & Kinsborne, 1987). Consistent with this idea, many left-handed individuals (like Moira) are also *ambidextrous*. That is, although they prefer their left hand, they sometimes use their right hand skillfully as well (McManus et al., 1988).

Handedness appears to be partly genetically determined, since similarity of hand preference is greater among biological than adoptive relatives (Carter-Saltzman, 1980). Hand preference also shows up early in development. By 5 to 6 months of age, more infants reach for objects with their right hand than with their left hand (McCormick & Maurer, 1988). But hand preference is not stable until about 2 years of age, and it increases during early and middle childhood. This indicates that specialization of brain regions strengthens during this time.

At this point, you may be wondering: What about children whose hand use suggests an unusual organization of brain functions? Do these youngsters develop normally? Perhaps you have heard that left-handedness is more frequent among severely retarded and mentally ill people than it is in the general population. While this is true, you also know that when two variables are correlated, this does not mean that one causes the other. Atypical lateralization is probably not responsible for the problems of these individuals. Instead, they may have suffered early brain damage to the left hemisphere, which caused their disabilities and, at the same time, led to a shift in handedness. In support of this idea, left-handedness is associated with a variety of prenatal and birth difficulties that can result in brain damage, including prolonged labor, prematurity, Rh incompatibility, and breech delivery (Coren & Halpern, 1991).

Research also indicates that right-handers live longer than left-handers, although estimates of this difference vary greatly, from as little 8 months to as much as 9 years (Coren & Halpern, 1991). The link between left-handedness and developmental problems undoubtedly contributes to this finding. Also, in a world built for the convenience of right-handed people, left-handers run a greater risk of physical injury. One study found that left-handed adults are five times more likely to die of accident-related causes (Halpern & Coren, 1990).

Finally, in considering the evidence on handedness and development, keep in mind that only a small number of left-handers show developmental problems of any kind. The great majority, like Moira, are normal in every respect. In fact, the unusual cortical lateralization of left-handed children may have certain advantages. Although we do not yet know why, left- and mixed-handed youngsters are more likely than their right-handed agemates to develop outstanding verbal and mathematical talents by adolescence (Benbow, 1986).

## Other Advances in Brain Development

Besides the cortex, several other areas of the brain make strides during early childhood. Figure 8.4 shows where each of these structures is located. As we look at these changes, you will see that they have one feature in common. They all involve establishing links between different parts of the brain, increasing the coordinated functioning of the central nervous system.

*Although left-handedness is associated with developmental problems, the large majority of left-handed children are completely normal.* (Gale Zucker/Stock Boston)

**Dominant cerebral hemisphere**
The hemisphere of the brain responsible for skilled motor action. The left hemisphere is dominant in right-handed individuals. In left-handed individuals, the right hemisphere may be dominant, or motor and language skills may be shared between the hemispheres.

**FIGURE 8.4** • Cross-section of the human brain, showing the location of three structures—the cerebellum, the reticular formation, and the corpus callosum—that undergo considerable development during early childhood. Also shown is the pituitary gland, which secretes hormones that control body growth (see page 287).

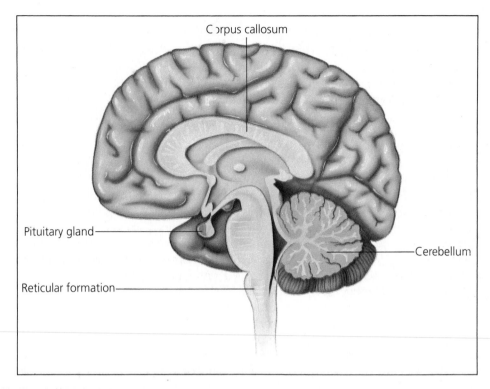

**Cerebellum**

A brain structure that aids in balance and control of body movements.

**Reticular formation**

A brain structure that maintains alertness and consciousness.

**Corpus callosum**

The large bundle of fibers that connects the two hemispheres of the brain.

At the rear and base of the brain is the **cerebellum,** a structure that aids in balance and control of body movement. Fibers linking the cerebellum to the cerebral cortex begin to myelinate after birth, but they do not complete this process until about age 4 (Tanner, 1978a). This change undoubtedly contributes to dramatic gains in motor control, so that by the end of the preschool years children can play a simple game of hopscotch, use their bodies to pump a playground swing, and throw a ball with a well-organized set of movements.

The **reticular formation,** a part of the brain that maintains alertness and consciousness, myelinates throughout early childhood, continuing its growth into adolescence. Neurons in the reticular formation send out fibers to other areas of the brain. Many go to the frontal lobe of the cortex (McGuinness & Pribram, 1980). Maturation of the reticular formation contributes to improvements in sustained, controlled attention that we will discuss in Chapters 9 and 12.

A final brain structure that undergoes major changes during early childhood is the **corpus callosum.** It is a large bundle of fibers that connects the two hemispheres so that they can communicate efficiently with one another. Myelinization of the corpus callosum does not begin until the end of the first year of life. By age 4 to 5, its development is fairly advanced (Spreen et al., 1984; Witelson & Kigar, 1988). By watching how young children solve certain problems, you can see evidence that the corpus callosum is developing. In one study, preschoolers played a matching game in which, with eyes closed, they felt a small textured pillow with one hand. While doing so, they had to tell whether a pillow rubbed across the other hand was made of the same fabric. Since each half of the brain receives information from only one side of the body, to match textures successfully, the hemispheres must communicate across the corpus callosum. Three-year-olds had great difficulty with this task, but by age 5 performance improved considerably (Galin et al., 1979).

BRIEF REVIEW   Compared to infancy, gains in body size take place more slowly during early childhood, and the child's body becomes more streamlined. The skeleton adds new epiphyses, and by the end of the preschool years children start to lose their primary teeth. Physical growth is an asynchronous process; different parts of the body have their own carefully timed patterns of maturation. During early childhood, the brain continues to grow more rapidly than the rest of the body. Hand preference strengthens, a sign of increasing brain lateralization. Although left-handedness is associated with developmental abnormalities and a shorter life span, the large majority of left-handed children show no developmental problems of any kind. The cerebellum, the reticular formation, and the corpus callosum undergo considerable development during early childhood, contributing to connections between different parts of the brain.

• *After graduating from dental school, Norm entered the Peace Corps and was assigned to rural India. He found that many Indian children had extensive tooth decay. In contrast, the young patients of his dental school friends in the United States had very little. What factors probably account for this difference?*

• *Crystal has a left-handed cousin who is mentally retarded. Recently she noticed that her 2-year-old daughter Shana is also left-handed. Crystal has heard that left-handedness is a sign of developmental problems, so she is worried about Shana. How would you respond to Crystal's concern?*

## FACTORS AFFECTING GROWTH AND HEALTH IN EARLY CHILDHOOD

In earlier chapters, we considered a wide variety of influences on physical growth during the prenatal period and infancy. In the sections below, as we discuss growth and health in early childhood, you will encounter a variety of familiar themes. While heredity remains powerfully important, environmental factors continue to play critical roles. Emotional well-being, good nutrition, and relative freedom from disease remain essential for healthy physical growth. Also, as Box 8.1 illustrates, environmental pollutants pose a serious threat to the physical health of hundreds of thousands of American children. Finally, we will see that like infant mortality, childhood mortality is largely preventable. Unintentional injuries are the leading cause of death during the preschool years.

### Hereditary and Hormonal Influences

The impact of heredity on physical growth is evident throughout childhood. Children's physical size and rate of growth (as measured by skeletal age) are related to their parents'. Genes influence growth by controlling the body's production of hormones. The most important hormones for human growth are released by the **pituitary gland,** which is located just below the front of the brain (return to Figure 8.4).

Two pituitary hormones are especially influential. The first is **growth hormone (GH),** the only pituitary secretion produced continuously throughout life. It affects the development of all body tissues, except the central nervous system and genitals. While GH does not seem to play a role in prenatal growth, it is necessary for physical development from birth on. Children who lack it reach an average mature height of only 4 feet, 4 inches, although they are normal in physical proportions and healthy in all other respects. When treated with injections of GH, such children show catch-up growth and then begin to grow at a normal rate. Reaching their genetically expected height depends on starting treatment early, before the epiphyses of the skeleton are very mature (D'Ercole & Underwood, 1986).

A second pituitary hormone affecting children's growth is **thyroid stimulating hormone (TSH).** It stimulates the thyroid gland (located in the neck) to release *thyroxin,* which is necessary for normal development of the nerve cells of the brain. Infants born with a deficiency of thyroxin must receive it at once, or they will be mentally retarded. At later ages, children with too little thyroxin show slow physical maturation. However, the central nervous system is no longer affected, since the

**Pituitary gland**

A gland located at the base of the brain that releases hormones affecting physical growth.

**Growth hormone (GH)**

A pituitary hormone that affects the development of almost all body tissues, except the central nervous system and genitals.

**Thyroid stimulating hormone (TSH)**

A pituitary hormone that stimulates the release of thyroxin from the thyroid gland. Thyroxin is necessary for normal brain development and body growth.

## SOCIAL ISSUES

### Box 8.1  *Lead Poisoning in Childhood*

*F*ive-year-old Desonia lives in an old, dilapidated tenement in a slum area of a large American city. Layers of paint applied over the years can be seen flaking off the inside walls and the back porch. The oldest paint chips are lead-based. As an infant and young preschooler, Desonia picked them up and put them in her mouth. The slightly sweet taste of the leaded flakes encouraged her to nibble more. Soon Desonia became listless, apathetic, and irritable. Her appetite dropped off, her stomach hurt, and she vomited frequently. When Desonia complained of constant headaches, began to walk with an awkward gait, and experienced repeated convulsions (involuntary muscle contractions), her parents realized that she had more than a passing illness. At a nearby public health clinic, Desonia's blood was analyzed and her bones X-rayed. The tests showed that she had severe lead poisoning, a condition that results in permanent brain damage and (if allowed to persist) early death (Friedman & Weinberger, 1990; Veerula & Noah, 1990).

Despite many years of public education, many parents remain unaware of the consequences of exposure to lead paint. In the United States, as many as 800,000 preschool children are believed to have dangerously high levels of lead in their bodies (American Academy of Pediatrics, 1987). Inner-city youngsters growing up in deteriorated housing are at greatest risk, but the problem is not limited to low-income families. Children of advantaged parents who purchase and restore old homes (built before 1950) can also be affected.

Severe lead poisoning like that experienced by Desonia has declined over the past two decades in the United States, following passage of laws restricting use of lead-based paint. But lead already present in home environments is difficult to remove. As a result, many children continue to receive low doses that lead to lasting cognitive and behavioral impairments. In one study, young children with varying degrees of low-level lead exposure were followed over an 11-year period. The more lead in their bodies during the early years of life, the lower their IQ scores and the more likely they were to have a wide variety of academic difficulties during the school years, including problems with reading, vocabulary, fine motor coordination, and sustained attention. During adolescence, they earned poorer grades than their agemates, and they were seven times more likely to drop out of high school (Needleman et al., 1979, 1990).

Childhood lead poisoning has been called "the silent epidemic of American cities" (Fee, 1990, p. 570). Children at risk for lead poisoning are those who live in or often visit old, run-down housing, those whose homes are located near lead processing plants, or those whose parents work in lead-related occupations. Such children should be tested for lead exposure regularly. Doctors and nurses should educate parents of all social classes about the hazards of lead. And communities should require that lead-based paint be removed from older housing before children become residents (American Academy of Pediatrics, 1987).

*RETURN TO CHAPTER 3*, page 110, and review the impact of lead exposure during the prenatal period on children's development. How is it similar to the findings described here?

Telephone a pediatrician's office or health clinic. Ask what kind of lead testing is routinely done (by law or otherwise) as part of children's physical exams in your community.

most rapid period of brain development is complete. With prompt treatment, such children catch up in body growth and eventually reach normal adult size (Tanner, 1978b).

### Emotional Well-Being

In Chapter 5, we showed that emotional well-being can have a profound effect on growth and health in infancy. During the childhood years, mind and body continue to be closely linked. Preschoolers with very stressful home lives (due to divorce, financial difficulties, or a change in their parents' employment status) suffer more

*Unpredictable appetites and picky eating are common during early childhood. At dinnertime, this 3-year-old girl seems more interested in playing than eating. Fortunately, her parents are sensitive to her nutritional needs. They offer a well-balanced meal and put only a small portion on her plate. (Joel Gordon)*

respiratory and intestinal illnesses as well as unintentional injuries (Beautrais, Fergusson, & Shannon, 1982).

When emotional deprivation is extreme, it can interfere with the production of growth hormone and lead to **deprivation dwarfism,** a growth disorder observed in children between 2 and 15 years of age. Lynette, the very small 4-year-old mentioned at the beginning of this chapter, was diagnosed as having this condition. Lynette had been taken from her parents' home and placed in foster care after child welfare authorities discovered that she spent most of her daytime hours by herself, unsupervised. Also, she may have been physically abused. To help her recover, she was enrolled in our laboratory preschool. Lynette showed the typical characteristics of deprivation dwarfism—very short stature, weight in proportion to her height, immature skeletal age, and decreased GH secretion. When such children are removed from their emotionally inadequate environments, their GH levels quickly return to normal, and they grow rapidly. But if treatment is delayed until late in development, the dwarfism can be permanent (Oates, Peacock, & Forrest, 1985).

## Nutrition

At the beginning of early childhood, there is often a dramatic change in the quantity and variety of foods that children will eat. Many children who, as toddlers, tried anything and everything, become picky eaters (Pelchat & Pliner, 1986). One father wistfully recalled his son's eager sampling of the cuisine at a Chinese restaurant during toddlerhood. "He ate rice, chicken chow mein, egg rolls, and more. Now, at age 3, the only thing he'll try is the ice cream!"

The decline in the young child's appetite is normal. It occurs because growth has slowed. And preschoolers' wariness of new foods may have adaptive value. Young children are still learning which items are safe to eat and which are not. By sticking to familiar foods, they are less likely to swallow dangerous substances when adults are not around to protect them (Rozin, 1990).

Because caloric intake is reduced, preschoolers need a high-quality diet. They require the same foods that make up a healthy adult diet—only smaller amounts. Milk and milk products, meat or meat alternatives (such as eggs, dried peas or beans,

**Deprivation dwarfism**
A growth disorder observed between 2 and 15 years of age. Characterized by very short stature, weight in proportion to height, immature skeletal age, and decreased GH secretion. Caused by emotional deprivation.

and peanut butter), vegetables and fruits, and breads and cereals should be included (Kendrick, Kaufmann, & Messenger, 1991). Although fats, oils, and salt are also needed, they should be kept to a minimum because of their link to high blood pressure and heart disease in adulthood (U.S. Department of Health and Human Services, 1988). Foods high in sugar should also be avoided. In addition to causing tooth decay, sugary cereals, cookies, cakes, soft drinks, and candy are high-energy items with little nutritional value that reduce young children's appetite for healthy foods.

The wide variety of foods eaten in cultures around the world indicates that the social environment has a powerful impact on young children's food preferences. For example, Mexican preschoolers eat chili peppers enthusiastically, while American children quickly reject them. What accounts for this difference? Children tend to imitate the food choices of people they admire—peers as well as adults. In Mexico, children often see family members delighting in the taste of peppery foods (Birch, Zimmerman, & Hind, 1980; Rozin & Schiller, 1980).

Repeated exposure to a new food (without any direct pressure to eat it) also increases children's acceptance. In one study, preschoolers were given one of three versions of a food they had never eaten before (sweet, salty, or plain tofu). After 8 to 15 exposures, they readily ate the food. But they preferred the version they had already tasted. For example, children in the "sweet" condition liked sweet tofu best, and those in the "plain" condition liked plain tofu best (Sullivan & Birch, 1990). These findings reveal that children's tastes are trained by foods they encounter repeatedly in the environment. Adding sugar or salt in hopes of increasing a young child's willingness to eat a healthy food is not necessary. It simply teaches the child to like a sugary or salty taste.

The emotional climate at mealtimes has a powerful impact on children's eating habits. For many parents, feeding preschoolers is a major source of anxiety, and meals become unpleasant and stressful. At times, food becomes a bribe. Parents coax their children by saying, "Finish your vegetables, and you can have an extra cookie." Unfortunately, trying to reinforce eating of healthy foods with treats causes children to like the healthy foods less and the treats more (Birch, 1987; Birch et al., 1987). There are many ways that parents, teachers, and caregivers can promote healthy, varied eating in young children. Table 8.1 offers some suggestions.

Finally, as we indicated in earlier chapters, many children in the United States and in developing countries are deprived of diets that support healthy growth. Hallie is a 5-year-old boy who was bused to our laboratory preschool from a poor neighborhood on the west side of town. His mother's welfare check was barely enough to cover cost of housing, let alone food. Hallie's diet was deficient in protein as well as a number of vitamins and minerals essential for healthy body growth and functioning—iron (to prevent anemia), calcium (to support development of bones and teeth), vitamin C (to facilitate iron absorption and wound healing), and vitamin A (to help maintain eyes, skin, and a variety of internal organs). These are the most common dietary deficiencies of the preschool years. Not surprisingly, Hallie was thin and pale, and he often seemed tired. By age 7 low-income children in the United States are, on the average, about 1 inch shorter than their middle-class counterparts (Goldstein, 1971). In contrast, there are no social class differences in body size in Sweden, where generous government food programs provide all children with access to nutritious diets (Children's Defense Fund, 1991b; Lindgren, 1976).

## Infectious Disease

Two weeks into the school year, I looked outside my window and noticed that Hallie was absent from the play yard. Several weeks passed; still, I did not see him. Finally, I asked Leslie, his preschool teacher, what had happened. "Hallie's been hospitalized

TABLE 8.1 • Ways to Encourage Good Nutrition in Early Childhood

Offer a well-balanced variety of nutritious foods that are colorful and attractively served.

Provide well-timed, predictable meals and several snacks each day. Young children's stomachs are small, and they may not be able to eat enough in three meals to satisfy energy requirements.

Offer small portions, and permit the child to ask for seconds. When too much food is put on the plate, the child may be overwhelmed and not even try to eat.

Introduce new foods early in the meal, before the child's appetite is satisfied. Let children see you eating and enjoying the new food. If the child rejects it, accept the refusal and serve it again at another meal. As foods become more familiar, they are more readily accepted.

Include the child in mealtime conversations. A pleasant, relaxed eating environment helps children develop positive attitudes toward healthy foods.

Avoid confrontations over disliked foods and table manners.

Avoid using food as a reward. Saying "No dessert until you clean your plate" tells children that they must eat regardless of how hungry they are and that dessert is the best part of the meal.

Avoid serving sugary desserts and foods as a regular part of meals and snacks.

*Source:* Kendrick, Kaufmann, & Messenger, 1991.

with the measles," she explained. "He's had a difficult time recovering—lost weight when there wasn't much to lose in the first place." In well-nourished children, ordinary childhood illnesses have no effect on physical growth. But when children are undernourished, disease interacts with malnutrition in a vicious spiral, and the consequences for physical growth can be severe.

Hallie's reaction to the measles is commonplace among children in developing nations, where a large proportion of the population lives in poverty. In these countries, many children are not immunized against childhood disease. Illnesses, such as measles and chicken pox, which typically do not appear until after age 3 in industrialized nations, occur much earlier in the Third World. This is because poor diet depresses the body's immune system, making children far more susceptible to disease (Eveleth & Tanner, 1976; Salomon, Mata, & Gordon, 1968). Disease, in turn, is a major cause of malnutrition and, through it, affects physical growth. Illness reduces appetite, and it limits the body's ability to absorb foods that children do eat.

Among children in industrialized nations, childhood diseases have declined dramatically during the past half century, largely due to widespread immunization of infants and young children. Hallie got the measles because, unlike his classmates from more advantaged homes, he did not receive a full program of immunizations during his first 2 years of life. Although the majority of preschoolers in the United States are immunized, a growing minority do not receive this protection until 5 or 6 years of age, when it is required for school entry (Williams, 1990). As a result, cases of preventable disease have increased in recent years. For example, in 1990 there were over 25,000 cases of measles, 16 times the number in 1983 (Children's Defense Fund, 1991e).

Figure 8.5 compares the immunization rates for preschoolers in the United States with those in a variety of European nations. The large number of low-income, racial minority youngsters who are not immunized is of special concern, since their overall poorer health makes them more vulnerable to complications when disease strikes. But note that immunization of white preschoolers also falls below the figures for other countries.

How is it that European nations (several of which also have large foreign-born and minority populations) manage to achieve high rates of immunization, while the

**FIGURE 8.5** • Immunization rates for preschool children in the United States and European nations, based on the most recent cross-national data. Children were immunized for diphtheria, tetanus, pertussis (whooping cough), measles, and polio. *(Adapted from Williams, 1990.)*

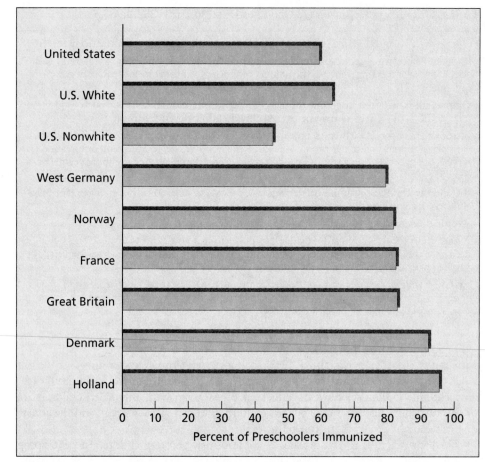

United States does poorly? In earlier chapters, we noted that many children in the United States do not have access to the medical care they need. Box 8.2 examines child health care in the United States and European nations. Experts agree that American public health services are in a state of crisis. A number one priority for the coming decade is the achievement of universal health insurance and high-quality medical care for all the nation's children (American Academy of Pediatrics, 1990; Children's Defense Fund, 1989; Colón & Colón, 1989).

A final point regarding communicable disease in early childhood deserves mention. In recent years, doctors, nurses, and parents have noticed that day-care attendance increases the potential for spread of infection. To explore this issue, turn to Box 8.3.

## Childhood Injuries

Three-year-old Tory caught my eye as I visited the preschool classroom one day. More than any other child, he had trouble sitting still and paying attention at story time. Outside, I saw him dart from one place to another, spending little time at a single activity. On a field trip to our campus museum, Tory ran across the street without holding his partner's hand, even though his teacher had just reminded the children of appropriate safety precautions. Later in the year, I read about Tory on the front page of our local newspaper:

> A 3-year-old boy escaped serious injury yesterday when he shifted his mother's car into gear while she was scraping its windows, causing the vehicle to roll over the side of an

## CULTURAL INFLUENCES

Box 8.2   *Child Health Care
in the United States and
European Nations*

In the United States, economically disadvantaged children are far less likely than well-off youngsters to receive basic health care. Because of the high cost of medical treatment, low-income children see a doctor only half as often as middle-class children with similar illnesses (Newacheck & Starfield, 1988). Recent estimates indicate that 60 percent of American children under age 5 who come from poor families are in less than excellent health (Children's Defense Fund, 1989).

American health insurance is an optional, employment-related fringe benefit. Many American businesses that rely on low-wage and part-time help do not insure their employees. If they do, they often do not cover other family members, including children. Although a variety of public health programs are available in the United States, they reach only the most needy individuals. This leaves nearly 12 million children from poor, low-income, and moderate-income families uninsured and, therefore, without affordable medical care (Oberg, 1988; Renner & Navarro, 1989).

The inadequacies of American child health care stand in sharp contrast to services provided in other industrialized nations, where medical insurance is government-sponsored and available to all citizens regardless of income. Let's take a look at two examples.

In Holland, each child receives free medical examinations from birth through adolescence. During the early years, health care also includes parental counseling in nutrition, disease prevention, and child development. Holland achieves its extraordinarily high childhood immunization rate (refer to Figure 8.5) by giving parents of every newborn baby a written schedule that shows exactly when and where the child should be immunized. If the child is not brought in at the specified time, a public health nurse calls the family (Verbrugge, 1990a, 1990b).

In Norway, federal law requires that well baby and child clinics be established in all communities and that examinations by physicians take place three times during the first year and at ages 2 and 4. Specialized nurses see children on additional occasions, monitoring their growth and development, providing immunizations, and counseling parents on physical and mental health. Although citizens pay a small fee for routine medical visits, hospital services are free of charge. Parents with a seriously ill hospitalized child are given leave from work with full salary, a benefit financed by the government (Lie, 1990).

In Chapter 2, we noted that Americans have historically been strongly committed to the idea that parents should assume total responsibility for the care and rearing of children. This belief, in addition to powerful economic interests in the medical community, has prevented government-sponsored health services from being offered to all children. In European nations, child health care is regarded as a fundamental human right, no different from the right to education (Williams, 1990).

overpass. Tory Flint was treated for bumps and bruises at Brokaw Hospital and released.

Police said his mother, 24-year-old Deborah Flint, parked her car in the driveway and put Tory in the front passenger seat. She told police she was outside the car scraping the windows free of ice when her son put the car into gear.

When the car moved forward, it went through a metal guardrail, took a nose dive over the side of a 10-foot concrete underpass, and hung there until rescue workers arrived. Police charged Mrs. Flint with a violation of state child restraint laws, which require use of child restraint seats for children under age 5.

Today, the greatest threat to children's health comes from a large collection of unintentional injuries—auto collisions, pedestrian accidents, drownings, poisonings, firearm wounds, burns, falls, swallowing of foreign objects, and others. Taken together, these events account for 40 to 50 percent of deaths in early and middle childhood and as many as 75 percent during adolescence. Approximately 22,000

## FROM RESEARCH TO PRACTICE

### Box 8.3  Day Care and Infectious Disease

During his first 12 months in day care, 3-year-old Zach caught five colds, had the flu on two occasions, experienced one bout of diarrhea, and developed an ear infection. His mother Madge, an assembly-line worker at a manufacturing plant, had to leave her job on the spur-of-the-moment five times to pick Zach up because of illness. Madge stayed home to care for Zach for a total of 15 days during the year. After using up her own sick leave of 7 days, she was forced to take nonpaid leave for the remainder. Madge thought to herself, "Missing extra days of work has already strained our limited family budget. Is day care increasing Zach's exposure to disease?"

In the past, infectious illnesses commonly occurred between 5 and 9 years of age, when children gathered together in large groups for the first time in school. Today, millions of children enroll in day care, creating earlier opportunities for children to come in close contact and increasing the exposure of infants and preschoolers to infection. Research in Europe and the United States indicates that childhood illness rises with day-care attendance. Diseases that spread most rapidly are respiratory infections (the most frequent illness suffered by young children) and diarrhea (Denny, Collier, & Henderson, 1987; Pickering, Bartlett, & Woodward, 1987). Childhood viral illnesses, such as measles, mumps, diptheria, and whooping cough, are not more common among day-care than home-reared children. The reason is that most licensed day-care settings require immunization. But as many as 10 to 20 percent of children attending day care are not immunized, so rapid transmission of these illnesses is still possible (Hinman, 1987).

Spread of communicable disease in day care can be controlled in the following ways:

1. Proper hygiene is essential. Illness rates decline when adults and children routinely wash their hands—before handling food, after toileting, and after handling clothing or objects contaminated with body secretions.

2. Regular cleaning of the day-care environment reduces the spread of illness. Because infants and young children often put toys in their mouths, these objects should be rinsed frequently with a disinfectant solution.

3. Design of the day-care setting can help control infection. Areas for food preparation and toileting should be physically separated. Spacious, well-ventilated rooms and small group sizes limit the spread of illness.

4. Children admitted to day care should have a full program of infant and early childhood immunization.

5. Isolation of children with communicable diseases that spread rapidly, such as viral illnesses and diarrhea, is important. As long as good hygiene is followed, children with mild respiratory infections (such as the common cold) can continue to attend day care with little impact on the health of other youngsters.

On the average, a day-care infant becomes sick 9 to 10 times a year, a day-care preschool child 6 to 7 times (Jordan, 1987). Unfortunately, most employed parents, like Madge, have no adequate solution to the problem of providing child care when their youngster is ill. A few day-care centers have special "get well" rooms for mildly ill children and care at separate sites for more seriously ill youngsters. Many parents need these backup systems, and they should be more widely available.

youngsters die from these incidents each year. And for each death, thousands of other injured children survive but suffer pain, brain damage, and permanent physical handicaps (Brooks & Roberts, 1990). As Figure 8.6 shows, auto accidents, fires, and drownings are the most common injuries during the early childhood years. Motor vehicle collisions are by far the most frequent source of injury at all ages. They are the leading cause of death among children over 1 year of age (Fawcett, Seekins, & Jason, 1987).

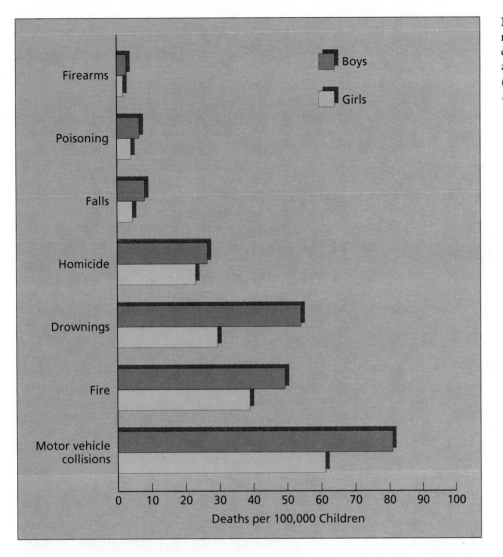

**FIGURE 8.6** • Rate of injury mortality in the United States for children between 1 and 4 years of age by type of injury and sex. *(Adapted from Williams & Kotch, 1990.)*

*Factors Related to Childhood Injuries.* We are used to thinking of childhood injuries as "accidental," a word that encourages us to believe that chance is responsible for them and that they cannot be prevented (Christophersen, 1989). But a close look at childhood injuries reveals that a variety of individual, environmental, and societal factors are related to them. This suggests that meaningful causes underlie childhood injuries, and we can, indeed, do something about them.

As Tory's case suggests, individual differences exist in the safety level of children's everyday behaviors. Because of their higher activity level and greater willingness to take risks during play, boys are more likely to be injury victims than are girls. (Look again at Figure 8.6.) Temperamental characteristics—irritability, inattentiveness, and negative mood—are also related to childhood injuries. As we saw in Chapter 7, children with these traits present parents with special child-rearing challenges. Where safety is concerned, these youngsters are likely to protest when placed in auto seat restraints, refuse to take a companion's hand when crossing the street, and disobey after repeated adult instruction and discipline (Matheny, 1987).

At the same time, families whose preschoolers get injured tend to have characteristics that increase the likelihood of exposure to danger. Poverty and low parental education are strongly associated with injury deaths. Parents who must cope with many daily stresses often have little time and energy to monitor the safety of their youngsters. And the homes and neighborhoods of such families pose further risks. Noise, crowding, and confusion characterize these households, and they tend to be located in run-down, inner-city neighborhoods where children have few places to play other than the streets (Matheny, 1987; Rivara & Barber, 1985).

Broad societal conditions also affect childhood injury. In Chapter 5, we pointed out that the United States has slipped down in the international rankings in infant mortality. Unfortunately, this pattern repeats itself for deaths due to childhood injuries. Among Western industrialized nations, the United States ranks among the highest in childhood injury mortality. Furthermore, although injury deaths have steadily declined in nearly all developed countries during the past 30 years, recent figures suggest that they may be on the rise in the United States (Williams & Kotch, 1990).

What factors probably account for this worrisome picture? Widespread poverty, a shortage of high-quality day care (to supervise children in their parents' absence), and an alarmingly high rate of births to teenagers (who are neither psychologically nor financially ready to raise a child) are believed to play important roles. But children from advantaged families are also at somewhat greater risk for injury in the United States than they are in European nations (Williams & Kotch, 1990). This indicates that besides reducing poverty and teenage pregnancy and upgrading the status of day care, additional steps must be taken to ensure the safety of American children.

***Preventing Childhood Injuries.***   Childhood injuries have many causes, so a variety of approaches are needed to control them. Laws prevent a great many injuries by requiring that young children ride in car safety seats, that medicine bottles have child-resistant caps, that clothing be flameproof, and that back-yard swimming pools (the site of 90 percent of early childhood drownings) be fenced. Communities can also help by modifying their physical environments. Inexpensive and widely available

*This father reduces his daughter's chances of injury by insisting that she ride in a car safety seat. In doing so, he also teaches her good safety practices.* (Sue Klemens/ Stock Boston)

public transportation can reduce the time that children spend in cars. Playgrounds, a common site of injury, can be covered with protective surfaces, such as rubber matting, sand, and wood chips (Wilson & Baker, 1987). Free, easily installed window guards can be given to families living in high-rise apartment buildings to prevent falls. And public education—in the form of widespread media campaigns and information distributed in doctors' offices, schools, and day-care centers—helps inform parents and children about safety issues (Pless & Arsenault, 1987).

Nevertheless, many dangers cannot be eliminated from the environment. And even though they know better, many parents and children continue to behave in ways that compromise safety. For example, 50 percent of parents (like Tory's mother) fail to place their infants and preschoolers in car safety seats (Wilson & Baker, 1987). Adults often leave caps off medicine bottles, neglect to replace batteries in home smoke detectors, and leave handguns within reach of children. In addition to the preventive measures described above, ways must be found to change human behavior.

A variety of programs based on the principles of behaviorism (modeling and reinforcement) have successfully improved the safety practices of adults and children alike. In one, counselors helped parents identify a variety of dangers in the home—fire hazards, objects that young children might swallow, poisonous substances, firearms, and others. Then they demonstrated specific ways to eliminate them (Tertinger, Greene, & Lutzker, 1984). In several other interventions, parents and children were rewarded with prizes if the youngsters arrived at day care or school each morning properly restrained in car seats (Roberts, Alexander, & Knapp, 1990; Roberts, Fanurik, & Wilson, 1988). Efforts like these have been remarkably successful in reducing the dangers to which children are exposed. They also add to the examples we have seen in earlier chapters of the practical usefulness of behaviorist theory.

*BRIEF REVIEW* Heredity influences physical growth by regulating the production of hormones. Two pituitary hormones, growth hormone (GH) and thyroid stimulating hormone (TSH), play important roles in children's growth. Many environmental factors affect growth and health in early childhood. Extreme emotional deprivation can interfere with the production of GH, resulting in deprivation dwarfism. Although appetites of preschoolers decline and they resist new foods, good nutrition remains important in early childhood. The emotional climate of mealtimes influences the quality and range of foods that young children will eat. Disease can interact with malnutrition to seriously undermine children's growth, an effect that is especially common in developing countries. Unintentional injuries are the leading cause of childhood mortality. Injuries rates are related to child and family characteristics as well as to broad societal conditions. Consequently, a variety of approaches are needed to prevent them.

• *One day, Leslie prepared a new snack to serve at preschool: celery stuffed with ricotta cheese and pineapple. The first time she served it, few of the children touched it. What techniques can Leslie use to encourage her pupils to accept the snack? What methods should she avoid?*

• *Chapter 1 introduced you to ecological systems theory, which shows how children's well-being is affected by several levels of the environment. Review ecological systems theory. Then list ways to reduce childhood injuries by intervening in the microsystem, mesosystem, and macrosystem.*

## MOTOR DEVELOPMENT IN EARLY CHILDHOOD

Visit a playground at a neighborhood park, preschool, or day-care center, and select several children between 2 and 6 years for observation. Jot down descriptions of their activities and movements, paying special attention to differences between the younger and older children. You will see that an explosion of new motor skills occurs in early childhood, each of which builds on the simpler movement patterns of toddlerhood.

The same principle that governs motor development during the first 2 years of life continues to operate during the preschool years. Children integrate previously acquired skills into more complex *systems of action* (return to Chapter 5, page 180 if you need to review this concept). Then they revise each new skill as their bodies become larger and stronger, their central nervous systems become better developed, and their environments present them with new challenges. Let's look closely at young children's gross and fine motor skills to illustrate this idea.

## Gross Motor Development

Toddlers walk with toes turned out, teetering from side to side and frequently toppling over. As children's bodies become more streamlined and less top-heavy, their center of gravity shifts downward, toward the trunk. As a result, balance improves greatly, a change that paves the way for new motor skills involving large muscles of the body (Ulrich & Ulrich, 1985). By age 2, the preschooler's gait becomes smooth and rhythmic—secure enough so that soon they leave the ground, at first by running and later by jumping, hopping, galloping, and skipping. As children become steadier on their feet, their arms and torsos are freed to experiment with new skills—throwing and catching balls, steering tricycles, and swinging on horizontal bars and rings. Then upper and lower body skills combine into more refined actions. Five- and 6-year-olds dash across the play yard to catch a ball, steer and peddle a tricycle at the same time, and flexibly move their whole body when hopping and jumping. Table 8.2 provides an overview of refinements in gross motor skills during the preschool years.

***Walking and Running.*** Ask a toddler to run for you. What you will see is a hurried walk, not a true run. Before age 2, children's feet are in constant contact with the floor, and their arms do not swing in opposition to their legs, helping to balance the body. During the third year, the left arm swings forward when the right foot steps, and children no longer need to keep their legs widely spaced to stay upright. As a result, feet come closer together and point straight ahead in a well-coordinated walk. Soon the child is airborne into a full-fledged run, lifting both feet off the ground during each stride. Gradually, preschoolers find that by contacting the ground with only the ball of the foot and vigorously thrusting the knees upward, they can run faster. Five-year-olds run about twice as quickly as they did at age 2—over 11 feet per second (Cratty, 1986).

Additional variations on the theme of walking appear as children experiment with movements and imitate the motor skills of playmates. Around age 4, gallops and one-step skips (in which a step on one foot is alternated with a step-shuffle on the other) appear. Older preschoolers can climb up and down ladders, scale jungle gyms, and walk balance beams easily. And around 6 years, they can skip in a well-coordinated fashion.

***Jumping and Hopping.*** As toddlers watch others jump, they try it themselves, but they are usually unsuccessful. One 18-month-old I observed bent her knees in preparation for lift-off but could not figure out what to do next! Not only is the appropriate body movement absent, but leg muscles probably lack the strength and power needed to overcome the child's weight. The first jumps, around age 2, are awkward. The young preschooler pushes off with one foot, while the other absorbs the shock of landing. During the middle of the third year, the first two-foot takeoffs and landings can be seen. The child can jump upward as well as forward, but movements of the arms are not yet used to propel the body (Roberton, 1984). For example, when asked to broad jump, the 3-year-old's arms move back into a wing position and remain there. In contrast, 6-year-olds move their arms forward during the jump, increasing the distance traveled.

Hopping shows a similar pattern of development. Initially, the child focuses only on the footwork. Between ages 2 and 3, children can hop a few times in succession, but they land flat-footed and hold the nonhopping leg still, usually in front of the

TABLE 8.2 • Changes in Gross Motor Skills During Early Childhood

| Age | Walking and Running | Jumping | Hopping | Throwing and Catching | Peddling and Steering |
|---|---|---|---|---|---|
| 2–3 years | Walks more rhythmically; widely spaced feet narrow; opposite arm-leg swing appears. Hurried walk changes to true run. | Jumps down from step. Jumps several inches off floor with both feet, no arm action. | Hops 1 to 3 times on same foot with stiff upper body and nonhopping leg held still. | Throws ball with forearm extension only; feet remain stationary. Awaits thrown ball with rigid arms outstretched. | Pushes riding toy with feet; does little steering. |
| 3–4 years | Walks up stairs, alternating feet. Walks downstairs, leading with one foot. Walks straight line. | Jumps off floor with coordinated arm action. Broad jumps about 1 foot. | Hops 4 to 6 times on same foot, flexing upper body and swinging nonhopping leg. | Throws ball with slight body rotation but little or no transfer of weight with feet. Flexes elbows in preparation for catching; traps ball against chest. | Peddles and steers tricycle. |
| 4–5 years | Walks downstairs, alternating feet. Walks circular line. Walks awkwardly on balance beam. Runs more smoothly. Gallops and skips with one foot. | Improved upward and forward jumps. Travels greater distance. | Hops 7 to 9 times on same foot. Improved speed of hopping. | Throws ball with increased body rotation and some transfer of weight forward. Catches ball with hands; if unsuccessful, may still trap ball against chest. | Rides tricycle rapidly, steers smoothly. |
| 5–6 years | Walks securely on balance beam. Increased speed of run. Gallops more smoothly. True skipping appears. | Jumps off floor about 1 foot. Broad jumps 3 feet. | Hops 50 feet on same foot in 10 seconds. Hops with rhythmical alternation (2 hops on one foot and 2 on the other). | Has mature throwing and catching pattern. Moves arm more and steps forward during throw. Awaits thrown ball with relaxed posture, adjusting body to path and size of ball. | Rides bicycle with training wheels. |

*Sources:* Cratty, 1986; Getchell & Roberton, 1989; Newborg, Stock, & Wnek, 1984; Roberton, 1984.

body. Over the next year, the entire motion becomes more flexible, as the child experiments with ways to allow a softer, more comfortable landing (Roberton & Halverson, 1988). Five- and 6-year-olds hop skillfully. They can repeat the motion many times, moving swiftly across the floor (Getchell & Roberton, 1989).

*Ball Skills.* Play a game of catch with a 2- or 3-year-old, and watch the child's body carefully. Young preschoolers stand still facing the target, throwing with their arms thrust forward. Once again, at first appearance of the skill, other parts of the body are not involved. Catching is equally awkward. Two-year-olds extend their arms and hands rigidly, using them as a single unit to trap the ball. By age 3, children flex their elbows enough to trap the ball against the chest. But if the ball arrives too quickly, younger preschoolers cannot adapt, and it may simply bounce off the child's body (Roberton, 1984).

**FIGURE 8.7** • Changes in catching during early childhood. At age 2, children extend their arms rigidly, and the ball tends to bounce off the body. At age 3, they flex their elbows in preparation for catching, trapping the ball against the chest. By ages 5 and 6, children involve the entire body, catching with the hands and fingers.

Gradually, children call on the shoulders, torso, trunk, and legs to support throwing and catching. By age 4, the body rotates as the child throws, and at 5 years preschoolers begin to shift their weight forward, stepping as they release the ball. As a result, the ball travels faster and farther. When the ball is returned, older preschoolers predict its place of landing by moving forward, backward, or sideways. Then they catch it with their hands and fingers, "giving" with arms and body to absorb the force of the ball (see Figure 8.7).

*Fine Motor Development*

Like gross motor development, fine motor skills take a giant leap forward during early childhood (see Table 8.3). Because control of the hands and fingers improves,

TABLE 8.3 • Changes in Fine Motor Skills During Early Childhood

| Age | Dressing | Feeding | Other |
|---|---|---|---|
| 2–3 years | Puts on and removes simple items of clothing. Zips and unzips large zippers. | Uses spoon effectively. | Opens door by turning knob. Strings large beads. |
| 3–4 years | Fastens and unfastens large buttons. | Serves self food without assistance. | Uses scissors to cut paper. Copies vertical line and circle. |
| 4–5 years | Dresses and undresses without assistance. | Uses fork effectively. | Cuts with scissors following line. Copies triangle, cross, and some letters. |
| 5–6 years | | Uses knife to cut soft food. | Ties single overhand knot; around age 6, ties shoes. Draws person with six parts. Copies some numerals and simple words. |

*Sources:* Furuno et al., 1987; Newborg, Stock, & Wnek, 1984.

young children at play put puzzles together, build structures out of small blocks, cut and paste, and string beads. To parents, the fine motor progress of the preschool years is most apparent in two areas: (1) children's increasing ability to care for their own bodies; and (2) the drawings and paintings that fill the walls at home, day care, and nursery school.

*Self-Help Skills.* During early childhood, children gradually become self-sufficient at dressing and feeding. Two-year-olds put on and take off simple items of clothing. By age 3, they do so well enough to take care of toileting needs by themselves. Between ages 4 and 5, children can dress and undress without supervision. At mealtimes, young preschoolers use a spoon well, and they can serve themselves. By age 4, they are adept with a fork, and around 5 to 6 years they can use a knife to cut soft foods. Roomy clothing with large buttons and zippers and child-sized eating utensils assist children in mastering these skills.

Preschoolers get great satisfaction from managing their own bodies. They are proud of their independence, and their new skills also make life easier for adults. But parents need to be patient about these abilities. When tired and in a hurry, young children often revert to eating with their fingers. And the 3-year-old who dresses himself in the morning sometimes ends up with his shirt on inside out, his pants on backward, and his left snow boot on his right foot! Perhaps the most complex self-help skill of early childhood is shoe tying, which children master around age 6. Success requires a longer attention span, memory for an intricate series of hand movements, and the dexterity to perform them. Shoe tying illustrates the close connection between cognitive and motor development. We will see additional examples of this relationship as we look at the development of young children's drawing and writing.

*Drawing and Writing.* When given crayon and paper, even young toddlers scribble in imitation of others, but their scrawls seem like little more than random tangles of lines. As the young child's ability to mentally represent the world expands, marks on the page take on definite meaning. At first, children's artful representation takes the form of gestures rather than pictures. For example, one 18-month-old took her crayon and hopped it around the page, explaining as she made a series of dots, "Rabbit goes hop-hop." By age 3, children's scribbles start to become pictures. Often this happens after they make a gesture with the crayon, notice that they have drawn a recognizable shape, and then decide to label it. In one case, a 2-year-old made some random marks on a page and then, realizing the resemblance between his scribbles and noodles, named the creation "chicken pie and noodles" (Winner, 1986).

A major milestone in children's drawing occurs when they begin to use lines to represent the boundaries of objects. This permits them to draw their first picture of a person by age 3 or 4. Look at the tadpole image on the left in Figure 8.8. It is a universal one in which the limits of the preschooler's fine motor skills reduce the figure down to the simplest form that still looks like a human being (Gardner, 1980; Winner, 1986).

Unlike many adults, young children do not demand that a drawing be realistic. As they get older, their fine motor control improves, and they learn to desire greater realism. As a result, they create more complex drawings, like the one shown on the right in Figure 8.8 made by a 6-year-old child. Still, children of this age are not very particular about mirroring reality in their pictures. There are perceptual distortions, since not until about age 9 do children figure out how to represent depth in their drawings (Winner, 1986).

As young children experiment with lines and shapes, notice print in storybooks, and observe the writing of others, they try to print letters and, later on, words. Often the first word printed is the child's name. Initially, it may be represented by a single

*To a preschooler, putting on clothing is challenging but rewarding. Young children enjoy a new sense of independence when they can dress themselves. (Mary Kate Denny/ PhotoEdit)*

**FIGURE 8.8** • Examples of young children's drawings. The universal tadpolelike shape that children use to draw their first picture of a person is shown on the left. The tadpole soon becomes an anchor for greater detail, as arms, fingers, toes, and facial features sprout from the basic shape. By the end of the preschool years, children produce more complex, differentiated pictures, like the one on the right drawn by a 6-year-old child. *(Tadpole drawings from* Artful scribbles: The significance of children's drawings, *by Howard Gardner, p. 64. Copyright © 1980 by Howard Gardner. Reprinted by permission of Basic Books, a division of HarperCollins Publishers, Inc. Six-year-old's picture from E. Winner, August 1986, "Where pelicans kiss seals,"* Psychology Today, *20(8), p. 35. Reprinted by permission.)*

letter. "How do you make a D?" my older son David asked at 3 years of age. When I printed a large uppercase D for him, he tried to copy. "D for David" he said as he wrote, quite satisfied with his backward, imperfect creation. A year later, David added several additional letters, and around age 5, he wrote his name clearly enough so that others could read it. In addition to gains in fine motor control, advances in perception contribute to the ability to form letters and words. Like many children, David continued to reverse some letters in his printing until well into second grade. When we take up early childhood perceptual development in the last section of this chapter, you will discover why these letter reversals are so common.

### Factors that Affect Early Childhood Motor Skills

We have been discussing motor milestones in terms of the average age at which children reach them, but, of course, there are wide individual differences. Many factors affect the motor progress of young children.

***Body Build, Race, and Sex***  Body build influences gross motor abilities. Compared to a short, stocky youngster, a tall, muscular child tends to move more quickly and acquire certain skills earlier. Researchers believe that body build contributes to the superior performance of African-American over Caucasian children in running and jumping. African-American youngsters tend to have longer limbs, so they have better leverage (Lee, 1980; Wakat, 1978).

Sex differences in motor skills are also evident in early childhood. Boys are slightly ahead of girls in skills that emphasize force and power. By age 5, they can jump slightly farther, run slightly faster, and throw a ball much farther (about 5 feet beyond the distance covered by girls). At the same time, girls have an edge in fine motor skills and in certain gross motor skills that require a combination of good balance and foot movement, such as hopping and skipping. Boys' greater muscle mass and (in the case of throwing) their slightly longer forearms may contribute to their skill advantages. And, in Chapter 5, we indicated that girls are ahead of boys in overall physical maturity. This difference may be partly responsible for girls' better balance and precision of movement.

From an early age, boys and girls are usually encouraged into different physical activities. For example, fathers often play catch in the backyard with their sons, but they seldom do so with their daughters. Baseballs and footballs are purchased for boys; jump ropes, hula hoops, and games of jacks for girls. As children get older, differences in motor skills between boys and girls get larger, yet sex differences in physical capacity remain small until adolescence. These trends suggest that social pressures for boys to be active and physically skilled and for girls to play quietly at fine motor activities may exaggerate small, genetically based differences that are there in the first place (Thomas & French, 1985).

*Enhancing Early Childhood Motor Development.* Today, many parents provide preschoolers with early training in motor skills, in the form of gymnastics, tumbling, and other lessons. These experiences offer excellent opportunities for physical exercise and social interaction. But aside from throwing (where direct instruction seems to make some difference), there is no evidence that preschoolers exposed to formal lessons are ahead in motor development. Instead, children seem to master the motor skills of early childhood naturally, as part of their everyday play (Espenschade & Eckert, 1980; Roberton, 1984).

Does this mean that adults can do little to promote motor development? The physical environment in which informal play takes place can make a difference in children's mastery of complex motor skills. When children have play spaces and equipment appropriate for running, climbing, jumping, and throwing, along with encouragement to use them, they respond eagerly to these challenges. But if balls are too large and heavy to be properly grasped and thrown, or jungle gyms, ladders, and horizontal bars are suitable for only the largest and strongest youngsters, then children's motor skills are likely to be poorly learned. Preschools, day-care centers, and city playgrounds need to accommodate a wide range of physical abilities by offering a variety of pieces of equipment that differ in size or that can be adjusted to fit the needs of individual children (Herkowitz, 1984).

*When play spaces are properly equipped for preschoolers and adults encourage children to use them, motor development is enhanced. (Erika Stone)*

*BRIEF REVIEW* Motor development proceeds at a rapid pace during early childhood. Improvements in balance support mastery of a variety of gross motor skills, including running, jumping, hopping, galloping, skipping, throwing, and catching. At first, new skills are awkward and involve only isolated regions of the body. Gradually, they become more flexible and include whole body action. Advances in fine motor development can be seen in children's ability to dress themselves and eat efficiently with utensils. Preschoolers also start to draw and print, making use of fine motor skills to represent the world through pictures and written symbols. Many factors are related to early childhood motor development, including body build, race, sex, and the richness and appropriateness of the child's play environment.

• *Mabel and Chad want to do everything they can to support their 3-year-old daughter's athletic development. What advice would you give them?*

## PERCEPTUAL DEVELOPMENT IN EARLY CHILDHOOD

Think back to our discussion of infant perceptual development in Chapter 5. The most striking changes occurred in vision, the sense on which humans depend most for obtaining information from environment. For infants, the initial perceptual task is one of figuring out how the space around them is organized. Once objects are located in space, infants begin to sort them out. For example, they start to discriminate faces as well as other visual patterns. Recall that Eleanor and James Gibson's *differentiation theory* helped us understand this process. Over time, infants search for invariant features (those that remain stable in a changing perceptual world), making finer and finer distinctions among stimuli (to review this theory, return to page 198).

During early childhood, the trends in perceptual development that began in infancy continue. Brain maturation contributes to better integration between the visual and motor systems. As a result, older preschoolers can visually track a thrown ball while moving to a nearby point to catch it. And, besides recognizing a number of geometric shapes and letters of the alphabet, 4- to 6-year-olds can copy them with reasonable accuracy.

Researchers have been especially interested in how detection of the fine-grained structure of visual patterns improves during early childhood, since it helps us understand how children go about the awesome task of discriminating written symbols as they learn to read. Eleanor Gibson has applied differentiation theory to this process. Her research shows that preschoolers begin by recognizing letters as a set of items. By age 3 or 4, they can tell writing from nonwriting (scribbling and pictures), even though they cannot yet identify very many individual letters of the alphabet. Then they go about discriminating particular letters. Those that are alike in shape are most difficult to tell apart. For example, because the invariant features of C and G, E and F, and M and W are very subtle, many preschoolers confuse these letter pairs (Gibson, 1970).

Letters that are mirror images of one another, such as b and d and p and q, are especially hard for young children to tell apart. This finding may remind you of a point made earlier in our discussion of preschoolers' writing. Until age 7 or 8, children print many letters backward. One reason is that until they learn to read,

*According to Eleanor Gibson, the early phase of learning to read involves detection of the invariant features of written symbols. At first, preschoolers distinguish letters from nonletters. Gradually they start to discriminate particular letters. (Tom Pollak/Monkmeyer Press)*

children do not find it especially useful to notice the difference between mirror-image forms. In everyday life, left–right reversals only occur when objects are twin aspects of the same thing. For example, two cups, one with a handle on the left and one with a handle on the right, are identical to young preschoolers. In contrast, children easily discriminate a cup turned upside-down, one placed right side up, and one turned over on its side, since they have many daily experiences in which objects must be placed right side up to be used effectively (Bornstein, 1988). Research reveals that the ability to tune into mirror images, as well as to scan a printed line carefully from left to right, depends in part on experience with reading materials (Casey, 1986). Thus, the very activity of learning to read helps children become sensitive to a variety of perceptual cues.

Of course, becoming a skilled reader is a very long developmental process, entailing much more than discriminating visual forms. Children must combine what they perceive on the printed page with a variety of information processing activities, including sustained attention, memory, comprehension, and inference making. But perceptual skills do seem to be essential, since children with advanced visual abilities read at higher levels (Fisher, Bornstein, & Gross, 1985; Kavale, 1982). We will consider other aspects of early literacy development when we take up the topic of cognitive development in the next chapter.

# SUMMARY

### Body Growth in Early Childhood

• Compared to infancy, gains in body size taper off into a slower pattern of growth in early childhood. Body fat also declines, and children become longer and leaner. New epiphyses appear in the skeleton, where cartilage gradually hardens into bone. Individual differences in body size and rate of physical growth become even more apparent during the preschool years.

• By the end of early childhood, children start to lose their primary teeth. Over the past two decades, improved dental care and water fluoridation have led to dramatic declines in childhood tooth decay. Low-income children, however, continue to suffer from poor dental health.

• Physical growth is an asynchronous process. Different parts of the body grow at different rates. The **general growth curve** describes change in overall body size—rapid during infancy, slower during early and middle childhood, rapid again during adolescence. Exceptions to this trend include the genitals, the lymph tissue, and the brain.

### Brain Development in Early Childhood

• During early childhood, the left cerebral hemisphere grows more rapidly than the right, supporting young children's rapidly expanding language skills.

• Hand preference indicates an individual's **dominant cerebral hemisphere.** Hand preference first appears in infancy and increases during early and middle childhood. Although left-handedness is associated with developmental problems and a shortened life span, the great majority of left-handed children show no abnormalities of any kind.

• During early childhood, connections are established among different brain structures. Fibers linking the **cerebellum** to the cerebral cortex myelinate, enhancing children's balance and motor control. The **reticular formation,** responsible for alertness and consciousness, and the **corpus callosum,** which connects the two cerebral hemispheres, also develop rapidly.

### Factors Affecting Growth and Health in Early Childhood

• Heredity influences physical growth by controlling the release of hormones from the **pituitary gland.** The most important pituitary hormones for childhood growth are **growth hormone (GH)** and **thyroid stimulating hormone (TSH).** Extreme emotional deprivation can affect the production of GH, resulting in **deprivation dwarfism.**

• Preschoolers' slower growth rate causes their appetites to decline, and often they become picky eaters. Young children's social environments have a powerful impact on food preferences. Modeling by others, repeated exposure to new foods, and a positive emotional climate at mealtimes can promote healthy, varied eating in young children.

• Malnutrition can combine with infectious disease to undermine healthy growth. In Third World countries, many children do not receive early immunizations that protect them from childhood illnesses. Immunization rates are lower in the United States than in other industrialized nations because many economically disadvantaged children do not have access to health insurance and good medical care.

• Unintentional injuries are the leading cause of childhood mortality. Injury victims are more likely to be boys, to be temperamentally irritable, inattentive, and negative in mood, and to be growing up in poor, inner-city families. A variety of approaches are needed to prevent childhood injuries. These include laws that promote child safety, modification of home and play environments, public education, and interventions designed to change parent and child behaviors.

*Motor Development in Early Childhood*

• During early childhood, children continue to integrate previously acquired motor skills into more complex systems of action. Body growth causes the child's center of gravity to shift toward the trunk, and balance improves, paving the way for an explosion of gross motor milestones. Preschoolers' gait becomes smooth and rhythmic, and they run, jump, hop, gallop, and eventually skip. These abilities, as well as throwing and catching, become better coordinated as movements of the entire body support each new skill.

• Gains in control of the hands and fingers lead to dramatic changes in fine motor skills. Preschoolers gradually become self-sufficient at dressing themselves and using a fork and knife at mealtimes. By age 3 children's scribbles become pictures. Their drawings increase in complexity with age.

Young children also try to print letters of the alphabet, an ability that gradually improves.

• A variety of factors affect early childhood motor development, including body build, race, and sex. Differences in motor skills between boys and girls are partly genetic, but environmental pressures seem to exaggerate them.

• Children master the motor skills of early childhood through informal play experiences. Richly equipped play environments that accommodate a wide range of physical abilities are important during the preschool years.

*Perceptual Development in Early Childhood*

• During early childhood, brain maturation contributes to improvements in integrating the visual and motor systems. The Gibsons' differentiation theory helps explain how children discriminate written symbols as they learn to read. Because preschoolers have little need to distinguish mirror-image forms in everyday life, left–right letter reversals are common in early childhood. Exposure to reading materials increases the variety of perceptual cues to which children are sensitive.

## IMPORTANT TERMS AND CONCEPTS

general growth curve (p. 284)
dominant cerebral hemisphere (p. 285)
cerebellum (p. 286)
reticular formation (p. 286)

corpus callosum (p. 286)
pituitary gland (p. 287)
growth hormone (GH) (p. 287)

thyroid stimulating hormone (TSH) (p. 287)
deprivation dwarfism (p. 289)

## FOR FURTHER INFORMATION AND SPECIAL HELP

**Infectious Disease in Childhood**

U.S. Centers for Disease Control
5600 Fishers Lane
Rockville, MD 20857
(301) 443-2610

Surveys national disease trends and environmental health problems. Has organized an agency network to address problems of infectious disease in day care, including distributing information to day-care staff on techniques that prevent the spread of infection.

American Academy of Pediatrics
P.O. Box 927
Elk Grove Village, IL 60007
(312) 228-5005

Provides public education on a variety of childhood health issues. Among the many pamphlets and publications available are written guidelines for effective control of infectious disease.

Child Care Information Exchange
Box 2890
Redmond, WA 98052
(206) 883-9394

A bimonthly publication written especially for day-care directors that addresses the practical issues of running a center. Articles discussing health and safety are often included.

U.S. Department of Health and Human Services
U.S. Government Printing Office
Superintendent of Documents
723 N. Capitol Street, N. W.
Washington, DC 20401
(202) 783-3283

Publishes *What to Do to Stop Disease in Child Day Care Centers: A Kit for Child Day Care Directors, Caregivers, and Parents,* document no. 017-023-00172-8. The kit includes handbooks, posters, and other items with specific advice on health-related issues.

**Childhood Injury Control**

U.S. Consumer Product Safety Commission
5401 Westbard Avenue
Bethesda, MD 20207
(800) 638-2772

Establishes and enforces product safety standards. Operates a hot line providing information on safety issues and recall of dangerous consumer products.

Safe Kids
111 Michigan Avenue, N.W.
Washington, DC 20010-2970
(202) 939-4993

A national organization with local and state affiliates devoted to improving child safety. Provides public education and promotes community intervention aimed at reducing five types of injuries: motor vehicle, burns, drownings, poisonings, and falls.

"The Young Artist," Li Cheng, 11 years, Taiwan.
Reprinted by permission from the International Museum of
Children's Art, Oslo, Norway.

# Cognitive Development in Early Childhood

**9**

Piaget's Theory: The Preoperational Stage
 *Advances in Mental Representation   Make-Believe Play   Limitations of Preoperational
 Thought   New Research on Preoperational Thought   Evaluation of the Preoperational
 Stage   Piaget and Education*

Further Challenges to Piaget's Ideas: Vygotsky's Sociocultural Theory
 *Piaget versus Vygotsky: Children's Private Speech   The Social Origins of Early Childhood
 Cognition   Vygotsky and Education*

Information Processing in Early Childhood
 *Attention   Memory   The Young Child's Theory of Mind   Early Literacy and
 Mathematical Development   A Note on Academics in Early Childhood*

Individual Differences in Mental Development During Early Childhood
 *Early Childhood Intelligence Tests   Home Environment and Mental Development   Preschool
 and Day Care   Educational Television*

Language Development in Early Childhood
 *Vocabulary Development   Grammatical Development   Becoming an Effective
 Conversationalist   Supporting Language Learning in Early Childhood*

O ne rainy morning, as I observed in our laboratory preschool, Leslie, the children's teacher, joined me at the back of the room to watch for a moment herself. "Preschoolers' minds are such a curious blend of logic, fantasy, and faulty reasoning," Leslie reflected. "Everyday, I'm startled by the maturity and originality of many things they say and do. Yet at other times, their thinking seems limited and inflexible."

Leslie's comments sum up the puzzling contradictions of early childhood cognition. Over the previous week, I had seen many examples as I followed the activities of 3-year-old Jason. That day, I found him at the puzzle table, moments after a loud clash of thunder occurred outside. Jason looked up, startled, then turned to Leslie and pronounced, "The man turned on the thunder!" Leslie patiently explained that people can't turn thunder on or off. But Jason persisted. "Then a lady did it," he stated with certainty.

In other respects, Jason's cognitive skills seemed surprisingly advanced. At snack time, he accurately counted, "One, two, three, four!" and then got four cartons of milk, giving one to each child at his table. Jason's keen memory and ability to categorize were also evident. As he sat in the reading corner, I heard him recite by heart *The Very Hungry Caterpillar* (Carle, 1969), a story he had heard many times before. Jason's favorite picture books were about animals, and he could name and group together dozens of them.

Still, Jason's cognitive skills seemed fragile and insecure. When more than four children joined his snack group, Jason's counting broke down. And some of his notions about quantity seemed as fantastic as his understanding of thunder. Across the snack table, Priti dumped out her raisins, and they scattered in front of her. "How come you got lots, and I only got this little bit?" asked Jason, failing to realize that he had just as many; they were simply all bunched up in a tiny red box.

In this chapter, we explore the many facets of early childhood cognition, drawing from three theories with which you are already familiar. We begin with Piaget's preoperational stage, which, for the most part, emphasizes preschool children's deficits rather than their strengths. New research on preoperational thought along with two additional perspectives—Vygotsky's sociocultural theory and information processing—extends our understanding of preschoolers' cognitive competencies. Then we turn to a variety of factors that contribute to individual differences in early childhood mental development—the home environment, the quality of preschool and day care, and the many hours young children spend watching television. Our chapter concludes with language development, the most awesome achievement of early childhood.

As our discussion proceeds, we will consider the controversial question of how language and thought are related. Do young children first master ideas and then translate them into words? Or does the capacity for language open new cognitive doors, permitting children to think in more mature ways? Major theorists differ sharply on this issue. We begin with Piaget's viewpoint in the next section.

## PIAGET'S THEORY: THE PREOPERATIONAL STAGE

As children move from the sensorimotor to the **preoperational stage,** the most obvious change is an extraordinary increase in representational, or symbolic, activity. Recall that toddlers have some ability to mentally represent the world. However, between the ages of 2 and 7, this capacity blossoms.

### Advances in Mental Representation

As I looked around the preschool classroom, signs of developing representation were present everywhere—in the children's drawings and paintings, in their re-creations of family life in the housekeeping area, and in their delight at storytime. Especially impressive were strides taking place in language skill. During free play, a hum of chattering voices rose from the classroom.

Piaget acknowledged that language is our most flexible means of mental representation. By detaching thought from action, it permits cognition to be far more efficient than it was during the sensorimotor stage. When we think in words, we overcome the limits of our momentary perceptions. We can deal with the past, present, and future all at once, creating larger, interconnected images of reality. And we can combine parts of the world in unique ways, as when we think about a hungry caterpillar eating bananas or monsters flying through the forest at night (Miller, 1989).

Yet despite the power of language, Piaget did not believe that it plays a major role in cognitive development. According to Piaget, language does not give rise to representational thought. Instead, sensorimotor activity provides the foundation that makes language possible, just as it gives rise to deferred imitation and make-believe play. Can you think of evidence that supports Piaget's view? Indeed, there is some. Recall from Chapter 6 that the first words toddlers use have a strong sensorimotor basis. In addition, toddlers acquire an impressive range of cognitive categories long before they use words to label them (see pages 219–220). These findings are consis-

**Preoperational stage**
Piaget's second stage, in which rapid growth in representation takes place. However, thought is not yet logical. Spans the years from 2 to 7.

tent with Piaget's belief that early language builds on advances in nonverbal cognitive skills, rather than the other way around. Still, Piaget's account of the link between language and thought is regarded by others as incomplete, as we will see later in this chapter.

## Make-Believe Play

Make-believe play provides another excellent example of the development of representation during the preoperational stage. Like language, it increases dramatically during early childhood (Singer & Singer, 1990). Piaget believed that through pretending, young children practice and strengthen newly acquired representational schemes. Drawing on his ideas, several investigators have traced changes in make-believe play during the preschool years.

**The Development of Make-Believe.** One day, Jason's 18-month-old brother Dwayne came to visit the classroom. Dwayne wandered around, picked up the receiver of a toy telephone, said, "Hi Mommy," and then dropped it. In the housekeeping area, he found a cup, pretended to drink, and then toddled off again.

In the meantime, Jason joined a group of children in the block area for a space shuttle launch. "That can be our control tower," he suggested to Vance, pointing to a corner by a bookshelf.

"Wait, I gotta get it all ready," said Lynette, who was still arranging the astronauts (two dolls and a teddy bear) inside a circle of large blocks, which represented the rocket.

"Countdown!" Jason announced, speaking into a small wooden block, his pretend walkie-talkie.

"Five, six, two, four, one, blastoff!" responded Vance, commander of the control tower.

Lynette made one of the dolls push a pretend button and reported, "Brrrm, brrrm, they're going up!"

A comparison of Dwayne's pretend with that of Jason and his classmates illustrates three important changes in make-believe, each of which reflects the preschool

During early childhood, make-believe play blossoms. This child uses objects as active agents in a complex play scene. (M. Siluk/The Image Works)

child's growing symbolic mastery. First, over time, play becomes increasingly detached from the real-life conditions associated with it. In early pretending, toddlers use only realistic objects—for example, a toy telephone to talk into or a cup to drink from. Around age 2, use of less realistic toys, such as a block for a telephone receiver, becomes more frequent. Sometime during the third year, children can imagine objects and events without support from the real world, as when Jason invented the control tower in a corner of the room. We can see that children's representations are becoming more flexible, since a play symbol no longer has to resemble the object for which it stands (Bretherton et al., 1984; Corrigan, 1987).

Second, the way in which the "child as self" participates in play changes with age. When make-believe first appears, it is directed toward the self—for example, Dwayne pretends to feed only himself. A short time later, children direct pretend actions toward other objects, as when the child feeds a doll. And early in the third year, they use objects as active agents, and the child becomes a detached participant who makes a doll feed itself or (in Lynette's case) push a button to launch a rocket. Here we can see how make-believe gradually becomes less self-centered, as children realize that agents and recipients of pretend actions can be independent of themselves (Corrigan, 1987; Ungerer et al., 1981).

Finally, over time play includes increasingly complex scheme combinations. For example, Dwayne can pretend to drink from a cup but he does not yet combine pouring and drinking. Later on, children combine schemes, especially in **sociodramatic play,** the make-believe with others that first appears around age 2 1/2 (Corrigan, 1987). Already, Jason and his classmates can create and coordinate several roles in an elaborate plot. By the end of early childhood, children have a sophisticated understanding of role relationships and story lines.

**Advantages of Make-Believe.**   Today, Piaget's view of make-believe as mere practice of representational schemes is regarded as too limited. Research indicates that play not only reflects, but also contributes to children's cognitive and social skills (Rubin, Fein, & Vandenberg, 1983). Sociodramatic play has been studied most thoroughly. In comparison to social nonpretend activities (such as drawing or putting puzzles together), during social pretend preschoolers' interactions last longer, show more involvement, draw larger numbers of children into the activity, and are more cooperative (Connolly, Doyle, & Reznick, 1988). When we consider these findings, it is not surprising that preschoolers who spend more time at sociodramatic play are advanced in cognitive development and are seen as more socially competent by their teachers (Burns & Brainerd, 1979; Connolly & Doyle, 1984). Young children who especially enjoy pretending also score higher on tests of imagination and creativity (Dansky, 1980; Pepler & Ross, 1981). We will return to the topic of early childhood play in Chapter 10.

## Limitations of Preoperational Thought

Aside from the development of representation, Piaget described preschool children in terms of what they *cannot,* rather than *can,* understand. The very name of the stage—*preoperational*—indicates that Piaget compared preschoolers to older, more capable concrete operational children. As a result, he discovered little of a positive nature about the young child's thinking. Later, when we discuss new research on preoperational thought, we will see that Piaget underestimated the cognitive competencies of early childhood. But first, let's consider young children's thinking from Piaget's point of view.

Concept Table 9.1 summarizes a set of concepts that Piaget used to describe young children's thought. As you look over these characteristics, you will see that for Piaget, **operations**—mental actions that obey logical rules—are where cognitive

**Sociodramatic play**

The make-believe play with others that first appears around age 2 1/2.

**Operations**

In Piaget's theory, mental actions that obey logical rules.

**CONCEPT TABLE 9.1 • Limitations of Preoperational Thought**

| Concept | Important Point | Example |
|---|---|---|
| Egocentrism | Preoperational children assume that others perceive, think, and feel just the way they do. This belief underlies all other limitations of the preoperational stage. | Three-year-old Josie turned on the TV in the living room while her father ate breakfast in the kitchen. "What's that boy doing?" called Josie while pointing to the screen, failing to realize that her father couldn't see the TV from where he was sitting. |
| Animistic thinking | Preoperational children regard inanimate objects as having lifelike qualities, just like the self. | Josie and her parents watched the sunset after spending a day at the seashore. As the sun started to sink below the horizon and the sky darkened, Josie remarked, "That sunshine's getting very sleepy." |
| Perception-bound thought | Preoperational children make judgments based on the immediate, perceptual appearance of objects. | Josie's mother handed her a large glass half full of lemonade and her brother a small glass filled to the top. "Fill mine up like Billie's so I'll have just as much," said Josie. |
| Centration | Preoperational children tend to center on one aspect of a situation to the neglect of other important features. | At preschool, it was Hallie's fourth birthday. Although Amy was only 3, Josie announced, "Amy's older 'cause she's taller," centering on height as a measure of age. |
| States versus transformations | Preoperational children focus on momentary states, failing to consider dynamic transformations between them. As a result, they have difficulty relating beginning and ending states in a situation. | Josie saw her little cousin Susie, whom she'd played with several times before, dressed up in a bathing suit and cap. "What's that baby's name?" Josie asked. Later, when Susie had her shirt and shorts on, Josie said, "Oh, it's Susie again." |
| Irreversibility | Preoperational children cannot think through a series of steps in a problem and then go backward, mentally returning to the starting point. | Josie's mother tried to explain, "When Susie puts on a bathing suit, she's still the same person." But Josie insisted that the bathing suit baby was not Susie. She failed to imagine Susie changing from her shorts and shirt into her suit and then back again. |
| Transductive reasoning | Preoperational children reason from particular to particular, rather than from particular to general (inductively) or general to particular (deductively). | "Why does it get dark at night?" Leslie asked the children at school one day. "Because we go to bed," responded Josie. |
| Lack of hierarchical classification | Preoperational children have difficulty grouping objects into hierarchies of classes and subclasses. | Leslie gave Josie some paper shapes to sort—red and blue squares and circles. Josie put all the red ones in one pile and the blue ones in another, but she had difficulty separating the groups further, by shape. |

development is going. In the preoperational stage, children are not capable of operations. Instead, their thinking is rigid, limited to one aspect of a situation at a time, and strongly influenced by the way things appear at the moment. When judged by adult standards, preoperational reasoning often seems distorted and incorrect.

*Egocentrism.* According to Piaget, the most serious deficiency of preoperational thinking, the one that underlies all others, is **egocentrism.** The word *ego* means self, and the term *egocentrism* suggests that preschoolers are self-centered. By this,

**Egocentrism**
The inability to distinguish viewpoints of others from one's own.

Piaget did not mean selfish or inconsiderate. Instead, he believed that when children first begin to mentally represent the world, they are egocentric with respect to their symbolic viewpoints. They are unaware of any perspectives other than their own, and they believe that everyone else perceives, thinks, and feels the same way they do (Piaget, 1950).

Piaget's most convincing demonstration of egocentrism involves a task called the *three mountains problem* (see Figure 9.1). A child is permitted to walk around a display of three mountains of different heights arranged on a table. Then the child stands on one side, and a doll is placed at various locations around the display. The child must choose a photograph that shows what the display looks like from the doll's perspective. Below the age of 6 or 7, most children simply select the photo that shows the mountains from their own point of view (Piaget & Inhelder, 1948/ 1956).

Egocentrism shows up in other aspects of children's reasoning as well. Recall Jason's firm insistence that someone must have turned on the thunder, in much the same way that he uses a switch to turn on a light or radio. Similarly, Piaget regarded egocentrism as responsible for preoperational children's **animistic thinking**—the belief that inanimate objects have lifelike qualities, such as thoughts, wishes, feelings, and intentions, just like themselves. The 3-year-old who charmingly explains that the sun is angry at the clouds and has chased them away is demonstrating this kind of reasoning.

**FIGURE 9.1** • Piaget's three mountains problem. Each mountain is distinguished by its color and by its summit. One has a red cross, another a small house, and the third a snow-capped peak. Children at the preoperational stage are egocentric. They cannot draw or select a picture that shows the mountains from the doll's perspective. They simply represent their own.

**Animistic thinking**
The belief that inanimate objects have lifelike qualities, such as thoughts, wishes, feelings, and intentions.

Piaget argued that egocentrism leads to the rigidity and illogical nature of young children's thinking. Thought proceeds so strongly from a single point of view that children do not *accommodate,* or revise their reasoning in response to their physical and social worlds. Egocentric thought is not reflective thought, which critically examines itself. But to fully appreciate these shortcomings of the preoperational stage, let's consider some additional tasks that Piaget presented to children.

***Inability to Conserve.***   Piaget's most important tasks are the conservation problems. **Conservation** refers to the idea that certain physical characteristics of objects remain the same, even when their outward appearance changes. At snack time, Jason revealed that he had difficulty with conservation of number. Priti and Jason each had identical boxes of raisins, but after Priti spread hers out on the table, Jason was convinced that she had more.

Another type of conservation task involves liquid. In this problem, the child is presented with two identical tall glasses of water and asked if they contain equal amounts. Once the child agrees, the water in one glass is poured into a short, wide container, changing the appearance of the water but not its amount. Then the child is asked whether the amount of water is still the same or whether it has changed. Preoperational children think that the quantity of water is no longer the same. They explain their reasoning in ways like this: "There is less now because the water is way down here" (that is, its level is so low in the short, wide container) or "There is more water now because it is all spread out." There are many types of Piagetian conservation tasks. You will find others in Figure 9.2 that you can try with children.

Preoperational children's inability to conserve highlights several related aspects of their thinking. First, their understanding is **perception-bound.** They are easily distracted by the concrete, perceptual appearance of objects (it *looks* like there is less water in the short, wide container, so there *must be* less water). Second, their thinking is *centered,* or characterized by **centration.** In other words, they focus on one aspect of a situation to the neglect of other important features. In the case of conservation of liquid, the child centers on the height of the water in the two containers, failing to realize that all changes in height of the liquid are compensated by changes in width. Third, children of this stage focus on *momentary states* in a situation rather than *dynamic transformations* between them. For example, in the conservation of liquid problem, they treat the initial and final states of the water as completely unrelated events. Another problem that Piaget presented to children dramatically illustrates this tendency to emphasize **states versus transformations.** A bar is allowed to fall freely from an upright position to a horizontal one. Then the child is asked either to draw or select a picture that shows what happened. Preoperational children focus only on the beginning and ending states, ignoring the bar's intermediate path of movement.

The most important illogical feature of preoperational thought is **irreversibility.** It refers to the inability to mentally go through a series of steps and then reverse direction, returning to the starting point. *Reversibility,* the opposite of this concept, is part of every logical operation. Notice how Jason cannot reverse after Priti spills her raisins. He does not think to himself, "I know that Priti doesn't have more raisins than I do. She just poured them out of that little red box, and if we put them back again, her raisins and my raisins would look just the same."

***Transductive Reasoning.***   Reversible thinking is flexible and well organized. Because preoperational children are not capable of it, their explanations are often collections of disconnected facts and contradictions. Piaget called this feature of young children's thought **transductive reasoning,** which means reasoning from one

**Conservation**

The understanding that certain physical characteristics of objects remain the same, even when their outward appearance changes.

**Perception-bound**

Being easily distracted by the concrete, perceptual appearance of objects.

**Centration**

The tendency to focus on one aspect of a situation to the neglect of other important features.

**States versus transformations**

The tendency to treat the initial and final states in a problem as completely unrelated.

**Irreversibility**

The inability to mentally go through a series of steps in a problem and then return to the starting point.

**Transductive reasoning**

Reasoning from one particular event to another particular event, instead of from general to particular or particular to general.

**FIGURE 9.2** • Some Piagetian conservation tasks. Children at the preoperational stage cannot yet conserve.

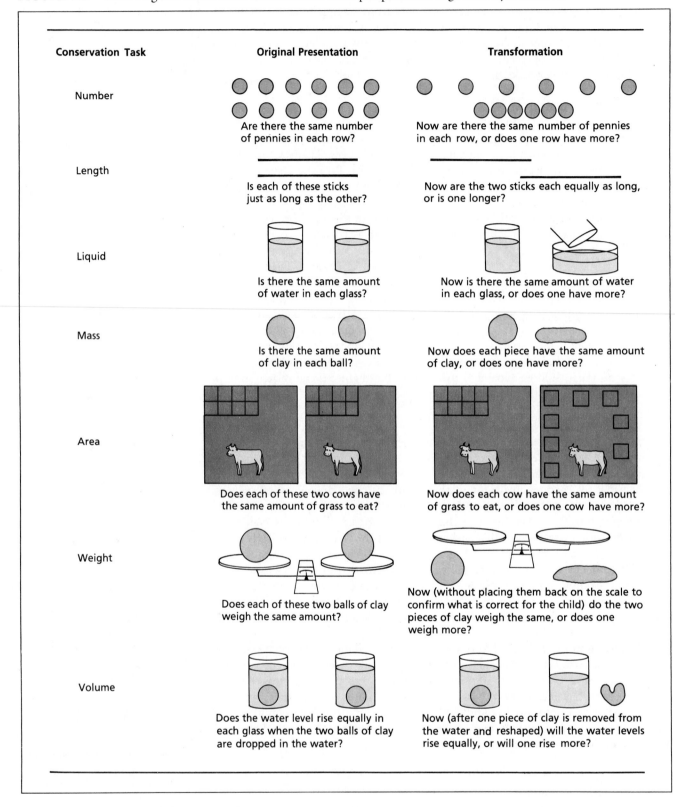

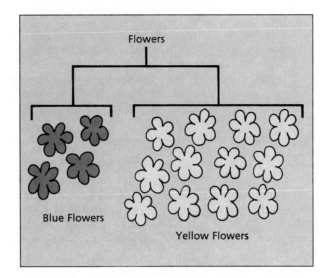

**FIGURE 9.3** • A Piagetian class inclusion problem. Children are shown 16 flowers, 4 of which are blue and 12 of which are yellow. Asked whether there are more yellow flowers or more flowers, the preoperational child responds, "More yellow flowers," failing to realize that both yellow and blue flowers are embedded in the category of "flowers."

particular event to another particular event. In other words, preschoolers link together two events that occur close in time and space in a cause and effect fashion. Sometimes this leads to some fantastic connections, as in the following interview that Piaget conducted with a young child about why the clouds move:

> You have already seen the clouds moving along? What makes them move?—*When we move along, they move along too.*—Can you make them move?—*Everybody can, when they walk.*—When I walk and you are still, do they move?—*Yes.*—And at night, when everyone is asleep, do they move?—*Yes.*—But you tell me that they move when somebody walks.—*They always move. The cats, when they walk, and then the dogs, they make the clouds move along.* (Piaget, 1929, p. 62)

True logical reasoning is not like this. It is either *inductive,* proceeding from a particular event to a general rule, such as: "We are walking right now, but the clouds are still. Therefore, our walking cannot make the clouds move." Or it can be *deductive,* proceeding from a general rule to a particular event. But it does not assume a causal association between two events simply because they occur at the same time or in the same place.

***Lack of Hierarchical Classification.*** Because preoperational children are not yet capable of logical operations, they have difficulty with **hierarchical classification.** That is, they cannot yet organize objects into hierarchies of classes and subclasses on the basis of similarities and differences. Piaget illustrated this with his famous *class inclusion problem.* Children are shown a set of common objects, such as 16 flowers, most of which are yellow and a few of which are blue (see Figure 9.3). When asked whether there are more yellow flowers or more flowers, preoperational children respond confidently, "More yellow flowers!" Their approach to the problem shows a tendency to center on the overriding perceptual feature of yellow and an inability to think reversibly by moving from the whole class (flowers) to the parts (yellow and blue) and back again.

***Summing Up Preoperational Thought.*** How can we combine the diverse characteristics of the preoperational stage into a unified description of what Piaget believed the young child's thought to be like? John Flavell, a well-known Piagetian scholar, suggests that Piaget viewed all these traits as expressions of a single, underlying cognitive orientation. Taken together, they reveal that preoperational thought

**Hierarchical classification**
The organization of objects into classes and subclasses on the basis of similarities and differences between the groups.

bears the impress of its sensory-motor origins. . . . It is extremely concrete . . . concerned more with immobile, eye-catching configurations than with more subtle, less obvious components . . . it is unconcerned with proof or logical justification and, in general, unaware of the effect of its communication on others. In short, in more respects than not, it resembles sensory-motor action which has simply been transposed to a new (symbolic) arena of operation. (Flavell, 1963, p. 162)

### New Research on Preoperational Thought

Over the past two decades, Piaget's account of a cognitively deficient preschool child has been seriously challenged. If researchers give his tasks in just the way that he originally designed them, indeed they find that preschoolers do perform poorly. But a close look at Piagetian problems reveals that many of them contain confusing or unfamiliar elements or too many pieces of information for young children to handle at once. As a result, preschoolers' responses do not reflect their true abilities. Piaget also missed many naturally occurring instances of preschoolers' effective reasoning. Let's look at some examples that illustrate these points.

**Egocentrism and Animism.** Are young children really so egocentric that they believe a person standing in a different location in a room sees the same thing that they see? Children's responses to Piaget's three mountains task suggest that the answer is "yes," but more recent studies say "no." When researchers change the nature of the visual display to include objects that are familiar to preschoolers, they perform quite maturely (Borke, 1975).

Nonegocentric responses also appear in young children's everyday interactions with people. For example, preschoolers adapt their speech to fit the needs of their listeners. Jason uses shorter, simpler expressions when talking to his little brother Dwayne than when speaking to his agemates or to adults (Gelman & Shatz, 1978). Also, in describing objects, children do not use such words as "big" and "little" in a rigid, egocentric fashion. Instead, they *adjust* their descriptions, taking account of the context. By age 3, children judge a 2-inch shoe as small when seen by itself (because it is much smaller than most shoes) but as big when asked about its appropriateness for a very tiny 5-inch doll (Gelman & Ebeling, 1989). These flexible communicative skills challenge Piaget's description of young children as strongly egocentric.

Recent studies also indicate that Piaget overestimated preschoolers' animistic beliefs because he asked children about objects with which they have little direct experience, such as the clouds, sun, and moon. Children as young as 3 rarely think that very familiar inanimate objects, such as rocks and crayons, are alive. They do make errors when questioned about certain vehicles, such as trains and airplanes. But these objects appear to be self-moving, a characteristic of almost all living things. And they also have some lifelike features—for example, headlights that look like eyes (Dolgin & Behrend, 1984; Richards & Siegler, 1986). Children's responses result from incomplete knowledge about some objects, not from a rigid belief that inanimate objects are alive. Experience contributes to preschoolers' grasp of other natural concepts as well—in particular, their understanding of death, as Box 9.1 reveals.

**Illogical Characteristics of Thought.** Many studies have reexamined the illogical characteristics that Piaget saw in the preoperational stage. Results show that when tasks are simplified and made relevant to preschoolers' everyday lives, they do better than Piaget might have expected.

For example, when a conservation of number task is scaled down to include only three items instead of six or seven, preschoolers perform well (Gelman, 1972). The ability to pay attention to transformations and think reversibly also shows up in other reasoning problems. In a recent study, children were shown "picture stories" of

## FROM RESEARCH TO PRACTICE

### Box 9.1  *Young Children's Understanding of Death*

*F*ive-year-old Miriam arrived at preschool the day after her dog Pepper died. Instead of running to play with the other children, she stayed close by Leslie's side. Leslie noticed Miriam's discomfort and asked, "What's wrong?"

"Daddy said Pepper had a sick tummy. He fell asleep and died." For a moment, Miriam looked hopeful, "When I get home, Pepper might be up."

Leslie answered directly, "No, Pepper won't get up again. He's not asleep. He's dead, and that means he can't sleep, eat, run, or play anymore."

Miriam wandered off. Later, she returned to Leslie and confessed, "I chased Pepper too hard," tears streaming from her eyes.

Leslie put her arm around Miriam. "Pepper didn't die because you chased him. He was very old and very sick," she explained.

Over the next few days, Miriam asked many more questions: "When I go to sleep, will I die?" "Can a tummy ache make you die?" "Does Pepper feel better now?" "Will Mommy and Daddy die?"

As adults we understand death in terms of three basic ideas: (1) *permanence:* once a living thing dies, it cannot be brought back to life; (2) *universality:* all living things eventually die; and (3) *nonfunctionality:* all living functions, including thought, movement, and vital signs, cease at death.

Without clear explanations, young children rely on the egocentric and magical thinking of Piaget's preoperational stage to make sense of death. They may believe, as Miriam did, that they are responsible for a relative or pet's death. (Return to the story of little Sam in Chapter 1, page 16, for another example). And they can easily come to incorrect conclusions—in Miriam's case, that sleeping or having a stomachache can cause someone to die.

Research shows that preschoolers master the three components of the death concept in a specific or-

der, with most children arriving at an adultlike understanding by age 7. Permanence, the notion that death cannot be reversed, is the first and most easily understood idea. When Leslie explained that Pepper would not get up again, Miriam accepted this fact quickly, perhaps because she had seen it in other less emotionally charged situations, such as the dead butterflies and beetles that she picked up and inspected while playing outside (Furman, 1990). Appreciation of universality comes slightly later. At first, children think that certain people do not die, especially those with whom they have close emotional ties or who are like themselves—other children. Finally, nonfunctionality is the most difficult component of death for children to grasp. Many preschoolers view dead things as retaining living capacities. When they first comprehend nonfunctionality, they do so in terms of its most visible aspects, such as heartbeat and breathing. Only later do they understand that thinking, feeling, and dreaming also cease (Speece & Brent, 1984; Stambrook & Parker, 1987).

Preschoolers' incompletely formed ideas about death are important to keep in mind when the death of a pet or relative occurs. Simple, direct explanations help children understand. Although parents often worry that discussing death with children will fuel their fears, this is not the case. Instead, children who have a good grasp of the facts of death have an easier time accepting it. When preschoolers ask very difficult questions—"Will I die?" "Will you die?"—parents can be truthful as well as comforting by taking advantage of children's sense of time. They can say something like, "Not for many, many years. First, I'm going to enjoy you as a grown-up and be a grandparent" (Furman, 1978). Open, honest discussions with children contribute not only to their cognitive appreciation of the concept, but also to their emotional well-being.

---

familiar experiences. In some, an object went from its basic state to a changed condition. For example, a cup became a wet cup. In others, it returned from its changed condition to its basic state. That is, a wet cup became a (dry) cup. Children were asked to pick an item from three choices (in this case, water, drying up cloth, or feather) that caused the object to change. Most 3-year-olds had difficulty; they picked water for both transformations. But 4-year-olds did well. They selected appropriate intermediate objects and reasoned effectively in either direction, from basic states to changed conditions and back again (Das Gupta & Bryant, 1989). This suggests that by age 4, preschoolers notice transformations, reverse their thinking, and understand causality in familiar contexts.

***Hierarchical Classification.*** Even though preschoolers have difficulty with Piagetian class inclusion tasks, their everyday knowledge seems to be organized into nested categories at an early age. A growing research literature reveals that, at first, children work on establishing *basic-level categories*—those at an intermediate level of generality, such as "chairs," "tables," "dressers," and "beds." Children's performance on object-sorting tasks indicates that by age 3 or 4, they can combine basic-level categories into more *general categories,* such as "furniture." They can also break them down into *subcategories,* such as "rocking chairs" and "desk chairs" (Mervis & Crisafi, 1982). Preschoolers' category systems are not yet very complex, and concrete operational reasoning facilitates their development (Ricco, 1989). But the capacity to classify hierarchically is present in early childhood.

***Appearance versus Reality.*** So far, we have seen that preschoolers show some remarkably advanced reasoning when presented with familiar situations and simplified problems. Yet new studies also reveal that in certain situations, young children are easily tricked by the outward appearance of things, just as Piaget suggested.

Recently, John Flavell and his colleagues took a close look at children's ability to distinguish appearance from reality. They presented children with objects that were disguised in various ways and asked what the items were, "really and truly." At age 3, children had some ability to separate the way an object appeared to feel from the way it truly felt. For example, they understood that even though an ice cube did not feel cold to their gloved finger, it "really and truly" was cold (Flavell, Green, & Flavell, 1989). But preschoolers were easily tricked by sights and sounds. When asked whether a white piece of paper placed behind a blue filter is "really and truly blue" or whether a can that sounds like a baby crying when turned over is "really and truly a baby," they often responded "yes!" Not until the very end of early childhood did children do well on these tasks (Flavell, Green, & Flavell, 1987).

How do children go about mastering distinctions between appearance and reality? Make-believe play may be important. Children can tell the difference between pretend play and real experiences long before they answer many appearance–reality problems correctly (DiLalla & Watson, 1988; Woolley & Wellman, 1990). During early childhood, children integrate a wide variety of objects into their make-believe themes. Often we hear them say such things as, "Pretend this block is a telephone," or "Let's use this box for a house." Experiencing the contrast between everyday and playful use of objects may help children refine their understanding of what is real and what is unreal in the surrounding world.

## Evaluation of the Preoperational Stage

How can we make sense of the contradictions between Piaget's conclusions and the findings of new research? The evidence as a whole indicates that Piaget was partly wrong and partly right about young children's cognitive capacities. When given simple tasks based on familiar experiences, preschoolers show the beginnings of logical operations long before the concrete operational stage. But their reasoning is not as well developed as that of the school-age child, since they fail Piaget's three mountains, conservation, and class inclusion tasks and have difficulty separating appearance from reality.

The fact that preschoolers have some logical understanding suggests that the attainment of logical operations is a gradual process. Operational thought is not absent at one point in time and suddenly present at another. Instead, children demonstrate mature reasoning at an early age, although it is fragile and incomplete. Evidence that preschool children can be trained to perform well on Piagetian problems, such as conservation and class inclusion, supports this idea (Beilin, 1978; McCabe & Siegel, 1987). It makes sense that children who possess part of a capacity will benefit from training, unlike those with no understanding at all.

Still, the idea that logical operations develop gradually poses a serious challenge to Piaget's stage concept, which assumes sudden and abrupt change toward logical reasoning around 6 or 7 years of age. Does a preoperational stage of development really exist? Some researchers no longer think so. They believe that children work out their understanding of each type of task separately. Their thinking is basically the same at all ages but just present to a greater or lesser extent (Gelman & Baillargeon, 1983). Recall from earlier chapters that this view of cognitive development as continuous is the basis for an alternative approach—information processing—which we take up shortly.

Other experts think the stage concept is still valid but that Piaget's definition of it needs to be refined. For example, Flavell (1982) argues for a less strict concept of stage, one in which certain capacities take a long time rather than a short time to develop. From this point of view, a stage simply refers to an extended period of related developmental changes. Flavell believes the stage idea is useful because it suggests that the young child's reasoning has a unique quality. In his words, "Perhaps what the field needs is another genius like Piaget to show us how, and to what extent, all those cognitive-developmental strands within the growing child are really knotted together" (Flavell, 1985, p. 297).

## Piaget and Education

Over the past 30 years, Piaget's theory has had a major impact on education, especially during early childhood. Leslie was greatly influenced by Piaget's work, which she studied in college. Three educational principles derived from his theory have become realities in her classroom:

1. *An emphasis on discovery learning.* Piaget believed that children learn best by acting directly on their world. In a Piagetian classroom, children are encouraged to discover for themselves through spontaneous interaction with the environment. Leslie has equipped her classroom with a rich variety of materials and play areas designed to promote exploration and discovery—art, puzzles, table games, dress-up clothing, building blocks, reading corner, woodworking, and more. For most of the morning, children choose freely from among these activities.

2. *Sensitivity to children's readiness to learn.* A Piagetian classroom does not try to speed up development. Instead, Piaget believed that appropriate learning experiences build on children's current level of thinking. Leslie watches and listens to her pupils, introducing experiences that permit them to practice newly discovered cognitive schemes and that are likely to challenge their incorrect ways of viewing the world. But she does not impose new skills before children indicate they are interested and ready, since this leads to superficial memorization of adult formulas rather than true understanding (Johnson & Hooper, 1982).

3. *Acceptance of individual differences.* Piaget's theory assumes that all children go through the same sequence of development, but they do so at different rates.

Leslie makes a special effort to plan activities for individual children and small groups, rather than for the total class (Ginsburg & Opper, 1988). In addition, since individual differences are expected, Leslie evaluates educational progress by comparing each child to his or her own previous course of development. She is less interested in how children measure up to normative standards, or the average performance of same-age peers (Gray, 1978).

Educational applications of Piaget's theory, like his stages, have met with criticism. Perhaps the greatest challenge has to do with his insistence that young children learn only through acting on the environment. In the next section, we see evidence that they also use language-based routes to knowledge, which Piaget deemphasized. In any case, Piaget's influence on education has been powerful and long-lasting. He gave teachers new ways to observe, understand, and enhance young children's development and offered strong theoretical justification for child-oriented approaches to classroom teaching and learning.

• *Recently, 2-year-old Brooke's father decided to shave off his thick beard and mustache. When Brooke saw him, she was very upset. Using Piaget's theory, explain why Brooke was distressed by her father's new appearance.*

**BRIEF REVIEW**   During Piaget's preoperational stage, mental representation flourishes, as indicated by growth in language and make-believe play. Aside from representation, Piaget's theory emphasizes the young child's cognitive limitations. Egocentrism underlies a variety of illogical features of preoperational thought, including animism, an inability to pass conservation tasks, transductive reasoning, and lack of hierarchical classification. New research reveals that when tasks are simplified and made relevant to children's everyday experiences, preschoolers show the beginnings of logical reasoning. These findings indicate that operational thought is not absent during early childhood, and they challenge Piaget's notion of stage. Piaget's theory has had a powerful influence on education, promoting discovery learning, sensitivity to children's readiness to learn, and acceptance of individual differences.

• *One weekend, 4-year-old Will went fishing with his family. When his father asked, "Why do you think the river is flowing along?" Will responded, "Because it's alive and wants to." Yet at home, Will understands very well that his tricycle isn't alive and can't move by itself. What explains this contradiction in Will's reasoning?*

• *Jason returned to preschool after several days of illness due to the flu. Leslie said, "Jason, I'm so glad you're back. Why were you sick?" "I was sick because I threw up," replied Jason. What kind of reasoning is Jason demonstrating, and why did he reason this way in response to Leslie's question?*

## FURTHER CHALLENGES TO PIAGET'S IDEAS: VYGOTSKY'S SOCIOCULTURAL THEORY

Piaget's deemphasis on language as an important source of cognitive development brought on yet another challenge, this time from Vygotsky's sociocultural theory. We have seen in earlier chapters that Vygotsky stressed the social context of cognitive development. During early childhood, rapid growth in language enhances children's ability to participate in social communication. Soon young children start to talk to themselves in much the same way that they converse with others, and this greatly enhances cognitive development. Let's see how this happens.

### Piaget versus Vygotsky: Children's Private Speech

Watch preschoolers as they go about their daily activities, and you will see that they frequently talk out loud to themselves as they play and explore the environment. For example, as Jason worked on a puzzle one day, I heard him say, "Where's the red piece? I need the red one. Now, a blue one. No, it doesn't fit. Try it here." On another occasion, Jason sat next to Mark on the rug and blurted out, "It broke," without explaining what or when.

Piaget (1923/1926) called these utterances *egocentric speech*, a term expressing his belief that they reflect the preoperational child's inability to imagine the perspectives of others. For this reason, Piaget said, young children's talk is often "talk for self" in which they run off thoughts in whatever form they happen to occur, regard-

*In a Piagetian classroom, children are encouraged to act directly on the environment. Activities are designed for individuals and small groups rather than for the total class. (Tony Freeman/PhotoEdit)*

less of whether it is understandable to a listener. Piaget believed that cognitive maturity and certain social experiences—namely, disagreements with peers—eventually bring an end to egocentric speech. Through arguments with agemates, children repeatedly see that others hold viewpoints different from their own. As a result, egocentric speech gradually declines and is replaced by social speech, in which children adapt what they say to their listeners.

Vygotsky (1934/1987) voiced a powerful objection to Piaget's conclusion that young children's language is egocentric and nonsocial. He reasoned that children speak to themselves for self-guidance and self-direction. Because language helps children think about their own behavior and plan courses of action, Vygotsky viewed it

*During the preschool years, children frequently talk to themselves as they play and explore the environment. Research supports Vygotsky's theory that children use private speech to guide their behavior when faced with challenging tasks. With age, private speech is transformed into silent, inner speech, or verbal thought. (Elizabeth Crews)*

as the foundation for all higher cognitive processes, including voluntary attention, memory, planning, problem solving, and self-reflection. As children get older and tasks become easier, their self-directed speech declines and is internalized as silent, *inner speech*—the verbal dialogues we carry on with ourselves while thinking and acting in everyday situations.

Over the past two decades, researchers have carried out many studies to determine which of these two views—Piaget's or Vygotsky's—is correct. Almost all the findings have sided with Vygotsky. As a result, children's speech-to-self is now referred to as **private speech** instead of egocentric speech. Research shows that children use more of it when tasks are difficult, after they make errors, or when they are confused about how to proceed (Berk, 1992a). Also, just as Vygotsky predicted, with age private speech goes underground, changing from utterances spoken out loud into whispers and silent lip movements (Frauenglass & Diaz, 1985). Finally, children who use private speech freely when faced with a challenging activity are more attentive and involved and show greater improvement in task performance than their less talkative peers (Bivens & Berk, 1990).

If private speech is a central force in cognitive development, where does it come from? Vygotsky's answer to this question highlights the social origins of cognition, his main difference of opinion with Piaget.

### The Social Origins of Early Childhood Cognition

Recall from Chapter 6 that Vygotsky stressed the role of social experience in cognitive development by conceiving of children's learning as taking place within the *zone of proximal development*—a range of tasks too difficult for the child to do alone but that can be accomplished with the help of others. During infancy, communication in the zone of proximal development is largely nonverbal. In early childhood, verbal dialogues are added as adults and more skilled peers help children master challenging activities. Consider the following example in which Jason's mother helped him put a difficult puzzle together:

> Jason: "I can't get this one in." (tries to insert a piece in the wrong place)
> Mother: "Which piece might go down here?" (points to the bottom of the puzzle)
> Jason: "His shoes." (looks for a piece resembling the clown's shoes but tries the wrong one)
> Mother: "Well, what piece looks like this shape?" (pointing again to the bottom of the puzzle)
> Jason: "The brown one." (tries it and it fits; then attempts another piece and looks at his mother)
> Mother: "Try turning it just a little." (gestures to show him)
> Jason: "There!" (puts in several more pieces as his mother watches)

Eventually, children take the language of these dialogues, make it part of their private speech, and use this speech to organize their independent efforts in the same way.

To be effective, the adult's communication must have certain features. It must offer a support system that helps the child master new skills (Wood, Bruner, & Ross, 1976). This requires careful coordination of the assistance offered with the current abilities of the child. Jason's mother offers help at just the right moment and in the right amount. As Jason becomes better able to handle the task himself, his mother permits him to take over her guiding role and apply it to his own activity.

Is there evidence to support Vygotsky's ideas on the social origins of private speech and cognitive development? One recent study found that mothers who used patient, sensitive communication in teaching their preschoolers how to solve a challenging puzzle had children who used more private speech while learning the task.

**Private speech**

Self-directed speech that children use to plan and guide their own behavior.

Such children were also more successful when asked to do a puzzle by themselves a week later (Behrend, Rosengren, & Perlmutter, 1992). Other research indicates that although young children benefit from working on tasks with same-age peers, their planning and problem solving show more improvement when their partner is either an "expert" peer (especially capable at the task) or an adult (Azmitia, 1988; Radziszewska & Rogoff, 1988). Also, conflict and disagreement between preschoolers (the feature of peer interaction emphasized by Piaget) does not seem to be as important in fostering cognitive development as the extent to which peers resolve their differences of opinion and cooperate with one another (Tudge, 1990).

### Vygotsky and Education

Today, educators are eager to use Vygotsky's ideas to enhance children's learning. Piagetian and Vygotskian classrooms clearly have features in common, such as opportunities for active participation and acceptance of individual differences in cognitive development. But a Vygotskian classroom goes beyond independent discovery learning. Instead, it promotes *assisted discovery*. Teachers guide children's learning with explanations, demonstrations, and verbal prompts, carefully tailoring their efforts to each child's zone of proximal development. Assisted discovery is also helped along by peer collaboration. Teachers arrange *cooperative learning* experiences, grouping together classmates whose abilities differ and encouraging them to teach and help one another (Gallimore & Tharp, 1990).

At this point, it is important to note that some of Vygotsky's ideas, like Piaget's, have been challenged. As Barbara Rogoff (1990) points out, verbal communication may not be the only means through which children's thinking develops, or even the most important one in some cultures. For example, the young child learning to sail a canoe in Micronesia or weave a garment on a foot loom in Guatemala may gain more from direct observation and practice than from joint participation with and verbal guidance by adults. It is possible that the kind of assistance offered to children varies greatly from one culture to another, depending on the tasks that must be mastered to become a contributing member of society. Thus, we are reminded once again that children learn in a great many ways, and as yet, no single theory provides a complete account of cognitive development.

**BRIEF REVIEW** Piaget and Vygotsky disagreed on the meaning of preschoolers' self-directed speech. Piaget regarded these utterances as egocentric and nonsocial. In contrast, Vygotsky viewed private speech as communication with the self for self-guidance and self-direction. According to Vygotsky, language provides the foundation for all higher cognitive processes. As adults and more skilled peers provide children with verbal guidance in the zone of proximal development, children incorporate these dialogues into their private speech and use them to guide their own behavior. Research supports Vygotsky's ideas. A Vygotskian classroom emphasizes assisted discovery rather than self-discovery. Verbal support from teachers and peer collaboration are important.

• *Tanisha sees her 5-year-old son Toby talking out loud to himself while he plays. She wonders whether she should discourage this behavior. Using Vygotsky's theory, explain why Toby talks to himself. How would you advise Tanisha?*

## INFORMATION PROCESSING IN EARLY CHILDHOOD

Return for just a moment to the model of information processing discussed on page 217 of Chapter 6. Recall that information processing focuses on *control processes,* or *mental strategies,* that children use to transform stimuli flowing into their mental systems. During early childhood, advances in representation and in children's ability to guide their own behavior lead to more efficient ways of manipulating information and solving problems. In the following sections, we look at how attention and memory change over the preschool years. We also examine children's growing awareness of their own mental life and its role in cognitive development. Finally, we see how young children begin to acquire academic skills that prepare them for learning in school.

## Attention

Parents and teachers are quick to notice that preschoolers spend only short times involved in tasks, have difficulty focusing on details, and are easily distracted. The capacity to sustain attention does improve during early childhood, and fortunately so, since children will rely on it greatly once they enter school. In one study, 3- to 6-year-olds were observed in preschool settings to find out what they did during free play. With age, they spent longer periods engaged in activities and moved more efficiently from one activity to the next. However, even 5- and 6-year-olds could not remain attentive for very long. The average time they spent involved in an activity was about 7 minutes (Stodolsky, 1974).

By the end of early childhood, attention also becomes more *planful,* as children's visual search behavior in familiar environments indicates. In one study, researchers had 3- to 5-year-olds look for a lost object in their preschool play yard. Each child was taken through the setting by an experimenter, who stopped at eight locations along the way to play a game (see Figure 9.4). In the third location, the adult took the child's picture, but by the seventh, the camera was missing. After reaching the eighth location, the child was asked to search for the camera. When 3-year-olds could

**FIGURE 9.4** • Layout of the playground in a study of children's visual search behavior. The children played games at eight locations. Each location was marked by a flag Ⓕ displaying a picture of the game played there. Red yarn stretching between the flags defined the path from locations 1 to 8, so children could easily retrace their steps during the search phase of the study. *(From H. M. Wellman, S. C. Somerville, & R. J. Haake, 1979, "Development of search procedures in real-life spatial environments,"* Developmental Psychology, *15, p. 532. Copyright 1979 by the American Psychological Association. Reprinted by permission of the author.)*

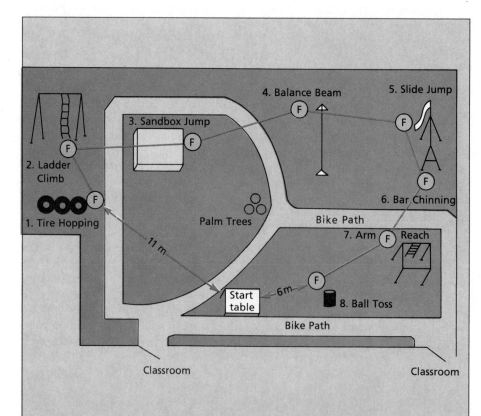

not find it at location 3, they gave up or searched outside the "critical area" (the path between location 3 where the picture was taken and location 7 where the camera was discovered missing). In contrast, older preschoolers were more likely to confine their search to the critical area and visit each possible location, searching systematically and exhaustively (Wellman, Somerville, & Haake, 1979).

Still, children's attentional strategies have a long way to go before they are very mature. When given detailed pictures or written materials, preschoolers fail to search thoroughly (Enns, 1990). As we will see in Chapter 12, attentional behavior on these tasks improves greatly during middle childhood.

## Memory

Unlike infants and toddlers, preschoolers have the language skills to describe what they remember, and they can follow directions on simple memory tasks. As a result, several aspects of memory development—recognition and recall, memory for every-day events, and the capacity to use remembered information in new situations—become easier to study in early childhood.

**Recognition and Recall.** Try showing a young child a set of 10 pictures or toys. Then mix them up with some unfamiliar items and ask the child to point to the ones in the original set. You will find that preschoolers' *recognition* memory (ability to tell whether a stimulus is the same or similar to one they have seen before) is remarkably good. It becomes even more accurate by the end of early childhood. In fact, 4- and 5-year-olds perform nearly perfectly. Now, give the child a more demanding task. While keeping the items out of view, ask the child to name the ones she saw. This requires *recall*—that the child generate a mental image of an absent stimulus. One of the most obvious features of young children's memories is their much poorer recall than recognition. At age 2, they can recall no more than 1 or 2 of the items, at age 4 only about 3 or 4 (Perlmutter, 1984).

Of course, recognition is much easier than recall for adults as well, but in comparison to adults, children's recall is quite deficient. The reason is that young children are less effective at using **memory strategies,** deliberate mental activities that improve our chances of remembering. For example, when you want to retain information, you might *rehearse,* or repeat the items over and over again. Or you might *organize* it, intentionally grouping together items that are alike so that you can easily retrieve them by thinking of the characteristic they share in common.

Preschoolers do show the beginnings of memory strategies. For example, when circumstances permit, they arrange items in space to aid their memories. In a study of 2- to 5-year-olds, an adult placed either an M&M or a wooden peg in each of 12 identical containers and handed them one by one to the child, who was asked to remember where the candy was hidden. By age 4, children put the candy containers in one place on the table and the peg containers in another, a strategy that almost always led to perfect recall (DeLoache & Todd, 1988). But preschoolers do not yet rehearse or organize items into categories (for example, all the vehicles together, all the animals together) when asked to recall a set of items. With intensive instruction they can be taught to do so, but training does not always improve their memory performance (Carr & Schneider, 1991; Lange & Pierce, 1992).

Perhaps young children are not very strategic memorizers because they see little need to remember information for its own sake, when there is no clear reason to retain it. In support of this explanation, the memory strategies that preschoolers do use are most effective when recall leads to a desired goal—for example, some M&Ms to eat, as in the research just described (Wellman, 1988b).

**Memory strategies**
Deliberate mental activities that improve the likelihood of remembering.

*Like adults, preschoolers remember familiar experiences in terms of scripts. After going to the grocery store with his father many times, this boy is unlikely to recall the details of a particular shopping trip. But he will be able to describe what typically happens when you go shopping. Scripts help children organize and interpret their everyday world. (Tony Freeman/PhotoEdit)*

**Script**

A general description of what occurs and when it occurs in a particular situation. A basic means through which children organize and interpret their everyday experiences.

***Memory for Everyday Experiences.*** Think about the difference in your recall of the listlike information discussed in the previous section and your memory for everyday experiences. In the former, you are asked to recall isolated pieces of information, and you try to reproduce them exactly as you originally learned them. In the latter, you must recall complex, meaningful events. Remembering this kind of information involves selecting experiences, relating them to one another, and interpreting them on the basis of previous knowledge. Do young children remember everyday experiences in these ways? The answer is clearly yes.

Like adults, preschoolers remember familiar experiences in terms of **scripts,** general descriptions of what occurs and when it occurs in a particular situation. For very young children, scripts begin as a general structure of main acts. For example, when asked to tell what happens when you go to a restaurant, a 3-year-old might say, "You go in, get the food, eat, and then pay." Children's first scripts contain only a few acts, but as long as events in a situation take place in a logical order, they are almost always recalled in correct sequence (Fivush, Kuebli, & Clubb, 1992). This is true even for 1- and 2-year-olds, who cannot yet verbally describe events but who act them out with toys (Bauer & Mandler, 1989, 1992). With increasing age, children's scripts become more elaborate, as in the following restaurant account given by a 5-year-old child: "You go in. You can sit in the booths or at a table. Then you tell the waitress what you want. You eat. If you want dessert, you can have some. Then you pay and go home" (Fivush, 1984; Nelson & Gruendel, 1981).

Scripts seem to be a basic means through which children organize and interpret their everyday world. For example, young children rely on scripted knowledge when listening to and telling stories. They recall more events from stories based on familiar event sequences than from stories based on unfamiliar ones (Hudson & Nelson, 1983). Preschoolers also use script structures for the stories they act out in play. Listen carefully to preschoolers' make-believe. You will hear everyday scripts reflected in their dialogues as they pretend to put the baby to bed, go on a trip, or play school.

Parents and teachers can enhance preschoolers' memory for everyday events by the way they talk about them with children. Children whose mothers converse about the past often, ask children many questions, and provide a great deal of elaborative information recount past events and stories in a more organized fashion and in much greater detail (Fivush, 1991; Hudson, 1990). In line with Vygotsky's ideas, these findings indicate that early social experiences play an important role in the development of memory skills.

***Generalizing Remembered Information to New Situations.*** Once information is stored in memory, children must learn to use it flexibly, applying it in new situations similar to the ones in which it was originally learned. Without the ability to generalize remembered information in this way, everything children learn would be limited to the context in which it was first acquired. There would be no general skills or knowledge (DeLoache, 1990).

To what extent can preschoolers take their memory for something experienced in one context and apply it to a new context? In one study, children of two ages—2 1/2 and 3—watched as a small toy (Little Snoopy) was hidden in a scale model of a room. Then they were asked to find a larger toy (Big Snoopy) hidden in the room that the model represented. The findings were startling. Although children of both ages remembered where the original object was hidden equally well, 2 1/2-year-olds were unable to transfer this knowledge to the new situation. But by age 3, most children could find the toy in the larger room (DeLoache, 1987).

These findings show that the capacity to generalize remembered information from one context to another improves rapidly over the third year of life. Advances in representation may account for this change. Although very young preschoolers can represent their world, they are just beginning to *represent relations* between stimuli. Between 2 1/2 and 3 years of age, children realize that the model is not just a toy room; it is both a room itself as well as a representation of another room. At first, this understanding is fragile. For example, 3-year-olds' performance depends on a high degree of similarity between the model and the room, such as furniture in the same position and covered with the same fabric (DeLoache, Kolstad, & Anderson, 1991). The more experience young children have with various forms of representation, the better they may be able to generalize remembered information. Exposure to picture books and make-believe play may increase the flexibility of memory.

## The Young Child's Theory of Mind

As their representation of the world and ability to remember and solve problems improve, children start to reflect on their own thought processes. They begin to construct a *theory of mind*, or set of beliefs about mental activities. This understanding is often called **metacognition.** The prefix *meta-*, meaning beyond or higher, is applied to the term because the central meaning of metacognition is "thinking about thought." As adults, we have a complex appreciation of our inner mental worlds. For example, you can tell the difference between a wide variety of cognitive activities, such as knowing, remembering, guessing, forgetting, and imagining, and you are aware of a great many factors that influence them. We rely on these understandings to interpret our own and others' behavior as well as to improve our performance of various tasks. How early are preschoolers aware of their mental lives, and how complete and accurate is their knowledge?

***Awareness of an Inner Mental Life.*** Children's conversations reveal that they can distinguish between an inner mental world and outer physical world at an early age. The words "think," "remember," and "pretend" are among the first verbs children add to their vocabularies, and after age 2 1/2, they use them appropriately to refer to internal states (Wellman, 1985). For example, one day, while looking for crayons and paper, Jason said, "I *thought* they were in the drawer, 'cept they weren't."

More convincing evidence that preschoolers grasp the difference between an inner mental and an outer physical world comes from games in which children are encouraged to mislead an adult. The findings show that by age 4, children understand that belief and reality can differ—in other words, that people can hold *false beliefs* (Harris, 1991; Perner, 1991). In one recent study, 2 1/2- to 4-year-olds were asked to hide the driver of a toy truck underneath one of five cups in a sandbox so that an adult, who happened to be out of the room, could not find it. An experimenter alerted the child to the fact that the truck, after delivering the driver to the cup, left telltale tracks in the sand as a sign of where it had been. Most 2- and 3-year-olds needed explicit prompts to hide the evidence—smoothing over the tracks and returning the truck to its starting place. In contrast, 4-year-olds thought of doing these things on their own. They were also more likely to trick the adult by laying false tracks or giving incorrect information about where the driver was hidden (Sodian et al., 1991).

Besides knowing that an internal cognitive system exists, preschoolers are aware of some factors that affect its functioning. For example, 3- and 4-year-olds understand that noise, lack of interest, and thinking about other things can interfere with attention to a task (Miller & Zalenski, 1982). And by age 5, most children realize that information briefly presented or that must be retained for a long time is more likely to be forgotten (Kreutzer, Leonard, & Flavell, 1975).

Is this early grasp of mentality unique to children growing up in industrialized nations, where adults frequently explain behavior in terms of inner beliefs and desires? A recent study of 2- to 6-year-olds among the Baka, a hunting and gathering people living in Cameroon, West Africa, addressed this question. The results showed that

**Metacognition**
Thinking about thought; awareness of mental activities.

Baka children grasp the notion of false belief between ages 4 and 5, about the time that it is achieved in the United States (Avis & Harris, 1991). The fact that reasoning about the mind emerges at about the same time in such different cultures strengthens the possibility that it is a universal feature of early childhood development.

***Limitations of the Young Child's Theory of Mind.*** Although surprisingly advanced, preschoolers' awareness of inner cognitive activities is far from complete. When questioned about subtle distinctions between mental states, children below age 5 often express confusion. For example, they believe that if you get an answer right, then you "knew" and "remembered," but if you get it wrong, then you "guessed" or "forgot" (Miscione et al., 1978; Moore, Bryant, & Furrow, 1989). Preschoolers do not yet realize that the meaning of these terms depends on people's *certainty about their knowledge,* not on their objective performance. In addition, young children believe that all events must be directly observed to be known. They do not understand that *mental inferences* can be a source of knowledge. For example, while a young child watches, show an adult a transparent jar of red balls (or other similar objects, all of the same color) and then, out of the adult's sight, put one ball in a paper bag. Next, inform the adult that a ball has been moved to the bag. Below age 6, most children insist that the adult has no way of knowing that the color of the missing ball is red (Sodian & Wimmer, 1987).

How, then, should we describe the difference between the young child's theory of mind and that of the older child? Preschoolers know that we have an internal mental life. But they seem to view the mind as a passive container of information. They believe physical experience with the environment determines mental experience. In contrast, older children view the mind as an active, constructive agent that selects and transforms information and affects how the world is perceived (Pillow, 1988; Wellman, 1988a). We will consider this change further in Chapter 12 when we take up metacognition in middle childhood.

## Early Literacy and Mathematical Development

Researchers have begun to study how children's information processing capacities affect the development of basic reading, writing, and mathematical skills that prepare them for school. The study of how preschoolers begin to master these complex activities provides us with additional information on their cognitive strengths and limitations. In addition, we can use this knowledge to find ways to foster early literacy and mathematical development.

***Early Childhood Literacy.*** One week, Leslie's pupils brought empty food boxes from home to place on special shelves in the classroom. Soon, a make-believe grocery store opened. Children labeled items with prices, made shopping lists, and wrote checks at the cash register. A sign at the entrance announced the daily specials: "APLS BNS 5¢" (apples bananas 5¢).

As their grocery store play reveals, preschoolers understand a great deal about written language long before they learn to read or write in conventional ways. This is not surprising when we consider that children in industrialized nations live in a world filled with written symbols. Each day, they observe and participate in activities involving storybooks, calendars, greeting cards, lists, and signs, to name just a few. As part of these experiences, children try to figure out how written symbols convey meaningful information, just as they strive to make sense of other aspects of their world.

Young preschoolers search for units of written language as they "read" memorized versions of stories and recognize familiar signs, such as ON and OFF on light switches and PIZZA at their favorite fast food counter. But their early ideas about how written language is related to meaning are quite different from our own. For example, many preschoolers think that a single letter stands for a whole word or that each letter in a person's signature represents a separate name. Often they believe that letters (just like pictures) look like the meanings they represent. One child explained that the word deer begins with the letter O because it is shaped like a deer; then he demonstrated by drawing an O and adding a set of antlers to it (Dyson, 1984).

Gradually children revise these ideas as their perceptual and cognitive capacities improve, as they encounter writing in many different contexts, and as adults help them with various aspects of written communication. Soon preschoolers become aware of some general characteristics of written language. As a result, they create symbols in their own writing that have many features of real print. Figure 9.5 shows a story and grocery list written by a 4-year-old. This child understands that stories are written from left to right, that print appears in rows, that letters have certain features, and that stories look different from shopping lists. He has begun to pay attention to many features of written language (McGee & Richgels, 1990).

By the end of early childhood, children make other discoveries. In their own writing, they combine letters. However, their first ideas about how letters contribute to larger units are usually incorrect. Children often think that each letter represents a syllable. For example, a child named Santiago wrote his name with three letters (SIO), which he read, "San-tia-go." At the same time, he had clearly taken an important step in recognizing that letters are parts of words. Soon children realize that letters and sounds are linked in systematic ways. You can see this in the invented spellings that are typical between ages 5 and 7. At first children rely heavily on the names of letters when deciding what to include in these spellings. A favorite example is ADE LAFWTS KRMD NTU A LAVATR (eighty elephants crammed into a[n] elevator). They do not use the standard spelling of adults, but their system is just as predictable. Over time, they will switch to conventional forms (Gentry, 1981; McGee & Richgels, 1989).

Literacy development builds on a broad foundation of spoken language and knowledge about the world. The more literacy-related experiences young children have in their everyday lives, the better prepared they are to tackle the complex tasks involved in becoming skilled readers and writers. Storybook reading with parents seems to be especially important. It is related to preschoolers' literacy knowledge and to later success in school (Crain-Thoreson & Dale, 1992; Wells, 1985). During early

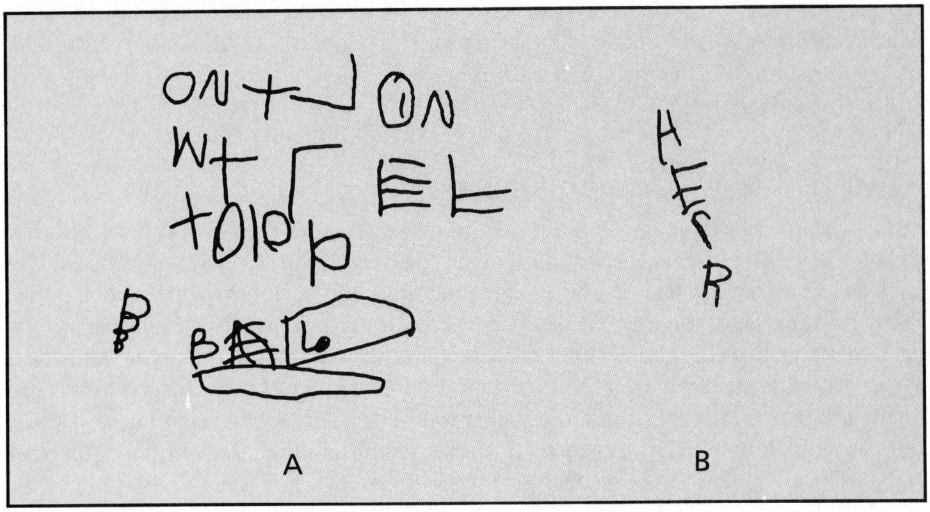

A                                    B

FIGURE 9.5 • A story (A) and a grocery list (B) written by a 4-year-old. This child's writing has many features of real print. It also reveals an awareness of different kinds of written expression. *(From L. M. McGee & D. J. Richgels, 1990,* Literacy's Beginnings, *Boston: Allyn and Bacon, p. 166. Reprinted by permission.)*

childhood, adults need not be overly concerned about the correctness of children's interpretations of written language. Instead, they can help most by accepting children's ideas and supporting their active efforts to revise and extend their knowledge.

***Young Children's Mathematical Reasoning.***   Mathematical reasoning, like literacy, builds on a foundation of informally acquired knowledge. In the early preschool period, children start to attach verbal labels (such as "lots," "little," "big," "small") to varying amounts and sizes of objects. They also begin to count. At first, counting is little more than a memorized routine. Some 2-year-olds can be heard reciting numbers in an undifferentiated string, like this: "Onetwothreefourfivesix!" Or they simply repeat a few number words while vaguely pointing in the direction of objects (Fuson, 1988).

Very soon their counting becomes more precise. By age 3, most children have established an accurate one-to-one correspondence between a short sequence of number words and the items they represent. Three-year-olds may not yet have memorized the appropriate number labels. For example, one child counted a sequence of three items by saying, "1, 6, 10." But her general method of counting was correct. She used only as many verbal tags as there were items to count (Gelman & Gallistel, 1986).

Sometime between 3 and 4, children grasp the vital **cardinality principle.** They understand that the last number in a counting sequence indicates the quantity of items in the set. If you return to the beginning of this chapter, you will see that Jason showed an appreciation of cardinality when he counted out milk cartons for his snack group. Mastery of cardinality helps children's counting become more flexible and efficient. By the late preschool years, children no longer need to start a counting sequence with the number "one." Instead, knowing that there are six items in one pile and some additional ones in another, they begin with the number "six" and *count up* to determine the total quantity. Eventually, they generalize this strategy and *count down* to find out how many items remain after some are taken away. Once they master these procedures, children start to manipulate numbers without requiring that countable objects be physically present (Fuson, 1988). At this point counting on fingers becomes an intermediate step on the way to automatically doing simple addition and subtraction.

Cross-cultural research suggests that the basic arithmetic knowledge just described emerges universally around the world (Resnick, 1989). Children may acquire this knowledge at different rates, depending on the extent to which counting experiences are available in their everyday lives. When adults provide many occasions and requests for counting, children probably construct these basic understandings sooner. Then they are solidly available as supports for the wide variety of mathematical skills they will be taught once they enter school.

## A Note on Academics in Early Childhood

Does preschoolers' developing grasp of reading and mathematical concepts mean that we should expose them to schoollike instruction aimed at accelerating these skills? Experts in early childhood education agree that it would be a serious mistake to do so. Premature academic training, which requires children to sit quietly for long periods of drill on reading, writing, and math facts does not fit with their developmental needs. These demands are likely to frustrate even the most patient of preschoolers and cause them to react negatively to school experiences. Formal academic training also takes time away from activities known to promote young children's cognitive and social

**Cardinality principle**
Principle stating that the last number in a counting sequence indicates the quantity of items in the set.

*In this preschool classroom, children have many opportunities to become familiar with written symbols in developmentally appropriate ways. Walls are colorfully decorated with pictures and printed labels, and children explore books with the encouragement and assistance of adults. These teachers seem to know that formal academic training is not for preschoolers. (Paul Conklin/ Monkmeyer Press)*

development, including play, peer interaction, and rich, stimulating conversations between adult and child (Greenberg, 1990).

How can we provide young children with the academic foundation they need? We can best do so by embedding written language and number concepts in everyday experiences. For example, in Leslie's classroom, play activities (such as the grocery store) provided opportunities for children to discover and practice academic-related knowledge. Around the room, names of pupils, labels for objects, and numbers appeared in large print so that children could become familiar with written symbols. Books and writing materials were always handy. As children explored them, they often came up with projects, such as writing a letter to a friend or relative with the teacher's help. Special techniques are needed to acquaint young children with academics if we are to do no harm:

> These methods keep academic content meaningful, integrate it into larger goals, allow for high levels of child choice and initiation, and provide for exploration and play. They also provide for high levels of supportive and responsive adult interaction, in situations where children want to know about and do what's beyond their independent reach. (Schickedanz et al., 1990, p. 12)

**BRIEF REVIEW** With age, preschoolers sustain attention for longer periods of time and search planfully for missing objects in familiar environments. By the end of early childhood, recognition memory is highly accurate. In contrast, recall improves slowly because preschoolers use memory strategies less effectively than do older children and adults. Like adults, young children remember everyday experiences in terms of scripts, which become more elaborate and complex with age. The capacity to generalize remembered information from one context to another improves rapidly during the third year. Around this time, children begin to construct a theory of mind. By age 4, it includes an understanding of false belief. Preschoolers also develop a basic understanding of written symbols and arithmetic concepts through informal experiences.

• *Piaget believed that because preschoolers are egocentric, they cannot reflect on their own mental activities. What evidence presented in the preceding sections would contradict this assumption?*

• *Lena notices that her 4-year-old son Gregor can recognize his name in print and count to twenty. She wonders why Gregor's preschool teacher permits him to spend so much time playing instead of teaching him academic skills. Gregor's teacher responds, "I am teaching him academics—through play." Explain how this is the case.*

## INDIVIDUAL DIFFERENCES IN MENTAL DEVELOPMENT DURING EARLY CHILDHOOD

So far in this chapter, we have not said much about individual differences. Preschoolers differ markedly in intellectual progress, just as they vary in physical growth and motor skills. Psychologists and educators typically measure how well preschoolers are developing cognitively by giving them intelligence tests. Scores are computed in the same way as they are for infants and toddlers (return to Chapter 6, page 224, to review). Test content, however, is markedly different than it was during the first 2 years of life. Instead of emphasizing perceptual and motor responses, tests for preschoolers sample a wide range of verbal and nonverbal cognitive abilities.

Child development specialists are interested in young children's mental test scores because by age 5 to 6, they become good predictors of later intelligence and academic achievement (Honzik, Macfarlane, & Allen, 1948; Siegler & Richards, 1982). In addition, understanding the link between early childhood experiences and test performance gives us ways to intervene in children's lives to support their cognitive growth.

### Early Childhood Intelligence Tests

Five-year-old Hallie, whom we introduced in Chapter 8, sat in a small, strange testing room while Sarah, an adult he met only a short while ago, gave him an intelligence test. The questions Sarah asked were of many kinds. Some were *verbal*. For example, Sarah held out a picture of shovel and said, "Tell me what this shows?", an item measuring vocabulary. Then she tested his memory by asking him to repeat sentences and lists of numbers back to her. Hallie's quantitative knowledge was probed by seeing if he could count and solve simple addition and subtraction problems. Other tasks Sarah gave were *nonverbal* and largely assessed spatial reasoning. Hallie copied designs with special blocks, figured out the pattern in a series of shapes, and indicated what a piece of paper folded and cut would look like when unfolded (Thorndike, Hagen, & Sattler, 1986).

Before Sarah began the test, she took special steps to ensure that Hallie's responses would accurately reflect his knowledge. Sarah was aware that Hallie came from an impoverished family background. When low-income and ethnic minority preschoolers are faced with an unfamiliar adult who bombards them with questions, they sometimes become anxious and afraid. Also, such children may not define the testing situation in achievement terms. Often they look for attention and approval from the examiner rather than focusing on the test questions themselves (Zigler & Seitz, 1982). Sarah spent time playing with Hallie before she began testing. In addition, she praised and encouraged him while the test was in progress. When testing conditions like these are used, low-income preschoolers improve in performance. In one study, they gained as much as 10 points, while middle-class children improved only slightly, about 3 points (Zigler, Abelson, & Seitz, 1973).

Perhaps you are wondering whether intelligence tests underestimate the abilities of minority children in other ways. The questions that Sarah asked Hallie tap knowledge and skills that not all children have had equal opportunity to learn. The issue of *cultural bias* in intelligence tests is a hotly debated topic that we will take up in Chapter 12. For now, keep in mind that intelligence tests do not sample the full range of human abilities, and performance is affected by cultural and situational factors. Nevertheless, test scores remain important because they predict school achievement, and this, in turn, is strongly related to vocational success in complex industrialized societies.

## Home Environment and Mental Development

Of all the settings in which preschoolers spend their days, their home environment is the most crucial. A special version of the *Home Observation for Measurement of the Environment (HOME)*, covered in Chapter 6, assesses aspects of 3- to 6-year-olds' home lives that support intellectual growth (see Table 9.1). In agreement with the theories of both Piaget and Vygotsky, physical surroundings and child-rearing practices play important roles. Preschoolers who develop well intellectually have parents who provide a home rich in toys and books, who are warm and affectionate, who stimulate language and academic knowledge, and who arrange outings to places where there are interesting things to see and do. Such parents also make reasonable demands for socially mature behavior—for example, that the child perform simple chores and behave courteously toward others. And when conflicts arise, these parents rely on reasoning to resolve them instead of physical force and punishment (Bradley & Caldwell, 1979).

Of course, relating to young children in these ways demands a great deal of time and patience. It also requires money—to provide children with the materials and experiences they need to develop at their best. As we saw in Chapter 2, the characteristics described here are less likely to be found in low-income and poor families where parents lead highly stressful lives. In instances in which low-income parents do manage, despite the pressures of their lives, to obtain high HOME scores, their youngsters do substantially better on measures of intelligence and school achievement (Bradley & Caldwell, 1979, 1981). These findings, along with additional evidence we will discuss in Chapter 12, indicate that quality of the home environment plays a major role in the generally poorer intellectual performance of low-income children in comparison to their middle-class peers.

TABLE 9.1 • Home Observation for the Measurement of the Environment (HOME): Early Childhood Subscales

| Subscale | Sample Item |
|---|---|
| Stimulation through toys, games, and reading material | Home includes toys that help child learn colors, sizes, and shapes. |
| Language stimulation | Parent teaches child about animals through books, games, and puzzles. |
| Organization of the physical environment | All visible rooms are reasonably clean and minimally cluttered. |
| Pride, affection, and warmth | Parent spontaneously praises child's qualities or behavior twice during observer's visit. |
| Stimulation of academic behavior | Child is encouraged to learn colors. |
| Modeling and encouragement of social maturity | Parent introduces interviewer to child. |
| Variety in daily stimulation | Family member takes child on one outing at least every other week (such as picnic, shopping). |
| Avoidance of physical punishment | Parent neither slaps nor spanks child during visit. |

*Source:* Bradley & Caldwell, 1979.

*Preschool and Day Care*

Even more than infants and toddlers, children between the ages of 2 and 6 spend considerable time away from their homes and parents, attending preschools and day care programs. Over the last 30 years, the number of young children enrolled in preschool or day care has steadily increased, a trend that is largely due to the dramatic rise in women participating in the labor force. Currently, 65 percent of American preschool-age children have mothers who are employed (Children's Defense Fund, 1991d). Figure 9.6 shows the varied ways in which preschoolers spend their days while their parents are at work.

The term *preschool* refers to half-day programs with planned educational experiences aimed at enhancing the development of 2- to 5-year-olds. In contrast, *day care* identifies a variety of arrangements for supervising children of employed parents, ranging from care in someone else's or the child's own home to some type of center-based program. But the line between preschool and day care is a fuzzy one. As Figure 9.6 indicates, parents often select a preschool as a child-care option. Many preschools (and public school kindergartens as well) have increased their hours to full days in response to the needs of employed parents (U.S. Department of Education, 1991). At the same time, today we know that good day care is not simply a matter of keeping children safe and adequately fed in their parents' absence. Day care should provide the same high-quality educational experiences that an effective preschool does, the only difference being that children attend for an extended day.

*Types of Preschool.* Preschool programs come in many forms, ranging along a continuum from child-centered to teacher-directed. In **child-centered preschools,** teachers provide a wide variety of activities from which children select, and most of the day is devoted to free play. In contrast, **academic preschools** are ones in which teachers structure the program. Children are taught letters, numbers, colors, shapes, and other academic skills through repetition and drill, and play is deemphasized. Despite grave concern about the appropriateness of this approach, preschool teachers have felt increased pressure to emphasize formal academic training. The trend is motivated by a widespread belief that providing academic instruction at earlier ages will improve the ultimate achievement of American youth. In contrast, in countries that outperform the United States in math and science achievement, such as Japan and Korea, children have a relaxed early childhood. They are not hurried into academic work during the preschool years (Song & Ginsburg, 1987).

Research on the consequences of preschool attendance indicates that, overall, middle-class children experience no more than small gains in test scores. A good preschool provides these youngsters with many extra and pleasurable opportunities to explore, solve problems, and develop socially, but it has little impact on mental development beyond the advantages provided by their privileged home lives (Zigler, 1987). But for low-income children, the benefits of preschool are considerable.

*Early Intervention for At-Risk Preschoolers.* In the 1960s, when the United States launched a "War on Poverty," a wide variety of preschool programs for disadvantaged children were initiated. The underlying assumption was that the learning problems of these youngsters were best treated early, before formal schooling begins. The most extensive of these experiments in early education is **Project Head Start,** begun by the federal government in 1965. A typical Head Start program provides children with a year or two of preschool education before they enter school, along with nutritional and medical services. Parent involvement is a central part of the Head Start philosophy. Parents serve on policy councils and contribute to program planning. They also work directly with children in classrooms, attend special programs on parenting and child development, and receive services directed at their own social, emotional, and vocational needs. Currently, over 1,300 Head Start centers

---

**Child-centered preschool**
Preschool in which teachers provide a wide variety of activities from which children select, and most of the day is devoted to free play.

**Academic preschool**
Preschool in which teachers structure the program, training children in academic skills through repetition and drill.

**Project Head Start**
Federal program providing low-income children with a year or two of preschool education before school entry and their parents with support services.

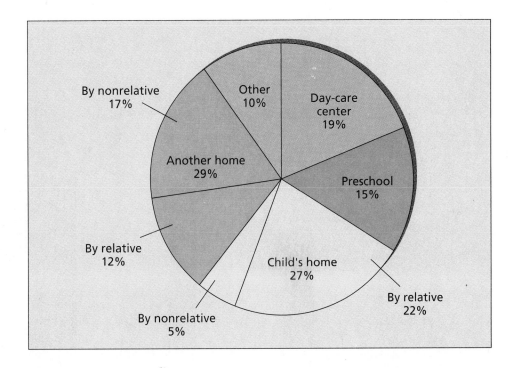

**FIGURE 9.6** • Who's minding America's preschoolers? The chart refers to settings in which 3- and 4-year-olds spend most time while their mothers are at work. The "other" category largely consists of children cared for by their mothers during working hours. Twenty-eight percent of 3- and 4-year-olds actually experience more than one type of child care, a fact not reflected in the chart. (From U.S. Bureau of the Census, 1990.)

located around the country serve about 600,000 children each year (Kantrowitz, 1992).

Two decades of research establishing the long-term benefits of preschool intervention have played a major role in the survival of Head Start. The most important of these studies combined data from seven university-based interventions. Results showed that children who attended the programs scored higher in IQ and school achievement than controls during the first 2 to 3 years of elementary school. After that time, differences in test scores declined. However, children who received intervention remained ahead on measures of real-life school adjustment into adolescence. As shown in Figure 9.7, they were less likely to be placed in special education or retained in grade, and a greater number graduated from high school. There were also lasting benefits in attitudes and motivation. Children who attended the programs were more likely to give achievement-related reasons (such as school or job accomplishments) for being proud of themselves, and their mothers held higher vocational aspirations for them (Lazar & Darlington, 1982).

Do these findings on the impact of outstanding university-based programs generalize to Head Start centers located in American communities? As long as programs are of high quality, the outcomes are much the same (Schweinhart & Weikart, 1986). In fact, as Box 9.2 indicates, immediate cognitive gains resulting from Head Start attendance are much greater than for other types of preschool. This suggests that the Head Start model, which combines early childhood education with parental support, is especially advantageous (Smith, 1991).

***Research on Day Care.*** We have seen that high-quality early intervention can enhance the development of disadvantaged children. At the same time, we noted in Chapter 6 that much day care in the United States is not of this high quality. Preschoolers exposed to poor-quality day care, regardless of whether they come from middle- or low-income homes, score lower on measures of cognitive and social skills (Howes, 1988b, 1990; Vandell & Powers, 1983). Inadequate day care can undermine the development of children from all walks of life. In contrast, good day care

338

**FIGURE 9.7** • Benefits of preschool early intervention programs. Low-income children who attended intervention programs fared better than controls on three real-life indicators of school adjustment. *(Adapted from Royce, Darlington, & Murray, 1983.)*

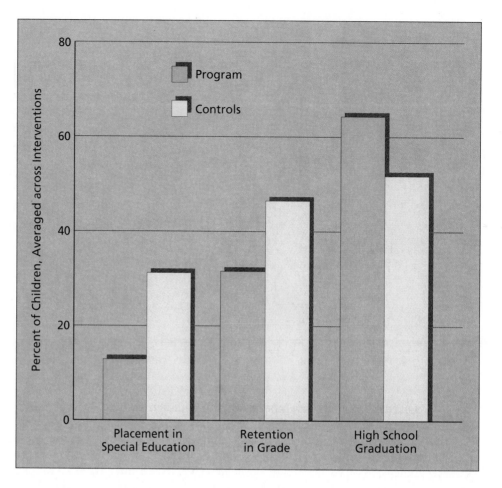

can reduce the negative impact of an underprivileged home life, and it sustains the benefits of growing up in an advantaged family.

What are the ingredients of high-quality day care in early childhood? Several large-scale studies of center- and home-based care reveal that three factors are especially important: group size (number of children in a single space), caregiver/child ratio, and the caregiver's educational preparation. When these characteristics are favorable, adults are more verbally stimulating and sensitive to children's needs, and children perform especially well on tests of intellectual, language, and social development (Divine-Hawkins, 1981; Howes, Phillips, & Whitebook, 1992; Ruopp et al., 1979). Other research shows that spacious, well-equipped environments and activities that meet the needs and interests of preschool-age children also contribute to positive outcomes (Burchinal, Lee, & Ramey, 1989; Howes, 1988b).

Table 9.2 summarizes characteristics of high-quality early childhood programs on the basis of current research. Taken together, they offer a set of worthy goals as our nation strives to expand and upgrade the educational services it offers to young children.

*Educational Television*

Besides home and preschool, young children spend a great deal of time in another learning environment: television. The average 2- to 6-year-old watches TV from 2 to 3 hours a day—a very long time in the life of a young child (Liebert & Sprafkin,

## SOCIAL ISSUES

### Box 9.2  *Project Head Start: A Social Policy Success Story*

The impact of Project Head Start on the lives of preschoolers has been questioned many times since the program began. Yet research reporting only minimal benefits is often biased by one very important factor: Because not all poor children can be served, Head Start typically enrolls the most disadvantaged youngsters. Controls to whom they are compared often do not come from such extremely impoverished families. A study of Head Start programs in two large cities took this into account. It also looked carefully at the effectiveness of Head Start by comparing it to other preschool alternatives as well as to no preschool at all (Lee, Brooks-Gunn, & Schnur, 1988).

Results showed that Head Start children, compared to "other preschool" and "no preschool" groups, had less educated mothers, came from more crowded households, and were more likely to be growing up in single-parent homes. Before entering preschool, they scored *well below* the other groups on mental tests. Yet a year later, Head Start children showed *greater gains* than the other groups.

These findings indicate that Head Start's unique model of combining high-quality education with efforts to help parents improve their own lives leads to large immediate test score gains. At the same time, we know that Head Start children do not emerge from the program with cognitive skills equal to those of children from advantaged backgrounds. And many studies show that initial test score gains wash away with time.

Yet we must keep in mind that it is unrealistic to expect a year or two of Head Start to make up for the early experiences of these youngsters. For intervention to be most effective, it must be continuous. Programs beginning in infancy and extending through adolescence would undoubtedly produce more permanent cognitive gains (Zigler & Berman, 1983). Yet the fact remains that a short-term Head Start experience can have lasting effects on children's ability to meet basic school requirements (refer to Figure 9.7). This result provides ample justification for expanding

*Disadvantaged preschoolers who experience the comprehensive early intervention of Project Head Start show greater short-term gains in IQ than do children who attend other types of preschools or no preschool at all. Although the IQ advantage diminishes over time, attending Head Start for a year or two can have a lasting impact on children's ability to meet basic school requirements. (J. Chenet/Woodfin Camp)*

the program. At present, Head Start reaches only 20 percent of eligible youngsters.

The success of Head Start has inspired a new federal program that promises to dramatically improve the nation's early intervention services. During the 1990s, public schools will be required to offer preschool intervention for 3- to 5-year-olds who either have or are at risk for serious developmental problems. Like Head Start, each school must take steps to ensure that parents participate in the education of their children (Gallagher, 1989). Involving and supporting parents increases the likelihood that the program's effects will be sustained. When parents feel better about their own lives and realize how much their children can learn, they teach and stimulate their youngsters more and hold higher expectations for their performance. These changes help prevent school failure in the years to come and translate into greater life success in adolescence and adulthood.

*Among the characteristics of high-quality early childhood programs are frequent interaction between teachers and parents about children's behavior and development.* (David Young-Wolff/PhotoEdit)

1988). Each afternoon, Jason looked forward to watching certain educational programs. The well-known "Sesame Street" was his favorite.

Find a time to watch an episode of "Sesame Street" yourself. The program was originally designed for the same population served by Head Start—low-income children who enter school academically behind their middle-class peers. Its founders

TABLE 9.2 • Signs of a Good-Quality Early Childhood Program

| Program Characteristics | Signs of Quality |
|---|---|
| Physical setting | Indoor environment is clean, in good repair, and well-ventilated. Classroom space is divided into richly equipped activity areas, including make-believe play, blocks, science, math, games and puzzles, books, art, and music. Fenced outdoor play space is equipped with swings, climbing equipment, tricycles, and sandbox. |
| Group size | In preschools and day-care centers, there are no more than 16 to 18 preschoolers with 2 teachers in a single space. |
| Teacher/child ratio | In preschools and day-care centers, teacher is responsible for no more than 8 children. In day-care homes, caregiver is responsible for no more than 6 children. |
| Daily activities | Most of the time, children work individually or in small groups. Children select many of their own activities and learn through experiences relevant to their own lives. Teachers facilitate children's involvement, accept individual differences, and adjust expectations to children's developing capacities. |
| Teacher training | Teacher has college-level specialized preparation in early childhood development/education. |
| Relationships with parents | Parents are encouraged to observe and participate. Teachers talk frequently with parents about children's behavior and development. |
| Licensing and accreditation | Program is licensed by the state. For a preschool or day-care center, accreditation by the National Academy of Early Childhood Programs is evidence of an especially high-quality program. |

*Source:* National Association for the Education of Young Children, 1984.

believed that using fast-paced action, lively sound effects, and humorous puppet characters to stress letter and number recognition, counting, vocabulary, and basic concepts might support children's academic development. Today, half of America's 2- to 5-year-olds regularly watch "Sesame Street," and it is broadcast in more than 40 countries around the world (Liebert & Sprafkin, 1988).

Research shows that "Sesame Street" works well as an academic tutor. The more children watch, the higher they score on tests designed to measure the program's learning goals (Bogatz & Ball, 1972; Rice et al., 1990). In other respects, however, the rapid-paced format of "Sesame Street" and other children's programs has been criticized. When different types of programs are compared, ones with slow-paced action and easy-to-follow story lines lead to more elaborate make-believe play. Those presenting quick, disconnected bits of information do not (Tower et al., 1979).

Some experts argue that because television presents such complete data to the senses, in heavy doses it encourages passive thinking. Too much television also takes up time children would otherwise spend reading, playing, and interacting with adults and peers (Singer & Singer, 1990). But television can support cognitive development as long as children's viewing is not excessive and programs meet their developmental needs. We will take up the impact of television on young children's emotional and social development in the next chapter.

*BRIEF REVIEW* By 5 to 6 years of age, IQ scores become good predictors of school achievement. A stimulating home environment, warm parenting, and reasonable demands for mature behavior are positively related to mental test scores. Project Head Start, an intervention for low-income children that combines preschool education with parental support, results in immediate gains in IQ and achievement. Although these decline over time, children show lasting benefits in real-life indicators of school adjustment. High-quality day care can serve as effective early intervention, while poor day care undermines the development of children from all social classes. Preschoolers who watch "Sesame Street" score higher on tests of academic knowledge, but too much TV watching takes time away from many cognitively stimulating, worthwhile activities.

• *Senator Smith heard that IQ gains resulting from Head Start do not last, so he plans to vote against funding for the program. Write a letter to Senator Smith explaining why he should support Head Start.*

## LANGUAGE DEVELOPMENT IN EARLY CHILDHOOD

Language is intimately related to virtually all the cognitive changes that we have discussed in this chapter. Through it, children express a wide variety of cognitive skills, and it also extends many aspects of cognitive development. Between the years of 2 and 6, advances in language are awesome and momentous. Preschoolers' remarkable achievements, as well as their mistakes along the way, indicate that they master their native tongue in an active, rule-oriented fashion.

### Vocabulary Development

At age 2, Jason had a vocabulary of 200 words. By age 6, he will have acquired around 14,000. To accomplish this extraordinary feat, Jason will learn an average of 9 new words each day (Clark, 1983). How do children build up their vocabularies so quickly? Researchers have discovered that they can connect a new word with an underlying concept after only a brief encounter, a process called **fast mapping.** In one study, an adult presented preschoolers with a novel nonsense word, "koob," in a game in which the object for which it stood (an oddly shaped plastic ring)

**Fast mapping**
Connecting a new word with an underlying concept after only a brief encounter.

was labeled only once. Children as young as 2 picked up the meaning of the word (Dollaghan, 1985).

Once children fast map a word, they often have to refine their first guess about its meaning. For example, Jason heard Leslie announce to the children one day that they would soon take a field trip. He excitedly told his mother at noon, "We're going on a field trip!" When she asked where the class would go, Jason responded matter-of-factly, "To a field, of course."

Jason's error suggests that young children fast map some words more accurately and easily than others, and, indeed, this is the case. Preschoolers acquire labels for objects the fastest because these refer to concrete items they already know much about from exploring their world (Gentner, 1982). Words for actions ("go," "run," "broke") are soon added in large numbers, as well as modifiers that refer to noticeable features of objects and people ("red," "round," "sad"). If modifiers are related to one another in meaning, they take somewhat longer to learn. For example, 2-year-olds grasp the general distinction between "big" and "small," but not until age 3 to 5 are more refined differences between "tall–short," "high–low," and "long–short" understood. Similarly, children acquire "now–then" before "yesterday–today–tomorrow" (Clark, 1983; Stevenson & Pollitt, 1987).

Preschoolers figure out the meanings of new words by relying on a special rule called the **principle of contrast.** They assume that each word they hear is unique, so when they hear a new label, they immediately try to tell what it means by contrasting it with ones they already know (Clark, 1987). Consistent with this idea, young children resist accepting two words for the same thing. When given a word for an object for which they already have a label—for example, "fep" for "dog"—they take the new word to mean a subset of the original category (a particular kind of dog). In this way, the principle of contrast not only assists children in figuring out word meanings, but also helps them build their first concept hierarchies (Taylor & Gelman, 1988, 1989).

Once preschoolers acquire new words, they use them creatively to fill in for ones they have not yet learned. As early as age 2, children coin new words, and they do so in systematic ways. For example, Jason said "plant-man" for gardener (created a compound word) and "crayoner" for a child using crayons (added the ending -er) (Clark & Hecht, 1982). Children's ability to invent these expressions is evidence for their remarkable, rule-governed approach to language at an early age.

Preschoolers also extend language meanings through metaphor. Some very clever metaphors appear in their everyday language. For example, one 3-year-old used the expression "fire engine in my tummy" to describe a recent stomachache (Winner, 1988). Not surprisingly, the metaphors preschoolers use and understand are based on concrete, sensory comparisons, such as "clouds are pillows" and "leaves are dancers." Once their vocabulary and knowledge of the world expand, they start to appreciate ones based on nonsensory comparisons as well, such as, "Friends are like magnets" (Karadsheh, 1991; Keil, 1986). Metaphors permit young children to communicate in especially vivid and memorable ways. And sometimes they are the only means we have to convey what we want to say.

## Grammatical Development

Grammar refers to the way we combine words into meaningful phrases and sentences. Between ages 2 and 3, English-speaking children use simple sentences that follow a subject–verb–object word order. This shows that they have a beginning grasp of the grammar of their language (Maratsos, 1983).

As young children conform to rules about word order, they also begin to make the small additions and changes in words that enable us to express meanings flexibly and efficiently—for example, adding "-s" to express plural (as in "cats"), applying

**Principle of contrast**
Principle that young children use to figure out the meaning of a new word—by contrasting it with word meanings they already know.

prepositions (such as "in" and "on"), and forming various tenses from the verb *to be* ("is," "are," "were," "has been," "will"). All English-speaking children master these grammatical markers in a regular sequence, starting with the ones that involve the simplest meanings and the fewest structural changes (Brown, 1973; De Villiers & De Villiers, 1973). For example, children master the plural form "*-s*" before they learn tenses of the verb *to be*. Pluralization requires just one distinction, the difference between one and more than one. In contrast, using tenses of the verb *to be* requires that children understand both number and time, and they must make several grammatical changes in a sentence at once.

By age 3 1/2, children have mastered a great many of these rules, and they apply them so consistently that they overextend the rules to words that are exceptions, a type of error called **overregularization.** "My toy car *breaked*," "I *runned* faster than you," and "We each have two *feets*," are common expressions among young preschoolers. As they listen to the language of those around them, children gradually revise their speech toward correct forms. But the mistakes they make provide yet another example of their systematic approach to language learning.

Between 3 and 6, children master even more complex grammatical forms, but once again, they make predictable errors along the way. In asking questions, preschoolers are reluctant to let go of the subject–verb–object structure that is so basic to the English language. At first, they form questions by failing to invert the subject and verb, as in "Mommy baking cookies?" and "What you are doing, Daddy?" (Tyack & Ingram, 1977). Other errors also occur because children tend to cling to a consistent word order. For example, some passive sentences give them trouble. When told to act out, "The car was pushed by the truck," preschoolers often make a toy car push a truck. By age 5, they understand expressions like these, but mastery of the passive form in its full range of possibilities is a long development that is not complete until the end of middle childhood (Horgan, 1978; Lempert, 1989).

Even though they make errors, preschoolers' grasp of grammar is impressive. For example, 3- and 4-year-olds link phrases and sentences together in ways that express causal relations, such as "*If* you take the medicine, *then* you feel better" or "She hit Joey *because* he took her doll." Although their reasoning is sometimes faulty (especially when discussing unfamiliar topics), preschoolers use these terms with the same degree of accuracy as adults (McCabe & Peterson, 1988). By age 4 to 5, they form embedded sentences ("I think *he will come*"), tag questions ("Dad's going to be home soon, *isn't he?*"), and indirect objects ("He showed *his friend* the present"). As the preschool years draw to a close, children use most of the grammatical constructions of their language competently (Tager-Flusberg, 1989).

## Becoming an Effective Conversationalist

Besides acquiring vocabulary and correct grammar, children must learn how to use language successfully in social contexts. For a conversation to go well, participants must take turns, stay on the same topic, and state their messages clearly. And they must conform to cultural rules that govern how individuals are supposed to interact—for example, that you use a different language style when talking to someone you do not know than to a close friend. This practical side of language is called **pragmatics,** and children make considerable headway in mastering it over the preschool years.

At the beginning of early childhood, children are already skilled conversationalists. In face-to-face interaction with peers, they take turns, respond appropriately to their partner's remarks, and maintain a topic over time (Garvey, 1975; Podrouzek & Furrow, 1988). The number of turns over which children can sustain interaction increases with age, but even 2-year-olds are capable of effective conversation. These

**Overregularization**
Application of regular grammatical rules to words that are exceptions.

**Pragmatics**
The practical, social side of language that is concerned with how to engage in effective dialogue with others.

surprisingly advanced abilities probably grow out of the interactional synchrony that children experience with caregivers from earliest infancy (see Chapter 7).

By age 4, children already know a great deal about culturally accepted ways of adjusting speech to fit the age, sex, and social status of speakers and listeners. In one study, 4- to 7-year-olds were asked to act out different roles with hand puppets. Children of all ages used more commands when playing both high status and male roles, such as doctor, teacher, and father. In contrast, they spoke more politely and used more indirect requests when acting out lower status and female roles, such as patient, pupil, and mother (Anderson, 1984). Older preschoolers also adjust their speech on the basis of how well they know their conversational partner. They give fuller explanations to a stranger than to someone with whom they share common experiences, such as a family member or friend (Menig-Peterson, 1975).

Preschoolers' conversational skills do break down occasionally. For example, have you tried talking on the telephone with a preschooler lately? Here is an excerpt of one 4-year-old's telephone conversation with his grandfather:

> Grandfather: "How old will you be?"
> John: "Dis many." (Holding up four fingers)
> Grandfather: "Huh?"
> John: "Dis many." (Again holding up four fingers)
> Grandfather: "How many is 'at?"
> John: "Four."
> John: "I'm gonna change ears, okay?"
> Grandfather: "Okay."
> John: "I'm back. I had ta change ears."
> Grandfather: "Okay. Was one of your ears gettin' tired?"
> John: "Yeah. This one is." (Points to his left ear) (Warren & Tate, 1992, pp. 259–260)

John used gestures that his grandfather could not see, and when his grandfather signaled that he could not understand ("Huh?"), John did not revise his message. While on the telephone, children cannot see their listeners' reactions or rely on typical conversational aids, such as toys and objects to talk about. Not until middle childhood do children interact effectively without these supports.

These findings indicate that preschoolers' communication does vary considerably across contexts. When talking face to face with familiar people about topics they know well, preschoolers make sophisticated language adjustments. Their conversations appear less mature when they cannot use gestures and other concrete props to help overcome the limits of their current knowledge, vocabulary, and memory (Warren-Leubecker & Bohannon, 1989). Recall the many examples we have seen in which preschoolers' cognitive capacities depend on the difficulty of the task. Research on children's conversational skills echoes this familiar theme.

## Supporting Language Learning in Early Childhood

From what you have learned so far, what experiences do you think would foster preschoolers' language growth? Perhaps you recall from Chapter 6 that interaction with more skilled speakers is especially important during toddlerhood. The same is true during the early childhood years. Opportunities for conversational give-and-take with adults, either at home or in preschool, are consistently related to general measures of language progress (Byrne & Hayden, 1980; McCartney, 1984).

Researchers have discovered that sensitive, caring adults use special techniques that promote language skills when talking to preschoolers. When children use words incorrectly or communicate unclearly, such adults give helpful, explicit feedback, such as, "There are several balls over there, and I can't tell exactly which one you want.

*Conversational give-and-take with adults, either at home or in preschool, promotes young children's language development.* (Rhoda Sidney/The Image Works)

Do you mean a large or small one or a red or green one?" (Robinson, 1981). At the same time, they do not overcorrect, especially when children make grammatical mistakes, because criticism discourages children from actively experimenting with language rules in ways that lead to new skills. Instead, the adult provides subtle, indirect feedback about grammar by using two techniques, often in combination: **expansions** and **recasts** (Bohannon & Stanowicz, 1988). For example, a parent hearing a child say, "Her gotted new red shoes," might respond, "Yes, she got those new red shoes at the store yesterday," *expanding* the complexity of the child's statement as well as *recasting* its incorrect features into mature form. Mothers who frequently expand and recast have preschoolers who make especially rapid progress in language development (Nelson et al., 1984).

Do these findings remind you once again of Vygotsky's theory? In language as in other aspects of intellectual growth, effective parents and teachers seem to interact with young children in ways that gently prompt them to take the next developmental step forward. They respond to children's natural desire to become competent speakers by listening attentively, elaborating on what they say, and stimulating them to talk further. In the next chapter we will see that this special combination of warmth and encouragement of mature behavior is at the heart of early childhood emotional and social development as well.

**Expansions**
Adult responses that elaborate on children's speech in ways that facilitate language development.

**Recasts**
Adult responses that restructure children's incorrect speech into a more mature form.

# SUMMARY

## Piaget's Theory: The Preoperational Stage

• Rapid advances in mental representation, including language and make-believe play, mark the beginning of the **preoperational stage.** With age, make-believe becomes increasingly complex, evolving into **sociodramatic play** with others. Preschoolers' make-believe supports many aspects of cognitive development.

• Aside from representation, Piaget described the young child in terms of deficits rather than strengths. Preoperational children are **egocentric**—unable to imagine the perspectives of others and reflect on their own thinking. Egocentrism leads to a variety of illogical features of thought. According to Piaget, preschoolers engage in **animistic thinking,** and their cognitions are **perception-bound, centered,** focused on **states rather than transformations,** and **irreversible.** In addition, preoperational children **reason transductively** as opposed to inductively or deductively. Because of these cognitive difficulties, they fail **conservation** and **hierarchical classification** tasks.

• When young children are given simplified problems relevant to their everyday lives, their performance appears much more mature. This indicates that operational thinking develops gradually over the preschool years, a finding that challenges Piaget's concept of stage.

• Piaget's theory has had a lasting impact on educational programs for young children. A Piagetian classroom promotes discovery learning, sensitivity to children's readiness to learn, and acceptance of individual differences.

## Further Challenges to Piaget's Ideas: Vygotsky's Sociocultural Theory

• In contrast to Piaget, who believed that language does not play a major role in cognitive development, Vygotsky regarded it as the foundation for all higher cognitive processes. According to Vygotsky, **private speech,** or self-directed language, emerges out of social communication as adults and more skilled peers help children master challenging tasks. Eventually private speech is internalized as inner, verbal thought.

• A Vygotskian classroom emphasizes assisted discovery. Verbal guidance from teachers and peer collaboration are important.

## Information Processing in Early Childhood

• Preschoolers spend only short times involved in tasks, have difficulty focusing on details, and are easily distracted. Attention gradually becomes more sustained and planful during early childhood.

• Young children's recognition memory is very accurate. Their recall for listlike information is much poorer than that of older children and adults because preschoolers use **memory strategies** less effectively.

• Like adults, preschoolers remember familiar experiences in terms of **scripts,** which become more elaborate with age.

The capacity to generalize remembered information from one situation to another improves rapidly around 3 years of age.

• Preschoolers begin to construct a theory of mind, indicating that they are capable of **metacognition,** or thinking about thought. Between ages 2 and 3, they distinguish between an inner mental and outer physical world, and by age 4 they understand that people can hold false beliefs. Young children regard the mind as a passive container of information rather than an active, constructive agent.

• Children understand a great deal about literacy long before they read or write in conventional ways. Preschoolers gradually revise incorrect ideas about the meaning of written symbols as their perceptual and cognitive capacities improve, as they encounter writing in many different contexts, and as adults help them make sense of written information. Children also experiment with counting strategies and discover basic mathematical concepts, including the **cardinality principle,** during the preschool years.

## Individual Differences in Mental Development During Early Childhood

• Intelligence tests in early childhood include a wide variety of verbal and nonverbal cognitive skills. When taking an intelligence test, low-income and ethnic minority children, especially, benefit from time to get to know the examiner and generous praise and encouragement.

• Children growing up in warm, stimulating homes with parents who make reasonable demands for mature behavior score higher on mental tests. Home environment plays a major role in the poorer intellectual performance of low-income children in comparison to their middle-class peers.

• Preschool programs come in great variety. **Child-centered preschools** emphasize free play. In **academic preschools,** teachers train academic skills through repetition and drill. Formal academic instruction, however, is inconsistent with young children's developmental needs.

• **Project Head Start** is the largest federally funded preschool program for low-income children in the United States. High-quality preschool intervention results in immediate test score gains and long-term improvements in school adjustment for disadvantaged children. The Head Start model, which combines early childhood education with parental support, has proven successful. Good day care can also serve as effective early intervention. Poor-quality day care undermines the development of children from all social classes.

## Language Development in Early Childhood

• Supported by **fast mapping,** children's vocabularies grow dramatically during early childhood. Preschoolers rely on the **principle of contrast** to figure out the meanings of new words. Once they learn words, children use them to extend language meanings, coining new words and creating metaphors.

• Between ages 2 and 3, children adopt the basic word order of their language. As they master additional grammatical rules, they engage in **overregularization,** applying the rules to words that are exceptions. By the end of the preschool years, children have acquired a wide variety of complex grammatical forms.

• **Pragmatics** refers to the social uses of language. In face-to-face interaction with peers, young preschoolers are already skilled conversationalists. By age 4, they modify their speech to fit the characteristics of their listeners in culturally accepted ways. In highly demanding contexts, however, preschoolers' communicative skills appear less mature.

• Opportunities for conversational give-and-take with more skilled speakers foster preschoolers' language skills. When adults provide explicit feedback on the clarity of children's utterances and use **expansions** and **recasts,** preschoolers show especially rapid progress in language development.

# IMPORTANT TERMS AND CONCEPTS

preoperational stage (p. 310)
sociodramatic play (p. 312)
operations (p. 312)
egocentrism (p. 313)
animistic thinking (p. 314)
conservation (p. 315)
perception-bound (p. 315)
centration (p. 315)
states versus transformations (p. 315)

irreversibility (p. 315)
transductive reasoning (p. 315)
hierarchical classification (p. 317)
private speech (p. 324)
memory strategies (p. 327)
script (p. 328)
metacognition (p. 329)
cardinality principle (p. 332)
child-centered preschool (p. 336)

academic preschool (p. 336)
Project Head Start (p. 336)
fast mapping (p. 341)
principle of contrast (p. 342)
overregularization (p. 343)
pragmatics (p. 343)
expansions (p. 345)
recasts (p. 345)

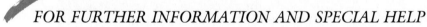

# FOR FURTHER INFORMATION AND SPECIAL HELP

**Early Childhood Development and Education**

Association for Childhood Education International (ACEI)
11141 Georgia Avenue, Suite 200
Wheaton, MD 20902
(301) 942-2443

Organization interested in promoting good educational practice from infancy through early adolescence. Student membership is available and includes a subscription to *Childhood Education,* a bimonthly journal covering research, practice, and public policy issues.

National Association for the Education of Young Children (NAEYC)
1834 Connecticut Avenue, N.W.
Washington, DC 20005
(202) 347-0308

Organization open to all individuals interested in acting on behalf of young children's needs, with primary focus on educational services. Student membership is available and includes a subscription to *Young Children,* a bimonthly journal covering theory, research, and practice in infant and early childhood development and education.

**Preschool Intervention**

National Head Start Association
1220 King Street
Alexandria, VA 22314
(703) 739-0875

Association of Head Start directors, parents, staff, and others interested in the Head Start program. Works to upgrade the quantity and quality of Head Start services.

High-Scope Foundation
600 N. River Street
Ypsilanti, MI 48198
(313) 485-2000

Devoted to improving development and education from infancy through adolescence. Conducts longitudinal research to determine the effects of early intervention on development.

**Day Care**

Child Care Resource and Referral, Inc.
2116 Campus Drive, S.E.
Rochester, MN 55904
(507) 287-2020

Represents more than 260 local agencies that work for high-quality day care and provide information on available services.

National Association for Family Day Care
815 15th Street, N.W., Suite 928
Washington, DC 20005
(202) 347-3356

Organization open to caregivers, parents, and other individuals involved or interested in family day care. Serves as a national voice that promotes high-quality day care.

*No title, Anne Marie, 15 years, Seychelles. Reprinted by permission from The National Museum of Children's Art, Oslo, Norway.*

# Emotional and Social Development in Early Childhood

# 10

Erikson's Theory: Initiative versus Guilt

Self-Development in Early Childhood
*Foundations of Self-Concept   Understanding Intentions   The Emergence of Self-Esteem*

Emotional Development in Early Childhood
*Understanding Emotion   Improvements in Emotional Self-Regulation   Changes in Complex Emotions   The Development of Empathy*

Peer Relations in Early Childhood
*Advances in Peer Sociability      First Friendships*

Foundations of Morality in Early Childhood
*The Psychoanalytic Perspective   Behaviorism and Social Learning Theory   The Cognitive-Developmental Perspective   The Other Side of Morality: The Development of Aggression*

The Development of Sex Typing in Early Childhood
*Preschoolers' Sex-Stereotyped Beliefs and Behavior   Genetic Influences on Sex Typing   Environmental Influences on Sex Typing   Sex-Role Identity   Raising Non-Sex-Stereotyped Children*

Child Rearing and Emotional and Social Development in Early Childhood
*Child-Rearing Styles   What Makes Authoritative Child Rearing So Effective?   Child Maltreatment*

*A*s the children in Leslie's classroom moved through the preschool years, their personalities took on clearer definition. By age 3, they voiced firm likes and dislikes as well as new ideas about themselves. "Stop bothering me," Jason said to Mark as he aimed a beanbag toward the mouth of a large clown face. "See, I'm great at this game," Jason announced with confidence, an attitude that kept him trying, even though he missed most of the throws.

The children's conversations also revealed their first notions about morality. Often they combined statements about right and wrong they had heard from adults with forceful attempts to defend their own desires. "You're 'posed to share," stated Mark while he grabbed a beanbag out of Jason's hand.

"I was here first! Gimme it back," demanded Jason, who pushed Mark while reaching for the beanbag. The two boys continued to struggle until Leslie intervened, provided an extra set of beanbags, and showed them how they could both play at once.

As Jason and Mark's interaction reveals, preschoolers are quickly becoming complex social beings. While arguments and aggression take place among all young children, cooperative exchanges are far more frequent. Between the years of 2 and 6, first friendships emerge in which children converse, act out complementary roles, and learn that their own desires for companionship and toys are best met when they consider the needs and interests of others.

Individual differences in sociability are also evident, becoming a distinct part of preschoolers' personalities. Jason was an assertive, outgoing child who organized many episodes of make-believe play with his classmates. In contrast, Shirley spent so much time by herself working puzzles and painting pictures that one day, her mother asked Leslie if this behavior was normal. Robbie's impulsive and distractible temperament made it difficult for him to make friends. He screamed and hit when he didn't get his way, and Leslie worked hard at showing him how to join play groups and settle conflicts successfully.

The children's play highlighted their developing understanding of their social world. Nowhere was this more apparent than in the attention they gave to the dividing line between male and female. While Lynette and Karen cared for a sick baby doll in the housekeeping area, Jason, Vance, and Mark transformed the block corner into a busy intersection. "Green light, go!" shouted police officer Jason as Vance and Mark pushed large wooden cars and trucks across the floor. Already, the children preferred to interact with same-sex peers, and their play themes mirrored the sex-typed standards of their cultural community.

This chapter is devoted to the many facets of emotional and social development in early childhood. We begin with the theory of Erik Erikson, which provides us with an overview of personality change during the preschool years. Then we consider children's concepts of themselves, their insights into their social and moral worlds, their increasing ability to manage their emotional and social behaviors, and factors that support these competencies. In the final sections of this chapter, we answer the question, "What is effective child rearing?" We also consider the complex conditions that support good parenting or lead it to break down. Today, child abuse and neglect rank among America's most serious national problems.

---

## ERIKSON'S THEORY: INITIATIVE VERSUS GUILT

**Initiative versus guilt**

In Erikson's theory, the psychological conflict of early childhood, which is resolved positively through play experiences that foster a healthy sense of initiative and through development of a superego, or conscience, that is not overly strict and guilt-ridden.

**Phallic stage**

Freud's psychosexual stage of early childhood, in which sexual impulses transfer to the genital region of the body and the Oedipal and Electra conflicts are resolved.

**Oedipal conflict**

The conflict of Freud's phallic stage in which the boy desires to possess his mother and feels hostile toward his father. Resolved by becoming like the father and forming a superego.

Erikson (1950) describes early childhood as a period of "vigorous unfolding" (p. 255). Once children have a sense of autonomy and feel secure about separating from parents, they become more relaxed and less contrary than they were as toddlers. Their energies are freed for tackling the critical psychological conflict of the preschool years: **initiative versus guilt.**

The word *initiative* means spirited, enterprising, and ambitious. It suggests that the young child has a new sense of purposefulness. Preschoolers are eager to tackle new tasks, join in activities with peers, and discover what they can do with the help of adults. At no time, comments Erikson, is the child "more ready to learn quickly and avidly . . . than during this period of his development" (p. 258).

Erikson regarded play as a central means through which young children find out about themselves and their social world. Play permits preschoolers to try out new skills with little risk of criticism and failure. It also creates a small social organization of children who must cooperate to achieve common goals. Make-believe, especially, offers unique opportunities for developing initiative. In cultures around the world, children act out family scenes and highly visible occupations—police officer, doctor, and nurse in our society, rabbit hunter and potter among the Hopi Indians, and hut builder and spear maker among the Baka of West Africa (Garvey, 1990). In this way, make-believe provides children with important insights into the link between self and wider society.

As you know from earlier chapters, Erikson's theory builds on Freud's psychosexual stages. Freud's **phallic stage** of early childhood is a time when sexual impulses transfer to the genital region of the body, and the well-known **Oedipal conflict** arises. The young boy wishes to have his mother all to himself and feels hostile and jealous of his father. Freud described a similar **Electra conflict** for girls, who want to possess their fathers and envy their mothers. These feelings soon lead to intense anxiety, since children fear they will lose their parents' love and be punished for their unacceptable wishes. To master the anxiety, avoid punishment, and maintain the affection of parents, children form a **superego,** or conscience, through **identification** with the same-sex parent. They take the parent's characteristics into their personality, and as a result, adopt the moral and sex-role standards of their society. In other words, they settle for the next best thing to replacing the envied parent: becoming *like* that parent. Finally, children turn the hostility previously aimed at the same-sex parent toward themselves, which leads to painful feelings of guilt each time the child disobeys the standards of conscience.

For Erikson, the negative outcome of early childhood is an overly strict superego, one that causes children to feel too much guilt because they have been threatened, criticized, and punished excessively by adults. When this happens, preschoolers' exuberant play and bold efforts to master new tasks break down. Their self-confidence is shattered, and they approach the world timidly and fearfully.

At this point, it is important to note that Freud's Oedipus and Electra conflicts are no longer regarded as satisfactory explanations of children's emotional, moral, and sex-role development. In later sections of this chapter, when we discuss these topics in detail, we will critically evaluate Freud's psychosexual ideas. At the same time, we will see that Erikson's image of initiative captures the diverse changes that take place in young children's emotional and social lives. The preschool years are, indeed, a time when children develop a confident self-image, more effective control over emotions, new social skills, the foundations of morality, and a clear sense of themselves as boy or girl. Now let's take a close look at each of these aspects of development.

*According to Freud and Erikson, preschoolers form a superego by identifying with the same-sex parent and, thereby, adopting the moral and sex-role standards of their society. This young boy displays a sense of initiative when he joins his father in making home repairs.* (Ann Hagen Griffiths/OPC)

## SELF-DEVELOPMENT IN EARLY CHILDHOOD

### Foundations of Self-Concept

Children emerge from toddlerhood with a firm awareness of their separateness from others. During the preschool years, new powers of representation permit them to reflect upon themselves. Preschoolers start to develop a **self-concept,** a set of beliefs about their own characteristics.

Ask a 3- to 5-year-old to tell you about him- or herself, and you will hear something like this:

> I'm Tommy. See, I got this new red T-shirt. I'm 4 years old. I can brush my teeth, and I can wash my hair all by myself. I have a new Tinkertoy set, and I made this big, big tower.

As these statements indicate, preschoolers' self-concepts, like other aspects of their thinking, are very concrete. Typically they mention observable characteristics, such as their name, physical appearance, possessions, and everyday behaviors (Keller, Ford, & Meacham, 1978).

Of course, as we saw in Chapter 9, as early as age 2 children are aware of their internal mental lives. As a result, preschoolers can describe themselves in terms of beliefs, emotions, and attitudes, but only as these are connected with specific experiences, such as "I wasn't happy about school today" (Eder, 1989). As yet they do not make reference to stable psychological characteristics, such as: "I'm helpful," "I'm friendly," or "I'm usually truthful." The ability to abstract these general ideas about

**Electra conflict**

The conflict of Freud's phallic stage in which the girl desires to possess her father and feels hostile toward her mother. Resolved by becoming like the mother and forming a superego.

**Identification**

In Freud's theory, the process leading to formation of the superego in which children take the same-sex parent's characteristics into their personality.

**Self-concept**

A set of beliefs about one's own characteristics.

the self from specific behaviors must wait for the greater cognitive maturity of middle childhood.

In fact, preschoolers' concepts of themselves are so bound up with particular possessions and actions that they spend much time asserting their rights to objects, as Jason did in the beanbag incident at the beginning of this chapter. In a study of the relationship between self-awareness and social behavior, 2-year-olds' ability to distinguish between self and other was assessed. For example, children were asked to perform actions that indicated they understood the difference between the personal pronouns *my* and *your,* as in "Touch my nose" and "Tickle your stomach." Then the experimenter observed each child interacting with a peer in a laboratory playroom. The stronger the children's self-definitions, the more possessive they were about objects, claiming them as "Mine!" This was despite the fact that the playroom contained duplicates of many toys (Levine, 1983). These observations suggest that young children's struggles over objects may not be a negative sign of selfishness. Instead, they seem to be a positive sign of developing selfhood, an effort to clearly mark off boundaries between self and others.

The ability to distinguish self from other underlies more than young children's disagreements. It also permits them to cooperate for the first time in resolving disputes over objects, playing games, and solving simple problems (Brownell & Carriger, 1990; Caplan et al., 1991). Adults might take both of these capacities into account when trying to promote friendly peer interaction. For example, teachers and parents can accept the young child's possessiveness as a sign of self-assertion ("Yes, that's your toy") and then encourage compromise ("but in a little while, can you give someone else a turn?"), rather than simply insisting on sharing.

## Understanding Intentions

As children learn more about themselves by reflecting on their own behavior, they start to distinguish actions that are deliberate and intentional from those that are accidental. By age 2, preschoolers already have intentions on their minds. In everyday conversations, they say "gonna," "hafta," and "wanna" to announce actions they are about to perform (Brown, 1973). Soon they use this grasp of purposefulness to defend themselves. After being scolded for bumping into a playmate or spilling a glass of milk, preschoolers often exclaim, "It was an accident!" or "I didn't do it on purpose!" (Shultz, 1980).

By 2 1/2 to 3 years of age, this understanding extends to others. Preschoolers become sensitive to cues that help them tell if another person is acting intentionally. At first, they focus on the person's statements. If a person says he is going to do something and then does it, 3-year-olds judge the behavior as deliberate. If statements and actions do not match, then the behavior was not intended (Astington, 1991). By the end of the preschool years, children use a much wider range of information to judge intentionality. For example, 5-year-olds note whether a person is concentrating on what he is doing, whether his action leads to positive or negative outcomes (negative ones are usually not intended), and whether some external cause can account for the person's behavior (Smith, 1978).

Interpreting others' behavior and responding to it appropriately often depend on being able to separate deliberate acts from accidental ones. Older preschoolers who get along well with peers make these judgments accurately and easily. When a playmate appears to have knocked down their block tower on purpose, they become angry and retaliate, but they do not do so if the behavior seems to be accidental. In contrast, highly aggressive children (whom we will discuss in a later section) have difficulty diagnosing intentions. They perceive hostile motives where they do not exist and, as a result, strike out even when the behavior of others is unintentional (Dodge, 1980; Dodge & Somberg, 1987). Such children require special help in learning how to interpret the behavior of others.

### The Emergence of Self-Esteem

Another aspect of self-concept emerges in early childhood: **self-esteem,** the judgments we make about our own worth or goodness. Take a moment to think about your own self-esteem. Besides a global appraisal of your worth as a person, you have a variety of separate self-judgments. For example, you may regard yourself as well liked by others, very good at school work, but only so-so at sports.

Preschoolers also have a sense of self-esteem, but it is not as well defined as that of older children and adults. Young children distinguish between how well others like them (social acceptance) and how "good" they are at doing things (competence). But before age 7, they do not discriminate competence at different activities. Also, when asked how well they can do something, they usually rate their own ability as extremely high and often underestimate the difficulty of the task (Harter, 1983, 1990). Jason's announcement that he was great at beanbag throwing despite his many misses of the target is a typical self-evaluation during the preschool years.

Preschoolers' high sense of self-esteem is adaptive during a period in which so many new skills must be mastered, and it contributes greatly to their sense of initiative. Young children's belief in their own capacities is probably supported by the special patience and encouragement of adults during early childhood. Most parents realize that their preschool youngsters are developing rapidly in a great many ways. They know that a child who has trouble riding a tricycle or cutting with scissors at age 3 is likely to be able to do so a short time later. Preschoolers, too, know that they are growing bigger and stronger, and they see that failure on one occasion often translates into success on another. In Chapter 13 we will see that once children enter school, they become much more aware of how well they are doing at tasks in comparison to their peers. As a result, self-esteem declines and becomes more differentiated during middle childhood.

*Most preschoolers have a high sense of self-esteem, a quality that encourages them to persist at new tasks during a period in which many new skills must be mastered. (Miro Vintoniu/Stock Boston)*

## EMOTIONAL DEVELOPMENT IN EARLY CHILDHOOD

Gains in representation, language, and self-concept support emotional development in early childhood. Between the ages of 2 and 6, children achieve a better understanding of their own and others' feelings. Their ability to regulate the expression of emotion improves as well. Self-development also contributes to a rise in *complex emotions*—shame, embarrassment, guilt, envy, and pride.

### Understanding Emotion

Preschoolers' vocabulary for talking about emotion expands rapidly, and they use it skillfully to reflect on their own and others' behavior. Here are some excerpts from everyday conversations in which 2-year-olds and 6-year-olds commented on emotionally charged experiences:

> Two-year-old: (After father shouted at child, she became angry, shouting back. ) "I'm mad at you, Daddy. I'm going away. Good-bye."

> Two-year-old: (Commenting on another child who refused to nap and cried.) "Mom, Annie cry. Annie sad."

**Self-esteem**
An aspect of self-concept that involves judgments about one's own worth or goodness.

Six-year-old:  (In response to mother's comment, "It's hard to hear the baby crying.") "Well, it's not as hard for me as it is for you." (When mother asked why) "Well, you like Johnny better than I do! I like him a little, and you like him a lot, so I think it's harder for you to hear him cry."

Six-year-old:  (Trying to comfort a small boy in church whose mother had gone up to communion) "Aw, that's all right. She'll be right back. Don't be afraid. I'm here." (Bretherton et al., 1986, pp. 536, 540, 541)

As these examples show, early in the preschool years, children refer to causes, consequences, and behavioral signs of emotion, and over time their understanding improves in accuracy and complexity. By age 4 to 5, children correctly judge the causes of many basic emotional reactions. When asked why a nearby playmate is happy, sad, or angry, they describe events similar to those identified by adults and that fit the emotion being expressed, such as "He's happy because he's swinging very high," "She's mad because he wouldn't share the toy," or "He's sad because he misses his mother." Preschoolers are also good at predicting what a playmate expressing a certain emotion might do next. For example, they know that an angry child might hit someone or grab a toy back and that a happy child is more likely to share (Russell, 1990). They are even aware that a lingering mood can affect a person's behavior for some time in the future (Bretherton et al., 1986).

If you look carefully at the examples given, you will see that young children use emotional language not just to comment on and explain the reactions of others, but also to guide and influence their companion's behavior. Preschoolers also come up with effective ways to relieve others' negative feelings. For example, they suggest physical comfort, such as hugging, to reduce sadness and giving a desired object to a playmate to reduce anger (Fabes et al., 1988). Overall, preschoolers have an impressive ability to interpret, predict, and change others' feelings—knowledge that is of great help in their efforts to get along with peers and adults.

At the same time, there are limits to young children's emotional understanding. They do not grasp abstract emotional terms, such as gratitude, envy, and pity. Also, in situations in which there are conflicting cues about how a person is feeling, preschoolers have difficulty making sense of what is going on. For example, when asked what might be happening in a picture showing a happy-faced child with a broken bicycle, 4- and 5-year-olds tended to rely only on the emotional expression ("He's happy because he likes to ride his bike"). Older children more often reconciled the two cues ("He's happy because his father promised to help fix his broken bike") (Gnepp, 1983). Much like their approach to Piagetian tasks, preschoolers focus on the most obvious aspect of a complex emotional situation to the neglect of other relevant information.

## Improvements in Emotional Self-Regulation

Language also contributes to preschoolers' improved *emotional self-regulation,* or ability to control the expression of emotion. By age 3 to 4, children verbalize a variety of strategies for adjusting their emotional arousal to a more comfortable level. For example, they know that emotions can be blunted by restricting sensory input (covering your eyes or ears in the face of a scary sight or sound), talking to yourself ("Mommy said she'll be back soon"), or changing your goals (deciding that you don't want to play anyway after being excluded from a game) (Thompson, 1990a).

Children's increasing awareness and use of these strategies means that intense emotional outbursts become less frequent over the preschool years. In fact, by age 3 children can even pose an emotion they do not feel, although these emotional "masks" are largely limited to the positive feelings of happiness and surprise. Children of all ages (and adults as well) find it more difficult to act sad, angry, or disgusted than to seem pleased (Lewis, Sullivan, & Vasen, 1987). Undoubtedly this is because most cultures encourage their members to communicate positive feelings and inhibit unpleasant ones as a way of promoting good interpersonal relations, and preschoolers try hard to conform to this rule.

By watching adults handle their own feelings, children pick up strategies for regulating their own emotions. When parents have difficulty controlling anger and hostility, children tend to have problems as well (Gottman & Katz, 1989). Adults' conversations with and instructions to children also provide information about cultural expectations for emotional control and techniques for regulating feelings. When parents prepare children for difficult experiences, such as a trip to the dentist's office or the first day of preschool, by describing what to expect and ways to handle anxiety, they offer coping strategies that children can later apply to themselves. Box 10.1 discusses several ways that parents can help young children manage fears that are a normal part of early childhood.

## Changes in Complex Emotions

One morning in Leslie's classroom, a group of children crowded around for a bread-baking activity. Leslie asked them to wait patiently while she got a baking pan. In the meantime, Jason reached for the dough to feel it, but the bowl came too close to the edge of the table, and the entire contents tumbled over the side. A chorus of "Uh-ohs!" arose from the children. When Leslie returned, Jason looked at her for a moment, covered his eyes with his hands, and said, "I did something bad." He was feeling ashamed and guilty.

As children's self-concepts become better developed, they become increasingly sensitive to the praise and blame of others or (in Jason's case) the possibility of such feedback. As a result, they experience complex emotions more often—feelings that involve injury to or enhancement of their sense of self (see Chapter 7).

As Jason's reaction indicates, preschoolers do not yet label complex emotions precisely. And they experience them under somewhat different conditions than do older children and adults. For example, young children are likely to feel guilty for any act that can be described as wrongdoing, even if it was accidental. In contrast, elementary school youngsters only report guilt for intentional misbehavior, such as ignoring chores, cheating, or lying (Graham, Doubleday, & Guarino, 1984). Also, the presence of an audience seems to be necessary for preschoolers to experience complex emotions. In the case of pride, children depend on a parent or teacher saying, "That's a great picture you drew" or "You did a good job picking up your toys today." And they are only likely to experience guilt and shame if their misdeeds are observed or detected by others (Harter & Whitesell, 1989).

Complex emotions play an important role in children's achievement-related and moral behavior. As children develop guidelines for good behavior, the presence of others will no longer be necessary to evoke these emotions. In addition, they will be limited to situations in which children feel personally responsible for an outcome (Lewis, 1992; Stipek, Recchia, & McClintic, 1992).

Already you may have noticed that current research does not support Freud's view of guilt as hostility toward the same-sex parent that is redirected toward the self. Instead, guilt is an emotion that, in mature form, is experienced each time we deliberately violate our own personal standards for right action (Campos et al., 1983; Hoffman, 1988). Because these standards take a long time to develop, the circumstances under which children experience guilt change considerably with age.

## The Development of Empathy

There is another complex emotion that occurs more often in early childhood—*empathy*. During the preschool years, the ability to recognize and respond sympatheti-

# FROM RESEARCH TO PRACTICE

## Box 10.1 *Helping Young Children Manage Fears*

Tonight was the third evening in a row that 5-year-old Hilary called from her bedroom after the lights had been turned out. "Mommy, Daddy, monsters are in my room again." Already, Hilary's parents had removed the animal pictures from her wall and the mobile that hung from the ceiling. Still, monsters lurked under the bed and in the closet.

Young children's vivid imaginations combined with their difficulty in separating appearance from reality (see Chapter 9) make fears common in early childhood. Preschoolers are likely to conjure up scary ghosts and bogeymen as shadows pass over the walls of their room at night, to fear the dark itself, and to express concern about being left alone. Other typical fears of this period include wariness of animals, anxiety about going to preschool or day care, resistance at getting into swimming pools, and apprehension of the doctor or dentist (Morris & Kratochwill, 1983).

Some fears are well founded and adaptive, and parents intentionally encourage them. Venturing into a busy street and going with strangers are examples. But Hilary's fear of monsters is unrealistic and irrational, causing her to avoid bedtime, lose sleep, and be irritable during the day. Hilary's parents wanted to ease her anxiety as quickly as possible.

Fortunately, most early childhood fears last no more than a few months. They are best dealt with through understanding and patience—acknowledging the child's feelings, encouraging the child to talk about them, offering reassurance, and waiting until the fear declines. Here are some techniques for handling specific fears:

*Monsters, Ghosts, and Darkness*—Reduce exposure to frightening stories in books and on TV until the child is better able to sort out appearance from reality. Make a thorough search of the room for monsters, showing the child that none are there. Leave a nightlight burning, sit by the child's bed until she falls asleep, and tuck in a favorite toy for protection.

*Preschool or Day Care*—Find out if the child fears separation from the parent or dislikes preschool itself. If the child resists getting up and preparing to go but seems content once there, then the fear is probably separation. Under these circumstances, provide a sense of warmth and caring while gently encouraging independence. If the child fears being at preschool, try to find out what is frightening—the teacher, the children, or perhaps a crowded, noisy environment. Provide extra support by accompanying the child at the beginning and lessening the amount of time you are present.

*Animals*—Do not force the child to approach a dog, cat, or other animal that arouses fear. Let the child move at his own pace. Demonstrate how to hold and pet the animal, showing the child that when treated gently the animal reacts in a friendly way. If the child is bigger than the animal, emphasize this: "You're so big. That kitty is probably afraid of you!"

*Swimming Pools*—Expose the child to water bit by bit. Begin with a sprinkler and gradually work up to a wading pool. Then move to the shallow end of a swimming pool, holding and playing with the child until she is ready to stand in the water independently. (Adapted from Feiner & Subak-Sharpe, 1988)

If a child's fear is very intense, persists for a long time, interferes with daily activities, and cannot be reduced in any of the ways suggested above, it has reached the level of a **phobia.** Sometimes phobias are linked to family problems, and special counseling is needed to reduce them. At other times, phobias simply diminish over time without treatment (DuPont, 1983).

Parents need to keep in mind that fears are normal throughout childhood. As the anxieties of one age period decline, others arise that are related to new developmental challenges. In later chapters, we will see that the haunting monsters of the preschool years are eventually replaced by more realistic concerns having to do with peer acceptance, performance in school, and frightening world events, such as the threat of nuclear war (Morris & Kratochwill, 1983). Some fears—of the dark and of being alone—continue for many years and are common across cultures (Robinson, Robinson, & Whetsell, 1988). Older children and adolescents simply develop more effective ways of managing them.

*As young children's language skills expand and their ability to take the perspective of others improves, expressions of empathy become more common. (Lora E. Askinazi/The Picture Cube)*

cally to the feelings of others is an important motivator of positive social behavior. Young children who react with empathy are more likely to share and help when they notice another person in distress (Eisenberg & Miller, 1987).

Recall from Chapter 6 that as toddlers become more self-aware, they display empathy for the first time. They offer comfort and reassurance when someone is sad or hurt. As language develops, children rely increasingly on words to console others, a change that indicates a more reflective level of empathy. One 6-year-old said this to his mother after noticing she was distressed at not being able to find a motel after a long day's travel: "You're pretty upset, aren't you, Mom? You're pretty sad. Well, I think it's going to be all right. I think we'll find a nice place and it'll be all right" (Bretherton et al., 1986, p. 540). As children's ability to take the perspective of others gradually improves, empathic responding increases over early and middle childhood.

The development of empathy depends on cognitive and language development, but it is also supported by early experience. Parents who are warm and encouraging and who show a sensitive, empathic concern for their children have preschoolers who are likely to react in a concerned way to the distress of others (Radke-Yarrow & Zahn-Waxler, 1984). This is not true for children who are repeatedly scolded and punished. In a recent study, researchers observed physically abused preschoolers at a day-care center to see how they reacted to other children's distress. Compared to nonabused youngsters, they rarely showed any signs of empathy. Instead, they responded with fear, anger, and physical attacks (Klimes-Dougan & Kistner, 1990). The children reacted to the suffering of others in the same way that their parents responded to them. Harsh, punitive parenting disrupts the development of empathy at a very early age.

**BRIEF REVIEW** Erikson's stage of initiative versus guilt provides an overview of the personality changes that take place in early childhood. During the preschool years, children develop a self-concept made up of concrete, observable characteristics, and they distinguish actions that are deliberate and intentional from those that are accidental. Preschoolers typically have a high sense of self-esteem, and it supports their enthusiasm for mastering new skills. Language for talking about

• *Reread the description of Jason and Mark's argument at the beginning of this chapter. On the basis of what you know about self-development, why was it a good idea for Leslie to resolve the dispute by providing an extra set of beanbags so that both boys could play at once?*

• *Four-year-old Tia had her face painted at a carnival. As she walked around with her mother, the heat of the afternoon caused her balloon to pop. When Tia started to cry, her mother said, "Oh, Tia, balloons aren't such a good idea when it's hot outside. We'll get another on a cooler day. If you cry, you'll mess up your beautiful face painting." What aspect of emotional development is Tia's mother trying to promote, and why is her intervention likely to be helpful to Tia?*

emotion grows rapidly. Young children have an accurate grasp of the causes and consequences of basic emotional states, and they verbalize a variety of strategies for regulating the expression of emotion. As self-awareness increases, children become more sensitive to the praise and criticism of others, and they experience complex emotions more often. Cognition, language, and warm, sensitive parenting support the development of empathy in early childhood.

## PEER RELATIONS IN EARLY CHILDHOOD

As children become increasingly self-aware, more skilled at communicating, and better at understanding the thoughts and feelings of others, their social skills improve rapidly. Nowhere is this more apparent than in their increasingly social play with peers.

Peer interaction provides young children with learning experiences that they can get in no other way. Because peers interact with one another on an equal footing, they must assume greater responsibility for keeping a conversation going, cooperating, planning, and setting goals for a play theme than when they associate with adults or older siblings. With peers, children form friendships—special relationships marked by attachment and common interests. In the following sections, we take a look at how peer interaction changes over the preschool years.

### Advances in Peer Sociability

**Phobia**
A fear that is very intense, persists for a long time, and cannot be reduced through reasoning and gentle encouragement.

**Nonsocial activity**
Unoccupied, onlooker behavior and solitary play.

**Parallel play**
A form of limited social participation in which the child plays near other children with similar materials but does not interact with them.

**Associative play**
A form of true social participation in which children are engaged in separate activities, but they interact by exchanging toys and commenting on one another's behavior.

**Cooperative play**
A form of true social participation in which children's actions are directed toward a common goal.

At 18 months, Jason's brother Dwayne interacted with peers, but he did so far less often than a preschool child. In a toddler play group, Dwayne spent much time standing and watching and orienting toward adults (Smith & Connolly, 1972). When he did play with a peer, he usually imitated the other child's actions—jumping, chasing, or banging a toy after a playmate did so. By age 2 1/2, children use words to affect a peer's behavior, as when they say "Want to jump?" or "Let's play chase." They also do things that complement one another's actions, such as "finding" a "hiding" child or feeding a doll that another child is holding (Eckerman, Davis, & Didow, 1989).

In the early part of this century, Mildred Parten (1932) noticed a dramatic rise over the preschool years in children's ability to engage in joint, interactive play. Observing 2- to 5-year-olds in nursery school, she concluded that social development proceeds in a three-step sequence. It begins with **nonsocial activity**—unoccupied, onlooker behavior and solitary play. Then it shifts to a limited form of social participation called **parallel play,** in which a child plays near other children with similar materials but does not try to influence their behavior. At the highest level, preschoolers engage in two forms of true social interaction. The first is **associative play,** in which children are involved in separate activities, but they interact by exchanging toys and commenting on one another's behavior. The second is **cooperative play**—a more advanced type of interaction in which children direct their action toward a common goal, such as acting out a make-believe theme or working on the same product—perhaps a sand castle or a painting (see Concept Table 10.1).

Find a time to observe young children of varying ages, noting how long they spend in each of these forms of play. You will probably discover, as current researchers have, that children do not follow the straightforward developmental sequence that Parten suggested. Although nonsocial activity does decline with age, it is still the most frequent form of behavior among 3- to 4-year-olds. Even among kindergartners it continues to take up as much as a third of children's free play time (refer to

*This girl engages in solitary play, the earliest form of play in Mildred Parten's developmental sequence. Yet her play should not be considered immature simply because she chooses to play alone. Instead, it is positive and constructive. Nonsocial activity remains common throughout early childhood, accounting for over one-third of children's play time. (Robert Brenner/Photo Edit)*

Concept Table 10.1). Also, solitary and parallel play remain fairly stable from 3 to 6 years of age, and together, these categories account for as much of the young child's play as does highly social, cooperative interaction. Social development during the preschool years is not just a matter of eliminating nonsocial and partially social activity from the child's behavior.

*These children are engaged in parallel play. Although they play side-by-side with similar materials, they do not try to influence one another's behavior. Parallel play remains stable over the preschool years, accounting for about one-fifth of children's play time. (George Goodwin/Monkmeyer Press)*

**CONCEPT TABLE 10.1 • Parten's Developmental Sequence of Social Play Categories**

| Concept | Important Point | Example |
|---|---|---|
| Nonsocial activity | The child is unoccupied, watches others, or plays alone. Remains frequent throughout the preschool years, accounting for about 40 percent of 3- to 4-year-olds' play time and 35 percent of 5- to 6-year-olds' play time. | During free play at preschool, 3-year-old Jason spends much time wandering around, observing other children's activities, and working puzzles by himself. |
| Parallel play | Limited social participation: The child plays near other children with similar materials but does not try to influence their behavior. Accounts for about 20 percent of 3- to 6-year-olds' play time. | Jason sits next to Hallie at the art table, cutting and pasting colored paper. Each child works on his own picture and does not interact with the other. |
| Associative play | True social interaction: Although involved in separate activities, children talk, trade toys, and comment on one another's behavior. They do not engage in joint efforts directed toward a common goal. | Jason digs a tunnel at one end of the sand table, while Shirley makes cupcakes at the other. The children converse and pass sand tools back and forth as they play. |
| Cooperative play | True social interaction: Children play *with*, rather than *beside*, one another. Their actions are directed toward a common goal. Along with associative play, accounts for about 40 percent of 3- to 4-year-olds' play time and 45 percent of 5- to 6-year-olds' play time. | "Let's play train," suggests Jason to Mark and Lynette. Together, the children line up several riding toys, climb aboard, and prepare to leave the station. |

*Sources:* Parten, 1932. Occurrences of play categories are averages of those reported by Barnes, 1971; Rubin, Maioni, & Hornung, 1976; Rubin, Watson, & Jambor, 1978; and Smith, 1978.

We now understand that it is the *type,* rather than the amount, of solitary and parallel play that changes during early childhood. In a detailed study of preschoolers' play behavior, researchers rated the *cognitive maturity* of nonsocial, parallel, and cooperative play by applying the categories shown in Concept Table 10.2. Within each of Parten's play types, 5-year-olds engaged in more cognitively mature behavior than did 4-year-olds (Rubin, Watson, & Jambor, 1978).

*As these preschoolers trade toys and comment on each other's activities at the sand table, they engage in a form of true social interaction called associative play.* (Mary Kate Denny/Photo Edit)

*In cooperative play, the most advanced form of social participation, children join in action directed toward a common goal. These boys develop an imaginative transportation scene in which one drives the vehicle while the other cooperates as passenger. By the end of early childhood, associative and cooperative play account for nearly half of children's play time. (Arlene Collins/Monkmeyer Press)*

These findings are helpful in responding to the concerns of Shirley's mother, raised at the beginning of this chapter. Often parents do wonder if a preschooler who spends large amounts of time playing alone is developing normally. Only *certain types* of nonsocial activity—aimless wandering and functional play involving immature, repetitive motor action—are cause for concern during the preschool years. Most nonsocial play of preschoolers is not of this kind. Instead, it is positive and constructive, and teachers encourage it when they set out art materials, puzzles, and building toys for children to choose during free play. Children like Shirley, who spend much time in these activities, are not maladjusted. Instead, they tend to be very bright youngsters, who, when they do play with peers, show socially skilled behavior (Rubin, 1982).

**CONCEPT TABLE 10.2 • Developmental Sequence of Cognitive Play Categories**

| Concept | Important Point | Example |
|---|---|---|
| Functional play | Play involving simple, repetitive motor movements with or without objects. Especially common during the first 2 years of life. | Running around a room, rolling a car back and forth, kneading clay with no intent to make something. |
| Constructive play | Play in which children create or construct something. Especially common between 3 and 6 years. | Making a house out of toy blocks, drawing a picture, putting together a puzzle. |
| Make-believe play | Play in which children act out everyday and imaginary roles. Especially common between 2 and 6 years. | Playing house, school, or police officer. Acting out fairytales or television characters. |

*Sources:* Rubin, Fein, & Vandenberg, 1983; Smilansky, 1968.

As we noted in Chapter 9, *sociodramatic play* (or make-believe with peers) be-comes an especially common type of cooperative play during the preschool years. It supports both emotional and social development. In joint make-believe, preschoolers act out and respond to one another's "pretend" feelings. As early as age 2, their play is rich in references to emotional states. Young children also explore and gain control of fear-arousing experiences when they play doctor or dentist or pretend to search for monsters in a magical forest. As a result, they are better able to understand the feelings of others and regulate their own. Finally, to collectively create and manage complex plots, preschoolers must resolve their disputes through negotiation and compromise—experiences that contribute greatly to their ability to get along with others (Garvey, 1990; Singer & Singer, 1990).

### First Friendships

As preschoolers interact, first friendships form that also serve as important contexts for emotional and social development. Take a moment to jot down what the word *friendship* means to you. You probably thought of a mutual relationship involving companionship, sharing, understanding of thoughts and feelings, and caring for and comforting one another in times of need. In addition, mature friendships endure over time and survive occasional conflicts.

Interviews with preschoolers show that they already understand something about the uniqueness of friendship. They know that a friend is someone "who likes you" and with whom you spend a lot of time playing (Youniss, 1980). Yet their ideas about friendship are far from mature. We have already seen that in early child-hood, children view themselves in concrete, activity-based terms. Their notion of friendship is much the same. Four- to 7-year-olds regard friendship as pleasurable play and sharing of toys. As yet, friendship does not have a long-term, enduring quality based on mutual trust (Damon, 1977; Selman, 1980). Indeed, Jason could be heard declaring, "Mark's my best friend" on days when the boys got along well. But he would state just the opposite—"Mark, you're not my friend!"—when a dis-pute arose that was not quickly settled.

Although the meaning of friendship is quite different in early childhood than it will be later on, interactions between friends already have a unique quality. Preschool-ers give twice as much reinforcement, in the form of greetings, praise, and compli-ance, to children whom they identify as friends, and they also receive more from them. Friends are also more emotionally expressive, talking, laughing, and looking at each other more often than nonfriends (Hartup, 1983). Apparently, sensitivity, spontaneity, and intimacy characterize friendships very early, although children are not able to say that these qualities are essential to a good friendship until much later.

As early as the preschool years, some children have difficulty making friends (Hartup, 1989; Howes, 1988a). In Leslie's classroom, Robbie was one of them. His demanding, aggressive behavior caused other children to actively dislike him. Wher-ever he happened to be, such comments as, "I don't want to sit next to Robbie," "Robbie ruined our block tower," and "Robbie hit me for no reason" could be heard. Robbie was, to begin with, a temperamentally difficult child, but he also experienced parenting practices that increased his hostility and aggressiveness. You will learn more about Robbie's problems as we take up the topic of moral development in the next section.

• *Three-year-old Bart lives in the country where there are no other preschoolers nearby. His parents wonder whether it is worth driv-ing Bart into town once a week to play with his 3-year-old cousin. What advice would you give Bart's parents, and why?*

**BRIEF REVIEW**   Beginning in early childhood, peer interaction provides an important context for the development of social skills. Over the preschool years, cooperative play becomes common, although solitary and parallel play are also frequent. First friendships form in early childhood. Although preschoolers do not have a mature understanding of friendship, interactions between friends are already more positive, emotionally expressive, and rewarding.

## FOUNDATIONS OF MORALITY IN EARLY CHILDHOOD

Preschoolers' first concepts of morality emerge in interactions with adults and peers. If you listen in on young children's conversations, you will find many examples of their developing moral sense. Two-year-olds can be heard saying such things as, "I naughty. I wrote on wall," or (after having been hit by another child) "Connie not nice to me." Late in the preschool years, children can state a great many moral rules, such as "You're not supposed to take things without asking" or "Tell the truth!" In addition, they argue over matters of justice, as when they say, "You sat there last time, so it's my turn" or "It's not fair. He got more!"

All theories of moral development recognize that conscience begins to take shape in early childhood. And most agree on the general direction of moral growth. At first, the child's morality is *externally controlled* by adults. Eventually, children *internalize* moral rules, taking over responsibility for their own moral conduct. **Internalization**—the shift from externally controlled responses to behavior that is based on inner standards—permits children to behave in a moral fashion in the absence of adult monitoring. The concept of internalization expresses a quality that most of us regard as essential for morality. Truly moral individuals do not just do the right thing when authority figures are around. Instead, they have adopted *principles of good conduct,* which they follow in a wide variety of situations.

Although points of agreement exist among major theories, there are also important differences. First, each emphasizes a different aspect of moral functioning. Psychoanalytic theory stresses the *emotional side* of conscience development—in particular, identification and guilt as motivators of good conduct. Behaviorism focuses on *moral behavior* and how it is learned through reinforcement and modeling. And the cognitive-developmental perspective emphasizes *thinking*—children's ability to reason about justice and fairness.

Second, these theories differ in the extent to which they view children as actively contributing to their own moral development. Think back to Chapter 1 and see if you can predict ahead of time which perspective regards the child as an active moral being who wonders about right and wrong and searches for moral truth. Then refer to Table 10.1 for a summary of each approach before we consider them in the following sections.

### The Psychoanalytic Perspective

From our discussion of psychoanalytic theory earlier in this chapter, you already know something about this approach to moral development. To briefly review, in Freud's Oedipal and Electra conflicts, children desire the opposite-sex parent, but they give up this wish because they fear punishment and loss of parental love. Instead, they form a *superego,* or conscience, by *identifying* with the same-sex parent, whose moral standards they take into their own personalities. Children obey the superego to avoid *guilt,* a painful emotion that arises each time they are tempted to misbehave. According to Freud, moral development is largely complete by 5 to 6 years of age, at the end of the phallic stage.

Although Freud's theory of conscience development is accepted by psychoanalysts, most child development researchers disagree with it. First, if you look carefully at the Oedipal and Electra conflicts, you will see that discipline promoting fear of

**Internalization**
The developmental shift from externally controlled responses to behavior that is controlled by inner standards.

TABLE 10.1 • An Overview of Three Theoretical Perspectives on Moral Development

| Theoretical Perspective | Brief Description |
|---|---|
| Psychoanalytic theory | To avoid punishment and loss of parental love, young children resolve Freud's Oedipal and Electra conflicts by forming a superego containing the same-sex parent's moral standards. Children obey the superego to avoid guilt. |
| Behaviorism and social learning theory | Modeling and reinforcement are powerful techniques for teaching young children to behave morally. When these experiences are positive and consistent, children internalize adults' moral standards and follow them in the absence of adults. |
| Cognitive-developmental theory | Young children actively think about right and wrong and construct their own principles of justice and fairness. |

**Induction**

A type of discipline in which the effects of the child's misbehavior on others are communicated to the child.

**Prosocial or altruistic behavior**

Responses that benefit another person without any expected reward for oneself.

punishment and loss of parental love should motivate young children to behave morally (Hoffman, 1988). Yet research shows that this is not the case. Children whose parents frequently use threats, commands, or physical force usually feel little guilt after harming others, and they show poor self-control. In the case of love withdrawal—for example, when a parent refuses to speak to or actually states a dislike for the child—children often respond with high levels of self-blame. They might think to themselves, "I'm no good, and nobody loves me." Eventually, these youngsters may protect themselves from overwhelming feelings of guilt by denying the emotion when they do something wrong. So they, too, develop a weak conscience (Zahn-Waxler et al., 1990).

In contrast to these techniques, a special type of discipline called **induction** does support conscience formation. It involves pointing out the effects of the child's misbehavior on others, by saying such things as, "If you keep pushing him he'll fall down and cry" or "She feels so sad because you won't give back her doll" (Hoffman, 1988). As long as the explanation matches the child's capacity to understand, induction is effective with children as young as 2 years of age. In one study, mothers who used inductive reasoning had preschoolers who were more likely to make up for their misdeeds. They also showed more **prosocial or altruistic behavior**—that is, responses that benefit another person without any expected reward for oneself. For example, they spontaneously gave hugs, toys, and verbal sympathy to others (Zahn-Waxler, Radke-Yarrow, & King, 1979).

Why is induction so effective? The reason is that it tells children how to behave so they can call on this information in future situations. Also, by pointing out the impact of the child's actions on others, parents encourage preschoolers to empathize, an emotion that promotes prosocial behavior. In contrast, discipline that relies too heavily on threats of punishment or love withdrawal produces such high levels of fear and anxiety that children cannot think clearly enough to figure out what they should do. These practices may stop unacceptable behavior temporarily, but in the long run they do not get children to internalize moral rules.

Finally, we will see in later chapters that, contrary to what Freud believed, moral development is not an abrupt event that is virtually complete by the end of early childhood. Instead, it is a much longer and more gradual process, beginning in the preschool years and extending into adulthood.

## Behaviorism and Social Learning Theory

According to the traditional behaviorist view, *operant conditioning* is regarded as an important way in which children pick up new responses. From this perspective, children start to behave in ways consistent with adult moral standards because parents and teachers follow up "good behavior" with *positive reinforcement* in the form of approval, affection, and other rewards.

***The Importance of Modeling.*** Some social learning theorists point out that operant conditioning is not enough for children to acquire many moral responses. Recall from Chapter 5 that for a behavior to be reinforced, it must first occur spontaneously and then be rewarded. Yet many prosocial behaviors, such as sharing, helping, or comforting an unhappy playmate, do not occur often enough at first for reinforcement to explain their rapid development in early childhood. Instead, social learning theorists believe that children largely learn to act morally through *modeling*—by observing and imitating models who demonstrate appropriate behavior (Bandura, 1977; Grusec, 1988). Once children acquire a moral response, such as sharing or telling the truth, reinforcement in the form of praise, along with adult reminders of the rules for moral behavior, increases its frequency (Mills & Grusec, 1989).

Many studies show that exposure to models who behave helpfully or generously increases young children's prosocial responses. In fact, models exert their most powerful effect on prosocial development during the preschool years. At the end of early childhood, children who have a history of consistent exposure to caring adults tend to behave prosocially regardless of whether a model is present. By that time, they have internalized prosocial rules from repeated experiences in which they have seen others help and give and been encouraged to behave in a similar way themselves (Mussen & Eisenberg-Berg, 1977).

A model's characteristics have a major impact on children's willingness to imitate their behavior. First, preschoolers are more likely to copy the prosocial actions of an adult who is warm and responsive than one who is cold and distant (Yarrow, Scott, & Waxler, 1973). Warmth may make children more receptive to the model and therefore more attentive to the model's behavior. Also, warm, affectionate responding is an example of altruism, and part of what children may be imitating is this aspect of the model's behavior. Second, children tend to select competent, powerful models to imitate—the reason that they are especially willing to copy the behavior of older peers and adults. Powerful individuals serve as effective models because children want to acquire their prestige for themselves (Bandura, 1977). A final characteristic that affects children's willingness to imitate is whether adults "practice what they preach." When models say one thing and do another—for example, announce that "it's important to help others" but do not help themselves—children generally choose the most lenient standard of behavior that adults demonstrate (Mischel & Liebert, 1966).

***Effects of Punishment.*** Undoubtedly you remember from earlier chapters that operant conditioning can involve *punishment*—scolding, criticism, spankings, and other outcomes that reduce the chances that an unacceptable behavior will occur again. The use of sharp reprimands or physical force to restrain or move a child from one place to another is justified when immediate obedience is necessary—for example, when a 3-year-old is about to run into the street or it is time to leave the house for an appointment and the child protests. In fact, parents are most likely to use forceful techniques under these conditions. When they are interested in fostering long-term goals, such as acting kindly toward others, they tend to rely on warmth and reasoning (Kuczynski, 1984).

These findings indicate that most parents are aware that the usefulness of punishment is limited and that it should be applied sparingly. Indeed, a great deal of research shows that punishment only promotes momentary compliance, not lasting changes in children's behavior. For example, Robbie's parents used punishment often, spanking, shouting, and criticizing when he engaged in an undesirable act. Robbie usually stopped misbehaving when his mother and father were around, but he displayed the behavior again as soon as they were out of sight and he thought he could get away with it. As a result, Robbie was especially unmanageable in settings away from home, such as preschool (Eron et al., 1974).

Harsh punishment also has undesirable side effects. First, it provides children with adult models of aggression. One reason that Robbie lashed out when he was frustrated was that he often saw his parents behaving this way (Emery, 1989). Second, children who are frequently punished soon learn to avoid the punishing adult. Each time Robbie's parents came into the room, Robbie braced himself for something unpleasant and kept his distance. When children avoid interacting with adults who are responsible for their upbringing, those adults have little opportunity to teach desirable behaviors to replace unacceptable responses (Redd, Morris, & Martin, 1975). Finally, as punishment "works" to stop children's misbehavior temporarily, it offers immediate relief to adults, and they are reinforced for using coercive discipline. For this reason, a punitive adult is likely to punish with greater frequency over time, a course of action that can spiral into serious abuse (Parke & Collmer, 1975).

***Alternatives to Harsh Punishment.*** Alternatives to criticism, slaps, and spankings can reduce the side effects of punishment. One is a technique called **time out,** in which children are removed from the immediate setting—for example, by sending them to their rooms—until they are ready to act appropriately. Time out usually requires only a few minutes to change children's behavior, and it also offers a "cooling off" period for parents, who may be very angry at the child. Another approach is *withdrawal of privileges,* such as playing outside or going to the movies. Removing privileges may generate some resentment in children, but it allows parents to avoid using harsh techniques that could easily intensify into violence (Parke, 1977).

*When parents rely on threats, commands, and physical force to discipline, children are exposed to models of aggressive behavior, experience high levels of fear and anxiety, and learn to avoid the punitive adult. Frequent use of harsh punishment interferes with conscience development.* (Brian Seed/Tony Stone Worldwide)

**Time out**

A form of mild punishment in which children are removed from the immediate setting until they are ready to act appropriately.

When parents do decide to use punishment, there are several ways in which they can increase its effectiveness. The first involves *consistency*. Punishment that is unpredictable is related to especially high rates of disobedience in children. When parents permit children to act inappropriately on some occasions but scold them on others, children are confused about how to behave, and the unacceptable act persists. Second, a *warm parent–child relationship* increases the effectiveness of an occasional punishment (Parke & Walters, 1967). Children of involved and caring parents find the interruption in parental affection that accompanies punishment to be especially unpleasant. As a result, they want to regain the warmth and approval of parents as quickly as possible. Third, punishment works best when it is accompanied by an *explanation* (Harter, 1983). Explanations increase the effectiveness of punishment because they help children recall the misdeed and relate it to expectations for future behavior (Walters & Andres, 1967).

Finally, parenting practices that do not wait for children to misbehave but that encourage and reward good conduct are the most effective forms of discipline. This means letting children know ahead of time how to act, serving as a good example, and praising children when they behave well. Adults can also reduce opportunities for misbehavior. For example, on a long car trip, parents can bring along back-seat activities that relieve children's restlessness and boredom. At the supermarket, where there are a great many exciting temptations, they can engage preschoolers in conversation and encourage them to help with the shopping rather than waiting for them to get into mischief before intervening (Holden, 1983; Holden & West, 1989). When adults help children acquire acceptable behaviors that they can use to replace forbidden acts, the need for punishment is greatly reduced.

### The Cognitive-Developmental Perspective

If you look back at the psychoanalytic and behaviorist approaches to morality that we have just discussed, you will see that they have one feature in common: Both focus on how children acquire ready-made standards of good conduct held by adults. The cognitive-developmental perspective on morality is different. It regards children as *active thinkers* about social rules. As early as the preschool years, children make moral judgments, deciding what is right or wrong on the basis of underlying concepts they have about justice and fairness (Rest, 1983).

Piaget's (1965) work served as the original inspiration for the cognitive-developmental approach to morality. We will consider his theory of moral development in Chapter 16 because it has important implications for adolescent moral understanding. Today, we know that Piaget underestimated young children's moral reasoning, just as he overlooked their ability to think logically about many aspects of their physical world (see Chapter 9). Young children already have some well-developed ideas about morality. For example, 3-year-olds respond that a child who intentionally knocks a playmate off a swing is worse than one who does so accidentally while trying to chase a ball, even though (as we saw earlier in this chapter) they report guilt for both types of acts (Yuill & Perner, 1988). They are also aware that disobeying *moral rules*, such as being kind to others and not taking someone else's possessions, is much more serious than violating *social conventions*, such as not saying "please" or "thank you" or eating messy food with fingers (Smetana & Braeges, 1990; Turiel, 1983).

How do young children come to make these distinctions? According to cognitive-developmental theorists, not through direct teaching, modeling, and reinforcement, since adults insist that children conform to social conventions just as often as they press for obedience to moral rules. Instead, children *actively make sense* of their experiences in moral and social-conventional situations. They observe that people respond differently to violations of moral rules than to breaks with social convention. When a moral offense occurs, children react emotionally, describe their own injury or loss, tell another child to stop, or retaliate. And an adult who intervenes is likely to call attention to the rights and feelings of the victim. In contrast, children are less likely to react to violations of social convention. And in these situations, adults tend to demand obedience without explanation, as when they state, "Say the magic word!" or "Don't eat with your fingers" (Nucci & Turiel, 1978; Smetana, 1989).

Young preschoolers are clearly off to a good start in appreciating that moral rules are important because they protect the rights and welfare of people. Their developing cognition and language supports this understanding. But children's social experiences also contribute. Disputes over rights, possessions, and property usually occur when children interact with peers and siblings. Interaction with other children provides preschoolers with important opportunities to work out their first ideas about justice and fairness. The way parents handle violations of rules and discuss moral issues with children also helps them reason about morality. Children who are advanced in moral thinking have parents who adapt their communications about fighting, honesty, and ownership to what their children can understand, respect the child's opinion, and gently stimulate the child to think further, without being hostile or critical (Walker & Taylor, 1991).

Preschoolers who are disliked by peers because of their aggressive approach to resolving conflict show difficulties with moral reasoning. They have trouble distinguishing between moral rules and social conventions, and they violate both kinds often (Sanderson & Siegal, 1988). Without special help, such children show long-term disruptions in moral development.

## The Other Side of Morality: The Development of Aggression

Beginning in late infancy, all children display aggression from time to time as they become better at identifying sources of anger and frustration. By the early preschool years, two forms of aggression are present. The most common type is **instrumental aggression.** In this form, children are not deliberately hostile. Instead, they want an object, privilege, or space and, in trying to get it, they push, shout at, or otherwise attack a person who is in the way. The other type, **hostile aggression,** is meant to hurt, as when the child hits, insults, or tattles on a playmate to injure the other person.

For most preschoolers, instrumental aggression declines with age as they learn to compromise over possessions. In contrast, hostile aggression increases between 4 and 7, although it is rare compared to children's friendly interactions (Shantz, 1987). This slight rise in hostile encounters occurs during an age period in which children become better at detecting others' intentions. Older preschoolers are more likely to recognize when another child is being deliberately malicious and to try to get even by attacking in return (Hartup, 1983).

Although children of both sexes show this general pattern of development, on the average boys are more aggressive than girls, a trend that appears in many cultures (Whiting & Edwards, 1988a). The sex difference is, in part, due to biological factors—in particular, male sex hormones, or androgens. In humans, androgens contribute to boys' higher rate of physical activity, which may increase their opportunities for aggressive encounters (Parsons, 1982). At the same time, the development of sex typing (a topic that we will take up shortly) is also important. As soon as 2-year-olds become dimly aware of sex-role standards—that males and females are expected to behave differently—aggression drops off in girls but is maintained in boys (Fagot & Leinbach, 1989). Then (as we will see shortly) parents' disciplining of boys and girls magnifies this effect.

We must keep in mind that an occasional aggressive exchange between young children is normal and to be expected. As we saw earlier in this chapter, preschoolers

**Instrumental aggression**
Aggression aimed at obtaining an object, privilege, or space with no deliberate intent to harm another person.

**Hostile aggression**
Aggressive acts intended to harm another individual.

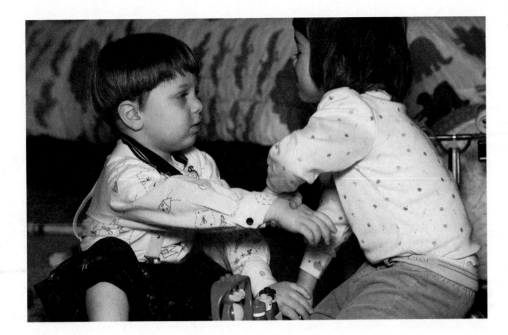

An occasional expression of aggression is normal in early childhood. These children display instrumental aggression as they struggle over an attractive toy. Instrumental aggression declines with age as preschoolers learn how to compromise and share. (Rita Mannini/Photo Researchers)

sometimes assert their developing sense of self through these encounters, which become important learning experiences as adults intervene and teach alternative ways of satisfying desires. But some preschoolers like Robbie show abnormally high rates of aggression. Researchers have traced their problems to strife-ridden families, poor parenting practices, and exposure to television violence—factors that often can be found together.

***The Family as Training Ground for Aggressive Behavior.*** "I can't control him, he's impossible," complained Nadine, Robbie's mother, at a conference with Leslie one day. When Leslie asked what might be going on at home that made it hard to handle Robbie, she discovered that Robbie's parents fought constantly. Their arguments led to high levels of family stress and a "spill over" of hostile communication into child rearing that stimulated and perpetuated Robbie's aggression (Holden & Ritchie, 1991; Patterson, DeBaryshe, & Ramsey, 1989).

Observations in families like Robbie's reveal that anger and punitiveness can quickly spread from one family member to another, creating a conflict-ridden family atmosphere and an "out-of-control" child (Patterson, 1982). The pattern begins with forceful discipline, which is made more likely by stressful life experiences, the parent's own personality, or a temperamentally difficult child. Once the parent threatens, criticizes, and punishes, then the child whines, yells, and refuses until the parent finds the child's behavior to be too much and "gives in." This sequence is likely to repeat itself in the future, since at the end of this exchange, both parent and child get relief for stopping the unpleasant behavior of the other. The next time the child misbehaves, the parent is even more coercive and the child more defiant, until one member of the pair again finds the other unbearable and "begs off." These cycles generate anxiety and irritability among other family members, who also imitate the hostile behavior. Aggressive children who are products of these family processes soon learn to view the world from a violent perspective. Because they expect others to react with anger and physical force, they see hostile intent where it does not exist. As a result, they make many unprovoked aggressive attacks, which contribute to the aggressive cycle.

For at least two reasons, boys are more likely than girls to become involved in family interactions that promote aggressive behavior. First, parents more often use commands and physical punishment with sons, which encourage them to adopt the same tactics (Lytton & Romney, 1991). Second, parents are less likely to interpret fighting among boys as aggressive, so they may overlook it more than they do with girls (Condry & Ross, 1985). In line with this idea, by middle childhood boys expect less parental disapproval and report feeling less guilty over aggression than do girls (Perry, Perry, & Weiss, 1989).

Unfortunately, highly aggressive children often have serious adjustment problems. Because of their hostile style of responding and their poor self-control, they tend to be rejected by peers, to fail in school, and (by adolescence) to seek out deviant peer groups, which lead them toward delinquency and adult criminality (see Chapter 16). These children need treatment early, before their antisocial behavior becomes so well practiced that it is difficult to change.

***Helping Children and Parents Control Aggression.*** Help for aggressive children must break the cycle of hostilities between family members, replacing it with effective interaction styles. Leslie suggested that Robbie's parents see a family therapist, who observed their inept practices, demonstrated alternatives, and had Nadine and her husband practice them. They learned not to give in to Robbie, to pair commands with reasons, and to replace verbal insults and spankings with more effective punishments, such as time out and withdrawal of privileges (Patterson, 1981).

At the same time, Leslie began teaching Robbie more successful ways of relating to peers. As opportunities arose, she encouraged Robbie to talk about a playmate's feelings and express his own. This helped Robbie take the perspective of others and empathize with them. Soon he showed greater willingness to share and cooperate (Feshbach & Feshbach, 1982). Robbie also participated in **social problem-solving training.** Over several months, he met with Leslie and a small group of preschoolers. The children used puppets to act out common conflicts, discussed effective and ineffective ways of resolving them, and tried out successful strategies in the classroom. Children who receive such training show improvements in social adjustment that are still present a year after the intervention (Spivack & Shure, 1974).

Finally, Robbie's parents got help with their marital problems. This, in addition to their improved ability to manage Robbie's behavior, greatly reduced stress and conflict in the household.

***Television, Aggression, and Other Aspects of Social Learning.*** Televised violence also encourages childhood aggression. In the United States, over 80 percent of programs broadcast contain at least some violence, with especially high levels in programs for children. Children's cartoons contain more acts of aggression than any other type of program—21 violent acts per hour (Gerbner et al., 1986).

Young children are especially likely to be influenced by television. One reason is that below age 8, children do not understand a great deal of what they see on TV. Because they have difficulty connecting separate scenes into a meaningful story line, they do not relate the actions of a TV character to motives or consequences (Collins et al., 1978). A villain who gets what he wants by punching, shooting, and killing may not be a "bad guy" to a preschooler, who fails to notice that the character was brought to justice in the end. Young children also find it hard to separate true-to-life from fantasized television content. They assume that TV reflects their world, unless extreme violations of reality occur, such as Superman dashing across the sky (Kelly, 1981). These misunderstandings increase young children's willingness to uncritically accept and imitate what they see on TV.

Hundreds of studies support the conclusion that TV violence increases children's aggressive behavior (Liebert & Sprafkin, 1988). Violent programming not only creates short-term difficulties in parent and peer relations, but has long-term effects as well. Longitudinal research reveals that highly aggressive children have a greater

**Social problem-solving training**

Training in which children are taught how to resolve common social conflicts.

appetite for violent TV. As they watch more, they become increasingly likely to resort to hostile ways of solving problems, a spiraling pattern of learning that contributes to serious antisocial acts by adolescence and young adulthood (Friedrich-Cofer & Huston, 1986; Huesmann, 1986). Television violence also "hardens" children to aggression, making them more willing to tolerate it in others. Heavy TV viewers begin to see the world as a mean and scary place where aggressive acts are a normal and acceptable means for solving problems (Parke & Slaby, 1983).

TV promotes conflict in a second way: through its advertising. Since preschoolers (and many older children as well) innocently believe that the promises of TV ads are true, they ask for products that they see. In the aisles of grocery and toy stores, adult refusals often lead to arguments between parents and children (Atkin, 1978). Commercials for sugary foods make up about 80 percent of advertising aimed at children. When parents give in to children's demands, young TV viewers come to prefer these snacks and are convinced by TV messages that they are healthy (Gorn & Goldberg, 1982).

Finally, television conveys racial and sex-role stereotypes that are common in American society. Although blacks are better represented on TV than they once were, too often they are segregated from whites in child- and adult-oriented programs. Other racial minorities rarely appear, and when they do, they tend to be depicted negatively, as villains or victims of violence (Gerbner et al., 1986). Similarly, women appear less often than men as main characters, and they are usually cast in "feminine" roles, such as wife, mother, nurse, teacher, or secretary (Macklin & Kolbe, 1984).

The ease with which television can manipulate the beliefs and behavior of children has resulted in strong public pressures to improve its content. Unfortunately, as Box 10.2 indicates, these efforts have not been very successful. At present, it is up to parents to regulate their children's exposure—a heavy burden, given that children find TV so attractive.

**BRIEF REVIEW** The young child's morality gradually shifts from externally controlled responses to internalized standards. Contrary to predictions from Freudian theory, power assertion and love withdrawal do not promote the development of conscience. Instead, induction is far more successful. Behaviorism and social learning theory have shown that modeling combined with reinforcement in the form of praise is very successful in encouraging prosocial acts. In contrast, harsh punishment only promotes temporary compliance, not lasting changes in children's behavior. Cognitive-developmental theory views children as active thinkers about justice and fairness. During the preschool years, children recognize that intentionally hurting someone is worse than doing so accidentally, and they distinguish between moral rules and social conventions. Hostile family atmospheres, poor parenting practices, and heavy television viewing promote childhood aggression, which can spiral into serious antisocial activity. TV also fosters a naive belief in the truthfulness of advertising and racial and sex-role stereotypes.

- *Alice and Wayne want their two young children to develop a strong, internalized conscience and to become generous, caring individuals. List as many parenting practices as you can that would promote these goals.*

- *Nanette told her 3-year-old son Darren not to go into the front yard without asking, since the house faces a very busy street. Darren disobeyed several times, and now Nanette thinks it's time to punish him. How would you recommend that Nanette discipline Darren, and why?*

## THE DEVELOPMENT OF SEX TYPING IN EARLY CHILDHOOD

Early in the preschool years, we can see sex-typed preferences and behavior among young children. In Leslie's classroom, children tended to play and form friendships with peers of their own gender. Girls spent more time in the housekeeping, art, and reading corners, while boys gathered more often in blocks, woodworking, and active

## SOCIAL ISSUES

### Box 10.2  *Regulating Children's Television*

*E*xposure to television is almost universal in the United States and other Western industrialized nations. Ninety-eight percent of American homes have at least one television set, and a TV is switched on in a typical household for a total of 7.1 hours a day. TV enters the lives of children at an early age, becoming a major teacher of undesirable attitudes and behavior. Yet television has as much potential for good as it does for ill. If the content of television were changed, it could promote prosocial attitudes and behavior and convey information about nonviolent aspects of the world, such as history, science, literature, fine arts, and other cultures (Huston, Watkins, & Kunkel, 1989).

Since the early days of television, high-quality programming for children has dropped off while advertising has risen as commercial broadcasting stations have tried to reach larger audiences and boost profits. Public broadcasting and cable TV offer some excellent programs for children. But government funding for public television has declined over the past two decades, and cable (which depends on user fees) is less available to low-income families. Furthermore, there are fewer restrictions today than there once were on program content and advertising for children. For example, a decade ago, characters in children's programs were not permitted to sell products. Today they commonly do—a strategy that greatly increases children's desire to buy. In addition, the amount of time devoted to commercials during child-oriented TV is no longer limited (Huston, Watkins, & Kunkel, 1989).

Professional organizations and citizens groups, such as *Action for Children's Television,* a 20,000-member association, have pressed for government regulation of TV. Many would like to see networks required to provide a certain amount of educational programming for children. And some believe that it would be best to ban advertising directed at children. But the First Amendment right to free speech has made the federal government reluctant to place limits on television content. And broadcasters, whose profits are at risk, are certainly against restrictions (Liebert & Sprafkin, 1988).

Until television does improve, protecting chil-

*Parents who watch TV with their children can help them interpret and evaluate televised messages. They can also encourage children to build on TV content in constructive ways—for example, through active play or a trip to the library to gather more information. (Sybil Shackman/Monkmeyer Press)*

dren from the impact of harmful TV rests in the hands of parents. Here are some strategies that they can use:

1.  Avoid using TV as a baby-sitter. Provide children with clear rules that limit the amount of time they can watch—for example, an hour a day and only certain programs—and stick to the rules.

2.  Do not use television as a reward or punishment, a practice that increases its attractiveness to children.

3.  Provide an effective model by avoiding excess television viewing yourself.

4.  Use parenting practices that promote social and moral maturity. Children who experience warmth and inductive discipline prefer programs with positive social content and are less attracted to violent TV (Abelman, 1985).

5.  Build on televised content in constructive ways, encouraging children to move away from the set into active engagement with their surroundings. For example, a program on animals might spark a trip to the zoo, a visit to the library for books

about animals, or new ways of observing and caring for the family pet.

6. As much as possible, watch with children, helping them understand what they see. When adults express disapproval of on-screen behavior, raise questions about the realism of televised information, and encourage children to talk about it,

they teach children to evaluate TV content rather than accept it uncritically (Collins, 1983).

*WATCH SEVERAL SATURDAY MORNING* cartoons, late-afternoon children's shows, and prime-time adult television programs. Count the number of prosocial and aggressive acts you see. Also note the roles that male and female characters play. How do the programs compare in terms of the social messages they send to children?

play spaces. As we saw in the previous section, television plays an important role in children's sex-typed learning, but sex typing develops so rapidly in early childhood that other powerful influences are clearly involved.

The same three theories that provide accounts of morality have been used to explain sex-role development. According to *psychoanalytic theory,* sex-typed beliefs and behaviors are adopted in the same way as other social standards—through identification with the same-sex parent as the Oedipal and Electra conflicts are resolved. Recall that Freud's ideas worked poorly in the area of morality. They also have difficulty accounting for sex typing. Research shows that the same-sex parent is only one of many influences in sex-role development. Opposite-sex parents, peers, teachers, and the broader social environment are important as well (Huston, 1983).

*Social learning theory,* with its emphasis on modeling and reinforcement, and *cognitive-developmental theory,* with its focus on children as active thinkers about their social world, are major current approaches to understanding children's sex typing (Ruble, 1988). We will see that neither has proved entirely adequate by itself. Consequently, a new perspective that combines elements of both, called *gender schema theory,* has recently arisen. In the following sections, we consider the early development of sex typing along with genetic and environmental factors that contribute to it.

### Preschoolers' Sex-Stereotyped Beliefs and Behavior

Recall from Chapter 7 that as early as age 2, children begin to categorize themselves and others on the basis of sex. As soon as basic gender categories are established, children start to sort out what they mean in terms of activities and behaviors. A wide variety of sex stereotypes are quickly mastered. Preschoolers associate many toys, articles of clothing, tools, household items, games, occupations, and even colors (pink and blue) with one sex as opposed to the other (Huston, 1983; Picariello, Greenberg, & Pillemer, 1990). Children's behavior falls in line with their sex-typed beliefs—not only in play preferences but in personality traits as well. We have already seen that boys tend to be more active, assertive, and aggressive. In contrast, girls tend to be more fearful, dependent, compliant, and emotionally sensitive (Jacklin & Maccoby, 1983).

Over the preschool years, children's sex-stereotyped beliefs become stronger—so much so that they operate like blanket rules rather than flexible guidelines (Weinraub et al., 1984; Martin, 1989). Once, when Leslie showed the children a picture of a Scottish bagpiper wearing a kilt, they insisted, "Men don't wear skirts!" During free play, they often exclaimed that girls don't drive fire engines and can't be police officers and boys don't take care of babies and can't be the teacher. These rigid ideas are the combined result of several factors—sex-typed information in the environment, preschoolers' cognitive tendency to exaggerate differences they observe, and their limited understanding of the biological basis of male and female. As we will see in greater detail later on, prominent observable characteristics—play activities, toy choices, occupations, hairstyles, and clothing—define gender for the majority of 3- to 5-year-olds. Most have not yet learned that genitals, hidden beneath clothing, determine a person's sex.

## Genetic Influences on Sex Typing

The sex differences that we have just described appear in many cultures around the world (Whiting & Edwards, 1988a). Certain of them—the preference for same-sex playmates as well as male activity level and aggression—are widespread among animal species as well (Meany, Stewart, & Beatty, 1985). So it is reasonable for us to ask whether sex typing might be influenced by genetic factors. We have already indicated that there is good evidence that aggression is indirectly linked to sex hormones in human children. That is, androgens promote active play among boys, increasing the likelihood of hostile encounters.

Eleanor Maccoby (1990) argues that hormonal differences between males and females have important consequences for sex typing. Early on, hormones affect play styles, leading to rough, noisy movements among boys and calm, gentle actions among girls. Then, as children begin to interact with peers, they naturally choose same-sex partners whose interests and behaviors are compatible with their own. Over the preschool years, girls increasingly seek out other girls because of their common preference for quieter activities. And boys come to prefer other boys, who respond positively to each other's desire to run, climb, play-fight, and build up and knock down. At age 4, children already spend three times as much time with same-sex as opposite-sex playmates. By age 6, this ratio has climbed to 11 to 1 (Maccoby & Jacklin, 1987).

In thinking about these preferences, we must be careful not to overemphasize the role of heredity in sex typing. As we will see in the next section, adults do a great deal to promote children's sex-stereotyped interests and behavior, and children's preference for same-sex peers provides further support for them. This suggests that environmental forces build on hereditary influences to increase children's sex-typed responding. Let's look at some research that supports this idea.

## Environmental Influences on Sex Typing

A wealth of evidence reveals that family influences, encouragement by teachers and peers, and examples in the broader social environment combine to promote the vigorous sex typing of early childhood.

**The Family.**   Beginning at birth, parents hold different perceptions and expectations of their sons and daughters (see Chapter 7), a trend that continues into the preschool years. Many parents state that they want their children to play with "sex-appropriate" toys, and they also believe that boys and girls should be raised differently. When asked about their child-rearing values, parents are likely to describe achievement, competition, and control of emotion as important for sons and warmth, "ladylike" behavior, and close supervision of activities as important for daughters (Brooks-Gunn, 1986; McGuire, 1988).

These beliefs carry over into actual parenting practices. Mothers and fathers are far more likely to purchase guns, cars, and footballs for boys and dolls, tea sets, and jump ropes for girls—toys that promote very different play styles. In addition, parents actively reinforce many sex-typed behaviors. For example, they react more positively when a young son as opposed to a daughter plays with cars and trucks, demands attention, or tries to take toys from others, thereby rewarding his active and assertive behavior (Fagot & Hagan, 1991). In contrast, they more often direct play activities, provide help, and discuss emotions with a daughter, encouraging her dependency and emotional sensitivity (Dunn, Bretherton, & Munn, 1987; Lytton & Romney, 1991).

These influences are major factors in children's sex-role learning, since parents who consciously avoid behaving in these ways have less sex-typed youngsters (Weisner & Wilson-Mitchell, 1990). Also, we must keep in mind that besides parents, other family members contribute to sex typing. For example, preschoolers with older, opposite-sex siblings have many more opportunities to imitate and participate in "cross-sex" play (Stoneman, Brody, & MacKinnon, 1986). In any case, of the two sexes, boys are clearly the more sex typed. One reason is that parents are far less tolerant of "cross-sex" behavior in their sons than in their daughters. They are much more concerned if a boy acts like a sissy than if a girl acts like a tomboy (Maccoby, 1980).

*Teachers.* Parents are not the only adults who encourage children's sex typing. Teachers do so as well. Several times, Leslie caught herself responding in ways that furthered sex segregation and stereotyping in her classroom. One day when the class was preparing to leave for a field trip, she called out, "Will the girls line up on one side and the boys on the other?" Then, as the class became noisy with excitement, she pleaded, "Boys, I wish you'd quiet down like the girls!"

As in their experiences at home, girls get more encouragement to participate in adult-structured activities at preschool. They can frequently be seen clustered around the teacher, following directions in an activity. In contrast, boys more often choose areas of the classroom where teachers are minimally involved. As a result, boys and girls practice very different social behaviors. Compliance and bids for help occur more often in adult-structured contexts, while assertiveness, leadership, and creative use of materials appear more often in unstructured pursuits (Carpenter, 1983).

*Peers.* Once formed, children's same-sex peer groups serve as powerful environments for strengthening stereotyped beliefs and behavior. By age 3, same-sex peers positively reinforce one another for sex-typed play by praising, imitating, or joining in the activity of an agemate who shows a "sex-appropriate" response (Fagot & Patterson, 1969). Similarly, when preschoolers engage in "gender-inappropriate" activities—for example, when boys play with dolls or girls with woodworking tools—they receive criticism from peers. Boys are especially intolerant of "cross-sex" play in their male companions (Fagot, 1977). A boy who frequently crosses gender lines is likely to be ignored by other boys even when he does engage in "masculine" activities!

Children also develop different styles of social influence in sex-segregated peer groups. To get their way with male peers, boys more often rely on commands, threats, and physical force. In contrast, girls learn to use polite requests and persuasion. These tactics succeed with other girls but not with boys, who pay little attention to them. Consequently, an additional reason that girls may stop interacting with boys is that they do not find it very rewarding to communicate with an unresponsive social partner (Maccoby, 1990).

*The Broader Social Environment.* A wide variety of examples of sex-typed behavior are available in children's everyday environments. Although American society has changed to some degree, children come in contact with many real people who conform to traditional sex-role expectations. As one writer points out:

> The average child sees women cooking, cleaning, and sewing; working in "female" jobs
> such as clerical, secretarial, sales, teaching, nursing; choosing to dance, sew, or play

bridge for recreation; and achieving in artistic or literary areas more often than in science and engineering. That same child sees men mowing the lawn, washing the car, or doing household repairs; working in "male" occupations . . . choosing team sports, fishing, and nights with "the boys" for recreation; and achieving in math, science, and technical areas more often than in poetry or art. In school, the teachers of young children are women; the teachers of older students and the administrators with power are usually men. . . . Hence, although there are some individual differences, most children are exposed continually in their own environments to models of sex-stereotyped activities, interests, and roles. (Huston, 1983, pp. 420–421)

As we will see in the next section, young children do not just imitate the many gender-linked responses they observe. They also start to view themselves and their environment in gender-biased ways, a perspective that can seriously limit their interests and skills.

## Sex-Role Identity

As adults, each of us has a **sex-role identity**—an image of oneself as relatively masculine or feminine in characteristics. By middle childhood, researchers can measure sex-role identity by asking children to rate themselves on personality traits, since at that time, self-concepts become based on psychological attributes rather than concrete behaviors.

Individuals differ considerably in the way that they respond to these questionnaires. A child or adult with a "masculine" identity scores high on traditionally masculine items (such as self-sufficient, ambitious, and forceful) and low on traditionally feminine ones (such as warm, soft-spoken, and cheerful). Someone with a "feminine" identity does just the reverse. Although the majority of individuals view themselves in sex-typed terms, a substantial minority (especially females) have a type of sex-role identity called **androgyny.** They score high on *both* masculine and feminine characteristics (Bem, 1974; Boldizar, 1991).

Research indicates that sex-role identity is a good predictor of psychological adjustment. Masculine and androgynous children and adults have a higher sense of self-esteem, while feminine individuals often think poorly of themselves, perhaps because many feminine traits are not highly valued in our society (Alpert-Gillis & Connell, 1989; Boldizar, 1991). Androgynous individuals have an additional advantage. In line with their flexible self-definitions, they are more adaptable in behavior—for example, able to show masculine independence or feminine sensitivity, depending on the situation (Bem, 1975). The concept of androgyny reveals that masculinity and femininity are not opposites, as many people believe. It is possible for children to acquire a mixture of positive qualities traditionally associated with each sex, a sex-role identity that may best help them realize their potential.

***The Emergence of Sex-Role Identity.***   How do children develop sex-role identities that consist of varying mixtures of masculine and feminine characteristics? Both social learning and cognitive-developmental answers to this question exist. According to *social learning theory,* behavior comes before self-perceptions. Preschoolers first acquire sex-typed responses through modeling and reinforcement, and only then do they organize these behaviors into gender-linked ideas about themselves. In contrast, *cognitive-developmental theory* regards the direction of development as the other way around. Over the preschool years, children first acquire a cognitive appreciation of their own gender. They develop **gender constancy,** the understanding that their sex is a permanent characteristic that remains the same even if clothing, hairstyle, and play activities change. Once formed, children use this idea to guide their behavior, and a preference for sex-typed activities appears (Kohlberg, 1966).

**Sex-role identity**

Image of oneself as relatively masculine or feminine in characteristics.

**Androgyny**

A type of sex-role identity in which the person scores high on both masculine and feminine personality characteristics.

**Gender constancy**

The understanding that one's own gender is permanent despite changes in clothing, hairstyle, and play activities.

Research indicates that gender constancy is not present in most children until the end of the preschool years. Shown a doll whose hairstyle and clothing are transformed before their eyes, a child younger than age 6 is likely to insist that the doll's sex has changed as well (McConaghy, 1979). And when asked such questions as "When you (a girl) grow up, could you ever be a daddy?" or "Could you be a boy if you wanted to?", young children freely answer yes (Slaby & Frey, 1975).

Yet a recent study showed that these responses are not due to preschoolers' cognitive immaturity, as cognitive-developmental theory assumes. Instead, they result from lack of knowledge about genital differences between the sexes. In many households in Western societies, young children do not see members of the opposite sex naked. Therefore, they distinguish males and females using the only information they do have—the way each sex dresses and behaves. Children as young as 3 who are aware of genital differences almost always answer gender constancy questions correctly (Bem, 1989).

Is cognitive-developmental theory correct that gender constancy is responsible for children's sex-typed behavior? From findings reviewed in earlier sections, perhaps you have already concluded that evidence for this assumption is weak. "Gender-appropriate" behavior appears so early in the preschool years that modeling and reinforcement must account for its initial appearance. But once children begin to reflect on these behaviors, they form basic gender categories that do strengthen sex-typed responding. A new theoretical perspective shows how this happens.

***Gender Schema Theory: A New Approach to Sex-Role Identity.*** **Gender schema theory** combines features of social learning and cognitive-developmental perspectives, emphasizing that both environmental pressures and children's cognitions work together to shape sex-role development (Bem, 1984; Martin & Halverson, 1981, 1987). Beginning at an early age, children respond to instruction from others, picking up sex-typed preferences and behavior. At the same time, they start to organize their experiences into *gender schemas,* or categories of maleness and femaleness, which they use to interpret their world. A young child who says, "Only boys can be doctors" or "Cooking is a girl's job" already has some well-formed gender schemas. As soon as preschoolers can label their own sex, they start to select gender schemas that are consistent with it, applying those categories to themselves (Fagot & Leinbach, 1989; Martin & Little, 1990). As a result, their self-perceptions become sex typed, and these serve as additional gender schemas that children use to guide their own behavior in a "gender-appropriate" direction.

Let's look at the example in Figure 10.1 to see exactly how this network of gender schemas strengthens sex-typed preferences and behavior. Our 3-year-old girl, Mandy, has been taught that "dolls are for girls" and "trucks are for boys." She also knows that she is a girl. Mandy uses this information to interpret the environment and make decisions about how to behave. Because her schemas lead her to conclude that "dolls are for me," when given a doll she approaches it, explores it, and learns more about it. In contrast, on seeing a truck, she uses her gender schemas to conclude that "trucks are not for me" and responds by avoiding the "sex-inappropriate" toy (Martin & Halverson, 1981).

## Raising Non-Sex-Stereotyped Children

How can adults help young children avoid developing rigid gender schemas that strengthen sex stereotypes and restrict their behavior and learning opportunities? Sandra Bem (1984) points out that gender-linked associations are so common in our environment that parents and teachers must work especially hard to prevent young children from absorbing them. Adults can begin by eliminating sex stereotyping from

**Gender schema theory**
A theory that combines features of social learning and cognitive-developmental perspectives to explain how environmental pressures and children's cognitions work together to shape sex-role development.

**FIGURE 10.1** • Effect of gender schemas on sex-typed preferences and behavior. Mandy's network of gender schemas leads her to approach and explore "feminine" toys, such as dolls, and to avoid "masculine" ones, such as trucks. *(From C. L. Martin & C. F. Halverson, 1981, "A schematic processing model of sex-typing and stereotyping in children," Child Development, 52, p. 1121. © The Society for Research in Child Development, Inc. Adapted by permission.)*

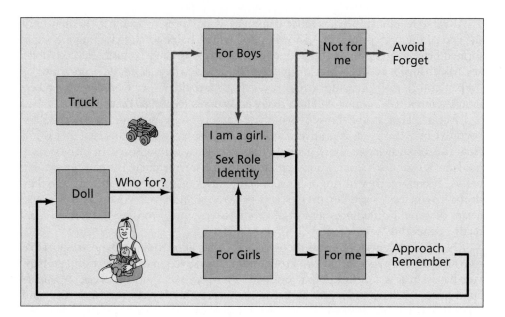

their own behavior and from the alternatives they provide for children. For example, mothers and fathers can take turns making dinner, bathing children, and driving the family car. They can provide sons and daughters with both trucks and dolls and pink and blue clothing. And teachers can make sure that all children spend some time each day in adult-structured and unstructured activities.

At the same time, adults can teach young children that anatomy and reproduction are the only characteristics that determine a person's sex. Because many preschoolers do not understand this idea, they mistakenly assume that arbitrary cultural practices are the basis of gender. Then, to preserve their own identity as boy or girl, they insist that these must be strictly obeyed.

Finally, once children notice the vast array of sex stereotypes in their society, parents and teachers can point out exceptions. For example, they can arrange for children to see males and females pursuing nontraditional careers. At the same time, adults can reason with children, explaining that interests and skills, not gender, should determine a person's occupation and activities. Recent evidence shows that such reasoning is very effective in reducing children's tendency to view the world in a gender-biased fashion (Bigler & Liben, 1990). And, as we will see in the next section, a rational approach to child rearing promotes healthy, adaptable functioning in many other areas as well.

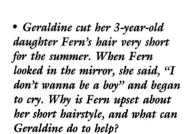

• *Geraldine cut her 3-year-old daughter Fern's hair very short for the summer. When Fern looked in the mirror, she said, "I don't wanna be a boy" and began to cry. Why is Fern upset about her short hairstyle, and what can Geraldine do to help?*

*BRIEF REVIEW* During the preschool years, children develop a wide variety of sex-typed beliefs, personality traits, and behaviors. Although heredity contributes to several aspects of sex typing, environmental forces play an especially powerful role. Parents view and treat boys and girls differently, and traditional sex-role learning receives further support from teachers, same-sex peers, and the wider social environment. Children gradually develop a sex-role identity, a view of themselves as masculine, feminine, or androgynous in characteristics. Neither the cognitive-developmental nor the social learning account of sex-role identity provides a complete explanation. Gender schema theory is a new approach that shows how environmental pressures and children's cognitions combine to affect sex-role development.

## CHILD REARING AND EMOTIONAL AND SOCIAL DEVELOPMENT IN EARLY CHILDHOOD

Throughout this chapter and the previous one, we have discussed many ways in which parents can foster children's development—by serving as warm models and positive reinforcers of mature behavior, by using reasoning, explanation, and inductive discipline, by avoiding harsh punishment, and by encouraging children to master new skills. As we conclude our discussion of early childhood, let's put these elements together into an overall view of effective parenting.

### Child-Rearing Styles

In a series of landmark studies, Diana Baumrind gathered information on child-rearing practices by watching parents interact with their preschoolers in a variety of situations. Two broad dimensions of parenting emerged from the observations. The first is *demandingness*. Some parents establish high standards for their children and insist that their youngsters meet those standards. Other parents demand very little and rarely try to influence their child's behavior. The second dimension is *responsiveness*. Some parents are accepting of and responsive to their children. They frequently engage in open discussion and verbal give-and-take. Others are rejecting and unresponsive.

As Table 10.2 shows, the various combinations of demandingness and responsiveness yield four types of parents. Baumrind's research focused on three of them.

**The Authoritative Parent.** **Authoritative parents** have the most adaptive style of child rearing. They make reasonable demands for maturity, and they enforce them by setting limits and insisting that the child obey. At the same time, they express warmth and affection, listen patiently to the child's point of view, and encourage their youngster to participate in family decision making. Authoritative parents use a rational, democratic approach that recognizes and respects the rights of both parents and children.

Baumrind's findings revealed that children of these parents were developing especially well. They were lively and happy in mood, self-confident in their mastery of new tasks, and self-controlled in their ability to resist engaging in disruptive behavior (Baumrind, 1967). These children also seemed less sex typed. Girls scored particularly high in independence and desire to master new tasks and boys in friendly, cooperative behavior (Baumrind & Black, 1967).

**The Authoritarian Parent.** **Authoritarian parents** are also demanding, but they place such a high value on conformity that they are unresponsive—even outright rejecting—when children are unwilling to obey. "Do it because I said so!" is the attitude of this type of parent. As a result, they engage in very little give-and-take

**Authoritative parent**
A parenting style that is demanding and responsive. A rational, democratic approach in which parents' and children's rights are respected.

**Authoritarian parent**
A parenting style that is demanding but low in responsiveness to children's rights and needs. Conformity and obedience are valued over open communication with the child.

TABLE 10.2 • A Two-Dimensional Classification of Parenting Styles

|  | Responsive | Unresponsive |
| --- | --- | --- |
| **Demanding** | Authoritative parent | Authoritarian parent |
| **Undemanding** | Permissive parent | Uninvolved parent |

*Source:* Adapted from E. E. Maccoby & J. A. Martin, 1983, "Socialization in the context of the family: Parent–child interaction," in E. M. Hetherington, ed., *Handbook of child psychology: Vol. 4. Socialization, personality, and social development*, 4th ed., p. 39. New York: Wiley, Copyright 1983 by John Wiley & Sons. Reprinted by permission.

with their youngsters. Instead, children are expected to accept their parent's word for what is right in an unquestioning manner. If they do not, authoritarian parents resort to force and punishment.

Baumrind found that preschoolers with authoritarian parents were anxious, withdrawn, and unhappy. When interacting with peers, they tended to react with hostility when frustrated (Baumrind, 1967). Boys, especially, showed high rates of anger and defiance. Girls were dependent and lacking in exploration, and they retreated from challenging tasks (Baumrind, 1971).

***The Permissive Parent.*** **Permissive parents** are nurturant and accepting, but they avoid making demands or imposing controls of any kind. Their children are allowed to make many of their own decisions at an age when they are not yet capable of doing so. They can eat meals and go to bed when they feel like it and watch as much television as they want. They do not have to learn good manners or do any household chores. While some permissive parents truly believe that this style of child rearing is good for children, many others lack confidence in their ability to influence their youngster's behavior and are disorganized and ineffective in running their households.

Baumrind reported that children of permissive parents were very immature. They had difficulty controlling their impulses and were disobedient and rebellious when asked to do something that conflicted with their momentary desires. They were also overly demanding and dependent on adults, and they showed less persistence on tasks at preschool. The link between permissive parenting and dependent, nonachieving behavior was especially strong for boys (Baumrind, 1971).

### What Makes Authoritative Child Rearing So Effective?

Since Baumrind's early work, a great many studies have confirmed her findings. Throughout childhood and adolescence, authoritative parenting is consistently associated with task persistence, social maturity, high self-esteem, internalized moral standards, and superior academic achievement (Denham, Renwick, & Holt, 1991; Maccoby & Martin, 1983; Steinberg, Elman, & Mounts, 1989).

Why does this approach to parenting work so well? There are a number of reasons. First, control that appears fair and reasonable to the child, not abrupt and arbitrary, is far more likely to be complied with and internalized. Second, nurturant parents who are secure in the standards they hold for their children provide models of caring concern as well as confident, assertive behavior. Finally, parents who are authoritative make demands that are reasonable in terms of their child's developing capacities. By adjusting expectations to fit children's ability to take responsibility for their own behavior, these parents let children know that they are competent individuals who can do things successfully for themselves. As a result, high self-esteem and mature, independent behavior are fostered (Kuczynski et al., 1987).

If you turn back to Table 10.2, you will see that we have not yet considered one pattern of parenting: the *uninvolved* style, which combines undemanding with indifferent, rejecting behavior. Uninvolved parents show little commitment to their role as caregivers beyond the minimum effort required to feed and clothe the child. Often these parents are so overwhelmed by the many pressures and stresses in their lives that they have little time and energy to spare for their children (Maccoby & Martin, 1983).

At its extreme, uninvolved parenting is a form of child maltreatment called *neglect*. Especially when it begins early, it disrupts virtually all aspects of development, including attachment, cognition, play, and social and emotional skills (Egeland & Sroufe, 1981; Radke-Yarrow et al., 1985). As we turn to the topic of child maltreatment in the final section of this chapter, we will see that effective child rearing

**Permissive parent**
A parenting style that is responsive but undemanding. An overly tolerant approach to parenting.

is sustained not just by the desire of mothers and fathers to be good parents. Almost all want to be. A great many factors, both within and outside the family, contribute to parents' capacity to be warm, consistent, and appropriately demanding. Unfortunately, when these vital supports for good parenting break down, children as well as their parents can suffer terribly.

## Child Maltreatment

Child maltreatment is as old as the history of humankind, but only recently has there been widespread acceptance that the problem exists, research aimed at understanding it, and programs directed at helping maltreated children and their families. Perhaps the increase in public concern is due to the fact that child maltreatment is especially common in large, industrialized nations (Gelles & Cornell, 1983). It occurs so often in the United States that a recent government committee called it "a national emergency." A total of 2.4 million cases were reported to juvenile authorities in 1989, an increase of 147 percent over the previous decade (Children's Defense Fund, 1991d). The true figure is surely much higher, since most cases, including ones in which children suffer serious physical injury, go unreported (Emery, 1989).

Child maltreatment takes the following forms:

1. *Physical abuse:* assaults on children that produce pain, cuts, welts, bruises, burns, broken bones, and other injuries.
2. *Sexual abuse:* sexual comments, fondling, intercourse, and other forms of exploitation.
3. *Physical neglect:* living conditions in which children do not receive enough food, clothing, medical attention, or supervision.
4. *Emotional neglect:* failure of caregivers to meet children's needs for affection and emotional support
5. *Psychological abuse:* actions that seriously damage children's emotional, social, or cognitive functioning.

Although all experts recognize that these five types exist, they do not agree on how frequent and intense an adult's actions must be to be called maltreatment. Definitions of abuse and neglect vary a great deal. The greatest problems arise in the case of subtle, ambiguous behaviors. While all of us can agree that broken bones, cigarette burns, and bite marks are abusive, the decision is harder to make in instances in which an adult touches or makes degrading comments to a child. Yet some experts regard sexual and psychological abuse as among the most frequent and destructive forms. The rate of psychological abuse may be the highest, since it accompanies most other types. About 210,000 cases of child sexual abuse are reported each year. Yet this statistic greatly underestimates the actual number, since affected children feel frightened, confused, and guilty and are usually pressured into silence (Hartman & Burgess, 1989). Although children of all ages are affected, the largest number of sexual abuse victims are identified in middle childhood. We will pay special attention to the devastating impact of this form of maltreatment in Chapter 13.

### The Origins of Child Maltreatment.
When child maltreatment first became a topic of research in the early 1960s, it was viewed as rooted in adult psychological disturbance. The first studies indicated that adults who abused or neglected their children usually had a history of maltreatment in their own childhoods, unrealistic expectations that children satisfy their own unmet emotional needs, and poor control of aggressive impulses (Kempe et al., 1962; Spinetta & Rigler, 1972).

But it soon became clear that although child abuse was more common among disturbed parents, a single "abusive personality type" did not exist. Sometimes, even "normal" parents harmed their children! Also, parents who were abused as children did not always repeat the cycle with their own youngsters (Hunter & Kilstrom, 1979; Simons et al., 1991).

For help in understanding child maltreatment, researchers turned to the *social systems perspective* on family functioning (see Chapter 2). They discovered that child abuse and neglect are affected by many interacting variables—at the family, community, and cultural levels. Table 10.3 provides a summary of factors associated with child maltreatment. The more of these risks that are present, the greater the likelihood that it will occur. Let's examine each set of influences in turn.

*The Family.* Within the family, parent and child often contribute jointly to child maltreatment. Certain kinds of children have an increased likelihood of becoming targets of abuse. These include premature or very sick babies and children who are temperamentally difficult, inattentive and overactive, or who have other developmental problems. But whether such children actually are maltreated depends on characteristics of parents (Pianta, Egeland, & Erickson, 1989). In one study, temperamentally difficult youngsters who were physically abused had mothers who believed that they could do little to control their child's behavior. They viewed the child as stubborn and bad, a perspective that led them to move quickly toward physical force when the child misbehaved (Bugental, Blue, & Cruzcosa, 1989).

Once child abuse gets started, it quickly becomes part of a self-sustaining family relationship. The small irritations to which abusive parents react—a fussy baby, a preschooler who knocks over a glass of milk, or a child who will not mind immediately—soon become bigger ones. Then the harshness of parental behavior increases as well. By the preschool years, abusive and neglectful parents seldom interact with their children. When they do, the communication is almost always negative (Trickett & Kuczynski, 1986). Maltreated children, in turn, engage in especially high rates of misbehavior, gradually developing serious learning and adjustment problems, including difficulties with peers, academic failure, substance abuse, and delinquency (Hotaling et al., 1988; Simons, Conger, & Whitbeck, 1988). These outcomes contribute to further mistreatment.

Most parents, however, have enough self-control not to respond to their children's misbehavior with abuse, and not all children with developmental problems are

TABLE 10.3 • Factors Related to Child Maltreatment

| | |
|---|---|
| Parent characteristics | Psychological disturbance; substance abuse; history of abuse as a child; belief in harsh, physical discipline; desire to satisfy unmet emotional needs through the child; unreasonable expectations for child behavior; young age (most under 30); low educational level |
| Child characteristics | Premature or very sick baby; difficult temperament; inattentiveness and overactivity; other developmental problems |
| Family characteristics | Low income; poverty; homelessness; marital instability; social isolation; physical abuse of mother by husband or boyfriend; frequent moves; large, closely spaced families; overcrowded living conditions; disorganized household; lack of steady employment; other signs of high life stress |
| Community | Characterized by social isolation; few parks, day-care centers, preschool programs, recreation centers, and churches to serve as family supports |
| Culture | Approval of physical force and violence as ways to solve problems |

*Sources:* Pianta, Egeland, & Erickson, 1989; Simons et al., 1991; Zigler & Hall, 1989.

mistreated. Other factors must combine with these conditions to prompt an extreme parental response. Research reveals that unmanageable parental stress is strongly associated with all forms of maltreatment. Such factors as low income, unemployment, marital conflict, overcrowded living conditions, frequent moves, and extreme household disorganization are common in abusive homes. These conditions increase the chances that parents will be so overwhelmed that they cannot meet basic child-rearing responsibilities or will vent their frustrations by lashing out at their children (Pianta, Egeland, & Erickson, 1989).

*The Community.*   The majority of abusive parents are also isolated from both formal and informal social supports in their communities. There are at least two causes of this social isolation. First, because of their own life histories, many of these parents have learned to mistrust and avoid others. They do not have the skills necessary for establishing and maintaining positive relationships with friends and relatives (Polansky et al., 1985). Second, abusive parents are more likely to live in neighborhoods that provide few links between family and community, such as parks, day-care centers, preschool programs, recreation centers, and churches (Garbarino & Sherman, 1980). For these reasons, they lack "lifelines" to others and have no one to turn to for help during particularly stressful times.

*The Larger Culture.*   One final factor—the values, laws, and customs of our culture—profoundly affects the chances that child maltreatment will occur when parents feel overburdened. Societies that view force and violence as appropriate ways to solve problems set the stage for child abuse. These conditions exist in the United States. Although all 50 states have laws designed to protect children from maltreatment, there is still strong support for the use of physical force in parent–child relations. For example, during the past 20 years, the United States Supreme Court has twice upheld the right of school officials to use corporal punishment to discipline children. Crime rates have risen in American cities, and television sets beam graphic displays of violence into family living rooms. In view of the widespread acceptance of violent behavior in American culture, it is not surprising that most parents use slaps and spankings at one time or another to discipline their children. In countries where physical punishment is not accepted, such as Luxembourg and Sweden, child abuse is rare (Zigler & Hall, 1989).

**Preventing Child Maltreatment.**   Since child maltreatment is embedded within families, communities, and society as a whole, efforts to prevent it must be directed at each of these levels. Many approaches have been suggested. These include interventions that teach high-risk parents effective child-rearing and disciplinary strategies, high school child development courses that include direct experience with children, and broad social programs that have as their goal better economic conditions for low-income families.

In earlier parts of this book, we saw that providing social supports to families is very effective in easing parental stress. It is not surprising that this approach sharply reduces child maltreatment as well. A recent study revealed that a trusting relationship with another person is the most important factor in preventing mothers with childhood histories of abuse from repeating the cycle with their own youngsters (Egeland, Jacobvitz, & Sroufe, 1988). *Parents Anonymous,* a national organization that has as its main goal helping child-abusing parents learn constructive parenting practices, does so largely through providing social supports to families. Each of its local chapters offers self-help group meetings, daily phone calls, and regular home visits to relieve social isolation and teach alternative child-rearing skills.

Other preventive approaches include announcements in newspapers and magazines and on television and radio that are designed to educate people about child

*Public service announcements help prevent child abuse by educating people about the problem and informing them of where to seek help. This poster reminds adults that degrading remarks can hit as hard as a fist. (Courtesy San Francisco Child Abuse Council)*

maltreatment and tell them where to seek help (Rosenberg & Reppucci, 1985). Besides these efforts, changes in the overall attitudes and practices of American culture are needed. Many experts believe that child maltreatment cannot be eliminated as long as violence is widespread and corporal punishment continues to be regarded as an acceptable child-rearing alternative (Gil, 1987; Zigler & Hall, 1989).

Although more cases reach the courts than in decades past, child maltreatment remains a crime that is difficult to prove. Most of the time, the only witnesses are the child victims themselves or other loyal family members. Even in court cases in which the evidence is strong, judges hesitate to impose the ultimate safeguard against further mistreatment: permanent removal of the child from the family.

The reasons for this reluctant attitude are many. First, in American society, government intervention into family life is viewed as a last resort, to be used only when there is near certainty that a child will be denied basic care and protection. Second, despite destructive family relationships, maltreated children and their parents are usually attached to one another. Most of the time, neither desires separation. Finally, the American legal system tends to regard children as parental property rather than as human beings in their own right, and this has also stood in the way of court-ordered protection (Hart & Brassard, 1987). Yet even with intensive treatment, some adults persist in their abusive acts. An average of 1,500 American children die of some form of maltreatment each year (Children's Defense Fund, 1991d). In cases in which parents are unlikely to change their behavior, taking the drastic step of separating parent from child and legally terminating parental rights is the only reasonable course of action.

Child maltreatment is a distressing and horrifying topic—a sad note on which to end our discussion of a period of childhood that is so full of excitement, awakening, and discovery. But there is reason to be optimistic. Great strides have been made in understanding and preventing child maltreatment over the last several decades. Although we still have a long way to go, the situation for abused and neglected children is far better now than it has been at any time in history (Kempe & Kempe, 1984).

## SUMMARY

### Erikson's Theory: Initiative versus Guilt

• According to Erikson, during early childhood children grapple with the psychological conflict of **initiative versus guilt.** A healthy sense of initiative depends on resolving the **Oedipal conflict** or the **Electra conflict** of Freud's **phallic stage,** in which the **superego,** or conscience, is formed. Although Freud's ideas are no longer widely accepted, Erikson's image of initiative captures the emotional and social changes that take place during this phase of development.

### Self-Development in Early Childhood

• A preschooler's **self-concept** largely consists of concrete, observable characteristics, such as possessions and behaviors. Young children's increasing self-awareness underlies their struggles over objects as well as first efforts to cooperate. Children show improved understanding of their own and others' intentions over the preschool years.

• During early childhood, **self-esteem** is not yet well-differentiated. Preschoolers' high self-esteem contributes to their mastery-oriented approach to the environment.

### Emotional Development in Early Childhood

• Young children have an impressive understanding of the causes and consequences of basic emotional reactions. By age 3 to 4, they are also aware of a variety of strategies that assist with emotional self-regulation.

• Complex emotions increase as children's self-concepts become better developed and they become more sensitive to the praise and criticism of others. Empathy becomes more common over the preschool years.

### Peer Relations in Early Childhood

• During early childhood, interactive play with peers increases. According to Parten, peer interaction begins with **nonsocial activity,** shifts to **parallel play,** and then moves to **associative play** and **cooperative play.** However, preschoolers do not follow this straightforward developmental sequence. Solitary play and parallel play remain common throughout early childhood. Sociodramatic play becomes especially frequent and supports many aspects of emotional and social development.

• Preschoolers view friendship in concrete, activity-based terms. Their interactions with friends are especially positive, emotionally expressive, and cooperative.

### Foundations of Morality in Early Childhood

• Most theories agree that a basic feature of moral development is **internalization.** In contrast to Freud's theory, discipline promoting fear of punishment and loss of parental love does not foster conscience development. Instead, **induction** is far more effective in encouraging self-control and **prosocial or altruistic behavior.**

• Behaviorism and social learning theory regard reinforcement and modeling as the basis for moral action. Effective adult models of morality are warm and powerful and practice what they preach. Harsh punishment is not effective in promoting moral internalization and socially desirable behavior.

• The cognitive-developmental perspective regards children as active thinkers about social rules. Preschoolers understand that disobeying moral rules is more serious than violating social conventions. Peer interaction provides children with important opportunities to work out their first ideas about justice and fairness. Parents who discuss moral issues with children help them reason about morality.

• All children display aggression from time to time. During early childhood, **instrumental aggression** declines while **hostile aggression** increases. Boys tend to be more aggressive than girls, a difference that may be linked to boys' higher activity level. Ineffective discipline and a conflict-ridden family atmosphere promote and sustain aggression in children. Teaching parents effective child-rearing practices and providing children with **social problem-solving training** are ways of reducing aggressive behavior. Television promotes childhood aggression, belief in the truthfulness of advertising, and racial and sex-role stereotypes.

### The Development of Sex Typing in Early Childhood

• Children start to acquire sex-typed beliefs and behavior in the early preschool years. Genetic factors are believed to play a role in boys' higher activity level and aggression and children's preference for same-sex playmates. At the same time, the environment provides powerful support for sex typing. Parents, teachers, peers, and the broader social environment encourage many sex-typed responses.

• Sex-role identity is measured by asking children and adults to rate themselves on sex-typed personality traits. While most people have traditional identities, some are **androgynous,** scoring high on both masculine and feminine characteristics.

• According to social learning theory, preschoolers first acquire sex-typed behavior and then organize it into cognitions about themselves. In contrast, cognitive-developmental theory suggests that **gender constancy** must be mastered before children develop sex-typed behavior. A new approach to sex-role identity, **gender schema theory,** combines social learning and cognitive-developmental features to explain how children develop sex-typed self-definitions, which they use to interpret their world.

### Child Rearing and Emotional and Social Development in Early Childhood

• Compared to **authoritarian parents** and **permissive parents, authoritative parents** have emotionally well-adjusted, socially mature children. Warmth, explanations, and reasonable demands for mature behavior account for the effectiveness of the authoritative style.

• Child maltreatment is related to factors within the family, community, and larger culture. Child and parent characteristics often feed on one another to produce abusive behavior. Unmanageable parental stress and social isolation greatly increase the chances that abuse and neglect will occur. When a society approves of force and violence as an appropriate means for solving problems, child abuse is fostered.

## IMPORTANT TERMS AND CONCEPTS

| | | |
|---|---|---|
| initiative versus guilt (p. 350) | parallel play (p. 358) | social problem-solving training (p. 370) |
| phallic stage (p. 350) | associative play (p. 358) | sex-role identity (p. 376) |
| Oedipal conflict (p. 350) | cooperative play (p. 358) | androgyny (p. 376) |
| Electra conflict (p. 351) | internalization (p. 363) | gender constancy (p. 376) |
| identification (p. 351) | induction (p. 364) | gender schema theory (p. 377) |
| self-concept (p. 351) | prosocial or altruistic behavior (p. 364) | authoritative parent (p. 379) |
| self-esteem (p. 353) | time out (p. 366) | authoritarian parent (p. 379) |
| phobia (p. 358) | instrumental aggression (p. 368) | permissive parent (p. 380) |
| nonsocial activity (p. 358) | hostile aggression (p. 368) | |

## FOR FURTHER INFORMATION AND SPECIAL HELP

**Children's Television**

Action for Children's Television
20 University Road
Cambridge, MA 02138
(617) 876-6620

A 20,000-member organization that works for quality TV programming for children and the elimination of commercials from children's TV. Publishes resource handbooks for parents and children, including the *TV-Smart Book for Kids*.

**Child Abuse and Neglect**

Child Help U.S.A., Inc.
6463 Independence Avenue
Woodland Hills, CA 91370
(818) 347-7280

Promotes public awareness of child maltreatment through publications, media campaigns, and a speakers' bureau. Supports the National Child Abuse Hotline, (800) 4-A-CHILD. Callers may request information about child abuse or speak with a crisis counselor.

Parents Anonymous
6733 S. Sepulveda, Suite 270
Los Angeles, CA 90045
(213) 410-9732

Dedicated to prevention and treatment of child abuse. Local groups provide support to child-abusing parents and training in nonviolent child-rearing techniques.

National Center on Child Abuse and Neglect
P.O. Box 1182
Washington, DC 20013
(703) 821-2086

Provides information to states and communities wishing to develop programs and activities that identify, prevent, and treat child abuse and neglect.

## MILESTONES OF DEVELOPMENT IN EARLY CHILDHOOD

| Age | Physical | Cognitive | Language | Emotional/Social |
|---|---|---|---|---|
| 2 years | Slower gains in height and weight than in toddlerhood. Balance improves, walking becomes better coordinated. Running, jumping, hopping, throwing, and catching appear. Puts on and removes some items of clothing. Uses spoon effectively. | Make-believe becomes less dependent on realistic toys, less self-centered, and more complex. Able to take the perspective of others in simple situations. Recognition memory well developed. Aware of the difference between inner mental and outer physical events. | Vocabulary increases rapidly. Sentences follow basic word order of native language; grammatical markers are added. Shows effective conversational skills, such as turn-taking and topic maintenance. | Begins to develop self-concept and self-esteem. Distinguishes intentional from unintentional acts. Peer cooperation and instrumental aggression appear. Understands causes and consequences of basic emotions. Empathy increases. Sex-typed beliefs and behavior increase. |
| 3–4 years | Running, jumping, hopping, throwing, and catching become better coordinated. Galloping and one-foot skipping appear. Rides tricycle. Uses scissors, draws first picture of person. Can tell the difference between writing and non-writing. | Notices transformations, reverses thinking, and has a basic understanding of causality in familiar situations. Classifies familiar objects hierarchically. Uses private speech to guide behavior when working on challenging tasks. Remembers familiar experiences in terms of scripts. Able to generalize remembered information from one situation to another. Understands that people can hold false beliefs. Aware of some meaningful features of written language. Counts small numbers of objects and grasps the cardinality principle. | Overextends grammatical rules to exceptions. Understands many culturally accepted ways of adjusting speech to fit the age, sex, and social status of speakers and listeners. | Emotional self-regulation improves. Complex emotions (shame, embarrassment, guilt, envy, and pride) increase. Nonsocial activity declines and joint, interactive play increases. Instrumental aggression declines and hostile aggression increases. First friendships form. Distinguishes moral rules and social conventions. Preference for same-sex playmates increases. |
| 5–6 years | Body is streamlined and longer-legged with proportions similar to that of adult. First permanent tooth erupts. Skipping appears. Gross motor skills increase in speed and endurance. Ties shoes, draws more elaborate pictures, writes name. Able to discriminate more fine-grained visual forms, such as letters of the alphabet. | Ability to distinguish appearance from reality improves. Time spent attending to tasks increases. Recall and scripted memory improve. Understands that letters and sounds are linked in systematic ways. Counts up and down, engaging in simple addition and subtraction. | Vocabulary reaches about 14,000 words. Has mastered many complex grammatical forms. | Bases understanding of people's intentions on a wider range of social cues. Ability to interpret, predict, and change others' emotions improves. Relies on language to express empathy. Has acquired many morally relevant rules and behaviors. Grasps genital basis of sex differences and shows gender constancy. |

*Sküng, Jiang Yen, 10 years, China. Reprinted by permission from The International Museum of Children's Art, Oslo, Norway.*

# Physical Development in Middle Childhood

**11**

Body Growth in Middle Childhood
> *Changes in Body Size and Proportions    Secular Trends in Physical Growth    Skeletal Growth    Brain Development*

Common Health Problems in Middle Childhood
> *Vision and Hearing    Malnutrition    Obesity    Type A Behavior    Bedwetting Illnesses    Unintentional Injuries*

Health Education in Middle Childhood

Motor Development and Play in Middle Childhood
> *New Motor Capacities    Organized Games with Rules    Shadows of Our Evolutionary Past    Physical Education*

"**I**'m on my way, Mom!" hollered 10-year-old Joey as he stuffed the last bite of toast into his mouth, slung his book bag over his shoulder, dashed out the door, jumped on his bike, and headed down the street for school. Joey's 8-year-old sister Lizzie followed next, quickly kissing her mother good-bye and hurrying to catch up with Joey. Off she raced, peddling furiously, until soon she was side by side with her older brother. Rena, the children's mother and one of my colleagues at the university, watched from the front porch as her son and daughter disappeared in the distance.

"They're branching out," Rena remarked to me over lunch that day as she described the children's expanding activities and relationships. Homework, household chores, soccer teams, music lessons, scouting, friends at school and in the neighborhood, and Joey's new paper route were all part of the children's routine. Commenting on how life was different from the way it had been a few years earlier, Rena said, "It seems as if the basics are all there; we don't have to monitor Joey and Lizzie so constantly anymore. But being a parent is still very challenging. Now it's more a matter of refinements—helping them become independent, competent, and productive individuals."

Joey and Lizzie have entered the phase of development called middle childhood, which spans the years from 6 to 11. Around the world, children of this age are assigned new responsibilities as they begin the process of entering the adult world. Joey and Lizzie, like other youngsters growing up in industrialized nations, spend many long hours in school—an institution designed to assist parents in preparing the young for adult roles in complex societies. Indeed, middle childhood has often been called the "school years," since its onset is marked by the start of formal schooling. In village and tribal cultures, the school may be a field or a jungle rather than a classroom. But universally, mature members of society guide children of this age period toward more realistic responsibilities that increasingly resemble those they will perform as adults (Erikson, 1950; Rogoff et al., 1975).

This chapter focuses on physical growth in middle childhood—changes that are less spectacular than those of the earlier years. By age 6, the brain has reached 90 percent of its adult size, and the body continues to grow slowly. In this way, nature grants school-age children the mental powers to master challenging tasks as well as added time to learn before reaching physical maturity. We begin our discussion by reviewing typical growth trends as well as special health concerns of middle childhood. Then we turn to children's rapid gains in motor abilities, which support practical everyday activities, athletic skills, and participation in organized games. We will see that each of these achievements is affected by and contributes to cognitive and social development. Our discussion will echo a familiar theme—that all areas of development are interrelated.

# BODY GROWTH IN MIDDLE CHILDHOOD

## Changes in Body Size and Proportions

*During middle childhood, the lower portion of the body is growing fastest. These 8-year-old girls are taller and longer legged than they were as preschoolers.* (Arnie Katz/Stock South)

The rate of physical growth during the school years is an extension of the pattern that characterized early childhood. Compared to the rapid height and weight gain of the first 2 years of life, growth is slow and regular. At age 6, the average child weighs 45 pounds and is 3 1/2 feet tall, with boys being slightly taller and heavier than girls. As shown in Figure 11.1, children continue to add about 2 to 3 inches in height and 5 pounds in weight each year. However, when researchers carefully track individual cases, growth is not quite as steady as these age-related norms suggest. A recent longitudinal study of 135 Scottish children who were followed between the ages of 3 and 10 revealed slight spurts in height. Girls tended to forge ahead at ages 4 1/2, 6 1/2, 8 1/2, and 10, boys slightly later, at 4 1/2, 7, 9, and 10 1/2. In between these spurts were lulls in which growth took place more slowly (Butler, McKie, & Ratcliffe, 1990).

Look again at Figure 11.1, and you will see that girls are slightly shorter and lighter than boys at ages 6 to 8. By age 9 this trend is reversed. Already, Rena noticed, Lizzie was starting to catch up with Joey in physical size. For many girls, the 10-year-old height spurt overlaps with the much more dramatic adolescent growth spurt, which takes place 2 years earlier in girls than it does in boys.

Because the lower portion of the body is growing fastest at this age period, Joey and Lizzie appeared longer-legged than they had in early childhood. Rena discovered that they grew out of their jeans more quickly than their jackets and frequently needed larger shoes. As in early childhood, girls have slightly more body fat and boys more muscle during the school years. After age 8, girls begin accumulating fat at a faster rate, and they will add even more during adolescence (Tanner & Whitehouse, 1975).

A glance into any elementary school classroom reveals that individual differences in body growth continue to be great in middle childhood. The diversity among children in physical size is especially apparent when we travel to different nations. Measurements of 8-year-olds living in many parts of the world reveal a 9-inch gap between the smallest and the largest youngsters. The shortest children tend to be found in South America, Asia, the Pacific Islands, and parts of Africa and include such ethnic groups as Colombian, Burmese, Thai, Vietnamese, Ethiopian, and Bantu. The tallest children reside in Australia, northern and central Europe, and the United States and consist of Czech, Dutch, Latvian, Norwegian, Swiss, and American black and white children (Meredith, 1978). These findings remind us that physical growth norms, such as those shown in Figure 11.1, need to be interpreted cautiously, espe-

**FIGURE 11.1** • Gains in height and weight during middle childhood among American youngsters. The slow rate of growth established in early childhood extends into the school years. Girls are slightly shorter and lighter than boys until age 9, at which time this trend is reversed as girls approach the adolescent growth spurt. Eight-year-old Lizzie is beginning to catch up with 10-year-old Joey in physical size. Wide individual differences in body size continue to exist, as the percentiles on these charts reveal.

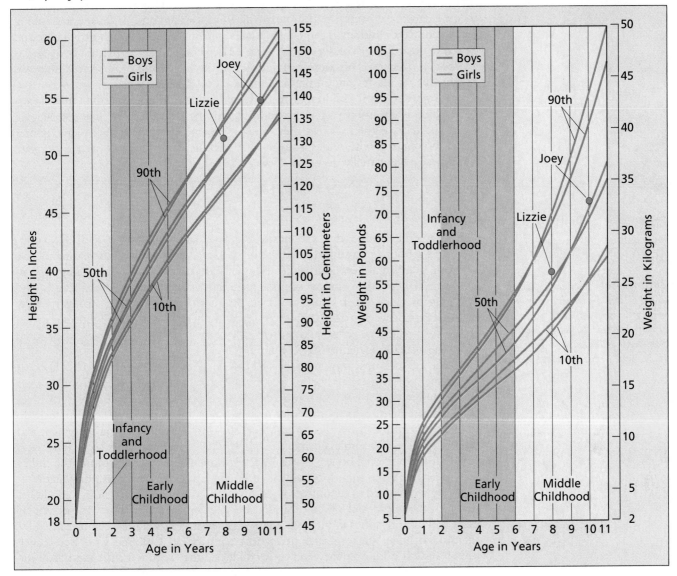

cially in countries like the United States, where so many racial and ethnic groups are represented.

What accounts for these vast differences in physical size? Both heredity and environment are involved. Body size is sometimes the result of evolutionary adaptations to a particular climate. For example, long, lean physiques are typical in hot, tropical regions and short stocky ones in cold, arctic areas. At the same time, children who grow tallest usually reside in developed countries where food is plentiful and infectious diseases are largely controlled. In contrast, small children tend to live in less developed regions, where poverty, hunger, and disease are common (Tanner, 1978b).

*This boy has the "toothless" smile typical of 6- and 7-year-olds. Two permanent lower front teeth have already erupted. The large, upper front teeth will be next to emerge. (L.L. Smith/Photo Researchers)*

**Secular trends in physical growth**
Changes in body size from one generation to the next.

**Malocclusion**
A condition in which the upper and lower teeth do not meet properly.

## Secular Trends in Physical Growth

Over the past century, **secular trends in physical growth**—changes in body size from one generation to the next—have taken place in industrialized nations. Joey and Lizzie are taller and heavier than their parents and grandparents were as children. These trends have been found in nearly all European nations, in Japan, and among black and white children in the United States. The difference appears early in life and becomes greater over childhood and early adolescence. Then, as mature body size is reached, it declines. This pattern suggests that the larger size of modern children is mostly due to a faster rate of physical maturation (Roche, 1979).

Why are so many children growing larger and maturing earlier than their ancestors? Once again, improved health and nutrition play major roles. The secular gain in height and weight is not as great among low-income groups, who have poorer diets. In countries with widespread poverty, famine, and disease, a secular decrease in body size has actually occurred (Tobias, 1975).

## Skeletal Growth

During middle childhood, the bones of the body lengthen and broaden. However, ligaments are not yet firmly attached to bones. This, combined with increasing muscle strength, grants children unusual flexibility of movement. School-age youngsters often seem like "physical contortionists," turning cartwheels, doing hand stands, and engaging in fancy break dance routines. As their bodies become stronger, many children experience a greater desire to engage in physical exercise. Nighttime "growing pains"—stiffness, aches, and muscle pulls—are common as muscles adapt to an enlarging skeleton (Sheiman & Slomin, 1988).

One of the most striking aspects of skeletal growth in middle childhood is replacement of primary or "baby" teeth with permanent teeth. Recall from Chapter 8 that children lose their first tooth at the end of early childhood. Between the ages of 6 and 12, all 20 primary teeth are replaced by permanent ones. The first teeth to go are the central incisors (lower and then upper front teeth), giving many first and second graders a "toothless" smile. For a while, permanent teeth seem much too large. Growth of facial bones, especially the jaw and chin, gradually causes the child's face to lengthen and mouth to widen, accommodating the newly erupting teeth.

About one-third of school-age youngsters suffer from **malocclusion,** a condition in which the upper and lower teeth do not meet properly. In about 14 percent of cases, serious difficulties in biting and chewing result. Malocclusion can be caused by thumb and finger sucking after permanent teeth erupt. Children who were eager thumb suckers during infancy and early childhood may require gentle but persistent encouragement to give up the habit by school entry. A second cause of malocclusion is crowding of permanent teeth. In some children, this problem clears up as the jaw grows. Others need braces, a common sight by the end of elementary school (Kilman & Helpin, 1983).

## Brain Development

During middle childhood, brain development largely involves more efficient functioning of various structures. The *frontal lobe* of the cortex (responsible for thought and consciousness) shows a slight increase in surface area between ages 5 and 7 due to continuing *myelinization* (Luria, 1973). In addition, *lateralization* of the cerebral hemispheres, already well-established in early childhood, becomes stronger over the school years (Thatcher, Walker, & Giudice, 1987).

Little information is available on how the brain changes in other ways during this age period. One idea is that development occurs at the level of **neurotransmitters,** chemicals that permit *neurons* to communicate across small gaps, or *synapses,* between them (see Chapter 5, page 169). Over time, neurons become increasingly selective, responding only to certain chemical messages. This change may contribute to more efficient and flexible thinking and behavior during middle childhood. Secretions of particular neurotransmitters are related to cognitive performance, social and emotional adjustment, and ability to withstand stress in children and adults. Children may suffer serious developmental problems, such as inattentiveness and overactivity, emotional disturbance, and epilepsy (an illness involving brain seizures and loss of motor control) when neurotransmitters are not present in appropriate balances (Shonkoff, 1984; Zametkin et al., 1990).

Researchers also believe that brain functioning may change during middle childhood because of the influence of hormones. Around age 7 to 8, an increase in *androgens* (male sex hormones), secreted by the adrenal glands located on top of the kidneys, occurs in children of both sexes. Androgens will rise further among boys at puberty, when the testes release them in large amounts. In many animal species, androgens affect brain organization and behavior, and they are believed to do so in human beings as well. Recall from Chapter 10 that androgens contribute to boys' higher activity level. They may also promote social dominance and play fighting, topics that we will take up at the end of this chapter (Maccoby, 1990).

*BRIEF REVIEW*   Body growth takes place slowly in middle childhood, at a pace similar to that of the preschool years. Gains in height occur in slight spurts followed by lulls; growth of the legs accounts for most of the increase. Large individual differences in body size result from both genetic and environmental factors. Children in industrialized nations are growing larger and reaching physical maturity earlier than they did in generations past because of better nutrition and health care. Between the ages of 6 and 12, all primary teeth are replaced by permanent ones. Brain development in middle childhood may involve neurotransmitter and hormonal influences.

*• How is body growth during the school years consistent with the cephalo-caudal trend of development that you studied in Chapter 5?*

*• Joey complained to his mother one evening that it wasn't fair that his younger sister Lizzie was almost as tall as he was. He worried that he wasn't growing fast enough. How should Rena respond to Joey's concern?*

## COMMON HEALTH PROBLEMS IN MIDDLE CHILDHOOD

Children like Joey and Lizzie, who come from advantaged homes, appear to be at their healthiest during middle childhood, full of energy and play. The cumulative effects of good nutrition, combined with rapid development of the body's immune system, offer greater protection against disease. Infections occur less often now than they did during early childhood. At the same time, growth in lung size permits more air to be exchanged with each breath, so children are better able to exercise vigorously without tiring.

Nevertheless, a variety of health problems do occur during the school years. We will see that many of them affect low-income children more than middle-class youngsters. Return for a moment to Box 8.2 on page 293 to review the status of children's health care in the United States. Because disadvantaged families often lack health insurance and cannot afford to pay for medical visits on their own, many youngsters continue to be deprived of regular access to a doctor. And a growing number also lack such basic necessities as a comfortable home and regular meals. Not surprisingly, poverty remains a powerful predictor of ill health during middle childhood.

**Neurotransmitters**
Chemicals that permit neurons to communicate across synapses.

## Vision and Hearing

The most common vision problem in middle childhood is **myopia**, or nearsightedness. By the end of the school years, nearly 25 percent of children are affected. The rate is slightly higher in girls than boys and about twice as great in white as black youngsters (Sperduto et al., 1983). Heredity contributes to myopia, since identical twins are more likely to both have the condition to a similar degree than are fraternals (Teikari et al., 1991). But myopia is also related to experience. Parents often warn their youngsters not to read in dim light or to sit too close to the TV set, exclaiming, "You'll ruin your eyes!" Their concern may be well founded. Myopia is one of the few health conditions that increases with family income and education, an association that is almost entirely explained by how people use their eyes. The more time people spend reading and doing other close-up work, the more likely they are to be myopic (Angle & Wissmann, 1980). Fortunately, for those youngsters who develop nearsightedness because they love reading, sewing, drawing, or model building, the condition can easily be corrected with glasses.

During middle childhood, the eustachian tube (canal that runs from the inner ear to the throat) becomes longer, narrower, and more slanted, preventing fluid and bacteria from traveling so easily from the mouth to the ear. As a result, ear infections become less frequent. Still, some children get ear infections that, if left untreated, can lead to permanent hearing defects. About 3 to 4 percent of the school-age population, and as many as 18 to 20 percent of low-income youngsters, develop some hearing loss for this reason (Mott, James, & Sperhac, 1990). Regular screening tests for both vision and hearing are important so that defects can be corrected before they lead to serious learning difficulties.

## Malnutrition

School-age children need a well-balanced, plentiful diet to provide energy for successful learning in school and increased physical activity. Many youngsters are so focused on play, friendships, and new activities that they spend little time at the table. Joey's hurried breakfast, described at the beginning of this chapter, is a common event during middle childhood. Readily available, healthy between-meal snacks—cheese, fruit, raw vegetables, and peanut butter—help meet nutritional needs during the school years.

As long as parents encourage healthy eating, the mild nutritional deficits that result from the child's busy daily schedule have no impact on development. But as we have seen in earlier chapters, a great many poverty-stricken youngsters in developing countries and in the United States suffer from serious and prolonged malnutrition. By middle childhood, the effects are apparent in retarded physical growth, low intelligence test scores, poor motor coordination, inattention, and distractibility. Research on animals reveals that diet affects the operation of neurotransmitters in the brain (Zeisel, 1986). The negative impact of malnutrition on learning and behavior may be extended during middle childhood in just this way.

Unfortunately, when malnutrition persists for many years, permanent damage is done. Prevention through government-sponsored food programs beginning in the early years and continuing throughout childhood and adolescence is necessary (Lozoff, 1989). Chronic hunger is painful and disabling. As one 10-year-old boy living with his family in a welfare hotel in New York City explained, "I just cannot think in school when I am hungry. My mind just stops thinking and this cannot go on forever . . . ." (Select Committee on Children, Youth, and Families, 1986, pp. 47–48).

## Obesity

Mona, a very overweight child in Lizzie's class at school, often stood on the side lines and watched during recess. When she did join in the children's games, she was

**Myopia**
Nearsightedness; inability to see distant objects clearly.

TABLE 11.1 • Factors Associated with Childhood Obesity

| Factor | Description |
|---|---|
| Heredity | Obesity runs in families. Obese children are likely to have at least one obese parent. |
| Social class | Obesity is more common in low-income than middle-income groups. |
| Early growth pattern | Infants who gain weight rapidly during the first year are at slightly greater risk for obesity. |
| Family eating habits | When parents purchase high-calorie treats and junk food and use them to reward children and reduce anxiety, their youngsters are more likely to be obese. |
| Responsiveness to food cues | Obese children often decide when to eat on the basis of external cues, such as taste, smell, sight, and time of day, rather than hunger. |
| Physical activity | Obese children are less physically active than their normal-weight peers. |
| Television viewing | Children who spend many hours watching television are more likely to become obese. |
| Traumatic events | Traumatic events, such as divorce, death of a family member, or child abuse and neglect, can trigger obesity. |

*Obesity is an emotionally painful and physically debilitating disorder. This boy has difficulty keeping up with his agemates in a gunnysack race. Because of peer rejection, fat children often lead lonely lives.* (Bob Daemmrich/Stock Boston)

slow and clumsy. On a daily basis, Mona was the target of unkind comments: "Move it, Tubs!" "Tree trunks for legs!" "No fatsoes allowed!" Although Mona was a good student, other children continued to reject her inside the classroom. When it was time to choose partners for a special activity, Mona was one of the last to be selected. On most afternoons, she walked home from school by herself while the other children gathered in groups, talking, laughing, and chasing. Once home and in the kitchen, Mona sought comfort in high calorie snacks, which promoted further weight gain.

Mona is one of about 27 percent of American children who suffer from **obesity,** a greater than 20 percent increase over average body weight, based on the child's age, sex, and physical build (Gortmaker et al., 1987). Overweight and obesity are growing problems in affluent nations like the United States. Childhood obesity has climbed steadily since the 1960s, with over 80 percent of youngsters like Mona retaining their overweight status as adults. These children have serious emotional and social difficulties and are at risk for lifelong health problems. High blood pressure and cholesterol levels along with respiratory abnormalities begin to appear in the early school years, symptoms that are powerful predictors of heart disease and early death (Taitz, 1983; Unger, Kreeger, & Christoffel, 1990). As you can see from Table 11.1, childhood obesity is a complex physical disorder with multiple causes.

*Causes of Obesity.* All children are not equally at risk for becoming overweight. Fat children tend to have fat parents, a relationship that could be due to heredity, environment, or (more likely) some combination of the two. We know that heredity plays some role, since the weights of adopted children are more strongly related to those of their biological than their adoptive parents (Stunkard et al., 1986). There is also good reason to believe that environment contributes to a child's weight. One indication is that social class and obesity are consistently related. Low-income youngsters in industrialized nations are not just at greater risk for malnutrition. They are also more likely to be overweight (Stunkard, d'Aquili, & Filion, 1972). Among the factors responsible are lack of knowledge about healthy diet; a tendency to buy high-fat, low-cost foods; and family stress, which prompts overeating in some individuals.

**Obesity**
A greater than 20 percent increase over average body weight, based on the child's age, sex, and physical build.

Recall from Chapter 5 that a slight relationship exists between very rapid weight gain in infancy and fatness in childhood. Although some researchers believe that the high protein, high fat content of formula made from cows' milk contributes to the chances that a child will become overweight (Kramer et al., 1985), most bottle-fed and chubby babies do not become obese. Other influences must also be present for later weight problems to appear. Parental feeding practices seem to play important roles. Some mothers interpret almost all the discomforts of their infants as a desire for food. They anxiously overfeed their babies and fail to help them learn the difference between hunger and other physical and emotional discomforts (Weil, 1975). Parents of older obese children can be seen using food as a reward and as a way to relieve the child's anxiety (Bruch, 1970). In families in which these practices are common, high-calorie treats gradually come to symbolize warmth, comfort, and relief of tension.

Perhaps because of these feeding experiences, obese children soon develop maladaptive eating habits. Research shows that they are more responsive to external stimuli associated with food—taste, sight, smell, and time of day—and less responsive to internal hunger cues than are normal-weight individuals. This difference is already present in middle childhood and may develop even earlier (Ballard et al., 1980; Constanzo & Woody, 1979). Overweight individuals also eat faster and chew their food less thoroughly, a behavior pattern that appears in overweight children as early as 18 months of age (Drabman et al., 1979).

Fat children do not just eat more; they are less physically active than their normal-weight peers. This inactivity is both cause and consequence of their overweight condition. Recent evidence indicates that the rise in childhood obesity in the United States over the past 30 years is in part due to television viewing. Next to already existing obesity, time spent in front of the TV set is the best predictor of future obesity among school-age children. In fact, the rate of obesity increases by 2 percent for each additional hour of TV watched per day (Dietz & Gortmaker, 1985; Gortmaker, Dietz, & Cheung, 1990). Television greatly reduces the time that children devote to physical exercise. At the same time, TV ads encourage them to eat fattening, unhealthy snacks—soft drinks, sweets, and salty chips and popcorn (Carruth, Goldberg, & Skinner, 1991).

One final factor can trigger childhood obesity: traumatic events, such as divorce, death of a family member, or child abuse and neglect. When children experience a sense of personal loss or feel unloved, they seek other sources of emotional support, and some turn to food. In one recent study, twelve cases of severe childhood obesity were linked to extreme family disorganization. Parents had psychological and substance-abuse problems, failed to supervise and discipline their children, and were hostile to professionals who tried to help. Once placed in foster homes, these children lost weight easily. Those who later returned to their disorganized home lives gained the weight back immediately (Christoffel & Forsyth, 1989).

***Treating Obesity.*** Overweight and obesity are best treated in childhood, before harmful eating patterns become well established. Yet childhood obesity is difficult to treat because it is a family disorder. Parents, who encourage, model, and reinforce behaviors that lead to overeating, must be willing to help their children change.

In Mona's case, the school nurse suggested that Mona and her obese mother enter a weight loss program together. But Mona's mother, unhappily married for many years, had her own reasons for continuing to overeat. She rejected this idea, claiming that Mona would eventually decide to lose weight on her own. Although many obese youngsters do try to slim down in adolescence, they usually do not choose sensible ways of doing so. Often they try crash diets that deprive them of essential nutrients during a period of rapid growth. These efforts can actually make matters worse. Temporary starvation leads to physical stress, discomfort, and fatigue.

Soon the child returns to old eating patterns, and weight rebounds to a higher level. Then, to protect itself, the body burns calories more slowly and becomes more resistant to future weight loss (Pinel, 1990).

When parents decide to seek treatment for an obese child, long-term changes in body weight do occur. A recent study found that the most effective interventions were family-based and focused on changing behaviors. Both parent and child revised eating patterns, exercised daily, and reinforced each other with praise and points for progress, which they exchanged for special activities and times together (Epstein et al., 1987). A follow-up after 5 years showed that children maintained their weight loss more effectively than did adults. This finding underscores the importance of intervening with obese children at an early age (Epstein et al., 1990).

## Type A Behavior

Besides obesity, another serious health problem also has roots in childhood and leads to later heart disease. Perhaps you have heard of the **Type A personality**—an adult who is overly competitive, impatient, restless, and time-conscious. Both on the job and during leisure time activities, Type A people are so focused on success that they become irritated and angry if anyone or anything hinders them. Their tense and driven approach to daily life is associated with high blood pressure and cholesterol levels and a rate of heart disease that is twice as high as that of more easygoing individuals (Friedman & Rosenman, 1959; Glass et al., 1980).

The Type A behavior pattern and its physical symptoms begin to emerge in early and middle childhood. Already, Joey's friend Terry showed signs of it. "Hurry up!" Terry complained as he waited for Joey to get his books from his locker after school one day. Terry paced, sighed, squirmed, and clicked his tongue with impatience until Joey was ready. Out on the playground, Terry constantly wanted to be first, challenged other children to competitive races, and became upset if he did not win. During class, he frequently interrupted other children, squirmed in his seat, and looked annoyed (Matthews & Angulo, 1980; Vega-Lahr et al., 1988).

An intense, determined temperamental style probably contributes to the early appearance of Type A behavior. But Type A characteristics do not become stable until the adolescent years (Steinberg, 1988b). Perhaps parenting practices lead this behavior pattern to continue in some children but not in others (Räikkönen, Keltikangas-Järvinen, & Pietikäinen, 1991; Weidner et al., 1988). When parents model impatience and competitiveness and set unrealistically high goals, Type A behaviors may be encouraged in children who are prone to be hard-driving and irritable in the first place.

Look carefully at the characteristics of the Type A personality, and you will see that it combines both prosocial and antisocial tendencies. On the positive side, Type A youngsters display a special potential for leadership and achievement. On the negative side, they are impatient, hostile, and inconsiderate of others (Steinberg, 1988b). Child development specialists hope to find ways to preserve the prosocial elements of the Type A personality while discouraging the antisocial ones as they experiment with ways to prevent this important cause of later heart disease.

## Bedwetting

One Friday afternoon, Terry called up Joey to see if he could sleep over, but Joey refused. "I can't," said Joey anxiously, without giving an explanation.

"Why not? We can take our sleeping bags out in the backyard. Come on, it'll be super!"

"My mom won't let me," Joey responded, unconvincingly. "I mean, well, I think we're busy, we're doing something tonight."

**Type A personality**
A personality characterized by excessive competitiveness, impatience, restlessness, and irritability. Associated with high blood pressure and cholesterol levels as well as heart disease in adulthood.

"Gosh, Joey, this is the third time you've said no. See if I'll ask *you* again!" snapped Terry as he hung up the phone.

Joey is one of 10 percent of American school-age children who suffer from **nocturnal enuresis,** or bedwetting during the night (Devlin, 1989). Enuresis evokes considerable distress in children and parents alike. For children, it restricts social activities and embarrasses them in front of family members. Most parents say that they worry about the problem and find the frequent night wakings and bedding changes annoying (Foxman, Valdez, & Brook, 1986). In one large-scale study, 36 percent admitted that they punished their children for wetting (Haque et al., 1981).

Although enuretic children show a slightly higher rate of psychological distress than their peers, this may be an outcome of the bedwetting itself. In the overwhelming majority of cases, the problem has biological roots. Heredity is a major contributing factor. Parents with a history of bedwetting are far more likely to have a child with the problem (McGuire & Savashino, 1984). Most often, it is caused by a failure of muscular responses that inhibit urination or a hormonal imbalance that permits too much urine to accumulate during the night (Houts, 1991). Punishing a school-age child for wetting is only likely to make matters worse.

To treat enuresis, doctors often prescribe antidepressant drugs, which reduce the amount of urine produced. But these gains are usually temporary. Once children stop taking the medication, they typically begin wetting again. Also, a small number of youngsters show side effects, such as anxiety, loss of sleep, and personality changes. The most effective treatment is a urine alarm that wakes the child at the first sign of dampness and works according to conditioning principles. Success rates of about 70 percent occur after 4 to 6 months of treatment. Most children who relapse achieve dryness after trying the alarm a second time (Rushton, 1989). Although many children outgrow enuresis without any form of intervention, it generally takes years for them to do so (Houts, 1991).

### Illnesses

Children experience a somewhat higher rate of illness during the first 2 years of elementary school than they will later on, due to exposure to sick children and the fact that their immune system is still developing. On the average, illness causes children to miss about 11 days of school per year, but most absences can be traced to a few students. These children tend to be low-income black and Hispanic youngsters with chronic health problems. Among children without diagnosed health difficulties, girls are more likely to miss school than boys. When a child shows symptoms of illness, sex-role standards may cause parents to perceive their daughters as more vulnerable than their sons (Kornguth, 1990).

Allergies, colds, influenza, muscle sprains, and bone fractures are common reasons for missing school. But the most frequent cause of school absence and childhood hospitalization is **asthma,** a condition in which the bronchial tubes (passages that connect the throat and lungs) are highly sensitive. In response to a variety of stimuli, such as cold weather, infection, exercise, or allergies, they fill with mucus and contract, leading to coughing, wheezing, and serious breathing difficulties. The number of children with asthma has increased by 50 percent over the last decade. Today, 2.5 percent of American youngsters are affected, and asthma-related deaths have risen in recent years (Gergen, Mullally, & Evans, 1988). Although heredity contributes to asthma, researchers believe that environmental factors are necessary to spark the illness. Boys, black children, and children who were born underweight, whose mothers smoke, and who live in poverty are at greatest risk (Weitzman, Gortmaker, & Sobol, 1990). Perhaps black and poverty-stricken youngsters experience a higher rate of asthma because of pollution in inner-city areas (which triggers allergic reactions), stressful home lives, and lack of access to good health care.

**Nocturnal enuresis**
Repeated bedwetting during the night.

**Asthma**
An illness in which highly sensitive bronchial tubes fill with mucus and contract, leading to episodes of coughing, wheezing, and serious breathing difficulties.

About 2 percent of American children have chronic illnesses that are more severe than asthma, such as cystic fibrosis (see Table 2.3, page 60), cancer, and acquired immune deficiency syndrome (AIDS). Painful medical treatments, physical discomfort, and changes in appearance often disrupt the sick child's daily life, making it difficult to concentrate in school and causing withdrawal from peers. As the illness worsens, family stress increases. Mothers, who typically bear the burden of caring for a very ill child, report more health problems of their own. For these reasons, chronically ill youngsters are at risk for academic, emotional, and social difficulties (Garrison & McQuiston, 1989). Many interventions have been found to improve their adjustment, including:

- family and health education, in which parents and children learn about the illness and get training in how to manage it;
- home visits by health professionals, who offer counseling and social support;
- disease-specific summer camps, which teach children self-help skills and grant parents time off from the demands of caring for an ill youngster;
- parent and peer support groups; and
- individual and family therapy.

## Unintentional Injuries

As we conclude our discussion of threats to children's health during the school years, let's return for a moment to the topic of unintentional injuries (discussed in detail in Chapter 8). As Figure 11.2 shows, the frequency of injuries increases steadily over

**FIGURE 11.2** • Rates of unintentional injury by age and sex of child in a sample of nearly 700 American families. Injuries increase steadily from 5 to 14 years of age, after which they decline. Boys experience more injuries than girls throughout childhood and adolescence. *(From E. L. Schor, 1987, "Unintentional Injuries,"* American Journal of Diseases of Children, *141, p. 1281. Reprinted by permission.)*

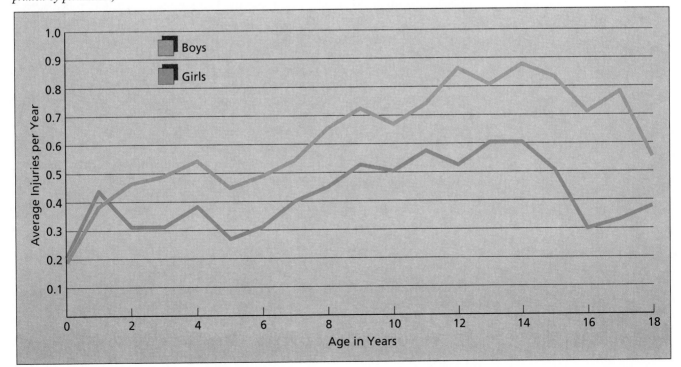

*Roller blading is a favorite pasttime for modern school-age children. Parents of these youngsters insist that they wear protective helmets and knee guards. Taking these precautions dramatically reduces the chances of serious injury. (David Young-Wolff/PhotoEdit)*

middle childhood into adolescence, with boys continuing to show a higher rate than girls. Auto and bicycle collisions account for most of this rise (Brooks & Roberts, 1990; Williams & Kotch, 1990).

As school-age children spend more time away from parents and range farther from home, safety education becomes especially important, along with incentives for following safety rules. Parents and teachers can enhance safety in middle childhood by continuing to make good use of the principles of behaviorism. For example, programs that reward children with prizes for arriving at school properly restrained in car seat belts are effective, just as they were in early childhood (Roberts & Fanurik, 1986). Insisting that children wear protective helmets while bicycling, roller skating, or skateboarding is also important. This simple safety precaution leads to an 85 percent reduction in the risk of head injury, a leading cause of permanent physical disability and death during the school years (Safe Kids, 1991).

Not all school-age children are likely to respond to efforts to increase their safety. By middle childhood, the greatest risk takers tend to be youngsters whose parents do not act as safety-conscious models or who try to enforce rules by using punitive or inconsistent discipline (Roberts, Elkins, & Royal, 1984). These child-rearing techniques, as we saw in Chapter 10, spark defiance in children, reduce their willingness to comply, and may actually promote high-risk behavior. The greatest challenge for injury control programs is how to reach these "more difficult-to-reach" youngsters, alter their family contexts, and reduce the dangers to which they are exposed (Brooks & Roberts, 1990).

## HEALTH EDUCATION IN MIDDLE CHILDHOOD

Child development specialists have become intensely interested in finding ways to help school-age youngsters understand how their bodies work, acquire mature conceptions of health and illness, and develop patterns of behavior that foster good health throughout life. Successfully targeting children for intervention on any health issue requires information on their current health-related knowledge. What informa-

# CULTURAL INFLUENCES

## Box 11.1  *Children's Understanding of Health and Illness*

Lizzie lay on the living-room sofa with a stuffy nose and sore throat, disappointed that she was missing her soccer team's final game and pizza party. "How'd I get this dumb cold anyhow?" she wondered aloud to Joey. "I probably did it to myself by playing outside without a hat the other day when it was freezing cold."

"No, no," Joey contradicted. "You can't get sick that way. Some creepy little viruses got into your bloodstream and attacked, just like an army."

"What're viruses? I didn't eat any viruses," answered Lizzie, puzzled.

"You don't eat them, silly, you breathe them in. Somebody probably sneezed them all over you at school. That's how you got sick!"

Lizzie and Joey are at different developmental levels in their understanding of health and illness—ideas that are influenced by cognitive development, exposure to biological knowledge, and cultural beliefs and practices. Researchers have asked 4- to 14-year-olds in Western cultures such questions as, "What does the word *health* mean?" or "What is a cold?" and "How do people get colds?"

During the preschool and early school years, children do not have much biological knowledge to bring to bear on their understanding of health and illness. For example, if you ask 4- to 8-year-olds to tell you what is inside their bodies, you will find that they know little about their internal organs and how they work. As a result, young children fall back on their rich knowledge of people's behavior to account for health and illness (Carey, 1985). Children of this age regard health as a matter of engaging in specific practices (eating the right foods, getting enough exercise, and wearing warm clothing on cold days) and illness as a matter of failing to follow these rules or coming too close to a sick person. Because of their limited knowledge, they sometimes view illness in superstitious ways—for example, as transmitted by magic or as punishment for doing something bad (Bibace & Walsh, 1980; Natapoff, 1978).

Over the course of middle childhood, children acquire more knowledge about their bodies and are cognitively better able to make sense of it. By age 9 or 10, they name a wide variety of internal organs and view them as interconnected, working as a system (Carey, 1985; Crider, 1981). Around this time, children's concepts of health and illness shift to biological explanations. Joey understands that illness can be caused by contagion—breathing in a harmful substance (a virus), which affects the operation of the body in some way.

By early adolescence, explanations become more elaborate and precise. Eleven- to 14-year-olds recognize health as a long-term condition that depends on the interaction of body, mind, and environmental influences (Hergenrather & Rabinowitz, 1991). And the adolescent's notions of illness involve clearly stated ideas about interference in normal body processes: "You get a cold when your sinuses fill up with mucus. Sometimes your lungs do, too, and you get a cough. Colds come from viruses. They get into the bloodstream and make your platelet count go down" (Bibace & Walsh, 1980).

School-age children everywhere are capable of grasping basic biological ideas, but whether or not they do so depends on information in their everyday environments along with cultural beliefs about health and disease. In Western society, a rational view of illness as disordered biological processes prevails, but the biological model is not accepted everywhere. A skin rash is likely to be understood very differently by a 10-year-old child growing up in a tribal society of believers in evil eyes and demons than in a middle-class family in the United States (Shonkoff, 1984).

The extent to which children in our own culture comprehend illness from a biological rather than magical point of view can be undermined by widely held attitudes in their social worlds. When certain diseases take on powerful symbolic meanings—for example, cancer as a malignant, destructive evil and AIDS as a sign of moral decay—even adults who have an accurate biological understanding of the illness irrationally expect bad things to happen from associating with affected people (Pryor et al., 1989). These beliefs are quickly picked up by children (Brown & Fritz, 1988), and they help explain the severe social rejection experienced by some youngsters with chronic diseases, such as AIDS and cancer.

tion can they understand? What reasoning processes do they use? What factors influence what they know? Box 11.1 summarizes findings on children's concepts of health and illness during middle childhood.

The school-age period may be an especially important time for fostering healthy life-styles because of the child's growing independence, increasing cognitive capacities, and rapidly developing self-concept, which includes perceptions of physical well-being (Harter, 1990). During middle childhood, children can learn a wide variety of health-related information—about the structure and functioning of their bodies, about good nutrition, and about the causes and consequences of many diseases (Shannon & Chen, 1988; Treiber, Schramm, & Mabe, 1986; Vessey, 1988).

Yet in virtually every effort to impart health concepts to children, researchers have found that health habits show little change. Why is there such a gap between health knowledge and practice in middle childhood? There are several related reasons. First, health is not an important goal to children. They are far more concerned about school work, friends, and play. Second, school-age youngsters, who feel good most of the time, do not perceive themselves as vulnerable to serious health problems. Third, children do not yet have an adultlike time perspective, which relates past, present, and distant future. Engaging in preventive behaviors is difficult when so much time intervenes between what children do now and its health consequences (Kalnins & Love, 1982). Finally, much health information that children get is contradicted by other sources, such as television advertising (see Chapter 10) and the examples of adults and peers.

This does not mean that teaching school-age youngsters health-related facts is unimportant. But information must be supplemented by other efforts. As we saw in earlier chapters, one effective way to foster children's health is to reduce hazards, such as pollution, inadequate medical care, and nonnutritious foods that are widely available in homes as well as school cafeterias (Children's Defense Fund, 1989; Shapiro, 1991). At the same time, since children's environments will never be totally free of health risks, parents and teachers should model and reinforce good health practices as much as possible (Friedman, Greene, & Stokes, 1991).

*BRIEF REVIEW*   Although many children are at their healthiest in middle childhood, a variety of health problems do occur. Most are more common among low-income youngsters, who are exposed to more health risks throughout development. Vision and hearing difficulties, malnutrition, overweight and obesity, Type A behavior, nighttime bedwetting, respiratory illnesses that result in school absences, and unintentional injuries are among the most frequent health concerns during the school years. Genetic and environmental factors combine to increase children's vulnerability to certain health problems, such as nearsightedness, obesity, Type A traits, and asthma. School-age children can learn a wide range of health information, but it has little impact on their everyday behavior. Interventions must also provide them with healthier environments and directly promote good health practices.

*• Rena discovered that Joey had stopped drinking milk in the school cafeteria because several of his friends no longer drank it. Also, he often skipped the main dish in favor of an extra dessert. Rena did not try to change Joey's eating practices at school. Instead, she encouraged him to eat a nutritious snack when he arrived home each day. Why is Rena's approach to handling this problem a sensible one? What should Joey's school be doing to foster good nutrition?*

## MOTOR DEVELOPMENT AND PLAY IN MIDDLE CHILDHOOD

Visit a city park on a pleasant weekend afternoon, watch several preschool and school-age children at play, and jot down their various physical activities. You will see that gains in body size and muscle strength support improved motor coordination during middle childhood. In addition, greater cognitive and social maturity permit older children to use their new motor skills in more complex ways. You are likely to notice a major change in children's play at this time.

## New Motor Capacities

**Gross Motor Skills.**    During middle childhood, running, jumping, hopping, and ball skills become more refined. At Joey and Lizzie's school one day, I watched during the third to sixth graders' recess. Children burst into sprints as they raced across the playground, jumped quickly over rotating ropes, engaged in intricate patterns of hopscotch, kicked and dribbled soccer balls, swung bats at balls pitched by their classmates, and balanced adeptly as they walked toe-to-toe across narrow ledges. Table 11.2 summarizes gross motor achievements between 6 and 12 years of age.

The diverse motor skills that improve during the school years reflect gains in four basic motor capacities. This first is *flexibility*. Compared to the movements of preschoolers, those of school-age children are more pliable and elastic, a difference that can be seen as children swing a bat, kick a ball, jump over a hurdle, or execute tumbling routines. Second, *balance* improves, both when the child is moving and when standing still. School-age children can walk a narrower balance beam than they could during early childhood, and their ability to remain in a one-foot stand increases. Improved balance supports advances in a great many athletic skills, including running, hopping, skipping, throwing, kicking, and the rapid changes of direction required in many team sports (Clark & Watkins, 1984). Third, children show marked gains in *agility*, or quickness and accuracy of movement. This change can be seen in the fancy footwork of jump rope and hopscotch, as well as in the forward, backward, and

TABLE 11.2 • Changes in Gross Motor Skills During Middle Childhood

| Skill | Developmental Change |
| --- | --- |
| Running | Running speed increases from 12 feet per second at age 6 to over 18 feet per second at age 12. |
| Other gait variations | Skipping improves. Sideways stepping appears around age 6 and becomes more continuous and fluid with age. |
| Vertical jump | Height jumped increases from 4 inches at age 6 to 12 inches at age 12. |
| Standing broad jump | Distance jumped increases from 3 feet at age 6 to over 5 feet at age 12. |
| Precision jumping and hopping (on a mat divided into squares) | By age 7 children can accurately move from square to square, a performance that improves until age 9 and then levels off. |
| Throwing | Throwing speed, distance, and accuracy increases for both sexes, but much more for boys than for girls. At age 6, a ball thrown by a boy travels 39 feet per second, one by a girl 29 feet per second. At age 12, a ball thrown by a boy travels 78 feet per second, one by a girl 56 feet per second. |
| Catching | Ability to catch small balls thrown over greater distances improves with age. |
| Kicking | Kicking speed and accuracy improve, with boys considerably ahead of girls. At age 6, a ball kicked by a boy travels 21 feet per second, one by a girl 13 feet per second. At age 12, a ball kicked by a boy travels 34 feet per second, one by a girl 26 feet per second. |
| Batting | Batting motions become more effective with age, increasing in speed and accuracy and involving the entire body. |
| Dribbling | Style of hand dribbling gradually changes, from awkward slapping of the ball to continuous, relaxed, even stroking. |

*Sources:* Cratty, 1986; Roberton, 1984.

*During middle childhood, gross motor skills become more refined. Gains in flexibility, balance, agility, and force permit this girl to jump faster, higher, and with fancier footwork than she could as a younger child.* (Roswell Angier/Stock Boston)

sideways motions older children use as they dodge opponents in tag and soccer. Finally, over the school years, children perform almost all movements with greater *force*. Older youngsters can throw and kick a ball harder and propel themselves further off the ground when running and jumping than they could at early ages (Cratty, 1986).

Although body growth contributes greatly to the improved motor performance of school-age children, more efficient information processing also plays an important role (Roberton, 1984). Steady improvements in *reaction time* occur during middle childhood, with 14-year-olds responding almost twice as quickly to a stimulus as 6-year-olds (Southard, 1985). As a result, younger children often have difficulty with skills that require immediate responding. When they dribble a ball, they often lose control, and when up at bat, they usually swing too late. Reaction time combines several cognitive skills that are critical for effective motor performance—time to recognize a stimulus, time to formulate an appropriate response, and time for the plan of action to reach the muscles (Cratty, 1986). The fact that speed of reaction is not yet well developed in younger school-age children has practical implications for physical education. Since 6- and 7-year-olds are seldom successful at batting a thrown ball, T-ball is more appropriate for them than baseball. And handball, four-square, and kickball should precede instruction in tennis, basketball, and football (Thomas, 1984).

*Fine Motor Skills.*   Fine motor development also improves steadily over the school years, a change that is apparent in the activities children of this age period enjoy. On rainy afternoons, Joey and Lizzie could be found experimenting with yo-yos, building model airplanes, weaving potholders on small looms, and working puzzles with hundreds of tiny pieces. Middle childhood is also the time when many children take up musical instruments, which demand considerable fine motor control.

Gains in fine motor skill are especially evident in children's writing and drawing, as you can see in Figure 11.3. By age 6, most children can print the alphabet, their first and last names, and the numbers from 1 to 10 with reasonable clarity. However, their writing tends to be quite large because they use the entire arm to make strokes rather than just the wrist and fingers. Children usually master uppercase letters first

**FIGURE 11.3** • Fine motor coordination improves over middle childhood, as these writing samples reveal. At age 5, Ted printed in large uppercase letters, asking for help in spelling the words. By age 7, he had mastered the lowercase alphabet, and his printing was small and evenly spaced. At age 9, he used cursive writing. Notice, also, how letter reversals and invented spellings decline with age. *(Ted's picture with label and space trip story from L. M. McGee & D. J. Richgels, 1990,* Literacy's beginnings, *Boston: Allyn and Bacon, pp. 240–312. Reprinted by permission of the authors. Ted's War of 1812 essay from D. J. Richgels, L. M. McGee, & E. A. Slaton, 1989, "Teaching expository text structure in reading and writing," in K. D. Muth, ed.,* Children's comprehension of text, *Newark, DE: International Reading Association, p. 180.)*

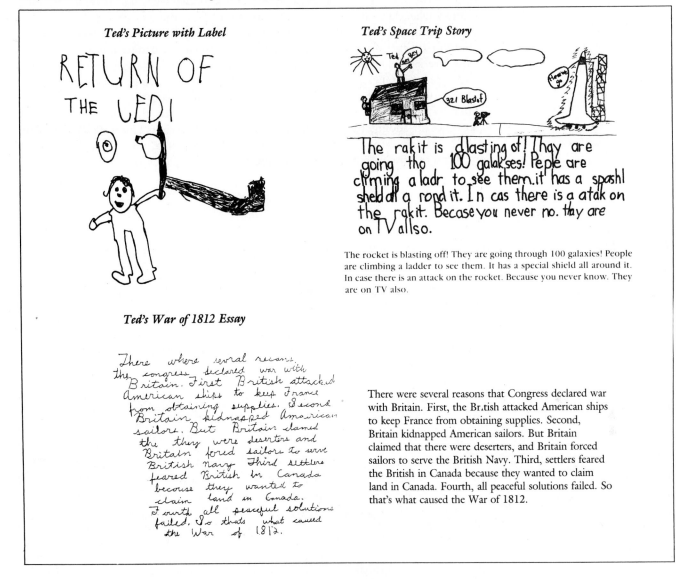

**Ted's Picture with Label**

RETURN OF THE UEDI

**Ted's Space Trip Story**

The rakit is dlasting of! Thay are going tho 100 galakses! Peple are clrming a ladr to see them. it has a spashl sheld all a rond it. In cas there is a atak on the rakit. Becase you never no. thay are on TV allso.

The rocket is blasting off! They are going through 100 galaxies! People are climbing a ladder to see them. It has a special shield all around it. In case there is an attack on the rocket. Because you never know. They are on TV also.

**Ted's War of 1812 Essay**

There were several reasons that Congress declared war with Britain. First, the Br.tish attacked American ships to keep France from obtaining supplies. Second, Britain kidnapped American sailors. But Britain claimed that there were deserters, and Britain forced sailors to serve the British Navy. Third, settlers feared the British in Canada because they wanted to claim land in Canada. Fourth, all peaceful solutions failed. So that's what caused the War of 1812.

because these rely on horizontal and vertical motions, which are easier for young children to control than the small curves of the lowercase alphabet. Legibility of writing gradually increases, not just because older children form letters more accurately, but also because they can produce letters of uniform height and spacing (Cratty, 1986). These improvements prepare children for mastering cursive writing by third grade.

Children's drawings show dramatic gains in organization, detail, and representation of depth during middle childhood. By the end of the preschool years, children can accurately copy many two-dimensional shapes, and they integrate these into their drawings. But when asked to copy a three-dimensional form, such as a cube or cylinder, most cannot do so before age 9 or 10. Around this time, the third dimension first appears in children's drawings. Older school-age youngsters start to master *linear perspective,* Western culture's system for creating the illusion of depth on a two-dimensional surface (Winner, 1986).

At first, children's efforts at three-dimensional drawing contain errors. In one study, 5- to 17-year-olds were seated in front of a table with objects on it and asked to draw what they saw. As you can see in Figure 11.4, the youngest children did not depict depth. They drew the table as a straight line or surface with the objects floating above or sitting on top of it. Around age 9, depth cues began to appear. Objects up close overlapped those further away, but the table top was incorrectly drawn as a rectangle or parallelogram. Not until adolescence did drawings accurately conform to the rules of perspective, with the sides of the table top represented as converging lines (Willats, 1977). All children do not follow precisely the same developmental sequence in adding the third dimension to their drawings (Nicholls & Kennedy, 1992). But once they notice that depth can be represented, they gradually solve the problem of how to put it down on paper.

**FIGURE 11.4** • Children ranging in age from 5 to 17 were asked to draw a table with objects on it. Below age 9, they did not represent perspective. When depth cues first appeared, children incorrectly drew the table as a parallelogram. Not until adolescence did their drawings conform to the rules of linear perspective. *(From J. Willats, 1977, "How children learn to represent three-dimensional space in drawings," in G. Butterworth, ed.,* The child's representation of the world, *New York: Plenum, pp. 189–202. Reprinted by permission.)*

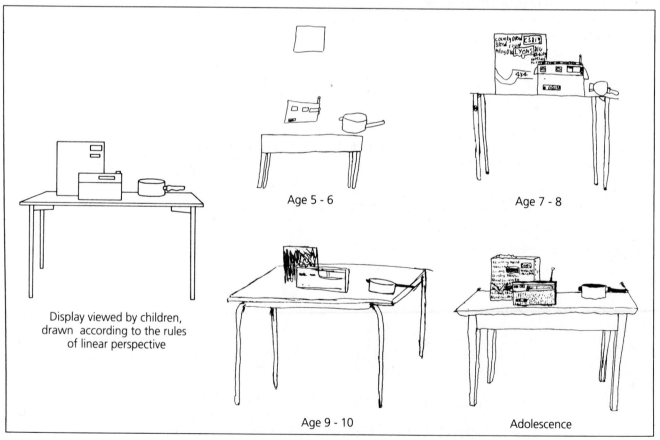

Display viewed by children, drawn according to the rules of linear perspective

Age 5 - 6

Age 7 - 8

Age 9 - 10

Adolescence

***Individual Differences.*** As was the case at younger ages, school-age children show marked individual differences in motor capacities that are influenced by both heredity and environment. Body build continues to affect gross motor performance, with the taller, more muscular child excelling on many tasks. At the same time, parents who encourage physical exercise tend to have youngsters who enjoy it more and who are also more skilled. Social class affects children's opportunities to develop a variety of physical abilities. Economically advantaged children are far more likely to have ballet, tennis, gymnastics, and music lessons than are youngsters from low-income families.

Sex differences in motor skills that began to appear during the preschool years extend into middle childhood and, in some instances, become more pronounced. Girls remain ahead in the fine motor area, including handwriting and drawing. They also continue to have an edge in gross motor skills that depend on balance and precision of movement, such as skipping, jumping, and hopping. But on all other skills listed in Table 11.2, boys outperform girls, and in the case of throwing and kicking, the difference is large (Cratty, 1986; Roberton, 1984; Thomas & French, 1985).

School-age boys' genetic advantage in muscle mass is not great enough to account for their superiority in so many gross motor skills. Instead, environment is believed to play a much larger role. Although women's participation in athletics has increased dramatically since the 1970s, it does not equal that of men (Coakley, 1990). Lizzie, for example, sees that her father reads magazines and watches TV programs about sports far more often than does her mother. In addition, almost all the participants in public sports events are men. Although Lizzie was encouraged to play in the city soccer league, both parents believed that Joey was better at athletics and that it was more critical for his development that he do well at sports.

A recent study of over 800 elementary school pupils found that parents hold higher expectations for boys' athletic performance, and children absorb these social messages at an early age. Kindergartners through third graders of both sexes viewed sports in a sex-stereotyped fashion—as much more important for boys. These attitudes affected children's physical self-images as well as their behavior. Girls saw themselves as having less talent at sports, and by sixth grade they devoted less time to athletics than did their male classmates (Eccles & Harold, 1991; Eccles, Jacobs, & Harold, 1990).

These findings indicate that special measures need to be taken to raise girls' confidence that they can do well at sports. Educating parents about the minimal differences in school-age boys' and girls' physical capacities and sensitizing them to unfair biases against girls' athletic ability may prove helpful. In addition, greater emphasis on skill training for girls along with increased attention to their athletic achievements in schools and communities is likely to improve their performance. Middle childhood may be a crucial time to take these steps, since during the school years children start to discover what they are good at and make some definite skill commitments.

## Organized Games with Rules

The physical activities of school-age children reflect an important advance in the quality of their play: Organized games with rules become common in middle childhood. In cultures around the world, the variety of children's spontaneous rule-based games is enormous. Some are variants on popular sports, such as soccer, baseball, basketball, and football. Others are well-known childhood games like tag, jacks, and hopscotch. Children have also invented hundreds of less well-known games and passed them from one generation to the next. Observing the spontaneous play of children in England and Israel, researchers identified over 2,000 games in each country. You may remember some of them from your own childhood, such as red rover, statues, blind man's buff, leap frog, one-o-cat, kick the can, and prisoner's base (Eifermann, 1971; Opie & Opie, 1969).

Gains in perspective-taking—in particular, children's ability to understand the roles of several players in a game—permit this transition to rule-oriented games. The contribution of these play experiences to development is great. Child-invented games usually rely on simple physical skills and involve a sizable element of luck. As a result, they rarely become contests of individual ability. Instead, they permit children to try out different styles of competing, winning, and losing with little personal risk. Also, in their efforts to organize a game, children discover why rules are necessary and which ones work well. Without rules that are fair and that keep things interesting for all participants, the game is likely to break apart. In fact, children often spend as much time working out the details of how a game should proceed as they do playing the game itself (Devereux, 1976). As we will see in Chapter 13, these experiences help children move toward more mature concepts of fairness and justice in middle childhood.

Because of their value for children's development, some researchers are concerned about the recent decline in child-organized games. Today, school-age youngsters spend less time gathering on sidewalks and playgrounds than they did in generations past. Children's attraction to television and video games accounts for some of this change. But adult-organized sports, such as Little League baseball and city soccer and hockey leagues, also fill many hours that children used to devote to spontaneous play. Are adult-structured athletics that mirror professional sports robbing children of critical learning experiences and endangering their development? For a look at this controversial issue, turn to Box 11.2.

## *Shadows of Our Evolutionary Past*

Besides a new level of structure and organization, some additional qualities of physical play become common in middle childhood. While watching children at your city park, notice how they occasionally wrestle, roll, hit, and run after one another while smiling and laughing. This friendly chasing and play fighting is called **rough-and-tumble play.** Research indicates that it is a good-natured, sociable activity that is quite distinct from aggressive fighting. Children in many cultures engage in it with peers whom they like especially well, and they continue interacting after a rough-and-tumble episode rather than separating, as they do at the end of an aggressive encounter. Sometimes parents and teachers mistake rough-and-tumble for real fighting and try to intervene. In these instances, children often respond, "It's all right, we're only playing!" School-age youngsters are quite good at telling the difference between playful wrestling and a true aggressive attack (Costabile et al., 1991; Smith & Boulton, 1990). Only those who have poor relations with peers sometimes confuse rough-and-tumble with hostility (Pellegrini, 1988).

Children's rough-and-tumble play is similar to the social behavior of young mammals of many species. Does it have some adaptive value? By age 11, children choose rough-and-tumble partners who are not only likable but similar in strength to themselves. In our evolutionary past, this form of interaction may have been important for the development of fighting skill (Humphreys & Smith, 1987). Rough-and-tumble play occurs more often among boys, but girls also display it. Girls' rough-and-tumble largely consists of running and chasing, while boys engage in more playful wrestling and hitting (Blurton Jones, 1972).

Rough-and-tumble tends to occur among children who are alike in physical capacity, but, as we have seen, children of the same age vary greatly in size and

**Rough-and-tumble play**

A form of peer interaction involving friendly chasing and play fighting that, in our evolutionary past, may have been important for the development of fighting skill.

## SOCIAL ISSUES

### Box 11.2 *Are Adult-Organized Sports Good for Children?*

The last several decades have witnessed a tremendous expansion of adult-organized sports for children. Today, youth programs in baseball, football, basketball, soccer, and hockey exist in many American cities. The largest of these is Little League Baseball, with nearly 50,000 teams and half a million children involved. Perhaps you participated in one of these sports during your own childhood. If so, what were your experiences like?

Adult-organized athletics for children has both critics and supporters. Critics make the following points:

1. When adults become involved in children's games, their focus becomes overly competitive— less on the process of playing and more on the product of winning. Children feel too much pressure from coaches and parents, who become overly critical when players make errors.

2. In adult-organized sports, children learn little about leadership, decision making, and fair play because adults control the game.

3. Assigning children to specific roles (for example, catcher, short stop, or outfielder) inhibits the experimentation and creativity common in child-organized games.

4. Highly structured, competitive sports are less fun; they resemble "work" more than "play."

Supporters argue this way:

1. Adult-structured athletics teaches children how to accept authority and prepares them for realistic competition—the kind they will one day face as adults.

2. Regularly scheduled practices and games ensure that children get plenty of exercise. They also fill free time that might otherwise be devoted to less constructive pursuits, such as watching television or hanging out.

3. Children get instruction in physical skills necessary for future success in athletics.

4. Adult-controlled sports enable parents and children to share an activity that both enjoy.

At present, the debate about the value of adult-organized sports is unresolved. Reviewing available research, one investigator concluded that there is little evidence that children's athletic leagues result in long-term psychological benefits or damage (Fine, 1987). But the arguments of critics are valid in some cases. When parents and coaches criticize rather than encourage and do not let players who have lost a game forget about defeat, a few children react to competitive sports with intense anxiety. Eventually, these youngsters may avoid athletics entirely (Horn, 1987).

*OBSERVE* A LITTLE LEAGUE BASEBALL or other adult-organized sports event in your community, and take note of the behavior of parents, coaches, and players during the game. How much pressure is placed on children to win? Do children seem to be enjoying the game?

strength. When children gather in groups for physical activity, social structures emerge on the basis of toughness and assertiveness. A **dominance hierarchy** is a stable ordering of individuals that predicts who will win when conflict arises between group members. Observations of arguments, threats, and physical attacks between children reveal a consistent lineup of winners and losers as early as the preschool years. This hierarchy becomes increasingly stable during middle childhood and adolescence, especially among boys (Pettit et al., 1990; Savin-Williams, 1979).

Like dominance relations among animals, those among human children serve the adaptive function of limiting aggression between group members. Once a dominance hierarchy is clearly established, hostility is rare. When it occurs, it is very restrained, often taking the form of playful verbal insults that can be accepted cheerfully by a play partner (Fine, 1980). For example, Joey rarely challenges Sean, a child much

**Dominance hierarchy**
A stable ordering of group members that predicts who will win under conditions of conflict.

*Rough-and-tumble play can be distinguished from aggression by its good-natured quality. In our evolutionary past, it may have been important for the development of fighting skill. (Nancy Sheehan/ The Picture Cube)*

larger than he, on the playground. But when he is unhappy about how things are going in a game, Joey is likely to tumble over humorously on the grass while saying something like this: "Hey, Sean, you've been up at bat so long you'll fall over dead if you swing at one more ball! Come on, give one of us a chance." This gradual replacement of direct hostility with friendly insults provides school-age children with an effective means of influencing their physically more powerful peers.

## Physical Education

In the preceding sections, we have seen that physical activity supports many aspects of children's development—the health of their bodies, their sense of self-worth as physically active and capable beings, and the cognitive and social skills necessary for getting along well with others. Physical education classes that provide regularly scheduled opportunities for exercise and play help ensure that all children have access to these benefits.

Yet physical education is not taught often enough in American schools. Only one-third of elementary school pupils have a daily physical education class; the average school-age child gets only 20 minutes of physical education a week (Committee on Labor and Human Resources, 1985). This means that children get most of their exercise outside of school. But on their own, American children often do not engage in enough vigorous physical activity. The growing fitness movement among adults has not yet filtered down to children, many of whom ride to and from school in buses and cars, sit in classrooms most of the day, and watch TV for 3 to 4 hours after they arrive home. The National Children and Youth Fitness Study, which tested thousands of schoolchildren on a variety of fitness items (such as pull-ups, sit-ups, and the one-mile run), revealed that only two-thirds of 10- to 12-year-old boys and about half of 10- to 12-year-old girls met basic fitness standards for children their age (Looney & Plowman, 1990).

These findings indicate that American schools need to do a better job of providing physical education. Besides offering more frequent classes, many experts believe that schools need to change the content of physical education programs. Training in competitive sports is often a high priority, but it is unlikely to reach the least physically fit youngsters, who draw back when an activity demands a high level of skill. Instead, programs should emphasize informal games that most children can perform well and individual exercise—walking, running, jumping, tumbling, and climbing. These athletic pursuits are also the ones most likely to last into later years.

Physical fitness builds upon itself. Children who are in good physical condition have more energy, and they take great pleasure in their rapidly developing motor skills and ability to control their own bodies. As a result, they seek out these activities in the future, developing rewarding interests in physical exercise that pave the way toward a lifelong commitment to an active and healthy life-style.

# SUMMARY

### Body Growth in Middle Childhood

• Gains in body size during middle childhood extend the pattern of growth established during the preschool period. On the average, children add about 5 pounds in weight and 2 to 3 inches in height each year. Growth is not steady; children show slight spurts in height followed by lulls over the school years. By age 9, girls overtake boys in physical size.

• Large individual differences in body growth exist, which are especially evident when children growing up in different parts of the world are compared. **Secular trends in physical growth** have occurred in industrialized nations. Because of improved health and nutrition, many children are growing larger and reaching physical maturity earlier than their ancestors.

• During the school years, bones continue to lengthen and broaden. Between the ages of 6 and 12, all 20 primary teeth are replaced by permanent ones. About one-third of school-age children suffer from **malocclusion**, a condition in which the upper and lower teeth do not meet properly. Braces are a common sight by the end of elementary school.

• Only a small increase in brain size occurs during middle childhood. Myelinization and lateralization of the cerebral hemispheres continue. Brain development during the school years is believed to involve **neurotransmitters** and hormonal influences.

### Common Health Problems in Middle Childhood

• Children from advantaged homes are at their healthiest during middle childhood, due to the cumulative effects of good nutrition combined with rapid development of the body's immune system. At the same time, a variety of health problems do occur, many of which are more common among low-income children.

• The most common visual problem in middle childhood is **myopia**, or nearsightedness. It is influenced by heredity as well as by how children use their eyes. Myopia is one of the few health conditions that increases with family education and income. Because of untreated ear infections, many low-income youngsters experience some hearing loss during the school years.

• Many poverty-stricken children in developing countries and in the United States continue to suffer from malnutrition during middle childhood. When malnutrition is allowed to persist for many years, its negative impact on physical growth, intellectual development, and motor performance is permanent.

• Overweight and **obesity** are growing problems in affluent nations like the United States. Although heredity contributes to obesity, parental feeding practices, maladaptive eating habits, and lack of exercise also play important roles. Obese children are often rejected by their classmates and display serious adjustment and behavior problems. Family-based interventions in which both parents and children revise eating patterns, engage in regular daily exercise, and reinforce one another's progress are the most effective approaches to treating childhood obesity.

• Signs of the **Type A personality**—competitiveness, impatience, irritation, and anger—begin to emerge in some children by early and middle childhood. An intense, determined temperamental style probably contributes to Type A behavior. However, Type A traits do not become stable until adolescence. Parenting practices may lead the behavior pattern to continue in some children but not in others.

• **Nocturnal enuresis**, or bedwetting during the night, affects 10 percent of American school-age children. In the majority of cases, it has biological roots. The most effective treatment involves use of a urine alarm that works according to conditioning principles.

• The most common cause of school absence and childhood hospitalization is **asthma**. It occurs more often among black and poverty-stricken children, perhaps because of pollution, stressful home lives, and lack of access to good health care. Children with severe chronic illnesses are at risk for academic, emotional, and social difficulties and benefit from a variety of interventions.

• The rate of unintentional injuries increases over middle childhood and adolescence, with auto and bicycle collisions accounting for most of the rise. Safety education and incentives for following safety rules are especially important in middle childhood.

### Health Education in Middle Childhood

• School-age children can successfully acquire a wide range of health-related information, but it seldom changes their health-related behavior. Besides educating children about good health, adults need to reduce health hazards to which children are exposed and model and reinforce good health practices.

### Motor Development and Play in Middle Childhood

• Gradual increases in body size and muscle strength support the refinement of many gross motor capacities in middle childhood. Gains in flexibility, balance, agility, and force occur. In addition, improvements in reaction time contribute to the athletic performance of school-age children.

• Fine motor development also improves during the school years. Children's writing becomes more legible, and their drawings show dramatic increases in organization, detail, and representation of depth.

• Children show wide individual differences in motor capacities that are influenced by both genetic and environmental factors. Adult encouragement of boys' athletic participation largely accounts for boys' superior performance on a wide range of gross motor skills in middle childhood.

• Organized games with rules become common in middle childhood. Children's spontaneous games support many aspects of development. Some features of children's physical activity reflect our evolutionary past. **Rough-and-tumble play** may have at one time been important for the development of fighting skill. **Dominance hierarchies** serve the adaptive function of limiting aggression among group members.

• Physical education classes help ensure that all children have access to the benefits of regular exercise and play. Yet physical education does not take place often enough in American schools. Many school-age youngsters do not meet basic physical fitness standards for children their age. Both the quantity and quality of physical education needs to be improved.

## IMPORTANT TERMS AND CONCEPTS

secular trends in physical growth (p. 392)

malocclusion (p. 392)

neurotransmitters (p. 393)

myopia (p. 394)

obesity (p. 395)

Type A personality (p. 397)

nocturnal enuresis (p. 398)

asthma (p. 398)

rough-and-tumble play (p. 408)

dominance hierarchy (p. 409)

## FOR FURTHER INFORMATION AND SPECIAL HELP

**Chronic Illness in Childhood**

Asthma and Allergy Foundation of America
1717 Massachusetts Avenue, Suite 305
Washington, DC 20036
(202) 265-0265

Devoted to solving health problems posed by allergic diseases, including asthma. Supports research and medical training and provides information to health professionals and the public.

Candlelighters Childhood Cancer Foundation
7910 Woodmont Avenue, Suite 460
Bethesda, MD 20814
(202) 659-5136

Increases public awareness of childhood cancer and provides information, guidance, and emotional support to parents with affected children. Has a crisis hotline, (800) 366-2223.

Cystic Fibrosis Foundation
6931 Arlington Road, Suite 200
Bethesda, MD 20814
(301) 951-4422

Supports research, education, and care centers to benefit children and young adults with cystic fibrosis.

Ryan White National Fund
c/o Athletes and Entertainers for Kids
P.O. Box 191 Building B
Gardena, CA 90248-0191
(213) 768-8493

Consists of corporations and individuals concerned about children with catastrophic illnesses, particularly AIDS. Provides assistance to children and families, including medical care and counseling. Operates Kids 'n AIDS National Program, which offers AIDS education in schools.

**Adult-Organized Sports for Children**

Little League Baseball
P.O. Box 3485
Williamsport, PA 17701
(717) 326-1921

Organizes baseball and softball programs for children 6 to 18 years of age. Operates a special division for handicapped children and sponsors an annual world series.

Soccer Association for Youth
5945 Ridge Avenue
Cincinnati, OH 45213
(513) 351-7291

Supports soccer programs for children between 6 and 18 years of age throughout the United States. Seeks to encourage widespread participation and offer equal opportunity regardless of ability or sex. Distributes supplies and support necessary to form teams.

*Birdwatching, S. Bapu Bhiva, 12 years, India. Reprinted by permission from The International Museum of Children's Art, Oslo, Norway.*

# Cognitive Development in Middle Childhood

# 12

Piaget's Theory: The Concrete Operational Stage
  *Operational Thought   Limitations of Concrete Operational Thought   New Research on Concrete Operational Thought   Evaluation of the Concrete Operational Stage*
Information Processing in Middle Childhood
  *Attention   Memory Strategies   The Knowledge Base and Memory Performance   Culture and Memory Strategies   The School-Age Child's Theory of Mind   Self-Regulation Applications of Information Processing to Academic Learning*
Individual Differences in Mental Development During Middle Childhood
  *Defining and Measuring Intelligence   Explaining Individual Differences in IQ   Overcoming Cultural Bias in Intelligence Tests*
Language Development in Middle Childhood
  *Vocabulary   Grammar   Pragmatics   Learning Two Languages at a Time*
Children's Learning in School
  *The Educational Philosophy   Teacher–Pupil Interaction   Computers in the Classroom   Teaching Children with Special Needs*
How Well Educated Are America's Children?

"Finally!" Lizzie exclaimed the day she entered first grade. "Now I get to go to *real* school just like Joey!" Rena remembered how 6-year-old Lizzie had walked confidently into her classroom, pencils, crayons, and writing pad in hand, ready for a more disciplined approach to learning than she had experienced in early childhood. As a preschooler, Lizzie had loved playing school, giving assignments as the "teacher" and pretending to read and write as the "pupil." Now she was there in earnest, eager to master the tasks that had sparked her imagination as a 4- and 5-year-old.

Lizzie entered a whole new world of challenging mental activities. In a single morning, she and her classmates wrote in journals, met in reading groups, worked on addition and subtraction, and sorted leaves gathered on the playground for a special science project. As Lizzie and Joey moved through the elementary school grades, they tackled increasingly complex tasks and gradually became more accomplished at reading, writing, math skills, and general knowledge of the world.

Cognitive development had prepared Joey and Lizzie for this new phase. We begin this chapter by returning to Piaget's theory and the information processing approach. Together, they provide us with an overview of cognitive change during the school years. Then we take an in-depth look at individual differences in mental development. We examine the genetic and environmental roots of IQ scores, which often enter into important educational decisions. Next our attention turns to language. Vocabulary, grammar, and communication skills continue to blossom during middle childhood, even though changes are less dramatic than they were during the preschool years. Finally, we consider the importance of schools in children's learning and development.

## PIAGET'S THEORY: THE CONCRETE OPERATIONAL STAGE

As a preschooler, Lizzie had once visited my child development class, where we watched her do several of Piaget's conservation problems (see Chapter 9, page 316). At age 4, Lizzie was easily confused by them. She was sure that after a row of six pennies had been placed in a pile, there were fewer of them. And when asked if the amount of water was still the same after it had been poured into a short wide container, she insisted that it was not.

At age 8, when Lizzie returned to my class for a second session, these problems were easy. "Of course it's the same," she said after the water had been poured in conservation of liquid, somewhat annoyed by this obvious question. "The water's shorter but it's also wider. Pour it back," she instructed the college student who was interviewing her. "You'll see, it's the same amount!" Lizzie's response indicates that she has entered Piaget's **concrete operational stage,** which spans the years from 7 to 11. During this period, thought is far more logical, flexible, and organized than it was during the preschool period. Concept Table 12.1 summarizes the major characteristics of the concrete operational stage.

### Operational Thought

**Conservation.** Piaget regarded *conservation* as the single most important achievement of the concrete operational stage. It provides clear evidence of *operations*—mental actions that obey logical rules. Notice how Lizzie coordinates several aspects of the task, rather than *centering* on only one as a preschooler would do. In other words, Lizzie is capable of **decentration;** she recognizes that a change in one aspect of the water (its height) is compensated for by a change in another aspect (its width). Lizzie also demonstrates **reversibility,** the capacity to mentally go through a series of steps in a problem and then reverse direction, returning to the starting point. Recall from Chapter 9 that reversibility is part of every logical operation. It is solidly achieved in middle childhood, as children's successful performance on a wide variety of Piagetian tasks reveals.

**Classification.** Operational thought permits school-age children to categorize more effectively. By the end of middle childhood, they pass Piaget's *class inclusion problem* (see page 317). They can group objects into hierarchies of classes and subclasses more effectively than they could at earlier ages (Achenbach & Weisz, 1975; Hodges & French, 1988). You can see this in children's play activities. Collections of all kinds of objects—stamps, coins, baseball cards, rocks, bottle caps, and more—become common in middle childhood. At age 10, Joey spent hours sorting and resorting his large box of baseball cards. At times he grouped them by league and team membership, at other times by playing position and batting average. He could separate the players into a variety of classes and subclasses and flexibly move back and forth between them. This understanding is beyond the grasp of preschoolers, who usually insist that a set of objects can be sorted in only one way.

**Seriation.** **Seriation** refers to the ability to arrange items along a quantitative dimension, such as length or weight. To test for it, Piaget asked children to arrange sticks of different lengths from shortest to longest. Older preschoolers can create the series, but they do so haphazardly. They put the sticks in a row but make many errors and take a long time to correct them. In contrast, 6- to 7-year-olds are guided by an orderly plan. They create the series efficiently by beginning with the smallest stick, then moving to the next smallest, and so on, until the ordering is complete.

**Concrete operational stage**
Piaget's third stage, during which thought is logical, flexible, and organized in its application to concrete information. However, the capacity for abstract thinking is not yet present. Spans the years from 7 to 11.

**Decentration**
The ability to focus on several aspects of a problem at once and relate them.

**Reversibility**
The ability to mentally go through a series of steps in a problem and then reverse direction, returning to the starting point.

**Seriation**
The ability to arrange items along a quantitative dimension, such as length or weight.

**CONCEPT TABLE 12.1 • Major Characteristics of the Concrete Operational Stage**

| Concept | Important Point | Example |
|---|---|---|
| Decentration | Concrete operational children coordinate several important features of a task rather than centering on only the perceptually dominant one. | After getting two glasses of lemonade from the kitchen, one for Joey and one for herself, Lizzie remarked, "Don't worry, I gave you just as much. My glass is tall but thin. Yours is short but wide." |
| Reversibility | Concrete operational children can think through the steps in a problem and then go backward, returning to the starting point. | Lizzie understands that addition and subtraction are reversible operations. In other words, when you add 7 plus 8 to get 15, then this tells you that 15 minus 8 must be 7. |
| Conservation | Concrete operational children recognize that certain physical characteristics of objects remain the same even when their outward appearance changes. | After spilling ten pennies stacked on her desk all over the floor, Lizzie bent down to search for them. "I know there have to be ten," she said to herself, "because that's how many I put in that little pile on my desk yesterday." |
| Hierarchical classification | Concrete operational children can flexibly group and regroup objects into hierarchies of classes and subclasses. | Lizzie discussed how to display her rock collection with her friend Marina. Marina suggested, "You could divide them up by size and then by color. Or you could use shape and color." |
| Seriation | Concrete operational children are guided by an overall plan when arranging items in a series. | Lizzie decided to arrange her rocks by size. She quickly lined up all 20 rocks in a row, selecting the smallest and then the next smallest from the pile, until the arrangement was complete. |
| Transitive inference | Concrete operational children can seriate mentally. After comparing A with B and B with C, they can infer the relationship between A and C. | "I saw Tina's new lunch box, and it's bigger than mine," Marina said while eating her sandwich with Lizzie one day. "Well, it must be bigger than mine, too, because look—my box isn't even as big as yours," said Lizzie. |
| Horizontal décalage | Children master logical concepts gradually over the course of middle childhood. | Lizzie understood conservation of number and liquid before she mastered conservation of area and weight. |

The concrete operational child's improved grasp of quantitative arrangements is also evident in a more challenging seriation problem—one that requires children to seriate mentally. This ability is called **transitive inference.** In a well-known transitive inference problem, Piaget showed children pairings of differently colored sticks. From observing that stick A is longer than stick B and stick B is longer than stick C, children must make the mental inference that A is longer than C. Not until age 7 or 8 do children perform well on this task (Chapman & Lindenberger, 1988; Piaget, 1967).

**Transitive inference**
The ability to seriate—or arrange items along a quantitative dimension—mentally.

*An improved ability to categorize underlies children's interest in collecting objects during middle childhood. This boy enjoys sorting his large rock collection into an elaborate structure of classes and subclasses.* (Blair Seitz/Photo Researchers)

***Distance, Time, and Speed.*** Piaget found that school-age youngsters have a more accurate understanding of space than they did during early childhood. For example, their comprehension of distance improves, as a special conservation task reveals. To give this problem, make two small trees out of modeling clay and place them apart on a table. Next, put a block or thick piece of cardboard between the trees. Then ask the child whether the trees are nearer together, farther apart, or still the same distance apart. Preschoolers say that the distance has become smaller. In other words, they do not understand that a filled up space has the same value as an empty space (Piaget, Inhelder, & Szeminska, 1948/1960). By the early school years, children grasp this idea easily. Although 4-year-olds can conserve distance when questioned about objects that are very familiar to them, their understanding is not as solid and complete as that of the school-age child (Miller & Baillargeon, 1990).

According to Piaget (1946/1970), concrete operational thinking permits children to combine distance with other physical concepts, such as time and speed. He reported that children first master the positive relationships between speed and distance (the faster you travel, the farther you go) and time and distance (the longer you travel, the farther you go). Only later do they grasp the negative relationship between speed and time (the faster you travel, the less time it takes to get to your destination). Other research confirms these findings. In one study, school-age children heard a story about a bunny and a skunk who raided a garden of cabbages. When frightened by a barking dog, the animals ran down a road and out of the garden. In telling the story, the adult provided information about two of the dimensions and asked the child to predict the third one—for example, "The bunny ran just as fast as the skunk, but the bunny ran farther. Did the bunny and skunk run for the same amount of time, or did one run longer?" First graders performed well when asked to coordinate speed with distance and time with distance. But not until third grade did they comprehend the negative association between speed and time (Acredolo, Adams, & Schmid, 1984).

## Limitations of Concrete Operational Thought

Because of their improved ability to conserve, classify, seriate, and deal with spatial concepts, elementary school children are far more capable problem solvers than they were during the preschool years. But concrete operational thinking suffers from one important limitation. Elementary school children think in an organized, logical fashion only when dealing with concrete information they can directly perceive. Their mental operations work poorly when applied to abstract ideas—ones not directly apparent in the real world.

Children's solutions to transitive inference problems provide a good illustration. When shown pairs of sticks of unequal length, Lizzie easily figured out that if stick A is longer than stick B and stick B is longer than stick C, then stick A is longer than stick C. But when given an entirely hypothetical version of this task, such as "Susan is taller than Sally and Sally is taller than Mary. Who is the tallest?" she had great difficulty. Not until age 11 or 12 can children solve this problem easily.

The fact that logical thought is at first tied to immediate situations helps account for a special feature of concrete operational reasoning. Perhaps you have already noticed that school-age children do not master all of Piaget's concrete operational tasks at once. Instead, they do so in a step-by-step fashion. For example, they usually grasp conservation problems in a certain order: first number; then length, mass, and liquid; and finally area and weight (Brainerd, 1978). Piaget used the term **horizontal décalage** (meaning development within a stage) to describe this gradual mastery of logical concepts. The horizontal décalage is another indication of the concrete operational child's difficulty with abstractions. School-age youngsters do not come up with the general principle of conservation and then apply it to all relevant situations. Rather, they seem to work out the logic of each problem they encounter separately.

## New Research on Concrete Operational Thought

From researchers' attempts to verify Piaget's assumptions about concrete operations, two themes emerge. The first has to do with the impact of specific experiences on the attainment of the concrete operational stage. The second deals with how best to explain children's sequential mastery of logical problems during middle childhood. Some theorists believe that the horizontal décalage can best be understood within an information processing framework.

**The Impact of Culture.** According to Piaget, brain maturation combined with experience in a rich and varied external world should lead children everywhere to reach the concrete operational stage. He did not believe that operational thinking depended on particular kinds of experiences. Yet recent evidence indicates that specific cultural practices have a great deal to do with children's mastery of Piagetian tasks (Rogoff, 1990).

A large body of evidence reveals that conservation develops at quite different times in different cultures. In non-Western societies, it is often greatly delayed. For example, among the Hausa of Nigeria, who live in small agricultural settlements and rarely send their children to school, even the most basic conservation tasks—number, length, and liquid—are not understood until age 11 or later (Fahrmeier, 1978). This suggests that for children to master conservation and other Piagetian concepts, they must take part in everyday activities that promote this way of thinking (Light & Perrett-Clermont, 1989). Joey and Lizzie, for example, have learned to think of fairness in terms of equal distribution—a value emphasized in their culture. They

**Horizontal décalage**
Development within a Piagetian stage. Gradual mastery of logical concepts during the concrete operational stage provides an example.

have frequent opportunities to divide materials, such as crayons, Halloween treats, and lemonade, equally among themselves and their friends. Because they often see the same quantity arranged in different ways, they grasp conservation early. For children who grow up in societies where equal sharing of goods is not common, conservation is unlikely to appear at the expected age.

These findings may remind you of a challenge to Piaget's theory we have mentioned several times before. Some investigators believe that conservation of number, mass, area, and weight are not natural forms of logic that emerge spontaneously in all children. Instead, they regard these concepts as socially generated—as outcomes of practical activities in particular cultures. This approach to cognitive development is much like Vygotsky's sociocultural theory, which we discussed in earlier chapters.

***An Information Processing View of the Horizontal Décalage.*** If you think carefully about the horizontal décalage, you will see that it too raises a familiar question about Piaget's theory: Is an abrupt stagewise transition to logical thought the best way to describe cognitive development in middle childhood? In Chapter 9, we showed that the beginnings of logical thinking are evident during the preschool years on simplified and familiar tasks. The horizontal décalage suggests that logical understanding continues to improve over the school years.

Some theorists argue that the development of operational thinking can best be understood in terms of gains in information processing capacity rather than a sudden shift to a new stage. For example, Robbie Case (1985, 1991b) proposes that as children repeatedly use cognitive schemes, they demand less attention and become more automatic. This frees up space in *working memory* (see page 217) so that children can focus on combining old schemes and generating new ones. For instance, the child confronted with water poured from one container to another recognizes that height of the liquid changes. As this understanding becomes routine, the child notices that width of the water changes as well. Soon the child coordinates both these observations, and conservation of liquid is achieved. Then, as this logical idea becomes well practiced, the child transfers it to more demanding situations, such as area and weight. A similar explanation of the horizontal décalage has been suggested by Kurt Fischer (1980), who believes that eventually school-age youngsters coordinate several context-specific skills into a general logical principle. At this point, thinking is highly efficient and abstract—the kind of change we will see when we discuss formal operational thought in Chapter 15.

## Evaluation of the Concrete Operational Stage

Piaget was indeed correct that school-age youngsters approach a great many problems in systematic and rational ways that were not possible just a few years before. But whether it is best to regard this period in terms of *continuous* improvement in logical skills or *discontinuous* restructuring of children's thinking (as Piaget's stage idea assumes) is still an issue about which there is little agreement. A growing number of researchers think that both types of change may be involved (Carey, 1985; Case, 1991b; Fischer, 1980; Sternberg & Odagaki, 1989). From early to middle childhood, children apply logical schemes to a much wider range of tasks. Yet in the process, their thought seems to undergo qualitative change—toward a more comprehensive grasp of the underlying principles of logical thought. Piaget himself seems to have recognized this possibility in the very concept of the horizontal décalage. So perhaps some blend of Piagetian and information processing ideas holds greatest promise for understanding cognitive development in middle childhood. With this thought in mind, let's take a closer look at what the information processing perspective has to say about cognitive change during the school years.

**BRIEF REVIEW** During the concrete operational stage, thought is more logical, flexible, and organized than it was during the preschool years. The ability to conserve indicates that children can decenter and reverse their thinking. School-age children also have an improved grasp of classification, seriation, and spatial concepts. However, they cannot yet think abstractly. Cross-cultural findings raise questions about Piaget's assumption that mastery of concrete operational tasks emerges spontaneously in all children. In addition, the gradual development of operational concepts challenges Piaget's notion of an abrupt stagewise transition to logical thought. A blend of Piagetian and information processing views may be the best way to understand cognitive change in middle childhood.

• *Mastery of the conservation problems provides one illustration of Piaget's horizontal décalage. Review the preceding sections. Then list as many additional examples as you can find to show-that operational reasoning develops gradually over middle childhood.*

## INFORMATION PROCESSING IN MIDDLE CHILDHOOD

In contrast to Piaget's theory, which focuses on overall changes in children's approach to solving problems and interpreting their world, the information processing perspective examines separate aspects of thinking. Attention and memory, which underlie every act of cognition, are central concerns in middle childhood, just as they were during infancy and the preschool years. In addition, researchers have been interested in finding out how children's growing knowledge of the world and awareness of their own mental activities affect these basic components of thinking. Finally, increased understanding of how children process information is being applied to their academic learning in school—in particular, to reading and mathematics.

### Attention

During middle childhood, attention changes in three ways. It becomes more controlled, adaptable, and planful.

*Control.* As Joey and Lizzie moved through the elementary school years, they became better at deliberately attending to just those aspects of a situation that were relevant to their task goals, ignoring other sources of information. Researchers study this increasing control of attention by introducing irrelevant stimuli into a task. Then they see how well children attend to its central elements (Lane & Pearson, 1982). In a typical experiment of this kind, school-age children and adults were asked to sort decks of cards as fast as possible on the basis of shapes appearing on each card—for example, circles in one pile and squares in another. Some decks contained no irrelevant information. Others included irrelevant stimuli, such as lines running across the shapes or stars appearing above or below them. Children's ability to ignore unnecessary information was determined by seeing how much longer it took them to sort decks with irrelevant stimuli. Their ability to keep attention focused on central features of the task improved sharply between 6 and 9 years of age (Strutt, Anderson, & Well, 1975).

*Adaptability.* Older children are also more adaptable; they flexibly adjust their attention to the momentary requirements of situations. For example, in judging whether pairs of stimuli are the same or different, sixth graders quickly shift their basis of judgment (from size to shape to color) when asked to do so. Second graders have trouble with this type of task (Pick & Frankel, 1974).

Older children also adapt their attention to changes in their own learning. When studying for a spelling test, 10-year-old Joey devoted most attention to the words he knew least well. Lizzie was much less likely to do so (Flavell, 1985).

*Planfulness.*   School-age children's attentional strategies become more planful. With age, they scan detailed pictures and written materials more thoroughly for similarities and differences (Vurpillot, 1968). And on complex tasks, they make decisions about what to do first and what to do next in an orderly fashion. In one study, 5- to 9-year-olds were given lists of 25 items to obtain from a play grocery store. Before starting on a shopping trip, older children more often took time to scan the store, and they also followed shorter routes through the aisles (Gauvain & Rogoff, 1989).

Why does attention improve so rapidly from early to middle childhood? At present, researchers are not sure. They do know that gains in attention are critical for successful performance in school. Unfortunately, some children have great difficulty focusing and sustaining attention during the school years. See Box 12.1 for a discussion of the serious learning and behavior problems of *attention-deficit hyperactivity disordered* children.

## Memory Strategies

As attention improves with age, so do *memory strategies,* the deliberate mental activities we use to store and retain information. During the school years, these techniques for holding information in working memory and transferring it to our long-term knowledge base take a giant leap forward (Kail, 1990).

When Lizzie had a list of things to learn, such as a phone number, the capitals of the United States, or the names of geometric shapes, she immediately used **rehearsal,** repeating the information to herself over and over again. This memory strategy first appears in the early grade-school years. Soon after, a second strategy becomes common: **organization.** Children group related items together (for example, all capitals in the same part of the country), an approach that improves recall dramatically (Bjorklund & Muir, 1988; Keeney, Canizzo, & Flavell, 1967).

Memory strategies require time and effort to perfect. At first, school-age children do not use them very effectively. For example, 8-year-old Lizzie rehearsed in a piecemeal fashion. After being given the word *cat* in a list of items, she said, "Cat, cat, cat." In contrast, 10-year-old Joey combined previous words with each new item, saying, "Desk, man, yard, cat, cat" (Kunzinger, 1985; Ornstein, Naus, & Liberty, 1975). Joey also organized more skillfully, grouping items into fewer categories. Not surprisingly, Joey retained much more information (Frankel & Rollins, 1985).

Children start to use a third memory strategy, **elaboration,** by the end of middle childhood. It involves creating a relationship, or shared meaning, between two or more pieces of information that are not members of the same category. For example, suppose the words *fish* and *pipe* are among those you want to learn. If, in trying to remember them, you generate a mental image of a fish smoking a pipe or recite a sentence expressing this relationship ("The fish puffed the pipe"), you are using elaboration. Once children discover this memory technique, they find it so effective that it tends to replace other strategies. Elaboration develops late because it requires a great deal of mental effort. To use it, children must translate items into images and think of a relationship between them. Elaboration becomes increasingly common during adolescence and young adulthood (Schneider & Pressley, 1989).

Because the strategies of organization and elaboration combine items into *meaningful chunks,* they permit children to hold on to much more information at once. As a result, the capacity of working memory expands. In addition, when children store a new item in long-term memory by linking it to information they already know, they can *retrieve* it easily by thinking of other items associated with it. As we will see in the next section, this is one reason that memory improves steadily during the school years.

---

**Attention-deficit hyperactivity disorder (ADHD)**

A childhood disorder involving inattentiveness, impulsivity, and excessive motor activity. Often leads to academic failure and social problems.

**Rehearsal**

The memory strategy of repeating information.

**Organization**

The memory strategy of grouping related items in a list.

**Elaboration**

The memory strategy of creating a relation between two or more items that are not members of the same category.

## FROM RESEARCH TO PRACTICE

### Box 12.1  *Attention-Deficit Hyperactivity Disordered Children*

While the other fifth graders worked quietly at their desks, Calvin squirmed in his seat, dropped his pencil, looked out the window, fiddled with his shoelaces, and talked out. "Hey Joey," he yelled over the top of several desks, "wanna play ball after school?" Joey didn't answer. He wasn't eager to play with Calvin. Out on the playground, Calvin was a poor listener and failed to follow the rules of the game. When up at bat, he had difficulty taking turns. In the outfield, he tossed his mitt up in the air and looked elsewhere when the ball came his way. Calvin's desk at school and his room at home were a chaotic mess. He often lost pencils, books, and other materials necessary for completing assignments.

Calvin is one of 3 to 5 percent of school-age children with **attention-deficit hyperactivity disorder (ADHD),** a problem that is 4 to 5 times more common among boys than girls (American Psychiatric Association, 1987). These youngsters have great difficulty staying on task for more than a few minutes. In addition, they often act impulsively, ignoring social rules and lashing out with hostility when frustrated. Many (but not all) are *hyperactive*. They charge through their days with excessive motor activity, leaving parents and teachers frazzled and other children annoyed. ADHD youngsters have few friends; they are soundly rejected by their classmates (Henker & Whalen, 1989).

The intelligence of ADHD children is normal, and they show no signs of serious emotional disturbance. Instead, attentional difficulties are at the heart of their problems. They do poorly on laboratory tasks requiring sustained attention, and they find it hard to ignore irrelevant information (Douglas, 1983; Landau, Milich, & Lorch, 1992). Although some outgrow these difficulties, most ADHD youngsters continue to have problems concentrating and finding friends into adolescence and adulthood.

ADHD does not have one single cause. Heredity plays some role, since identical twins tend to share the disorder more often than do fraternals. Also, an adopted child who is inattentive and hyperactive is likely to have a biological parent (but not an adoptive parent) with similar symptoms (Alberts-Corush, Firestone, & Goodman, 1986; O'Connor et al., 1980). At the same time, ADHD is associated with a variety of environmental factors. These children are somewhat more likely to come from homes in which marriages are unhappy and family stress is high (Whalen, 1983). Also, recall from earlier chapters that prenatal teratogens (including alcohol and smoking) as well as exposure to lead are linked to later attentional problems. Dietary causes, such as food additives and sugar, have been suggested, but there is little evidence that these play important roles (Henker & Whalen, 1989; Milich & Pelham, 1986).

Calvin's doctor eventually prescribed stimulant medication, the most common treatment for ADHD. As long as dosage is carefully regulated, these drugs reduce activity level and improve attention, academic performance, and peer relations for 70 percent of children who take them (Barkley, 1990). Researchers do not know precisely why stimulants are helpful. Some believe that ADHD children are chronically underaroused. That is, normal levels of stimulation do not engage their interest and attention. They seek excitement anywhere and everywhere, attending to irrelevant features of the environment and engaging in high rates of motor activity. Stimulant drugs may work because they have an alerting effect on the central nervous system. As a result, they decrease the child's need to engage in off-task and self-stimulating behavior.

Drug treatment by itself does not eliminate all these children's difficulties. Recent evidence suggests that combining medication with interventions that model and reinforce appropriate academic and social behavior may be the most effective approach to helping children with ADHD (Barkley, 1990). Teachers can also create conditions in classrooms that support these pupils' special learning needs. Short work periods followed by a chance to get up and move around help them concentrate. Finally, family intervention is particularly important. Inattentive, overactive children strain the patience of parents, who are likely to react punitively and inconsistently in return—a child-rearing style that strengthens inappropriate behavior. Breaking this cycle is as important for ADHD children as it is for the defiant, aggressive youngsters we discussed in Chapter 10. In fact, 50 percent of the time these two sets of behavior problems occur together (Henker & Whalen, 1989).

## The Knowledge Base and Memory Performance

During middle childhood, the long-term knowledge base grows larger and becomes better organized. Children arrange the vast amount of information in their memories into increasingly elaborate, hierarchically structured networks (Ford & Keating, 1981). Some researchers believe that this rapid growth of knowledge helps children use strategies and remember. In other words, knowing more about a particular topic makes new information more meaningful and familiar so it is easier to store and retrieve (Bjorklund & Muir, 1988; Chi & Ceci, 1987).

If children's growing knowledge base does account for better memory performance, then in areas in which children are more knowledgeable than adults, they should show better recall. To test this idea, Michelene Chi (1978) looked at how well third- through eighth-grade chess experts could remember complex chessboard arrangements. The youngsters were compared to adults who knew how to play chess but were not especially knowledgeable. Just as expected, the children could reproduce the chessboard configurations considerably better than the adults could. These findings cannot be explained by the selection of very bright youngsters with exceptional memories. On a standard memory span task in which the subjects had to recall a list of numbers, the adults did better than the children (see Figure 12.1). The children showed superior memory performance only in the domain of knowledge in which they were expert.

Although knowledge clearly plays an important role in memory development, it may have to be quite broad and well-structured before it can facilitate the use of strategies and recall. A brief series of lessons designed to increase knowledge in a particular area does not affect children's ability to remember new information in that domain (DeMarie-Dreblow, 1991). Until children have enough knowledge and have had time to connect it into stable, well-formed hierarchies, they may not be able to apply it to new memory problems (Chi & Ceci, 1987).

Finally, we must keep in mind that knowledge is not the only important factor in children's strategic memory processing. Children who are expert in a particular area, whether it be chess, math, social studies, or spelling, are usually highly motivated. Faced with new material, they say to themselves, "What can I do to clarify the meaning of this information so I can learn it more easily?" As a result, they not only

**FIGURE 12.1** • Performance of skilled child chess players and adults on two tasks: memory for complex chessboard arrangements and numerical digits. The child chess experts recalled more on the chess task, the adults on the digit task. These findings show that size of the knowledge base contributes to memory performance. (*Adapted from Chi, 1978.*)

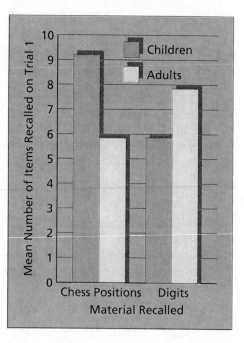

acquire knowledge more quickly, but they *actively use what they already know* to add more. Research indicates that academically successful and unsuccessful fifth graders differ in just this way. Poor students fail to approach memory tasks by asking how previously stored information can clarify new material. This, in turn, interferes with the development of a broad knowledge base (Bransford et al., 1981; Brown et al., 1983). So at least by the end of the school years, knowledge acquisition and use of memory strategies are intimately related and mutually support one another.

## Culture and Memory Strategies

Think, for a moment, about the kinds of situations in which the strategies of rehearsal, organization, and elaboration are useful. People usually employ these techniques when they need to remember information for its own sake. On many other occasions, they participate in daily activities that produce excellent memory as a natural by-product of the activity itself. For example, Joey can spout off a wealth of facts about baseball teams and players—information he picked up from watching the game, discussing it, and trading baseball cards with his friends.

A repeated finding of cross-cultural research is that people in non-Western cultures who have no formal schooling do not use or benefit from instruction in memory strategies (Cole & Scribner, 1977; Rogoff, 1990). This suggests that experiences associated with going to school promote these conscious memorizing techniques. Tasks that require children to recall isolated bits of information for their own sake are common in classrooms. In fact, Western children get so much practice with this type of learning that they do not refine other techniques for remembering that rely on spatial location and arrangement of objects, cues that are readily available in everyday life. Australian aboriginal and Guatemalan Mayan children are considerably better at these memory skills (Kearins, 1981; Rogoff, 1986). Looked at in this way, the development of memory strategies is not just a matter of a more competent information processing system. It is also a product of task demands and cultural circumstances.

## The School-Age Child's Theory of Mind

During middle childhood, children's *theory of mind,* or set of beliefs about mental activities, becomes much more elaborate and refined. You may recall from Chapter 9 that this awareness of cognitive processes is often referred to as *metacognition.* School-age children's improved ability to reflect on their own mental life is another reason for the advances in thinking and problem solving that take place at this time.

Unlike preschoolers, who view the mind as a passive container of information, older children regard it as an active, constructive agent capable of selecting and transforming information (Pillow, 1988; Wellman, 1988a). Consequently, they have a much better understanding of the impact of psychological factors on cognitive performance. They know, for example, that doing well on a task depends on focusing attention—concentrating on it, wanting to do it, and not being tempted by anything else (Miller & Bigi, 1979). They are also aware that in studying material for later recall, it is helpful to devote most effort to items that you know least well. And when asked, elementary school pupils show that they know quite a bit about effective memory strategies. Witness this 8-year-old's response to the question of what she would do to remember a phone number:

> Say the number is 663-8854. Then what I'd do is—say that my number is 663, so I won't have to remember that, really. And then I would think now I've got to remember 88. Now I'm 8 years old, so I can remember, say, my age two times. Then I say how old my brother is, and how old he was last year. And that's how I'd usually remember that phone number. [Is that how you would most often remember a phone number?] Well, usually I write it down. (Kreutzer, Leonard, & Flavell, 1975, p. 11)

*School-age children have an improved ability to reflect on their own mental life. This child is aware that external aids to memory are often necessary to ensure that information will be retained.* (Frank Siteman/The Picture Cube)

This child clearly understands the importance of establishing connections between new information and existing knowledge. And she also recognizes that she can use external aids to enhance memory—in this case, writing the phone number down.

Once children become conscious of the many factors that influence how well they do on a task, they combine these into an integrated understanding of mental activity. School-age youngsters are far more likely than preschoolers to take account of *interactions* among variables—how age and motivation of the learner, effective use of strategies, and nature and difficulty of the task work together to affect cognitive performance (Wellman, 1985). In this way, metacognition truly becomes a comprehensive theory during middle childhood.

## Self-Regulation

Although metacognition expands, school-age youngsters often have difficulty putting what they know about thinking into action. They are not yet good at **self-regulation,** the process of continuously monitoring progress toward a goal, checking outcomes, and redirecting unsuccessful efforts. For example, Lizzie is aware that she should group items together in a memory task and that she should read a complicated paragraph more than once to make sure she understands it. But she does not always do these things when working on an assignment (Brown et al., 1983).

It is not surprising that the capacity for self-regulation develops slowly. Monitoring learning outcomes is a cognitively demanding activity itself, requiring moment-by-moment evaluation of effort and progress. Self-regulation does not become well developed until adolescence. By then it is a strong predictor of academic success. Students who do well in school know when they possess a skill and when they do not. If they run up against obstacles, such as poor study conditions, a confusing text passage, or a class presentation that is unclear, they take steps to organize the learning environment, review the material, or seek other sources of support. This active, purposeful approach contrasts sharply with the passive orientation of students who do poorly (Borkowski et al., 1990; Zimmerman, 1990).

**Self-regulation**
The process of continuously monitoring progress toward a goal, checking outcomes, and redirecting efforts that prove unsuccessful.

Parents and teachers can foster children's self-regulatory skills by pointing out the special demands of tasks, indicating how use of strategies will improve performance, and emphasizing the value of self-correction. Many studies show that providing children with instructions to check and monitor their progress toward a goal has a substantial impact on how well they do (Pressley & Ghatala, 1990).

Children who acquire effective self-regulatory skills succeed at challenging tasks. As a result, they develop confidence in their own ability—a belief that supports the use of self-regulation in the future (Paris & Newman, 1990; Schunk, 1990). Unfortunately, some children receive messages from parents and teachers that seriously undermine their academic self-esteem and self-regulatory skills. We will consider the special problems of these *learned helpless* youngsters, along with ways to help them, in Chapter 13.

### Applications of Information Processing to Academic Learning

Joey entered first grade able to recognize only a handful of written words. By fifth grade, he was a proficient reader. His eyes moved quickly across the page, and his hand flew up when the teacher asked questions that probed how well the children understood an assignment. Similarly, at age 6 Joey had an informally acquired knowledge of number concepts. By age 10, he could add, subtract, multiply, and divide with ease, and he had begun to master fractions and percentages.

Over the past decade, fundamental discoveries about the development of information processing have been applied to children's learning of reading and mathematics. Researchers have begun to identify the cognitive ingredients of skilled performance, trace their development, and distinguish good from poor learners by pinpointing the cognitive skills in which they are deficient. They hope, as a result, to design teaching methods that will help children master these essential skills.

**Reading.** While reading, we use a large number of skills at once, taxing all aspects of our information processing systems. We must perceive single letters and letter combinations, translate them into speech sounds, hold chunks of text in working memory while interpreting their meaning, and combine the meanings of various parts of a text passage into an understandable whole. In fact, reading is such a demanding process that most or all of these skills must be done automatically. If one or more are poorly developed, they will compete for space in our limited working memories, and reading performance will decline (Perfetti, 1988).

Researchers do not yet know how children manage to acquire and combine all these varied skills into fluent reading. Currently, psychologists and educators are engaged in a "great debate" about how to teach beginning reading. On one side are those who take a **whole language approach** to reading instruction. They argue that reading should be taught in a way that parallels natural language learning. From the very beginning, children should be exposed to text in its complete form—stories, poems, letters, posters, and lists—so they can appreciate the communicative function of written language. According to these experts, as long as reading is kept whole and meaningful, children will be motivated to discover the specific skills they need as they gain experience with the printed word (Goodman, 1986; Watson, 1989). On the other side of the debate are those who advocate a **basic skills approach.** According to this view, children should be given simplified text materials. At first, they should be coached on *phonics*—the basic rules for translating written symbols into sounds. Only later, after they have mastered these skills, should they get complex reading material (Rayner & Pollatsek, 1989; Samuels, 1985).

As yet, research does not show clear-cut superiority for either of these approaches (McKenna, Robinson, & Miller, 1990). In fact, a third group of experts believes that children may learn best when they receive a balanced mixture of both (Barr, 1991).

**Whole language approach**

An approach to beginning reading instruction that parallels children's natural language learning and keeps reading materials whole and meaningful.

**Basic skills approach**

An approach to beginning reading instruction that emphasizes training in phonics—the basic rules for translating written symbols into sounds—and simplified reading materials.

Learning the basics—relationships between letters and sounds—enables children to decipher words that they have never seen before. As this process becomes more automatic, it releases children's attention to the higher-level activities involved in comprehending the text's meaning. But if practice in basic skills is overemphasized, children may lose sight of the goal of reading—understanding. Many teachers report cases of pupils who can read aloud fluently but who register little or no meaning. These children might have been spared serious reading problems if they had been exposed to rich early childhood literacy experiences (see Chapter 9) followed by meaning-based instruction that included attention to basic skills.

***Mathematics.*** Once children enter elementary school, they apply their rich informal knowledge of number concepts and counting to more complex mathematical skills (Resnick, 1989). For example, children first understand multiplication as a kind of repeated addition. When given the following problem, "Sue has 5 books. Joe has 3 times as many. How many books does Joe have?", Lizzie thought to herself, "What's 5 × 3?" When she had difficulty remembering the answer, she said, "Okay, it's got to be 5 books + 5 books + 5 books. I know, it's 15!" Lizzie's use of addition strengthened her understanding of multiplication. It also helped her recall a multiplication fact that she had been trying to memorize.

Mathematics as taught in many classrooms, however, does not make good use of children's basic grasp of number concepts. Children are given procedures for solving problems without linking these to their informally acquired understandings. Consequently, they often apply a rule that is close to what they have been taught but that yields a wrong answer. Their mistakes indicate that they have tried to memorize a method, but they do not comprehend the basis for it. For example, look at the following subtraction errors made by two of Lizzie's classmates:

$$
\begin{array}{r}
427 \\
-138 \\
\hline
311
\end{array}
\qquad
\begin{array}{r}
{}^{6\ \ 1} \\
7002 \\
-5445 \\
\hline
1447
\end{array}
$$

In the first problem, the child consistently subtracts a smaller from a larger digit, regardless of which is on top. In the second, columns with zeros are skipped in a borrowing operation, and whenever there is a zero on top, the bottom digit is written as the answer. Some researchers believe that drill-oriented math instruction that provides children with little information on the reasons behind procedures is at the heart of these difficulties (Fuson, 1990; Resnick, 1989).

Arguments about how to teach early mathematics closely resemble the positions we considered earlier in the area of reading. Drill in computational skills is pitted against "number sense" or understanding. Yet once again, a blend of the two is probably most beneficial. Research indicates that conceptual knowledge serves as a vital base for the development of accurate, efficient computation in middle childhood (Byrnes & Wasik, 1991). Yet comparisons of the math achievement of American and Asian children indicate that math instruction in the United States may have gone too far in emphasizing memorization over number concepts. As we will see later in this chapter, Japanese and Taiwanese children are considerably ahead of American pupils in mathematical development. In Asian classrooms, much more time is spent exploring underlying concepts and much less time is spent on drill and repetition (Stigler, Lee, & Stevenson, 1990).

**BRIEF REVIEW** Over the school years, attention becomes more controlled, adaptable, and planful, and memory strategies become more effective. An expanding knowledge base contributes to improved memory performance. However, children's

• *One day, the children in Lizzie and Joey's school saw a slide show about endangered species. They were told to remember as many animal names as they could. Fifth and sixth graders recalled considerably more than did second and third graders. What factors might account for this difference?*

• *Lizzie knows that if you have difficulty learning part of a task, you should devote most of your attention to that aspect. But she plays each of her piano pieces from beginning to end instead of picking out the hard parts for extra practice. What explains Lizzie's failure to apply what she knows?*

willingness to use what they know when learning new information is also important. Metacognition moves from a passive to an active view of mental functioning during middle childhood. Only gradually does it affect task performance. An important reason is that children have difficulty with self-regulation. Information processing has been applied to children's academic learning in school. Instruction that combines meaning and understanding with training in basic skills may be most effective in reading and mathematics.

## INDIVIDUAL DIFFERENCES IN MENTAL DEVELOPMENT DURING MIDDLE CHILDHOOD

During middle childhood, intelligence tests become an increasingly important means for assessing individual differences in mental development. Most children take these tests frequently—as often as every two or three years in school. Around age 6, IQ becomes more stable than it was at earlier ages, and it correlates well with academic achievement, from .40 to .70 (Siegler & Richards, 1982). Because IQ predicts school performance, it plays an important role in educational decisions. Children with low IQs who do poorly in school are often assumed to have limited potential to learn. Consequently, these pupils (a great many of whom come from low-income ethnic minority homes) may be placed in slower educational tracks, assigned to remedial classrooms, or held back in grade.

Do intelligence tests provide an accurate indication of the school-age child's ability to profit from instruction? In the following sections, we take a close look at this controversial issue.

### Defining and Measuring Intelligence

Take a moment to jot down a list of behaviors that you regard as typical of a highly intelligent school-age child. Did you come up with just one or two or a great many? Virtually all intelligence tests provide an overall score (the IQ), which is taken to represent *general intelligence* or reasoning ability. Yet a diverse array of tasks appear on most tests for children. Today, there is widespread agreement that intelligence is a collection of a great many mental capacities.

Test designers use a complicated statistical technique called *factor analysis* to identify the various abilities measured by questions on an intelligence test. This procedure determines which sets of items on the test correlate strongly with one another. Those that do are assumed to measure a similar ability and, therefore, are designated as a separate factor. To understand the types of intellectual factors measured in middle childhood, let's look at some representative intelligence tests and how they are administered.

**Some Representative Intelligence Tests.** Intelligence tests for children come in great variety. Those that Joey and Lizzie take every so often in school are *group administered tests*. They permit large numbers of pupils to be tested at once and require very little training of teachers who give them. Group tests are useful for instructional planning and identifying children who require more extensive evaluation with *individually administered tests*. Unlike group tests, individually administered ones demand considerable training and experience to give well. The examiner not only considers the child's answers but also carefully observes the child's behavior, noting such things as attentiveness to and interest in the tasks and wariness of the adult. These reactions provide insight into whether the test score is accurate or underestimates the child's abilities.

Two individual tests are most often used to identify highly intelligent children and diagnose those with learning problems. As we look briefly at these, refer to Figure 12.2, which shows some of the items that typically appear on intelligence tests for children.

*The Stanford-Binet Intelligence Scale.*   The modern descendent of Alfred Binet's first successful intelligence test is the **Stanford-Binet Intelligence Scale,** which is appropriate for individuals between 2 and 18 years of age. Its newest version, which appeared in 1986, measures both overall IQ and four intellectual factors: verbal reasoning, quantitative reasoning, spatial reasoning, and short-term memory (Thorndike, Hagen, & Sattler, 1986). Within these factors are 15 subtests that permit a detailed analysis of each child's mental abilities. The verbal and quantitative factors emphasize culturally loaded, fact-oriented information, such as the child's knowledge of vocabulary and comprehension of sentences. In contrast, the spatial reasoning factor is believed to be less culturally biased because it demands little in the way of specific information. Instead, it tests children's ability to see complex relationships, as illustrated by the spatial visualization item shown in Figure 12.2.

Like many new tests, the Stanford-Binet is designed to be sensitive to minority and handicapped children and to reduce sex bias. Pictures of children from different racial groups, a child in a wheelchair, and "unisex" figures that can be interpreted as male or female are included. One serious drawback is that this test takes an especially long time to give—up to 2 hours for some children (Sattler, 1988).

*The Wechsler Intelligence Scale for Children–III.*   The **Wechsler Intelligence Scale for Children–III (WISC-III)** is the third edition of a widely used test for 6- through 16-year-olds. A downward extension of it—the *Wechsler Preschool and Primary Scale of Intelligence–Revised (WPPSI–R)*—is appropriate for children 3 through 8 (Wechsler, 1989, 1991). The Wechsler tests offered both an overall IQ and a variety of separate factor scores long before the Stanford-Binet. As a result, over the past two decades, psychologists and educators have come to prefer the WISC and WPPSI.

Both the WISC–III and the WPPSI–R assess two broad intellectual factors: verbal and performance. Each contains 6 subtests, yielding 12 separate scores in all. Performance items (see examples in Figure 12.2) require the child to arrange materials rather than talk to the examiner. Consequently, these tests provided one of the first means through which non-English-speaking children and children with speech and language disorders could demonstrate their intellectual strengths.

The Wechsler tests were also the first to be standardized on samples representing the total population of the United States, including racial and ethnic minorities. Their broadly representative standardization samples have served as models for many other tests, including the recent version of the Stanford-Binet.

*Other Intelligence Tests.*   Although the Stanford-Binet and the Wechsler scales are the most well-known intelligence tests, others based on alternative approaches do exist. For example, several Piagetian tests for school-age children include a variety of conservation and classification problems (Goldschmid & Bentler, 1968; Humphreys, Rich, & Davey, 1985). Performance on these measures correlates well with IQ and achievement. But Piagetian tests have not caught hold strongly, largely because they do not sample as wide a range of mental abilities as the Stanford-Binet and Wechsler scales.

Perhaps the most innovative effort to measure children's intelligence in recent years is the **Kaufman Assessment Battery for Children (K-ABC).** It is the first major test to be grounded in information processing theory. Published in 1983, the K-ABC measures the intelligence of children from age 2 1/2 through 12 on the basis of two broad types of information processing skills. The first, *simultaneous processing,* demands that children integrate a variety of stimuli at the same time, as when they recall the placement of objects on a page presented only briefly. The second, *sequential processing,* refers to problems that require children to think in a step-by-step fashion.

---

**Stanford-Binet Intelligence Scale**

An individually administered intelligence test that is the modern descendent of Alfred Binet's first successful test for children. Measures overall IQ and four factors: verbal reasoning, quantitative reasoning, spatial reasoning, and short-term memory.

**Wechsler Intelligence Scale for Children–III (WISC–III)**

An individually administered intelligence test that includes both an overall IQ and a variety of verbal and performance scores.

**Kaufman Assessment Battery for Children (K-ABC)**

An individually administered intelligence test that measures two broad types of information processing skills: sequential and simultaneous processing. The first major test to be grounded in information processing theory.

| Item Type | **TYPICAL VERBAL ITEMS** |
|---|---|
| Vocabulary | Tell me what "carpet" means. |
| General Information | How many ounces make a pound?<br>What day of the week comes right after Thursday? |
| Verbal Comprehension | Why are policemen needed? |
| Verbal Analogies | A rock is hard; a pillow is _____ . |
| Logical Reasoning | Five girls are sitting side by side on a bench. Jane is in the middle and Betty sits next to her on the right. Alice is beside Betty, and Dale is beside Ellen, who sits next to Jane. Who are sitting on the ends? |
| Number Series | Which number comes next in the series?<br>**4   8   6   12   10   ____** |

**TYPICAL NONVERBAL ITEMS**

| | |
|---|---|
| Picture Oddities | Which picture does not belong with the others? |

| | |
|---|---|
| Spatial Visualization | Which of the boxes on the right can be made from the pattern shown on the left? |

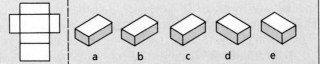

| | |
|---|---|
| Picture Series | Put the pictures in the right order so that what is happening makes sense. |

| | |
|---|---|
| Puzzles | Put these pieces together so they make a wagon. |

**FIGURE 12.2** • Sample items similar to those that appear on common intelligence tests for children. In contrast to verbal items, nonverbal items do not require reading or direct use of language. Performance items are also nonverbal, but they require the child to draw or construct something rather than merely give a correct answer. As a result, they appear only on individually administered intelligence tests. (*Logical reasoning, picture oddities, and spatial visualization examples are adapted with permission of The Free Press, a Division of Macmillan, Inc., from Arthur R. Jensen, 1980, Bias in mental testing, New York: Free Press, pp. 150, 154, 157.*)

Examples include repeating a series of digits or hand movements presented by the examiner. The K-ABC also makes a special effort to respond to the needs of culturally different children. If a child fails one of the first three items on any subtest, the examiner is permitted to "teach the task." The tester can use alternative wording and gestures and may even communicate in a language other than English (Kaufman & Kaufman, 1983).

The K-ABC is not without its critics. Some point out that the test samples a very narrow range of information processing skills and that there is little research support for the simultaneous/sequential processing distinction (Goetz & Hall, 1984; Sternberg, 1984). Nevertheless, the K-ABC is responsive to a new trend to define intelligence in terms of cognitive processes, as we will see in the following section.

*Recent Developments in Defining Intelligence.*   As the K-ABC suggests, researchers have started to combine the factor analytic approach to defining intelligence with information processing. Those involved in this effort believe that factors on intelligence tests are of limited usefulness unless we can identify the cognitive processes responsible for them. Once we understand the underlying basis of IQ, we will know much more about why a particular child does well or poorly and what capacities must be worked on to improve performance. These researchers conduct *componential analyses* of children's IQ scores. This means that they look for relationships between aspects (or components) of information processing and intelligence test scores (Sternberg, 1985b). Preliminary findings reveal that the speed with which individuals can perceive information and manipulate it in working memory is related to IQ (Jensen, 1985a, 1988; Larson, 1989).

The componential approach has one major shortcoming: It regards intelligence as entirely due to causes within the child. Yet throughout this book, we have seen how cultural and situational factors profoundly affect children's cognitive skills. Recently, Robert Sternberg expanded the componential approach into a comprehensive theory that regards intelligence as a product of both inner and outer forces.

*Sternberg's Triarchic Theory.*   As shown in Figure 12.3, Sternberg's (1985a, 1988a) **triarchic theory of intelligence** is made up of three interacting subtheories. The first, the *componential subtheory*, spells out the information processing skills that underlie intelligent behavior. You are already familiar with its main elements—strategy application, knowledge acquisition, metacognition, and self-regulation.

According to Sternberg, children's use of these components is not just a matter of internal capacity. It is also a function of the conditions under which intelligence is assessed. The *experiential subtheory* states that highly intelligent individuals, in comparison to less intelligent ones, process information more skillfully in novel situations. When given a relatively new task, the bright person learns rapidly, making strategies automatic so working memory is freed for more complex aspects of the situation.

Think, for a moment, about the implications of this idea for measuring children's intelligence. To accurately compare children in brightness—in ability to deal with novelty and learn efficiently—all children would need to be presented with equally unfamiliar test items. Otherwise, some children will appear more intelligent than others simply because of their past experiences, not because they are really more cognitively skilled. These children start with the unfair advantage of prior practice on the tasks.

This point brings us to the third part of Sternberg's model, his *contextual subtheory*. It proposes that intelligent people skillfully *adapt* their information processing skills to fit with their personal desires and the demands of their everyday worlds. When they cannot adapt to a situation, they try to *shape*, or change it to meet their needs. If they cannot shape it, they *select* new contexts that are consistent with their goals. The contextual subtheory emphasizes that intelligent behavior is never culture-

**Triarchic theory of intelligence**
Sternberg's theory, which states that information processing skills, prior experience with tasks, and contextual factors interact to determine intelligent behavior.

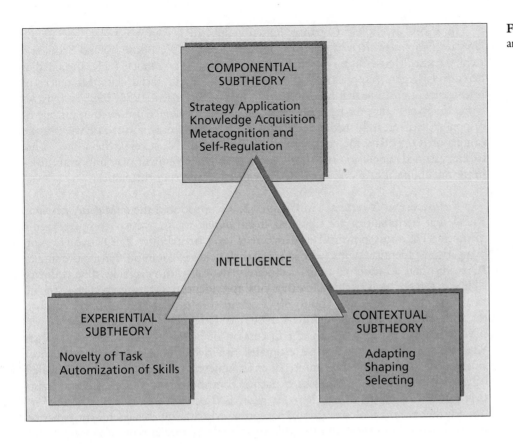

**FIGURE 12.3** • Sternberg's tri-archic theory of intelligence.

free. Because of their backgrounds, some children come to value behaviors required for success on intelligence tests, and they easily adapt to the tasks and testing conditions. Others with different life histories misinterpret the testing context or reject it entirely because it does not suit their needs. Yet such children may display very sophisticated abilities in daily life—for example, telling stories, engaging in complex artistic activities, or interacting skillfully with other people (Sternberg, 1988a).

Sternberg's theory emphasizes the complexity of intelligent behavior and the wide variety of human mental skills, all of which are not included on intelligence tests. As you can already see, his ideas are relevant to the controversy surrounding cultural bias in IQ testing. In the following sections, we turn to genetic and environmental influences on the IQ score.

### Explaining Individual Differences in IQ

When we compare individuals in terms of academic achievement, years of education, and the status of their occupations, it quickly becomes clear that certain sectors of the population are advantaged over others. In trying to explain these differences, researchers have examined the intelligence test performance of children from different ethnic and social class backgrounds. Many studies show that American black children score, on the average, 15 IQ points below American white children (Brody, 1985). Social class differences in IQ also exist. The gap between middle-income and low-income children is about 9 points (Jensen & Figueroa, 1975). These figures are, of course, averages. There is considerable variation *within* each race and social class. Still, racial and social class differences in IQ are large enough and of serious enough consequence that they cannot be ignored.

In 1969, psychologist Arthur Jensen published a controversial article in the *Harvard Educational Review* entitled, "How Much Can We Boost IQ and Scholastic Achievement?" Jensen's answer to this question was "not much." He argued that heredity is largely responsible for individual, racial, and social class differences in intelligence, a position that he continues to maintain (Jensen, 1980, 1985a). Jensen's work received widespread public attention. It was followed by an outpouring of responses and research studies, leading to a heated nature–nurture debate on the origins of IQ. Today, the controversy has died down. Most researchers have come to the reasoned conclusion that both heredity and environment play important roles in mental ability. Let's look carefully at evidence addressing this issue.

***Nature versus Nurture.***   In Chapter 2, we introduced the *heritability estimate*. Recall that heritabilities are obtained from *kinship studies,* which compare family members. The most powerful evidence regarding heritability of IQ involves twin comparisons. Identical twins (who share all their genes in common) have more similar IQ scores than do fraternal twins (who are genetically no more alike than ordinary siblings). On the basis of this and other kinship evidence, current researchers estimate the heritability of IQ to be about .50 (Loehlin, 1989). This means that about half the differences in IQ among children can be traced to their genetic makeup. However, if you return for a moment to our discussion of heritability in Chapter 2 (pages 82–84), you will see that these estimates risk overestimating genetic influences and underestimating the importance of environment. Although heritability research offers convincing evidence that genetic factors contribute to IQ, disagreement persists over just how large the role of heredity really is (Ceci, 1990).

Furthermore, a widespread misconception exists that if a characteristic is heritable, then the environment can do little to affect it. A special type of kinship study, involving adopted children and their biological and adoptive relatives, shows that this assumption is untrue. In one investigation of this kind, children of two extreme groups of biological mothers, those with IQs below 95 and those with IQs above 120, were chosen for special study. All the children were adopted at birth by parents who were well above average in income and education. When tested during the school years, children of the low-IQ biological mothers scored above average in IQ, indicating that test performance can be greatly improved by an advantaged home life! At the same time, they did not do as well as children of brighter natural mothers placed in similar adoptive families. Adoption research confirms the balanced position that both heredity and environment affect IQ scores (Horn, 1983; Willerman, 1979).

Some intriguing adoption research also sheds light on the origins of the black–white IQ gap. Black children placed into well-to-do white homes during the first year of life also score high on intelligence tests. In two such studies, adopted black children attained mean IQs of 110 and 117, well above average and 20 to 30 points higher than the typical scores of children growing up in low-income black communities (Moore, 1986; Scarr & Weinberg, 1983). These findings reveal that genetic factors cannot be responsible for the lower IQs of black children! Instead, the destructive impact of poverty depresses the intelligence of large numbers of ethnic minority youngsters. And in many other cases, unique cultural values and practices do not prepare these children for the kinds of intellectual tasks that are sampled by intelligence tests and valued in school.

***Cultural Influences.***   Jermaine, a black child in Lizzie's third-grade class, participated actively in class discussion and wrote complex, imaginative stories. But he did not enter first grade feeling so comfortable with classroom life. At the beginning, Jermaine responded, "I don't know," to the simplest of questions, including "What's your name?" Fortunately, Jermaine's teacher understood his uneasiness. Slowly and gently, she helped him build a bridge between the learning style fostered by his cultural background and the style necessary for academic success. A growing body of evidence reveals that IQ scores are affected by specific learning experiences, including exposure to certain language customs and knowledge.

*Language Customs.* Ethnic minority subcultures often foster unique language skills that do not fit the expectations of most classrooms and testing situations. Shirley Brice Heath (1982, 1989), an anthropologist who has spent many hours observing in low-income black homes in a southeastern American city, found that black children were asked very different kinds of questions than is typical in white middle-class families. From an early age, white parents ask knowledge-training questions, such as "What color is it?" and "What's this story about?", that resemble the questioning style of tests and classrooms. In contrast, the black parents asked only "real" questions—ones that they themselves did not know the answer to. Often these were analogy questions ("What's that like?") or story-starter questions ("Didja hear Miss Sally this morning?") that called for elaborate responses about whole events and had no single right answer. The black children developed complex verbal skills at home, such as storytelling and exchanging quick-witted remarks. Unfortunately, these worked poorly when they got to school. The children were confused by the questions in classrooms and often withdrew into silence.

When faced with the strangeness of the testing situation, the minority child may look to the examiner for cues about how to respond. Yet most intelligence tests permit tasks to be presented in only one way, and they allow no feedback to children. Consequently, minority children may simply give the first answer that comes to mind, not one that truly represents what they know. For example, look at the following responses of a black child to a series of test questions:

> Tester: "How are wood and coal alike? How are they the same?"
> Child: "They're hard."
> Tester: "An apple and a peach?"
> Child: "They taste good."
> Tester: "A ship and an automobile?"
> Child: "They're hard."
> Tester "Iron and silver?"
> Child: "They're hard." (Miller-Jones, 1989, p. 362)

Earlier in the testing session, this child asked whether she was doing all right but got no reply. She probably repeated her first answer because she had trouble figuring out the task's meaning, not because she was unable to classify objects. Had the tester prompted her to look at the questions in a different way, she might have done better.

*Familiarity of Item Content.* Many researchers argue that IQ scores are affected by specific information acquired as part of middle-class upbringing. Even nonverbal test items (believed to be less culturally loaded) seem to depend on subtle learning opportunities. In one study, children's performance on a spatial reasoning task was related to the extent to which they had played a popular but expensive game sold in toy stores that (like the test item) required them to arrange blocks to duplicate a design as quickly as possible (Dirks, 1982). Low-income minority children, who are often raised in homes that are more "people-oriented" than "object-oriented," may lack opportunities to use games and objects that promote certain intellectual skills (Sternberg, 1988a).

That specific experiences affect performance on intelligence tests is also supported by a large body of evidence indicating that the amount of time a child spends in school is a strong predictor of IQ. When children of the same age who are in different grades are compared, those who have been in school longer score higher on intelligence tests. Similarly, dropping out of school leads to a decrease in IQ. The earlier children leave school, the greater their loss of IQ points. Taken together, these findings indicate that a more intelligent child may come to school with a greater ability to profit from instruction. But teaching children the factual knowledge and ways of thinking valued in classrooms has a sizable impact on their intelligence test performance (Ceci, 1990, 1991).

### Overcoming Cultural Bias in Intelligence Tests

While not all experts agree, today there is greater acknowledgment than ever before that IQ scores can underestimate the intelligence of children not reared in the culture of the tests and schools. A special concern exists about incorrectly labeling minority children as slow learners and assigning them to remedial classes, which are far less stimulating than regular school experiences (Landesman & Ramey, 1989). Jane Mercer (1979), a leader in the movement to create culture-fair tests, suggests that extra IQ points be added to the minority child's scores to compensate for lack of exposure to school-relevant knowledge. She also recommends that intellectual assessments include measures of adaptive behavior—children's ability to cope with the demands of their everyday environments. The child who does poorly on an IQ test yet plays a complex game on the playground, figures out how to rewire a broken TV, or cares for younger siblings responsibly is unlikely to be mentally deficient. As we will see later, current definitions of mental retardation do include both IQ and adaptive behavior. Although the notion of an adjusted IQ score is controversial, these proposals remind us that special precautions are needed in evaluating minority children.

A few experts believe intelligence tests are so biased that they should be banned entirely. Most regard this solution as unacceptable, since important educational decisions would be based only on subjective impressions. This policy actually increases the discriminatory placement of minority children! Intelligence tests are useful measures when interpreted carefully by examiners who are sensitive to the impact of culture on test performance (Reschly, 1981). The current effort to include culturally relevant materials and to permit examiners to adapt testing procedures to the needs of minorities is a positive one. The K-ABC, for example, cut the typical black–white IQ gap in half and nearly equalized the scores of Hispanic and white youngsters (Kaufman, Kamphaus, & Kaufman, 1985). Despite their limitations, IQ scores continue to be fairly accurate measures for the majority of Western children.

• *Desiree, a low-income black child, was quiet and withdrawn while taking an intelligence test. Later she remarked to her mother, "I can't understand why that lady asked me all those questions, like what a ball and stove are for. She's a grown-up. She must* know *what a ball and stove are for!" Using Sternberg's triarchic theory, explain Desiree's reaction to the testing situation. Why is Desiree's score likely to underestimate her intelligence?*

**BRIEF REVIEW** Intelligence tests for children measure overall IQ as well as a variety of separate intellectual factors. The Stanford-Binet Intelligence Scale and the Wechsler Intelligence Scale for Children–III (WISC–III) are commonly used tests in middle childhood. The Kaufman Assessment Battery for Children (K-ABC) is the first major test to be grounded in information processing theory. Recently, researchers have combined the factor analytic approach to defining intelligence with information processing in an effort to discover the cognitive processes underlying IQ scores. Sternberg has expanded this componential approach into a triarchic theory of intelligence. It states that information processing skills, prior experience with the tasks, and contextual factors (the child's cultural background and interpretation of the testing situation) interact to determine IQ. Heritability and adoption research shows that both genetic and environmental factors contribute to individual differences in intelligence. Because of different language customs and unfamiliar item content, the IQ scores of low-income minority children often do not reflect their true abilities.

## LANGUAGE DEVELOPMENT IN MIDDLE CHILDHOOD

Language continues to develop in middle childhood, although the changes that take place are less obvious than those that occurred at earlier ages. Vocabulary, grammar, and pragmatics expand and become more refined. In addition, children's attitude toward language undergoes a fundamental shift. School-age children attend to language much more directly. They develop *language awareness*.

### Vocabulary

Because the average 6-year-old's vocabulary is already quite large (about 14,000 words), parents and teachers usually do not notice rapid gains during the school years. Between the start of elementary school and young adulthood, vocabulary more than doubles, eventually reaching about 30,000 words. In addition (as we saw earlier in this chapter), the conceptual knowledge that underlies school-age children's vocabulary becomes better organized and hierarchically arranged. This change permits them to use words more precisely and to think about them differently than they did at younger ages.

If you look carefully at children's word definitions, you will see examples of this change. Five- and 6-year-olds give very concrete descriptions that refer to functions or appearance—for example, knife: "when you're cutting carrots"; bicycle: "it's got wheels, a chain, and handlebars." By the end of elementary school, their definitions emphasize more general, socially shared information. Synonyms and explanations of categorical relationships appear—for example, knife: "something you could cut with. A saw is like a knife. It could also be a weapon" (Litowitz, 1977; Wehren, DeLisi, & Arnold, 1981). This advance reflects the older child's ability to deal with word meanings on an entirely verbal plane. Fifth and sixth graders no longer need to be shown what a word refers to in order to understand it. They can add new words to their vocabulary simply by being given a definition (Dickinson, 1984).

School-age children's more reflective and analytical approach to language permits them to appreciate the multiple meanings of words. For example, they recognize that a great many words, such as "sharp" or "cool," have psychological as well as physical meanings: "What a *cool* shirt!" or "That movie was really *neat!*" This grasp of double meanings permits 8- to 10-year-olds to comprehend more subtle metaphors than they could at earlier ages, such as "sharp as a tack," "spilling the beans," and "left high and dry" (Waggoner & Palermo, 1989; Winner, 1988). It also leads to a change in children's humor. In middle childhood, riddles and puns requiring children to go back and forth between different meanings of the same key word are common:

> "Hey, did you take a bath?" "No! Why, is one missing?"
> "Order! Order in the court!" "Ham and cheese on rye, your honor?"
> "Why did the old man tiptoe past the medicine cabinet?" "Because he didn't want to wake up the sleeping pills."

Preschoolers may laugh at these statements because they are nonsensical. But they cannot tell a good riddle or pun, nor do they understand why these jokes are funny (McGhee, 1979).

### Grammar

Although children have mastered most of the grammar of their language by the time they enter school, use of complex grammatical constructions improves. The passive voice is one example. Preschoolers spontaneously produce some passive sentences. Most of these are abbreviated, as in "It got broken" or "They got lost." During middle childhood, children use the passive more frequently, and it expands into full statements, such as "The glass was broken by Mary" (Horgan, 1978). Older children also apply their understanding of the passive voice to a wider range of nouns and verbs. Preschoolers comprehend the passive best when the subject of the sentence is an animate being and the verb is an action word ("The *boy* is *kissed* by the girl"). During the school years, inanimate subjects, such as *drum* or *hat,* and experiential verbs, such as *like* or *know,* are included (Lempert, 1989; Pinker, Lebeaux, & Frost, 1987).

Another grammatical achievement of middle childhood is the understanding of infinitive phrases, such as the difference between "John is eager to please" and "John is easy to please" (Chomsky, 1969). Like gains in vocabulary, children's appreciation of these subtle grammatical distinctions is supported by their grasp of complex relationships and ability to deal with language on an entirely verbal plane. During middle childhood, children can judge the grammatical correctness of a sentence even if its meaning is false or senseless, whereas preschoolers cannot (Bialystok, 1986).

## Pragmatics

Improvements in pragmatics, the communicative side of language, take place in middle childhood. One of the most obvious gains is the ability to adapt to the needs of listeners in challenging communicative situations. In one study, 3- to 10-year-olds were brought into a laboratory and shown eight objects, all of which were similar in size, shape, and color. The children were asked to indicate which object they liked best as a birthday present for an imaginary friend. Preschoolers gave ambiguous descriptions, such as "the red one." In contrast, school-age youngsters referred to the objects in much more precise ways—for example, "the round red one with stripes on it" (Deutsch & Pechmann, 1982). On tasks like this one, older school-age children are also better at increasing the detail of their descriptions when told that the listener is a stranger who has never played with the objects before (Sonnenschein, 1986).

Conversational strategies also become more refined in middle childhood. For example, older children have a more advanced appreciation of how to phrase things to get their way. When faced with an adult who refuses to hand over a desired object, 9-year-olds, but not 5-year-olds, state their second requests more politely (Axia & Baroni, 1985). School-age children are also more sensitive than preschoolers to distinctions between the form and meaning of utterances. For example, the day after she forgot to take the garbage out, Lizzie knew that her mother's statement, "The garbage is beginning to smell," really meant, "Take that garbage out!" Making subtle inferences about the relationship between an utterance and its context is beyond the ability of preschoolers (Ackerman, 1978).

## Learning Two Languages at a Time

Like most American children, Joey and Lizzie speak only one language, their native tongue of English. Yet throughout the world, a great many children grow up as *bilinguals.* They learn two languages, and sometimes more than two, during the childhood years. Current estimates indicate that 2.5 million American school-age children speak a language other than English at home. This figure is expected to double by the year 2000 (Hakuta & Garcia, 1989).

Children can become bilingual in two ways: (1) by acquiring both languages at the same time in early childhood or (2) by learning a second language after mastering the first. Children of bilingual parents who teach them both languages in early childhood show no special problems with language development. For a time, they appear to develop more slowly because they mix the vocabulary and grammar of the two systems. But once they become aware that they are dealing with two separate languages, each develops independently. These children acquire normal native ability in

*Several million American school-age children speak a language other than English in their homes and neighborhoods. Research shows that bilingualism enhances many aspects of cognitive and language development. (Chet Seymour/The Picture Cube)*

the language of their surrounding community and good to native ability in the second language, depending on their exposure to it. When children acquire a second language after they already speak a first language, it generally takes them about a year to become as fluent in the second language as native-speaking agemates (Reich, 1986).

A large body of research shows that bilingualism has a positive impact on cognitive development. Children who are fluent in two languages do better than others on tests of analytical reasoning, concept formation, and cognitive flexibility (Hakuta, Ferdman, & Diaz, 1987). In addition, bilingual children are advanced in their ability to reflect on language. They are more conscious of language structure and detail, more aware that words are arbitrary symbols for objects and actions, and better at noticing errors of grammar and meaning in spoken and written prose (Bialystok, 1986; Galambos & Goldin-Meadow, 1990). This sensitivity to language as a system is a strong predictor of other measures of cognitive, language, and literacy development.

The advantages of bilingualism provide strong justification for bilingual education programs in American schools. Box 12.2 describes the current controversy over bilingual education in the United States. As you will see, bilingual children rarely receive support for their native language in classrooms. Yet bilingualism provides one of the best examples of how language, once learned, becomes an important tool of the mind and fosters cognitive growth. In fact, the goals of schooling could reasonably be broadened to include helping all children become bilingual, thereby fostering the cognitive, language, and cultural enrichment of the entire nation (Hakuta, 1986; Ruiz, 1988).

**BRIEF REVIEW** During the school years, vocabulary continues to increase rapidly, and children develop a more precise and flexible understanding of word meanings. Mastery of complex grammatical constructions becomes more refined. School-age children express themselves well in challenging communicative situations, and they acquire more subtle conversational strategies. Bilingualism has a positive impact on cognitive development and language awareness.

*• Ten-year-old Shana arrived home from school after a long day, sank into the living-room sofa, and commented, "I'm totally wiped out!" Megan, her 5-year-old sister, looked puzzled and asked, "What did'ya wipe out, Shana?" Explain Shana and Megan's different understandings of the meaning of this expression.*

## SOCIAL ISSUES

### Box 12.2  *Bilingual Education in the United States*

Vincente, a 7-year-old boy who recently immigrated from Mexico to the United States, attends a bilingual education classroom in a large American city. His teacher, Serena, is fluent in both Spanish and English. At the beginning of the year, Serena instructed Vincente and his classmates in their native tongue. As the children mixed with English-speaking youngsters at school and in the community, they quickly picked up English phrases, such as "My name is . . .," "I wanna," and "Show me." Serena reinforced her pupil's first efforts to speak English, helping them feel confident about communicating in a second language. Gradually, she introduced more English into classroom learning experiences. At the same time, she continued to strengthen the children's native language and culture.

Vincente is enrolled in one of many bilingual education programs serving the growing number of American children with limited proficiency in English. Although state and federal funding for bilingual education has increased in recent years, the question of how Vincente and his classmates should be taught continues to be hotly debated.

On one side of the controversy are those who believe that Vincente should be instructed only in English. According to this view, time spent communicating in the child's native tongue subtracts from English language achievement, which is crucial for success in the world of school and work. On the other side are educators like Serena, who are committed to truly *bilingual* education—developing Vincente's native language while fostering his mastery of English. Supporters of this view believe that providing instruction in the native tongue lets minority children know that their heritage is respected (McGroarty, 1992). In addition, by avoiding abrupt submersion in an English-speaking environment, bilingual education prevents *semilingualism*, or inadequate proficiency in both languages. When minority children experience a gradual loss of the first language as a result of being taught the second, they end up limited in both languages for a period of time, a circumstance that leads to serious academic difficulties. Semilingualism is one factor believed to contribute to the high rates of school failure and dropout among low-income Hispanic youngsters, who make up nearly

*When bilingual education programs provide instruction in both the child's native language and in English, children are more involved in learning and show superior language development. These native Spanish-speaking pupils receive reading instruction in Spanish. Bulletin boards in the classroom reveal that the children are also being introduced to English. (Bob Daemmrich/ Stock Boston)*

50 percent of the American language minority population (August & Garcia, 1988; Ruiz, 1988).

At present, public opinion sides with the first of these two viewpoints. Many states have passed laws declaring English to be their official language, creating conditions in which schools have no obligation to teach minority pupils in languages other than English. Yet research underscores the value of instruction in the child's native tongue. In classrooms where both languages are integrated into the curriculum, minority children are more involved in learning, participate more actively in class discussions, and acquire the second language more easily. In contrast, when teachers speak only in a language their pupils can barely understand, children display frustration, boredom, and withdrawal (Cazden, 1984; Wong-Fillmore et al., 1985).

*ASK SEVERAL PEOPLE* you know for their opinion on the value of bilingual education for ethnic minority children. Which side does each take on the controversy described here? For those who think children should be taught only in English, describe research findings on the benefits of bilingualism. Did any change their minds?

## CHILDREN'S LEARNING IN SCHOOL

Throughout this chapter, we have touched on evidence indicating that schools are vital forces in children's cognitive development, affecting their modes of remembering, reasoning, problem solving, and language skills. How do schools exert such a powerful impact? Research looking at schools as complex social systems—their educational philosophies, teacher–pupil interaction patterns, and the larger cultural context in which they are embedded—provides important insights into this question.

### The Educational Philosophy

Each teacher brings to the classroom an educational philosophy that plays a major role in children's learning experiences. Two philosophical approaches have been studied in American education. They differ in what children are taught, the way they are believed to learn, and how their progress is evaluated.

**Traditional versus Open Classrooms.** In a **traditional classroom,** children are relatively passive in the learning process. The teacher is the sole authority for knowledge, rules, and decision making and does most of the talking. Children spend most of the time seated at their desks, listening, responding when called on, and completing teacher-assigned tasks. Their progress is evaluated by how well they keep pace with a uniform set of standards for all pupils in their grade.

In contrast, in an **open classroom,** children are viewed as active agents in their own development. The teacher assumes a flexible authority role, sharing decision making with pupils, who learn at their own pace. Children are evaluated by considering their progress in relation to their own prior development. How well they compare to same-age pupils is of lesser importance. A glance inside the door of an open classroom reveals richly equipped learning centers, small groups of pupils working on tasks they choose themselves, and a teacher who moves from one area to another, guiding and supporting in response to children's individual needs (Minuchin & Shapiro, 1983).

Over the past 30 years, the pendulum in American education has swung back and forth between these two views. In the 1960s and early 1970s, open education gained in popularity, inspired by Piaget's vision of the child as an active, motivated learner. Then, as high school students' scores on the Scholastic Aptitude Test (SAT) declined over the 1970s, a "back to basics" movement arose. Classrooms returned to traditional, teacher-directed instruction, which remains the dominant approach today.

The combined results of many studies reveal that children in traditional classrooms have a slight edge in terms of academic achievement. At the same time, open settings are associated with other benefits. Open-classroom pupils are more independent, and they value and respect individual differences in their classmates more. Pupils in open environments also like school better than those in traditional classrooms, and their attitudes toward school become increasingly positive as they spend more time there (Hedges, Giaconia, & Gage, 1981; Walberg, 1986).

**New Philosophical Directions.** The philosophies of some teachers are neither traditional nor open. Instead, they fall somewhere in between. These teachers want to foster high achievement as well as independence, positive social relationships, and excitement about learning. New experiments in elementary education, grounded in Vygotsky's sociocultural theory, represent this intermediate point of view. One that has received widespread attention is the Kamehameha Elementary Education Program (KEEP). Vygotsky's concept of the *zone of proximal development*—a range of challenging tasks that the child is ready to master with the help of a more skilled partner (see Chapter 6)—serves as the foundation for KEEP's theory of instruction.

**Traditional classroom**
Elementary school classrooms based on the educational philosophy that children are passive learners who acquire information presented by teachers. Pupils are evaluated on the basis of how well they keep up with other pupils in their grade.

**Open classroom**
Elementary school classrooms based on the educational philosophy that children are active agents in their own development and learn at different rates. Teachers share decision making with pupils. Pupils are evaluated in relation to their own prior development.

To spur development forward, KEEP combines a variety of strategies that have traditionally belonged to other theories:

- *modeling,* to introduce children to unfamiliar skills;
- *instructing,* to direct children toward the next specific act they need to learn in order to move through the zone of proximal development;
- *verbal feedback* (or reinforcement), to let children know how well they are progressing in relation to reasonable standards of performance;
- *questioning,* to encourage children to think about the task; and
- *explaining,* to provide strategies and knowledge necessary for thinking in new ways.

These techniques are applied in activity settings specially designed to enhance opportunities for teacher–child and child–child dialogue. In each setting, children work on a project that ensures that their learning will be active and directed toward a meaningful goal. For example, they might read a story and discuss its meaning or draw a map of the playground to promote an understanding of geography. Sometimes activity settings include the whole class. More often, they involve small groups that foster cooperative learning and permit teachers to stay in touch with how well each child is doing. The precise organization of each KEEP classroom is adjusted to fit the unique learning styles of its pupils, creating culturally responsive environments (Gallimore & Tharp, 1990; Tharp & Gallimore, 1988).

Thousands of low-income minority children have attended KEEP classrooms in the public schools of Hawaii. So far, research suggests that the approach is highly effective. In KEEP schools, minority pupils performed at their expected grade level in reading achievement, much better than children of the same background enrolled in traditional schools (see Figure 12.4). Classroom observations also showed that KEEP pupils participated actively in class discussion, used elaborate language structures, frequently supported one another's learning, and were more attentive and involved than were non-KEEP controls (Tharp & Gallimore, 1988). As the KEEP model becomes more widely applied, perhaps it will prove successful with all types of children because of its comprehensive goals and effort to meet the learning needs of a wide range of pupils.

### Teacher-Pupil Interaction

In all classrooms, teachers vary in the way they interact with children—differences that are consistently related to academic achievement. Lizzie's third-grade teacher, for example, organized the learning environment so that activities ran smoothly, transitions were brief and orderly, and there were few disruptions and discipline problems. Teachers who are effective classroom managers have pupils who spend more time learning, and this is reflected in higher achievement test scores (Brophy, 1986).

The quality of teachers' instructional messages also affects children's involvement and achievement. Although Lizzie's teacher was well-organized and efficient, she usually emphasized factual knowledge. She seldom encouraged the children to think critically about what they had learned or apply their knowledge to new situations. Down the hall in Joey's class, higher-level questions were common. Joey's teacher asked, "Why is the main character in this story a hero?" and "Now that you are good at division, let's use what we know. How many teams should we have at recess? How many children on each team?" In an observational study of fifth-grade social studies and math lessons, students were far more attentive when teachers encouraged higher-level thinking rather than limiting instruction to simple memory exercises (Stodolsky, 1988).

*When teachers emphasize competition, make public evaluations of pupils, and are overly critical of those who do poorly, negative self-fulfilling prophecies can be set in motion that undermine children's self-esteem and achievement.* (Mac Donald Photography/Envision)

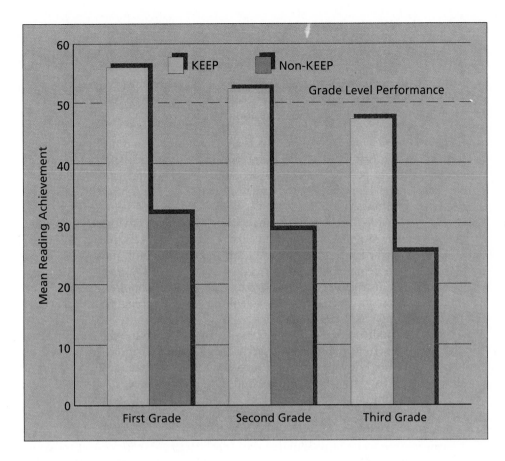

**FIGURE 12.4** • Reading achievement of KEEP-instructed and traditionally instructed first-through third-grade low-income minority pupils. The KEEP children performed at grade level; the non-KEEP pupils performed substantially below grade level. (*Adapted from R. G. Tharp and R. Gallimore, 1988,* Rousing minds to life: Teaching, learning, and schooling in social context, *New York: Cambridge University Press, p. 116. Adapted by permission.*)

Teachers do not interact in the same way with all children. Some get more attention and praise than others. Well-behaved, high-achieving pupils experience positive interactions with their teachers. In contrast, teachers especially dislike children who achieve poorly and who are also disruptive in the classroom. These unruly pupils are often criticized and are rarely called on to contribute to class discussion. When they seek special help or permission, their requests are usually denied (Brophy & Good, 1974).

Unfortunately, once teachers' attitudes toward pupils are established, they are in danger of becoming more extreme than is warranted by children's behavior. A special concern is that an educational **self-fulfilling prophecy** can be set in motion. In other words, children may adopt teachers' positive or negative views and start to live up to them. Many studies show that during the school years, children become increasingly aware of teacher opinion, and it can influence their performance (Harris & Rosenthal, 1985). This effect is especially strong in certain classrooms—those in which teachers emphasize competition and frequently make public comparisons among children (Weinstein et al., 1987).

In many schools, pupils are *ability grouped* or *tracked* into classes in which children of similar achievement levels are taught together. Some researchers believe that teachers' treatment of different ability groups may be an especially powerful source of self-fulfilling prophecies (Brophy, 1983; Corno & Snow, 1986). In low-ability groups, pupils get more drill on basic facts and skills, a slower learning pace, and less time on academic work. Gradually, children in low groups show a drop in self-esteem and are viewed by themselves and others as "not smart." Not surprisingly, ability grouping widens the gap between high and low achievers (Slavin, 1987).

**Self-fulfilling prophecy**
The idea that children may adopt teachers' positive or negative attitudes toward them and start to live up to these views.

## Computers in the Classroom

Besides teachers, another interactive aid to learning can be found in many modern classrooms. In each of the rooms in Joey and Lizzie's school, a computer sat in a quiet corner. Children took turns working on special assignments, sometimes by themselves and at other times with their classmates. A growing research literature reveals that computers can have rich educational benefits.

**Advantages of Computers.**   Computers are typically used in three different ways in classrooms. The first is *computer-assisted instruction,* in which specially designed educational software permits children to acquire new knowledge and practice basic skills. For example, Lizzie and her classmates often used the computer to practice multiplication and division. They could begin at their current level of mastery, and the computer provided immediate feedback and extra practice with problems that they missed. Other programs contain gamelike activities that teach new concepts. In one, Lizzie operated a lemonade stand and learned about economic principles of cost, profit, supply, and demand in a familiar context. Gains in achievement occur when computer-assisted instruction is a regular part of children's school experiences. The benefits are greatest for younger pupils and those who are doing poorly in school (Kulik, 1986; Lepper & Gurtner, 1989).

As soon as children begin to read and write, they can also use the computer for *word processing.* It permits them to write freely and experiment with letters and words without being slowed down by the fine motor task of handwriting. When children use the computer to write stories, letters, and other text material, they are less concerned about making mistakes because they can easily revise and polish their work. As a result, their written products are longer and of higher quality (Levin, Boruta, & Vasconcellos, 1983).

Finally, *programming* offers children the highest degree of control over the computer, since they must tell it just what to do. Specially designed computer languages are available to introduce children to programming skills. As long as teachers encourage and support children's efforts, computer programming leads to improvements in a variety of cognitive abilities, including concept formation, problem solving, and creativity (Clements, 1991; Degelman et al., 1986; Pea & Kurland, 1984). In addition, because children must detect errors in their programs to get them to work, programming helps them think about their own thought processes. Several studies report gains in metacognition and self-regulation as a result of a programming experience (Clements, 1986, 1990). Finally, children who know how to program are more aware of the uses of computers and how they function. They are better prepared to participate in a society in which computers are becoming increasingly important in everyday life.

**Concerns About Computers.**   Although computers provide children with many learning advantages, they raise serious concerns as well. Computers appear most often in schools that serve economically well-off pupils. Parents of these children are far more likely to buy computers and extend their educational benefits into the home. As a result, some experts believe that computers are widening the intellectual performance gap between lower- and middle-income children (Laboratory of Comparative Human Cognition, 1989).

Furthermore, by the end of middle childhood, boys spend much more time with computers than do girls, both in and out of school. Because of sex-typed expectations, adults encourage this difference. Parents of sons are twice as likely as parents of daughters to install a computer in the home. Even when girls have ready access to computers, much of the software is unappealing to them because it emphasizes themes of war, violence, and male-dominated sports (Lepper, 1985). Girls' reduced involvement with computers may contribute to sex differences in mathematical

*Special steps are needed to ensure that girls and minority pupils have equal access to computers during the school years. Without teacher intervention, boys can dominate computer environments in classrooms.* (Bill Aron/Photo Researchers)

achievement and interest in scientific careers that emerge by adolescence (see Chapter 15). Yet research suggests that girls' tendency to retreat from computers can be overcome. When teachers present computers in the context of cooperative rather than competitive learning activities and software is designed with sensitivity to the interests and reactions of girls, they become enthusiastic users (Hawkins & Sheingold, 1986; Linn, 1985).

Finally, computers are especially attractive to children because of their multiple communication modes. Color graphics, lively animation, voice, music, and text all combine to sustain children's interest. Critics worry that children might become too dependent on this highly stimulating, entertaining format. Will children be able to generalize the academic skills they acquire from the computer to other contexts? At present, this unanswered question awaits further research.

### Teaching Children with Special Needs

So far, we have seen that effective teachers flexibly adjust their teaching strategies to accommodate pupils with a wide range of abilities and characteristics. But such adjustments are increasingly difficult to make at the very low and high ends of the ability distribution. How do schools serve children with special learning needs?

***Mainstreaming Children with Learning Difficulties.*** In 1975, Congress passed the *Education for All Handicapped Children Act* (Public Law 94–142). It required that schools place handicapped children in the "least restrictive" environments that can meet their educational needs. The law led to a rapid increase in **mainstreaming** of many pupils who otherwise would have been served in special education classes. Instead, they were integrated into regular classrooms for part or all of the school day, a practice designed to better prepare them for participation in a nonhandicapped social world. Most mainstreamed pupils are mildly retarded or learning disabled. Let's take a brief look at the characteristics of these youngsters.

*Mildly Mentally Retarded Children.* About 1.5 percent of the child population suffers from **mental retardation,** or substantially below-average intellectual performance. Approximately 85 percent of these children are mildly mentally retarded—the highest

**Mainstreaming**
The integration of handicapped pupils into regular classrooms for part or all of the school day.

**Mental retardation**
Substantially below-average intellectual functioning.

TABLE 12.1 · Classification of Mental Retardation

| Level of Retardation | Approximate IQ Range | Description |
|---|---|---|
| Mild | 55–70 | Can be educated to about the sixth-grade level by late adolescence. In adulthood, can live independently and hold a routine job. Requires extra support when under stress. |
| Moderate | 40–54 | Can be educated to about fourth-grade level by late adolescence. In adulthood, usually requires living arrangements with moderate supervision. Can be employed in a sheltered workshop or unskilled job. |
| Severe | 25–39 | Can learn to talk and be trained in basic health habits, but cannot acquire academic skills. In adulthood, requires extensive supervision. |
| Profound | Below 25 | Develops only minimal speech and motor functioning. Little capacity to profit from training of any kind. Requires complete care and supervision. |

*Sources:* Grossman, 1983; Sloan & Birch, 1955.

functioning category (see Table 12.1). Their IQs fall between 55 and 70, and they also show problems in adaptive behavior (social and self-help skills in everyday life). Typically, a mildly mentally retarded child can be educated to the level of an average sixth grader. In adulthood, most can live independently and hold routine jobs, although they require extra guidance and support during times of stress (American Psychiatric Association, 1987; Grossman, 1983).

As you know from earlier chapters, the depressed intellectual functioning that characterizes mentally retarded children can develop in many ways. Hereditary defects, a faulty prenatal environment, birth complications, childhood injuries, a severely impoverished home life, or some combination of these factors are common causes.

*Learning Disabled Children.* The largest number of mainstreamed children have **learning disabilities.** About 5 to 10 percent of school-age children are affected. These youngsters obtain average or above-average IQ scores. Nevertheless, they have great difficulty with one or more aspects of learning. As a result, their achievement is considerably behind what would be expected on the basis of their IQ. The problems of these children cannot be traced to any obvious physical handicap, emotional problem, or environmental disadvantage. Instead, faulty brain functioning is believed to underlie their difficulties (Hammill, 1990). Some of the disorders run in families, suggesting that they are at least partly genetic (Pennington & Smith, 1988). In most instances, the cause is unknown.

Learning disabled children display a wide variety of cognitive processing deficits. Usually, the basic area of difficulty is noted. A problem with reading is called *dyslexia,* one with arithmetic, *dyscalculia,* and one with writing, *dysgraphia.* But within each, impairments are varied. For example, one child might have difficulty interpreting visual stimuli. The letters *d, b, p, q,* and *g* are confused, so that "dog" is read as "god" and "ball" as "gall." Another child might have trouble tracking from left to right and, as a result, read the same line twice, jump over words, or skip lines. Some children cannot integrate information appropriately. After reading a story, they mix up the sequence of events. In retelling it, they start in the middle, go to the beginning, and then shift to the end. Serious memory problems can contribute to spelling and math difficulties. A child might study a spelling list or math concept, know it well, but

**Learning disabilities**
Specific learning disorders that lead children to achieve poorly in school, despite an average or above-average IQ. Believed to be due to faulty brain functioning.

forget it completely an hour or two later. Finally, sometimes the muscles of the hand fail to work together, resulting in extremely slow, unclear handwriting (Silver, 1989a).

The learning problems of these children are so frustrating that they can lead to serious emotional, social, and family difficulties (Silver, 1989b). Yet those who are treated with patience and understanding and who receive appropriate educational intervention have a good chance of making a satisfactory adjustment in adulthood. Although the disability usually persists, these individuals find ways to compensate for it. Often they select college majors and careers that do not rely heavily on the skill in which they are deficient. The majority of learning disabled adults manage to equal or exceed the average educational and occupational attainment of the general population (Horn, O'Donnell, & Vitulano, 1983).

*How Effective Is Mainstreaming?* Does mainstreaming accomplish its two goals— providing more appropriate academic experiences for mildly handicapped children as well as integrated participation with normal classmates? At present, research findings are not positive on either of these points. Achievement differences between mainstreamed pupils and those taught in self-contained classrooms are not great (MacMillan, Keogh, & Jones, 1986). Furthermore, both retarded and learning disabled children are frequently rejected by peers. Retarded pupils are overwhelmed by the social skills of normal agemates. They cannot interact quickly or adeptly in a conversation or game. And the processing deficits of some learning disabled children lead to problems in social awareness and responsiveness as well (Rourke, 1988; Taylor, Asher, & Williams, 1987).

Does this mean that mainstreaming is not a good way to meet the educational needs of mildly handicapped children? This extreme conclusion is not warranted. Many regular classroom teachers do not have the specialized training or the time to give handicapped pupils all the help that they need. Often these children do best when they receive instruction in a *resource room* for part of the day and in the regular classroom for the remainder. In the resource room, a special education teacher works with pupils on an individual and small-group basis. Then, depending on their abilities, children are mainstreamed for different subjects and amounts of time. This flexible approach makes it more likely that the unique academic needs of each handicapped child will be served (Keogh, 1988; Lerner, 1989).

Once handicapped children enter the regular classroom, special steps must be taken to promote their acceptance by normal peers. When instruction is carefully individualized and teachers minimize comparisons with higher-achieving classmates, handicapped pupils show gains in self-esteem and achievement (Madden & Slavin, 1983). Also, cooperative learning experiences in which a handicapped child and several normal peers work together on the same task have been found to promote friendly interaction and social acceptance (Nastasi & Clements, 1991).

### Gifted Children.

In Joey and Lizzie's school, some children were **gifted.** They displayed exceptional intellectual strengths. Like handicapped pupils, their characteristics were diverse. In every grade were one or two pupils with IQ scores above 130, the standard definition of giftedness based on intelligence test performance (Horowitz & O'Brien, 1986). High IQ children, as we have seen, are particularly quick at academic work. They have keen memories and an exceptional capacity to analyze a challenging problem and efficiently move toward a correct solution.

Yet earlier in this chapter we noted that intelligence tests do not sample the entire range of human mental skills. Over the past two decades, recognition of this fact has led to an expanded conception of giftedness in public schools.

*Creativity.* Besides general intelligence, high *creativity* can result in a child being designated as gifted. Tests that measure it tap a form of cognition called **divergent**

**Giftedness**

Exceptional intellectual ability. Includes high IQ, creativity, and specialized talent.

**Divergent thinking**

The generation of multiple and unusual possibilities when faced with a task or problem. Associated with creativity.

**FIGURE 12.5** • Responses of a highly creative 8-year-old to a figural measure of creativity. This 8-year-old was asked to make as many pictures as she could from the circles on the page. The titles she gave her drawings, from left to right, are as follows: "dracula," "one-eyed monster," "pumpkin," "hula-hoop," "poster," "wheelchair," "earth," "moon," "planet," "movie camera," "sad face," "picture," "stoplight," "beach ball," "the letter O," "car," "glasses." (*Test form copyright © 1980 by Scholastic Testing Service, Inc. Reprinted by permission of Scholastic Testing Service, Inc., from* The Torrance Tests of Creative Thinking *by E. P. Torrance.*)

**Convergent thinking**
The generation of a single correct answer to a problem. Type of cognition emphasized on intelligence tests.

thinking—the generation of multiple and unusual possibilities when faced with a task or problem. Divergent thinking contrasts sharply with **convergent thinking,** which involves arriving at a single correct answer—the type of cognition emphasized on intelligence tests (Guilford, 1985).

Both verbal and figural measures of divergent thinking exist. A verbal measure might ask children to name as many uses for common objects (such as a newspaper) as they can. A figural measure might ask them to come up with as many drawings based on a circular motif as possible (Torrance, 1980). Responses can be scored for the number of ideas generated as well as their originality. For example, saying that a newspaper can be used "as handgrips for a bicycle" would be more unusual than saying it can be used "to clean things." Figure 12.5 displays the responses of a highly creative 8-year-old in Lizzie's class to a figural creativity test.

Research reveals that parents of creative children value nonconformity, emphasize intellectual curiosity and freedom of exploration, and are highly accepting of their youngster's individual characteristics. Creative children are, in turn, broad in their interests, attracted by complexity, and relatively unconcerned about conventional social norms (Wallach, 1985). Because of these characteristics, creative children are often not well liked by teachers—especially those with rigid expectations for how pupils should respond in class. Creative pupils often interpret assignments in novel and humorous ways, as you can see in the following autobiography written by a youngster who scored high in divergent thinking:

> I was transferred from another world or "hatched" as you might call it, at a very young age (0 for a fact). I called my mammy and she came runnin'. Den dat dok came an' he done took me and ah' squealed with fright. O' course I couldn' see anythin' any-hoo. . . . Den a grown up fur' three (3) yer' before my brudder was bornded. He is de' durndest critter ah' eveh' saw podnah'. At this time in my life you can see I played cowboy, with my mudder as injun. She never was the same cause ah used to hit her with a frin' pan. . . . (Getzels & Jackson, 1962, p. 100)

Unfortunately, many teachers are annoyed rather than intrigued by this inventive reformulation of a problem.

*Talent.* Tests of divergent thinking have turned out to be imperfect predictors of real-life creative accomplishments (Kogan, 1983; Wallach, 1985). Partly for this reason, modern definitions of giftedness have been extended to include *specialized talent.* There is clear evidence that outstanding performances in particular areas, such as mathematics, science, music, art, athletics, and leadership, have roots in specialized skills that first appear in childhood (Gardner, 1983; Gardner & Hatch, 1989).

At the same time, we now know that natural ability is not enough for the development of talent. It must be nurtured in a favorable environment. Studies of highly accomplished musicians, mathematicians, and Olympic athletes show that they had deeply committed parents and inspiring teachers who encouraged them from an early age. In addition, as children these individuals displayed extraordinary dedication, devoting many long hours to practice—much more than they gave to any other activity (Bloom, 1985; Feldman, 1991). These findings suggest that the most effective way to foster creativity is to provide talented pupils with training aimed at helping them reach the limits of a particular field and then move beyond.

*Educating the Gifted.* Teaching gifted children with such a wide range of capacities is, indeed, a monumental task. Enrichment activities in regular classrooms and pull-out programs in which bright youngsters are gathered together for special instruction have been common ways of serving the gifted for decades. Yet these approaches are of limited value, since they usually provide the same experience to all pupils without considering each child's unique talents and skills.

Current trends in gifted education place greater emphasis on building each child's special abilities. Enrichment might include mentorship programs in which a highly skilled adult tutors the gifted pupil in a relevant field, such as art or public speaking (Kornhaber, Krechevsky, & Gardner, 1991). Another approach is to provide accelerated learning programs in which gifted pupils are given fast-paced instruction in a particular subject or are advanced to a higher grade. Acceleration is a controversial practice because of concerns that bright youngsters might suffer socially if they are placed with older pupils. Yet when children are carefully selected on the basis of their maturity, acceleration is highly successful. Longitudinal studies of accelerated students indicate that they continue to be socially well adjusted while demonstrating outstanding academic accomplishments (Brody & Benbow, 1987).

Today, the educational needs of gifted children are commanding greater attention, and other innovative techniques for teaching them are being tried. These include gifted resource rooms, cluster groups that bring children with similar talents together, and special after-school and Saturday programs. In some states, Governor's Schools provide advanced instruction in both academic and artistic fields. A promising outcome of these efforts is that some of the practices designed to stimulate complex problem solving and creativity in the gifted are spilling over into regular classrooms, extending learning opportunities for all pupils (Reis, 1989).

## CULTURAL INFLUENCES

### Box 12.3  *Education in Japan, Taiwan, and the United States*

Why do Asian children perform so well academically? Recent research examining societal, school, and family conditions in Japan, Taiwan, and the United States provides some answers:

#### *Cultural Valuing of Academic Achievement.*

In Japan and Taiwan, natural resources are limited. Progress in science and technology is essential for economic well-being. Because a well-educated work force is necessary to meet this goal, children's mastery of academic skills is of central importance. In the United States, attitudes toward academic achievement are far less unified. Many Americans believe that it is more important to encourage children to feel good about themselves and to explore various areas of knowledge than to perform well in school.

#### *Emphasis on Effort.*

Japanese and Taiwanese parents and teachers believe that all children have the potential to master challenging academic tasks if they work hard enough. In contrast, many more of their American counterparts regard native ability as the key to academic success. These differences in attitude may contribute to the fact that American parents are less likely to encourage activities at home that might improve school performance. Japanese and Taiwanese children spend more free time reading and playing ac-

ademic-related games than do children in the United States (Stevenson & Lee, 1990).

#### *Involvement of Parents in Education.*

Asian parents devote many hours to helping their children with homework. American parents spend very little time helping with homework and, at least while their children are in elementary school, do not regard homework as especially important. Overall, American parents hold much lower standards for their children's academic performance and are far less concerned about how well their youngsters are doing in school (Chen & Stevenson, 1989; Stevenson & Lee, 1990).

#### *High Quality Education for All.*

Unlike teachers in the United States, Japanese and Taiwanese teachers do not make early educational decisions on the basis of achievement. There are no separate ability groups or tracks in elementary schools. Instead, all pupils receive the same high-quality instruction. Academic lessons are particularly well-organized and presented in ways that capture children's attention. Topics in mathematics are treated in greater depth, and there is less repetition of material taught the previous year (McKnight et al., 1987; Stevenson & Lee, 1990).

---

• *Saul, a third-grade teacher, places stars by the names of children who get A's on assignments. Children who earn at least ten stars each week are called "all stars." What effect is this practice likely to have on children who achieve poorly, and why?*

• *How might the current broad definition of giftedness improve the educational experiences of low-income minority children?*

**BRIEF REVIEW**  Schools are powerful forces in children's cognitive development. Pupils who attend traditional classrooms are slightly advantaged in academic achievement; those in open classrooms are more independent, tolerant of individual differences, and excited about learning. The Kamehameha Elementary Education Program (KEEP), an approach grounded in Vygotsky's theory, has resulted in both academic and social benefits. Teachers who are effective classroom managers and who provide cognitively stimulating activities enhance children's involvement and learning. Self-fulfilling prophecies are likely to occur when teachers emphasize competition and make public comparisons among pupils. Computers lead to rich educational benefits in classrooms, but they reach affluent children and boys more effectively than low-income children and girls. To be effective, mainstreaming must be carefully tailored to meet the academic and social needs of mildly retarded and learning disabled children. Today, giftedness means more than high IQ; it includes creativity and specialized talent. Gifted children are best served by educational programs that build on their unique strengths.

***More Time Devoted to Instruction.*** In Japan and Taiwan, the school year is over 50 days longer than in the United States, and much more of the day is devoted to academic pursuits, especially mathematics.

***Communication between Teachers and Parents.*** Japanese and Taiwanese teachers come to know their pupils especially well. They teach the same children for two or three years and make visits to the home once or twice a year. Continuous communication between teachers and parents takes place with the aid of small notebooks that children carry back and forth every day and in which messages about assignments, academic performance, and behavior are written. No such formalized system of frequent teacher–parent communication exists in the United States (Stevenson & Lee, 1990).

Do Japanese and Taiwanese children pay a price for the pressure placed on them to succeed? By high school, academic work often displaces other experiences important for healthy development, since Asian adolescents must pass a highly competitive entrance exam to gain admission to college. Yet the American approach seems to err in the other direction—by placing too little emphasis on diligence and excellence. Awareness of the ingredients of Asian success has prompted Americans to rethink current educational practices.

*Japanese pupils achieve considerably better than their American counterparts for a variety of reasons. Their culture stresses the importance of working hard to master academic skills. Their parents help more with homework and communicate more often with teachers, and their schools devote more time to high-quality instruction. (Karen Kasmauski/Woodfin Camp)*

## HOW WELL EDUCATED ARE AMERICA'S CHILDREN?

Our discussion of schooling has largely focused on what teachers can do in classrooms to support the education of children. Yet a great many factors, both within and outside schools, affect children's learning. Societal values, school resources, quality of teaching, and parental encouragement all play important roles. Nowhere are these multiple influences more apparent than when schooling is examined in cross-cultural perspective.

Perhaps you are aware from recent news reports that American children fare poorly when their achievement is compared to that of children in other industrialized nations. In international studies of mathematics and science achievement, American students score no better than at the mean of participating countries, and often they fall at the bottom of the pack (International Education Association, 1988; McKnight et al., 1987). These trends emerge early in development. In a comparison of elementary school children in Japan, Taiwan, and the United States, large differences in mathematics achievement were present in kindergarten and became greater with increasing grade. Less extreme gaps occurred in reading, in which Taiwanese children scored highest, Japanese children lowest, and American children in between (Stevenson & Lee, 1990). As we will see in Chapter 15, there is now clear evidence that too many American youngsters manage to complete their education with weak reading, writing, and mathematical skills (Mullis et al., 1991).

Why do American children fall behind in academic accomplishments? To find out, researchers have looked closely at learning environments in top-performing Asian nations—especially Japan and Taiwan. A common assumption is that Asian children are high achievers because they are "smarter," but this is not true. They do not score better on intelligence tests than do American children (Stevenson et al., 1985). Instead, as box Box 12.3 indicates, a variety of social forces combine to foster a strong commitment to learning in Asian families and schools.

Japan and Taiwan have established broad cultural climates for achievement. However, the educational system of one society cannot simply be transplanted to cure the ills of another. The United States faces challenges that are different from those in Asian countries—among them, the problem of how to educate children from a great many ethnic backgrounds for successful participation in a common culture (Leetsma et al., 1987). Yet members of diverse ethnic groups are in strong agreement about one thing: the importance of education and the need to improve it in the United States (Stevenson & Lee, 1990).

The Japanese and Taiwanese examples underscore that families, schools, and the larger society must work together to upgrade American education. Already, progress is being made. Throughout the country, academic standards and teacher certification requirements are being strengthened. Many schools are also making an effort to increase parent involvement in children's education. Parents who create stimulating learning environments at home, monitor their youngster's academic progress, help with homework, and communicate often with teachers have children who consistently show superior academic progress (Bradley, Caldwell, & Rock, 1988; Dossey et al., 1988; Stevenson & Baker, 1987). The current educational reform movement is an encouraging sign. It reflects the firm desire of many educators and concerned citizens to rebuild an educational system capable of preparing American children for a prosperous and civilized adulthood in a complex, changing world.

# SUMMARY

### Piaget's Theory: The Concrete Operational Stage

• During the **concrete operational stage,** thought is far more logical and organized than it was during the preschool years. The ability to conserve indicates that children can **decenter** and **reverse** their thinking. In addition, they are better at hierarchical classification, **seriation,** and **transitive inference.** School-age youngsters have an improved understanding of distance, and they can combine it with other physical concepts, such as time and speed.

• Concrete operational thought is limited in that children can reason logically only about concrete, tangible information; they have difficulty with abstractions. Piaget used the term **horizontal décalage** to describe the school-age child's gradual mastery of logical concepts, such as conservation.

• Recent evidence indicates that specific cultural practices affect children's mastery of Piagetian tasks. Some researchers believe that the horizontal décalage can best be understood within an information processing framework.

### Information Processing in Middle Childhood

• Attention becomes much more controlled, adaptable, and planful during middle childhood. Children become better at ignoring irrelevant information, adjusting their attention to task demands and changes in their own learning, and scanning stimuli systematically.

• During the school years, children use memory strategies more often. **Rehearsal** appears first, followed by **organization** and then **elaboration.**

• Development of the long-term knowledge base facilitates strategic memory processing. Children's willingness to use what they know also contributes to memory development. Memory strategies are promoted by learning activities in school.

• Metacognition expands over middle childhood. School-age children regard the mind as an active, constructive agent, and they combine their metacognitive knowledge into an integrated theory of mind.

• School-age children are not yet good at **self-regulation.** Providing children with instructions to monitor their cognitive activity improves self-regulatory skills and task performance.

• Skilled reading draws on all aspects of the information processing system. Experts disagree on whether a **whole language approach** or **basic skills approach** should be used to teach reading. A balance between the two may be most effective. An overemphasis on drill rather than understanding limits children's mastery of mathematics in school.

### Individual Differences in Mental Development During Middle Childhood

• During the school years, IQ becomes more stable, and it correlates strongly with academic achievement. Most intelligence tests yield an overall score as well as scores for separate intellectual factors. Current widely used intelligence tests for children are the **Stanford-Binet Intelligence Scale,** the **Wechsler Intelligence Scale for Children–III (WISC–III),** and the **Kaufman Assessment Battery for Children (K-ABC).**

• To search for the precise mental processes underlying mental ability factors, researchers have combined the factor analytic approach to defining intelligence with information processing. Sternberg's **triarchic theory of intelligence** extends this effort. Intelligence is viewed as a complex interaction of information processing skills, specific experiences, and contextual influences.

• Heritability estimates and adoption research reveal that intelligence is a product of heredity and environment. Studies of black children adopted into white middle-class homes indicate that the black-white IQ gap is environmentally determined.

• IQ scores are affected by specific learning experiences, including exposure to certain language customs and familiarity with the kind of knowledge sampled by the test. Cultural bias in intelligence tests has contributed to overlabeling of low-income minority children as slow learners. Special precautions need to be taken when evaluating the mental abilities of these children.

### Language Development in Middle Childhood

• During middle childhood, vocabulary continues to grow rapidly, and children have a more precise and flexible understanding of the meanings of words. Improvement in children's grasp of complex grammatical constructions also takes place. School-age children can handle challenging communicative situations, and their conversational strategies become more refined.

• Historically, Americans have held negative attitudes toward learning two languages in childhood. Research shows that bilingual children are advanced in cognitive development and language awareness.

### Children's Learning in School

• Schools exert powerful influences on children's cognitive development. Pupils in **traditional classrooms** are advantaged in terms of academic achievement. Those in **open classrooms** tend to be independent learners who respect individual differences and have more positive attitudes toward school. The Kamehameha Elementary Education Program (KEEP) is a balanced philosophical viewpoint based on Vygotsky's sociocultural theory. It promotes academic achievement, positive social relationships, and excitement about learning.

• Patterns of teacher–pupil interaction affect children's academic progress. Teachers who are effective classroom managers have pupils who achieve especially well. Instruction that encourages higher-level thinking fosters children's interest and involvement. **Self-fulfilling prophecies,** in which children start to live up to the opinions of their teachers, are most likely to occur in classrooms that emphasize competition and public evaluation.

• Computers can have rich educational benefits. Gains in academic performance result from computer-assisted instruction and word processing. Programming promotes complex cognitive skills and knowledge of how computers function. However, computers may widen intellectual gaps between the social classes and sexes.

• Teachers face special challenges in meeting the needs of children at the very low and high ends of the ability distribution. Pupils with mild **mental retardation** and **learning disabilities** are often integrated into regular classrooms. The success of **mainstreaming** depends on efforts by teachers to provide individualized instruction and promote positive peer relations.

• **Giftedness** includes high IQ, high creativity, and exceptional talent. Gifted children are best served by educational programs that build on their special strengths. Academic acceleration is a controversial practice, but when carefully implemented, it is highly successful.

### How Well Educated Are America's Children?

• American children fare poorly when their achievement is compared to that of children in other industrialized nations. In contrast, children from Japan and Taiwan are consistently among the top performers. A strong cultural commitment toward learning is responsible for the academic success of Asian pupils.

## IMPORTANT TERMS AND CONCEPTS

concrete operational stage (p. 416)
decentration (p. 416)
reversibility (p. 416)
seriation (p. 416)
transitive inference (p. 417)
horizontal décalage (p. 419)
attention-deficit hyperactivity disorder (ADHD) (p. 422)
rehearsal (p. 422)

organization (p. 422)
elaboration (p. 422)
self-regulation (p. 426)
whole language approach (p. 427)
basic skills approach (p. 427)
Stanford-Binet Intelligence Scale (p. 430)
Wechsler Intelligence Scale for Children–III (WISC–III) (p. 430)
Kaufman Assessment Battery for Children (K-ABC) (p. 430)

triarchic theory of intelligence (p. 432)
traditional classroom (p. 441)
open classroom (p. 441)
self-fulfilling prophecy (p. 443)
mainstreaming (p. 445)
mental retardation (p. 445)
learning disabilities (p. 446)
giftedness (p. 447)
divergent thinking (p. 447)
convergent thinking (p. 448)

## FOR FURTHER INFORMATION AND SPECIAL HELP

**Attention-Deficit Hyperactivity Disorder**

Children with Attention-Deficit Disorders
499 N.W. 70th Avenue, Suite 308
Plantation, FL 33317
(305) 587-3700

Provides support and education to families of children with attention-deficit hyperactivity disorder. Encourages schools and health care professionals to be responsive to their needs.

**Bilingual Education**

National Association for Bilingual Education
810 First Street, N.E.
Third Floor
Washington, DC 20002
(202) 898-1829

An organization of educators, public citizens, and students aimed at increasing public understanding of the importance of bilingual education.

**Computers**

National Center for Computer Equity
99 Hudson Street
New York, NY 10013
(212) 925-6635

Works to resolve problems in equal access to computer education for girls. Sponsored by the National Organization for Women (NOW).

**Mental Retardation**

Division on Mental Retardation of the Council for Exceptional Children
245 Cedar Springs Drive
Athens, GA 30605
(404) 546-6132

An organization of teachers of the mentally retarded. Seeks to advance education, research, and public understanding. Publishes the journal, *Education and Training in Mental Retardation.*

**Learning Disabilities**

Learning Disabilities Association of America
4156 Library Road
Pittsburgh, PA 15234
(412) 341-1515

A 60,000-member organization of parents of learning disabled children and interested professionals. Local groups provide parent support and education and sponsor recreational programs and summer camps for children.

**Giftedness**

The Association for the Gifted of the Council for Exceptional Children
920 Association Drive
Reston, VA 22091
(216) 672-2477

An organization of educators and parents aimed at stimulating interest in program development for gifted children. Publishes *Journal for the Education of the Gifted*.

National Association for Gifted Children
1155 15th Street N.W., No. 1002
Washington, DC 20005
(202) 785-4268

Association of scholars, educators, and librarians devoted to advancing education for gifted children. Distributes information and sponsors institutes. Publishes the journal, *Gifted Child Quarterly*.

*Fishing, Tang Chong Min, 9 years, Singapore. Reprinted by permission from The International Museum of Children's Art, Oslo, Norway.*

# Emotional and Social Development in Middle Childhood

# 13

Erikson's Theory: Industry versus Inferiority

Self-Development in Middle Childhood
  *Changes in Self-Concept   Development of Self-Esteem   Influences on Self-Esteem*

Emotional Development in Middle Childhood

Understanding Others
  *Selman's Stages of Perspective-Taking   Perspective-Taking and Social Behavior*

Moral Development in Middle Childhood
  *Learning About Justice Through Sharing   Changes in Moral and Social Conventional Understanding*

Peer Relations in Middle Childhood 000
  *Peer Groups   Friendships   Peer Acceptance*

Sex Typing in Middle Childhood
  *School-Age Children's Sex-Stereotyped Beliefs   Sex-Role Identity and Behavior   Cultural Influences on Sex Typing*

Family Influences in Middle Childhood
  *Parent–Child Relationships   Siblings   Divorce   Remarriage   Maternal Employment*

Some Common Problems of Development
  *Fears and Anxieties   Child Sexual Abuse*

Stress and Coping in Middle Childhood

O ne late afternoon, Rena heard Joey dash through the front door, run upstairs, and call up his best friend Terry. "Terry, gotta talk to you," pleaded Joey, out of breath from running home. "Everything was going great until that word I got—*porcupine*," remarked Joey, referring to the fifth-grade spelling bee that had taken place at school that day. "Just my luck! P-o-r-k, that's how I spelled it! I can't believe it. Maybe I'm not so good at social studies," Joey confided, "but I *know* I'm better at spelling than that stuck-up Belinda Brown. Gosh, I knocked myself out studying those spelling lists. Then *she* got all the easy words. Did'ya see how snooty she acted after she won? If I *had* to lose, why couldn't it be to a nice person, anyhow?"

Joey's conversation reflects a whole new constellation of emotional and social capacities. First, Joey shows evidence of *industriousness*. By entering the spelling bee, he energetically pursued meaningful achievement in his culture—a major change of the middle childhood years. At the same time, Joey's social understanding has greatly expanded. He can size up himself and others in terms of strengths, weaknesses, and personality characteristics—a capacity that was beyond him during the preschool years. Furthermore, friendship means something quite different to Joey than it did at younger ages. Terry is not just a convenient playmate; he is a best friend whom Joey counts on for understanding and emotional support.

*When Joey and Belinda Brown competed in the spelling bee, they showed evidence of industriousness by pursuing meaningful achievement in their culture. According to Erikson, developing a sense of industry is the critical psychosocial task of middle childhood. (Charles Gupton/ Stock Boston)*

We begin this chapter by returning to Erikson's theory for an overview of the personality changes of middle childhood. Then we take a close look at a variety of aspects of emotional and social development. We will see how, as children reason more effectively and spend more time in school and with peers, their views of themselves, of others, and of social relationships become more complex.

Although school-age children spend less time with parents than they did at earlier ages, the family remains a powerful context for development. Joey and Lizzie, along with many children of their generation, are growing up in homes profoundly affected by social change. Rena, unlike her own mother, has been employed since her children were preschoolers. In addition, Joey and Lizzie's home life has been disrupted by family discord; Rena is divorced. The children's personal experiences in adjusting to these departures from traditional family arrangements will help us appreciate the vital role of family relationships in all aspects of child development.

Finally, when stress is overwhelming and social support lacking, school-age youngsters experience serious adjustment difficulties. Our chapter concludes with a discussion of some common emotional problems of middle childhood.

## ERIKSON'S THEORY: INDUSTRY VERSUS INFERIORITY

**Latency stage**

Freud's psychosexual stage of middle childhood, when the sexual instincts lie dormant.

According to Erikson (1950), the personality changes of the school years build on Freud's **latency stage,** a period in which the sexual instincts lie dormant after the Oedipus and Electra conflicts of early childhood are resolved. In Chapter 10, we noted that Freud's Oedipal theory is no longer widely accepted. Yet when experiences with caregivers have been positive, children enter middle childhood with the calm confidence that Freud intended when he used the word *latency* to describe this stage. Their energies are redirected from the make-believe of early childhood into realistic accomplishment.

According to Erikson, the combination of adult expectations and children's drive toward mastery sets the stage for the critical psychological conflict of middle childhood: **industry versus inferiority.** Industry means developing competence at useful skills and tasks. In cultures everywhere, children's improved physical and cognitive capacities mean that adults impose new demands. Children, in turn, are ready to meet these challenges and benefit from them:

- Among the Baka of Cameroon, 5- to 7-year-olds begin to fetch and carry water, bathe and mind younger siblings, and accompany adults on food-gathering missions. Behind the main camp stands a miniature village. There, in this "school" of the Baka hunting-and-gathering society, children practice the arts of hut building, spear shaping, and fire making (Avis & Harris, 1991).

- The Ngoni of Malawi, Central Africa, believe that children are ready for a different kind of life when they shed their first teeth. Between ages 6 and 7, they stop their childish games and start skill training. Boys move out of the huts of family members into dormitories, where they enter a system of male domination and instruction. At that time, children are expected to show independence and are held personally accountable for irresponsible and disrespectful behavior (Read, 1968; Rogoff et al., 1975).

In industrialized nations, the transition to middle childhood is marked by the beginning of formal schooling. With it comes literacy training, which provides children with the widest possible preparation for the vast array of specialized careers in complex societies. In school, children engage in productive work beside and with other children. They become aware of their own and others' unique capacities, learn the value of division of labor, and develop a sense of moral commitment and responsibility. The danger at this stage is *inferiority,* reflected in the sad pessimism of some children who have come to believe they will never be good at anything. This profound sense of inadequacy can develop when family life has not prepared children for school life or when experiences with teachers and peers are so negative that they destroy children's feelings of competence and mastery.

Erikson's sense of industry combines several critical developments of middle childhood: a positive but realistic self-concept, pride in doing things well, moral responsibility, and cooperative participation with agemates. Let's look at how these aspects of self and social relationships change over the school years.

## SELF-DEVELOPMENT IN MIDDLE CHILDHOOD

In middle childhood, several transformations in self-understanding take place. First, children become capable of describing themselves in terms of psychological traits. Second, they start to compare their own characteristics to those of their peers. Finally, they speculate about the causes of their strengths and weaknesses. These new capacities for thinking about the self have a major impact on children's developing sense of self-esteem.

### Changes in Self-Concept

During the school years, children's self-concepts change from a list of concrete, observable characteristics to an emphasis on general dispositions, with a major change taking place between ages 8 and 11. The following responses of two children, who

**Industry versus inferiority**
In Erikson's theory, the psychological conflict of middle childhood, which is resolved positively when experiences lead children to develop a sense of competence at useful skills and tasks.

were asked to tell about themselves, reflect this change:

> *A boy age 7:* I am 7 and I have hazel eyes and brown hair and my hobby is stamp collecting. I am good at football and I am quite good at sums and my favourite game is football and I love school and I like reading books and my favourite car is an Austin. (Livesley & Bromley, 1973, p. 237)

> *A girl age 11 1/2:* My name is A. I'm a human being. I'm a girl. I'm a truthful person. I'm not pretty. I do so-so in my studies. I'm a very good cellist. I'm a very good pianist. I'm a little bit tall for my age. I like several boys. I like several girls. I'm old-fashioned. I play tennis. I am a very good swimmer. I try to be helpful. I'm always ready to be friends with anybody. Mostly I'm good, but I lose my temper. I'm not well-liked by some girls and boys. I don't know if I'm liked by boys or not. (Montemayor & Eisen, 1977, pp. 317–318)

Notice that the younger child does not refer to any psychological traits. Although the older one mentions her physical appearance and activities, she also describes her personality. For example, she notes that she is truthful, old-fashioned, helpful, friendly, and short-tempered.

A second change in self-concept takes place in middle childhood. School-age children begin to make *social comparisons*. In other words, they judge their appearance, abilities, and behavior in relation to those of others. Return to Joey's comments about the spelling bee at the beginning of this chapter. You will see that he expressed some thoughts about how good he was compared to Belinda Brown—better at spelling but not so great at social studies. Children younger than 7 practically never include social comparison information in their self-descriptions (Ruble, 1988).

What factors are responsible for these revisions in self-concept? Early in this century, sociologist George Herbert Mead (1934) described the self as a blend of what important people in our lives think of us. He believed that a well-organized psychological self emerges when children can imagine the attitude that others take toward them. In other words, *perspective-taking* skills emerging during middle childhood—in particular, an improved ability to imagine what other people are thinking—play a crucial role in the development of a psychological self. Indeed, as we will see later in this chapter, perspective-taking improves greatly over the school years.

During middle childhood, children look to more people for information about themselves as they enter a wider range of settings in school and community. This is reflected in children's frequent reference to social groups in their self-descriptions (Livesley & Bromley, 1973). "I'm a Boy Scout, a paper boy, and a Prairie City soccer player," Joey remarked when asked to describe himself. Gradually, as children move toward adolescence, their sources of self-definition become more selective. Although parents remain influential, between the ages of 8 and 15 peers become more important. And over time, self-concept becomes increasingly vested in the feedback children receive from their close friends (Rosenberg, 1979).

## Development of Self-Esteem

Self-esteem, the judgments children make about their own worth, is also reorganized in middle childhood. Recall from Chapter 10 that most preschoolers have extremely high self-esteem. As children move into middle childhood, they get much more feedback about their performance in different activities compared to that of their peers. As a result, self-esteem differentiates, and it also adjusts to a more realistic level (Stipek & Mac Iver, 1989).

***A Hierarchically Structured Self-Esteem.*** Susan Harter (1982) asked children to indicate the extent to which a variety of statements, such as "I am good at homework," "I'm usually the one chosen for games," and "Most kids like me," are true of

*During the school years, children's self-concepts expand to include feedback from a wider range of people as they spend more time in settings beyond the home. Girl scouting and its associated qualities of friendliness, helpfulness, and kindness are probably important aspects of the self-definitions of these two girls. (Joel Gordon)*

themselves. Her findings, and those of other researchers, reveal that by age 7 to 8 children have formed at least three separate self-esteems: cognitive competence, physical ability, and social self-worth. Gradually, they combine these separate self-evaluations into a general psychological image of themselves, an overall sense of self-worth. Consequently, by the mid-elementary school years, self-esteem takes on the hierarchical structure shown in Figure 13.1 (Harter, 1990; Marsh, 1989a).

*Changes in Level of Self-Esteem.*    As children evaluate themselves in various areas, they lose the sunny optimism of early childhood. Self-esteem drops during the

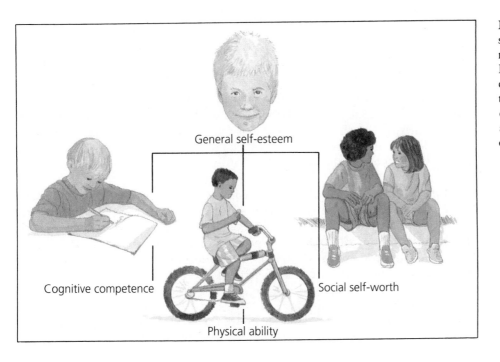

General self-esteem

Cognitive competence

Physical ability

Social self-worth

**FIGURE 13.1** • Hierarchical structure of self-esteem in the mid-elementary school years. From their experiences in different settings, children form at least three separate self-esteems— cognitive, physical, and social— and then combine them into an overall sense of self-worth.

first few years of elementary school (Stipek & Mac Iver, 1989). This decline can be explained by the fact that children gradually adjust their self-judgments to fit the opinions of others as well as their objective performance.

Typically, the drop in self-esteem is not great enough to be harmful. Most (but not all) children appraise their characteristics and competencies realistically while maintaining an attitude of self-acceptance and self-respect. In fact, from fourth to sixth grade, self-esteem rises for the majority of youngsters (Nottelmann, 1987; Wallace, Cunningham, & Del Monte, 1984). As we will see in Chapter 16, self-esteem will decline again when children enter junior high school and encounter many new experiences and expectations.

### Influences on Self-Esteem

From middle childhood on, strong relationships exist between self-esteem and everyday behavior. For example, cognitive self-esteem predicts children's school achievement as well as their willingness to try hard at challenging tasks (Marsh, Smith, & Barnes, 1985). Children with high social self-esteem are consistently better liked by their peers (Harter, 1982). And as we saw in Chapter 11, boys come to believe they have more athletic talent than do girls, and they are also more advanced in a wide variety of physical skills.

Because self-esteem is so powerfully related to individual differences in behavior, researchers have been intensely interested in finding out exactly which social influences cause it to be high for some children and low for others. If ways can be found to improve children's sense of self-worth, then many aspects of child development might be enhanced as well.

**Child-Rearing Practices.** School-age children whose parents are warm and responsive and who provide firm but reasonable expectations for behavior—that is, who use an *authoritative* child-rearing style (see Chapter 10)—feel especially good about themselves (Bishop & Ingersoll, 1989; Coopersmith, 1967). If you think carefully about this finding, you will see that it makes perfect sense. Warm, positive parenting lets children know that they are accepted as competent, worthwhile human beings. And firm but appropriate expectations, backed up with explanations, seem to help children make sensible choices and evaluate their own behavior against realistic standards.

Although parental acceptance and maturity demands are undoubtedly important ingredients of high self-esteem, we must keep in mind that these findings are correlational. We cannot really tell the extent to which child-rearing styles cause or result from children's characteristics and behavior. Research focusing on the precise content of adults' messages to children has been far more successful at isolating factors that affect children's sense of self-worth. Let's see how these communicative forces mold children's evaluations of themselves.

**Making Attributions: Reasoning About the Causes of Success and Failure.** **Attributions** are our common, everyday explanations for the causes of behavior—the answers we provide to the question, "Why did I (or another person) do that?" Look back at Joey's conversation about the spelling bee at the beginning of this chapter. Notice how he attributes his second-place performance to *luck* (Belinda got all the easy words) and his usual success at spelling to *ability* (he *knows* he's a better speller than Belinda). Joey also appreciates that *effort* makes a difference; he "knocked himself out studying those spelling words."

Cognitive development permits children to recognize and separate all these variables in explaining performance—something they could not do during the preschool

**Attributions**
Common, everyday explanations for the causes of behavior.

*Children who receive feedback from others that attributes their successes to high ability and their failures to insufficient effort are likely to be mastery-oriented youngsters who approach difficult tasks with enthusiasm and persistence.* (Dennis MacDonald/The Picture Cube)

years (Chapman & Skinner, 1989; Dweck & Leggett, 1988). Yet school-age children differ greatly in the extent to which they account for their successes and failures in healthy and adaptive ways. Children who are high in academic self-esteem develop **mastery-oriented attributions** (see Concept Table 13.1). They believe their successes are due to ability—a characteristic they can count on in the future when faced with new challenges. And when failure occurs, they attribute it to factors about themselves or the environment that can be changed and controlled, such as insufficient effort or a very difficult task. So regardless of whether these children succeed or fail, they take an industrious, persistent, and enthusiastic approach to learning.

Unfortunately, other children, who develop **learned helplessness,** hold far less flattering explanations for their performance. They attribute their failures, not their successes, to ability. And unlike their mastery-oriented counterparts, they have come to believe that ability is a fixed characteristic of the self that cannot be changed. They do not think that competence can be improved by trying hard. So when a task is difficult, these children experience an anxious loss of control—in Erikson's terms, a pervasive sense of inferiority. They quickly give up, saying "I can't do this," before they have really tried (Dweck & Elliott, 1983).

What accounts for the very different attributions of mastery-oriented and learned helpless children? The feedback they receive from parents and teachers plays a key role. In one study, children who displayed a learned helpless approach in math had parents who believed they were less capable and had to work harder to succeed. The children, in turn, adopted these beliefs (Parsons, Adler, & Kaczala, 1982). In another study, researchers manipulated the feedback that fourth and fifth graders received after they failed at a task. Once again, those receiving negative messages about their competence more often attributed failure to lack of ability than did children who were told that they had not tried hard enough (Dweck et al., 1978).

Some children are especially likely to have their performance undermined by the kind of feedback they receive from adults. Girls more often than boys blame their ability for poor performance. Girls also tend to receive messages from teachers and parents that their ability is at fault when they do not do well (Dweck & Elliott, 1983). Low-income ethnic minority children are also vulnerable to learned helplessness. In most studies comparing teacher communication with black and white pupils, black

**Mastery-oriented attributions**

Attributions that credit success to high ability and failure to insufficient effort. Leads to high self-esteem and a willingness to approach challenging tasks.

**Learned helplessness**

A pattern of attributions in which failures are credited to lack of ability. Leads to anxious loss of control in the face of challenging tasks.

**CONCEPT TABLE 13.1 • An Attributional Approach to Success and Failure in Middle Childhood**

| Concept | Important Point | Example |
|---|---|---|
| Mastery-oriented attributions | Children with mastery-oriented attributions interpret success as due to ability and failure as the result of lack of effort. Because they regard outcomes as controllable, they approach challenging tasks with effort and enthusiasm. | Roy received a D on his recent math test. When his parents inquired about the low grade, Roy said, "I guess I wasn't really trying. I know I can do these problems." Roy reworked the ones he missed. |
| Learned helplessness | Children with learned helplessness attribute their failures to ability. When faced with challenging tasks, they experience an anxious loss of control and give up without really trying. | After Adrian did poorly on a math test, he said to his parents, "I just can't understand this stuff! No matter what I do, I keep getting bad grades. Let's face it, I'm stupid at math." |

children received less favorable treatment (Aaron & Powell, 1982; Hillman & Davenport, 1978; Irvine, 1986). Also, when ethnic minority children observe that adults in their own family are not rewarded by society for their achievement efforts, they may give up themselves. Many African-American children may come to believe that even if they do try in school, social prejudice will prevent them from succeeding in the end (Ogbu, 1988).

*Supporting Children's Self-Esteem.* Attribution research suggests that even adults who are, on the whole, warm and supportive may send subtle messages to children that undermine their competence. **Attribution retraining** is an approach to intervention that encourages learned helpless youngsters to believe that they can overcome failure if only they exert more effort. Most often, children are asked to work on tasks that are hard enough so that some failure experiences are bound to occur. Then they get repeated feedback that helps them revise their attributions, such as, "You can do it if you try harder." Children are also taught to view their successes as due to both ability and effort, rather than chance factors, by giving them additional feedback after they succeed, such as, "You're really good at this" or "You really tried hard on that one." These procedures are remarkably effective in helping children believe in themselves and persist in the face of task difficulty (Dweck, 1975; Schunk, 1983).

To work well, attribution retraining may need to begin in middle childhood, before children's views of themselves become hard to change. An even better approach is to prevent low self-esteem before it happens—by minimizing comparisons among children, helping them overcome failures, and designing school environments that accommodate individual differences in development and styles of learning. Finally, extra measures should be taken to support the self-esteem of girls and ethnic minority children—by providing role models of adult success, fostering ethnic pride, and ensuring equality of opportunity in society at large.

• *Return to page 407 of Chapter 11 and review the messages that parents send to girls about their athletic talent. On the basis of what you know about children's attributions for success and failure, why do school-age girls perform more poorly and spend less time at sports than do boys?*

• *In view of Joey's attributions for his spelling bee performance, is he likely to enter the next spelling bee and try hard to do well? Why or why not?*

**BRIEF REVIEW** Erikson's stage of industry versus inferiority indicates that when family, school, and peer experiences are positive, school-age children develop an industrious approach to productive work and feelings of competence and mastery.

During middle childhood, psychological traits and social comparisons appear in children's self-descriptions. A differentiated, hierarchically organized self-esteem emerges, and children's sense of self-worth declines as they adjust their self-judgments to fit the opinions of others and their objective performance. Parental warmth and reasonable maturity demands are related to high self-esteem. Attribution research has identified adult communication styles that affect children's explanations for success and failure and, in turn, their self-esteem and task performance.

## EMOTIONAL DEVELOPMENT IN MIDDLE CHILDHOOD

Greater self-awareness and social sensitivity spur emotional development forward in middle childhood. Gains take place in children's experiencing of complex emotions, their awareness of emotional states, and emotional self-regulation.

In middle childhood, the complex emotions of pride and guilt become clearly integrated with personal responsibility. Unlike preschoolers, 6- to 11-year-olds experience these feelings in the absence of adult monitoring. A teacher or parent does not have to be present for a new accomplishment to spark a glowing sense of pride or for a transgression to arouse painful pangs of guilt (Harter, Wright, & Bresnick, 1987). Also, school-age youngsters do not report guilt for any mishap, as they did at younger ages, but only for intentional wrongdoing, such as ignoring responsibilities, cheating, or lying (Graham, Doubleday, & Guarino, 1984).

School-age children are also much more aware of the diversity of emotional experiences. By the end of middle childhood, children recognize that individuals can experience more than one emotion at a time—in other words, they can have "mixed feelings" (Gnepp, McKee, & Domanic, 1987; Harter & Buddin, 1987). For example, recalling the birthday present he received from his grandmother, Joey reflected, "I was happy that I got something but sad that I didn't get just what I wanted." Similarly, Joey appreciates that emotional reactions need not reflect a person's true feelings. Consequently, he is much better at hiding his own emotions when it is socially appropriate to do so. "I got all excited and told grandma I liked that dumb plastic toy train," Joey said to Rena one day, "but I really don't. It's too babyish for a 10-year-old" (Saarni, 1989).

Rapid gains in emotional self-regulation occur in middle childhood as children come up with many more ways to handle emotionally arousing situations. In several studies, 5- to 11-year-olds were told stories about positive and negative events, such as having to wait before receiving an attractive prize, getting a shot at the doctor's office, or receiving a bad grade on a test. Then they were asked what could be done to control emotions under these conditions. With age, children were less likely to mention complete avoidance, such as leaving the scene or going to sleep—a form of coping that is usually counterproductive. And while children of all ages were aware that they could distract themselves through behavioral techniques, such as reading or watching TV, older children more often mentioned cognitive strategies for handling feelings. When an event could not be changed, they came up with ways of reinterpreting it that enabled them to accept current conditions (Altshuler & Ruble, 1989; Band & Weisz, 1988). For example, to getting a shot, one child suggested, "Think happy thoughts. Remind yourself it'll be over soon." To a bad grade on a test, another redefined the event by saying, "Things could be worse. There'll be another test."

School-age children are not just better at recognizing and responding to their own feelings. They are also more aware of the thoughts and feelings of others, as we will see in the next section.

**Attribution retraining**

An approach to intervention in which attributions of learned helpless children are modified through feedback that encourages them to believe in themselves and persist in the face of task difficulty.

## UNDERSTANDING OTHERS

By the mid-elementary school years, children discover consistencies in the behavior of people they know. As with their self-descriptions, they begin to describe other people in terms of psychological traits (Barenboim, 1977; Eder, 1989). This increases their awareness that others may react differently than they do to social situations. Middle childhood brings with it major advances in **perspective-taking**—the capacity to imagine what other people may be thinking and feeling.

### Selman's Stages of Perspective-Taking

Robert Selman has developed a five-stage model describing major changes in children's perspective-taking skill. He asked preschool through adolescent-age youngsters to respond to social dilemmas in which the characters have differing information and opinions about an event. Here is one example:

> Holly is an 8-year-old girl who likes to climb trees. She is the best tree climber in the neighborhood. One day while climbing down from a tall tree she falls off the bottom branch but does not hurt herself. Her father sees her fall. He is upset and asks her to promise not to climb trees anymore. Holly promises.
>    Later that day, Holly and her friends meet Sean. Sean's kitten is caught up in a tree and cannot get down. Something has to be done right away or the kitten may fall. Holly is the only one who climbs trees well enough to reach the kitten and get it down, but she remembers her promise to her father. (Selman & Byrne, 1974, p. 805)

After the dilemma is presented, children answer questions that highlight their ability to interpret the story from varying points of view, such as:

> Does Sean know why Holly cannot decide whether or not to climb the tree?
> What will Holly's father think? Will he understand if she climbs the tree?
> Does Holly think she will be punished for climbing the tree? Should she be punished for doing so?

Table 13.1 summarizes Selman's five stages of perspective-taking. As you can see, children gradually include a wider range of information in their understanding of others' viewpoints. At first, they have only a limited idea of what other people might be thinking and feeling. Over time, they become more conscious of the fact that people can interpret the same event in quite different ways. Soon, they can "step in another person's shoes" and reflect on how that person might regard their own thoughts, feelings, and behavior. Finally, they can examine the relationship between two peoples' perspectives simultaneously, at first from the vantage point of a disinterested spectator and, finally, by making reference to societal values.

Both cross-sectional and longitudinal research provides support for Selman's stages (Gurucharri & Selman, 1982; Selman, 1980). Even so, perspective-taking skill varies greatly among children of the same age. These individual differences have to do with cognitive development as well as everyday experiences in which adults and peers clarify their own viewpoints, encouraging children to look at situations from another's perspective (Dixon & Moore, 1990; Krebs & Gillmore, 1982).

### Perspective-Taking and Social Behavior

Children's developing ability to appreciate the perspectives of others helps them get along with other people. When we anticipate another person's point of view, social relationships become more predictable. Each individual can plan actions with some knowledge of what the other person is likely to do in return. In addition, when

**Perspective-taking**
The capacity to imagine what other people may be thinking and feeling.

TABLE 13.1 • Selman's Five Stages of Perspective-Taking

| Stage | Age | Description | Typical Response to the "Holly" Dilemma |
|---|---|---|---|
| Undifferentiated perspective-taking | 3–6 | Children recognize that the self and others can have different thoughts and feelings, but they frequently confuse the two. | The child predicts that Holly will save the kitten because she does not want it to get hurt and believes that Holly's father will feel just as she does about her climbing the tree: "Happy, he likes kittens." |
| Social-informational perspective-taking | 5–9 | Children understand that different perspectives may result because people have access to different information. | When asked how Holly's father will react when he finds out that she climbed the tree, the child responds, "If he didn't know anything about the kitten, he would be angry. But if Holly shows him the kitten, he might change his mind." |
| Self-reflective perspective-taking | 7–12 | Children can "step in another person's shoes" and view their own thoughts, feelings, and behavior from the other person's perspective. They also recognize that others can do the same. | When asked whether Holly thinks she will be punished, the child says, "No. Holly knows that her father will understand why she climbed the tree." This response assumes that Holly's point of view is influenced by her father being able to "step in her shoes" and understand why she saved the kitten. |
| Third-party perspective-taking | 10–15 | Children can step outside a two-person situation and imagine how the self and other are viewed from the point of view of a third, impartial party. | When asked whether Holly should be punished, the child says, "No, because Holly thought it was important to save the kitten. But she also knows that her father told her not to climb the tree. So she'd only think she shouldn't be punished if she could get her father to understand why she had to climb the tree." This response steps outside the immediate situation to view both Holly's and her father's perspectives simultaneously. |
| Societal perspective-taking | 14–Adult | Individuals understand that third-party perspective-taking can be influenced by one or more systems of larger societal values. | When asked if Holly should be punished, the individual responds, "No. The value of humane treatment of animals justifies Holly's action. Her father's appreciation of this value will lead him not to punish her." |

*Sources:* Selman, 1976; Selman & Byrne, 1974.

children recognize that other people may have thoughts and feelings different from their own, they can respond to the momentary needs of others more effectively.

It is not surprising that perspective-taking is related to a wide variety of social skills in middle childhood. Good perspective-takers are more likely to display empathy and compassion (Eisenberg et al., 1987). In addition, they are better at *social problem solving,* or thinking of effective ways to handle difficult social situations (Marsh, Serafica, & Barenboim, 1981). In fact, once children are capable of self-reflective perspective-taking (see Table 13.1), they often rely on it to clear up everyday misunderstandings. For example, one day when Joey happened to tease Terry in a friendly way, Terry took offense. Joey made use of advanced perspective-taking to patch up the situation. "Terry, I didn't mean it," he explained, "I *thought you would think* I was just kidding when I said that."

Children with very poor social skills—in particular, those with the angry, aggressive styles that we discussed in Chapter 10—have great difficulty imagining the thoughts and feelings of others. They often mistreat adults and peers without feeling the guilt and remorse that is engendered by awareness of another's point of view (MacQuiddy, Maise, & Hamilton, 1987). Interventions that provide these children with coaching and practice in perspective-taking are helpful in reducing antisocial behavior and increasing empathy and prosocial responding (Chalmers & Townsend, 1990; Chandler, 1973).

## MORAL DEVELOPMENT IN MIDDLE CHILDHOOD

Recall from Chapter 10 that preschoolers pick up a great many morally relevant behaviors through modeling and reinforcement. By the time they enter middle childhood, they have had time to reflect on these experiences, putting them together into rules for good conduct, such as, "It's good to help others in trouble" or "It's wrong to take something that doesn't belong to you." Consequently, school-age children can follow internalized standards, even when behaviors consistent with them are not being demonstrated or rewarded by others at the moment.

These changes lead children to become considerably more independent and trustworthy. During middle childhood, they can take on many more responsibilities, from running an errand at the supermarket to making sure a younger sibling does not wander into the street. Of course, these advances only take place when children have had much time to profit from the consistent guidance and example of caring adults in their lives.

In Chapter 10, we also saw that children do not just copy their morality from those around them. As the cognitive-developmental approach emphasizes, from an early age they actively think about right and wrong. Children's expanding social world and their increasing ability to take the perspective of others leads moral understanding to improve greatly in middle childhood.

### Learning About Justice Through Sharing

In everyday life, children frequently experience situations that involve **distributive justice**—beliefs about how to divide up material goods fairly. Heated discussions often take place over how much weekly allowance is to be given to siblings of different ages, who has to sit where in the family car on a long trip, and in what way an eight-slice pizza is to be shared by six hungry playmates. William Damon (1977, 1988) has studied children's changing concepts of distributive justice over early and middle childhood.

Even 4-year-olds recognize the importance of sharing, but their reasons for doing so often seem contradictory and self-serving. When asked why they gave some of their toys to a playmate, preschoolers typically say something like this: "I shared because if I didn't, she wouldn't play with me" or "I let her have some, but most are for me because I'm older."

As children enter middle childhood, they start to express more mature notions of distributive justice (see Table 13.2). At first, these ideas of fairness are based on *equality*. Children in the early school grades are intent on making sure that each

**Distributive justice**
Beliefs about how to divide up material goods fairly.

TABLE 13.2 • Damon's Sequence of Distributive Justice Reasoning

| Basis of Reasoning | Age | Description |
|---|---|---|
| Equality | 5–6 | Fairness involves strictly equal distribution of goods. Special considerations like merit and need are not taken into account. |
| Merit | 6–7 | Fairness is based on deservingness. Children recognize that some people should get more because they have worked harder. |
| Benevolence | 8 | Fairness includes giving special consideration to those who are disadvantaged. More should be given to those who are in need. |

person gets the same amount of a treasured resource, such as money, turns in a game, or a delicious treat.[1]

A short time later, children start to view fairness in terms of *merit*. Extra rewards should be given to someone who has worked especially hard or otherwise performed in an exceptional way. Finally, around age 8, children can reason on the basis of *benevolence*. They recognize that special consideration should be given to those in a condition of disadvantage, like the needy or the handicapped. Older children indicate that an extra amount might be given to a child who cannot produce as much or who does not get any allowance from his parents.

According to Damon (1988), parental advice and encouragement support these developing standards of justice, but the give-and-take of peer interaction is especially important. Peer disagreements, along with efforts to resolve them, make children more sensitive to others' perspectives, and this, in turn, supports their developing ideas of justice. Indeed, mature distributive justice reasoning shows many of the same relationships to everyday social behavior as perspective-taking. For example, it is associated with more effective social problem solving and a greater willingness to help and share with others (Blotner & Bearison, 1984; McNamee & Peterson, 1986).

## Changes in Moral and Social Conventional Understanding

As their ideas about justice advance, children clarify and create linkages between moral rules and social conventions. During middle childhood, they realize that situations do arise when the two overlap. Sometimes, violations of social conventions are moral matters! For example, saying "thank you" after receiving a present is an arbitrary practice arrived at by social agreement. At the same time, not doing so can injure others by hurting their feelings (Turiel, 1983).

As children think about the connections between social conventions and moral rules, they also come to realize that certain conventions, which they took as absolute truths during preschool years, are far more arbitrary than they formerly believed. Sex-stereotyped beliefs are an example. We will see later in this chapter that school-age youngsters have a more flexible appreciation of the activities and occupations appropriate for males and females—a development that parallels their improved understanding of the distinction between moral rules and social conventions (Carter & Patterson, 1982).

At this point, you may be wondering: As children work out their ideas about morality, are their discoveries universal ones arrived at by children everywhere? Box 13.1 presents some intriguing cross-cultural evidence that bears on this issue.

*BRIEF REVIEW* In middle childhood, complex emotions become clearly linked to personal responsibility. Children's awareness of emotional experience expands, and they become better at emotional self-regulation. Perspective-taking undergoes major advances and is related to a wide variety of positive social skills. Moral understanding also improves. Children develop more advanced notions of distributive justice, and they begin to appreciate the overlap between moral rules and social conventions.

• *Return to Joey's description of Belinda Brown at the beginning of this chapter. How does it reflect changes in children's understanding of others during middle childhood?*

• *When given the "Holly" dilemma and asked, "Does Holly think she will be punished for climbing the tree?" Lizzie responded, "No, Holly knows that her father will understand how sad she would feel if she let that kitten fall out of the tree." Which of Selman's perspective-taking stages is Lizzie at?*

[1]Recall from Chapter 12 that in some cultures, equal sharing of goods among children is not common, and conservation is greatly delayed (see page 419). It is possible that Damon's sequence of distributive justice reasoning does not represent children's concepts of fairness in all societies.

## CULTURAL INFLUENCES

### Box 13.1  *Children's Moral Concepts in India and the United States*

A re there universal moral imperatives, such as truth, justice, and the value of human life, that all children appreciate in much the same way? Or does the understanding and acceptance of moral beliefs depend on cultural context? Interviews with 8- to 10-year-olds in India and the United States revealed that children's notions of morality are far more diverse than researchers previously thought (Shweder, Mahapatra, & Miller, 1990). The Indian children were Hindus, members of the dominant religion of India. For centuries, Hinduism has had a powerful influence on Indian culture. It regards a wide variety of moral and social rules as part of a natural world order, not as invented by human beings.

The children were asked to rank a large number of social and moral concerns from most serious to least serious. Indian and American youngsters differed sharply in their moral beliefs. Indian children regarded certain food and politeness transgressions as more serious than selfish behavior or even family violence. For example, they thought that eating chicken a day after a father's death or calling parents by their first names was much worse than a man beating his wife or his son for misbehavior. American children, in contrast, condemned wife and child beating but thought eating forbidden foods and referring to parents on a first-name basis were perfectly all right.

These findings suggest that the Western tendency to separate morality from social conventions is not shared by all cultures. In India, as in many Third World countries, culturally specific practices have profound moral and religious significance. For example, one Indian mother explained that not taking a bath and changing clothes before eating breakfast would be considered an unfavorable sign—an indication that something bad might happen to the family. In her opinion, wearing the proper clothes at the right time is not arbitrary. "It has something to do with respect

*In Hindu culture, moral rules and social conventions are less distinct than they are in the United States. Unlike most Americans, Hindus regard violating certain food and politeness customs as serious moral transgressions. (Rameshwar Das/ Monkmeyer Press)*

for oneself, for others, for one's station in life, for God, and for the rhythms of nature" (Shweder, 1990, p. 2063).

Finally, Indian and American children did not differ with respect to all moral beliefs. Both agreed that it is wrong to ignore beggars, break promises, destroy another person's property, kick harmless animals, and steal flowers. These responses may reflect a common basis of morality—a sense of justice that will become increasingly abstract and rational during adolescence and young adulthood. Although American children grapple with the relationship between moral rules and social conventions, never are the two as closely linked as they are for Indian children. There seem to be both cultural universals and diversity in moral thought.

## PEER RELATIONS IN MIDDLE CHILDHOOD

In Chapter 10, we saw how peer interaction expands during the preschool years, supported by cognitive and language development as well as parental encouragement and example. In middle childhood, the society of peers becomes an increasingly important context for development.

## Peer Groups

If you watch children in the school yard or neighborhood, you will see that groups of three to a dozen or more often gather. The organization of these collectives changes greatly with age. By the end of middle childhood, children display a strong desire for group belongingness. Together, they generate unique values and standards for behavior. They also create a social structure of leaders and followers that ensures group goals will be met. When these characteristics are present, a **peer group** has formed (Hartup, 1983).

The practices of these informal groups lead to a "peer culture" that typically consists of a specialized vocabulary, dress code, and place to "hang out" during leisure hours. For example, Joey formed a club with three other boys. The children met in the treehouse in Joey's backyard, called each other by nicknames, and wore a "uniform" consisting of T-shirts, jeans, and tennis shoes. Calling themselves "the pack," the boys developed a secret handshake and chose Joey as their leader. Their activities included improving the clubhouse, trading baseball cards, making trips to the video arcade, and—just as important—keeping girls and adults out!

As children develop these exclusive associations, the codes of dress and behavior that grow out of them become more broadly influential. At school, children who deviate are often rebuffed by their peers. "Kissing up" to teachers, wearing the wrong kind of shirt or shoes, tattling on classmates, or carrying a strange-looking lunch box are grounds for critical glances and comments until a child's behavior is brought in line with group expectations.

These special customs bind peers together, creating a sense of group identity. In addition, by participating in peer groups, children acquire many valuable social skills. The group provides a context in which children practice cooperation, leadership, and followership and develop a sense of loyalty to collective goals. Through these experiences, children experiment with and learn much about social organizations.

The beginning of peer group ties is also a time in which some of the "nicest children begin to behave in the most awful way" (Redl, 1966, p. 395). During their

Peer groups first form in middle childhood. These boys have probably established a social structure of leaders and followers as they gather often for joint activities, such as bike riding and basketball. Their body language suggests that they feel a strong sense of group belonging. (R. Sidney/The Image Works)

**Peer group**
Peers who form a social unit by generating shared values and standards of behavior and a social structure of leaders and followers.

10-year-old daughter's slumber party, two parents I know listened in on a stream of petty, malicious remarks about several uninvited classmates. The parents vowed to never permit their daughter to have friends sleep over again! From fourth grade on, gossip, rumor spreading, and exclusion rise among girls, who (because of sex-role expectations) express aggression in subtle, indirect ways (Cairns et al., 1989). Boys are more straightforward in their hostility toward the "outgroup." Prank playing, such as egging a house, making a funny phone call, or ringing a door bell and running away, often occurs among small groups of boys, who provide one another with temporary social support for these mildly antisocial behaviors (Fine, 1980).

The school-age child's desire for group belongingness can also be satisfied through formal group ties—Girl Scouts, Boy Scouts, 4-H, church groups, and other associations. Adult involvement holds in check the negative behaviors associated with children's informal peer groups. In addition, children gain much from these memberships as they work on joint projects and help in their communities. Those who participate are advanced in social and moral understanding (Harris, Mussen, & Rutherford, 1976; Keasey, 1971).

## Friendships

While peer groups provide children with insight into larger social structures, close, one-to-one friendships contribute to the development of trust and sensitivity. During the school years, children's concepts of friendship become more complex and psychologically based. Compare the following answers of a 5-year-old and an 8-year-old to questions about what makes a best friend:

> (five-year-old). Why is Amy your best friend? *I like her. I knew her in . . . [preschool] and I knew her before I came to school.* How did you meet Amy? *We sat on the bus, we played together. . . .* Would you let Amy ride your bike? *Yes, if she came over to my house.* Why would Amy come over to your house? *Because I want her to. . . .* How do you make a friend? *You say, "Hi, what's your name," and that's all.*

> (eight-year-old). Who's your best friend? *Shelly.* Why is Shelly your best friend? *Because she helps me when I'm sad, and she shares. . . .* What makes Shelly so special? *I've known*

*In schools and neighborhoods where interracial contact is common, many children form close cross-race friendships.* (Tony Freeman/PhotoEdit)

*her longer, I sit next to her and got to know her better. . . .* How come you like Shelly better than anyone else? *She's done the most for me. She never disagrees, she never eats in front of me, she never walks away when I'm crying, and she helps me on my homework. . . .* How do you get someone to like you? *. . . . If you're nice to [your friends], they'll be nice to you.* (Damon, 1988, pp. 80–81)

As these responses show, during middle childhood friendship is no longer just a matter of engaging in the same activities. Instead, it becomes a mutually agreed on relationship in which children like each other's personal qualities and respond to one another's needs and desires. Since friendship is a matter of both children wanting to be together, getting it started takes more time and effort than it did at earlier ages. And once a friendship is formed, *trust* becomes its defining feature. School-age children state that a good friendship is based on acts of kindness that signify each person can be counted on to support the other. Consequently, events that break up a friendship are quite different than they were during the preschool years. Older children regard violations of trust, such as not helping when others need help, breaking promises, and gossiping behind the other's back, as serious breaches of friendship (Damon, 1977; Selman, 1980).

Because of these features, school-age children are more selective about their friendships. Preschoolers say they have lots of friends—sometimes, everyone in their class! By age 8 or 9, children have only a handful of people they call friends and, very often, only one best friend. Girls, especially, are likely to be exclusive in their friendships because they demand greater closeness in the relationship than do boys (Berndt, 1986). In addition, throughout childhood friends tend to be of the same age, sex, race, and social class. Note, however, that characteristics of schools and neighborhoods affect friendships. For example, in integrated schools, as many as 50 percent of pupils report at least one close cross-race friend (DuBois & Hirsch, 1990).

Through friendship, children learn the importance of emotional commitment. They come to realize that close relationships can survive disagreements if both parties are secure in their liking for one another (Nelson & Aboud, 1985). Friendships remain fairly stable over middle childhood. Most last for several years. But as children approach puberty, their varying rates of development and changing interests cause many friendships to break up and new ones to be established (Berndt, 1988). As we will see in Chapter 16, the basis of friendship will change further in adolescence.

## Peer Acceptance

As we all know from our own childhoods, some children make friends and enter peer groups far more easily than others. In Chapters 11 and 12, we saw that obese and handicapped youngsters often have great difficulty with peer acceptance. Yet there are other children whose appearance and intellectual abilities are quite normal; still, their classmates despise them.

Researchers assess peer acceptance with **sociometric techniques.** These are self-report measures that ask peers to evaluate one another's likability. For example, children may be asked to nominate several peers in their class whom they especially like or dislike, to indicate for all possible pairs of classmates which one they prefer to play with, or to rate each peer on a scale from "like very much" to "like very little" (Asher & Hymel, 1981). Children's responses reveal four different categories of social acceptance: **popular children,** who get many positive votes; **rejected children,** who are actively disliked; **controversial children,** who get a large number of positive and negative votes; and **neglected children,** who are seldom chosen, either positively or negatively. About two-thirds of pupils in a typical elementary school classroom fit one of these categories. The remaining one third are *average* in peer acceptance; they do not receive extreme scores (Coie, Dodge, & Coppotelli, 1982).

Peer acceptance is a powerful predictor of current as well as later psychological

**Sociometric techniques**
Self-report measures that ask peers to evaluate one another's likability.

**Popular children**
Children who get many positive votes on sociometric measures of peer acceptance.

**Rejected children**
Children who are actively disliked and get many negative votes on sociometric measures of peer acceptance.

**Controversial children**
Children who get a large number of positive and negative votes on sociometric measures of peer acceptance.

**Neglected children**
Children who are seldom chosen, either positively or negatively, on sociometric measures of peer acceptance.

adjustment. Rejected children, especially, are unhappy, alienated, poorly achieving children with a low sense of self-esteem (French & Waas, 1985). Both teachers and parents rate them as having a wide range of emotional and social problems. Peer rejection in middle childhood is also strongly associated with dropping out of school and delinquency in adolescence and criminality in young adulthood (Parker & Asher, 1987).

***Determinants of Peer Acceptance.*** What causes one child to be liked and another to be rejected? A wealth of research reveals that social behavior plays a powerful role. Popular children have very positive social skills. They communicate with peers in sensitive, friendly, and cooperative ways. When they do not understand another child's reaction, they ask for an explanation. If they disagree with a play partner in a game, they go beyond voicing their displeasure; they suggest what the other child could do instead. When they want to enter an ongoing play group, they adapt their behavior to the flow of the activity (Dodge et al., 1983; Gottman, Gonso, & Rasmussen, 1975; Ladd & Price, 1987).

Rejected children, in contrast, display high rates of conflict, aggression, and immature play (Coie & Koeppl, 1990). They grab belongings and bully their classmates—behaviors that worsen with age. Over time, these children seem to learn that by intimidating others, they can get their way (Coie et al., 1991). Rejected children are also deficient in social understanding, including perspective-taking and the ability to think of effective ways to solve social problems (Rubin & Daniels-Bierness, 1983). And they often misinterpret the innocent behaviors of peers as hostile. A classmate who cracks a friendly joke or accidently bumps into them is in store for an intense retaliation because these youngsters cannot judge the intentions of others accurately (Waas, 1988).

Consistent with the mixed peer opinion they engender, controversial children display a blend of positive and negative social behaviors. Like rejected youngsters, they are active and disruptive, but they also engage in high rates of positive, prosocial acts (Coie, Dodge, & Coppotelli, 1982). As yet, researchers know very little about the causes of this behavior style or its consequences for long-term adjustment. It is not clear whether the positive social skills of controversial children offset the negative ones, reducing their chances of developing later problems.

Finally, perhaps the most surprising finding on peer acceptance is that neglected children, once thought to be in need of treatment, are usually well adjusted. Although these youngsters engage in low rates of interaction and are considered shy by their classmates, the majority are just as socially skilled as average children. They do not report feeling especially lonely, and when they want to, they can break away from their usual pattern of playing by themselves (Asher & Wheeler, 1985; Coie & Kupersmidt, 1983). Neglected children remind us that there are other paths to emotional well-being besides the outgoing, gregarious personality style that is so highly valued in our culture.

***Helping Rejected Children.*** A variety of interventions aimed at improving the rejected child's peer relations and psychological adjustment have been developed. Most involve coaching, modeling, and reinforcement of positive social skills, such as how to begin interacting with a peer, cooperate in play, and respond to another child with friendly emotion and approval. Several of these programs have produced lasting gains in social competence and peer acceptance (Bierman, 1986; Mize & Ladd, 1990).

Some researchers believe that these interventions might be made even more effective by combining them with other treatments. Often rejected children are poor students, and their low cognitive self-esteem magnifies their negative reactions to teachers and classmates. Intensive academic tutoring has been shown to improve both their school achievement and social acceptance (Coie & Kreihbel, 1984). Other interventions focus on training in perspective-taking and social problem solving (Ladd & Mize, 1983). Still another approach is to increase rejected children's expectations for social success. Many conclude, after repeated rebuffs from peers, that no matter how hard they try, they will never be liked. Rejected youngsters make better use of the social skills they do have when they believe peers will accept them (Rabiner & Coie, 1989).

## SEX TYPING IN MIDDLE CHILDHOOD

Children's understanding of sex roles broadens in middle childhood, and their sex-role identities (views of themselves as relatively masculine or feminine) change as well. We will see that the direction of development is different for boys and girls, and it can vary considerably across cultures.

### School-Age Children's Sex-Stereotyped Beliefs

During the school years, children extend the sex-stereotyped beliefs they acquired in early childhood. As soon as they can think about people as personalities, they label some traits as more typical of one sex rather than the other. For example, school-age youngsters regard "tough," "aggressive," "rational," and "dominant" as masculine and "gentle," "sympathetic," "excitable," and "affectionate" as feminine, in much the same way adults do (Best et al., 1977).

Not long after children enter elementary school, they figure out which academic subjects and skill areas are more "for boys" and which ones are more "for girls." Throughout the school years, children tend to regard reading, art, and music as feminine and mathematics, athletics, and mechanical skills as masculine (Huston, 1983). This form of stereotyping influences children's preferences for certain subjects and, in turn, how well do at them. In a study in which children in Japan, Taiwan, and the United States were asked to name the school subject they liked best, in all three countries girls were more likely to prefer reading while boys tended to

*During middle childhood, girls feel freer than boys to engage in "opposite-sex" activities. These girls participate in a team sport typically reserved for boys and men.* (Tony Freeman/PhotoEdit)

prefer mathematics. Asked to predict their future performance, boys thought they would do better in math. In contrast, no sex difference emerged in predictions about reading (Lummis & Stevenson, 1990). As we will see in Chapter 15, these beliefs become realities in adolescence.

Of course, just because children are aware of stereotypes does not mean that they endorse them. Some evidence suggests that school-age youngsters (unlike pre-schoolers) do not necessarily approve of sex-typed distinctions (Kelly & Smail, 1986). In middle childhood, children begin to realize that boys and girls often do certain things because, as one child put it, "it is the way we have been brought up," not because of physical differences between the sexes. This view is more common among girls than boys. Throughout childhood and adolescence, boys hold more sex-typed beliefs, and they are also more likely to think sex differences are due to biological rather than social causes (Smith & Russell, 1984).

### Sex-Role Identity and Behavior

Boys' and girls' sex-role identities follow different paths of development in middle childhood. From third to sixth grade, boys strengthen their identification with the masculine role. In contrast, girls' identification with feminine traits declines. Although girls still lean toward the feminine side, they begin to describe themselves as having some "opposite-sex" characteristics (Hall & Halberstadt, 1980). You can see this difference in the activities children choose in middle childhood. While boys usually stick to "masculine" pursuits, girls feel free to experiment with a wider range of options. Besides cooking, sewing, and baby-sitting, they join organized sports teams, take up science projects, and build forts in the backyard (Huston-Stein & Higgins-Trenk, 1978).

In Chapter 10, we saw that parents encourage sex-typed activities and behaviors, and they are far less tolerant when sons as opposed to daughters cross gender lines. These child-rearing influences play important roles in the developmental trends we have just described. Peers are also influential. A tomboyish girl can make her way into boys' activities without losing status with her female peers, but a boy who hangs out with girls is likely to be ridiculed and rejected. Finally, perhaps school-age girls realize that society attaches greater prestige to "masculine" characteristics. As a result, they want to try some of the activities and behaviors associated with the more highly valued sex role (Ullian, 1976).

### Cultural Influences on Sex Typing

Although the sex differences described here are typical in Western nations, they do not apply to children everywhere. Girls are less likely to experiment with "masculine" activities in cultures in which the gap between male and female roles is especially strong. And when social and economic conditions make it necessary for boys to take over "feminine" tasks, their personalities and behaviors become less stereotyped.

To clarify how cultures shape sex-typed behavior, Beatrice Whiting and Carolyn Edwards (1988a, 1988b) collected detailed information on the daily activities of children in 12 communities around the world. Their findings revealed that in most societies, boys were dominant and aggressive and girls were dependent, compliant, and nurturant. But striking exceptions emerged in communities in which children were given "cross-sex" assignments as part of their daily responsibilities.

One such community is Nyansongo, a small agricultural settlement in Kenya. Nyansongo mothers, who work four to five hours a day in the gardens, assign the care of young children, the tending of the cooking fire, and the washing of dishes to older siblings in the family. Half the boys between ages 5 and 8 take care of infants, and half help with household chores. As a result, girls are relieved of total responsibil-

*This Kenyan boy is often assigned "feminine" tasks, such as caring for infants and helping with household chores. Compared to boys in other cultures, he is likely to be less sex-stereotyped in personality characteristics. (Paul Conklin/Monkmeyer Press)*

ity for "feminine" tasks and have more idle time to interact with agemates. Compared to children of other cultures, Nyansongo youngsters display less conformity to traditional sex roles. Girls' greater freedom and independence leads them to score high in dominance, assertiveness, and playful roughhousing. Boys' caregiving responsibilities mean that they frequently engage in help-giving and emotional support.

Although these findings might be taken to suggest that boys in Western cultures be assigned more "cross-sex" tasks, the consequences of doing so are not so straightforward. Recent evidence shows that when fathers hold traditional sex-role beliefs and their sons engage in "feminine" housework, boys experience strain in the father–child relationship, feel stressed by their responsibilities, and judge themselves to be less competent (McHale et al., 1990). So parental values may need to be consistent with task assignments for children to benefit from them.

*BRIEF REVIEW* During middle childhood, children become members of peer groups, through which they learn much about the functioning of larger social structures. Friendships change, emphasizing mutual trust and assistance. Peer acceptance is a powerful predictor of current and future psychological adjustment. Popular children interact positively, rejected children behave antisocially, and controversial children display a mixture of the two. Neglected children tend to be socially competent youngsters who prefer solitary activities. Programs that train effective social skills, improve academic performance, and increase social understanding have been used to treat rejected children.

Over the school years, children extend their sex-typed beliefs to personality characteristics and achievement areas. Boys' masculine sex-role identities strengthen, while girls' identities become more flexible. However, cultural values and practices can modify these developmental trends.

- *Apply your understanding of attributions to rejected children's social self-esteem. How are rejected children likely to explain their failure to gain peer acceptance? What impact on future efforts to get along with agemates are these attributions likely to have?*

- *Return to Chapter 10, page 376, and review the concept of androgyny. Which of the two sexes is more androgynous in middle childhood, and why?*

## FAMILY INFLUENCES IN MIDDLE CHILDHOOD

As children move out into school, peer, and community contexts, the parent–child relationship changes. At the same time, the school-age child's developing sense of competence continues to depend on the quality of family interaction. We will see that recent changes in the American family—high rates of divorce, remarriage, and maternal employment—can have positive as well as negative effects on children.

### Parent–Child Relationships

During middle childhood, the amount of time children spend with parents declines dramatically. In a study in which parents were asked to keep diaries of family activities, they reported spending less than half as much time in caregiving, teaching, reading, and playing with 5- to 12-year-olds as they did with preschoolers (Hill & Stafford, 1980).

**New Child-Rearing Issues.** The school-age child's growing independence means that parents must deal with new issues. "I've struggled with how many chores to demand of them, how much allowance for what kinds of work, and whether their friends are good influences," noted Rena. "And then there's the problem of how to keep track of them when they're out of the house or even when they're home and I'm not there to see what's going on." Rena worried, especially, about too much television viewing. Indeed, the amount of time children spend in front of the set rises over the school years, from 3 hours a day at age 6 to more than 4 hours at age 11 (Liebert & Sprafkin, 1988). Rena also became concerned over Joey's passion for video games, largely because of their highly violent content. Yet at present, we do not know if video games are as detrimental to children's well-being as televised violence (see Chapter 10, pages 370–371) (Delphi Communication Sciences, 1990).

Besides wondering how to promote responsible behavior and constructive use of leisure time, parents must figure out how to deal with children's problems at school. This task is especially difficult for low-income and ethnic minority parents, who often feel alienated from the school environment. Finally, American parents worry about how much to become involved in their youngster's homework, although (as we saw in Chapter 12) their support plays an important role in children's school success (Maccoby, 1984a).

***Parent–Child Communication.*** Although parents face a new set of concerns, child rearing actually becomes easier for those who established an authoritative style during the early years (Maccoby, 1984b). Reasoning works more effectively with school-age children because of their more logical approach to the world. Nevertheless, older children sometimes use their cognitive powers to bargain and negotiate—a circumstance that can try their parents' patience. "Mom," Joey pleaded for the third time, "if you let Terry and me go to the mall to see that car show tonight, I'll rake all the leaves in the yard, I promise."

Fortunately, parents can appeal to the child's better developed sense of self-esteem, humor, and morality to resolve these difficulties. "Joey, you know it's a school night, and you have a test tomorrow," Rena responded. "You'll be unhappy at the results if you stay out late and don't study. Come on, no more wheeler-dealering!" Perhaps because parents and children have, over time, learned how to resolve conflicts, coercive discipline declines over the school years (Maccoby, 1984a).

As children demonstrate that they can manage daily activities and responsibilities, effective parents gradually shift control from adult to child. But before they let go entirely, parents engage in **coregulation,** a transitional form of supervision in which they exercise general oversight, while permitting children to be in charge of moment-by-moment decision making. Coregulation supports and protects children, who are not yet ready for total independence. At the same time, it prepares them for adolescence, when youngsters will need to make many important decisions themselves.

Coregulation grows out of a cooperative relationship between parent and child—one based on give-and-take and mutual respect. Here is a summary of its critical ingredients:

> The parental tasks . . . are threefold: First, they must monitor, guide, and support their children at a distance—that is, when their children are out of their presence; second, they must effectively use the times when direct contact does occur; and third, they must strengthen in their children the abilities that will allow them to monitor their own behavior, to adopt acceptable standards of good (conduct), to avoid undue risks, and to know when they need parental support and guidance. Children must be willing to inform parents of their whereabouts, activities, and problems so that parents can mediate and guide when necessary. (Maccoby, 1984a, pp. 191–192)

Although school-age children often press for greater independence, they also know how much they need their parents' continuing support. In one study, fourth graders described parents as the most influential people in their lives. They often turned to mothers and fathers for affection, advice, enhancement of self-worth, and assistance with everyday problems (Furman & Buhrmester, 1992).

## Siblings

In addition to parents and friends, siblings are important sources of support to school-age youngsters. Siblings provide one another with companionship, help with

**Coregulation**

A transitional form of supervision in which parents exercise general oversight, while permitting children to be in charge of moment-by-moment decision making.

difficult tasks, and comfort during times of emotional stress (Furman et al., 1989). Yet as everyone with a brother or sister knows, sibling relationships are marked by conflict as well as caring. Over middle childhood, sibling rivalry tends to increase. As children participate in a wider range of activities, parents often compare their youngsters' abilities. The child who gets less parental admiration, more disapproval, and fewer rewards and material resources is likely to resent the one who receives more favorable treatment (McHale & Pawletko, 1992; Stocker, Dunn, & Plomin, 1989).

When siblings are close in age and of the same sex, comparisons take place more frequently, and more quarreling and antagonism results. Siblings often take steps to reduce this rivalry by striving to be different from one another (Huston, 1983). For example, two brothers I know deliberately selected different school subjects, athletic pursuits, and music lessons. At age 7, the younger one said, "What can I play that's *not* the piano [his brother's instrument]?" If the older one did especially well at an activity, the younger one did not want to try it. Of course, parents can reduce these effects by making a special effort not to compare children. But some feedback about their competencies is inevitable, and as siblings strive to win recognition for their own uniqueness, they shape important aspects of each other's development.

Birth order clearly plays an important role in sibling experiences. For a period of time, oldest children have their parents' attention all to themselves. Even after brothers and sisters are born, they receive greater pressure for mature behavior from parents. For this reason, the oldest child is slightly advantaged in IQ and school achievement (Paulhus & Shaffer, 1981; Zajonc, Markus, & Markus, 1979). Younger siblings, in contrast, tend to be more popular with agemates (Miller & Maruyama, 1976). Perhaps as the result of learning to get along with larger, more powerful brothers and sisters, they become especially skilled at negotiating and compromising.

### Divorce

Sibling interaction is affected by other aspects of family life. Joey and Lizzie's relationship, Rena told me, had been particularly negative only a few years before. Joey pushed, hit, taunted, and called Lizzie names. The arguments usually ended with Lizzie running in tears to her mother. Joey and Lizzie's fighting coincided with Rena and her husband's growing marital unhappiness. When Joey was 8 and Lizzie 5, their father Drake moved out.

The children were not alone in having to weather this traumatic event. Between 1960 and 1980, the divorce rate in the United States tripled and then stabilized. Currently, it is the highest in the world, nearly doubling that of the second-ranked country, Sweden. Over one million American children experience the separation and divorce of their parents each year. At any given time, about one-fourth of American youngsters live in single-parent households. The large majority (89 percent) reside with their mothers (U.S. Bureau of the Census, 1991a).

Children spend an average of 5 years in a single-parent home, or almost a third of their total childhood. For many, divorce eventually leads to new family relationships. About two-thirds of divorced parents marry a second time (Glick & Lin, 1987). Half of these children eventually experience a third major change—the breakup of their parent's second marriage (Bumpass, 1984).

These figures reveal that divorce is not a single event in the lives of parents and children. Instead, it is a transition that leads to a variety of new living arrangements, accompanied by changes in housing, income, and family roles and responsibilities (Wallerstein, 1991). Since the 1960s, many studies have reported that marital breakup is quite stressful for children. But the research also reveals great individual differences in how children respond. Among factors that make a difference are the custodial parent's psychological health, the child's characteristics, and social supports

*Although sibling rivalry tends to increase in middle childhood, siblings also provide one another with emotional support and help with difficult tasks. (Erika Stone)*

TABLE 13.3 • Factors Related to Children's Adjustment to Divorce

| Factor | Description |
|---|---|
| Custodial parents' psychological health | A mature, well-adjusted parent is better able to handle stress, shield the child from conflict, and engage in authoritative parenting. |
| Child characteristics | |
|   Age | Preschool and early elementary-school children often blame themselves and show intense separation anxiety. Older children may also react strongly by engaging in disruptive, antisocial acts. However, some display unusually mature, responsible behavior. |
|   Sex | Boys in mother-custody households experience more severe and longer-lasting problems than do girls. |
|   Temperament | Children with difficult temperaments are less able to withstand stress and show longer-lasting difficulties. |
| Social supports | The ability of divorced parents to set aside their hostilities, contact with the noncustodial parent, and positive relationships with extended family members, teachers, and friends lead to improved outcomes for children. |

within the family and surrounding community. As we look at evidence on the impact of divorce, you may find it helpful to refer to the summary in Table 13.3.

***Immediate Consequences.*** "Things were worst during the period in which Drake and I decided to separate," Rena reflected. "We fought over everything—from custody of the children to the living-room furniture. I guess it was all an expression of our raging anger at one another, and the kids really suffered. Lizzie would burst into tears for what seemed like no reason. Once, sobbing, she told me she was 'sorry she made Daddy go away.' Joey kicked and threw things at home. At school, his teacher complained that he was distracted and often didn't do his work. In the midst of everything, I could hardly deal with their problems. We had to sell the house; there was no way I could afford it alone. And I needed a better-paying job. I had to change from teaching part-time to full-time at the university or start looking."

Rena's description captures conditions in many newly divorced households. Family conflict often rises for a period of time as parents try to settle disputes over children and personal belongings. Once one parent moves out, additional events threaten supportive interactions between parents and children. Mother-headed households generally experience a sharp drop in income. Many divorced women lack the education and experience needed to obtain well-paid jobs. To make matters worse, the majority of ex-husbands fail to meet their child support obligations (Children's Defense Fund, 1991d). Mother-headed families often have to move to new housing for economic reasons, reducing supportive ties to neighbors and friends.

These life circumstances often lead to a highly disorganized family situation called "minimal parenting" (Wallerstein & Kelly, 1980). "Meals and bedtimes were at all hours, the house didn't get cleaned, and I stopped taking Joey and Lizzie on weekend outings," said Rena. As children react with distress and anger to their less secure home lives, discipline may become harsh and inconsistent as mothers try to recapture control of their upset youngsters. Fathers usually spend more time with children immediately after divorce, but often this contact decreases over time. When fathers see their children only occasionally, they are inclined to be permissive and indulgent. This often conflicts with the mother's style of parenting and makes her task of managing the child on a day-to-day basis even more difficult (Furstenberg & Nord, 1985; Hetherington, Cox, & Cox, 1982).

In view of these changes, it is not surprising that children experience painful emotional reactions during the period surrounding divorce. But the intensity of their feelings and the way these are expressed varies with the child's age and sex.

*Age of the Child.* Five-year-old Lizzie's fear that she had caused her father to leave home is not unusual. The limited cognitive understanding of preschool and early elementary-school children makes it difficult for them to grasp the reasons behind their parents' separation. Younger children often blame themselves and take the marital breakup as a sign that they could be abandoned by both parents. They may whine and cling, displaying intense separation anxiety. Preschoolers are especially likely to fantasize that their parents will get back together (Wallerstein, 1983; Wallerstein, Corbin, & Lewis, 1988). For example, when playing with her dolls, Lizzie made the mother and father hug and kiss. Then she said to Rena, "That's how I want it. You and Daddy love each other again."

In contrast, older children are better able to understand the reasons behind their parents' divorce. They recognize that strong differences of opinion, incompatible personalities, and lack of caring for one another are responsible (Neal, 1983). The ability to accurately assign blame may reduce some of the pain that children feel. Still, many school-age and adolescent youngsters react strongly to the end of their parents' marriage. Some enter into undesirable peer activities that provide an escape from their unpleasant home lives. Skipping school, running away from home, school discipline problems, and delinquent behavior are common (Dornbusch et al., 1985).

However, not all older children react this way. For some—especially the oldest child in the family—divorce can trigger more mature behavior. These youngsters may willingly take on extra burdens, such as household tasks, care and protection of younger siblings, and emotional support of a depressed, anxious mother. But if these demands are too great, older children may eventually become resentful and withdraw from the family into some of the more destructive behavior patterns just described (Hetherington, Stanley-Hagan, & Anderson, 1989; Wallerstein & Kelly, 1980).

*Sex of the Child.* Girls sometimes respond to divorce as Lizzie did, with internalizing reactions, such as crying, self-criticism, and withdrawal. More often, they show some demanding, attention-getting behavior. In mother-custody families, boys experience more serious adjustment problems. They typically react with high levels of hostility and disobedience. Consequently, coercive interaction between divorced mothers and their sons becomes common (Hetherington, Cox, & Cox, 1982). As Joey's behavior toward Lizzie illustrates, these negative behaviors soon spread to sibling relations as well (MacKinnon, 1989). Recall from Chapter 10 that boys are more assertive and noncompliant than girls to begin with. They seem to display these behaviors even more strongly in the midst of parental conflict and harsh discipline. Because boys become so hard to manage, mothers, teachers, and peers provide them with less emotional support. This, in turn, compounds their difficulties. Children of both sexes show declines in school achievement during the aftermath of divorce, but school problems are greater for boys (Guidubaldi & Cleminshaw, 1985).

**Long-Term Consequences.** Rena eventually found full-time work at the university and gained control over the daily operation of the household. Her own feelings of anger and rejection over the divorce also declined. And after several meetings with a counselor, Rena and Drake realized the harmful impact of their quarreling on Joey and Lizzie. They resolved to keep the children out of future disagreements. Drake visited regularly and handled Joey's unruliness with firmness and consistency. Soon Joey's school performance improved, his behavior problems subsided, and both children seemed calmer and happier.

Like Joey and Lizzie, many children show improved adjustment by two years after divorce. Yet a significant number continue to have serious difficulties for many years. Boys and children with difficult temperaments are especially likely to experience lasting emotional problems. The reason is that they are more often exposed to ineffective child rearing, which further undermines their coping skills (Hetherington & Clingempeel, 1992). Among girls, the major long-term effects have to do with heterosexual behavior—a rise in sexual activity at adolescence, short-lived sexual relationships in early adulthood, and lack of self-confidence in associations with men (Kalter et al., 1985; Wallerstein & Corbin, 1989).

The overriding factor in positive adjustment following divorce is parental functioning—in particular, how well the custodial parent handles stress, shields the child from family conflict, and engages in authoritative parenting (Buchanan, Maccoby, & Dornbusch, 1991; Hetherington, 1989). Contact with fathers is also important. For girls, a good father–child relationship appears to contribute to heterosexual development. For boys, it seems to play a critical role in overall psychological well-being. In fact, several studies indicate that outcomes for sons are better when the father is the custodial parent (Camara & Resnick, 1988; Santrock & Warshak, 1986). Fathers are more likely than mothers to praise a boy's good behavior and less likely to ignore his disruptiveness. The father's image of greater power and authority may also help him obtain more compliance from sons.

Although divorce is painful for children, there is clear evidence that remaining in a stressed intact family is much worse than making the transition to a low-conflict, single-parent household (Block, Block, & Gjerde, 1988; Hetherington, Cox, & Cox, 1982). When divorcing couples put aside their disagreements and support one another in their parenting roles, children have the best chance of adapting well to a single-parent household and growing up competent, stable, and happy. Caring extended family members, teachers, and friends also play important roles in reducing the likelihood that divorce will result in long-term disruption (Hetherington, Stanley-Hagan, & Anderson, 1989).

***Divorce Mediation, Joint Custody, and Child Support.*** Awareness that divorce is a highly stressful event has led to interventions aimed at helping families through this difficult time. One is **divorce mediation.** It consists of a series of meetings between divorcing adults and a trained professional, who tries to help them settle disputes, such as child custody and property division. Its purpose is to avoid legal battles that intensify conflict within the family. In some states, divorce mediation is voluntary. In others, it must be attempted before a case is heard by a judge. Research reveals that it increases out-of-court settlements, compliance with these agreements, and feelings of well-being among divorcing parents. By reducing family hostilities, it probably has great benefits for children (Emery & Wyer, 1987).

A relatively new child custody option tries to keep both parents involved with children. In **joint custody,** the court grants the mother and father equal say in important decisions about the child's upbringing. Yet many experts have raised questions about the advisability of this practice. Joint custody results in a variety of living arrangements. In most instances, children reside with one parent and see the other on a fixed schedule, much like the typical sole custody situation. But in other cases, parents share physical custody, and children must move between homes and sometimes schools and peer groups as well. These transitions are likely to be especially hard on younger children (Johnston, Kline, & Tschann, 1989; Kline et al., 1989). The success of joint custody requires a cooperative relationship between divorcing parents. If they continue to quarrel, it prolongs children's exposure to a hostile family atmosphere (Steinman, Zemmelman, & Knoblauch, 1985).

Finally, for many single-parent families, child support from the absent parent is necessary to relieve financial strain. In response to a new federal law, all states have recently established procedures for withholding wages from parents who fail to make these court-ordered payments. Although child support is usually not enough to lift

**Divorce mediation**

A series of meetings between divorcing adults and a trained professional, who tries to help them settle disputes. Aimed at reducing family conflict during the period surrounding divorce.

**Joint custody**

A child custody arrangement following divorce in which the court grants both parents equal say in important decisions about the child's upbringing.

a single-parent family out of poverty, it can ease its burdens substantially (Children's Defense Fund, 1991d).

### Remarriage

"If you get married to Wendell and Daddy gets married to Carol," Lizzie wondered aloud to Rena, "then I'll have two sisters and one more brother. And let's see, how many grandmothers and grandfathers? Gosh, a lot!" exclaimed Lizzie. "But what will I call them all?" she asked, looking worried.

For many children, life in a single-parent family is temporary. Their parents remarry within a few years. As Lizzie's comments indicate, entry into these *blended* or *reconstituted families* leads to a complex set of new relationships. For some children, this expanded family network is a positive turn of events that brings with it greater adult attention. But for most, it presents difficult adjustments (Bray, 1988; Hetherington, Cox, & Cox, 1985). Stepparents often use different child-rearing practices than the child was used to, and having to switch to new rules and expectations can be stressful for children (Lutz, 1983). In addition, children often regard steprelatives as "intruders" into the family. Indeed, their arrival does change interaction with the natural parent. But how well children adapt is, once again, related to the overall quality of family functioning. This often depends on which parent remarries as well as the age and sex of the child. As we will see, older children and girls seem to have the hardest time (see Table 13.4).

#### Mother/Stepfather Families.

The most frequent form of blended family is a mother/stepfather arrangement, since mothers generally retain custody of the child. Under these conditions, boys usually adjust quickly. They welcome a stepfather who is warm and responsive and who offers relief from the coercive cycles of interaction that tend to build with their divorced mothers. Mothers' friction with sons declines for other reasons as well—greater economic security, another adult to share household tasks, and an end to loneliness. One study found that less than two years after remarriage, boys living in mother/stepfather households were doing almost as well as those living in nondivorced families (Hetherington, Cox, & Cox, 1985). In contrast, girls adapt less favorably when custodial mothers remarry. Stepfathers disrupt the close ties many girls established with mothers in a single-parent family, and girls often react to the new arrangement with "sulky, resistant, ignoring, critical behavior" (Hetherington, 1989, p. 7; Vuchinich et al., 1991).

TABLE 13.4 • Factors Related to Children's Adjustment to Remarriage

| Factor | Description |
| --- | --- |
| Form of blended family | Children living in father/stepmother families display more adjustment difficulties than those in mother/stepfather families, perhaps because father-custody children start out with more problems. |
| Child characteristics | |
| Age | Older children are more aware of the impact of remarriage on their own life circumstances and find it harder to adjust. |
| Sex | Girls display more severe reactions than do boys because of interruptions in close bonds with custodial parents and greater conflict with stepmothers. |
| Social supports | (See Table 13.3) |

Note, however, that age affects these findings. Older school-age and adolescent youngsters of both sexes find it harder to adjust to blended families (Hetherington & Anderson, 1987; Hobart, 1987). Perhaps because they are more aware of the impact of remarriage on their own lives, they challenge some aspects of it that younger children simply accept, creating more relationship issues with their step-relatives.

*Father/Stepmother Families.* Although only a few studies have focused on father/stepmother families, research consistently reveals more confusion for children under these circumstances. In the case of noncustodial fathers, remarriage often leads to reduced contact. They tend to withdraw from their "previous" families, even more so if they have daughters rather than sons (Hetherington, Cox, & Cox, 1982). When fathers have custody, children typically react negatively to remarriage. One reason is that children living with fathers often start out with more problems. Perhaps the biological mother could no longer handle the unruly child (usually a boy), so the father and his new wife are faced with a youngster with serious behavior problems. In other instances, the father is granted custody because of a very close relationship to the child, and his remarriage disrupts this bond (Brand, Clingempeel, & Bowen-Woodward, 1988).

Girls, especially, have a hard time getting along with their stepmothers (Hobart & Brown, 1988). Sometimes (as just mentioned) this occurs because the girl's relationship with her father is threatened by the remarriage. In addition, girls often become entangled in loyalty conflicts between their two mother figures. Noncustodial mothers (unlike fathers) are likely to maintain regular contact with children, but frequent visits by the mother are associated with less favorable stepmother–stepdaughter relations. The longer girls live in father/stepmother households, the more positive their interaction with stepmothers becomes. With time and patience they do adjust, and eventually girls benefit from the support of a second mother figure (Brand, Clingempeel, & Bowen-Woodward, 1988).

## Maternal Employment

For many years, divorce has been associated with a high rate of maternal employment, due to financial strains experienced by mothers responsible for maintaining their own families. But as we have seen, women of all sectors of the population—not just those who are single and poor—have gone to work in increasing numbers. Today, single and married mothers are in the labor market in nearly equal proportions, and over 70 percent of those with school-age children are employed (U.S. Bureau of the Census, 1991a).

*Maternal Employment and Child Development.* In Chapter 7, we saw that the impact of maternal employment on infant development depends on the quality of substitute care and the continuing parent–child relationship. This same conclusion applies during later years. In addition, many studies agree that a host of factors—the mother's work satisfaction, the support she receives from her husband, the sex of the child, and the social class of the family—have a bearing on whether children show benefits or problems from growing up in an employed-mother family.

Children of mothers who enjoy their work and remain committed to parenting show especially positive adjustment—a higher sense of self-esteem, more positive family and peer relations, and less sex-stereotyped beliefs (Hoffman, 1989). These benefits undoubtedly result from parenting practices. Employed mothers who value their parenting role are more likely to use an authoritative child-rearing style (Greenberger & Goldberg, 1989). They schedule special times to devote to their children and also encourage greater responsibility and independence. A modest increase in fathers' involvement in child-care and household duties also accompanies maternal employment (Hoffman, 1986). More contact with the father is related to higher IQ and achievement test scores, mature social behavior, and flexible sex-role attitudes in both boys and girls (Baruch & Barnett, 1986; Gottfried, Gottfried, & Bathurst, 1988).

But there are some qualifiers to these encouraging findings. First, daughters show more favorable outcomes than do sons. Girls, especially, profit from the image of female competence. Daughters of employed mothers have higher educational aspirations and, in college, are more likely to choose nontraditional careers, such as law, medicine, and physics (Hoffman, 1974). In contrast, boys are sometimes adversely affected. Sons in low-income families tend to be less admiring of their fathers and to interact more negatively with them. These findings are probably due to a lingering belief in many lower-class homes that when a mother works, the father has failed in his provider role (Hoffman, 1989). And when employment places heavy demands on the mother's schedule, younger children especially are at risk for ineffective parenting. A recent study found that employed mothers who spent little time in shared activities with their first graders had youngsters who were developing less positively, both cognitively and socially (Moorehouse, 1991).

*Child Care for School-Age Children.*   The impact of maternal employment is also related to the quality of child care for school-age youngsters. In recent years, much concern has been voiced about the millions of "latchkey" children who regularly look after themselves during after-school hours. While many of these youngsters return home to an empty house, others "hang out" with peers in the neighborhood or in nearby shopping malls during late afternoons and evenings.

Research on latchkey children reveals inconsistent findings. Some studies indicate that they suffer from low self-esteem, poor academic achievement, and fearfulness, while others show no such effects (Padilla & Landreth, 1989). Why these contradictions? The way latchkey children spend their time is most likely the critical

*In the United States, millions of "latchkey" children care for themselves during after-school hours. A history of authoritative child rearing and parental monitoring from a distance help protect the safety and adjustment of these youngsters. (Jeff Dunn/The Picture Cube)*

factor. Children who have a history of authoritative child rearing, are monitored from a distance by parental telephone calls, and have regular after-school chores appear responsible and well-adjusted. In contrast, those left to their own devices are more likely to bend to peer pressures and engage in antisocial behavior (Steinberg, 1986, 1988a).

Unfortunately, when children express discomfort with the latchkey arrangement or are not mature enough to handle it, many employed parents have no alternative. After-school programs for 6- to 13-year-olds are rare in American communities. Enrolling a child in poor-quality after-school care may do more harm than good. One study found that third graders who attended crowded day-care centers with inadequately trained staff fared worse in academic achievement and social competence than children who reported to a sitter or took care of themselves (Vandell & Corasaniti, 1988).

***Support for Employed Mothers and Their Families.*** The research we have reviewed indicates that maternal employment need not be detrimental. To the contrary, as long as mothers have the necessary supports to engage in effective child rearing, it offers children many benefits. In a dual-earner family, the husband's involvement in family responsibilities is crucial. Today, men assist to a greater extent than they did in decades past, but women still shoulder most of the burden of household and parenting tasks (Robinson, 1988). If the father helps very little or not at all, the mother carries a double load, at home and at work, leading to fatigue, distress, and reduced time and energy for children.

Besides fathers, work settings and communities can help employed mothers in their child-rearing roles. Part-time employment and time off when children are ill would help many women juggle the demands of work and child rearing. Equal pay and equal employment opportunities for women are also important. Because they enhance financial status and morale, they improve the way mothers feel and behave when they arrive home. Finally, high-quality child care is vital for parents' peace of mind and children's well-being at all ages, even during the middle childhood years.

*BRIEF REVIEW* During the school years, child rearing shifts toward co-regulation, a transitional form of supervision in which parents exercise general oversight while granting children more decision-making power. Sibling rivalry tends to increase, and children often take steps to reduce it by striving to be different from one another. Large numbers of American children experience the divorce of their parents. Although many adjust well by two years after the divorce, boys and temperamentally difficult children are likely to experience lasting emotional problems. Effective child rearing is the most important factor in helping children adapt to life in a single-parent family. When parents remarry, children living in father/stepmother families, and daughters especially, display more adjustment difficulties. Maternal employment is related to high self-esteem, reduced sex stereotyping, and mature social behavior during the school years. However, these outcomes vary with children's sex and social class, the demands of the mother's job, and the father's participation in child rearing.

- *"How come you don't study hard and get good grades like your sister?" a mother exclaimed in exasperation after seeing her son's poor report card. What impact do remarks like this have on sibling interaction, and why?*

- *What advice would you give a divorcing couple with two school-age sons about how to help their children adapt to life in a single-parent family?*

- *Eight-year-old Bobby's mother has just found employment, so Bobby takes care of himself after school. What factors are likely to affect Bobby's adjustment to this arrangement?*

## SOME COMMON PROBLEMS OF DEVELOPMENT

Throughout our discussion, we have considered a variety of stressful experiences that place children at risk for future problems. In the following sections, we touch on two more areas of concern: school-age children's fears and anxieties and the devastating

TABLE 13.5 • Common Fears in Middle Childhood

| Age | Fears |
|---|---|
| 6 years | Supernatural beings (ghosts, witches, "Darth Vader"), bodily injuries, thunder and lightning, dark, sleeping or staying alone, separation from parent |
| 7–8 years | Supernatural beings, bodily injuries, dark, staying alone, media events |
| 9–12 years | Bodily injuries, thunder and lightning, tests and grades in school, physical appearance, death, nuclear war |

*Sources:* Goldberg et al., 1985; Morris & Kratochwill, 1983.

consequences of child sexual abuse. Finally, we sum up factors that help children cope effectively with stress and those that predispose them to long-term psychological dysfunction.

## Fears and Anxieties

Although fears of the dark, of thunder and lightning, and of supernatural beings (often stimulated by movies and television) persist into middle childhood, children's anxieties are also directed toward new concerns. As Table 13.5 shows, school-age youngsters worry about academic performance, physical appearance, staying alone, and bodily injuries. In addition, as children begin to understand the realities of the wider world, media events often trouble them. During the Persian Gulf War, a major American newspaper ran a hotline for children. The majority of callers were 8- to 11-year-olds, who asked about the bruised faces of prisoners of war, whether bombs and terrorists might reach the United States, what might happen to relatives who were in the Middle East, and whether nuclear war was possible (DeAngelis, 1991b).

Most children handle their fears constructively, by talking about them with parents, teachers, and friends and relying on the more sophisticated emotional self-regulation strategies that develop in middle childhood. But about 20 percent of school-age youngsters develop an intense, unmanageable anxiety of some kind (Beidel, 1991). **School phobia** is an example. Typically, children with this disorder are middle-class youngsters whose achievement is average or above. Still, they feel severe apprehension about attending school, often accompanied by physical complaints (dizziness, nausea, stomachaches, and vomiting) that disappear once they are allowed to remain home. About one-third are 5- to 7-year-olds, most of whom do not fear school so much as separation from the mother. The difficulty can often be traced to a troubled parent–child relationship in which the mother does not want to let go and encourages clinginess and dependency. Intensive family therapy is necessary help these children (Leung, 1989; Pilkington & Piersel, 1991).

Most cases of school phobia appear later, around 11 to 13, during the transition from middle childhood to adolescence (Last et al., 1987; Rutter & Hersov, 1985). These older children usually do not suffer from separation anxiety, as was once believed. Instead, they find a particular aspect of school experience frightening—an overcritical teacher, a school bully, a threatening gang, being called on in class, the jeering remarks of insensitive peers, or too much parental pressure for school success. Treating this form of school phobia may require a change in school environment or parenting practices (Pilkington & Piersel, 1991). Firm insistence that the child return to school along with training in how to cope with difficult situations is also helpful (Klungness, 1990).

Severe childhood anxieties may also arise from harsh living conditions. A great many children live in the midst of constant violence. In inner-city ghettos and in

**School phobia**
Severe apprehension about attending school, often accompanied by physical complaints that disappear once the child is allowed to remain home.

war-torn areas of the world, they learn to drop to the floor at the sound of gunfire and witness the wounding and killing of friends and relatives. These youngsters typically suffer from long-term emotional distress, learning impairments, and sleep disturbances. They worry about the safety of themselves and family members and are often preoccupied with catastrophic events (DeAngelis, 1991a; Garbarino, Kostelny, & Dubrow, 1991). Finally, as we saw in our discussion of child abuse in Chapter 10, too often violence and other destructive acts become part of adult–child relationships. During middle childhood, child sexual abuse increases, and the damage done to children can be profound and long-lasting.

### Child Sexual Abuse

Until very recently, child sexual abuse was viewed as a rare occurrence. When children did come forward and report it, adults often thought that they fantasized the experience, and their claims were not taken seriously. In the 1970s, efforts by professionals along with widespread media attention caused child sexual abuse to be recognized as a serious national problem. Although several hundred thousand cases are reported each year (see Chapter 10), studies in which adults have been asked about their own childhoods suggest that, in actuality, a great many more are victimized. For example, in one recent telephone survey of over 2,000 people, 22 percent reported experiencing sexual abuse as children—27 percent of the women and 16 percent of the men (Crewdson, 1988).

**Characteristics of Abusers and Victims.** Child sexual abuse is committed against children of both sexes, but more often against girls than boys. The most likely victims are between the ages of 9 and 11. However, sexual abuse also occurs at younger and older ages, and few children experience only a single incident. For some, the abuse begins early in life and continues for many years (Finkelhor, 1984; Gomez-Schwartz, Horowitz, & Cardarelli, 1990; Russell, 1983).

Generally, the abuser is a male—a parent or someone whom the parent knows well. Often it is a father, stepfather, or live-in boyfriend, somewhat less often, an uncle or older brother. In a few instances, mothers are the offenders, more often with sons than daughters. If it is a nonrelative, it is usually a person whom the child has come to know and trust (Alter-Reid et al., 1986; Pierce & Pierce, 1985).

In the overwhelming majority of cases, the abuse is serious. Children are subjected to vaginal or anal intercourse, oral–genital contact, fondling, and forced stimulation of the adult. Abusers make the child comply in a variety of distasteful ways, including deception, bribery, verbal intimidation, and aggressive acts, such as physical force and threats with weapons. Sexually abusing relatives are just as likely as nonrelatives to resort to violence to get the child to submit (Gomez-Schwartz, Horowitz, & Cardarelli, 1990).

At this point, you may be wondering how any adult—especially, a parent or close relative—could possibly violate a child sexually. Many offenders deny their own responsibility. They blame the abuse on the willing participation of a seductive youngster. Yet children are not capable of making a deliberate, informed decision to enter into a sexual relationship! Even at older ages, they are not free to say yes or no (Finkelhor, 1984). Instead, abusers tend to have characteristics that predispose them toward sexual exploitation of children. As Table 13.6 shows, they have great difficulty controlling their impulses, may suffer from psychological disorders, and are often addicted to alcohol or drugs. Often they pick out children who are unlikely to defend themselves—those who are physically weak, emotionally deprived, and socially isolated.

Reported cases of child sexual abuse are strongly linked to poverty, marital instability, and the resulting weakening of family ties. Children who live in homes

TABLE 13.6 • Factors Related to Child Sexual Abuse

| Factor | Description |
|---|---|
| Abuser | Usually a male and a member of the child's family. Finds children sexually arousing, has difficulty controlling impulses, rationalizes that the victim wants sex and will enjoy it, and has learned to believe that sexual use of others is appropriate. May have a history of alcohol or drug addiction, serious psychological disturbance, or sexual abuse as a child. |
| Victim | More often female than male. Abusers tend to select children that seem like easy targets—ones who are physically weak, compliant in personality, emotionally needy, and socially isolated. |
| Family | Often associated with poverty and repeated marital breakup. However, also occurs in relatively stable middle-class families. |

*Sources:* Faller, 1990; Finkelhor, 1984.

where there is a history of constantly changing characters—repeated marriages, separations, and new partners—are especially vulnerable. But community surveys reveal that middle-class children in relatively stable homes are also victims. Economically advantaged families are simply more likely to escape detection (Gomez-Schwartz, Horowitz, & Cardarelli, 1990).

***Consequences for Children.*** Virtually all children are emotionally distressed at the time sexual abuse occurs. Long-term consequences can be prevented if the abuse is stopped after only a few instances and children are assured that caring, nonabusive adults will support and protect them. Unfortunately, the outcomes for a great many youngsters are not so favorable. Sexually abused children often become known to authorities only after they have developed extreme behavioral symptoms. Perhaps a school official suspects abuse, or a parent observes the child's emotional difficulties and seeks professional help (Faller, 1990).

The adjustment problems of child-sexual-abuse victims are severe. Depression, low self-esteem, mistrust of adults, feelings of anger and hostility, and difficulties in getting along with peers are common. Younger children often react with sleep difficulties, loss of appetite, and generalized fearfulness. Adolescents sometimes show runaway and suicidal reactions (Alter-Reid et al., 1986; Haugaard & Reppucci, 1988).

Sexually abused children frequently display sexual knowledge and behavior beyond that which is appropriate for their age. They have learned from their abusers that sexual overtures are acceptable ways to get attention and rewards. As they move toward young adulthood, abused girls often enter into unhealthy relationships. Many become promiscuous, believing that their bodies are for the use of others. When they marry, they are likely to choose husbands who are abusive toward themselves and their children (Faller, 1990). And as mothers, they often show poor parenting skills, abusing and neglecting their youngsters (Pianta, Egeland, & Erickson, 1989). In these ways, the harmful impact of sexual abuse is transmitted to the next generation.

***Prevention and Treatment.*** Treating child sexual abuse is difficult. Once it is revealed, the reactions of family members—anxiety about harm to the child, anger toward the abuser, and sometimes hostility toward the victim for telling—can increase children's distress. Sensitive work with parents is critical to helping the abused child. Since sexual abuse typically appears in the midst of other serious family problems, long-term therapy with children and families is usually necessary (Gomez-Schwartz, Horowitz, & Cardarelli, 1990).

The best way to reduce the suffering of victims of child sexual abuse is to prevent it from continuing in our society. Today, courts are prosecuting abusers (especially nonrelatives) more rigorously. As Box 13.2 indicates, children's testimony is being taken more seriously, and new ways have been devised to help children tell about their experiences without suffering additional emotional harm. In schools, sex education programs can help children recognize inappropriate sexual advances and encourage them to report these actions. Finally, educating teachers, caregivers, and other adults who work with children about the signs and symptoms of sexual abuse can help ensure that victimized children are identified early and receive the help that they need.

## STRESS AND COPING IN MIDDLE CHILDHOOD

Throughout middle childhood—and other phases of development as well—children are confronted with challenging and sometimes threatening situations that demand that they cope with psychological stress. In this trio of chapters, we have considered such topics as chronic illness, learning disabilities, divorce, and child sexual abuse. Each taxes children's coping resources, creating serious risks for development.

At the same time, many studies indicate that only a modest relationship exists between stressful life experiences and psychological disturbance in childhood (Compas et al., 1989; Dubow et al., 1991; Rutter, 1979). If you recall our discussion of the consequences of birth complications in Chapter 4, we noted that some children manage to defy all the odds, overcoming the combined effects of birth trauma, poverty, and a deeply troubled family life. The same is true when we look at research on family transitions, school difficulties, and child maltreatment.

Research on stress-resistant children highlights three broad factors that consistently protect against maladjustment (Garmezy, 1983):

1. Personal characteristics of children—an easy temperament, high self-esteem, and a mastery-oriented approach to new situations.

2. A family environment that provides warmth, closeness, and order and organization to the child's life.

3. A person outside the immediate family—perhaps a grandparent, teacher, or close friend—who develops a special relationship with the child, offering a support system and a positive coping model.

Any one of these ingredients can account for why one child fares well and another poorly when exposed to extreme hardship. Yet most of the time, personal and environmental resources are interconnected (Compas, 1987). Throughout this book, we have seen many examples of how unfavorable life experiences increase the chances that parents and children will act in ways that expose them to further hardship, magnifying stress and diminishing their ability to cope effectively. Children can usually handle one stressor in their lives, even if it is chronic. But when negative conditions pile up, such as marital discord, poverty, crowded living conditions, and parental psychological disorder, the rate of maladjustment is multiplied (Rutter, 1979).

Social supports are especially important during periods of developmental transition—when children are more vulnerable because they are faced with many new tasks (Rutter, 1987). One such turning point is the beginning of middle childhood, a time of new challenges in academic work and peer relations. We have seen how families, schools, communities, and society as a whole can enhance or undermine the school-age child's developing sense of competence. Another major turning point is the transition to adolescence. As the next three chapters will reveal, young people whose experiences have helped them learn how to overcome obstacles and strive for self-direction meet the challenges of this new phase quite well.

## FROM RESEARCH TO PRACTICE

### Box 13.2   *Children's Eyewitness Testimony*

Renata, a physically abused and neglected 8-year-old, was taken from her parents and placed in foster care. There, she was seen engaging in sexually aggressive behavior toward other children, including grabbing their sex organs and using obscene language. Renata's foster mother suspected that sexual abuse had taken place in her natural home. She informed the child protective service worker, who met with Renata to gather information. But Renata appeared distraught and frightened. She did not want to answer any questions.

Increasingly, children are being called on to testify in court cases involving child abuse and neglect, child custody, and other matters. Having to provide such information can be traumatic. Most of the time, children are asked to give testimony against a parent or other relative to whom they have strong feelings of loyalty or who has threatened to punish them if they speak out. In addition, children are faced with a strange and unfamiliar situation—at the very least an interview in the judge's chambers and at most an open courtroom with judge, jury, spectators, and the possibility of unsympathetic cross-examination. Nevertheless, children's testimony is often essential. For example, in instances of child abuse, the child is often the only witness to the crime.

When testimony is important, judgments must be made about the child's competence to provide it. It is rare for children under age 5 to be asked to testify, while those age 6 and older often are (Saywitz, 1987). These guidelines make good sense in terms of what we know about cognitive development. Compared to preschoolers, school-age children are better able to give detailed descriptions of past experiences and make accurate inferences about others' motives and intentions. They are also more resistant to suggestion by opposing attorneys, who may want to influence the content of the child's response (Goodman, Aman, & Hirschman, 1987; Wells, Turtle, & Luus, 1989).

Nevertheless, when properly questioned, even preschoolers can recall their experiences with considerable accuracy. To ease the stress of providing information, special interviewing methods have been developed for children. In Renata's case, a professional used puppets to ask questions and had Renata respond through them. Also, Renata was asked to demonstrate with dolls and a dollhouse what had happened and where it had happened (Faller, 1990).

Child witnesses need to be prepared so that they understand the courtroom process and know what to expect. Below age 8, children have little grasp of the differing roles of judge, attorney, and police officer. Many regard the court negatively, as "a room you pass through on your way to jail" (Saywitz, 1989, p. 149). In some places, "court schools" exist in which children are taken through the setting and given an opportunity to role-play court activities. As part of this process, children can be encouraged to admit not knowing an answer rather than guessing or going along with what an adult expects of them (Cole & Loftus, 1987).

If the child is likely to experience emotional trauma or later punishment (in a family dispute), then courtroom procedures can be adapted to protect them. For example, Renata eventually testified over closed circuit TV so she would not have to face her abusive father. When it is not wise for a child to participate directly, expert witnesses can provide testimony that reports on the child's psychological condition and includes important elements of the child's story (Bulkley, 1989).

# SUMMARY

### Erikson's Theory: Industry versus Inferiority

• According to Erikson, the personality changes of the school years build on Freud's **latency stage.** Children who successfully resolve the critical psychological conflict of **industry versus inferiority** develop a sense of competence at useful skills and tasks.

### Self-Development in Middle Childhood

• During middle childhood, children's self-concepts include personality traits and social comparisons. Self-esteem becomes hierarchically organized and declines over the early school years as children adjust their self-judgments to feedback from the environment.

• Studies of children's **attributions** have identified adult communication styles that affect self-esteem. Children with **mastery-oriented attributions** credit their successes to high ability and their failures to insufficient effort. In contrast, those with **learned helplessness** attribute failures to low ability. Children who receive negative feedback about their ability develop the learned helpless pattern. **Attribution retraining** encourages learned helpless children to revise their failure-related attributions, thereby improving their self-esteem.

### Emotional Development in Middle Childhood

• In middle childhood, the complex emotions of pride and guilt become integrated with personal responsibility. School-age children also recognize that people can experience more than one emotion at a time. Emotional self-regulation improves as children use cognitive strategies for controlling feelings.

### Understanding Others

• **Perspective-taking** improves greatly over middle childhood. According to Selman, children move through five perspective-taking stages. Good perspective-takers show more positive social skills.

### Moral Development in Middle Childhood

• By middle childhood, children have internalized a wide variety of moral rules. Consequently, they are less dependent on modeling and reinforcement for morally relevant behavior than they were at younger ages.

• Children's concepts of **distributive justice** change over middle childhood, from equality to merit to benevolence. School-age children also begin to grasp the linkage between moral rules and social conventions.

### Peer Relations in Middle Childhood

• By the end of the school years, children organize themselves into **peer groups.** Friendships develop into mutual relationships based on trust.

• **Sociometric techniques** are used to distinguish four types of peer acceptance: (1) **popular children,** who are liked by many agemates; (2) **rejected children,** who are actively disliked; (3) **controversial children,** who are both liked and disliked; and (4) **neglected children,** who are seldom chosen, either positively or negatively. Rejected children often experience lasting adjustment difficulties. Interventions that provide coaching in social skills, academic tutoring, and training in social understanding have been used to help rejected youngsters.

### Sex Typing in Middle Childhood

• School-age children extend their awareness of sex stereotypes to personality characteristics and academic subjects. Over middle childhood, boys strengthen their identification with the masculine role, while girls feel free to experiment with "opposite-sex" activities. Cultures shape sex-typed behavior through the daily activities assigned to children.

### Family Influences in Middle Childhood

• Effective parents of school-age youngsters engage in **coregulation,** exerting general oversight while permitting children to be in charge of moment-by-moment decision making. Coregulation depends on a cooperative relationship between parent and child.

• During middle childhood, sibling rivalry increases as children participate in a wider range of activities and parents compare their abilities. Older siblings tend to be advantaged in IQ and school achievement. Younger siblings are more popular.

• Divorce is common in the lives of American children. Although most experience painful emotional reactions, younger children and boys in mother-custody homes tend to react more strongly. Boys and children with difficult temperaments are more likely to show lasting psychological problems. The overriding factor in positive adjustment following divorce is good parenting. Contact with noncustodial fathers is also important. Because **divorce mediation** helps parents resolve their disputes, it can reduce children's exposure to conflict. **Joint custody** is a controversial practice that may create additional strains for children.

• Many divorced parents remarry, a transition that also creates difficulties for children. Children in father/step-mother families, and girls especially, display the greatest adjustment problems.

• Maternal employment is associated with positive outcomes for children, including a higher sense of self-esteem, better family and peer relations, and less sex-stereotyped beliefs. However, boys in low-income homes sometimes show adverse effects. Latchkey children who are monitored from a distance and experience authoritative parenting appear responsible and well-adjusted. High-quality after-school child care and fathers' involvement in family responsibilities help mothers balance the multiple demands of work and child rearing effectively.

### Common Problems of Development

• During middle childhood, children's fears are directed toward new concerns having to do with achievement, physical appearance, physical safety, and media events. Some children develop intense, unmanageable fears, such as **school phobia.** Severe anxiety can also result from harsh living conditions.

• Child sexual abuse is generally committed by male family members, more often against girls than boys. Abusers have characteristics that predispose them toward sexual exploitation of children. Reported cases are strongly associated with poverty and marital instability. Adjustment problems of abused children are often severe.

### Stress and Coping in Middle Childhood

• Overall, only a modest relationship exists between stressful life experiences and psychological disturbance in childhood. Personal characteristics of children; a warm, well-organized home life; and social supports outside the family are consistently related to childhood resilience in the face of stress.

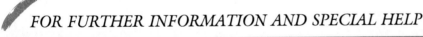

# IMPORTANT TERMS AND CONCEPTS

latency stage (p. 458)
industry versus inferiority (p. 459)
attributions (p. 462)
mastery-oriented attributions (p. 463)
learned helplessness (p. 463)
attribution retraining (p. 465)

perspective-taking (p. 466)
distributive justice (p. 468)
peer group (p. 471)
sociometric techniques (p. 473)
popular children (p. 473)
rejected children (p. 473)

controversial children (p. 473)
neglected children (p. 473)
coregulation (p. 478)
divorce mediation (p. 482)
joint custody (p. 482)
school phobia (p. 487)

# FOR FURTHER INFORMATION AND SPECIAL HELP

**Divorce**

Parents Without Partners
8807 Colesville Road
Silver Spring, MD 20910
(301) 588-9354

Organization of custodial and noncustodial single parents that provides support in the upbringing of children. Many local groups exist throughout the United States.

**Remarriage**

Stepfamily Association of America
215 Centennial Mall South, Suite 212
Lincoln, NE 68508
(402) 477-7837

Association of families interested in stepfamily relationships. Organizes support groups and offers education and children's services.

Stepfamily Foundation
333 West End Avenue
New York, NY 10023
(212) 877-3244

Organization of remarried parents, interested professionals, and divorced individuals. Arranges group counseling sessions for stepfamilies and provides training for professionals.

**Child Sexual Abuse**

Committee for Children
172 20th Avenue
Seattle, WA 98122
(206) 322-5050

Develops programs for preschool, elementary, and high school students that can be used in schools to help prevent child sexual abuse. Also conducts training programs for teachers. Supports legislation benefitting victims. Publishes the journal, *Connections in the Prevention of Child Sexual Abuse.*

Parents United
c/o Institute for Community as Extended Family
P.O. Box 952
San Jose, CA 95108
(408) 453-7616

Organization of individuals who have experienced child sexual abuse. Assists families affected by incest and other types of sex-

ual abuse by providing information and arranging for medical and legal counseling.

Society's League Against Molestation
P.O. Box 346
Collingswood, NJ 08108
(609) 858-7800

A 100,000-member organization that works to prevent child sexual abuse through public education. Offers counseling and assistance to victims and their families.

| Milestones of Development in Middle Childhood | | | | |
| --- | --- | --- | --- | --- |
| Age | Physical | Cognitive | Language | Emotional/Social |
| 6–8 years | Slow gains in height and weight continue until adolescent growth spurt. Gradual replacement of primary teeth by permanent teeth throughout middle childhood. Writing becomes smaller and more legible. Letter reversals decline. Drawings become more organized and detailed. Organized games with rules and rough-and-tumble play become common. Dominance hierarchies become more stable, especially among boys. | Thought becomes more logical, as shown by the ability to pass Piagetian conservation, class inclusion, and seriation problems. Understanding of spatial concepts and ability to integrate distance, time, and speed improve. Attention becomes more focused, adaptable, and planful. Memory strategies of rehearsal and organization appear. Awareness of importance of memory strategies and psychological factors (attention, motivation) in task performance improves. | Vocabulary continues to increase rapidly throughout middle childhood. Word definitions are concrete, referring to functions and appearance. Language awareness improves over middle childhood. | Self-esteem differentiates, becomes hierarchically organized, and declines to a more realistic level. Distinguishes ability, effort, and luck in attributions for success and failure. Understands that access to different information often causes people to have different perspectives. Becomes more responsible and independent. Distributive justice reasoning changes from equality to merit to benevolence. Pride and guilt are integrated with personal responsibility. |
| 9–11 years | Adolescent growth spurt begins 2 years earlier for girls than boys. Gross motor skills of running, jumping, throwing, catching, kicking, batting, and dribbling are executed more quickly and with better coordination. Reaction time improves, contributing to motor skill development. Depth cues appear in drawings. | Logical thought remains tied to concrete situations until end of middle childhood. Piagetian tasks continue to be mastered in a step-by-step fashion. Memory strategies of rehearsal and organization become more effective. Memory strategy of elaboration appears. Long-term knowledge base grows larger and becomes better organized. Self-regulation of cognitive performance improves. | Word definitions emphasize synonyms and categorical relations. Understanding of complex grammatical forms improves. Grasps double meanings of words, as reflected in comprehension of metaphors and humor. Adapts messages to the needs of listeners in complex communicative situations. Conversational strategies become more refined. | Self-concept includes personality traits and social comparisons. Self-esteem tends to rise. Recognizes that individuals can experience more than one emotion at a time. Emotional self-regulation includes cognitive strategies. Can "step in another's shoes" and view the self from that person's perspective. Later, can view the relationship between self and other from the perspective of a third, impartial party. Appreciates the linkage between moral rules and social conventions. Peer groups emerge. Friendships are defined by mutual trust. Academic subjects and personality traits become sex-stereotyped, but children (especially girls) view the capacities of males and females more flexibly. Sibling rivalry tends to increase. |

# GLOSSARY

**AB Search error.** The error made by 8- to 12-month-olds after an object is moved from hiding place A to hiding place B. Infants in Piaget's Substage 4 search for it only in the first hiding place (A).

**Academic preschool.** Preschool in which teachers structure the program, training children in academic skills through repetition and drill. Distinguished from *child-centered preschool*.

**Accommodation.** That part of adaptation in which new schemes are created and old ones adjusted to create a better fit with the environment. Distinguished from *assimilation*.

**Acquired Immune Deficiency Syndrome (AIDS).** A relatively new viral infection that destroys the immune system. Spread through transfer of body fluids from one person to another, usually through sexual contact or sharing of needles by illegal drug users. Can be transmitted prenatally.

**Adaptation.** In Piaget's theory, the process of acting directly on the environment and being influenced by it as a result. Made up of two complementary processes: *assimilation* and *accommodation*.

**Adolescent initiation ceremony.** A ritual or rite of passage announcing to the community that a young person is making the transition into adolescence or full adulthood.

**Age of viability.** The age at which the fetus can first survive if born early. Occurs sometime between 22 and 26 weeks.

**Allele.** Each of two forms of a gene located at the same place on the autosomes.

**Amnion.** The inner membrane that forms a protective covering around the prenatal organism.

**Amniotic fluid.** The fluid that fills the amnion, helping to keep temperature constant and to provide a cushion against jolts caused by the mother's movement.

**Anal stage.** Freud's second psychosexual stage, in which toddlers take pleasure in retaining and releasing urine and feces at will.

**Analgesia.** A mild pain-relieving drug.

**Androgyny.** A type of sex-role identity in which the person scores high on both masculine and feminine personality characteristics.

**Anesthesia.** A strong painkilling drug that blocks sensation.

**Animistic thinking.** The belief that inanimate objects have lifelike qualities, such as thoughts, wishes, feelings, and intentions. Believed by Piaget to characterize children in the preoperational stage.

**Anorexia nervosa.** An eating disorder in which individuals (usually females) starve themselves because of a compulsive fear of getting fat.

**Apgar Scale.** A rating used to assess the newborn baby's physical condition immediately after birth.

**Assimilation.** That part of adaptation in which the external world is interpreted in terms of current schemes. Distinguished from *accommodation*.

**Associative play.** A form of true social participation in which children are engaged in separate activities, but they interact by exchanging toys and commenting on one another's behavior. Distinguished from *nonsocial activity, parallel play,* and *cooperative play*.

**Asthma.** An illness in which highly sensitive bronchial tubes (passages that connect the throat and lungs) fill with mucous and contract, leading to episodes of coughing, wheezing, and serious breathing difficulties.

**Attachment.** The strong, affectional tie that humans feel toward special people in their lives.

**Attention-deficit hyperactivity disorder (ADHD).** A childhood disorder involving inattentiveness, impulsivity, and excessive motor activity. Often leads to academic failure and social problems.

**Attribution retraining.** An approach to intervention in which attributions of learned helpless children are modified through feedback that encourages them to believe in themselves and persist in the face of task difficulty.

**Attributions.** Common, everyday explanations for the causes of behavior.

**Authoritarian parent.** A parenting style that is demanding but low in responsiveness to children's rights and needs. Conformity and obedience are valued over open communication with the child. Distinguished from *authoritative* and *permissive parents*.

**Authoritative parent.** A parenting style that is demanding and responsive. A rational, democratic approach in which parents' and children's rights are respected. Distinguished from *authoritarian* and *permissive parents*.

**Autonomous morality.** Piaget's second stage of moral development, in which children view rules as flexible, socially agreed on principles that can be revised when there is a need to do so. Begins around age 10.

**Autonomy versus shame and doubt.** In Erikson's theory, the psychological conflict of toddlerhood, which is resolved positively if parents provide young children with suitable guidance and appropriate choices.

**Autosomes.** The 22 matching chromosome pairs in each human cell.

**Avoidant attachment.** The quality of insecure attachment characterizing infants who are usually not distressed by maternal separation and who avoid the mother when she returns. Distinguished from *secure, resistant,* and *disorganized/disoriented attachment*.

**Babbling.** Repetition of consonant-vowel combinations in long strings, beginning around 6 months of age.

**Basic emotions.** Emotions that can be directly inferred from facial expressions, such as happiness, interest, surprise, fear, anger, sadness, and disgust.

**Basic skills approach.** An approach to beginning reading instruction that emphasizes training in phonics—the basic rules for translating written symbols into sounds—and simplified reading materials. Distinguished from *whole language approach*.

**Basic trust versus mistrust.** In Erikson's theory, the psychological conflict of infancy, which is resolved positively if caregiving, especially during feeding, is sympathetic and loving.

**Behavior modification.** A set of practical procedures that combine reinforcement, modeling, and the manipulation of situational cues to change behavior.

**Behaviorism.** An approach that views directly observable events—stimuli and responses—as the appropriate focus of study and the development of behavior as taking place through classical and operant conditioning.

**Blastocyst.** The zygote four days after fertilization, when the tiny mass of cells forms a hollow, fluid-filled ball.

**Body image.** Conception of and attitude toward one's physical appearance.

**Bonding.** Parents' feelings of affection and concern for the newborn baby.

**Breech position.** A position of the baby in the uterus that would cause the buttocks or feet to be delivered first.

**Bulimia.** An eating disorder in which individuals (mainly females) go on eating binges followed by deliberate vomiting, other purging techniques such as heavy doses of laxatives, and strict dieting.

**Canalization.** The tendency of heredity to restrict the development of some characteristics to just one or a few outcomes.

**Cardinality principle.** Principle stating that the last number in a counting sequence indicates the quantity of items in the set.

**Carrier.** A heterozygous individual who can pass a recessive gene to his or her children.

**Catch-up growth.** Physical growth that returns to its genetically determined path after being delayed by environmental factors.

**Centration.** The tendency to focus on one aspect of a situation to the neglect of other important features. A characteristic of Piaget's preoperational stage. Distinguished from *decentration*.

**Cephalo-caudal trend.** An organized pattern of physical growth that proceeds from head to tail.

**Cerebellum.** A brain structure that aids in balance and control of body movements.

**Cerebral cortex.** The largest structure of the human brain that accounts for the highly developed intelligence of the human species.

**Cerebral palsy.** A general term for a variety of problems, all of which involve muscle coordination, that result from brain damage before, during, or just after birth.

**Cesarean delivery.** A surgical delivery in which the doctor makes an incision in the mother's abdomen and lifts the baby out of the uterus.

**Child development.** A field of study devoted to understanding all aspects of human growth from conception through adolescence.

**Child-centered preschool.** Preschool in which teachers provide a wide variety of activities from which children select, and most of the day is devoted to free play. Distinguished from *academic preschool*.

**Chorion.** The outer membrane that forms a protective covering around the prenatal organism. Sends out tiny fingerlike villi, from which the placenta begins to emerge.

**Chromosomes.** Rodlike structures in the cell nucleus that store and transmit genetic information.

**Circular reaction.** In Piaget's theory, a means of building schemes in which infants try to repeat a chance event caused by their own motor activity.

**Classical conditioning.** A form of learning that involves associating a neutral stimulus with a stimulus that leads to a reflexive response.

**Clinical interview.** A method in which the researcher uses a flexible, conversational style to probe for the subject's point of view.

**Clinical method.** A method in which the researcher attempts to understand the unique individual child by combining interview data, observations, and sometimes test scores.

**Clique.** A small group of about 5 to 7 members who are either close or good friends.

**Co-dominance.** A pattern of inheritance in which both alleles, in a heterozygous combination, are expressed.

**Cognitive-developmental theory.** An approach introduced by Piaget that views the child as actively building psychological structures and cognitive development as taking place in stages.

**Cohort effects.** Effects of cultural-historical change on the accuracy of findings. Due to the fact that children born in one period of time are influenced by particular cultural and historical conditions.

**Colostrum.** The sticky yellowish fluid produced by the mother's breast before the milk comes in that is especially high in antibodies.

**Complex emotions.** Emotions that blend two or more basic emotional states and involve injury to or enhancement of the sense of self. Examples are shame, embarrassment, guilt, envy, and pride.

**Compliance.** Voluntary obedience to adult requests and commands.

**Comprehension.** In language development, the words and word combinations that children understand. Distinguished from *production*.

**Concordance rates.** The percentage of instances in which both members of a twin pair show a trait when it is present in one pair member. Used to study the the role of heredity in traits that can be judged as either present or absent, such as emotional and behavior disorders.

**Concrete operational stage.** Piaget's third stage, during which thought is logical, flexible, and organized in its application to concrete information. However, the capacity for abstract thinking is not yet present. Spans the years from 7 to 11.

**Conditioned response (CR).** In classical conditioning, an originally reflexive response that is produced by a conditioned stimulus (CS).

**Conditioned stimulus (CS).** In classical conditioning, a neutral stimulus that, through pairing with an unconditioned stimulus (UCS), leads to a new response (CR).

**Conservation.** In Piaget's theory, the understanding that certain physical characteristics of objects remain the same, even when their outward appearance changes.

**Continuous development.** A view that regards development as a cumulative process of adding on more of the same types of skills that were there to begin with. Distinguished from *discontinuous development*.

**Contrast sensitivity.** A general principle accounting for early pattern preferences, which states that if babies can detect a difference in contrast between two patterns, they will prefer the one with more contrast.

**Control processes, or mental strategies.** In information processing, procedures that operate on and transform information, increasing the efficiency of thinking as well as the chances that information will be retained for later use.

**Controversial children.** Children who get a large number of positive and negative votes on sociometric measures of peer acceptance. Distinguished from *popular*, *neglected*, and *rejected children*.

**Conventional level.** Kohlberg's second level of moral development, in which moral understanding is based on conforming to social rules to ensure positive human relationships and societal order.

**Convergent thinking.** The generation of a single correct answer to a problem. Type of cognition emphasized on intelligence tests. Distinguished from *divergent thinking*.

**Cooing.** Pleasant vowel-like noises made by infants beginning at about 2 months of age.

**Cooperative play.** A form of true social participation in which children's actions are directed toward a common goal. Distinguished from *nonsocial activity, parallel play,* and *associative play*.

**Coregulation.** A transitional form of supervision in which parents exercise general oversight, while permitting children to be in charge of moment-by-moment decision making.

**Corpus callosum.** The large bundle of fibers that connects the two hemispheres of the brain.

**Correlation coefficient.** A number, ranging from −1.00 to +1.00, that describes how two measures, or variables, are associated with one another. The size of the number shows the strength of the relationship. The sign of the number (+ or −) refers to the direction of the relationship.

**Correlational design.** A research design that gathers information without altering subjects' experiences and that cannot determine cause and effect.

**Critical period.** A limited period of time in which a part of the body or a behavior is biologically prepared to undergo rapid development and is especially sensitive to the environment.

**Cross-sectional design.** A research design in which groups of subjects of different ages are studied at the same point in time. Distinguished from *longitudinal design*.

**Crossing over.** Exchange of genes between chromosomes next to each other during meiosis.

**Crowd.** The joining of several cliques into a larger group of peers. Provides a supportive context for adolescent boys and girls to get to know each other.

**Decentration.** The ability to focus on several aspects of a problem at once and relate them. In Piaget's theory, a characteristic of operational thought. Distinguished from *centration*.

**Deferred imitation.** The ability to remember and copy the behavior of models who are not immediately present.

**Deoxyribonucleic acid (DNA).** Long, double-stranded molecules that make up chromosomes, segments of which are genes.

**Dependent variable.** The variable that the researcher expects to be influenced by the independent variable in an experiment.

**Deprivation dwarfism.** A growth disorder observed between 2 and 15 years of age. Characterized by very short stature, weight in proportion to height, immature skeletal age, and decreased GH secretion. Caused by emotional deprivation.

**Developmental quotient, or DQ.** A score on an infant intelligence test, based primarily on perceptual and motor responses. Computed in the same manner as an IQ.

**Diethylstilbestrol (DES).** A hormone widely used between 1945 and 1970 to prevent miscarriage. Increases the chances of genital tract abnormalities and cancer of the vagina and testes in adolescence and young adulthood.

**Differentiation theory.** The view that perceptual development involves the detection of increasingly fine-grained invariant features in the environment.

**Difficult child.** A child whose temperament is such that he or she is irregular in daily routines, is slow to accept new experiences, and tends to react negatively and intensely. Distinguished from *easy child* and *slow-to-warm-up child*.

**Dilation and effacement of the cervix.** Widening and thinning of the cervix during the first stage of labor.

**Discontinuous development.** A view in which new and different modes of interpreting and responding to the world emerge at particular time periods. Assumes that development takes place in stages. Distinguished from *continuous development*.

**Dishabituation.** Increase in responsiveness after stimulation changes.

**Disorganized/disoriented attachment.** The quality of insecure attachment characterizing infants who respond in a confused, contradictory fashion when reunited with their mothers. Distinguished from *secure, avoidant,* and *resistant attachment*.

**Distributive justice.** Beliefs about how to divide up material goods fairly.

**Divergent thinking.** The generation of multiple and unusual possibilities when faced with a task or problem. Associated with creativity. Distinguished from *convergent thinking*.

**Divorce mediation.** A series of meetings between divorcing adults and a trained professional, who tries to help them settle disputes. Aimed at reducing family conflict during the period surrounding divorce.

**Dizygotic twins.** See fraternal twins.

**Dominance hierarchy.** A stable ordering of group members that predicts who will win under conditions of conflict.

**Dominant cerebral hemisphere.** The hemisphere of the brain responsible for skilled motor action. The left hemisphere is dominant in right-handed individuals. In left-handed individuals, the right hemisphere may be dominant, or motor and language skills may be shared between the hemispheres.

**Dominant–recessive inheritance.** A pattern of inheritance in which, under heterozygous conditions, the influence of only one allele is apparent.

**Drive reduction account of attachment.** A behaviorist view that regards the mother's satisfaction of the baby's hunger (primary drive) as the basis for the infant's preference for her (secondary drive).

**Easy child.** A child whose temperament is such that he or she quickly establishes regular routines in infancy, is generally cheerful, and adapts easily to new experiences. Distinguished from *difficult child* and *slow-to-warm-up child*.

**Ecological systems theory.** Bronfenbrenner's approach, which views the child as developing within a complex system of relationships affected by multiple levels of the environment, from immediate settings of family and school to broad cultural values and programs.

**Ego.** In Freud's theory, the part of the personality that directs the id's urges so they are discharged on appropriate objects and at acceptable times and places.

**Egocentrism.** The inability to distinguish viewpoints of others from one's own.

**Elaboration.** The memory strategy of creating a relation between two or more items that are not members of the same category.

**Electra conflict.** The conflict of Freud's phallic stage in which the girl desires to possess her father and feels hostile toward her mother. Resolved by becoming like the mother and forming a superego.

**Embryo.** The prenatal organism from 2 to 8 weeks after conception, during which time the foundations of all body structures and internal organs are laid down.

**Embryonic disk.** A small cluster of cells on the inside of the blastocyst, from which the embryo will develop.

**Emotional self-regulation.** Strategies for adjusting our emotional state to a comfortable level of intensity.

**Empathy.** The ability to understand and respond sympathetically to the feelings of others.

**Engrossment.** The father's experience of intense involvement and interest in the newborn baby.

**Epiphyses.** Growth centers in the bones where new cartilage cells are produced and gradually harden.

**Episiotomy.** A small incision made during childbirth to increase the size of the vaginal opening.

**Equilibration.** In Piaget's theory, back-and-forth movement between cognitive equilibrium and disequilibrium throughout development, which leads to more effective schemes. Describes how assimilation and accommodation work together to produce cognitive change.

**Ethological theory of attachment.** A theory formulated by Bowlby, which views the infant's emotional tie to the familiar caregiver as an evolved response that promotes survival.

**Ethology.** An approach concerned with the adaptive or survival value of behavior and its evolutionary history.

**Expansions.** Adult responses that elaborate on children's speech in ways that facilitate language development.

**Experimental design.** A research design in which subjects are randomly assigned to treatment conditions. Since the researcher directly manipulates changes in an independent variable and observes their effects on a dependent variable, permits inferences about cause and effect.

**Expressive style.** A style of early language learning in which toddlers use language mainly to talk about the feelings and needs of themselves and other people. Initial vocabulary emphasizes pronouns and social formulas.

**Extended family household.** A household in which parent and child live with one or more adult relatives.

**Extinction.** In classical conditioning, decline of the CR, as a result of presenting the CS enough times without the UCS.

**Fantasy period.** The period of vocational development in which young children fantasize about career options through make-believe play. Spans early and middle childhood.

**Fast mapping.** Connecting a new word with an underlying concept after only a brief encounter.

**Fetal alcohol effects (FAE).** The condition of children who display some but not all of the defects of fetal alcohol syndrome. Usually their mothers drank alcohol in smaller quantities during pregnancy.

**Fetal alcohol syndrome (FAS).** A pattern of defects that results when pregnant women consume large amounts of alcohol during most or all of pregnancy. Includes mental retardation, slow physical growth, and facial abnormalities.

**Fetal monitors.** Electronic instruments that track the baby's heart rate during labor.

**Fetus.** The prenatal organism from the beginning of the third month to the end of pregnancy, during which time completion of body structures and dramatic growth in size takes place.

**Fontanels.** Six soft spots that separate the bones of the skull at birth.

**Forceps.** A metal device placed around the baby's head that is used to pull the infant from the birth canal.

**Formal operational stage.** Piaget's final stage, in which adolescents develop the capacity for abstract, scientific thinking. Begins around 11 years of age.

**Fraternal or dizygotic twins.** Twins resulting from the release and fertilization of two ova. They are genetically no more alike than ordinary siblings.

**Functional play.** A type of play involving pleasurable motor activity with or without objects. Enables infants and toddlers to practice sensorimotor schemes.

**Gametes.** Human sperm and ova, which contain half as many chromosomes as a regular body cell.

**Gender constancy.** The understanding that one's own gender is permanent despite changes in clothing, hairstyle, and play activities.

**Gender intensification.** Increased sex stereotyping of attitudes and behavior. Occurs in early adolescence.

**Gender schema theory.** A theory that combines features of social learning and cognitive-developmental perspectives to explain how environmental pressures and children's cognitions work together to shape sex-role development.

**Gene.** A segment of a DNA molecule that contains hereditary instructions.

**General growth curve.** Curve that represents overall changes in body size—rapid growth during infancy, slower gains in early and middle childhood, and rapid growth once more during adolescence.

**Genetic counseling.** Counseling that helps couples assess the likelihood of giving birth to a baby with a hereditary disorder.

**Genetic–environmental correlation.** The idea that heredity influences the environments to which individuals are exposed.

**Genital stage.** Freud's psychosexual stage of adolescence, when instinctual drives are reawakened and shift to the genital region, upsetting the delicate balance between id, ego, and superego established during middle childhood.

**Genotype.** The genetic makeup of the individual.

**Giftedness.** Exceptional intellectual ability. Includes high IQ, creativity, and specialized talent.

**Glial cells.** Brain cells serving the function of myelinization.

**Goodness-of-fit.** An effective match between child-rearing practices and a child's temperament, leading to favorable adjustment.

**Growth hormone (GH).** A pituitary hormone that affects the development of almost all body tissues, except the central nervous system and genitals.

**Growth spurt.** The rapid gain in height and weight during adolescence.

**Habituation.** A gradual reduction in the strength of a response as the result of repetitive stimulation.

**Heritability estimate.** A statistic that measures the extent to which continuous traits, such as intelligence or personality, can be traced to heredity.

**Heteronomous morality.** Piaget's first stage of moral development, in which children view moral rules as permanent features of the external world that are handed down by authorities and cannot be changed. Extends from about 5 and 10 years of age.

**Heterozygous.** Having two different alleles at the same place on a pair of chromosomes. Distinguished from *homozygous*.

**Hierarchical classification.** The organization of objects into classes and subclasses on the basis of similarities and differences between the groups.

**Home Observation for Measurement of the Environment (HOME).** A checklist for gathering information about the quality of children's homelives through observation and parental interview.

**Homozygous.** Having two identical alleles at the same place on a pair of chromosomes. Distinguished from *heterozygous*.

**Horizontal décalage.** Development within a Piagetian stage. Gradual mastery of logical concepts during the concrete operational stage provides an example.

**Hostile aggression.** Aggressive acts intended to harm another individual. Distinguished from *instrumental aggression*.

**Human development.** A field of study that includes all changes human beings experience throughout the life span.

**Hypothetico-deductive reasoning.** A formal operational problem-solving strategy in which adolescents begin with a general theory of all possible factors that could affect an outcome in a problem and deduce specific hypotheses, which they test in an orderly fashion.

**Id.** In Freud's theory, the part of the personality that is the source of basic biological needs and desires.

**Identical or monozygotic twins.** Twins that result when a zygote, during the early stages of cell duplication, divides in two. They have the same genetic makeup.

**Identification.** In Freud's theory, the process leading to formation of the superego in which children take the same-sex parent's characteristics into their personality.

**Identity.** A well-organized conception of the self made up of values, beliefs, and goals to which the individual is solidly committed.

**Identity achievement.** The identity status of individuals who have explored and committed themselves to self-chosen values and occupational goals. Distinguished from *moratorium, identity diffusion,* and *identity foreclosure.*

**Identity diffusion.** The identity status of individuals who do not have firm commitments to values and goals and are not actively trying to reach them. Distinguished from *identity achievement, moratorium,* and *identity foreclosure.*

**Identity foreclosure.** The identity status of individuals who have accepted ready-made values and goals that authority figures have chosen for them. Distinguished from *identity achievement, moratorium,* and *identity diffusion.*

**Identity versus identity diffusion.** In Erikson's theory, the psychological conflict of adolescence, which is resolved positively when adolescents attain an identity after a period of exploration and inner soul-searching.

**Imaginary audience.** Adolescents' belief that they are the focus of everyone else's attention and concern.

**Imitation.** Learning by copying the behavior of another person. Also called modeling or observational learning.

**Implantation.** Attachment of the blastocyst to the uterine lining seven to nine days after fertilization.

**Independent variable.** The variable manipulated by the researcher in an experiment.

**Induced labor.** A labor started artificially by breaking the amnion and giving the mother a hormone that stimulates contractions.

**Induction.** A type of discipline in which the effects of the child's misbehavior on others are communicated to the child.

**Industry versus inferiority.** In Erikson's theory, the psychological conflict of middle childhood, which is resolved positively when experiences lead children to develop a sense of competence at useful skills and tasks.

**Infant mortality.** The number of deaths in the first year of life per 1,000 live births.

**Information processing.** An approach that views the human mind as a symbol-manipulating system through which information flows and that regards cognitive development as a continuous process.

**Initiative versus guilt.** In Erikson's theory, the psychological conflict of early childhood, which is resolved positively through play experiences that foster a healthy sense of initiative and through development of a superego, or conscience, that is not overly strict and guilt-ridden.

**Inorganic failure to thrive.** A growth disorder usually present by 18 months of age that is caused by lack of affection and stimulation.

**Instrumental aggression.** Aggression aimed at obtaining an object, privilege, or space with no deliberate intent to harm another person. Distinguished from *hostile aggression.*

**Intelligence quotient, or IQ.** A score that permits an individual's performance on an intelligence test to be compared to the performances of individuals the same age.

**Intentional, or goal directed behavior.** A sequence of actions in which infants combine schemes deliberately to solve a sensorimotor problem.

**Interactional synchrony.** A sensitively tuned "emotional dance," in which the mother responds to infant signals in a well-timed, appropriate fashion and both partners match emotional states, especially the positive ones. Promotes secure attachment.

**Intermodal perception.** Perception that combines information from more than one sensory system.

**Internalization.** The developmental shift from externally controlled responses to behavior that is controlled by inner standards.

**Invariant features.** Features that remain stable in a constantly changing perceptual world.

**Irreversibility.** The inability to mentally go through a series of steps in a problem and then return to the starting point. A characteristic of Piaget's preoperational stage. Distinguished from *reversibility.*

**Joint custody.** A child custody arrangement following divorce in which the court grants both parents equal say in important decisions about the child's upbringing.

**Just community.** Kohlberg's approach to moral education, in which a small society of teachers and students practice a democratic way of life.

**Kaufman Assessment Battery for Children (K-ABC).** An individually administered intelligence test that measures two broad types of information processing skills: sequential and simultaneous processing. The first major test to be grounded in information processing theory.

**Kinship studies.** Studies comparing the characteristics of family members to determine the importance of heredity in complex human characteristics.

**Kwashiorkor.** A disease usually appearing between 1 and 3 years of age that is caused by a diet low in protein. Symptoms include an enlarged belly, swollen feet, hair loss, skin rash, and irritable and listless behavior.

**Language acquisition device (LAD).** An innate ability that permits children, as soon as they have picked up enough words, to combine them into grammatically correct expressions.

**Lanugo.** A white, downy hair that covers the entire body of the fetus, helping the vernix stick to the skin.

**Latency stage.** Freud's psychosexual stage of middle childhood, when the sexual instincts lie dormant.

**Lateralization.** Specialization of functions of the two hemispheres of the cortex.

**Learned helplessness.** A pattern of attributions in which failures are credited to lack of ability. Leads to anxious loss of control in the face of challenging tasks.

**Learning disabilities.** Specific learning disorders that lead children to achieve poorly in school, despite an average or above average IQ. A problem with reading is called *dyslexia,* one with arithmetic *dyscalculia,* and one with writing *dysgraphia.* Believed to be due to faulty brain functioning.

**Long-term memory.** In information processing, the permanent knowledge base of the mental system.

**Longitudinal design.** A research design in which one group of subjects is studied repeatedly at different ages. Distinguished from *cross-sectional design.*

**Longitudinal-sequential design.** A research design with both longitudinal and cross-sectional components in which groups of subjects born in different years are followed over time.

**Mainstreaming.** The integration of handicapped pupils into regular classrooms for part or all of the school day.

**Make-believe play.** A type of play in which children pretend, acting out everyday and imaginary activities.

**Malocclusion.** A condition in which the upper and lower teeth do not meet properly.

**Marasmus.** A disease usually appearing in the first year of life that is caused by a diet low in all essential nutrients. Leads to a wasted condition of the body.

**Mastery-oriented attributions.** Attributions that credit success to high ability and failure to insufficient effort. Leads to high self-esteem and a willingness to approach challenging tasks.

**Maturation.** A genetically determined, naturally unfolding course of growth.

**Mechanistic theory.** A theory that regards the child as a passive reactor to environmental inputs. Distinguished from *organismic theory.*

**Meiosis.** The process of cell division through which gametes are formed and in which the number of chromosomes in each cell is halved.

**Memory strategies.** Deliberate mental activities that improve the likelihood of remembering.

**Menarche.** First menstruation.

**Mental representation.** An internal image of an object or event not present.

**Mental retardation.** Substantially below-average intellectual functioning.

**Metacognition.** Thinking about thought; awareness of mental activities.

**Mitosis.** The process of cell duplication, in which each new cell receives an exact copy of the original chromosomes.

**Monozygotic twins.** See identical twins.

**Moratorium.** The identity status of individuals who are exploring alternatives in an effort to find values and goals to guide their life. Distinguished from *identity achievement, identity diffusion,* and *identity foreclosure.*

**Motherese.** A form of language used by adults to speak to young children that consists of short sentences with exaggerated expression and very clear pronunciation.

**Mutation.** A sudden but permanent change in a segment of DNA.

**Myelinization.** A process in which neural fibers are coated with an insulating fatty sheath that improves the efficiency of message transfer.

**Myopia.** Nearsightedness; inability to see distant objects clearly.

**Natural or prepared childbirth.** An approach designed to reduce pain and medical intervention and to make childbirth a rewarding experience for parents.

**Naturalistic observation.** A method in which the researcher goes into the natural environment to observe the behavior of interest.

**Nature–nurture controversy.** Disagreement among theorists about whether genetic or environmental factors are the most important determinants of development and behavior.

**Neglected children.** Children who are seldom chosen, either positively or negatively, on sociometric measures of peer acceptance. Distinguished from *popular, rejected,* and *controversial children.*

**Neonatal Behavioral Assessment Scale (NBAS).** A test developed by Brazelton to assess the behavior of the infant during the newborn period. Considers reflexes, state changes, responsiveness to physical and social stimuli, motor abilities, and other reactions.

**Neonatal mortality.** The number of deaths in the first month of life per 1,000 live births.

**Neural tube.** The primitive spinal cord that develops from the ectoderm, the top of which swells to form the brain.

**Neurons.** Nerve cells that store and transmit information in the brain.

**Neurotransmitter.** Chemicals that permit neurons to communicate across synapses.

**Niche-picking.** A type of genetic-environmental correlation in which individuals actively choose environments that complement their heredity.

**Noble savage.** Rousseau's view of the child as naturally endowed with an innate plan for orderly, healthy growth.

**Nocturnal enuresis.** Repeated bedwetting during the night.

**Non-rapid-eye-movement (NREM) sleep.** A "regular" sleep state in which the body is quiet and heart rate, breathing, and brain wave activity are slow and regular.

**Nonsocial activity.** Unoccupied, onlooker behavior and solitary play. Distinguished from *parallel, associative,* and *cooperative play.*

**Normative approach.** An approach in which age-related averages are computed to represent the typical child's development.

**Obesity.** A greater than 20 percent increase over average body weight, based on the child's age, sex and physical build.

**Object permanence.** The understanding that objects continue to exist when they are out of sight.

**Oedipal conflict.** The conflict of Freud's phallic stage in which the boy desires to possess his mother and feels hostile toward his father. Resolved by becoming like the father and forming a superego.

**Open classroom.** Elementary school classroom based on the educational philosophy that children are active agents in their own development and learn at different rates. Teachers share decision making with pupils. Pupils are evaluated in relation to their own prior development.

**Operant conditioning.** A form of learning in which the infant's responses determine the kind of stimuli (reinforcer or punisher) received.

**Operations.** In Piaget's theory, mental actions that obey logical rules.

**Oral stage.** Freud's first psychosexual stage, during which infants obtain pleasure through the mouth.

**Organismic theory.** A theory that assumes the existence of psychological structures inside the child that underlie and control development. Distinguished from *mechanistic theory.*

**Organization.** In Piaget's theory, the internal rearrangement and linking together of schemes so that they form a strongly interconnected cognitive system. In information processing, the memory strategy of grouping related items in a list.

**Overextension.** An early vocabulary error in which a word is applied too broadly, to a wider collection of objects and events than is appropriate. Distinguished from *underextension.*

**Overregularization.** Applying regular grammatical rules to words that are exceptions. For example, saying "mouses" instead of "mice."

**Parallel play.** A form of limited social participation in which the child plays near other children with similar materials but does not interact with them. Distinguished from *nonsocial activity, associative play,* and *cooperative play.*

**Peer group.** Peers who form a social unit by generating shared values and standards of behavior and a social structure of leaders and followers.

**Perception-bound.** Being easily distracted by the concrete, perceptual appearance of objects. In Piaget's theory, a characteristic of preoperational thought.

**Permissive parent.** A parenting style that is responsive but undemanding. An overly tolerant approach to parenting. Distinguished from *authoritative* and *authoritarian parents.*

**Personal fable.** Adolescents' belief that they are special and unique. Leads them to conclude that others cannot possibly understand their thoughts and feelings and that they are invulnerable to danger.

**Perspective-taking.** The capacity to imagine what other people may be thinking and feeling.

**Phallic stage.** Freud's psychosexual stage of early childhood, in which sexual impulses transfer to the genital region of the body and the Oedipal and Electra conflicts are resolved.

**Phenotype.** The individual's physical and behavioral characteristics, which are determined by both genetic and environmental factors.

**Phobia.** A fear that is very intense, persists for a long time, and cannot be reduced through reasoning and gentle encouragement.

**Pincer grasp.** The well-coordinated grasp emerging at the end of the first year, involving thumb and forefinger opposition.

**Pituitary gland.** A gland located at the base of the brain that releases hormones affecting physical growth.

**Placenta.** The organ that separates the mother's bloodstream from the embryo or fetal bloodstream but permits exchange of nutrients and waste products.

**Plasticity.** The ability of other parts of the brain to take over functions of damaged regions.

**Polygenic inheritance.** A pattern of inheritance in which many genes determine a characteristic.

**Popular children.** Children who get many positive votes on sociometric measures of peer acceptance. Distinguished from *rejected, controversial,* and *neglected children.*

**Postconventional level.** Kohlberg's highest level of moral development, in which individuals define morality in terms of abstract principles and values that apply to all situations and societies.

**Postpartum depression.** Feelings of sadness and withdrawal that appear shortly after childbirth and that continue for weeks or months.

**Postterm.** Infants who spend a longer than average time period in the uterus—more than 42 weeks.

**Pragmatics.** The practical, social side of language that is concerned with how to engage in effective dialogue with others.

**Preconventional level.** Kohlberg's first level of moral development, in which moral understanding is based on rewards, punishments, and the power of authority figures.

**Preformationism.** Medieval view of the child as a miniature adult.

**Prenatal diagnostic methods.** Medical procedures that permit detection of problems before birth. Includes amniocentesis, chorionic villi biopsy, ultrasound, fetoscopy, and maternal blood analysis.

**Preoperational stage.** Piaget's second stage, in which rapid growth in representation takes place. However, thought is not yet logical. Spans the years from 2 to 7.

**Prereaching.** The poorly coordinated primitive reaching movements of newborn babies.

**Preterm.** Infants born several weeks or more before their due date. Although small in size, their weight may still be appropriate for the time they spent in the uterus. Distinguished from *small for dates.*

**Primary sexual characteristics.** Physical features that involve the reproductive organs directly (ovaries, uterus, and vagina in females; penis, scrotum, and testes in males).

**Principle of contrast.** Principle that young children use to figure out the meaning of a new word—by contrasting it with word meanings they already know.

**Private speech.** Self-directed speech that children use to plan and guide their own behavior.

**Production.** In language development, the words and word combinations that children say. Distinguished from *comprehension.*

**Project Head Start.** Federal program providing low-income children with a year of preschool education before school entry and their parents with support services.

**Propositional thought.** A type of formal operational reasoning in which adolescents evaluate the logic of verbal statements without making reference to real-world circumstances.

**Prosocial or altruistic behavior.** Responses that benefit another person without any expected reward for oneself.

**Proximo-distal trend.** An organized pattern of physical growth that proceeds from the center of the body outward.

**Psychoanalytic theory.** A perspective introduced by Freud that emphasizes the importance of sexual and aggressive drives and the unique developmental history of each child.

**Puberty.** Biological changes at adolescence that lead to an adult-sized body and sexual maturity.

**Public policies.** Laws and government programs.

**Punishment.** In operant conditioning, removing a desirable stimulus or presenting an unpleasant one to decrease the occurrence of a response.

**Range of reaction.** Each person's unique, genetically determined response to a range of environmental conditions.

**Rapid-eye-movement (REM) sleep.** An "irregular" sleep state in which brain wave activity is similar to that of the waking state; eyes dart beneath the lids, heart rate, blood pressure, and breathing are uneven; and slight body movements occur.

**Realistic period.** The period of vocational development in which young people focus on a general career category and, slightly later, settle on a single occupation. Spans late adolescence and young adulthood.

**Recall.** A type of memory that involves remembering a stimulus that is not present. Distinguished from *recognition.*

**Recasts.** Adult responses that restructure children's incorrect speech into a more mature form.

**Recognition.** A type of memory that involves noticing whether a stimulus is identical or similar to one previously experienced. Distinguished from *recall.*

**Referential style.** A style of early language learning in which toddlers use language mainly to label objects.

**Reflex.** An inborn, automatic response to a particular form of stimulation.

**Rehearsal.** The memory strategy of repeating information.

**Reinforcer.** In operant conditioning, a stimulus that increases the occurrence of a response.

**Rejected children.** Children who are actively disliked and get many negative votes on sociometric measures of peer acceptance. Distinguished from *popular, controversial,* and *neglected children.*

**Resistant attachment.** The quality of insecure attachment characterizing infants who remain close to the mother before departure and display angry, resistive behavior when she returns. Distinguished from *secure, avoidant,* and *disorganized/disoriented attachment.*

**Respiratory distress syndrome.** A disorder of preterm infants in which the lungs are so immature that the air sacs collapse, causing serious breathing difficulties. Otherwise known as *hyaline membrane disease.*

**Reticular formation.** A brain structure that maintains alertness and consciousness.

**Reversibility.** The ability to mentally go through a series of steps in a problem and then reverse direction, returning to the starting point. In Piaget's theory, part of every logical operation. Distinguished from *irreversibility.*

**Rh Factor.** A protein that, when present in the fetus's blood but not in the mother's, can cause the mother to build up antibodies. If these return to the fetus's system, they destroy red blood cells, reducing the oxygen supply to organs and tissues.

**Rooming in.** An arrangement in which the newborn baby stays in the mother's hospital room all or most of the time.

**Rough-and-tumble play.** A form of peer interaction involving friendly chasing and play-fighting that, in our evolutionary past, may have been important for the development of fighting skill.

**Rubella.** Three-day German measles. Causes a wide variety of prenatal abnormalities, especially when it strikes during the embryonic period.

**Scheme.** In Piaget's theory, a specific structure, or organized way of making sense of experience, that changes with age.

**School phobia.** Severe apprehension about attending school, often accompanied by physical complaints that disappear once the child is allowed to remain home.

**Script.** A general description of what occurs and when it occurs in a particular situation. A basic means through which children organize and interpret their everyday experiences.

**Secondary sexual characteristics.** Features visible on the outside of the body that serve as signs of sexual maturity but do not involve the reproductive organs (for example, breast development in females, appearance of underarm and pubic hair in both sexes).

**Secular trends in physical growth.** Changes in body size from one generation to the next.

**Secure attachment.** The quality of attachment characterizing infants who are distressed by maternal separation and easily comforted by the mother when she returns. Distinguished from *resistant, avoidant,* and *disorganized/disoriented attachment.*

**Secure base.** The use of the familiar caregiver as a base from which the infant confidently explores the environment.

**Self-concept.** A set of beliefs about one's own characteristics.

**Self-control.** The capacity to resist an impulse to engage in socially disapproved behavior.

**Self-esteem.** An aspect of self-concept that involves judgments about one's own worth or goodness.

**Self-fulfilling prophecy.** The idea that children may adopt teachers' positive or negative attitudes toward them and start to live up to these views.

**Self-regulation.** The process of continuously monitoring progress toward a goal, checking outcomes, and redirecting efforts that prove unsuccessful.

**Sensorimotor stage.** Piaget's first stage, during which infants and toddlers "think" with their eyes, ears, hands, and other sensorimotor equipment. Spans the first 2 years of life.

**Sensory register.** In information processing, that part of the mental system in which sights and sounds are held briefly before they decay or get transferred to working or short-term memory.

**Separation anxiety.** An infant's distressed reaction to the departure of the familiar caregiver.

**Separation-individuation.** In Mahler's theory, the process of separating from the mother and becoming aware of the self, which is triggered by crawling and walking.

**Seriation.** The ability to arrange items along a quantitative dimension, such as length or weight.

**Sex chromosomes.** The 23rd pair of chromosomes, which determines the sex of the child. In females, called XX; in males, called XY.

**Sex-role identity.** Image of oneself as relatively masculine or feminine in characteristics.

**Short-term memory.** See working memory.

**Skeletal age.** An estimate of physical maturity based on development of the bones of the body.

**Slow-to-warm-up child.** A child whose temperament is such that he or she is inactive, shows mild, low-key reactions to environmental stimuli, is negative in mood, and adjusts slowly when faced with new experiences. Distinguished from *easy child* and *difficult child.*

**Small for dates.** Infants whose birth weight is below normal when length of pregnancy is taken into account. May be full term or *preterm.*

**Social learning theory.** An approach that emphasizes the role of modeling, or observational learning, in the development of behavior.

**Social problem-solving training.** Training in which children are taught how to resolve common social conflicts.

**Social referencing.** Relying on a trusted person's emotional reaction to decide how to respond to an uncertain situation.

**Social smile.** The smile evoked by the stimulus of the human face. First appears between 6 and 10 weeks.

**Social systems perspective.** A view of the family as a complex system in which the behaviors of each family member affect those of others.

**Sociocultural theory.** Vygotsky's approach, in which children acquire the ways of thinking and behaving that make up a community's culture through cooperative dialogues with more knowledgeable members of that society.

**Sociodramatic play.** The make-believe play with others that first appears around age 2 1/2.

**Sociometric techniques.** Self-report measures that ask peers to evaluate one another's likability.

**Spermarche.** First ejaculation of seminal fluid.

**Stage.** Qualitative changes in thinking, feeling, and behaving that characterize particular time periods of development.

**Stanford-Binet Intelligence Scale.** An individually administered intelligence test that is the modern descendent of Alfred Binet's first successful test for children. Measures overall IQ and four factors: verbal reasoning, quantitative reasoning, spatial reasoning, and short-term memory.

**States of arousal.** Different degrees of sleep and wakefulness.

**States versus transformations.** The tendency to treat the initial and final states in a problem as completely unrelated. In Piaget's theory, a characteristic of preoperational thought.

**Strange Situation.** A procedure involving short separations from and reunions with the mother that assesses the quality of the attachment bond.

**Stranger anxiety.** The infant's expression of fear in response to unfamiliar adults. Appears in many babies after 7 months of age.

**Structured interview.** A method in which the researcher asks each subject the same questions in the same way.

**Structured observation.** A method in which the researcher sets up a cue for the behavior of interest and observes that behavior in the laboratory.

**Subculture.** Groups of people with beliefs and customs that differ from those of the larger culture.

**Sudden infant death syndrome (SIDS).** Death of a seemingly healthy baby, who stops breathing during the night, without apparent cause.

**Superego.** In Freud's theory, the part of the personality that is the seat of conscience and is often in conflict with the id's desires.

**Symbiosis.** In Mahler's theory, the baby's intimate sense of oneness with the mother, encouraged by warm, physical closeness and gentle handling.

**Synapse.** The gap between neurons, across which chemical messages are sent.

**System of action.** In motor development, the combination of previously acquired skills to produce a more advanced skill.

**Tabula rasa.** Locke's view of the child as a blank slate whose character is shaped by experience.

**Telegraphic speech.** Toddlers' two-word utterances that, like a telegram, leave out smaller and less important words.

**Temperament.** Stable individual differences in quality and intensity of emotional reaction.

**Tentative period.** Period of vocational development in which adolescents weigh vocational options against their interests, abilities, and values. Spans early and middle adolescence.

**Teratogen.** Any environmental agent that causes damage during the prenatal period.

**Thalidomide.** A sedative widely available in Europe, Canada, and South America in the early 1960s. When taken by mothers between the fourth to sixth week after conception, it produced gross deformities of the baby's arms and legs.

**Theory.** An orderly, integrated set of statements that describes, explains, and predicts behavior.

**Thyroid stimulating hormone (TSH).** A pituitary hormone that stimulates the release of thyroxin from the thyroid gland. Thyroxin is necessary for normal brain development and body growth.

**Time out.** A form of mild punishment in which children are removed from the immediate setting until they are ready to act appropriately.

**Toxemia.** An illness of pregnancy in which the mother's blood pressure increases sharply and her face, hands, and feet swell. If untreated, can cause convulsions in the mother and death of the baby.

**Toxoplasmosis.** A parasitic disease caused by eating raw or undercooked meat or contact with the feces of infected cats. During the first trimester, it leads to eye and brain damage.

**Traditional classroom.** Elementary school classroom based on the educational philosophy that children are passive learners who acquire information presented by teachers. Pupils are evaluated on the basis of how well they keep up with other pupils in their grade.

**Transductive reasoning.** Reasoning from one particular event to another particular event, instead of from general to particular or particular to general.

**Transition.** Climax of the first stage of labor, in which the frequency and strength of contractions are at their peak and the cervix opens completely.

**Transitive inference.** The ability to seriate—or arrange items along a quantitative dimension—mentally.

**Triarchic theory of intelligence.** Sternberg's theory, which states that information processing skills, prior experience with tasks, and contextual factors interact to determine intelligent behavior.

**Trimesters.** Three equal time periods in the prenatal period, each of which lasts three months.

**Type A personality.** A personality characterized by excessive competitiveness, impatience, restlessness, and irritability. Associated with high blood pressure and cholesterol levels as well as heart disease in adulthood.

**Ulnar grasp.** The clumsy grasp of the young infant, in which the fingers close against the palm.

**Umbilical cord.** The long cord connecting the prenatal organism to the placenta that delivers nutrients and removes waste products.

**Unconditioned response (UCR).** In classical conditioning, a reflexive response that is produced by an unconditioned stimulus (UCS).

**Unconditioned stimulus (UCS).** In classical conditioning, a stimulus that leads to a reflexive response.

**Underextension.** An early vocabulary error in which a word is applied too narrowly, to a smaller number of objects and events than is appropriate. Distinguished from *overextension*.

**Vacuum extractor.** A plastic cup attached to a suction tube that is used to deliver the baby.

**Vernix.** A white, cheeselike substance covering the fetus and preventing the skin from chapping due to constant exposure to the amniotic fluid.

**Visual acuity.** Fineness of visual discrimination.

**Wechsler Intelligence Scale for Children–III (WISC-III).** An individually administered intelligence test that includes both an overall IQ and a variety of verbal and performance scores.

**Whole language approach.** An approach to beginning reading instruction that parallels children's natural language learning and keeps reading materials whole and meaningful. Distinguished from *basic skills approach*.

**Working or short-term memory.** In information processing, the conscious part of the mental system, where we actively "work" on a limited amount of information to ensure that it will be retained.

**X-linked inheritance.** A pattern of inheritance in which a recessive gene is carried on the X chromosome. Males are more likely to be affected.

**Zone of proximal development.** In Vygotsky's theory, a range of tasks that the child cannot yet handle alone but can do with the help of more skilled partners.

**Zygote.** The union of sperm and ovum at conception.

# REFERENCES

AARON, R., & POWELL, G. (1982). Feedback practices as a function of teacher and pupil race during reading groups instruction. *Journal of Negro Education, 51*, 50–59.

AARONSON, L. S., & MACNEE, C. L. (1989). Tobacco, alcohol, and caffeine use during pregnancy. *Journal of Obstetrics, Gynecology, and Neonatal Nursing, 18*, 279–287.

ABEL, E. L. (1988). Fetal alcohol syndrome in families. *Neurotoxicology and Teratology, 10*, 1–2.

ABELMAN, R. (1985). Styles of parental disciplinary practices as a mediator of children's learning from prosocial television portrayals. *Child Study Journal, 15*, 279–287.

ABRAVANEL, E., & SIGAFOOS, A. D. (1984). Exploring the presence of imitation during early infancy. *Child Development, 55*, 381–392.

ACHENBACH, T. M. (1978). *Research in developmental psychology: Concepts, strategies, and methods.* New York: Free Press.

ACHENBACH, T. M., PHARES, V., HOWELL, C. T., RAUH, V. A., & NURCOMBE, B. (1990). Seven-year outcome of the Vermont program for low-birthweight infants. *Child Development, 61*, 1672–1681.

ACHENBACH, T. M., & WEISZ, J. R. (1975). A longitudinal study of developmental synchrony between conceptual identity, seriation, and transitivity of color, number, and length. *Child Development, 46*, 840–848.

ACKERMAN, B. P. (1978). Children's understanding of speech acts in unconventional frames. *Child Development, 49*, 311–318.

ACREDOLO, C., ADAMS, A., & SCHMID, J. (1984). On the understanding of the relationships between speed, duration, and distance. *Child Development, 55*, 2151–2159.

ADAMS, G. R., ABRAHAM, K. G., & MARKSTROM, C. A. (1987). The relations among identity development, self-consciousness, and self-focusing during middle and late adolescence. *Developmental Psychology, 23*, 292–297.

ADCOCK, A. G., NAGY, S. N., & SIMPSON, J. A. (1991). Selected risk factors in adolescent suicide attempts. *Adolescence, 26*, 817–828.

AINSWORTH, M. D. S., BLEHAR, M. C., WATERS, E., & WALL, S. (1978). *Patterns of attachment.* Hillsdale, NJ: Erlbaum.

ALBERTS-CORUSH, J., FIRESTONE, P., & GOODMAN, J. T. (1986). Attention and impulsivity characteristics of the biological and adoptive parents of hyperactive and normal control children. *American Journal of Orthopsychiatry, 56*, 413–423.

ALESSANDRI, S. M., & WOZNIAK, R. H. (1987). The child's awareness of parental beliefs concerning the child: A developmental study. *Child Development, 58*, 316–323.

ALPERT-GILLIS, L. J., & CONNELL, J. P. (1989). Gender and sex-role influences on children's self-esteem. *Journal of Personality, 57*, 97–114.

ALTEMEIER, W. A., O'CONNOR, S. M., SHERROD, K. B., & VIETZE, P. M. (1984). Prospective study of antecedents for nonorganic failure to thrive. *Journal of Pediatrics, 106*, 360–365.

ALTER-REID, K., GIBBS, M. S., LACHENMEYER, J. R., SIGAL, J., & MASSOTH, N. A. (1986). Sexual abuse of children: A review of empirical findings. *Clinical Psychology Review, 6*, 249–266.

ALTSHULER, J. L., & RUBLE, D. N. (1989). Developmental changes in children's awareness of strategies for coping with uncontrollable stress. *Child Development, 60*, 1337–1349.

AMERICAN ACADEMY OF PEDIATRICS (1984). Report of the task force on the assessment of the scientific evidence relating to infant-feeding practices and infant health. *Pediatrics, 74*, 579–762.

AMERICAN ACADEMY OF PEDIATRICS (1987). Statement on childhood lead poisoning. *Pediatrics, 79*, 457–465.

AMERICAN ACADEMY OF PEDIATRICS, Committee on Sports Medicine (1989). Anabolic steroids and the adolescent athlete. *Pediatrics, 83*, 127–128.

AMERICAN ACADEMY OF PEDIATRICS (1990). Presidential address delivered on April 30, 1990, at the spring meeting of the American Academy of Pediatrics. *Pediatrics, 86* (6, Pt. 2), 1025–1027.

AMERICAN COLLEGE OF SPORTS MEDICINE (1984). Position stand on the use of anabolic-androgenic steroids in sports. *Medical Science and Sports, 19*, 534–539.

AMERICAN PSYCHIATRIC ASSOCIATION (1987). *Diagnostic and statistical manual of mental disorders* (3rd ed., rev.). Washington, DC: Author.

AMERICAN PSYCHOLOGICAL ASSOCIATION, Division on Developmental Psychology (1968). Ethical standards for research with children. *Newsletter*, 1–3.

ANAND, K. J. S., PHIL, D., & HICKEY, P. R. (1987). Pain and its effects in the human neonate and fetus. *New England Journal of Medicine, 317*, 1321–1329.

ANDERSON, E. S. (1984). The acquisition of sociolinguistic knowledge: Some evidence from children's verbal role play. *Western Journal of Speech Communication, 48*, 125–144.

ANDERSON, J. E., KANN, L., HOLTZMAN, D., ARDAY, S., TRUMAN, B., & KOLBE, L. (1990). HIV/AIDS knowledge and sexual behavior among high school students. *Family Planning Perspectives, 22*, 252–255.

ANDERSSON, B-E. (1989). Effects of public day-care—a longitudinal study. *Child Development, 60*, 857–866.

ANDERSSON, B-E. (1992). Effects of day-care on cognitive and socio-emotional competence of thirteen-year-old Swedish schoolchildren. *Child Development, 63*, 20–36.

ANDREWS, L. B. (1987). Ethical and legal aspects of in vitro fertilization and artificial insemination by donor. *Urologic Clinics of North America, 14*, 633–643.

ANGLE, J., & WISSMANN, D. A. (1980). The epidemiology of myopia. *American Journal of Epidemiology, 111*, 220–228.

APGAR, V. (1953). A proposal for a new method of evaluation in the newborn infant. *Current Research in Anesthesia and Analgesia, 32*, 260–267.

APPLETON, T., CLIFTON, R., & GOLDBERG, S. (1975). The development of behavioral competence in infancy. In F. D. Horowitz (Ed.), *Review of child development research* (Vol. 4, pp. 101–186). Chicago: University of Chicago Press.

ARCHER, S. L. (1982). The lower age boundaries of identity development. *Child Development, 53*, 1551–1556.

ARCHER, S. L. (1989a). Gender differences in identity development: Issues of process, domain, and timing. *Journal of Adolescence, 2*, 117–138.

ARCHER, S. L. (1989b). The status of identity: Reflections on the need for intervention. *Journal of Adolescence, 12*, 345–359.

ARCHER, S. L., & WATERMAN, A. S. (1990). Varieties of identity diffusions and foreclosures: An exploration of subcategories of the identity statuses. *Journal of Adolescent Research, 5*, 96–111.

ARIES, P. (1962). *Centuries of childhood.* New York: Random House.

ARNOLD, K., & DENNY, T. (1985). *The lives of academic achievers: The career aspirations of male and female high school valedictorians and salutatorians.* Paper presented at the annual meeting of the American Educational Research Association, Chicago.

ARTERBERRY, M. E., & YONAS, A. (1988). Infants' sensitivity to kinetic information for three-dimensional object shape. *Perception and Psychophysics, 44*, 1–6.

ASHER, S. R., & HYMEL, S. (1981). Children's social competence in peer relations: Sociometric and behavioral assessment. In J. D. Wine & W. D. Smye (Eds.), *Social competence* (pp. 125–157). New York: Guilford Press.

ASHER, S. R., & WHEELER, V. A. (1985). Children's loneliness: A comparison of rejected and neglected peer status. *Journal of Consulting and Clinical Psychology, 53,* 500–505.

ASHMEAD, D. H., & PERLMUTTER, M. (1980). Infant memory in everyday life. In M. Perlmutter (Ed.), *New directions for child development* (Vol. 10, pp. 1–16). San Francisco: Jossey-Bass.

ASHMEAD, D. H., DAVIS, D. L., WHALEN, T., & ODOM, R. D. (1991). Sound localization and sensitivity to interaural time differences in human infants. *Child Development, 62,* 1211–1226.

ASLIN, R. N. (1987). Visual and auditory development in infancy. In J. D. Osofsky (Ed.), *Handbook of infant development* (2nd ed., pp. 5–97). New York: Wiley.

ASLIN, R. N., PISONI, D. B., & JUSCZYK, P. W. (1983). Auditory development and speech perception in infancy. In M. M. Haith & J. J. Campos (Eds.), *Handbook of child psychology: Vol. 2. Infancy and developmental psychobiology* (4th ed., pp. 573–687). New York: Wiley.

ASTINGTON, J. W. (1991). Intention in the child's theory of mind. In C. Moore & D. Frye (Eds.), *Children's theories of mind* (pp. 157–172). Hillsdale, NJ: Erlbaum.

ASTLEY, S. J., CLARREN, S. K., LITTLE, R. E., SAMPSON, P. D., & DALING, J. R. (1992). Analysis of facial shape in children gestationally exposed to marijuana, alcohol, and/or cocaine. *Pediatrics, 89,* 67–77.

ATKIN, C. (1978). Observation of parent-child interaction in supermarket decision making. *Journal of Marketing, 42,* 41–45.

ATKINSON, J., & BRADDOCK, O. (1989). Development of basic visual functions. In A. Slater & G. Bremner (Eds.), *Infant development* (pp. 7–41). Hillsdale, NJ: Erlbaum.

ATKINSON, R. C., & SHIFFRIN, R. M. (1968). Human memory: A proposed system and its control processes. In K. W. Spence & J. T. Spence (Eds.), *Advances in the psychology of learning and motivation* (Vol. 2, pp. 90–195). New York: Academic Press.

ATTIE, I., & BROOKS-GUNN, J. (1989). Development of eating problems in adolescent girls: A longitudinal study. *Developmental Psychology, 25,* 70–79.

AUGUST, D., & GARCIA, E. E. (1988). *Language minority education in the United States.* Springfield, IL: Charles C. Thomas.

AVIS, J., & HARRIS, P. (1991). Belief-desire reasoning among Baka children: Evidence for a universal conception of mind. *Child Development, 62,* 460–467.

AXIA, G., & BARONI, R. (1985). Linguistic politeness at different age levels. *Child Development, 56,* 918–927.

AZMITIA, M. (1988). Peer interaction and problem solving: When are two heads better than one? *Child Development, 59,* 87–96.


BAHRICK, L. E. (1983). Infants' perception of substance and temporal synchrony in multimodal events. *Infant Behavior and Development, 6,* 429–451.

BAHRICK, L. E. (1988). Intermodal learning in infancy: Learning on the basis of two kinds of invariant relations in audible and visible events. *Child Development, 59,* 197–209.

BAILEY, R. C. (1990). Growth of African pygmies in early childhood. *New England Journal of Medicine, 323,* 1146.

BAILLARGEON, R. (1987). Object permanence in 3 1/2- and 4 1/2-month-old infants. *Developmental Psychology, 23,* 655–664.

BAILLARGEON, R., & GRABER, M. (1988). Evidence of location memory in 8-month-old infants in a nonsearch AB task. *Developmental Psychology, 24,* 502–511.

BAIRD, P. A., & SADOVNICK, A. D. (1987). Maternal age-specific rates for Down syndrome: Changes over time. *American Journal of Medical Genetics, 29,* 917–927.

BAKEMAN, R., ADAMSON, L. B., KONNER, M., & BARR, R. G. (1990). !Kung infancy: The social context of object exploration. *Child Development, 61,* 794–809.

BAKER, D., & STEVENSON, D. (1986). Mothers' strategies for school achievement: Managing the transition to high school. *Sociology of Education, 59,* 156–167.

BALLARD, B. D., GIPSON, M. T., GUTTENBERG, W., & RAMSEY, K. (1980). Palatability of food as a factor influencing obese and normal-weight children's eating habits. *Behavior Research and Therapy, 18,* 598–600.

BANCROFT, J., AXWORTHY, D., & RATCLIFFE, S. (1982). The personality and psycho-sexual development of boys with 47 XXY chromosome constitution. *Journal of Child Psychology and Psychiatry, 23,* 169–180.

BAND, E. B., & WEISZ, J. R. (1988). How to feel better when it feels bad: Children's perspectives on coping with everyday stress. *Developmental Psychology, 24,* 247–253.

BANDURA, A. (1977). *Social learning theory.* Englewood Cliffs, NJ: Prentice-Hall.

BANDURA, A. (1986). *Social foundations of thought and action: A social cognitive theory.* Englewood Cliffs, NJ: Prentice-Hall.

BANDURA, A. (1989). Social cognitive theory. In R. Vasta (Ed.), *Annals of child development* (Vol. 6, pp. 1–60). Greenwich, CT: JAI Press.

BANE, M. J., & ELLWOOD, D. T. (1989). One fifth of the nation's children: Why are they poor? *Science, 245,* 1047–1053.

BANKS, M. S. (1980). The development of visual accommodation during early infancy. *Child Development, 51,* 646–666.

BANKS, M. S., & GINSBURG, A. P. (1985). Early visual preferences: A review and new theoretical treatment. In H. W. Reese (Ed.), *Advances in child development and behavior* (Vol. 19, pp. 207–246). New York: Academic Press.

BANKS, M. S., & SALAPATEK, P. (1981). Infant pattern vision: A new approach based on the contrast sensitivity function. *Journal of Experimental Child Psychology, 31,* 1–45.

BANKS, M. S., & SALAPATEK, P. (1983). Infant visual perception. In M. M. Haith & J. J. Campos (Eds.), *Handbook of child psychology: Vol. 2. Infancy and developmental psychobiology* (4th ed., pp. 435–571). New York: Wiley.

BARANOWSKI, T., RASSIN, D. K., RICHARDSON, C. J., BROWN, J. P., & BEE, D. E. (1986). Attitudes toward breastfeeding. *Developmental and Behavioral Pediatrics, 7,* 367–372.

BARDEN, R. C., FORD, M. E., JENSEN, A. G., ROGERS-SALYER, M., & SALYER, K. E. (1989). Effects of craniofacial deformity in infancy on the quality of mother-infant interactions. *Child Development, 60,* 819–824.

BARENBOIM, C. (1977). Developmental changes in the interpersonal cognitive system from middle childhood to adolescence. *Child Development, 48,* 1467–1474.

BARKER, R. G. (1955). *Midwest and its children.* Stanford, CA: Stanford University Press.

BARKLEY, R. A. (1990). *Attention deficit hyperactivity disorder: A handbook for diagnosis and treatment.* New York: Guilford.

BARNES, K. E. (1971). Preschool play norms: A replication. *Developmental Psychology, 5,* 99–103.

BARNES, S., GUTFREUND, M., SATTERLY, D., & WELLS, D. (1983). Characteristics of adult speech which predict children's language development. *Journal of Child Language, 10,* 65–84.

BARNETT, M. (1982). Infant outcome in relation to second stage labor pushing method. *Birth, 9,* 221–228.

BAROL, B. (1986, July 28). Cocaine babies: Hooked at birth. *Newsweek, 58* (4), 56–57.

BARR, H. M., STREISSGUTH, A. P., DARBY, B. L., & SAMPSON, P. D. (1990). Prenatal exposure to alcohol, caffeine, tobacco, and aspirin: Effects on fine and gross motor performance in 4-year-old children. *Developmental Psychology, 26,* 339–348.

BARR, R. (1991, May). Toward a balanced perspective on beginning reading. *Educational Researcher, 20* (4), 30–32.

BARRERA, M. E., & MAURER, D. (1981a). Discrimination of strangers by the three-month-old. *Child Development, 52,* 559–563.

BARRERA, M. E., & MAURER, D. (1981b). Recognition of mother's photographed face by the three-month-old infant. *Child Development, 52,* 714–716.

BARRETT, D. E., & YARROW, M. R. (1977). Prosocial behavior, social inferential ability, and assertiveness in children. *Child Development, 48,* 475–481.

BARRETT, K. C., & CAMPOS, J. J. (1987). Perspectives on emotional development: II. A functionalist approach to emotion. In J. D. Osofsky (Ed.), *Handbook of infant development* (2nd ed., pp. 1101–1149). New York: Wiley.

BARUCH, G. K., & BARNETT, R. C. (1986). Fathers' participation in family work and children's sex-role attitudes. *Child Development, 57,* 1210–1223.

BATES, E. (1979). *The emergence of symbols: Cognition and communication in infancy.* New York: Academic Press.

BATES, E., BRETHERTON, I., & SNYDER, L. (1988). *From first words to grammar.* Cambridge, England: Cambridge University Press.

BATES, J. E. (1987). Temperament in infancy. In J. D. Osofsky (Ed.), *Handbook of infant development* (2nd ed., pp. 1101–1149). New York: Wiley.

BATES, J. E., & BAYLES, K. (1988). Attachment and the development of behavior problems. In J. Belsky & T. Nexworski (Eds.), *Clinical implications of attachment* (pp. 253–294). Hillsdale, NJ: Erlbaum.

BAUER, P. J., & MANDLER, J. M. (1989). One thing follows another: Effects of temporal structure on 1- to 2-year-olds' recall of events. *Developmental Psychology, 25,* 197–206.

BAUER, P. J., & MANDLER, J. M. (1992). Putting the horse before the cart: The use of temporal order in recall of events by one-year-old children. *Developmental Psychology, 28,* 441–452.

BAUMEISTER, R. F. (1990). Identity crisis. In R. M. Lerner, A. C. Petersen, & J. Brooks-Gunn (Eds.), *The encyclopedia of adolescence* (Vol. 1, pp. 518–521). New York: Garland.

BAUMRIND, D. (1967). Child care practices anteceding three patterns of preschool behavior. *Genetic Psychology Monographs, 75,* 43–88.

BAUMRIND, D. (1971). Current patterns of parental authority. *Developmental Psychology Monograph, 4* (No. 1, Pt. 2).

BAUMRIND, D. (1983). Rejoinder to Lewis's reinterpretation of parental firm control effects: Are authoritative families really harmonious? *Psychological Bulletin, 94,* 132–142.

BAUMRIND, D. (1991). The influence of parenting style on adolescent competence and substance use. *Journal of Early Adolescence, 11,* 56–95.

BAUMRIND, D., & BLACK, A. E. (1967). Socialization practices associated with dimension of competence in preschool boys and girls. *Child Development, 38,* 291–327.

BAYLEY, N. (1969). *Bayley Scales of Infant Development.* New York: Psychological Corporation.

BEAUTRAIS, A. L., FERGUSSON, D. M., & SHANNON, F. T. (1982). Life events and childhood morbidity: A prospective study. *Pediatrics, 70,* 935–940.

BEEGHLEY, L., & SELLERS, C. (1986). Adolescents and sex: A structural theory of premarital sex in the United States. *Deviant Behavior, 7,* 313–336.

BEHREND, D. (1988). Overextensions in early language comprehension: Evidence from a signal detection approach. *Journal of Child Language, 15,* 63–75.

BEHREND, D. A., ROSENGREN, K. S., & PERLMUTTER, M. (1992). The relation between private speech and parental interactive style. In R. M. Diaz & L. E. Berk (Eds.), *Private speech: From social interaction to self-regulation* (pp. 85–100) Hillsdale, NJ: Erlbaum.

BEHRMAN, R. E., & VAUGHAN, V. C. (1987). *Nelson textbook of pediatrics* (13th ed.). Philadelphia: Saunders.

BEIDEL, D. (1991). Social phobia and overanxious disorder in school-age children. *Journal of the American Academy of Child and Adolescent Psychiatry, 30,* 545–552.

BEILIN, H. (1978). Inducing conservation through training. In G. Steiner (Ed.), *Psychology of the twentieth century* (Vol. 7, pp. 260–289). Munich: Kindler.

BEILIN, H. (1989). Piagetian theory. In R. Vasta (Ed.), *Annals of child development* (Vol. 6, pp. 85–131). Greenwich, CT: JAI Press.

BEILIN, H. (1992). Piaget's enduring contribution to developmental psychology. *Developmental Psychology, 28,* 191–204.

BELL, A., WEINBERG, M., & HAMMERSMITH, S. (1981). *Sexual preference: Its development in men and women.* Bloomington, IN: Indiana University Press.

BELLINGER, D., LEVITON, A., WATERNAUX, C., NEEDLEMAN, H., & RABINOWITZ, M. (1987). Longitudinal analysis of prenatal and postnatal lead exposure and early cognitive development. *New England Journal of Medicine, 316,* 1037–1043.

BELSKY, J. (1988). The "effects" of infant day care reconsidered. *Early Childhood Research Quarterly, 3,* 235–272.

BELSKY, J., & BRAUNGART, J. M. (1991). Are insecure-avoidant infants with extensive day-care experience less stressed by and more independent in the Strange Situation? *Child Development, 62,* 567–571.

BELSKY, J., GOODE, M. K., & MOST, R. K. (1980). Maternal stimulation and infant exploratory competence: Cross-sectional, correlational, and experimental analyses. *Child Development, 51,* 1163–1178.

BELSKY, J., ROVINE, M., & TAYLOR, D. G. (1984). The Pennsylvania Infant and Family Development Project: III. The origins of individual differences in infant-mother attachment: Maternal and infant contributions. *Child Development, 55,* 718–728.

BELSKY, J., SPANIER, G. B., & ROVINE, M. (1983). Stability and change in marriage across the transition to parenthood. *Journal of Marriage and the Family, 45,* 567–577.

BEM, S. L. (1974). The measurement of psychological androgyny. *Journal of Consulting and Clinical Psychology, 42,* 155–162.

BEM, S. L. (1975). Sex role adaptability: One consequence of psychological androgyny. *Journal of Personality and Social Psychology, 31,* 634–643.

BEM, S. L. (1984). Androgyny and gender schema theory: A conceptual and empirical integration. In R. A. Dienstbier & T. B. Sondregger (Eds.), *Nebraska Symposia on Motivation* (Vol. 34, pp. 179–226). Lincoln, NB: University of Nebraska Press.

BEM, S. L. (1989). Genital knowledge and gender constancy in preschool children. *Child Development, 60,* 649–662.

BENACERRAF, B. R., GREEN, M. F., SALTZMAN, D. H., BARSS, V. A., PENSO, C. A., NADEL, A. S., HEFFNER, L. J., STRYKER, J. M., SANDSTROM, M. M., & FRIGOLETTO, F. D., JR. (1988). Early amniocentesis for prenatal cytogenetic evaluation. *Radiology, 169,* 709–710.

BENBOW, C. P. (1986). Physiological correlates of extreme intellectual precocity. *Neuropsychologia, 24,* 719–725.

BENBOW, C. P. (1988). Sex differences in mathematical reasoning ability in intellectually talented preadolescents: Their nature, effects, and possible causes. *Behavioral and Brain Sciences, 11,* 169–232.

BENBOW, C. P., & ARJMAND, O. (1990). Predictors of high academic achievement in mathematics and science by mathematically talented students: A longitudinal study. *Journal of Educational Psychology, 82,* 430–441.

BENBOW, C. P., & STANLEY, J. C. (1980). Sex differences in mathematical ability: Fact or artifact? *Science, 210,* 1262–1264.

BENBOW, C. P., & STANLEY, J. C. (1983). Sex differences in mathematical reasoning: More facts. *Science, 222,* 1029–1031.

BENCH, R. J., COLLYER, Y., MENTZ, L., & WILSON, I. (1976). Studies in infant behavioural audiometry: I. Neonates. *Audiology, 15,* 85–105.

BENEDICT, R. (1934a). Anthropology and the abnormal. *Journal of Genetic Psychology, 10,* 59–82.

BENEDICT, R. (1934b). *Patterns of culture.* Boston: Houghton Mifflin.

BEREZIN, J. (1990). *The complete guide to choosing child care.* New York: Random House.

BERG, M., & MEDRICH, E. A. (1980). Children in four neighborhoods: The physical environment and its effects on play and play patterns. *Environment and Behavior, 12,* 320–348.

BERG, W. K., & BERG, K. M. (1987). Psychophysiological development in infancy: State, startle, and attention. In J. Osofsky (Ed.), *Handbook of infant development* (2nd ed., pp. 238–317). New York: Wiley.

BERK, L. E. (1985). Relationship of caregiver education to child-oriented attitudes, job satisfaction, and behaviors toward children. *Child Care Quarterly, 14,* 103–129.

BERK, L. E. (1992a). Children's private speech: An overview of theory and the status of research. In R. M. Diaz & L. E. Berk (Eds.), *Private speech: From social interaction to self-regulation* (pp. 17–53). Hillsdale, NJ: Erlbaum.

BERK, L. E. (1992b). The extracurriculum. In P. W. Jackson (Ed.), *Handbook of research on curriculum* (pp. 1002–1043). New York: Macmillan.

BERKO GLEASON, J. (1989). Studying language development. In J. Berko Gleason (Ed.), *The development of language* (pp. 1–34). Columbus, OH: Merrill.

BERKOWITZ, M. W., & GIBBS, J. C. (1983). Measuring the developmental features of moral discussion. *Merrill-Palmer Quarterly, 29,* 399–410.

BERMAN, P. (1980). Are women more responsive than men to the young? A review of developmental and situational variables. *Psychological Bulletin, 88,* 668–695.

BERMAN, P. W., & PEDERSEN, F. A. (Eds.). (1987). *Men's transition to parenthood: Longitudinal studies and early family experience.* Hillsdale, NJ: Erlbaum.

BERNDT, T. J. (1986). Children's comments about their friendships. In M. Perlmutter (Ed.), *Cognitive perspectives on children's social and behavioral development* (pp. 189–212). Hillsdale, NJ: Erlbaum.

BERNDT, T. J. (1988). The nature and significance of children's friendships. In R. Vasta (Ed.), *Annals of child development* (Vol. 5, pp. 155–186). Greenwich, CT: JAI Press.

BERNDT, T. J., & PERRY, T. B. (1990). Distinctive features and effects of early adolescent friendships. In R. Montemayor, G. R. Adams, & T. P. Gullotta (Eds.), *From childhood to adolescence: A transitional period?* (pp. 269–287). Newbury Park, CA: Sage.

BERTENTHAL, B. I., & CAMPOS, J. J. (1987). New directions in the study of early experience. *Child Development, 58,* 560–567.

BERTENTHAL, B. I., CAMPOS, J. J., & BARRETT, K. (1984). Self-produced locomotion: An organizer of emotional, cognitive, and social development in infancy. In R. Emde & R. Harmon (Eds.), *Continuities and discontinuities in development* (pp. 174–210). New York: Plenum.

BERTENTHAL, B. I., CAMPOS, J. J., & HAITH, M. (1980). Development of visual organization: The perception of subjective contours. *Child Development, 51,* 1077–1080.

BERTENTHAL, B. I., PROFFITT, D. R., KRAMER, S. J., & SPETNER, N. B. (1987). Infants' encoding of kinetic displays varying in relative coherence. *Developmental Psychology, 23,* 171–178.

BERTENTHAL, B. I., PROFFITT, D. R., SPETNER, N. B., & THOMAS, M. A. (1985). The development of infant sensitivity to biomechanical motions. *Child Development, 56,* 531–543.

BEST, D. L., WILLIAMS, J. E., CLOUD, J. M., DAVIS, S. W., ROBERTSON, L. S., EDWARDS, J. R., GILES, H., & FOWLES, J. (1977). Development of sex-trait stereotypes among young children in the United States, England, and Ireland. *Child Development, 48,* 1375–1384.

BEUNEN, G. P., MALINA, R. M., VAN'T HOF, M. A., SIMONS, J., OSTYN, M., RENSON, R., & VAN GERVEN, D. (1988). *Adolescent growth and motor performance.* Champaign, IL: Human Kinetics.

BIALYSTOK, E. (1986). Factors in the growth of linguistic awareness. *Child Development, 57,* 498–510.

BIBACE, R., & WALSH, M. E. (1980). Development of children's concepts of illness. *Pediatrics, 66,* 912–917.

BIERMAN, K. L. (1986). Process of change during social skills training with preadolescents and its relation to treatment outcome. *Child Development, 57,* 230–240.

BIGLER, R. S., & LIBEN, L. S. (1990). The role of attitudes and interventions in gender-schematic processing. *Child Development, 61,* 1440–1452.

BIRCH, L. L. (1987). Children's food preferences: Developmental patterns and environmental influences. In G. Whitehurst & R. Vasta (Eds.), *Annals of child development* (Vol. 4, pp. 171–208). Greenwich, CT: JAI Press.

BIRCH, L. L. (1990). Development of food acceptance patterns. *Developmental Psychology, 26,* 515–519.

BIRCH, L. L., MCPHEE, L., SHOBA, B. C., STEINBERG, L., & KREH-BIEL, R. (1987). "Clean up your plate": Effects of child feeding practices on the development of intake regulation. *Learning and Motivation, 18,* 301–317.

BIRCH, L. L., ZIMMERMAN, S., & HIND, H. (1980). The influence of social-affective context on preschool children's food preferences. *Child Development, 51,* 856–861.

BIRNHOLZ, J. C., & BENACERRAF, B. R. (1983). The development of human fetal hearing. *Science, 222,* 516–518.

BISHOP, S. M., & INGERSOLL, G. M. (1989). Effects of marital conflict and family structure on the self-concepts of pre- and early adolescents. *Journal of Youth and Adolescence, 18,* 25–38.

BIVENS, J. A., & BERK, L. E. (1990). A longitudinal study of the development of elementary school children's private speech. *Merrill-Palmer Quarterly, 36,* 443–463.

BJORKLUND, D. F., & MUIR, J. E. (1988). Children's development of free recall memory: Remembering on their own. In R. Vasta (Ed.), *Annals of child development* (Vol. 5, pp. 79–123). Greenwich, CT: JAI Press.

BLANCHARD, M., & MAIN, M. (1979). Avoidance of the attachment figure and social-emotional adjustment in day-care infants. *Developmental Psychology, 15,* 445–446.

BLASI, A. (1983). Moral cognition and moral action: A theoretical perspective. *Developmental Review, 3,* 178–210.

BLASS, E. M., GANCHROW, J. R., & STEINER, J. E. (1984). Classical conditioning in newborn humans 2–48 hours of age. *Infant Behavior and Development, 7,* 223–235.

BLATT, M., & KOHLBERG, L. (1975). The effects of classroom moral discussion upon children's moral judgment. *Journal of Moral Education, 4,* 129–161.

BLAUBERGS, M. S. (1980, March). Sex-role stereotyping and gifted girls'

experience and education. *Roeper Review, 2* (3), 13–15.

BLOCK, J. H. (1984). *Sex role identity and ego development.* San Francisco: Jossey-Bass.

BLOCK, J., BLOCK, J. H., & GJERDE, P. F. (1988). Parental functioning and home environment in families of divorce: Prospective and concurrent analyses. *Journal of the American Academy of Child and Adolescent Psychiatry, 27,* 207–213.

BLOOM, B. S. (Ed.). (1985). *Developing talent in young people.* New York: Ballantine Books.

BLOTNER, R., & BEARISON, D. J. (1984). Developmental consistencies in socio-moral knowledge: Justice reasoning and altruistic behavior. *Merrill-Palmer Quarterly, 30,* 349–367.

BLUEBOND-LANGER, M. (1977). Meanings of death to children. In H. Feifel (Ed.), *New meanings of death* (pp. 47–66). New York: McGraw-Hill.

BLURTON JONES, N. (1972). Categories of child-child interaction. In N. Blurton Jones (Ed.), *Ethological studies of child behaviour* (pp. 97–127). Cambridge, England: Cambridge University Press.

BLYTH, D., HILL, J., & THIEL, K. (1982). Early adolescents' significant others: Grade and gender differences in perceived relationships with familial and nonfamilial adults and young people. *Journal of Youth and Adolescence, 11,* 425–450.

BLYTH, D. A., SIMMONS, R. G., & ZAKIN, D. F. (1985). Satisfaction with body image for early adolescent females: The impact of pubertal timing within different school environments. *Journal of Youth and Adolescence, 14,* 207–225.

BOBAK, I. M., JENSEN, M. D., & ZALAR, M. K. (1989). *Maternity and gynecologic care.* St. Louis: Mosby.

BOGATZ, G. A., & BALL, S. (1972). *The second year of Sesame Street: A continuing evaluation.* Princeton, NJ: Educational Testing Service.

BOHANNON, J. N., III, & STANOWICZ, L. (1988). The issue of negative evidence: Adult responses to children's language errors. *Developmental Psychology, 24,* 684–689.

BOHANNON, J. N., III, & WARREN-LEUBECKER, A. (1988). Recent developments in child-directed speech: We've come a long way, baby-talk. *Language Sciences, 10,* 89–110.

BOHANNON, J. N., III, & WARREN-LEUBECKER, A. (1989). Theoretical approaches to language acquisition. In J. Berko Gleason (Ed.), *The development of language* (2nd ed., pp. 167–223). Columbus, OH: Merrill.

BOLDIZAR, J. P. (1991). Assessing sex typing and androgyny in children: The children's sex role inventory. *Developmental Psychology, 27,* 505–515.

BORGHRAEF, M., FRYNS, J. P., DIELKENS, A., PYCK, K., & VAN DEN BERGHE, H. (1987). Fragile (X) syndrome: A study of the psychological profile of 23 prepubertal patients. *Clinical Genetics, 32,* 179–186.

BORKE, H. (1975). Piaget's mountains revisited: Changes in the egocentric landscape. *Developmental Psychology, 11,* 240–243.

BORKOWSKI, J. G., CARR, M., RELLINGER, E., & PRESSLEY, M. (1990). Self-regulated cognition: Interdependence of metacognition, attributions, and self-esteem. In B. F. Jones & L. Idol (Eds.), *Dimensions of thinking and cognitive instruction* (pp. 57–92). Hillsdale, NJ: Erlbaum.

BORNSTEIN, M. H. (1988). Perceptual development across the life cycle. In M. H. Bornstein & M. E. Lamb (Eds.), *Developmental psychology: An advanced textbook* (pp. 151–204). Hillsdale, NJ: Erlbaum.

BORNSTEIN, M. H., & SIGMAN, M. D. (1986). Continuity in mental development from infancy. *Child Development, 57,* 251–274.

BORSTELMANN, L. J. (1983). Children before psychology: Ideas about children from antiquity to the late 1800s. In W. Kessen (Ed.), *Handbook of child psychology: Vol. 1: History, theory, and methods* (4th ed., pp. 1–40). New York: Wiley.

BOSSARD, J. S. S., & BOLL, E. S. (1956). *The large family system.* Philadelphia: University of Pennsylvania Press.

BOUCHARD, T. J., JR., & MCGUE, M. (1981). Familial studies of intelligence: A review. *Science, 212,* 1055–1058.

BOUCHARD, T. J., JR., LYKKEN, D. T., MCGUE, M., SEGAL, N. L., & TELLEGEN, A. (1990). Sources of human psychological differences: The Minnesota Study of Twins Reared Apart. *Science, 250,* 223–228.

BOUKYDIS, C. F. Z. (1985). Perception of infant crying as an interpersonal event. In B. M. Lester & C. F. Z. Boukydis (Eds.), *Infant crying* (pp. 187–215). New York: Plenum.

BOUKYDIS, C. F. Z., & BURGESS, R. L. (1982). Adult physiological response to infant cries: Effects of temperament of infant, parental status and gender. *Child Development, 53,* 1291–1298.

BOWLBY, J. (1969). *Attachment and loss: Vol. 1: Attachment.* New York: Basic Books.

BOWLBY, J. (1980). *Attachment and loss: Vol. 3: Loss.* New York: Basic Books.

BRACKBILL, Y., MCMANUS, K., & WOODWARD, L. (1985). *Medication in maternity: Infant exposure and maternal information.* Ann Arbor: University of Michigan Press.

BRADLEY, R. H., & CALDWELL, B. M. (1979). Home Observation for Measurement of the Environment: A revision of the preschool scale. *American Journal of Mental Deficiency, 84,* 235–244.

BRADLEY, R. H., & CALDWELL, B. M. (1981). The HOME Inventory: A validation of the preschool scale for black children. *Child Development, 52,* 708–710.

BRADLEY, R. H., & CALDWELL, B. M. (1982). The consistency of the home environment and its relation to child development. *International Journal of Behavioral Development, 5,* 445–465.

BRADLEY, R. H., CALDWELL, B. M., & ROCK, S. L. (1988). Home environment and school performance: A ten-year follow-up and examination of three models of environmental action. *Child Development, 59,* 852–867.

BRADLEY, R. H., CALDWELL, B. M., ROCK, S. L., RAMEY, C. T., BARNARD, D. E., GRAY, C., HAMMOND, M. A., MITCHELL, S., GOTTFRIED, A., SIEGEL, L., & JOHNSON, D. L. (1989). Home environment and cognitive development in the first 3 years of life: A collaborative study involving six sites and three ethnic groups in North America. *Developmental Psychology, 25,* 217–235.

BRAINE, M. D. S. (1976). Children's first word combinations. *Monographs of the Society for Research in Child Development, 41* (1, Serial No. 164).

BRAINERD, C. J. (1978). *Piaget's theory of intelligence.* Englewood Cliffs, NJ: Prentice-Hall.

BRAND, E., CLINGEMPEEL, W. G., & BOWEN-WOODWARD, K. (1988). Family relationships and children's psychological adjustment in stepmother and stepfather families: Findings and conclusions from the Philadelphia Stepfamily Research Project. In E. M. Hetherington & J. D. Arasteh (Eds.), *Impact of divorce, single-parenting, and stepparenting on children* (pp. 299–324). Hillsdale, NJ: Erlbaum.

BRANSFORD, J. D., STEIN, B. S., SHELTON, T. S., & OWINGS, R. A. (1981). Cognition and adaptation: The importance of learning to learn. In J. Harvey (Ed.), *Cognition, social behavior, and the environment* (pp. 93–110). Hillsdale, NJ: Erlbaum.

BRAUNGART, J. M., PLOMIN, R. DeFRIES, J. C., & FULKER, D. W. (1992). Genetic influence on tester-rated infant temperament as assessed by Bayley's Infant Behavior Record: Nonadoptive and adoptive siblings and twins. *Developmental Psychology, 28,* 40–47.

BRAY, J. H. (1988). Children's development during early remarriage. In E. M. Hetherington & J. D. Arasteh (Eds.), *Impact of divorce, single parenting, and stepparenting on children* (pp. 279–298). Hillsdale, NJ: Erlbaum.

BRAZELTON, T. B. (1962). A child-oriented approach to toilet-training. *Pediatrics, 29,* 121–128.

BRAZELTON, T. B. (1984). *Neonatal Behavioral Assessment Scale.* Philadelphia: Lippincott.

BRAZELTON, T. B., KOSLOWSKI, B., & TRONICK, E. (1976). Neonatal behavior among urban Zambians and Americans. *Journal of the American Academy of Child Psychiatry, 15,* 97–107.

BRAZELTON, T. B., NUGENT, J. K., & LESTER, B. M. (1987). Neonatal Behavioral Assessment Scale. In J. D. Osofsky (Ed.), *Handbook of infant development* (2nd ed., pp. 780–817). New York: Wiley.

BRENNAN, W. M., AMES, E. W., & MOORE, R. W. (1966). Age differences in infants' attention to patterns of different complexities. *Science, 151,* 354–356.

BRETHERTON, I. (1990). Open communication and internal working models: Their role in the development of attachment relationships. In R. A. Thompson (Ed.), *Nebraska Symposium on Motivation* (Vol. 36, pp. 57–113). Lincoln, NB: University of Nebraska Press.

BRETHERTON, I., FRITZ, J., ZAHN-WAXLER, C., & RIDGEWAY, D. (1986). Learning to talk about emotions: A functionalist perspective. *Child Development, 57,* 529–548.

BRETHERTON, I., O'CONNELL, B., SHORE, C., & BATES, E. (1984). The effect of contextual variation on symbolic play: Development from 20 to 28 months. In I. Bretherton (Ed.), *Symbolic play and the development of social understanding* (pp. 271–298). New York: Academic Press.

BRINDLEY, B. A., & SOKOL, R. J. (1988). Induction and augmentation of labor: Basis and methods for current practice. *Obstetrics and Gynecology Survey, 43,* 730–743.

BRODY, G. H., STONEMAN, Z., & BURKE, M. (1987). Child temperaments, maternal differential behavior, and sibling relationships. *Developmental Psychology, 23,* 354–362.

BRODY, L. E., & BENBOW, C. P. (1987). Accelerative strategies: How effective are they for the gifted? *Gifted Child Quarterly, 3,* 105–110.

BRODY, L. R., ZELAZO, P. R., & CHAIKA, H. (1984). Habituation-dishabituation to speech in the neonate. *Developmental Psychology, 20,* 114–119.

BRODY, N. (1985). The validity of tests of intelligence. In B. B. Wolman (Ed.), *Handbook of intelligence* (pp. 353–389). New York: Wiley.

BROMAN, S. H. (1983). Obstetric medications. In C. C. Brown (Ed.), *Childhood learning disabilities and prenatal risk* (pp. 56–64). New York: Johnson & Johnson.

BRONFENBRENNER, U. (1979). *The ecology of human development: Experiments by nature and design.* Cambridge, MA: Harvard University Press.

BRONFENBRENNER, U. (1989). Ecological systems theory. In R. Vasta (Ed.), *Annals of child development* (Vol. 6, pp. 187–251). Greenwich, CT: JAI Press.

BRONFENBRENNER, U., & CROUTER, A. C. (1983). The evolution of environmental models in developmental research. In W. Kessen (Ed.), *Handbook of child psychology, Vol. 1: History, theory and methods* (4th ed., pp. 357–476). New York: Wiley.

BRONSON, G. W. (1991). Infant differences in rate of visual encoding. *Child Development, 62,* 44–54.

BROOKS, P. H., & ROBERTS, M. C. (1990, Spring). Social science and the prevention of children's injuries. *Social Policy Report of the Society for Research in Child Development, 4* (No. 1).

BROOKS-GUNN, J. (1986). The relationship of maternal beliefs about sex typing to maternal and young children's behavior. *Sex Roles, 14,* 21–35.

BROOKS-GUNN, J. (1988a). Antecedents and consequences of variations in girls' maturational timing. *Journal of Adolescent Health Care, 9,* 365–373.

BROOKS-GUNN, J. (1988b). The impact of puberty and sexual activity upon the health and education of adolescent girls and boys. *Peabody Journal of Education, 64,* 88–113.

BROOKS-GUNN, J., BOYER, C. B., & HEIN, K. (1988). Preventing HIV infection and AIDS in children and adolescents. *American Psychologist, 43,* 958–964.

BROOKS-GUNN, J., & FURSTENBERG, F. F., JR. (1989). Adolescent sexual behavior. *American Psychologist, 44,* 249–257.

BROOKS-GUNN, J., & PETERSEN, A. C. (1991). Studying the emergence of depression and depressive symptoms during adolescence. *Journal of Youth and Adolescence, 20,* 115–119.

BROOKS-GUNN, J., & REITER, E. O. (1990). The role of pubertal processes in the early adolescent transition. In S. Feldman & G. Elliott (Eds.), *At the threshold: The developing adolescent* (pp. 16–53). Cambridge, MA: Harvard University Press.

BROOKS-GUNN, J., & RUBLE, D. N. (1980). Menarche: The interaction of physiology, cultural, and social factors. In A. J. Dan, E. A. Graham, & C. P. Beecher (Eds.), *The menstrual cycle: A synthesis of interdisciplinary research* (pp. 141–159). New York: Springer-Verlag.

BROOKS-GUNN, J., & RUBLE, D. N. (1983). The experience of menarche from a developmental perspective. In J. Brooks-Gunn & A. C. Petersen (Eds.), *Girls at puberty* (pp. 155–177). New York: Plenum.

BROOKS-GUNN, J., & WARREN, M. P. (1989). Biological and social contributions to negative affect in young adolescent girls. *Child Development, 60,* 40–55.

BROOKS-GUNN, J. WARREN, M. P., SAMELSON, M., & FOX, R. (1986). Physical similarity of and disclosure of menarcheal status to friends: Effects of grade and pubertal status. *Journal of Early Adolescence, 6,* 3–14.

BROPHY, J. E. (1983). Research on the self-fulfilling prophecy and teacher expectations. *Journal of Educational Psychology, 75,* 631–661.

BROPHY, J. E. (1986). Teacher influences on student achievement. *American Psychologist, 41,* 1069–1077.

BROPHY, J. E., & GOOD, T. L. (1974). *Teacher-student relationships: Causes and consequences.* New York: Holt, Rinehart and Winston.

BROWN, A. L., BRANSFORD, J. D., FERRARA, R. A., & CAMPIONE, J. C. (1983). Learning, remembering and understanding. In J. H. Flavell & E. M. Markman (Eds.), *Handbook of child psychology: Vol. 3. Cognitive development* (4th ed., pp. 77–166). New York: Wiley.

BROWN, B. B., LOHR, M. J., & McCLENAHAN, E. L. (1986). Early adolescents' perceptions of peer pressure. *Journal of Early Adolescence, 6,* 139–154.

BROWN, B. B., CLASEN, D., & EICHER, S. (1986). Perceptions of peer pressure, peer conformity dispositions, and self-reported behavior among adolescents. *Developmental Psychology, 22,* 521–530.

BROWN, B. B., EICHER, S., & PETRIE, S. (1986). The importance of peer group ("crowd") affiliation in adolescence. *Journal of Adolescence, 9,* 73–96.

BROWN, J. W. (1988). Should eligibility standards go beyond minimum requirements? *NASSP Bulletin, 72,* 46–49.

BROWN, L. K., & FRITZ, G. K. (1988). Children's knowledge and attitudes about AIDS. *Journal of the American Academy of Child and Adolescent Psychiatry, 27,* 504–508.

BROWN, R. W. (1973). *A first language: The early stages.* Cambridge, MA: Harvard University Press.

BROWNELL, C. A., & CARRIGER, M. S. (1990). Changes in cooperation and self-other differentiation during the second year. *Child Development, 61,* 1164–1174.

BRUCH, H. (1970). Juvenile obesity: Its courses and outcome. In C. V. Rowlan (Ed.), *Anorexia and obesity* (pp. 231–254). Boston: Little Brown.

BRUMBERG, J. J. (1988). *Fasting girls.* Cambridge, MA: Harvard University Press.

BRUNER, J. (1990). *Acts of meaning.* Cambridge, MA: Harvard University Press.

BRYANT, B. K. (1985). The neighborhood walk: Sources of support in middle childhood. *Monographs for the Society for Research in Child Development, 50* (3, Serial No. 210).

BRYANT, D. M., & RAMEY, C. T. (1987). An analysis of the effectiveness of early intervention programs for environmentally at-risk children. In M. J. Guralnick & F. C. Bennett (Eds.), *The effectiveness of early intervention for at-risk handicapped children* (pp. 33–78). Orlando, FL: Academic Press.

BUCHANAN, C. M., MACCOBY, E. E., & DORNBUSCH, S. M. (1991). Caught between parents: Adolescents' experience in divorced homes. *Child Development, 62,* 1008–1029.

BUCK, G. M., COOKFAIR, D. L., MICHALEK, A. M., NASCA, P. C., STANDFAST, S. J., SEVER, L. E., & KRAMER, A. A. (1989). Intrauterine growth retardation and risk of sudden infant death syndrome (SIDS). *American Journal of Epidemiology, 129,* 874–884.

BUGENTAL, D. B., BLUE, J., & CRUZCOSA, M. (1989). Perceived control over caregiving outcomes: Implications for child abuse. *Developmental Psychology, 25,* 532–539.

BUHRMESTER, D., & FURMAN, W. (1987). The development of companionship and intimacy. *Child Development, 58,* 1101–1115.

BUHRMESTER, D., & FURMAN, W. (1990). Perceptions of sibling relationships during middle childhood and adolescence. *Child Development, 61,* 1387–1398.

BUKOWSKI, W. M., & KRAMER, T. L. (1986). Judgments of the features of friendship among early adolescent boys and girls. *Journal of Early Adolescence, 6,* 331–338.

BULATAO, R. A., & ARNOLD, F. (1977). *Relationships between the value and cost of children and fertility: Cross-cultural evidence.* Paper presented at the General Conference of the International Union for the Scientific Study of Population, Mexico City.

BULKLEY, J. A. (1989). The impact of new child witness research on sexual abuse prosecutions. In S. J. Ceci, D. F. Ross, & M. P. Toglia (Eds.), *Perspectives on children's testimony* (pp. 208–229). New York: Springer-Verlag.

BULLOCK, M., & LUTKENHAUS, P. (1990). Who am I? The development of self-understanding in toddlers. *Merrill-Palmer Quarterly, 36,* 217–238.

BUMPASS, L. L. (1984). Children and marital disruption: A replication and update. *Demography, 21,* 71–82.

BURCHINAL, M., LEE, M., & RAMEY, C. (1989). Type of day care and preschool intellectual development in disadvantaged children. *Child Development, 60,* 128–137.

BURNS, S. M., & BRAINERD, C. J. (1979). Effects of constructive and dramatic play on perspective taking in very young children. *Developmental Psychology, 15,* 512–521.

BUSHNELL, E. W. (1985). The decline of visually guided reaching during infancy. *Infant Behavior and Development, 8,* 139–155.

BUSS, A. H., & PLOMIN, R. (1984). *Temperament: Early developing personality traits.* Hillsdale, NJ: Erlbaum.

BUTLER, G. E., McKIE, M., & RATCLIFFE, S. G. (1990). The cyclical nature of prepubertal growth. *Annals of Human Biology, 17,* 177–198.

BYRNE, M. C., & HAYDEN, E. (1980). *Topic maintenance and topic establishment in mother-child dialogue.* Paper presented at the meeting of the American Speech and Hearing Association, Detroit, MI.

BYRNES, J. P., & WASIK, B. A. (1991). Role of conceptual knowledge in mathematical procedural learning. *Developmental Psychology, 27,* 777–786.

CAINE, N. (1986). Behavior during puberty and adolescence. In G. Mitchell & J. Erwin (Eds.), *Comparative primate biology: Vol. 2A. Behavior, conservation, and ecology* (pp. 327–361). New York: Alan R. Liss.

CAIRNS, R. B. (1983). The emergence of developmental psychology. In W. Kessen (Ed.), *Handbook of child psychology: Vol. 1. History, theory, and methods* (4th ed., pp. 41–102). New York: Wiley.

CAIRNS, R. B., CAIRNS, B. D., & NECKERMAN, H. J. (1989). Early school dropout: Configurations and determinants. *Child Development, 60,* 1437–1452.

CAIRNS, R. B., CAIRNS, B. D., NECKERMAN, H. J., FERGUSON, L. L., & GARIÉPY, J-L. (1989). Growth and aggression: 1. Childhood to early adolescence. *Developmental Psychology, 25,* 320–330.

CALDERA, Y. M., HUSTON, A. C., & O'BRIEN, M. (1989). Social interactions and play patterns of parents and toddlers with feminine, masculine, and neutral toys. *Child Development, 60,* 70–76.

CAMARA, K. A., & RESNICK, G. (1988). Interparental conflict and cooperation: Factors moderating children's post-divorce adjustment. In E. M. Hetherington & J. D. Arasteh (Eds.), *Impact of divorce, single parenting, and stepparenting on children* (pp. 169–195). Hillsdale, NJ: Erlbaum.

CAMPBELL, F. A., & RAMEY, C. T. (1991). *The Carolina Abecedarian Project.* Paper presented at the biennial meeting of the Society for Research in Child Development, Seattle, WA.

CAMPOS, J. J., CAPLOVITZ, K. B., LAMB, M. E., GOLDSMITH, H. H., & STENBERG, C. (1983). Socioemotional development. In M. M. Haith & J. J. Campos (Eds.), *Handbook of child psychology: Vol. 2. Infancy and developmental psychobiology* (4th ed., pp. 783–915). New York: Wiley.

CAMPOS, J., & BERTENTHAL, B. (1989). Locomotion and psychological development. In F. Morrison, K. Lord, & D. Keating (Eds.), *Applied developmental psychology* (Vol. 3, pp. 229–258). New York: Academic Press.

CAMPOS, R. G. (1989). Soothing pain-elicited distress in infants with swaddling and pacifiers. *Child Development, 60,* 781–792.

CAPELLI, C. A., NAKAGAWA, N., & MADDEN, C. M. (1990). How children understand sarcasm: The role of context and intonation. *Child Development, 61,* 1824–1841.

CAPLAN, M., VESPO, J., PEDERSEN, J., & HAY, D. F. (1991). Conflict and its resolution in small groups of one-and two-year-olds. *Child Development, 62,* 1513–1524.

CAPUZZI, D. (1989). *Adolescent suicide prevention.* Ann Arbor, MI: ERIC Counseling and Personnel Services Clearinghouse.

CAREY, S. (1985). *Conceptual change in childhood.* Cambridge, MA: MIT Press.

CARLE, E. (1969). *The very hungry caterpillar.* New York: Philomel.

CARLSON, C., HSU, J., & COOPER, C. (1990, March). *Predicting school achievement in early adolescence: The role of family process.* Paper presented at the Conference on Human Development, Atlanta, GA.

CARLSON, V., CICCHETTI, D., BARNETT, D., & BRAUNWALD, K. (1989). Disorganized/disoriented attachment relationship in maltreated infants. *Child Development, 25,* 525–531.

CARON, R. F., CARON, A. J., & MYERS, R. S. (1982). Abstraction of invariant face expressions in infancy. *Child Development, 53,* 1008–1015.

CARPENTER, C. J. (1983). Activity structure and play: Implications for socialization. In M. Liss (Eds.), *Social and cognitive skills: Sex roles and children's play* (pp. 117–145). New York: Academic Press.

CARR, M., & SCHNEIDER, W. (1991). Long-term maintenance of organizational strategies in kindergarten children. *Contemporary Educational Psychology, 16,* 61–75.

CARRUTH, B. R., GOLDBERG, D. L., & SKINNER, J. D. (1991). Do parents and peers mediate the influence of television advertising on food-related purchases? *Journal of Adolescent Research, 6,* 253–271.

CARTER, D. B., & PATTERSON, C. J. (1982). Sex roles as social conventions: The development of children's conceptions of sex-role stereotypes. *Developmental Psychology, 18,* 812–824.

CARTER-SALTZMAN, L. (1980). Biological and socio-cultural effects on handedness: Comparison between biological and adoptive families. *Science, 209,* 1263–1265.

CASE, R. (1985). *Intellectual development: A systematic reinterpretation.* New York: Academic Press.

CASE, R. (1991a). Stages in the development of the young child's first sense of self. *Developmental Review, 11,* 210–230.

CASE, R. (1991b). *The mind's staircase: Exploring the conceptual underpinnings of children's thought and knowledge.* Hillsdale, NJ: Erlbaum.

CASEY, M. B. (1986). Individual differences in selective attention among prereaders: A key to mirror-image confusions. *Developmental Psychology, 22,* 824–831.

CASKEY, T., & McKUSICK, V. A. (1990). Medical genetics. *Journal of the American Medical Association, 283,* 2654–2657.

CASPI, A., ELDER, G. H., JR., & BEM, D. J. (1987). Moving against the world: Life-course patterns of explosive children. *Developmental Psychology, 23,* 308–313.

CASPI, A., ELDER, G. H., JR., & BEM, D. J. (1988). Moving away from the world: Life-course patterns of shy children. *Developmental Psychology, 24,* 824–831.

CATES, W., JR., & RAUH, J. L. (1985). Adolescents and sexually transmitted diseases: An expanding problem. *Journal of Adolescent Health Care, 6,* 1–5.

CATON, C. L. M. (1990). *Homeless in America.* New York: Oxford University Press.

CAUDILL, W. (1973). Psychiatry and anthropology: The individual and his nexus. In L. Nader & T. W. Maretzki (Eds.), *Cultural illness and health: Essays in human adaptation* (Anthropological Studies 9, pp. 67–77). Washington, DC: American Anthropological Association.

CAUDILL, W., & FROST, L. (1975). A comparison of maternal care and infant behavior in Japanese-American, American, and Japanese families. In U. Bronfenbrenner & M. A. Mahoney (Eds.), *Influences on human development* (2nd ed., pp. 329–342). Hinsdale, IL: Dryden.

CAZDEN, C. (1984). *Effective instructional practices in bilingual education.* Washington, DC: National Institute of Education.

CECI, S. J. (1990). *On intelligence . . . More or less.* Englewood Cliffs, NJ: Prentice-Hall.

CECI, S. J. (1991). How much does schooling influence general intelligence and its cognitive components? A reassessment of the evidence. *Developmental Psychology, 27,* 703–722.

CERNOCH, J. M., & PORTER, R. H. (1985). Recognition of maternal axilary odors by infants. *Child Development, 56,* 1593–1598.

CHALMERS, J. B., & TOWNSEND, M. A. R. (1990). The effects of training in social perspective taking on socially maladjusted girls. *Child Development, 61,* 178–190.

CHANDLER, M. J. (1973). Egocentrism and antisocial behavior: The assessment and training of social perspective-taking skills. *Developmental Psychology, 9,* 326–332.

CHAPMAN, M., & LINDENBERGER, U. (1988). Functions, operations, and décalage in the development of transitivity. *Developmental Psychology, 24,* 542–551.

CHAPMAN, M., & SKINNER, E. A. (1989). Children's agency beliefs, cognitive performance, and conceptions of effort and ability: Individual and developmental differences. *Child Development, 60,* 1229–1238.

CHASNOFF, I. J., GRIFFITH, D. R., MacGREGOR, S., DIRKES, K., & BURNS, K. S. (1989). Temporal patterns of cocaine use in pregnancy: Perinatal outcome. *Journal of the American Medical Association, 261,* 1741–1744.

CHEN, C., & STEVENSON, H. W. (1989). Homework: A cross-cultural examination. *Child Development, 60,* 551–561.

CHERLIN, A. J., & FURSTENBERG, F. F., JR. (1986). *The new American grandparent.* New York: Basic Books.

CHI, M. T. H. (1978). Knowledge structures and memory development. In R. S. Siegler (Ed.), *Children's thinking: What develops?* (pp. 73–96). Hillsdale, NJ: Erlbaum.

CHI, M. T. H., & CECI, S. J. (1987). Content knowledge: Its role, representation, and restructuring in memory development. In H. W. Reese (Ed.), *Advances in child development and behavior* (Vol. 20, pp. 91–142). Orlando, FL: Academic Press.

CHILDREN'S DEFENSE FUND (1989). *The health of America's children.* Washington, DC: Author.

CHILDREN'S DEFENSE FUND (1990a). *A children's defense budget.* Washington, DC: Author.

CHILDREN'S DEFENSE FUND (1990b). *Children 1990.* Washington, DC: Author.

CHILDREN'S DEFENSE FUND (1990c, July). School barriers hamper efforts to educate homeless children. *CDF Reports, 11* (11), 1–3.

CHILDREN'S DEFENSE FUND (1990d, September). Women, children get squeezed out of food program. *CDF Reports, 12* (1), pp. 1, 6.

CHILDREN'S DEFENSE FUND (1991a). *A children's defense fund budget.* Washington, DC: Author.

CHILDREN'S DEFENSE FUND (1991b, April). Hunger in America. *CDF Reports, 12* (7), 4–5.

CHILDREN'S DEFENSE FUND (1991c). *The adolescent and young adult fact book.* Washington, DC: Author.

CHILDREN'S DEFENSE FUND (1991d). *The State of America's Children: 1991.* Washington, DC: Author.

CHILDREN'S DEFENSE FUND (1991e, May). Vaccine shortages causing immunization crisis. *CDF Reports, 12* (8), 3, 12.

CHILDS, C. P., & GREENFIELD, P. M. (1982). Informal modes of learning and teaching: The case of Zinacanteco weaving. In N. Warren (Ed.), *Advances in cross-cultural psychology* (Vol. 2, pp. 269–316). London: Academic Press.

CHIPMAN, S. F., & WILSON, D. M. (1985). Understanding mathematics course enrollment and mathematics achievement: A synthesis of the research. In S. F. Chipman, L. R. Brush, & D. M. Wilson (Eds.), *Women and mathematics: Balancing the equation* (pp. 275–328). Hillsdale, NJ: Erlbaum.

CHISHOLM, J. S. (1989). Biology, culture, and the development of temperament: A Navajo example. In J. K. Nugent, B. M. Lester, & T. B. Brazelton (Eds.), *Biology, culture, and development* (Vol. 1, pp. 341–364). Norwood, NJ: Ablex.

CHOMSKY, C. (1969). *The acquisition of syntax in children from five to ten.* Cambridge, MA: MIT Press.

CHOMSKY, N. (1957). *Syntactic structures.* The Hague: Mouton.

CHONG, G. L., & THIBODEAU, S. N. (1990). A simple assay for the screening of the cystic fibrosis allele in carriers of the $Phe^{508}$ deletion mutation. *Mayo Clinic Proceedings, 65,* 1072–1076.

CHRISTOFFEL, K. K., & FORSYTH, B. W. (1989). Mirror image of environmental deprivation: Severe childhood obesity of psychosocial origin. *Child Abuse and Neglect, 13,* 249–256.

CHRISTOPHERSEN, E. R. (1989). Injury control. *American Psychologist, 44,* 237–241.

CHURCHILL, S. R. (1984). Disruption: A risk in adoption. In P. Sachdev (Ed.), *Adoption: Current issues and trends* (pp. 115–127). Toronto: Butterworth.

CICCHETTI, D., & ABER, J. L. (1986). Early precursors of later depression: An organizational perspective. In L. P. Lipsitt & C. Rovee-Collier (Eds.), *Advances in infancy research* (Vol. 4, pp. 87–137). Norwood, NJ: Ablex.

CLARK, E. V. (1983). Meanings and concepts. In J. H. Flavell & E. M. Markman (Eds.), *Handbook of child psychology: Vol. 3. Cognitive development* (4th ed., pp. 787–840). New York: Wiley.

CLARK, E. V. (1987). The principle of contrast: A constraint on language acquisition. In B. MacWhinney (Ed.), *Mechanisms of language acquisition* (pp. 1–33). Hillsdale, NJ: Erlbaum.

CLARK, E. V., & HECHT, B. F. (1982). Learning to coin agent and instrument nouns. *Cognition, 12,* 1–24.

CLARK, J. T., & WATKINS, D. L. (1984). Static balance in young children. *Child Development, 55,* 133–139.

CLARKE-STEWART, K. A. (1973). Interactions between mothers and their young children: Characteristics and consequences. *Monographs of the Society for Research in Child Development, 38* (6–7, Serial No. 153).

CLARKE-STEWART, K. A. (1989). Infant day care: Maligned or malignant? *American Psychologist, 44,* 266–273.

CLAUDY, J. G. (1984). The only child as a young adult: Results from Project Talent. In T. Falbo (Ed.), *The single-child family* (pp. 211–252). New York: Guilford Press.

CLAUSEN, J. A. (1975). The social meaning of differential physical and sexual maturation. In S. E. Dragastin & G. H. Elder (Eds.), *Adolescence in the life cycle: Psychological change and the social context* (pp. 25–47). New York: Halsted.

CLEMENTS, D. H. (1986). Effects of Logo and CAI environments on cognition and creativity. *Journal of Educational Psychology, 78,* 309–318.

CLEMENTS, D. H. (1990). Metacomponential development in a Logo programming environment. *Journal of Educational Psychology, 82,* 141–149.

CLEMENTS, D. H. (1991). Enhancement of creativity in computer environments. *American Educational Research Journal, 28,* 173–187.

COAKLEY, J. (1990). *Sport and society: Issues and controversies* (4th ed.). St. Louis: Mosby.

COATES, T. J., & THORESON, C. E. (1978). Treating obesity in children and adolescents: A review. *American Journal of Public Health, 68,* 143–151.

COCHI, S. L., EDMONDS, L. E., DYER, K., GREAVES, W. L., MARKS, J. S., ROVIRA, E. Z., PREBLUD, S. R., & ORENSTEIN, W. A. (1989). Congenital rubella syndrome in the United States, 1970–1985: On the verge of elimination. *American Journal of Epidemiology, 129,* 349–361.

COHEN, F. L. (1984). *Clinical genetics in nursing practice.* Philadelphia: Lippincott.

COHEN, S. E., & PARMELEE, A. H. (1983). Prediction of five-year Stanford-Binet scores in preterm infants. *Child Development, 54,* 1242–1253.

COHEN-OVERBEEK, W. C. J., HOP, M., OUDEN, M. DEN, PIPERS, L., JAHODA, M. G. J., & WLADIMIROFF, J. W. (1990). Spontaneous abortion rate and advanced maternal age: Consequences for prenatal diagnosis. *Lancet, 336,* 27–29.

COHN, J. F., CAMPBELL, S. B., MATIAS, R., & HOPKINS, J. (1990). Face-to-face interactions of postpartum depressed and nondepressed mother-infant pairs at 2 months. *Developmental Psychology, 26,* 15–23.

COIE, J. D., DODGE, K. A., COPPOTELLI, H. (1982). Dimensions and types of social status: A cross-age perspective. *Developmental Psychology, 18,* 557–570.

COIE, J. D., DODGE, K. A., TERRY, R., & WRIGHT, V. (1991). The role of aggression in peer relations: An analysis of aggression episodes. *Child Development, 62,* 812–826.

COIE, J. D., & KOEPPL, G. K. (1990). Adapting intervention to the problems of aggressive and disruptive rejected children. In S. R. Asher & J. D. Coie (Eds.), *Peer rejection in childhood* (pp. 309–337). New York: Cambridge University Press.

COIE, J. D., & KREHBIEL, G. (1984). Effects of academic tutoring on the social status of low-achieving, socially rejected children. *Child Development, 55,* 1465–1478.

COIE, J. D., & KUPERSMIDT, J. B. (1983). A behavioral analysis of emerging social status in boys' groups. *Child Development, 54,* 1400–1416.

COLBY, A., KOHLBERG, L., GIBBS, J., & LIEBERMAN, M. (1983). A longitudinal study of moral judgment. *Monographs of the Society for Research in Child Development, 48* (1–2, Serial No. 200).

COLE, C. B., & LOFTUS, E. F. (1987). The memory of children. In S. J. Ceci, M. P. Toglia, & D. F. Ross (Eds.), *Children's eyewitness memory* (pp. 178–208). New York: Springer-Verlag.

COLE, J. R., & ZUCKERMAN, H. (1987, February). Marriage, motherhood, and research performance in science. *Scientific American, 256* (2), 119–125.

COLE, M., & SCRIBNER, S. (1977). Cross-cultural studies of memory and cognition. In R. V. Kail, Jr. & J. W. Hagen (Eds.), *Perspectives on the development of memory and cognition* (pp. 239–271). Hillsdale, NJ: Erlbaum.

COLEMAN, J. (1961). *The adolescent society.* Glencoe, IL: Free Press.

COLLEA, J. V., CHEIN, C., & QUILLIGAN, E. J. (1980). The randomized management of term frank breech presentations: A study of 208 cases. *American Journal of Obstetrics and Gynecology, 137,* 235–244.

COLLINS, W. A. (1983). Children's processing of television content: Implications for prevention of negative effects. *Prevention in Human Services, 2,* 53–66.

COLLINS, W. A., WELLMAN, H., KENISTON, A. H., & WESTBY, S. D. (1978). Age-related aspects of comprehension and inference from a televised dramatic narrative. *Child Development, 49,* 389–399.

COLMAN, L. L., & COLMAN, A. D. (1991). *Pregnancy: The psychological experience.* New York: Noonday Press.

COLÓN, P. A., & COLÓN, A. R. (1989). The health of America's children. In F. J. Macchiarola & A. Gartner (Eds.), *Caring for America's children* (pp. 45–57). New York: The Academy of Political Science.

COMER, J. P. (1986). Parent participation in the schools. *Phi Delta Kappan, 67,* 442–444.

COMMITTEE ON LABOR AND HUMAN RESOURCES, UNITED STATES SENATE (1985). *Examining problems confronting the physical condition of our children and ways to help them.* Washington, DC: U.S. Government Printing Office.

COMPAS, B. E. (1987). Stress and life events during childhood and adolescence. *Clinical Psychology Review, 7,* 275–302.

COMPAS, B. E., HOWELL, D. C., PHARES, V., WILLIAMS, R. A., & LEDOUX, N. (1989). Parent and child stress symptoms: An integrative analysis. *Developmental Psychology, 25,* 550–559.

CONDRY, J., & ROSS, D. F. (1985). Sex and aggression: The influence of gender label on the perceptions of aggression in children. *Child Development, 56,* 225–233.

CONNOLLY, J. A., & DOYLE, A. B. (1984). Relations of social fantasy play to social competence in preschoolers. *Developmental Psychology, 20,* 797–806.

CONNOLLY, J. A., DOYLE, A. B., & REZNICK, E. (1988). Social pretend play and social interaction in preschoolers. *Journal of Applied Developmental Psychology, 9,* 301–313.

CONNOLLY, K., & DAGLEISH, M. (1989). The emergence of tool-using skill in infancy. *Developmental Psychology, 25,* 894–912.

CONSTANZO, P. R., & WOODY, E. Z. (1979). Externality as a function of obesity in children: Pervasive style or eating-specific attribute? *Journal of Personality and Social Psychology, 37,* 2286–2296.

COOKE, R. A. (1982). The ethics and regulation of research involving children. In B. B. Wolman (Ed.), *Handbook of developmental psychology* (pp. 149–172). Englewood Cliffs, NJ: Prentice-Hall.

COOPER, R. P., & ASLIN, R. N. (1990). Preference for infant-directed speech in the first month after birth. *Child Development, 61,* 1584–1595.

COOPERSMITH, S. (1967). *The antecedents of self-esteem.* San Francisco: Freeman.

CORAH, N. L., ANTHONY, E. J., PAINTER, P., STERN, J. A., & THURSTON, D. L. (1965). Effects of perinatal anoxia after seven years. *Psychological Monographs 79* (3, Whole No. 596).

COREN, S., & HALPERN, D. F. (1991). Left-handedness: A marker for decreased survival fitness. *Psychological Bulletin, 109,* 90–106.

CORMAN, H. H., & ESCALONA, S. K. (1969). Stages of sensorimotor development: A replication study. *Merrill-Palmer Quarterly, 15,* 351–360.

CORNELL, E. H., & GOTTFRIED, A. W. (1976). Intervention with premature human infants. *Child Development, 47,* 32–39.

CORNELL, E. H., & McDONNELL, P. M. (1986). Infants' acuity at twenty feet. *Investigative Ophthalmology and Visual Science, 27,* 1417–1420.

CORNO, L., & SNOW, R. E. (1986). Adapting teaching to individual differences among learners. In M. C. Wittrock (Ed.), *Handbook of research on teaching* (3rd ed., pp. 214–229). New York: Macmillan.

CORRIGAN, R. (1987). A developmental sequence of actor–object pretend play in young children. *Merrill-Palmer Quarterly, 33,* 87–106.

COSTABILE, A., SMITH, P. K., MATHESON, L., ASTON, J., HUNTER, T., & BOULTON, M. (1991). Cross-national comparison of how children distinguish serious and playful fighting. *Developmental Psychology, 27,* 881–887.

COTTON, P. (1990). Sudden infant death syndrome: Another hypothesis offered but doubts remain. *Journal of the American Medical Association, 263,* 2865, 2869.

COWAN, C. P., & COWAN, P. A. (1988). Changes in marriage during the transition to parenthood: Must we blame the baby? In G. Y. Michaels & W. A. Goldberg (Eds.), *The transition to parenthood* (pp. 114–154). New York: Cambridge University Press.

COWAN, C. P., COWAN, P. A., HEMING, G., GARRETT, E., COYSH, W. S., CURTIS-BOLES, H., & BOLES, A. J. (1985). Transition to parenthood: His, hers, and theirs. *Journal of Family Issues, 6,* 461–481.

COX, K., & SCHWARTZ, J. D. (1990). *The well-informed patient's guide to caesarean births.* New York: Dell.

COX, M. J., OWEN, M., LEWIS, J. M., & HENDERSON, V. K. (1989). Marriage, adult adjustment, and early parenting. *Child Development, 60,* 1015–1024.

COX, T. (1983). Cumulative deficit in culturally disadvantaged children. *British Journal of Educational Psychology, 53,* 317–376.

CRAIK, F. I. M., & LOCKHART, R. S. (1972). Levels of processing: A framework for memory research. *Journal of Verbal Learning and Verbal Behavior, 11,* 671–684.

CRAIN-THORESON, C., & DALE, P. S. (1992). Do early talkers become early readers? Linguistic precocity, preschool language, and emergent literacy. *Developmental Psychology, 28,* 421–429.

CRATTY, B. J. (1986). *Perceptual and motor development in infants and children* (3rd ed.). Englewood Cliffs, NJ: Prentice-Hall.

CREWDSON, J. (1988). *By silence betrayed.* New York: Harper & Row.

CRIDER, C. (1981). Children's conceptions of the body interior. In R. Bibace & M. Walsh (Eds.), *New directions in child development* (No. 14, pp. 49–65). San Francisco: Jossey-Bass.

CROCKENBERG, S. B. (1981). Infant irritability, mother responsiveness, and social support influences on the security of mother-infant attachment. *Child Development, 52,* 857–865.

CROCKENBERG, S. B. (1986). Are temperamental differences in babies associated with predictable differences in care-giving? In J. V. Lerner & R. M. Lerner (Eds.), *New directions for child development* (No. 30, pp. 75–88). San Francisco: Jossey-Bass.

CROCKENBERG, S., & LITMAN, C. (1990). Autonomy as competence in 2-year-olds: Maternal correlates of child defiance, compliance, and self-assertion. *Developmental Psychology, 26,* 961–971.

CROCKETT, L. J. (1990). Sex role and sex-typing in adolescence. In R. M. Lerner, A. C. Petersen, & J. Brooks-Gunn (Eds.), *The encyclopedia of adolescence* (Vol. 2, pp. 1007–1017). New York: Garland.

CROOK, C. K. (1978). Taste perception in the newborn infant. *Infant Behavior and Development, 1,* 52–69.

CROOK, C. K., & LIPSITT, L. P. (1976). Neonatal nutritive sucking: Effects of taste stimulation upon sucking rhythm and heart rate. *Child Development, 47,* 518–522.

CSIKSZENTMIHALYI, M., & LARSON, R. (1984). *Being adolescent: Conflict and growth in the teenage years.* New York: Basic Books.

CUMMINGS, E. M., IANNOTTI, R. J., & ZAHN-WAXLER, C. (1985). Influence of conflict between adults on the emotions and aggression of young children. *Developmental Psychology, 21,* 495–507.

CUNNINGHAM, F. G., MacDONALD, P.C., & GANT, N. F. (1989). *Williams obstetrics* (18th ed.). Norwalk, CT: Appleton & Lange.

CURRAN, D. K. (1987). *Adolescent suicidal behavior.* Washington, DC: Hemisphere.

CURTISS, S. (1977). *Genie: a psycholinguistic study of a modern-day "wild child."* New York: Academic Press.

CYTRYN, L., McKNEW, D. H., ZAHN-WAXLER, C., & GERSHON, E. S. (1986). Developmental issues in risk research: The offspring of affectively ill parents. In M. Rutter, C. E. Izard, & P. B. Read (Eds.), *Depression in young people: Developmental and clinical perspectives* (pp. 163–188). New York: Guilford.

DAMON, W. (1977). *The social world of the child.* San Francisco: Jossey-Bass.

DAMON, W. (1988). *The moral child.* New York: The Free Press.

DAMON, W. (1990). Self-concept, adolescent. In R. M. Lerner, A. C. Petersen, & J. Brooks-Gunn (Eds.), *The encyclopedia of adolescence* (Vol. 2, pp. 87–91). New York: Garland.

DAMON, W., & HART, D. (1988). *Self-understanding in childhood and adolescence.* Cambridge, MA: Cambridge University Press.

DANNEMILLER, J. L., & STEPHENS, B. R. (1988). A critical test of infant pattern preference models. *Child Development, 59,* 210–216.

DANSKY, J. L. (1980). Make-believe: A mediator of the relationship between play and associative fluency. *Child Development, 51,* 576–579.

DARWIN, C. (1877). *Biographical sketch of an infant. Mind, 2,* 285–294.

DARWIN, C. (1936). *On the origin of species by means of natural selection.* New York: Modern Library. (Original work published 1859)

DAS GUPTA, P., & BRYANT, P. E. (1989). Young children's causal inferences. *Child Development, 60,* 1138–1146.

DAVID, H. P., DYTRYCH, Z., MATEJCEK, Z., & SCHÜLLER, V. (1988). *Born unwanted.* New York: Springer-Verlag.

DeANGELIS, T. (1991a, January). Living with violence: Children suffer, cope. *APA Monitor, 22* (11), 26–27.

DeANGELIS, T. (1991b, March). Psychologists take calls from kids about the war. *APA Monitor, 22* (11), 8.

DeCASPER, A. J., & SPENCE, M. J. (1986). Prenatal maternal speech influences newborns' perception of speech sounds. *Infant Behavior and Development, 9,* 133–150.

DeFRAIN, J., TAYLOR, J., & ERNST, L. (1982). *Coping with sudden infant death.* Lexington, MA: Heath.

DEGELMAN, D., FREE, J. U., SCARLATO, M., BLACKBURN, J. M., & GOLDEN, T. (1986). Concept learning in preschool children: Effects of a short-term Logo experience. *Journal of Educational Computing Research, 2,* 199–205.

DELECKI, J. (1985). Principles of growth and development. In P. M. Hill (Ed.), *Human growth and development throughout life* (pp. 33–48). New York: Wiley.

DELGADO, H. L., VALVERDE, V. E., MARTORELL, R., & KLEIN, R. E. (1982). Relationship of maternal and infant nutrition to infant growth. *Early Human Development, 6,* 273–286.

DELGADO-GAITAN, C. (1986). Adolescent peer influence and differential school performance. *Journal of Adolescent Research, 1,* 449–462.

DELLAS, M., & JERNIGAN, L. P. (1990). Affective personality characteristics associated with undergraduate ego identity formation. *Journal of Adolescent Research, 5,* 306–324.

DeLISI, R., & STAUDT, J. (1980). Individual differences in college students' performance on formal operational tasks. *Journal of Applied Developmental Psychology, 1,* 201–208.

DeLOACHE, J. S. (1987). Rapid change in symbolic functioning of very young children. *Science, 238,* 1556–1557.

DeLOACHE, J. S. (1990). Young children's understanding of models. In R. Fivush & J. Hudson (Eds.), *Knowing and remembering in young children* (pp. 94–126). New York: Cambridge University Press.

DeLOACHE, J. S., KOLSTAD, V., & ANDERSON, K. N. (1991). Physical similarity and young children's understanding of scale models. *Child Development, 62,* 111–126.

DeLOACHE, J. S., & TODD, C. M. (1988). Young children's use of spatial categorization as a mnemonic strategy. *Journal of Experimental Child Psychology, 46,* 1–20.

DELPHI COMMUNICATION SCIENCES (1990). *Video game use symposium.* Los Angeles, CA: Author.

DeMARIE-DREBLOW, D. (1991). Relation between knowledge and memory: A reminder that correlation does not imply causality. *Child Development, 62,* 484–498.

DENHAM, S. A., RENWICK, S. M., & HOLT, R. W. (1991). Working and playing together: Prediction of preschool social-emotional competence from mother-child interaction. *Child Development, 62,* 242–249.

DENNIS, M., & WHITAKER, H. A. (1976). Language acquisition following hemidecortication: Linguistic superiority of the left over the right hemisphere. *Brain and Language, 3,* 404–433.

DENNIS, W. (1960). Causes of retardation among institutionalized children: Iran. *Journal of Genetic Psychology, 96,* 47–59.

DENNIS, W., & DENNIS, M. G. (1940). The effect of cradling practices upon the onset of walking in Hopi children. *Journal of Genetic Psychology, 56,* 77–86.

DENNY, F. W., COLLIER, A. M., & HENDERSON, F. W. (1987). Acute respiratory infections in day care. In M. T. Osterholm, J. O. Klein, S. S. Aronson, & L. K. Pickering (Eds.), *Infectious diseases in child day care* (pp. 15–20). Chicago: University of Chicago Press.

D'ERCOLE, A. J., & UNDERWOOD, L. E. (1986). Regulation of fetal growth by hormones and growth factors. In F. Falkner & J. M. Tanner (Eds.), *Human growth* (2nd ed., Vol. 1, pp. 327–338). New York: Plenum.

DEUTSCH, F. M., RUBLE, D. N., FLEMING, A., BROOKS-GUNN, J., & STANGOR, C. (1986, April). *Becoming a mother: Information-seeking and self-definitional processes.* Paper presented at the annual meeting of the Eastern Psychological Association, New York, NY.

DEUTSCH, W., & PECHMANN, T. (1982). Social interaction and the development of definite descriptions. *Cognition, 11,* 159–184.

DEVEREUX, E. C. (1976). Backyard versus Little League Baseball: The impoverishment of children's games. In D. M. Landers (Ed.), *Social problems in athletics* (pp. 37–56). Urbana: University of Illinois Press.

DE VILLIERS, J. G., & DE VILLIERS, P. A. (1973). A cross-sectional study of the acquisition of grammatic morphemes in child speech. *Journal of Psycholinguistic Research, 2,* 267–278.

DEVLIN, J. B. (1989). Childhood nocturnal enuresis: A descriptive analysis. *Irish Journal of Medical Science, 158,* 29–32.

DIAMOND, A. (1988). Abilities and neural mechanisms underlying AB performance. *Child Development, 59,* 523–527.

DIAZ, R. M., & BERNDT, T. J. (1982). Children's knowledge of a best friend: Fact or fancy. *Developmental Psychology, 18,* 787–794.

DICK-READ, G. (1959). *Childbirth without fear.* New York: Harper & Brothers.

DICKENSON, G. (1975). Dating behavior of black and white adolescents before and after desegregation. *Journal of Marriage and the Family, 37,* 602–608.

DICKINSON, D. K. (1984). First impressions: Children's knowledge of words gained from a single exposure. *Applied Psycholinguistics, 5,* 359–373.

DIETZ, W. H., JR., & GORTMAKER, S. L. (1985). Do we fatten our children at the television set? Obesity and television viewing in children and adolescents. *Pediatrics, 75,* 807–812.

DILALLA, L. F., & WATSON, M. W. (1988). Differentiation of fantasy and reality: Preschoolers' reactions to interruptions in their play. *Developmental Psychology, 24,* 286–291.

DIRKS, J. (1982). The effect of a commercial game on children's Block Design scores on the WISC-R test. *Intelligence, 6,* 109–123.

DIRKS, J., & GIBSON, E. (1977). Infants' perception of similarity between live people and their photographs. *Child Development, 48,* 124–130.

DITTRICHOVA, J., BRICHACEK, V., PAUL, K., & TAUTERMANNOVA, M. (1982). The structure of infant behavior: An analysis of sleep and waking in the first months of life. In W. W. Hartup (Ed.), *Review of child development research* (Vol. 6, pp. 73–100). Chicago: University of Chicago Press.

DIVINE-HAWKINS, P. (1981). *Family day care in the United States: National Day Care Home Study final report, executive summary.* Washington, DC: U.S. Government Printing Office.

DIXON, J. A., & MOORE, C. F. (1990). The development of perspective taking: Understanding differences in information and weighting. *Child Development, 61,* 1502–1513.

DIXON, R. A., & LERNER, R. M. (1988). A history of systems in developmental psychology. In M. Bornstein & M. Lamb (Eds.), *Developmental psychology: An advanced textbook* (2nd ed., pp. 3–50). Hillsdale, NJ: Erlbaum.

DODGE, K. A. (1980). Social cognition and children's aggressive behavior. *Child Development, 51,* 162–170.

DODGE, K. A. (1989). Coordinating responses to aversive stimuli: Introduction to a special section on the development of emotional regulation. *Developmental Psychology, 25,* 339–342.

DODGE, K. A., SCHLUNDT, D. C., SCHOCKEN, L., & DELUGACH, J. D. (1983). Social competence and children's sociometric status: The role of peer group entry strategies. *Merrill-Palmer Quarterly, 29,* 309–336.

DODGE, K. A., & SOMBERG, D. R. (1987). Hostile attributional biases among aggressive boys are exacerbated under conditions of threats to the self. *Child Development, 58,* 213–224.

DODWELL, P. C., HUMPHREY, G. K., & MUIR, D. W. (1987). Shape and pattern perception. In P. Salapatek & L. Cohen (Eds.), *Handbook of infant perception* (Vol. 2, pp. 1–77). Orlando, FL: Academic Press.

DOI, L. T. (1973). *The anatomy of dependence* (J. Bester, Trans.). Tokyo: Kadansha International.

DOLGIN, K. G., & BEHREND, D. A. (1984). Children's knowledge about animates and inanimates. *Child Development, 55,* 1646–1650.

DOLLAGHAN, C. (1985). Child meets word: "Fast mapping" in preschool children. *Journal of Speech and Hearing Research, 28,* 449–454.

DONTAS, C., MARATSOS, O., FAFOUTIS, M., & KARANGELIS, A. (1985). Early social development in institutionally reared Greek infants: Attachment and peer interaction. In I. Bretherton & E. Waters (Eds.), Growing points of attachment theory and research. *Monographs of the Society for Research in Child Development, 50* (1–2, Serial No. 209).

DORNBUSCH, S. M., CARLSMITH, J. M., BUSHWALL, S. J., RITTER, P. L., LEIDERMAN, H., HASTORF, A. H., & GROSS, R. T. (1985). Single parents, extended households, and the control of adolescents. *Child Development, 56,* 326–341.

DORNBUSCH, S. M., CARLSMITH, J., GROSS, R., MARTIN, J., JENNINGS, D., ROSENBERG, A., & DUKE, P. (1981). Sexual development, age, and dating: A comparison of biological and social influences upon one set of behaviors. *Child Development, 52,* 179–185.

DORNBUSCH, S. M., RITTER, P. L., LEIDERMAN, P. H., ROBERTS, D. F., & FRALEIGH, M. J. (1987). The relation of parenting style to adolescent school performance. *Child Development, 58,* 1244–1257.

DORRIS, M. (1989). *The broken cord.* New York: Harper & Row.

DOSSEY, J. A., MULLIS, I. V. S., LINDQUIST, M. M., & CHAMBERS, D. L. (1988). *The Mathematics Report Card: Are we measuring up?* Princeton, NJ: Educational Testing Service.

DOUGLAS, V. I. (1983). Attentional and cognitive problems. In M. Rutter (Ed.), *Developmental neuropsychiatry* (p. 280–329). New York: Guilford.

DOUVAN, E., & ADELSON, J. (1966). *The adolescent experience.* New York: Wiley.

DOWNS, A. C., & LANGLOIS, J. H. (1988). Sex typing: Construct and measurement issues. *Sex Roles, 18,* 87–100.

DRABMAN, R. S., CORDUA, G. D., HAMMER, D., JARVIE, G. J., & HORTON, W. (1979). Developmental trends in eating rates of normal and overweight preschool children. *Child Development, 50,* 211–216.

DRAPER, P., & CASHDAN, E. (1988). Technological change and child behavior among the !Kung. *Ethnology, 27,* 339–365.

DREYER, P. (1982). Sexuality during adolescence. In B. Wolman (Ed.), *Handbook of developmental psychology* (pp. 559–601). Englewood Cliffs, NJ: Prentice-Hall.

DROTAR, D., & STURM, L. (1988). Prediction of intellectual development in young children with early histories of nonorganic failure-to-thrive. *Journal of Pediatric Psychology, 13,* 281–296.

DUBOIS, D. L., & HIRSCH, B. J. (1990). School and neighborhood friendship patterns of black and whites in early adolescence. *Child Development, 61,* 524–536.

DUBOW, E. F., TISAK, J., CAUSEY, D., HRYSHKO, A., & REID, G. (1991). A two-year longitudinal study of stressful life events, social support, and social problem-solving skills: Contributions to children's behavioral and academic adjustment. *Child Development, 62,* 583–599.

DUNCAN, P., RITTER, P., DORNBUSCH, S., GROSS, R., & CARLSMITH, J. (1985). The effects of pubertal timing on body image, school behavior, and deviance. *Journal of Youth and Adolescence, 14,* 227–236.

DUNCAN, S. W., & MARKMAN, H. J. (1988). Intervention programs: Prevention perspective. In G. Y. Michaels & W. A. Goldberg (Eds.), *The transition to parenthood* (pp. 270–310). New York: Cambridge University Press.

DUNFORD, F. W., & ELLIOTT, D. S. (1984). Identifying career offenders using self-reported data. *Journal of Research in Crime and Delinquency, 21,* 57–86.

DUNHAM, P., & DUNHAM, F. (1992). Lexical development during middle infancy: A mutually driven infant-caregiver process. *Developmental Psychology, 28,* 414–420.

DUNN, J. (1989). Siblings and the development of social understanding in early childhood. In P. G. Zukow (Ed.), *Sibling interaction across cultures* (pp. 106–116). New York: Springer-Verlag.

DUNN, J., BRETHERTON, I., & MUNN, P. (1987). Conversations about feeling states between mothers and their young children. *Developmental Psychology, 23,* 132–139.

DUNN, J., & KENDRICK, C. (1982). *Siblings: Love, envy and understanding.* Cambridge, MA: Harvard University Press.

DUNPHY, D. C. (1963). The social structure of urban adolescent peer groups. *Sociometry, 26,* 230–246.

DuPONT, R. L. (1983). Phobias in children. *Journal of Pediatrics, 102,* 999–1002.

DUSEK, J. B. (1987). Sex roles and adjustment. In D. B. Carter (Ed.), *Current conceptions of sex roles and sex typing* (pp. 211–222). New York: Praeger.

DWECK, C. S. (1975). The role of expectations and attributions in the alleviation of learned helplessness. *Journal of Personality and Social Psychology, 31,* 674–685.

DWECK, C. S., DAVIDSON, W., NELSON, S., & ENNA, B. (1978). Sex differences in learned helplessness: III. An experimental analysis. *Developmental Psychology, 14,* 268–276.

DWECK, C. S., & ELLIOTT, E. S. (1983). Achievement motivation. In E. M. Hetherington (Ed.), *Handbook of child psychology: Vol. 4. Socialization, personality, and social development* (4th ed., pp. 643–691). New York: Wiley.

DWECK, C. S., & LEGGETT, E. L. (1988). A social-cognitive approach to motivation and personality. *Psychological Review, 95,* 256–273.

DYE-WHITE, E. (1986). Environmental hazards in the work setting: Their effect on women of child-bearing age. *American Association of Occupational Health and Nursing Journal, 34,* 76–78.

DYSON, A. H. (1984). Emerging alphabetic literacy in school contexts: Toward defining the gap between school curriculum and child mind. *Written Communication, 1,* 5–55.

EAST, P. L., & ROOK, K. S. (1992). Compensatory patterns of support among children's peer relationships: A test using school friends, nonschool friends, and siblings. *Developmental Psychology, 28,* 168–172.

EASTERBROOKS, M. A. (1989). Quality of attachment to mother and to father: Effects of perinatal risk status. *Child Development, 60,* 831–837.

ECCLES, J. (1987). Adolescence: Gateway to gender-role transcendence. In D. B. Carter (Ed.), *Current conceptions of sex roles and sex typing: Theory and research* (pp. 225–241). New York: Praeger.

ECCLES, J. S. (1990). Academic achievement. In R. M. Lerner, A. C. Petersen, & J. Brooks-Gunn (Eds.), *The encyclopedia of adolescence* (pp. 1–5). New York: Garland.

ECCLES, J. S., & HAROLD, R. D. (1991). Gender differences in sport involvement: Applying the Eccles' expectancy-value model. *Journal of Applied Sport Psychology, 3,* 7–35.

ECCLES, J.S., JACOBS, J., & HAROLD, R. D. (1990). Gender-role stereotypes, expectancy effects, and parents' role in the socialization of gender differences in self-perceptions and skill acquisition. *Journal of Social Issues, 46,* 183–201.

ECCLES, J. S., & MIDGLEY, C. (1989). Stage environment fit: Developmentally appropriate classrooms for young adolescents. In R. E. Ames & C. Ames (Eds.), *Research in motivation in education* (Vol. 3, pp. 139–186). New York: Academic Press.

ECKERMAN, C. O., DAVIS, C. C., & DIDOW, S. M. (1989). Coordination of size standards by young children. *Child Development, 59,* 888–896.

ECKSTROM, R. B., GOERTZ, M. E., POLLACK, J. M., & ROCK, D. A. (1986). Who drops out of school and why? Findings from a national study. *Teachers College Record, 87,* 356–373.

EDER, D., & PARKER, S. (1987). The cultural production and reproduction of gender: The effect of extracurricular activities on peer-group culture. *Sociology of Education 60,* 200–213.

EDER, R. A. (1989). The emergent personologist: The structure and content of 3 1/2-, 5 1/2-, and 7 1/2-year-olds' concepts of themselves and other persons. *Child Development, 60,* 1218–1228.

EGELAND, B., JACOBVITZ, D., & SROUFE, L. A. (1988). Breaking the cycle of abuse. *Child Development, 59,* 1080–1088.

EGELAND, B., & SROUFE, L. A. (1981). Developmental sequelae of maltreatment in infancy. In R. Rizley & D. Cicchetti (Eds.), *New directions for child development* (No. 11, pp. 77–92). San Francisco: Jossey-Bass.

EIFERMANN, R. R. (1971). Social play in childhood. In R. E. Herron & B. Sutton-Smith (Eds.), *Child's play* (pp. 270–297). New York: Wiley.

EISENBERG, L. (1984). The epidemiology of suicide in adolescents. *Pediatric Annals, 13,* 47–54.

EISENBERG, N. (1982). The development of reasoning regarding prosocial behavior. In N. Eisenberg (Ed.), *The development of prosocial behavior* (pp. 219–249). New York: Academic Press.

EISENBERG, N., & MILLER, P. A. (1987). The relation of empathy to prosocial and related behaviors. *Psychological Bulletin, 101,* 91–119.

EISENBERG, N., SHELL, R., PASTERNACK, J., LENNON, R., BELLER, R., & MATHY, R. M. (1987). Prosocial development in middle childhood: A longitudinal study. *Developmental Psychology, 23,* 712–718.

EKMAN, P., & FRIESEN, W. (1972). Constants across culture in the face and emotion. *Journal of Personality and Social Psychology, 17,* 124–129.

ELARDO, R., & BRADLEY, R. H. (1981). The Home Observation for Measurement of the Environment (HOME) Scale: A review of research. *Developmental Review, 1,* 113–145.

ELBERS, L., & TON, J. (1985). Play pen monologues: The interplay of words and babbles in the first words period. *Journal of Child Language, 12,* 551–565.

ELDREDGE, L., & SALAMY, A. (1988). Neurobehavioral and neurophysiological assessment of healthy and "at-risk" full-term infants. *Child Development, 59,* 186–192.

ELKIND, D. (1984). *All grown up and no place to go: Teenagers in crisis.* Reading, MA: Addison-Wesley.

ELKIND, D. (1991, August). Attitudes toward homosexuality (14-through 18-year-olds). *Parents, 66* (8), 140.

ELKIND, D., & BOWEN, R. (1979). Imaginary audience behavior in children and adolescents. *Developmental Psychology, 15,* 33–44.

EMDE, R. N., GAENSBAUER, T. J., & HARMON, R. J. (1976). Emotional expression in infancy: A biobehavioral study. *Psychological Issues, 10* (No. 37). New York: International Universities Press.

EMDE, R. N., & KOENIG, K. L. (1969). Neonatal smiling and rapid eye movement states. *American Academy of Child Psychiatry, 8,* 57–67.

EMERY, R. E. (1989). Family violence. *American Psychologist, 44,* 321–328.

EMERY, R. E., & WYER, M. M. (1987). Divorce mediation. *American Psychologist, 42,* 472–480.

EMORY, E. K., & TOOMEY, K. A. (1988). Environmental stimulation and human fetal responsibility in late pregnancy. In W. P. Smotherman & S. R. Robinson (Eds.), *Behavior of the fetus* (pp. 141–161). Caldwell, NJ: Telford.

ENGEL, N. (1989). An American experience of pregnancy and childbirth in Japan. *Birth, 16,* 81–86.

ENNS, J. T. (Ed.) (1990). *The development of attention: Research and theory.* Amsterdam: North-Holland.

ENRIGHT, R. D., LAPSLEY, D. K., & SHUKLA, D. (1979). Adolescent egocentrism in early and late adolescence. *Adolescence, 14,* 687–695.

EPSTEIN, J. L. (1983a). Selection of friends in differently organized schools and classrooms. In J. L. Epstein & N. Karweit (Eds.), *Friends in school* (pp. 73–92). New York: Academic Press.

EPSTEIN, J. L. (1983b). The influence of friends on achievement and affective outcomes. In J. L. Epstein & N. L. Karweit (Eds.), *Friends in school* (pp. 177–200). New York: Academic Press.

EPSTEIN, L. H., McCURLEY, J., WING, R. R., & VALOSKI, A. (1990). Five-year follow-up of family-based treatments for childhood obesity. *Journal of Consulting and Clinical Psychology, 58,* 661–664.

EPSTEIN, L. H., WING, R. R., KOESKE, R., & VALOSKI, A. (1987). Long-term effects of family-based treatment of childhood obesity. *Journal of Consulting and Clinical Psychology, 55,* 91–95.

Erikson, E. (1950). *Childhood and society.* New York: Norton.

ERIKSON, E. H. (1968). *Identity, youth, and crisis.* New York: Norton.

ERNHART, C. B., WOLF, A. W., FILIPOVICH, H. F., KENNARD, M. J., ERHARD, P., & SOKOL, R. J. (1985). Intrauterine lead exposure. *Teratology, 31,* 7B–8B.

ERON, L. D., WALDER, L. O., HUESMANN, L. R., & LEFKOWITZ, N. M. (1974). The convergence of laboratory and field studies of the development of aggression. In J. deWit & W. W. Hartup (Eds.), *Determinants of the origins of aggressive behavior* (pp. 347–380). The Hague: Mouton.

ESCALONA, S. K., & CORMAN, H. (1969). *Albert Einstein Scales of Sensorimotor Development.* New York: Albert Einstein College of Medicine, Yeshiva University.

ESPENSCHADE, A., & ECKERT, H. (1974). Motor development. In W. R. Johnson & E. R. Buskirk (Eds.), *Science and medicine of exercise and sport* (pp. 322–333). New York: Harper & Row.

ESPENSCHADE, A., & ECKERT, H. (1980). *Motor development.* Columbus, OH: Merrill.

EVELETH, P. B., & TANNER, J. M. (1976). *Worldwide variation in human growth.* Cambridge, England: Cambridge University Press.

FABES, R. A., EISENBERG, N., McCORMICK, S. E., & WILSON, M. S. (1988). Preschoolers' attributions of the situational determinants of others' naturally occurring emotions. *Developmental Psychology, 24,* 376–385.

FAGAN, J. F., III. (1971). Infants' recognition memory for a series of visual stimuli. *Journal of Experimental Child Psychology, 11,* 244–250.

FAGAN, J. F., III. (1973). Infants' delayed recognition memory and forgetting. *Journal of Experimental Child Psychology, 16,* 424–450.

FAGAN, J. F., III. (1977). Infant recognition memory: Studies in forgetting. *Child Development, 45,* 351–356.

FAGAN, J. F., III, & MONTIE, J. E. (1988). The behavioral assessment of cognitive well-being in the infant. In J. Kavanagh (Ed.), *Understanding mental retardation* (pp. 207–221). Baltimore: Paul H. Brookes.

FAGAN, J. F., III, SHEPHERD, P. A., & KNEVEL, C. R. (1991). *Predictive validity of the Fagan Test of Infant Intelligence.* Paper presented at the biennial meeting of the Society for Research in Child Development, Seattle, WA.

FAGAN, J., SLAUGHTER, E., & HARTSTONE, E. (1987). Blind justice? The impact of race on the juvenile justice process. *Crime & Delinquency, 33,* 259–286.

FAGOT, B. I. (1977). Consequences of moderate cross-gender behavior in preschool children. *Child Development, 48,* 902–907.

FAGOT, B. I. (1978). The influence of sex of child on parental reactions to toddler children. *Child Development, 49,* 459–465.

FAGOT, B. I., & HAGAN, R. I. (1991). Observations of parent reactions to sex-stereotyped behaviors: Age and sex effects. *Child Development, 62,* 617–628.

FAGOT, B. I., & KAVANAUGH, K. (1990). The prediction of antisocial behavior from avoidant attachment classifications. *Child Development, 61,* 864–873.

FAGOT, B. I., & LEINBACH, M. D. (1989). The young child's gender schema: Environmental input, internal organization. *Child Development, 60,* 663–672.

FAGOT, B. I., & PATTERSON, G. R. (1969). An in vivo analysis of reinforcing contingencies for sex-role behaviors in the preschool child. *Developmental Psychology, 1,* 563–568.

FAHRMEIER, E. D. (1978). The development of concrete operations among the Hausa. *Journal of Cross-Cultural Psychology, 9,* 23–44.

FALBO, T., & POLIT, D. (1986). A quantitative review of the only child literature: Research evidence and theory development. *Psychological Bulletin, 100,* 176–189.

FALLER, K. C. (1990). *Understanding child sexual maltreatment.* Newbury Park, CA: Sage.

FANTZ, R. L. (1961, May). The origin of form perception. *Scientific American, 204* (5), 66–72.

FANTZ, R. L. (1963). Pattern vision in newborn infants. *Science, 140,* 296–297.

FARRINGTON, D. P. (1987). Epidemiology. In H. C. Quay (Ed.), *Handbook of juvenile delinquency* (pp. 33–61). New York: Wiley.

FAUST, M. S. (1977). Somatic development of adolescent girls. *Monographs of the Society for Research in Child Development, 42* (1, Serial No. 169).

FAWCETT, S. B., SEEKINS, T., & JASON, L. A. (1987). Policy research and child passenger safety legislation: A case study and experimental evaluation. *Journal of Social Issues, 43,* 133–148.

FEATHERMAN, D. (1980). Schooling and occupational careers: Constancy and change in worldly success. In O. Brim, Jr., & J. Kagan (Eds.), *Constancy and change in human development* (pp. 675–738). Cambridge, MA: Harvard University Press.

FEDELE, N. M., GOLDING, E. R., GROSSMAN, F. K., & POLLACK, W. S. (1988). Psychological issues in adjustment to first parenthood. In G. Y. Michaels & W. A. Goldberg (Eds.), *The transition to parenthood* (pp. 85–113). New York: Cambridge University Press.

FEE, E. (1990). Public health in practice: An early confrontation with the 'silent epidemic' of childhood lead paint poisoning. *Journal of the History of Medicine and Allied Sciences, 45,* 570–606.

FEINER, J., & SUBAK-SHARPE, G. (1988, November). Understanding children's fears. *Parents, 63* (11), 101–105.

FEINGOLD, A. (1988). Cognitive gender differences are disappearing. *American Psychologist, 43,* 95–103.

FELDLAUFER, H., MIDGLEY, C., & ECCLES, J. S. (1988). Student,

teacher, and observer perceptions of the classroom environment before and after the transition to junior high school. *Journal of Early Adolescence, 8,* 133–156.

FELDMAN, D. H. (1991). *Nature's gambit: Child prodigies and the development of human potential.* New York: Teachers College Press.

FENZEL, L. M., BLYTH, D. A., & SIMMONS, R. G. (1990). School transitions: Secondary. In R. M. Lerner, A. C. Petersen, & J. Brooks-Gunn (Eds.), *The encyclopedia of adolescence* (Vol. 2, pp. 970–973). New York: Garland.

FERGUSON, L. R. (1978). The competence and freedom of children to make choices regarding participation in research: A statement. *Journal of Social Issues, 34,* 114–121.

FERGUSSON, D. M., HORWOOD, L. J., & SHANON, F. T. (1987). Breastfeeding and subsequent social adjustment in six- to eight-year-old children. *Journal of Child Psychology and Psychiatry, 28,* 378–386.

FERNALD, A., TAESCHNER, T., DUNN, J., PAPOUSEK, M., BOYSSEN-BARDIES, B., & FUKUI, I. (1989). A cross-language study of prosodic modifications in mothers' and fathers' speech to preverbal infants. *Journal of Child Language, 16,* 477–502.

FESHBACH, N. D., & FESHBACH, S. (1982). Empathy training and the regulation of aggression: Potentialities and limitations. *Academic Psychology Bulletin, 4,* 399–413.

FIELD, T. M., SCHANBERG, S. M., SCAFIDI, F., BAUER, C. R., VEGA-LAHR, N., GARCIA, R. NYSTROM, J., & KUHN, C. M. (1986). Effects of tactile/kinesthetic stimulation on preterm neonates. *Pediatrics, 77,* 654–658.

FIELD, T. M., WOODSON, R., GREENBERG, R., & COHEN, D. (1982). Discrimination and imitation of facial expressions by neonates. *Science, 218,* 179–181.

FIESE, B. (1990). Playful relationships: A contextual analysis of mother-toddler interaction and symbolic play. *Child Development, 61,* 1648–1656.

FINE, G. A. (1980). The natural history of preadolescent male friendship groups. In H. C. Foot, A. J. Chapman, & J. R. Smith (Eds.), *Friendship and social relations in children* (pp. 293–320). Chichester, England: Wiley.

FINE, G. A. (1987). *With the boys: Little League Baseball and preadolescent culture.* Chicago: University of Chicago Press.

FINE, M. (1986). Why urban adolescents drop into and out of public high school. *Teacher's College Record, 87,* 393–409.

FINKELHOR, D. (1984). *Child sexual abuse: New theory and research.* New York: The Free Press.

FISCHER, K. W. (1980). A theory of cognitive development: The control and construction of hierarchies of skills. *Psychological Review, 87,* 477–531.

FISCHER, K. W., & PIPP, S. L. (1984). Processes of cognitive development: Optimal level and skill acquisition. In R. J. Sternberg (Ed.), *Mechanisms of cognitive development* (pp. 45–80). New York: Freeman.

FISHER, C. B., BORNSTEIN, M. H., & GROSS, G. G. (1985). Left-right coding skills related to beginning reading. *Journal of Developmental and Behavioral Pediatrics, 6,* 279–283.

FIVUSH, R. (1984). Learning about school: The development of kindergartners' school scripts. *Child Development, 55,* 1697–1709.

FIVUSH, R. (1991). The social construction of personal narratives. *Merrill-Palmer Quarterly, 37,* 59–81.

FIVUSH, R., KUEBLI, J., & CLUBB, P. A. (1992). The structure of events and event representations: A developmental analysis. *Child Development, 63,* 188–201.

FLAVELL, J. H. (1963). *The developmental psychology of Jean Piaget.* New York: Van Nostrand.

FLAVELL, J. H. (1982). Structures, stage and sequences in cognitive development. In W. A. Collins (Ed.), *Minnesota Symposia on Child Psychology* (Vol. 15, pp. 1–28). Hillsdale, NJ: Erlbaum.

FLAVELL, J. H. (1985). *Cognitive development* (2nd ed.). Englewood Cliffs, NJ: Prentice-Hall.

FLAVELL, J. H., GREEN, F. L., & FLAVELL, E. R. (1987). Development of knowledge about the appearance-reality distinction. *Monographs of the Society for Research in Child Development, 51* (1, Serial No. 212).

FLAVELL, J. H., GREEN, F. L., & FLAVELL, E. R. (1989). Young children's ability to differentiate appearance-reality and level 2 perspectives in the tactile modality. *Child Development, 60,* 201–213.

FLEMING, P. J., GILBERT, R., AZAZ, Y., BERRY, P. J., RUDD, P. T., STEWART, A., & HALL, E. (1990). Interaction between bedding and sleep position in sudden infant death syndrome: A population based-control study. *British Medical Journal, 301,* 85–89.

FOGEL, A. TODA, S., & KAWAI, M. (1988). Mother-infant face-to-face interaction in Japan and the United States: A laboratory comparison using 3-month-old infants. *Developmental Psychology, 24,* 398–406.

FOOD RESEARCH AND ACTION CENTER (1991). *Community Childhood Hunger Identification Project.* Washington, DC: Author.

FORD, C., & BEACH, F. (1951). *Patterns of sexual behavior.* New York: Harper & Row.

FORD, M. E., & KEATING, D. P. (1981). Development and individual differences in long-term memory retrieval: Process and organization. *Child Development, 52,* 234–241.

FORDHAM, S., & OGBU, J. U. (1986). Black students' school success: Coping with the "burden of 'acting white.'" *Urban Review, 18,* 176–206.

FORREST, J. D., & SINGH, S. (1990). The sexual and reproductive behavior of American women, 1982–1988. *Family Planning Perspectives, 22,* 206–214.

FOX, N. A. (1991). If it's not left, it's right: Electroencephalograph asymmetry and the development of emotion. *American Psychologist, 46,* 863–872.

FOX, N. A., & DAVIDSON, R. J. (1986). Taste-elicited changes in facial signs of emotion and the asymmetry of brain electrical activity in newborn infants. *Neuropsychologia, 24,* 417–422.

FOXMAN, B., VALDEZ, R. B., & BROOK, R. H. (1986). Childhood enuresis: Prevalence, perceived impact, and prescribed treatments. *Pediatrics, 77,* 482–487.

FRANCIS, P. L., & MCCROY, G. (1983). *Bimodal recognition of human stimulus configurations.* Paper presented at the biennial meeting of the Society for Research in Child Development, Detroit.

FRANK, D. A., ZUCKERMAN, B. S., AMARO, H., ABOAGYE, K., BAUCHNER, H., CABRAL, H., FRIED, L., HINGSON, R., KAYNE, H., LEVENSON, S. M., PARKER, S., REECE, H., & VINCI, R. (1988). Cocaine use during pregnancy: Prevalence and correlates. *Pediatrics, 82,* 888–895.

FRANK, S. J., PIRSCH, L. A., & WRIGHT, V. C. (1990). Late adolescents' perceptions of their relationships with their parents: Relationships among deidealization, autonomy, relatedness, and insecurity and implications for adolescent adjustment and ego identity status. *Journal of Youth and Adolescence, 19,* 571–588.

FRANKEL, E. (1979). *DNA: The ladder of life.* New York: McGraw-Hill.

FRANKEL, K. A., & BATES, J. E. (1990). Mother-toddler problem solving: Antecedents in attachment, home behavior, and temperament. *Child Development, 61,* 810–819.

FRANKEL, M. T., & ROLLINS, H. A. (1985). Associative and categorical hypotheses of organization in the free recall of adults and children. *Journal of Experimental Child Psychology, 40,* 304–318.

FRAUENGLASS, M. H., & DIAZ, R. M. (1985). Self-regulatory functions of children's private speech: A critical analysis of recent challenges to Vygotsky's theory. *Developmental Psychology, 21,* 357–364.

FREEDMAN, D. G. (1976). *Developmental psychobiology: The significance of infancy.* Hillsdale, NJ: Erlbaum.

FREEDMAN, D. G., & FREEDMAN, N. (1969). Behavioral differences between Chinese-American and European-American newborns. *Nature, 224,* 1227.

FREEMAN, D. (1983). *Margaret Mead and Samoa: The making and unmaking of an anthropological myth.* Cambridge, MA: Harvard University Press.

FRENCH, D. C., & WAAS, G. A. (1985). Behavior problems of peer-neglected and peer rejected elementary age children: Parent and teacher perspectives. *Child Development, 56,* 246–252.

FREUD, S. (1973). *An outline of psychoanalysis.* London: Hogarth. (Original work published 1938)

FREUD, S. (1974). *The ego and the id.* London: Hogarth. (Original work published 1923)

FRIED, M. N., & FRIED, M. H. (1980). *Transitions: Four rituals in eight cultures.* New York: Norton.

FRIED, P. A., WATKINSON, B., DILLON, R. F., & DULBERG, C. S. (1987). Neonatal neurological status in a low-risk population after prenatal exposure to cigarettes, marijuana, and alcohol. *Journal of Developmental and Behavioral Pediatrics, 8,* 318–326.

FRIEDMAN, A. G., GREENE, P. G., & STOKES, T. (1991). Improving dietary habits of children: Effects of nutrition education and correspondence training. *Behavior Therapy and Experimental Psychiatry, 21,* 263–268.

FRIEDMAN, J. A., & WEINBERGER, H. L. (1990). Six children with lead poisoning. *American Journal of Diseases of Children, 144,* 1039–1044.

FRIEDMAN, M., & ROSENMAN, R. H. (1959). Association of specific overt behavior patterns with blood and cardiovascular findings. *Journal of the American Medical Association, 169,* 1286–1296.

FRIEDRICH-COFER, L., & HUSTON, A. C. (1986). Television violence and aggression: The debate continues. *Psychological Bulletin, 100,* 364–371.

FRISCH, R. E., GOTZ-WELBERGEN, A., MCARTHUR, J. W., ALBRIGHT, T., WITSCHI, J., BULLEN, B., BIRNHOLZ, J. REED, R. B., & HERMANN, H. (1981). Delayed menarche and amenorrhea of college athletes in relation to age of onset of training. *Journal of the American Medical Association, 246,* 1559–1563.

FRODI, A. (1985). When empathy fails: Aversive infant crying and child abuse. In B. M. Lester & C. F. Z. Boukydis (Eds.), *Infant crying: Theoretical and research perspectives* (pp. 263–277). New York: Plenum.

FROGGATT, P., BECKWITH, J. B., SCHWARTZ, P. J., VALDES-DAPENA, M., & SOUTHALL, D. P. (1988). Cardiac and respiratory mechanisms that might be responsible for sudden infant death syndrome. In P. J. Schwartz, D. P. Southall, & M. Valdes-Dapena (Eds.), *The sudden infant death syndrome* (Annals of the New York Academy of Sciences, Vol. 533, pp. 421–426). New York: The New York Academy of Sciences.

FUCHS, I., EISENBERG, N., HERTZ-LAZAROWITZ, R., & SHARABANY, R. (1986). Kibbutz, Israeli city, and American children's moral reasoning about prosocial moral conflicts. *Merrill-Palmer Quarterly, 32,* 37–50.

FURMAN, E. (1978, May). Helping children cope with death. *Young Children, 33* (4), 25–32.

FURMAN, E. (1990, November). Plant a potato—learn about life (and death). *Young Children, 46* (1), 15–20.

FURMAN, W., & BUHRMESTER, D. (1992). Age and sex differences in perceptions of networks of personal relationships. *Child Development, 63,* 103–115.

FURMAN, W., JONES, L., BUHRMESTER, D., & ADLER, T. (1989). Children's, parents', and observers' perspectives on sibling relationships. In P. G. Zukow (Ed.), *Sibling interaction across cultures* (pp. 165–183). New York: Springer-Verlag.

FURROW, D., & NELSON, K. (1984). Environmental correlates of individual differences in language acquisition. *Journal of Child Language, 11,* 523–534.

FURSTENBERG, F. F., JR., BROOKS-GUNN, J., & CHASE-LANSDALE, L. (1989). Teenaged pregnancy and childbearing. *American Psychologist, 44,* 313–320.

FURSTENBERG, F. F., JR., BROOKS-GUNN, J., & MORGAN, S. P. (1987). *Adolescent mothers and their children in later life.* Cambridge: Cambridge University Press.

FURSTENBERG, F. F., JR., & CRAWFORD, D. B. (1978). Family support: Helping teenagers to cope. *Family Planning Perspectives, 10,* 322–333.

FURSTENBERG, F. F., JR., LEVINE, J. A., & BROOKS-GUNN, J. (1990). The children of teenage mothers: Patterns of early childbearing in two generations. *Family Planning Perspectives, 22,* 54–61.

FURSTENBERG, F. F., JR., MORGAN, S. P., MOORE, K. A., & PETERSON, J. L. (1987). Race differences in the timing of adolescent intercourse. *American Sociological Review, 52,* 511–518.

FURSTENBERG, F. F., JR., & NORD, C. W. (1985). Parenting apart: Patterns of childrearing after marital disruption. *Journal of Marriage and the Family, 47,* 893–904.

FURUNO, S., O'REILLY, K., INATSUKA, T., HOSAKA, C., ALLMAN, T., & ZEISLOFT-FALBEY, B. (1987). *Hawaii Early Learning Profile.* Palo Alto, CA: VORT Corporation.

FUSON, K. (1990). Issues in place-value and multidigit addition and subtraction learning and teaching. *Journal for Research in Mathematics Education, 21,* 273–280.

FUSON, K. C. (1988). *Children's counting and concepts of number.* New York: Springer-Verlag.

GADDINI, R., & GADDINI, E. (1970). Transitional objects and the process of individuation: A study in three different social groups. *Journal of the American Academy of Child Psychiatry, 9,* 347–365.

GADDIS, A., & BROOKS-GUNN, J. (1985). The male experience of pubertal change. *Journal of Youth and Adolescence, 14,* 61–69.

GAGAN, R. J. (1984). The families of children who fail to thrive: Preliminary investigations of parental deprivation among organic and nonorganic cases. *Child Abuse and Neglect, 8,* 93–103.

GALAMBOS, S. J., & GOLDIN-MEADOW, S. (1990). The effects of learning two languages on levels of metalinguistic awareness. *Cognition, 34,* 1–56.

GALIN, D., JOHNSTONE, J., NAKELL, L., & HERRON, J. (1979). Development of the capacity for tactile information transfer between hemispheres in normal children. *Science, 204,* 1330–1332.

GALLAGHER, J. J. (1989). A new policy initiative: Infants and toddlers with handicapping conditions. *American Psychologist, 44,* 387–392.

GALLER, J. R., RAMSEY, F., & SOLIMANO, G. (1985a). A follow-up study of the effects of early malnutrition on subsequent development: I. Physical growth and sexual maturation during adolescence. *Pediatric Research, 19,* 524–527.

GALLER, J. R., RAMSEY, F., & SOLIMANO, G. (1985b). A follow-up study of the effects of early malnutrition on subsequent development: II. Fine motor skills in adolescence. *Pediatric Research, 19,* 524–527.

GALLER, J. R., RAMSEY, F., SOLIMANO, G., KUCHARSKI, L. T., & HARRISON, R. (1984). The influence of early malnutrition on subsequent behavioral development: IV. Soft neurological signs. *Pediatric Research, 18,* 826–832.

GALLIMORE, R., & THARP, R. (1990). Teaching mind in society: Teaching, schooling, and literate discourse. In L. C. Moll (Ed.), *Vygotsky and education* (pp. 175–205). New York: Cambridge University Press.

GALLUP, G. (1987). More today than in 1985 say premarital sex is wrong. *The Gallup Report, 263,* 20.

GALOTTI, K. M., KOZBERG, S. F., & FARMER, M. C. (1991). Gender and developmental differences in adolescents' conceptions of moral reasoning. *Journal of Youth and Adolescence, 20,* 13–30.

GARBARINO, J., KOSTELNY, K., & DUBROW, N. (1991). *No place to be a child: Growing up in a war zone.* Lexington, MA: Heath.

GARBARINO, J., & SHERMAN, D. (1980). High-risk neighborhoods and high-risk families: The human ecology of child maltreatment. *Child Development, 51,* 188–198.

GARDNER, H. (1980). *Artful scribbles: The significance of children's drawings.* New York: Basic Books.

GARDNER, H. (1983). *Frames of mind: The theory of multiple intelligences.* New York: Basic Books.

GARDNER, H., & HATCH, T. (1989, November). Multiple intelligences go to school. *Educational Researcher, 18* (8), 4–10.

GARDNER, M.J., SNEE, M. P., HALL, A. J., POWELL, C. A., DOWNES, S., & TERRELL, J. D. (1990). Leukemia cases linked to fathers' radiation dose. *Nature, 343,* 423–429.

GARMEZY, N. (1983). Stressors of childhood. In N. Garmezy & M. Rutter (Eds.), *Stress, coping, and development in children* (pp. 43–84). New York: McGraw-Hill.

GARRICK, J. G., & REQUA, R. H. (1978). Injuries in high school sports. *Pediatrics, 61,* 465–469.

GARRISON, C., SCHLUCHTER, M., SCHOENBACH, V., & KAPLAN, B. (1989). Epidemiology of depressive symptoms in young adolescents. *Journal of the American Academy of Child and Adolescent Psychiatry, 28,* 343–351.

GARRISON, W. T., & McQUISTON, S. (1989). *Chronic illness during childhood and adolescence.* Newbury Park, CA: Sage.

GARVEY, C. (1975). Requests and responses in children's speech. *Journal of Child Language, 2,* 41–63.

GARVEY, C. (1990). *Play.* Cambridge, MA: Harvard University Press.

GARWOOD, S. G., PHILLIPS, D., HARTMAN, A., & ZIGLER, E. F. (1989). As the pendulum swings: Federal agency programs for children. *American Psychologist, 44,* 434–440.

GAUVAIN, M., & ROGOFF, B. (1989). Collaborative problem solving and children's planning skills. *Developmental Psychology, 25,* 139–151.

GELLATLY, A. R. H. (1987). Acquisition of a concept of logical necessity. *Human Development, 30,* 32–47.

GELLES, R. J., & CORNELL, C. P. (1983). International perspectives on child abuse. *Child Abuse & Neglect, 7,* 375–386.

GELMAN, R. (1972). Logical capacity of very young children: Number invariance rules. *Child Development, 43,* 75–90.

GELMAN, R., & BAILLARGEON, R. (1983). A review of some Piagetian concepts. In J. H. Flavell & E. M. Markman (Eds.), *Handbook of child psychology: Vol. 3. Cognitive development* (4th ed., pp. 167–230). New York: Wiley.

GELMAN, R., & GALLISTEL, C. R. (1986). *The child's understanding of number.* Cambridge, MA: Harvard University Press.

GELMAN, R., & SHATZ, M. (1978). Appropriate speech adjustments: The operation of conversational constraints on talk to two-year-olds. In M. Lewis & L. A. Rosenblum (Eds.), *Interaction, conversation, and the development of language* (pp. 27–61). New York: Wiley.

GELMAN, S. A., & EBELING, K. S. (1989). Children's use of nonegocentric standards in judgments of functional size. *Child Development, 60,* 920–932.

GELMAN, S. A., & MARKMAN, E. M. (1987). Young children's inductions from natural kinds: The role of categories and appearances. *Child Development, 58,* 1532–1541.

GENTNER, D. (1982). Why nouns are learned before verbs: Linguistic relativity versus natural partitioning. In S. A. Kuczaj, II (Ed.), *Language development: Vol. 2. Language, thought, and culture* (pp. 301–322). Hillsdale, NJ: Erlbaum.

GENTRY, J. R. (1981, January). Learning to spell developmentally. *The Reading Teacher, 35* (2), 378–381.

GERBNER, G., GROSS, L., SIGNORELLI, N., & MORGAN, M. (1986). *Television's mean world: Violence Profile No. 14–15.* Philadelphia, PA: Annenberg School of Communications, University of Pennsylvania.

GERGEN, P. J., MULLALLY, D. I., & EVANS, R. (1988). National survey of prevalence of asthma among children in the United States, 1976–1980. *Pediatrics, 81,* 1–7.

GERSHON, E. S., TARGUM, S. D., KESSLER, L. R., MAZURE, C. M., & BUNNEY, W. E., JR. (1977). Genetics studies and biologic strategies in affective disorders. *Progress in Medical Genetics, 2,* 103–164.

GESELL, A. (1933). Maturation and patterning of behavior. In C. Murchison (Ed.), *A handbook of child psychology.* Worcester, MA: Clark University Press.

GESELL, A., & ILG, F. L. (1949). The child from five to ten. In A. Gesell & F. Ilg (Eds.), *Child development* (pp. 394–454). New York: Harper & Row. (Original work published 1946)

GESELL, A., & ILG, F. L. (1949). The infant and child in the culture of today. In A. Gesell & F. Ilg (Eds.), *Child Development* (pp. 1–393). New York: Harper & Row. (Original work published 1943)

GETCHELL, N., & ROBERTON, M. A. (1989). Whole body stiffness as a function of developmental level in children's hopping. *Developmental Psychology, 25,* 920–928.

GETZELS, J. W., & JACKSON, P. W. (1962). *Creativity and intelligence.* New York: Wiley.

GIBSON, E. J. (1970). The development of perception as an adaptive process. *American Scientist, 58,* 98–107.

GIBSON, E. J., & SPELKE, E. S. (1983). The development of perception. In J. H. Flavell & E. M. Markman (Eds.), *Handbook of child psychology: Vol. 3. Cognitive development* (4th ed., pp. 1–76). New York: Wiley.

GIBSON, E. J., & WALK, R. D. (1960). The "visual cliff." *Scientific American, 202,* 64–71.

GIBSON, J. J. (1979). *The ecological approach to visual perception.* Boston: Houghton Mifflin.

GIBSON, K. (1977). Brain structure and intelligence. In S. Chevalier-Skolnikoff & F. Porter (Eds.), *Primate bio-social development* (pp. 113–157). New York: Garland Press.

GIL, D. G. (1987). Maltreatment as a function of the structure of social systems. In M. R. Brassard, R. Germain, & S. N. Hart (Eds.), *Psychological maltreatment of children and youth* (pp. 159–170). New York: Pergamon Press.

GILBERT, E. H., & DeBLASSIE, R. R. (1984). Anorexia nervosa: Adolescent starvation by choice. *Adolescence, 76,* 839–846.

GILLIGAN, C. F. (1982). *In a different voice.* Cambridge, MA: Harvard University Press.

GILLIGAN, C. F., & ATTANUCCI, J. (1989). Two moral orientations: Gender differences and similarities. *Merrill-Palmer Quarterly, 34,* 223–237.

GILLIGAN, C. F., & BELENKY, M. F. (1980). A naturalistic study of abortion decisions. In R. L. Selman & R. Yando (Eds.), *New directions for child development* (Vol. 7, pp. 69–90). San Francisco: Jossey-Bass.

GINSBURG, H. P., & OPPER, S. (1988). *Piaget's theory of intellectual development* (3rd ed.). Englewood Cliffs, NJ: Prentice-Hall.

GINZBERG, E. (1972). Toward a theory of occupational choice: A restatement. *Vocational Guidance Quarterly, 20,* 169–176.

GINZBERG, E. (1988). Toward a theory of occupational choice. *Career Development Quarterly, 36,* 358–363.

GLASS, D. C., KRAKOFF, L. R., CONTRADA, R., HILTON, W. F., KEHOE, K., MANNUCCI, E. G., COLLINS, C., SNOW, B., & ELTING, E. (1980). Effect of harassment and competition upon cardiovascular and plasma catecholamine responses in Type A and Type B individuals. *Psychophysiology, 17,* 453–463.

GLICK, P. C., & LIN, S. (1987). Remarriage after divorce: Recent changes and demographic variations. *Sociological Perspectives, 30,* 162–179.

GLIDDEN, L. M., & PURSLEY, J. T. (1989). Longitudinal comparisons of families who have adopted children with mental retardation. *American Journal on Mental Retardation, 94,* 272–277.

GNEPP, J. (1983). Children's social sensitivity: Inferring emotions from conflicting cues. *Developmental Psychology, 19,* 805–814.

GNEPP, J., McKEE, E., & DOMANIC, J. A. (1987). Children's use of situational information to infer emotion: Understanding emotionally equivocal situations. *Developmental Psychology, 23,* 114–123.

GOETZ, E. T., & HALL, R. J. (1984). A critical analysis of the psychometric properties of the K-ABC. *Journal of Special Education, 18,* 281–296.

GOFFIN, S. G. (1988, March). Putting our advocacy efforts into a new context. *Young Children, 43* (3), 52–56.

GOLDBERG, S. (1983). Parent-infant bonding: Another look. *Child Development, 54,* 1355–1382.

GOLDBERG, S., BRACHFELD, S., & DiVITTO, B. (1980). Feeding, fussing, and play: Parent-infant interaction in the first year as a function of prematurity and perinatal medical problems. In T. M. Field (Ed.), *High-risk infants and children* (pp. 133–153). New York: Academic Press.

GOLDBERG, S., LaCOMBE, S., LEVINSON, D., PARKER, K. R., ROSS, C., & SOMMERS, F. (1985). Thinking about the threat of nuclear war: Relevance to mental health. *American Journal of Orthopsychiatry, 55,* 503–512.

GOLDFIELD, B. A. (1987). Contributions of child and caregiver to referential and expressive language. *Applied Psycholinguistics, 8,* 267–280.

GOLDFIELD, B. A., & REZNICK, J. S. (1990). Early lexical acquisition: Rate, content, and the vocabulary spurt. *Journal of Child Language, 17,* 171–183.

GOLDIN-MEADOW, S., & MORFORD, M. (1985). Gesture in early language: Studies of deaf and hearing children. *Merrill-Palmer Quarterly, 31,* 145–176.

GOLDMAN-RAKIC, P. S. (1987). Development of cortical circuitry and cognitive function. *Child Development, 58,* 601–622.

GOLDSCHMID, M. L., & BENTLER, P. M. (1968). *Manual: Concept Assessment Kit—Conservation.* San Diego, CA: Educational and Industrial Testing Service.

GOLDSMITH, H. H. (1987). Roundtable: What is temperament? Four approaches. *Child Development, 58,* 505–529.

GOLDSMITH, H. H., & GOTTESMAN, I. I. (1981). Origins of variation in behavioral style: A longitudinal study of temperament in young twins. *Child Development, 52,* 91–103.

GOLDSTEIN, A. P. (1990). *Delinquents on delinquency.* Champaign, IL: Research Press.

GOLDSTEIN, H. (1971). Factors influencing the height of seven-year-old children: Results from the National Child Development Study. *Human Biology, 43,* 92–111.

GOMEZ-SCHWARTZ, B., HOROWITZ, J. M., & CARDARELLI, A. P. (1990). *Child sexual abuse: Initial effects.* Newbury Park, CA: Sage.

GOODLAD, J. I. (1984). *A place called school.* New York: McGraw-Hill.

GOODMAN, G. S., AMAN, C., & HIRSCHMAN, J. (1987). Child sexual and physical abuse: Children's testimony. In S. J. Ceci, M. P. Toglia, & D. F. Ross (Eds.), *Children's eyewitness memory* (pp. 1–23). New York: Springer-Verlag.

GOODMAN, K. S. (1986). *What's whole in whole language?* Portsmouth, NH: Heinemann.

GOODMAN, R. A., & WHITAKER, H. A. (1985). Hemispherectomy: A

review (1928–1981) with special reference to the linguistic abilities and disabilities of the residual right hemisphere. In R. A. Goodman & H. A. Whitaker (Eds.), *Hemispheric functions and collaboration in the child* (pp. 121–155). New York: Academic Press.

GOPNIK, A., & MELTZOFF, A. N. (1986). Relations between semantic and cognitive development in the one-word stage: The specificity hypothesis. *Child Development, 57,* 1040–1053.

GOPNIK, A., & MELTZOFF, A. N. (1987a). The development of categorization in the second year and its relation to other cognitive and linguistic developments. *Child Development, 58,* 1523–1531.

GOPNIK, A., & MELTZOFF, A. N. (1987b). Language and thought in the young child: Early semantic developments and their relationships to object permanence, means-ends understanding, and categorization. In K. Nelson & A. Van Kleeck (Eds.), *Children's language* (Vol. 6, pp. 191–212). Hillsdale, NJ: Erlbaum.

GORDON, S., & GILGUN, J. F. (1987). Adolescent sexuality. In V. B. Van Hasselt & M. Hersen (Eds.), *Handbook of adolescent psychology* (pp. 147–167). New York: Pergamon Press.

GORN, G. J., & GOLDBERG, M. E. (1982). Behavioral evidence of the effects of televised food messages on children. *Journal of Consumer Research, 9,* 200–205.

GORTMAKER, S. L., DIETZ, W. H., & CHEUNG, L. W. Y. (1990). Inactivity, diet, and the fattening of America. *Journal of the American Dietetic Association, 90,* 1247–1252.

GORTMAKER, S. L., DIETZ, W. H., SOBOL, A. M., & WEHLER, C. A. (1987). Increasing pediatric obesity in the United States. *American Journal of Diseases of Children, 141,* 535–540.

GOTLIB, I. H., WHIFFEN, V. E., MOUNT, J. H., MILNE, K., & CORDY, N. I. (1989). Prevalence rates and demographic characteristics associated with depression in pregnancy and postpartum. *Journal of Consulting and Clinical Psychology, 57,* 269–274.

GOTTESMAN, I. I. (1963). Genetic aspects of intelligent behavior. In N. Ellis (Ed.), *Handbook of mental deficiency* (pp. 253–296). New York: McGraw-Hill.

GOTTFRIED, A. E., GOTTFRIED, A. W., & BATHURST, K. (1988). Maternal employment, family environment, and children's development: Infancy through the school years. In A. E. Gottfried & A. W. Gottfried (Eds.), *Maternal employment and children's development: Longitudinal research* (pp. 11–58). New York: Plenum.

GOTTLIEB, G. (1991). Experiential canalization of behavioral development: Theory. *Developmental Psychology, 27,* 4–13.

GOTTMAN, J. M., & KATZ, L. F. (1989). Effects of marital discord on young children's peer interaction and health. *Developmental Psychology, 25,* 373–381.

GOTTMAN, J. M., GONSO, J., & RASMUSSEN, B. (1975). Social interaction, social competence, and friendship in children. *Child Development, 46,* 709–718.

GOULD, M. S., (1990). Cluster suicides. In R. M. Lerner, A. C. Petersen, & J. Brooks-Gunn (Eds.), *The encyclopedia of adolescence* (Vol. 2, pp. 1117–1122). New York: Garland.

GRAHAM, F. K., ERNHART, C. B., THURSTON, D. L., & CRAFT, M. (1962). Development three years after perinatal anoxia and other potentially damaging newborn experiences. *Psychological Monographs, 76* (3, Whole No. 522).

GRAHAM, L., & HAMDAN, L. (1987). *Youth trends: Capturing the $200 billion youth market.* New York: St. Martin's Press.

GRAHAM, S., DOUBLEDAY, C., & GUARINO, P. A. (1984). The development of relations between perceived controllability and the emotions of pity, anger, and guilt. *Child Development, 55,* 561–565.

GRANT, J. P. (1990). *The state of the world's children.* New York: Oxford University Press (in cooperation with UNICEF).

GRANTHAM-McGREGOR, S., SCHOFIELD, W., & POWELL, C. (1987). Development of severely malnourished children who received psychosocial stimulation: Six-year follow-up. *Pediatrics, 79,* 247–254.

GRAU, P. N. (1985). Counseling the gifted girl. *Gifted Child Today, 38,* 8–11.

GRAY, W. M. (1978). A comparison of Piagetian theory and criterion-referenced measurement. *Review of Educational Research, 48,* 223–250.

GREEN, J. A., GUSTAFSON, G. E., & WEST, M. J. (1980). Effects of infant development on mother-infant interactions. *Child Development, 51,* 199–207.

GREEN, J. A., JONES, L. E., & GUSTAFSON, G. E. (1987). Perception of cries by parents and nonparents: Relation to cry acoustics. *Developmental Psychology, 23,* 370–382.

GREEN, R. (1987). *The 'sissy boy' syndrome and the development of homosexuality.* New Haven: Yale University Press.

GREENBERG, M., & MORRIS, N. (1974). Engrossment: the newborn's impact upon the father. *American Journal of Orthopsychiatry, 44,* 520–531.

GREENBERG, P. (1990, February). Why not academic preschool? *Young Children, 45* (2), 70–80.

GREENBERGER, E., & GOLDBERG, W. A. (1989). Work, parenting, and the socialization of children. *Developmental Psychology, 25,* 22–35.

GREENBERGER, E., & STEINBERG, L. (1986). *When teenagers work.* New York: Basic Books.

GREENBOWE, T., HERRON, J. D., LUCAS, C., NURRENBERN, S., STAVER, J. R., & WARD, C. R. (1981). Teaching preadolescents to act as scientists: Replication and extension of an earlier study. *Journal of Educational Psychology, 73,* 705–711.

GREENO, J. G. (1989). A perspective on thinking. *American Psychologist, 44,* 134–141.

GREENOUGH, W. T., BLACK, J. E., & WALLACE, C. S. (1987). Experience and brain development. *Child Development, 58,* 539–559.

GREIF, E. B., & ULMAN, K. (1982). The psychological impact of menarche on early adolescent females: A review. *Child Development, 53,* 1413–1430.

GRIMES, D. A., & MISHELL, D. R., JR. (1988). Congenital limb reduction deformities and oral contraceptives [letter]. *American Journal of Obstetrics and Gynecology, 158,* 439–440.

GROSS, S. J., GELLER, J., & TOMARELLI, R. M. (1981). Composition of breast milk from mothers of preterm infants. *Pediatrics, 68,* 480–493.

GROSSMAN, H. D. (Ed.) (1983). *Classification in mental retardation.* Washington, DC: American Association on Mental Deficiency.

GROSSMAN, L. K., FITZSIMMONS, S. M., LARSEN-ALEXANDER, J. B., SACHS, L., & HARTER, C. (1990). The infant feeding decision in low and upper income women. *Clinical Pediatrics, 29,* 30–37.

GROSSMANN, K., GROSSMANN, K. E., SPANGLER, G., SUESS, G., & UNZNER, L. (1985). Maternal sensitivity and newborns' orientation responses as related to quality of attachment in Northern Germany. In I. Bretherton & E. Waters (Eds.), Growing points of attachment theory and research. *Monographs of the Society for Research in Child Development, 50* (1–2, Serial No. 209).

GROTEVANT, H. D., & COOPER, C. R. (1981). *Assessing adolescent identity in the areas of occupation, religion, politics, friendships, dating, and sex roles: Manual for administration and coding of the interview.* Austin, TX: University of Texas.

GROTEVANT, H. D., & COOPER, C. R. (1985). Patterns of interaction in family relationships and the development of identity exploration in adolescence. *Child Development, 56,* 415–428.

GROTEVANT, H., & COOPER, C. (1988). The role of family experience in career exploration during adolescence. In P. Baltes, D. Featherman, & R. Lerner (Eds.), *Life-span development and behavior* (Vol. 8, pp. 231–258). Hillsdale, NJ: Erlbaum.

GROTEVANT, H., & DURRETT, M. (1980). Occupational knowledge and career development in adolescence. *Journal of Vocational Behavior, 17,* 171–182.

GRUSEC, J. E. (1988). *Social development: History, theory, and research.* New York: Springer-Verlag.

GUIDUBALDI, J., & CLEMINSHAW, H. K. (1985). Divorce, family health and child adjustment. *Family Relations, 34,* 35–41.

GUILFORD, J. P. (1985). The structure-of-intellect model. In B. B. Wolman (Ed.), *Handbook of intelligence* (pp. 225–266). New York: Wiley.

GUMP, P. V. (1975). *Ecological psychology and children.* Chicago: University of Chicago Press.

GURUCHARRI, C., & SELMAN, R. L. (1982). The development of interpersonal understanding during childhood, preadolescence, and adolescence: A longitudinal follow-up study. *Child Development, 53,* 924–927.

GUSTAFSON, G. E., & HARRIS, K. L. (1990). Women's responses to young infants' cries. *Developmental Psychology, 26,* 144–152.

HAAN, N., AERTS, E., & COOPER, B. (1985). *On moral grounds: The search for practical morality.* New York: New York University Press.

HAAN, N., SMITH, M. B., & BLOCK, J. (1968). Moral reasoning of young adults: Political-social behavior, family background, and personality correlates. *Journal of Personality and Social Psychology, 10,* 183–201.

HAGLUND, B., & CNATTINGIUS, S. (1990). Cigarette smoking as a risk factor for sudden infant death syndrome: A population-based study. *American Journal of Public Health, 80,* 29–32.

HAHN, W. K. (1987). Cerebral lateralization of function: From infancy through childhood. *Psychological Bulletin, 101,* 376–392.

HAINLINE, L. (1985). Oculomotor control in human infants. In R. Groner, G. W., McConkie, & C. Menz (Eds.), *Eye movements and human information processing* (pp. 71–84). Amsterdam: Elsevier.

HAKUTA, K. (1986). *Mirror of language.* New York: Basic Books.

HAKUTA, K., FERDMAN, B. M., & DIAZ, R. M. (1987). Bilingualism and cognitive development: Three perspectives. In S. Rosenberg (Ed.), *Advances in applied psycholinguistics: Vol. 2. Reading, writing, and language learning* (pp. 284–319). New York: Cambridge University Press.

HAKUTA, K., & GARCIA, E. E. (1989). Bilingualism and education. *American Psychologist, 44,* 374–379.

HALL, G. S. (1904). *Adolescence* (Vols. 1–2). New York: Appleton-Century-Crofts.

HALL, J. A., & HALBERSTADT, A. G. (1980). Masculinity and femininity in children: Development of the Children's Attributes Questionnaire. *Developmental Psychology, 16,* 270–280.

HALL, J. G., SYBERT, V. P., WILLIAMSON, R. A., FISHER, N. L., & REED, S. D. (1982). Turner's syndrome. *West Journal of Medicine, 137,* 32–44.

HALL, W. S. (1989). Reading comprehension. *American Psychologist, 44,* 157–161.

HALMI, K. A. (1987). Anorexia nervosa and bulimia. In V. B. Van Hasselt & M. Hersen (Eds.), *Handbook of adolescent psychology* (pp. 265–287). New York: Pergamon.

HALPERN, D. F., & COREN, S. (1990). *Hand preference and life span.* Unpublished manuscript.

HALVERSON, H. M. (1931). An experimental study of prehension in infants by means of systematic cinema records. *Genetic Psychology Monographs, 10,* 107–286.

HAMILTON, S. F. (1986). Raising standards and reducing dropout rates. *Teacher's College Record, 86,* 410–429.

HAMILTON, S. F. (1990). *Apprenticeship for adulthood: Preparing youth for the future.* New York: The Free Press.

HAMMILL, D. D. (1990). On defining learning disabilities: An emerging consensus. *Journal of Learning Disabilities, 23,* 74–84.

HANIGAN, W. C., MORGAN, A. M., STAHLBERG, L. K., & HILLER, J. L. (1990). Tentorial hemorrhage associated with vacuum extraction. *Pediatrics, 85,* 534–539.

HAQUE, M., ELLERSTEIN, N. S., GUNDY, J. H., SHELOV, S. P., WEISS, J. C., McINTIRE, M. S., OLNESS, K. N., JONES, D. J., HEAGARTY, M. C., & STARFIELD, B. H. (1981). Parental perceptions of enuresis. *American Journal of Diseases of Children, 135,* 809–811.

HARLOW, H. F., & ZIMMERMAN, R. (1959). Affectional responses in the infant monkey. *Science, 130,* 421–432.

HARRIS, G., & BOOTH, A. (1987). Infants' preference for salt in food: Its dependence upon recent dietary experience. *Journal of Reproductive and Infant Psychology, 5,* 97–104.

HARRIS, M. J., & ROSENTHAL, R. (1985). Mediation of interpersonal expectancy effects: 31 meta-analyses. *Psychological Bulletin, 97,* 363–386.

HARRIS, P. L. (1983). Infant cognition. In M. M. Haith & J. J. Campos (Eds.), *Handbook of child psychology: Vol. 2. Infancy and developmental psychobiology* (4th ed., pp. 689–782). New York: Wiley.

HARRIS, P. L. (1991). The work of the imagination. In A. Whiten (Ed.), *Natural theories of mind* (pp. 283–304). Oxford: Blackwell.

HARRIS, R. T. (1991, March/April). Anorexia nervosa and bulimia nervosa in female adolescents. *Nutrition Today, 26* (2), 30–34.

HARRIS, S., MUSSEN, P. H., & RUTHERFORD, E. (1976). Some cognitive, behavioral, and personality correlates of maturity of moral judgment. *Journal of Genetic Psychology, 128,* 123–135.

HARRISON, A. O., WILSON, M. N., PINE, C. J., CAN, S. Q., & BURIEL, R. (1990). Family ecologies of ethnic minority children. *Child Development, 61,* 127–137.

HART, S. N., & BRASSARD, M. R. (1987). A major threat to children's mental health. *American Psychologist, 42,* 160–165.

HARTER, S. (1982). The perceived competence scale for children. *Child Development, 53,* 87–97.

HARTER, S. (1983). Developmental perspectives on the self-system. In E. M. Hetherington (Ed.), *Handbook of child psychology: Vol. 4. Socialization, personality, and social development* (4th ed., pp. 275–385). New York: Wiley.

HARTER, S. (1990). Issues in the assessment of the self-concept of children and adolescents. In A. LaGreca (Ed.), *Through the eyes of a child* (pp. 292–325). Boston: Allyn and Bacon.

HARTER, S., & BUDDIN, B. J. (1987). Children's understanding of the simultaneity of two emotions: A five-stage developmental acquisition sequence. *Developmental Psychology, 23,* 388–399.

HARTER, S., & WHITESELL, N. (1989). Developmental changes in children's understanding of simple, multiple, and blended emotion concepts. In C. Saarni & P. Harris (Eds.), *Children's understanding of emotion* (pp. 81–116). Cambridge, England: Cambridge University Press.

HARTER, S., WRIGHT, K., & BRESNICK, S. (1987). *A developmental sequence of the emergence of self affects.* Paper presented at the biennial meeting of the Society for Research in Child Development, Baltimore.

HARTMAN, C. R., & BURGESS, A. W. (1989). Sexual abuse of children: Causes and consequences. In D. Cicchetti & V. Carlson (Eds.), *Child maltreatment* (pp. 95–128). New York: Cambridge University Press.

HARTUP, W. W. (1983). Peer relations. In E. M. Hetherington (Ed.), *Handbook of child psychology: Vol. 4. Socialization, personality, and social development* (4th ed., pp. 103–196). New York: Wiley.

HARTUP, W. W. (1989). Social relationships and their developmental significance. *American Psychologist, 44,* 120–126.

HAUGAARD, J. J., & REPPUCCI, N. D. (1988). *The sexual abuse of children.* San Francisco: Jossey-Bass.

HAVILAND, J., & LELWICA, M. (1987). The induced affect response: 10-week-old infants' responses to three emotion expressions. *Developmental Psychology, 23,* 97–104.

HAWKE, S., & KNOX, D. (1978). The one-child family: A new life-style. *The Family Coordinator, 27,* 215–219.

HAWKINS, D. J., & LAM, T. (1987). Teacher practices, social development, and delinquency. In J. D. Burchard & S. N. Burchard (Eds.), *Prevention of delinquent behavior* (pp. 241–274). Newbury Park, CA: Sage.

HAWKINS, J., & SHEINGOLD, K. (1986). The beginnings of a story: Computers and the organization of learning in classrooms. In J. A. Culbertson & L. L. Cunningham (Eds.), *Microcomputers and education* (85th Yearbook of the National Society for the Study of Education, pp. 40–58). Chicago: University of Chicago Press.

HAWKINS, J., PEA, R. D., GLICK, J., & SCRIBNER, S. (1984). "Merds that laugh don't like mushrooms": Evidence for deductive reasoning by preschoolers. *Developmental Psychology, 20,* 584–594.

HAYES, C. (ED.). (1987). *Risking the future: Adolescent sexuality, pregnancy, and childbearing* (Vol. 1). Washington, DC: National Academy Press.

HAYES, R. M. (1989). Homeless children. In F. J. Macchiarola & A. Gartner (Eds.), *Caring for America's children* (pp. 58–69). New York: The Academy of Political Science.

HAYGHE, H. V. (1990, March). Family members in the work force. *Monthly Labor Review.* Washington, DC: U.S. Government Printing Office.

HAYNE, H., ROVEE-COLLIER, C., & PERRIS, E. E. (1987). Categorization and memory retrieval by three-month-olds. *Child Development, 58,* 750–767.

HAYNES, C. F., CUTLER, C., GRAY, J., O'KEEFE, K., & KEMPE, R. S. (1983). Nonorganic failure to thrive: Implications of placement through analysis of videotaped interactions. *Child Abuse and Neglect, 7,* 321–328.

HEATH, S. B. (1983). *Ways with words: Language, life, and work in communities and classrooms.* Cambridge, England: Cambridge University Press.

HEATH, S. B. (1989). Oral and literate traditions among black Americans living in poverty. *American Psychologist, 44,* 367–373.

HEATH, S. B. (1990). The children of Trackton's children: Spoken and written language in social change. In J. Stigler, G. Herdt, & R. A. Shweder (Eds.), *Cultural psychology: Essays on comparative human development* (pp. 496–519). New York: Cambridge University Press.

HEDGES, L. V., GIACONIA, R. M., & GAGE, N. L. (1981). *Meta-analysis of the effects of open and traditional instruction.* Stanford, CA: Stanford University, Program on Teaching Effectiveness.

HEINL, T. (1983). *The baby massage book.* London: Coventure.

HEINONEN, O. P., SLONE, D., & SHAPIRO, S. (1977). *Birth defects and drugs in pregnancy.* Littleton, MA: PSG Publishing Company.

HENGGELER, S. W. (1989). *Delinquency in adolescence.* Newbury Park, CA: Sage.

HENKER, B., & WHALEN, C. K. (1989). Hyperactivity and attention deficits. *American Psychologist, 44,* 216–223.

HERGENRATHER, J. R., & RABINOWITZ, M. (1991). Age-related differences in the organization of children's knowledge of illness. *Developmental Psychology, 27,* 952–959.

HERKOWITZ, J. (1984). Developmentally engineered equipment and playgrounds. In J. R. Thomas (Ed.), *Motor development during childhood and adolescence* (pp. 139–173). Minneapolis: MN: Burgess.

HETHERINGTON, E. M. (1989). Coping with family transitions: Winners, losers, and survivors. *Child Development, 60,* 1–14.

HETHERINGTON, E. M., & ANDERSON, E. R. (1987). The effects of divorce and remarriage on early adolescents and their families. In M. D. Levine & E. R. McArney (Eds.), *Early adolescent transitions* (pp. 49–67). Lexington, MA: Heath.

HETHERINGTON, E. M., & CLINGEMPEEL, W. G. (1992). Coping with marital transitions: A family systems perspective. *Monographs of the Society for Research in Child Development, 57* (2–3, Serial No. 227).

HETHERINGTON, E. M., COX, M., & COX, R. (1982). Effects of divorce on parents and children. In M. E. Lamb (Ed.), *Nontraditional families: Parenting and child development* (pp. 233–288). Hillsdale, NJ: Erlbaum.

HETHERINGTON, E. M., COX, M., & COX, R. (1985). Long-term effects of divorce and remarriage on the adjustment of children. *Journal of the American Academy of Child Psychiatry, 24,* 518–530.

HETHERINGTON, E. M., STANLEY-HAGAN, M., & ANDERSON, E. R. (1989). Marital transitions: A child's perspective. *American Psychologist, 44,* 303–312.

HETHERINGTON, S. E. (1990). A controlled study of the effect of prepared childbirth classes on obstetric outcomes. *Birth, 17,* 86–90.

HILL, C. R., & STAFFORD, F. P. (1980). Parental care of children: Time diary estimate of quantity, predictability, and variety. *Journal of Human Resources, 15,* 219–239.

HILL, J. P. (1988). Adapting to menarche: Familial control and conflict. In M. Gunnar & W. A. Collins (Eds.), Development during the transition to adolescence. *Minnesota Symposia on Child Psychology* (Vol. 21, pp. 43–77). Hillsdale, NJ: Erlbaum.

HILL, J. P., & HOLMBECK, G. N. (1987). Family adaptation to biological change during adolescence. In R. M. Lerner & T. T. Foch (Eds.), *Biological-psychosocial interactions in early adolescence* (pp. 207–224). Hillsdale, NJ: Erlbaum.

HILL, J. P., & LYNCH, M. E. (1983). The intensification of gender-related role expectations during early adolescence. In J. Brooks-Gunn & A. C. Petersen (Eds.), *Girls at puberty: Biological and psychological perspectives* (pp. 201–228). New York: Plenum.

HILL, P. M., & HUMPHREY, P. (1982). *Human growth and development throughout life: A nursing perspective.* New York: Delmar.

HILLMAN, S. B., & DAVENPORT, G. G. (1978). Teacher-student interactions in desegregated schools. *Journal of Educational Psychology, 70,* 545–553.

HINDE, R. A. (1989). Ethological and relationships approaches. In R. Vasta (Ed.), *Annals of child development* (Vol. 6, pp. 251–285). Greenwich, CT: JAI Press.

HINMAN, A. R. (1987). Vaccine-preventable diseases and child day care. In M. T. Osterholm, J. O. Klein, S. S. Aronson, & L. K. Pickering (Eds.), *Infectious diseases in child day care* (pp. 61–71). Chicago: University of Chicago Press.

HIRSH-PASEK, K., KEMLER NELSON, D. G., JUSCZYK, P. W., CASSIDY, K. W., DRUSS, B., & KENNEDY, L. (1987). Clauses are perceptual units for young infants. *Cognition, 26,* 269–286.

HISCOCK, M., & KINSBOURNE, M. (1987). Specialization of the cerebral hemispheres: Implications for learning. *Journal of Learning Disabilities, 20,* 130–143.

Ho, H., Glahn, T. J., & Ho, J. (1988). The fragile-X syndrome. *Developmental Medicine and Child Neurology, 30,* 257–261.

Hobart, C. (1987). Parent-child relations in remarried families. *Journal of Family Issues, 8,* 259–277.

Hobart, C., & Brown, D. (1988). Effects of prior marriage children on adjustment in remarriages: A Canadian study. *Journal of Comparative Family Studies, 19,* 381–396.

Hock, E., & DeMeis, D. (1987). *Depression in mothers of infants: The role of maternal employment.* Paper presented at the biennial meeting of the Society for Research in Child Development, Baltimore, MD.

Hodges, J., & Tizard, B. (1989). Social and family relationships of ex-institutional adolescents. *Journal of Child Psychology and Psychiatry, 30,* 77–97.

Hodges, R. M., & French, L. A. (1988). The effect of class and collection labels on cardinality, class-inclusion, and number conservation tasks. *Child Development, 59,* 1387–1396.

Hoff-Ginsburg, E. (1986). Function and structure in maternal speech: Their relation to the child's development of syntax. *Developmental Psychology, 22,* 155–163.

Hoffman, L. W. (1974). Effects of maternal employment on the child: A review of the research. *Developmental Psychology, 10,* 204–228.

Hoffman, L. W. (1984). Work, family, and the socialization of the child. In R. D. Parke (Ed.), *Review of child development research* (Vol. 7, pp. 223–282). Chicago: University of Chicago Press.

Hoffman, L. W. (1986). Work, family, and the child. In M. S. Pallak & R. O. Perloff (Eds.), *Psychology and work: Productivity, change, and employment* (pp. 173–220). Washington, DC: American Psychological Association.

Hoffman, L. W. (1989). Effects of maternal employment in the two-parent family. *American Psychologist, 44,* 283–292.

Hoffman, L. W., Thornton, A., & Manis, J. D. (1978). The value of children to parents in the United States. *Journal of Population, 1,* 91–131.

Hoffman, M. L. (1984). Interaction of affect and cognition in empathy. In C. E. Izard, J. Kagan, & R. B. Zajonc (Eds.), *Emotions, cognition, and behavior* (pp. 103–131). Cambridge, England: Cambridge University Press.

Hoffman, M. L. (1988). Moral development. In M. H. Bornstein & M. E. Lamb (Eds.), *Developmental psychology: An advanced textbook* (2nd ed., pp. 497–548). Hillsdale, NJ: Erlbaum.

Hofsten, C. von (1984). Developmental changes in the organization of prereaching movements. *Developmental Psychology, 20,* 378–388.

Hofsten, C. von (1989). Motor development as the development of systems: Comments on the special section. *Developmental Psychology, 25,* 950–953.

Holden, C. (1986). Youth suicide: New research focuses on a growing social problem. *Science, 233,* 839–841.

Holden, G. W. (1983). Avoiding conflict: Mothers as tacticians in the supermarket. *Child Development, 54,* 233–240.

Holden, G. W., & Ritchie, K. L. (1991). Linking extreme marital discord, child rearing, and child behavior problems: Evidence from battered women. *Child Development, 62,* 311–327.

Holden, G. W., & West, M. J. (1989). Proximate regulation by mothers: A demonstration of how differing styles affect young children's behavior. *Child Development, 60,* 64–69.

Holmbeck, G. N., Waters, K. A., & Brookman, R. R. (1990). Psychosocial correlates of sexually transmitted diseases and sexual activity in black adolescent females. *Journal of Adolescent Research, 5,* 431–448.

Hong, K., & Townes, B. (1976). Infants' attachment to inanimate objects. *Journal of the American Academy of Child Psychiatry, 15,* 49–61.

Honzik, M. P. (1983). Measuring mental abilities in infancy: The value and limitations. In M. Lewis (Ed.), *Origins of intelligence* (2nd ed., pp. 67–105). New York: Plenum.

Honzik, M. P., Macfarlane, J. W., & Allen, L. (1948). The stability of mental test performance between two and eighteen years. *Journal of Experimental Education, 17,* 309–329.

Hook, E. B. (1980). Genetic counseling dilemmas: Down syndrome, paternal age, and recurrence risk after remarriage. *American Journal of Medical Genetics, 5,* 145.

Hook, E. B. (1988). Evaluation and projection of rates of chromosome abnormalities in chorionic villus studies (c.v.s.). *American Journal of Human Genetics Supplement, 43,* A108.

Hopkins, B., & Westra, T. (1988). Maternal handling and motor development: An intracultural study. *Genetic, Social and General Psychology Monographs, 14,* 377–420.

Horan, J. J., & Straus, L. K. (1987). Substance abuse in adolescence. In V. B. Ban Hasselt & M. Hersen (Eds.), *Handbook of adolescent psychology* (pp. 313–331). New York: Pergamon Press.

Horgan, D. (1978). The development of the full passive. *Journal of Child Language, 5,* 65–80.

Horn, J. M. (1983). The Texas Adoption Project: Adopted children and their intellectual resemblance to biological and adoptive parents. *Child Development, 54,* 268–275.

Horn, T. S. (1987). The influence of teacher-coach behavior on the psychological development of children. In D. Gould & M. R. Weiss (Eds.), *Advances in pediatric sport sciences* (Vol. 2, pp. 121–142). Champaign, IL: Human Kinetics.

Horn, W. F., O'Donnell, J. P., & Vitulano, L. A. (1983). Long-term follow-up studies of learning disabled persons. *Journal of Learning Disabilities, 16,* 542–555.

Horner, T. M. (1980). Two methods of studying stranger reactivity in infants: A review. *Journal of Child Psychology and Psychiatry, 21,* 203–219.

Hornik, R., Risenhoover, N., & Gunnar, M. (1987). The effects of maternal positive, neutral, and negative affective communications on infant responses to new toys. *Child Development, 58,* 937–944.

Horowitz, F. D. (1987). *Exploring developmental theories: Toward a structural/behavioral model of child development.* Hillsdale, NJ: Erlbaum.

Horowitz, F. D., & O'Brien, M. (1986). Gifted and talented children: State of knowledge and directions for research. *American Psychologist, 41,* 1147–1152.

Hotaling, G. T., Finkelhor, D., Kirkpatrick, J. T., & Strauss, M. A. (Eds.). (1988). *Family abuse and its consequences: New directions in research.* Newbury Park, CA: Sage.

Houts, A. C. (1991). Nocturnal enuresis as a biobehavioral problem. *Behavior Therapy, 22,* 133–151.

Howard, M., & McCabe, J. B. (1990). Helping teenagers postpone sexual involvement. *Family Planning Perspectives, 22,* 21–26.

Howe, N., & Ross, H. S. (1990). Socialization, perspective-taking, and the sibling relationship. *Developmental Psychology, 26,* 160–165.

Howes, C. (1988a). Peer interaction of young children. *Monographs of the Society for Research in Child Development, 53* (1, Serial No. 217).

Howes, C. (1988b). Relations between early child care and schooling. *Developmental Psychology, 24,* 53–57.

Howes, C. (1990). Can the age of entry into child care and the quality of child care predict adjustment in kindergarten? *Developmental Psychology, 26,* 292–303.

Howes, C., Phillips, D. A., & Whitebook, M. (1992). Thresholds of quality: Implications for the social development of children in center-based child care. *Child Development, 63,* 449–460.

Howes, C., Rodning, C., Galluzzo, D. C., & Myers, L. (1988). Attachment and child care: Relationships with mother and caregiver. *Early Childhood Research Quarterly, 3,* 403–416.

Howes, P., & Markman, H. J. (1989). Marital quality and child functioning: A longitudinal investigation. *Child Development, 60,* 1044–1051.

Hoyseth, K. S., & Jones, P. J. H. (1989). Ethanol induced teratogenesis: Characterization, mechanisms, and diagnostic approaches. *Life Sciences, 44,* 643–649.

Hubel, D. H., & Wiesel, T. N. (1970). The period of susceptibility to the physiological effects of unilateral eye closure in kittens. *Journal of Physiology, 206,* 419–436.

Hudson, J. A. (1990). The emergence of autobiographic memory in mother-child conversations. In R. Fivush & J. A. Hudson (Eds.), *Knowing and remembering in young children* (pp. 166–196). New York: Cambridge University Press.

Hudson, J. A., & Nelson, K. (1983). Effects of script structure on children's story recall. *Developmental Psychology, 19,* 625–635.

Huesmann, L. R. (1986). Psychological processes promoting the relation between exposure to media violence and aggressive behavior by the viewer. *Journal of Social Issues, 42,* 125–139.

Humphreys, A. P., & Smith, P. K. (1987). Rough and tumble, friendship, and dominance in schoolchildren: Evidence for continuity and change with age. *Child Development, 58,* 201–212.

HUMPHREYS, L. G., RICH, S. A., & DAVEY, T. C. (1985). A Piagetian test of general intelligence. *Developmental Psychology, 21,* 871–877.

HUNTER, R. S., & KILSTROM, N. (1979). Breaking the cycle in abusive families. *American Journal of Psychiatry, 136,* 1320–1322.

HUSTON, A. C. (1983). Sex-typing. In E. M. Hetherington (Ed.), *Handbook of child psychology: Vol. 4. Socialization, personality, and social development* (4th ed., pp. 387–467). New York: Wiley.

HUSTON, A. C., & ALVAREZ, M. M. (1990). The socialization context of gender role development in early adolescence. In R. Montemayor, G. R. Adams, & T. P. Gullotta (Eds.), *From childhood to adolescence: A transitional period?* (pp. 156–179). Newbury Park, CA: Sage.

HUSTON, A. C., WATKINS, B. A., & KUNKEL, D. (1989). Public policy and children's television. *American Psychologist, 44,* 424–433.

HUSTON-STEIN, A., & HIGGINS-TRENK, A. (1978). Development of females from childhood through adulthood: Career and feminine role orientations. In P. B. Baltes (Ed.), *Life-span development and behavior* (Vol. 1, pp. 257–296). New York: Academic Press.

HUTTENLOCHER, J., HAIGHT, W., BRYK, A., SELTZER, M., & LYONS, T. (1991). Early vocabulary growth: Relation to language input and gender. *Developmental Psychology, 27,* 236–248.

HWANG, K. (1986). Behavior of Swedish primary and secondary caretaking fathers in relation to mother's presence. *Developmental Psychology, 22,* 739–751.

HYDE, J. S., & LINN, M. C. (1988). Gender differences in verbal ability: A meta-analysis. *Psychological Bulletin, 104,* 53–69.

HYMES, J. L., JR. (1991). *The year in review: A look at 1990.* Washington, DC: National Association for the Education of Young Children.

INHELDER, B., & PIAGET, J. (1958). *The growth of logical thinking from childhood to adolescence: An essay on the construction of formal operational structures.* New York: Basic Books. (Original work published 1955)

INTERNATIONAL EDUCATION ASSOCIATION (1988). *Science achievement in seventeen countries: A preliminary report.* Oxford, England: Pergamon Press.

IRVINE, J. J. (1986). Teacher-student interactions: Effects of student race, sex, and grade level. *Journal of Educational Psychology, 78,* 14–21.

ISABELLA, R., & BELSKY, J. (1991). Interactional synchrony and the origins of infant-mother attachment: A replication study. *Child Development, 62,* 373–384.

ISTVAN, J. (1986). Stress, anxiety, and birth outcomes: A critical review of the evidence. *Psychological Bulletin, 100,* 331–348.

IZARD, C. E. (1979). *The maximally discriminative facial movement scoring system.* Unpublished manuscript, University of Delaware.

IZARD, C. E., HEMBREE, E. A., & HUEBNER, R. R. (1987). Infant's emotion expressions to acute pain. *Developmental Psychology, 23,* 105–113.

JACKLIN, C. N., & MACCOBY, E. E. (1983). Issues of gender differentiation in normal development. In M. D. Levine, W. B. Carey, A. C. Crocker, & R. T. Gross (Eds.), *Developmental-behavioral pediatrics* (pp. 175–184). Philadelphia: Saunders.

JACKLIN, C. N., SNOW, M. E., GAHART, M., & MACCOBY, E. E. (1980). Sleep pattern development from 6 to 33 months. *Journal of Pediatric Psychology, 5,* 295–303.

JACOBS, F. H., & DAVIES, M. W. (1991). Rhetoric or reality? Child and family policy in the United States. *Social Policy Report of the Society for Research in Child Development, 5* (No. 4).

JACOBSON, J. L., & WILLE, D. E. (1986). The influence of attachment pattern on developmental changes in peer interaction from the toddler to the preschool period. *Child Development, 57,* 338–347.

JACOBSON, J. L., JACOBSON, S. W., & HUMPHREY, H. E. B. (1990). Effects of in utero exposure to polychlorinated biphenyls on cognitive functioning in young children. *Journal of Pediatrics, 116,* 38–45.

JACOBSON, J. L., JACOBSON, S. W., FEIN, G., SCHWARTZ, P. M., & DOWLER, J. (1984). Prenatal exposure to an environmental toxin: A test of the multiple effects model. *Developmental Psychology, 20,* 523–532.

JACOBSON, J. L., JACOBSON, S. W., PADGETT, R. J., BRUMITT, G. A., & BILLINGS, R. L. (1992). Effects of prenatal PCB exposure on cognitive processing efficiency and sustained attention. *Developmental Psychology, 28,* 297–306.

JACOBSON, S. W., FEIN, G. G., JACOBSON, J. L., SCHWARTZ, P. M., & DOWLER, J. (1985). The effect of intrauterine PCB exposure on visual recognition memory. *Child Development, 56,* 853–860.

JENCKS, C. (1972). *Inequality: A reassessment of the effect of family and schooling in America.* New York: Basic Books.

JENSEN, A. R. (1969). How much can we boost IQ and scholastic achievement? *Harvard Educational Review, 39,* 1–123.

JENSEN, A. R. (1980). *Bias in mental testing.* New York: Free Press.

JENSEN, A. R. (1985a). Methodological and statistical techniques for the chronometric study of mental abilities. In C. R. Reynolds & V. L. Willson (Eds.), *Methodological and statistical advances in the study of individual difference* (pp. 51–116). New York: Plenum.

JENSEN, A. R. (1985b). The nature of the black-white difference on various psychometric tests: Spearman's hypothesis. *Behavioral and Brain Sciences, 8,* 193–219.

JENSEN, A. R. (1988). Speed of information processing and population differences. In S. H. Irvine & J. W. Berry (Eds.), *Human abilities in cultural context* (pp. 105–145). New York: Cambridge University Press.

JENSEN, A. R., & FIGUEROA, R. A. (1975). Forward and backward digit-span interaction with race and IQ: Predictions from Jensen's theory. *Journal of Educational Psychology, 67,* 882–893.

JOHNSON, C. L., STUCKEY, M. K., LEWIS, L. D., & SCHWARTZ, D. M. (1983). A survey of 509 cases of self-reported bulimia. In P. L. Darby (Ed.), *Anorexia nervosa: Recent developments in research* (pp. 159–171). New York: Alan R. Liss.

JOHNSON, J. E., & HOOPER, F. E. (1982). Piagetian structuralism and learning: Two decades of educational application. *Contemporary Educational Psychology, 7,* 217–237.

JOHNSON, J. S., & NEWPORT, E. L. (1989). Critical period effects in second language learning: The influence of maturational state on the acquisition of English as a second language. *Cognitive Psychology, 21,* 60–99.

JOHNSTON, J. R., KLINE, M., & TSCHANN, J. M. (1989). Ongoing post-divorce conflict. *American Journal of Orthopsychiatry, 57,* 587–600.

JONES, C. P., & ADAMSON, L. B. (1987). Language use in mother-child and mother-child-sibling interactions. *Child Development, 58,* 356–366.

JONES, E. F., FORREST, J. D., GOLDMAN, N., HENSHAW, S. K., LINCOLN, R., ROSOFF, J. I., WESTOFF, C. F., & WULF, D. (1985). Teenage pregnancy in developed countries: Determinants and policy implications. *Family Planning Perspectives, 17,* 53–63.

JONES, G. P., & DEMBO, M. H. (1989). Age and sex role differences in intimate friendships during childhood and adolescence. *Merrill-Palmer Quarterly, 35,* 445–462.

JONES, M. C. (1965). Psychological correlates of somatic development. *Child Development, 36,* 899–911.

JONES, M. C., & BAYLEY, N. (1950). Physical maturing among boys as related to behavior. *Journal of Educational Psychology, 41,* 129–148.

JONES, M. C., & MUSSEN, P. H. (1958). Self-conceptions, motivations, and interpersonal attitudes of early- and late-maturing girls. *Child Development, 29,* 491–501.

JONES, S. S., & RAAG, T. (1989). Smile production in older infants: The importance of a social recipient for the facial signal. *Child Development, 60,* 811–818.

JOOS, S. K., POLLITT, K. E., MUELLER, W. H., & ALBRIGHT, D. L. (1983). The Bacon Chow Study: Maternal nutritional supplementation and infant behavioral development. *Child Development, 54,* 669–676.

JORDAN, A. E. (1987). The unresolved child care dilemma: Care for the acutely ill child. In M. T. Osterholm, J. O. Klein, S. S. Aronson, & L. K. Pickering (Eds.), *Infectious diseases in child day care* (pp. 114–118). Chicago: University of Chicago Press.

JORDAN, B. (1980). *Birth in four cultures.* Montreal: Eden.

JORDAN, P. L. (1990). Laboring for relevance: Expectant and new parenthood. *Nursing Research, 39,* 11–16.

KAGAN, J. (1989). *Unstable ideas: Temperament, cognition, and self.* Cambridge, MA: Harvard University Press.

KAGAN, J. KEARSLEY, R. B., & ZELAZO, P. R. (1978). *Infancy: Its place in human development.* Cambridge, MA: Harvard University Press.

KAGAN, J., & MOSS, J. (1962). *Birth to maturity*. New York: Wiley.

KAGAN, J., REZNICK, J. S., & GIBBONS, J. (1989). Inhibited and uninhibited types of children. *Child Development, 60,* 838–845.

KAGAN, J., REZNICK, J. S., & SNIDMAN, N. (1988). Biological bases of childhood shyness. *Science, 240,* 167–171.

KAGAN, J., & SNIDMAN, N. (1991). Temperamental factors in human development. *American Psychologist, 46,* 856–862.

KAIL, R. (1990). *The development of memory in children* (3rd ed.). New York: Freeman.

KAINULAINEN, K., STEINMAN, B., COLLINS, F., DIETZ, H. C., FANCOMANO, C. A., CHILD, A., KILPATRICK, M. W., BROCK, D. J. H., KESTON, M., PYERITZ, R. E., & PELTONEN, L. (1991). Marfan syndrome: No evidence for heterogeneity in different populations, and more precise mapping of the gene. *American Journal of Human Genetics, 49,* 662–667.

KAITZ, M., GOOD, A., ROKEM, A. M., & EIDELMAN, A. I. (1987). Mothers' recognition of their newborns by olfactory cues. *Developmental Psychobiology, 20,* 587–591.

KAITZ, M., GOOD, A., ROKEM, A. M., & EIDELMAN, A. I. (1988). Mothers' and fathers' recognition of their newborns' photographs during the postpartum period. *Journal of Developmental and Behavioral Pediatrics, 9,* 223–226.

KAITZ, M., LAPIDOT, P., BRONNER, R., & EIDELMAN, A. I. (1992). Parturient women can recognize their infants by touch. *Developmental Psychology, 28,* 35–39.

KAITZ, M., MESCHULACH-SARFATY, O., AUERBACH, J., & EIDELMAN, A. (1988). A reexamination of newborns' ability to imitate facial expressions. *Developmental Psychology, 24,* 3–7.

KALER, S. R., & KOPP, C. B. (1990). Compliance and comprehension in very young toddlers. *Child Development, 61,* 1997–2003.

KALNINS, I., & LOVE, R. (1982). Children's concepts of health and illness—and implications for health education: An overview. *Health Education Quarterly, 9,* 104–115.

KALTER, N. RIEMER, B., BRICKMAN, A., & CHEN, J. W. (1985). Implications of parental divorce for female development. *Journal of the American Academy of Child Psychiatry, 24,* 538–544.

KAMMERMAN, S. B. (1991). Child care policies and programs: An international overview. *Journal of Social Issues, 47,* 179–196.

KANDEL, D. B. (1978). Homophily, selection, and socialization in adolescent friendships. *American Journal of Sociology, 84,* 427–436.

KANDEL, D. B., & DAVIES, M. (1986). Adult sequelae of adolescent depressive symptoms. *Archives of General Psychiatry, 43,* 255–262.

KANDEL, D. B., RAVEIS, V. H., & DAVIES, M. (1991). Suicidal ideation in adolescence: Depression, substance use, and other risk factors. *Journal of Youth and Adolescence, 20,* 289–309.

KANDEL, D., & LESSER, G. S. (1972). *Youth in two worlds*. San Francisco: Jossey-Bass.

KANNER, A. D., FELDMAN, S. S., WEINBERGER, D. A., & FORD, M. E. (1987). Uplifts, hassles, and adaptational outcomes in early adolescents. *Journal of Early Adolescence, 7,* 371–394.

KANTOR, D., & LEHR, W. (1975). *Inside the family*. San Francisco: Jossey-Bass.

KANTROWITZ, B. (1990, February 12). The crack children. *Newsweek, 65* (7), 62–63.

KANTROWITZ, B. (1992, January 27). A Head Start does not last. *Newsweek, 69* (4), 44–45.

KAPLAN, B. J. (1972). Malnutrition and mental deficiency. *Psychological Bulletin, 78,* 321–334.

KARADSHEH, R. (1991). *This room is a junkyard!: Children's comprehension of metaphorical language*. Paper presented at the biennial meeting of the Society for Research in Child Development, Seattle, WA.

KATCHADOURIAN, H. (1977). *The biology of adolescence*. San Francisco: Freeman.

KATCHADOURIAN, H. (1990). Sexuality. In S. S. Feldman & G. R. Elliott (Eds.), *At the threshold: The developing adolescent* (pp. 330–351). Cambridge, MA: Harvard University Press.

KAUFMAN, A. S., & KAUFMAN, N. L. (1983). *Kaufman Assessment Battery for Children: Administration and scoring manual*. Circle Pines, MN: American Guidance Service.

KAUFMAN, A. S., KAMPHAUS, R. W., & KAUFMAN, N. L. (1985). New directions for intelligence testing: The Kaufman Assessment Battery

for Children (K-ABC). In B. B. Wolman (Ed.), *Handbook of intelligence* (pp. 663–698). New York: Wiley.

KAVALE, K. (1982). Meta-analysis of the relationship between visual perceptual skills and reading achievement. *Journal of Learning Disabilities, 15,* 42–51.

KAYE, K., ELKIND, L., GOLDBERG, D., & TYTUN, A. (1989). Birth outcomes for infants of drug abusing mothers. *New York State Journal of Medicine, 89,* 256–261.

KAYE, K., & MARCUS, J. (1981). Infant imitation: The sensory-motor agenda. *Developmental Psychology, 17,* 258–265.

KAYE, K., & WELLS, A. J. (1980). Mothers' jiggling and the burst-pause pattern in neonatal feeding. *Infant Behavior and Development, 3,* 29–46.

KEARINS, J. M. (1981). Visual spatial memory in Australian aboriginal children of desert regions. *Cognitive Psychology, 13,* 434–460.

KEASEY, C. B. (1971). Social participation as a factor in the moral development of preadolescents. *Developmental Psychology, 5,* 216–220.

KEATING, D. (1979). Adolescent thinking. In J. Adelson (Ed.), *Handbook of adolescent psychology* (pp. 211–246). New York: Wiley.

KEENEY, T. J., CANIZZO, S. R., & FLAVELL, J. H. (1967). Spontaneous and induced verbal rehearsal in a recall task. *Child Development, 38,* 953–966.

KEIL, F. (1986). Conceptual domains and the acquisition of metaphor. *Cognitive Development, 1,* 73–96.

KELLER, A., FORD, L. H., & MEACHAM, J. A. (1978). Dimensions of self-concept in preschool children. *Developmental Psychology, 14,* 483–489.

KELLY, A., & SMAIL, B. (1986). Sex stereotypes and attitudes to science among eleven-year-old children. *British Journal of Educational Psychology, 56,* 158–168.

KELLY, H. (1981). Viewing children through television. In H. Kelly & H. Gardner (Eds.), *New directions for child development* (No. 13, pp. 59–71). San Francisco: Jossey-Bass.

KEMPE, C. H., SILVERMAN, B. F., STEELE, P. W., DROEGEMUELLER, P. W., & SILVER, H. K. (1962). The battered-child syndrome. *Journal of the American Medical Association, 181,* 17–24.

KEMPE, R. S., & KEMPE, C. H. (1984). *The common secret: Sexual abuse of children and adolescents*. New York: Freeman.

KENDLER, K. S., & ROBINETTE, C. D. (1983). Schizophrenia in the National Academy of Sciences–National Research Council twin registry: A 16-year update. *American Journal of Psychiatry, 140,* 1551–1563.

KENDRICK, A. S., KAUFMANN, R., & MESSENGER, K. P. (1991). *Healthy young children: A manual for programs*. Washington, DC: National Association for the Education of Young Children.

KEOGH, B. K. (1988). Improving services for problem learners. *Journal of Learning Disabilities, 21,* 6–11.

KERMOIAN, R., & CAMPOS, J. J. (1988). Locomotor experience: A facilitator of spatial cognitive development. *Child Development, 59,* 908–917.

KERR, B. A. (1983). Raising the career aspirations of gifted girls. *Vocational Guidance Quarterly, 32,* 37–43.

KESSEN, W. (1967). Sucking and looking: Two organized congenital patterns of behavior in the human newborn. In H. W. Stevenson, E. H. Hess, & H. L. Rheingold (Eds.), *Early behavior: Comparative and developmental approaches* (pp. 147–179). New York: Wiley.

KILBOURNE, B. W., BUEHLER, J. W., & ROGERS, M. F. (1990). AIDS as a cause of death in children, adolescents, and young adults. *American Journal of Public Health, 80,* 499.

KILBRIDE, J. E., & KILBRIDE, P. L. (1975). Sitting and smiling behavior of Baganda infants. *Journal of Cross-Cultural Psychology, 6,* 88–107.

KILMAN, C., & HELPIN, M. L. (1983). Recognizing dental malocclusion in children. *Pediatric Nursing, 9,* 204–208.

KINSMAN, C. A., & BERK, L. E. (1979). Joining the block and housekeeping areas: Changes in play and social behavior. *Young Children, 35,* 66–75.

KISER, L. J., BATES, J. E., MASLIN, C. A., & BAYLES, K. (1986). Mother-infant play at six months as a predictor of attachment security at thirteen months. *Journal of the American Academy of Child Psychiatry, 25,* 68–75.

KISKER, E. E. (1985). Teenagers talk about sex, pregnancy, and contraception. *Family Planning Perspectives, 17,* 83–90.

KLAHR, D. (1989). Information-processing approaches. In R. Vasta

(Ed.), *Annals of child development* (Vol. 6, pp. 133–185). Greenwich, CT: JAI Press.

KLAUS, M. H., & KENNELL, J. H. (1982). *Parent-infant bonding.* St. Louis: Mosby.

KLIMES-DOUGAN, B., & KISTNER, J. (1990). Physically abused preschoolers' responses to peers' distress. *Developmental Psychology, 26,* 599–602.

KLINE, M., TSCHANN, J. M., JOHNSTON, J. R., & WALLERSTEIN, J. S. (1989). Children's adjustment in joint and sole physical custody families. *Developmental Psychology, 25,* 430–438.

KLINMAN, D. G., SANDER, J. H., ROSEN, J. L., & LONGO, K. R. (1986). The Teen Father Collaboration: A demonstration and research model. In A. B. Elster & M. E. Lamb (Eds.), *Adolescent fatherhood* (pp. 155–170). Hillsdale, NJ: Erlbaum.

KLUNGNESS, L. (1990). Diagnosis and behavioral treatment of children who refuse to attend school. In P. A. Keller & S. R. Heyman (Eds.), *Innovations in clinical practice: A source book* (Vol. 9, pp. 107–118). Sarasota, FL: Professional Resource Exchange, Inc.

KNITTLE, J. L., & HIRSCH, J. (1968). Effect of early nutrition on the development of rat epididymal fat pads: Cellularity and metabolism. *Journal of Clinical Investigation, 47,* 2091–2098.

KNOBLOCH, H., & PASAMANICK, B. (Eds.). (1974). *Gesell and Amatruda's Developmental Diagnosis.* Hagerstown, MD: Harper & Row.

KNOBLOCH, H., STEVENS, F., & MALONE, A. F. (1980). *Manual of developmental diagnosis.* Hagerstown, MD: Harper & Row.

KODROFF, J. K., & ROBERGE, J. J. (1975). Developmental analysis of the conditional reasoning abilities of primary-grade children. *Developmental Psychology, 11,* 21–28.

KOGAN, N. (1983). Stylistic variation in childhood and adolescence: Creativity, metaphor, and cognitive style. In J. H. Flavell & E. M. Markman (Eds.), *Handbook of child psychology:* Vol. 3. Cognitive development (4th ed., pp. 630–708). New York: Wiley.

KOHLBERG, L. (1966). A cognitive-developmental analysis of children's sex-role concepts and attitudes. In E. E. Maccoby (Ed.), *The development of sex differences* (pp. 82–173). Stanford, CA: Stanford University Press.

KOHLBERG, L. (1969). Stage and sequence: The cognitive-developmental approach to socialization. In D. A. Goslin (Ed.), *Handbook of socialization theory and research* (pp. 347–480). Chicago: Rand McNally.

KOHLBERG, L., LEVINE, C., & HEWER, A. (1983). *Moral stages: A current formulation and a response to critics.* Basel, Switzerland: Karger.

KOHN, B., & DENNIS, M. (1974). Selective impairments of visuo-spatial abilities in infantile hemiplegics after right cerebral hemidecortication. *Neuropsychologia, 12,* 505–512.

KOHN, M. L. (1977). *Class and conformity: A study in values* (rev. ed.). Chicago: University of Chicago Press.

KOHN, M. L. (1979). The effects of social class on parental values and practices. In D. Reiss & H. A. Hoffman (Eds.), *The American family: Dying or developing* (pp. 45–68). New York: Plenum.

KOJIMA, H. (1986). Childrearing concepts as a belief-value system of the society and the individual. In H. Stevenson, H. Azuma, & K. Hakuta (Eds.), *Child development and education in Japan* (pp. 39–54). New York: Freeman.

KOLATA, G. B. (1989, May 14). Operating on the unborn. *The New York Times Magazine,* pp. 34–35, 46–48.

KOPP, C. (1983). Risk factors in development. In M. M. Haith & J. J. Campos (Eds.), *Handbook of child psychology: Vol. 2. Infancy and developmental psychobiology* (4th ed., pp. 1081–1188). New York: Wiley.

KOPP, C. B. (1987). The growth of self-regulation: Caregivers and children. In N. Eisenberg (Ed.), *Contemporary topics in developmental psychology* (pp. 34–55). New York: Wiley.

KOPP, C. B. (1989). Regulation of distress and negative emotions: A developmental view. *Developmental Psychology, 25,* 343–354.

KOPP, C. B., & KALER, S. R. (1989). Risk in infancy. *American Psychologist, 44,* 224–230.

KOPP, C. B., & KRAKOW, J. B. (1982). *The child: Development in a social context.* Reading, MA: Addison-Wesley.

KORNER, A. F., HUTCHINSON, C. A., KOPERSKI, J. A., KRAEMER, H. C., & SCHNEIDER, P. A. (1981). Stability of individual differences of neonatal motor and crying pattern. *Child Development, 52,* 83–90.

KORNGUTH, M. L. (1990). School illnesses: Who's absent and why? *Pediatric Nursing, 16,* 95–99.

KORNHABER, M., KRECHEVSKY, M., & GARDNER, H. (1991). Engaging intelligence. *Educational Psychologist, 25,* 177–199.

KORTE, D., & SCAER, R. (1990). *A good birth, a safe birth.* New York: Bantam.

KOZOL, J. (1991). *Savage inequalities.* New York: Crown.

KOZULIN, A. (1990). *Vygotsky's psychology: A biography of ideas.* Cambridge, MA: Harvard University Press.

KRAMER, M. S., BARR, R. G., LEDUC, D. G., BIOSJOLY, C., & PLESS, I. B. (1985). Infant determinants of childhood weight and adiposity. *Journal of Pediatrics, 107,* 104–107.

KREBS, D., & GILLMORE, J. (1982). The relationship among the first stages of cognitive development, role-taking abilities, and moral development. *Child Development, 53,* 877–886.

KREIPE, R. E., CHURCHILL, B. H., & STRAUSS, J. (1989). Long-term outcome of adolescents with anorexia nervosa. *American Journal of Diseases of Children, 143,* 1322–1327.

KREMENITZER, T. P., VAUGHAN, H. G., KURTZBERG, D., & DOWLING, K. (1979). Smooth-pursuit eye movements in the newborn infant. *Child Development, 50,* 441–448.

KREUTZER, M. A., LEONARD, C., & FLAVELL, J. H. (1975). An interview study of children's knowledge about memory. *Monographs of the Society for Research in Child Development, 40* (1, Serial No. 159).

KRICKER, A., ELLIOTT, J. W., FORREST, J., M., & McCREDIE, J. (1986). Congenital limb reduction deformities and use of oral contraceptives. *American Journal of Obstetrics and Gynecology, 155,* 1072–1078.

KUCZAJ, S. A., II. (1986). Thoughts on the intentional basis of early object word extension: Evidence from comprehension and production. In S. A. Kuczaj, II, & M. D. Barrett (Eds.), *The development of word meaning* (pp. 99–120). New York: Springer-Verlag.

KUCZYNSKI, L. (1984). Socialization goals and mother-child interaction: Strategies for long-term and short-term compliance. *Developmental Psychology, 20,* 1061–1073.

KUCZYNSKI, L., KOCHANSKA, G., RADKE-YARROW, M., & GIRNIUS-BROWN, O. (1987). A developmental interpretation of young children's noncompliance. *Developmental Psychology, 23,* 799–806.

KUHN, D. (1988). Cognitive development. In M. H. Bornstein & M. E. Lamb (Eds.), *Developmental psychology: An advanced textbook* (2nd ed., pp. 205–260). Hillsdale, NJ: Erlbaum.

KUHN, D., Ho, V., & ADAMS, C. (1979). Formal reasoning among pre- and late adolescents. *Child Development, 50,* 1128–1135.

KULIK, J. A. (1986). Evaluating the effects of teaching with computers. In P. F. Campbell & G. G. Fein (Eds.) *Young children and microcomputers* (pp. 103–128). Englewood Cliffs, NJ: Prentice-Hall.

KUNZINGER, E. L., III. (1985). A short-term longitudinal study of memorial development during early grade school. *Developmental Psychology, 21,* 642–646.

LABORATORY OF COMPARATIVE HUMAN COGNITION (1983). Culture and cognitive development. In W. Kessen (Ed.), *Handbook of child psychology: Vol. 1. History, theory, and methods* (4th ed., pp. 295–356). New York: Wiley.

LABORATORY OF COMPARATIVE HUMAN COGNITION (1989). Kids and computers: A positive vision of the future. *Harvard Educational Review, 59,* 73–86.

LADD, G. W., & MIZE, J. (1983). A cognitive-social learning model of social skill training. *Psychological Review, 90,* 127–157.

LADD, G. W., & PRICE, J. M. (1978). Predicting children's social and school adjustment following the transition from preschool to kindergarten. *Child Development, 58,* 1168–1189.

LAGERCRANTZ, H., & SLOTKIN, T. A. (1986). The "stress" of being born. *Scientific American, 254,* 100–107.

LAMAZE, F. (1958). *Painless childbirth.* London: Burke.

LAMB, M. E. (1976). Interaction between eight-month-old children and their fathers and mothers. In M. E. Lamb (Ed.), *The role of the father in child development* (pp. 307–327). New York: Wiley.

LAMB, M. E. (1987). *The father's role: Cross-cultural perspectives.* Hillsdale, NJ: Erlbaum.

LAMB, M. E., THOMPSON, R. A., GARDNER, W., CHARNOV, E. L., &

CONNELL, J. P. (1985). Infant-mother attachment: The origins and developmental significance of individual differences in the Strange Situation: Its study and biological interpretation. *Behavioral and Brain Sciences, 7,* 127–147.

LANDAU, E. (1986). *Sexually transmitted diseases.* Hillside, NJ: Enslow.

LANDAU, S., MILICH, R., & LORCH, E. P. (1992). Visual attention to and comprehension of television in attention-deficit hyperactivity disordered and normal boys. *Child Development, 63,* 928–937.

LANDESMAN, S., & RAMEY, C. (1989). Developmental psychology and mental retardation: Integrating scientific principles with treatment practices. *American Psychologist, 44,* 409–415.

LANE, D. M., & PEARSON, D. A. (1982). The development of selective attention. *Merrill-Palmer Quarterly, 28,* 317–337.

LANGE, G., & PIERCE, S. H. (1992). Memory-strategy learning and maintenance in preschool children. *Developmental Psychology, 28,* 453–462.

LANGLOIS, J. H., & STEPHAN, C. W. (1981). Beauty and the beast: The role of physical attractiveness in peer relationships and social behavior. In S. S. Brehm, S. M. Kassin, & S. X. Gibbons (Eds.), *Developmental social psychology: Theory and research* (pp. 152–168). New York: Oxford University Press.

LAOSA, L. M. (1981). Maternal behavior: Sociocultural diversity in modes of family interaction. In R. W. Henderson (Ed.), *Parent-child interaction: Theory, research, and prospects* (pp. 125–167). New York: Academic Press.

LAPSLEY, D. K. (1985). Elkind on egocentrism. *Developmental Review, 5,* 227–236.

LAPSLEY, D. K. (1990). Egocentrism theory and the "new look" at the imaginary audience and personal fable in adolescence. In R. M. Lerner, A. C. Petersen, & J. Brooks-Gunn (Eds.), *The encyclopedia of adolescence* (pp. 281–286). New York: Garland.

LAPSLEY, D. K., ENRIGHT, R., & SERLIN, R. (1989). Moral and social education. In F. Danner & J. Worell (Eds.), *The adolescent as a decision-maker: Applications to development and education* (pp. 111–141). New York: Academic Press.

LAPSLEY, D. K., FITZGERALD, D., RICE, K., & JACKSON, S. (1989). Separation-individuation and the "new look" at the imaginary audience and personal fable: A test of an integrative model. *Journal of Adolescent Research, 4,* 483–505.

LAPSLEY, D. K., JACKSON, S., RICE, K., & SHADID, G. (1988). Self-monitoring and the "new look" at the imaginary audience and personal fable: An ego-developmental analysis. *Journal of Adolescent Research, 3,* 17–31.

LAPSLEY, D. K., MILSTEAD, M., QUINTANA, S., FLANNERY, D., & BUSS, R. (1986). Adolescent egocentrism and formal operations: Tests of a theoretical assumption. *Developmental Psychology, 22,* 800–807.

LAPSLEY, D. K., RICE, K. G., & FITZGERALD, D. P. (1990). Adolescent attachment, identity, and adjustment to college: Implications for the continuity of adaptation hypothesis. *Journal of Counseling and Development, 68,* 561–565.

LAROSSA, R., & LAROSSA, M. M. (1981). *Transition to parenthood: How infants change families.* Beverly Hills, CA: Sage.

LARSON, G. (1989). Cognitive correlates of general intelligence: Toward a process theory of G. *Intelligence, 13,* 5–31.

LARSON, R., & LAMPMAN-PETRAITIS, C. (1989). Daily emotional states as reported by children and adolescents. *Child Development, 60,* 1250–1260.

LAST, C. G., FRANCIS, G., HERSEN, M., KAZDIN, A. E., & STRAUSS, C. C. (1987). Separation anxiety and school phobia: A comparison using DSM-III criteria. *American Journal of Psychiatry, 144,* 653–657.

LAWRENCE, R. A. (1983). Early mothering by adolescents. In E. R. McAnarney (Ed.), *Premature adolescent pregnancy and parenthood* (pp. 207–218). New York: Grune & Stratton.

LAZAR, I., & DARLINGTON, R. (1982). Lasting effects of early education: a report from the Consortium for Longitudinal Studies. *Monographs of the Society for Research in Child Development, 47* (2–3, Serial No. 195).

LEACH, P. (1989). *Babyhood* (2nd ed.). New York: Knopf.

LEE, A. M. (1980). Child-rearing practices and motor performance of black and white children. *Research Quarterly for Exercise and Sport, 51,* 494–500.

LEE, C. L., & BATES, J. E. (1985). Mother-child interaction at age two years and perceived difficult temperament. *Child Development, 56,* 1314–1325.

LEE, V. E., BROOKS-GUNN, J., & SCHNUR, E. (1988). Does Head Start work? A 1-year follow-up of disadvantaged children attending Head Start, no preschool. *Developmental Psychology, 24,* 210–222.

LEETSMA, R., AUGUST, R. L., GEORGE, B., & PEAK, L. (1987). *Japanese education today: A report from the U.S. Study of Education in Japan.* Washington, DC: U.S. Government Printing Office.

LEHMAN, D. R., & NISBETT, R. E. (1990). A longitudinal study of the effects of undergraduate training on reasoning. *Developmental Psychology, 26,* 952–960.

LEIFER, M. (1980). *Psychological aspects of motherhood: A study of first pregnancy.* New York: Praeger.

LEMING, J. (1978). Intrapersonal variations in stage of moral reasoning among adolescents as a function of situational context. *Journal of Youth and Adolescence, 7,* 405–416.

LEMIRE, R. J., LOESER, J. D., LEECH, R. W., & ALVORD, E. C. (1975). *Normal and abnormal development of the human nervous system.* New York: Harper & Row.

LEMPERT, H. (1989). Animacy constraints on preschoolers' acquisition of syntax. *Child Development, 60,* 237–245.

LENNEBERG, E. H. (1967). *Biological foundations of language.* New York: Wiley.

LEONARD, M. F., RHYMES, J. P., & SOLNIT, A. J. (1986). Failure to thrive in infants: A family problem. *American Journal of Diseases of Children, 111,* 600–612.

LEPPER, M. R. (1985). Microcomputers in education: Motivational and social issues. *American Psychologist, 40,* 1–18.

LEPPER, M. R., & GURTNER, J-L. (1989). Children and computers: Approaching the twenty-first century. *American Psychologist, 44,* 170–178.

LERNER, J. W. (1989). Educational interventions in learning disabilities. *Journal of the American Academy of Child and Adolescent Psychiatry, 28,* 326–331.

LESTER, B. M. (1985). Introduction: There's more to crying than meets the ear. In B. M. Lester & C. F. Z. Boukydis (Eds.), *Infant crying* (pp. 1–27). New York: Plenum.

LESTER, B. M. (1987). Developmental outcome prediction from acoustic cry analysis in term and preterm infants. *Pediatrics, 80,* 529–534.

LESTER, B. M., & DREHER, M. (1989). Effects of marijuana use during pregnancy on newborn cry. *Child Development, 60,* 765–771.

LESTER, B. M., KOTELCHUCK, M., SPELKE, E., SELLERS, M. J., & KLEIN, R. E. (1974). Separation protest in Guatemalan infants: Cross-cultural findings. *Developmental Psychology, 10,* 79–85.

LEUNG, A. K. C. (1989). School phobia: Sometimes a child or teenager has a good reason. *Postgraduate Medicine, 85,* 281–289.

LEVENO, K. J., CUNNINGHAM, F. G., NELSON, S., ROARK, M., WILLIAMS, M. L., GUZICK, D., DOWLING, S., ROSENFELD, C. R., & BUCKLEY, A. (1986). A prospective comparison of selective and universal electronic fetal monitoring in 34,995 pregnancies. *New England Journal of Medicine, 315,* 615–619.

LEVIN, J. A., BORUTA, M. J., & VASCONCELLOS, M. T. (1983). Microcomputer-based environments for writing: A writer's assistant. In A. C. Wilkinson (Ed.), *Classroom computers and cognitive science* (pp. 219–232). New York: Academic Press.

LEVINE, L. E. (1983). Mine: Self-definition in 2-year-old boys. *Developmental Psychology, 19,* 544–549.

LEVY, G. D., & CARTER, D. B. (1989). Gender schema, gender constancy, and gender-role knowledge: The roles of cognitive factors in preschoolers' gender-role stereotype attributions. *Developmental Psychology, 25,* 444–449.

LEVY-SHIFF, R., & ISRAELASHVILI, R. (1988). Antecedents of fathering: Some further exploration. *Developmental Psychology, 24,* 434–440.

LEWIS, C. C. (1981). The effects of parental firm control: A reinterpretation of findings. *Psychological Bulletin, 90,* 547–563.

LEWIS, M. (1991). Ways of knowing: Objective self-awareness or consciousness. *Developmental Review, 11,* 231–243.

LEWIS, M. (1992). The self in self-conscious emotions (commentary on Self-evaluation in young children). *Monographs of the Society for Research in Child Development, 57* (Serial No. 226, No. 1).

LEWIS, M., & BROOKS-GUNN, J. (1979). *Social cognition and the acquisition of self.* New York: Plenum.

LEWIS, M., & McGURK, H. (1972). Evaluation of infant intelligence. *Science, 178,* 1174–1177.

LEWIS, M., & SULLIVAN, M. W. (1985). Infant intelligence and its assessment. In B. B. Wolman (Ed.), *Handbook of infant intelligence* (pp. 505–599). New York: Wiley.

LEWIS, M., SULLIVAN, M. W., STANGER, C., & WEISS, M. (1989). Self development and self-conscious emotions. *Child Development, 60,* 146–156.

LEWIS, M., SULLIVAN, M. W., & VASEN, A. (1987). Making faces: Age and emotion differences in the posing of emotional expressions. *Developmental Psychology, 23,* 690–697.

LIE, S. O. (1990). Children in the Norwegian health care system. *Pediatrics, 86* (6, Pt. 2), 1048–1052.

LIEBERT, R. M., & SPRAFKIN, J. (1988). *The early window: Effects of television on children and youth* (3rd ed.). New York: Pergamon Press.

LIGHT, P., & PERRET-CLERMONT, A.-N. (1989). Social context effects in learning and testing. In A. Gellatly, D. Rogers, & J. Sloboda (Eds.), *Cognition and social worlds* (pp. 99–112). Oxford: Clarendon Press.

LINDE, E. V., MORRONGIELLO, B. A., & ROVEE-COLLIER, C. (1985). Determinants of retention in 8-week-old infants. *Developmental Psychology, 21,* 601–613.

LINDELL, S. G. (1988). Education for childbirth: A time for change. *Journal of Obstetrics, Gynecology, and Neonatal Nursing, 17,* 108–112.

LINDGREN, G. (1976). Height, weight, and menarche in Swedish urban school children in relation to socio-economic and regional factors. *Annals of Human Biology, 3,* 501–528.

LINN, M. C. (1985). Fostering equitable consequences from computer learning environments. *Sex Roles, 13,* 229–240.

LINN, M. C., & HYDE, J. S. (1989). Gender, mathematics, and science. *Educational Researcher, 18,* 17–27.

LINN, M. C., & PETERSEN, A. C. (1985). Emergence and characterization of sex differences in spatial ability: A meta-analysis. *Child Development, 56,* 1479–1498.

LINN, S., LIEBERMAN, E., SCHOENBAUM, S. C., MONSON, R. R., STUBBLEFIELD, P. G., & RYAN, K. J. (1988). Adverse outcomes of pregnancy in women exposed to diethylstilbestrol in utero. *Journal of Reproductive Medicine, 33,* 3–7.

LIPSITT, L. P. (1982). Infant learning. In T. M. Field, A. Huston, H. C. Quay, L. Troll, & G. E. Finley (Eds.), *Review of human development* (pp. 62–78). New York: Wiley.

LIPSITT, L. P. (1986). Learning in infancy: Cognitive development in babies. *Journal of Pediatrics, 109,* 172–182.

LIPSITT, L. P. (1990). Learning and memory in infants. *Merrill-Palmer Quarterly, 36,* 53–66.

LIPSITT, L. P., STURNER, W. Q., & BURKE, P. (1979). Perinatal indicators and subsequent crib death. *Infant Behavior and Development, 2,* 325–328.

LITOWITZ, B. (1977). Learning to make definitions. *Journal of Child Language, 8,* 165–175.

LITTLE, B. B., SNELL, L. M., KLEIN, V. R., & GILSTRAP, L. C., III. (1989). Cocaine abuse during pregnancy: Maternal and fetal implications. *Obstetrics and Gynecology, 73,* 157–160.

LIVESLEY, W. J., & BROMLEY, D. B. (1973). *Person perception in childhood and adolescence.* London: Wiley.

LIVSON, N., & PESKIN, H. (1980). Perspectives on adolescence from longitudinal research. In J. Adelson (Ed.), *Handbook of adolescent psychology* (pp. 47–98). New York: Wiley.

LOCKE, J. (1892). Some thoughts concerning education. In R. H. Quick (Ed.), *Locke on education* (pp. 1–236). Cambridge, England: Cambridge University Press. (Original work published 1690)

LOEHLIN, J. C. (1989). Partitioning environmental and genetic contributions to behavioral development. *American Psychologist, 44,* 768–778.

LOEHLIN, J. C., WILLERMAN, L., & HORN, J. M. (1988). Human behavior genetics. *Annual Review of Psychology, 38,* 101–133.

LOONEY, M. A., & PLOWMAN, S. A. (1990). Passing rates of American children and youth on the FITNESSGRAM criterion-referenced physical fitness standards. *Research Quarterly of Exercise and Sport, 61,* 215–223.

LORENZ, K. (1952). *King Solomon's ring.* New York: Thomas Y. Crowell.

LORENZ, K. Z. (1943). Die angeborenen Formen möglicher Erfahrung. *Zeitschrift für Tierpsychologie, 5,* 235–409.

LOUIE, R., BRUNELLE, J. A., MAGGIORE, E. D., & BECK, R. W. (1990). Caries prevalence in Head Start children. *Journal of Public Health Dentistry, 50,* 299–305.

LOZOFF, B. (1989). Nutrition and behavior. *American Psychologist, 44,* 231–236.

LUMMIS, M., & STEVENSON, H. W. (1990). Gender differences in beliefs about achievement: A cross-cultural study. *Developmental Psychology, 26,* 254–263.

LURIA, A. R. (1973). *The working brain.* New York: Basic Books.

LUSTER, T., RHOADES, K., & HAAS, B. (1989). The relation between parental values and parenting behavior. *Journal of Marriage and the Family, 51,* 139–147.

LUTZ, P. (1983). The stepfamily: An adolescent perspective. *Family Relations, 32,* 367–375.

LYTTON, H., & ROMNEY, D. M. (1991). Parents' sex-related differential socialization of boys and girls: A meta-analysis. *Psychological Bulletin, 109,* 267–296.

MACCOBY, E. E. (1980). Sex differences and sex typing. In E. Maccoby (Ed.), *Social development: Psychological growth and the parent-child relationship* (pp. 203–250). San Diego: Harcourt Brace Jovanovich.

MACCOBY, E. E. (1984a). Middle childhood in the context of the family. In W. A. Collins (Ed.), *Development during middle childhood* (pp. 184–239). Washington, DC: National Academy Press.

MACCOBY, E. E. (1984b). Socialization and developmental change. *Child Development, 55,* 317–328.

MACCOBY, E. E. (1990). Gender and relationships. *American Psychologist, 45,* 513–520.

MACCOBY, E. E., & JACKLIN, C. N. (1987). Gender segregation in childhood. In E. H. Reese (Ed.), *Advances in child development and behavior* (Vol. 20, pp. 239–287). New York: Academic Press.

MACCOBY, E. E., & MARTIN, J. A. (1983). Socialization in the context of the family: Parent-child interaction. In E. M. Hetherington (Ed.), *Handbook of child psychology: Vol. 4. Socialization, personality, and social development* (4th ed., pp. 1–101). New York: Wiley.

MACFARLANE, J. (1975). Olfaction in the development of social preferences in the human neonate. In *Parent-infant interaction* (Ciba Foundation Symposium No. 33, pp. 103–117). Amsterdam: Elsevier.

MACFARLANE, J., SMITH, D. M., & GARROW, D. H. (1978). The relationship between mother and neonate. In S. Kitzinger (Ed.), *The place of birth* (pp. 185–200). New York: Oxford University Press.

MACFARLANE, J. W. (1971). From infancy to adulthood. In M. C. Jones, N. Bayley, J. W. Macfarlane, & M. P. Honzik (Eds.), *The course of human development* (pp. 406–410). Waltham, MA: Xerox College Publishing.

MACKINNON, C. E. (1989). An observational investigation of sibling interactions in married and divorced families. *Developmental Psychology, 25,* 36–44.

MACKLIN, M. C., & KOLBE, R. H. (1984). Sex role stereotyping in children's advertising: Current and past trends. *Journal of Advertising, 13,* 34–42.

MACMILLAN, D. L., KEOGH, B. K., & JONES, R. L. (1986). Special educational research on mildly handicapped learners. In M. C. Wittrock (Ed.), *Handbook of research on teaching* (3rd ed., pp. 686–724). New York: Macmillan.

MACQUIDDY, S. L., MAISE, S. J., & HAMILTON, S. B. (1987). Empathy and affective perspective taking skills in parent identified conduct disordered boys. *Journal of Clinical Child Psychology, 16,* 260–268.

MADDEN, N., & SLAVIN, R. (1983). Mainstreaming students with mild handicaps: Academic and social outcomes. *Review of Educational Research, 53,* 519–659.

MAHALSKI, P. A., SILVA, P. A., & SPEARS, G. F. S. (1985). Children's attachment to soft objects at bedtime, child rearing, and child development. *Journal of the American Academy of Child Psychiatry, 24,* 442–446.

MAHLER, M. S., PINE, F., & BERGMAN, A. (1975). *The psychological birth of the human infant.* New York: Basic Books.

MAIN, M., KAPLAN, N., & CASSIDY, J. (1985). Security in infancy, childhood, and adulthood: A move to the level of representation.

*Monographs of the Society for Research in Child Development, 50* (1–2, Serial No. 209).

MAIN, M., & SOLOMON, J. (1986). Discovery of an insecure-disorganized/disoriented attachment pattern. In T. B. Brazelton & M. W. Yogman (Eds.), *Affective development in infancy* (pp. 95–124). Norwood, NJ: Ablex.

MAKIN, J. W., & PORTER, R. H. (1989). Attractiveness of lactating females' breast odors to neonates. *Child Development, 60,* 803–810.

MAKINSON, C. (1985). The health consequences of teenage fertility. *Family Planning Perspectives, 17,* 132–139.

MALATESTA, C. Z., CULVER, C., TESMAN, J. R., & SHEPARD, B. (1989). The development of emotion expression during the first two years of life. *Monographs of the Society for Research in Child Development, 54* (1–2, Serial No. 219).

MALATESTA, C. Z., GRIGORYEV, P., LAMB, C., ALBIN, M., & CULVER, C. (1986). Emotion socialization and expressive development in preterm and full-term infants. *Child Development, 57,* 316–330.

MALATESTA, C. Z., & HAVILAND, J. M. (1982). Learning display rules: The socialization of emotion expression in infancy. *Child Development, 53,* 991–1003.

MALINA, R. M. (1975). *Growth and development: The first twenty years in man.* Minneapolis: Burgess.

MALINA, R. M. (1990). Physical growth and performance during the transitional years (9–16). In R. Montemayor, G. R. Adams, & T. P. Gullotta (Eds.), *From childhood to adolescence: A transitional period?* (pp. 41–62). Newbury Park, CA: Sage.

MALONEY, M., & KRANZ, R. (1991). *Straight talk about eating disorders.* New York: Facts on File.

MANCHESTER, D. (1988). Prehensile development: A contrast of mature and immature patterns. In J. E. Clark & J. H. Humphrey (Eds.), *Advances in motor development research* (pp. 165–199). New York: AMS Press.

MANGELSDORF, S., GUNNAR, M., KESTENBAUM, R., LANG, S., & ANDREAS, D. (1990). Infant proneness-to-distress temperament, maternal personality, and mother-infant attachment: Associations and goodness of fit. *Child Development, 61,* 820–831.

MANNINO, F. (1988). Neonatal complications of postterm gestation. *Journal of Reproductive Medicine, 33,* 271–276.

MARATSOS, M. (1983). Some current issues in the study of the acquisition of grammar. In J. H. Flavell & E. M. Markman (Eds.), *Handbook of child psychology: Vol. 3. Cognitive development* (4th ed., pp. 707–786). New York: Wiley.

MARATSOS, M. P., & CHALKLEY, M. A. (1980). The internal language of children's syntax: The ontogenesis and representation of syntactic categories. In K. Nelson (Ed.), *Children's language* (Vol. 2, pp. 127–214). New York: Gardner Press.

MARCELLA, S., & McDONALD, B. (1990). The infant walker: An unappreciated household hazard. *Connecticut Medicine, 54,* 127–129.

MARCIA, J. E. (1980). Identity in adolescence. In J. Adelson (Ed.), *Handbook of adolescent psychology* (pp. 159–187). New York: Wiley.

MARCIA, J. E. (1988). Common processes underlying ego identity, cognitive/moral development, and individuation. In D. K. Lapsley & F. P. Clark (Eds.), *Self, ego, and identity* (pp. 211–225). New York: Springer-Verlag.

MARCIA, J. E. (1989). Identity and intervention. *Journal of Adolescence, 12,* 401–410.

MARCUS, L. C. (1983). Preventing and treating toxoplasmosis. *Drug Therapy, 13,* 129–144.

MARION, R. W., WIZNIA, A. A., HUTCHEON, R. G., & RUBINSTEIN, A. (1986). Human T-cell lymphotropic virus Type III (HTLV-III) embryopathy. *American Journal of Diseases of Children, 140,* 638–640.

MARKMAN, E. M. (1979). Realizing that you don't understand: Elementary school children's awareness of inconsistencies. *Child Development, 50,* 643–655.

MARKMAN, E. M. (1989). *Categorization and naming in children.* Cambridge, MA: MIT Press.

MARKOVITS, H., & VACHON, R. (1989). Reasoning with contrary-to-fact propositions. *Journal of Experimental Child Psychology, 47,* 398–412.

MARKOVITS, H., SCHLEIFER, M., & FORTIER, L. (1989). Development of elementary deductive reasoning in young children. *Developmental Psychology, 25,* 787–793.

MARKOVITS, H., & VACHON, R. (1990). Conditional reasoning, representation, and level of abstraction. *Developmental Psychology, 26,* 942–951.

MARSH, D. T., SERAFICA, F. C., & BARENBOIM, C. (1981). Interrelationships among perspective taking, interpersonal problem solving, and interpersonal functioning. *Journal of Genetic Psychology, 138,* 37–48.

MARSH, H. W. (1989a). Age and sex effects in multiple dimensions of self-concept: preadolescence to early adulthood. *Journal of Educational Psychology, 81,* 417–430.

MARSH, H. W. (1989b). Sex differences in the development of verbal and mathematics constructs: The high school and beyond study. *American Educational Research Journal, 26,* 191–225.

MARSH, H. W., SMITH, I. D., & BARNES, J. (1985). Multidimensional self-concepts: Relations with sex and academic achievement. *Journal of Educational Psychology, 77,* 581–596.

MARSHALL, W. A., & TANNER, J. M. (1969). Variations in the pattern of pubertal changes in girls. *Archives of Disease in Childhood, 44,* 291–303.

MARTIN, C. L. (1989). Children's use of gender-related information in making social judgments. *Developmental Psychology, 25,* 80–88.

MARTIN, C. L., & HALVERSON, C. F. (1981). A schematic processing model of sex typing and stereotyping in children. *Child Development, 52,* 1119–1134.

MARTIN, C. L., & HALVERSON, C. F. (1987). The role of cognition in sex role acquisition. In D. B. Carter (Ed.), *Current conceptions of sex roles and sex typing: Theory and research* (pp. 123–137). New York: Praeger.

MARTIN, C. L., & LITTLE, J. K. (1990). The relation of gender understanding to children's sex-typed preferences and gender stereotypes. *Child Development, 61,* 1427–1439.

MARTIN, G. B., & CLARK, R. D., III. (1982). Distress crying in neonates: Species and peer specificity. *Developmental Psychology, 18,* 3–9.

MARTIN, J. A. (1981). A longitudinal study of the consequences of early mother-infant interaction: A microanalytic approach. *Monographs of the Society for Research in Child Development, 46* (3, Serial No. 190).

MARTIN, J. B. (1987). Molecular genetics: Applications to the clinical neurosciences. *Science, 298,* 765–772.

MARTIN, R. M. (1975). Effects of familiar and complex stimuli on infant attention. *Developmental Psychology, 11,* 178–185.

MARTIN, S. L., RAMEY, C. T., & RAMEY, S. (1990). The prevention of intellectual impairment in children of impoverished families: Findings of a randomized trial of educational day care. *American Journal of Public Health, 80,* 844–847.

MASCIELLO, A. L. (1990). Anesthesia for neonatal circumcision: Local anesthesia is better than dorsal penile nerve block. *Obstetrics and Gynecology, 75,* 834–838.

MASSAD, C. M. (1981). Sex role identity and adjustment during adolescence. *Child Development, 52,* 1290–1298.

MATAS, L., AREND, R., & SROUFE, L. A. (1978). Continuity of adaptation in the second year: The relationship between quality of attachment and later competence. *Child Development, 49,* 547–556.

MATHENY, A. P., JR. (1987). Psychological characteristics of childhood accidents. *Journal of Social Issues, 43,* 45–60.

MATHEWS, K. A., & ANGULO, J. (1980). Measurement of the Type A behavior pattern in children: Assessment of children's competitiveness, impatience, anger, and aggression. *Child Development, 51,* 466–475.

MATUTE-BIANCHI, M. E. (1986). Ethnic identities and patterns of school success and failure among Mexican-descent and Japanese-American students in a California high school: An ethnographic analysis. *American Journal of Education, 95,* 233–255.

MAURER, D. (1985). Infants' perception of facedness. In T. Fields & N. Fox (Eds.), *Social perception in infants* (pp. 73–100). Norwood, NJ: Ablex.

McCABE, A. E., & PETERSON, C. (1988). A comparison of adults' versus children's spontaneous use of *because* and *so. Journal of Genetic Psychology, 149,* 257–268.

McCABE, A. E., & SIEGEL, L. S. (1987). The stability of training effects In young children's class inclusion reasoning. *Merrill-Palmer Quarterly, 33,* 187–194.

McCABE, M. P. (1984). Toward a theory of adolescent dating. *Adolescence, 19,* 159–170.

McCALL, R. B., APPELBAUM, M. I., & HOGARTY, P. S. (1973). Developmental changes in mental performance. *Monographs of the Society for Research in Child Development, 42* (3, Serial No. 171).

MCCARTNEY, K. (1984). The effect of quality of day care environment upon children's language development. *Developmental Psychology, 20*, 244–260.

MCCARTNEY, K., SCARR, S., PHILLIPS, D., & GRAJEK, S. (1985). Day care as intervention: Comparisons of varying quality programs. *Journal of Applied Developmental Psychology, 6*, 247–260.

MCCLAIN, C. S. (1987). Some social network differences between women choosing home and hospital birth. *Human Organization, 46*, 146–152.

MCCONAGHY, M. J. (1979). Gender permanence and the genital basis of gender: Stages in the development of constancy of gender identity. *Child Development, 50*, 1223–1226.

MCCORMICK, M. C., GORTMAKER, S. L., & SOBOL, A. M. (1990). Very low birth weight children: Behavior problems and school difficulty in a national sample. *Journal of Pediatrics, 117*, 687–693.

MCCORMICK, C. M., & MAURER, D. M. (1988). Unimanual hand preferences in 6-month-olds: Consistency and relation to familial-handedness. *Infant Behavior and Development, 11*, 21–29.

MCGEE, L. M., & RICHGELS, D. J. (1989, December). "K is Kristen's": Learning the alphabet from a child's perspective. *The Reading Teacher, 43* (3), 216–225.

MCGEE, L. M., & RICHGELS, D. J. (1990). *Literacy's beginnings: Supporting young readers and writers.* Boston: Allyn and Bacon.

MCGHEE, P. E. (1979). *Humor: Its origin and development.* San Francisco: Freeman.

MCGINTY, M. J., & ZAFRAN, E. I. (1988). *Surrogacy: Constitutional and legal issues.* Cleveland, OH: The Ohio Academy of Trial Lawyers.

MCGOWAN, J. D., ALTMAN, R. E., & KANTO, W. R., JR. (1988). Neonatal withdrawal symptoms after chronic maternal ingestion of caffeine. *Southern Medical Journal, 81*, 1092–1094.

MCGROARTY, M. (1992, March). The societal context of bilingual education. *Educational Researcher, 21* (2), 7–9.

MCGUINNESS, D., & PRIBRAM, K. H. (1980). The neuropsychology of attention: Emotional and motivational controls. In M. C. Wittcock (Ed.), *The brain and psychology* (pp. 95–139). New York: Academic Press.

MCGUIRE, E. J., & SAVASHINO, J. A. (1984). Urodynamic studies in enuresis and the non-neurogenic-neurogenic bladder. *Journal of Neurology, 132*, 299–302.

MCGUIRE, J. (1988). Gender stereotypes of parents with two-year-olds and beliefs about gender differences in behavior. *Sex Roles, 19*, 233–240.

MCHALE, S. M., BARTKO, W. T., CROUTER, A. C., & PERRY-JENKINS, M. (1990). Children's housework and psychosocial functioning: The mediating effects of parents' sex-role behaviors and attitudes. *Child Development, 61*, 1413–1426.

MCHALE, S. M., & PAWLETKO, T. M. (1992). Differential treatment of siblings in two family contexts. *Child Development, 63*, 68–81.

MCKENNA, M. C., ROBINSON, R. D., & MILLER, J. W. (1990, November). Whole language: A research agenda for the nineties. *Educational Researcher, 19* (8), 3–6.

MCKENZIE, B., & OVER, R. (1983). Young infants fail to imitate facial and manual gestures. *Infant Behavior and Development, 6*, 85–95.

MCKNIGHT, C. C., CROSSWHITE, F. J., DOSSEY, J. A., KIFER, E., SWAFFORD, J. O., TRAVERS, K. J., & COONEY, T. J. (1987). *The underachieving curriculum: Assessing U.S. school mathematics from an international perspective.* Champaign, IL: Stipes.

MCKUSICK, V. A. (1988). *Mendelian inheritance in man: Catalogs of autosomal dominant, autosomal recessive, and X-linked phenotypes* (7th ed.). Baltimore: The Johns Hopkins University Press.

MCLOYD, V. C. (1990). The impact of economic hardship on black families and children: Psychological distress, parenting, and socioemotional development. *Child Development, 61*, 311–346.

MCMANUS, I. C., SIK, G., COLE, D. R., MELLON, A. F., WONG, J., & KLOSS, J. (1988). The development of handedness in children. *British Journal of Developmental Psychology, 6*, 257–273.

MCNAMEE, S., & PETERSON, J. (1986). Young children's distributive justice reasoning, behavior, and role taking: Their consistency and relationship. *Journal of Genetic Psychology, 146*, 399–404.

MCWILLIAMS, M. (1986). *The parents' nutrition book.* New York: Wiley.

MEAD, G. H. (1934). *Mind, self, and society.* Chicago: University of Chicago Press.

MEAD, M. (1928). *Coming of age in Samoa.* Ann Arbor, MI: Morrow.

MEAD, M., & NEWTON, N. (1967). Cultural patterning of perinatal behavior. In S. Richardson & A. Guttmacher (Eds.), *Childbearing: Its social and psychological aspects* (pp. 142–244). Baltimore: Williams & Wilkins.

MEANY, M. J., STEWART, J., & BEATTY, W. W. (1985). Sex differences in social play: The socialization of sex roles. In J. S. Rosenblatt, C. Bear, C. M. Busnell, & P. Slater (Eds.), *Advances in the study of behavior* (Vol. 15, pp. 1–58). New York: Academic Press.

MEDNICK, B. R., BAKER, R. L., & SUTTON-SMITH, B. (1979). Teenage pregnancy and perinatal mortality. *Journal of Youth and Adolescence, 8*, 343–357.

MEDRICH, E. A., ROSEN, J., RUBIN, V., & BUCKLEY, S. (1982). *The serious business of growing up.* Berkeley: University of California Press.

MEEHAN, A. M. (1984). A meta-analysis of sex differences in formal operational thought. *Child Development, 55*, 1110–1124.

MEILMAN, P. W. (1979). Cross-sectional age changes in ego identity status during adolescence. *Developmental Psychology, 15*, 230–231.

MELTZOFF, A. N. (1988a). Infant imitation after a 1-week delay: Long-term memory for novel acts and multiple stimuli. *Developmental Psychology, 24*, 470–476.

MELTZOFF, A. N. (1988b). Infant imitation and memory: Nine-month-olds in immediate and deferred tests. *Child Development, 59*, 217–255.

MELTZOFF, A. N., & BORTON, R. W. (1979). Intermodal matching by human neonates. *Nature, 282*, 403–404.

MELTZOFF, A. N., & MOORE, M. K. (1977). Imitation of facial and manual gestures by human neonates. *Science, 198*, 75–78.

MELTZOFF, A. N., & MOORE, M. K. (1989). Imitation in newborn infants: Exploring the range of gestures imitated and the underlying mechanisms. *Developmental Psychology, 25*, 954–962.

MENIG-PETERSON, C. L. (1975). The modification of communicative behavior in preschool-aged children as a function of the listener's perspective. *Child Development, 46*, 1015–1018.

MERCER, J. R. (1979). *System of Multicultural Pluralistic Assessment: Technical manual.* New York: Psychological Corporation.

MEREDITH, N. V. (1978). *Human body growth in the first ten years of life.* Columbia, SC: State Printing.

MERVIS, C. (1985). On the existence of prelinguistic categories: A case study. *Infant Behavior and Development, 8*, 293–300.

MERVIS, C. B., & CRISAFI, M. A. (1982). Order of acquisition of subordinate-, basic-, and superordinate-level categories. *Child Development, 53*, 258–266.

MICHAELS, G. Y. (1988). Motivational factors in the decision and timing of pregnancy. In G. Y. Michaels & W. A. Goldberg (Eds.), *The transition to parenthood: Current theory and research* (pp. 23–61). New York: Cambridge University Press.

MICHALS, K., AZEN, C., ACOSTA, P., KOCH, R., & MATALON, R. (1988). Blood phenylalanine levels and intelligence of 10-year-old children with PKU in the National Collaborative Study. *Journal of the American Dietetic Association, 88*, 1226–1229.

MICHEL, C. (1989). Radiation embryology. *Experientia, 45*, 69–77.

MICHELI, L. J., & KLEIN, J. D. (1991). Sports injuries in children and adolescents. *British Journal of Sports Medicine, 25*, 6–9.

MIDGLEY, C., FELDLAUFER, H., & ECCLES, J. S. (1989). Student/teacher relations and attitudes toward mathematics before and after the transition to junior high school. *Child Development, 60*, 981–992.

MILICH, R., & PELHAM, W. E. (1986). The effects of sugar ingestion on the classroom and play group behavior of attention deficit disordered boys. *Journal of Consulting and Clinical Psychology, 54*, 714–718.

MILLER, B. C., & OLSON, T. D. (1988). Sexual attitudes and behavior of high school students in relation to background and contextual factors. *Journal of Sex Research, 24*, 194–200.

MILLER, C. A. (1987). A review of maternity care programs in Western Europe. *Family Planning Perspectives, 19*, 207–211.

MILLER, K. F., & BAILLARGEON, R. (1990). Length and distance: Do preschoolers think that occlusion brings things together? *Developmental Psychology, 26*, 103–114.

MILLER, N., & MARUYAMA, G. (1976). Ordinal position and peer popularity. *Journal of Personality and Social Psychology, 33*, 123–131.

MILLER, P. H. (1989). *Theories of developmental psychology* (2nd ed.). New York: Freeman.

MILLER, P. H., & BIGI, L. (1979). The development of children's understanding of attention. *Merrill-Palmer Quarterly, 25*, 235–250.

MILLER, P. H., & ZALENSKI, R. (1982). Preschoolers' knowledge about attention. *Developmental Psychology, 18,* 871–875.

MILLER, S. A. (1987). *Developmental research methods.* Englewood Cliffs, NJ: Prentice-Hall.

MILLER-JONES, D. (1989). Culture and testing. *American Psychologist, 44,* 360–366.

MILLS, J., HARLAP, S., & HARLEY, E. E. (1981). Should coitus late in pregnancy be discouraged? *Lancet, 2,* 136–138.

MILLS, R., & GRUSEC, J. (1989). Cognitive, affective, and behavioral consequences of praising altruism. *Merrill-Palmer Quarterly, 35,* 299–326.

MILLSTEIN, S. G., & IRWIN, C. E. (1987). Concepts of health and illness: Different constructs or variations on a theme? *Health Psychology, 6,* 515–524.

MILLSTEIN, S. G., & IRWIN, C. E. (1988). Accidentrelated behaviors in adolescents: A biosocial view. *Alcohol, Drugs, and Driving, 4,* 21–29.

MILLSTEIN, S. G., & LITT, I. F. (1990). Adolescent health. In S. S. Feldman & G. R. Elliott (Eds.), *At the threshold: The developing adolescent* (pp. 431–456). Cambridge, MA: Harvard University Press.

MINKOFF, H., DEEPAK, N., MENEZ, R., & FIKRIG, S. (1987). Pregnancies resulting in infants with acquired immunodeficiency syndrome of AIDS-related complex: Follow-up of mothers, children, and subsequently born siblings. *Obstetrics and Gynecology, 69,* 288–291.

MINUCHIN, P. P. (1988). Relationships within the family: A systems perspective on development. In R. A. Hinde & J. Stevenson-Hinde (Eds.), *Relationships within families: Mutual influences* (pp. 7–26). New York: Oxford University Press.

MINUCHIN, P. P., & SHAPIRO, E. K. (1983). The school as a context for social development. In E. M. Hetherington (Ed.), *Handbook of child psychology: Vol. 4. Socialization, personality, and social development* (4th ed., pp. 197–274). New York: Wiley.

MISCHEL, W., & LIEBERT, R. M. (1966). Effects of discrepancies between observed and imposed reward criteria on their acquisition and transmission. *Journal of Personality and Social Psychology, 3,* 45–53.

MISCIONE, J. L., MARVIN, R. S., O'BRIEN, R. G., & GREENBERG, M. T. (1978). A developmental study of preschool children's understanding of the words "know" and "guess." *Child Development, 48,* 1107–1113.

MIYAKE, K., CHEN, S., & CAMPOS, J. J. (1985). Infant temperament, mother's mode of interaction, and attachment in Japan: An interim report. In I Bretherton & E. Waters (Eds.), Growing points in attachment theory and research. *Monographs of the Society for Research in Child Development, 50* (1–2, Serial No. 209).

MIZE, J., & LADD, G. W. (1990). A cognitive-social learning approach to social skill training with low-status preschool children. *Developmental Psychology, 26,* 388–397.

MOERK, E. L. (1989). The LAD was a lady and the tasks were ill-defined. *Developmental Review, 9,* 21–57.

MOFFITT, T. E., CASPI, A., BELSKY, J., & SILVA, P. A. (1992). Childhood experience and the onset of menarche: A test of a sociobiological model. *Child Development, 63,* 47–58.

MOILANEN, I. (1989). The growth, development, and education of Finnish twins: A longitudinal follow-up study in a birth cohort from pregnancy to nineteen years of age. *Growth, Development and Aging, 18,* 302–306.

MONROE, S., GOLDMAN, P., & SMITH, V. E. (1988). *Brothers: Black and poor—a true story of courage and survival.* New York: Morrow.

MONTEMAYOR, R., & EISEN, M. (1977). The development of self-conceptions from childhood to adolescence. *Developmental Psychology, 13,* 314–319.

MOORE, C., BRYANT, D., & FURROW, D. (1989). Mental terms and the development of certainty. *Child Development, 60,* 167–171.

MOORE, E. G. J. (1986). Family socialization and the IQ test performance of traditionally and transracially adopted black children. *Developmental Psychology, 22,* 317–326.

MOORE, K. L. (1989). *Before we are born* (3rd ed.). Philadelphia: Saunders.

MOORE, K., PETERSON, J., & FURSTENBERG, F. F., JR. (1986). Parental attitudes and the occurrence of early sexual activity. *Journal of Marriage and the Family, 48,* 777–782.

MOOREHOUSE, M. J. (1991). Linking maternal employment patterns to mother-child activities and children's school competence. *Developmental Psychology, 27,* 295–303.

MORRIS, R., & KRATOCHWILL, T. (1983). *Treating children's fears and phobias: A behavioral approach.* Elmsford, NY: Pergamon.

MORRONGIELLO, B. A. (1986). Infants' perception of multiple-group auditory patterns. *Infant Behavior and Development, 9,* 307–319.

MORRONGIELLO, B. A. (1988). Infants' localization of sounds in the horizontal plane: Estimates of minimum audible angle. *Developmental Psychology, 24,* 8–13.

MOTT, F. L., & MARSIGLIO, W. (1985). Early childbearing and completion of high school. *Family Planning Perspectives, 17,* 234–237.

MOTT, S. R., JAMES, S. R., & SPERHAC, A. M. (1990). *Nursing care of children and families.* Redwood City, CA: Addison-Wesley.

MULLIS, I. V. S., DOSSEY, J. A., FOERTSCH, M. A., JONES, L. R., & GENTILE, C. A. (1991). *Trends in academic progress.* Washington, DC: U.S. Government Printing Office.

MULLIS, I. V. S., DOSSEY, J. A., OWEN, E. H., & PHILLIPS, G. W. (1991). *The state of mathematics achievement: Executive summary* (NAEP's 1990 assessment of the nation and the trial assessment of the states). Princeton, NJ: Educational Testing Service.

MUNRO, G., & ADAMS, G. R. (1977). Ego identity formation in college students and working youth. *Developmental Psychology, 13,* 523–524.

MURRAY, A. D. (1985). Aversiveness is in the mind of the beholder. In B. M. Lester & C. F. Z. Boukydis (Eds.), *Infant crying* (pp. 217–239). New York: Plenum.

MURRAY, A. D., DOLBY, R. M., NATION, R. L., & THOMAS, D. B. (1981). Effects of epidural anesthesia on newborns and their mothers. *Child Development, 52,* 71–82.

MURRETT-WAGSTAFF, S., & MOORE, S. G. (1989). The Hmong in America: Infant behavior and rearing practices. In J. K. Nugent, B. M. Lester, & T. B. Brazelton (Eds.), *Biology, culture, and development* (Vol. 1, pp. 319–339). Norwood, NJ: Ablex.

MUSSEN, P., & EISENBERG-BERG, N. (1977). *Roots of caring, sharing, and helping.* San Francisco: Freeman.


NAEYE, R. L., & PETERS, E. C. (1984). Mental development of children whose mothers smoked during pregnancy. *Obstetrics and Gynecology, 64,* 601–607.

NAEYE, R. L., BLANC, W., & PAUL, C. (1973). Effects of maternal nutrition on the human fetus. *Pediatrics, 52,* 494–503.

NANEZ, J. (1987). Perception of impending collision in 3- to 6-week-old infants. *Infant Behavior and Development, 11,* 447–463.

NASH, J. E., & PERSAUD, T. V. N. (1988). Embryopathic risks of cigarette smoking. *Experimental Pathology, 33,* 65–73.

NASTASI, B. K., & CLEMENTS, D. H. (1991). Research on cooperative learning: Implications for practice. *School Psychology Review, 20,* 110–131.

NATAPOFF, J. (1978). Children's views of health: A developmental study. *American Journal of Public Health, 68,* 995–1000.

NATIONAL ASSOCIATION FOR THE EDUCATION OF YOUNG CHILDREN (1984). *Accreditation criteria and procedures of the National Academy of Early Childhood Programs.* Washington, DC: Author.

NATIONAL CENTER FOR HEALTH STATISTICS (1991). *Advance Report of Final Natality Statistics* (Vol. 42). Washington, DC: U.S. Government Printing Office.

NATIONAL COMMISSION FOR THE PROTECTION OF HUMAN SUBJECTS (1977). *Report and recommendations: Research involving children.* Washington, DC: U.S. Government Printing Office.

NATIONAL COMMISSION TO PREVENT INFANT MORTALITY (1988). *Death before life: The tragedy of infant mortality.* Washington, DC: Author.

NATIONAL COMMITTEE FOR INJURY PREVENTION AND CONTROL (1989). *Injury prevention: Meeting the challenge.* New York: Oxford University Press.

NEAL, J. H. (1983). Children's understanding of their parents' divorces. In L. A. Kurdek (Ed.), *New directions for child development* (Vol. 19, pp. 3–14). San Francisco: Jossey-Bass.

NEEDLEMAN, H. L., GUNNOE, C., LEVITON, A., REED, R., PERESIE, H., MAHER, C., & BARRETT, B. S. (1979). Deficits in psychologic and classroom performance of children with elevated dentine lead levels. *New England Journal of Medicine, 300,* 689–695.

NEEDLEMAN, H. L., SCHELL, A., BELLINGER, D., LEVITON, A., & ALLRED, E. N. (1990). The long-term effects of exposure to low doses of lead in childhood. *New England Journal of Medicine, 322,* 83–88.

NELSON, J., & ABOUD, F. E. (1985). The resolution of social conflict between friends. *Child Development, 56,* 1009–1017.

NELSON, K. (1973). Structure and strategy in learning to talk. *Monographs of the Society for Research in Child Development, 38* (1–2, Serial No. 149).

NELSON, K. (1981). Individual differences in language development: Implications for development and language. *Developmental Psychology, 17,* 170–187.

NELSON, K., & GRUENDEL, J. (1981). Generalized event representations: Basic building blocks of cognitive development. In M. Lamb & A. Brown (Eds.), *Advances in developmental psychology* (Vol. 1, pp. 131–158). Hillsdale, NJ: Erlbaum.

NELSON, K. E., DINNINGER, M., BONVILLIAN, J., KAPLAN, B., & BAKER, N. (1984). Maternal adjustments and non-adjustments as related to children's linguistic advances and language acquisition theories. In A. Pelligrini & T. Yawkey (Eds.), *The development of oral and written languages: Readings in developmental and applied linguistics* (pp. 31–56). Norwood, NJ: Ablex.

NELSON-LE GALL, S. A. (1985). Motive-outcome matching and outcome foreseeability: Effects on attribution of intentionality and moral judgments. *Developmental Psychology, 21,* 332–337.

NETLEY, C. T. (1986). Summary overview of behavioural development in individuals with neonatally identified X and Y aneuploidy. *Birth Defects, 22,* 293–306.

NEWACHECK, P. W., & STARFIELD, B. (1988). Morbidity and use of ambulatory care services among poor and nonpoor children. *American Journal of Public Health, 78,* 927–933.

NEWBORG, J., STOCK, J. R., & WNEK, L. (1984). *Battelle Developmental Inventory.* Allen, TX: LINC Associates, Inc.

NEWCOMB, M. D., & BENTLER, P. M. (1988). Consequences of adolescent substance use on young adult health status and utilization of health services: A structural equation model over four years. *Social Science and Medicine, 24,* 71–82.

NEWCOMB, M. D., & BENTLER, P. M. (1989). Substance use and abuse among children and teenagers. *American Psychologist, 44,* 242–248.

NEWCOMB, M. D., MADDAHIAN, E., & BENTLER, P. M. (1986). Risk factors for drug use among adolescents: Concurrent and longitudinal analyses. *American Journal of Public Health, 76,* 525–531.

NEWPORT, E. L., GLEITMAN, H., & GLEITMAN, L. R. (1977). Mother, I'd rather do it myself: Some effects and non-effects of maternal speech style. In C. A. Ferguson & C. E. Snow (Eds.), *Talking to children* (pp. 109–149). New York: Cambridge University Press.

NICHOLLS, A. L., & KENNEDY, J. M. (1992). Drawing development: From similarity of features to direction. *Child Development, 63,* 227–241.

NIDORF, J. F. (1985). Mental health and refugee youths: A model for diagnostic training. In T. C. Owen (Ed.), *Southeast Asian mental health: Treatment, prevention, services, training, and research* (pp. 391–427). Washington, DC: National Institute of Mental Health.

NILSSON, L., & HAMBERGER, L. (1990). *A child is born.* New York: Delacorte.

NORBECK, J. S., & TILDEN, V. P. (1983). Life stress, social support, and emotional disequilibrium in complications of pregnancy: A prospective, multivariate study. *Journal of Health and Social Behavior, 24,* 30–46.

NOTTELMANN, E. D. (1987). Competence and self-esteem during transition from childhood to adolescence. *Developmental Psychology, 23,* 30–46.

NOTTELMANN, E. D., INOFF-GERMAIN, G., SUSMAN, E. J., & CHROUSOS, G. P. (1990). Hormones and behavior at puberty. In J. Bancroft & J. M. Reinisch (Eds.), *Adolescence and puberty* (pp. 88–123). New York: Oxford University Press.

NOTZON, F. C. (1990). International differences in the use of obstetric interventions. *Journal of the American Medical Association, 263,* 3286–3291.

NOVICK, B. E. (1989). Pediatric AIDS: A medical overview. In J. M. Seibert & R. A. Olson (Eds.), *Children, adolescents, and AIDS* (pp. 1–23). Lincoln, NB: University of Nebraska Press.

NOWAKOWSKI, R. S. (1987). Basic concepts of CNS development. *Child Development, 58,* 568–595.

NUCCI, L. P., & TURIEL, E. (1978). Social interactions and the development of social concepts in preschool children. *Child Development, 49,* 400–407.

NUCKOLLS, K. B., CASSEL, J., & KAPLAN, B. H. (1972). Psychosocial assets, life crisis, and the prognosis of pregnancy. *American Journal of Epidemiology, 95,* 431–441.

OAKES, J., GAMORAN, A., & PAGE, R. N. (1992). Curriculum differentiation: Opportunities, outcomes, and meanings. In P. W. Jackson (Ed.), *Handbook of research on curriculum* (pp. 570–608). New York: Macmillan.

OATES, R. K. (1984). Similarities and differences between nonorganic failure to thrive and deprivation dwarfism. *Child Abuse and Neglect, 8,* 438–445.

OATES, R. K., PEACOCK, A., & FORREST, D. (1985). Long-term effects of nonorganic failure to thrive. *Pediatrics, 75,* 36–40.

OBERG, C. N. (1988, Spring). Children and the uninsured. *Social Policy Report of the Society for Research in Child Development, 3* (No. 1).

OBLER, L. K. (1989). Language beyond childhood. In J. Berko Gleason (Ed.), *The development of language* (pp. 275–301). Columbus, OH: Merrill.

O'CONNOR, M., FOCH, T., SHERRY, T., & PLOMIN, R. (1980). A twin study of specific behavioral problems of socialization as viewed by parents. *Journal of Abnormal Child Psychology, 8,* 189–199.

OFFER, D. (1988). *The teenage world: Adolescents' self-image in ten countries.* New York: Plenum.

OFFICE OF EDUCATIONAL RESEARCH AND IMPROVEMENT (1988). *Youth indicators 1988: Trends in the well-being of American youth.* Washington, DC: U.S. Government Printing Office.

OGBU, J. (1988). Black education: A cultural-ecological perspective. In H. P. McAdoo (Ed.), *Black families* (pp. 169–186). Beverly Hills, CA: Sage.

OLLER, D. K., & EILERS, R. E. (1988). The role of audition in infant babbling. *Child Development, 59,* 441–449.

OMER, H., & EVERLY, G. S. (1988). Psychological factors in preterm labor: Critical review and theoretical synthesis. *American Journal of Psychiatry, 145,* 1507–1513.

OPIE, I., & OPIE, P. (1969). *Children's games in street and playground.* Oxford: Clarendon Press.

ORNSTEIN, P. A., NAUS, M. J., & LIBERTY, C. (1975). Rehearsal and organizational processes in children's memory. *Child Development, 46,* 818–830.

OSHERSON, D. N., & MARKMAN, E. M. (1975). Language and the ability to evaluate contradictions and tautologies. *Cognition, 2,* 213–226.

O'SULLIVAN, M., FUMIA, F., HOLSINGER, K., & MCLEOD, A. G. W. (1981). Vaginal delivery after cesarean section. *Clinics in Perinatology, 8,* 131–143.

OTAKI, M., DURRETT, M., RICHARDS, P., NYQUIST, L., & PENNEBAKER, J. (1986). Maternal and infant behavior in Japan and America: A partial replication. *Journal of Cross-Cultural Psychology, 17,* 251–268.

OWEN, M. T., & COX, M. (1988). Maternal employment and the transition to parenthood. In A. E. Gottfried & A. W. Gottfried (Eds.), *Maternal employment and children's development: Longitudinal research* (pp. 85–119). New York: Plenum.

OWENS, T. (1982). Experience-based career education: Summary and implications of research and evaluation findings. *Child and Youth Services Journal, 4,* 77–91.

PADGHAM, J. J., & BLYTH, D. A. (1990). Dating during adolescence. In R. M. Lerner, A. C. Petersen, & J. Brooks-Gunn (Eds.), *The encyclopedia of adolescence* (Vol. 1, pp. 196–198). New York: Garland.

PADILLA, M. L., & LANDRETH, G. L. (1989). Latchkey children: A review of the literature. *Child Welfare, 68,* 445–454.

PAGE, D. C., MOSHER, R., SIMPSON, E. M., FISHER, E. M. C., MARDON, G., POLLACK, J., MCGILLIVRAY, B., DE LA CHAPELLE, A., & BROWN, L. G. (1987). The sex-determining region of the human Y chromosome encodes a finger protein. *Cell, 51,* 1091–1104.

PAGE, E. B., & GRANDON, G. M. (1979). Family configuration and mental ability: Two theories contrasted with U.S. data. *American Educational Research Journal, 16,* 257–272.

PAIKOFF, R. L., & BROOKS-GUNN, J. (1991). Do parent-child relationships change during puberty? *Psychological Bulletin, 110,* 47–66.

PALKOVITZ, R., & COPES, M. (1988). Changes in attitudes, beliefs and expectations associated with the transition to parenthood. *Marriage and Family Review, 6,* 183–199.

PALLIKKATHAYIL, L., & FLOOD, M. (1991). Adolescent suicide: Prevention, intervention, and postvention. *Nursing Clinics of North America, 26,* 623–634.

PAPINI, D. R., MICKA, J. C., & BARNETT, J. K. (1989). Perceptions of intrapsychic and extrapsychic functioning as bases of adolescent ego identity statuses. *Journal of Adolescent Research, 4,* 462–482.

PAREKH, U. C., PHERWANI, A., UDANI, P. M., & MUKHERJEE, S. (1970). Brain weight and head circumference in fetus, infant and children of different nutritional and socio-economic groups. *Indian Pediatrics, 7,* 347–358.

PARIS, S. G., & NEWMAN, R. S. (1990). Developmental aspects of self-regulated learning. *Educational Psychologist, 25,* 87–102.

PARK, K. A., & WATERS, E. (1989). Security of attachment and preschool friendships. *Child Development, 60,* 1076–1081.

PARKE, R. D. (1977). Punishment in children: Effects, side effects, and alternative control strategies. In H. Hom, Jr., & A. Robinson (Eds.), *Early childhood education: A psychological perspective* (pp. 71–97). New York: Academic Press.

PARKE, R. D., & COLLMER, C. W. (1975). Child abuse: An interdisciplinary analysis. In E. M. Hetherington (Ed.), *Review of child development research* (Vol. 5, pp. 264–283). Chicago: University of Chicago Press.

PARKE, R. D., & SLABY, R. G. (1983). The development of aggression. In E. M. Hetherington (Ed.), *Handbook of child psychology: Vol. 4. Socialization, personality, and social development* (Vol. 4, pp. 547–641). New York: Wiley.

PARKE, R. D., & TINSLEY, B. R. (1981). The father's role in infancy: Determinants of involvement in caregiving and play. In M. E. Lamb (Ed.), *The role of the father in child development* (pp. 429–458). New York: Wiley.

PARKE, R. D., & WALTERS, R. H. (1967). Some factors determining the efficacy of punishment for inducing response inhibition. *Monographs of the Society for Research in Child Development, 32* (1, Serial No. 109).

PARKER, J. G., & ASHER, S. R. (1987). Peer relations and later personal adjustment: Are low-accepted children at risk? *Psychological Bulletin, 102,* 357–389.

PARMELEE, A., WENNER, W., AKIYAMA, Y., STERN, E., & FLESCHER, J. (1967). Electroencephalography and brain maturation. In A. Minkowski (Ed.), *Symposium on regional development of the brain in early life.* Philadelphia: Davis.

PARRISH, L. H. (1991). Community resources and dropout prevention. In L. L. West (Ed.), *Effective strategies for dropout prevention of at-risk youth* (pp. 217–232). Gaithersburg, MD: Aspen Publishers.

PARSONS, J. E. (1982). Biology, experience, and sex-dimorphic behaviors. In W. R. Gove & G. R. Carpenter (Eds.), *The fundamental connection between nature and nurture* (pp. 137–170). Lexington, MA: Lexington Books.

PARSONS, J. E. (1983). Expectancies, values, and academic behaviors. In J. T. Spence (Ed.), *Achievement and achievement motives: Psychological and sociological approaches* (pp. 75–146). San Francisco: Freeman.

PARTEN, M. (1932). Social participation among preschool children. *Journal of Abnormal and Social Psychology, 27,* 243–269.

PASS, R. F. (1985). Epidemiology and transmission of cytomegalovirus. *Journal of Infectious Diseases, 152,* 243–248.

PASSMAN, R. H. (1976). Arousal reducing properties of attachment objects: Testing the functional limits of the security blanket relative to the mother. *Developmental Psychology, 12,* 468–469.

PASSMAN, R. H. (1987). Attachment to inanimate objects: Are children who have security blankets insecure? *Journal of Consulting and Clinical Psychology, 55,* 825–830.

PATTERSON, G. R. (1981). Mothers: the unacknowledged victims. *Monographs of the Society for Research in Child Development, 45* (5, Serial No. 186).

PATTERSON, G. R. (1982). *Coercive family processes.* Eugene, OR: Castilla Press.

PATTERSON, G. R. (1988). Stress: A change agent for family process. In N. Garmezy & M. Rutter (Eds.), *Stress, coping, and development in children* (pp. 235–264). Baltimore: Johns Hopkins University Press.

PATTERSON, G. R., DEBARYSHE, B. D., & RAMSEY, E. (1989). A developmental perspective on antisocial behavior. *American Psychologist, 44,* 329–335.

PAULHUS, D., & SHAFFER, D. R. (1981). Sex differences in the impact of number of older and number of younger siblings on scholastic aptitude. *Social Psychology Quarterly, 44,* 363–368.

PEA, R. D., & KURLAND, D. M. (1984). On the cognitive effects of learning computer programming. *New Ideas in Psychology, 2,* 137–168.

PEARSON, J. L., HUNTER, A. G., ENSMINGER, M. E., & KELLAM, S. G. (1990). Black grandmothers in multigenerational households: Diversity in family structure and parenting involvement in the Woodlawn community. *Child Development, 61,* 434–442.

PEDERSEN, F. A., CAIN, R., ZAZLOW, M., & ANDERSON, B. (1980). *Variation in infant experience associated with alternative family role organization.* Paper presented at the International Conference on Infant Studies, New Haven, CT.

PELCHAT, M. L., & PLINER, P. (1986). Antecedents and correlates of feeding problems in young children. *Journal of Nutritional Education, 18,* 23–29.

PELLEGRINI, A. D. (1988). Elementary-school children's rough-and-tumble play and social competence. *Developmental Psychology, 24,* 802–806.

PENNINGTON, B. F., BENDER, B., PUCK, M., SALBENBLATT, J., & ROBINSON, A. (1982). Learning disabilities in children with sex chromosome abnormalities. *Child Development, 53,* 1182–1192.

PENNINGTON, B. F., & SMITH, S. D. (1988). Genetic influences on learning disabilities: An update. *Journal of Consulting and Clinical Psychology, 56,* 817–823.

PEPLER, D. J., & ROSS, H. S. (1981). The effects of play on convergent and divergent problem solving. *Child Development, 52,* 1202–1210.

PERFETTI, C. A. (1988). Verbal efficiency in reading ability. In M. Daneman, G. E. MacKinnon, & T. G. Waller (Eds.), *Reading research: Advances in theory and practice* (Vol. 6, pp. 109–143). San Diego, CA: Academic Press.

PERLMUTTER, M. (1984). Continuities and discontinuities in early human memory: Paradigms, processes, and performances. In R. V. Kail, Jr., & N. R. Spear (Eds.), *Comparative perspectives on the development of memory* (pp. 253–287). Hillsdale, NJ: Erlbaum.

PERNER, J. (1991). *Understanding the representational mind.* Cambridge, MA: Bradford/MIT Press.

PERRY, D. G., PERRY, L. C., & WEISS, R. J. (1989). Sex differences in the consequences that children anticipate for aggression. *Developmental Psychology, 25,* 312–319.

PESHKIN, A. (1978). *Growing up American: Schooling and the survival of the community.* Chicago: University of Chicago Press.

PETERSEN, A. (1985). Pubertal development as a cause of disturbance: Myths, realities, and unanswered questions. *Genetic, Social, and General Psychology Monographs, 111,* 205–232.

PETERSEN, A. C., SARIGIANI, P. A., & KENNEDY, R. E. (1991). Adolescent depression: Why more girls? *Journal of Youth and Adolescence, 20,* 247–271.

PETTIT, G. S., BAKSHI, A., DODGE, K. A., & COIE, J. D. (1990). The emergence of social dominance in young boys' play groups: Developmental differences and behavioral correlates. *Developmental Psychology, 26,* 1017–1025.

PHILLIPS, D. A., MCCARTNEY, K., & SCARR, S. (1987). Child-care quality and children's social development. *Developmental Psychology, 23,* 537–543.

PHINNEY, J. S. (1989). Stages of ethnic identity development in minority group adolescents. *Journal of Early Adolescence, 9,* 34–49.

PHINNEY, J., & ALIPURIA, L. (1990). Ethnic identity in college students from four ethnic groups. *Journal of Adolescence, 13,* 171–183.

PIAGET, J. (1926). *The language and thought of the child.* New York: Harcourt, Brace & World. (Original work published 1923)

PIAGET, J. (1929). *The child's conception of physical causality.* New York: Harcourt, Brace & World. (Original work published 1926)

PIAGET, J. (1930). *The child's conception of the world.* New York: Harcourt, Brace, & World. (Original work published 1926)

PIAGET, J. (1950). *The psychology of intelligence.* New York: International Universities Press.

PIAGET, J. (1951). *Play, dreams, and imitation in childhood.* New York: Norton. (Original work published 1945)

PIAGET, J. (1952). *The origins of intelligence in children.* New York: International Universities Press. (Original work published 1936)

PIAGET, J. (1965). *The moral judgment of the child.* New York: The Free Press. (Original work published 1932)

PIAGET, J. (1967). *Six psychological studies*. New York: Vintage.

PIAGET, J. (1970). *The child's conception of movement and speed*. London: Routledge & Kegan Paul. (Original work published 1946)

PIAGET, J. (1971). *Biology and knowledge*. Chicago: University of Chicago Press.

PIAGET, J. (1978). *Success and understanding*. Cambridge, MA: Harvard University Press.

PIAGET, J. (1985). *The equilibration of cognitive structures: The central problem of intellectual development*. Chicago: University of Chicago Press.

PIAGET, J., & INHELDER, B. (1956). *The child's conception of space*. London: Routledge & Kegan Paul. (Original work published 1948)

PIAGET, J., INHELDER, B., & SZEMINSKA, A. (1960). *The child's conception of geometry*. New York: Basic Books. (Original work published 1948)

PIANTA, R., EGELAND, B., & ERICKSON, M. F. (1989). The antecedents of maltreatment: Results of the Mother-Child Interaction Research Project. In D. Cicchetti & V. Carlson (Eds.), *Child maltreatment* (pp. 203–253). New York: Cambridge University Press.

PICARIELLO, M. L., GREENBERG, D. N., & PILLEMER, D. B. (1990). Children's sex-related stereotyping of colors. *Child Development, 61,* 1453–1460.

PICK, A. D., & FRANKEL, G. W. (1974). A developmental study of strategies of visual selectivity. *Child Development, 45,* 1162–1165.

PICK, H. L., JR. (1989). Motor development: The control of action. *Developmental Psychology, 25,* 867–870.

PICKERING, L. K., BARTLETT, A. V., & WOODWARD, W. E. (1987). Acute infectious diarrhea among children in day care: Epidemiology and control. In M. T. Osterholm, J. O. Klein, S. S. Aronson, & L. K. Pickering (Eds.), *Infectious diseases in child day care* (pp. 27–35). Chicago: University of Chicago Press.

PIERCE, R., & PIERCE, L. H. (1985). The sexually abused child: A comparison of male and female victims. *Child Abuse and Neglect, 9,* 191–199.

PIETZ, J., BENNINGER, C., SCHMIDT, H., SCHEFFNER, D., & BICKEL, H. (1988). Long-term development of intelligence (IQ) and EEG in 34 children with phenylketonuria treated early. *European Journal of Pediatrics, 147,* 361–367.

PILKINGTON, C. L., & PIERSEL, W. C. (1991). School phobia: A critical analysis of the separation anxiety theory and an alternative conceptualization. *Psychology in the Schools, 28,* 290–303.

PILLOW, B. H. (1988). The development of children's beliefs about the mental world. *Merrill-Palmer Quarterly, 34,* 1–32.

PINEL, J. P. J. (1990). *Biopsychology*. Boston: Allyn and Bacon.

PINKER, S., LEBEAUX, D. S., & FROST, L. A. (1987). Productivity and constraints in the acquisition of the passive. *Cognition, 26,* 195–267.

PIPES, P. L. (1989). *Nutrition in infancy and childhood* (4th ed.). St. Louis: Mosby.

PLESS, I. B., & ARSENAULT, L. (1987). The role of health education in the prevention of injuries to children. *Journal of Social Issues, 43,* 87–104.

PLOMIN, R. (1986). *Development, genetics and psychology*. Hillsdale, NJ: Erlbaum.

PLOMIN, R. (1989). Environment and genes: Determinants of behavior. *American Psychologist, 44,* 105–111.

PODROUZEK, W., & FURROW, D. (1988). Preschoolers' use of eye contact while speaking: The influence of sex, age, and conversational partner. *Journal of Psycholinguistic Research, 17,* 89–93.

POINDRON, P., & LE NEINDRE, P. (1980). Endocrine and sensory regulation of maternal behavior in the ewe. In J. S. Rosenblatt , R. A. Hinde, C. Beer, & M. Busnel (Eds.), *Advances in the study of behavior* (pp. 76–119). New York: Academic Press.

POLANSKY, N. A., GAUDIN, J. M., AMMONS, P. W., & DAVIS, K. B. (1985). The psychological ecology of the neglectful mother. *Child Abuse & Neglect, 9,* 265–275.

POLLOCK, L. (1987). *A lasting relationship: Parents and children over three centuries*. Hanover, NH: University Press of New England.

PORTER, F. L., PORGES, S. W., & MARSHALL, R. E. (1988). Newborn pain cries and vagal tone: Parallel changes in response to circumcision. *Child Development, 59,* 495–505.

POWER, F. C., HIGGINS, A., & KOHLBERG, L. (1989). *Lawrence Kohlberg's approach to moral education*. New York: Columbia University Press.

POWERS, S. I., HAUSER, S. T., & KILNER, L. A. (1989). Adolescent mental health. *American Psychologist, 44,* 200–208.

PRECHTL, H. F. R. (1958). Problems of behavioral studies in the newborn infant. In D. S. Lehrmann, R. A. Hinde, & E. Shaw (Eds.), *Advances in the study of behavior* (Vol. 1, pp. 75–98). New York: Academic Press.

PRECHTL, H. F. R., & BEINTEMA, D. (1965). *The neurological examination of the full-term newborn infant*. London: William Heinemann Medical Books.

PREISSER, D. A., HODSON, B. W., & PADEN, E. P. (1988). Developmental phonology: 18–29 months. *Journal of Speech and Hearing Disorders, 53,* 125–130.

PRENTICE, A., & LIND, T. (1987). Fetal heart rate monitoring during labor—too frequent intervention, too little benefit? *Lancet, 2,* 1375–1377.

PRESSLEY, M. (1979). Increasing children's self-control through cognitive interventions. *Review of Educational Research, 49,* 319–370.

PRESSLEY, M., & GHATALA, E. S. (1990). Self-regulated learning: Monitoring learning from text. *Educational Psychologist, 25,* 19–34.

PREYER, W. (1888). *The mind of the child* (2 vols.). New York: Appleton. (Original work published 1882)

PRYOR, J. B., REEDER, G. D., VINACCO, R. J., & KOTT, T. L. (1989). The instrumental and symbolic functions of attitudes toward persons with AIDS. *Journal of Applied Social Psychology, 19,* 377–404.

QUAY, H. C. (1987). Institutional treatment. In H. C. Quay (Ed.), *Handbook of juvenile delinquency* (pp. 244–265). New York: Wiley.

RABINER, D., & COIE, J. (1989). Effect of expectancy inductions on rejected children's acceptance by unfamiliar peers. *Developmental Psychology, 25,* 450–457.

RADKE-YARROW, M., CUMMINGS, E. M., KUCZYNSKI, L., & CHAPMAN, M. (1985). Patterns of attachment in two- and three-year-olds in normal families with parental depression. *Child Development, 56,* 884–893.

RADKE-YARROW, M., & ZAHN-WAXLER, C. (1984). Roots, motives, and patterns in children's prosocial behavior. In J. Reykowski, J. Karylowski, D. Bar-Tel, & E. Staub (Eds.), *The development and maintenance of prosocial behaviors: International perspectives on positive morality* (pp. 81–99). New York: Plenum.

RADZISZEWSKA, B., & ROGOFF, B. (1988). Influence of adult and peer collaboration on the development of children's planning skills. *Developmental Psychology, 24,* 840–848.

RAFFERTY, Y., & SHINN, M. (1991). The impact of homelessness on children. *American Psychologist, 46,* 1170–1179.

RAGOZIN, A. S., BASHAM, R. B., CRNIC, K. A., GREENBERG, M. T., & ROBINSON, N. M. (1982). Effects of maternal age on parenting role. *Developmental Psychology, 18,* 627–634.

RÄIKKÖNEN, K., KELTIKANGAS-JÄRVINEN, L., & PIETIKÄINEN, M. (1991). Type A behavior and its determinants in children, adolescents, and young adults with and without parental coronary heart disease: A case-control study. *Journal of Psychosomatic Research, 35,* 273–280.

RAMEY, C. T., & CAMPBELL, F. A. (1984). Preventive education for high-risk children: Cognitive consequences of the Carolina Abecedarian Project. *American Journal of Mental Deficiency, 88,* 515–523.

RAMEY, C. T., & FINKELSTEIN, N. W. (1981). Psychosocial mental retardation: A biological and social coalescence. In M. Begab (Ed.), *Psychosocial influences and retarded performance: Strategies for improving social competence* (Vol. 1, pp. 65–92). Baltimore: University Park Press.

RATNER, N., & BRUNER, J. S. (1978). Social exchange and the acquisition of language. *Journal of Child Language, 5,* 391–402.

RAYNER, K., & POLLATSEK, A. (1989). *The psychology of reading*. Englewood Cliffs, NJ: Prentice-Hall.

READ, C. R. (1991). Achievement and career choices: Comparisons of males and females. *Roeper Review, 13,* 188–193.

READ, M. (1968). *Children of their fathers: Growing up among the Ngoni of Malawi*. New York: Holt, Rinehart & Winston.

REDD, W. H., MORRIS, E. K., & MARTIN, J. A. (1975). Effects of positive and negative adult-child interaction on children's social preferences. *Journal of Experimental Child Psychology, 19,* 153–164.

REDL, F. (1966). *When we deal with children*. New York: The Free Press.

REICH, P. A. (1986). *Language development*. Englewood Cliffs, NJ: Prentice-Hall.

REICH, T., VAN EERDEWEGH, P., RICHE, J., JULLANEY, J., ENDICOTT, J., & KLERMAN, G. L. (1987). The familial transmission of primary major depressive disorder. *Archives of General Psychology, 41*, 441–447.

REIS, S. M. (1989). Reflections on policy affecting the education of gifted and talented students: Past and future perspectives. *American Psychologist, 44*, 399–408.

REIS, S. M. (1991). The need for clarification in research designed to examine gender differences in achievement and accomplishment. *Roeper Review, 13*, 193–198.

REISER, J., YONAS, A., & WIKNER, K. (1976). Radial localization of odors by human neonates. *Child Development, 47*, 856–859.

REISMAN, J. E. (1987). Touch, motion, and proprioception. In P. Salapatek & L. Cohen (Eds.), *Handbook of infant perception: Vol. 1. From sensation to perception* (pp. 265–303). Orlando, FL: Academic Press.

REISSLAND, N. (1988). Neonatal imitation in the first hour of life: Observations in rural Nepal. *Developmental Psychology, 24*, 464–469.

RENNER, C., & NAVARRO, V. (1989). Why is our population of uninsured and underinsured persons growing? In L. Breslow, J. E. Fielding, & L. B. Lave (Eds.), *Annual review of public health* (Vol. 10, pp. 85–94). Palo Alto, CA: Annual Reviews.

RESCHLY, D. J. (1981). Psychological testing in educational classification and placement. *American Psychologist, 36*, 1094–1102.

RESNICK, L. B. (1989). Developing mathematical knowledge. *American Psychologist, 44*, 162–169.

RESNICK, R. (1988). Introduction to Postterm Gestation: A Symposium. *Journal of Reproductive Medicine, 33*, 249–251.

REST, J. R. (1979). *Development in judging moral issues*. Minneapolis: University of Minnesota Press.

REST, J. R. (1983). Morality. In J. H. Flavell & E. M. Markman (Eds.), *Handbook of child psychology: Vol. 3. Cognitive development* (4th ed., pp. 556–629). New York: Wiley.

REST, J. R., & THOMA, S. J. (1985). Relation of moral judgment to formal education. *Developmental Psychology, 21*, 709–714.

REZNICK, J. S., & GOLDFIELD, B. A. (1992). Rapid change in lexical development in comprehension and production. *Developmental Psychology, 28*, 406–413.

RHOADS, G. G., JACKSON, L. G., SCHLESSELMAN, S. E., DE LA CRUZ, F. F., DESNICK, R. J., GOLBUS, M. S., LEDBETTER, D. H., LUBS, H. A., MAHONEY, M. J., & PERGAMENT, E. (1989). The safety and efficacy of chorionic villus sampling for early prenatal diagnosis of cytogenetic abnormalities. *New England Journal of Medicine, 320*, 609–617.

RICCO, R. B. (1989). Operational thought and the acquisition of taxonomic relations involving figurative dissimilarity. *Developmental Psychology, 25*, 996–1003.

RICE, F. P. (1993). *The adolescent: Development, relationships, and culture* (7th ed.). Boston: Allyn and Bacon.

RICE, M. L., HUSTON, A. C., TRUGLIO, R., & WRIGHT, J. (1990). Words from "Sesame Street": Learning vocabulary while viewing. *Developmental Psychology, 26*, 421–428.

RICHARDS, D. D., & SIEGLER, R. S. (1986). Children's understandings of the attributes of life. *Journal of Experimental Child Psychology, 42*, 1–22.

RICHARDSON, P. (1983). Women's perceptions of change in relationships shared with their husbands during pregnancy. *Maternal-Child Nursing Journal, 12*, 1–19.

RICHARDSON, S. A. KOLLER, H., & KATZ, M. (1986). Factors leading to differences in the school performance of boys and girls. *Developmental and Behavioral Pediatrics, 7*, 49–55.

RIEDER, M. J., SCHWARTZ, C., & NEWMAN, J. (1986). Patterns of walker use and walker injury. *Pediatrics, 78*, 488–493.

RIESE, M. L. (1987). Temperament stability between the neonatal period and 24 months. *Developmental Psychology, 23*, 216–222.

RIVARA, F. P., & BARBER, M. (1985). Demographic analysis of childhood pedestrian injuries. *Pediatrics, 76*, 375–381.

ROBERTON, M. A. (1984). Changing motor patterns during childhood. In J. R. Thomas (Ed.), *Motor development during childhood and adolescence* (pp. 48–90). Minneapolis, MN: Burgess.

ROBERTON, M. A., & HALVERSON, L. E. (1988). The development of locomotor coordination: Longitudinal change and invariance. *Journal of Motor Behavior, 20*, 197–241.

ROBERTS, K. (1988). Retrieval of a basic-level category in prelinguistic infants. *Developmental Psychology, 24*, 21–27.

ROBERTS, M. C., & FANURIK, D. (1986). Rewarding elementary schoolchildren for their use of safety belts. *Health Psychology, 5*, 185–196.

ROBERTS, M. C., ALEXANDER, K., & KNAPP, L. G. (1990). Motivating children to use safety belts: A program combining rewards and "flash for life." *Journal of Community Psychology, 18*, 110–119.

ROBERTS, M. C., ELKINS, P. D., & ROYAL, G. P. (1984). Psychological applications to the prevention of accidents and injuries. In M. C. Roberts & L. Peterson (Eds.), *Prevention of problems in childhood: Psychological research and applications* (pp. 173–199). New York: Wiley.

ROBERTS, M. C., FANURIK, D., & WILSON, D. R. (1988). A community program to reward children's use of seat belts. *American Journal of Community Psychology, 16*, 395–407.

ROBINSON, B. (1988). *Teenage fathers*. Lexington, MA: Lexington Books.

ROBINSON, E. H., III, ROBINSON, S. L., & WHETSELL, M. V. (1988). A study of children's fears. *Journal of Humanistic Education and Development, 27*, 84–95.

ROBINSON, E. J. (1981). The child's understanding of inadequate messages and communication failure: A problem of ignorance or egocentrism? In W. P. Dickson (Ed.), *Children's oral communication skills* (pp. 167–188). New York: Academic Press.

ROBINSON, J. P. (1988). Who's doing the housework? *American Demographics, 10*, 24–63.

ROCHAT, P. (1989). Object manipulation and exploration in 2- to 5-month-old infants. *Developmental Psychology, 25*, 871–884.

ROCHE, A. F. (1979). Secular trends in stature, weight, and maturation. In A. F. Roche (Ed.), Secular trends in human growth, maturation, and development. *Monographs of the Society for Research in Child Development, 44* (3–4, Serial No. 179).

ROCHE, A. F. (1981). The adipocyte-number hypothesis. *Child Development, 52*, 31–43.

ROFFWARG, H. P., MUZIO, J. N., & DEMENT, W. C. (1966). Ontogenetic development of the human sleep-dream cycle. *Science, 152*, 604–619.

ROGOFF, B. (1986). The development of strategic use of context in spatial memory. In M. Perlmutter (Ed.), *Perspectives on intellectual development* (pp. 107–123). Hillsdale, NJ: Erlbaum.

ROGOFF, B. (1990). *Apprenticeship in thinking: Cognitive development in social context*. New York: Oxford University Press.

ROGOFF, B., MALKIN, C., & GILBRIDE, K. (1984). Interaction with babies as guidance in development. In B. Rogoff & J. V. Wertsch (Eds.), *New directions for child development* (No. 23, pp. 31–44). San Francisco: Jossey-Bass.

ROGOFF, B., & MORELLI, G. (1989). Culture and American children: Section introduction. *American Psychologist, 44*, 341–342.

ROGOFF, B., SELLERS, M., PIRROTTA, S., FOX, N., & WHITE, S. (1975). Age of assignment of roles and responsibilities in children: A cross-cultural survey. *Human Development, 18*, 353–369.

ROHLEN, T. P. (1983). *Japan's high schools*. Berkeley, CA: University of California Press.

ROHNER, R. P., & ROHNER, E. C. (1981). Parental acceptance-rejection and parental control: Cross-cultural codes. *Ethnology, 20*, 245–260.

ROMAINE, S. (1984). *The language of children and adolescents: The acquisition of communicative competence*. Oxford: Blackwell.

ROOPNARINE, J. L., TALUKDER, E., JAIN, D., JOSHI, P., & SRIVASTAV, P. (1990). Characteristics of holding, patterns of play, and social behaviors between parents and infants in New Delhi, India. *Developmental Psychology, 26*, 667–673.

ROOSA, M. W. (1984). Maternal age, social class, and the obstetric performance of teenagers. *Journal of Youth and Adolescence, 13*, 365–374.

ROSCOE, B., DIANA, M. S., & BROOKS, R. H. (1987). Early, middle, and late adolescents' views on dating and factors influencing partner selection. *Adolescence, 22*, 59–68.

ROSE, S. A. (1980). Enhancing visual recognition memory in preterm infants. *Developmental Psychology, 16*, 85–92.

ROSE, S. A., FELDMAN, J. F., & WALLACE, I. F. (1988). Individual differences in infant information processing: Reliability, stability, and prediction. *Child Development, 59*, 1177–1197.

ROSENBERG, M. (1979). *Conceiving the self.* New York: Basic Books.

ROSENBERG, M. S., & REPPUCCI, N. D. (1985). Primary prevention of child abuse. *Journal of Consulting and Clinical Psychology, 53,* 576–585.

ROSENBERG, M., SCHOOLER, C., & SCHOENBACH, C. (1989). Self-esteem and adolescent problems: Modeling reciprocal effects. *American Sociological Review, 54,* 1004–1018.

ROSENBERG, R. N., & PETTIGREW, J. W. (1983). Genetic neurologic diseases. In R. N. Rosenberg (Ed.), *The clinical neurosciences* (pp. 33–165). New York: Churchill Livingstone.

ROSENBLATT, J. S., & LEHRMAN, D. (1963). Maternal behavior of the laboratory rat. In H. R. Rheingold (Ed.). *Maternal behavior in mammals* (pp. 8–57). New York: Wiley

ROSENTHAL, D. A. (1987). Ethnic identity development in adolescents. In J. S. Phinney & M. J. Rotheram (Eds.), *Children's ethnic socialization* (pp. 156–179). Newbury Park, CA: Sage.

ROSS, G. S. (1980). Categorization in 1- to 2-year-olds. *Developmental Psychology, 16,* 391–396.

ROTHBART, M. K. (1981). Measurement of temperament in infancy. *Child Development, 52,* 569–578.

ROTHERAM-BORUS, M. J. (1989). Ethnic differences in adolescents' identity status and associated behavior problems. *Journal of Adolescence, 12,* 361–374.

ROTHERAM-BORUS, M. J. (in press). Bicultural reference group orientation and adjustment. In M. Bernal & G. Knight (Eds.), *Ethnic identity.* Albany, NY: State University of New York Press.

ROURKE, B. P. (1988). Socioemotional disturbances of learning disabled children. *Journal of Consulting and Clinical Psychology, 56,* 801–810.

ROUSSEAU, J. J. (1955). *Emile.* New York: Dutton. (Original work published 1762)

ROVEE-COLLIER, C. K. (1984). The ontogeny of learning and memory in human infancy. In R. Kail & N. E. Spear (Eds.), *Comparative perspectives on the development of memory* (pp. 103–134). Hillsdale, NJ: Erlbaum.

ROVEE-COLLIER, C. K. (1987). Learning and memory. In J. D. Osofsky (Ed.), *Handbook of infant development* (2nd ed., pp. 98–148). New York: Wiley.

ROVEE-COLLIER, C., PATTERSON, J., & HAYNE, H. (1985). Specificity in the reactivation of infant memory. *Developmental Psychobiology, 18,* 559–574.

ROYCE, J. M., DARLINGTON, R. B., & MURRAY, H. W. (1983). Pooled analyses: Findings across studies. In Consortium for Longitudinal Studies (Ed.), *As the twig is bent: Lasting effects of preschool programs* (pp. 411–459). Hillsdale, NJ: Erlbaum.

ROZIN, P. (1990). Development in the food domain. *Developmental Psychology, 26,* 555–562.

ROZIN, P., & SCHILLER, D. (1980). The nature and acquisition of a preference for chili pepper by humans. *Motivation and Emotion, 4,* 77–101.

RUBIN, D. H., KRASILNIKOFF, P. A., LEVENTHAL, J. M., WEILE, B., & BERGET, A. (1986). Effects of passive smoking on birth weight. *Lancet, 2,* 415–417.

RUBIN, J. Z., PROVENZANO, F. J., & LURIA, Z. (1974). The eye of the beholder: Parents' views on sex of newborns. *American Journal of Orthopsychiatry, 44,* 512–519.

RUBIN, K. H. (1982). Nonsocial play in preschoolers: Necessarily evil? *Child Development, 53,* 651–657.

RUBIN, K. H., & DANIELS-BIERNESS, T. (1983). Concurrent and predictive correlates of sociometric status in kindergarten and grade one children. *Merrill-Palmer Quarterly, 29,* 337–352.

RUBIN, K. H., FEIN, G. G., & VANDENBERG, B. (1983). Play. In E. M. Hetherington (Ed.), *Handbook of child psychology: Vol. 4. Socialization, personality, and social development* (4th ed., pp. 693–744). New York: Wiley.

RUBIN, K. H., MAIONI, T. L., & HORNUNG, M. (1976). Free play behaviors in middle- and lower-class preschoolers: Parten and Piaget revisited. *Child Development, 47,* 414–419.

RUBIN, K. H., WATSON, K. S., & JAMBOR, T. W. (1978). Free-play behaviors in preschool and kindergarten children. *Child Development, 49,* 539–536.

RUBLE, D. N. (1988). Sex-role development. In M. H. Bornstein & M. E. Lamb (Eds.), *Developmental psychology: An advanced textbook* (2nd ed., pp. 411–460). Hillsdale, NJ: Erlbaum.

RUFF, H. A., LAWSON, K. R., PARRINELLO, R., & WEISSBERG, R. (1990). Long-term stability of individual differences in sustained attention in the early years. *Child Development, 61,* 60–75.

RUGH, R., & SHETTLES, L. B. (1971). *From conception to birth: The drama of life's beginnings.* New York: Harper & Row.

RUIZ, R. (1988). Bilingualism and bilingual education in the United States. In C. B. Paulston (Ed.), *International handbook of bilingualism and bilingual education* (pp. 539–560). New York: Greenwood Press.

RUMBERGER, R. W. (1990). Second chance for high school dropouts: The costs and benefits of dropout recovery programs in the United States. In D. Inbar (Ed.), *Second chance in education: An interdisciplinary and international perspective* (pp. 227–250). Philadelphia: Falmer.

RUMBERGER, R. W., GHATAK, R., POULOS, G., RITTER, P. L., & DORNBUSCH, S. M. (1990). Family influences on dropout behavior in one California high school. *Sociology of Education, 63,* 283–299.

RUOPP, R., TRAVERS, J., GLANTZ, F., & COELEN, C. (1979). *Children at the center: Final report of the National Day Care Study.* Cambridge, MA: Abt Books.

RUSHTON, H. G. (1989). Nocturnal enuresis: Epidemiology, evaluation, and currently available treatment options. *Journal of Pediatrics, 114,* 691–696.

RUSSELL, D. E. H. (1983). The incidence and prevalence of intrafamilial and extrafamilial sexual abuse of female children. *Child Abuse and Neglect, 7,* 133–146.

RUSSELL, J. A. (1990). The preschooler's understanding of the causes and consequences of emotion. *Child Development, 61,* 1872–1881.

RUTTER, M. (1979). Protective factors in children's responses to stress and disadvantage. In M. W. Kent & J. Rolf (Eds.), *Primary prevention of psychopathology. Vol III: Social competence in children* (pp. 49–74). Hanover, NH: University Press of New England.

RUTTER, M. (1983). School effects on pupil progress: Research findings and policy implications. *Child Development, 54,* 1–29.

RUTTER, M. (1986). The developmental psychology of depression: Issues and perspectives. In M. Rutter, C. E. Izard, & P. B. Read (Eds.), *Depression in young people: Clinical and developmental perspectives* (pp. 3–30). New York: Guilford.

RUTTER, M. (1987). Psychosocial resilience and protective mechanisms. *American Journal of Orthopsychiatry, 57,* 316–331.

RUTTER, M., & GARMEZY, N. (1983). Developmental psychopathology. In E. M. Hetherington (Ed.), *Handbook of child psychology: Vol. 4. Socialization, personality, and social development* (4th ed., pp. 775–911). New York: Wiley.

RUTTER, M., & HERSOV, L. (Eds.). (1985). *Child and adolescent psychiatry: Modern approaches* (2nd ed.). London: Blackwell Press.

RUTTER, M., GRAHAM, P., CHADWICK, O. F. D., & YULE, W. (1976). Adolescent turmoil: Fact or fiction. *Journal of Child Psychology and Psychiatry, 17,* 35–56.

RUTTER, M., & MADGE, N. (1976). *Cycles of disadvantage.* London: Heinemann.

RYAN, K. J. (1989). Ethical issues in reproductive endocrinology and infertility. *American Journal of Obstetrics and Gynecology, 160,* 1415–1417.


SAARNI, C. (1989). Children's understanding of strategic control of emotional expression in social transactions. In C. Saarni & P. L. Harris (Eds.), *Children's understanding of emotion* (pp. 181–208). Cambridge, England: Cambridge University Press.

SADLER, L. S. (1991). Depression in adolescents: Context, manifestations, and clinical management. *Nursing Clinics of North America, 26,* 559–572.

SADLER, T. W. (1990). *Langman's medical embryology* (6th ed.). Baltimore: Williams & Wilkins.

SAFE KIDS (1991). *National Safe Kids Campaign: 1991 Public Policy Priorities.* Washington, DC: Author.

SALAPATEK, P. (1975). Pattern perception in early infancy. In L. B. Cohen & P. Salapatek (Eds.), *Infant perception: From sensation to cognition* (pp. 133–248). New York: Academic Press.

SALAPATEK, P., & COHEN, L. (Eds.). (1987). *Handbook of infant perception: Vol. 2. From perception to cognition.* Orlando, FL: Academic Press.

SALOMON, J. B., MATA, L. J., & GORDON, J. E. (1968). Malnutrition and the common communicable diseases of childhood in rural Guatemala. *American Journal of Health, 58*, 505–516.

SAMSON, L. F. (1988). Perinatal viral infections and neonates. *Journal of Perinatal Neonatal Nursing, 1*, 56–65.

SAMUELS, M., & SAMUELS, N. (1986). *The well pregnancy book*. New York: Summit.

SAMUELS, S. J. (1985). Toward a theory of automatic information processing in reading: Updated. In H. Singer & R. B. Ruddell (Eds.), *Theoretical models and processes of reading* (3rd ed., pp. 719–721). Newark, DE: International Reading Association.

SANDBERG, D. E., EHRHARDT, A. A., INCE, S. E., & MEYER-BAHLBERG, H. F. L. (1991). Gender differences in children's and adolescents' career aspirations. *Journal of Adolescent Research, 6*, 371–386.

SANDERSON, J. A., & SIEGAL, M. (1988). Conceptions of moral and social rules in rejected and nonrejected preschoolers. *Journal of Clinical Child Psychology, 17*, 66–72.

SANFORD, J. P. (1985). *Comprehension-level tasks in secondary classrooms*. Austin, TX: Research and Development Center for Teacher Education, University of Texas at Austin.

SANTROCK, J. W., & WARSHAK, R. A. (1986). Development of father custody relationships and legal/clinical considerations in father-custody families. In M. E. Lamb (Ed.), *The father's role: Applied perspectives* (pp. 135–166). New York: Wiley.

SATTLER, J. M. (1988). *Assessment of children's intelligence and special abilities* (3rd ed.). San Diego: Author.

SAVIN-WILLIAMS, R. C. (1979). Dominance hierarchies in groups of early adolescents. *Child development, 50*, 923–935.

SAVIN-WILLIAMS, R. C., & BERNDT, T. J. (1990). Friendship and peer relations. In S. S. Feldman & G. R. Elliott (Eds.), *At the threshold: The developing adolescent* (pp. 277–307). Cambridge, MA: Harvard University Press.

SAXE, G. B. (1988, August-September). Candy selling and math learning. *Educational Researcher, 17 (6)*, 14–21.

SAYWITZ, K. J. (1987). Children's testimony: Age-related patterns of memory errors. In S. J. Ceci, M. P. Toglia, & D. F. Ross (Eds.), *Children's eyewitness memory* (pp. 36–52). New York: Springer-Verlag.

SAYWITZ, K. J. (1989). Children's conceptions of the legal system: "Court is a place to play basketball." In M. P. Toglia (Eds.), *Perspectives on children's testimony* (pp. 131–157). New York: Springer-Verlag.

SCARR, S. (1988). How genotypes and environments combine: Development and individual differences. In N. Bolger, A. Caspi, G. Downey, & M. Moorehouse (Eds.), *Persons in context: Developmental processes* (pp. 217–244). Cambridge, England: Cambridge University Press.

SCARR, S., & KIDD, K. K. (1983). Developmental behavior genetics. In M. M. Haith & J. J. Campos (Eds.), *Handbook of child psychology: Vol. 2. Infancy and developmental psychobiology* (4th ed., pp. 345–433). New York: Wiley.

SCARR, S., & MCCARTNEY, K. (1983). How people make their own environments: A theory of genotype → environment effects. *Child Development, 54*, 424–435.

SCARR, S., PHILLIPS, D. A., & MCCARTNEY, K. (1990). Facts, fantasies, and the future of child care in America. *Psychological Science, 1*, 26–35.

SCARR, S., & WEINBERG, R. A. (1983). The Minnesota Adoption Studies: Genetic differences and malleability. *Child Development, 54*, 260–267.

SCHACHTER, F. F., & STONE, R. K. (1985). Difficult sibling-easy sibling: Temperament and the within-family environment. *Child Development, 56*, 1335–1344.

SCHAEFER, M., HATCHER, R. P., & BARGELOW, P. D. (1980). Prematurity and infant stimulation. *Child Psychiatry and Human Development, 10*, 199–212.

SCHAFFER, H. R., & EMERSON, P. E. (1964). The development of social attachments in infancy. *Monographs of the Society for Research in Child Development, 29* (3, Serial No. 94).

SCHAIVI, R. C., THEILGAARD, A., OWEN, D., & WHITE, D. (1984). Sex chromosome anomalies, hormones, and aggressivity. *Archives of General Psychiatry, 41*, 93–99.

SCHANBERG, S., & FIELD, T. M. (1987). Sensory deprivation stress and supplemental stimulation in the rat pup and preterm human neonate. *Child Development, 58*, 1431–1447.

SCHICKEDANZ, J. A., CHAY, S., GOPIN, P., SHENG, L. L., SONG, S., & WILD, N. (1990, November). Preschoolers and academics: Some thoughts. *Young Children, 46* (1), 4–13.

SCHINKE, S. P., BLYTHE, B. J., & GILCHRIST, D. (1981). Cognitive-behavioral prevention of adolescent pregnancy. *Journal of Counseling Psychology, 28*, 451–454.

SCHLEGEL, A., & BARRY, H., III. (1980). The evolutionary significance of adolescent initiation ceremonies. *American Ethnologist, 7*, 696–715.

SCHLEGEL, A., & BARRY, H., III. (1991). *Adolescence: An anthropological inquiry*. New York: The Free Press.

SCHNEIDER, W., & PRESSLEY, M. (1989). *Memory development between 2 and 20*. New York: Springer-Verlag.

SCHNEIRLA, T. C., ROSENBLATT, J. S., & TOBACH, E. (1963). Maternal behavior in the cat. In H. R. Rheingold (Ed.), *Maternal behavior in mammals* (pp. 122–168). New York: Wiley.

SCHOR, E. L. (1987). Unintentional injuries. *American Journal of Diseases of Children, 141*, 1280–1284.

SCHRAG, S. G., & DIXON, R. L. (1985). Occupational exposures associated with male reproductive dysfunction. *Annual Review of Pharmacology and Toxicology, 25*, 567–592.

SCHRAMM, W., BARNES, D., & BAKEWELL, J. (1987). Neonatal mortality in Missouri home births. *American Journal of Public Health, 77*, 930–935.

SCHULTZ, D. P. (1975). *A history of modern psychology*. New York: Academic Press.

SCHUNK, D. H. (1983). Ability versus effort attributional feedback: Differential effects on self-efficacy and achievement. *Journal of Educational Psychology, 75*, 848–856.

SCHUNK, D. H. (1990). Goal setting and self-efficacy during self-regulated learning. *Educational Psychologist, 25*, 71–86.

SCHWARTZ-BICKENBACH, D., SCHULTE-HOBEIN, B., ABT, S., PLUM, C., & NAU, H. (1987). Smoking and passive smoking during pregnancy and early infancy: Effects on birth weight, lactation period, and cotinine concentrations in mother's milk and infant's urine. *Toxicology Letters, 35*, 73–81.

SCHWEINHART, L. J., & WEIKART, D. P. (1986, January). What do we know so far? A review of the Head Start Synthesis Project. *Young Children, 41* (2), 49–55.

SCRIBNER, S. (1977). Modes of thinking and ways of speaking: Culture and logic reconsidered. In P. N. Johnson-Laird & P. C. Wason (Eds.), *Thinking: Readings in cognitive science* (pp. 483–500). London: Cambridge University Press.

SEARS, R. R. (1975). *Your ancients revisited: A history of child development*. Chicago: University of Chicago Press.

SEBALD, H. (1986). Adolescents' shifting orientation toward parents and peers: A curvilinear trend over recent decades. *Journal of Marriage and the Family, 48*, 5–13.

SELECT COMMITTEE ON CHILDREN, YOUTH, AND FAMILIES, House of Representatives (1986). Testimony of David Bright. *Hearing on Hunger*. Washington, DC: U. S. Government Printing Office.

SELIGMAN, M. E. P. (1975). *Helplessness: On depression, development, and death*. San Francisco: Freeman.

SELIGMANN, J. (1991, December 9). Condoms in the classroom. *Newsweek, 118* (24), 61.

SELMAN, R. L. (1976). Social-cognitive understanding: A guide to educational and clinical practice. In T. Likona (Ed.), *Moral development and behavior: Theory, research, and social issues* (pp. 299–316). New York: Holt, Rinehart and Winston.

SELMAN, R. L. (1980). *The growth of interpersonal understanding*. New York: Academic Press.

SELMAN, R. L., & BYRNE, D. F. (1974). A structural-developmental analysis of levels of role taking in middle childhood. *Child Development, 45*, 803–806.

SELTZER, V., & BENJAMIN, F. (1990). Breast-feeding and the potential for human immunodeficiency virus transmission. *Obstetrics and Gynecology, 75*, 713–715.

SEVER, J. L. (1983). Maternal infections. In C. C. Brown (Ed.), *Childhood learning disabilities and prenatal risk* (pp. 31–38). New York: Johnson & Johnson.

SEXTON, M., & HEBEL, J. R. (1984). A clinical trial of change in maternal smoking and its effect on birth weight. *Journal of the American Medical Association, 251*, 911–915.

SHAFFER, D. (1985). Depression, mania, and suicidal acts. In M. Rutter & L. Hersov (Eds.), *Child and adolescent psychiatry: Modern approaches* (pp. 698–719). New York: Guilford Press.

SHAFFER, D., GARLAND, A., GOULD, M., FISHER, P., & TRAUTMAN,

P. (1988). Preventing teenage suicide: A critical review. *Journal of the American Academy of Child and Adolescent Psychiatry, 27,* 675–687.

SHAHAR, S. (1990). *Childhood in the Middle Ages.* London: Routledge & Kegan Paul.

SHAINESS, N. (1961). A re-evaluation of some aspects of femininity through a study of menstruation: A preliminary report. *Comparative Psychiatry, 2,* 20–26.

SHANNON, B., & CHEN, A. W. (1988). A three-year school based nutrition education study. *Journal of Nutrition Education, 20,* 114–123.

SHANNON, D. C., KELLY, D. H., AKSELROD, S., & KILBORN, K. M. (1987). Increased respiratory frequency and variability in high risk babies who die of sudden infant death syndrome. *Pediatric Research, 22,* 158–162.

SHANTZ, C. U. (1987). Conflicts between children. *Child Development, 58,* 283–305.

SHAPIRO, L. (1991, Summer). What's in a lunch? *Newsweek (special issue), 117* (26), 66–68.

SHAVER, P., FURMAN, W., & BUHRMESTER, D. (1985). Transition to college: Network changes, social skills, and loneliness. In S. Duck & D. Perlman (Eds.), *Understanding personal relationships: An interdisciplinary approach* (pp. 193–219). London: Sage.

SHEDLER, J., & BLOCK, J. (1990). Adolescent drug use and psychological health: A longitudinal inquiry. *American Psychologist, 45,* 612–630.

SHEIMAN, D. L., & SLOMIN, M. (1988). *Resources for middle childhood.* New York: Garland.

SHERMAN, M., HERTZIG, M., AUSTRIAN, R., & SHAPIRO, T. (1981). Treasured objects in school-aged children. *Pediatrics, 68,* 379–386.

SHERMAN, T. (1985). Categorization skills in infants. *Child Development, 56,* 1561–1573.

SHIELDS, J. W. (1972). *The trophic function of lymphoid elements.* Springfield, IL: Charles C. Thomas.

SHIELDS, P. J., & ROVEE-COLLIER, C. (1992). Long-term memory for context-specific category information at six months. *Child Development, 63,* 245–259.

SHIFFRIN, R. M., & ATKINSON, R. C. (1969). Storage and retrieval processes in long-term memory. *Psychological Review, 76,* 179–193.

SHILLER, V., IZARD, C. E., & HEMBREE, E. A. (1986). Patterns of emotion expression during separation in the Strange Situation. *Developmental Psychology, 22,* 378–382.

SHIME, J. (1988). Influence of prolonged pregnancy on infant development. *Journal of Reproductive Medicine, 33,* 277–284.

SHINN, M. W. (1900). *The biography of a baby.* Boston: Houghton Mifflin.

SHIPMAN, G. (1971). The psychodynamics of sex education. In R. Muuss (Ed.), *Adolescent behavior and society* (pp. 326–339). New York: Random House.

SHONKOFF, J. P. (1984). The biological substrate and physical health in middle childhood. In W. A. Collins (Ed.), *Development during middle childhood* (pp. 24–69). Washington, DC: National Academic Press.

SHULTZ, T. R. (1980). Development of the concept of intention. In W. A. Collins (Ed.), *Minnesota Symposia on Child Psychology* (Vol. 13, pp. 131–164). Hillsdale, NJ: Erlbaum.

SHWEDER, R. A. (1990). In defense of moral realism: Reply to Gabennesch. *Child Development, 61,* 2060–2067.

SHWEDER, R. A., MAHAPATRA, M., & MILLER, J. G. (1990). Culture and moral development. In J. Stigler, R. A. Shweder, & G. Herdt (Eds.), *Cultural psychology: Essays on comparative human development* (pp. 130–204). New York: Cambridge University Press.

SIEBERT, J. M., GARCIA, A., KAPLAN, M., & SEPTIMUS, A. (1989). Three model pediatric AIDS programs: Meeting the needs of children, families, and communities. In J. M. Siebert & R. A. Olson (Eds.), *Children, adolescents, and AIDS* (pp. 25–60). Lincoln, NB: University of Nebraska Press.

SIEGLER, R. S. (1976). Three aspects of cognitive development. *Cognitive Psychology, 8,* 481–520.

SIEGLER, R. S. (1978). The origins of scientific reasoning. In R. S. Siegler (Ed.), *Children's thinking: What develops?* (pp. 109–149). Hillsdale, NJ: Erlbaum.

SIEGLER, R. S. (1981). Developmental sequences within and between concepts. *Monographs of the Society for Research in Child Development, 46* (2, Serial No. 189).

SIEGLER, R. S. (1983a). Five generalizations about cognitive development. *American Psychologist, 38,* 263–277.

SIEGLER, R. S. (1983b). Information processing approaches to development. In W. Kessen (Ed.), *Handbook of child psychology: Vol. 1. History, theory, and methods* (4th ed., pp. 129–212). New York: Wiley.

SIEGLER, R. S. (1988). Mechanisms of cognitive development. *Annual Review of Psychology, 40,* 353–379.

SIEGLER, R. S. (1992). The other Alfred Binet. *Developmental Psychology, 28,* 179–190.

SIEGLER, R. S., & RICHARDS, D. D. (1982). The development of intelligence. In R. J. Sternberg (Ed.), *Handbook of human intelligence* (pp. 897–971). Cambridge, England: Cambridge University Press.

SILVER, L. B. (1989a). Learning disabilities. *Journal of the American Academy of Child and Adolescent Psychiatry, 28,* 309–313.

SILVER, L. B. (1989b). Psychological and family problems associated with learning disabilities: Assessment and intervention. *Journal of the American Academy of Child and Adolescent Psychiatry, 28,* 319–325.

SILVER, M., & WOLFE, S. (1989). *Unnecessary cesarean sections: How to cure a national epidemic.* Washington, DC: Citizen's Health Research Group.

SILVERBERG, S. B., & STEINBERG, L. (1990). Psychological well-being of parents with early adolescent children. *Developmental Psychology, 26,* 658–666.

SIMKIN, P., WHALLEY, J., & KEPPLER, A. (1984). *Pregnancy, childbirth, and the newborn.* New York: Meadowbrook.

SIMMONS, R. G., & BLYTH, D. A. (1987). *Moving into adolescence.* New York: Aldine De Gruyter.

SIMMONS, R. G., BURGESON, R., CARLTON-FORD, S., & BLYTH, D. (1987). The impact of cumulative change in early adolescence. *Child Development, 58,* 1220–1234.

SIMONS, R. L., CONGER, R. D., & WHITBECK, L. B. (1988). A multistage social learning model of the influences of family and peers upon adolescent substance use. *Journal of Drug Issues, 18,* 293–316.

SIMONS, R. L., WHITBECK, L. B., CONGER, R. D., & CHYI-IN, W. (1991). Intergenerational transmission of harsh parenting. *Developmental Psychology, 27,* 159–171.

SINGER, D. G., & SINGER, J. L. (1990). *The house of make-believe.* Cambridge, MA: Harvard University Press.

SIRIGNANO, S. W., & LACHMAN, M. E. (1985). Personality change during the transition to parenthood: The role of perceived infant temperament. *Developmental Psychology, 21,* 558–567.

SKINNER, B. F. (1957). *Verbal behavior.* New York: Appleton-Century-Crofts.

SLABY, R. G., & FREY, K. S. (1975). Development of gender constancy and selective attention to same-sex models. *Child Development, 46,* 849–856.

SLADE, A. (1987). A longitudinal study of maternal involvement and symbolic play during the toddler period. *Child Development, 58,* 367–375.

SLAVIN, R. E. (1987). Ability grouping and student achievement in elementary schools: A best-evidence synthesis. *Review of Educational Research, 57,* 293–336.

SLOAN, W., & BIRCH, J. W. (1955). A rationale for degrees of retardation. *American Journal of Mental Deficiency, 60,* 258–264.

SMEEDING, T., TORREY, B. B., & REIN, M. (1988). Patterns of income and poverty: Economic status of children and the elderly in eight countries. In J. L. Palmer & I. V. Sawhill (Eds.), *The vulnerable* (pp. 89–119). Washington, DC: The Urban Institute Press.

SMETANA, J. (1988). Concepts of self and social convention: Adolescents' and parents' reasoning about hypothetical and actual family conflicts. In M. Gunnar & W. A. Collins (Eds.), *Minnesota Symposia on Child Psychology* (Vol. 21, pp. 79–122). Hillsdale, NJ: Erlbaum.

SMETANA, J. G. (1989). Toddlers' social interactions in the context of moral and conventional transgressions in the home. *Developmental Psychology, 25,* 499–508.

SMETANA, J. G., & BRAEGES, J. L. (1990). The development of toddlers' moral and conventional judgments. *Merrill-Palmer Quarterly, 36,* 329–346.

SMILANSKY, S. (1968). *The effects of sociodramatic play on disadvantaged children: Preschool children.* New York: Wiley.

SMITH, C., & LLOYD, B. (1978). Maternal behavior and perceived sex of infant: Revisited. *Child Development, 49,* 1263–1266.

SMITH, J., & RUSSELL, G. (1984). Why do males and females differ? Children's beliefs about sex differences. *Sex Roles, 11,* 1111–1119.

SMITH, M. C. (1978). Cognizing the behavior stream: The recognition of intentional action. *Child Development, 49,* 736–743.

SMITH, P. K. (1978). A longitudinal study of social participation in preschool children: Solitary and parallel play reexamined. *Developmental Psychology, 14,* 517–523.

SMITH, P. K., & BOULTON, M. (1990). Rough-and-tumble play, aggression and dominance: Perception and behavior in children's encounters. *Human Development, 33,* 271–282.

SMITH, P. K., & CONNOLLY, K. J. (1980). *The ecology of preschool behaviour.* Cambridge, England: Cambridge University Press.

SMITH, S. (1991, Spring). Two-generation program models: A new intervention strategy. *Social Policy Report of the Society for Research in Child Development, 5* (No. 1).

SMOLUCHA, F. (1992). Social origins of private speech in pretend play. In R. M. Diaz & L. E. Berk (Eds.), *Private speech: From social interaction to self-regulation* (pp. 123–141). Hillsdale, NJ: Erlbaum.

SNAREY, J. R., REIMER, J., & KOHLBERG, L. (1985). The development of social-moral reasoning among kibbutz adolescents: A longitudinal cross-cultural study. *Developmental Psychology, 21,* 3–17.

SNOW, C. E., & HOEFNAGEL-HÖHLE, M. (1978). The critical period for language acquisition: Evidence from second language learning. *Child Development, 49,* 1114–1128.

SNOWDEN, L. R., SCHOTT, T. L., AWALT, S. J., & GILLIS-KNOX, J. (1988). Marital satisfaction in pregnancy: Stability and change. *Journal of Marriage and the Family, 50,* 325–333.

SNYDER, J., & PATTERSON, G. R. (1987). Family interaction and delinquent behavior. In H. C. Quay (Ed.), *Handbook of juvenile delinquency* (pp. 216–243). New York: Wiley.

SOBESKY, W. E. (1983). The effects of situational factors on moral judgments. *Child Development, 54,* 575–584.

SOCIETY FOR RESEARCH IN CHILD DEVELOPMENT, Committee for Ethical Conduct in Child Development Research (1990, Winter). SRCD ethical standards for research with children. *SRCD Newsletter.* Chicago: Author.

SOCKETT, H. (1992). The moral aspects of the curriculum. In P. W. Jackson (Ed.), *Handbook of research on curriculum* (pp. 543–569). New York: Macmillan.

SODIAN, B., & WIMMER, H. (1987). Children's understanding of inference as a source of knowledge. *Child Development, 58,* 424–433.

SODIAN, B., TAYLOR, C., HARRIS, P. L., & PERNER, J. (1991). Early deception and the child's theory of mind: False trails and genuine markers. *Child Development, 62,* 468–483.

SOKOLOFF, B. Z. (1987). Alternative methods of reproduction: Effects on the child. *Clinical Pediatrics, 26,* 11–17.

SOMMERVILLE, J. (1982). *The rise and fall of childhood.* Beverly Hills, CA: Sage.

SONENSTEIN, F. L., PLECK, J. H., & KU, L. C. (1989). Sexual activity, condom use and AIDS awareness among adolescent males. *Family Planning Perspectives, 21,* 152–154.

SONG, M., & GINSBURG, H. P. (1987). The development of informal and formal mathematical thinking in Korean and U.S. children. *Child Development, 58,* 1286–1296.

SONNENSCHEIN, S. (1986). Development of referential communication skills: How familiarity with a listener affects a speaker's production of redundant messages. *Developmental Psychology, 22,* 549–552.

SORCE, J., EMDE, R., CAMPOS, J., & KLINNERT, M. (1985). Maternal emotional signaling: Its effect on the visual cliff behavior of 1-year-olds. *Developmental Psychology, 21,* 195–200.

SOSA, R., KENNELL, J., KLAUS, M., ROBERTSON, S., & URRUTIA, J. (1980). The effect of a supportive companion on perinatal problems, length of labor, and mother-infant interaction. *New England Journal of Medicine, 303,* 597–600.

SOUTHARD, B. (1985). Interlimb movement control and coordination in children. In J. E. Clark & J. E. Humphrey (Eds.), *Motor development* (Vol. 1, pp. 55–66). Princeton, NJ: Princeton Press.

SPEARS, R. A. (1991). *Contemporary American slang.* Lincolnwood, IL: National Textbook Company.

SPEECE, M. W., & BRENT, S. B. (1984). Children's understanding of death: A review of three components of a death concept. *Child Development, 55,* 1671–1686.

SPELKE, E. S. (1987). The development of intermodal perception. In P. Salapatek & L. Cohen (Eds.), *Handbook of infant perception: Vol. 2.*

*From perception to cognition* (pp. 233–273). Orlando, FL: Academic Press.

SPELLACY, W. N., MILLER, S. J., & WINEGAR, A. (1986). Pregnancy after 40 years of age. *Obstetrics and Gynecology, 68,* 452–454.

SPENCE, M. J., & DECASPER, A. J. (1987). Prenatal experience with low-frequency maternal voice sounds influences neonatal perception of maternal voice samples. *Infant Behavior and Development, 10,* 133–142.

SPENCER, M. B., & DORNBUSCH, S. M. (1990). Challenges in studying minority youth. In S. Feldman & G. R. Elliott (Eds.), *At the threshold: The developing adolescent* (pp. 123–146). Cambridge, MA: Harvard University Press.

SPERDUTO, R. D., SEIGEL, D., ROBERTS, J., & ROWLAND, M. (1983). Prevalence of myopia in the United States. *Archives of Ophthalmology, 101,* 405–407.

SPINETTA, J., & RIGLER, D. (1972). The child-abusing parent: A psychological review. *Psychological Bulletin, 77,* 296–304.

SPIRITO, A., BROWN, L., OVERHOLSER, J., & FRITZ, G. (1989). Attempted suicide in adolescence: A review and critique of the literature. *Child Psychology Review, 9,* 336–363.

SPITZ, R. A. (1945). Hospitalism: An inquiry into the genesis of psychiatric conditions in early childhood. *Psychoanalytic Study of the Child, 1,* 113–117.

SPITZ, R. A. (1946). Anaclitic depression. *Psychoanalytic Study of the Child, 2,* 313–342.

SPIVACK, G., & SHURE, M. B. (1974). *Social adjustment of young children: A cognitive approach to solving real life problems.* San Francisco: Jossey-Bass.

SPOCK, B., & ROTHENBERG, M. B. (1985). *Dr. Spock's baby and child care.* New York: Pocket Books.

SPREADBURY, C. L. (1982). First date. *Journal of Early Adolescence, 2,* 83–89.

SPREEN, O., TUPPER, D., RISSER, A., TUOKKO, H., & EDGELL, D. (1984). *Human developmental neuropsychology.* New York: Oxford University Press.

SROUFE, L. A. (1979). Socioemotional development. In J. D. Osofsky (Ed.), *Handbook of infant development* (pp. 462–516). New York: Wiley.

SROUFE, L. A. (1983). Infant-caregiver attachment and patterns of adaptation in preschool: The roots of maladaptation. In M. Perlmutter (Ed.), *Minnesota Symposia on Child Psychology* (Vol. 16, pp. 41–83). Hillsdale, NJ: Erlbaum.

SROUFE, L. A. (1985). Attachment classification from the perspective of infant-caregiver relationships and infant temperament. *Child Development, 56,* 1–14.

SROUFE, L. A. (1988). A developmental perspective on day care. *Early Childhood Research Quarterly, 3,* 283–292.

SROUFE, L. A., & WATERS, E. (1976). The ontogenesis of smiling and laughter: A perspective on the organization of development in infancy. *Psychological Review, 83,* 173–189.

SROUFE, L. A., & WUNSCH, J. P. (1972). The development of laughter in the first year of life. *Child Development, 43,* 1324–1344.

STAMBROOK, M., & PARKER, K. C. H. (1987). The development of the concept of death in childhood: A review of the literature. *Merrill-Palmer Quarterly, 33,* 133–157.

STANBURY, J. B., WYNGAARDEN, J. B., & FREDERICKSON, D. S. (1983). *The metabolic basis of inherited disease.* New York: McGraw-Hill.

STANHOPE, L., BELL, R. Q., & PARKER-COHEN, N. Y. (1987). Temperament and helping behavior in preschool children. *Developmental Psychology, 23,* 347–353.

STANITSKI, C. L. (1989). Common injuries in preadolescent and adolescent athletes. *Sports Medicine, 7,* 32–41.

STARK, L. J., ALLEN, K. D., HURST, M., NASH, D. A., RIGNEY, B., & STOKES, T. F. (1989). Distraction: Its utilization and efficacy with children undergoing dental treatment. *Journal of Applied Behavior Analysis, 22,* 297–307.

STATTIN, H., & MAGNUSSON, D. (1990). *Pubertal maturation in female development.* Hillsdale, NJ: Erlbaum.

STECHLER, G., & HALTON, A. (1982). Prenatal influences on human development. In B. B. Wolman (Ed.), *Handbook of developmental psychology* (pp. 175–189). Englewood Cliffs, NJ: Prentice-Hall.

STEIN, A. (1983). Pregnancy in gravidas over age 35 years. *Journal of Nurse-Midwifery, 28,* 17–20.

STEIN, Z., SUSSER, M., SAENGER, G., & MAROLLA, F. (1975). *Famine and human development: The Dutch hunger winder of 1944–1945.* New York: Oxford.

STEINBERG, L. (1984). The varieties and effects of work during adolescence. In M. Lamb, A. Brown, & B. Rogoff (Eds.), *Advances in developmental psychology* (pp. 1–37). Hillsdale, NJ: Erlbaum.

STEINBERG, L. (1986). Latchkey children and susceptibility to peer pressure: An ecological analysis. *Developmental Psychology, 22,* 433–439.

STEINBERG, L. (1987). The impact of puberty on family relations: Effects of pubertal status and pubertal timing. *Developmental Psychology, 23,* 451–460.

STEINBERG, L. (1988a). Simple solutions to a complex problem: A response to Rodman, Pratto, & Nelson. *Developmental Psychology, 24,* 295–296.

STEINBERG, L. (1988b). Stability of Type A behavior from early childhood to young adulthood. In P. B. Baltes, D. L. Featherman, & R. M. Lerner (Eds.), *Life-span development and behavior* (Vol. 8, pp. 129–161). Hillsdale, NJ: Erlbaum.

STEINBERG, L. (1989). *Adolescence* (2nd ed.). New York: McGraw-Hill.

STEINBERG, L. D. (1990). Interdependence in the family: Autonomy, conflict, and harmony in the parent-adolescent relationship. In S. S. Feldman & G. R. Elliott (Eds.), *At the threshold: The developing adolescent* (pp. 255–276). Cambridge, MA: Harvard University Press.

STEINBERG, L., & DORNBUSCH, S. M. (1991). Negative correlates of part-time employment during adolescence: Replication and elaboration. *Developmental Psychology, 27,* 304–313.

STEINBERG, L., ELMAN, J. D., & MOUNTS, N. S. (1989). Authoritative parenting, psychosocial maturity, and academic success among adolescents. *Child Development, 60,* 1424–1436.

STEINBERG, L., & SILVERBERG, S. (1986). The vicissitudes of autonomy in early adolescence. *Child Development, 57,* 841–851.

STEINER, J. E. (1979). Human facial expression in response to taste and smell stimulation. In H. W. Reese & L. P. Lipsitt (Eds.), *Advances in child development and behavior* (Vol. 13, pp. 257–295). New York: Academic Press.

STEINER, M. (1990). Postpartum psychiatric disorders. *Canadian Journal of Psychiatry, 35,* 89–95.

STEINMAN, S. B., ZEMMELMAN, S. E., & KNOBLAUCH, T. M. (1985). A study of parents who sought joint custody following divorce: Who reaches agreement and sustains joint custody and who returns to court? *Journal of the American Academy of Child and Adolescent Psychiatry, 24,* 554–562.

STENE, J., STENE, E., & STENGEL-RUTKOWSKI, S. (1981). Paternal age and Down's syndrome. Data from prenatal diagnosis (DFG). *Human Genetics, 59,* 119–124.

STEPHENSON, M. G., LEVY, A. S., SASS, N. L., & MCGARVEY, W. E. (1987). 1985 NHIS findings: Nutrition knowledge and baseline data for the weight-loss objectives. *Public Health Reports, 102,* 61–67.

STERN, D. N. (1985). *The interpersonal world of the infant: A view from psychoanalysis and developmental psychology.* New York: Basic Books.

STERNBERG, R. J. (1984). Evaluation of the Kaufman Assessment Battery for Children from an information processing perspective. *Journal of Special Education, 18,* 269–279.

STERNBERG, R. J. (1985a). *Beyond IQ: A triarchic theory of human intelligence.* New York: Cambridge University Press.

STERNBERG, R. J. (1985b). Cognitive approaches to intelligence. In B. B. Wolman (Ed.), *Handbook of intelligence* (pp. 59–118). New York: Wiley.

STERNBERG, R. J. (1988a). A triarchic view of intelligence in cross-cultural perspective. In S. H. Irvine & J. W. Berry (Eds.), *Human abilities in cultural context* (pp. 60–85). New York: Cambridge University Press.

STERNBERG, R. J. (1988b). Intellectual development: Psychometric and information-processing approaches. In M. H. Bornstein & M. E. Lamb (Eds.), *Developmental psychology: An advanced textbook* (2nd ed., pp. 261–295). Hillsdale, NJ: Erlbaum.

STERNBERG, R. J., & ODAGAKI, L. (1989). Continuity and discontinuity in intellectual development are not a matter of 'either-or.' *Human Development, 32,* 159–166.

STEVENS, J. H. (1984). Black grandmothers' and black adolescent mothers' knowledge about parenting. *Developmental Psychology, 20,* 1017–1025.

STEVENSON, H. W., & BAKER, D. P. (1987). The family-school relation and the child's school performance. *Child Development, 58,* 1348–1357.

STEVENSON, H. W., & LEE, S-Y. (1990). Contexts of achievement: A study of American, Chinese, and Japanese children. *Monographs of the Society for Research in Child Development, 55* (1–2, Serial No. 221).

STEVENSON, H. W., STIGLER, J. W., LEE, S-Y., LUCKER, G. W., LITAMURA, S., & HSU, C. (1985). Cognitive performance and academic achievement of Japanese, Chinese, and American children. *Child Development, 56,* 718–734.

STEVENSON, R., & POLLITT, C. (1987). The acquisition of temporal terms. *Journal of Child Language, 14,* 533–545.

STEWART, D. A. (1982). *Children with sex chromosome aneuploidy: Follow-up studies.* New York: Alan R. Liss.

STEWART, R. B. (1983). Sibling attachment relationships: Child-infant interactions in the Strange Situation. *Developmental Psychology, 19,* 192–199.

STIGLER, J. W., LEE, S-Y., & STEVENSON, H. W. (1990). *The mathematical knowledge of Japanese, Chinese, and American elementary school children.* Reston, VA: National Council of Teachers of Mathematics.

STILLMAN, R. J. (1982). In utero exposure to diethylstilbestrol: Adverse effects on the reproductive tract and reproductive performance in male and female offspring. *American Journal of Obstetrics and Gynecology, 142,* 905–921.

STINI, W. A., WEBER, C. W., KEMBERLING, S. R., & VAUGHAN, L. A. (1980). Lean tissue growth and disease susceptibility in bottle-fed versus breast-fed infants. In L. S. Greene & F. E. Johnson (Eds.), *Social and biological predictors of nutritional status, physical growth, and neurological development* (pp. 61–79). New York: Academic Press.

STIPEK, D. J. (1981). Children's perceptions of their own and their classmates' ability. *Journal of Educational Psychology, 73,* 404–410.

STIPEK, D. J., GRALINSKI, J. H., & KOPP, C. B. (1990). Self-concept development in the toddler years. *Developmental Psychology, 26,* 972–977.

STIPEK, D., & MAC IVER, D. (1989). Developmental change in children's assessment of intellectual competence. *Child Development, 60,* 531–538.

STIPEK, D., RECCHIA, S., & MCCLINTIC, S. (1992). Self-evaluation in young children. *Monographs of the Society for Research in Child Development, 57* (Serial No. 226, No. 1).

STOCH, M. B., SMYTHE, P. M., MOODIE, A. D., & BRADSHAW, D. (1982). Psychosocial outcome and CT findings after growth undernourishment during infancy: A 20-year developmental study. *Developmental Medicine and Child Neurology, 24,* 419–436.

STOCKER, C., & DUNN, J. (1990). Sibling relationships in adolescence. In R. M. Lerner, A. C. Petersen, & J. Brooks-Gunn (Eds.), *The encyclopedia of adolescence* (Vol. 2, pp.1046–1048). New York: Garland.

STOCKER, C., DUNN, J., & PLOMIN, R. (1989). Sibling relationships: Links with child temperament, maternal behavior, and family structure. *Child Development, 60,* 715–727.

STODOLSKY, S. S. (1974). How children find something to do in preschools. *Genetic Psychology Monographs, 90,* 245–303.

STODOLSKY, S. S. (1988). *The subject matters.* Chicago: University of Chicago Press.

STOEL-GAMMON, C., & OTOMO, K. (1986). Babbling development of hearing-impaired and normal hearing subjects. *Journal of Speech and Hearing Disorders, 51,* 33–41.

STONE, L. (1977). *The family, sex, and marriage in England, 1500–1800.* New York: Harper & Row.

STONEMAN, Z., BRODY, G. H., & MACKINNON, C. E. (1986). Same-sex and cross-sex siblings: Activity choices, roles, behavior, and gender stereotypes. *Sex Roles, 15,* 495–511.

STRASBURGER, V. C. (1989). Adolescent sexuality and the media. *Adolescent Gynecology, 36,* 747–773.

STRAUSS, S., & LEVIN, I. (1981). Commentary on Siegler's "Developmental sequences within and between concepts." *Monographs of the Society for Research in Child Development, 46* (2, Serial No. 189).

STREISSGUTH, A. P., BARR, H. M., SAMPSON, P. D., DARBY, B. L., & MARTIN, D. C. (1989). IQ at age 4 in relation to maternal alcohol use and smoking during pregnancy. *Developmental Psychology, 25,* 3–11.

STREISSGUTH, A. P., MARTIN, D. C., BARR, H. M., SANDMAN, B. M., KIRCHNER, G. L., & DARBY, B. L. (1984). Intrauterine alcohol and nicotine exposure: Attention and reaction time in 4-year-old children. *Developmental Psychology, 20,* 533–541.

STREISSGUTH, A. P., TREDER, R., BARR, H. M., SHEPARD, T., BLEYER, W. A., SAMPSON, P. D., & MARTIN, D. (1987). Aspirin and acetaminophen use by pregnant women and subsequent child IQ and attention decrements. *Teratology, 35,* 211–219.

STREITMATTER, J. L., & PATE, G. S. (1989). Identity status development and cognitive prejudice in early adolescents. *Journal of Early Adolescence, 9,* 142–152.

STROBER, M., MCCRACKEN, J., & HANNA, G. (1990). Affective disorders. In R. M. Lerner, A. C. Petersen, & J. Brooks-Gunn (Eds.), *The encyclopedia of adolescence* (Vol. 1, pp. 18–25). New York: Garland.

STRUTT, G. F., ANDERSON, D. R., & WELL, A. D. (1975). A developmental study of the effects of irrelevant information on speeded classification. *Journal of Experimental Child Psychology, 20,* 127–135.

STUNKARD, A. J., D'AQUILI, E., & FILION, R. D. L. (1972). Influence of social class on obesity and thinness in children. *Journal of the American Medical Association, 221,* 579–584.

STUNKARD, A. J., SORENSON, T. I. A., HANIS, C., TEASDALE, T. W., CHAKRABORTY, R., SCHULL, W. J., & SCHULSINGER, F. (1986). An adoption study of human obesity. *New England Journal of Medicine, 314,* 193–198.

SULLIVAN, H. S. (1953). *The interpersonal theory of psychiatry.* New York: Norton.

SULLIVAN, J. W., & HOROWITZ, F. D. (1983). The effects of intonation on infant attention: The role of the rising intonation contour. *Journal of Child Language, 10,* 521–534.

SULLIVAN, L. W. (1987). The risks of the sickle-cell trait: Caution and common sense. *New England Journal of Medicine, 317,* 830–831.

SULLIVAN, S. A., & BIRCH, L. L. (1990). Pass the sugar, pass the salt: Experience dictates preference. *Developmental Psychology, 26,* 546–551.

SUOMI, S. (1982). Biological foundations and developmental psychobiology. In C. B. Kopp & J. B. Krakow (Eds.), *The child: Development in a social context* (pp. 42–91). Reading, MA: Addison-Wesley.

SUPER, C. M. (1980). Cognitive development: Looking across at growing up. In C. Super & M. Harkness (Eds.), *New directions for child development* (Vol. 8, pp. 59–69). San Francisco: Jossey-Bass.

SUPER, C. M. (1981). Behavioral development in infancy. In R. H. Monroe, R. L. Monroe, & B. B. Whiting (Eds.), *Handbook of cross-cultural human development* (pp. 181–270). New York: Garland.

SUPER, C. M., & HARKNESS, S. (1982). The infant's niche in rural Kenya and metropolitan America. In L. L. Adler (Ed.), *Cross-cultural research at issue* (pp. 247–255). New York: Academic Press.

SUPER, D. (1980). A life-span, life-space approach to career development. *Journal of Vocational Behavior, 16,* 282–298.

SUSANNE, C. (1975). Genetic and environmental influences in morphological characteristics. *Annals of Human Biology, 2,* 279–287.


TAGER-FLUSBERG, H. (1989). Putting words together: Morphology and syntax in the preschool years. In J. Berko Gleason (Ed.), *The development of language* (pp. 135–165). Columbus, OH: Merrill.

TAITZ, L. S. (1983). *The obese child.* Boston: Blackwell.

TAKAHASHI, K. (1990). Are the key assumptions of the "Strange Situation" procedure universal? A view from Japanese research. *Human Development, 33,* 23–30.

TAMIS-LEMONDA, C. S., & BORNSTEIN, M. H. (1989). Habituation and maternal encouragement of attention in infancy as predictors of toddler language, play, and representational competence. *Child Development, 60,* 738–751.

TANNER, J. M. (1962). *Growth at adolescence* (2nd ed.). Oxford, England: Blackwell.

TANNER, J. M. (1978a). *Education and physical growth.* New York: International Universities Press.

TANNER, J. M. (1978b). *Fetus into man.* Cambridge, MA: Harvard University Press.

TANNER, J. M., & WHITEHOUSE, R. H. (1975). Revised standards for triceps and subscapular skinfolds in British children. *Archives of Disease in Childhood, 50,* 142–145.

TANNER, J. M., WHITEHOUSE, R. H., CAMERON, N., MARSHALL, W. A., HEALEY, M. J. R., & GOLDSTEIN, H. (1983). *Assessment of skeletal maturity and prediction of adult height* (TW2 method) (2nd ed.). New York: Academic Press.

Task Force on Pediatric AIDS (1989). Pediatric AIDS and human immunodeficiency virus infection. *American Psychologist, 44,* 258–264.

TAYLOR, A. R., ASHER, S. R., & WILLIAMS, G. A. (1987). The social adaptation of mainstreamed mildly retarded children. *Child Development, 58,* 1321–1334.

TAYLOR, M., & GELMAN, S. A. (1988). Adjectives and nouns: Children's strategies for learning new words. *Child Development, 59,* 411–419.

TAYLOR, M., & GELMAN, S. A. (1989). Incorporating new words into the lexicon: Preliminary evidence for language hierarchies. *Child Development, 60,* 625–636.

TEBERG, A. J., WALTHER, F. J., & PENA, I. C. (1988). Mortality, morbidity, and outcome of the small-for-gestational-age infant. *Seminar in Perinatology, 12,* 84–94.

TEIKARI, J. M., O'DONNELL, J. O., KAPRIO, J., & KOSKENVUO, M. (1991). Impact of heredity in myopia. *Human Heredity, 41,* 151–156.

TELLER, D. Y., & BORNSTEIN, M. H. (1987). Infant color vision and color perception. In P. Salapatek & L. Cohen (Eds.), *Handbook of infant perception* (2nd ed., pp. 185–236). Orlando, FL: Academic Press.

TERMINE, N. T., & IZARD, C. E. (1988). Infants' responses to their mothers' expressions of joy and sadness. *Developmental Psychology, 24,* 223–229.

TERTINGER, D. A., GREENE, B. F., & LUTZKER, J. R. (1984). Home safety: Development and validation of one component of an ecobehavioral treatment program for abused and neglected children. *Journal of Applied Behavior Analysis, 17,* 159–174.

THARP, R. G., & GALLIMORE, R. (1988). *Rousing minds to life: Teaching, learning, and schooling in social context.* Cambridge: Cambridge University Press.

THATCHER, R. W., WALKER, R. A., & GIUDICE, S. (1987). Human cerebral hemispheres develop at different rates and ages. *Science, 236,* 1110–1113.

THELEN, E. (1989). The (re)discovery of motor development: Learning new things from an old field. *Developmental Psychology, 25,* 946–949.

THELEN, E., FISHER, D. M., & RIDLEY-JOHNSON, R. (1984). The relationship between physical growth and a newborn reflex. *Infant Behavior and Development, 7,* 479–493.

THEORELL, K., PRECHTL, H., & VOS, J. (1974). A polygraphic study of normal and abnormal newborn infants. *Neuropaediatrie, 5,* 279–317.

THOMA, S. J. (1986). Estimating gender differences in the comprehension and preference of moral issues. *Developmental Review, 6,* 165–180.

THOMAS, A., & CHESS, S. (1977). *Temperament and development.* New York: Brunner/Mazel.

THOMAS, A., CHESS, S., & BIRCH, H. G. (1970, August). The origins of personality. *Scientific American, 223* (2), 102–109.

THOMAS, J. R. (1984). Children's motor skill development. In J. R. Thomas (Ed.), *Motor development during childhood and adolescence* (pp. 91–104). Minneapolis, MN: Burgess.

THOMAS, J. R., & FRENCH, K. E. (1985). Gender differences across age in motor performance: A meta-analysis. *Psychological Bulletin, 98,* 260–282.

THOMPSON, R. A. (1988). The effects of infant day care through the prism of attachment theory: A critical appraisal. *Early Childhood Research Quarterly, 3,* 273–282.

THOMPSON, R. A. (1990a). On emotion and self-regulation. In R. A. Thompson (Ed.), *Nebraska Symposia on Motivation* (Vol. 36, pp. 383–483). Lincoln, NB: University of Nebraska Press.

THOMPSON, R. A. (1990b). Vulnerability in research: A developmental perspective on research risk. *Child Development, 61,* 1–16.

THOMPSON, R. A., & LIMBER, S. (1991). "Social anxiety" in infancy: Stranger wariness and separation distress. In H. Leitenberg (Ed.), *Handbook of social and evaluation anxiety* (pp. 85–137). New York: Plenum.

THOMPSON, R. A., LAMB, M., & ESTES, D. (1982). Stability of infant-mother attachment and its relationship to changing life circumstances in an unselected middle-class sample. *Child Development, 53,* 144–148.

THOMPSON, R. A., TINSLEY, B. R., SCALORA, M. J., & PARKE, R. D. (1989). Grandparents' visitation rights: Legalizing the ties that bind. *American Psychologist, 44,* 1217–1222.

THORNDIKE, R. L., HAGEN, E. P., & SATTLER, J. M. (1986). *The Stanford-Binet Intelligence Scale.* Chicago: Riverside Publishing.

TIZARD, B., & HODGES, J. (1978). The effect of early institutional rearing on the development of eight year old children. *Journal of Child Psychology and Psychiatry, 19,* 99–118.

TIZARD, B., & REES, J. (1975). The effect of early institutional rearing on the behaviour problems and affectional relationships of four-year-old children. *Journal of Child Psychology and Psychiatry, 16,* 61–73.

TOBIAS, P. V. (1975). Anthropometry among disadvantaged people: Studies in Southern Africa. In E. S. Watts, F. E. Johnston, & G. W. Lasker (Eds.), *Biosocial interrelations in population adaptation: World anthropology series* (pp. 287–305). The Hague: Mouton.

TOLSON, T. F. J., & WILSON, M. N. (1990). The impact of two- and three-generational black family structure on perceived family climate. *Child Development, 61,* 416–428.

TOMASELLO, M. (1990). The role of joint attentional processes in early language development. *Language Sciences, 10,* 69–88.

TOMASELLO, M., MANNLE, S., & KRUGER, A. C. (1986). Linguistic environment of 1- to 2-year-old twins. *Developmental Psychology, 22,* 169–176.

TORFS, C. P., BERG, B. VAN DEN, OECHSLI, F. W., & CUMMINS, S. (1990). Prenatal and perinatal factors in the etiology of cerebral palsy. *Journal of Pediatrics, 116,* 615–619.

TORRANCE, E. P. (1980). *Torrance Tests of Creative Thinking.* New York: Scholastic Testing Service.

TOUWEN, B. C. L. (1984). Primitive reflexes—Conceptual or semantic problem? In H. F. R. Prechtl (Ed.), *Continuity of neural functions from prenatal to postnatal life* (Clinics in Developmental Medicine No. 94, pp. 115–125). Philadelphia: Lippincott.

TOWER, R. B., SINGER, D. G., SINGER, J. L., & BIGGS, A. (1979). Differential effects of television programming on preschoolers' cognition, imagination, and social play. *American Journal of Orthopsychiatry, 49,* 265–281.

TREIBER, F. A., SCHRAMM, L., & MABE, P. A. (1986). Children's knowledge and concerns toward a peer with cancer: A workshop intervention approach. *Child Psychiatry and Human Development, 16,* 249–260.

TRICKETT, P. K., & KUCZYNSKI, L. (1986). Children's misbehaviors and parental discipline strategies in abusive and nonabusive families. *Developmental Psychology, 22,* 115–123.

TRONICK, E. Z. (1989). Emotions and emotional communication in infants. *American Psychologist, 44,* 112–119.

TRONICK, E. Z., COHN, J., & SHEA, E. (1986). The transfer of affect between mothers and infants. In T. B. Brazelton & M. W. Yogman (Eds.), *Affect development in infancy* (pp. 11–25). Norwood, NJ: Ablex.

TUDGE, J. (1990). Vygotsky, the zone of proximal development, and peer collaboration: Implications for classroom practice. In L. C. Moll (Ed.), *Vygotsky and education* (pp. 155–172). New York: Cambridge University Press.

TURIEL, E. (1983). *The development of social knowledge: Morality and convention.* New York: Cambridge University Press.

TURIEL, J. (1991a, February 3). At the survival borderline. *San Francisco Examiner,* pp. D13–D14.

TURIEL, J. (1991b, February 10). Life-and-death battle. *San Francisco Examiner,* pp. D13–D14.

TURKHEIMER, E., & GOTTESMAN, I. I. (1991). Individual differences and the canalization of human behavior. *Developmental Psychology, 27,* 18–22.

TYACK, D., & INGRAM, D. (1977). Children's production and comprehension of questions. *Journal of Child Language, 4,* 211–224.


UDRY, J. R. (1990). Hormonal and social determinants of adolescent sexual initiation. In J. Bancroft & J. M. Reinisch (Eds.), *Adolescence and puberty* (pp. 70–87). New York: Oxford University Press.

ULLIAN, D. Z. (1976). The development of conceptions of masculinity and femininity. In B. Loyd & J. Archer (Eds.), *Exploring sex differences* (pp. 25–47). London: Academic Press.

ULRICH, B. D., & ULRICH, D. A. (1985). The role of balancing in performance of fundamental motor skills in 3-, 4-, and 5-year-old children. In J. E. Clark & J. H. Humphrey (Eds.), *Motor development* (Vol. 1, pp. 87–98). Princeton, NJ: Princeton Books.

UNGER, R., KREEGER, L., & CHRISTOFFEL, K. K. (1990). Childhood obesity: Medical and familial correlates and age of onset. *Clinical Pediatrics, 29,* 368–372.

UNGERER, J. A., ZELAZO, P. R., KEARSLEY, R. B., & O'LEARY, K. (1981). Developmental changes in the representation of objects in symbolic play from 19–34 months of age. *Child Development, 52,* 186–195.

U.S. BUREAU OF THE CENSUS (1991a). *Current population reports, Series P-20.* Washington, DC: U.S. Government Printing Office.

U.S. BUREAU OF THE CENSUS (1991b). *Statistical abstract of the United States* (111th ed.) Washington, DC: U.S. Government Printing Office.

U.S. CENTERS FOR DISEASE CONTROL (1991, January). *HIV/AIDS surveillance.* Atlanta, GA: Author.

U.S. DEPARTMENT OF EDUCATION, NATIONAL CENTER FOR EDUCATION STATISTICS (1991). *Digest of Education Statistics 1990.* Washington, DC: U.S. Government Printing Office.

U.S. DEPARTMENT OF HEALTH AND HUMAN SERVICES (1988). *The Surgeon General's report on nutrition and health.* Washington, DC: U.S. Government Printing Office.

U.S. DEPARTMENT OF HEALTH AND HUMAN SERVICES, NATIONAL INSTITUTE ON DRUG ABUSE (1990a). *Drug abuse among youth: Findings from the 1988 national household survey on drug abuse.* Washington, DC: U.S. Government Printing Office.

U.S. DEPARTMENT OF HEALTH AND HUMAN SERVICES, NATIONAL INSTITUTE ON DRUG ABUSE (1990b). *Drug use among American high school seniors, college students and young adults, 1975–1990* (Vol. 1). Washington, DC: U.S. Government Printing Office.

U.S. DEPARTMENT OF HEALTH AND HUMAN SERVICES (1990c). *Vital and health statistics, Series 24 (No. 4).* Washington, DC: U.S. Government Printing Office.

U.S. DEPARTMENT OF HEALTH AND HUMAN SERVICES (1991a). *Healthy people 2000.* Washington, DC: U.S. Government Printing Office.

U.S. DEPARTMENT OF HEALTH AND HUMAN SERVICES (1991b). *Vital Statistics of the United States, 1988.* Washington, DC: U.S. Government Printing Office.

U.S. DEPARTMENT OF JUSTICE (1991). *Crime in the United States.* Washington, DC: U.S. Government Printing Office.

U.S. DEPARTMENT OF LABOR, BUREAU OF LABOR STATISTICS (1990, January). *Employment and earnings* (Vol. 37, No. 1). Washington, DC: U.S. Government Printing Office.

U.S. DEPARTMENT OF LABOR, BUREAU OF LABOR STATISTICS (1992, January). *CPI detailed report.* Washington, DC: U.S. Government Printing Office.

U.S. GENERAL ACCOUNTING OFFICE (1986). *School dropouts: The extent and nature of the problem.* Washington, DC: Author.

UŽGIRIS, I. C. (1973). Patterns of cognitive development in infancy. *Merrill-Palmer Quarterly, 19,* 181–204.

UŽGIRIS, I. C., & HUNT, J. McV. (1975). *Assessment in infancy: Ordinal scales of psychological development.* Urbana: University of Illinois Press.


VALLEROY, L. A., HARRIS, J. R., & WAY, P. O. (1990). The impact of HIV infection on child survival in the developing world. *AIDS, 4,* 667–672.

VAN DYKE, D. C., LANG, D. J., HEIDE, F., VAN DUYNE, S., & SOUCEK, M. J. (Eds.). (1990). *Clinical perspectives in the management of Down syndrome.* New York: Springer-Verlag.

VAN IJZENDOORN, M. H., & KROONENBERG, P. M. (1988). Cross-cultural patterns of attachment: A meta-analysis of the Strange Situation. *Child Development, 59,* 147–156.

VANDELL, D. L., & CORASANITI, M. A. (1988). The relation between third graders' after-school care and social, academic, and emotional functioning. *Child Development, 59,* 868–875.

VANDELL, D., & POWERS, C. (1983). Day care quality and children's free play activities. *American Journal of Orthopsychiatry, 53,* 293–300.

VANFOSSEN, B., JONES, J., & SPADE, J. (1987). Curriculum tracking and status maintenance. *Sociology of Education, 60,* 104–122.

VAUGHN, B. E., KOPP, C. B., & KRAKOW, J. B. (1984). The emergence and consolidation of self-control from eighteen to thirty months of age: Normative trends and individual differences. *Child Development, 55,* 990–1004.

VAUGHN, B. E., LEFEVER, B. G., SEIFER, R., & BARGLOW, P. (1989). Attachment behavior, attachment security, and temperament during infancy. *Child Development, 60,* 728–737.

VEERULA, G. R., & NOAH, P. K. (1990). Clinical manifestations of childhood lead poisoning. *Journal of Tropical Medicine and Hygiene, 93,* 170–177.

VEGA-LAHR, N., FIELD, T., GOLDSTEIN, S., & CARRAN, D. (1988). Type A behavior in preschool children. In T. M. Field, P. M. McCabe, & N. Schneiderman (Eds.), *Stress and coping across development* (pp. 89–107). Hillsdale, NJ: Erlbaum.

VENTURA, S. J. (1989). Trends and variations in first births to older women in the United States, 1970–86. *Vital and Health Statistics* (Series 21). Hyattsville, MD: U.S. Department of Health and Human Services.

VERBRUGGE, H. P. (1990a). The national immunization program of the Netherlands. *Pediatrics, 86* (6, Pt. 2), 1060–1063.

VERBRUGGE, H. P. (1990b). Youth health care in the Netherlands: A bird's eye view. *Pediatrics, 86* (6, Pt. 2), 1044–1047.

VERHULST, F. C., ALTHAUS, M., & VERSLUIS-DEN BIEMAN, H. J. M. (1990). Problem behavior in international adoptees: I. An epidemiological study. *Journal of the American Academy of Child and Adolescent Psychiatry, 29,* 94–103.

VESSEY, J. A. (1988). Comparison of two teaching methods on children's knowledge of their internal bodies. *Nursing Research, 37,* 262–267.

VILLAR, J., & GONZALEZ-COSSIO, T. (1986). Nutritional factors associated with low birth weight and short gestational age. *Clinical Nutrition, 5,* 78–85.

VINOVSKIS, M. A. (1988). *An "epidemic" of adolescent pregnancy?* New York: Oxford University Press.

VOHR, B. R., & GARCIA-COLL, C. T. (1988). Follow-up studies of high-risk low-birth-weight infants: Changing trends. In H. E. Fitzgerald, B. M. Lester, & M. W. Yogman (Eds.), *Theory and research in behavioral pediatrics* (pp. 1–65). New York: Plenum.

VORHEES, C. V. (1986). Principles of behvioral teratology. In E. P. Riley & C. V. Vorhees (Eds.), *Handbook of behavioral teratology* (pp. 23–48). New York: Plenum.

VORHEES, C. V., & MOLLNOW, E. (1987). Behavioral teratogenesis: Long-term influences on behavior from early exposure to environmental agents. In J. D. Osofsky (Ed.), *Handbook of infant development* (2nd ed., pp. 913–971). New York: Wiley.

VOYDANOFF, P., & DONNELLY, B. W. (1990). *Adolescent sexuality and pregnancy.* Newbury Park, CA: Sage.

VUCHINICH, S., HETHERINGTON, E. M., VUCHINICH, R. A., & CLINGEMPEEL, W. G. (1991). Parent-child interaction and gender differences in early adolescents' adaptation to stepfamilies. *Developmental Psychology, 27,* 618–626.

VURPILLOT, E., RUEL, J., & CASTREC, A. (1977). L'organization perceptive chez le nourrisson: Résponse au tout au ses éléments. *Bulletin de Psychologie, 327,* 396–405.

VYGOTSKY, L. S. (1978). *Mind in society: The development of higher psychological processes.* Cambridge, MA: Harvard University Press. (Original works published 1930, 1933, and 1935)

VYGOTSKY, L. S. (1987). Thinking and speech. In R. W. Rieber, A. S. Carton (Eds.), & N. Minick (Trans.), *The collected works of L. S. Vygotsky: Vol. 1. Problems of general psychology* (pp. 37–285). New York: Plenum. (Original work published 1934)

WAAS, G. A. (1988). Social attributional biases of peer-rejected and aggressive children. *Child Development, 59,* 969–975.

WACHS, T. D., (1975). Relation of infants' performance on Piagetian scales between twelve and twenty-four months and their Stanford-Binet performance at thirty-one months. *Child Development, 46,* 929–935.

WACHS, T. D., UŽGIRIS, I. C., & HUNT, J. McV. (1971). Cognitive development in infants of different age levels and from different environmental backgrounds: An explanatory investigation. *Merrill-Palmer Quarterly, 17,* 283–317.

WADDINGTON, C. H. (1957). *The strategy of the genes.* London: Allen and Unwin.

WAGGONER, J. E., & PALERMO, D. S. (1989). Betty is a bouncing bubble: Children's comprehension of emotion-descriptive metaphors. *Developmental Psychology, 25,* 152–163.

WAGNER, M. E., SCHUBERT, H. J. P., & SCHUBERT, D. S. P. (1985). Family size effects: A review. *Journal of Genetic Psychology, 146,* 65–78.

WAKAT, D. K. (1978). Physiological factors of race and sex in sport. In L. K. Bunker & R. J. Rotella (Eds.), *Sport psychology: From theory to practice* (pp. 194–209). Charlotte, VA: University of Virginia. (Proceedings of the 1978 Sport Psychology Institute)

WALBERG, H. J. (1986). Synthesis of research on teaching. In M. C. Wittrock (Ed.), *Handbook of research on teaching* (3rd ed., pp. 214–229). New York: Macmillan.

WALDEN, T. A., & OGAN, T. A. (1988). The development of social referencing. *Child Development, 59,* 1230–1240.

WALK, R. D., & GIBSON, E. J. (1961). A comparative and analytic study of visual depth perception. *Psychological Monographs, 75* (15, Whole No. 519).

WALKER, L. J. (1988). The development of moral reasoning. In R. Vasta (Ed.), *Annals of child development* (Vol. 5, pp. 33–78). Greenwich, CT: JAI Press.

WALKER, L. J. (1989). A longitudinal study of moral reasoning. *Child Development, 60,* 157–166.

WALKER, L. J., & DE VRIES, B. (1985). *Moral stages/moral orientations: Do the sexes really differ?* Paper presented at the annual meeting of the American Psychological Association, Los Angeles.

WALKER, L. J., & TAYLOR, J. H. (1991). Family interactions and the development of moral reasoning. *Child Development, 62,* 264–283.

WALLACE, J. R., CUNNINGHAM, T. F., & DEL MONTE, V. (1984). Change and stability in self-esteem between late childhood and early adolescence. *Journal of Early Adolescence, 4,* 253–257.

WALLACH, M. A. (1985). Creativity testing and giftedness. In F. D. Horowitz & M. O'Brien (Eds.), *The gifted and talented: Developmental perspectives* (pp. 99–123). Washington, DC: American Psychological Association.

WALLERSTEIN, J. S. (1983). Children of divorce: The psychological tasks of the child. *American Journal of Orthopsychiatry, 53,* 230–243.

WALLERSTEIN, J. S. (1991). The long-term effects of divorce on children: A review. *Journal of the American Academy of Child and Adolescent Psychiatry, 30,* 349–360.

WALLERSTEIN, J., & CORBIN, S. B. (1989). Daughters of divorce: Report from a ten-year follow-up. *American Journal of Orthopsychiatry, 59,* 593–604.

WALLERSTEIN, J. S., CORBIN, S. G., & LEWIS, J. M. (1988). Children of divorce: A ten-year study. In E. M. Hetherington & J. Arasteh (Eds.), *Impact of divorce, single parenting, and stepparenting on children* (pp. 198–214). Hillsdale, NJ: Erlbaum.

WALLERSTEIN, J. S., & KELLY, J. B. (1980). *Surviving the break-up: How children and parents cope with divorce.* New York: Basic Books.

WALTERS, R. H., & ANDRES, D. (1967). *Punishment procedures and self-control.* Paper presented at the annual meeting of the American Psychological Association, Washington, DC.

WARREN, A. R., & TATE, C. S. (1992). Egocentrism in children's telephone conversations. In R. M. Diaz & L. E. Berk (Eds.), *Private speech: From social interaction to self-regulation* (pp. 245-264). Hillsdale, NJ: Erlbaum.

WARREN, S. F., & KAISER, A. P. (1988). Research in early language intervention. In S. L. Odom & M. B. Karnes (Eds.), *Early intervention for infants and children with handicaps* (pp. 89–108). Baltimore, MD: Paul H. Brookes.

WARREN-LEUBECKER, A., & BOHANNON, J. N., III. (1989). Pragmatics: Language in social contexts. In J. Berko Gleason (Ed.), *The development of language* (pp. 327–368). Columbus, OH: Merrill.

WATERMAN, A. S. (1985). Identity in context of adolescent psychology. In A. S. Waterman (Ed.), *New directions for child development* (No. 30, pp. 5–24). San Francisco: Jossey-Bass.

WATERMAN, A. S. (1989). Curricula interventions for identity change: Substantive and ethical considerations. *Journal of Adolescence, 12,* 389–400.

WATSON, D. J. (1989). Defining and describing whole language. *Elementary School Journal, 90,* 129–141.

WATSON, J. B., & RAYNOR, R. (1920). Conditioned emotional reactions. *Journal of Experimental Psychology, 3,* 1–14.

WATSON, J. D., & CRICK, R. H. C. (1953). Molecular structure of nucleic acids. *Nature, 171,* 737–738.

WECHSLER, D. (1989). *Manual for the Wechsler Preschool and Primary Scale of Intelligence-Revised.* New York: Psychological Corporation.

WECHSLER, D. (1991). *Manual for the Wechsler Intelligence Test for Children-III.* New York: Psychological Corporation.

WEGMAN, M. E. (1991). Annual summary of vital statistics—1990. *Pediatrics, 88,* 1081–1092.

WEHREN, A., DeLisi, R., & Arnold, M. (1981). The development of noun definition. *Journal of Child Language, 8,* 165–175.

WEIDEGER, P. (1976). *Menstruation and menopause.* New York: Knopf.

WEIDNER, G. Sexton, G., Matarazzo, J. D., Pereira, C., & Friend, R. (1988). Type A behavior in children, adolescents, and their parents. *Developmental Psychology, 24,* 118–121.

WEIL, W. B. (1975). Infant obesity. In M. Winick (Ed.), *Childhood obesity* (pp. 61–72). New York: Wiley.

WEINRAUB, M., & Lewis, M. (1977). The determinants of children's responses to separation. *Monographs of the Society for Research in Child Development, 42* (4, Serial No. 172).

WEINSTEIN, R. S., Marshall, H. H., Sharp, L., & Botkin, M. (1987). Pygmalion and the student: Age and classroom differences in children's awareness of teacher expectations. *Child Development, 58,* 1079–1093.

WEISNER, T. S., & Gallimore, R. (1977). My brother's keeper: Child and sibling caretaking. *Current Anthropology, 18,* 169–190.

WEISNER, T. S., & Wilson-Mitchell, J. E. (1990). Nonconventional family life-styles and sex typing in six-year-olds. *Child Development, 61,* 1915–1933.

WEITZMAN, M., Gortmaker, S., & Sobol, A. (1990). Racial, social, and environmental risks for childhood asthma. *American Journal of Diseases of Children, 144,* 1189–1194.

WELLMAN, H. M. (1985). The child's theory of mind: The development of conceptions of cognition. In S. R. Yussen (Ed.), *The growth of reflection in children* (pp. 169–206). San Diego, CA: Academic Press.

WELLMAN, H. M. (1988a). First steps in the child's theorizing about mind. In J. W. Astington, P. L. Harris, & D. R. Olson (Eds.), *Developing theories of mind* (pp. 64–92). Cambridge, England: Cambridge University Press.

WELLMAN, H. M. (1988b). The early development of memory strategies. In F. F. Weinert & M. Perlmutter (Eds.), *Memory development: Universal changes and individual differences* (pp. 3–29). Hillsdale, NJ: Erlbaum.

WELLMAN, H. M., Cross, D., & Bartsch, K. (1987). Infant search and object permanence: A meta-analysis of the A-not-B error. *Monographs of the Society for Research in Child Development, 51* (3, Serial No. 214).

WELLMAN, H. M., Somerville, S. C., & Haake, R. J. (1979). Development of search procedures in real-life spatial environments. *Developmental Psychology, 15,* 530–542.

WELLS, G. (1985). Preschool literacy-related activities and success in school. In D. R. Olson, N. Torrance, & A. Hildyard (Eds.), *Literacy, language, and learning* (pp. 229–255). Cambridge, England: Cambridge University Press.

WELLS, G. L., Turtle, J. W., & Luus, C. A. E. (1989). The perceived credibility of child eyewitnesses: What happens when they use their own words? In S. J. Ceci, D. F. Ross, & M. P. Toglia (Eds.), *Perspectives on children's testimony* (pp. 23–36). New York: Springer-Verlag.

WENTZEL, K., & Feldman, S. (1990, March). *The relationship between family functioning, classroom self-restraint, and academic achievement.* Paper presented at the Conference on Human Development, Atlanta, GA.

WERKER, J. F. (1989). Becoming a native listener. *American Scientist, 77,* 54–59.

WERNER, E. E. (1989, April). Children of the garden island. *Scientific American, 260* (4), 106–111.

WERNER, E. E., & Smith, R. S. (1982). *Vulnerable but invincible: A study of resilient children.* New York: McGraw-Hill.

WERNER, S. J., & Siqueland, E. R. (1978). Visual recognition memory in the preterm infant. *Infant Behavior and Development, 1,* 79–94.

WEST, L. L. (1991). Introduction. In L. L. West (Ed.), *Effective strategies for dropout prevention of at-risk youth* (pp. 1–42). Gaithersburg, MD: Aspen Publishers.

WHALEN, C. K. (1983). Hyperactivity, learning problems, and the attention deficit disorders. In T. H. Ollendick & M. Hersen (Eds.), *Handbook of child psychopathology* (pp. 155–199). New York: Plenum.

WHIFFEN, V. E. (1988). Vulnerability to postpartum depression: A prospective multivariate study. *Journal of Abnormal Psychology, 97,* 467–474.

WHIFFEN, V. E., & Gotlib, I. H. (1989). Infants of postpartum depressed mothers: Temperament and cognitive status. *Journal of Abnormal Psychology, 98,* 274–279.

WHISNANT, L., & Zegans, L. (1975). A study of attitudes toward menarche in white middle-class American adolescent girls. *American Journal of Psychiatry, 132,* 809–814.

WHITE, B., & Held, R. (1966). Plasticity of sensorimotor development in the human infant. In J. F. Rosenblith & W. Allinsmith (Eds.), *The causes of behavior* (pp. 60–70). Boston: Allyn and Bacon.

WHITE, S. H. (1992). G. Stanley Hall: From philosophy to developmental psychology. *Developmental Psychology, 28,* 25–34.

WHITEHURST, G. J. (1982). Language development. In B. B. Wolman (Ed.), *Handbook of developmental psychology* (pp. 367–386). New York: Wiley.

WHITEHURST, G. J., Fischel, J. E., Caulfield, M. B., DeBaryshe, B. D., & Valdez-Menchaca, M. C. (1989). Assessment and treatment of early expressive language delay. In P. R. Zelazo & R. Barr (Eds.), *Challenges to developmental paradigms: Implications for assessment and treatment* (pp. 113–135). Hillsdale, NJ: Erlbaum.

WHITEHURST, G. J., & Vasta, R. (1975). Is language acquired through imitation? *Journal of Psycholinguistic Research, 4,* 37–59.

WHITING, B., & Edwards, C. P. (1988a). *Children in different worlds.* Cambridge, MA: Harvard University Press.

WHITING, B., & Edwards, C. P. (1988b). A cross-cultural analysis of sex differences in the behavior of children aged 3 through 11. In G. Handel (Ed.), *Childhood socialization* (pp. 281–297). New York: Aldine de Gruyter.

WHITING, J. W. M., Burbank, V. K., & Ratner, M. S. (1986). The duration of maidenhood across cultures. In J. B. Lancaster & B. Hamburg (Eds.), *School-age pregnancy and parenthood: Biosocial dimensions* (pp. 273–302). New York: Aldine De Gruyter.

WILENSKY, H. L. (1983). Evaluating research and politics: Political legitimacy and consensus as missing variables in the assessment of social policy. In E. Spiro & E. Yuchtman-Yaar (Eds.), *Evaluating the welfare state: Social and political perspectives* (pp. 51–74). New York: Academic Press.

WILLATS, J. (1977). How children learn to represent three-dimensional space in drawings. In G. Butterworth (Ed.), *The child's representation of the world* (pp. 189–202). New York: Plenum.

WILLERMAN, L. (1979). Effects of families on intellectual development. *American Psychologist, 34,* 923–929.

WILLIAMS, B. C. (1990). Immunization coverage among preschool children: The United States and selected countries. *Pediatrics, 86* (6, Pt. 2), 1052–1055.

WILLIAMS, B. C., & Kotch, J. B. (1990). Excess injury mortality among children in the United States: Comparison of recent international statistics. *Pediatrics, 86* (6, Pt. 2), 1067–1073.

WILSON, A. L., & Neidich, G. (1991). Infant mortality and public policy. *Social Policy Report of the Society for Research in Child Development, 5* (No. 2).

WILSON, M., & Baker, S. (1987). Structural approach to injury control. *Journal of Social Issues, 43,* 73–86.

WILSON, M. N. (1986). The black extended family: An analytical consideration. *Developmental Psychology, 22,* 246–258.

WILSON, M. N. (1989). Child development in the context of the black extended family. *American Psychologist, 44,* 380–385.

WILSON, M. N., & Tolson, T. F. J. (1985). *An analysis of adult-child interaction patterns in three-generational black families.* Unpublished manuscript, University of Virginia.

WILSON, R., & Cairns, E. (1988). Sex-role attributes, perceived competence and the development of depression in adolescence. *Journal of Child Psychology and Psychiatry, 29,* 635–650.

WILSON, R. S. (1976). Concordance in physical growth for monozygotic and dizygotic twins. *Annals of Human Biology, 3,* 1–10.

WILSON, R. S. (1983). The Louisville Twin Study: Developmental synchronies in behavior. *Child Development, 54,* 298–316.

WILSON, W. J. (1987). *The truly disadvantaged.* Chicago: University of Chicago Press.

WINICK, M., & Noble, A. (1966). Cellular response in rats during malnutrition at various ages. *Journal of Nutrition, 89,* 300–306.

WINICK, M., Rosso, P., & Waterlow, J. (1970). Cellular growth of cerebrum, cerebellum, and brain stem in normal and marasmic children. *Experimental Neurology, 26,* 393–400.

WINN, S., Tronick, E. Z., & Morelli, G. A. (1989). The infant and the group: A look at Efe caretaking. In J. K. Nugent, B. M. Lester, & T. B. Brazelton (Eds.), *Biology, culture, and development* (Vol. 1, pp. 87–109). Norwood, NJ: Ablex.

WINNER, E. (1986, August). Where pelicans kiss seals. *Psychology Today, 20 (8)*, 25–35.

WINNER, E. (1988). *The point of words: Children's understanding of metaphor and irony*. Cambridge, MA: Harvard University Press.

WINSTON, M. H., & SHALITA, A. R. (1991). Acne vulgaris: Pathogenesis and treatment. *Pediatric Clinics of North America, 38*, 889–903.

WITELSON, S. F., & KIGAR, D. L. (1988). Anatomical development of the corpus callosum in humans: A review with reference to sex and cognition. In D. L. Molfese & S. J. Segalowitz (Eds.), *Brain lateralization in children* (pp. 35–57). New York: Guilford Press.

WOLFF, P. H. (1963). Observations on the early development of smiling. In B. M. Foss (Ed.), *Determinants of infant behavior* (Vol. 2, pp. 113–138). London: Methuen.

WOLFF, P. H. (1966). The causes, controls and organization of behavior in the neonate. *Psychological Issues, 5* (1, Serial No. 17).

WONG-FILLMORE, L., AMMON, P., McLAUGHLIN, B., & AMMON, M. S. (1985). *Learning English through bilingual instruction*. Rosslyn, VA: National Clearinghouse for Bilingual Education.

WOOD, D. J., BRUNER, J. S., & ROSS, G. (1976). The role of tutoring in problem solving. *Journal of Child Psychology and Psychiatry, 17*, 89–100.

WOODSON, E. M., WOODSON, R. H., BLURTON-JONES, N. G., POLLOCK, S. B., & EVANS, M. A. (1980). *Maternal smoking and newborn behavior*. Paper presented at the International Conference on Infant Studies, New Haven, CT.

WOOLLEY, J. D., & WELLMAN, H. M. (1990). Young children's understanding of realities, nonrealities, and appearances. *Child Development, 61*, 946–961.

WOROBEY, J., & BLAJDA, V. M. (1989). Temperament ratings at 2 weeks, 2 months, and 1 year: Differential stability of activity and emotionality. *Developmental Psychology, 25*, 257–263.

WRIGHT, J. (1991). Poverty, homelessness, health, nutrition, and children. In J. H. Kryder-Coe, L. M. Salamon, & J. M. Molnar (Eds.), *Homeless children and youth: A new American dilemma* (pp. 71–104). New Brunswick, NJ: Transaction.


YARROW, A. L. (1991). *Latecomers: Children of parents over 35*. New York: The Free Press.

YARROW, M. R., SCOTT, P. M., & WAXLER, C. Z. (1973). Learning concern for others. *Developmental Psychology, 8*, 240–260.

YESALIS, C. E., STREIT, A. L., VICARY, J. R., FRIEDL, K. E., BRANNON, D., & BUCKLEY, W. (1989). Anabolic steroid use: Indications of habituation among adolescents. *Journal of Drug Education, 19*, 103–116.

YOGMAN, M. W. (1981). Development of the father-infant relationship. In H. Fitzgerald, B. Lester, & M. W. Yogman (Eds.), *Theory and research in behavioral pediatrics* (Vol. 1, pp. 221–279). New York: Plenum.

YONAS, A., GRANRUD, E. C., ARTERBERRY, M. E., & HANSON, B. L. (1986). Infants' distance perception from linear perspective and texture gradients. *Infant Behavior and Development, 9*, 247–256.

YOUNG, C., McMAHON, J. E., BOWMAN, V., & THOMPSON, D. (1989). Maternal reasons for delayed prenatal care. *Nursing Research, 38*, 242–243.

YOUNG, K. T. (1990). American conceptions of infant development from 1955 to 1984: What the experts are telling parents. *Child Development, 61*, 17–28.

YOUNGER, B. A. (1985). The segregation of items into categories by ten-month-old infants. *Child Development, 56*, 1574–1583.

YOUNISS, J. (1980). *Parents and peers in social development: A Piagetian-Sullivan perspective*. Chicago: University of Chicago Press.

YOUNISS, J., & SMOLLAR, J. (1986). *Adolescent relations with mothers, fathers, and friends*. Chicago: University of Chicago Press.

YUILL, N., & PERNER, J. (1988). Intentionality and knowledge in children's judgments of actor's responsibility and recipient's emotional reaction. *Developmental Psychology, 24*, 358–365.


ZAHN-WAXLER, C., KOCHANSKA, G., KRUPNICK, J., & McKNEW, D. (1990). Patterns of guilt in children of depressed and well mothers. *Developmental Psychology, 26*, 51–59.

ZAHN-WAXLER, C., RADKE-YARROW, M., & KING, R. M. (1979). Child-rearing and children's prosocial initiations toward victims of distress. *Child Development, 50*, 319–330.

ZAHN-WAXLER, C., RADKE-YARROW, M., WAGNER, E., & CHAPMAN, M. (1992). Development of concern for others. *Developmental Psychology, 28*, 126–136.

ZAJONC, R. B., MARKUS, H., & MARKUS, G. B. (1979). The birth order puzzle. *Journal of Personality and Social Psychology, 37*, 1325–1341.

ZAMETKIN, A. J., NORDAHL, T. E., GROSS, M., KING, A. C., SEMPLE, W. E., RUMSEY, J., HAMBURGER, S., & COHEN, R. M. (1990). Cerebral glucose metabolism in adults with hyperactivity of childhood onset. *New England Journal of Medicine, 323*, 1413–1415.

ZEISEL, S. H. (1986). Dietary influences on neurotransmission. *Advances in Pediatrics, 33*, 23–48.

ZELAZO, P. R. (1983). The development of walking: New findings on old assumptions. *Journal of Motor Behavior, 2*, 99–137.

ZESKIND, P. S., & LESTER, B. M. (1978). Acoustic features and auditory perception of the cries of newborns with prenatal and perinatal complications. *Child Development, 49*, 580–589.

ZESKIND, P. S., & LESTER, B. M. (1981). Analysis of cry features in newborns with differential fetal growth. *Child Development, 52*, 207–212.

ZESKIND, P. S., & RAMEY, C. T. (1978). Fetal malnutrition: An experimental study of its consequences on infant development in two caregiving environments. *Child Development, 49*, 1155–1162.

ZESKIND, P. S., & RAMEY, C. T. (1981). Preventing intellectual and interactional sequelae of fetal malnutrition: A longitudinal, transactional, and synergistic approach to development. *Child Development, 52*, 213–218.

ZIEGLER, C. B., DUSEK, J. B., & CARTER, D. B. (1984). Self-concept and sex-role orientation: An investigation of multidimensional aspects of personality development in adolescence. *Journal of Early Adolescence, 4*, 25–39.

ZIGLER, E. F. (1987). Formal schooling for four-year-olds? No. *American Psychologist, 42*, 254–260.

ZIGLER, E. F., ABELSON, W. D., & SEITZ, V. (1973). Motivational factors in the performance of economically disadvantaged children on the Peabody Picture Vocabulary Test. *Child Development, 44*, 294–303.

ZIGLER, E. F., & BERMAN, W. (1983). Discerning the future of early childhood intervention. *American Psychologist, 38*, 894–906.

ZIGLER, E. F., & FINN-STEVENSON, M. E. (1988). Applied developmental psychology. In M. H. Bornstein & M. E. Lamb (Eds.), *Developmental psychology: An advanced textbook* (2nd ed., pp. 595–634). Hillsdale, NJ: Erlbaum.

ZIGLER, E. F., & HALL, N. W. (1989). Physical child abuse in America: Past, present, and future. In D. Cicchetti & V. Carlson (Eds.), *Child maltreatment* (pp. 203–253). New York: Cambridge University Press.

ZIGLER, E. F., & SEITZ, V. (1982). Social policy and intelligence. In R. J. Sternberg (Ed.), *Handbook of human intelligence* (pp. 586–641). Cambridge, England: Cambridge University Press.

ZIMMERMAN, B. J. (1990). Self-regulation learning and academic achievement: An overview. *Educational Psychologist, 25*, 3–18.

ZIPORYN, T. (1992, February). Postpartum depression: True blue? *Harvard Health Letter, 17* (4), 1–3.

ZUKOW, P. G. (1986). The relationship between interaction with the caregiver and the emergence of play activities during the one-word period. *British Journal of Developmental Psychology, 4*, 223–234.

ZUKOW, P. G. (1989). Siblings as effective socializing agents: Evidence from central Mexico. In P. G. Zukow (Ed.), *Sibling interaction across cultures* (pp. 79–105). New York: Springer-Verlag.

# Name Index

Aaron, R., 464
Aaronson, L. S., 105, 107, 108
Abel, E. L., 116
Abelman, R., 372
Aber, J. L., 187
Ableson, W. D., 334
Aboud, F. E., 473
Abraham, K. G., 574
Abravanel, E., 190
Achenbach, T. M., 39, 143, 416
Ackerman, P. B., 438
Acredolo, C., 419
Adams, A., 419
Adams, C., 539
Adams, G. R., 573, 574
Adamson, L. B., 237
Adcock, A. G., 597
Adelson, J., 592
Adler, T. F., 463
Aerts, E., 583
Ainsworth, M. D. S., 261, 262n, 264
Alberts-Corush, J., 423
Alessandri, S. M., 543
Alexander, K., 297
Alipuria, L., 577
Allen, L., 334
Alpert-Gillis, L. J., 376
Altemeier, W. A., 177
Alter-Reid, K., 488, 489
Althaus, M., 69
Altman, R. E., 105
Altshuler, J. L., 465
Alvarez, M. M., 586
Alvord, E. C., 170n
Aman, C., 491
American Academy of Pediatrics, 173, 288, 292, 531
American College of Sports Medicine, 531
American Psychiatric Association, 423, 446, 521
American Psychological Association, 43, 43n
Ames, E. W., 195
Anand, K. J. S., 150
Anderson, D. R., 421
Anderson, E. R., 481, 482, 484
Anderson, E. S., 344
Anderson, J. E., 526
Anderson, K. N., 329
Andersson, B-E., 227
Andres, D., 367
Andrews, L. B., 66
Angle, J., 394.
Angulo, J., 397

Apgar, V., 129, 130n
Applebaum, M. I., 225
Appleton, T., 152, 192
Archer, S. L., 573, 575
Arend, R., 270
Aries, P., 7
Arjmand, O., 562
Arnold, F., 268
Arnold, K., 562
Arnold, M., 437
Arsenault, L., 297
Arterberry, M. E., 193
Asher, S. R., 447, 473, 474
Ashmead, D. H., 152, 219
Aslin, R. N., 152, 153, 237
Astington, J. W., 352
Astley, S. J., 108
Atkin, C., 371
Atkinson, J., 192
Atkinson, R. C., 23, 217, 217n, 218
Attanucci, J., 585
Attie, I., 516
August, D., 440
Avis, J., 330, 459
Axia, G., 438
Axworthy, D., 64n
Azmitia, M., 325

Bahrick, L. E., 197
Bailey, R. C., 280
Baillargeon, R., 22, 213, 214n, 321, 418
Baird, P. A., 62, 63
Bakeman, R., 30
Baker, D. P., 76, 452, 553
Baker, R. L., 116
Baker, S., 297
Bakewell, J., 135
Ball, S., 341
Ballard, B. D., 396
Bancroft, J., 64n
Band, E. B., 465
Bandura, A., 17, 18, 365
Bane, M. J., 75
Banks, M. S., 152, 192, 193, 195, 195n
Baranowski, T., 175n
Barber, M., 296
Barenboim, C., 466, 467, 572
Bargelow, P. D., 143
Barkley, R. A., 423
Barker, R. G., 77
Barnes, D., 135
Barnes, J., 462

Barnes, K. E., 360n
Barnes, S., 237
Barnett, J. K., 575
Barnett, M., 132
Barnett, R. C., 268, 485
Barol, B., 106
Baroni, R., 438
Barr, H. M., 105, 108
Barr, R., 427
Barrera, M. E., 197
Barrett, D. E., 32
Barrett, K. C., 194, 246
Barry, H., III, 500, 511
Bartlett, A. V., 294
Bartsch, K., 213
Baruch, G. K., 268, 485
Bates, E., 233, 236
Bates, J. E., 252, 257, 270
Bathurst, K., 485
Bauer, P. J., 328
Baumeister, R. F., 571
Baumrind, D., 72, 73, 379, 380, 587, 594
Bayles, K., 270
Bayley, N., 179n, 184n, 189, 224, 513
Beach, F., 518
Bearison, D. J., 469
Beatty, W. W., 374
Beautrais, A. L., 289
Beeghley, L., 518
Behrend, D. A., 234, 318, 325
Behrman, R. E., 61n
Beidel, D., 487
Beilin, H., 18, 19, 321
Beintema, D., 148n
Belenky, M. F., 582
Bell, A., 521
Bell, R. Q., 33
Bellinger, D., 110
Belsky, J., 120, 222, 264, 265, 267
Bem, D. J., 40, 253
Bem, S. L., 376, 377
Benacerraf, B. R., 67n, 102
Benbow, C. P., 285, 449, 547, 562
Bench, R. J., 152
Benedict, R., 250, 518
Benjamin, F., 174
Bentler, P. M., 430, 526, 528
Berezin, J., 228n
Berg, K. M., 177
Berg, M., 76
Berg, W. K., 177
Bergman, A., 244
Berk, L. E., 33, 324, 531, 559

Berko Gleason, J., 236
Berkowitz, M. W., 583
Berman, P. W., 129, 157
Berman, W., 339
Berndt, T. J., 473, 588, 589, 590
Best, D. L., 475
Bertenthal, B. I., 194, 196, 197n
Beunen, G. P., 530
Bialystok, E., 438, 439
Bibace, R., 401
Bierman, K. L., 474
Bigi, L., 425
Bigler, R. S., 378
Birch, H. G., 253n
Birch, J. W., 446n
Birch, L. L., 175, 290
Birnholz, J. C., 102
Bishop, S. M., 462
Bivens, J. A., 324
Bjorklund, D. F., 422, 424
Black, A. E., 379
Black, J. E., 169
Blajda, V. M., 252
Blanc, W., 113
Blanchard, M., 262
Blasi, A., 585
Blass, E. M., 186
Blatt, M., 584
Blaubergs, M. S., 562
Block, Jeanne H., 482, 586
Block, Jack, 482, 527, 528, 585
Bloom, B. S., 449
Blotner, R., 469
Blue, J., 382
Blurton Jones, N., 408
Blyth, D. A., 513, 550, 551n, 552, 573,
    588, 592
Blythe, B. J., 524
Bobak, I. M., 111, 132
Bogatz, G. A., 341
Bohannon, J. N., III, 232, 237, 344, 345
Boldizar, J. P., 376
Boll, E. S., 269
Booth, A., 175
Borghraef, M., 64n
Borke, H., 318
Borkowski, J. G., 426
Bornstein M. H., 305, 153, 192, 219, 222
Borstelmann, L. J., 7
Borton, R. W., 197
Boruta, M. J., 444
Bossard, J. S. S., 269
Bouchard, T. J., Jr., 82, 86
Boukydis, C. F. Z., 155
Boulton, M., 408
Bowen, R., 543
Bowen-Woodward, K., 484
Bowlby, J., 24, 259, 261, 266
Boyer, C. B., 525
Brachfeld, S., 142
Brackbill, Y., 137
Braddock, O., 192
Bradley, R. H., 226, 226n, 227, 335, 335n,
    452
Braeges, J. L., 367

Braine, M. D. S., 234
Brainerd, C. J., 312, 419, 536, 538
Brand, E., 484
Bransford, J. D., 425
Brassard, M. R., 384
Bray, J. H., 483
Braungart, J. M., 83, 267
Brazelton, T. B., 137, 156, 157, 184
Brennan, W. M., 195
Brent, S. B., 319
Bresnick, S., 465
Bretherton, I., 236, 251, 261, 312, 354,
    357, 375
Brindley, B. A., 138
Brody, G. H., 269, 375
Brody, L. E., 449
Brody, L. R., 152
Brody, N., 433
Broman, S. H., 137
Bromley, D. B., 460
Bronfenbrenner, U., 25, 28, 71, 83
Bronson, G. W., 196
Brook, R. H., 398
Brookman, R. R., 525
Brooks, P. H., 294, 400
Brooks, R. H., 592
Brooks-Gunn, J., 68, 271, 272, 339, 374,
    505, 508, 509, 511, 513, 514, 516,
    519, 522, 523, 525, 594
Brophy, J. E., 442, 443
Brown, A. L., 425, 426, 546
Brown, B. B., 591, 593, 593n
Brown, D., 484
Brown, L. K., 401
Brown, R. W., 232, 234, 235n, 343, 352
Brownell, C. A., 352
Bruch, H., 396
Brumberg, J. J., 516
Bruner, J. S., 221, 233, 324
Bryant, B. K., 76
Bryant, Dana, 330
Bryant, Donna M., 229, 330
Bryant, P. E., 320
Buchanan, C. M., 482
Buck, G. M., 188
Buddin, B. J., 465
Buehler, J. W., 525
Bugental, D. B., 382
Buhrmester, D., 41, 478, 588, 590, 592
Bukowski, W. M., 590
Bulatao, R. A., 268
Bulkley, J. A., 491
Bullock, M., 271
Bumpass, L. L., 479
Burbank, V. K., 500
Burchinal, M., 338
Burgess, A. W., 381
Burgess, R. L., 155
Burke, M., 269
Burke, P., 188
Burns, S. M., 312
Bushnell, E. W., 181
Buss, A. H., 252
Butler, G. E., 390
Byrne, D. F., 466, 467n

Byrne, M. C., 344
Byrnes, J. P., 428


Caine, N., 511
Cairns, B. D., 558n
Cairns, E., 596
Cairns, R. B., 10, 472, 558n
Caldera, Y. M., 273
Caldwell, B. M., 226, 335, 335n, 452
Camara, K. A., 482
Cameron, N., 282n
Campbell, F. A., 230, 231n
Campos, J. J., 177, 194, 196, 197n, 246,
    247, 249, 254, 263, 355
Campos, R. G., 156n
Canizzo, S. R., 422
Capelli, C. A., 548
Caplan, M., 352
Capuzzi, D., 598n
Cardarelli, A. P., 488, 489
Carey, S., 401, 420
Carle, E., 309
Carlson, C., 553
Carlson, V., 265
Caron, A. J., 219
Caron, R. F., 219
Carpenter, C. J., 375
Carr, M., 327
Carriger, M. S., 352
Carruth, B. R., 396
Carter, D. B., 469, 586
Carter-Saltzman, L., 285
Case, R., 22, 221, 272, 420, 540
Casey, M. B., 305
Cashdan, E., 30, 78
Caskey, T., 68
Caspi, A., 40, 253
Cassel, J., 115
Cassidy, J., 120
Cates, W., Jr., 525
Caton, C. L. M., 75
Caudill, W., 182, 254, 255
Cazden, C., 440
Ceci, S. J., 424, 434, 436
Cernoch, J. M., 151
Chaika, H., 152
Chalkley, M. A., 232, 234
Chalmers, J. B., 467
Chandler, M. J., 467
Chapman, M., 417, 463
Chase-Landsdale, L., 68, 523
Chasnoff, I. J., 106
Chein, C., 139
Chen, A. W., 402
Chen, C., 450
Chen, S., 177, 263
Cherlin, A. J., 72
Chess, S., 252, 253n, 256, 257
Cheung, L. W. Y., 396
Chi, M. T. H., 424, 424n
Children's Defense Fund, 28, 75, 114, 117,
    144, 227, 290, 291, 292, 293, 336,
    381, 384, 402, 480, 483, 522, 523,
    525, 529, 556, 559, 565

Childs, C. P., 29
Chipman, S. F., 547
Chisholm, J. S., 156
Chomsky, C., 438
Chomsky, N., 231
Christoffel, K. K., 395, 396
Christophersen, E. R., 295
Churchill, B. H., 517
Churchill, S. R., 69
Cicchetti, D., 187
Clark, E. V., 234, 341, 342
Clark, J. T., 403
Clark, R. D., III, 155
Clarke-Stewart, K. A., 37, 267
Clasen, D., 593
Claudy, J. G., 93
Clausen, J. A., 513
Clements, D. H., 444, 447
Cleminshaw, H. K., 481
Clifton, R., 152, 192
Clingempeel, W. E., 482, 484
Clubb, P. A., 328
Cnattingius, S., 188
Coakley, J., 407
Cochi, S. L., 111
Cohen, F. L., 57n, 61, 61n, 64n, 67n, 110n
Cohen, L., 199
Cohen, S. E., 142
Cohen-Overbeek, W. C. J., 95
Cohn, J. F., 158, 265
Coie, J. D., 473, 474, 475
Colby, A., 579, 582
Cole, C. B., 491
Cole, J. R., 562
Cole, M., 425
Coleman, J., 553
Collea, J. V., 139
Collier, A. M., 294
Collins, W. A., 370, 373
Collmer, C. W., 366
Colman, A. D., 119, 120, 159
Colman, L. L., 119, 120, 159
Colón, A. R., 292
Colón, P. A., 292
Comer, J. P., 559
Committee on Labor and Human
    Resources, 410
Compas, B. E., 75, 490
Condry, J., 370
Conger, R. D., 382
Connell, J. P., 376
Connolly, J. A., 312
Connolly, K. J., 180, 358
Constanzo, P. R., 396
Cooke, R. A., 44
Cooper, B., 583
Cooper, C. R., 553, 561, 573, 575
Cooper, R. P., 237
Coopersmith, S., 462
Copes, M., 159
Coppotelli, H., 473, 474
Corah, N. L., 140
Corasaniti, M. A., 486
Corbin, S. G., 481, 482
Coren, S., 285

Corman, H. H., 215, 226
Cornell, C. P., 381
Cornell, E. H., 143, 152
Corno, L., 443
Corrigan, R., 312
Costabile, A., 408
Cotton, P., 188
Cowan, C. P., 120, 159
Cowan, P. A., 159
Cox, K., 139
Cox, M., 72, 267, 480, 481, 482, 483, 484
Cox, R., 480, 481, 482, 483, 484
Cox, T., 228
Craik, F. I. M., 23
Crain-Thoreson, C., 331
Cratty, B. J., 298, 299n, 403n, 404, 405,
    407
Crawford, D. B., 79
Crewdson, J., 488
Crick, R. H. C., 50
Crider, C., 401
Crisafi, M. A., 320
Crockenberg, S. B., 257, 266, 273
Crockett, L. J., 586
Crook, C. K., 151
Cross, D., 213
Crouter, A. C., 83
Cruzcosa, M., 382
Csikszentmihalyi, M., 509, 512n, 545, 588,
    589, 589n
Cummings, E. M., 38
Cunningham, F. G., 137
Cunningham, T. F., 462
Curran, D. K., 598
Curtiss, S., 549
Cytryn, L., 158


Dagleish, M., 180
Dale, P. S., 331
Damon, W., 362, 468, 469, 473, 572
Daniels-Bierness, T., 474
Dannemiller, J. L., 196
Dansky, J. L., 312
d'Aquili, E., 395
Darlington, R. B., 337, 338n
Darwin, C., 9, 10
Das Gupata, P., 320
Davenport, G. G., 464
Davey, T. C., 430
David, H. P., 69
Davidson, R. J., 172
Davies, Margery W., 81, 227
Davies, M., 595, 597
Davis, C. C., 358
De Villiers, J. G., 343
De Villiers, P. A., 343
De Vries, B., 585
DeAngelis, T., 487, 488
DeBaryshe, B. D., 72, 369, 601n
DeBlassie, R. R., 516, 517
DeCasper, A. J., 102, 152
DeFrain, J., 188
Degelman, D., 444
Del Monte, V., 462

Delecki, J., 168
Delgado-Gaitan, C., 553
DeLisi, R., 437, 540
Dellas, M., 574
DeLoache, J. S., 327, 328, 329
Delphi Communication Sciences, 478
DeMarie-Dreblow, D., 424
Dembo, M. H., 590
DeMeis, D., 267
Dement, W. C., 154
Denham, S. A., 380
Dennis, M. G., 172, 180
Dennis, W., 180
Denny, F. W., 294
Denny, T., 562
D'Ercole, A. J., 287
Deutsch, F. M., 119
Deutsch, W., 438
Devereux, E. C., 408
Devlin, J. B., 398
Diamond, A., 214
Diana, M. S., 592
Diaz, R. M., 324, 439, 590
Dick-Read, G., 132
Dickenson, G., 592
Dickinson, D. K., 437
Didow, S. M., 358
Dietz, W. H., Jr., 396
DiLalla, L. F., 320
Dirks, J., 197, 435
Dittrichova, J., 154
Divine-Hawkins, P., 338
DiVitto, B., 142
Dixon, J. A., 466
Dixon, R. A., 10
Dixon, R. L., 59
Dodge, K. A., 250, 353, 473, 474
Dodwell, P. C., 195
Doi, L. T., 255
Dolgin, K. G., 318
Dollaghan, C., 342
Domanic, J. A., 465
Donnelly, B. W., 520, 522, 525
Dontas, C., 147
Dornbusch, S. M., 79, 481, 482, 552, 553,
    565, 577, 592
Dorris, M., 107, 116
Dossey, J. A., 452, 555
Doubleday, C., 355, 465
Douglas, V. I., 423
Douvan, E., 592
Doyle, A. B., 312
Drabman, R. S., 396
Draper, P., 30, 78
Dreher, M., 107
Dreyer, P., 520
Drotar, D., 177
DuBois, D. L., 473
Dubow, E. F., 490
Dubrow, N., 488
Duncan, P., 514
Duncan, S. W., 118, 120
Dunford, F. W., 599
Dunham, F., 233
Dunham, P., 233

Dunn, J., 251, 268, 269, 269n, 272, 375, 479, 588
Dunphy, D. C., 592
DuPont, R. L., 356
Durrett, M., 562
Dusek, J. B., 586
Dweck, C. S., 463, 464
Dye-White, E., 110
Dyson, A. H., 331

East, P. L., 588
Easterbrooks, M. A., 265
Ebeling, K. S., 318
Eccles, J. S., 407, 550, 553, 556, 586
Eckerman, C. O., 358
Eckert, H., 303, 530n
Eckstrom, R. B., 558n
Eder, D., 531
Eder, R. A., 351, 466
Edwards, C. P., 368, 374, 476
Egeland, B., 380, 382, 382n, 383, 489
Eicher, S., 591, 593
Eifermann, R. R., 408
Eilers, R. E., 233
Eisen, M., 460
Eisenberg, L., 599
Eisenberg, N., 357, 467, 582
Eisenberg-Berg, N., 365
Ekman, P, 246
Elardo, R., 226n
Elbers, L., 233
Elder, G. H., Jr., 40, 253
Elkind, D., 521, 543, 544, 545
Elkins, P. D., 400
Elliot, E. S., 463
Elliott, D. S., 599
Ellwood, D. T., 75
Elman, J. D., 380
Emde, R. N., 247, 248
Emerson, P. E., 258
Emery, R. E., 27, 366, 381, 482
Emory, E. K., 128
Engel, N., 120
Enns, J. T., 327
Enright, R. D., 544, 584
Epstein, J. L., 553, 590
Epstein, L. H., 397
Erickson, E., 458
Erickson, M. F., 382, 382n, 383, 489
Erikson, E. H., 12, 16, 242, 350, 389, 570, 575
Ernhart, C. B., 110
Ernst, L., 188
Eron, L. D., 366
Escalona, S. K., 215, 226
Espenschade, A., 303, 530n
Estes, D., 266
Evans, R., 398
Eveleth, P. B., 291, 507
Everly, G. S., 115

Fabes, R. A., 354
Fagan, J., 599

Fagan, J. F., III, 218, 225
Fagot, B. I., 255, 270, 273, 368, 375, 377
Fahmeier, E. D., 419
Falbo, T., 93
Faller, K. C., 489, 489n, 491
Fantz, R. L., 195, 196
Fanurik, D., 297, 400
Farmer, M. C., 585
Farrington, D. P., 599
Fawcett, S. B., 294
Featherman, D., 561
Fedele, N. M., 121
Fee, E., 288
Fein, G. G., 312, 361
Feiner, J., 356
Feingold, A., 546
Feldlaufer, H., 553
Feldman, D. H., 449
Feldman, J. F., 225
Feldman, S., 553
Fenzel, L. M., 552
Ferdman, B. M., 439
Ferguson, L. R., 44
Fergusson, D. M., 174, 289
Fernald, A., 236
Feshbach, N. D., 370
Feshbach, S., 370
Field, T. M., 143, 189, 190n
Fiese, B., 223, 227
Figueroa, R. A., 433
Filion, R. D. L., 395
Fine, G. A., 409, 472
Fine, M., 558, 558n
Finkelhor, D., 488, 489n
Finkelstein, N. W., 228
Finn-Stevenson, M. E., 81
Firestone, P., 423
Fischer, K. W., 22, 420, 540
Fisher, C. B., 305
Fisher, D. M., 149
FitzGerald, D. P., 575
Fivush, R., 328
Flavell, E. R., 320
Flavell, J. H., 206, 213, 318, 320, 321, 329, 421, 422, 425
Flemming, P. J., 188
Flood, M., 598
Fogel, A., 255
Food Research and Action Center, 176
Ford, C., 518
Ford, L. H., 351
Ford, M. E., 424
Fordham, S., 553
Forrest, D., 289
Forrest, J. D., 518
Forsyth, B. W., 396
Fortier, L., 539
Fox, N. A., 172, 247
Foxman, B., 398
Francis, P. L., 219
Frank, D. A., 105
Frank, S. J., 574
Frankel, E., 51n
Frankel, G. W., 421
Frankel, K. A., 270

Frankel, M. T., 422
Frauenglass, M. H., 324
Frederickson, D. S., 61n
Freedman, D. G., 156, 254
Freedman, N., 156
Freeman, D., 500
French, D. C., 474
French, K. E., 303, 407
French, L. A., 416
Freud, S., 13
Frey, K. S., 377
Fried, M. H., 510
Fried, M. N., 510
Fried, P. A., 107
Friedman, A. G., 402
Friedman, J. A., 288
Friedman, M., 397
Friedrich-Cofer, L., 371
Friesen, W., 246
Frisch, R. E., 501
Fritz, G. K., 401
Frodi, A., 155
Froggatt, P., 188
Frost, Lois, 254, 255
Frost, Loren Ann, 438
Fuchs, I., 583
Furman, E., 319
Furman, W., 41, 478, 479, 588, 590, 592
Furrow, D., 236, 330, 343
Furstenberg, F. F., Jr., 68, 72, 79, 480, 519, 520, 522, 523
Furuno, S., 300n
Fuson, K. C., 332, 428

Gaddini, E., 259
Gaddini, R., 259
Gaddis, A., 508
Gaensbauer, T. J., 248
Gagan, R. J., 177
Gage, N. L., 441
Galambos, S. J., 439
Galin, D., 286
Gallagher, J. J., 229, 339
Galler, J. R., 176
Gallimore, R., 78, 325, 442, 443n
Gallistel, C. R., 332
Gallup, G., 518
Galotti, K. M., 585
Gamoran, A., 554
Gant, N. F., 137
Garbarino, J., 75, 383, 488
Garcia, E. E., 438, 440
Garcia-Coll, C. T., 140, 141
Gardner, H., 301, 302n, 449
Gardner, M. J., 61
Garmezy, N., 490, 595
Garrick, J. G., 529
Garrison, C., 595
Garrison, W. T., 390
Garrow, D. H., 147
Garvey, C., 343, 350, 362
Garwood, S. G., 80
Gauvain, M., 422
Gellatly, A. R. H., 540

Geller, J., 174
Gelles, R. J., 381
Gelman, R., 22, 318, 321, 332
Gelman, S. A., 318, 342
Gentner, D., 342
Gentry, J. R., 331
Gerbner, G., 370, 371
Gergen, P. J., 398
Gershon, E. S., 83
Gesell, A., 10
Getchell, N., 299, 299n
Getzels, J. W., 449
Ghatala, E. S., 427
Giaconia, R. M., 441
Gibbons, J., 253
Gibbs, J. C., 583
Gibson, E. J., 192, 197, 199, 215, 304
Gil, D. G., 384
Gilbert, E. H., 516, 517
Gilchrist, D., 524
Gilgun, J. F., 518, 520, 521
Gilligan, C. F., 582, 584, 585
Gillmore, J., 466
Ginsburg, A. P., 195
Ginsburg, H. P., 205, 322, 336
Ginzberg, E., 560
Giudice, S., 284, 392
Gjerde, P. F., 482
Glahn, T. J., 64, 64n
Glass, D. C., 397
Gleitman, H., 236
Gleitman, L. R., 236
Glick, P. C., 479
Glidden, L. M., 69
Gnepp, J., 354, 465
Goetz, E. T., 432
Goffin, S. G., 77
Goldberg, D. L., 396
Goldberg, M. E., 371
Goldberg, S., 142, 147, 152, 192, 487n
Goldberg, W. A., 484
Goldfield, B. A., 234, 236
Goldin-Meadow, S., 233, 439
Goldman, P., 576
Goldman-Rakic, P. S., 214
Goldschmid, M. L., 430
Goldsmith, H. H., 252, 253
Goldstein, A. P., 601
Goldstein, H., 282n, 290
Gomez-Schwartz, B., 488, 489
Gonso, J., 474
Gonzalez-Cossio, T., 114
Good, T. L., 443
Goode, M. K., 222
Goodlad, J. I., 76
Goodman, G. S., 491
Goodman, J. T., 423
Goodman, K. S., 427
Goodman, R. A., 172
Gopnik, A., 220, 234
Gordon, J. E., 291
Gordon, S., 518, 520, 521
Gorn, G. J., 371
Gortmaker, S. L., 141, 395, 396, 398
Gotlib, I. H., 158

Gottesman, I. I., 84, 85n, 86, 253
Gottfried, A. E., 485
Gottfried, A. W., 143, 485
Gottlieb, G., 85
Gottman, J. M., 355, 474
Gould, M. S., 599
Graber, M., 213
Graham, F. K., 140
Graham, L., 504
Graham, S., 355, 465
Gralinski, J. H., 273
Granchrow, J. R., 186
Grandon, G. M., 93
Grant, J. P., 120, 174
Grantham-McGregor, S., 114
Grau, P. N., 562
Gray, W. M., 322
Green, F. L., 320
Green, J. A., 73, 155
Green, R., 521
Greenberg, D. N., 373
Greenberg, M., 147
Greenberg, P., 333
Greenberger, E., 484, 565
Greenbowe, T., 539
Greene, B. F., 297
Greene, P. G., 402
Greenfield, P. M., 29
Greeno, J. G., 24
Greenough, W. T., 169
Greif, E. B., 508
Grimes, D. A., 109
Gross, G. G., 305
Gross, S. J., 174
Grossman, H. D., 446, 446n
Grossman, L. K., 175n
Grossmann, K., 263
Grotevant, H. D., 561, 573, 562, 575
Gruendel, J., 328
Grusec, J. E., 365
Guarino, P. A., 355, 465
Guidubaldi, J., 481
Guilford, J. P., 448
Gump, P. V., 77
Gunnar, M., 249
Gurtner, J-L., 444
Gurucharri, C., 466
Gustafson, G. E., 73, 155


Haake, R. J., 326n, 327
Haan, N., 583, 585
Haas, B., 73
Hagan, R. I., 375
Hagen, E. P., 334, 430
Haglund, B., 188
Hahn, W. K., 172
Hainline, L., 192
Haith, M., 196, 197n
Hakuta, K., 438, 439
Halberstadt, A. G., 476
Hall, G. S., 10, 498
Hall, J. A., 476
Hall, J. G., 63, 64n
Hall, N. W., 382n, 383, 384

Hall, R. J., 432
Hall, W. S., 24
Halmi, K. A., 516, 517
Halpern, D. F., 285
Halton, A., 140
Halverson, C. F., 377, 378n
Halverson, H. M., 181
Halverson, L. E., 299
Hamberger, L., 55, 96n, 99, 100, 111
Hamdan, L., 504
Hamilton, S. B., 467
Hamilton, S. F., 556, 558, 563, 564n
Hammersmith, S., 521
Hammill, D. D., 446
Hanigan, W. C., 137
Hanna, G., 595
Haque, M., 398
Harkness, S., 177
Haynes, C. F., 177
Harlap, S., 120
Harley, E. E., 120
Harlow, H. F., 258
Harmon, R. J., 248
Harold, R. D., 407
Harris, G., 175
Harris, J. R., 112
Harris, K. L., 155
Harris, M. J., 443
Harris, P. L., 215, 329, 330, 459
Harris, R. T., 516, 517
Harris, S., 472, 585
Harrison, A. O., 78
Hart, D., 572
Hart, S. N., 384
Harter, S., 353, 355, 402, 460, 461, 462,
   465, 573
Hartman, C. R., 381
Hartstone, 599
Hartup, W. W., 362, 368, 471, 591
Hatch, T., 449
Hatcher, R. P., 143
Haugaard, J. J., 489
Hauser, S. T., 499, 573
Haviland, J. M., 249, 251
Hawke, S., 94n
Hawkins, D. J., 601
Hawkins, J., 445, 539
Hayden, E., 344
Hayes, C. D., 519, 519n, 520, 522, 525
Hayes, R. M., 75
Hayghe, H. V., 78
Hayne, H., 219
Haynes, C. F., 177
Healey, M. J. R., 282n
Heath, S. B., 74, 76, 77, 435
Hebel, J. R., 107
Hecht, B. F., 342
Hedges, L. V., 441
Hein, K., 525
Heinl, T., 156n
Heinonen, O. P., 116
Held, R., 181
Helpin, M. L., 392
Hembree, E. A., 248
Henderson, F. W., 294
Henggeler, S. W., 599, 601

Henker, B., 423
Hergenrather, J. R., 401
Herkowitz, J., 303
Hersov, L., 487
Hetherington, E. M., 480, 481, 482, 483, 484
Hetherington, S. E., 132
Hewer, A., 579
Hickey, P. R., 150
Higgins, A., 584
Higgins-Trenk, A., 476
Hill, C. R., 477
Hill, J. P., 511, 586, 587, 588, 591
Hill, P. M., 168n
Hillman, S. B., 464
Hind, H., 290
Hinde, R. A., 24, 25
Hinman, A. R., 294
Hirsch, B. J., 473
Hirsch, J., 174
Hirschman, J., 491
Hirsh-Pasek, K., 191
Hiscock, M., 285
Ho, H., 64, 64n
Ho, J., 64, 64n
Ho, V., 539
Hobart, C., 484
Hock, E., 267
Hodges, J., 147, 264
Hodges, R. M., 416
Hoefnagel-Höhle, M., 549
Hoff-Ginsburg, E., 237
Hoffman, L. W., 92, 272, 484, 485
Hoffman, M. L., 74, 155, 355, 364
Hofsten, C. von, 180, 181
Hogarty, P. S., 225
Holden, C., 597
Holden, G. W., 367, 369
Holmbeck, G. N., 525, 587, 591
Holt, R. W., 380
Hong, K., 259
Honzik, M. P., 225, 334
Hook, E. B., 63, 65
Hooper, F. E., 321
Hopkins, B., 182, 183n
Horan, J. J., 527
Horgan, D., 343, 438
Horn, J. M., 83, 434
Horn, T. S., 409
Horn, W. F., 447
Horner, T. M., 248
Hornick, R., 249
Hornung, M., 360n
Horowitz, F. D., 18, 152, 447
Horowitz, J. M., 488, 489
Horwood, l. J., 174
Hotaling, G. T., 382
Houts, A. C., 398
Howard, M., 524
Howe, N., 269, 269n
Howes, C., 227, 267, 337, 338, 362
Howes, P., 72
Hoyseth, K. S., 108
Hsu, J., 553
Hubel, D. H., 169

Hudson, J. A., 328
Huebner, R. R., 248
Huesmann, L. R., 371
Humphrey, G. K., 195
Humphrey, H. E. B., 110
Humphrey, P., 168n
Humphrey, T., 150
Humphreys, A. P., 408
Humphreys, L. G., 430
Hunt, J. McV., 74, 215, 226
Hunter, R. S., 382
Huston, A. C., 273, 371, 372, 373, 376, 475, 479, 586
Huston-Stein, A., 476
Huttenlocher, J., 237
Hwang, K., 268
Hyde, J. S., 546, 547
Hymel, S., 473
Hymes, J. L., Jr., 80

Iannotti, R. J., 38
Ilg, F. L., 10
Ingersoll, G. M., 462
Ingram, D., 343
Inhelder, B., 314, 418, 536, 543
International Education Association, 450
Irvine, J. J., 464
Irwin, C. E., 529
Isabella, R., 264, 265
Israelashvili, R., 268
Istvan, J., 115
Izard, C. E., 247n, 248, 249

Jacklin, C. N., 177, 235, 254, 373, 374
Jackson, P. W., 449
Jacobs, F. H., 81, 227
Jacobs, J., 407
Jacobson, J. L., 110
Jacobson, S. W., 110
Jacobvitz, D., 383
Jambor, T. W., 360, 360n
James, S. R., 169, 175, 280, 283, 394, 515
Jason, L. A., 294
Jencks, C., 74
Jensen, A. R., 83, 431n, 432, 433, 434
Jensen, M. D., 111, 132
Jernigan, L. P., 574
Johnson, C. L., 517
Johnson, J. E., 321
Johnson, J. S., 549
Johnston, J. R., 482
Jones, C. P., 237
Jones, E. F., 519, 522
Jones, G. P., 590
Jones, J., 554
Jones, L. E., 155
Jones, M. C., 513
Jones, P. J. H., 108
Jones, R. L., 447
Jones, S. S., 248
Joos, S. K., 114
Jordan, A. E., 294
Jordan, B., 131n, 135

Jordan, P. L., 157
Jusczyk, P. W., 152

Kaczala, C. M., 463
Kagan, J., 252, 253, 254, 261n, 266
Kail, R., 422
Kainulainen, K., 61n
Kaiser, A. P., 236
Kaitz, M., 147, 190
Kaler, S. R., 105, 141, 273
Kalnins, I., 402
Kalter, N., 482
Kammerman, S. B., 227
Kamphaus, R. W., 436
Kandel, D. B., 590, 593, 595, 597
Kanner, A. D., 590
Kanto, W. R., Jr., 105
Kantor, D., 71
Kantrowitz, B., 106, 337
Kaplan, B. H., 115
Kaplan, N., 120
Karadsheh, R., 342
Katchadourian, H., 503, 506, 523
Katz, L. F., 355
Katz, M., 61, 254
Kaufman, A. S., 432, 436
Kaufman, N. L., 432, 436
Kaufmann, R., 290, 291n
Kavale, K., 305
Kavanaugh, K., 270
Kawai, M., 255
Kaye, K., 106, 150, 210
Kearins, J. M., 425
Kearsley, R. B., 261n
Keasey, C. B., 472
Keating, D. P., 424, 539
Keeney, T. J., 422
Keil, F., 342
Keller, A., 351
Kelly, A., 476
Kelly, H., 370
Kelly, J. B., 480, 481
Keltikangas-Järvinen, L., 397
Kempe, C. H., 381, 384
Kempe, R. S., 384
Kendler, K. S., 83
Kendrick, A. S., 290, 291n
Kendrick, C., 268, 269, 269n
Kennedy, J. M., 406
Kennedy, R. E., 595
Kennell, J. H., 147
Keogh, B. K., 447
Keppler, A., 116
Kermoian, R., 194
Kerr, B. A., 562
Kessen, W., 149
Kidd, K. K., 83, 254
Kigar, D. L., 286
Kilbourne, B. W., 525
Kilbride, J. E., 182
Kilbride, P. L., 182
Kilman, C., 392
Kilner, L. A., 499, 573
Kilstrom, N., 382

King, R. M., 364
Kinsborne, M., 285
Kinsman, C. A., 33
Kiser, L. J., 264
Kisker, E. E., 520
Kistner, J., 357
Klahr, D., 22, 216
Klaus, M. H., 147
Klein, J. D., 529
Klimes-Dougan, B., 357
Kline, M., 482
Klinman, D. G., 525
Klungness, L., 487
Knapp, L. G., 297
Knevel, C. R., 225
Knittle, J. L., 174
Knoblauch, T. M., 482
Knobloch, H., 11n, 148n, 149
Knox, D., 94n
Kodroff, J. K., 539
Koenig, K. I., 247
Koeppl, G. K., 474
Kogan, N., 449
Kohlberg, L., 376, 579, 580, 581, 583, 584
Kohn, B., 172
Kohn, M. L., 74, 561
Kojima, H., 255
Kolata, G. B., 67
Kolbe, R. H., 371
Koller, H., 61, 254
Kolstad, V., 329
Kopp, C. B., 27n, 63, 105, 141, 250, 273, 274n
Korner, A. F., 253
Kornguth, M. L., 398
Kornhaber, M., 449
Korte, D., 137, 139n
Koslowski, B., 156
Kostelny, K., 488
Kotch, J. B., 295n, 296, 400
Kozberg, S. F., 585
Kozol, J., 554
Kozulin, A., 28
Krakow, J. B., 27n, 273, 274n
Kramer, M. S., 396
Kramer, T. L., 590
Krantz, R., 516
Kratochwill, T., 356, 487n
Krebs, D., 466
Krechevsky, M., 449
Kreeger, L., 395
Kreihbel, G., 475
Kreipe, R. E., 517
Kremenitzer, T. P., 153
Kreutzer, M. A., 329, 425
Kricker, A., 109
Kroonenberg, P. M., 263, 263n
Kruger, A. C., 237
Ku, L. C., 519
Kuczaj, S. A., II, 235
Kuczynski, L., 273, 365, 380, 382
Kuebli, J., 328
Kuhn, D., 19, 216, 539, 542
Kulick, J. A., 444
Kunkel, D., 372

Kunzinger, E. L., III, 422
Kupersmidt, J. B., 474
Kurland, D. M., 444

Laboratory of Comparative Human
    Cognition, 29, 444
Lachman, M. E., 252
Ladd, G. W., 474, 475
Lagercrantz, H., 128
Lam, T., 601
Lamaze, F., 132
Lamb, M. E., 266, 268, 270
Landau, E., 526n
Landau, S., 423
Landesman, S., 436
Landreth, G. L., 485
Lane, D. M., 421
Lange, G., 327
Langlois, J. H., 513
Laosa, L. M., 73
Lapman-Petraitis, C., 509
Lapsley, D. K., 544, 575, 584
LaRossa, M. M., 159
LaRossa, R., 159
Larson, G., 432
Larson, R., 509, 512n, 545, 588, 589, 589n
Last, C. G., 487
Lawrence, R. A., 523
Lazar, I., 337
Le Neindre, P., 147
Leach, P., 184
Lebeaux, D. S., 438
Lee, A. M., 303
Lee, C. L., 257
Lee, M., 338
Lee, S-Y., 78, 428, 450, 451, 452
Lee, V. E., 339
Leech, R. W., 170n
Leetsma, R., 452
Leggett, E. L., 463
Lehman, D. R., 542
Lehr, W., 71
Lehrman, D., 147
Leifer, M., 119
Leinbach, M. D., 273, 368, 377
Lelwica, M., 249
Leming, J., 582
Lemire, R. J., 170n
Lempert, H., 343, 438
Lenneberg, E. H., 171
Leonard, C., 329, 425
Leonard, M. F., 176
Lepper, M. R., 444
Lerner, J. W., 447
Lerner, R. M., 10
Lesser, G. S., 593
Lester, B. M., 107, 137, 155, 156, 156n, 157, 260
Leung, A. K. C., 487
Leveno, K. J., 136
Levin, H., 258
Levin, I., 542
Levin, J. A., 444
Levine, C., 579

Levine, J. A., 523
Levine, L. E., 352
Levy-Shiff, R., 268
Lewis, C. C., 72
Lewis, J. M., 481
Lewis, M., 225, 249, 271, 272, 354, 355
Liben, L. S., 378
Liberty, C., 422
Lie, S. O., 293
Liebert, R. M., 338, 341, 365, 370, 372, 477
Light, P., 419
Limber, S., 248
Lin, S., 479
Lind, T., 136
Linde, E. V., 219
Lindell, S. G., 130, 132
Lindenberger, U., 417
Lindgren, G., 290
Linn, M. C., 445, 546, 547
Linn, S., 109
Lipsitt, L. P., 188, 189, 151, 219
Litman, C., 273
Litowitz, B., 437
Litt, I. F., 515
Little, B. B., 105, 106
Little, J. K., 377
Livesley, W. J., 460
Livson, N., 514
Lloyd, B., 255
Locke, J., 8
Lockhart, R. S., 23
Loehlin, J. C., 82, 83, 434
Loeser, J. D., 170n
Loftus, E. F., 491
Lohr, M. J., 593, 593n
Looney, M. A., 410
Lorch, E. P., 423
Lorenz, K. Z., 24, 129
Louie, R., 283
Love, R., 402
Lozoff, B., 113, 176, 394
Lummis, M., 476
Luria, A. R., 392
Luria, Z., 255
Luster, T., 73
Lutkenhaus, P., 271
Lutz, P., 483
Lutzker, J. R., 297
Luus, C. A. E., 491
Lynch, M. E., 586
Lytton, H., 370, 375

Mabe, P. A., 402
Mac Iver, D., 460, 462
Maccoby, E. E., 235, 254, 258, 373, 374, 375, 379n, 380, 393, 478
MacDonald, P. C., 137
MacFarlane, J., 147, 151
Macfarlane, J. W., 334, 514
MacKinnon, C. E., 375, 481
Macklin, M. C., 371
MacMillan, D. L., 447
MacNee, C. L., 105, 107, 108

MacQuiddy, S. L., 467
Maddahian, E., 528
Madden, C. M., 548
Madden, N., 447
Madge, N., 93
Magnusson, D., 514
Mahalski, P. A., 259
Mahapatra, M., 470
Mahler, M. S., 244
Main, M., 120, 261, 262
Maioni, T. L., 360n
Maise, S. J., 467
Makin, J. W., 151
Makinson, C., 523
Malatesta, C. Z., 247, 251, 265
Malina, R. M., 501, 502, 504n, 515
Malone, A. F., 11n
Maloney, M., 516
Manchester, D., 180
Mandler, J. M., 328
Mangelsdorf, S., 266
Manis, J. D., 92
Mannino, F., 146
Mannle, S., 237
Maratsos, M. P., 232, 234, 342
Marcella, S., 194
Marcia, J. E., 571, 574, 579
Marcus, J., 210
Marcus, L. C., 111
Marion, R. W., 112
Markman, E. M., 538
Markman, H. J., 72, 118, 120
Markovits, H., 539
Markstrom, C. A., 574
Markus, G. B., 479
Markus, H., 479
Marsh, D. T., 467
Marsh, H. W., 461, 462, 547
Marshall, R. E., 150
Marshall, W. A., 282n, 505
Marsiglio, W., 523
Martin, C. L., 373, 377, 378n
Martin, G. B., 155
Martin, J. A., 37, 366, 379n, 380
Martin, J. B., 61n
Martin, R. M., 218
Martin, S. L., 230
Maruyama, G., 479
Masciello, A. L., 150
Massad, C. M., 586
Mata, L. J., 291
Matas, L., 270
Matheny, A. P., Jr., 295, 296
Matthews, K. A., 397
Matute-Bianchi, M. E., 577
Maurer, D. M., 196, 197, 285
McCabe, A. E., 321,343
McCabe, J. B., 524
McCabe, M. P., 592
McCall, R. B., 225
McCartney, K., 86, 227, 267, 344
McClain, C. S., 134
McClenahan, E. L., 593, 593n
McClintic, S., 355
McConaghy, M. J., 377

McCormick, C. M., 285
McCormick, M. C., 141
McCracken, J., 595
McCroy, G., 219
McDonald, B., 194
McDonnell, P. M., 152
McGee, L. M., 331, 331n, 405n
McGhee, P. E., 437
McGinty, M. J., 66
McGowan, J. D., 105
McGroarty, M., 440
McGue, M., 82
McGuinness, D., 286
McGuire, E. J., 398
McGuire, J., 374
McGurk, H., 225
McHale, S. M., 477, 479
McKee, E., 465
McKenna, M. C., 427
McKenzie, B., 190
McKie, M., 390
McKnight, C. C., 450, 451
McKusick, V. A., 59n, 61n, 62, 68
McLoyd, V. C., 75, 79
McManus, I. C., 172, 285
McManus, K., 137
McNamee, S., 469
McQuiston, S., 390
McWilliams, M., 515
Meacham, J. A., 351
Mead, G. H., 131, 460, 500
Meany, M. J., 374
Mednick, B. R., 116
Medrich, E. A., 76
Meehan, A. M., 549
Meilman, P. W., 573
Meltzoff, A. N., 189, 190, 197, 214, 215, 220, 234
Menig-Peterson, C. L., 344
Mercer, J. R., 436
Meredith, N. V., 390
Mervis, C. B., 219, 320
Messenger, K. P., 290, 291n
Michaels, G. Y., 92, 93n
Michals, K., 58
Michel, C., 109
Micheli, L. J., 529
Micka, J. C., 575
Midgley, C., 550, 553
Milich, R., 423
Miller, B. C., 518
Miller, J. G., 470
Miller, J. W., 427
Miller, K. F., 418
Miller, N., 479
Miller, P. A., 357
Miller, P. H., 25, 310, 329, 425
Miller, S. A., 32, 144
Miller, S. J., 116
Miller-Jones, D., 435
Mills, J., 120
Mills, R., 365
Millstein, S. G., 515, 529
Minkoff, H., 112
Minuchin, P. P., 71, 76, 441

Mischel, W., 365
Miscione, J. L., 330
Mishell, D. R., Jr., 109
Miyake, K., 177, 263
Mize, J., 474, 475
Moerk, E. L., 232
Moffitt, T. E., 501
Moilanen, I., 56
Mollnow, E., 105, 106, 108, 109
Monroe, S., 576
Montemayor, R., 460
Montie, J. E., 225
Moore, Colleen F., 466
Moore, Chris, 330
Moore, E. G. J., 434
Moore, Keith L., 68n, 96n, 96, 98n, 99, 101n, 101, 104n, 105, 169
Moore, Kristin, 520
Moore, M. K., 189, 190
Moore, R. W., 195
Moore, S. G., 156
Moorehouse, M. J., 485
Morelli, G. A., 77, 78
Morford, M., 233
Morgan, S. P., 523
Morris, E. K., 366
Morris, N., 147
Morris, R., 356, 487n
Morrongiello, B. A., 152, 191, 219
Moss, J., 253
Most, R. K., 222
Mott, F. L., 523
Mott, S. R., 169, 175, 280, 283, 394. 515
Mounts, N. S., 380
Muir, D. W., 195
Muir, J. E., 422, 424
Mullally, D. I., 398
Mullis, I. V. S., 452, 555
Munn, P., 251, 375
Munro, G., 573
Murett-Wagstaff, S., 156
Murray, A. D., 137, 155
Murray, H. W., 338n
Mussen, P. H., 365, 472, 513, 585
Muzio, J. N., 154
Myers, R. S., 219


Naeye, R. L., 107, 113
Nagy, S. N., 597
Nakagawa, N., 548
Nanez, J., 193
Nash, J. E., 107
Nastasi, B. K., 447
Natapoff, J., 401
National Association for the Education of Young Children, 228n, 340n
National Center for Health Statistics, 173
National Commission to Prevent Infant Mortality, 144
National Committee for Injury Prevention and Control, 529
Naus, M. J., 422
Navarro, V., 293
Neal, J. H., 481

Neckerman, H. J., 558n
Needleman, H. L., 288
Neidich, G., 188
Nelson, J., 473
Nelson, Keith E., 345
Nelson, Katherine, 234, 235, 236, 237, 328
Nelson-Le Gall, S. A., 579
Netley, C. T., 63, 64n
Newacheck, P. W., 293
Newborg, J., 299n, 300n
Newcomb, M. D., 526, 528
Newman, J., 194
Newman, R. S., 427
Newport, E. L., 236, 549
Newton, N., 131n
Nicholls, A. L., 406
Nidorf, J. F., 577
Nilsson, L., 55, 96n, 99, 100, 111
Nisbett, R. E., 542
Noah, P. K., 288
Noble, A., 174
Norbeck, J. S., 115
Nord, C. W., 480
Nottelmann, E. D., 462, 509, 573
Notzon, F. C., 135
Novick, B. E., 112
Nowakowski, R. S., 99, 100, 108, 169
Nucci, L. P., 368
Nuckolls, K. B., 115
Nugent, J. K., 137, 156, 157

O'Brien, M., 273, 447
O'Connor, M., 423
O'Donnell, J. P., 447
O'Sullivan, M., 139
Oakes, J., 554
Oates, R. K., 176, 289
Oberg, C. N., 293
Obler, L. K., 548, 549
Odagaki, L., 420
Offer, D., 573
Office of Educational Research and
    Improvement, 558
Ogan, T. A., 249
Ogbu, J. U., 464, 553
Oller, D. K., 233
Olson, T. D., 518
Omer, H., 115
Opie, I., 408
Opie, P., 408
Opper, S., 205, 322
Ornstein, P. A., 422
Osherson, D. N., 538
Otaki, M., 255
Otomo, K., 233
Over, R., 190
Owen, M. T., 267
Owens, T., 565

Padgham, J. J., 592
Padilla, M. L., 485
Page, D. C., 56
Page, E. B., 93

Page, R. N., 554
Paikoff, R. L., 511
Palermo, D. S., 437
Palkovitz, R., 159
Pallikkathayil, L., 598
Papini, D. R., 575
Parekh, U. C., 113
Paris, S. G., 427
Park, K. A., 73, 270
Parke, R. D., 147, 268, 366, 367, 371
Parker, G. J., 474
Parker, K. C. H., 319
Parker, S., 531
Parker-Cohen, N. Y., 33
Parmelee, A. H., 142, 154
Parrish, L. H., 555
Parsons, J. E., 368, 463
Parten, M., 358, 360n
Pasamanick, B., 148n, 149
Pass, R. F., 526n
Passman, R. H., 259
Pate, G. S., 575
Patterson, C. J., 469
Patterson, G. R., 18, 72, 75, 369, 370, 375,
    599, 601n
Patterson, J., 219
Paul, C., 113
Paulhus, D., 479
Pawletko, T. M., 479
Pea, R. D., 444
Peacock, A., 289
Pearson, D. A., 421
Pearson, J. L., 79
Pechmann, T., 438
Pedersen, F. A., 157, 268
Pelchat, M. L., 289
Pelham, W. E., 423
Pellegrini, A. D., 408
Pena, I. C., 141
Pennington, B. F., 63, 64n, 446
Pepler, D. J., 312
Perfetti, C. A., 427
Perlmutter, M., 219, 325, 327
Perner, J., 329, 367, 579
Perret-Clermont, A-N., 419
Perris, E. E., 219
Perry, D. G., 370
Perry, L. C., 370
Perry, T. B., 589, 590
Persaud, T. V. N., 107
Peshkin, A., 76
Peskin, H., 514
Peters, E. C., 107
Petersen, A. C., 513, 547, 594, 595
Peterson, C., 343
Peterson, J., 469, 520
Petrie, S., 591
Pettigrew, J. W., 63
Pettit, G. S., 409
Phil, D., 150
Phillips, D. A., 227, 267, 338
Phinney, J. S., 576, 577
Piaget, J., 18, 35, 181, 189, 206, 209, 210,
    212, 314, 317, 322, 367, 417, 418,
    536, 543, 546, 578

Pianta, R., 382, 382n, 383, 489
Picariello, M. L., 373
Pick, A. D., 421
Pick, H. L., Jr., 180
Pickering, L. K., 294
Pierce, L. H., 488
Pierce, R., 488
Pierce, S. H., 327
Piersel, W. C., 487
Pietikäinen, M., 397
Pietz, J., 58
Pilkington, C. L., 487
Pillemer, D. B., 373
Pillow, B. H., 330, 425
Pine, F., 244
Pinel, J. P. J., 397
Pinker, S., 438
Pipes, P. L., 173
Pipp, S. L., 22
Pirsch, L. A., 574
Pisoni, D. B., 152
Pleck, J. H., 519
Pless, I. B., 297
Pliner, P., 289
Plomin, R., 83, 86, 252, 254, 255, 269,
    479
Plowman, S. A., 410
Podrouzek, W., 343
Poindron, P., 147
Polansky, N. A., 383
Polit, D., 93
Pollatsek, A., 427
Pollitt, C., 342
Pollock, L., 8
Porges, S. W., 150
Porter, F. L., 150
Porter, R. H., 151
Powell, C., 114
Powell, G., 464
Power, F. C., 584
Powers, C., 337
Powers, S. I., 499, 573
Prechtl, H. F. R., 148n, 149, 155
Prentice, A., 136
Pressley, M., 274, 422, 427
Preyer, W., 10
Pribram, K. H., 286
Price, J. M., 474
Provezano, F. J., 255
Pryor, J. B., 401
Pursley, J. T., 69

Quay, H. C., 601
Quilligan, E. J., 139

Raag, T., 248
Rabiner, D., 475
Rabinowitz, M., 401
Radke-Yarrow, M., 265, 357, 364, 380
Radziszewska, B., 325
Rafferty, Y., 75
Ragozin, A. S., 95
Räikkönen, K., 397

Ramey, C. T., 114, 228, 229, 230, 231n, 338, 436
Ramey, S., 230
Ramsey, E., 72, 369, 601n
Ramsey, F., 176
Rasmussen, B., 474
Ratcliffe, S. G., 64n, 390
Ratner, M. S., 500
Ratner, N., 233
Rauh, J. L., 525
Raveis, V. H., 597
Rayner, K., 427
Raynor, R., 17
Read, C. R., 562
Read, M., 459
Recchia, S., 355
Redd, W. H., 366
Redl, F., 471
Rees, J., 264
Reich, P. A., 439
Reich, T., 83
Reimer, J., 583
Rein, M., 80n
Reis, S. M., 449, 561, 562
Reiser, J., 151
Reisman, J. E., 155, 156n
Reissland, N., 190
Reiter, E. O., 505, 508
Renner, C., 293
Renwick, S. M., 380
Reppucci, N. D., 384, 489
Requa, R. H., 529
Reschly, D. J., 436
Resnick, G., 482
Resnick, L. B., 24, 332, 428
Resnick, R., 146
Rest, J. R., 367, 578, 581, 582, 583, 585
Reznick, E., 312
Reznick, J. S., 234, 253, 254
Rhoades, K., 73
Rhoads, G. G., 67n
Rhymes, J. P., 176
Ricco, R. B., 320
Rice, F. P., 561
Rice, K. G., 575
Rice, M. L., 341
Rich, S. A., 430
Richards, D. D., 318, 334, 429
Richardson, P., 121
Richardson, S. A., 61, 254
Richgels, D. J., 331, 331n, 405n
Ridley-Johnson, R., 149
Rieder, M. J., 194
Riese, M. L., 253
Rigler, D., 381
Risenhoover, N., 249
Ritchie, K. L., 369
Rivara, F. P., 296
Roberge, J. J., 539
Roberton, M. A., 298, 299, 299n, 303, 403n, 404, 407
Roberts, K., 219
Roberts, M. C., 294, 297, 400
Robinette, C. D., 83
Robinson, B., 525

Robinson, E. H., III, 356
Robinson, E. J., 345
Robinson, J. P., 486
Robinson, R. D., 427
Robinson, S. L., 356
Rochat, P., 181, 184n
Roche, A. F., 175, 392, 507
Rock, S. L., 452
Roffwarg, H. P., 154
Rogers, M. F., 525
Rogoff, B., 77, 221, 325, 389, 419, 422, 425, 459
Rohlen, T. P., 556
Rohner, E. C., 73
Rohner, R. P., 73
Rollins, H. A., 422
Romaine, S., 548
Romney, D. M., 370, 375
Rook, K. S., 588
Roopnarine, J. L., 268
Roosa, M. W., 116
Roscoe, B., 592
Rose, S. A., 189, 225
Rosenberg, Mindy S., 384
Rosenberg, Morris, 460, 573
Rosenberg, R. N., 63
Rosenblatt, J. S., 147
Rosengren, K. S., 325
Rosenman, R. H., 397
Rosenthal, D. A., 577
Rosenthal, R., 443
Ross, D. F., 370
Ross, G. S., 219, 324
Ross, H. S., 269, 269n, 312
Rosso, P., 113
Rothbart, M. K., 252
Rothenberg, M. B., 269n
Rotheram-Borus, M. J., 576, 577
Rouke, B. P., 447
Rousseau, J. J., 8, 498
Rovee-Collier, C. K., 185, 187, 219
Rovine, M., 120, 264
Royal, G. P., 400
Royce, J. M., 338n
Rozin, P., 289, 290
Rubin, D. H., 107
Rubin, J. Z., 255
Rubin, K. H., 312, 360, 360n, 361, 361n, 474
Ruble, D. N., 373, 460, 465, 508
Ruff, H. A., 253
Rugh, R., 54, 62, 97
Ruiz, R., 439, 440
Rumberger, R. W., 558, 558n, 559
Ruopp, R., 338
Rushton, H. G., 398
Russell, D. E. H., 488
Russell, G., 476
Russell, J. A., 354
Rutherford, E., 472, 585
Rutter, M., 93, 487, 490, 499, 554, 595
Ryan, K. J., 66

Saarni, C., 465
Sadler, L. S., 595

Sadler, T. W., 53, 96
Safe Kids, 400
Salomon, J. B., 291
Salapatek, P., 193, 195, 195n, 196, 196n, 199
Samson, L. F., 110n, 111
Samuels, M., 109, 111, 117, 120, 126, 133n
Samuels, N., 109, 111, 117, 120, 126, 133n
Samuels, S. J., 427
Sanderson, J. A., 368
Sandovnick, A. D., 62, 63
Sanford, J. P., 554
Santrock, J. W., 482
Sarigiani, P. A., 595
Sattler, J. M., 334, 430
Savashino, J. A., 398
Savin-Williams, R. C., 409, 588, 590
Saxe, G. B., 29
Saywitz, K. J., 491
Scaer, R., 137, 139n
Scarr, S., 81, 83, 84, 86, 227, 254, 267, 434
Schachter, F. F., 255
Schaefer, M., 143
Schaffer, H. R., 258
Schaivi, R. C., 64n
Schanberg, S., 143
Schickedanz, J. A., 333
Schiller, D., 290
Schinke, S. P., 524
Schlegel, A., 500, 511
Schleifer, M., 539
Schmid, J., 419
Schneider, W., 327, 422
Schneirla, T. C., 147
Schnur, E., 339
Schoenbach, C., 573
Schofield, W., 114
Schooler, C., 573
Schor, E. L., 399n
Schrag, S. G., 59
Schramm, L., 402
Schramm, W., 135
Schubert, D. S. P., 93
Schubert, H. J. P., 93
Schultz, D. P., 16
Schunk, D. H., 427, 464
Schwartz, C., 194
Schwartz, J. D., 139
Schwartz-Bickenbach, D., 107
Schweinhart, L. J., 337
Scott, P. M., 39, 365
Scribner, S., 425, 540
Sears, R. R., 16, 258
Sebald, H., 593
Seekins, T., 294
Seitz, V., 334
Select Committee on Children, Youth, and Families, 394
Seligman, M. E. P., 187
Seligmann, J., 525
Sellers, C., 518
Selman, R. L., 362, 466, 467n, 473

Seltzer, V., 174
Serafica, F. A., 467
Serlin, R., 584
Sever, J. L., 110n
Sexton, M., 107
Shaffer, D., 598, 599
Shaffer, D. R., 479
Shahar, S., 7
Shainess, N., 508
Shalita, A. R., 504
Shannon, B., 402
Shannon, D. C., 188
Shannon, F. T., 289
Shanon, F. T., 174
Shantz, C. U., 368
Shapiro, E. K., 76, 441
Shapiro, L., 402
Shapiro, S., 116
Shatz, M., 318
Shaver, P., 592
Shea, E., 265
Shedler, J., 527, 528
Sheiman, D. L., 392
Sheingold, K., 445
Shepherd, P. A., 225
Sherman, D., 75, 383
Sherman, M., 259
Sherman, T., 219
Shettles, L. B., 54, 62, 97
Shields, J. W., 284
Shields, P. J., 219
Shiffrin, R. M., 23, 217, 217n, 218
Shiller, V., 248
Shime, J., 146
Shinn, Millicent W., 10
Shinn, Marybeth, 75
Shipman, G., 508
Shonkoff, J. P., 393, 401
Shukla, D., 544
Shultz, T. R., 352
Shure, M. B., 370
Shweder, R. A., 470
Siebert, J. M., 112
Siegal, M., 368
Siegel, L. S., 321
Siegler, R. S., 11, 24, 216, 218, 318, 334,
    429, 540, 541n, 542
Sigafoos, A. D., 190
Sigman, M. D., 219
Silva, P. A., 259
Silver, L. B., 447
Silver, M., 138, 139
Silverberg, S., 587, 588
Simkin, P., 116
Simmons, R. G., 513, 550, 551, 551n, 552,
    573
Simons, R. L., 382, 382n
Simpson, J. A., 597
Singer, D. G., 311, 341, 362
Singer, J. L., 311, 341, 362
Singh, S., 518
Siqueland, E. R., 189, 218
Sirignano, S. W., 252
Skinner, E. A., 463
Skinner, J. D., 396

Slaby, R. G., 371, 377
Slade, A., 223
Slaton, E. A., 405n
Slaughter, E., 599
Slavin, R. E., 443, 447
Sloan, W., 446n
Slomin, M., 392
Slone, D., 116
Slotkin, T. A., 128
Smail, B., 476
Smeeding, T., 80n
Smetana, J. G., 367, 368
Smilansky, S., 361
Smith, C., 255
Smith, D. M., 147
Smith, I. D., 462
Smith, J., 476
Smith, M. B., 585
Smith, M. C., 352
Smith, P. K., 358, 360n, 408
Smith, R. S., 75, 146
Smith, Shelley D., 446
Smith, Shiela, 337
Smith, V. E., 576
Smollar, J., 590
Smolucha, F., 223
Snarey, J. R., 583
Snidman, N., 252, 254
Snow, C. E., 549
Snow, R. E., 443
Snowden, L. R., 121
Snyder, J., 599
Snyder, L., 236
Sobesky, W. E., 582
Sobol, A. M., 141, 398
Society for Research in Child Development,
    43, 43n
Sockett, H., 584
Sodian, B., 329, 330
Sokol, R. J., 138
Sokoloff, B. Z., 66
Solimano, G., 176
Solnit, A. J., 176
Solomon, J., 261
Somberg, D. R., 353
Somerville, S. C., 326n, 327
Sommerville, J., 7
Sonenstein, F. L., 519
Song, M., 336
Sonnenschein, S., 438
Sorce, J., 249
Sosa, R., 134
Southard, B., 404
Spade, J., 554
Spanier, G. B., 120
Spears, G. F. S., 259
Spears, R. A., 548
Speece, M. W., 319
Spelke, E. S., 197, 215
Spellacy, W. N., 116
Spence, M. J., 102, 152
Spencer, M. B., 577
Sperduto, R. D., 394
Sperhac, A. M., 169, 175, 280, 283, 394,
    515

Spinetta, J., 381
Spirito, A., 598
Spitz, R. A., 264
Spivack, G., 370
Spock, B., 269n
Sprafkin, J., 338, 341, 370, 372, 477
Spreadbury, C. L., 592
Spreen, O., 169, 171, 286
Sroufe, L. A., 73, 247, 248, 249, 266, 267,
    270, 380, 383
Stafford, F. P., 477
Stambrook, M., 319
Stanbury, J. B., 61n
Stanhope, L., 33
Stanitski, C. L., 529
Stanley, J. C., 547
Stanley-Hagan, M., 481, 482
Stanowicz, L. 345
Starfield, B., 293
Stark, L. J., 18
Stattin, H., 514
Staudt, J., 540
Stechler, G., 140
Stein, A., 116
Stein, Z., 113
Steinberg, L., 380, 397, 486, 500, 511,
    565, 587, 588
Steiner, J. E., 151, 186
Steiner, M., 158
Steinman, S. B., 482
Stene, E., 63
Stene, J., 63
Stengel-Rutkowski, S., 63
Stephan, C. W., 513
Stephens, B. R., 196
Stephenson, M. G., 174
Stern, D. N., 264
Sternberg, R. J., 420, 432, 433, 435, 542
Stevens, F., 11n
Stevens, J. H., 79
Stevenson, D., 553
Stevenson, H. W., 76, 78, 428, 450, 451,
    452, 476
Stevenson, R., 342
Stewart, D. A., 63
Stewart, J., 374
Stewart, R. B., 269
Stigler, J. W., 428
Stillman, R. J., 109
Stini, W. A., 173
Stipek, D. J., 273, 355, 460, 462
Stoch, M. B., 176
Stock, J. R., 299n, 300n
Stocker, C., 269, 479, 588
Stodolsky, S. S., 326, 442
Stoel-Gammon, C., 233
Stokes, T., 402
Stone, L., 7
Stone, R. K., 255
Stoneman, Z., 269, 375
Strasburger, V. C., 518
Straus, L. K., 527
Strauss, J., 517
Strauss, S., 542
Streissguth, A. P., 105, 107, 108

Streitmatter, J. L., 575
Strober, M., 595
Strutt, G. F., 421
Stunkard, A. J., 173, 395
Sturm, L., 177
Sturner, W. Q., 188
Subak-Sharpe, G., 356
Sullivan, H. S., 590
Sullivan, J. W., 152
Sullivan, L. W., 59
Sullivan, M. W., 225, 354
Sullivan, S. A., 290
Suomi, S., 170
Super, C. M., 78, 177, 182
Super, D., 560
Susanne, C., 173
Sutton-Smith, B., 116
Szeminska, A., 418

Tager-Flusberg, H., 343
Taitz, L. S., 395
Takahashi, K., 263
Tamis-LeMonda, C. S., 222
Tanner, J. M., 165, 166, 167n, 168, 280,
    282n, 283n, 284, 286, 288, 291, 390,
    391, 501, 502, 503, 505, 506, 506n,
    507
Task Force on Pediatric AIDS, 112
Tate, C. S., 344
Taylor, A. R., 447
Taylor, D. G., 264
Taylor, Jacque 188
Taylor, John H., 368, 583
Taylor, M., 342
Teberg, A. J., 141
Teikari, J. M., 394
Teller, D. Y., 153, 192
Termine, N. T., 249
Tertinger, D. A., 297
Tharp, R. G., 325, 442, 443n
Thatcher, R. W., 284, 392
Thelen, E., 149, 180
Theorell, K., 155
Thiel, K., 588
Thoma, S. J., 583, 585
Thomas, A., 252, 253n, 256, 257
Thomas, J. R., 303, 404, 407
Thompson, R. A., 44, 78, 248, 250, 266,
    267, 354
Thorndike, R. L., 334
Thorndike, R. L., 430
Thornton, A., 92
Tilden, V. P., 115
Tinsley, B. R., 147, 268
Tizard, B., 147, 264
Tobach, E., 147
Tobias, P. V., 392
Toda, S., 255
Todd, C. M., 327
Tolson, T. F. J., 79
Tomarelli, R. M., 174
Tomasello, M., 233, 237
Ton, J., 233
Toomey, K. A., 128

Torfs, C. P., 140
Torrance, E. P., 448, 448n
Torrey, B. B., 80n
Touwen, B. C. L., 150
Tower, R. B., 341
Townes, B., 259
Townsend, M. A. R., 467
Treiber, F. A., 402
Trickett, P. K., 382
Tronick, E. Z., 78, 156,158, 249, 265
Tschann, J. M., 482
Tudge, J., 325
Turiel, E., 367, 368, 469
Turiel, J., 141, 143
Turkheimer, E., 86
Turtle, J. W., 491
Tyack, D., 343


U.S. Bureau of the Census, 93, 144, 337n,
    479, 484, 561, 562n
U.S. Centers for Disease Control, 525
U.S. Department of Education, 336
U.S. Department of Health and Human
    Services, 94n, 290, 526n, 527, 527n,
    528, 597, 597n
U.S. Department of Justice, 599, 600n
U.S. Department of Labor, 92n, 557n
U.S. General Accounting Office, 559
Udry, J. R., 517
Ullian, D. Z., 476
Ulman, K., 508
Ulrich, B. D., 298
Ulrich, D. A., 298
Underwood, L. E., 287
Unger, R., 395
Ungerer, J. A., 312
Užgiris, I. C., 74, 213, 215, 226


Vachon, R., 539
Valdez, R. B., 398
Valleroy, L A., 112
Van Dyke, D. C., 63
van IJzendoorn, M. H., 263, 263n
Vandell, D. L., 337, 486
Vandenberg, B., 312, 361n
Vanfossen, B., 554
Vasconcellos, M. T., 444
Vasen, A., 354
Vasta, R., 230
Vaughan, V. C., 61n
Vaughn, B. E., 266, 273, 274n
Veerula, G. R., 288
Vega-Lahr, N., 397
Ventura, S. J., 94n, 95
Verbrugge, H. P., 293
Verhulst, F. C., 69
Versluis-Den Bieman, H. J. M., 69
Vessey, J. A., 402
Villar, J., 114
Vinovskis, M. A., 522
Vitulano, L. A., 447
Vohr, B. R., 140, 141
Vorhees, C. V., 105, 106, 108, 109, 110n

Vos, J., 155
Voydanoff, P., 520, 522, 525
Vuchinich, S., 483
Vurpillot, E., 422
Vygotsky, L. S., 28, 221, 323


Waas, G. A., 474
Wachs, T. D., 74, 226
Waddington, C. H., 85
Waggoner, J. E., 437
Wagner, M. E., 93
Wakat, D. K., 303
Walberg, H. J., 441
Walden, T. A., 249
Walk, R. D., 192
Walker, L. J., 368, 582, 583, 585
Walker, R. A., 284, 392
Wallace, C. S., 169
Wallace, I. F., 225
Wallace, J. R., 462
Wallach, M. A., 448, 449
Wallerstein, J. S., 479, 480, 481, 482
Walsh, M. E., 401
Walters, R. H., 367
Walther, F. J., 141
Warren, A. R., 344
Warren, M. P., 509
Warren, S. F., 236
Warren-Leubecker, A., 232, 237, 344
Warshak, R. A., 482
Wasik, B. A., 428
Waterlow, J., 113
Waterman, A. S., 575
Waters, E., 73, 247, 270
Waters, K. A., 525
Watkins, D. L., 403
Watson, B. A., 372
Watson, D. J., 427
Watson, J. B., 17
Watson, J. D., 50
Watson, K. S., 360, 360n
Watson, M. W., 320
Waxler, C. Z., 39, 365
Way, P. O., 112
Wechsler, D., 430
Wegman, M. E., 144, 145n
Wehren, A., 437
Weidner, G., 397
Weikart, D. P., 337
Weil, W. B., 396
Weinberg, M., 521
Weinberg, R. A., 83, 84, 86, 434
Weinberger, H. L., 288
Weinraub, M., 373
Weinstein, R. S., 443
Weisner, T. S., 78, 375
Weiss, R. J., 370
Weisz, J. R., 465
Weitzman, M., 398
Weiz, J. R., 416
Well, A. D., 421
Wellman, H. M., 213, 320, 326n, 327, 329,
    330, 425, 426
Wells, A. J., 150

Wells, G. L., 331, 491
Wentzel, K., 553
Werker, J. F., 191
Werner, E. E., 75, 146
Werner, S. J., 189, 218
West, L. L., 558
West, M. J., 73, 367
Westra, T., 182, 183n
Whalen, C. K., 423
Whalley, J., 116
Wheeler, V. A., 474
Whetsell, M. V., 356
Whiffen, V. E., 158
Whisnant, L., 509
Whitaker, H. A., 172
Whitbeck, L. B., 382
White, B., 181
White, S. H., 10
Whitebook, M., 338
Whitehouse, R. H., 166, 282n, 390
Whitehurst, G. J., 18, 229, 230
Whitesell, N., 355
Whiting, B., 368, 374, 476
Whiting, J. W. M., 500
Wiesel, T. N., 169
Wikner, K., 151
Wilensky, H. L., 80
Willats, J., 406, 406n
Willerman, L., 83, 434
Williams, B. C., 291, 292n, 293, 295n, 296, 400
Williams, G. A., 447
Wilson, A. L., 188

Wilson, D. M., 547
Wilson, D. R., 297
Wilson, Melvin N., 79
Wilson, Modena, 297
Wilson, Ronnie, 596
Wilson, Ronald S., 86, 173
Wilson-Mitchell, J. E., 375
Wimmer, H., 330
Winegar, A., 116
Winick, M., 113, 174
Winn, S., 78
Winner, E., 301, 302n, 342, 406, 437, 548
Winston, M. H., 504
Wissmann, D. A., 394
Witelson, S. F., 286
Wnek, L., 299n, 300n
Wolfe, S., 138, 139
Wolff, P. H., 154n, 247
Wong-Fillmore, L., 440
Wood, D. J., 324
Woodson, E. M., 107
Woodward, L., 137
Woodward, W. E., 294
Woody, E. Z., 396
Woolley, J. D., 320
Worobey, J., 252
Wozniak, R. H., 543
Wright, J., 75
Wright, K., 465
Wright, V. C., 574
Wunsch, J. P., 248
Wyer, M. M., 482
Wyngaarden, J. B., 61n

Yarrow, A. L., 95
Yarrow, M. R., 32, 39, 365
Yesalis, C. E., 530
Yogman, M. W., 268
Yonas, A., 151, 193
Young, C., 117
Younger, B. A., 219
Youniss, J., 362, 590
Yuill, N., 367, 579


Zafran, E. I., 66
Zahn-Waxler, C., 38, 272, 357, 364
Zajonc, R. B., 479
Zalar, M. K., 111, 132
Zalenski, R., 329
Zametkin, A. J., 393
Zegans, L., 509
Zeisel, S. H., 394
Zelazo, P. R., 261n, 149, 152
Zemmelman, S. E., 482
Zeskind, P. S., 114, 155
Ziegler, C. B., 586
Zigler, E. F., 81, 334, 336, 339, 382n, 383, 384
Zimmerman, B. J., 426
Zimmerman, R., 258
Zimmerman, S., 290
Ziporyn, T., 158
Zuckerman, H., 562
Zukow, P. G., 223

# Subject Index

Ability
  attribution and, 463
  physical, 461, 572
Ability grouping, 443, 554
Abortion
  choice of, 68–69, 522
  ethics of, 69
  legalization of, 65
  spontaneous, 61
AB search error, 210, 211, 213
Abstract reasoning, 19, 538, 539–540, 544
  consequences of, 542–546
Abuse. *See* Child maltreatment; Child sexual
  abuse
Abusive personality type, 381–382
Academic achievement
  in adolescence, 549, 552–556
  of Asian children, 78, 450–452
  child-rearing practices and, 552–553
  cultural valuing of, 451
  IQ and, 429
  peer influences on, 553, 590
  school characteristics and, 553–556
  self-esteem and, 462
  teacher-pupil interaction and, 553–554
Academic learning, information processing
  applied to, 427–429
Academic performance. *See* Academic
  achievement
Academic preschools, 336
Academics
  in early childhood, 332–333
  sex differences in, 444–445, 475–476,
    546–547
Accelerated learning programs, 449
Accommodation, 205, 206, 315
Acne, 504
Acquired immune deficiency syndrome
  (AIDS), 111, 112, 399, 525, 526
Active genetic-environmental correlation, 86
Adaptability, of attention, 421
Adaptation, 18
  evolutionary, 391
  in information processing, 432–433
  in Piaget's theory, 205, 206
Adaptive behaviors, 24, 25, 207
Addiction, in newborns, 106
Adolescence
  cognitive development in, 535–565
  conceptions of, 498–500
  emotional and social development in,
    569–602
  and extended families, 79

language development in, 547–549
physical development in, 497–531
pregnancy in (*see* Teenage pregnancy)
problems of development in, 594–601
Adolescent initiation ceremonies, culture
  and, 509, 510, 511
Adopted children
  and IQ scores, 434
  and obesity, 395
Adopted siblings, 86
Adoption, 69–70, 522
Adoption studies
  of depression, 83
  of intelligence, 83, 434
  of schizophrenia, 83
Adoptive parents, 147, 264, 395
Adrenal androgens, 501
Adrenal glands, 393, 501
Adulthood
  childbearing in, 94–95
  transition to, 501–507, 602
Advertising, on TV, 371, 372
Affection, and physical development,
  176–177
African Americans
  assessment of newborns, 129
  average body growth, 165
  cultural values of, 79
  extended families of, 78, 79
  identity development of, 576
  infant mortality rates, 144
  inherited diseases in, 58–59
  learned helplessness of, 464
  motor skills of, 302
  performance on IQ tests, 433, 434, 435
  sexual activity of, 519, 520
  stereotypes of, 371
African infants, motor development in, 182
Age of viability, 101
Aggression
  adult models of, 366
  anger and, 38
  causes of, 369
  development of, 368–371
  in early childhood, 352
  family and, 369–370
  friendship and, 362
  helping parents and children control, 370
  hostile, 368, 369
  instrumental, 368
  in middle childhood, 472
  and moral reasoning, 368
  sex differences in, 368, 369–370, 472

Agility, 403
AIDS. *See* Acquired immune deficiency
  syndrome
Alcohol abuse, 108, 526
  in pregnancy, 107–108, 108, 116
Alleles, 56
  dominant, 56, 57, 58
  recessive, 56, 57, 58, 59
Altruistic behavior, 364, 365
Ambidextrous, 285
American Psychological Association, 43
American values, 77–78, 80
Amniocentesis, 65, 67, 68
Amnion, 95–96
  breaking of the, 137
Amniotic fluid, 96, 100, 128, 146
Anabolic steroids, 530
Analgesias, 136
Anal stage, 14, 243
Androgens, 108, 374, 501
  and aggression, 368
  and brain functioning, 393
Androgyny, 376, 586, 590, 595–596
Anesthesias, 136, 139, 150
Anger
  and aggression, 38
  cognitive development and, 248
  in infants, 248
Animals
  caregiving behaviors, 147
  chromosomes in, 50
  fears about, 356
  multiple births in, 56
  survival behaviors of, 24
Animistic thinking, 314, 318
Anorexia nervosa, 516–517
Anthropology, 29
Antidepressant drugs, in treatment of
  enuresis, 398
Antisocial behavior, 593, 599–601
  in adolescence, 370, 371
Anxiety
  hormones released in, 115
  in middle childhood, 487–488
  separation, 260, 261, 481
  *see also* Fears
Apgar Scale, 129–130
Appearance versus reality, 320
Apprenticeship program, in West Germany,
  564, 565
Argumentativeness, 543
Arousal, states of, 153, 154
  changing, 177–178

Asian children
  academic achievement of, 78, 450–452
  identity development of, 576
Assessment, neonatal, 129–130, 150,
    155–157. See also Intelligence testing;
    Intelligence tests
Assimilation, 205, 206
Assisted discovery, 325
Associative play, 358, 360
Asthma, 398
Athletics, 86. See Games; Physical education;
    Sports
At-risk infants and toddlers, 228–229, 265
At-risk preschoolers, 336–337
Attachment, 256
  avoidant, 262
  behaviorist drive reduction view of,
    257–261
  cultural variations in, 262–263
  development of, 256–270, 260
  disorganized/disoriented, 262
  ethological theory of, 24–25, 259–261
  factors affecting the security of, 263–266
  family circumstances and, 266
  fathers and, 266–268
  infant characteristics and, 265–266
  insecure, 261–262, 264, 265, 267, 270
  and later development, 269–270
  multiple, 266–269
  psychoanalytic view of, 257, 258–259
  quality of caregiving and, 264–265
  resistant, 262
  secure, 261–262, 265, 270
  siblings and, 269
  to soft objects, 258, 259
Attention
  in early childhood, 326–327
  in infancy, 218, 233
  and memory, 217, 218–219
  in middle childhood, 421–422
Attention-deficit hyperactivity disorder
    (ADHD), 422, 423
Attribution retraining, 464, 465
Attributions, 462–464
  and learned helplessness, 463
  mastery-oriented, 463
Australian aborigines, 425
Authoritarian parent, 379–380
Authoritative parent, 379, 380–381, 462,
    478, 486, 552, 587
Autism, 64
Autonomous morality, 578
Autonomy, 244, 570. See also Independence
Autonomy versus shame and doubt, 15,
    243–244, 244
Autosomal diseases, 60, 63
Autosomes, 55, 56, 63
Avoidant attachment, 262


Babbling, 230, 232–233
Baby biographies, 9–10
Back to basics movement, in education, 441
Bacterial diseases, and pregnancy, 111
Baganda, motor development in, 182

Baka children, 329–330, 459
Balance, development of, 298, 403
Ball skills, 299, 303, 403, 404
Basic emotions, 246–248
Basic-level categories, 320
Basic skills approach, to teaching reading,
    427–428
Basic trust versus mistrust, 15, 242–243
Bayley Scales of Infant Development, 224
Bedwetting, 397–398
Behaviorism, 8, 16–18, 31, 187
Behaviorist perspective
  of attachment, 257–261
  in language development, 230
  of moral development, 363
Behavior modification, 18, 517
Benevolence, in distributive justice
    reasoning, 469
Bias
  cultural, in intelligence tests, 334, 430,
    434–436
  in the juvenile justice system, 599
  sex, in intelligence tests, 430, 433
Bidirectional influences, in family
    relationships, 26, 105
Bilingual education, 439, 440
Bilingualism, 438–439, 549
Binocular depth cues, 193
Biological perspective, on adolescence, 498,
    500
Birth. See Childbirth
Birth canal, 126, 137, 146
Birth centers, 130–132
Birth control. See Contraceptives
Birth control pills, 109, 525
Birth defects, 112, 116. See also Brain
    damage
Birth order, 479
Births, multiple, 56
Birth weight, low, 106, 107, 140–143,
    144
Bisexuals, 112
Black Americans. See African Americans
Blastocyst, 95
Blended families, 483
Blindness, color, 61
Blood type, Rh factor, 115–116
Bloody show (labor), 126
Body build, and motor skills, 302–303
Body fat, 390, 501, 503
Body growth
  in adolescence, 501, 515
  asynchronies in, 283–284
  in early childhood, 280–284, 287–297
  factors affecting, 172–177, 287–297
  hereditary and hormonal influences on,
    287
  in infancy and toddlerhood, 164–169
  in middle childhood, 390–393, 404
  trends in, 165–166, 167, 392, 502–503,
    507
Body image, 513
  distorted, 516
Body proportions
  in adolescence, 502–503

  in early childhood, 280
  in infancy and toddlerhood, 128–129,
    165–166
  in middle childhood, 390–391
  in prenatal period, 101, 165–166
Body size
  in adolescence, 501, 502–503
  in early childhood, 280
  evolutionary adaptations in, 391
  in infancy and toddlerhood, 164–165
  in middle childhood, 390–391
  secular trends in, 392
  twins and, 172
Body weight. See Weight
Bonding, 147
Bones. See Skeletal growth
Bottle-feeding, 173–174, 175
Bowel and bladder control, 181–184
Bowlby's theory. See Ethological theory
Brain
  cerebral cortex, 170–172, 197
  hemispheres of, 171, 284, 392
  lateralization of, 171–172, 284–285, 392
  neurons, 169–170
  plasticity, 171
  prenatal development of, 99, 100, 102
  see also Brain development
Brain damage
  with forceps delivery, 137
  lead poisoning and, 288
  and left-handedness, 285
  mercury exposure and, 109
  in newborns, 140, 141, 172
  and reflexes, 150
  teratogens and, 111
Brain development
  critical period in, 169
  in early childhood, 284–287
  in infancy and toddlerhood, 170–172,
    197
  in middle childhood, 392–393
  prenatal, 99, 100, 102
Brain seizures, 106, 107, 172
Brain waves, 171
Breast development, 501, 505
Breast-feeding, 157
  versus bottle-feeding, 173–174, 175
  drugs and, 174
Breech position, 138–139
Bulimia, 517


Caffeine, 105
Canalization, 84, 85–86
Cancer, 61, 109, 399
Carbon monoxide, 107
Cardinality principle, in mathematical
    reasoning, 332
Career decisions. See Vocational choice;
    Vocational development
Caregiving
  collective, 78
  in day-care centers, 33–39
  and preterm infants, 142
  quality of, and attachment, 264–265

sibling, 78
training parents in, 143
see also Infant-caregiver relationship
Caring reasoning, in moral development,
584–585
Carolina Abecedarian Project, 228, 230–231
Carriers, genetic, 57
Cartilage, 167
Cartoons, aggression in, 370
Case study approach, 36. See also Clinical
method
Catch-up growth, 173, 176, 177
Categories
basic-level, 320
general, 320
social, 273
sub-, 320
Categorization skills
in memory, 218, 219–220
in play, 219–220
Categorizing the self, 273
Cause and effect relationships, in research,
38
Cell division, 53
Cell duplication, 96, 108. See also Mitosis
Cells, 50. See also Sex cells
Central nervous system
damage to, 106, 107, 113
disorders of, 58
Centration, 315
Cephalo-caudal trend, 166, 167, 178, 503
Cerebellum, 286
Cerebral cortex, 102, 170
development of, 170–172, 197
lateralization of, 171–172
Cerebral palsy, 140
Cervix, 54
dilation and effacement of, 126–127
Cesarean delivery, 136, 138–139
Chessboard configurations, 424
Childbearing
in adolescence, 505, 521, 525
age of mother and, 51, 63, 65, 94
surrogate, 66
see also Pregnancy
Childbirth
breech, 138–139
cesarean delivery, 136, 138–139
complications, 135, 136, 138–139,
140–146
cultural differences in, 130–131, 135
first moments after, 147
home delivery, 130, 132, 133, 134
hospital delivery, 130, 133, 147
induced labor, 137–138
medical interventions, 135–139
natural, 132–133, 173
positions for, 132
stages of, 126–130, 137
trauma of, 128
Childbirth education programs, 111
Child-centered preschools, 336
Child development
as an interdisciplinary, applied field, 2–3
basic themes and issues, 3–6

comparing theories in, 29–31
defined, 2
as a legitimate discipline, 12
Child health care, 292, 293
Childhood. See Early childhood; Middle
childhood; Toddlerhood
Childhood illness. See Illness
Childhood injuries. See Injuries
Child maltreatment, 75, 380, 381–384
attachment problems and, 265
causes of, 366
court cases, 384
and development of empathy, 357
factors related to, 382
forms of, 381
of infants, 155
origins of, 381–383
preventing, 383–384
see also Child sexual abuse
Child rearing
and academic achievement, 552–553
cultural differences in, 15, 73, 77–78, 177
early adjustments, 73
effective, 73
fathers and, 485, 486
historical perspective, 7
of identical twins, 86
issues of middle childhood, 477–478
level of education and, 74
of mentally retarded children, 63
and morality, 583
non-sex-stereotyped children, 377–378
poverty and, 74–75
responsibility for, 78
and self-esteem, 462
sex-typed beliefs and, 255
and sex typing, 374–375
social class and, 73–74, 78
temperament and, 255–256
see also Parenting; Home environment
Child-rearing styles, 72, 379–380, 478, 486,
552, 587
Children, decision to have, 91–95, 120
Children's research rights, 43
Child sexual abuse, 488–490
characteristics of abusers and victims,
488–489
consequences for children, 489
prevention and treatment for, 489–490
see also Child maltreatment
Child support, 482–483
Chinese infants, temperament of, 254
Cholesterol levels, 395
Chorion, 96
Chorionic villi biopsy, 65, 67, 68, 97n
Chromosomal abnormalities, 62–65
Chromosomes, 50–54, 56, 64
pairs of, 50
sex, 55–56
Circular reactions, 207, 208–211
Circumcision, 150
City life, influence on development, 76–77
Classical conditioning, 16–17, 185–187
Classification, 416, 417, 430
hierarchical, 317, 320, 416, 417

Class inclusion problem, 317, 416
Classrooms
computers in, 444
traditional versus open, 441
Cleft palate, 115
Clinical interviews, 19, 34–35, 579
Clinical method, 15–16, 19, 34, 36, 246
Cliques, 591–592
Cloning, 67
Close ties to others, 241
Cocaine, in pregnancy, 105, 106
Codominance, 58–59
Cognition, 18
Cognitive development
in adolescence, 535–565
in early childhood, 309–345, 334–341
environmental influences on, 226
fear and anger and, 248
home environment and, 226–227, 335
individual differences in, 224–230,
334–341, 429–436
in infancy and toddlerhood, 203–237,
248
information processing theory of (see
Information processing)
and language, 204, 310 (see also Language
development)
in middle childhood, 415–452, 429–436
Piaget's theory of (see Piaget's theory of
cognitive development)
social experience and, 221–223, 324
testing (see Intelligence testing;
Intelligence tests)
voluntary reaching and, 181
Vygotsky's theory of (see Sociocultural
theory)
Cognitive psychology, 22
Cognitive stages. See Piaget's theory of
cognitive development
Cohort effects, 40, 41
Cohorts, 40
Color blindness, 61
Color vision, 153, 192
Colostrum, 173
Communicable disease. See Infectious
diseases
Communication
adult-infant, 233
conversational, 343–344
interactional synchrony, 264–265
teacher-parent, 78, 452
Community(s)
family and, 75–77
social support in, 383
urban, 77
Complex emotions, 249–250, 272, 353,
355, 465
adult instruction and, 249
audience and, 355
defined, 249
in early childhood, 353
labeling, 355
in middle childhood, 465
Compliance, 273
Componential analyses, 432

Componential subtheory, Sternberg's, 432
Comprehension, language, 235
Computer-assisted instruction, 444
Computers, advantages and disadvantages of, 444–445
Conception, 49, 53–55
Concordance rates, 83–84
Concrete operational stage, 19, 20, 416–421, 537, 540, 544
  defined, 416
  evaluation of, 420
  impact of culture and, 419–420
  limitations in, 419
  major characteristics of, 417
  new research on, 419–420
  operational thought, 416–419
Conditioned response (CR), 186
Conditioned stimulus (CS), 186
Conditioning. See Classical conditioning; Operant conditioning
Conformity, in adolescence, 592–594
Conscience
  in early childhood, 363
  Freud's theory of, 13, 351
  see also Moral development
Consent for research
  informed, 43, 44
  parental, 44
Conservation, 315, 416, 417, 419, 430
  of liquid, 315
  of number, 315, 318, 420
Contexts for development, 24
  cultural, 77–81
  environmental, 70–81
Contextual subtheory, Sternberg's, 432
Continuous development, 4, 8
  versus discontinuous, 4–5, 31, 420
Contraceptives
  access to, 525
  use of, 92, 93, 520, 523, 524
Contractions, 126, 127, 128, 137
  in induced labor, 137
  stimulation of, 137
Contrast, principle of, 342
Contrast sensitivity, 195
Control, of attention, 421
Control processes or mental strategies, 217
Controversial children, 473, 474
Conventional level, of moral understanding, 580, 581
Convergent thinking, 448
Conversational skills, 343–344, 438
Cooing, 233
Cooley's anemia, 60
Cooperation, 352
Cooperative learning, 325
Cooperative play, 358, 360, 362
Coregulation, 478
Corpus callosum, 286
Corpus luteum, 54
Correlation genetic-environmental
  active, 86
  evocative, 86
  passive, 86
Correlational design, 37–38, 39

Correlation coefficient, 37
Cortex, 284. See also Cerebral cortex
Counseling
  genetic, 65, 70
  marital, 158–159
Counting, 332
Crack, in pregnancy, 106
Crawling, 178, 180
  and cognitive development, 215
  and depth cues, 192–193, 194
  and individuation, 245
Creativity, 447–449
Critical periods, 24
  in brain development, 169
  in language development, 549
  in prenatal development, 103–104, 113
Cross-cultural research, 28–29. See also Cultural differences
Crossing over, 51, 53
Cross-sectional design, 39, 41
Crowds, 592
Crowning, in childbirth, 128
Crying, infant, 155, 156, 248
Cultural bias, in intelligence tests, 334–335, 430, 436
Cultural differences
  in attachment, 262–263
  in body growth, 280–281, 390–391
  in childbirth, 130–131, 135
  in child rearing, 73, 77–78, 177
  in cognitive development, 419–420, 540
  in development, 28
  in education, 78, 450–451, 563–564
  in identity development, 576–577
  in maternal roles, 120
  in memory strategies, 425
  in moral reasoning, 470, 583
  in motor development, 180, 181
  in newborn behavior, 156
  in psychosocial development, 14–15
  in temperament, 255
  in toys, 30
Cultural influences. See Culture
Culturally specific practices, 28
Culture, 28
  acquiring, 30
  and adolescent initiation ceremonies, 509
  and child maltreatment, 383
  and concrete operational stage, 419–420
  and formal operational stage, 540
  and IQ, 434–435
  and memory strategies, 425
  and moral reasoning, 470, 583
  peer, 471
  and sex typing, 476–477
  and sexual activity, 518
Cuna Indians, 131
Custody
  fathers and, 482, 484
  joint, 482
Cystic fibrosis, 60, 68, 399
Cytomegalovirus, 111

Dark, fear of the, 356
Darwin's theory. See Evolution, theory of

Dating, 586, 592
Day care, 336–338
  caregivers and, 33, 39
  fears about, 356
  good quality, 227, 228, 230, 336–338, 340
  inadequate, 337
  for infants, 227, 267
  infectious disease and, 294
  poor quality, 227, 267
  for preschoolers, 336, 337–338
  publicly supported, 78
  for school-age children, 485–486
  as a threat to attachment security, 267
Death, child's understanding of, 319. See also Mortality
Debriefing, in research, 44
Decentration, 416
Decision making, 546
Deductive reasoning, 317
Deferred imitation, 212, 214–215
Delinquency, 599–601
  factors related to, 599–600
  prevention and treatment, 601
Delivery, 127–128
  cesarean, 136
  cultural differences in, 131
  home, 130, 132, 133
  instrument, 137
  medications during, 136–137, 191
Demandingness, by parents, 379
Deoxyribonucleic acid (DNA), 50–52, 59
Dependent variable, 38
Depression
  in adolescence, 594–596
  postpartum, 158–159
  twin studies of, 83
Deprivation dwarfism, 289
Deprivation, maternal, 264
Depth cues
  binocular, 193
  crawling and, 192–193, 194
  motion and, 192–193
  pictorial, 193, 406
  reaching and, 192, 193
Depth perception, 192–194
  development of, 192–194
  independent movement and, 193–194
DES. See Diethylstilbestrol
Development
  contexts for, 24–29, 70–81
  life-span nature of, 14
  see also Child development
Developmental research designs, 39, 40–42
  improving, 41–42
Diabetes
  and obesity, 174
  and pregnancy, 117
Diagnosis. See Prenatal diagnostic methods
Diarrhea, 294
Diet
  in adolescence, 515
  in early childhood, 289–291
  in infancy, 173–175
  in middle childhood, 394
  and prenatal development, 113

Diethylstilbestrol (DES), 109
Dieting, 516
  adolescents and, 515
  infants and, 175
  obese children and, 396–397
Diets
  to control PKU, 58
  crash, 396
  fad, 515
  vegetarian, 515
Differentiation theory, 198, 304–305
Difficult children, 252, 257
Dilation and effacement of the cervix,
    126–127
Discipline, parental, 72
  and aggression, 369
  inconsistent, 480
  with threats of punishment, 364
Discontinuous development, 5
Discontinuous versus continuous
    development, 4–5, 31
Diseases
  bacterial, 111
  as cause of malnutrition, 291
  dominant, 58, 59, 60
  immunization against, 291, 293
  infectious, 110, 290–292, 294
  maternal, in pregnancy, 110–111
  in middle childhood, 398–399
  parasitic, 111
  recessive, 58, 60, 61
  sexually transmitted, 518, 525–526
  viral, 111, 112, 294
  see also Illness
Disequilibrium, 206
Dishabituation, 189, 213, 218, 219
Disorganized/disoriented attachment,
    262
Distance, concept of, 418–419
Distributive justice, 468
Divergent thinking, 447–448
Divorce, 479–483
  age of child and, 481
  custody arrangements, 482
  and family relationships, 479
  immediate consequences of, 480–481
  long-term consequences of, 481–482
  sex of child and, 481
  stress of, 72
Divorce mediation, 482
DNA. See Deoxyribonucleic acid
Dominance hierarchy, 409
Dominant alleles, 56
Dominant cerebral hemisphere, 285
Dominant diseases, 58, 59, 60
Dominant-recessive inheritance, 56–57
Donor insemination, 66
Double standard of sexual behavior,
    518
Down syndrome, 62–63
Drawing, three-dimensional, 406
Drawing skills, 301, 404–406
Dreams, understanding of, 34–35
Drive reduction theory, 17
  of attachment, 257–258

Drives
  channeling, 244
  primary, 17, 257
  secondary or learned, 17, 257
  sex, 17, 517
Dropping out, 556–559
  factors related to, 556–558
  prevention of, 558–559
Drug abuse, 525, 526–528, 530
Drugs
  in adolescence, 525–528, 530
  analgesias, 136
  anesthesias, 136, 139, 150
  antidepressant, 398
  and breast-feeding, 174
  fertility, 56
  illegal, 105–107
  for labor and delivery, 136–137, 191
  mood-altering, 105, 106
  for newborns, 150
  nonprescription, 105
  pain-relieving, 136–137
  in pregnancy, 105
  to prevent miscarriage, 109
Drug treatment
  for ADHD, 423
  for enuresis, 398
Duchenne muscular dystrophy, 61, 68
Dyscalculia, 446
Dysgraphia, 446
Dyslexia, 446

Ear infections, 394
Early childhood
  cognitive development in, 309–345
  emotional and social development in,
    349–384
  milestones of development in, 387
  motor development in, 297–303
  physical development in, 279–305
Easy child, 252
Eating disorders, 515–517
Eating habits
  adaptive value of, 396
  in adolescence, 515
  in early childhood, 290
  encouraging good, 175
  and obesity, 395
Eclampsia, 117
Ecological systems theory, 25–28, 31, 71
Ectoderm, 98, 99
Education
  acceleration programs, 449
  bilingual, 439, 440
  childbirth, 111
  cross-cultural perspective, 450–452
  cultural differences in, 78, 450–452, 475,
    556
  health, 400–402, 517
  of homeless children, 75
  and information processing, 24
  involving parents in, 76, 451
  moral, 584
  new philosophical directions in, 441–442
  physical, 410–411

Piaget's theory of, 321–322, 441
  safety, 400
  sex, 490, 518, 520, 522, 523, 524,
    525–526
  and social class differences, 74
  for special needs children, 445–449
  teenage mothers and, 523
  Vygotsky's theory of, 325, 441
  see also Schools
Educational television, 338–341
Education for All Handicapped Children Act
    (Public Law 94–142), 445
Efe, 78, 280–281
Ego, 13
Egocentric speech, 322–323
Egocentrism, 313–315, 318, 543
Ego integrity versus despair, 15
Ejaculation, 506
Elaboration, as memory strategy, 422
Electra conflict, 351, 363, 373, 458
Embarrassment, 249, 250, 353
Embryo, 97, 169
  deformities of, 105
  period of the, 97–99, 104
Embryonic disk, 95, 98
Emotional commitment, in friendships, 473
Emotional deprivation, 176–177, 264, 289
Emotional development
  in adolescence, 569–602
  in early childhood, 349–384
  in infancy and toddlerhood, 241–276
  in middle childhood, 457–491
  temperament and, 251–256
Emotional expression
  controlling, 354
  in infancy, 247, 249
  regulating, 250–251, 354–355, 465
Emotional neglect, 380, 381. See also Child
    maltreatment
Emotional reactions
  individual differences in, 252
  judging the causes of, 354
Emotional self-regulation, 250
  in early childhood, 354–355
  in infancy and toddlerhood, 250–251
  language and, 251
  in middle childhood, 465
Emotional well-being, 288–289
Emotions
  basic, 246–248
  complex, 249–250, 272, 353, 355, 465
  infant's reactions to, 249
  survival value of, 248
  understanding, 353–354
Empathy, 272, 467
  child maltreatment and, 357
  development of, 355–357, 370
Endoderm, 98
Engrossment, 147
Enlightenment, 8–9
Enuresis, 398
Environment
  choosing (niche-picking), 86
  and heredity, 49, 81, 84
  home, 226, 228, 335

Environmental influences, 6
    context and, 24, 70–81
    on depression, 595
    and ecological systems theory, 25–28
    on food preferences, 290
    on health, 173–177, 288–297, 398,
        400–402, 515–517, 525–529
    on intelligence, 85, 226–230, 335–341,
        434–436, 547
    on language development, 236–237,
        344–345, 438–440, 549
    on morality, 364–367, 368, 582–583
    on motor skills, 180–181, 182, 303, 407,
        410–411
    in mutations, 59
    on obesity, 395
    on sex typing, 373, 374–376, 476–477
    on teeth, 283
    on temperament, 255–257
    see also Mechanistic theories
Environmental perspective, on adolescence,
    499–500
Environmental pollution
    and health, 287
    in pregnancy, 109–110
Envy, 249, 353
Epilepsy, 393
Epiphyses, 167–168, 280–281, 502
Episiotomy, 128
Equality, in distributive justice reasoning,
    468–469
Equilibration, 206
Equilibrium, 19, 205, 206
Erikson's theory. See Psychosocial
    development
Estrogens, 501
Ethical guidelines, for research, 43, 44
Ethic of care, in moral development,
    584–585
Ethics
    of abortion, 69
    in research, 42–44
Ethnic minorities. See Minorities
Ethological theory of attachment, 24–25,
    259–261
Ethology, 24–25, 31
European countries, 291, 293, 296, 556
Eustachian tube, 394
Evocative genetic-environmental correlation,
    86
Evolution, theory of, 9, 498
Exercise
    in pregnancy, 111–113
    and weight gain, 175, 396
Exosystem, 26–27, 28
Expansions, of children's language, 345
Experiential subtheory, Sternberg's, 432
Experimental designs, 38, 39
Experiments
    field, 38–39
    laboratory, 38
    natural, 38–39
    see also Research designs; Research
        methods
Explaining, as educational strategy, 442

Exploration, and identity development, 571,
    575
Expressive style, of language development,
    235
Extended family, 78, 79
Extinction, 186
Extracurricular activities, 559
Eye movements, in newborns, 153
Eyewitness testimony, 491

Face perception, 196–197, 198
    development of, 198
Facial abnormalities, 108
    and Down syndrome, 63
    and fetal alcohol syndrome, 108
    and prenatal AIDS exposure, 112
Facial expressions
    cues to emotions, 246
    infants' response to, 249
Factor analysis, 429, 432
FAE. See Fetal alcohol effects
Failure, attributions and, 462
Failure to thrive, 176–177
Fallopian tubes, 54, 66
False labor, 126
Family(s)
    in adolescence, 575, 586–588, 599–601
    blended or reconstituted, 483–484
    and community, 75–77
    conflict-ridden, 369
    divorce and, 479–483
    extended, 78, 79
    homeless, 75
    influence in middle childhood, 477–486
    influence on aggressive behavior, 369
    influence on development, 70–73
    one-child, 93, 94
    poverty in, 74–75
    reconstituted or blended, 483
    and sex typing, 374–375
    and social class, 73–74
    as a social system, 71–73
    and vocational choice, 561
Family size, 92–93
Family system, 71–73
Fantasy period, of vocational development,
    560
FAS. See Fetal alcohol syndrome
Fast mapping, 341–342
Fat, body, 166, 390, 501, 503
Fat cells, 174–175
Fathers
    attachment behaviors of, 266–268
    child rearing and, 485, 486
    as custodial parents, 482
    and divorce, 480, 482
    expectant, 119
    of newborns, 147, 157, 158
    sex-role beliefs of, 477
    teenage, 525
Father/stepmother families, 484
Fats, in human milk, 173
Fear(s)
    adaptive value of, 356

    cognitive development and, 248, 356
    conditioning of, 17, 186–187
    in early childhood, 355, 356
    of heights, 248
    helping children manage, 356
    hormones released in, 115
    and imagination, 356
    in infants, 248
    and memory, 248
    in middle childhood, 487–488
    see also Phobias
Federal government. See Public policy
Feeding, infant, 258, 259, 260
Feelings. See Emotions
Fertility, and age, 95
Fertility drugs, 56
Fertilization, 53, 54, 56
    in vitro, 66
Fetal alcohol effects (FAE), 108
Fetal alcohol syndrome (FAS), 108, 116
Fetal medicine, 65–68
Fetal monitoring, 135–136, 138
Fetal monitors, 135–136
Fetoscopy, 100
Fetus, 99
    age of viability, 101
    period of the, 99–102, 104
    sex of, 100
Field experiments, 38–39
Fine motor skills
    in early childhood, 279, 300–302
    in infancy and toddlerhood, 178, 179,
        180, 181–183
    in middle childhood, 404–406
Firearms, and injuries, 529, 598
Fitness, 410. See also Physical education
Fixation, in psychoanalytic theory, 13
Flexibility, in motor development, 403
Focusing, visual, in infancy, 152, 192
Fontanels, 168
Food preferences, 151, 290
Force, in motor development, 404
Forceps, 137
Formal operational stage, 19, 20, 536–
    540
    hypothetico-deductive reasoning,
        536–537
    new research on, 539
    propositional thought, 538–539
Fragile X syndrome, 64
France, 522
Fraternal or dizygotic twins, 56, 57, 82,
    83
    developmental patterns in, 86
    and IQ scores, 434
    maternal factors linked to, 57
    physical development in, 172
    temperamental traits of, 254
Free-standing birth centers, 130–132
Freud's theory
    criticisms of, 13–14, 351
    of moral development, 363–364, 373
    of psychosexual development, 12–14,
        350–351, 363, 458–459, 499
    see also Psychoanalytic theory

Friendships
in adolescence, 589–590
cross-race, 473
in early childhood, 362
in middle childhood, 457, 472–473
selectivity in, 473
sex differences in, 590
see also Peer relations
Frontal lobe, 170, 392
Functional play, 212

Games
adult-structured, 408, 409
child-organized, 408
with infants, 268
in medieval times, 6
rule-oriented, 407–408
Gametes, 52, 53, 56
Gender constancy, 376–377
Gender intensification, 586, 595
Gender schemas, 377
Gender schema theory, 373, 377
and sex-role identity, 377
General growth curve, 284
Generation gap, 545
Generativity versus stagnation, 15
Genes, 50–51
cloning, 67
Gene splicing, 68
Genetic code, 50–51, 61
Genetic counseling, 65, 70
Genetic disorders, 57–61, 62–64
Genetic engineering, 67
Genetic-environmental correlation, 84,
86–87
Genetic factors
in body growth, 287
in depression, 595
in homosexuality, 521
in intelligence, 82–83, 434
in obesity, 395
in schizophrenia, 83
in sex typing, 374
in temperament and personality, 83, 254
in vision, 394
see also Heredity
Genetics, 49–62
basic principles of, 50
disorders of, 57–61, 62–64
Genitals, growth of, 100, 284, 505
Genital stage, 14, 499
Genotype, 49
German infants, attachment behavior of,
262–263
Ghosts, fear of, 356
Gifted children, 447–449, 546
Glial cells, 100, 169
Goal-directed (intentional) behavior, in
Piaget's sensorimotor stage, 210
"Good boy-good girl" orientation, of moral
understanding, 580
Goodness-of-fit model, 255–256, 266
child rearing and, 256–257
Governmental programs. See Public policies

Governor's Schools, 449
Grammar, 231–232
Grammatical development, 245
in adolescence, 547–548
in early childhood, 342–343
in middle childhood, 437–438
Grandparents, 78, 79, 248
Grasp
pincer, 182, 183
ulnar, 181, 183
Grasp reflex, 149
Gross motor skills
in early childhood, 279, 298–300
in infancy and toddlerhood, 178, 179
in middle childhood, 403–404, 407
Group administered intelligence tests, 429
Growing pains, 392
Growth hormone (GH), 287, 289, 501
Growth spurt, 501, 502, 505, 506
Guilt, 249, 465
in early childhood, 355
Freud's view of, 355, 363, 364
initiative versus, 15, 350–351
self-development and, 353

Habituation, 189
Habituation-dishabituation response, 213,
214, 218, 219
Hair
body and facial, 501, 506
pubic, 501, 506
Hair color, 56–57
Handedness, lateralization and, 284–285
Handicapped children, 445–447
adoption of, 69
Handicapped infants, 140
Handwriting, 407
Happiness, in infants, 247–248
Hausa, 419
Head Start. See Project Head Start
Health
in adolescence, 401, 507, 514–529
and childbirth, 135–139
children's understanding of, 401
in early childhood, 287
emotional well-being and, 288–289
environmental pollutants and, 287
of homeless children, 75
in infancy and toddlerhood, 173–177
in middle childhood, 393–400
poverty and, 393
prenatal, 103–118
Health care
child, 292, 293, 393
prenatal, 116–117
Health care programs, 144
Health education, 400–402, 517
Health insurance, 117, 292
national system of, 144
Hearing
in infancy, 191
in middle childhood, 394
of newborns, 152

Hearing-impaired infants, language
development in, 233, 236
Hearing loss, 141
Heartbeat, fetal, 135–136
Heart disease, 174
Heinz dilemma, 579, 582, 584
Hemispheres of the brain, 171, 284, 392
Hemophilia, 61
Heredity, 6
and environment, 49, 81, 84
patterns of genetic inheritance, 56–62
and physical development, 172–173
studies of, 81–84
see also Genetic factors; Nature-nuture
controversy
Heritability estimates, 82–83, 434
limitations of, 83–84
twin studies of, 82–83, 254, 434
Heroin, in pregnancy, 105, 106
Herpes viruses, 526
in pregnancy, 110, 111
Heteronomous morality, 578
Heterosexual development, 482
Heterozygous pattern of genetic inheritance,
56, 57, 59
Hierarchical classification, 317, 320, 416, 417
lack of, 317
High blood pressure, 395
obesity and, 174
in pregnancy, 117
Hindus, 470
Hispanics
bilingual education for, 440
drop-out rate, 556
identity development of, 576
Historical foundations of child development,
3, 6–12
Darwin's theory of evolution, 9
Historical perspective, 3, 6–12
Darwin's theory of evolution, 9
early scientific beginnings, 9–12
Enlightenment, 8–9
medieval times, 6–7
mid-twentieth century influences, 12–22
modern theories, 22–29
Reformation, 7–8
Holland, 293, 522
Home delivery, 130, 132, 133, 134
Home environment, and mental
development, 226, 228, 335
Homeless families, 75
Home Observation for Measurement of the
Environment (HOME), 226, 335
defined, 226
Homework, 478
Homosexuality, 112, 521, 525
Homozygous pattern of genetic inheritance,
56, 57
Hopi Indians, motor development in, 180
Hopping, 298, 403
Horizontal décalage, 417, 419
information processing view of, 420
Hormones, 54
in adolescence, 501
after childbirth, 157

Hormones (continued)
  and body growth, 287, 501
  and brain functioning, 393
  fear and anxiety and, 115
  female sex, 501
  male sex, 108, 368, 501
  and sex typing, 374
  stimulation of labor contractions with,
    137
  stress, 115, 128, 139
  synthetic, 109
  taking, in pregnancy, 108–109
Hospital birth centers, 130–132, 133
Hostile aggression, 368, 369
Hostility, and friendship, 362. *See also*
    Aggression
Human development, 2
Humor, 437
Hunger, 17
  chronic, 394
  in infants, 155, 248, 257, 258
Hunters and gatherers, 30, 78
Huntington disease, 58, 60, 68
Hyaline membrane disease, 140
Hygiene, and infectious disease in day care,
    294
Hyperactivity, 422, 423
Hypothesis, 32
Hypothetico-deductive reasoning, 536–537


Id, 13
Idealism, of adolescents, 544–545
Identical or monozygotic twins, 56–57, 82,
    83
  developmental patterns in, 86
  and IQ scores, 434
  physical development in, 172
  reared apart, 86
  tempermental traits of, 254
Identification, 351, 363
  with same-sex parent, 351
Identity
  in adolescence (*see* Identity development)
  Erikson's theory of, 15, 570–571
  group, 471
  paths to, 573
  sex-role, 376–377, 475, 476
  sexual, 521
  *see also* Self-development
Identity achievement, 573, 574
Identity crisis, 570–571
Identity development, 498, 570
  of ethnic minorities, 576–577
  factors that affect, 575
  *see also* Self-development
Identity diffusion, 571, 573, 574–575
Identity foreclosure, 573, 574–575
Identity statuses, 573–574
  personality characteristics and, 574–575
Identity versus identity diffusion, 15,
    570–571
Illness
  childhood, 290–292, 293, 294, 398–
    399

children's understanding of, 401
  school phobia and, 487
  *see also* Diseases
Imaginary audience, 543, 544
Imagination, and fears, 356
Imitation, 189
  deferred, 212, 214–215
  in infancy, 210, 211, 215
  in language development, 230
  and learning, 189
  by newborns, 189–190
  *see also* Modeling; Observational learning
Immune system
  AIDS and, 112
  development of, 102, 284
Immunization, 291, 293
Implantation, of blastocyst, 95–96
Imprinting, 24, 25, 259
Independence
  in middle childhood, 478
  in toddlerhood, 244
  *see also* Autonomy
Independent variable, 38
India, moral concepts in, 470
Individual differences
  in body growth, 280, 390
  in cognitive development, 429–436
  in development, 12
  in emotional reaction, 252
  genetic influences on, 62
  in IQ, 433–436
  in language development, 235–236
  in learning, 321–322
  in mental development, 334–341
  in motor development, 178, 407
  in sibling relationships, 269
  in sociability, 349–350
  in temperament and personality,
    241–242, 254
Individually administered intelligence tests,
    429
Individuation, in infancy and toddlerhood,
    245
Induced labor, 137–138, 146
Induction, 364
Inductive reasoning, 317
Industry, 457, 459, 570
Industry versus inferiority, 15, 458–459
Infancy and toddlerhood
  cognitive development in, 203–237
  emotional and social development in, 241,
    246–251
  milestones of development in, 277
  physical development in, 163–199
  *see also* Infants; *specific topics*
Infant day care, 227, 267
Infantile autism, 64
Infant intelligence tests, 224–226
  computing scores on, 224–225
  predicting later performance from, 224,
    225–226
  *see also* Intelligence tests
Infant mortality, 143, 144, 145, 294, 295,
    296
  and poverty, 144

Infants
  appearance of newborns, 128–129
  attachment behavior of, 260, 261–262
  cognitive development of, 206–210,
    213–215, 218–219, 221–223
  cultural differences in behavior, 156
  factors affecting growth in, 172–177
  failure-to-thrive, 177
  handicapped, 140
  individual differences in intelligence of,
    224–230
  language development of, 233
  low birth weight, 106, 107, 140–143,
    144
  maltreated, 265
  neonatal assessment, 129–130, 150,
    155–157
  newborns, 147–150, 153–155
  newborn states, 153–155
  personality development of, 242–243,
    244–245
  postterm, 143–146
  premature, 56, 106, 141–142
  preterm, 140–143, 154
  rapid weight gain in, 396
  reflexes of, 148–150
  sleep and wakefulness patterns in,
    153–155, 177
  social world of, 269
  *see also* specific topics
Infectious diseases
  day care and, 294
  during pregnancy, 110
  in early childhood, 290–292
Inference
  mental, 330
  transitive, 417, 419
Inferiority, 459
Infertility, new reproductive technologies
    for, 66
Infinitive phrases, 433
Information processing, 22–24, 31
  in adolescence, 540–542
  application to academic learning, 427–
    429
  in early childhood, 325–333
  and education, 24
  and horizontal décalage, 420
  in infancy and toddlerhood, 204, 215,
    216–221
  in middle childhood, 421–429
  models, 23, 216–218
  Siegler's rule-assessment approach,
    540–542
Information processing theory, evaluation
    of, 220–221
Informed consent, 43, 44
Inheritance
  dominant-recessive, 56–57
  polygenic, 62
  X-linked, 61–62
  *see also* Genetic factors; Heredity
Inhibited children, 252
Initiative, 350, 570
Initiative versus guilt, 15, 350–351

Injuries
  in adolescence, 529
  automobile, 529
  causes of, 295–296, 529
  in early childhood, 292–297
  in middle childhood, 399–400
  preventing, 296–297
  sports-related, 529
  unintentional, 292–297, 399–400, 529
Inner mental life, awareness of, 329–330
Inner speech, 324
Inorganic failure to thrive, 176–177
Insecure attachment, 261–262, 264, 265, 267
  continuity of caregiving and, 270
  day care and, 267
Instructing, as educational strategy, 442
Instrumental aggression, 368
Instrumental purpose orientation, in moral
    understanding, 580–581
Intelligence
  adoption studies of, 82–83
  defining, 11, 429–433
  environmental influences on, 85,
    226–230, 335–341, 434–436, 547
  general, 429
  genetic factors in, 82–83, 434
  kinship studies of, 82–83, 434
  measuring, 224, 334, 429–433
  predicting, 156, 225, 334
  prenatal development and, 105, 107, 108,
    113
  racial differences in, 83–84
  recent developments in defining, 432
  triarchic theory of, 432–433
  twin studies of, 82, 434
  see also Intelligence testing; Intelligence
    tests
Intelligence quotient (IQ), 224–225
  cultural influences on, 434–435
  individual differences in, 433–436
  and infant-toddler intervention, 230–231
  as predictor of school performance, 429
  sex differences in, 546–547
  social class and, 433, 434
  stability of, 225, 429
  see also Intelligence
Intelligence testing
  history of, 11–12
  in early childhood, 334
  in middle childhood, 429–436
  in infancy, 224–226
  prediction with, 11–12, 224, 225
  purpose of, 224
  see also Intelligence; Intelligence tests
Intelligence tests, 429
  cultural bias in, 334–335, 430, 433, 436
  early childhood, 334
  group administered, 429
  individually administered, 429
  infant, 224–226
  Piagetian, 430–431
  representative, 429–430
  sex bias in, 430
  see also Intelligence; Intelligence testing;
    Test scores

Intentional (goal-directed) behavior, in
    Piaget's sensorimotor stage, 210
Intentions, understanding, 352–353
Interactional synchrony, 264–265, 266, 344
Interactionist perspective, in language
    development, 232, 236
Intermodal perception, 197, 198
Internalization, and moral development, 363
Interpersonal cooperation, morality of, 581
Interviews
  clinical, 19, 34–35, 579
  research, 34–36
Intimacy
  in dating, 592
  development of, 571, 573
  in friendships, 589
Intimacy versus isolation, 15
Invariant features, and perceptual
    development, 198, 304
In vitro fertilization, 66
Ionizing radiation, 59–60
IQ. See Intelligence quotient (IQ); Test
    scores
Iron deficiency, 515
Irony, 548
Irreversibility, 315
Isolette, 142

Japanese children
  education of, 450–452, 475, 556
  language development in, 191
  rate of body growth, 165
  temperament of, 254
Japanese mothers
  caregiving, 263
  child-rearing practices, 177, 255
  effect of radiation on, 109
  pregnancy and, 120
Jarara, 131
Joint custody, 482
Jumping, 298, 403
Just community, 584
Justice, distributive, 468–470
Justice reasoning, in moral development,
    584–585
Juvenile justice system, 599

Kamehameha Elementary Education
    Program (KEEP), 441–442
Kauai study, 146
Kaufman Assessment Battery for Children
    (K-ABC), 430, 432, 436
Kibbutzim, 583
Kinship studies, 82, 83
  of intelligence, 434
Kipsigis, motor development in, 182
Klinefelter syndrome, 63, 64
Knowledge, and memory performance,
    424–425
!Kung, 30, 78, 510
Kwashiorkor, 176

Labor
  false, 126
  induced, 137–138, 146
  medications during, 136–137, 191
  stages of, 126–130, 134, 137
Laboratory experiments, 38
Language
  bilingualism, 438–439, 549
  and cognitive development, 310,
    322–324, 538
  conversational, 343–344
  expressing emotions through, 251, 354
  semilingualism, 440
  understanding written, 330–332
  see also Language development
Language acquisition device (LAD), 231
Language awareness, 437
Language customs, and intelligence testing,
    435
Language development
  in adolescence, 547–549
  adult-child communication and, 233,
    344–345
  behaviorist perspective, 231
  brain and, 284, 285
  comprehension versus production, 235
  cooing and babbling, 232–233
  critical period of, 24, 549
  in early childhood, 341–345
  first words, 233–234
  getting ready to talk, 232–233
  individual differences in, 235–236
  in infancy and toddlerhood, 191, 229–237
  interactionist perspective, 232, 236
  in middle childhood, 437–439
  milestones of, 232
  nativist perspective, 231–232
  and self-control, 273
  social class and, 74
  styles of, 235–236
  in twins, 237
  two-word utterance phase, 234–235
  see also Grammatical development;
    Vocabulary development
Language disorders, 236
Lanugo, 100
Latchkey children, 485
Latency stage, 14, 458
Lateralization, brain, 171–172, 284–285, 392
  atypical, 285
  and handedness, 284–285
Laughter, in infants, 247–248
Lead poisoning, 110, 288
Learned drives, 17
Learned helplessness, 427, 463
Learning
  academic, 427–429
  cooperative, 325, 447
  discovery, 321
  individual differences in, 321–322
  in infancy and toddlerhood, 185–191
  observational, 17
  in school, 441–450, 549–559
  sex-role, 374–376, 377
  see also Education

Learning disabilities, 446–447
Left-handedness, 285
Legal system, and child maltreatment, 384
Lens (eye), 152
Letters
  combining, 331
  discriminating, 304–305
  learning, 404
  and sounds, 428
Life changes, effect on attachment, 266
Life-span nature of development, 14
Life-style, in adolescence, 515
Lightening (labor), 126
Linear perspective, in children's drawings, 406
Literacy, in early childhood, 330–332
Locke's philosophy, 8
Logical reasoning, in Piaget's theory, 312–313, 315, 317, 320–321, 416–418
Longitudinal design, 39, 40–41
Longitudinal-sequential design, 39, 41
Long-term memory, 217, 218
Love withdrawal discipline, 364
Loyalty, in friendships, 589
Lungs, 393, 503
  of newborns, 140
Luxembourg, 383
Lymph system, 284

Macrosystem, 27–28
Mahler's theory. See Separation-individuation
Mainstreaming, 445–447
Make-believe play
  advantages of, 312
  development of, 212, 223, 311–312
  in early childhood, 311–312, 320, 350, 361, 362
  parent-toddler interaction and, 223
Malnutrition, 113, 114, 394
  in adolescence, 516
  disease and, 291
  effect on cognitive functioning and the brain, 516
  and low birth weight, 141
  and physical development, 175–176
  prenatal, 141, 176
Malocclusion, 392
Maltreated children, 382. See also Child maltreatment
Maltreated infants, 265. See also Child maltreatment
Marasmus, 176
Marfan syndrome, 60
Marijuana, 106, 526–527
Marital relationship
  effect on child's development, 72
  and parenthood, 120–121
  and postpartum depression, 158–159
Mastery-oriented attributions, 463
Matching, in research, 38
Maternal age, 116
  and child rearing, 94
  and Down syndrome, 63
  and pregnancy complications, 116

Maternal blood analysis, in prenatal diagnosis, 65, 67
Maternal deprivation, and attachment, 264
Maternal diseases, in pregnancy, 110–111
Maternal employment, 93, 159, 484–486
  and adolescent autonomy, 587–588
  and attachment, 267
  and caregiving styles, 268
  and child development, 484–485
  and day care, 485–486
  divorce and, 480, 484
  influence on vocational choice, 561
  public support for, 486
Mathematical development, 428
  in adolescence, 546–547
  cross-cultural research on, 332
  in early childhood, 330–332
  in middle childhood, 428–429
  sex differences in, 546–547
Maturation, 8
  early versus late, 507, 513–514
  and motor development, 180–181
Mayan children, 131, 425
Mechanistic theory, 4
Media events, anxiety about, 487
Medications. See Drugs
Medieval times, 6–7
Meiosis, 51–53, 62, 63
Memory
  attention and, 217, 218–219
  in early childhood, 327–329
  for everyday experiences, 328
  fear and, 248
  generalizing remembered information to new situations, 328–329
  in infancy, 213, 218–219, 225
  knowledge base and, 424–425
  long-term, 217, 218
  recognition, 219, 327, 225, 235, 327
  retrieval, 218, 422
  working or short-term, 217–218, 420
Memory strategies, 217–218, 327, 422
  culture and, 425
  elaboration, 422
  organization, 327, 422
  rehearsal, 327, 422, 425
Menarche, 505
  delayed, 501, 507
  girls' reaction to, 508
  in other cultures, 510
Menstrual cycle, 54
Menstruation, 54, 501, 505, 516
Mental inferences, as a source of knowledge, 330
Mental representation, 207, 211
  in Piaget's theory, 211–213
Mental retardation, 436, 445–446
  causes of, 58, 62–63, 64, 108, 140, 446
Mental testing movement, 11. See also Intelligence testing; Intelligence tests
Mercury, in pregnancy, 109
Merit, in distributive justice reasoning, 469
Mesoderm, 98
Mesosystem, 26
Metacognition, 329, 425–426, 432, 444

Metaphors, understanding of, 342, 548
Methadone, 106
Mexican Americans, identity development of, 577
Microsystem, 26
Middle childhood
  cognitive development in, 415–452
  emotional and social development in, 457–491
  milestones of development in, 495
  physical development in, 389–411
Midwives, 134
Mind, young children's theory of. See Theory of mind
Minorities
  education of, 442
  identity development among, 576–577
  immunization of, 291–292, 294
  learned helplessness of, 463–464
  performance on intelligence tests, 334
  and poverty, 75
  and intelligence testing situations, 435–436
  see also names of groups
Miscarriage, 63, 67, 95, 105, 522
  drugs to prevent, 109
Mitosis, 50–51
Modeling, 17–18
  as educational strategy, 442
  and moral development, 365
  see also Imitation
Monkeys, attachment in, 258
Monsters, fear of, 356, 362
Moodiness, in adolescence, 509, 594
Moral development
  behaviorist perspective of, 363, 365–367
  cognitive-developmental perspective of, 363, 367–368, 578–579
  psychoanalytic perspective of, 363–364
  social learning perspective of, 365–367
  see also Morality
Moral dilemmas, 579, 580
Moral education, 584
Morality
  in adolescence, 577–585
  autonomous, 578
  cultural influences on, 470, 593
  in early childhood, 363–371
  environmental influences on, 582–583
  heteronomous, 578
  Kohlberg's theory of, 579–586
  longitudinal studies of, 582
  in middle childhood, 468–469
  Piaget's theory of, 363, 367–368, 578–579
  punishment and, 582
  relationship to behavior, 585
  self-control and, 273
  sex differences in, 584–585
  see also Moral development
Moratorium, 573, 574–575
Moro reflex, 149
Mortality, injuries and, 294, 295. See also Infant mortality; Neonatal mortality
Motherese, 236–237

Mother-infant relationship
  and attachment, 258, 264–265
  cesarean delivery and, 139
  medications during labor and, 137
  postpartum depression and, 158–159
  and preterm infants, 142
  symbiosis and, 244–245
  see also Attachment; Bonding;
    Parent-infant relationship
Mother/stepfather families, 483–484
Motion, as depth cue, 192–193
Motor development
  in adolescence, 530–531
  cephalo-caudal trend, 166, 167, 178, 503
  cultural differences in, 180, 182
  in early childhood, 297–303
  enhancing, 303
  fine, 178, 179
  gross, 178, 179
  in infancy and toddlerhood, 178–184
  maturation and experience and, 180–181
  in middle childhood, 402–411
  proximo-distal trend, 166, 167, 178
  sequence of, in infancy and toddlerhood,
    178–180
Motor skills
  cognitive development and, 215
  as complex systems of action, 180
  early training in, 303
  factors that affect, 180–181, 182,
    302–303, 407, 410–411
  fine (see Fine motor skills)
  in the first two years, 179
  gross (see Gross motor skills)
  reflexes and, 149
  as systems of action, 297
Motor tasks, on infant tests, 224, 225
Multiple births, 56
Muscle-fat makeup, 166, 173, 501,
  503–504
Muscular dystrophy, 61, 68
Mutation, 59–61
Myelinization, 169–170, 176, 284, 286,
  392
Myelin sheath, 169–170
Myopia, 394


National Children and Youth Fitness Study,
  410
Nation's Report Card, 555
Native Americans, 108, 156
Nativist perspective, in language
  development, 230–232
Natural experiments, 38–39
Naturalistic observation, 32, 34
Natural or prepared childbirth, 132–133
Nature, 5. See also Nature-nurture
  controversy
Nature-nurture controversy, 5–6, 31, 81, 86
  and intelligence, 434
  and motor development, 180
Nearsightedness. See Myopia
Neglect, physical and emotional, 381. See
  also Child maltreatment

Neglected children, 473, 474
Neighborhoods, 75–76
Neonatal Behavioral Assessment Scale
  (NBAS), 155–157
Neonatal mortality, 144, 145
Nervous system, prenatal development of, 99
Neural tube, 99, 169
Neurons, 99, 169, 393
  development of, 169–170
  stimulation of, 169
Neurotransmitters, 393
Neutral stimulus, in classical conditioning,
  17, 186
Newborns. See Infants
New York Longitudinal Study, 252, 257
Ngoni, 459
Niche-picking, 86
Nicotine, in pregnancy, 107
Noble savage, 8
Nocturnal enuresis, 398
Non-rapid-eye-movement (NREM) sleep,
  154
Normal or bell-shaped curve, 224
Normative approach, 10, 12
Norms, 224
Norway, 293
NREM sleep. See Non-rapid-eye-movement
  (NREM) sleep
Nucleus, cell, 50
Nurse-midwives, 134
Nurture, 5, 8. See also Nature-nurture
  controversy
Nutrition
  in adolescence, 507, 515
  and breast- versus bottle-feeding,
    173–174, 175
  in early childhood, 289–290, 291
  in infancy and toddlerhood, 173–175
  in middle childhood, 394
  and obesity, 174–175
  in pregnancy, 113–115
  ways to encourage good, 291
  see also Malnutrition
Nyansongo, 476–477


Obesity, 395
  causes of, 395–396
  early chubbiness and, 174–175
  factors associated with, 395
  fat cells and, 174–175
  health risks, 174
  and menstruation, 501
  in middle childhood, 394–397
  and pregnancy, 115
  social class and, 395
  treating, 396–397
Object-hiding tasks, Piaget's, 210, 211, 212,
  213
Object permanence, 207, 210, 212,
  213–214, 215, 226
Observation
  naturalistic, 32–33, 34
  structured, 33
  systematic, 32–34

Observational learning, 17
Occupational choice. See Vocational choice;
  Vocational development
Odor preference, in newborns, 151
Oedipal conflict, 350–351, 363, 373, 458
One-child families, 93
Open classrooms, 441
Operant conditioning, 187, 213, 219
  and language development, 230
  and moral development, 365
  punishment and, 365
Operational thought, in Piaget's theory,
  321, 416–419
Operations, in Piaget's theory, 312
Oral stage, 14, 242–243, 259
Organismic theory, 4
Organization, 422
  of long-term memory, 218
  as memory strategy, 327, 422
  in Piaget's theory, 205, 206
Ovaries, 51, 54, 56
Overextension, 234
Overregularization, 343
Overweight. See Obesity
Ovulation, 51
Ovum, 51, 54–55, 66, 109
Oxygen deprivation, during childbirth, 138,
  140, 146
Oxytocin, 137


Pacifiers, 197
Pain
  during childbirth, 132, 136–137
  newborn's sensitivity to, 150
Parallel play, 358, 360
Parasitic diseases, and pregnancy, 111
Parental consent, for research participation, 44
Parent-child relationship, 73
  in adolescence, 511–513, 545, 587–588
  coregulation, 478
  in middle childhood, 477–478
  punishment and, 367
  see also Mother-infant relationship;
    Parent-infant relationship
Parenthood
  adjustment to, 157–159
  benefits and costs of, 93
  marital relationship and, 120
  models of effective, 119–120
  motivations for, 91–95, 120
  preparing for, 118–121
  seeking information on, 119
  stress of new, 158, 159
Parent-infant relationship, 113, 114, 118
  and language development, 233
  see also Mother-infant relationship
Parenting
  in early childhood, 353
  of employed mothers, 484–485
  minimal, 480
  punishment and, 365–367
  social networks and, 27
  work schedules and, 27
  see also Child rearing

Parenting styles. *See* Child-rearing styles
Parents
    adoptive, 147, 264, 395
    authoritarian, 379–380
    authoritative, 379, 380–381.
    de-idealizing, 587
    and education, 76, 451–452, 552–553
    feeding practices of, 396
    permissive, 380
    and sex typing, 377, 378
    teenage, 522–523, 525
    training in caregiving skills, 143
    training in child rearing, 228
    uninvolved, 380
Parents' Anonymous, 383
Passive genetic-environmental correlation,
    86
Passive voice, in language development,
    437–438
Pattern perception, 189, 194–195
    brain development and, 197
    development of, 198
    invariant features in, 198
Pavlov's theory. *See* Classical conditioning
Pedigree, 65
Peer acceptance, 473–475
    determinants of, 474
Peer groups, 471
    in adolescence, 513–514, 548, 591
    cliques and crowds, 591–592
    influence on academic achievement, 553
    maturational timing and, 513–514
    in middle childhood, 471–472
    same-sex, 375
Peer pressure
    in adolescence, 592–594
    on latchkey children, 485
Peer relations
    in adolescence, 513–514, 548, 588–594,
        591
    in early childhood, 352, 358–363
    in middle childhood, 460, 469, 470–475
Peers. *See* Friendships; Peer relations
Peer sociability, 358–362
Pendulum problem, and Piaget's formal
    operational stage, 537
Penis, 55, 505, 506
Perception
    color, 192
    depth, 192–194
    face, 196–197, 198
    intermodal, 197, 198
    pattern, 194–196
Perception-bound thought, and Piaget's
    preoperational stage, 315
Perceptual development, 191–199
    differentiation theory, 198
    in early childhood, 304–305
    hearing, 191
    in infancy, 191–199, 304
    invariant features and, 198
Perceptual tasks, on infant tests, 225
Permissive parents, 380
Personal fable, 543–544, 598

Personality development
    biological foundations of, 254
    Erikson's theory of, 14–16, 242–244,
        245–246, 350–351, 458–459,
        570–571
    Freud's theory of, 13–14, 242–243,
        350–351, 458–459, 499
    genetic factors in, 83, 254
    and language development, 235
    Mahler's theory of, 244–246
    stability of, 40
Perspective-taking, 408, 466–467
    in adolescence, 544, 580
    and self-concept in middle childhood, 460
    Selman's stages of, 466, 580
    and social behavior, 466–467
Phallic stage, 14, 350
Phenotype, 49
Phenylketonuria (PKU), 58, 60
Phobia(s), 356, 358
    school, 487
    *see also* Fears
Physical abuse, 381. *See also* Child
    maltreatment; Child sexual abuse
Physical attractiveness, and maturational
    timing in adolescence, 513
Physical development
    in adolescence, 497–531
    affection and stimulation and, 176–177
    catch-up growth, 173
    in early childhood, 279–305
    growth disorders, 176
    heredity and, 172–173, 287–288
    in infancy and toddlerhood, 163–199
    malnutrition and, 175–176, 291, 394,
        516–517
    in middle childhood, 389–411
    nutrition and, 173–175
    rate of, 167
    *see also* Body growth
Physical education, 410–411. *See also* Sports
Physical fitness, 410
Physically handicapped. *See* Handicapped
    children; Handicapped infants
Physical neglect, 380, 381. *See also* Child
    maltreatment
Piaget's theory of cognitive development,
    18–22, 31, 204–206
    concrete operational stage, 416–421, 537,
        540
    contributions and limitations of, 20–22,
        215, 322–325
    and education, 321–322
    formal operational stage, 536–540
    key concepts, 204–206
    methods of study, 19, 34–35
    preoperational stage, 310–322
    schemes, 204
    sensorimotor stage, 206–216
    Vygotsky's challenge to, 28–29, 322–325
    *see also* names of stages
Piaget's theory of moral development, 363,
    367–368, 578–579
Pictorial depth cues, 193

Pincer grasp, 181, 183
Pituitary gland, 287, 501
PKU. *See* Phenylketonuria
Placenta, 96–97, 132, 137
    birth of, 128
Planning, development of, 422, 546
Plasticity, brain, 171
Play
    associative, 358, 360
    categorization skills in, 219–220
    constructive, 361
    cooperative, 358, 360, 362
    developmental sequence of cognitive, 361
    developmental sequence of social, Parten's,
        358–361
    in early childhood, 279, 350
    father-infant, 268
    functional, 212, 361
    make-believe, 212–213, 223, 311–312,
        320, 350, 361, 362
    in middle childhood, 402–411
    with older siblings, 223, 375
    parallel, 358, 360
    rough-and-tumble, 408
    sex-typed, 33, 350, 371–372, 373, 374
    sociodramatic, 312, 362
    solitary, 223, 358, 361
Pollution, environmental, and pregnancy, 109–110
Polychlorinated-biphenyls (PCBs), and
    pregnancy, 110
Polygenic inheritance, 62
Popular children, 473
Postconventional level, of moral
    understanding, 581–582
Postpartum depression, 158–159
Postponing Sexual Involvement, 524
Postterm infants, 143–146
Poverty
    and AIDS, 112
    and child rearing, 74–75
    and delayed menarche, 507
    ethnic minorities and, 78
    and health, 393
    and infant mortality, 144
    and injuries, 295, 296
    and intelligence test scores, 228–229, 434
    and malnutrition, 113, 114
    and prenatal care, 108, 117
    public policy and, 78–80
    stress of, 79
    and teenage parenthood, 523
Pragmatics, 343, 438, 548
Precentral gyrus, 170
Preconventional level, of moral
    understanding, 580–581
Prediction
    with hypotheses, 32
    with intelligence tests, 11–12, 156, 224,
        334
    with theories, 3
Preformationism, 6
Pregnancy
    age and, 53, 65, 94, 116
    alcohol in, 107–108, 116

drugs in, 105
emotional state in, 115
exercise in, 111–112
healthy, dos and don'ts, 117, 118
length of, 143
new reproductive technologies, 66
number of previous births and, 116
nutrition in, 113–115
physical changes in, 111, 119
psychological challenges of, 118, 119
radiation in, 59, 109
Rh factor and, 115–116
sexual intercourse in, 120
smoking in, 107
teenage, 116, 520, 521–525
termination of, 68–69 (see also Abortion)
see also Prenatal care; Prenatal
development
Prelabor, 126
Premarital sex, 518–520
Premature infants, 56, 106, 141–142
abuse of, 382
Prenatal care, 116–117
Prenatal development, 95–102
AIDS and, 112
body proportions in, 101, 165
critical periods in, 103, 104, 113
environmental influences, 102–117
major milestones of, 96
maternal factors in, 111–116
nutrition and, 113
in other species, 9
period of the embryo, 97–99, 104
period of the fetus, 99–102, 104
period of the zygote, 95–97, 104
skeletal growth, 167
teratogens and, 103
trimesters in, 96, 169
see also Pregnancy
Prenatal diagnostic methods, 65–68, 97n,
100, 119
Preoperational stage, 19, 20, 310–322
advances in mental representation,
310–311
evaluation of, 320–321
limitations in, 312–318
make-believe play, 311–312
new research on, 318–320
Prereaching, 181, 183
Preschools, 336–338
academic, 336
child-centered, 336
fears about, 356
parental involvement in, 336
see also Day care
Preterm infants, 140–143, 154
and breast milk, 174
caregiving and, 142
characteristics of, 142
habituation and dishabituation in, 218,
219
intervening with, 142–143
versus small for dates, 141–142
stimulation of, 143

Pride, 249, 250, 353, 355, 459, 465, 573
Primary drives, 17, 257
Primary sexual characteristics, 504
Principle of contrast, 342
Privacy, children's right to, 43
Private speech, 322–323, 324
Privileges, withdrawal of, 366
Problem solving, in information processing,
22
Production, language, 235
Programming skills, computer, 444
Project Head Start, 336, 339
Proportions, body. See Body proportions
Propositional thought, 538–539
Prosocial behavior, 364, 365
Protestantism, 7
Proximo-distal trend, 166, 167, 178
Psychoanalysis, 19
Psychoanalytic perspective
of attachment, 257, 258–259
of sex-role development, 373
Psychoanalytic theory, 12–16, 31
contributions and limitations of, 15–16
Erikson's theory, 14–16, 242–244,
245–246, 350–351, 458–459,
570–571
Freud's theory, 13–14, 242–243,
350–351, 458–459, 499
Psychological abuse, 381. See also Child
maltreatment
Psychosexual development, Freud's theory
of, 13–14, 242–243, 350–351,
458–459, 499
Psychosexual stages, 13, 14
Psychosocial development, Erikson's theory
of, 14–16, 242–244, 245–246,
350–351, 458–459, 570–571
Puberty, 393, 498, 501–507
body size and proportion changes, 502
delayed, 63
emotional and social behavior and,
509–513
group differences in, 507
hormonal changes in, 501, 517
muscle-fat makeup, 501, 503–504
parent-child relationships and, 511–513
psychological impact of, 507–514
reactions to, 508–509
secular trends in, 507
sexual maturation, 501, 504–506,
513–514
Public health programs, 292, 293
Public policies, 78
and athletics, 531
and bilingual education, 440
and child development, 78–81
and child maltreatment, 383–384, 490
and childhood injuries, 296–297, 529
and day care, 78, 227, 267, 337–338
and delinquency, 601
and early intervention, 336–337, 339
and education, 450–452, 531, 555
and health services, 117, 144, 288, 293
and mainstreaming, 445, 447

and maternal employment, 486
and teenage pregnancy and child bearing,
523, 525
and vocational training, 558, 565
see also United States
Pukapukans, 131
Punishment, 187
accompanied by explanation, 367
alternatives to, 366–367
consistency in, 367
corporal, 383
effect on moral development, 365, 582
parental, 72–73
physical, 7, 8, 72, 73, 370
side effects of, 366
threat of, 364
Punishment and obedience orientation, of
moral understanding, 580
Puritanism, 7–8
Pyloric stenosis, 115

Quantitative reasoning, 430
Questioning, as educational strategy, 442
Questionnaires, 10, 34–36

Racial differences
in body growth, 165, 280–281
in intelligence, 83–84
in motor skills, 302–303
in skeletal age, 168
in temperament, 254–255
Racial minorities. See Minorities
Racial stereotypes, 371
Radiation, 59–60
in pregnancy, 109
Random assignment, in research, 38, 39
Range of reaction, 84–85
Rapid-eye-movement (REM) sleep, 154
Reaching, 178, 180
depth cues and, 192, 193
prereaching, 181
visually guided, 181
voluntary, 181–183
Reaction range, 84–85
Reaction time, 404
Readiness, to learn, 321
Reading, 304
information processing and, 427–428
with parents, 331
Realistic period, of vocational development,
560
Reality, appearance versus, 320
Reasoning
abstract, 19, 538, 539–540, 544
in adolescence, 536
deductive, 317
hypothetico-deductive, 536–537
inductive, 317
mathematical, 332, 428, 546–547
moral, 367–368, 468–469, 578–585
propositional, 538
quantitative, 334, 430
with school-age children, 478

Reasoning (continued)
  spatial, 334, 430
  transductive, 315–317
  verbal, 334, 430, 538
  *see also* Attributions
Recall, 219, 327
Recasts, of children's language, 345
Recessive alleles, 56–59
Recessive characteristics and disorders,
  57–59
Reciprocity, 579, 580, 581
Recognition memory, 219, 225, 235,
  327
Reconstituted families, 483
Red-green color blindness, 61
Referential style, of language development,
  235
Reflex(es), 148
  assessing, 150
  and early social relationships, 149–150
  grasping, 149, 181–183
  Moro or embracing, 149
  and motor skill development, 149
  newborn, 148–150, 185, 188
  rooting, 148
  stepping, 149
  sucking, 148, 149, 150, 151, 152
  survival value of, 148–149
  tonic neck, 149
Reformation, 7–8
Rehearsal, as memory strategy, 327, 422,
  425
Reinforcement
  in discipline, 365
  in friendships, 362
  in language development, 231
Reinforcers, 17, 187
Rejected children, 473
  helping, 474–475
Relaxation techniques, for childbirth, 132
Remarriage, 483–484
  factors related to children's adjustment to,
  483
REM sleep. *See* Rapid-eye-movement
  (REM) sleep
Representation, mental, 207, 211, 213
Reproduction, 54
Reproductive choices, 65–70
  abortion, 68–69
  adoption, 69–70
  fetal medicine advances and, 65–68
  genetic counseling, 65
  new technologies, 66
  prenatal diagnosis, 65–68
Reproductive disorders
  female, 66
  male, 66
Reproductive organs, 54, 55, 98, 504–505
Reproductive technologies, 66
Research
  deception in, 44
  ethics in, 42–44
  federally funded, 44
Research designs, 32, 37–39
  correlational, 37–38, 39

cross-sectional, 41
developmental, 39, 40–42
experimental, 38, 39
field experiments, 38–39
general, 37–39
longitudinal design, 40
modified experimental designs, 38–39
natural experiments, 38–39
strengths and weaknesses of common, 39
Research methods, 32–44
  common, 32–37
  clinical method, 16, 36
  concordance rates, 82–83
  heritability estimates, 82–83
  self-reports, 34–36
  systematic observation, 32–34
  strengths and weaknesses of, 34, 83–84
Resistant attachment, 262
Resource rooms, for children with special
  educational needs, 447, 449
Respiratory distress syndrome, 140, 141
Respiratory infections, 294
Responsiveness, by parents, 379
Reticular formation, 286
Retina, 152
Retrieval, 218, 422
Reversibility, 315, 416
Rh factor, 115–116
RhoGam, 116
Risk-taking, adolescent, 529, 544, 602
Rite of passage, 509
Rooming in, 147
Rooting reflex, 148–149
Rough-and-tumble play, 408
Rousseau's philosophy, 8–9
Rubella, 110
Rule-assessment approach, Siegler's,
  540–542
Running, 298, 403

Safety education, 400
Samoan adolescents, 499–500
Sarcasm, 548
Schemes, 204, 205, 206
  building, 209
  changes with age, 207
  modifying, 206
  reflexive, 207, 208
Schizophrenia, 69n
  twin studies of, 83
Scholastic Aptitude Test (SAT), 441, 547, 555
Schooling
  formal, 459
  years of, and moral reasoning, 583
School performance. *See* Academic
  achievement
School phobia, 487
Schools
  computers in, 444–445
  influence on development, 76
  integrated, 473
  learning experiences in, 441–450,
  553–554, 575
  mainstreaming in, 447

punishment in, 383
teacher-parent interaction, 76, 452
teacher-pupil interaction, 442–443
traditional versus open classrooms, 441
*see also* Education
School transitions, 550–552
Science, child study as, 9–12
Scientific verification, theories and, 3
Scottish children, 390
Screening, for developmental problems, 225
Scripts, 328
Scrotum, 55, 505
Sebaceous glands, 504
Secondary or learned drives, 17, 257
Secondary sexual characteristics, 504
Secular trends in physical growth, 392, 507
Secure attachment, 262, 270
Secure base, 260
Seizures
  brain, 172
  epileptic, 393
Self
  categorizing the, 273
  sense of, 241, 244, 249
  *see also* Identity; Self-concept; Self-esteem
Self-awareness, 245, 272
Self-concept
  in adolescence, 572
  in early childhood, 351–352, 355
  in middle childhood, 459–460
Self-confidence, 573
  negative, 351
Self-consciousness, in adolescence, 543–544
Self-control, 273, 517
  emergence of, 273–274
  and language development, 273
  and morality, 273
Self-development, 242
  in adolescence, 572–577
  in early childhood, 351–353
  in infancy and toddlerhood, 270–274
  in middle childhood, 459–465
Self-esteem, 353, 459, 460–464, 489
  academic, 463, 474
  in adolescence, 551, 572–573
  adult support of, 464
  changes in level of, 572–573, 461–
  462
  emergence of, 353
  hierarchically structured, 460–461
  influences on, 462–464
  in middle childhood, 474
  sex differences in, 551
  and sex-role identity, 376
  and social class, 573
Self-focusing, in adolescence, 543–544
Self-fulfilling prophecy, 443
Self-help skills, 301
Self-recognition, 271–272
Self-regulation, 426–427
  in adolescence, 546
  computer programming and, 444
  emotional, 250, 354–355, 465
  information processing and, 432
  language and, 250

Self-reports, 34–36
Semilingualism, 440
Sensation, 191. *See also* Perceptual
  development
Sense of agency, 271
Sense of self, 241, 244, 249
Senses, in newborns, 150–153
Sensorimotor stage, 19, 20, 204, 206–
  213
  circular reaction, 207
  evaluation of, 215
  mental representation, 211–213
  new research, 213–215
  object permanence, 213–214
  substages of, 206, 207
Sensory register, 217
Separation anxiety, 260, 261, 481
Separation-individuation, Mahler's theory of,
  244–245
Sequential processing, 430
"Sesame Street," 341
Seriation, 416–417
Sex bias, in intelligence tests, 430, 433
Sex cells, 51–53
  age and, 63
  male, 61
Sex chromosomes, 55–56
  abnormalities of, 63–64
Sex determination, 55–56, 100
Sex differences
  in academics, 444–445, 475–476,
    546–547
  in aggression, 368, 369–370, 472
  in body growth, 165, 280–281, 390–
    391
  in body size, 280–281
  in cognitive abilities, 546–547, 562
  in depression, 595
  in emotional expression, 251
  in friendships, 590
  in moral reasoning, 584–585
  in motor development, 302–303, 407,
    462, 530–531
  in muscle-fat makeup, 166, 503–504
  in pubertal maturation, 501
  in self-esteem, 551
  in sex typing, 476–477
  in shyness, 40
  in skeletal age, 168
  in suicide, 597
  in temperament, 254–255
  in vocational development, 561–562
  in X-linked diseases, 61–62
Sex drive, 17, 517
Sex education, 490, 518, 520, 522–526
Sex hormones, 501, 504, 509
  female, 501
  male, 108, 368, 501
Sex-role development, theories of, 373,
  376–377
Sex-role identity, 376–377, 475
  androgynous, 376, 586
  and behavior, 476
Sex roles, 377–378
  awareness of, 368

traditional, 375, 477
  *see also* Sex typing
Sex-role stereotypes
  in the social environment, 375–376
  on television, 371
  *see also* Sex typing
Sex-typed behavior, 33
  in adolescence, 586
  in early childhood, 373–374
  in middle childhood, 476
Sex-typed beliefs, 469
  in adolescence, 586
  and child-rearing, 255
  in early childhood, 373–374
  in middle childhood, 475
Sex typing
  in adolescence, 586
  adults and, 374
  cultural influences on, 476–477
  in early childhood, 371–378
  in middle childhood, 475–477
  and sports, 407, 531
Sexual abuse, 381. *See* Child maltreatment;
  Child sexual abuse
Sexual activity, adolescent, 517–521, 523,
  524
  contraceptive use, 520
  double standard of behavior, 518
  homosexuality, 521
  impact of culture on, 518
  pregnancy and parenthood, 520, 521–
    525
  premarital, 518–520
  and sexually transmitted diseases,
    525–526
Sexual identity, 521, 570
Sexual intercourse, 54
  in pregnancy, 120
Sexually transmitted diseases (STD), 518,
  525–526, 526
Sexual maturation, 501, 504–506, 517
  in boys, 505–506
  in girls, 501, 505
Shame, 249, 250, 353
Sharing, justice through, 468
Short-term memory. *See* Working or
  short-term memory
Shyness, 252, 474
  biological basis of, 254
  sex differences in, 40
  stability of, 40, 253–254, 256
Sibling relationships, 71
  in adolescence, 588
  adopted children and, 86
  caregiving and, 78
  infants and, 268–269
  inherited characteristics and, 53, 56
  in middle childhood, 478–479
Sibling rivalry, 479
Sickle cell anemia, 58–59, 60
Sickle cell trait, 58
Simultaneous processing, 430
Single-parent households, 479, 480, 482
  maternal employment and, 484–485
  *see also* Divorce

Single parenthood, stress of, 79
Sitting, 178
Skeletal age, 167, 281
Skeletal growth, 167–169
  in adolescence, 501, 503
  in early childhood, 280–283
  general, 167–168
  in middle childhood, 392
  skull, 168, 169
  teeth, 169
Skin, of newborns, 129
Skull, growth of, 168, 169
Slang, teenage, 548
Sleep
  in infants, 153–154, 177
  NREM, 154
  REM, 154
Slow-to-warm-up child, 252
Small-for-dates infants, 141
  versus preterm, 141–142
Smell, sense of, in newborns, 151
Smiles
  of infants, 247–248
  social, 247
  of toddlers, 248
Smoking, 526–527
  in pregnancy, 107
Sociability
  peer, 358–362
  stability of, 253–254, 256
Social acceptance, 353
  categories of, 473
Social class
  and child rearing, 73–74, 78
  and cognitive development, 74
  and family functioning, 73–74
  and IQ, 433, 434
  and language development, 74
  and self-esteem, 573
Social cognitive approach, 18
Social comparisons, in self concept, 460
Social contract orientation, of moral
  understanding, 581–582
Social conventions, 367, 469
Social development, 17–18
  in adolescence, 569–602
  in early childhood, 349–384
  in infancy and toddlerhood, 241–276
  in middle childhood, 457–491
Social dilemmas, and perspective-taking, 466
Social learning theory, 17–18, 31
  and moral behavior, 365–367
  and sex-role development, 373
  and sex-role identity, 376–377
Social networks, 27
Social-order-maintaining orientation, of
  moral understanding, 581
Social problem solving, 370, 467
Social programs, 80–81. *See also* Public
  policies; United States
Social referencing, 249
Social skills
  and peer acceptance, 474
  perspective-taking and, 466–467
Social smile, 247

Social systems perspective, on family functioning, 71–73
  on child maltreatment, 382
  direct and indirect influences, 71–72
  dynamics of, 72–73
Society for Research in Child Development, 43
Sociocultural theory, 28–29, 31
  early childhood cognition, 310, 322–325
  and education, 325
  infant and toddler cognition, 204, 221–223
  private speech, 322–324
Sociodramatic play, 312, 362
Sociometric techniques, 473
Sounds
  letters and, 428
  newborn's response to, 152
  perception of, in infancy, 191
Space, understanding of, 192–194, 418
Spatial skills, 63, 334, 430, 547
  brain and, 171
  development of, 284, 285
Specialized talent, 449
Special needs children, 445–449
Speech
  egocentric, 322–323
  inner, 324
  perception of, in infancy, 191
  private, 322–323
  telegraphic, 234
  see also Language development
Speech sounds, newborn's response to, 152
Speed, concept of, 418–419
Sperm, 51, 53, 54, 55, 66, 109
Spermarche, 506
  boys' reactions to, 508–509
Spinal cord, prenatal development of, 99
Spontaneous abortion, 61
Sports
  in adolescence, 529, 530–531
  adult-organized, 409
  competitive, 410
  see also Athletics; Games; Physical education
Sports injuries, 529
Stage, concept of, 5, 8
Stage theories, 5. See also names of theories
Stanford-Binet Intelligence Scale, 11–12, 429, 430
States of arousal, 153, 154
States versus transformations, in Piaget's theory, 315
Stepfathers, 483
Stepmothers, 484
Stepping reflex, 149
Stereotypes
  racial, 371
  sex-role, 371
  on television, 371
  see also Sex typing
Stimulation
  of neurons, 169
  overstimulation, in infancy, 181, 250

and physical development, 176–177
  of preterm infants, 143
Strange Situation, 261, 262, 265–266
Stress
  of divorce, 72
  maternal, 128
  in middle childhood, 490
  of parenthood, 158, 159
  in pregnancy, 115
Stress hormones, 139
Stress-resistant children, 490
Structured interviews, 34, 35
Structured observations, 33, 34
Subcultures, 78
Substance use and abuse, 526–528
  correlates and consequences of, 528
  experimenters and abstainers, 527
  prevention strategies, 528
Sucking reflex, 148, 149, 150, 151, 152, 187, 197
Sudden infant death syndrome (SIDS), 188
Suicide, 596–599
  factors related to, 597
  prevention and treatment, 598–599
Superego, 13, 351, 363. See also Conscience
Surrogate motherhood, 66
Sweden, 290, 383, 522
Swimming pools, fears about, 356
Symbiosis, in Mahler's theory, 244–245
Synapses, 169, 393
Synchrony, interactional, 264–265, 266, 344
Systematic observation, 32–34
Systems of action, in motor development, 180, 297

Tabula rasa, 8
Taiwanese children, 450–452, 475
Talent, 449
Taste, in newborns, 151
Tay-Sachs disease, 60, 65, 70
Teacher-parent communication, 452
Teacher-pupil interaction, 442–443
  and school performance, 553–554
Teachers
  educational philosophies of, 441–442
  influence on vocational choice, 561
  and sex typing, 375
Teenage fathers, 525
Teenage mothers, 79, 116
Teenage parenthood, 522–523
Teenage pregnancy, 68, 116, 520, 521–525
  correlates and consequences of, 522–523
  preventing, 523–525
Teeth, 283
  appearance of, 169
  cultural heritage and, 283
  permanent, 283, 392
  primary, 283, 392
Telegraphic speech, 234
Television
  advertising on, 371, 372
  children's, regulation of, 372
  educational, 338–341

and obesity, 396
  prosocial attitudes on, 372
  sex on, 518
  violence on, 370–371, 383
Temperament, 252
  and attachment security, 265–266
  biological foundations of, 254
  and child rearing, 255–256
  dimensions of, 252–253
  and emotional development, 252–256
  environmental influences on, 255
  individual differences in, 241–242, 254
  and injuries, 295
  measuring, 252
  and sibling relationships, 269
  stability of, 253–254, 255
Temperature change, 155
  newborn reaction to, 150
Temper tantrums, 245
Temptation, resistance to, 273, 274
Tentative period, of vocational development, 560
Teratogens, 103–111
  factors affecting the impact of, 103
Testes, 54, 393, 501, 505
  cancer of, 109
Testosterone, 501
Tests. See Intelligence testing; Intelligence tests
Thalidomide, 105
Theories, 3
  comparing child development, 29–31
  continuity versus discontinuity, 4–5, 31
  importance of, 3
  nature versus nurture, 5–6, 31
  organismic versus mechanistic, 4, 31
  specific verification of, 3
  stage, 5
  see also names of theories
Theory of mind
  in early childhood, 329–330
  in middle childhood, 425–426
Three-dimensional drawings, 406
Three mountains problem, 314
Thumb sucking, 392
Thyroid gland, 287
Thyroid stimulating hormone (TSH), 287
Thyroxin, 287, 501
Tikopians, 510
Time, concept of, 418–419
Time out, 366
Toddlerhood. See Infancy and toddlerhood; Toddlers
Toddlers
  attachment behavior of, 260
  cognitive development of, 211–212, 219–220
  complex emotions in, 249, 272
  emotional self-regulation in, 251
  language development of, 234–235
  parent interaction and make-believe play, 223
  personality development of, 243–244, 245
  self-control in, 273–274

*see also* Infancy and toddlerhood; specific topics
Toilet training, 181–184, 244
Tonic neck reflex, 149
Touch
 in newborns, 150–151
 preterm newborns and, 143
Town life, influence on development, 76–77
Toxemia, 117
Toxoplasmosis, 111
Toys, 216
 cultural differences in, 30
 for infants and toddlers, 216
 Medieval times, 6
 sex-appropriate, 374
Tracking
 in school, 443, 554–556
 visual, in infancy, 192
Traditional classrooms, 441
Transductive reasoning, 315–317
Transition, in childbirth, 127
Transitive inference, 417, 419
Traumatic events
 divorce, 479
 obesity and, 396
Triarchic theory of intelligence, Sternberg's, 432–433
Trimesters, of prenatal development, 96, 100–102, 169
Triple X syndrome, 63, 64
Trobriand Islanders, 518
Trust, 244, 245, 258, 260, 473, 570, 590
 basic, 242–243
Turner syndrome, 63, 64
Twins
 fraternal, 56, 57 (*see also* Fraternal twins)
 identical, 56, 57 (*see also* Identical twins)
 language development in, 237
 physical development in, 172
 rate of development, 56
Twin studies
 of depression, 83
 of intelligence, 82, 434
 of schizophrenia, 83
 of temperament, 254
Type A personality, 397

Ulnar grasp, 181, 183
Ultrasound, 65, 67, 68, 100, 119
Umbilical cord, 96–97, 128, 138, 140
Unconditioned response (UCR), 186
Unconditioned stimulus (UCS), 186
Underextension, 234
United States
 abortion in, 522
 education in, 554, 555
 moral concepts in, 470
 substance abuse in, 526–527
 vocational development in, 565
 *see also* Public policies; Social programs
Universal ethical principle orientation, of moral understanding, 582

Uterus, 54, 66, 100, 109, 501
 contractions of, 126, 127, 128

Vaccines, for Rh negative mothers, 116. *See also* Immunization
Vacuum extractor, 137
Vagina, 55, 501
 cancer of, 109
Values
 American, 77, 80
 cultural, 79
Variables
 dependent, 38
 independent, 38
Vas deferens, 54
Verbal feedback, as educational strategy, 442
Verbal skills, 63, 334, 430
 brain and, 171
 development of, 284, 285
 sex differences in, 235, 546
Vernix, 100
Video games, 478
Vietnam War, 575
Villi, 96–97
 chorionic, 65, 67, 96–97
Violence
 anxiety about, 487–488
 on television, 370–371, 383
 in video games, 478
 *see also* Aggression; Child sexual abuse; Child maltreatment
Viral diseases, 294
 and pregnancy, 111, 112
 *see also* Acquired immune deficiency syndrome
Vision
 color, 153
 in infancy, 192–197
 in middle childhood, 394
 in newborns, 152–153
 *see also* Perception; Perceptual development; Visual development
Visual acuity, 152, 192
Visual cliff, 192–193, 194, 215, 248, 249
Visual development
 contrast sensitivity, 195
 depth perception, 192–194
 face perception, 196–197
 intermodal perception, 197, 198
 pattern perception, 194–195, 196–197
Visually-guided reaching, 181
Visual scanning, 196
Vocabulary development, 234–235
 in adolescence, 547–548
 in early childhood, 341–342, 353–354
 in middle childhood, 437
 overextensions and underextensions, 234
 *see also* Language development
Vocational choice, 560–562, 575
 factors influencing, 560–562
 family influence on, 561
 teachers and, 561

Vocational development, 559–565
 phases of, 560
 sex differences in, 561–562
 transition from school to work, 563–565
Vocational information, access to, 562
Vocational training, 558, 575
Voice change, in adolescence, 506
Voluntary reaching, 181–183
Vomiting, 517
Vygotsky's theory. *See* Sociocultural theory

Walkers, for infants, 194
Walking, 180, 298
 and individuation, 245
Watson's theory. *See* Behaviorism
Wechsler Intelligence Scale for Children-III (WISC), 430
Wechsler Preschool and Primary Scale of Intelligence-Revised (WPPSI-R), 430
Weight
 heredity and, 173
 low birth, 106–107, 140–143, 144
Weight gain
 in adolescence, 503
 in early childhood, 280
 exercise and, 175
 from infancy to toddlerhood, 164–165
 in middle childhood, 390
Weight loss, and anorexia, 516
West Germany, apprentice system, 563, 564
West Indian infants, motor development in, 182
Whole language approach, 427–428
Withdrawal symptoms, in drug-addicted newborns, 105, 106
Word processing, and computers, 444
Working or short-term memory, 217–218, 420
Work-study programs, 564, 565
Writing skills
 in early childhood, 301, 331
 in middle childhood, 404–405

X-linked diseases, 61
X-linked inheritance, 61–62
X-rays, 109, 168
XYY syndrome, 63, 64

Yolk sac, 96, 99
Yurok Indians, 14

Zambian infants, 156
Zinacanteco Indians, 29
Zone of proximal development, 221, 237, 324, 441
Zuni Indians, 250
Zygote, 55
 period of the, 95–97, 104